Financial Accounting and Reporting

Second Edition

Financial Accounting and Reporting
A Global Perspective

Second Edition

Hervé Stolowy & Michel J. Lebas

Australia • Canada • Mexico • Singapore • Spain • United Kingdom • United States

Financial Accounting and Reporting – A Global Perspective, Second Edition
Hervé Stolowy and Michel J. Lebas

Publishing Director
John Yates

Publisher
Pat Bond

Editorial Assistant
Alice Rodgers

Senior Production Editor
Alissa Chappell

Manufacturing Manager
Helen Mason

Marketing Manager
Katie Thorn

Typesetter
Gray Publishing, Tunbridge Wells

Production Controller
Maeve Healy

Printer
Canale, Italy

Cover Design
Adam Renvoize

Text Design
Design Deluxe, Bath

For more information, contact
Thomson Learning,
High Holborn House;
50-51 Bedford Row,
London WC1R 4LR

or visit us on the World Wide Web at:
http://www.thomsonlearning.co.uk

ISBN-13: 978-1-84480-250-0
ISBN-10: 1-84480-250-7

This edition published 2006 by Thomson Learning.

British Library Cataloguing-in-Publication Data
A catalogue record for this book is available from the British Library

Dedication

To Nicole, Natacha, and Audrey
For their indefatigable support and immense patience

To my wife Michael Adler and to Alfie
They both know how important a role they played in this project

Brief contents

Contents

List of real companies referenced

Company name	Country	Chapters
4Kids Entertainment	USA	Chapter 15
Adidas-Salomon	Germany	Chapter 3
Alliance Unichem	UK	Chapter 12
Aluminum Corporation of China	China	Chapters 8, 9, 11, 14
Aracruz Celulose	Brazil	Chapter 3
Asda (Wal-Mart UK)	UK	Chapter 12
Atos Origin	France	Chapters 6, 7
Baltimore Technologies	UK	Chapter 8
Barloworld	South Africa	Chapters 11, 12
Bayer	Germany	Chapters 6, 7, 8, 10
Benihana	USA	Chapters 9, 14
Boc	UK	Chapter 10
Boots	UK	Chapter 12
Bosch	Germany	Chapters 9, 10
Bull	France	Chapters 6, 8, 10
Carrefour	France	Chapter 3
CeWe Color	Germany	Chapter 8
China Eastern Airlines	China	Chapters 12, 13, 15
China International Marine Container	China	Chapter 13
China Petroleum & Chemical Corporation	China	Chapters 7, 10
China Unicom	China	Chapter 6
Chugoku Power Electric Company	Japan	Chapter 15
Club Méditerranée	France	Chapters 7, 8, 11, 12, 15
Cobham	UK	Chapter 12
Coles Myer	Australia	Chapter 14
Creaton	Germany	Chapter 15
Dave & Buster's	USA	Chapter 9
Diedrich Coffee	USA	Chapter 9
Easyjet	UK	Chapter 3
Easynet	UK	Chapter 12
Eircom	Ireland	Chapter 7
Electrolux	Sweden	Chapter 5
Elkem	Norway	Chapters 7, 10, 12, 15
EMI	UK	Chapter 8
Ericsson	Sweden	Chapters 6, 9, 10, 11, 14, 15
EVN	Austria	Chapters 8, 13
Fiat	Italy	Chapter 10
Fielmann	Germany	Chapter 12
Frisch's Restaurants	USA	Chapter 9
Gerry Weber	Germany	Chapter 11
Go Sport	France	Chapter 3

Heineken	Netherlands	Chapter 7
Hewlett-Packard	USA	Chapter 9
Hilton Group	UK	Chapter 11
Holcim	Switzerland	Chapter 3
Holmen	Sweden	Chapters 10, 11
Honda Motor	Japan	Chapters 7, 13
Iberia	Spain	Chapters 10, 12
Interbrew	Belgium	Chapters 7, 8
Irish Continental	Ireland	Chapters 7, 9, 15
ISS	Denmark	Chapters 7, 8, 10, 12
J Sainsbury	UK	Chapter 12
Kerry Group	Ireland	Chapters 9, 11
L'Oreal	France	Chapter 9
Marks and Spencer	UK	Chapter 12
McDonald's	USA	Chapter 9
Meritage Hospitality Group	USA	Chapters 5, 9
Metro	Germany	Chapter 3
Michelin	France	Chapter 3
Microsoft	USA	Chapter 6
Mitsubishi Electric	Japan	Chapters 12, 14
Mittal Steel	Netherlands	Chapters 11, 12
Morton's Restaurant	USA	Chapters 9, 12
Mountain Province Diamonds	Canada	Chapter 12
Nokia	Finland	Chapters 3, 11
Norsk Hydro	Norway	Chapter 9
Ona Group	Morocco	Chapter 3
Orkla	Norway	Chapter 3
Pernod Ricard	France	Chapter 10
Philips	Netherlands	Chapters 5, 7, 8, 9, 10
Pirelli	Italy	Chapters 5, 7, 8, 9
Procter & Gamble	USA	Chapters 6, 8, 11, 14, 15
Rare Hospitality International	USA	Chapters 9, 10
RC2 corporation	USA	Chapters 8, 10
Repsol YPF	Spain	Chapters 6, 7, 8, 9, 11, 12
Rio Tinto	UK	Chapter 1
Roche	Switzerland	Chapter 8
Rottneros	Sweden	Chapter 11
RWE	Germany	Chapter 1
Saint-Gobain	France	Chapters 7, 8, 13
Sandvik	Sweden	Chapters 3, 8, 11, 12
Sanofi-Aventis	France	Chapters 3, 8
Sauer-Danfoss	USA	Chapter 9
Saurer	Switerland	Chapters 6, 9, 10
Scania Trucks	Sweden	Chapter 1
SEB	France	Chapter 9
Securitas	Sweden	Chapters 7, 8
Serono	Switzerland	Chapter 13
Siemens	Germany	Chapters 7, 9
Sinopec	China	Chapters 12, 14
Skis Rossignol	France	Chapter 3
Smith & Nephew	UK	Chapter 1
Sony	Japan	Chapters 9, 10, 12
Stora Enso	Finland	Chapters 2, 7, 10, 12, 13, 14
Suez	France	Chapter 3

Sulzer	Switzerland	Chapters 10, 12
Taylor Nelson Sofres	UK	Chapters 7, 9
Telefónica	Spain	Chapters 3, 9
Temple-Inland	USA	Chapter 7
Tesco UK	UK	Chapter 12
Thales	France	Chapters 12, 13
Toray Industries	Japan	Chapters 9, 11, 15
Toyota	USA	Chapter 9
Trigano	France	Chapter 3
Unilever	Netherlands	Chapter 9
Vermont Teddy Bear	USA	Chapter 14
Vimpel Communications	Russia	Chapters 8, 15
Volvo Group	Sweden	Chapters 8, 9, 11
Volvo Trucks	Sweden	Chapter 1
Waitrose	UK	Chapter 12
Weyerhaeuser	USA	Chapter 7
Wipro	India	Chapter 3
Wm Morrison	UK	Chapter 12

About the authors

Hervé Stolowy is Professor of Accounting at the HEC School of Management (Jouy-en-Josas, France). He holds a degree in business administration (ESCP–Paris Graduate School of Management), a master's degree in private law (University Paris-Val de Marne), a BA in Russian and American studies (University Paris-Sorbonne), a PhD in financial accounting (University Paris-Panthéon-Sorbonne) and an *'habilitation à diriger des recherches'* (which certifies him as a qualified doctoral dissertation adviser). He is a certified *'expert comptable'* (French equivalent of a chartered accountant or certified public accountant).

He has authored and co-authored nine books, chapters in 10 collective works and published over 65 articles in academic and applied journals, such as *Accounting Auditing & Accountability Journal, Advances in International Accounting, Comptabilité – Contrôle – Audit,* the *European Accounting Review, Finance – Contrôle – Stratégie, The International Journal of Accounting, Les Echos,* the *Review of Accounting and Finance*, the *Revue de Droit Comptable* and the *Revue Française de Comptabilité*.

Professor Stolowy's research and teaching interests span financial and international accounting, and focus more specifically on intangibles, accounts manipulation, and design and use of cash flow statements. He is a member of the Association Francophone de Comptabilité (AFC), European Accounting Association (EAA), American Accounting Association (AAA), and Canadian Academic Accounting Association (CAAA). He is a past treasurer, current vice-president, and president-elect of AFC.

Hervé Stolowy teaches financial accounting in the different graduate programs of the HEC School of Management: introduction to financial accounting and financial statement analysis (HEC-MBA Program and HEC Master of Science in Management – *Grande Ecole*), and both advanced accounting and international accounting (HEC MSc in Management *Grande Ecole*). He also teaches in the HEC doctoral program (research in financial accounting).

Michel J. Lebas is Emeritus Professor of Management Accounting and Management Control at the HEC School of Management. He was educated both in France (HEC) and in the United States (Tuck School at Dartmouth College and Stanford University Graduate School of Business). After a brief career as an economic analyst for a US multinational and later as a staff consultant in the New York office of the then Price Waterhouse, he joined the academic profession while maintaining a freelance consulting practice. He is now a freelance consultant and executive education trainer, working mainly for multinational companies.

Professor Lebas' field of research and consulting concentrates on advanced practices in management accounting and performance management systems. He is one of the academic research associates in the Beyond Budgeting Round Table Program of the Consortium for Advanced Manufacturing–International (CAM-I); from July 1992 to July 2000 he represented the *French Ordre des Experts Comptables* and the *Compagnie des Commissaires aux Comptes* on the then 'Financial and Management Accounting Committee' (FMAC) (currently 'Accountant in Business Committee') of the International Federation of Accountants (IFAC). He is the founder, and was from 1992 until 1996 co-editor of the management accounting section of the *Revue Française de Comptabilité*. His publications, in addition to this textbook, include chapters in major international collective works, co-authorship/editorship of a *Glossary of Accounting English*, co-authorship of a *Management Accounting Glossary*, as well as a management accounting textbook. He co-authored a CAM-I monograph on *Best Practices in World Class Organizations* with Ken Euske and C.J. McNair. His numerous articles have been published in many academic and professional journals including *Administracion de Empresas* (Argentina), *Cahiers Français* (France), *De Accountant* (Netherlands), *European Accounting Review* (UK), *European Management Journal* (UK), *International Journal of Production Economics* (Netherlands), *Journal of Management Studies* (UK), *Management Accounting Research* (UK), *Performances Humaines et Techniques* (France), *Problemi di Gestione* (Italy), *Revue Française de Comptabilité* (France), *Revue Française de Gestion Industrielle* (France), *Sviluppo & Organizzazione* (Italy), *Travail* (France), and in the publications of IFAC.

Beside Lebas' research, consulting and executive education teaching, he has been teaching for the past 15 years in several executive MBA programs in Europe, Asia, North America and Africa. He has been Associate Dean for Academic Affairs of the HEC *Grande Ecole* (1986–9), and holds or has held visiting appointments at Aarhus Business School, SDA Bocconi in Milan, INSEAD, the Mediterranean School of Business in Tunis, the Darden Graduate School of Business at the University of Virginia, and at the University of Washington School of Business.

The author team is a reflection of the spirit and the tone of the text. Hervé Stolowy brings the accounting and reporting practitioner/researcher and external financial analyst viewpoint, while Michel Lebas brings the internal and managerial preoccupations in the design of information systems and the interpretation of accounting information.

Preface

A book to meet changing student and faculty expectations

The success of the first edition of this award-winning book confirmed that our market analysis was correct: most students of Financial Accounting in European universities or schools, especially in the best programs, no longer focus solely on local reporting practices in their local language or cultural environment.

It is even more the case now, than in 2002 when the first edition was published, that individual countries retaining their own accounting standards is becoming irrelevant. Financial Accounting and Reporting courses today recognize both the diversity of national traditions and also the trend towards accounting harmonization.

The student profile in graduate and undergraduate business programs in Europe and beyond has changed.

- Student bodies, in every institution, from India to China, from Tunisia to Finland, from Lebanon to Brazil, from Canada to Australia, or from France to Russia are now true melting pots with participants from many countries.
- To these students, English has become the *lingua franca* of business and more and more business programs are being taught in part or completely in International English.
- These mobile and 'delocalized' students have only rarely been exposed to the Financial Accounting and Reporting practices of their home country.
- Most of these students know they will, on graduation and even more so than four years ago, work in an international context (i.e. not where they grew up, and, often, not even where they were educated). The ever-growing intra-European mobility of executives and students, amplified by the recent enlargement of the EU towards Eastern Europe, has only increased the relevance of our a-national approach.
- Students and managers want therefore to be trained to appreciate, understand and analyze a variety of Accounting and Reporting problems from a theoretical and generic point of view, rather than just memorize the local regulatory solution prescribed in any given country or context. They know they will have to adapt and apply their understanding of generic Accounting and Reporting principles and practices to the local circumstances they will face.
- Students want both to know the common principles and to familiarize themselves with financial information as it is presented in a variety of cultural contexts. They must be able to decode, without error, signals and messages about the economic performance of a business that come in an assortment of formats.

A book with multiple perspectives on financial accounting and reporting

This book recognizes the needs created by the *international* audiences of business courses (graduate and undergraduate — MBA, Masters of Accounting or BA — as well as post experience executive programs). The authors conceived their work to allow the teaching of

Financial Accounting and Reporting to a non-specialist audience with the following four perspectives in mind:

- First, it definitely takes a user-orientation position throughout, whether it is when explaining principles or in the practice of analyzing financial statements.
- Second, it provides an a-*national* approach in that the issues are explained as natural business and common-sense problems with multiple possible solutions and positions. In as much as possible, all likely solutions are examined with their own logic and pros and cons.
- Third, it takes on an *international point of view* because national practices have rapidly evolved in response to complex external (foreign in many cases) pressures coming from International Accounting/Financial Reporting Standards (IASC, now IASB), US GAAP, and regulations promulgated by Financial Market regulators such as IOSCO or SEC and its national or regional equivalents.
- Finally, it continuously offers the possibility to *position the rules and practices of different countries in a generic a-national format.* The students need to familiarize themselves with comparative accounting and be able to interpret signals or information coming from a diversity of international or national practices, rules and standards.

Purpose of this text

This book offers an introduction to Financial Accounting and Reporting. It is designed:

- for business students following their course of studies in institutions where knowledge of a single (national) accounting system is recognized as being insufficient preparation for the world where the graduates will work; and,
- for non-financial business executives who wish to understand the financial performance of enterprises and their reporting to the outside world.

Our approach derives from the characteristics of our targeted audience

The approach is based on the following ideas:

- We adopted a *user*, rather than a preparer perspective. Our choice results from our deeply held belief that business 'students' (graduate, undergraduate, or executive), regardless of the area of specialization they will select, or the career they will embrace, will be first and foremost, and on a regular basis, users of financial statements.

  Whether they will use accounting and financial information as internal managers or executives, or as external users (investors, credit analysts, etc.) they will need to interpret accounting data.

  Their knowledge of the preparation of accounting and reporting numbers need only encompass enough comprehension of key principles to allow the user to not be at the mercy of the information preparer.
- The book is based on real-world examples and illustrations. It incorporates a profusion of extracts from the annual reports of well-known firms and excerpts from the financial press. Some of these elements of annual reports are commented on in details, in order to prepare the students with reading and interpreting annual reports and articles in the financial press.
- Rather than providing a regulatory (technical) solution to a (simple or complex) reporting or measurement issue, we have chosen to first examine the economic logic of the problem and second identify generic possible solutions and what impact each might have on a company's or decision maker's decisions.
- Throughout the book and whenever appropriate, we cite and explain the latest IASB standards (IFRS/IAS). We strongly believe that, in many situations, the IASB recommendations, with the leeway and flexibility they contain, offer a good *a-national*

approach, but we do not hesitate to highlight the areas where the debate is still open, or where we feel in disagreement, always taking the point of view of the user, with aspects of a currently 'recommended' solution.

- In each chapter, we are providing a clear difference between what we feel is essential and what, in our opinion, might be considered more advanced or specialized knowledge. Each chapter is divided into seven parts giving instructors great flexibility in defining their own customized approach: (1) Core issues, (2) Advanced issues, (3) Key points, (4) Review, (5) Assignments, (6) References and (7) Further reading. A Glossary of key terms is provided at the end of the book.
- The term 'Advanced issues' does not mean that the topics are not important or are outside the scope of a basic course. It only means that these topics could be covered after the core issues, at a later date, or not at all, depending on the instructor's preference.
- The comparative accounting aspects of the text follow a topical (issue oriented) approach, rather than a country-by-country approach. They include, however, comparative tables that are structured by countries.
- The authors have written this text with the intention of showing that quality accounting reports are essential to decision makers. Accounting statements are as essential to managers as reading newspapers. Good accounting, like good journalism, follows rules and is limited only by professionalism, culture, ethics, and tradition. The talent of the journalist like that of the accountant rests in his or her ability to choose the right descriptors that will give a true and fair view of events. Accounting describes the economic reality of enterprises by using a dedicated language. We hope this book will demystify the world of financial reporting.

A few practical considerations

- As the choice of currency unit has no bearing on the logic of our arguments or presentation, we use, throughout the book, a generic Currency Unit (or CU), except when we refer to real-life examples in which case the original currency is always used.
- All reviews and assignments based on actual business organizations are identified with an asterisk next to the name of the company to highlight the 'real-life' origin of the review or assignment.
- In some tables, based on real-life examples, the use of parentheses is equivalent to a negative sign, as it is a common practice in many countries.
- Tables and figures are numbered by chapter. Those in appendices are referred to with a letter A after the number (For example: Table 12.1A would be in the web based appendices to Chapter 12, while Table 12.1 would be in Chapter 12 in the textbook you hold in your hands).

Level of the text

The text is pitched at an 'introductory level' for graduate students with business experience (MBA, essentially), undergraduate students with minimal business experience and executive education participants who originate from functions distant from financial techniques and information. Because of the dual level of complexity in each chapter, the book can also be used in intermediate courses on Financial Statement Analysis, Financial Reporting or International Accounting.

Supplementary support materials for students and teachers

Supplementary support material is available for both students and instructors and teachers on the book's dedicated website (at the following address: http: //www.thomsonlearning.co.uk/stolowylebas2).

For students

- Excel files with the text of a certain number of assignments.
- Appendices.

For instructors and teachers

- Multilingual glossary of accounting terms (English, French, German, Italian, Spanish).
- PowerPoint slides of the figures and tables included in the text.
- Additional PowerPoint presentation slides.
- Solutions to the end-of-chapter assignments. We have sometimes written special notes to the instructor indicating the frequently made mistakes and alternative solutions.
- Additional assignments and solutions.
- Excel file solutions.
- Multiple-choice questions with solutions.

The supplementary material may be found on the Internet at the following address: http://www.thomsonlearning.co.uk/stolowylebas2

Access will be given to academics through several levels of password protection.

New features of the second edition

In addition to updating the first edition throughout for latest developments in the IFRS program and bringing the IAS up to date, and using the most recently available financial statements at the time of writing, the second edition offers:

- New and updated real-life examples included from companies operating in a range of countries throughout the world.
- Conformity with current IFRS/IAS.
- Expansion and updating of ratio analysis content in Chapter 15, including residual income and EVA.
- Ample developments in Chapter 15 on Governance and Ethics.
- Glossary of key terms added at the end of the book.
- Solutions for reviews placed at the end of the book.
- More and updated exercise material at end of chapters increased in quantity.
- Streamlining and simplification to the bare minimum of bookkeeping (preparer) issues in Chapter 4.
- An enriched provision of materials on the faculty website, which instructors can share, if needed, with their students.

Acknowledgments

Jennifer Pegg, our commissioning editor at Thomson Learning for the first edition, provided us with constant and caring support. She played an essential role in the birth of the first edition of this book.

Patrick (Pat) Bond, our editor for the second edition, showed us the same warm, constructive, and positive attitude. His wisdom and patience allowed him to give the authors, at times, the prodding, supporting, cuddling, and comforting they needed.

Our appreciation also goes to all the staff at Thomson who have contributed to the creation of this book and especially to Robert Gray and Alissa Chappell.

Anonymous reviewers and adopters of the first edition played a significant role in shaping the second edition. Their constructive comments helped us narrow down or focus our views and, we believe, improve the pedagogical approach in this second edition. They 'kept us honest' by telling us where our pet-topics had led to outsized sections or had led us to overlook a critical issue. Adopters and reviewers helped us create what we feel is now a better balanced text. Some of these evaluators, who also, often, helped us in the design of the first edition have accepted to lose their anonymity and we gladly acknowledge in person these friends and kindred souls:

Ignace de Beelde, University of Gent
Axel Haller, University of Regensburg
Begoñia Giner Inchausti, University of Valencia
Ann Jorissen, University of Antwerp
Josephine Maltby, University of Sheffield
Pat Sucher, Royal Holloway College, University of London
Anne Ullathorne, University of Birmingham
Stefano Zambon, University of Ferrara
Peter Walton, ESSEC
Charles P. van Wymeersch, University of Namur.

Our students, whether in the HEC MBA Program, the HEC *Master of Science in Management* program or in other institutions or international settings, and users from all over the world, have been our often toughest evaluators. They have criticized and commented on the first edition of this book. Our greatest appreciation goes to these truly international students for their patience and tolerance with our occasional lack of clarity and weaknesses and for their generally constructive comments.

We wish to recognize Nils Clotteau, our student-assistant on the first edition. Special thanks and recognition go to Sophie Marmousez, our research assistant who helped us immensely on the second edition and became a dedicated advocate for the future readers. Our students' and assistants' work has allowed us to create this better balanced and updated second edition.

The multilingual glossary (available on the instructor's section of the website) is a collective work and we are pleased to acknowledge our co-authors: Eva Eberhartinger (Professor, Chair of Accounting and Auditing, University of Vienna, Austria), José Antonio Gonzalo (Professor of Accounting and Financial Economics, Department of Managerial

Science, University of Alcalá, Spain), and Stefano Zambon (Professor of Business Economics, Faculty of Economics, University of Ferrara, Italy).

Lastly and certainly not the least, we wish to thank Georges Langlois who has translated and adapted this second edition for the French speaking markets. Translation is a very unforgiving test for the authors as any lack of clarity becomes perfectly obvious once the sentences are translated, even by a brilliantly competent translator/adaptor. George was kind enough to accept to work with us in a sort of a shuttle system, where we received his comments in real time. We were able to clarify our English text and he helped us make sure we remained on the straight and narrow of our objectives.

We warmly thank all these contributors for the generosity of their time and intelligence.

The authors, nonetheless, assume full responsibility for the ideas expressed and for any errors or omissions.

We will appreciate any and all comments from readers and users.

Hervé Stolowy, Jouy-en-Josas, France
Michel J. Lebas, Seattle, USA
June 2006

Contact:
stolowy@hec.fr
lebas@u.washington.edu

Walk through tour

Chapter 3

Financial statements presentation

Learning objectives

After studying this chapter, you will understand:

- That the balance sheet and income statement can be presented in different ways but that the logic of their construction remains the same and the informational content is often not affected by differences in presentation.
- That the balance sheet can be presented vertically or horizontally, single step or multiple step, and with a classification of assets and liabilities by nature or by term.
- That the income statement can be presented vertically or horizontally, single step or multiple step, and with a classification of expenses by nature or by function.
- That neither presentation is intrinsically 'better'.
- The main purpose and content of the notes to financial statements.
- The objective of the cash flow statement.
- How the cash flow statement relates to the balance sheet and income statement.
- The content of the annual report.
- The common formats for the presentation of the balance sheet and the income statement.
- That the accounting terminology may differ between US English and UK English.

In the first two chapters we briefly introduced three of the main documents called financial statements that are part of the managerial information set. These documents report the financial situation of the firm. The accounting information contained in the balance sheet, the income statement, and the notes to financial statements is essential for decision-makers and all stakeholders. The 4th European Directive (EU 1978) specifies in its article 2 that: 'The annual accounts shall comprise the balance sheet, the profit and loss account and the notes on the accounts'. A large majority of countries, whether part of the European Union or not, require at least these three documents. Many countries add the cash flow statement (see below and Chapter 14) and/or a statement of changes in shareholders' equity (see Chapter 11) to the required reporting package to be sure investors, shareholders, and other accounting information users are well informed about the situation of a business.

In its Accounting Standard No. 1 (IASB 2003: § 8), the International Accounting Standards Board (IASB) offers a definition of **financial statements** by stating that 'a complete set of financial statements comprises:

(a) a balance sheet;

(b) an income statement;

(c) a statement of changes in equity showing either:

– all changes in equity; or

– changes in equity other than those arising from capital transactions with equity

97

Chapter opening page

◀ Learning objectives set out concisely what is to be learned in the chapter, and ultimately link in to the Key points at the end of the chapter

Introductory text expands on the learning objectives and shows how the chapter fits in with other chapters. This helps readers to put the chapter in context and see the 'big picture'.

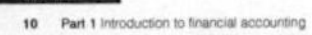

10 Part 1 Introduction to financial accounting

1 Core issues

1.1 Definition of financial accounting

1.1.1 Accounting

Accounting is about information. To count is to measure and quantify. To account for something is to acknowledge its existence and describe it. Accounting does both: it is a method of counting and a method of accounting for economic parameters describing the life of an enterprise (be it 'for' or 'not-for' profit). Accounting is about providing users with information (i.e., more than just data) about the economic and financial aspects of the life of an enterprise.

Broadly speaking, accounting information is an essential decision-support tool. Most decisions in a business are about resource planning, resource acquisition, and resource allocation in order to fulfill the firm's strategic intent (see, for example Lebas 1999: 54). These decisions are based on financial and non-financial (i.e., operational) information.

Such information is the output of an ongoing process of identifying, capturing, managing, analyzing, interpreting, and distributing data and information describing the economic activity of the firm.

Accounting has two key missions:

- To facilitate value creation by supporting resource acquisition and allocation decision-making. Value can be reduced to economic wealth if one refers only to shareholders who are looking for a financial return on their investment. However, we will keep using the term 'value' because it refers to the broader concept of being 'better off' for a variety of stakeholders whose utility preference functions may not be expressed solely in economic or monetary terms.
- To measure and report to stakeholders the amount of value created during a given period.

Although accounting is a complete discipline, this duality of missions has traditionally led to separating it in two (although closely interactive) subclasses on the basis of the different users who have access to its output:

- The first is called **managerial accounting**. It deals with a rather detailed account of how resources (which may include non-financial resources such as employee or customer loyalty or ability to create a network of resource providers) are acquired, managed, and used in the various business processes constituting the firm and is thus of particular interest to managers inside the firm.
- The second one is called regulated, legacy, or **financial accounting**. It is the focus of this text. It is aimed at reporting, in a somewhat aggregated way, the (economic) performance of the firm to essential external users such as shareholders, bankers, creditors, customers, unions, tax authorities, etc. Financial accounting focuses on the financial or monetary aspects of performance. Since its output will be used by outside investors and stakeholders to allocate their own resources, accounting information is a social good and therefore is generally regulated so that all classes of users receive signals of equivalent significance.

As we will see later, such a distinction between the accounting subclasses is somewhat artificial and often causes debates as to where the frontier should be placed between them.

1.1.2 Financial accounting

Financial accounting is a **process** of description of the various events that take place in the life of a firm. These events are essentially **transactions** between the firm and outside

Core issues

▲ The Core issues section explains the essential material in the chapter. This helps readers focus on acquiring key knowledge.

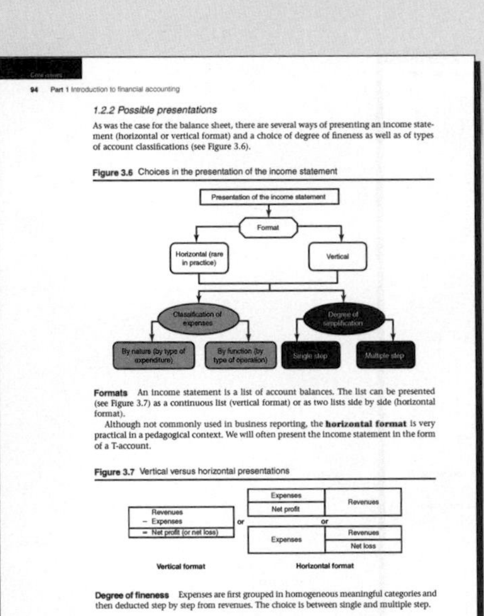

94 Part 1 Introduction to financial accounting

1.2.2 Possible presentations

As was the case for the balance sheet, there are several ways of presenting an income statement (horizontal or vertical format) and a choice of degree of fineness as well as of types of account classifications (see Figure 3.6).

Figure 3.6 Choices in the presentation of the income statement

Formats An income statement is a list of account balances. The list can be presented (see Figure 3.7) as a continuous list (vertical format) or as two lists side by side (horizontal format).

Although not commonly used in business reporting, the **horizontal format** is very practical in a pedagogical context. We will often present the income statement in the form of a T-account.

Figure 3.7 Vertical versus horizontal presentations

Degree of fineness Expenses are first grouped in homogeneous meaningful categories and then deducted step by step from revenues. The choice is between single and multiple step.

Single step It is the most simplified version of the income statement. Expenses and revenues are each considered as one category (see, for example, the left panel of Figure 3.7).

Multiple step Revenue and expense categories are paired so as to highlight the components of total net income (see Table 3.5). For example, trading (or operating) revenues and trading

Diagrams and figures

◀ These are exceptionally clear to help the reader conceptualise abstract ideas such as income statement formats

Tables

► Basic definitions and clarification of key terms are given in a glossary section at the end of the book.

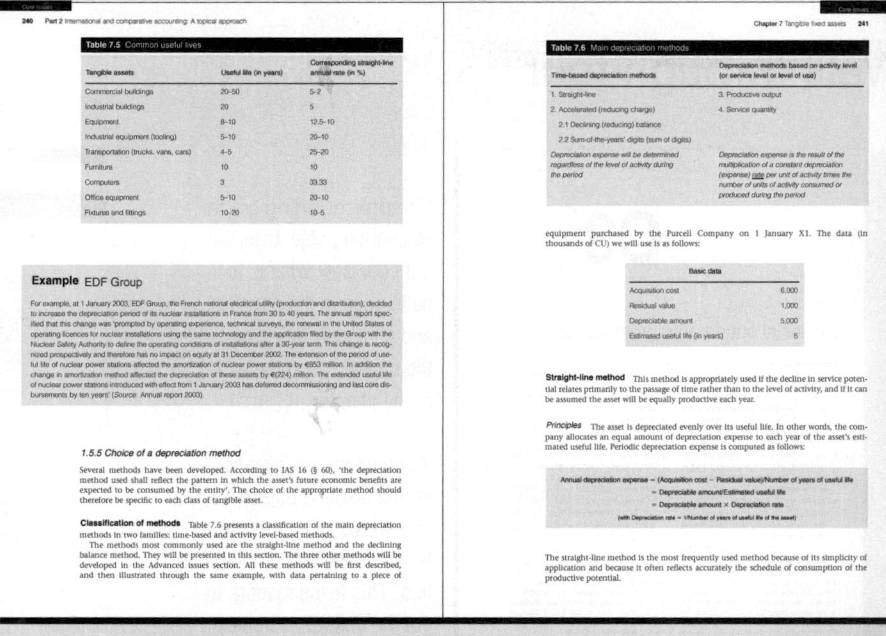

Examples

▲ Examples are frequently used to illustrate issues in the text, most of the time using real companies

Real-life examples

▼ Extracts from the financial statements of companies from around the world help bring the learning points to life

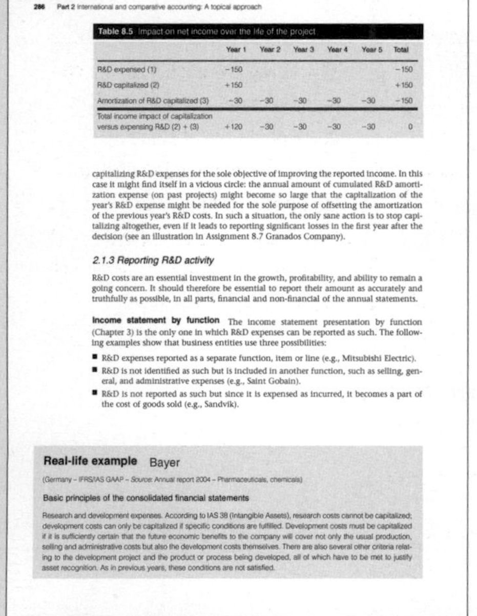

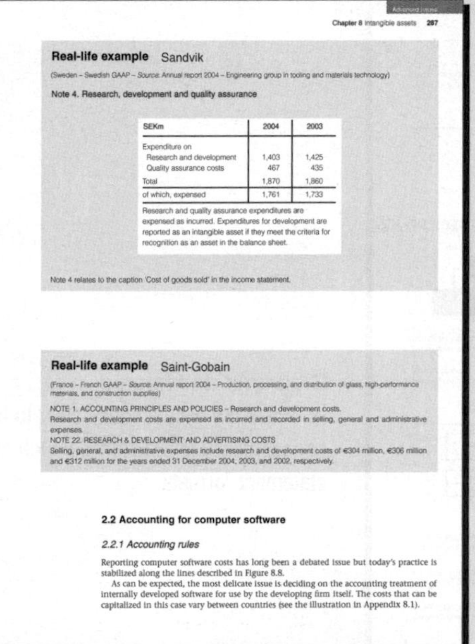

2 Advanced issues

Earlier sections of this chapter dealt with the general principles of revenue recognition. We will now examine the specific revenue recognition issues raised by some business practices.

2.1 Long-term contracts

As shown earlier in this chapter, long-term contracts represent a very common situation in which the revenue and cost recognition principles find all their usefulness.

2.1.1 Principles

Long-term contracts are referred to by IASB as 'construction contracts' (IAS 11, IASB 1993a). We will, however, keep using the expression long-term contracts since contracts that span several accounting periods include many other categories of contracts than construction contracts. For example, research contracts, contracts for the delivery of a series of locomotives or aircraft, facilities management contracts, computer service contracts, law suits, consulting contracts, etc., are all long-term contracts which span several accounting periods.

This section is largely inspired by IAS 11, which states the problems arising with the accounting for long-term contracts in a very clear way. The primary issue with long-term contracts is the allocation of contract revenues and contract costs to the accounting periods in which work is performed. The general rules of revenue recognition introduced in the 'Core issues' section of this chapter apply.

IAS 11 (§ 3) distinguishes two types of long-term contracts based on the revenue determination formula:

- A *fixed price contract* is one 'in which the contractor agrees to a fixed contract price, or a fixed rate per unit of output, which in some cases is subject to cost escalation clauses' to reflect inflation on the cost of resources consumed.
- A *cost plus contract* is one 'in which the contractor is reimbursed for allowable or otherwise defined costs, plus a "margin" represented by a percentage of these costs or a fixed fee'.

'When the outcome of a [long-term contract] can be estimated reliably, contract revenue and contract costs associated with [this] contract shall be recognized as revenue and expenses respectively by reference to the stage of completion of the contract activity at the balance sheet date' (IAS 11: § 22). The IASB and a majority of countries prefer the 'percentage of completion method' over any other. It consists in recording costs and revenues associated with the contract in increments linked (generally proportionally) to the degree of completion of the contract during the period.

The IASB endorses this method if several stated conditions are met. In the case, for example, of a fixed price contract (see IAS 11: § 23), 'the outcome of the contract can be considered to have been reliably estimated when all the conditions mentioned earlier for recognition of services are satisfied'. If any one of these conditions cannot be met, IAS 11 recommends a prudent approach for the recognition of revenue, which is a variation on the percentage of completion method (IAS 11: § 32):

(a) 'Revenue shall be recognized only to the extent of contract costs incurred that it is probable will be recoverable; and

Advanced issues

◀ This section of the chapter covers more-technical refinements of the basic material

2.8.2 Grants related to income

These grants are defined by IAS 20 (§ 3) as government grants other than those related to assets. In practice, they are also called operating grants or subsidies. They include capacity development grants when the capacity refers to the development of competences or skills. An example of an operating subsidy could be that of an incentive grant awarded to a business that creates new jobs or provides gainful employment to certain categories of unemployed persons. Grants related to income are included in the income statement when they are received, as an income (in the category 'other income') or as a deduction of the related expense.

2.8.3 Forgivable loans and repayable grants

These loans are defined as loans for which the lender accepts to waive repayment under certain prescribed conditions such as, for example, the effective creation within a specified time span of a given number of jobs. If the conditions are not met, the grant is, in principle, repayable. Other grants are repayable in case of success, such as, for example, a grant to help in research and development or a grant to help develop a new market. These grants are recorded in the balance sheet (on the liabilities side) until the condition has been met or it is established that the conditions will not be met. They are recorded under the special caption 'conditional advances received from the state' that lists these grants immediately next to shareholders' equity. At the end of the life of such a grant, if the conditions are not met the grant is repayable and will be handled exactly as would a normal loan. If, conversely, the conditions are met, an operating revenue or an exceptional revenue will be recorded.

Key points

- The issue of revenue recognition deals with when and how much revenue to recognize.
- Criteria for recognition vary according to the type of transaction: sales of goods, rendering of services, or use of enterprise assets yielding interest, royalties, or dividends.
- Revenue from the sale of goods should be recognized when several conditions have been satisfied, and mainly when the enterprise has transferred to the buyer the significant risks and rewards of ownership of the goods.
- When the outcome of a transaction involving the rendering of services spanning several accounting periods (such as in long-term contracts) can be estimated reliably, revenue and costs associated with the transaction should be recognized on the balance sheet date as a function of the stage or percentage of completion of the transaction.
- There may be some divergences between tax regulation and accounting rules. When these differences relate to the timing of the recognition they are called 'temporary differences'.
- Deferred tax assets or liabilities are created when the income tax expense is based on the pre-tax reported income (defined according to accounting rules) and not on the taxable income (based on the tax rules).
- The 'percentage of completion method', which consists of recording costs and revenue associated with the contracts as the work proceeds, is the preferred method for the recognition of profit in long-term contracts.
- Accounting standards stipulate that for an income statement to be useful in terms of evaluation of performance and permitting extrapolations, it must present separately and distinctly what pertains to 'normal' and recurrent business activities, and what pertains to actions, decisions, and events that are occasional and unusual.
- The comprehensive income includes revenue and expenses that are usually excluded from net income (e.g., unrealized gains and losses on short-term investments). This concept aims at showing the global performance of the company.
- Government assistance (grants, subsidies, subventions or premiums) raises revenue recognition issues.

Key points

► Key points conclude the chapter and highlight the core learning points covered. They link in to the learning objectives introduced at the start of the chapter. They are a useful reminder for a reader who is reviewing the chapter.

Key points

- Financial statements include, as a minimum, a balance sheet, an income statement, and notes to financial statements. Additionally, they tend to also comprise a cash flow statement and a statement of changes in shareholders' equity.
- The several possibilities of presentation that exist for the balance sheet do not affect its generic content.
- There are several ways of presenting an income statement. They all provide the same bottom line.
- The choice between a presentation by nature or by function is always debatable.
- The notes to the financial statements (often called 'footnotes') are an essential component of the information provided through financial statements.
- The cash flow statement reflects the timing difference existing between the recognition of revenues and expenses and their impact on cash, as well as any transaction affecting cash but not the income statement.
- An annual report includes information on the activity of a company as well as financial information.

Review (solutions are at the back of the book)

Review 3.1 Orkla*

Topic: Constructing a balance sheet
Related part of the chapter: Core issues

Orkla is a Norwegian-based group operating in the branded consumer goods, chemicals, and financial investment sectors. Listed below are in alphabetical order items and amounts taken from the group's consolidated balance sheet for the accounting year ended on 31 December 2004. All numbers are in millions of NOK (*source*: Annual report 2004). The consolidated financial statements have been prepared in accordance with laws and regulations, as well as Norwegian GAAP.

Accumulated profit	24,068	Other financial long-term assets	4,919
Cash and cash equivalents	2,232	Other short-term liabilities	8,223
Equity	26,304	Paid-in equity	2,007
Equity and liabilities	41,755	Portfolio investments, etc.	12,837
Intangible assets	3,647	Provisions	1,657
Inventories	2,869	Receivables	4,449
Investments in associates	1,716	Short-term assets	22,387
Long-term assets	19,368	Short-term interest-bearing liabilities	199
Long-term interest-bearing liabilities	5,372	Short-term liabilities	8,422
Long-term liabilities and provisions	7,029	Tangible assets	9,086
Minority interests	229	Total assets	41,755

Note:
- Minority interests represent the part of the net assets of a subsidiary attributable to interests, which are not owned, directly or indirectly through subsidiaries, by the parent company (minority shareholders). This item will be presented in a more detailed manner in the Chapter 13 devoted to Consolidation.
- 'Provisions' are assimilated to long-term liabilities.

Required

1. Reconstruct the balance sheet in a vertical, single-step and increasing liquidity/maturity format (check figure: total assets in balance sheet = 41,755).
2. Is the balance sheet organized by nature or by term?

Review 3.2 Holcim*

Topic: Constructing an income statement
Related part of the chapter: Core issues

Holcim is a Swiss-based group producing and selling cement and clinker, as well as aggregates. It is closely linked to the building industry. Listed below are in alphabetical order items and amounts taken from the group's consolidated statement of income for the accounting year ended on 31 December 2004. All numbers are in millions of Swiss Francs (*source*: Annual report 2004). The consolidated financial statements have been prepared in accordance with International Financial Reporting Standards (IFRS).

Administration expenses	(1,050)	Net income before minority interests	1,153
Distribution and selling expenses	(2,980)	Net income before taxes	1,663
EBIT (Earnings Before Interest and Taxes)	2,175	Net sales	13,215
Financial expenses net	(512)	Operating profit	2,251
Gross profit	6,598	Other depreciation and amortization	(317)
Income taxes	(510)	Other income (expenses)	(76)
Minority interests	(239)	Production cost of goods sold	(6,617)
Net income after minority interests	914		

Note: Minority interests, see note to Review 3.1.

Required

1. Prepare the income statement in a multiple-step format (check figure: bottom line = 914).
2. Is the income statement organized by nature or by function?

Review 3.3 Beethoven Company

Topic: Link between balance sheet, income statement and cash flow statement
Related part of the chapter: Core issues

Beethoven Company, a limited liability company that was incorporated in X1, has a commercial activity. It buys and sells books and CDs devoted to the learning of foreign languages. (The founder of the Company speaks at least 10 languages fluently.)

The balance sheet as at 31 December X1 is presented below.

Balance sheet as at 31 December X1 (in 000 CU)

ASSETS		SHAREHOLDERS' EQUITY AND LIABILITIES	
Fixed assets		*Shareholders' equity*	
Equipment (net value)	800	Capital	710
		Reserves	300
		Net income for X1 (a)	216
Current assets		*Liabilities*	
Merchandise inventory	150	Financial debt	110
Accounts receivable (b)	400	Accounts payable (c)	120
Cash at bank	250	Income tax payable (c)	144
Total	1,600	Total	1,600

(a) to be appropriated in X2: one third will be distributed.
(b) to be received in X2.
(c) to be paid in X2.

The following budgeted activities are envisaged for the year X2 (in 000 CU):

1. Sales budget: 1,600 (1,400 will be received from customers during the year).
2. Purchases budget (merchandise): 510 (400 will be paid to suppliers during the year).
3. Planned merchandise-ending inventory: 130.
4. Finance budget: repayment of financial debt for 80.
5. Salaries and social expenses budget: 430 (paid during the year)

Review

◀ The Review section at the end of the chapter contains questions, the solutions to which are found at the back of the book. Readers are encouraged to attempt the questions without first looking at the solutions.

Assignments

► The numerous Assignments test a range of issues covered in the chapter. Solutions are provided on the companion website and are available only to lecturers adopting the book.

Review (solutions are at the back of the book)

Review 13.1 Mater & Filia

Topic: Consolidated balance sheet (three methods)
Related part of the chapter: Core issues

The balance sheet of the Mater & Filia companies, as of 31 December X1, are given in the following table (Mater Co. is the parent company and Filia Co. is the subsidiary company).

Balance sheets as of 31 December X1 (in thousands of CU)

	Mater	Filia
Assets		
Fixed assets (net)	1,500	550
Investment in Filia Company (1)	160	–
Inventories	930	510
Other current assets	1,210	740
Total Assets	3,800	1,800
Liabilities and shareholders' equity		
Capital	500	200
Retained earnings and reserves	780	600
Net income (2)	220	150
Debts	2,300	850
Total Liabilities and shareholders' equity	3,800	1,800

(1) Mater acquired 80% of the capital of Filia when the latter was first incorporated.
(2) Net income will not be distributed.

Required

Prepare the consolidated balance sheet by each of the following methods:

- Full consolidation
- Proportionate consolidation
- Equity method.

Assignments

Assignment 13.1
Multiple-choice questions

Related part of the chapter: Core issues

Select the right answer (one possible answer, unless otherwise mentioned).

1. The percentage of interest
   (a) Is used to define the dependency link
   (b) Is used to decide about the inclusion of a company in the consolidation scope
   (c) Reflects the interests that are controlled directly and indirectly
   (d) None of these
2. In the situation described in the diagram below, the percentage of control (voting rights, vote) of P in C2 is:

   P —70%→ C1 —10%→ C2; P —20%→ C2

   (a) 10%
   (b) 20%
   (c) 30%
   (d) 27%
   (e) None of these
3. In the diagram of question 2 above, the percentage of interest (ownership, stake) is:
   (a) 10%
   (b) 20%
   (c) 30%
   (d) 27%
   (e) None of these
4. Minority interests can be reported (several possible answers):
   (a) As a part of shareholders' equity
   (b) As a part of long-term liabilities
   (c) As a part of current liabilities
   (d) Between shareholders' equity and long-term liabilities
   (e) As a negative liability within financial fixed assets
   (f) None of these
   (g) All of these
5. Associate and affiliate are often considered as synonymous
   (a) True
   (b) False
6. The only possibility to hold control of a company is to own more than 50% of the voting rights of this entity
   (a) True
   (b) False
7. Minority interests are reported when which method is used?
   (a) Full consolidation
   (b) Equity method
   (c) Proportionate consolidation
   (d) None of these
8. Goodwill is the difference between the purchase price (cost of investment) of shares and the book value of these shares
   (a) True
   (b) False
9. Before the adoption and implementation of SFAS 141 and IFRS 3, the study of annual reports showed that goodwill was generally amortized over 20 or 40 years
   (a) True
   (b) False
10. The equity method should be used when the percentage of control is more than 30% and less than 50%
   (a) True
   (b) False

Assignment 13.2
Mutter & Tochter

Topic: Preparation of a consolidated balance sheet
Related part of the chapter: Core issues

The balance sheet of Mutter and Tochter companies, as of 31 December X1, is given in the following table (Mutter Co. is the parent and Tochter Co. is the subsidiary).

Balance sheet as at 31 December X1 (000 CU)

	Mutter		Tochter	
Fixed assets (net)	22,000		16,000	
Investment in Tochter Company	10,000	(1)	–	
Inventories	34,000		10,000	
Other current assets	25,700	(2)	9,200	
Total assets	91,700		35,200	
Capital	40,000		15,000	
Retained earning/Reserves	14,000		6,000	
Net income	7,000		4,000	
Debts	30,700		10,200	(3)
Total shareholders' equity and liabilities	91,700		35,200	

(1) When Mutter acquired 60% of the capital of Tochter, the shareholders' equity (capital, retained earnings/reserves and net income) of the subsidiary was valued at 16,000.
(2) Includes a loan to Tochter — 1,000
(3) Includes a debt to Mutte — 1,000

References and Further reading

▼ These provide directions to further sources of information

Assignment 15.7
4Kids Entertainment, Inc.*

Topic: Earnings per share
Related part of the chapter: Advanced issues

4Kids Entertainment is a US company that receives revenues from a number of sources, principally through licensing and media buying. It represents such well-known properties as Pokémon and Nintendo. The company's common stock is traded on the NASDAQ. The annual report 2004 (for the year ended 31 December) contains the following information. The company applies SFAS No. 128, which requires the computation and presentation of earnings per share (EPS) to include basic and diluted EPS. Basic EPS is computed based solely on the weighted average number of common shares outstanding during the period. Diluted EPS reflects all potential dilution of common stock.

The number of common shares, in 2004, is 13,683,756 and the number of stock options granted is 651,587 (if exercised, each option entitles the holder to one share of common stock). The income statement shows net income to be US $12,730,000.

Required

Prepare a statement showing the computation of basic and diluted earnings per share for the year 2004.

References

Altman, E. I. (1968) Financial ratios, discriminant analysis and the prediction of corporate bankruptcy. *The Journal of Finance*, (23), September, 589–609.

Altman, E. I., and McGough, T. P. (1974) Evaluation of a company as a going concern. *Journal of Accountancy*, December, 50–57.

ASB (1998) Financial Reporting Standard No. 14: Earnings Per Share, London, UK.

Baker, C. R., Ding, Y., and Stolowy, H. (2005) Using 'statement of intermediate balances' as tool for international financial statement analysis in airline industry. *Advances in International Accounting*, 18, 169–98.

Barnea, A., Ronen, J., and Sadan, S. (1975) The implementation of accounting objectives: An application to extraordinary items. *The Accounting Review*, January, 58–68.

Barnea, A., Ronen, J., and Sadan, S. (1976) Classificatory smoothing of income with extraordinary items. *The Accounting Review*, January, 110–22.

Black, E. L., Sellers, K. F., and Manly, T. S. (1998) Earnings management using asset sales: An international study of countries allowing noncurrent asset revaluation. *Journal of Business Finance & Accounting*, 25(9) & (10), 1287–317.

Copeland, R. M. (1968) Income smoothing. *Journal of Accounting Research, Empirical Research in Accounting, Selected Studies*, 6, Supplement, 101–16.

FASB (1997) Statement of Financial Accounting Standard No. 128: Earnings Per Share, Norwalk, CT.

FASB (1997) Statement of Financial Accounting Standard No. 131: Disclosures About Segments of an Enterprise and Related Information, Norwalk, CT.

Fern, R. H., Brown, B., and Dickey, S. W. (1994) An empirical test of politically-motivated income smoothing in the oil refining industry. *Journal of Applied Business Research*, 10(1) Winter, 92.

Griffiths, I. (1986) *Creative Accounting*, Irwin, London.

Griffiths, I. (1995) *New Creative Accounting*, Macmillan.

IASB (1997) International Accounting Standard No. 14: Segment Reporting, London.

IASB (2003) International Accounting Standard No. 33: Earnings Per Share, London.

Lebas, M. (ed.) (1999) *Management Accounting Glossary*, ECM, Paris and CIMA London.

Mathews, M. R., and Perera, M. H. B. (1996) *Accounting Theory and Development*, Nelson – ITPC, Melbourne.

Moore, M. L. (1973) Management changes and discretionary accounting decisions. *Journal of Accounting Research*, (Spring), 100–107.

Ronen, J., and Sadan, S. (1975) Classificatory smoothing: Alternative income models. *Journal of Accounting Research*, (Spring), 133–49.

Smith, A. (2003) *The Wealth of Nations (1776)*, New Edition Bantam Classics, New York.

Smith, T. (1996) *Accounting for Growth – Stripping the Camouflage From Company Accounts*, 2nd edn, Century Business, London.

Stolowy, H., and Breton, G. (2004) Accounts manipulation: A literature review and proposed conceptual framework, *Review of Accounting and Finance*, 3(1), 5–65.

Sutton, T. (2004) *Corporate Financial Accounting and Reporting*, 2nd edn, Financial Times Prentice Hall, London.

Further reading

Alford, A., Jones, J., Leftwich, R., and Zmijewski, M. (1993) The Relative Informativeness of Accounting Disclosures in Different Countries. *Journal of Accounting Research*, 31(Supplement), 183–223.

Cote, J. M., and Latham, C. K. (1999) The merchandising ratio: A comprehensive measure of working capital strategy. *Issues in Accounting Education*, 14(2), 255–67.

Deppe L. (2000) Disclosing disaggregated information. *Journal of Accountancy*, 190(3), 47–52.

Haller, A., and Park, P. (1994) Regulation and practice of segmental reporting in Germany. *European Accounting Review*, 3(3), 563–80.

Haller, A., and Stolowy, H. (1998) Value added in financial accounting: A comparative study of Germany and France. *Advances in International Accounting*, 11, 23–51.

Lainez, J. A., and Callao, S. (2000) The effect of accounting diversity on international financial analysis: empirical evidence. *International Journal of Accounting*, 35(1), 65–83.

Prather-Kinsey, J., and Meek, G. K. (2004) The effect of revised IAS 14 on segment reporting by IAS companies. *European Accounting Review*, 13(2), 213–34.

Prencipe, A. (2004) Proprietary costs and determinants of voluntary segment disclosure: Evidence from Italian listed companies *European Accounting Review*, 13(2), 319–40.

Street D. L., Nichols N. B., and Gray S. J. (2000) Segment disclosures under SFAS No. 131: Has business segment reporting improved? *Accounting Horizons*, 14(3), September, 259–85.

Additional material on the website

Go to http://www.thomsonlearning.co.uk/stolowylebas2 for further information.

The following appendices to this chapter are available on the dedicated website:

Appendix 15.1: Value added
Appendix 15.2: Working capital need in sales days
Appendix 15.3: Complementary remarks on ratios computation
Appendix 15.4: Business newspapers and magazines – specialized magazines
Appendix 15.5: Databases and statistics publications
Appendix 15.6: Filing of financial statements
Appendix 15.7: Scoring models

Notes

1. We distinguish data from information. A piece of data is a fact, a number, a descriptor. It has no specific meaning in and of itself. It is descriptive of something. Information is the result of a process applied to data (comparison with other pieces of data such as the construction of a ratio, calculation of the trend of the evolution over time of a given measure, replacing the piece of data in its historical or competitive context, etc.) that yields (potentially useful) metrics that can effectively be used in a decision model. These useful metrics are called information. Information has the *potential* of leading the decision maker to modify the decision he or she would have taken before the 'new' piece of information was provided. Data do not have such potential.
2. SARS or 'severe acute respiratory syndrome' is a health epidemic that caused a dramatic reduction in air travel within and towards South East Asia during the year 2003.
3. Assumed to be calculated for one year – should a different duration prove to be useful, replace 'year', where appropriate, by 'period'.
4. Current assets include cash.
5. Current liabilities include bank overdrafts.
6. 'Debt' represents long-term and short-term interest-bearing liabilities.
7. Average equity = (Beginning Shareholders' equity + Ending Shareholders' equity)/2.
8. The relevance of extraordinary items in the determination of the income integrated in the EPS computation has been discussed and the practice differs a lot.
9. We take here the meaning of 'earnings quality' to mean that it describes fairly and accurately the situation of the firm. Financial market analysts sometimes use the same expression but, in that case, they refer to the fact the earnings variance is proportionately small, thus that earnings are easily predictable and, most of the time, that the trend of earnings over time is ascending. We limit our analysis here to the formal quality (accurate descriptiveness) of the reported figures.
10. The *beta* (β) is a measure of the risk of the company's shares. It relates the variance of earnings of a company with the average variance of earnings of the market.
11. The Report on the Financial Aspects of Corporate Governance, 1992.
12. Sir Adrian Cadbury: 'Corporate governance: a Framework for Implementation', World Bank.
13. Information Systems Audit and Control Foundation, 2001.
14. 'Governance for young leaders: Understanding corporate governance', March 23, 2004.
15. For a quick introduction to Altman's Z score, see: 'Z scores – a guide to failure prediction', by Gregory J. Eidleman, *The CPA Journal*, February 1995 (The CPA Journal Online).

Companion website

Visit the *Financial Accounting and Reporting* companion website at www.thomsonlearning.co.uk/stolowylebas2 to find valuable teaching and learning material including:

For students

- Appendices for each chapter
- Excel files for selected assignments

For lecturers

- A secure, password-protected site with teaching material
- PowerPoint slides to be used in your lectures
- Multilingual glossary
- Solutions to all assignments as Word files and, when appropriate, as Excel files
- Addional assignments with solutions (Word files and, when appropriate, Excel files)

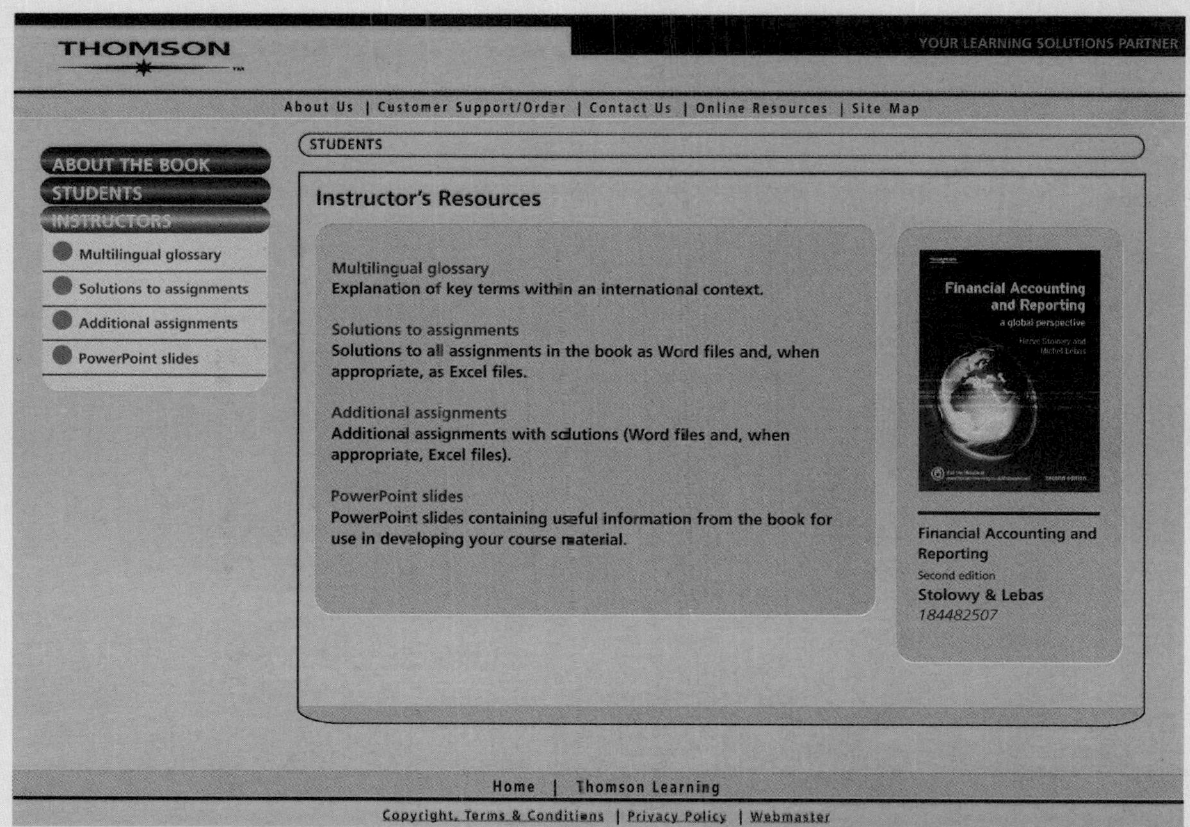

Part 1

Introduction to financial accounting

1 Accounting: The language of business
2 Introduction to financial statements
3 Financial statements presentation
4 The accounting process
5 Accounting principles and end-of-period adjustments

Chapter 1

Accounting: The language of business

Learning objectives

After studying this chapter, you will understand:

- That accounting is a language that helps modeling business activity.
- What accounting, financial accounting, and managerial accounting represent.
- That financial accounting is based on a set of rules and accounting standards, also called financial reporting standards.
- That financial accounting is, in practice, a process.
- That reporting on the financial condition of the firm through financial statements is the end product of this process.
- That different users are interested in financial accounting information.
- The role of the International Accounting Standards Board (IASB) in harmonizing accounting rules and standards between countries to make financial statements more comparable.
- How basic transactions are recorded and impact the financial statements.
- What are the characteristics and roles of each financial statement.
- That accounting, historically, is a very old decision-making tool.

Accounting is inseparable from business and management. In this book on accounting and reporting we will be discussing business issues and decisions by management and investors. 'Accounting is the language of business' is a frequently heard expression. Let us see what is behind what has, by now, become a banal expression.

A model of business activity

Business is about action (transformation of resources) and involves transactions between several people (Robinson Crusoe, alone on his island, may have had undertakings but could not have had a business).

Business involves both suppliers and customers but also a variety of people, each bringing to the business a specialized skill set that will be used in the enterprise's transformation process.

Business is about transforming resources into something else (product or service, tangible or intangible) that will meet a customer's expectation and create 'profit' in doing so. Each skill set provided by individuals or groups of individuals (marketing, R&D, purchasing, manufacturing, selling, hiring, coordinating, managing, measuring, etc.) contributes to the transformation process of resources into making available and delivering effectively a product or service value proposition to a (solvent) customer base.

Business decisions involve how resources will be acquired, allocated to each skill set, and utilized (i.e., transformed) to serve customers. All decisions in an enterprise are therefore built on a *representation* of the transformation process that includes a description of the role of each skill set. Each firm has its own vision of its transformation process (and therefore about its allocation of resources): it is its specific strategy. The strategy of Scania Trucks is, for example, different from that of Volvo Trucks. Both firms try to provide customers with the ability to find the truck that serves their needs as perfectly as possible. They have, however, opted for very different business processes. Scania opted, more than 20 years ago, for a modular design of its products that allows great possibilities for customization while limiting complexity at the manufacturing level, at the expense of a large investment in upfront research for flexibility and compatibility. Meanwhile, Volvo Trucks, having grown largely through external acquisitions, has a rich product offering coming from a much more complex transformation process to create a great diversity of discrete truck models, thus creating a market offering that is about as rich as Scania's. Both enterprises are leaders in their markets and accounting must be able to compare them. Accounting must, therefore, be generic enough to be applicable to a variety of situations and business models.

A generic representation of the activity of any business is shown in Figure 1.1 as the 'cash pump' cycle. In this cycle, resources are transformed into a value proposition, physically 'packaged' in goods or services delivered to customers. These, in turn, exchange cash for said goods and that cash is, in due course, used for the acquisition of additional resources. The 'cash pump' cycle is essentially endless, as long as the enterprise can acquire resources and continues to give satisfaction to customers (at least better than competitors) and receives more cash from customers than it must give to all suppliers (including labor) that allows the transformation cycle to continue to take place.

This cycle needs to be monitored by the managers of the firm. Every transaction (between suppliers and the enterprise or between the enterprise and its customers, but also inside the transformation process) needs to be recorded in order to serve as a basis for analysis over time (for example: does the enterprise need more or fewer resources than during the previous period in order to find a customer?) and comparatively to competitors (does the enterprise require more resources than its competitor to find a reliable supplier of a resource?).

The only way for the various managers and actors in the firm (actors in the 'cash pump') to be able to analyze transactions and take any action required to maintain the competitiveness of the firm is to agree on shared rules for describing transactions so they can communicate with one another. In other words, they need to share a language with is vocabulary, grammar, and syntax to describe events and transactions that need to be examined in order to manage the 'cash pump'. That language is called accounting.

Figure 1.1 The generic business model is an 'cash pump' cycle

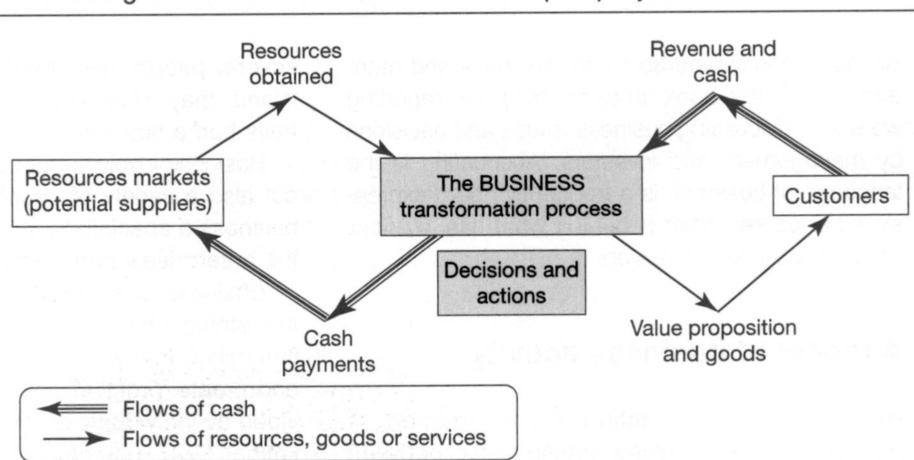

Accounting: A language for business

Accounting is a specialized language that has the specificity of being able to:

- Describe a state or a result (such as: 'the sales revenue obtained from customers in the month of October amounted to 12 million currency units (CU)').
- Describe the events that led to that result (such as: 'An advertising campaign worth 750,000 CU was run on TV in the first week of October; sales increased by 10% between October 1 and October 31; prices were reduced by 5% on October 1 from what they had been since last year; additional customers were acquired, etc.').
- Provide a rank ordering of results allowing evaluators of accounting signals to be able to say 'This result – be it for a time period or for a market or a responsibility center – is better (or worse) than that result'.

Figure 1.1 must, therefore, be amended to show that accounting is needed to support decision making. Figure 1.2 illustrates such amendment.

Accounting records all flows through the 'cash pump' of the business cycle. Accounting records principally economic variables using monetary units. It can, however, also describe non-financial parameters, as in a physical balance of the weight of materials consumed that must be equal to the weight of finished goods plus waste. Accounting is an integral part of the life of business. It is as inseparable from business activity as the shadow is to the illuminated object. Accounting helps managers know what was done so they can modify their future actions in order for the future to yield results that are more coherent with their intent.

However the reader will remember that the title of this book is Financial Accounting and **Reporting.** Why reporting?

Business creates an agency relationship that calls for reporting

Business is about delegation. Delegation from the capital providers to the managers in charge of creating wealth with the capital they were awarded; and delegation within the organization to specialized managers to work in a coordinated and coherent way to create wealth (among other things for capital providers, but also for other participants in the business process). Delegation means control that the devolution and autonomy granted was used appropriately. Control means that information be provided about what the 'delegatee' (or agent) did and what results were achieved. This flow of information, allowing control by the 'delegator' (or principal), is called reporting. Reporting is accounting for what the subordinate or delegatee has done with the resources she or he has received from her or his superior or principal. A 'report' may document effort or results or both. If effort is reported, accounting will be detailed and will provide the values of those parameters needed to describe the business

Figure 1.2 Accounting describes – and is linked to – all parts of the activity of the firm

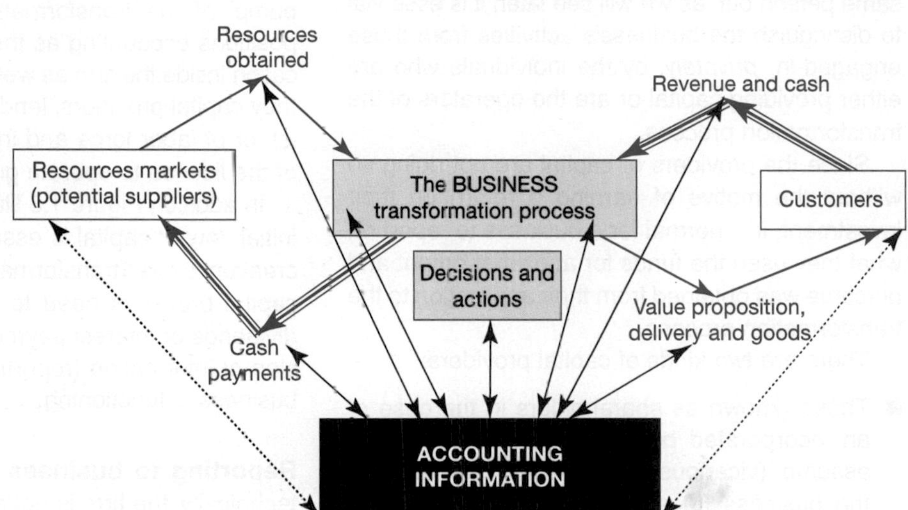

processes transforming resources into a value proposition and its delivery. Reporting on effort will be business specific (we will later call it 'managerial accounting'). If, on the contrary, only results are reported, the report may be generic since the financial information users' questions are essentially the same regardless of the nature of the business (this type of report will be the focus of this text and is part of what we will call 'financial accounting'). The questions (or informational needs) are about: (a) whether the business has created value (i.e., a comparatively positive return on investment, given a certain level of risk) – and will continue to do so – for capital providers (current or potential); and (b) whether the business is viable for the future (this question being of prime importance for employees, customers and suppliers, among many stakeholders[1] in the business).

Reporting to capital providers The 'cash pump' cycle described in Figure 1.1 is not completely operational. Like any pump, this one must be primed. How can the business acquire resources to feed its transformation process unless there is already some cash in the enterprise before it starts to operate? Suppliers might extend credit to prime the pump, but the operating (transformation) cycle might be much longer than the duration of the credit the suppliers are willing to extend.

There must be capital providers who provide initial financial resources that will be used to prime the transformation cycle. The business manager is therefore the agent of the capital provider: she or he has received the mandate to use the capital to earn a positive return within acceptable risk-taking practices. In some cases the entrepreneur/manager and the capital provider might be one and the same person but, as we will see later, it is essential to distinguish the business's activities from those engaged-in, *privately*, by the individuals who are either providing capital or are the operators of the transformation process.

Since the providers of capital are not doing so without the motive of earning a return on their investment, it is normal for a business to report on what they used the funds for and what output and outcome was obtained from their application to the transformation process.

There are two kinds of capital providers:

- Those (known as shareholders in the case of an incorporated business) who are willing to assume (vicariously or directly) the risks of the business (in exchange for a variable but hopefully large return) and who are investing capital for an unspecified term.
- Those (known as lenders) who are not willing to assume much of the risks of the business and want a guaranteed return on their provision of funds within a specified short, medium or long term.

Each category has specific needs in terms of reporting, which the accounting information system will need to satisfy. Lenders are mainly interested in being kept informed about the ability of the business to reimburse the money it has borrowed. The emphasis is therefore on the cash generation potential of the firm.

Shareholders, by way of contrast, are interested in two types of information: on the one hand, from a fiduciary point of view, shareholders want to know periodically what the firm they have invested in owns (and what their share of ownership is) and be sure that appropriate controls are in place to avoid inappropriate disbursement of resources (we call the accounting report that serves this purpose the **balance sheet** or **statement of financial position);** on the other hand, they are interested in knowing how much residual wealth was created in the transformation process that they can claim as theirs (we call the accounting report that serves this purpose the **income statement** or **profit and loss account)**.

In addition, both lenders and capital providers are interested in knowing more about the plans of the business and the dynamics of the evolution of the relevant and specifically defined 'cash pump'.

Figure 1.2 can now be enriched again to recognize the complexity of all processes behind the life of an enterprise. Figure 1.3 illustrates not only a representation of the business cycle (the 'cash pump' of the transformation process), but also positions accounting as the medium of communication inside the firm as well as with its partners, be they capital providers, lenders, suppliers of material, or of labor force and intelligence, or providers of the license to operate granted to the business.

In addition Figure 1.3 illustrates the fact that an initial flow of capital is essential to start the value creation cycle (transformation process) and that capital providers need to be rewarded by either dividends or interest payment, but also by a provision of information (reporting) about how well the business is functioning.

Reporting to business 'partners' Although, technically, the firm is not an agent of employees, customers, or suppliers (the firm has not received a mandate from them), it is normal, if the relationships with these actors are to be durable, that they be kept informed since they are de facto 'partners' in the future success of the firm. All others who need to evaluate the risks of a business and the likelihood of its survival will use, for that purpose, accounting reports that were originally prepared mainly for capital providers. These other users will do so by surmising the business model and looking at tell-tale ratios or metrics describing the 'health' of the 'cash pump' process both in terms of efficiency and relevance, but also in terms of security of provision of funds by capital providers (we call this **financial statement analysis** and Chapter 15 is devoted entirely to such activity).

Reporting to superiors and peers Accounting describes transactions and results of actions and decisions. It is normal (and convenient, since the information already has been captured to satisfy capital providers) that a superior uses accounting information to verify the subordinate discharged her or his responsibility appropriately. If the superior is only interested in results, information in a format similar to the one used to report to capital providers might prove to be sufficient (financial accounting is 'results oriented'), while, if the superior is interested in evaluating the effort of the subordinate, she or he might be interested in the detailed steps undertaken by the subordinate in fulfilling her or his mission. In this case the accounting report will be more process oriented and will be called, as already mentioned, 'managerial accounting'.

Accounting is a living language

As we have seen, accounting describes what actors in the transformation process of the firm do. The process of the 'cash pump' is one of value creation. Business makes sense only if more resources (in the broad sense of the term resources, i.e., financial and non-financial) are created as the outcome of the transformation process than were consumed in its course.

The process of doing business changes over time (the application of the generic 'cash pump' changes continuously). Business relationships are affected by technology. For example, the introduction of the Internet has greatly modified the way the transformation process is organized. Web-based

Figure 1.3 A generic representation of the operations of a business and the role of accounting

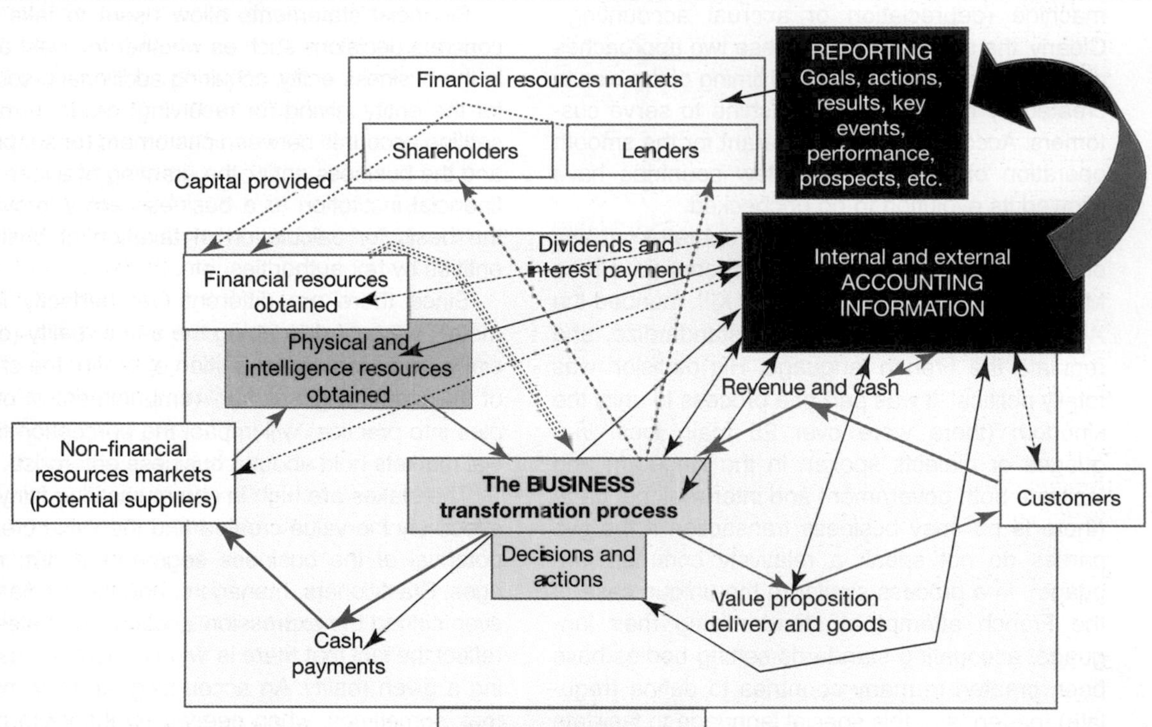

market places and speed of communication change the relationships between enterprises, suppliers, and customers. Similarly, new issues appear with the evolution of society. For example, 75 years ago few businesses paid significant attention to the possible creation of a retirement income for their former employees. New business issues are born every day that accounting must be able to describe. The new description must be an enrichment that is added to previously established modes of description of economic reality. The reality that accounting describes is alive and evolving continuously. The accounting language must therefore be very strong and flexible and rest on solid principles that will allow that flexibility.

Accounting is a language and its 'words' are symbols that reflect a certain view of the world. Just like our everyday language evolves continuously, accounting must be able to adapt to the needs of the time.

Accounting is a very special language in that the way it describes the world of business affects the timing and measurement of wealth creation. Just to give a brief example, when one buys a machine, one could offset the purchase against the revenue generated by the use of the machine during the first year (cash accounting) or one could consider that the machine will be useful to generate sales over several years and therefore one would offset in the first year only a part of the cost of the machine (depreciation or accrual accounting). Clearly, the choice between these two approaches will affect greatly the perceived timing of the wealth created by the use of the machine to serve customers. Accounting is so important for the smooth operation of a society that few countries have allowed its evolution to go unchecked.

Language is essential to the operation of any organized society. Cardinal de Richelieu, Prime Minister to the French King Louis XIII, founded the *Académie Française* to create, standardize, and regulate the French language. His decision was totally political. It was part of a process to unify the kingdom (there were over 25 main local languages or dialects spoken in the kingdom) and facilitate both government and inter-regional trade (there is no easy business transaction if the two parties do not speak a relatively common language). In a process similar to the unique case of the French attempt at standardizing their language, accounting standards-setting bodies have been created in many countries to define (regulate) the terms of this special language to facilitate measurement of wealth creation and therefore open exchanges and facilitate the support financial markets provide to the development of businesses.

Today, regulation of the accounting language is carried out at the global level because businesses trade globally, and also because financial markets span the globe (see later, in 'Core issues').

Accounting is a language with some maneuvering room

Accounting, because of the variety of requirements placed on its applicability and evolution, remains, by necessity, built on very generic principles and leaves some room for customizing the representations it creates to the specific needs of businesses or classes of users of accounting information. The accounting language must be able to describe any business activity. It must allow any user (also defined in 'Core issues') to shape their opinion about an economic entity by looking at the entity's financial statements. These statements are like the 'final product' of the accounting business process.

The users' opinion is built on several aspects of a business entity's potential: financial situation (through the balance sheet), sales performance, and efficiency in its consumption of resources for the generation of sales (through the income statement), and cash generation (through the cash flow statement).

Financial statements allow users to take very concrete decisions such as whether to invest or not in the business entity, acquiring additional resources for the entity, giving (or receiving) credit terms for settling accounts between customers (or suppliers) and the business entity, the granting of a loan by a financial institution to a business entity, providing the basis for calculation of taxation of business entities by tax authorities, etc.

Since there are different (yet perfectly legitimate[2]) ways of describing the same reality (especially the timing of recognition of profit), the choice of an accounting 'solution' (embodiment of principles into practice) will impact the perception financial markets hold about a business enterprise.

The stakes are high in communicating fairly and effectively the value created and the value creation potential of the business segments a firm manages. Practitioners, managers, and the media have even coined the expression 'accounting strategy' to reflect the fact that there is 'wiggle room' in describing a given reality. An accounting strategy means that, sometimes, when needed (in theory to better serve the users), one can alter the accounting representation to achieve better the purpose of communicating at that time. Clearly, that maneuvering space has to be regulated (see 'Core issues'). Although room exists for variations in measurement, timing, and classification of a given reality, over the long run the results are always the same (but the decisions of the users of accounting information may have been affected in the meantime). Some quotes illustrate this point.

> RWE AG, a German company based in Essen, which supplies electricity, gas, and water in Europe and the US, said its 2004 net profit more than doubled, lifted by an accounting change. Most of the gain came from an accounting change, under which RWE no longer has to take systematic goodwill amortization charges. Without that effect, bottom-line growth would have been 11% (adapted from: Joe Flint, *Wall Street Journal Europe*, 25–27 February 2005, p. A4).

Here the change in accounting method was related to the amortization of goodwill (a concept that will be more fully covered in Chapters 8 and 13). In short, goodwill equals the excess amount paid to acquire a firm over the fair value of this firm's net assets. It mainly represents future economic benefits expected from the acquisition (it represents such intangible elements as the value of brands, the location of stores or the remaining duration of their leasehold, the quality of personnel, the pipeline of R&D projects, the opportunities for standardization of product platforms, or the effects of the increased purchasing power of the new entity, etc.). In the past, this difference was 'amortized', i.e., considered 'consumed' over several years, which generated a recurring reduction of income (since the consumption of a resource is an expense that must be offset against the revenue it helped generate). A new rule states that goodwill is no longer automatically amortized, but is subject to an 'impairment' test (has the intangible value acquired been properly managed and maintained or has it 'evaporated'?), which could lead to a reduction (impairment) of the goodwill only if necessary. In the absence of such a reduction, the new rule leads to higher reported income than previously.

> British mining company Rio Tinto's earnings could swing by million of dollars when it issues its first set of results under IFRS later this year. Rio Tinto has operations in Africa, Europe, the Americas, Australasia, and the Pacific rim and is exposed to fluctuations in exchange rates because of its geographic spread and the link between commodity prices and currency values. New reporting standards will change how foreign-exchange gains on debt and derivatives are dealt with, which will have a significant impact on how the mining multinational manages the risk of foreign-exchange variations (adapted from: Nicholas Neveling, *Accountancy Age*, 11 February 2005).

> Smith & Nephew, a British company based in London, has noted that IFRS would take 1.5% off the company's earnings per share figure for the year ending 31 December 2004. The reduction came as a result of accounting for share-based payments under IFRS which took £5.7 m off the bottom line. The company also noted that accounting for the year under IFRS would increase net debt (adapted from: *Accountancy Age*, 11 February 2005).

These two examples illustrate the impact of the implementation of a new International Financial Reporting Standards (IFRS) topic, covered later in this chapter. If the change has a real, but directionally unspecified, impact on the reported income of Rio Tinto, the impact of the same rule is clearly detrimental in the case of Smith & Nephew. This apparent paradox can easily be explained: the set of IFRS is extremely wide. Depending on the topic covered and the firm's circumstances, the impact on individual companies' accounts can vary widely.

These examples also illustrate the fact that accounting is never deterministic. This is why the field has drawn so much interest for so long: within a limited set of rules and principles the language of accounting is there to serve the users by giving the most useful, true, and fair description of a sometimes ambiguous reality (especially when it comes to the timing of the recognition of expenses and revenues).

This chapter's Core issues section defines financial accounting, introduces the various users of financial information, and describes the international accounting standards-setting process as well as some elements of the accounting process.

The Advanced issues section revisits the distinction between reporting issues to shareholders and to third parties (financial accounting) and issues of efficiency in the use of resources (managerial accounting) we briefly touched on in the introduction. This section also emphasizes that accounting is almost as old as human economic activity. We therefore provide a short overview of the history and evolution of accounting over the years. Accounting, being the language of business, is an open language. It can be used to describe different visions of business, just as there are many ways artists can create a portrait of their model.

1 Core issues

1.1 Definition of financial accounting

1.1.1 Accounting

Accounting is about information. To count is to measure and quantify. To account for something is to acknowledge its existence and describe it. Accounting does both: it is a method of counting and a method of accounting for economic parameters describing the life of an enterprise (be it 'for' or 'not-for' profit). Accounting is about providing users with information (i.e., more than just data) about the economic and financial aspects of the life of an enterprise.

Broadly speaking, accounting information is an essential decision-support tool. Most decisions in a business are about resource planning, resource acquisition, and resource allocation in order to fulfill the firm's strategic intent (see, for example Lebas 1999: 54). These decisions are based on financial and non-financial (i.e., operational) information.

Such information is the output of an ongoing process of identifying, capturing, managing, analyzing, interpreting, and distributing data and information describing the economic activity of the firm.

Accounting has two key missions:

- To facilitate value creation by supporting resource acquisition and allocation decision-making. Value can be reduced to economic wealth if one refers only to shareholders who are looking for a financial return on their investment. However, we will keep using the term 'value' because it refers to the broader concept of being 'better off' for a variety of stakeholders whose utility preference functions may not be expressed solely in economic or monetary terms.
- To measure and report to stakeholders the amount of value created during a given period.

Although accounting is a complete discipline, this duality of missions has traditionally led to separating it in two (although closely interactive) subclasses on the basis of the different users who have access to its output:

- The first is called **managerial accounting**. It deals with a rather detailed account of how resources (which may include non-financial resources such as employee or customer loyalty or ability to create a network of resource providers) are acquired, managed, and used in the various business processes constituting the firm and is thus of particular interest to managers inside the firm.
- The second one is called regulated, legacy, or **financial accounting**. It is the focus of this text. It is aimed at reporting, in a somewhat aggregated way, the (economic) performance of the firm to essential external users such as shareholders, bankers, creditors, customers, unions, tax authorities, etc. Financial accounting focuses on the financial or monetary aspects of performance. Since its output will be used by outside investors and stakeholders to allocate their own resources, accounting information is a social good and therefore is generally regulated so that all classes of users receive signals of equivalent significance.

As we will see later, such a distinction between the accounting subclasses is somewhat artificial and often causes debates as to where the frontier should be placed between them.

1.1.2 Financial accounting

Financial accounting is a **process** of description of the various events that take place in the life of a firm. These events are essentially **transactions** between the firm and outside partners (suppliers of resources and customers of the firm's output). The description of each elemental transaction is **materialized** by source documents that contain both financial and non-financial elements to allow a **valuation** of that transaction. These are **recorded**, classified, and **analyzed** so as to allow for the **periodic** creation of synthetic reports called **financial statements.** These generally comprise an income statement, a balance sheet, notes, and, in several countries, a cash flow statement. Financial statements are established periodically and it is traditional to create these synthetic documents at least once every year, generally around a date when sales activity (and, logically, inventories) is the slowest.

The origin of the annual nature of financial statements can probably be traced back to the cycle of nature as it applies to economic undertakings such as hunting or farming. After the harvest was completed, the farmer calculated the amount of wealth created before it could be distributed between the various stakeholders according to the contract binding the partners (owner of the land and provider of the labor force that created the harvest) in such formats as sharecropping (shared risks, alas not always in the fairest of ways), farming (the landowner takes no risk since he or she will receive a rent from the operator of the agricultural business), or salaried labor force (the landowner takes all the business risks). It was traditional to close the 'books' on the harvest, at the end of the production cycle, i.e., at the end of the year. Therefore many countries have retained a preference for a civil 'year-end' closing. However, in businesses such as retail sales, home electronics, toys, or gifts sales, and many more, a civil year-end closing would not make much sense as that is a period of boom. It would be more logical to close (i.e., prepare the synthetic financial statements), for example in February for a toy retailer, when business is slack, inventories are low, and the wealth or value created by the business cycle is pretty well definitively acquired. (A toy retailer expects few returns more than two months after the year-end boom sales.) The topic of the choice of a closing date is developed further in Appendix 1.1.

From the above definition of financial accounting several keywords merit attention:

- **Process**: The method of describing events and transactions and collecting the descriptors is organized by what is called the accounting process. It is a set of rules and practices, supported by dedicated hardware and software, and coordinated by the activities of a variety of people, extending well beyond the staff of the accounting department.
- **Transactions** include such events as the acquisition of resources, selling the firm's output, securing work space through the signing of a lease, payment of the monthly rent, obtaining a loan from a financial institution, etc. Financial accounting only recognizes transactions that have or will have monetary implications, i.e., which will result in an exchange of cash at some point. However, rules that govern financial accounting create certain exceptions such as depreciation in which the cash transaction (acquisition of the fixed assets) takes place before the recognition of the value creation event (recognition of the consumption of the value creation potential of a piece of equipment or an asset) (see Chapters 2 and 7).
- **Materialization of transactions:** Each transaction is materialized by a concrete document (invoice, bank statement, voucher, receipt, etc.). If a transaction is not documented, the accountant cannot recognize it and record it. For example, if a business were to acquire a resource without a corresponding invoice, it would be impossible to record it.
- **Analysis** of transactions consists in defining the category or class they belong to so they may be aggregated into homogeneous classes. This step in the accounting process (described in Chapter 4) is often manual (with the possibility of human errors and inconsistencies). This classification and aggregation tends, however, to be replaced by automated procedures, for example by the definition of bar codes placed on types of documents corresponding to certain transactions, or by linking software such as the accounting recording and invoicing software so that transactions are automatically recorded in the appropriate category.

- **Recording** is generally carried out on a regular periodic basis (most frequently, daily), and in chronological order. This may explain why the record of these transactions is called the **journal** (from the root 'jour' meaning 'day') (see Chapter 4).
- **Valuation** consists in giving a monetary value to the transaction so it can be recorded. It is often easy to place a monetary value when there is an invoice, but often it is more subjective as in the case of an exchange of assets or of the recording in the acquirer's books of the purchase price of an acquired business that is comprised of both physical assets and a loyal clientele.
- **Financial statements** also called 'accounts' or 'annual accounts': They provide a synthesis of the performance of the firm in terms of value creation. The balance sheet describes the 'stock' of resources of the firm and the claims on that stock. The income statement describes how and how much value was created between two 'balance sheet' dates. Notes that explain choices made by the firm and give more details about some transactions and the cash flow statement describe the cash situation, and how it changed during the period.
- **Periodicity** of financial statements has been generally agreed to be at least one calendar year (IAS 1, IASB 2003a: § 49), but these can be established for any shorter period duration, if it is useful for decision makers.

1.2 Users of financial accounting

Financial accounting reflects the economic activity of the firm. Its purpose is to allow users to understand its situation in global and synthetic ways. It produces information for managers as well as for third-party stakeholders. Financial accounting is also often used to document tax obligations and is therefore subject to regulation and control by tax authorities. Creditors expect from financial accounting that it will help them better understand the profitability of the firm as well as its ability to generate cash in the future to repay its lenders. Customers, suppliers, and employees alike look to financial accounting for information about the ongoing nature of the business.

There are many users of financial accounting and they have, by definition, different needs and expectations. The first user of financial accounting information is the firm itself. Managers need to have a synthetic view of their collective performance. It is impossible to create a hierarchy of users. Such rank ordering would be context and culture specific. Figure 1.4 illustrates a generic structure of potential financial accounting users and is not meant to carry any idea of rank ordering.

The diversity of needs of the different users is analyzed in further detail in Table 1.1[3] that illustrates how each class of users may employ financial statements for their own purposes.

While all the information needs of these users cannot conceivably be met by only one set of financial statements, there are needs that are common to all users. As investors are providers of risk capital to the enterprise, the provision of financial statements that meet their needs and expectations will also likely meet many or most of the needs of other users who are interested in estimating risks and potential rewards attached to the operations of a given enterprise (see Conceptual framework, IASB 1989: § 10).

Limited liability companies must periodically file financial statements with a regulatory organization such as the Registrar in the UK, the Commercial Register in Spain, or the Commercial Courts in France (see Appendix 15.6 to Chapter 15). Such filings are required in each European Union member country for the protection of third parties. The European Union reinforced such an obligation by the 1st (9 March 1968) and 4th Directives (25 July 1978). The EU Directive No. 90-605 (8 November 1990) essentially extends to all incorporated businesses, whatever their legal structure, the requirement to file financial statements.

Figure 1.4 A set of financial accounting users

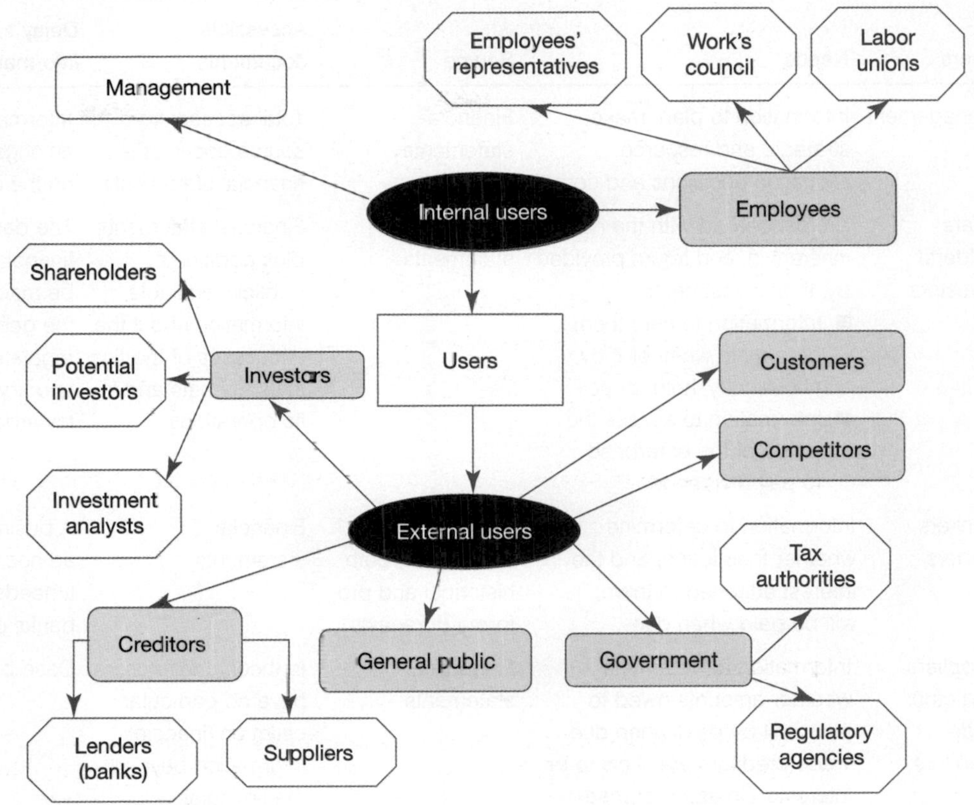

1.3 Financial reporting standards

1.3.1 Necessity of financial reporting standards

The various (and numerous) users of financial statements mentioned in the previous section need to understand financial information is the result of a unique coding of events. For that reason, within each country, local regulations issue **generally accepted accounting principles (GAAP)**[4] that are called **accounting standards** or **financial reporting standards**.

Accounting standards are authoritative statements of how particular types of transactions and other events should be reflected in financial statements. These standards include specific principles, bases, conventions, rules, and practices necessary to prepare the financial statements.

In each country, regulatory bodies (such as the Accounting Standards Board in the UK or the Deutsches Rechnungslegungs Standards Committee – German Accounting Standards Committee – in Germany) and/or the professional accountancy bodies promulgate financial reporting standards. Each national official source of regulation issues pronouncements, which include standards, laws, doctrines, etc.

Because of differences in culture and traditions, taxation policy, sources of financing, importance and recognition of the accounting profession, nature of accounting regulation, etc., there are differences of form and content between the published financial reporting standards of most countries. However, comparability of financial information is a key issue in an international environment. The various users act more and more globally and should be able to understand, and also trust, the financial statements issued in any country of the world. Further, lack of commonly accepted standards can increase the preparation costs for

Table 1.1 Users and their different needs

Users	Needs	Source	Accessible documents	Delay to obtain information
Management	Information to plan, make strategic and resource allocation decisions and control	Financial statements	Total access, from source documents to financial statements	Information is accessible on an ongoing basis. It depends on the organization itself
Shareholders/ Investors	Are concerned with the risk inherent in, and return provided by, their investments: ■ Information to help them determine whether they should buy, hold, or sell ■ Information to assess the ability of the enterprise to pay dividends	Financial statements	Financial statements plus additional publicly available information about the successes of the firm in its markets and in its operations	The date on which the financial statements must be made available before the general assembly is regulated in each and every country. The trend is towards earlier publication
Bankers, lenders	Information to determine whether their loans, and the interest attached to them, will be paid when due	Financial statements, both historical and pro-forma (forecasts)	Financial statements	A business will produce the ad hoc documents whenever it needs to raise funds from banks or on the market
Suppliers and other trade creditors	Information to determine whether amounts owed to them will be paid when due. Trade creditors are likely to be interested in an enterprise over a shorter period than lenders unless they are dependent upon the continuation of the enterprise as a major customer	Financial statements	In theory these users have no particular claim on financial information beyond the financial statements but, by benchmarking and comparative analysis plus an organized intelligence watch, they can interpret financial information in a detailed manner	Case by case
Customers	Information about the going concern nature of an enterprise, especially when they have a long-term involvement with, or are dependent on, the enterprise. Customers are especially interested in evaluating the viability of the firm as an ongoing supplier	Financial statements	Just like suppliers, customers will ask information directly and cross-reference it to be able to have leading signals indicating possible opportunities or problems	Case by case
Competitors	To compare relative performance	Financial statements	Competitive analysis will be the output of large databases of financial statements, cross-referenced with business intelligence and a good understanding of the economic sector	Case by case, as a function of the amount of resources dedicated to information gathering

(*continued*)

Table 1.1 *(continued)*

Users	Needs	Source documents	Accessible information	Delay to obtain information
Employees	Information about the stability and profitability of their employers Information to assess the ability of the enterprise to provide remuneration, retirement benefits, and employment opportunities	Financial statements	Access is regulated through legislation in every country	Case by case moderated by local legislation
Government, regulatory agencies, tax authorities	Are interested in resource allocation and, therefore, want to know about the activities of enterprises. Also use information in decisions to stimulate the economy, and to determine taxation policies and assessments. Also use some or all the information in the calculation of national economic statistics	Financial statements, often recast in a predefined tax-based format possibly following different rules	On a recurring basis the tax-formatted financial statements plus, in the case of a tax audit, access to all source documents	Each country has specific rules. For example, in the UK, most companies are required to pay corporation tax nine months and a day after the end of an accounting period
General public	Enterprises affect members of the public individually and collectively. For example, enterprises may make a substantial contribution to the local economy in many ways, including the number of people they employ and their patronage of local suppliers. Financial statements may assist the public by providing information about the trends and recent developments in the prosperity of the enterprise and the range of its activities	Financial statements	Regulated access	Case by case

financial reports: for instance, a multinational group having to prepare financial statements in multiple countries, and following different accounting standards in each, would incur a much higher cost of preparation (and a possible loss of quality of the aggregate description of the whole business) than would be incurred had there been one single set of standards. The relationship between internal and external reporting would also militate in favor of accounting harmonization. More precisely, an international group having harmonized its internal measures of performance could also want to harmonize its external reporting.

1.3.2 The International Accounting Standards Board

In this context, the International Accounting Standards Board (IASB) is an independent, private sector body, formed in 1973, under the name of International Accounting Standards

Committee (IASC), and restructured in 2001 when the name was changed to IASB. Its main objective is to promote convergence of accounting principles that are used by businesses and other organizations for financial reporting around the world.

Objectives of the IASB The IASB is the standards-setting body of the IASC Foundation. The objectives of the IASC Foundation, as stated in its new constitution (IASB 2005: § 2), are:

(a) 'to develop, in the public interest, a single set of high quality, understandable and enforceable global accounting standards that require high quality, transparent and comparable information in financial statements and other financial reporting to help participants in the world's capital markets and other users make economic decisions;

(b) to promote the use and rigorous application of those standards; and

(c) to bring about convergence of national accounting standards and International Accounting Standards and International Financial Reporting Standards to high quality solutions'.

History of the IASB The confidence crisis which began in 1998 in certain Asian countries and spread to other regions of the world showed the need for reliable and transparent accounting to support sound decision making by investors, lenders, and regulatory authorities. This led to a restructuring process that culminated on 1 April 2001, when the IASB assumed accounting standards-setting responsibilities from its predecessor body, the IASC.

Structure In March 2001, the IASC Foundation, a not-for-profit corporation incorporated in the State of Delaware, USA, was formed and is the parent entity of the IASB, which is based in London, UK. The new structure has the following main features: the IASC Foundation is an independent organization having two main bodies, the Trustees, coming from the accounting and financial community, and the IASB, supplemented by the Standards Advisory Council and the International Financial Reporting Interpretations Committee. The IASC Foundation Trustees appoint the IASB members, exercise oversight, and raise the funds needed, whereas IASB, which consists of 14 individuals (12 full-time members and two part-time members), has sole responsibility for setting accounting standards. The Standards Advisory Council provides a formal vehicle for groups and individuals having diverse geographic and functional backgrounds to give advice to the IASB and, at times, to advise the trustees. The International Financial Reporting Interpretations Committee (IFRIC) assists the IASB in establishing and improving standards. Its role is to provide timely guidance on newly identified financial reporting issues not specifically addressed in the IASB's standards or issues where unsatisfactory or conflicting interpretations have developed, or seem likely to develop.

Figure 1.5 summarizes this structure.

Past international accounting standards In April 2001, the IASB approved that 'all standards and interpretations issued under previous constitutions continue to be applicable unless and until they are amended or withdrawn'. These standards adopted by the IASC are named 'International Accounting Standards' (IAS for one standard – when referring to several standards, some authors use the plural form IASs. But, for the sake of simplification, we will use IAS to refer to one or several standards).

New terminology The IASB also announced in April 2001 that the IASC Foundation trustees have agreed that accounting standards issued by IASB shall be designated 'International Financial Reporting Standards' (IFRS for one standard – or IFRSs in the plural form; for the same reason as mentioned above, we will only use the term IFRS). In the introduction to

Figure 1.5 The IASB Structure (*Source*: adapted from the IASB website, www.iasb.org)

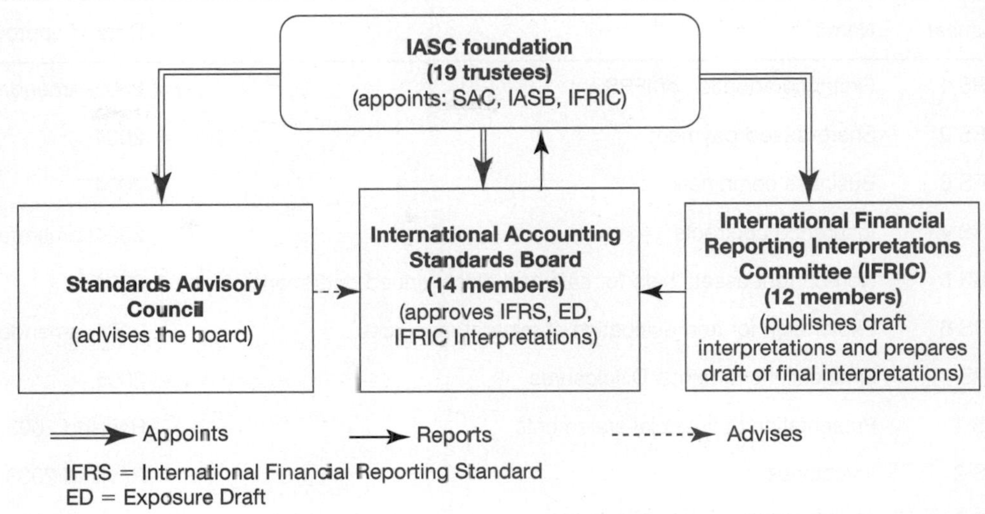

the bound volume of its accounting standards (IASB 2005: 8), the IASB states that 'the term "International Financial Reporting Standards" [in a broad sense, we should add], includes IFRS, IFRIC Interpretations, IAS and SIC [Standing Interpretations Committee, predecessor of the IFRIC] Interpretations'.

It should be noted that the terminology adopted by the European Union texts (see below) is not consistent with that of the IASB. The European regulation 1606/2002 refers to 'International Accounting Standards' to include IAS and IFRS.

Consequently, in order to reduce a possible confusion for the reader, arising from this unfortunate inconsistency, we adopt in this book the following principles: when we mention in a row IFRS and IAS, we make a distinction between IFRS in the strict sense (i.e., standards adopted by the new IASB) and IAS (i.e., standards adopted by the IASC). When we need to mention the set of all accounting standards, we use the term 'IFRS/IAS'.

List of standards Table 1.2 provides a list of the International Financial Reporting Standards and the International Accounting Standards issued as of 30 September 2005.

Implementation of International Financial Reporting (Accounting) Standards (IFRS or IAS) The IASB has no authority to require compliance with its accounting standards. However, many countries already endorsed, require, or recommend IFRS and IAS as their own reporting standards either without amendment, or with minor additions or deletions (as was the case for Armenia, Barbados, Botswana, Croatia, Cyprus, the Czech Republic, Egypt, Georgia, Hungary, Kenya, Latvia, Lesotho, Macedonia, Malta, Nepal, and the Philippines).

Furthermore, important developments have taken place in the world: a European regulation (EC No. 1606/2002) adopted on 19 July 2002 by the European Parliament and published on 11 September 2002, requires the application of 'International Accounting Standards' (i.e., IFRS and IAS) in consolidated financial statements of approximately 7,000 listed companies for each financial year starting on or after 1 January 2005. Australia and Russia have adopted a similar requirement also enforceable in 2005.

The European Union requires the application of IFRS/IAS, but only once these have been endorsed by the European Parliament after a positive recommendation by the European Accounting Regulatory Committee (ARC). So far, the procedure of endorsement has been straightforward, with the major exception of the standard referring to financial instruments,

Table 1.2 List of IFRS and IAS

Number	Name	Date of approval or revision
IFRS 1	First-time adoption of IFRS	2003, amended June 2005
IFRS 2	Share-based payment	2004
IFRS 3	Business combinations	2004
IFRS 4	Insurance contracts	2004, amended August 2005
IFRS 5	Non-current assets held for sale and discontinued operations	2004
IFRS 6	Exploration for and evaluation of mineral resources	2004, amended June 2005
IFRS 7	Financial instruments: Disclosures	2005
IAS 1	Presentation of financial statements	Revised 2003, amended 2005
IAS 2	Inventories	Revised 2003
IAS 3	(Superseded by IAS 27 and 28)	–
IAS 4	(Superseded by IAS 16, 22 and 38)	–
IAS 5	(Superseded by IAS 1)	–
IAS 6	(Superseded by IAS 15)	–
IAS 7	Cash flow statements	Revised 1992
IAS 8	Accounting policies, changes in accounting estimates and errors	Revised 2003
IAS 9	(Superseded by IAS 38)	–
IAS 10	Events after the balance sheet date	Revised 2003
IAS 11	Construction contracts	Revised 2003
IAS 12	Income taxes	Revised 2000
IAS 13	(Superseded by IAS 1)	–
IAS 14	Segment reporting	Revised 1997
IAS 15	(Superseded by IAS 29)	–
IAS 16	Property, plant and equipment	Revised 2003
IAS 17	Leases	Revised 2003
IAS 18	Revenue	1993
IAS 19	Employee benefits	Revised 2002, amended December 2004
IAS 20	Accounting for government grants and disclosure of government assistance	Revised 1994
IAS 21	The effects of changes in foreign exchange rates	Revised 2003
IAS 22	(Superseded by IFRS 3)	–
IAS 23	Borrowing costs	Revised 1993
IAS 24	Related party disclosures	Revised 2003

(*continued*)

Table 1.2 *(continued)*

Number	Name	Date of approval or revision
IAS 25	(Superseded by IAS 39 and 40)	–
IAS 26	Accounting and reporting by retirement benefit plans	1987
IAS 27	Consolidated and separate financial statements	Revised 2003
IAS 28	Investments in associates	Revised 2003
IAS 29	Financial reporting in hyperinflationary economies	1989
IAS 30	Disclosures in the financial statements of banks and similar financial institutions	Revised 1999, superseded by IFRS 7, August 2005, effective 2007
IAS 31	Interests in joint ventures	Revised 2003
IAS 32	Financial instruments: Disclosure and presentation	Revised 2003, partly superseded by IFRS 7, August 2005
IAS 33	Earnings per share	Revised 2003
IAS 34	Interim financial reporting	1998
IAS 35	(Superseded by IFRS 5)	–
IAS 36	Impairment of assets	Revised 2004
IAS 37	Provisions, contingent liabilities and contingent assets	1998
IAS 38	Intangible assets	Revised 2004
IAS 39	Financial instruments: Recognition and measurement	Revised 2004, amended 2005
IAS 40	Investment property	Revised 2003
IAS 41	Agriculture	2001

about which the European Union strongly disagrees with the approach taken by the IASB (see more on this subject in Chapter 13). The resolution of this opposition is currently under negotiation with a likely positive outcome in the near future.

Future impact of IASB The next few years will be crucial for IASB, as its success will depend on the attitude of the stock markets regulators, and, in particular, of the United States' Securities and Exchange Commission (SEC), towards the IFRS/IAS. The SEC is currently working through the International Organization of Securities Commissions (IOSCO), which is the representative body of the world's securities markets regulators[5], with the IASB. The SEC has already accepted use of IFRS/IAS by foreign companies with reconciliation to US GAAP. The major remaining issue to be settled is the following: will the SEC accept the filing in the US of financial statements prepared according to the IFRS/IAS *without* any reconciliation to US GAAP? It seems to be the case as, on 22 April 2005, top officials of the EU Commission and the SEC, meeting in the context of the EU–US Financial Markets Regulatory Dialogue, reached agreement on a 'roadmap' toward equivalence between IFRS/IAS and US GAAP. The roadmap sets out steps the SEC will take to eliminate the need for companies using IFRS/IAS to reconcile to US GAAP possibly as soon as 2007, but no later than 2009.

In parallel to this evolution, the IASB and the FASB (Financial Accounting Standards Board, the US standards-setting body) have developed closer relationships. A common program of revision of several standards has been initiated, leading to a likely convergence of the two sets of standards.

1.4 Introduction to the accounting process

An illustration will show how the need for accounting arises from a simple set of transactions between persons or corporations and how the accounting process is created to monitor and record these transactions.

Let us assume we are at the end of the 15th century in Venice. Mantzaros, a young merchant of Greek origin, wants to become rich and powerful. A quick survey of his environment leads him to the conclusion that the most effective way for him to achieve his objective is to trade with the Orient. His family had endowed him with some 120 gold ducats. In order not to mix his own 'estate' with the risky venture he is considering, Mantzaros, as an individual, creates a separate entity he calls 'Venture Mantzaros' or VM for short. Mantzaros decides to invest 100 of his ducats in this entity (VM). Mantzaros, as the sole investor in this business venture, holds claim to all the profit the venture might create in the future. He is a 100% owner or 'shareholder'.

However, if profit is to be created, this endowment of 100 ducats is not enough to buy and commission a ship to start trading with the Orient. Such an activity would require about 1,000 ducats. Thus, Mantzaros, now as the *manager* of the venture, visits a Florentine banker who agrees to lend the venture the 900 additional ducats it needs for the acquisition and outfitting of a ship. The loan will be for not more than five years and will carry an annual interest rate of 10%. The interest is to be paid in one lump sum on the date of the return of the ship or at the end of the five-year term, when the principal must be reimbursed, whichever comes first.

The venture must record that it has entered into two obligations: it has agreed to refund the money it received from the banker (the principal of the loan) not later than five years from now, and it has agreed to pay an interest charge of 10% a year for as many years as the money will be borrowed. In a blank notebook, let us call it a 'journal', Mantzaros, as manager of VM, records the commitments the venture has made. If VM were to 'take stock' of its wealth at that moment, it would show on one side the cash it holds (the original 100 ducats provided by Mantzaros, the individual, plus the cash received from the banker), and it also would record the debt commitment that, if – and when – the loan were called by the bank, would diminish the wealth of the venture.

Essentially, VM's 'net situation' has evolved this way:

- Situation before the agreement of the banker: Wealth or 'net worth' = 100 ducats.
- Situation after the agreement with the banker: Wealth = 100 ducats plus 900 ducats received minus a debt of 900 ducats = 100 ducats.

Borrowing, in itself, does not create wealth. It is what the money will be used for that, eventually, creates wealth.

The 'wealth account' of the venture at this stage is presented in Table 1.3.

Accounting alone (i.e., recording) does not create wealth[6]. It only keeps track of what the economic entity (here it is the Venture Mantzaros) does with its resources and what claims (here, from the lender and from the investor) exist, at any point in time, on the resources of the business. The owner's (or capitalist's) claim is equal, at any moment, to the net worth of the enterprise, i.e., the sum of the resources minus the claims from the lender(s). Since the venture has done nothing so far to create wealth (there has been neither 'productive transformation' activity nor trading of output with third parties), the claim of Mantzaros, the individual, is still equal to the 100 gold ducats he invested in the business.

Mantzaros (as the manager of VM) then uses the cash resource (1,000 ducats) to buy a good ship, outfit it, staff it, and load its hold with cargo and merchandise that the captain of the ship will trade in the Orient (actually the 'Near Orient' or Middle East, at the Eastern

Table 1.3 VM's 'Wealth account' at step 1

Venture Mantzaros owns		Venture Mantzaros owes	
Cash in hand (100 + 900)	1,000 ducats	Owed to banker	900 ducats
Total	1,000 ducats	Total	900 ducats
		'Net worth' of Venture Mantzaros (conceptually, it is 'owed' by VM to Mantzaros, the individual capitalist)	100 ducats

end of the Mediterranean). Venture Mantzaros' wealth has not changed. Cash has simply been changed into tangible goods. If VM were in a perfect market, whether it holds cash or merchandise should not make any difference. Both are resources that VM, as an economic entity, can and will use to try to create future economic benefits, i.e., wealth.

The VM 'wealth account' after the expedition is about ready to depart reads like Table 1.4.

Since VM owns goods, a ship, and cash worth 1,000 ducats but owes 900 ducats, its net wealth (or net worth) is still 100 ducats. Not only does Table 1.4 show VM's net worth, it also lists all that the venture owns, structured in different classes or categories. Such a document is of great importance for 'controlling' the efforts of the captain (Venture Mantzaros' representative or agent) in his efforts to create more wealth. It can also be used to verify that no pilferage takes place (internal control). At any time, Mantzaros, or someone else, can verify the physical existence of what the venture owns.

The fact that Mantzaros was able to select a good captain, a good crew, and a solid ship is very important: the likelihood of success rests on the quality of the captain and his or her crew. Mantzaros (as an individual) now not only represents the reality of what he owns (he is the sole proprietor of VM), but that ownership now represents a potential profit to come if and when the ship returns and is sold along with its cargo for more than VM owes the banker. His hope and intention is that the captain of his venture will bring back more than just one ship. He has encouraged him or her to behave as a privateer and capture as many 'enemy' ships and place them under his (her) control. Mantzaros is looking forward to the success of the VM expedition.

Table 1.4 'Wealth account' after step 2

Venture Mantzaros owns		Venture Mantzaros owes	
Cash in hand (petty cash)	10 ducats	Owed to banker	900 ducats
Cash in the hands of the captain for sailors' future wages, maintenance of the ship, and trading	150 ducats		
Inventory of food and supplies on board	330 ducats		
Inventory of merchandise to be traded	350 ducats		
Ship and equipment	160 ducats		
Total	1,000 ducats	Total	900 ducats
		'Net worth' of Venture Mantzaros	100 ducats

Mantzaros is expecting it will take four years before the ship can be expected to return, hopefully loaded with more valuable merchandise than it sailed out with. Mantzaros needs resources to live on while the venture runs its course. He realizes that not only has he handed over most of his cash to the venture, but, also, he is not even entirely confident in its success. He wants to obtain more cash to live on (as an individual) and hedge his bet (i.e., diversify his risks). He therefore seeks partners who are willing to share the risks and the returns of his planned 'expedition'. He finds a wealthy friend who agrees Mantzaros has bought a solid ship and hired an excellent and entrepreneurial captain who is likely to return with valuable goods. This friend buys, in exchange for 500 ducats in cash, a half 'share' of the rights and claims Mantzaros (as an individual) holds over the venture: i.e., half of the net worth today, which includes the right to receive 50% of the possible profit realized if and when the ship returns. Essentially, Mantzaros (individual) sold privately a state conditional claim (50% of future profits, whatever they will be) for 500 ducats, thus reducing his own claim on future profits from 100% to 50%.

The wealth of the venture remains at 100 ducats, although the wealth of Mantzaros, the individual, has been modified by his receiving 500 ducats in cash. The fundamental advantage of having created Venture Mantzaros is that the 'shares' (i.e., unit claims on future profits) can be sold privately by 'shareholders'. Such a sale has no impact on the situation of the venture itself. Mantzaros' claim on the future profit of the venture has been reduced to 50% while it used to be 100% before his private transaction with his friend. Mantzaros' personal wealth before the sale of a half of his share was '20 ducats in hand – he had handed over most of his cash wealth to the venture – plus a 100% claim on the profits of the venture'.

His wealth after the private sale of a 50% interest in the venture is now '520 ducats in hand plus an only 50% interest in the future profits of the venture'. Mantzaros traded his rights to 100% of an uncertain reward (future profits) for 500 ducats in hand plus only 50% of the uncertain future reward. He has diversified his risk but reduced the possible high return he would eventually claim from the venture when it is concluded.

The wealth account of VM integrating the fact Mantzaros sold half his personal contingent claim on future profit is summarized in Table 1.5. As the reader can see, the sale of Mantzaros' half-interest in the venture is completely external to the venture itself. It is a private matter between the two partners, both now 'shareholders'. The only element recorded is that if the venture were to be liquidated or earn profit, there are now two equal claimants on the net worth or profit, where there was only one before.

Table 1.5 'Wealth account' of VM after step 3

Venture Mantzaros owns		Venture Mantzaros owes	
Cash in hand	10 ducats	Owed to banker	900 ducats
Cash given to the captain for wages	150 ducats		
Inventory of food and supplies	330 ducats		
Inventory of merchandise to be traded	350 ducats		
Ship and equipment	160 ducats		
Total	1,000 ducats	Total	900 ducats
		'Net worth' of the venture	100 ducats
		Share of 'net worth' held by Mantzaros	50%
		Share held by friend	50%

It can be noticed that the claim held by the 'share' holders is not recorded in the same way as the amount payable to the banker. Although the shareholders (Mantzaros and his friend) certainly hope to recover their capital, it will not be by reimbursement but by sharing in the profit of the venture. Each 'share' holder has a right over the future profits. The 500 ducats the friend paid were part of the net worth of Mantzaros the individual, not part of the venture's net worth. The change in the ownership structure of the venture does not create wealth for the venture[7]. If we were to look at the immediate net worth accruing to each shareholder, it would be half of the net worth of the venture or 50 ducats each. The friend essentially bought from Mantzaros for 500 ducats what is immediately worth only 50 but also includes a claim on future returns to be obtained in the next few years. The friend paid 450 gold ducats more than the 'book value' of what he holds because he thinks future returns will be greater than the 'premium' he paid.

Mantzaros' personal wealth is now 520 ducats plus a claim of only 50% on the future profit of the venture. The venture is a separate entity from Mantzaros as a person. It is essential in accounting to know exactly the perimeter of the economic entity of which one speaks. From now on, we will speak only of the 'venture' as the relevant economic entity. We can record the situation for the 'sailing/trading expedition' by saying it 'owns' physical or tangible resources (or 'assets') in the amount of 1,000 ducats and owes 900 ducats. The net worth of the venture to date (and at any point in the future until the contract between Mantzaros and his partner is ended) is to be distributed half to his partner and half to him. When the ship returns, hopefully within the time frame originally intended, the merchandise the ship (ships) carries (carry) will be sold. Any profit will be calculated after the interest on the loan has been paid to the banker, and any bonuses have been paid to the captain and the crew, etc., i.e., all operating expenses of the venture have been offset against the venture's revenues.

Let us assume that, after only four years, the captain of Venture Mantzaros' expedition brings back three ships, and that the merchandise they hold is sold and brings in 10,008 ducats in cash.

Given the great success of the expedition[8], Mantzaros decides to grant a bonus of 1,000 ducats to the captain and his or her crew, over and above the agreed upon salary of 150 ducats.

The banker also considers the venture a success, and thinks highly of its manager. He/she offers Mantzaros the possibility to extend the term of the loan, at the same interest rate, if he and his shareholder friend decide to continue their business venture, even in another line of trade. The banker therefore accepts that the principal of the loan be repaid at a later date (to be renegotiated and which will be after the end of our story). However, of course, the venture must pay the 418 ducats of interest that have accrued over the four years on the principal of the loan ($900 \times 1.10^4 - 900 = 417.69$, which we choose to round up to 418 ducats for the sake of simplicity). The interest is an expense.

Mantzaros, with the approval of his shareholder friend, decides to continue the venture and not dissolve or liquidate the business. However, the shareholders decide to shift the venture's focus towards a less risky business. They plan to reorient their venture towards agricultural production, a more predictable, although still risky, business. Since the venture no longer needs the ships, the three vessels are sold. This will give Mantzaros, manager of the venture, a very clear vision of the liquidities the venture can invest in acquiring a large farm and its equipments.

The first ship's original value of 160 ducats has been reduced to, say, 100 ducats due to wear and tear. If the venture had continued its activities in the shipping–privateering–trading business, we would need to recognize the loss of value of that ship (i.e., its loss of sailing potential) as an operating expense known as 'depreciation' (amounting, here, to 60 ducats, i.e., the original 160 ducats minus the 100 ducats resale value) and charge it against the revenues in the calculation of the operating profit of the venture. However, since the venture changes completely the nature of its business, the situation can be simplified. We can actually ignore this operating expense since the original ship is sold and we can record an expense of 160 ducats, its original cost, and a revenue of 100 ducats for the sale of the ship. The other two ships are sold for 75 ducats for one and for 125 ducats for the other. Thus, the sale of the three ships brings, in total, 300 ducats in cash.

In order to summarize the elements related to the expedition and its 'final outcome', we prepare Table 1.6, called 'income statement' or report of the business activity.

The positive elements creating wealth are called 'revenues' and the negative ones consuming (destroying) wealth or resources are called 'expenses'. The difference between the revenues and the expenses represents the income generated (or the wealth created) by the business.

The ending cash balance is computed in Table 1.7.

Table 1.7, which displays the determination of the ending cash balance, can be rearranged in the format shown in Table 1.8, distinguishing the three sources and uses of cash: operations, investing, and financing.

Table 1.8 offers an analytical view of the cash flow generation. The net cash flow is divided into three sections: (1) operations (including the interest expense, because the operating cash flow includes all elements related to wealth creation and destruction); (2) investments (here, we have the purchase and sale of the ships); and (3) financing. This table, named 'cash flow statement' will be studied in more details in Chapters 3 and 14.

We can also see the evolution of the 'wealth account' in Table 1.9.

Compared to the original net worth of 100 ducats, the net worth of VM has increased by 7,900 ducats (8,000 − 100). This difference represents the profit of the venture. Since we are not looking at the accounts of the Venture Mantzaros over its complete life cycle, net worth and ending cash balance do not show the same amount. It would be extremely unusual, in the real world, to be able to look at the complete life cycle of any business venture. Most businesses are created in the belief of their ongoing nature, without any specified predetermined liquidation date (a business venture with a specified date of 'birth' and date of 'end' is generally called a campaign or project, not an enterprise). Thus, in

Table 1.6 Report on the activity of the Venture Mantzaros for the four years of its activity

Revenues	
Sales of merchandise	10,008
Sale of the ships*	300
Total revenues	10,308
Expenses	
Wages and expenses (covered by the original cash)	−150
Bonus paid to the captain and crew	−1,000
Consumption of inventory of food and supplies	−330
Consumption of inventory of merchandise to be traded	−350
Interest expense paid to banker	−418
Value of the original ship	−160
Total expenses	−2,408
Income	7,900

*The reader will notice that by counting the original ship at its original cost of 160 ducats in the expenses and for the 100 ducats its sale brings in the revenues, we are, in fact, charging the venture with a depreciation expense equal to 160 − 100 = 60 ducats.

Table 1.7 Ending cash balance

Beginning cash balance (1)	100
Receipts	
Sales of merchandise	10,008
Amount received from the banker	900
Sale of ships	300
Total receipts (2)	11,208
Payments or disbursements	
Different payments (cash for wages, inventory, food, ship)	−990
Payment of bonus to captain and crew	−1,000
Interest expense	−418
Total payments (3)	−2,408
Ending cash balance (1) + (2) + (3)	8,900
Cash flow generated during the period (2) + (3)	8,800

Table 1.8 Cash flow statement

Beginning cash balance (1)	100
Operating cash flows	
Sales of merchandise	10,008
Different payments (cash for wages, inventory, food) (excluding the ship)	−830
Payment of bonus to captain and crew	−1,000
Interest expense	−418
Total operating cash flows (2)	*7,760*
Investing cash flows	
Acquisition of one ship	−160
Sale of ships	300
Total investing cash flows (3)	*140*
Financing cash flows	
Amount received from the banker	900
Total financing cash flows (4)	*900*
Cash flow generated during the period (5) = [(2) + (3) + (4)]	8,800
Ending cash balance (1) + (5)	8,900

Table 1.9 'Wealth account' after step 4 (return of the expedition)

Venture Mantzaros owns		Venture Mantzaros owes	
Cash in hand (see Table 1.7)	8,900 ducats	Owed to banker	900 ducats
Total	8,900 ducats	Total	900 ducats
		Net 'worth' of the venture	8,900 – 900 = 8,000 ducats
		Percentage of the net worth owned by Mantzaros himself	50%
		Percentage of the net worth owned by the shareholder friend	50%

general, and as shown in the Mantzaros example, cash in hand and net worth will never be the same (more on this in Chapters 2 and 3).

The profit earned during the period (7,900 ducats) could be distributed as 'dividends' to the 'shareholders' Mantzaros and his friend (one half to each of any amount not to exceed 7,900 ducats), or retained, in total or in part, in the venture (hence the term of 'retained earnings'). Profit can be retained, partially or completely, in order to finance future operations. Since VM intends to start a new operation in agriculture, the shareholders know that they need to have a significant amount of available funds to acquire a good property. Since VM has the cash in hand, it could avoid having to borrow additional money to finance its growth and development. If we assume that a good farm and its equipment can be bought for about 5,000 ducats, not all the cash would be required for the ongoing business activity, VM could still be able to distribute a significant dividend to its two shareholders without endangering its ability to be a 'going concern'. This way Mantzaros (the individual shareholder) could receive a cash dividend of 1,450 ducats (and his friend the same amount) [(7,900 – 5,000)/2 = 1,450], without endangering the business's capability to prosper. The concepts of profit and retained earnings will be developed in Chapters 2 and 11.

In this short story, we have shown the need to:

- Record the financial position or the condition of an economic entity called the 'venture' (we will call this a balance sheet and we established one at the beginning [see Table 1.3], one at the end [see Table 1.9] and two in between [see Tables 1.4 and 1.5]).
- Acknowledge the business entity as being separate from its shareholders.
- Record the composition of the resources of the business entity at any time.
- Record the sharing of future profit.
- Establish the baseline against which wealth creation will be calculated.
- Establish rules about how wealth created will be calculated before it can be shared.
- Establish a synthetic document recording how much value was created by the economic activity of the venture (the income statement).
- Understand how the captain (a manager or an agent acting on behalf of the two co-owners of the venture) came about to have three fully loaded ships upon her or his return so as to allow Mantzaros (the initiator of this venture and potentially future ventures) to learn about patterns of how the expedition could have been run more efficiently or where additional resources would have facilitated the process of value creation. Looking at a 'journal' in which the captain would have recorded every transaction that took place during the four years of the 'campaign' would be very helpful.

- Provide proof of the success of the business concept to secure, if needed, more funds from bankers or from other potential partners for a continuation or expansion of the venture.

We can also notice that:

- The income of the period and the cash flow of the period are not the same. This situation is not exceptional. It happens because some cash inflows are not revenues. For example, in the case of venture Mantzaros, the loan received from the banker is not a revenue but a debt. Such a situation is common for most businesses as the timing of revenues and costs and of cash inflows and outflows are generally different if one spans a period of a year or less. Most businesses are conceived as 'going concerns', that, theoretically, and if well managed, should never cease their activity. The relationship between profit and cash in an ongoing business will be studied in more details in Chapters 3 and 14.
- The profit computed directly from the activity is equal to the change in net wealth. This situation is no coincidence, as we will show in Chapter 2.

Accounting is the whole process of recording, analyzing, and reporting relevant information, whether with the intention of helping settle the claims at the end of the business venture or for a better understanding (and thus better management of) the business processes leading to value creation.

2 Advanced issues

2.1 Financial accounting and managerial accounting

As mentioned earlier, accounting is separated between financial (external reporting) and managerial (internal) components to reflect the distinction between the users, either mainly external or mainly internal.

Managerial accounting deals with the informational needs of decision makers inside the organization. It therefore deals with complex issues such as detailed business process cost analyses or the diffusion of information inside the firm to create a mobilization of the energies of all members of the personnel and staff. It spans a wide range of fields from cost issues to management of performance, including anticipatory management, motivation, and commitment building, and the analysis of deviations from plans.

Financial accounting and managerial accounting use the same basic information (economic events occurring with the purpose of creating current or future economic benefits) for different purposes. They cannot describe events in different ways. Simply put, financial accounting tends to be a 'recording' of historical events, while managerial accounting uses the same information to forecast future situations through a fine modeling of business processes. In the end, both types of information processing should (and do) lead to the very same *ex post* measure of value created.

Aside from being linked at the beginning (one single basic record of the same event serves as input for both) and at the end (one single income statement), financial and managerial accounting are also linked during the data analysis processes itself in that the costing aspect of managerial accounting, although used primarily for product and customer portfolio management, is also used, by financial accounting, for the valuation of inventories of finished or semi-finished goods and of work in progress. Table 1.10 below presents some key differences between financial accounting and managerial accounting.

Table 1.10 Differences between managerial and financial accounting

	Managerial accounting	Financial accounting
Purpose	Understand how value is created in detail so as to assist internal decisions	Measure the performance of the firm as a whole and report it to external decision makers
Principal users of the output	Managers and decision makers at all levels inside the firm and in a responsibility orientation	Essentially external users who look at the firm as a whole: investors, banks, customers, personnel, etc.
Regulatory context	None, but focus on continuous progress in a philosophy of balancing costs and benefits	Financial accounting information is a social good and is therefore regulated at least by the bodies regulating financial markets, by tax authorities, and by the profession itself in a spirit of true and fair view
Behavioral implications	Aimed at mobilizing energies inside the firm by the distribution of the appropriate information after ad hoc analyses	Does not attempt to influence behavior and even, on the contrary, tries to be as fair as possible to all parties involved
Time frame	Oriented toward anticipation (based on fine modeling of internal and market-linked business processes) and analysis of deviations between anticipated and observed results	An objective record of what was actually realized, thus mainly oriented towards the past but the comparison of periods allows for extrapolation
Time horizon	Flexible and continuous. Information is collected on any time period deemed interesting to the decision maker	Less flexible in that financial statements must be made available at fixed intervals
Orientation	Detailed units of analysis such as: business processes, activities, functions, knowledge sets, markets, customers, products, resources, etc.	A process of systematic aggregation of records of discrete simple and elemental events to create categories of like transactions and create, in the end, financial statements that give a synthetic view of the situation of the firm on a given date
Fineness	Accent is placed on interactions and on the operation of business models	Aggregate and *ex post facto* vision
Frontiers	Defined by the usefulness of the data: importance of commercial, strategic, behavioral, and economic aspects in decision-making aspects. It is totally normal in managerial accounting to extend the analysis beyond the legal borders of the entity	Often defined and constrained by the regulatory and legal context, financial accounting is limited to be within the definition of the legal (or otherwise specified) perimeter of the entity

It is very important to remember that there is only one discipline called accounting. Although each approach deals with a specific angle of analysis, in the end they must be reconciled to give the same figure for the increase in the net worth, i.e., the amount of value created.

Figure 1.6 illustrates how the same data are processed according to two parallel but different approaches. They give, however, the same figure in the end. The types of decisions that are taken on the basis of either approach differ, of course, because of the degree of fineness of both the data and the analysis, which is vastly different between the two approaches.

Figure 1.6 The unity of accounting: different but coherent approaches

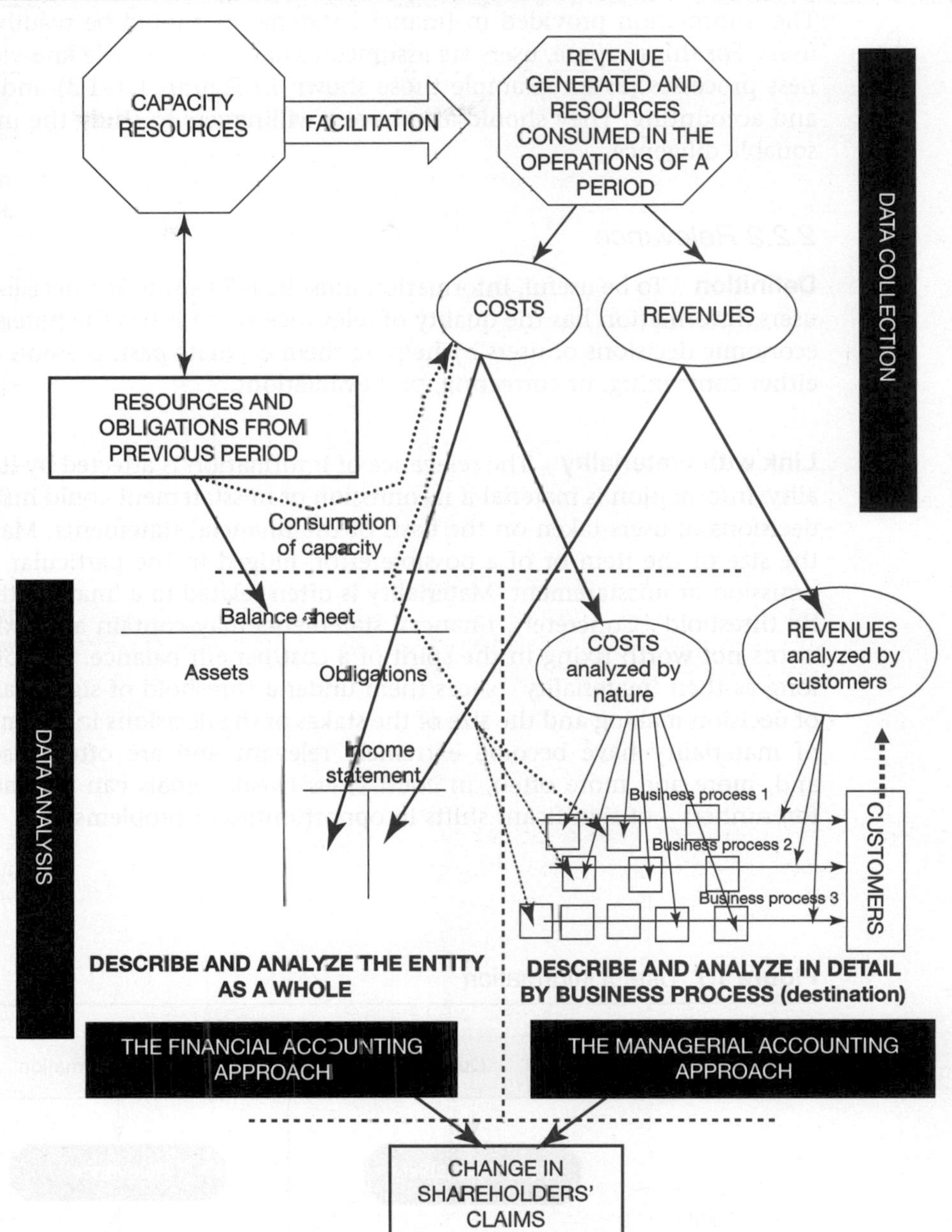

2.2 Qualitative characteristics of useful financial statements

According to the IASB (Conceptual framework, 1989: § 24), the qualitative characteristics of useful financial statements are 'the attributes that make the information provided in financial statements relevant to users'. Figure 1.7 highlights the characteristics of useful financial information and the constraints it must satisfy.

The four principal qualitative characteristics are understandability, relevance, reliability and comparability. They drive a series of principles guiding recording practices that ensure these four characteristics can be met.

2.2.1 Understandability

The information provided in financial statements should be readily understandable by users. For this purpose, users are assumed to have a reasonable knowledge of generic business processes (as for example those shown in Figures 1.1–1.3) and economic activities and accounting. They should also have a willingness to study the information with reasonable diligence.

2.2.2 Relevance

Definition To be useful, information must be relevant to the decision-making process of users. Information has the quality of relevance when it has the potential to influence the economic decisions of users by helping them evaluate past, present, or future events and either confirming, or correcting, past evaluations.

Link with materiality The relevance of information is affected by its nature and materiality. Information is material if its omission or misstatement could influence the economic decisions of users taken on the basis of the financial statements. Materiality depends on the size of the item or of a possible error, judged in the particular circumstances of its omission or misstatement. Materiality is often related to a 'materiality level' or 'materiality threshold'. Concretely, financial statements may contain approximations and minor errors not worth fixing in the spirit of a cost/benefit balance. It is of no consequence as long as their 'materiality' places them under a threshold of significance. With the speed of decision making and the size of the stakes of the decisions in the 'new economy', issues of materiality have become extremely relevant and are often discussed in the press and, more and more often, in court cases (weak signals can be leading indicators – or forerunners – of significant shifts in opportunities or problems).

Figure 1.7 Useful information

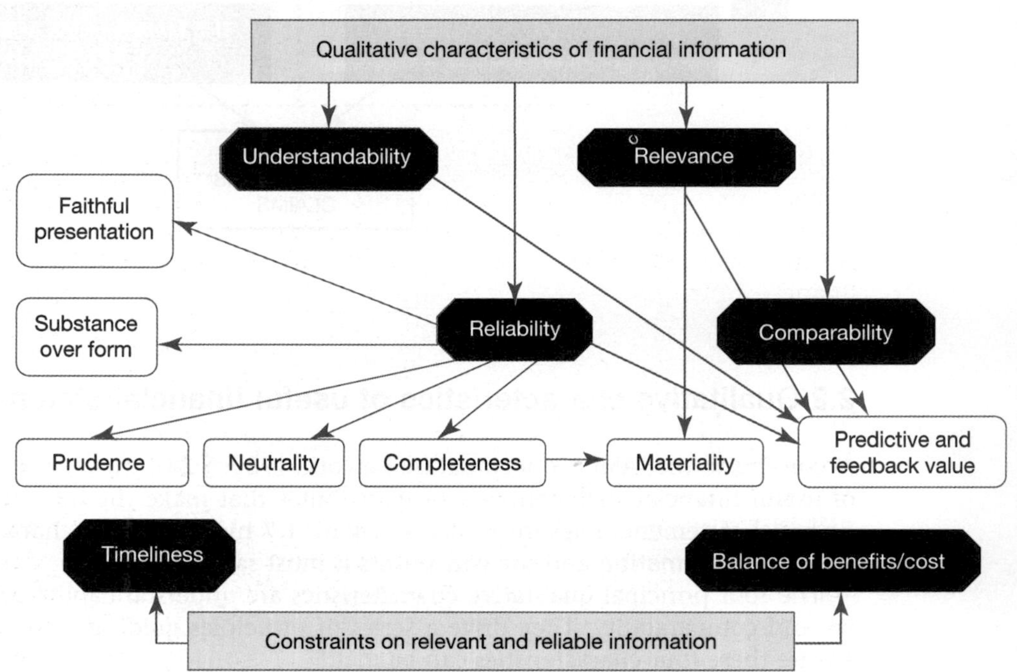

2.2.3 Reliability

To be useful, information should also be 'reliable, in that financial statements:

1. represent faithfully the financial position, financial performance, and cash flows of the entity;
2. reflect the economic substance of transactions, other events and conditions, and not merely the legal form;
3. are neutral, i.e., free from bias;
4. are prudent; and
5. are complete in all material respects' (IAS 8, IASB 2003b: § 10).

These aspects will be developed later in Chapter 5.

2.2.4 Comparability

Users must be able to compare the financial statements of an enterprise through time in order to identify trends in its financial position and performance. Hence, the measurement and display of the financial effect of like transactions and other events must be carried out in a consistent way throughout an enterprise and over time.

Users also would like to be able to compare the financial statements of different enterprises in order to evaluate their relative financial position, performance, and changes in financial position. However, comparability is often in contradiction with the requirement of relevance. The need to choose a common coding process (between firms) for like events may lead to the choice of a 'lowest common denominator', i.e., a very 'coarse' description of events or their consequences through which, in the end, very little is learned. For example, without reporting by segment of business (by types of markets or technology), total revenues measures may be misleading because revenues from a booming, but narrow, market may hide, temporarily, the declining revenues from one larger market that is dying. Total revenues as a signal is difficult to exploit and compare unless more than the bare minimum is reported. If left to their own devices, each management team would probably be inclined to code events in a way they feel gives the 'best' description of the very strategic view they hold of their firm's business processes and results. The debate about the pros and cons of common coding of events and common presentation of accounts between firms is never closed. France, for one, right after World War II, opted for a common presentation and imposed a constraining chart of accounts (see Chapter 4) on all businesses. This is not the case in most of Europe (although Spain and Belgium also have a standardized chart of accounts).

Given that enterprises generally do not follow exactly the same format as other firms in the same sector, there is a need for an informational arbitraging business provided, generally, as a sellable service by analysts, stockbrokers, banks, consulting firms, or semi-governmental agencies that use sophisticated models and additional information to recast financial statements into industry specific formats fitting the business model applicable to any particular industrial sector.

2.2.5 Predictive and feedback value

Accounting information is useful both to account for what was done and for anticipating what decisions will be taken or modified, if any.

It is, therefore, important to remember that the rules and principles such as understandability, relevance, comparability, prudence, neutrality, completeness, materiality, etc. need to be subjected to the filter that, in the end, information is useful only if it helps understand the past (and particularly how agents have discharged their responsibility) and predict the future (by extrapolation or other more sophisticated models).

2.2.6 Constraints on useful information

Timeliness If there is undue delay in the reporting of information, it may lose its relevance. Management may need to balance the relative merits of timely reporting (including the cost of the information technology allowing such timely reporting) and of the provision of reliable information to decision makers. Balancing timeliness and relevance is a day-to-day issue for all businesses. Timely information is expensive, but missing an opportunity may be even more expensive. The issue is therefore: What is best? A piece of information that may be timely but not reliable, or reliable information that may not be timely? Each management team has its set of ad hoc answers.

Benefits/cost relation The benefits derived from information should exceed the cost of providing it.

2.2.7 Balance between qualitative characteristics

In practice, a balancing, or trade-off, between qualitative characteristics is often necessary. Generally, the aim is to achieve an appropriate balance among the characteristics in order to meet the objective of financial statements. The relative importance of the characteristics in different cases is a matter of professional judgment.

2.3 History of accounting: from Sumer to Luca Pacioli

Accounting is not the 'new kid on the block'. Some historians (Colasse 2005: 18) assert that marks found on bones dating as far back as 20,000 or 30,000 years ago were a form of accounting, recording claims of various tribe members on the result of hunting expeditions. Let us see how modern accounting originated from before the time of the Hammurabi Code in the times of ancient Sumer (Hammurabi ruled Babylon from 1795 to 1750 BC) to the founding work of Fra Luca Pacioli (1494) that recorded the accounting practices of Venetian merchants and allowed for the development of modern accounting[9].

2.3.1 Sumerian times

The origins of accounting are often traced to the times of Sumer, in Mesopotamia, starting in the 4th millennium BC. The Sumerian civilization pre-dates that of ancient Egypt by a few centuries. Archeological explorations in the region between the Tigris and Euphrates rivers have unearthed innumerable vestiges of accounting documents recorded on stone or clay tablets. The very fragility of the material was the guarantee of the security of the record because any attempt at falsification would have caused its destruction. The efforts to protect these tablets were commensurate with the likely desire to uphold the contracted commitment and the corresponding counting.

As far back as the 3rd millennium BC, during the Ur Dynasty, accounting entries became both more complex and precise. All features of a modern account were recorded on clay tablets: nature of objects being transacted, names of the parties to the contract, quantities of goods, and their equivalent value in other goods or currency. Some tablets even carry over the balance of the previous period, separate increases from decreases, and also show the end of period balance.

In some cases, rules were discovered that required use of materials such as stone, more sturdy than clay, to record official or sacred accounts or statements. One such example is the Hammurabi Code, which dates back to the 18th century BC. This 'document' reflects societal rules in Babylon. This text, essentially about contracts and family law, contains notions of accounting and management that refer to an agency contract. This implies that the agent keep clear accounts or, more likely, that some specified transactions be recorded in the form of accounts. Accounting, then and since, has always been placed in an agency context: the issue is to define the profit resulting from transactions carried by the agent (manager) in the name of the principal (owner) and provide the basis for sharing it between the principal and the agent.

Surprisingly, this first 'accounting civilization' seems to have rapidly disappeared when the cuneiform language[10] it used was supplanted by the 'more efficient' Aramaic and Phoenician languages and writing techniques.

2.3.2 Accounting in Egypt

Accounting was well developed in ancient Egypt. Scribes had a simplified script (less complex than hieroglyphics) dedicated to home and business economics. They were required to know both arithmetic and bookkeeping. They kept their records on papyrus, a lighter and more flexible medium but more vulnerable than stone or clay tablets. Transactions were registered first in draft form before being recopied carefully in 'definitive' chronological records. From time to time, and at least once a year, chronological records were summarized in synthetic documents. Accounts had all the characteristics of 'universal accounts': name of the account, date, and amount. Receipts were distinguished from disbursements. From 300 BC, Egyptians, who were then part of the Greek cultural universe, adopted the Greek language and practices in banking. These include account-to-account transfers, which are an essential step in the development of modern accounting as it provides a way to add to or subtract from any account without actually going through a cash transaction.

2.3.3 Accounting in Greece

Greek accounting was, as already mentioned, very advanced. Some historians believe that temples were the first organizations to need accounting (and, incidentally, to play the role of bankers). Exactly as was the case in ancient Babylon or in Egypt, offerings to the gods were recorded on marble or limestone tablets. Greek bankers kept thorough accounts. The complexity of the banking network led to the development of accounting control systems, the predecessors of auditing. As far back as 300 BC, Athens had an audit court comprised of 10 'logists'[11] who had the responsibility of controlling accounts. The set of practices, including completeness of records, thorough controls and existence of public records, and accountability, obvious signs of democracy, vanished with its demise.

2.3.4 Accounting in Rome

In Rome, each family (a much broader concept than the nuclear family of the 21st century AD – a family included all parents from all generations plus uncles and aunts and a multitude of servants and slaves) was, in fact, an economic entity with its own production and trading systems. Keeping books was the responsibility of the head of the household (*pater familias*) as it is the responsibility today of a person heading an enterprise. According to Cicero (143–106 BC), who described the set of books kept in his time, the main document was the *Codex Accepti et Expansi* or journal of receipts and payments. Entries were first recorded in a draft before being organized in the *Codex*. The *Codex Rationum* was the permanent document with value of proof. It was the predecessor of what we now call the General Ledger (see Chapter 4). The demise of the Roman civilization caused the disappearance of this body of accounting knowledge.

2.3.5 Accounting in the Middle Ages

Although the so-called Barbarians overran and destroyed the western part of the Roman Empire early on, the eastern part of the empire, including Greece, Constantinople, and the Middle East, remained untouched for a while. The Greek accounting expertise was preserved in the Byzantine Empire. The development of the Arab civilization and its intense trading activity capitalized on the accounting knowledge of the territories it conquered and developed it even further by incorporating refinements derived from mathematics and astronomy.

It is not clear whether the western European merchants learned from their Byzantine and Arab partners or whether they actually rediscovered administrative and accounting practices. The fact is accounting underwent a rebirth in western Europe, mainly in northern Italy, the Netherlands and Flanders as early as the 13th century.

Whether merchants formed large, multi-establishment 'companies' (the predecessors of our multinational corporations), or dealt through mercantile or commissioned agents, they needed rigorous accounting. Accounting recorded the transactions and the wealth created and transferred between establishments. This allowed agents to be accountable for their activity. The development of international trade, of companies, and of agency contracts is the major cause of the re-emergence of accounting in the Middle Ages. This extended period or resurgence has known three sequential phases: memorial, single entry, and double entry bookkeeping.

Memorial The 'memorial' is essentially a journal recording a business entity's transactions on a daily basis without any attempt at regrouping transactions of similar nature. It is essentially the same rudimentary practice that was predominant in early Antiquity.

Single entry bookkeeping Single entry bookkeeping is a significant improvement to the simplistic memorial method. The growing complexity of the operations of medieval merchants led to the partitioning of the memorial into separate accounts of similar nature (such as purchases, payment to labor, sales to a given customer, etc.). Each type of transaction or establishment is recorded in its own coherent table keeping track of all relevant specific events, thus forming an account.

Double entry bookkeeping Double entry bookkeeping marks the birth of modern accounting. Each transaction is recorded by entries in two accounts: one entry 'credits' one account and the other one 'debits' another one. The earliest record of double entry bookkeeping is found in the books of the *Massari* (treasurers of the city state of Genoa) around 1340 AD. However, it is the Franciscan monk, Luca Pacioli, who formalized and extensively described these procedures in his 1494 mathematics text entitled *Summa de arithmetica, geometria, proportioni et proportionalita*. Incidentally, his purpose in inserting a chapter on accounting in his book was not to write a business text, but to illustrate one way of handling the concept of 'zero' which had been lost to western European mathematicians (although not to Arabic ones, but the western European merchants and the Arabic ones were not exactly on 'friendly terms' at the time). In effect, the fundamental equation of accounting 'debits = credits' or 'assets = obligations to outside parties + shareholders' claims' shows that, if this is true, the balance has to be zero, i.e., 'nothing', a very difficult concept to apprehend at the time. It was especially important for accountants to be able to show, for example, a debt had been paid back or extinguished and that the borrower in fact owed 'nothing', but the record of both the debt and its payment should not be lost in the settlement. This was done easily by crediting (reducing) cash and debiting the debt account where the borrower's debt was recorded (i.e., eliminating the debt – since debt and cash are on opposite sides of the financial situation account, the terms debit and credit work in opposite ways). (More on this in Chapter 4.) Modern accounting was born with Luca Pacioli, and this text will deal only with double entry bookkeeping and with the accounting that derives from such practice.

Key points

- Accounting is a language that allows any person interested in the economic life of a business to communicate with others with the same interest about the past, present, and future of the business as an economic entity.
- Broadly speaking, accounting information is an essential decision-support tool. Most decisions in a business are about resource planning, acquisition, and resource allocation in order to fulfill the firm's strategic intent.
- Accounting information is the output of an ongoing process of identifying, capturing, managing, analyzing, interpreting, and distributing data and information describing the economic transactions of the firm.
- Accounting is inseparable from and necessary to any business activity. It allows any user to shape their opinion about the economic aspects of an economic entity by looking at its financial statements.
- Financial statements are the synthetic 'final product' of the accounting business process. These generally include an income statement, a balance sheet, notes (which explain choices made by the firm and provide more detail regarding some complex or critical transactions), and, in several countries, a cash flow statement.
- Financial statements are established periodically and it is traditional to create these synthetic documents at least once every year, generally around a date when the sales activity is the least active in the year.
- The various (and numerous) users of financial statements need to understand the financial information in the same way. For that reason, within each country, local regulations issue generally accepted accounting principles (GAAP) that are called accounting standards or financial reporting standards, which include specific principles, bases, conventions, rules, and practices necessary to prepare the financial statements.
- The International Accounting Standards Board's main objective is to promote convergence of accounting principles that are used by businesses and other organizations for financial reporting around the world.
- Accounting is separated between financial (external reporting) and managerial components to reflect the distinction between the decision needs of users, either mainly external or mainly internal.
- Financial statements relevant to users meet four criteria: understandability, relevance, reliability, and comparability.

Review (solutions are at the back of the book)

Review 1.1 Multiple-choice questions

Related part of the chapter: Core issues

Select the right answer (one possible answer, unless otherwise mentioned).

1. In general, financial statements are comprised of the following documents (several possible answers)
   (a) Balance sheet
   (b) Cash flow statement
   (c) Notes to financial statements
   (d) Income statement
   (e) Value added statement
   (f) Value created statement
2. Only an event with a monetary implication (potential impact on the cash situation) must be recorded in financial accounting
   (a) True
   (b) False
3. Financial accounting offers the great advantage of being completely objective and thus leaves no room for being subjective
   (a) True
   (b) False

4. Bookkeeping is a subset of ...
   (a) Management accounting
   (b) Financial accounting
   (c) Auditing

Review 1.2 Discussion questions

Related part of the chapter: Core/Advanced issues

1. Why do decision makers use accounting information and for what purpose?
2. Why have standards of reporting emerged that constrain the way events are recorded in accounting?
3. What distinguishes financial accounting and reporting, from managerial accounting?

Assignments

Assignment 1.1 Multiple-choice questions

Related part of the chapter: Core issues

Select the right answer (one possible answer, unless otherwise mentioned).

1. The objectives of financial reporting for a business entity are based on which element
   (a) Generally Accepted Accounting Principles.
   (b) The need of users.
   (c) The need for managers to be accountable to owners.
   (d) The principles of prudence and conservatism.
   (e) Tax policies formulated by the tax authorities of the country.

2. Which of the following statements best describes the purpose of financial reporting (Explain why you chose your answer and why you rejected the others)
   (a) Provide a listing of an enterprise's resources and obligations.
   (b) Provide an estimate of future cash flows on the basis of past cash flows.
   (c) Provide an estimate of the market value of the enterprise.
   (d) Provide a fair description of how wealth was created in the past as a basis for estimating future wealth creation.

3. The operating cycle of a business is defined by
   (a) Tax authorities
   (b) Seasons
   (c) The time it takes for cash consumed (or committed) to acquire resources to be returned to cash through sales.
   (d) Each industry trade association.

4. For a manufacturing firm, the choice of reporting date (date at which the books are 'closed' and the balance sheet, income statement and cash flow are established) is based largely on
   (a) Tax constraints
   (b) Time at which the inventory of finished goods is at its lowest.
   (c) The timing of the major vacation period for personnel.
   (d) The availability of time for the accountants.

5. In the following list of qualitative characteristics of accounting data, choose the two that seem to you to be the most important ones (Explain your choice):
   (a) Verifiable
   (b) Fair and true
   (c) Precise
   (d) Relevant
   (e) Unambiguous
   (f) Reliable
   (g) Consistent
   (h) Comparable
   (i) Neutral
   (j) Material
   (k) Conservative
   (l) Timely

6. An accounting datum is considered 'material' if (explain your choice)
   (a) It refers to raw materials.
   (b) It is relevant to the decisions considered.
   (c) It is more than a previously defined percentage of net income.
   (d) It refers to transactions that are critical in the customer-oriented supply chain.

(e) Its nature and magnitude have the potential of changing the decision of a user in a given context.
(f) It is declared to be so by the tax authorities.
(g) It exceeds a previously defined amount.

Assignment 1.2
Discussion questions

Related part of the chapter: Core issues

1. Should managers of a company (i.e., decision makers who are inside the business entity) be considered to be part of the population of 'users' of financial accounting?
2. Are there possible conflicts of interests between the various users of financial information?
3. How can a decision maker obtain a copy of a firm's financial statements if the latter does not make them public (for example, an unlisted business or of a closely held competitor)? Identify concrete examples in a given country.
4. Why are suppliers and customers interested in studying the financial statements of a company?
5. What sources of information on a business' economic situation, other than financial statements, are available to the general public?

Assignment 1.3
Xenakis

Topic: Financial situation
Related part of the chapter: Core issues

Xenakis, a young Greek person, arrives on the first day of summer in Byblos, a Phoenician harbor city. His parents, respectable rich merchants in Athens have sent him on a 'world' journey to discover himself and learn about business. They have given him some material goods and a little money. Xenakis brought these goods and some of the cash to a venture he set up for the purpose of trading. This business venture is called Venture Xenakis.

When he arrives in Byblos for a planned 10-day stay, Venture Xenakis' wealth is as follows:

- Six gold flatware pieces, worth 50 drachmas each;
- 10 crystal glassware pieces, worth 15 drachmas each;
- 102 drachmas in cash (down from the 150 drachmas he left home with – his sea passage had cost him 48 drachmas).

As soon as he sets foot on land, he rents a room at the Cedar Inn. The innkeeper offers full room and board for 10 days for one drachma a day. Once settled in, he goes out looking for the Phoenician merchants his parents have recommended to him. As he ambles along the narrow streets and sunny piazzas, he reminisces about the basic rule his tutor had taught him: 'keep a detailed account of all operations and transactions you engage in'.

Xenakis met a merchant who agreed to buy all of Xenakis' six pieces of golden flatware for 70 drachmas each. Next, Xenakis sold his crystal pieces for 25 drachmas each. He bought a dozen amphorae of assorted spices and he paid 45 drachmas for each. He also bought two pieces of silk fabric for 90 drachmas each. Very happy with his transactions, he bought his return fare to Athens for which he paid 50 drachmas in cash. Feeling a little short of cash to be able to live until his departure in the style he was accustomed to, he asked a Greek friend he had met on the wharf to lend him 10 drachmas. As soon as he was back in Athens he sold all the merchandise he had brought back at the locally accepted prices:

- 60 drachmas per amphora of assorted spices;
- 120 drachmas per silk piece.

Required

1. Describe Venture Xenakis' 'net worth' on the day of his departure from Athens for Byblos.
2. How much cash does the Venture Xenakis have after he sold all his merchandise after his return to Athens?
3. Compute the income generated by the Venture Xenakis on his round trip.
4. Describe the Venture Xenakis' 'net worth' after his return to Athens.

Assignment 1.4
Theodorakis

Topic: Users of financial information
Related part of the chapter: Core issues

Required

Identify at least five classes of users (including at least one non-profit organization) of financial information about a given business (specify clearly the characteristics of the business you chose) and list on what specific aspects of the life of the business (including short and long term if necessary) each class of users might like to be informed. Show whether accounting, as described in the chapter, is likely to satisfy these classes of users. If you feel accounting statements do not provide all the relevant information needed, elaborate on at least three legitimate reasons why accounting information falls short of expectation of this or these classes.

Assignment 1.5
Horn of Abundance

Topic: Users of financial information
Related part of the chapter: Core

The following list contains data or information that might be provided about a business.

1. List of managers and directors.
2. Compensation package of directors and managers.
3. List of major competitors by markets and by product groups.
4. Allocation of responsibility in the business.
5. Age distribution pyramid of employees and managers.
6. Result of labor union elections in the establishments of the business.
7. Social climate in each department of the business.
8. Financial statements (balance sheet, income statement, notes, cash flow statement).
9. Map of the layout of the plant and the warehouse.
10. Location, size, and staffing of all points of sale.
11. Evolution of sales of each key product group over the past three years.
12. Age distribution of products (products still sold launched one, two, or three years ago or more).
13. Number of employees.
14. Distribution of shares ownership (with major shareholders and percentage they own as well as percentage of total shares traded in a normal month).
15. Details of the loans received (amounts and reimbursement schedule).
16. Cost of capital (weighted current average cost of capital).
17. Opportunities for investments in the business and their expected rate of return.
18. Major capital investment projects approved over the last three years.
19. Partition of assets between owned and leased.
20. Percent of completion of investment projects started in the last three years.
21. Outside expert report on the technological and physical obsolescence of assets owned by the business.
22. Details on the incentive plans implemented in this business (including stock options).
23. Evolution of the share price of the business on the Euronext Stock markets over the past three years (including a comparison with other firms in the same economic sector).
24. Description of the sales technology and techniques used in each of the markets in which the products are sold.
25. Amount spent on acquiring new customers and creating demand (marketing, advertising, promotion, and sales expenses).
26. Tax filings for the past three years and amount of taxes still owed.

Cash or liquid assets position.

…escription of key customers with length of relation-…nd evolution of percentage each represents in …s' total sales.

29. Opinion of the senior management team about how they see the future of the firm and its markets.
30. Amounts spend on R&D, structured by types of research.
31. Evolution of the duration of R&D projects until success or abandonment and percentage of successful projects in the last 10 years.
32. Percentage of sales (per product group) carried out in currencies other than that of the home country of the business. Percent of physical volume of sales exported.
33. Existence, details, and status of any court litigation against the business or which the business has originated against others.
34. A summary of the history of the business.
35. By-laws or articles of incorporation.
36. Existence, value, and relevance of proprietary technology owned by the business (own research or purchased?).
37. Percent of total expenses spent on humanitarian or not-for-profit activities (and the list of these activities).
38. Environmental report by an external independent agency evaluating the effect of the business on noise, air, and water quality, as well as the health environment of both workers and citizens in a 10-kilometer radius around the plant.
39. Statistics of the work related injuries and deaths over the past ten years.
40. Partnership agreements with suppliers and customers.
41. List of subsidiaries and affiliates.
42. Percentage of employees (structured by homogeneous classes) connected effectively via a broadband intranet/internet system.

Required

From the list above select the 10 most important items you feel an investor might want to find, for her or his analysis and review, in a business' annual report. Explain why you selected these and rejected the others. Examine whether the items you wish to provide to investors originate in the accounting or in other information systems. If they do not originate in the accounting systems, explain which aspect of accounting regulation or practice may explain why these items have been excluded from the traditional reach of accounting.

Assignment 1.6
Kalomiris Construction

Topic: Useful information
Related part of the chapter: Core issues

Kalomiris Construction, Inc. is a locally very important construction company listed in a regional stock exchange.

Its main market is building single-family homes, either for individuals or for developers. At the end of X2, it announces that the full year's profit will, in all likelihood, exceed that of X1 by a third. It also reports that its net cash has been depleted by 50% from what it was at the beginning of the year.

Required

What information would the following parties be interested in, in the financial statements of Kalomiris Construction for this year and the previous three years, and what actions might they take on the basis of that information?

- current stockholders,
- potential investors,
- creditors,
- customers having a contract with Kalomiris Construction,
- tax authorities,
- bankers,
- regional association of real estate developers,
- national associations of suppliers of lumber and construction materials,
- regional government,
- industrial council (representing all employees of Kalomiris Construction).

Assignment 1.7
Nikopoulos

Topic: Book value versus market value
Related part of the chapter: Core issues

Elisabeth Rossiter, the single proprietor of Nikopoulos, Inc., a successful manufacturer of advanced microchips for computer gaming consoles, is seeking new long-term capital to finance the growth of her business. The net worth of the company to date is 500,000 CU.

Required

You are considering buying a 20% stake in the company. Why might you be willing to offer Elisabeth more than 100,000 CU for such an investment?

References

Chatfield, M., and Vangermersch, R. (eds) (1996) *The History of Accounting, an International Encyclopedia*, Garland Publishing, New York & London.

Colasse, B. (2005) *Comptabilité générale*, 9th edn, Economica, Paris.

Degos, J. G. (1998) *Histoire de la comptabilité, Que-sais-je?* No. 3398, PUF, Paris.

IASB (1989) Framework for the Preparation and Presentation of Financial Statements, London.

IASB (2003a) International Accounting Standard No. 1: Presentation of Financial Statements, London.

IASB (2003b) International Accounting Standard No. 8: Accounting Policies, Changes in Accounting Estimates and Errors, London.

IASB (2005) Constitution in *International Financial Reporting Standards*, (bound volume), London.

Lebas, M. J. (ed) (1999) *Management Accounting Glossary*, ECM, Paris and CIMA, London.

Further reading

Aiken, M., and Lu, W. (1998) The evolution of bookkeeping in China: Integrating historical trends with western influences. *Abacus*, 34(2), 220–42.

Haller, A. (2002) Financial accounting developments in the European union: Past events and future prospects. *European Accounting Review*, 11(1), 153–90.

Murphy, A. B. (2000) Firm characteristics of Swiss companies that utilize international accounting standards, *International Journal of Accounting*, 34(1), 121–31.

Street, D. L., Gray, S. J., and Bryant, S. M. (1999) Acceptance and observance of international accounting standards: An empirical study of companies claiming to comply with IASs. *International Journal of Accounting*, 34(1), 11–48.

Tarca, A. (2004). International convergence of accounting practices: Choosing between IAS and US GAAP. *Journal of International Financial Management and Accounting*, 15(1), 60–91.

Additional material on the website

Go to http://www.thomsonlearning.co.uk/stolowylebas2 for further information.

The following appendix to this chapter is available on the dedicated website:

Appendix 1.1: The reporting period.

Notes

1. Stakeholders are any party that has a 'stake' in the outcome and output resulting from the activity of an enterprise. They include a variety of parties. A far from exhaustive list may include the following stakeholders in addition to the obvious capital providers which, in the western economies, tend to be seen as the major stakeholders (see also Figure
   - Employees whose interest is in the long-term s their employment and/or in the ability for maintain the employability of its person of employment outside the firm as well
   - Customers who want to be certain able to serve them in the future

of security and of efficiency because finding a good supplier is expensive.

- Suppliers whose interest is to have a long-lasting buyer for their output. (It is costly to find a good customer.)
- Health authorities, as the economic activity of the enterprise can impact on the health of employees, of the community surrounding the plants, of the community of users of the output, etc.
- Government authorities who are looking at the effect of the economic activity of the firm on the country's balance of payment (net importer or net exporter) or employment level.
- Social watchdog organizations looking for the enforcement of evolving societal values like 'no child labor' or 'no prisoner labor', 'no discrimination in employment' or sourcing or selling, etc.

2. A German and a North American user may not require that the same reality, for example income, be couched in the same format and terms. The German user of accounting information, coming from a culture where business, banks and labor unions are quite intermingled, may tend to have a long-term view of business and probably would support wholeheartedly an accounting language that would smooth-over peaks and valleys in the reporting and timing of value creation. Her or his North American counterpart, coming from a culture of rapid movement and short-term investment decisions where 'a dollar today is always better than a dollar tomorrow', might, on the other hand, be more short-term minded and might support an accounting language that would be as reactive as possible and would not allow smoothing of good or bad events or news.
3. For *investors, lenders, suppliers, customers, employees, government* and the *general public* the needs listed in Table 1.1 are adapted from the IASB conceptual framework (1989: § 9).
4. The AICPA (American Institute of Certified Public Accountants) in its APB Statement No. 4 Basic Concepts and Accounting Principles Underlying Financial Statements of Business Enterprises (New York, 1970) defines a GAAP as encompassing 'conventions, rules and procedures necessary to define accepted accounting practice at a particular time. It includes not only broad guidelines of general application but also detailed practices and procedures. Those conventions, rules and procedures provide a standard by which to measure financial presentations'. Every country, every culture, or society creates its own GAAP, adapted to its tradition, principles, values, and practices.
5. Members include among others the Australian Securities and Investments Commission, the members of the Canadian Securities Administrators (CSA), the French *Autorité des Marchés Financiers* (AMF), the Italian *Commissione Nazionale per le Società e la Borsa* (CONSOB), the UK's Financial Services Authority (FSA), and the United States Securities and Exchange Commission (SEC).
6. But wealth and wealth creation cannot be measured unless assets, obligations, and transactions are recorded and 'accounts' drawn.
7. Here the capital or endowment of the venture was not modified by the private sale of shares. We will see in Chapter 11 how a business can issue shares and increase its capital.
8. And also because of the honesty of the captain that is attested by an examination of the log or journal he kept of his periodic authorization of payments, trades, and transactions.
9. This section draws heavily, by permission of the author, on Degos (1998). This short abstract is, however, our entire responsibility. The reader can also refer to Chatfield and Vangermersch (1996).
10. Cuneiform refers to a scripture based on a combination of wedge-shaped marks resembling 'little nails', thus its name from the Latin *cuneus* or nail.
11. The 'logists' were selected by random drawing from the 500 members of the *Boulé*, or parliament (50 representatives per tribe) to audit the accounts of the elected city-state officials at the end of their mandate.

C2

Chapter 2
Introduction to financial statements

Learning objectives

After studying this chapter, you will understand:

- That basic financial statements comprise the balance sheet, the income statement, and the notes to both of these (explaining details about assumptions, principles, or figures).
- How these financial statements are defined and constructed.
- That the balance sheet is a representation of the 'business equation', the fundamental building block of accounting.
- That the equilibrium in this equation must always be respected when recording all transactions.
- What double entry accounting is.
- How the income statement is derived from the basic business equation and is interlaced with the balance sheet.
- What the concept of depreciation represents.
- How profit is appropriated, i.e., divided between dividends (distributed) and retained earnings (kept in the business, as a de facto increase in the financial commitment of shareholders).
- How purchases of goods (merchandise, raw materials, and finished products) are recorded.
- How transactions involving inventories are recorded, during the year and at year-end.

We have seen in the previous chapter that **financial statements** are one of the key 'outputs' of the financial accounting process. They form the reporting package and are comprised of several documents:

- The balance sheet, the income statement, and notes to these documents (common to all countries' accounting standards).
- One or more of the following: a cash flow statement (or funds flow statement – developed in Chapters 3 and 14), a statement of retained earnings (developed in Chapter 11), and a statement of changes in equity (required in some, but not all countries – developed in Chapter 11).

This chapter introduces the minimum set of documents: balance sheet, income statement, and their relevant notes. In doing so, we introduce the 'basic business equation' also known as the 'balance sheet equation' or 'accounting equation'. In the 'Advanced issues' section, we introduce important concepts, which are developed in later chapters such as depreciation, profit appropriation, and inventory.

1 Core issues

The 'basic' financial statements are the balance sheet, the income statement, and the notes to financial statements.

1.1 Balance sheet or statement of financial position

As any good sailor knows, any business' manager (captain or pilot) needs to know the ship's position at any given time in order to decide how to allocate resources and create value for its owners (achieve its destination or objective). She or he therefore needs to know what the business' resources are, and what its obligations to third parties are.

The very term **balance sheet** contains a message about its format. It is a set of two lists: resources on one side (also called assets) and obligations to external parties on the other side (liabilities to creditors and the 'net worth', conceptually owed to shareholders or owners). The totals of the two lists, expressed in monetary terms as we have stated in Chapter 1, must be equal or balanced.

In languages other than English, the term used for balance sheet emphasizes more the *status* of the firm's position at a particular point in time than the *balancing* aspect of the statement. For example, *Bilanz* in German or *bilan* in French imply drawing a statement of up-to-date information – rather like a photograph – but the idea of equilibrium between resources and obligations is not explicitly present.

The balance sheet, also called '**statement of financial position**', shows, by offsetting resources and obligations to third parties (i.e., other than shareholders), the 'net worth' of a business at a given point in time. It is the document that allows a netting of what the firm possesses, i.e., its resources to engage in the fulfillment of its 'strategic intent' to create value, and what it owes, i.e., what obligations it has contracted in order to obtain these resources.

The obligation side is generally separated in two parts: the *liabilities* and the *shareholders' equity*. **Liabilities** represent what is owed (with certainty) to third parties that are not participants in the ownership of the business (and therefore are not sharing the risks taken by the business venture). The **equity** (or 'net worth') is what remains when resources (assets) are offset against the external obligations (liabilities). Shareholders' equity represents the obligation the firm has towards its shareholders or, conversely, it is the claim the owners of the business collectively hold over the firm's current 'net worth' and potential future wealth. Each shareholder's claim is proportional to his or her contribution to the capital. Since: (a) the amount of equity is conditional on the success of the business; and (b) the shareholders are committed to supporting the business without any specified deadline, the nature of the shareholders' claim is different from that of lenders. It is, thus, recorded separately.

The business equation or balance sheet equation is therefore as follows:

Resources (or assets) = Obligations to third parties (liabilities) *plus* Equity (shareholders' claim)

or

Assets *minus* liabilities = Net assets = Shareholders' equity (or 'net worth')

We choose to qualify this equation as the 'business equation' rather than calling it 'balance sheet equation' because it anchors accounting in the domain of business modeling, i.e., the identification and reporting of a dynamic set of relationships, flows, and stocks which, when appropriately coordinated, create value for the owners.

The balance sheet is a table that records in detail all resources and all obligations that have definite monetary implications and for which an amount can be determined without ambiguity.

A balance sheet is a snapshot[1] of the status of the financial position of a business entity at a given point in time. It focuses on the composition of its financial position (see Figure 2.1 and Table 2.1).

The list of obligations and resources can be structured either in increasing or decreasing order of liquidity. Although the rank ordering of resources and obligations in terms of relative liquidity does not change anything of substance in the situation of the firm, the behavioral implications may be meaningful in the sense that what appears on the top of a list is often considered, at least in the western world, to be the most important item(s). If the firm wishes to focus the attention of the reader on its potential for future value creation, management may prefer to show buildings, machinery, and inventories on the top of the asset list. If, on the contrary, a business wishes to communicate its ability to pay its short-term obligations, it might choose to present its cash balance and marketable securities at the top of the list of assets.

Continental European tradition tends to favor reporting the 'stock' of assets (long-term resources) first, thus emphasizing the long-term potential; on the other hand, the North American tradition tends to favor reporting first the data that help understand the short-term survival potential of the firm, i.e., resources are listed in decreasing order of liquidity.

In Table 2.1, assets are ordered from least liquid to most liquid ('increasing liquidity'), and liabilities are presented with longer term liabilities first and shorter term last (increasing degree of maturity). Some countries, such as the United States and Canada, use the reverse order (see Table 2.2).

Chapter 3, devoted to financial statements, will explore further the pros and cons of each presentation. At this point, the way the balance sheet is presented is not important. Whatever the order of the various elements, what matters is that both sides be balanced and that the basic business equation be respected. Any imbalance between the two sides

Figure 2.1 Financial position

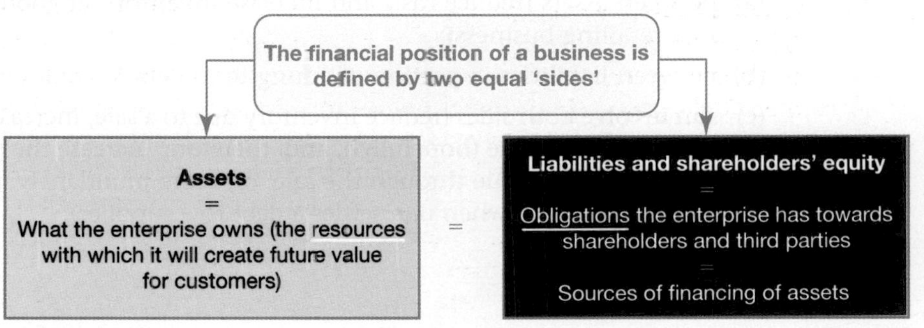

Table 2.1 Balance sheet (continental European presentation)

000 Currency Units or CU[2]			
Assets		**Shareholders' equity and liabilities**	
Land and equipment	200	Shareholders' equity	400
Inventories	150		
Accounts receivable	100		
Cash	50	Liabilities	100
Total	500	Total	500

Table 2.2 Balance sheet (North American presentation)

000 CU			
Assets		**Liabilities and shareholders' equity**	
Cash	50	Liabilities	100
Accounts receivable	100		
Inventories	150		
Land and equipment	200	Shareholders' equity	400
Total	500	Total	500

would mean that the shareholders' equity would need to be adjusted (up or down, reflecting a gain or a loss) until balance is regained.

1.2 The basic business equation or balance sheet equation

1.2.1 Basic principle

Any transaction in a business affects some elements of the balance sheet. Even though the total of each side of the balance sheet may be modified, the net effect of the transaction is that there will always be a perfect balance between the two sides. This principle is part of the very foundation of modern accounting.

Each transaction will impact the basic equation in at least two opposite ways that will keep the equation balanced. This system is known as 'double entry accounting'.

Transactions can take place:

(a) between assets (reduce cash and increase inventory of goods for sale, for example, in a retailing business);
(b) between liabilities (a portion of a long-term debt becomes current or payable); or
(c) can involve both sides (reduce inventory due to a sale, increase in cash for more than the inventory value (hopefully!), and, therefore, increase the shareholders' equity, by the creation of value through the sale, or, more mundanely, reduce cash and reduce accounts payable when one settles a debt to a supplier).

1.2.2 Terminology

Assets An **asset** is a 'resource controlled by an entity as a result of past events and from which future economic benefits are expected to flow to the entity' (Conceptual framework, IASB 1989: § 49).

Liabilities A **liability** is a 'present obligation of the entity arising from past events, the settlement of which is expected to result in an outflow [at an agreed upon date] from the entity of resources embodying economic benefits' (IASB 1989: § 49).

Shareholders' equity *or* equity capital **Equity** is a claim, a right or an interest one has over some 'net worth'. Equity, taken globally, represents the claim of all shareholders. Equity is generally represented by some form of 'shares' indicating how much of the total claim accrues to each of the parties comprising the group of shareholders.

Equity is defined (IASB 1989: § 49) as 'the residual interest in the assets of the entity after deducting all its liabilities':

Assets − Liabilities = Shareholders' equity

Shareholders' equity is itself composed of two components, identical in nature (they represent claims shareholders have over the firm's 'net worth') but not in their origin. They are 'share capital' and 'retained earnings'.

Share capital is the historical value of the contributions to the firm shareholders have made in the beginning and during the life of the firm by making external resources available to the firm and giving up control over these resources (cash, effort or ideas, physical assets, etc.).

Retained earnings (also called **reserves**) represent that part of the value created through the firm's operations that shareholders have chosen not to take out of the firm. It is a de facto increase in their contribution to the ongoing activity of the firm. Unlike share capital, which remains constant until shareholders decide to increase it, retained earnings is an account that fluctuates each period with the accumulation of the results of the operations of the firm (profit or loss) and the decisions of shareholders to withdraw the wealth created in the form of dividends.

Earnings **Revenues** represent 'the gross inflow of economic benefits during the period arising in the course of the ordinary activities of an entity when those inflows result in increases in equity, other than increases relating to contributions from equity participants' (IAS 18, IASB 2003c: § 7). In other terms, revenues are an increase in shareholders' equity that originates from the business of the company such as a sale of goods or services or interest received from short-term investments.

Expenses represent 'decreases in economic benefits during the accounting period in the form of outflows or depletion of assets or incurrence of liabilities that result in decreases in equity, other than those relating to distributions to equity participants' (IASB 1989: § 70). Expenses originate from activities of the firm such as purchase of services, payment of salaries, or remuneration to employees, payment of rent for the use of certain physical facilities, wear and tear on equipment, royalties for the right to use someone else's idea, etc. In other words, expenses result from the consumption of resources, and represent a decrease in shareholders' equity that originates from carrying out the business of the company.

Earnings (or **net income** or **period earnings**) is thus the difference between the resources created by the economic activity of the business (total revenues) and the resources consumed in operating the firm (total expenses). It represents the profit or loss of a period. In essence, earnings are the net increase (profit) or decrease (loss) of the shareholders' equity due to the operations of the business. They describe the value created through the activity of the business. The following equation applies:

Earnings (net income) (period t) = Shareholders' equity (at the end of period t) **minus** Shareholders' equity (at the beginning of period t) (all things being otherwise equal)

The net income is generally calculated in a separate and subsidiary account called 'Income Statement' (in US accounting terms) or 'Profit and Loss Account' (P&L) (in British accounting terms)[3]. This special account or statement will be further developed later in this chapter. The income statement allows managers to follow revenues and expenses separately without measuring changes in shareholders' equity at each transaction. The balance of the income statement (or P&L) is the net income, i.e., the amount that describes the net effect of one period's activity on the shareholders' equity.

1.2.3 Transactions

The operation of the basic business equation is illustrated by looking at several illustrative transactions. As a convention, we have chosen to follow the rank ordering of items on the balance sheet where the most liquid items are listed first, and the least liquid are listed last. It is important to remind the reader at this point that the rank ordering preferences have no impact on the output of accounting. One important element to keep in mind is that the rank ordering preference must apply homogeneously to both assets, on the one hand, and liabilities and equity, on the other.

Transaction 1 – Initial investment by shareholders Stefania, a professional photographer, and her life partner Stefano, a graphic-design artist, decide to create an advertising agency on 1 January X1. The financial resources they wish to invest in their business venture amount to 90 CU. They create their business (company) with a capital contribution of 90 CU. It is agreed between them that Stefania receives 60 shares with a nominal par value of 1 CU (implying she contributed two-thirds of the initial capital), while Stefano receives 30 shares. They choose to name their business venture 'Verdi' and open a bank **account**[4] in that name. Each shareholder deposits the agreed upon amount of cash on the bank account. Once in Verdi's bank account, the funds now belong to neither Stefania nor Stefano. They are now part of the 'net worth' of Verdi. Stefania has a claim of two-thirds over that 'net worth', while Stefano has a claim of one-third. The personal 'net worth' of the 'shareholders' is always (at least conceptually) distinct from that of the business in which they have invested. Various legal structures exist that reinforce the separation of 'net worth' of the entity from that of the individual shareholders – limited liability companies for example – or weaken the separation – individual entrepreneur for example. These will be covered in Chapter 11.

Figure 2.2 illustrates the effect of the company's creation as a separate economic entity on the basic equation.

Figure 2.2 Transaction 1

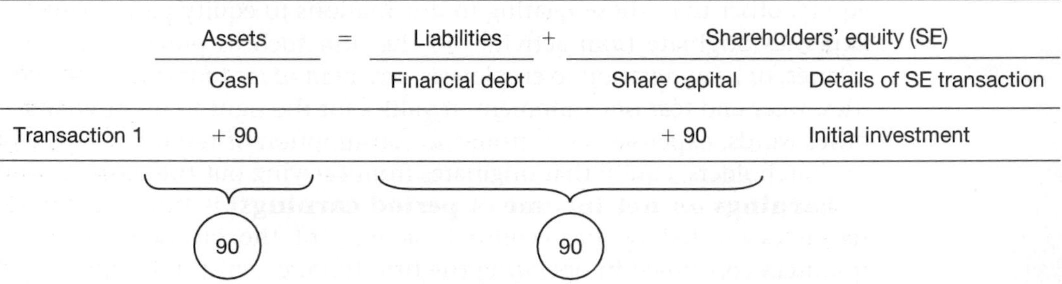

The transaction results in an increase by the same amount (from zero to 90) in both assets and shareholders' equity. Investments by shareholders do not represent revenues and are excluded from the determination of net income. 'Cash' and 'share capital' will eventually have to be set up as individual 'accounts' so as to allow the tracing of the many transactions that will impact on their balance in the normal course of the life of the agency.

The equation is balanced because the 'assets' side equals the 'liabilities plus equity' side. Equity will, in time, and as we will see below in this chapter, become more complex and income will be added to the capital brought initially by shareholders. The shareholders' equity will eventually be equal to share capital plus income from previous years reinvested by shareholders (retained earnings/reserves) plus income of the most recently concluded period.

The net income for the period is zero since, in this transaction, no value or wealth was created (wealth or value is only created through transactions with customers) and no value or wealth was destroyed (value is destroyed by consumption of resources).

Income corresponds to a period of time, while the balance sheet corresponds to an instant in time. Net income is calculated at the end of a period of any duration. Conceptually, income (or change in shareholders' equity) could be calculated for each transaction but it would be very cumbersome to do so. Net income is generally required to be reported to shareholders at least once a year for the previous year, but management and, increasingly, other users and financial markets require more frequent reporting of net income to help managers, users, and investors alike evaluate the performance trend on which a given firm operates. Managers will be interested in adjusting the course of action they have selected, on the basis of the confrontation between expected and observed results and also on the basis of the evolution of the external competitive conditions under which the firm operates. Shareholders, meanwhile, will essentially use the information to review their investment decision.

Transaction 2 – Verdi obtains a loan Early in January X1, Verdi obtains a 60 CU loan from its bank (or from another financial institution – the nature of the lender has no bearing on our accounting for it). The principal of the loan is deposited in Verdi's bank account. The contract specifies the interest shall be paid, at the end of each period, on the remaining principal.

When the business contracts the loan, it actually 'acquires' an obligation to repay 60 CU in the future, and also the obligation to pay interest on the principal outstanding. Since obtaining the loan increases Verdi's external obligations, the record of liabilities will increase by 60 CU (interest is not due until the end of the period, thus only the principal will be recorded). Of course, the counterbalancing event is that the cash balance increased by the same amount. Since we have increased both sides of the equation, the impact on equity is zero. Borrowing in itself does not create nor destroy value or wealth; at least not until we consider the passage of time and the fact we will have to pay interest (paying interest reduces cash or creates another obligation to pay in the future). Interest payable increases the obligations of the firm to a third party (the bank), thus the only way to keep the equation balanced is to reduce shareholders' equity. At the time when interest payable is effectively paid, the reduction of the liability to the bank will be settled by reducing the cash owned by Verdi, and this will not affect shareholders' equity. In other words, interest is an expense as defined earlier. We will not, however, record the interest expense at this stage since we have opted for a chronological sequence of transactions and the interest is not due until the end of the period.

This borrowing transaction will increase both the cash and the liabilities of Verdi Company as recorded in Figure 2.3.

Figure 2.3 Transaction 2

	Assets	=	Liabilities	+	Shareholders' equity (SE)
	Cash		Financial debt		Share capital
Beginning balance	90				90
Transaction 2	+ 60		+ 60		
Ending balance	150	=	60	+	90
	(150)		(150)		

Figure 2.3 shows the cumulative effect of the previous transactions, the specific effect of the current transaction, and the cumulative effect of all transactions. After this transaction, net income is still zero. No value was created by the simple acquisition of additional funding.

Transaction 3 – Purchase of equipment in exchange for liquidity In the first half of January X1 Verdi acquires some equipment (a computer, a color printer, and an art/drawing software program). These resources or assets cost 125 CU in total. The supplier is paid for this purchase with a check drawn on Verdi's bank account.

This equipment will be used in the future to create (or contribute to the creation of) services that will be sold to customers in keeping with the chosen strategy. Such equipment has the potential of creating future streams of revenues (i.e., economic benefits). It is now a resource of the business, i.e., an asset.

An interesting question is the definition of the 'value' at which the resources will be recognized in Verdi's balance sheet. The need to keep the 'business equation' in balance gives us the answer: since the equipment originally cost 125 CU (consumption of another resource, i.e., cash), the assets will be valued at the invoiced price (or cost of acquisition, also known as its historical cost). The substitution of a resource for another does not, in itself, create (or consume) value or wealth: value creation (consumption) happens only when there is increase (decrease) in the equity the shareholders have in the business. Clearly, a resource substitution does not, in itself, create (nor consume) value. Even if the asset substitution modifies the potential of future value creation, the prudence rule calls for ignoring the modification until the use of the new resource actually generates additional resources through the sale of the output of the consumption of the resources.

The acquired equipment increases Verdi's assets by 125 CU and simultaneously, because of the payment to the supplier, the bank account is decreased by 125 CU, and thus the event 'acquisition of a piece of equipment' has the following net effect: (+125) + (−125) = 0, i.e., no effect on total assets nor on equity.

The business has neither gained nor lost wealth or value due to this investment in physical equipment. However, this will not be the case in the future, as two sequences of events will normally take place: (a) a stream of revenues will derive (directly or indirectly) from the sales generated by the use of the equipment, i.e., additional resources will be created; and (b) the equipment will be consumed, i.e., its future ability to create resources will be diminished and thus its value in the list of resources of the firm will have to be decreased. Thus, in the future, the *net* effect of the use of the equipment will be either to create resources – that is to create profit, or to destroy resources – which is called a loss.

In summary, the asset acquisition transaction results in an equal increase and decrease in total assets and does not change the magnitude of total assets, liabilities or shareholders' equity of Verdi Company. Figure 2.4 shows that this transaction only changed the composition of the company's assets by increasing equipment and decreasing cash.

Figure 2.4 Transaction 3

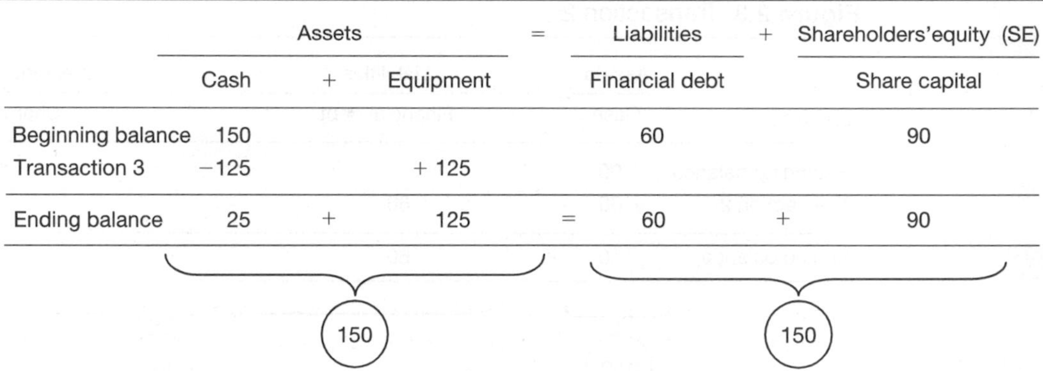

	Assets			=	Liabilities	+	Shareholders'equity (SE)
	Cash	+	Equipment		Financial debt		Share capital
Beginning balance	150				60		90
Transaction 3	−125		+ 125				
Ending balance	25	+	125	=	60	+	90
	150				150		

Transaction 4 – Services rendered Sam Suffit, a retailer, approaches Verdi on 14 January and contracts for an advertising campaign to be carried out in February for his spring season products. After discussion about the content and format of the campaign, Sam Suffit agrees to pay 250 CU for the service Verdi will render. He also agrees to pay the full amount 30 days after he receives the invoice, which will be sent after the advertising campaign has been implemented. Therefore, he agrees to pay the full amount no later than 31 March. Verdi has thus engaged in a transaction that will generate sales revenue of 250 CU, which will be recognizable on 1 March when Verdi invoices Sam (to recognize a revenue – or an expense – is to record it formally and officially in the accounts that will serve in preparing the financial statements). The likelihood that Sam will actually give the promised cash is extremely high and we can anticipate the future cash inflow. Simply, we will recognize the

250 CU sale as 'potential cash' under the name of **accounts receivable**. It is not really cash, but represents a claim on Sam Suffit that Verdi will exercise on 31 March. In fact, such claim could be sold for cash now (at a discount of course, because of the time value of money – see this concept in Chapter 12), just like any other resource.

Since this transaction creates an increase in the resources side of the business equation, there must be a counterbalancing entry, which can either be an increase in the equity component of the 'net worth' (which will be called income) or a reduction in other resources. It could even be a combination of both (as we will see after Transaction 6).

At this stage, in this simplistic example, let us assume, for the time being, there are no costs attached to the actual execution of the advertising campaign. The net effect on the balance sheet is that, on the left-hand side, the claim on the customer (accounts receivable) has increased by 250 CU (increase in assets: the account receivable is a resource that could be exchanged or transformed to create different or more resources) while, on the right-hand side, equity has increased by the same amount (liabilities were not affected).

Revenues increase shareholders' equity. Because the 'sale of services' is not for cash, assets other than cash will increase: this is done through the recognition of the accounts receivable. Revenues are included in the determination of net income (see Figure 2.5).

Figure 2.5 Transaction 4

	Assets			= Liabilities +	Shareholders' equity (SE)		
	Cash +	Equipment +	Accounts receivable	Financial debt	Share + capital	Earnings	Detail of SE transaction
Beginning balance	25	125		60	90		
Transaction 4			250			250	Service revenue
Ending balance	25 +	125 +	250 =	60 +	90 +	250	
	400			400			

To simplify our understanding of the effect of all transactions on equity, one must separate the shareholders' equity in two parts:

(a) 'Share capital', which recognizes the initial amount brought in by the investors (two investors in Verdi's case); and

(b) 'Earnings', which record the net cumulative effect on equity of any and all transactions.

Earnings are, in fact, the property of the owners of the firm (shareholders). If they choose not to withdraw the earnings over which they have a claim, these earnings become 'retained earnings' (i.e., retained in the business to allow it to conserve its resources pool – especially cash – and allow the shareholders to increase their stake in the firm while supporting its ability to grow).

- *Remark 1*: Shareholders' equity increased by 250 CU. Because we have (for the time being) assumed there were no costs attached to the creation of the revenues, the sale is plainly an increase in the shareholders' equity. This is so because the accounts receivable have increased the left-hand side of the balance sheet but there is no counterpart other than 'sales revenue', which is, in fact, a subsidiary account of shareholders' equity (revenues minus costs equals income or increase – or decrease – in shareholders' equity). When net additional resources enter the financial position of the firm without resources being decreased or new obligations created to third parties, value is created.
- *Remark 2*: The balance sheet remains balanced (by recognizing the income the equilibrium is maintained).

- *Remark 3*: The cash position has not been modified because the customer has not paid yet. This sale was on credit, and this fact is reflected in the 'accounts receivable' account. Such an account is clearly an asset (or a resource) since Verdi has a legal claim on Sam Suffit to request payment and can even go to court to collect if Sam Suffit were to fail to pay on the due date.

Transaction 5 – Receipt of cash in settlement of the accounts receivable When Sam Suffit sends a check to pay 180 CU of the 250 CU debt to Verdi, this check is immediately deposited in Verdi's bank account on 31 March. The claim is only partially settled.

As was the case in Transaction 3, this transaction results in an equal increase and decrease in assets and does not change the total assets, liabilities, and shareholders' equity of Verdi Company. It changes the composition of the company's assets by increasing cash and decreasing accounts receivable. However, the accounts receivable transaction related to the transaction between Sam Suffit and Verdi is not entirely completed. The new balances are as shown in Figure 2.6.

Figure 2.6 Transaction 5

	Assets			=	Liabilities	+	Shareholders' equity (SE)	
	Cash +	Equipment +	Accounts receivable		Financial debt		Share capital +	Earnings
Beginning balance	25	125	250		60		90	250
Transaction 5	180		−180					
Ending balance	205 +	125 +	70	=	60	+	90 +	250
	400				400			

As the 180 CU actual payment of the revenue has already been 'earned' (included in Transaction 4), it cannot increase shareholders' equity a second time. The new balance of accounts receivable (here it is 70 CU, since the original balance was 250 CU and the customer paid 180 CU) represents the amount that still remains to be collected.

Transaction 6 – Expenses either in cash or on account In order to carry out the advertising campaign mentioned in Transaction 4, Verdi had to pay wages to employees in the amount of 101 CU, including social contributions and fringe benefits. For the sake of simplicity, we will assume here that the wage cost plus social contributions and fringe benefits are paid in one single operation. This payment will be carried out by writing a check. In addition, the lending institution withdraws at the end of the period the interest accrued which amounts to 4 CU. Lastly, Verdi has received an invoice from a supplier (a subcontracted special effects artist) who worked on specific aspects of the Sam Suffit campaign. The invoice is in the amount of 85 CU and is due within 60 days of receipt.

Services purchased from suppliers, or work realized by employees, are not free of charge. They are the foundation of claims by these parties on the resources of the enterprise. The recognition of these claims creates what we call expenses (i.e., consumption of resources). When the claims will eventually be settled (extinguished), it will be by paying cash. The conclusion of these transactions will reduce Verdi's cash account balance (i.e., reduce resources).

When the claim by a supplier is not settled immediately for cash, it is first recognized under the name of '**accounts payable**' (a debt owed by Verdi) before finally being settled through a transfer of cash, at a later date, in the hands of the creditors – supplier and employee in this case.

For example, Verdi Company has consumed 85 CU worth of resources to acquire and consume external services from a supplier (this consumption is called 'external expenses').

That amount has a direct impact on equity. Even if the invoice were to be paid in two installments, for example of 80 and 5 CU, the way the claim is settled has no impact on equity (see Transaction 7 for details).

When the financial institution lent money to Verdi, it was expecting both repayment of the principal (the nominal amount lent) and the periodic payment of interest on any remaining balance on the loan at scheduled intervals. The **interest** represents the fee for having the right to use the money that belongs to the bank. That 'rental fee' will be settled by giving up (consuming) resources (cash) in favor of the bank. Interest is, therefore, an expense and will be recognized on the agreed upon anniversary dates. This is called a 'financial expense'.

> An expense is the recognition of a consumption of resources creating a claim on current or future cash (with the exception of depreciation, which reflects the consumption of the productive potential of an existing long-term asset already acquired, whether for cash or on credit – see more on depreciation later in this chapter).
>
> An expense is equivalent to a reduction in the equity of the business.

The way the bank's claim is settled (now or later) does not affect the equity of the firm. The interest expense is a reduction in the equity of Verdi, i.e., an expense. However, if Verdi were to repay all or part of the principal of the loan, this transaction would have no impact on equity because there is a simultaneous reduction of cash, on the asset side, and of the debt payable, on the liability side (see Transaction 8 below).

To sum up, any expense (with the exception of depreciation) will eventually be settled in cash. The recognition of an expense causes a reduction in equity in a way symmetrical to the recognition of revenue, which, as we have seen, causes an increase in the equity of the firm (see, for example, Transaction 4). The way the expense is actually settled does not affect equity.

The effect of these transactions on the basic equation is shown in Figure 2.7.

Figure 2.7 Transaction 6

	Assets			=	Liabilities		+	Shareholders' equity (SE)		
	Cash +	Equipment +	Accounts receivable		Accounts + payable	Financial debt		Share + capital	Earnings	Detail of SE transaction
Beginning balance	205	125	70			60		90	250	
Transaction 6	−101								−101	Salaries expense
	−4								−4	Interest expense
					85				−85	External expense
Ending balance	100 +	125 +	70	=	85 +	60 +		90 +	60	
	295				295					

Transaction 7 below shows how the settlement of a delayed claim affects the books. The three types of expenses listed above are completely consumed in the course of Verdi's activity. It confirms the common wisdom that it is generally necessary to consume resources in order to create revenues. (For example, in old Dutch the saying goes: *De cost gaet for de baet* or 'the cost is what "gets" – i.e., drives – the [sales] revenue'.)

Both expenses and revenues affect equity (earnings). It might be interesting to regroup expenses by homogeneous type so as to gain a better understanding of how the business model of the firm actually creates wealth or value. Here, we distinguished expenses by their nature (operational or financial), but we will see in Chapter 3 that they could also usefully be regrouped by function or destination (be it products or services, customers, markets, or even departments). The expense classification is secondary to understanding the impact of the expenses on earnings and shareholders' equity.

Transaction 7 – Settlement of accounts payable Verdi only settles 80 out of the 85 CU supplier's claim (accounts payable) on the due date. The remaining 5 CU will be settled at a later date. The supplier's invoice has been previously recorded (see Transaction 6) as an account payable. This payment will decrease both assets (cash) and liabilities (accounts payable). The effect of this transaction on the equation is illustrated in Figure 2.8.

Figure 2.8 Transaction 7

	Assets						=	Liabilities			+	Shareholdersíequity (SE)		
	Cash	+	Equipment	+	Accounts receivable			Accounts payable	+	Financial debt		Share capital	+	Earnings
Beginning balance	100	+	125	+	70		=	85	+	60	+	90	+	60
Transaction 7	−80							−80						
Ending balance	20	+	125	+	70		=	5	+	60	+	90	+	60
			215								215			

When 80 CU are paid in cash to the supplier, there is simultaneously a reduction of the asset side of the basic equation and a reduction of the claim amount recognized in the accounts payable on the right-hand (liabilities) side. Thus, since both sides are decremented by exactly the same amount there is no impact on equity. The fact that an amount of 5 CU remains unsettled simply means we have to recognize it as a residual claim to be settled in the future.

No value was created nor destroyed by this operation. The impact on equity was already recorded in Transaction 6 and cannot be recorded a second time.

Transaction 8 – Repayment of a debt Verdi partially reimburses the lender by returning 15 CU out of the loan principal of 60 CU:

- The assets side will be reduced by 15 CU (reduction of cash).
- Debt is also, simultaneously, reduced by 15 CU.

By reimbursing part of its debt, Verdi did not create value. It neither gained nor lost wealth! Since the reimbursement affects simultaneously both the assets and liabilities sides by the same amount, there is no impact on equity.

Here we see an important limitation of accounting. Although the statement that Verdi neither gained nor lost wealth is arithmetically (and accounting-wise) perfectly correct, the leverage effect would lead us to think otherwise. Hopefully, the business could have used, as an alternative, the cash represented by the reimbursement to generate a sale activity that might have yielded a return that would have exceeded the interest expense avoided through the early reimbursement of the principal. Thus, if the firm had opportunities that could have yielded more income or earnings than the avoided interest rate on the same amount of resources, it should not have reimbursed the principal early. Reimbursing early, when more profitable alternative uses of cash exist, deprives the shareholders of potential future earnings, therefore making them lose an opportunity to earn more wealth. If, on the contrary, no such opportunity had existed, it was definitely best for the shareholders to have Verdi reimburse the principal on the loan because the interest expense avoided is greater than the earnings that would have been generated through the use of these resources. When no more profitable alternative use of cash exists, early reimbursement of a debt actually avoids future expenses and is therefore equivalent to a future (or potential) creation of wealth. Accounting, however, will not recognize these possible opportunities because they are not known with certainty.

Accounting is essentially prudent and only recognizes or considers elements that are certain and for which the amount is perfectly known, i.e., that are historical (or contractually defined) or not set in an uncertain (state conditional) future.

Transaction 8 is very close in nature to the previous one: decrease in assets (cash) and decrease in liabilities (financial debt). Figure 2.9 illustrates the effect of this transaction on the business equation.

Figure 2.9 Transaction 8

	Assets					=	Liabilities			+	Shareholders' equity (SE)		
	Cash	+	Equipment	+	Accounts receivable		Accounts payable	+	Financial debt		Share capital	+	Retained earnings
Beginning balance	20	+	125	+	70	=	5	+	60	+	90	+	60
Transaction 8	−15								−15				
Ending balance	5	+	125	+	70	=	5	+	45	+	90	+	60
	200						200						

Summary A summary of the eight transactions affecting Verdi Company is presented in Figure 2.10.

Figure 2.10 Summary table

Transaction	Cash	+ Equipment	+ Accounts receivable	= Accounts payable	+ Financial debt	+ Share capital	+ Earnings	Detail of SE transaction
	Assets			Liabilities		Shareholders' equity (SE)		
1	+90					+ 90		Initial investment
2	+60				+60			
3	−125	+125						
4			+250				+250	Service revenue
5	+180		−180					
6	−101						−101	Salaries expense
	−4						−4	Interest expense
6				85			−85	External expense
7	−80			−80				
8	−15				−15			
Ending balance	5 +	125 +	70 =	5 +	45 +	90 +	60	
	200			200				

After all these transactions have been recorded, the synthetic financial position account (the balance sheet) appears as shown in Table 2.3.

Conclusion – some key points The previous transactions illustrate the following points.

1. *Both sides of the business equation must always be balanced with one another.*
2. *Each transaction must be analyzed specifically to identify its possible impact on shareholders' equity.*

Table 2.3 Balance sheet on 30 April X1

Assets			Equity and liabilities		
Fixed assets			**Shareholders' equity**		150
Equipment	125		Capital	90	
			Earnings (net income)	60	
Current assets			**Liabilities**		
Accounts receivable	70		Financial debt		45
Cash at bank	5		Accounts payable		5
Total assets	200		**Total equity and liabilities**		200

3. *The end result of all transactions that create or consume value (i.e., create profit or loss) ultimately impacts the 'retained earnings' account, a subsidiary account of shareholders' equity in a way that can be described by the following formula:*

(Beginning retained earnings balance) + (Profit or loss from the period) − (Dividends) = (Ending retained earnings balance)

In our example, since there have been no dividends paid, the change in the amount of the retained earnings at the end of a period is equal to the net income of that period (here, it is +60).

Since income belongs to the shareholders, part or all of it can be distributed in the form of dividends. Income (or loss) for a period is only reflective of what happened during that period. If the shareholders decide to withdraw some of the wealth created (either this period or during previous periods), it is their right and therefore the ending balance of the earnings retained in any balance sheet (accumulating in the retained earnings account) is given by the formula above.

The **retained earnings** account (also called **reserves**) reflects the cumulated effect of the earnings the shareholders have chosen not to withdraw from the business.

4. *What creates income?*

There was no income (impact on shareholders' equity) until Transaction 4 (sale of services). This transaction was the first operation in our illustrative sequence that created profit (i.e., affected positively the shareholders' equity) and therefore, ultimately, affected the retained earnings account. Any transaction that affects either assets and/or liabilities (excluding shareholders' equity, of course) in uneven or unbalanced ways affects earnings (the balance of all transactions is what we call net income). Any transaction that only affects assets and/or liabilities in even or balanced ways is not a source of value creation. Only transactions with outside customers are susceptible to create revenues, and transactions with outside customers always require the consumption of resources, i.e., consume or destroy 'value'.

Income is the difference between the value created in customer-based transactions and the value destroyed by consuming resources to serve customers.

5. *Net income is different from cash*

Since our example only looked at the first period of existence of Verdi, and no dividend payment has been decided, the net income of the period and the retained earnings show, by definition, identical amounts, namely +60 CU. The cash balance (in the bank) went from 0 CU (beginning of the story) to +5, i.e., a fluctuation of plus 5 CU. The variation in the cash balance is in no way connected to the magnitude of the income of the period. Two main explanations for the difference can be proposed.

- Some transactions only have an impact on the bank's cash balance and not on earnings: e.g., Transaction 2 (obtaining a loan) and Transaction 3 (acquisition of an asset or equipment).
- The fact that some sales lead to extending credit to customers (and, conversely, some acquisitions of resources lead to credit being extended by the supplier) creates a situation in which the earnings account is modified when the transaction takes place and not when it is finally settled through payment from the customer or to the supplier. This was the case in Transaction 4 (sale of services) in which earnings were increased but not the cash account. Similarly, Transaction 6 (purchasing resources or services from an outside supplier) generated a reduction in earnings without modifying the bank balance at the same moment.

The effect on earnings (and the counterbalancing claim) is recognized when the triggering event (transaction) takes place. There is no need to take into account this transaction when the claim is actually settled by the exchange of cash or other commodity.

The timing difference between cash and profit is crucial, especially in a fast growing business. Let us build a simple example to illustrate the situation. Assume there is a business whose sales double each period. Expenses are 80% of revenues. Customers pay two periods after the sales take place and suppliers require payment within one period after the delivery. The resources are acquired in the same period when the sales take place (see Table 2.4).

Table 2.4 Cash versus profit

Period	1	2	3	4	5	6	7
Sales	10	20	40	80	160	320	640
Expenses	8	16	32	64	128	256	512
Profit	**2**	**4**	**8**	**16**	**32**	**64**	**128**
Opening cash	0	0	−8	−14	−26	−50	−98
Cash inflow	0	0	10	20	40	80	160
Cash outflow	0	8	16	32	64	128	256
Ending cash	**0**	**−8**	**−14**	**−26**	**−50**	**−98**	**−194**

We have here a business which is clearly extremely profitable, but for which the cash situation is dramatically dangerous and probably will lead to bankruptcy unless something is done, such as obtaining more starting cash (upfront capital or borrowing), changing the credit terms given to customers (not always possible for a start-up business), or obtaining better credit terms from the suppliers (here again, not an easy task for the small enterprise). Many fast growing businesses actually go bankrupt because they cannot generate enough long-term capital to provide stable resources to keep the firm alive through this fast growth phase.

The cash flow statement (see Chapters 3 and 14) describes in detail the relationship between the income and cash situation.

6. *The order in which items are listed on the balance sheet is not random*

Each national or enterprise culture lists items in a sequential order that matches their value system. Chapter 3 shows that some countries go as far as defining a standard rank order. One of the reputed advantages of a normalized rank ordering is that it facilitates comparability of financial statements between comparable enterprises. The opposite is, of course, that comparability is useless if it is obtained at the detriment of the quality and descriptive flexibility of accounting. Most multinational companies have imposed on their subsidiaries, all over the globe, the obligation to report (to the parent) in similar formats (regardless of the locally required format) and also to use the same definition of terms so as to facilitate the comparative evaluation of the value creation potential of each subsidiary by senior management in the headquarters. Similarly, financial analysts and investment advisors are interested in homogeneous reporting so as to facilitate their task of identifying superior performers in an industrial sector.

1.2.4 Typical transactions

Table 2.5 below lists some typical transactions and their impact on assets, liabilities, and shareholders' equity. This table is in no way exhaustive and we have deliberately focused on the most common transactions. However, it aims to show that the knowledge of a relatively limited number of transactions allows one to understand the impact (on the elements of the business equation) of almost any 'ordinary' transaction realized by a firm.

Table 2.5 Impact of most common transactions

Example	Assets	=	Liabilities	+	Shareholders' equity
Creation of the company by capital contribution	+				+C
Purchase of equipment for cash	+ and −				
Purchase of equipment on credit	+		+		
Sales revenue for cash or on account	+				+E
Collection of accounts receivable	+ and −				
Expense for cash	−				−E
Expense on account			+		−E
Payment of a liability (e.g., accounts payable)	−		−		
Obtaining a loan (recording of a debt)	+		+		
Repayment of a debt	−		−		
Conversion of a debt into share capital			−		+C
Reduction of capital (repayment of the capital)	−				−C

The shareholders' equity account is separated between: C = capital and E = earnings

1.3 Income statement (or I/S or profit and loss account, also known as P&L)

In the previous section, revenues and expenses generated by each transaction were recorded through their impact on shareholders' equity and, more specifically, the '[retained] earnings' account. This choice was made to show the fundamental mechanism of the business equation. The number of transactions in the life of a business is, however, so large that it would be extremely cumbersome to record each change individually in the [retained] earnings account or to handle the revenue and expense accounts as a subsidiary account of shareholders' equity in the balance sheet. Dealing with each transaction individually as it affects equity would also make it difficult to carry out analyses of transactions to understand the business model of value creation during the period (remember that the balance of retained earnings reflects the cumulated impact of all transactions – including distribution of income to shareholders – since the firm was created).

In practice, transactions will be recorded in specific accounts opened only for a given period of time. These accounts will form the 'income statement'. These allow us to analyze the processes through which income of the period was created, and thus how [retained] earnings will be modified. For each period, only the income statement's net balance at the end of the period (i.e., net income of the period) will be transferred to the balance sheet account (as part of the shareholders' equity, pending decision by shareholders of dividend payment or incorporation in the retained earnings). The income statement will be the record of what happened during the period that caused the observed income (profit or loss). This separate record of actions can be subjected to analysis so as to identify which decisions can be modified to create even more profit for the next period.

The balance sheet will remain a 'snapshot' of the financial position of the firm, while the income statement will record the dynamics of how such position changed during a period of time. In a way, if the balance sheet is a snapshot, the income statement is like the 'film' of the 'activity' of the business during a given period that explains how the beginning balance sheet became the ending balance sheet.

Some key terms have been introduced here:

- **Activity**: This term refers to both the industrial or commercial sector in which a business operates, and the level of intensity of its transactions (level of activity). The term activity refers to what the firm does. The income statement reflects the activity of the firm. It gives a view of how it went from one balance sheet to the next. The income statement, therefore, does not give the financial position (or a record of the 'net worth' of the firm). It provides a view of what the firm did during the period. It records the consumption of resources and the creation of revenues. Resources can be short-lived, as would be the case for salaries, supplies, energy, etc., or can be long-lived such as tangible or physical assets (land, buildings, machinery, fixtures, office equipment, etc.) or intangible assets (e.g., patents). In the case of long-lived assets we will only record the reduction of their potential to create future economic benefits due to usage (wear and tear, obsolescence, etc.).
- **During a given period**: The income statement is a recapitulation of all transactions linked to serving customers during a given period of time called the 'accounting period', as defined in Chapter 1.

The income statement allows managers and accounting information users to track revenues (conventionally placed on the right-hand side of the I/S account, to mimic the fact that revenues are equivalent to an increase in shareholders' equity) and the expenses or costs (conventionally placed on the left-hand side). The income statement is a temporary account that will be 'closed' at the end of the period by the transfer of its balance to the shareholders' equity and ultimately to the 'retained earnings' account on the balance sheet. If revenues are greater than expenses, there is profit, i.e., an increase in shareholders' equity. Income (difference between revenues and expenses, whether positive [profit], or negative [loss]) is the amount required to balance both sides of the income statement. Thus, when closing the income statement at the end of the period 'profit' will appear on the left-hand side of the income statement, and the counterbalancing entry will be the recognition of the increase in the shareholders' equity, on the right-hand side of the balance sheet. If there had been a loss (expenses exceed revenues), the loss would have appeared on the right-hand side of the income statement and the counterbalancing entry, at closing, would have been a reduction of shareholders' equity. Such reduction, conceptually on the left-hand side of the balance sheet, would appear as a negative impact on shareholders' equity.

This co-temporal recognition of related revenues and expenses, called the **accrual principle**, is essential for financial statements to be useful. This principle means that revenue (expense) is recorded in the income statement at the time of the transaction that causes it and not at the time of the cash inflow (or outflow, for an expense). Both managers and outside information users can read directly from the income statement (established on an accrual basis) how much of the business' resources must be mobilized to create revenues. By comparing several successive periods, these users can also see whether the 'productivity' of the business' resources is improving or deteriorating (due to any combination of quality of management, changes in competitive conditions, relevance of value offering to customers, etc.).

1.3.1 Business equation and income statement

Figure 2.11 illustrates the link between the basic business (balance sheet or accounting) equation and the income statement.

Figure 2.11 Link between the balance sheet and the income statement

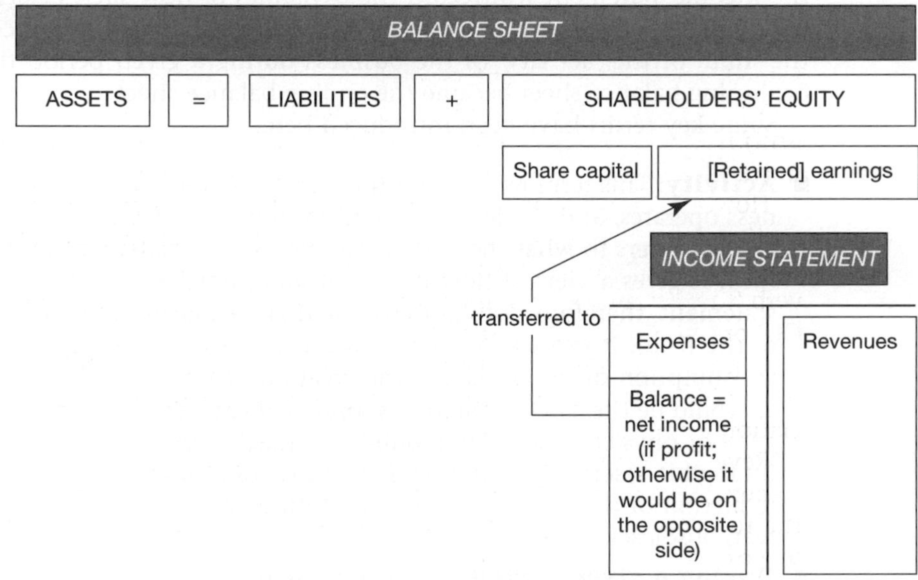

1.3.2 Elements of the income statement

Revenues A revenue is an influx of economic resources for the firm, coming from third parties and whose origin is generally a commercial transaction. A revenue is always an increase in shareholders' equity.

The ultimate purpose of an enterprise is to create profit so as to give a positive return to (or increase the wealth of) its shareholders. The way an enterprise creates profit is by satisfying its customers. The **sales** revenue (or sales turnover) is the metric that reflects how successful the firm is at creating and delivering a customer value proposition at any given point. Note that the concept of value offering or value proposition includes provision of goods or services as well as rental of facilities, technologies, or goods. The concept of rental revenue recognition is of increasing interest in the 'new economy' and will be further explored in Chapter 6. The rate of growth of the sales revenue is an even better indicator of the appreciation by the customers of the firm's value proposition or value offering than the absolute value of the sales revenue, as is shown in Chapter 15. Sales are measured in accounting by the recording of some form of invoice, which is the material proof of the existence of the transaction.

Accounting records the sale based on the assumption that the customer will pay the invoice on the agreed upon date. It is therefore critical to understand that 'revenue' and 'receipt of funds' are very different. The actual receipt of funds may happen: (1) earlier than when the revenue is recognized (as in the case of a down payment); (2) simultaneously with the revenue recognition (as in the case of a cash sale); or (3) later than the revenue recognition (as in the case of a credit sale or sale on account).

Revenues may also come from a financial investment made by the firm (interest or return on investment). For example, if a retailer receives cash from a customer 30 days before the supplier must be paid, the retailer can invest the cash received for 30 days and earn additional revenue on the sale in the form of interest revenue. Retail distributors (such as Wal-Mart, Carrefour, H&M, and many others) are known to significantly rely on this time lag to generate financial revenue, which often represents a significant share of their net income and thus allows them to keep trading margins at a low level (see further developments in Chapter 15).

Expenses An expense is a consumption of resources, i.e., a reduction in shareholders' equity. The term 'cost' refers to the amount of value exchanged to acquire a resource and, by extension, the total value of resources (singly or collectively) consumed when the object, product, or service is created through the consumption of said resources. We therefore could legitimately say the cost of acquisition of a product component is 100 CU for 20 units, the component expense (in the course of production) is 5 CU per unit consumed, and the cost of the objects assembled (assuming each consumes 3 components and 1.5 hour of labor that costs 20 CU per hour, and requires overhead costs of 14 CU per unit) is 59 CU ($3 \times 5 + 1.5 \times 20 + 14$). So as to not complicate the vocabulary, we will, however, use the terms 'cost' and 'expense' as synonyms in this text.

However, it is important to realize that the corresponding verbs, 'to expense' and 'to cost', are not equivalent. The verb 'to expense' is dynamic and active in its meaning. It is equivalent to 'recognize the consumption of a resource in the accounting process'. The verb 'to cost', however, implies the creation of a result, as in 'this resource costs so many CU' or 'these products cost this much'.

Expenses can be separated between cash expenses (out-of-pocket expenses or expenses on credit that will be settled with cash eventually) and non-cash expenses such as depreciation expense.

Revenues generated by a business are the representation of the exchange value customers place on the value offering or value proposition of the firm. The value offering is the result of an efficient and coordinated use of resources (consumption). Resources are diverse. Accounting only considers those resources that can be expressed in terms of cash equivalents. Resources include workers' labor, employees and staff (materialized by salaries that consume cash), supplies or services provided by third parties (they eventually consume cash directly, or indirectly if bartered), information and information systems, raw materials or products for sale (consume inventory that was purchased for cash, and eventually cash for replenishment of the inventory level), equipment, such as machinery, computers, telephone systems, commercial facilities (the value of an asset is equal to the net present value of the future cash flows it will generate; the 'consumption' of a fixed asset recognizes the fact that usage and obsolescence reduce future cash flows), etc.

One critical issue in revenue and expense recognition is their '**matching**' in the proper time period. The matching principle, derived from the accrual principle, stipulates that when revenues are recorded, all expenses that contributed to the generation of these revenues should be reported in the same period. Implementing this principle is not always easy. For example, resource consumption for research and development, for acquiring customers, for developing a market, or for promoting a new product may not take place in the same period as the revenue that will result from these cash outlays and/or resource consumption. Accounting will pay great attention to the 'matching' of revenues and expenses. An income statement will attempt to show side by side the revenues and the expenses corresponding to the same business activity for a given period. Matching will be further addressed in Chapter 5.

Income or 'bottom line' Every year (or at the end of any 'accounting period' or 'accounting year') the balance between all revenues and expenses is drawn. This is done by balancing out all of the increases and decreases in shareholders' equity that result from normal business operations. As mentioned before, the difference between revenues and expenses is called [net] income. If revenues are greater than expenses, shareholders' equity has a net increase and income is called profit. If, however, revenues of the period are not enough to cover expenses, it means shareholders' equity has been reduced during the period, and income is then a loss. The profit or loss appears as the last line (bottom line) of the two lists of revenues and expenses, when the income statement is presented vertically (see below) and thus it has become colloquially acceptable to refer to a period's profit or loss as the period's 'bottom line'.

In summary, during any given period we have the following equation:

Revenues − Expenses = Income (profit or loss)

1.3.3 Application to Verdi

During the year X1, Verdi Company has recognized net sales or net revenue of 250 CU. This means it has produced invoices in the amount of 250 CU. It has concurrently consumed resources (services and supplies) that outside suppliers invoiced to Verdi for a total amount of 85 CU. In addition Verdi consumed the labor force of its employee and incurred for such consumption an expense of 101 CU (salaries, and fringe and social benefits). Lastly, Verdi was able to generate the 250 CU of revenue because it had been able to use its resources, including some that have been financed through the acquisition of financial debt. The interest expense of 4 CU is thus a relevant operational cost that must be matched against the revenue of 250.

The operations of Verdi Company are summarized in Table 2.6.

Table 2.6 Income statement of Verdi Company for accounting year X1 (vertical format)

Total revenues		**250**
Sales	250	
Total expenses		**190**
Services and supplies	85	
Personnel expenses	101	
Interest expenses	4	
Income (revenues − expenses)		**+60**

During X1, Verdi's business activities have created a profit of 60 CU (before income tax). In the statement, revenues and expenses have been presented in a vertical list (vertical format) and the income is truly the 'bottom line' (see above).

The business transactions could also have been shown as a subset of the shareholders' equity account, i.e., using the convention of showing increases in shareholders' equity on the right-hand side and decreases on the left-hand side. Such a format is known as the horizontal format and is illustrated in Table 2.7.

Table 2.7 Income statement for the year X1 (horizontal format)

Expenses		Revenues	
Purchases and external expenses	85	Sales	250
Personnel expenses	101		
Interest expenses	4		
Profit	*60*		
Total	250	Total	250

In the Verdi example, expenses are listed by nature, simply summarizing transactions of a similar nature, without any other calculations besides simple additions. Some countries, such as the United States and Canada, have chosen to present expenses by grouping them further by destination (or function). In their model, expenses are shown in 'blocks' grouping expenses that have the same purpose (and the details of these expenses are not considered useful for the decider), such as cost of sales or cost of goods sold, cost of acquiring and servicing customers, general and administrative expenses, etc.

The functional approach distinguishes at least between four categories of costs: 'cost of goods sold', 'cost of selling' (which, most of the time, includes marketing costs as well as the costs of delivering the goods or services), 'cost of administering' the firm, and 'cost of financing'. This aspect will be further developed in Chapter 3, which is devoted to the format of financial statements. At this point, the format of presentation of the income statement is not important for our purpose.

In the previous format of the income statement 'profit' appears to be in the same column as expenses or costs. It is simply the result of the fact that the net income is the balance of revenues minus expenses and would be written as a way to update the shareholders' equity account (see Figure 2.12).

Figure 2.12 Link between profit and shareholders' equity

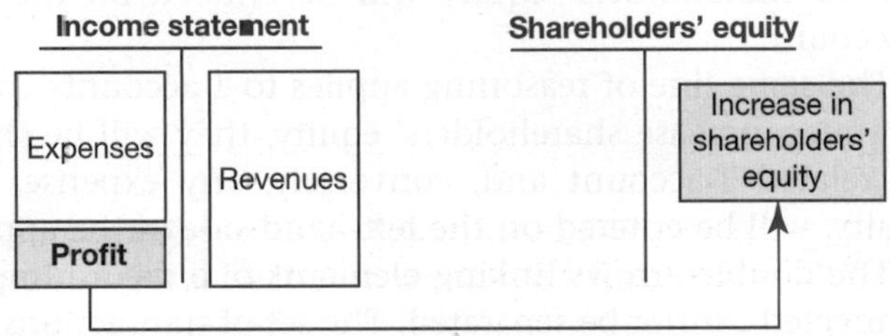

Of course, if there had been a loss (i.e., expenses exceed revenues), the net income would have been shown on the right-hand side of the income statement because the counterpart would have been a decrease in shareholders' equity.

1.3.4 Impact of transactions on financial statements

So far, we have recorded transactions, one by one, by applying the basic business equation (Assets = Liabilities + Shareholders' equity). We will now focus on the transactions that impact the financial statements as a stand-alone document. The income statement will no longer be considered being a subpart of shareholders' equity at each step, but will be connected to the balance sheet only at the end of the period (see Figure 2.13). This will

Figure 2.13 Impact on financial statements

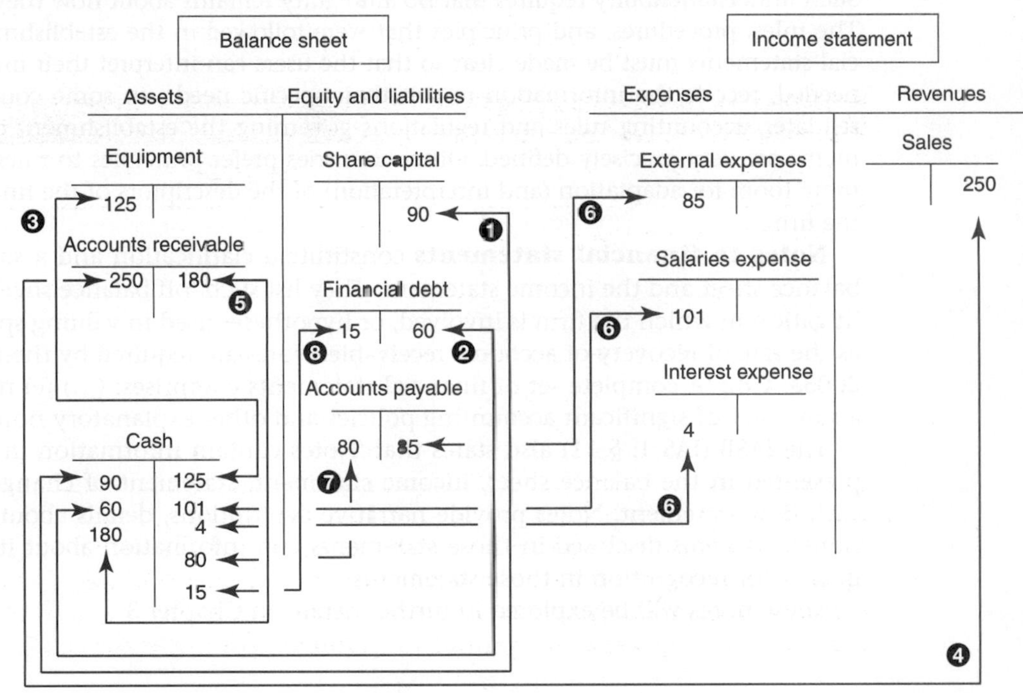

thus create the income statement as a document that records all transactions and only the ending balance (of the I/S) will be carried over to the balance sheet as a modification of shareholders' equity.

From now on, we will use this T-account based format to illustrate the handling of transactions. The reader will have noticed that T-accounts operate like miniature versions of the basic business equation (Assets = Liabilities plus Shareholders' Equity). Since assets are on the left-hand side of the equal sign in the business equation, an increase in assets will be shown on the left side of the corresponding T-account and, conversely, a decrease in assets will be on the right-hand side of the appropriate T-account. Since liabilities and shareholders' equity are on the right-hand side of the equal sign in the business equation, an increase in liabilities or shareholders' equity will be entered on the right-hand side of the corresponding T-account, while a reduction in liabilities or shareholders' equity will be entered on the left-hand side of the appropriate T-account.

The same line of reasoning applies to T-accounts used in the income statement. Since revenues increase shareholders' equity, they will be shown on the right-hand side of an I/S related T-account and, conversely, any expense, i.e., a reduction in shareholders' equity, will be entered on the left-hand side of the appropriate I/S related T-account.

The double arrows linking elements of a record imply that the two or more elements connected cannot be separated. The set of transactions records will always be balanced by definition.

1.3.5 Balance sheet and value creation

Appendix 2.1 shows how the change between two balance sheets can be related to value creation.

1.4 Notes to financial statements

The accounting system must provide relevant information with as much precision and reliability as possible so that users of the financial statements trust their informational content. Such understandability requires that no ambiguity remains about how they were developed. The rules, procedures, and principles that were followed in the establishment of the financial statements must be made clear so that the users can interpret their implications and, if needed, recode the information to suit their specific needs. In some countries, as we will see later, accounting rules and regulations governing the establishment of financial statements are very precisely defined. Other countries prefer principles to rules. Principles leave more room for adaptation (and interpretation) of the descriptors of the financial position of the firm.

Notes to financial statements constitute a clarification and a supplement to the balance sheet and the income statement. They list such 'off balance sheet' information as litigation in which the firm is involved, or hypotheses used in valuing specific assets such as the rate of recovery of accounts receivable. Notes are required by the IASB (IAS 1, IASB 2003a: § 8): 'A complete set of financial statements comprises: (...) (e) notes, comprising a summary of significant accounting policies and other explanatory notes'.

The IASB (IAS 1: § 11) also states that 'Notes contain information in addition to that presented in the balance sheet, income statement, statement of changes in equity and cash flow statement. Notes provide narrative descriptions, details about – or disaggregations of – items disclosed in those statements and information about items that do not qualify for recognition in those statements'.

These notes will be explored in further details in Chapter 3.

2 Advanced issues

2.1 Notion of depreciation

2.1.1 Principle

In order to fulfill its mission of creating value for shareholders by providing value to customers (in the form of goods or services) a business needs to invest in permanent 'means of production'. These can be in the form of plant, machinery, warehouses, retail facilities, fixtures, computers, vehicles, distribution systems, etc. Most of these assets have a useful life that exceeds the duration of the accounting period. They are called 'fixed assets' to distinguish them from the 'current assets', which are acquired and consumed within the duration of the operating cycle or the accounting period (whichever is the shortest).

Fixed assets gradually lose value (i.e., lose their potential to create future economic benefits, or sellable goods or services in the future) due to usage, aging, or obsolescence. They must be replaced periodically to maintain the value creation ability of the business. The loss of value of such a 'fixed' asset due to any of the previously mentioned causes is considered as a cost since it is an actual 'consumption' of an asset. The consumption of a fixed asset is called '**depreciation expense**' since it reflects the gradual loss of value of this asset.

Depreciation is the process of adjusting (downwards) the value of an asset by recognizing that it is consumed in a way that does not completely eliminate the resource. It would have been a violation of the matching principle to recognize the full value of the equipment as being consumed in the very period when it was acquired since benefits will continue to be derived in the future years from owning the asset. (Verdi knew their equipment would create a flow of revenues for several years.) Depreciation is the procedure that allows a business to match revenues and fixed asset resource consumption, when the asset will benefit several periods. Rather than trying to estimate the actual consumption of the fixed assets in the creation of revenues of a period, always difficult to determine, the original depreciable value of the asset (generally its cost of acquisition and installation minus the resale value – if the latter can be estimated) is allocated according to pre-agreed rules over the productive life of the asset. IAS 16 (IASB 2003b: § 6) defines depreciation as 'the systematic allocation of the depreciable amount of an asset over its useful life' (see further developments in Chapter 7).

Carrying amount (often called 'book value' or 'net value' in practice) is 'the amount at which an asset is recognized after deducting any accumulated depreciation and accumulated impairment losses' (IAS 16: § 6).

In many cases, the **accumulated depreciation** expense of any fixed asset will eventually be equal to the amount initially paid to acquire it and bring it into the productive stream. The fixed asset will then be recorded as 'fully depreciated' and have a zero book (or net) value (see more on this in Chapter 7).

A **depreciation expense** is recognized every year (or period) in the income statement just as supplies or salary expenses are. Depreciation, however, will be recognized at the end of the period and not each time the asset is used.

2.1.2 Application to Verdi

Verdi had acquired fixed assets (a computer, a color printer, and an art/drawing software) at the beginning of the period for 125 CU. Let us assume these assets have an expected useful life of five years (i.e., they will be able to contribute to the generation of economic benefits for five years). This means that, in five years, they will be worthless and will no longer be productive assets. Verdi will have consumed the fixed assets completely over five years. If we choose a simple approach, we may recognize that these fixed assets lose 20% of their value every year. We will see in Chapter 7 that methods other than this '**straight-line**' approach (proportional to the passage of time) are possible. The choice of method however, although it modifies the timing of recognition of the depreciation expense, does not modify the principle of depreciation: all outputs created by using a fixed asset must bear a part of the cost of the depreciation of the asset.

In Verdi's case the depreciation expense for the year is thus 25 CU (for each year since we selected a method – straight-line depreciation – that creates an equal amount of depreciation each year). At the end of the first period, the book (or net) value of these fixed assets would now be 125 CU minus 25 CU or 100 CU. The yearly depreciation expense of 25 CU is another expense in the income statement. It will be offset against revenues to help determine the income for the period. Thus, for the next four years, an annual expense of 25 CU will also be recognized in the annual income statement to acknowledge the consumption of the productive capacity. At the end of the five years, the book (net) value of the equipment will be zero. In theory the equipment will have to be replaced at the end of the five-year period if the exhaustion of the value creation potential of the asset is also physical, in addition to being financial.

An 'improved', i.e., more complete, representation of the situation of Verdi Company appears as Figure 2.14. It is important to notice that the balance sheet reports 'accumulated depreciation' while the income statement reports the 'depreciation expense' of the period. Since we have only one period of activity the two amounts are (exceptionally) identical, but it must be clear that, as early as period 2, the two balances will no longer be identical: accumulated depreciation (in the balance sheet) is the sum of the depreciation expenses (in the successive income statements) of each of the consecutive years or periods during which the depreciable asset is detained.

The balance sheet (assuming no other transactions between April and December) is adjusted as shown in Table 2.8.

The income statement is also modified (see Table 2.9).

Remark: Had we chosen the *vertical* presentation of the income statement, the latter would look as described in Table 2.10.

Figure 2.14 Recording the depreciation

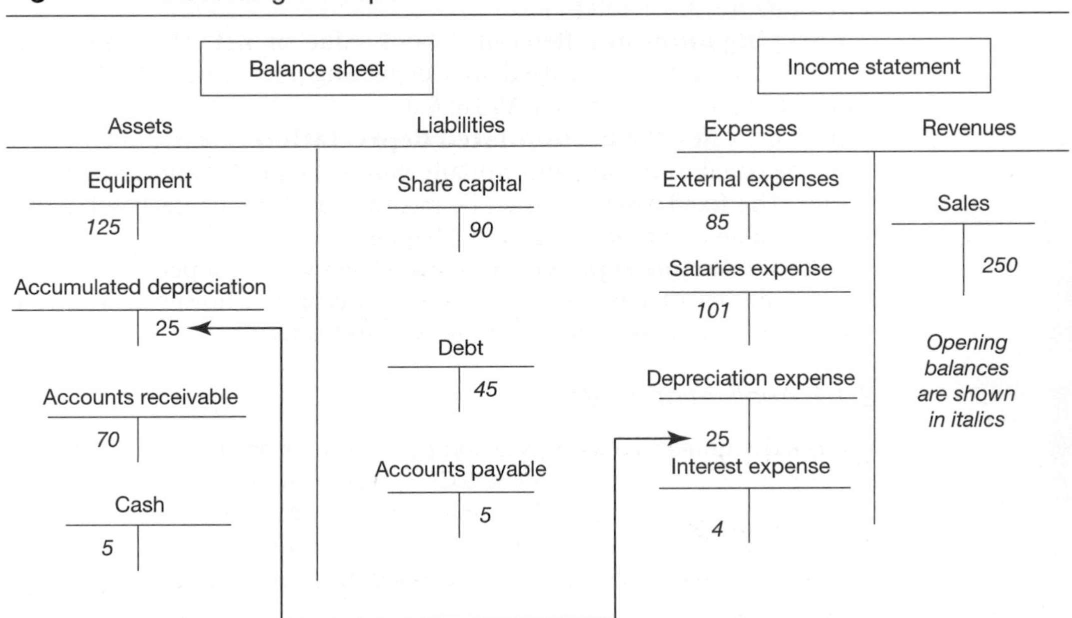

Table 2.8 Balance sheet after depreciation

Balance sheet on 31 December X1				
Assets			**Equity and liabilities**	
Equipment			Shareholders' equity	
Gross value	125	100	Capital	90
−Acc. depreciation	25		Earnings	35
Accounts receivable		70	Liabilities	
Cash		5	Debt	45
			Accounts payable	5
Total assets		175	Total liabilities	175

Table 2.9 Income statement after depreciation

Income statement for the period ending 31 December X1			
Expenses		**Revenues**	
External expenses (services purchased from third parties)	85	Sales	250
Salaries expense	101		
Depreciation expense	25		
Interest expense	4		
Profit	35		
	250		250

Table 2.10 Vertical income statement for the period ending 31 December X1

Revenues	
Sales	250
Total revenues	250
Expenses	
External expenses	85
Salaries expense	101
Depreciation expense	25
Interest expense	4
Total expenses	215
Income (revenues − expenses)	35

2.2 Profit appropriation

2.2.1 Principle

The income (profit or loss) calculated in the balance sheet is an increase or a reduction of shareholders' equity and reflects whether the business created any net additional wealth. When shareholders contribute their own personal resources to create a business (cash, intellectual property, effort, or transfer control of a physical asset, for example), these contributions form the capital from the point of view of the business. They are considered as an investment (shareholders' viewpoint). The latter expect a return on their investment.

As we said earlier, profit represents the increase in wealth created by the operation of the firm and literally belongs to the shareholders. The shareholders can choose to take out of the business in the form of dividends (i.e., appropriate to themselves) all or part of that increase in their equity. Whatever part of the profit is not distributed is considered to be 'retained' earnings.

In a limited liability company (public or private limited company in the UK, *société anonyme* or *société à responsabilité limitée* in France, *Aktiengesellschaft* or *GmbH* in Germany, *SpA* in Italy, etc.) there are generally many shareholders and it would be difficult to allow each individual shareholder to decide whether or not they wish to withdraw their share of the added wealth to which they are personally entitled (based on the percentage of their contribution to the share capital and opening balance of earnings retained from previous periods). The decision is, therefore, made by a vote of the general assembly of the shareholders and their decision applies uniformly to all shareholders.

Practically, the decision regarding what to do with profit of the period consists of choosing from among any of three possibilities:

1. Distribute the profit entirely to the shareholders as dividends.
2. Distribute the profit partially to the shareholders as dividends and the balance is considered to be an increase of the investment of the shareholders in the business, in the proportion of their previous contributions.
3. Not distribute profit at all and the investors (shareholders) reinvest their claim in its entirety in the business.

The debate about whether or not to distribute the profit implies an arbitration between the individual needs of shareholders for cash income (and the opportunities they have to privately earn a return on that cash by investing it elsewhere) and the medium- to long-term interest of the firm. When dividends are paid out, there is a reduction in shareholders' equity, and a simultaneous reduction in cash. If the drain on the cash of the firm is too high it may create a serious limitation of the ability of the firm to pursue its operations (remember that profit and cash flow are often disconnected – see Table 2.4). The issue is generally to balance any partition of the profit of the firm between owners and the firm itself (retained earnings) in such a way that the shareholders receive enough cash for their needs, and the firm is not drained out of cash, which is the fuel for its smooth operation and growth.

After the shareholders have approved the terms of distribution, the part of the profit that will be paid out as dividends is first recognized as a short-term debt to shareholders (dividends payable). When the dividend is actually paid out, the debt is canceled and cash is reduced appropriately.

The profit retained in the business is aggregated to the shareholders' equity but remains, often for legal or regulatory reasons, distinct from the strictly defined 'capital'. Profit retained in the business is called either 'retained earnings' (for example, in the United States or in Canada) or 'reserves' (for example, in the Nordic countries, Germany, France, or the UK).

It should be clear that retained earnings (or reserves) are in no way equivalent to available cash. Since income and cash are disconnected through credit terms and different timings of revenue flows and expense flows, a business can be in a situation where there is a lot of profit (and potentially a large addition to the retained earnings) but a negative cash position (see, for example, Tables 2.4 and 2.11).

The topic of **profit appropriation** will be further developed in Chapter 11 and reporting for retained earnings and reserves is presented in Appendix 2.2.

2.2.2 Application to Verdi

The shareholders of Verdi Company observe their business results during the recently closed accounting period and determine that they made a profit of 35 CU (after depreciation and if we ignore taxes, for the time being). They decide to award themselves a dividend of 3 CU or, in other words, they decide to keep in the business 32 CU (of a profit amounting to 35 CU) as retained earnings (or as a 'reserve'). In fact, this is equivalent to their reinvesting that same amount into the business (with the significant personal tax advantage that since the amount reinvested was never distributed, the shareholders will not be individually taxed on the investment income they now choose to reinvest). The shareholders' decision to pay a dividend will be recorded by recognizing the immediate liability to the shareholders under the name of 'dividends payable'. The impact on cash, however, will not take place until the actual payout takes place (here, we can assume it will take place in the early part of X2).

The transaction of 'declaring dividends' results in a decrease in retained earnings and creation of a liability for the same amount. On the date of payment, this liability account is canceled and cash is decreased. We show below the impact on the basic financial statements. Because the intermediate step using the 'dividends payable' account is not necessary for the understanding of profit appropriation, we don't disclose it in Figure 2.15. For the sake of simplification, we have also ignored the tax implications in the above illustration. In the 'real world', before recording it on the balance sheet, income would first have been subject to taxation according to the rules of the country where Verdi is operating. Depending on the country or the company, retained earnings (or reserves) can be reported in two different ways (for more details see Appendix 2.2).

Figure 2.15 Recording of profit appropriation

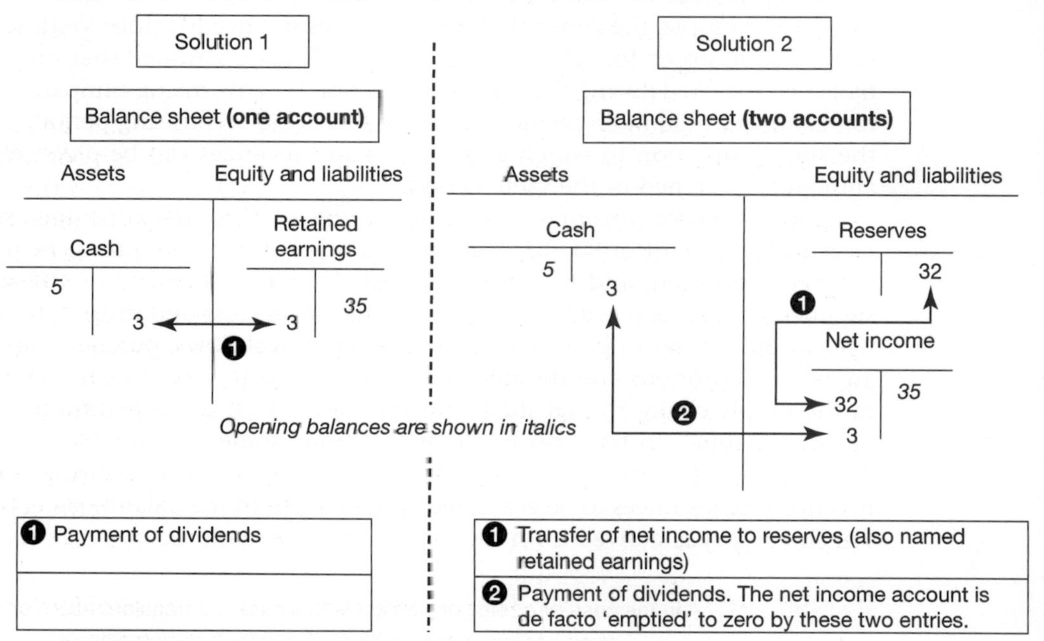

2.2.3 Cash, profit, and reserves

The terms 'reserves' or 'retained earnings' prove to be misleading at times to students (and executives alike) who do not fully grasp the distinction between profit and cash balance. As was shown earlier (and in Table 2.4 especially), a business can be very profitable but be extremely cash poor, or the converse can be true as illustrated in Table 2.11 for a business whose unprofitable sales double each period. For each currency unit of revenue the cost is 1.1 CU. However, the customers pay immediately but the business does not have to pay the supplier(s) until two periods after the cash sale was realized.

Table 2.11 Cash versus profit

Period	1	2	3	4	5	6	7
Sales	10	20	40	80	160	320	640
Expenses	11	22	44	88	176	352	704
Income (here a loss)	**(1)**	**(2)**	**(4)**	**(8)**	**(16)**	**(32)**	**(64)**
Opening cash	0	10	30	59	117	233	465
Cash inflow	10	20	40	80	160	320	640
Cash outflow	0	0	11	22	44	88	176
Ending cash	**10**	**30**	**59**	**117**	**233**	**465**	**929**

We can see from this illustration that this business is a cash-generating machine, although it is actually 'losing money' on every sale. In Table 2.11, if we ignore that the cash generated could be invested profitably (which could yield a substantial return), the business is literally destroying the capital. Losses are reducing equity and if the business were to keep on going under these conditions, the capital could be entirely destroyed as negative retained earnings are created. Negative retained earnings are no more equivalent to a cash shortage than retained earnings or (positive) reserves are equivalent to available cash.

2.3 Consumption of resources and inventory

We will introduce the subject only briefly here as it is further developed in Chapter 9. In the Verdi example, the concept of inventory was not needed since Verdi sold a service that could not be stored for sale at a later date. Further, we assumed that no preparation work had been incurred during the accounting period for advertising campaigns ordered by customers that would be implemented in the following accounting period. Thus, we were in the simple situation in which all expenses and revenues can be physically, and without ambiguity, matched in the same period.

Expenses reflect consumed resources. During X1 Verdi has consumed supplies and services to an amount of 80 CU. The supplies (paper, toner, etc.) must be purchased before their consumption, and it is probably best to have on hand some '**inventory**' of such supplies so as to never run out (which might mean a lost opportunity to serve a customer who would not be willing to wait). The two physical flows, purchases and consumption, are not synchronous and the role of an inventory is to serve as a buffer against incidents in the supply chain, so that stock-outs do not occur. It is most common, even in a world of 'just in time', to have on hand, at any time, some consumable resources physically stored ahead of consumption. Therefore, at the end of the accounting period, there is an inventory of resources to be evaluated and recorded in the balance sheet on the asset side. This inventory is derived from the following two equations:

In the case of a retail or wholesale business (no transformation) or of an intermediate workshop in a manufacturing plant:

Beginning inventory + Acquired consumable resources = Resources available for consumption

Resources available for consumption − Resources consumed = Ending inventory

In the case of a manufacturing firm and for finished products (FP):

Beginning inventory + Cost of finished goods manufactured = Finished products available for sale

Finished products available for sale − Cost of finished products sold = Ending inventory of FP

Let us illustrate the impact of inventories on the financial statements through the case illustration of Puccini & Co., an umbrella manufacturer.

2.3.1 Goods purchased for resale (merchandise) or for use in a transformation process (raw materials and parts)

Assume that Puccini & Co. acquires, with cash for 100 CU, the raw materials and parts necessary for the manufacturing of umbrellas (ribs, handles, mechanical parts, fabric, thread, sheaths, etc.). During the accounting period, Puccini & Co. consumed only 80 CU worth of materials. It, therefore, still holds 20 CU worth of parts and materials at the end of the period.

Two different approaches exist for recording this situation. The first one (called 'perpetual inventory system') creates a record each time goods (materials and parts) are consumed in order to satisfy customer orders (i.e., each time resources are withdrawn from inventory). The second one (known as 'periodic inventory system') calculates the total consumption at the end of the period by measuring what remains on hand (i.e., knowing the ending balance, the beginning balance, and purchases or additions means that the consumption can be deducted).

Method 1 – Purchases recorded as inventory in the balance sheet (perpetual system) In this method withdrawals from inventory or consumption to satisfy customers are recorded as they occur. The parts and materials purchased are considered to enter first in the inventory of Puccini & Co. before they can be withdrawn and consumed. Therefore the consequence of the purchase is an increase in the 'inventory' account on the asset side of the balance sheet and either a decrease in cash or an increase in payables. When parts and materials are required for the manufacturing of umbrellas (probably on several occasions during the period), the plant manager (or the retail store manager, if we had not been in a manufacturing context) issues a requisition and the goods (parts and materials, here) are withdrawn from inventory. These are, therefore, withdrawn for immediate consumption. Their value will be recognized, each time a withdrawal takes place, as both an expense (consumption of a resource) and a reduction of the asset amount listed under the heading 'inventory'. The total of all withdrawals will be either: (a) recognized under the name of 'cost of merchandise sold' if there is only a resale without transformation; or (b) considered as a component of the 'cost of goods manufactured' (and, eventually, of 'cost of goods sold' as products manufactured are sold).

We can summarize this process very simply:

	Beginning inventory
Plus	Purchases (sum of all invoices of the period)
Minus	*Consumption (sum of all recorded material or merchandise requisitions)*
Equals	Ending inventory (which can be validated by a physical stocktaking – i.e., counting what really and physically exists in the inventory)

In X1, a period in which there was no beginning inventory, the impact of inventories, carried under this first method, on the financial statements is as shown in Figure 2.16. (Here we assume that production takes place after the customers orders have been received and thus the consumption of parts and materials can flow directly to the 'cost of goods sold' since there is no need for a finished goods inventory.)

The impact on the basic business equation is shown in Appendix 2.3.

Suppose that during X2 Puccini & Co. purchases supplies for an amount of 200 CU. The value of the 'supplies available' for consumption in the normal operations of the firm is 200 CU *plus* the existing beginning inventory of 20 CU, which means a total available for use worth 220 CU. Consumption (i.e., sum of the withdrawals) during the year equals 211 CU. As a consequence, the ending inventory (computed by difference) is 9 CU (i.e. [20 + 200 − 211]). The impact on the financial statements is shown in Figure 2.17.

Figure 2.16 Impact on financial statements – Year X1

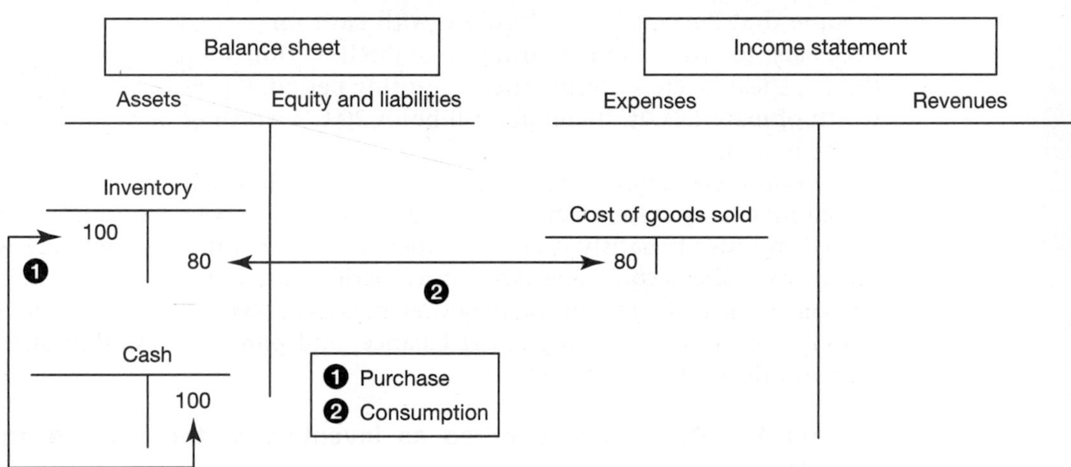

Figure 2.17 Impact on financial statements – Year X2

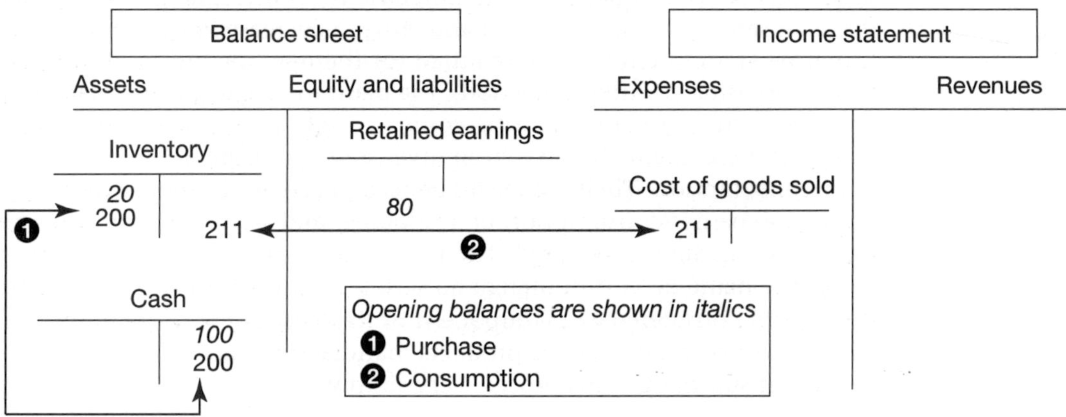

Method 2 – Purchases are recorded as an expense in the income statement (periodic system) This approach, instead of assuming all materials or parts acquired for future production are going through an inventory account before being consumed, makes the hypothesis that all that is purchased (100 CU worth in Puccini & Co.'s case) is meant to be consumed in the current period (either through resale or consumed in the manufacturing process) and is therefore considered to be expensed for the full amount at the time of purchase.

At the end of the period, when Puccini & Co. orders a physical stocktaking, it will observe that the hypothesis of exhaustive consumption of materials and parts may not have been quite correct. In our example, there are still 20 CU worth of goods left in inventory. Expenses (consumption of parts and materials) have, therefore, been overestimated in our simplifying hypothesis. They must be adjusted *ex post* to recognize (the matching principle strikes again) only that part of the 'materials and parts' that have been consumed in order to match them against revenues from sales.

This second method is very simple to apply and relatively less expensive than the first inventory-based approach (here, there is no need for record keeping of withdrawals from inventory during the period) but does not give the same control over consumption or the same fineness of information (which managers and external users of information may want to have in their resource allocation decision). Computerization, the generalization of barcodes, or the emerging Radio Frequency Identification of articles tends to make the periodic system approach obsolete since it has become rather economical today to record every movement of goods, materials, or parts. However, physical inventory taking is still a necessity in order to validate the quality of the computerized recording process of withdrawals and to detect and prevent pilferage and human (or software) errors.

When purchases are assumed to be consumed in the same period, the equation defining the relation between beginning and ending inventories is modified. Instead of having the unknown be the ending inventory, the unknown becomes the consumption of materials.

	Beginning inventory
Plus	Purchases (sum of all invoices of the period)
Equals	Available for consumption to satisfy customers
Minus	*Ending inventory (which results from a physical stocktaking)*
Equals	Consumption

At the end of the period, the physical stocktaking carried out shows the final inventory to be worth 20 CU (physical quantities multiplied by the unit purchase cost of the items found in inventory). The amount recorded as an expense must therefore be adjusted so as to reflect the correct value for the consumption of materials and parts. We create an 'ending inventory account' which takes on the value of 20 CU. If we want to use a crude physical illustration of what happens, the inventory is taken out of the 'plant' (the income statement), where it was 'temporarily' stored (under the name of expense) and stored in a 'warehouse' (the inventory account in the balance sheet).

Figure 2.18 illustrates how accounting records the transaction under this approach. The impact of inventories on the financial statements is as follows (since there is no impact on liabilities, they can be ignored).

In this method, since purchases were assumed to have been immediately consumed (i.e., turned into expenses or costs to be deducted from revenues) the ending inventory

Figure 2.18 Impact on financial statements – Year X1

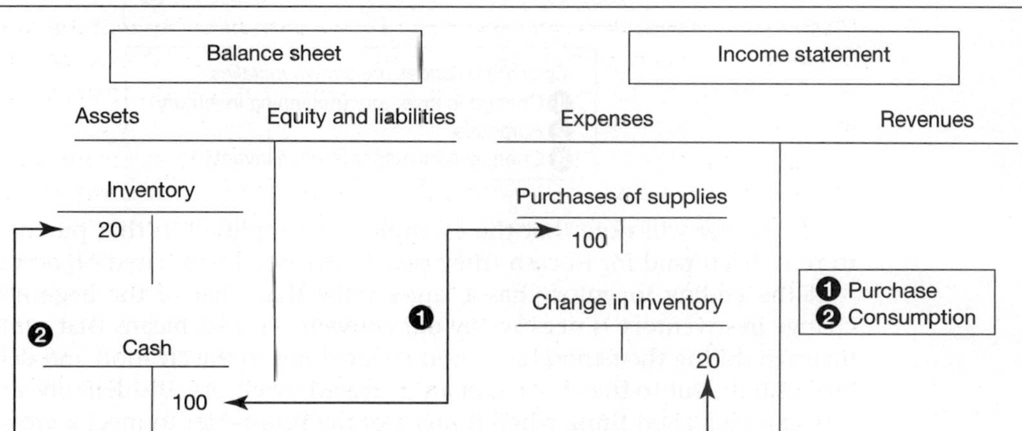

Note that in this example, we have made the hypothesis that purchases have an immediate impact on income and that the consumption is adjusted *ex post* via a physical checking of inventory. We have seen above, and we will also see in greater detail in Chapter 9, that another approach exists.

must be deducted from the expenses recognized so far, in order to create the cost reflecting the actual consumption of parts and materials.

To further understand the entries recorded in the income statement, let us see what happens the following year. During the following year, purchases are 200 CU and the final inventory measured by stocktaking at the end of the year is estimated to be worth 9 CU.

The beginning inventory (BI) (ending inventory of the previous period) was worth 20 CU. The ending inventory (EI) is valued at 9 CU. The accounting change in inventory is therefore +11 CU (i.e., BI − EI, or 20 − 9), and the cost of materials consumed to satisfy customers is the full 200 CU purchased plus the reduction of inventory, or 200 + 11 = 211 CU.

	Purchases	200
Plus	Beginning inventory	20
Minus	Ending inventory	−9
Equals	Total consumed supplies	211

Note that accountants define 'variations in inventory level' or 'changes in inventory' of raw materials, supplies and merchandise as the difference: beginning inventory (BI) minus ending inventory (EI). By convention, the change in inventory level of purchased goods (raw materials, supplies, and merchandise) is always shown on the expenses side of the income statement (see further developments on finished products below and in Chapter 9).

The impact of inventory on the financial statements for X2 appears in Figure 2.19.

Figure 2.19 Impact on financial statements – Year X2

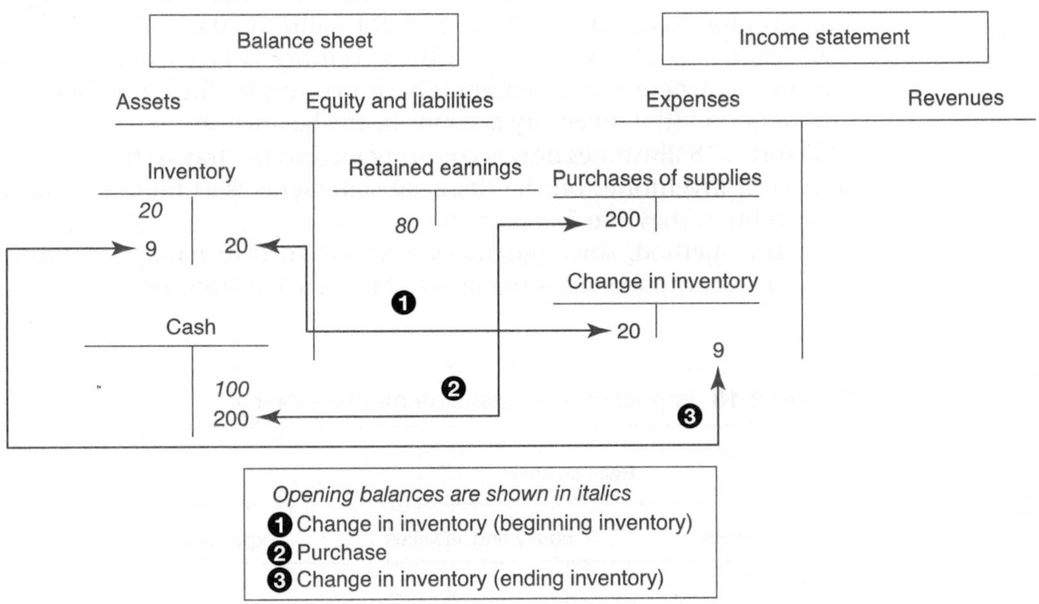

The reader will note that the example was simplified in that purchases were assumed to have been paid for in cash (they could have been purchased on account).

If the ending inventory has a larger value than that of the beginning inventory, the change in inventory is negative by our convention. This means that some of the resources incurred during the period have been devoted not to the creation and delivery of the value proposition, but to the creation of an increased inventory. Incidentally, an increased inventory can be a good thing when it prepares the firm better to meet a growing demand with short response time. Since in this (continental European) approach the current expenses recognized on the left-hand side of the income statement include all purchases, creating a 'change in inventory' account reduces (or increases) the expenses of the period so that the balance is equal to the costs that needs to be matched with revenues. The way of calculating the 'change in inventory' as 'BI – EI' adjusts the accounts automatically to recognize the amount of materials (or components or parts) expenses that matches the revenues, regardless of when these were acquired.

Intuitively (more logically, maybe?), we could have written:

Consumption = Purchases *minus* Increase (or *plus* Decrease) in inventories

where increase and decrease are defined as the difference (ending minus beginning inventories) that leads us to define consumption as being equal to 'purchases' minus (ending inventory – beginning inventory).

The choice between the perpetual and periodic inventory methods depends on the tradition of each country and on the resources and needs of each enterprise. The two methods give exactly the same results in a non-inflationary world. If there are many purchases and there is serious inflation, under the perpetual method the cost of resources consumed may reflect better the current prices of the resources.

The main difference between the two methods is the reporting of one account ('cost of goods sold') versus two accounts ('purchases' and 'change in inventory') in the income statement. Thus, it is a question of fineness of information in the income statement and that is an issue which affects the users.

2.3.2 Goods manufactured

The main objective of Puccini & Co. is to manufacture and sell umbrellas. It could also offer a service of maintenance and repairs on its umbrellas. Service cannot, by definition, be stored. At the end of any period Puccini & Co. may, however, happen to have the following types of inventories:

- Inventory of finished umbrellas, ready for sale.
- Inventory of semi-finished umbrellas. For example, the mechanical parts of the umbrella and the fabric may be manufactured in two different workshops before final assembly in a third workshop. Each workshop may create an inventory of partially finished umbrellas or umbrella subsystems (they are called semi-finished).
- Work in progress (umbrellas or subsystems that are still being worked on when the period ends). They are neither finished nor semi-finished but somewhere in between. In industries where the transformation process is very long (such as ship building or assembly or aircraft), this inventory may be very significant and its correct evaluation may be essential to the estimation of the income of the period.
- 'Inventory' of development projects (R&D, engineering, development of new machinery by the manufacturing personnel themselves, etc.).

For all these 'inventories', the logic of valuation is absolutely similar to the one followed above for raw materials, goods, merchandise, or parts and components for consumption or resale. Instead of being consumed to satisfy customers request directly, raw materials and parts are first consumed in a production process and then the finished products are made available to customers and are, hopefully, sold.

The following diagram illustrates the process (see Figure 2.20).

In each box the same equation applies: Beginning inventory plus new 'Entries' minus 'Withdrawals' equals 'Ending inventory'.

Logically, given that there are two methods for inventory accounting, there are two different but perfectly compatible income statement presentations, as illustrated in Figure 2.21.

If the income statement is prepared according to the perpetual method for inventory recording, the users will only have available the cost of goods sold and the selling, general,

Figure 2.20 The process of inventory accounting

RAW MATERIALS	MANUFACTURING	FINISHED GOODS	INCOME STATEMENT
Beginning inventory of raw materials **Plus** purchases **Minus** consumption in production **Equals** ending inventory of raw materials	Beginning inventory of work in progress **Plus** resources consumed (includes cost of materials consumed, labor, depreciation, energy, etc.) **Minus** transfers to finished products inventory **Equals** ending inventory of work in progress	Beginning inventory of finished goods **Plus** transfers received from manufacturing **Minus** transfers to income statement (cost of goods sold) **Equals** ending inventory of finished goods	REVENUES **Minus** cost of sales (i.e., manufacturing cost of goods sold) **Minus** other costs such as selling, marketing, and administrative costs **Equals** profit

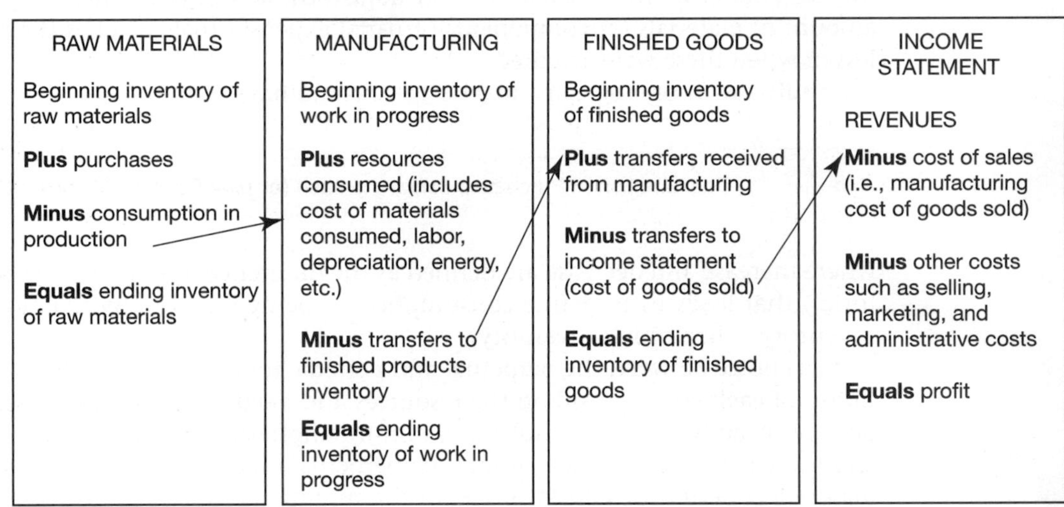

Figure 2.21 Income statement and inventory

Income statement using the periodic inventory system (Method 2) for inventory recording	**Income statement using the perpetual inventory system (Method 1) for inventory recording**
Beginning inventory of raw materials + Purchases of raw materials − Ending inventory of raw materials = **Cost of raw materials consumed (CoMC)**	
Revenues Sales revenue	**Revenues** Sales revenue
Expenses Beginning inventory of raw materials + Purchases of raw materials − Ending inventory of raw materials	**Expenses**
+ Beginning inventory of finished products + Expenses by nature incurred for production + Depreciation expense of productive equipment − Ending inventory of finished products	+ Beginning inventory of finished products + Manufacturing expenses including CoMC incurred for production + Depreciation expense of productive equipment − Ending inventory of finished products
	= Cost of goods sold
− Selling, general, and administrative expenses (SG&A), including depreciation expense of commercial and administrative equipment	− Selling, general, and administrative expenses (SG&A) including depreciation expense of commercial and administrative equipment
= Net income	= Net income

ALTERNATIVELY

Revenues Sales revenue + Change in inventory of finished products	**Revenues** Sales revenue
Expenses Purchases of raw materials +Change in inventory of raw materials +Expenses by nature pertaining to manufacturing +Depreciation expenses of productive equipment +Selling, general, and administrative expenses (by nature) (generally abbreviated SG&A) including depreciation expense of commercial and administrative equipment	**Expenses** Cost of goods sold Selling, general, and administrative expenses (SG&A) (structured functionally and not necessarily by nature) including depreciation expense of commercial and administrative equipment
= Net income	= Net income

and administrative expenses, which might or might not be reported in some detail, however inventory levels will only be found by looking at the balance sheet.

If, on the contrary, the periodic method of recording inventories is followed, the income statement will in principle provide more details, in that both purchases and inventories will be provided. (Some companies, e.g., in Germany, report in the expenses one line 'Materials consumed' which represents the netting of purchases of raw materials and of the change in inventory of raw materials, whereas the change in inventory of finished products is displayed in the revenues side of the income statement. These cases, even if they indicate the probable use of the periodic method, show that some businesses feel the need to disclose only one line of expenses for the consumption of raw materials and rely on the balance sheet to provide the complementary information that will fully enlighten the users.)

Regardless of the method, any change in inventory is automatically reported, either by: (a) a one-line item (the cost of goods consumed); or (b) by reporting purchases and the net change in inventory; or (c) by providing the three components that define the balance, i.e., purchases and beginning and ending inventories. In recent years the choice appears to have been limited to the first two positions, thus relegating, in any case, the absolute value of inventories to the balance sheet.

Whether or not to report the balance of the change in inventory in the income statement is a question of choice and of uses of the financial statement. It may appear interesting to some users to be able to find a measure of the evolution of inventories over the period (i.e., a measure of the preparedness of the firm for subsequent periods) in the income statement, next to information pertaining to the profitability of current sales. Others may find the information redundant since ending and beginning inventories are in the balance sheet. What matters is that both the perpetual and the periodic approaches provide a good matching of expenses with revenues. The income for the period is, of course, the same, regardless of the method used (in a non-inflationary world).

2.4 Financial statement analysis

Financial statements are prepared by businesses and used by different stakeholders in their decision making. Investors are looking for: (a) an understanding concerning how profit was created (analysis of the income statement); and (b) being able to build an evaluation of the prognosis for the future of the firm. In this context, ratios (i.e., a metric that describes the relation between two variables that are key to the success of the firm) may prove to be useful in providing a quick idea about the soundness of the financial structure and the quality of the financial performance of the company. Although financial statement analysis will be revisited in almost all of the following chapters, and specifically in Chapters 14 and 15, we wanted to introduce some basic ratios right now to reinforce the message of usefulness of financial statements.

2.4.1 Balance sheet ratios

Short-term liquidity ratios The following ratios assess the firm's ability to finance its day-to-day operations and to pay its liabilities as they fall due.

Current ratio = Current assets/Current liabilities (amounts falling due within one year)

The current ratio shows the firm's ability to pay its current liabilities from its current assets, i.e., the probability that a slowdown in the economy or in the operating cycle will place the firm in a difficult liquidity position.

Cash ratio = (Cash + Marketable securities)/Current liabilities

The objective of the cash ratio is to evidence the firm's ability to pay its current liabilities from its cash and cash equivalents (i.e., the ability of the firm to cover its short-term obligations even without having to wait until the end of the operating cycle).

Average collection period = [(Accounts receivable Year 2 + Accounts receivable Year 1)/2 × 365]/Sales

The average length of time to collect accounts receivable is an important indicator relating to the management of receivables, but is also a metric describing part of the operating cycle. The longer the collection period, the longer the cycle is that transforms cash into cash again. The longer the operating cash to cash cycle is, the more long-term financing the firm needs.

Long-term solvency ratios The objective is now to determine the firm's ability to pay its long-term liabilities.

Long-term debt to equity ratio = Long-term debt/Equity

This ratio is often known as the degree of financial leverage. A firm that has a large equity to debt ratio is said to be 'overcapitalized' or 'underleveraged'. Conversely, a firm that has a very small equity and large debt is called 'undercapitalized' or 'highly leveraged'.

If two, nearly equivalent, firms differ only on their value of this debt to equity ratio, the one with the highest leverage will provide the better return to their shareholders (interest expense is not proportional to sales but to the level of indebtedness, all things being equal). But, of course, that firm is also the one that takes a higher risk because it has more external debt than the lesser leveraged firm. If a firm is too leveraged, capital providers may feel the situation is risky for lenders and thus charge a higher rate of interest than they would have otherwise. The interest expense that arises from the long-term debt may place the highly leveraged firm in a difficult position in terms of profitability. Overleveraged firms are generally undercapitalized and must dedicate an often undue proportion of their cash flow to meeting their interest expense, thus depriving the firm of the possibility of investing in developing products or markets.

Conversely, overcapitalized firms may not avail themselves of the opportunity of using borrowed capital effectively. External capital is generally obtained at a cost that is lower than the cost of shareholder capital. As long as the business invests in projects that return more than the cost of financing, the shareholders receive wealth without having had to provide the capital. The level of leverage appropriate for a business is a question beyond the scope of this textbook. Each managerial team will decide on the leverage they feel suits best the interests of their shareholders.

2.4.2 Income statement ratios

The main ratios are known as 'profitability ratios' as they measure the firm's performance.

Return on sales (net profit margin) = Net income/Sales

This ratio computes the percentage of each sales currency unit that contributes to net income. It can be used internally to compare markets or customers, and externally to compare the firm with others in the same sector (same risk and opportunities environment).

Return on shareholders' equity (ROE) = Net income/Average equity[5] (or Earnings before interest and tax (EBIT)/Average equity)

This ratio emphasizes the return to shareholders, i.e., the profit generated during a period on the capital invested by the shareholders. The 'or' in the definition does not mean that the concepts are strictly equivalent but that there are two alternative ways to compute the ROE. Each definition provides a different ratio but these are equivalent in terms of informational content.

Return on investment (ROI) (return on capital employed or **ROCE)** = Net income/(Average long-term liabilities + Average equity) = Net income/Capital employed (or Earnings before interest and tax (EBIT)/Capital employed)

This ratio measures the income earned on invested capital.

Return on assets (ROA) = Net income/[(Assets Year 2 + Assets Year 1)/2]

This ratio measures the firm's ability to use its assets to create profits.

Key points

- Financial statements include a minimum set of documents: balance sheet, income statement, and notes. Additionally, they may comprise a cash flow statement and a statement of changes in equity.
- A balance sheet is a set of two lists of resources on one side (also called assets) and of obligations to external parties on the other side (liabilities to creditors and residual interest due to the shareholders or owners). The two lists must be equal in value or balanced.
- Shareholders' equity represents the obligation the firm has towards its shareholders or the claim the owners of the business have collectively over the firm's current 'net worth' and potential future wealth.
- The balance sheet can be represented by an equation: Assets (resources) = Liabilities (obligations to third parties) + Equity (claims of shareholders).
- An asset is a resource controlled by an enterprise as a result of past events and from which future economic benefits are expected to flow to the enterprise.
- A liability is a present obligation of the enterprise arising from past events. Its settlement is expected to result in an outflow from the enterprise of resources generating economic benefits.
- An income statement describes the processes through which income of the period was created and thus how retained earnings have been modified.
- Revenues represent an increase in shareholders' equity that originates from the business of the company such as a sale of goods or services or interest received from short-term investment.
- Expenses are decreases in shareholders' equity that originate from the business of the company such as services purchased, salaries paid to the employees, rent paid for the use of certain physical facilities, wear and tear on equipment, etc.
- Net income is thus the difference between total revenues and total expenses recorded during a period.
- Retained earnings represent that part of the value created through the firm's operations that shareholders have chosen not to take out of the firm.
- Net income is different from cash.
- Notes to financial statements constitute a clarification of – and a supplement to – the balance sheet, income statement, and cash flow statement (when reported).
- Depreciation is the recognition of the consumption of a fixed asset.
- Profit appropriation is the decision taken by the shareholders to distribute entirely, partially, or not to distribute the profit of the year.

Review (solutions are at the back of the book)

Review 2.1 Vivaldi Company (1)

Topic: Transactions and the business equation
Related part of the chapter: Core/Advanced issues

Vivaldi Company is a retailer. During the year X1 it carried the following transactions:

(A) Creation of the business and provision by shareholders of tangible assets in the amount of 40 and of cash for 60 CU.

(B) Purchase of merchandise for resale: 40 CU (on account).

(C) Advertising expense: 7 CU (on account).

(D) Sale of merchandise to customers (on account): 120 CU. The purchase price of the merchandise that was sold is 30 CU.

(E) Personnel expenses for the period: salaries 30 CU, social charges and fringe benefits 15 CU (these will be paid out in cash during the next period).

(F) Miscellaneous business taxes: 20 CU (will be paid in cash during the next period).

(G Cash received from customers (who had bought on account): 60 CU.

(H) Payment to the merchandise suppliers: 35 CU.

(I) Payment of salaries: 30 CU.

(J) The assets brought as a capital contribution when the business was created are expected to have a useful life of 10 years. The loss of value of the asset is expected to be the same each year for 10 years.

(K) The purchase value of the merchandise on hand at the end of the year (ending inventory) is 10 CU.

Required

1. Show the impact of each event on the basic business equation (recording the purchase of merchandise in expenses).
2. Prepare the year-end balance sheet reflecting the events listed in A–K above.
3. Prepare the income statement for the period reflecting the events listed in A–K above.

Review 2.2 Vivaldi Company (2)

Topic: Transactions and impact on the financial statements
Related part of the chapter: Core/Advanced issues

Refer to the Vivaldi (1) exercise above.

Required

Record the transactions in the appropriate accounts.

Review 2.3 Albinoni Company

Topic: Transactions and the business equation
Related part of the chapter: Core issues

Albinoni Company is a retailer. During one accounting period, it carried the following transactions:

1. Creation of the business and provision by shareholders of a piece of equipment for the amount of 80 CU, and of cash for 30 CU.
2. A loan was received from the banker: 200 CU.

3. Miscellaneous business taxes: 40 CU (paid cash during the period).
4. Purchase of merchandise for resale: 50 CU (on account).
5. Legal fees: 10 CU (cash outflow during the period).
6. Personnel expenses for the period: salaries and social charges: 30 CU (paid cash during the period).
7. Sale of merchandise to customers: 80 CU (on account) and 20 CU (cash sales). The merchandise that was sold had been purchased for 40 CU.
8. Payment to the merchandise suppliers: 30 CU.
9. Cash received from customers: 70 CU.
10. The assets brought as a capital contribution when the business was created are expected to have a useful life of four years. The loss of value of the asset is expected to be the same each year for four years.
11. The value of the merchandise on hand at the end of the year (ending inventory) is 10 CU.

Required

Show the impact of each event on the balance sheet equation. You have the following choice:

1. To record the purchases of merchandise as inventory ('perpetual inventory system') or
2. To record these purchases as expenses ('periodic inventory system'). Please mention clearly your choice.

Use the format presented in Appendix 1.

Appendix 1: Balance sheet

Please identify your choice of inventory carrying method: purchases recorded as inventory ('perpetual inventory system') or purchases recorded as expenses ('periodic inventory system')

	Assets			=	Liabilities	+	Shareholders' equity (SE)	
	+	+	+	=	+	+	+	Details of SE transactions
(1)								
(2)								
(3)								
(4)								
(5)								
(6)								
(7)								
(8)								
(9)								
(10)								
(11)								
Ending balance								

Assignments

Assignment 2.1
Multiple-choice questions

Related part of the chapter: Core/Advanced issues

Select the right answer (only one possible answer unless otherwise stated).

1. Raw materials and merchandise purchased can be included in (two solutions)
   (a) Cash
   (b) Expenses
   (c) Fixed assets
   (d) Current assets
   (e) None of these

2. Obtaining a long-term debt affects which of the following accounts
   (a) Operating liabilities
   (b) Financial liabilities
   (c) Shareholders' equity
   (d) Retained earnings
   (e) None of these

3. Land, buildings, furniture and computers are included in
   (a) Current assets
   (b) Fixed assets
   (c) Cash
   (d) Inventory
   (e) None of these

4. The document reporting all the expenses and revenues for a given period is the
   (a) Balance sheet
   (b) Cash flow statement
   (c) Income statement
   (d) Notes to financial statement
   (e) Statement of changes in equity
   (f) None of these

5. A balance sheet is presented
   (a) Only after profit appropriation
   (b) Only before profit appropriation
   (c) Before and after profit appropriation
   (d) None of these

6. An income statement is presented
   (a) Only after profit appropriation
   (b) Only before profit appropriation
   (c) Before and after profit appropriation
   (d) None of these

7. Advance payments received from customers are included in
   (a) Revenues
   (b) Assets
   (c) Liabilities
   (d) Shareholders' equity
   (e) Expenses
   (f) None of these

8. Advance payments to suppliers are included in
   (a) Revenues
   (b) Assets
   (c) Liabilities
   (d) Shareholders' equity
   (e) Expenses
   (f) None of these

9. The depreciation recorded in the balance sheet includes
   (a) Accumulated depreciation for past years
   (b) Depreciation for the current year
   (c) Both
   (d) None of these

10. An example of an item that is not a current asset is
    (a) Accounts receivable
    (b) Inventory
    (c) Equipment
    (d) Cash
    (f) None of these

Assignment 2.2
Vivaldi Company (3)

Topic: Transactions and the business equation
Related part of the chapter: Core/Advanced issues

Please refer to the Vivaldi Company (1) exercise above.

Required

1. Show the impact of each event on the accounting equation (recording the purchases of merchandise in inventory in the balance sheet).

2. Prepare the year-end balance sheet reflecting the events listed in A–K above.
3. Prepare the income statement for the period reflecting the events listed in A–K above.

Assignment 2.3
Busoni Company

Topic: Transactions and the financial statements
Related part of the chapter: Core/Advanced issues

Busoni Company is a wholesaler. During one accounting period, it carried the following transactions (in thousands of CU):

1. Creation of the business and provision by shareholders of a piece of equipment in the amount of 100 CU, and of cash for 40 CU.
2. Merchandise for resale were purchased: 60 CU (on account).
3. A debt was received from the banker: 100 CU.
4. Personnel expenses were incurred for the period: salaries and social charges: 35 CU (paid cash).
5. Merchandise was sold to customers: 50 CU (on account) and 40 CU (paid cash). The merchandise that was sold had been purchased for 38 CU.
6. Cash was received from customers: 42 CU.
7. Merchandise suppliers were given a partial payment: 55 CU.
8. The assets brought as a capital contribution when the business was created are expected to have a useful life of five years. The loss of value of the asset is expected to be the same each year.
9. The value of the merchandise on hand at the end of the year (ending inventory) is 22 CU.

Required

Show the impact of each event on the financial statements with T-accounts. You have the following choice:

1. To record the purchases of merchandise as inventory ('perpetual inventory system') or
2. To record these purchases as expenses ('periodic inventory system'). Please mention clearly your choice.

Use the following structure.

Balance sheet		Income statement	
Assets	Equity and liabilities	Expenses	Revenues

Assignment 2.4
Corelli Company (1)

Topic: Classification of accounts
Related part of the chapter: Core issues

Corelli Company provides below a list (in alphabetical order) of all the accounts it uses (far left-hand column). For each line you are provided five choices of families of accounts to which the account listed on the left can be related.

Required

Indicate by a checkmark in the appropriate column to which account family each account is related. It should be noted that the accounts should be related to one column only (one 'family'), because one account is only one part of a double entry.

	Assets	Shareholders' equity	Liabilities	Revenues	Expenses
Accounts payable					
Accounts receivable					
Administrative expense					
Advance payments received from customers					
Advance payments to suppliers					
Buildings					
Cash at bank					
Cash in hand					
Computing equipment					
Financial debts					
Income tax expense					
Income tax payable					
Industrial equipment					
Insurance expense					
Interest expense					
Interest revenue					
Loans					
Marketable securities					
Repair and maintenance expense					
Salaries payable					
Salary expense					
Sales of merchandise					
Selling expense					
Share capital					
Social security payable					

Assignment 2.5
Corelli Company (2)

Topic: Classification of accounts
Related part of the chapter: Advanced issues

Corelli Company provides below a listing (in alphabetical order) of all the accounts it uses (far left-hand column). For each line you are provided five choices of families of accounts to which the account listed on the left can be related.

Required

Indicate by a checkmark in the appropriate column to which account family or families each account is related. It should be noted that the accounts should be related to one column only (one 'family'), because one account is only one part of a double entry.

	Assets	Shareholders' equity	Liabilities	Revenues	Expenses
Accumulated depreciation					
Cost of goods sold					
Finished products					
Merchandise					
Purchases of merchandise					
Purchases of supplies					
Raw materials					
Reserves					
Retained earnings					

Assignment 2.6
Stora Enso*

Topic: Financial statement analysis
Related part of the chapter: Advanced issues

Stora Enso is a Finnish company involved in paper production. From its annual reports 1997 through 2004, we extracted the following balance sheets and income statements, which have been prepared in accordance with International Accounting Standards. (Figures for 1997 have been converted from Finnish Markka to Euros at the rate of 5.94573 Markka = €1.00.)

Consolidated balance sheet

€ millions – as at 31 December	1997	1998	1999	2000	2001	2002	2003	2004
Assets								
Fixed assets and other long-term investments								
Goodwill	509.4	540.5	466.4	2,228.6	2,276.0	1,055.5	902.6	787.9
Intangible fixed assets	42.2	42.0	60.3	89.2	89.6	73.3	80.4	108.1
Property, plant, and equipment	10,731.5	10,424.6	10,721.7	12,785.6	12,335.6	10,812.1	9,964.5	9,754.8
Biological assets	0.0	0.0	0.0	0.0	0.0	0.0	1,587.8	64.6
Investments in associated companies	317.9	334.1	165.5	213.6	306.7	211.7	319.0	568.1
Listed securities	37.9	48.0	49.3	132.3	197.4	169.2	227.7	220.1
Unlisted shares	57.0	128.8	280.4	177.2	181.0	148.5	140.8	132.8
Non-current loan receivables	77.8	90.1	66.8	486.3	505.4	480.6	44.3	233.1
Deferred tax assets	11.6	7.8	5.9	11.7	28.1	52.7	12.1	11.4
Other non-current assets	78.6	79.2	88.6	254.5	257.9	241.1	170.3	210.5
	11,863.9	**11,695.1**	**11,904.9**	**16,379.0**	**16,177.7**	**13,244.7**	**13,449.5**	**12,091.4**
Current assets								
Inventories	1,289.1	1,332.3	1,265.6	1,589.5	1,600.0	1,565.0	1,623.5	1,771.3
Tax receivables	0.3	3.4	71.9	153.0	224.3	243.1	182.5	160.9
Short-term receivables	2,040.5	1,783.4	2,090.5	2,360.7	1,976.3	1,902.4	1,703.3	1,865.3
Current portion of loan receivables	110.0	3.9	63.0	96.2	333.1	1,090.5	781.8	248.7
Cash and cash equivalents	249.7	595.0	642.2	744.4	247.0	168.5	201.5	274.3
	3,689.6	**3,718.0**	**4,133.2**	**4,943.8**	**4,380.7**	**4,969.5**	**4,492.6**	**4,320.5**
Total assets	**15,553.5**	**15,413.1**	**16,038.1**	**21,322.8**	**20,558.4**	**18,214.2**	**17,942.1**	**16,411.9**

(*continued*)

Consolidated balance sheet (*continued*)

€ millions – as at 31 December	1997	1998	1999	2000	2001	2002	2003	2004
Shareholders' equity and liabilities								
Shareholders' equity								
Share capital	1,277.5	1,277.5	1,277.6	1,576.3	1,541.5	1,529.6	1,469.3	1,423.3
Share premium fund	0.0	0.0	379.6	1,823.2	1,641.9	1,554.0	1,237.4	1,009.2
Treasury shares	0.0	0.0	0.0	−173.7	−125.5	−314.9	−258.0	−180.8
Other comprehensive income	0.0	0.0	0.0	0.0	58.6	233.4	114.6	67.6
Cumulative translation adjustment	0.0	0.0	15.7	−69.6	−52.5	−144.4	−197.1	−218.9
Restricted equity	736.1	704.6	0.0	0.0	0.0	0.0	0.0	0.0
Retained earnings	3,090.5	3,093.2	3,537.2	3,979.6	4,998.7	5,417.8	5,448.8	5,211.0
Net profit for the period	409.0	191.0	746.4	1,435.0	926.3	−240.7	137.9	739.7
	5,513.1	**5,266.3**	**5,956.5**	**8,570.8**	**8,989.0**	**8,034.8**	**7,952.9**	**8,051.1**
Minority interests	**271.7**	**278.8**	**202.0**	**149.4**	**50.2**	**30.4**	**60.3**	**136.1**
Long-term liabilities								
Pension and post-employment benefit provisions	564.0	569.6	575.5	771.8	774.0	919.0	911.9	637.8
Other provisions	121.5	256.0	186.5	173.4	153.6	194.5	97.1	60.9
Deferred tax liabilities	1,373.8	1,326.6	1,489.7	2,247.5	2,011.0	1,737.4	1,777.3	1,320.6
Long-term debt	4,209.1	4,294.1	3,846.2	5,514.7	5,182.0	4,525.2	3,404.6	3,328.1
Other long-term liabilities	84.4	90.7	87.0	92.6	51.4	36.9	77.7	153.2
	6,352.8	**6,537.0**	**6,184.9**	**8,800.0**	**8,172.0**	**7,413.0**	**6,268.6**	**5,500.6**
Current liabilities								
Current portion of long-term debt	1,202.1	1,218.4	446.7	262.8	230.0	306.5	359.5	102.1
Interest-bearing liabilities	590.1	475.4	1,476.6	1,078.0	997.5	343.9	1,410.1	597.4
Short-term operative liabilities	1,485.6	1,451.7	1,507.8	1,890.6	1,631.0	1,547.9	1,538.3	1,673.1
Tax liabilities	138.1	185.5	263.6	571.2	488.7	537.7	352.4	351.5
	3,415.9	**3,331.0**	**3,694.7**	**3,802.6**	**3,347.2**	**2,736.0**	**3,660.3**	**2,724.1**
Total shareholders' equity and liabilities	**15,553.5**	**15,413.1**	**16,038.1**	**21,322.8**	**20,558.4**	**18,214.2**	**17,942.1**	**16,411.9**

Consolidated income statement

€ millions – year ended 31 December	1998	1999	2000	2001	2002	2003	2004
Sales	10,489.6	10,635.7	13,017.0	13,508.8	12,782.6	12,172.3	12,395.8
Other operating income	44.9	77.9	96.1	63.2	218.6	39.3	146.7
Changes in inventories of finished goods and work in progress	41.8	−119.4	−51.1	38.4	30.3	63.5	39.0
Gain on disposal of discontinued operations, energy	0.0	48.2	524.8	0.0	0.0	0.0	0.0
Change in net value of biological assets	0.0	0.0	0.0	0.0	0.0	11.6	7.1
Materials and services	−5,033.5	−4,826.4	−6,037.8	−6,547.8	−6,415.7	−6,202.5	−6,573.6
Freight and sales commissions	−1,016.0	−993.5	−1,282.2	−1,234.0	−1,240.9	−1,286.8	−1,367.8
Personnel expenses	−1,805.2	−1,754.3	−1,995.7	−2,234.4	−2,308.1	−2,297.6	−1,937.3

(*continued*)

Consolidated income statement (*continued*)

Other operating expenses	−861.5	−757.5	−770.4	−839.7	−802.6	−828.0	−831.8
Depreciation, amortization, and impairment, charges	−1,151.4	−911.1	−1,129.4	−1,267.6	−2,441.9	−1,200.4	−1,172.0
Operating profit	**708.7**	**1,399.6**	**2,371.3**	**1,486.9**	**−177.7**	**471.4**	**706.1**
Share of results in associated companies	9.9	9.7	20.6	79.6	14.6	−23.0	38.9
Net financial items	−379.2	−266.6	−292.9	−343.5	−206.2	−237.7	−106.0
Profit before tax and minority items	**339.4**	**1,142.7**	**2,099.0**	**1,223.0**	**−369.3**	**210.7**	**639**
Income tax expense	−148.2	−391.8	−650.3	−299.6	128.5	−67.0	108.8
Profit/(loss) after tax	**191.2**	**750.9**	**1,448.7**	**923.4**	**−240.8**	**143.7**	**747.8**
Minority interests	−0.2	−4.5	−13.7	2.9	0.1	−5.8	−8.1
Net profit/loss for the period	**191.0**	**746.4**	**1,435.0**	**926.3**	**−240.7**	**137.9**	**739.7**

Required

1. Compute the ratios you feel are important for the evaluation of the business for the years 1998 through 2004.
2. Evaluate the evolution of the context (you may either use your common sense or visit the Stora Enso web site at www.storaenso.com) and of the performance of the firm on the basis of these ratios. What risks seem to be increasing?

Please notice that minority interests[6] are often included in equity in the computation of ratios based on this concept.

References

IASB (1989) Framework for the Preparation and Presentation of Financial Statements, in International Financial Reporting Standards (bound volume, annual edition), London.

IASB (2003a) International Accounting Standard No. 1: Presentation of Financial Statements, London.

IASB (2003b) International Accounting Standard No. 16: Property, Plant and Equipment, London.

IASB (2003c) International Accounting Standard No. 18: Revenue, London.

Additional material on the website

Go to http://www.thomsonlearning.co.uk/stolowylebas2 for further information.

The following appendices to this chapter are available on the dedicated website:

Appendix 2.1: Balance sheet and value creation

Appendix 2.2: Reporting for retained earnings and reserves

Appendix 2.3: Recording of inventory – Impact on the basic business equation

Notes

1. The snapshot, however, represents the picture only at its 'historical' value. For example, a piece of land will be shown at its purchase price, even if events subsequent to the purchase may have modified the potential resale value of the land. If, for example, the development of a shopping area next to the plot has increased its value, such a change in value will not be recorded in the accounts. Accounting must be credible without ambiguity or debate. Since the value of a resource (exchange or resale value or potential to create sellable objects or services in the future) changes continuously, accounting practitioners have chosen long ago to prefer reliability over accuracy.
2. As indicated in the preface, the choice of the currency unit has no bearing on the logic of our presentation. We will specify the currency only when presenting real cases.
3. It should be noted that the expression 'P&L' is also used in a North American environment where the term 'Income statement' is the official name of the document. 'P&L' is then a simple way to refer to the 'income statement'.
4. Each amount is recorded in an 'account', i.e., a table with several columns that classifies entries between increases or decreases. There is an account for every type of resource or obligation, and therefore for revenues and expenses (cash, capital, accounts payable, etc.). By convention, accounts are often presented in the form of a T (thus the term T-account), separating movement in homogeneous categories on either side of the vertical bar of the T (see further illustrations in Chapter 4).
5. Average equity = (Beginning shareholders' equity + Ending shareholders' equity)/2.
6. They represent the part of the net results of operations of a subsidiary attributable to interests that are not owned, directly or indirectly through subsidiaries, by the parent company (minority shareholders). This item will be presented in a more detailed manner in Chapter 13, devoted to Consolidation.

C3

Chapter 3
Financial statements presentation

Learning objectives

After studying this chapter, you will understand:

- That the balance sheet and income statement can be presented in different ways but that the logic of their construction remains the same and the informational content is often not affected by differences in presentation.
- That the balance sheet can be presented vertically or horizontally, single step or multiple step, and with a classification of assets and liabilities by nature or by term.
- That the income statement can be presented vertically or horizontally, single step or multiple step, and with a classification of expenses by nature or by function.
- That neither presentation is intrinsically 'better'.
- The main purpose and content of the notes to financial statements.
- The objective of the cash flow statement.
- How the cash flow statement relates to the balance sheet and income statement.
- The content of the annual report.
- The common formats for the presentation of the balance sheet and the income statement.
- That the accounting terminology may differ between US English and UK English.

In the first two chapters we briefly introduced three of the main documents called financial statements that are part of the managerial information set. These documents report the financial situation of the firm. The accounting information contained in the balance sheet, the income statement, and the notes to financial statements is essential for decision-makers and all stakeholders. The 4th European Directive (EU 1978) specifies in its article 2 that: 'The annual accounts shall comprise the balance sheet, the profit and loss account and the notes on the accounts'. A large majority of countries, whether part of the European Union or not, require at least these three documents. Many countries add the cash flow statement (see below and Chapter 14) and/or a statement of changes in shareholders' equity (see Chapter 11) to the required reporting package to be sure investors, shareholders, and other accounting information users are well informed about the situation of a business.

In its Accounting Standard No. 1 (IASB 2003: § 8), the International Accounting Standards Board (IASB) offers a definition of **financial statements** by stating that 'a complete set of financial statements comprises:

(a) a balance sheet;

(b) an income statement;

(c) a statement of changes in equity showing either:

- all changes in equity; or
- changes in equity other than those arising from capital transactions with equity

holders acting in their capacity as equity holders;

(d) a cash flow statement; and

(e) notes, comprising a summary of significant accounting policies and other explanatory notes'.

The purpose of this chapter is to develop further the three core components of financial statements (balance sheet, income statement, and notes), and to briefly introduce the cash flow statement, which will be fully developed in Chapter 14.

As mentioned earlier, the issue of comparability of financial situation of firms is essential for accounting information users. However, this objective of ease of comparability is far from being achieved today. Many countries have either encouraged, or required, or accepted a diversity of formats of presentation of the key documents. Each presentation emanates from a certain vision of the business model financial statements are supposed to describe. Chapter 2 already mentioned that the order in which assets and liabilities are listed in a balance sheet depends on the choice of the image the firm wants to give to information users (or the regulatory authorities want businesses to provide). For example, a firm may be deemed to be 'secure' or 'solid' either because: (a) it has a strong productive capacity (it wants to show off its physical and intellectual assets first to a reader from a western culture who reads from the top to the bottom and left to right); or (b) because it is very liquid (it wants to highlight its ability to pay its debt by presenting liquid assets first). Neither position is intrinsically better. Each is coherent with a certain philosophy and communication approach.

A good understanding of the different formats of financial statements is, however, necessary. Each format will be, as we will show in Chapter 15, more or less supportive of certain financial statement analysis tools, or will require additional reformatting of the data to be able to derive certain ratios perceived as important by analysts. Furthermore, the knowledge of the different formats will allow the user to analyze almost any type of financial statements published by any company from any country in the world.

This chapter will be an opportunity to explore the different presentations of a content that is essentially the same. We will focus on the format of the statements and not on specific accounts, which will only be introduced in later chapters.

1 Core issues

As mentioned in the IASB Conceptual Framework (IASB 1989: § 47): 'financial statements portray the financial effects of transactions and other events by grouping them into broad classes according to their economic characteristics. These broad classes are termed the elements of financial statements'.

1.1 Balance sheet

1.1.1 Definition

The **balance sheet** shows the financial position of a business on a given date. The IASB specifies that 'the elements directly related to the measurement of financial position are assets, liabilities and equity' (IASB 1989: § 49).

1.1.2 Possible presentations

The key choices are essentially pertaining to format of the list (horizontal or vertical), to the degree of fineness (single or multiple-step), and to the type of classification of assets and liabilities (by term or by nature, see Figure 3.1).

Formats The balance sheet is a list of account balances. The list can be continuous (vertical format, see Figure 3.2), or presented as two lists side by side (horizontal format, see Figure 3.3).

The 'horizontal' format is often represented as two blocks as in Figure 3.4.

Figure 3.1 Presentation of the balance sheet

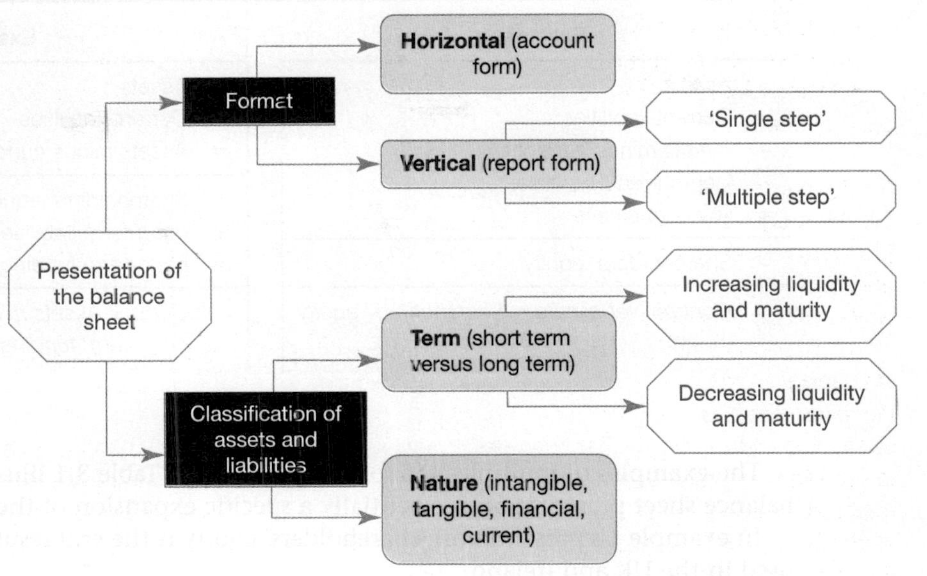

Figure 3.2 Vertical format

Figure 3.3 Horizontal format

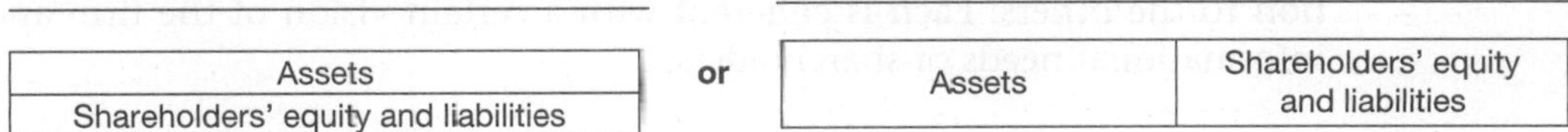

Figure 3.4 Balance sheet horizontal format

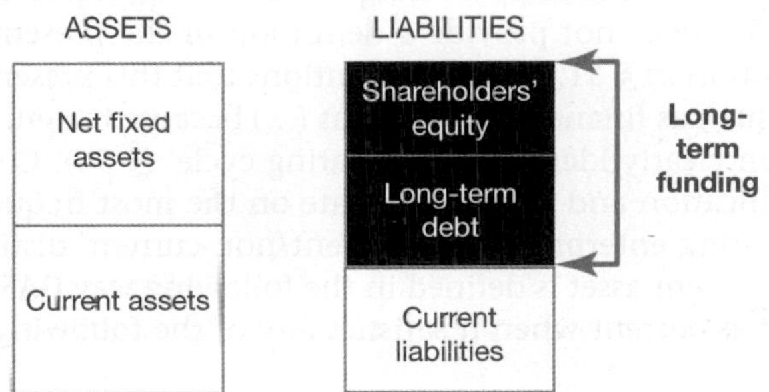

Degree of fineness in the vertical format The **'single-step' format** provides a simple list of accounts with very little detail or value added by the presentation, while the **'multiple-step' format** creates a list of subsets of the main categories of assets and liabilities, and identifies managerially useful subtotals by subtracting relevant other subcategories of assets or liabilities.

The single-step and the multiple-step approaches reflect different readings of the basic business equation and different perspectives on the firm's position:

Single step →	Assets = Liabilities + Shareholders' equity
Multiple step →	Assets − Liabilities = Shareholders' equity

Table 3.1 Balance sheet examples using the 'multiple-step' vertical format

Example 1	Example 2
Assets – Current liabilities = Assets minus current liabilities – Non-current liabilities = Total net assets	Assets – Current liabilities = Assets minus current liabilities
= Shareholders' equity	Shareholders' equity + Long-term liabilities = Long-term funding
Control: Net assets = Shareholders' equity	*Control: Assets minus Current liabilities = Long-term funding*

The examples of multiple-step format provided in Table 3.1 illustrate the fact that any balance sheet presentation is essentially a specific expansion of the business equation.

In example 1's presentation, shareholders' equity is the end result. It is a format widely used in the UK and Ireland.

The format illustrated by example 2 focuses attention on long-term funding of the firm. It is found in some Dutch (e.g., Royal Vopak) and Indian (e.g., Wipro) annual reports.

Neither one of the two illustrated formats provides an intrinsically superior presentation to the others. Each is coherent with a certain vision of the firm and the perceived informational needs of shareholders.

Classifications of assets and liabilities IAS 1 (IASB 2003: § 51) states that 'an entity shall present current and non-current assets, and current and non-current liabilities (...) except when a presentation based on liquidity provides information that is reliable and is more relevant. When that exception applies, all assets and liabilities shall be presented broadly in order of [increasing or decreasing] liquidity'.

IAS 1 does not provide a definition of the presentation 'by liquidity' described as an exception in § 51. It simply mentions that this presentation could be used 'for some entities, such as financial institutions (...) because the entity does not supply goods or services within clearly identifiable operating cycle' (§ 54). Consequently, we will not discuss this classification and will concentrate on the most frequent practice for commercial or manufacturing enterprises, the 'current/non-current' distinction.

A current asset is defined in the following way (IASB 2003: § 57): 'An asset shall be classified as current when it satisfies any of the following criteria:

(a) it is expected to be realized in, or intended for sale or consumption in, the entity's normal operating cycle;

(b) it is held primarily for the purpose of being traded;

(c) it is expected to be realized within twelve months after the balance sheet date; or

(d) it is cash or a cash equivalent (...) unless it is restricted from being exchanged or used to settle a liability for at least twelve months after the balance sheet date.

All other assets shall be classified as non-current'.

A symmetric definition is provided for current liabilities (IASB 2003: § 60): 'A liability shall be classified as current when it satisfies any of the following criteria:

(a) it is expected to be settled in the entity's normal operating cycle;

(b) it is held primarily for the purpose of being traded;

(c) it is due to be settled within twelve months after the balance sheet date; or

(d) the entity does not have an unconditional right to defer settlement of the liability for at least twelve months after the balance sheet date.

All other liabilities shall be classified as non-current'.

In the definitions provided in §§ 57 and 60 of IAS 1, the list of 'any of the following criteria' can be summarized as two main alternative criteria emerge: (a) the realization/settlement in the operating cycle; or (b) the realization/settlement within 12 months after the balance sheet date.

In practice, when looking at the financial reporting of companies around the world, it appears that companies are consistent in their choice of classification of assets and liabilities: the same classification is adopted on both sides of the balance sheet.

In summary, two types of references, coherent with IAS 1, can be used to classify assets and liabilities that are:

- Reference to the duration of the operating cycle: we call this classification 'by nature' (financial versus operating).
- Reference to the 12 months after the balance sheet date realization/settlement time horizon: we call this second classification 'by term' (short term versus long term).

Even if IAS 1 appears to rank the operating cycle in the first place (see § 53), a cursory observation of financial reporting practices leads to the conclusion that the presentation 'by term' is actually the one most frequently used. We will therefore start our presentation with this classification.

Classification of assets and liabilities 'by term' (short term versus long term) Assets and liabilities are split, respectively, between items that should be recovered/settled in more than 12 months after the balance sheet date (which we call 'long term') and other items that will be recovered/settled within 12 months (called 'short term'). For example, liabilities can be classified in the following subsets:

- Long-term (non-current) liabilities (amounts falling due after more than 12 months):
  - financial debts (long-term portion);
  - accounts payable (for payables due in more than 12 months).
- Short-term (current) liabilities (amounts falling due within 12 months after the balance sheet date):
  - financial debts (short-term portion);
  - bank overdrafts;
  - accounts payable (for which the due date is typically less than 12 months from the balance sheet date).

A parallel classification must also be applied to assets: long-term assets will be recognized as fixed assets (the stream of economic benefits they create for the firm extends beyond one year) and will be distinguished from short-term or current assets which are recovered within 12 months after the balance sheet date.

When the balance sheet is presented according to the 'term' (short term versus long term), two approaches exist: increasing (Table 3.2) or decreasing (Table 3.3) order of liquidity and maturity. Each approach, once again, emphasizes a different point: long-term strength or short-term liquidity. Neither one is, however, intrinsically superior to the other.

The decreasing liquidity approach is most commonly used in North America and in countries that follow the American model. The increasing liquidity approach is most commonly used in continental Europe.

Table 3.2 Increasing liquidity and maturity

Assets	Shareholders' equity and liabilities
Fixed assets	Shareholders' equity
Current assets ■ Inventory ■ Accounts receivable ■ Cash	Liabilities ■ Long term (non-current) ■ Short term (current)

Table 3.3 Decreasing liquidity and maturity

Assets	Liabilities and shareholders' equity
Current assets ■ Cash ■ Accounts receivable ■ Inventory	Liabilities ■ Short term (current) ■ Long term (non-current)
Fixed assets	Shareholders' equity

Classification of assets and liabilities 'by nature' (tangible versus intangible, financial versus operating/trading) This classification emphasizes the nature of the assets and liabilities and their role in the operating cycle or operations of the business illustrated in Figure 3.5.

Figure 3.5 Example of an operating cycle

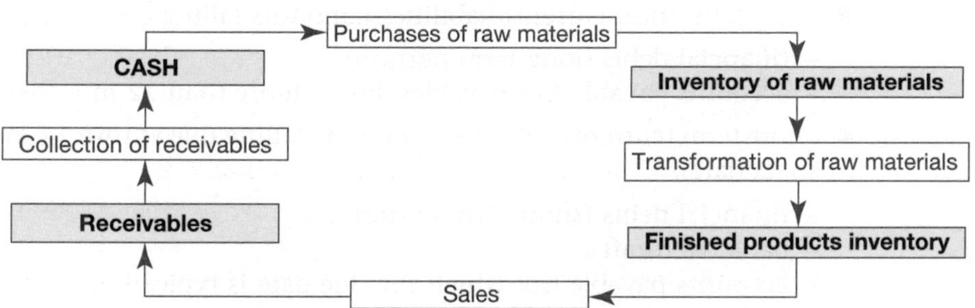

The four current assets in Figure 3.5 are chronologically: cash, inventory of raw materials, finished goods inventory, and accounts receivable. Of course, the purchases of raw materials are not necessarily paid for in cash and may be obtained on credit, which leads to the creation of a debt or accounts payable, a fact that delays the outflow of cash. (We will deal with this issue later.)

Liabilities can be, in the by-nature approach, structured as:

- Financial liabilities (regardless of their due date):
  - debts to financial institutions (long-term and short-term portions of loans obtained);
  - bank overdrafts.

- Trading (or operating) liabilities (debts linked to trading and relations with other partners):
  - advance payments received from customers on contracts to be delivered in the future;
  - accounts payable (debts contracted from suppliers in the course of running the business);
  - debts to tax authorities.

On the asset side a parallel distinction will apply. Financial assets generally are financial investments or loans to business associates (such as key suppliers), while operating or trading assets are connected to the cycle of operations. Inventories and accounts receivable are considered to be operating or trading assets (see Table 3.4).

Operating and trading liabilities and operating and trading assets are generally referred to as 'current liabilities' or 'current assets'. In this context, the term 'current' means 'related to the operating cycle of the business'.

In summary, there is an ambiguity relating to the use of the terminology 'current/non-current' which has, across companies, a dual meaning: based on the context, it either refers to the distinction short term/long term or to the distinction operating/financial. This ambiguity arises from the flexibility given by IAS 1 in its definitions of current assets and liabilities (see above).

IAS 1 (IASB 2003: § 52) also specifies that: 'whichever method of presentation is adopted, for each asset and liability line item that combines amounts expected to be recovered or settled (a) no more than 12 months after the balance sheet date and (b) more than 12 months after the balance sheet date, an entity shall disclose the amount expected to be recovered or settled after more than 12 months'.

Table 3.4 Classification of assets and liabilities 'by nature'

Assets	Shareholders' equity and liabilities
Fixed assets ■ Intangible assets ■ Tangible assets ■ Financial fixed assets	Shareholders' equity
Current assets ■ Inventory ■ Accounts receivable ■ Cash	Liabilities ■ Financial (including the current portion) ■ Operating (due within the time horizon of the operating cycle)

1.2 Income statement

1.2.1 Definition

The **income statement** reports the revenues and expenses incurred during a period and serves to establish the net income. Net income is the remainder after all expenses have been deducted from revenues. It is a measure of the wealth created by an economic entity (increased shareholders' equity) during an accounting period. The income statement reports how the company's financial performance was achieved.

1.2.2 Possible presentations

As was the case for the balance sheet, there are several ways of presenting an income statement (horizontal or vertical format) and a choice of degree of fineness as well as of types of account classifications (see Figure 3.6).

Figure 3.6 Choices in the presentation of the income statement

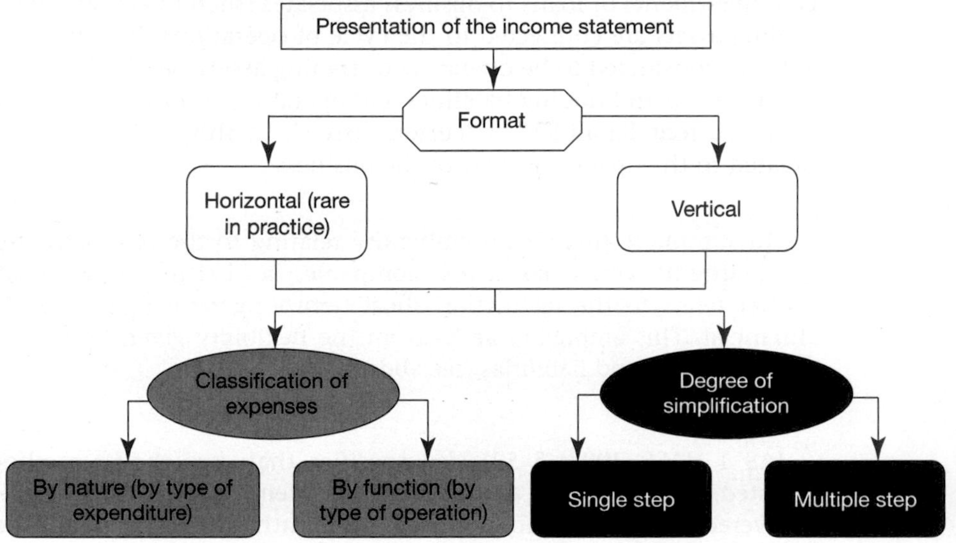

Formats An income statement is a list of account balances. The list can be presented (see Figure 3.7) as a continuous list (vertical format) or as two lists side by side (horizontal format).

Although not commonly used in business reporting, the **horizontal format** is very practical in a pedagogical context. We will often present the income statement in the form of a T-account.

Figure 3.7 Vertical versus horizontal presentations

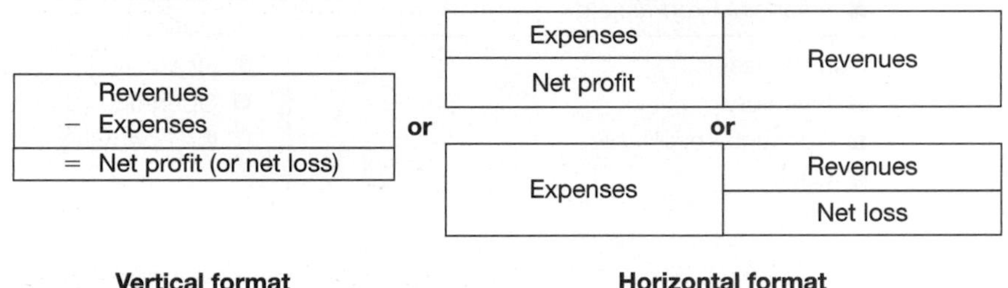

Degree of fineness Expenses are first grouped in homogeneous meaningful categories and then deducted step by step from revenues. The choice is between single and multiple step.

Single step It is the most simplified version of the income statement. Expenses and revenues are each considered as one category (see, for example, the left panel of Figure 3.7).

Multiple step Revenue and expense categories are paired so as to highlight the components of total net income (see Table 3.5). For example, trading (or operating) revenues and trading

Table 3.5 Example of multiple-step income statement (vertical)

	Operating revenues
−	Operating expenses
=	Operating income (or margin) (1)
	Financial revenues
−	Financial expenses
=	Financial income (or margin) (2)
=	Net income (1) + (2)

(or operating) expenses will be grouped to create the trading (or operating) income. Financial revenues and expenses will be offset against one another to inform the users about the role of the financial activity in total net income. This format is also used in reporting income by segments such as types of business, products, markets, regions, etc. (see Chapter 15).

This rich format of reporting income is the most commonly used in business reports because it is more informative than the single-step approach. Its usefulness rests on the ability for the firm to separate revenues and expenses on sound and meaningful bases, without using rules of allocation that would create doubt about the usefulness for decision making of the subcategories of the net income.

Classification of expenses IASB (2003: § 88) states that: 'an entity shall present an analysis of expenses using a classification based on either the nature of expenses or their function within the entity, whichever provides information that is reliable and more relevant'. This standard adds (§ 90) that 'expenses are subclassified to highlight components of financial performance that may differ in terms of frequency, potential for gain or loss and predictability'. This information is provided either by nature or by function. Classification issues are especially important for operating expenses. Thus, in the development below we do not explore classification schemes beyond those of operating income, as most other sources of income are self-explanatory.

Classification by nature (or 'nature of expense method') In this approach, expenses are aggregated in the income statement directly according to their nature: for example, purchases of materials, transportation costs, taxes other than income tax, salaries, social contribution expenses, fringe benefits (the latter can be aggregated to form the category 'remuneration expenses' or 'labor and personnel expenses'), depreciation, etc. (see Table 3.6). This method

Table 3.6 Income statement by nature (vertical presentation)

	Net sales
+	Other operating revenues
−	Purchases of merchandise
−	Change in inventories of merchandise
−	Labor and personnel expense
−	Other operating expenses
−	Depreciation expense
=	Operating income

is simple to apply, even in small enterprises, because no allocation or partition of expenses or costs is required (see IASB 2003: § 91). The structure follows the nature of source documents such as invoices or payment vouchers.

Classification by function (or 'cost of sales method') This method classifies expenses according to their role in the determination of income (cost of goods sold, commercial, distribution, or administrative expenses are common distinctions in this case) (see Table 3.7).

Table 3.7 Income statement by function (vertical presentation)

	Net sales
−	Cost of goods sold (cost of sales)
=	Gross margin
−	Commercial and distribution expenses
−	Administrative expenses
−	Other operating expenses
=	Operating income

Choice of a classification approach The criteria 'degree of fineness' and 'classification of expenses' are not exclusionary and can form a 2 × 2 matrix. For example, an income statement by nature can be presented according to the single- or the multiple-step method. An income statement prepared according to the functional approach can be either single or multiple step. The 'horizontal × functional' approach is, however, rather rare and thus is ignored here.

No single format of the multiple-step approach appears to be dominating in practice. Each firm chooses the representation that best communicates its intended emphasis on specific points and messages.

- Preference for a classification by nature often reflects pressure exercised by some governmental statistics agency to ease their own work of consolidation of income and expenses in their preparation of the national accounts (this is often the case in continental and eastern European countries[1]). Such a presentation is often difficult to decipher by users, especially if they want, as is the purpose of financial reporting, to make forecasts.
- Preference for a functional presentation often reflects an emphasis on the income creation process. It is the preferred method in North America and is also used by most firms quoted on the New York Stock Exchange. The informational content of such annual statements is easily understandable and usable by ordinary users.

The IASB chooses sides by stating that the presentation by function 'provides more relevant information to users than the classification of expenses by nature' (IASB 2003: § 92). However, it draws the attention of the report preparer, in the very same paragraph, to the fact that 'allocating costs to functions may require arbitrary allocations and involve considerable judgment'. However paragraph 94 recognizes that 'the choice between the function of expense method and the nature of expense method depends on historical and industry factors and the nature of the entity. Both methods provide an indication of those costs that might vary, directly or indirectly, with the level of sales or production of the entity'.

Proponents of the classification by nature highlight the fact that this method may allow for a user-specific analysis of the performance of the firm. They point out that, in theory, the cost of goods sold (or the cost of sales) can be reconstructed to suit the analysis of the user. However, most reports presented by nature fail to offer any partition of key natures of expenses between manufacturing, selling, and administration. Proponents of the classification by function highlight the fact that gross profit (revenues minus manufacturing cost of goods sold) and the commercial and distribution expenses are two key figures in monitoring the performance of a business and are easily understandable by any user.

In conclusion, we will not choose sides and will agree with IASB that 'each method of presentation has merit for different types of entities' (IASB 2003: § 94). We will go further and acknowledge the fact that the choice between classifications must be in favor of that which most fairly presents the elements of the entity's performance.

However, 'because information on the nature of expenses is useful in predicting future cash flows, additional disclosure is provided when the function of expense classification is used' (IAS 1: § 94). Depreciation and amortization (concept equivalent to depreciation and applied to intangible assets – see Chapter 8) must critically be disclosed in a footnote or in the cash flow statement. It can prove useful for forecasting purposes, especially in internal reporting, to break up the cost of goods sold through a local application of the by nature approach, distinguishing consumption of consumables, raw materials, manufacturing labor, and services purchased from third parties. Employee benefits expense should also be disclosed.

In the second part of this chapter we will sketch the landscape of practice in the domain of income statement presentation in several countries.

1.3 Notes to financial statements

Since the purpose of the financial statements is to give a true and fair view of a business' financial performance, the **notes** (often called 'notes to the financial statements' or 'footnotes') are essential. They provide any additional information the format of presentation selected failed to communicate since no format of presentation is actually perfect or serves the interests of all parties.

The European Union emphasizes this point in stating in article 2 of the 4th European Directive that 'these documents' (the financial statements, including the notes) 'shall constitute a composite whole'. The notes should not be forgotten or omitted by preparers, a practice that was quite common on the part of medium and small enterprises before the publication of the 4th Directive.

IAS 1 (IASB 2003: § 103) states that the notes shall:

(a) 'present information about the basis of preparation of the financial statements and the specific accounting policies used in accordance with paragraphs 108–115 [which deal with "Disclosure of Accounting Policies"];

(b) disclose information required by IFRSs that is not presented on the face of the balance sheet, income statement, statement of changes in equity or cash flow statement; and

(c) provide additional information that is not presented on the face of the balance sheet, income statement, statement of changes in equity or cash flow statement but is relevant to an understanding of any of them'.

Notes to the statements are a set of qualitative and quantitative comments or specification of hypotheses required to provide a really 'true and fair view' of both the financial position of the firm and of its financial performance over the previous period and periods. They state the valuation hypotheses used and principles followed by management in establishing the figures that are in the financial statements.

Notes should not, however, become so cumbersome to use that they defeat their purpose of clarification. They should be reserved for remarks that are significant and may have a material effect on the meaning of figures.

Table 3.8 offers a list of some commonly found remarks in notes to financial statements.

Table 3.8 Example of information found in the notes

Qualitative Information	Quantitative Information
Accounting policies: ■ Accounting principles ■ Basis of consolidation Measurement bases Specific accounting policy	Fixed assets – movements for the year Depreciation – movements for the year Amortization and provision – movements for the year Analysis of debt by maturity

A real-life example (notes to Sandvik's financial statements) is provided opposite.

1.4 Cash flow statement

Although the **cash flow statement** is a required component of financial statements only in some countries, our position is that it constitutes an essential document for understanding the financial life of a business. The vision given through both balance sheet and income statement may appear to be restrictive because:

- the balance sheet offers only a static vision of the financial position; and
- the income statement, based on accruals (see this concept below in Section 1.4.1), fails to show the importance of cash in the operation of the firm.

Cash is the blood of any organization as shown, for example, in Figure 3.5. Neither the balance sheet nor the income statement emphasizes the dynamics of the cash flowing in and out of the business. Comparing two consecutive balance sheets certainly allows the user to calculate the net change in cash position. However that is not sufficient to understand *how* this change happened. Operations bring in and take out cash, but plenty of other events affect the cash balance such as additional cash contributions by shareholders, payment of dividends, acquisition or disposal of fixed assets, acquisition or granting of rights to operate specific technologies, etc. All these events need to be understood before the full meaning of the ending cash balance can be understood. Where did cash come from and what was it used for are the two key questions the cash flow statement addresses.

We will only present here a brief outline of this statement and Chapter 14 will give us the opportunity to explore this document further. We will emphasize here the relations between the three documents: balance sheet, income statement, and cash flow statement.

1.4.1 Accrual basis of accounting

The need for the cash flow statement arises from the choice made of the **accrual** approach for the recognition of revenues and expenses. IAS 1 (IASB 2003: § 25) states: 'an entity shall prepare its financial statements, except for cash flow information, under the accrual basis of accounting'. Under this method, transactions and events are recognized when they occur (and not as cash or its equivalent is received or paid) and they are recognized

Real-life example Sandvik

The structure of the notes to the 2004 financial statements of Sandvik, a Swedish engineering company is presented below (*Source*: Annual report 2004).

Accounting principles

- Basis of presentation
- Consolidation principles
  - Subsidiaries
  - Associated companies
  - Purchase price allocation: goodwill, etc.
  - Elimination of transactions between group companies
- Currency rate effects
  - Transactions in foreign currency
  - Translation of the group's foreign companies' financial reports
- Financial assets and liabilities, recognition, and derecognition
- Financial assets and liabilities, measurement
- Intangible fixed assets
  - Goodwill
  - Research and development
  - Other intangible assets
  - Subsequent expenditure
  - Amortization of intangible assets
- Tangible fixed assets
  - Owned assets
  - Leased assets
  - Subsequent expenditure
  - Depreciation of tangible fixed assets
- Financial fixed assets
- Impairment losses
- Inventories
- Receivables
- Shareholders' equity
  - Repurchased own shares
  - Group contributions and shareholders' contributions
- Employee benefits
  - Pensions and sickness benefits
  - Share-related benefits
- Provisions
  - Warranties
  - Restructuring
  - Onerous contracts
- Contingent liabilities
- Revenues
  - Sales and service revenue
  - Construction contracts
  - Other revenues
- Expenses
  - Net financing costs
  - Income taxes
- Segment reporting
- Cash flow statement
- Effects of new international accounting standards

Notes to the consolidated accounts (excerpts)

Information on business areas/market areas
Categories of revenues
Personnel information and remuneration to management and auditors
Research, development and quality assurance
Depreciation/amortization of tangible and intangible fixed assets
Fees for finance and operating leases
Income from investments held as fixed assets
Other interest income and expense
Appropriations
Taxes
Balance sheet items with recovery or settlement time exceeding 12 months
Consolidated tangible and intangible fixed assets
Shares in group companies
Investments in associated companies
Other investments held as fixed assets
Inventories
Special information on shareholders' equity
Provision for pensions and other long-term post-employment benefits
Other provision
Convertible debenture loans
Accrued expenses and deferred income
Contingent liabilities
Exchange rated differences
Supplementary information to the group's cash flow statement
Earnings per share

in the accounting records and reported in the financial statements of the periods to which they relate. Such a principle distinguishes modern accounting from cash basis accounting in which transactions and events are recorded at the time of the flow of cash they trigger. Accrual accounting creates a timing difference between recognition of revenues or expenses and their cash implications. The cash flow statement explains this timing difference.

1.4.2 Evolution

After many years of diversity of orientation and presentation, the cash flow statement has become a relatively standardized document. The requirement to publish one has spread rapidly since the mid-1980s. Canada was first in requiring a cash flow statement in 1985, followed by the USA (1987), France (1988), and the UK (1991). Most importantly, the cash flow statement became part of the standard reporting package required under IASB rules in 1992 reflecting an international generally accepted model. It offers a template that allows each country and tradition the possibility of attaching some specific (but minor) modifications to serve their local needs.

According to IAS 7 (IASB 1992: § 10): 'the cash flow statement shall report cash flows during the period classified by operating, investing and financing activities'. This creates a document structured to distinguish three fundamental phases of life in an enterprise: operations, investing, and financing. Table 3.9 offers an illustration of the IASB model cash flow statement.

Practically speaking, and without changing the logic of the approach, the cash flow statement can start with the opening cash balance and conclude with the closing balance. Then, using the same figures as above, we can present the cash flow statement for the period as illustrated below (see Table 3.10).

Table 3.9 Illustrative cash flow statement

Cash flows from operating activities		
Cash received from customers		80
Cash paid to suppliers and employees		−30
Net cash from operating activities	*(1)*	*50*
Cash flows from investing activities		
Purchase of property, plant and equipment		−15
Proceeds from sale of equipment		5
Net cash used in investing activities	*(2)*	*−10*
Cash flows from financing activities		
Proceeds from issuance of share capital		35
Proceeds from long-term borrowings		10
Dividends paid		−20
Net cash from financing activities	*(3)*	*25*
Net increase in cash and cash equivalents	(4) = (1) + (2) + (3)	65
Cash and cash equivalents at beginning of year	(5)	5
Cash and cash equivalents at end of year	(6)	70
Change in cash	(7) = (6) − (5)	65
Control	(4) = (7)	

Table 3.10 Cash flow statement – alternative presentation

Cash and cash equivalents at beginning of year	(1)	5
Net cash from operating activities	(2)	50
Net cash used in investing activities	(3)	−10
Net cash from financing activities	(4)	25
Cash and cash equivalents at end of year	(5) = (1) + (2) + (3) + (4)	70

1.4.3 Link between balance sheet, income statement, and cash flow statement

The balance sheet, the income statement, and the cash flow statement are totally linked, as is shown in Figure 3.8. They form a closed system in which everything that happens in the life of the business is recorded so that the user of accounting information can understand very well how value was created (income statement) and how the liquidity of the firm (availability of cash) has been affected by operations and decisions during the period (cash flow statement). The balance sheet records the situation that is the outcome of the previously mentioned transactions recorded in the other two documents of the financial statements.

Each key relation is explored in further detail below. (Each number refers to the numbers in Figure 3.8.)

Figure 3.8 Link between balance sheet, income statement, and cash flow statement

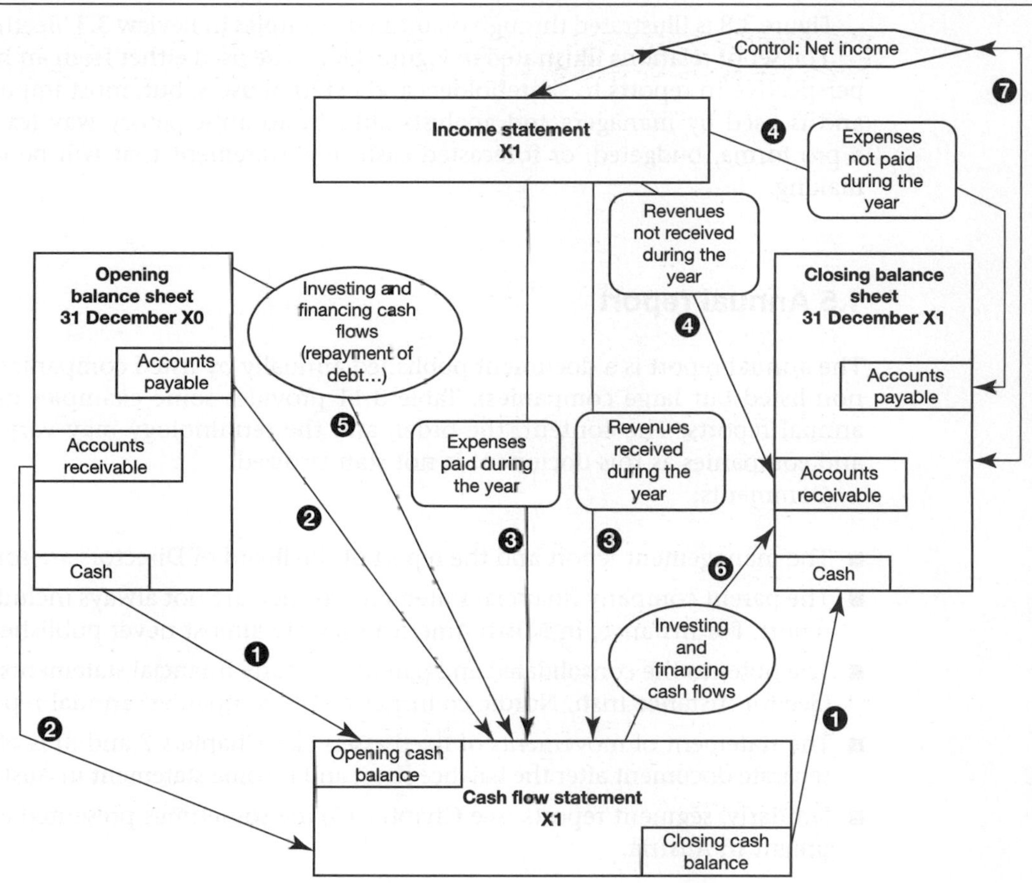

❶ The cash balance in the opening balance sheet is the opening cash balance in the cash flow statement. This transfer from the balance sheet is not a flow of cash per se but only an accounting entry that is used to start the cash flow statement. The same line of reasoning will be used to transfer back the closing cash balance in the cash flow statement to the closing balance sheet.

❷ Revenues and expenses of the previous year that were not collected or paid during that year (and recorded as accounts receivable or accounts payable) will, in principle, be collected or paid during the current year. They will impact the cash flow statement.

❸ The income statement impact on the cash flow statement is through revenues and expenses collected or paid during the year.

❹ Conversely, if revenues and expenses of the current period are not collected or paid during this period, they will, in all likelihood, be collected or paid in the following period. They are recognized as part of the receivables and payables balances in the closing balance sheet.

❺ Items in the opening balance sheet that are connected to investment or financing may also have an impact on the cash flow statement. For example, repaying all or part of the principal of a debt will generate a cash outflow, whereas proceeds from the sale of a fixed asset will create a cash inflow.

❻ Some investing or financing cash flows will also impact on the closing balance sheet. They can, for example, be the floatation of a new bond issue or the issuance of new share capital.

❼ When the income statement and closing balance sheet have been prepared, it is critical to double-check that the net income is the same in both documents. This is the closing relation to make sure the system is truly comprehensive and 'balanced'.

Figure 3.8 is illustrated through quantified examples in Review 3.3 'Beethoven Company'.

The set of relations illustrated in Figure 3.8 can be used either from an historical (*ex post*) perspective in reports to shareholders and external users, but, most importantly, it can be and is used by managers and analysts alike in an anticipatory way (*ex ante*) to prepare a pro forma, budgeted, or forecasted cash flow statement that will be used for decision making.

1.5 Annual report

The annual report is a document published annually by listed companies (as well as some non-listed but large companies). Table 3.11 provides some examples of items found in annual reports. The content, the order, and the terminology may vary across countries and companies as this document is not standardized.

Comments:

- The management report and the report of the Board of Directors are sometimes merged.
- The parent company financial statements as such are not always included in the annual report. For instance, in North America they are almost never published.
- The notes to the consolidated and parent company financial statements are often mixed. (See for instance Irish, Nordic countries or UK companies' annual reports.)
- The statement of movements of fixed assets (see Chapters 7 and 8) is often reported as a separate document after the balance sheet and income statement in Austria and Germany.
- Similarly, segment reports (see Chapter 15) are sometimes presented as a separate document in Austria.

Table 3.11 Illustrative components of an annual report

First part: Business reporting

- Key financial information (or financial highlights – the year in brief)
- Letters from the President and/or from the CEO (also called Review by the President)
- Management report (or Review of operations): Overview of the group and divisional reviews, personnel, research and development
- Report of the Board of Directors (or financial review – management discussion and analysis): markets evolution, changes in group composition, earnings, production, personnel, capital expenditure, research and development, financing, shares, outlook for the following year, dividend

Second part: Financial reporting

- Consolidated financial statements: balance sheet, income statement, cash flow statement, statement of changes in equity
- Notes to the consolidated financial statements
- Parent company financial statements: balance sheet, income statement, cash flow statement
- Notes to the parent company financial statements
- Information on shares (shareholder information)
- Report of the auditors
- Composition of the executive board (directors and corporate officers)

2 Advanced issues

2.1 Balance sheet

This section provides illustrations of the various presentations of the balance sheet we introduced in Core issues.

2.1.1 International 'model'

IAS 1 (2003: § IG4) includes an *illustrative* balance sheet showing one way in which a balance sheet distinguishing between current and non-current items may be presented. This example corresponds to the format 'by term' (see Table 3.12).

Table 3.12 IASB format

XYZ Group – Balance sheet as at 31 December X2 (in thousands of currency units)	X2	X1
ASSETS		
Non-current assets		
Property, plant, and equipment	X	X
Goodwill	X	X
Other intangible assets	X	X
Investments in associates	X	X
Available-for-sale investments	X	X
	X	X
Current assets		
Inventories	X	X
Trade receivables	X	X
Other current assets	X	X
Cash and cash equivalents	X	X
	X	X
Total assets	X	X
EQUITY AND LIABILITIES		
Equity attributable to equity holders of the parent		
Share capital	X	X
Other reserves	X	X
Retained earnings	X	X
	X	X
Minority interest	X	X
Total equity	X	X
Non-current liabilities		
Long-term borrowings	X	X
Deferred tax	X	X
Long-term provisions	X	X
Total non-current liabilities	X	X
Current liabilities		
Trade and other payables	X	X
Short-term borrowings	X	X
Current portion of long-term borrowings	X	X
Current tax payable	X	X
Short-term provisions	X	X
Total current liabilities	X	X
Total liabilities	X	X
Total equity and liabilities	X	X

2.1.2 European 'models'

Practice in European countries is shaped by the 4th European Directive, which was issued in July 1978 (EU 1978). In the United Kingdom, for example, limited companies must use one of the two formats prescribed in the Companies Act. The two formats are illustrated in Tables 3.13 and 3.14 and are variations on the 'vertical balance sheet'.

In practice, most UK companies have adopted format 1 while most continental European firms tend to report under format 2.

Table 3.13 UK format 1 – Multiple-step vertical balance sheet

Fixed assets	(1)	100
Current assets	(2)	70
Creditors (amounts falling due within one year)	(3)	−60
Net current assets/(liabilities)	(4) = (2 + 3)	10
Total assets less current liabilities	(5) = (1 + 4)	110
Creditors (amounts falling due after more than one year)	(6)	−20
Provisions for liabilities and charges	(7)	−10
Total net assets	(8) = (5 + 6 + 7)	80
Capital and reserves	(9)	80
Total equity	(10) = (9)	80

The balance sheet balances with (10) = (8)

Table 3.14 UK format 2 – Single-step vertical balance sheet

Fixed assets	(1)	100
Current assets	(2)	70
Total assets	(3) = (1 + 2)	170
Capital and reserves	(4)	80
Provisions for liabilities and charges	(5)	10
Creditors	(6)	80
Total equity and liabilities	(7) = (4 + 5 + 6)	170

The balance sheet balances with (7) = (3)

2.1.3 US 'model'

As opposed to a continental European balance sheet that reflects a patrimonial approach and thus lists fixed assets at the top, a North American approach tends to emphasize the short-term liquidity of the firm and thus lists assets in the order of decreasing liquidity with fixed assets at the bottom of the list. Table 3.15 illustrates a 'typical' North American balance sheet structure.

Table 3.15 A typical US balance sheet

ASSETS	
Current assets	
Cash and cash equivalents Accounts receivable Inventories Prepaid expenses and other current assets *Total current assets* ***Fixed assets*** Investments Property, plant and equipment Intangible assets *Total fixed assets*	 *(1)* *(2)*
Total assets	(3) = (1) + (2)
LIABILITIES AND STOCKHOLDERS' EQUITY	
Current liabilities	
Accounts payable Income taxes payable Accrued expenses Dividends payable Current portion of long-term debt *Total current liabilities*	 *(4)*
Long-term debt	
Borrowings Other long-term liabilities *Total long-term debt*	 *(5)*
Stockholders' equity	
Capital stock Capital in excess of par value of stock Retained earnings *Total stockholders' equity*	 *(6)*
Total liabilities and stockholders' equity	(7) = (4) + (5) + (6)
Balance	(3) = (7)

2.2 Income statement

2.2.1 International 'models'

IAS 1 (2003: § IG4) provides two income statements to illustrate the alternative classification of revenues and expenses, by nature and by function (see Tables 3.16 and 3.17).

Table 3.16 IASB income statement format by nature

Revenue	x
Other operating income	x
Changes in inventories of finished goods and work in progress	(x)
Work performed by the enterprise and capitalized	x
Raw material and consumables used	(x)
Employee benefits expense	(x)
Depreciation and amortization expense	(x)
Impairment of property, plant and equipment	(x)
Other expenses	(x)
Finance costs	(x)
Share of profit of associates	x
Profit before tax	x
Income tax expense	(x)
Profit for the period	x
Attributable to:	
Equity holders of the parent	x
Minority interest	x

Table 3.17 IASB income statement format by function

Revenue	x
Cost of sales	(x)
Gross profit	x
Other income	x
Distribution costs	(x)
Administrative expenses	(x)
Other expenses	(x)
Finance cost	(x)
Share of profit of associates	x
Profit before tax	x
Income tax expense	(x)
Profit for the period	x
Attributable to:	
Equity holders of the parent	x
Minority interest	x

2.2.2 European 'models'

The 4th European Directive (EU 1978) allows four formats by crossing, in a 2 × 2 matrix, the horizontal/vertical option with the nature/function option. Table 3.18 summarizes the principles underlying these formats.

In the UK for example, where the income statement is called Profit and Loss account (P&L), businesses are allowed to use one of the four formats prescribed in the Companies Act, which are the four EU sanctioned formats. Tables 3.19 and 3.20 illustrate some of the most commonly found formats in the UK and in Europe in general.

In Table 3.20 we did not go beyond the level of profit before interest and taxation as the remaining lines of the income statement are identical to what is shown in Table 3.19.

Table 3.18 Income statement formats

Article of the 4th EU directive	Vertical or horizontal format	Presentation by nature or by function
23	Vertical	Nature
24	Horizontal	Nature
25	Vertical	Function
26	Horizontal	Function

Table 3.19 Article 25 format (vertical and by function)

Turnover [sales revenue]	(1)	100
Cost of sales [cost of goods sold]	(2)	−65
Gross profit (loss)	(3) = (1 + 2)	35
Commercial and distribution costs	(4)	−5
Administrative expenses	(5)	−21
Other operating income	(6)	9
Profit before interest and taxation [operating profit] [*EBIT = earnings before interest and taxation*]	(7) = (3 + 4 + 5 + 6)	18
Net interest income (charge)	(8)	−5
Profit on ordinary activities before taxation	(9) = (7 + 8)	13
Taxation on profit on ordinary activities	(10)	−8
Profit on ordinary activities after taxation	(11) = (9 + 10)	5
Extraordinary profit (loss)	(12)	3
Taxation on profit on extraordinary activities	(13)	−1
Profit (loss) for the financial year	(14) = (11 + 12 + 13)	7

Table 3.20 Article 23 format (vertical and by nature)

Turnover [sales revenue]	100
Change in inventories of finished goods and in work in progress	5
Own work capitalized	3
Other operating income	9
Raw materials and consumables consumed	−20
Other external charges	−25
Staff [labor] costs	−30
Depreciation and other amounts written off tangible and intangible fixed assets	−10
Exceptional amounts written off current assets	−4
Other operating charges	−10
Profit (earnings) before interest and taxation [operating profit] [*EBIT*]	18

2.2.3 US 'model'

Table 3.21 illustrates a commonly found multiple-step income statement.

Table 3.21 US multiple-step income statement

Net sales	(1)
Cost of goods sold	(2)
Gross profit	(3) = (1)−(2)
Selling and distribution expenses	(4)
Administrative expenses	(5)
Operating income	(6) = (3)−(4)−(5)
Interest revenue and expenses	(7)
Gain or loss on sale of equipment	(8)
Pretax income from continuing operations	(9) = (6)−(7) ± (8)
Income tax expense	(10)
Income from continuing operations	(11) = (9)−(10)
Discontinued operations (gain or loss on disposal)	(12)
Extraordinary items	(13)
Cumulative effect of change in accounting principle	(14)
Net income	(15) = (11) + (12) ± (13) ± (14)

2.2.4 Cost of goods sold

Expenses in the income statement by function are divided in three or four main categories:

- cost of sales (or **cost of goods sold**) (this concept is further developed in Appendix 3.1);
- selling and distribution expenses;
- administrative expenses;
- some companies add research & development (R&D) expenses to this list.

In order to compare presentations of an income statement by nature and by function, let us look at a quantified example. Brahms Company is a retailer. Its beginning inventory of merchandise is valued at 2,000 (all figures are in thousands of CU). During the period we are considering, Brahms Co. incurred total purchases of 8,000 and recorded invoicing customers for 17,000. The cost of goods sold pertaining to these sales was 9,000 (the 2,000 CU worth of beginning inventory plus 7,000 CU of the newly purchased merchandise – we assume here that oldest merchandise is sold first so as to avoid holding obsolete products on the shelves). Thus, the ending inventory of merchandise is 1,000 (i.e., 2,000 + 8,000 = goods available for sale minus 9,000 withdrawn to meet demand, i.e., the cost of sales). Labor and personnel expenses include the compensation of the sales force (4,000) and of the accounting and administration staff (2,000). The depreciation of administrative equipment for the period was estimated at 1,000.

Table 3.22 shows, side by side, the calculation of the operating income by nature and by function. The net operating income we find under either approach will, mechanically, be exactly the same. The potential for interpretation and uses of the information contained in the income statement may, however, be different.

Table 3.22 Comparison between income statement by nature and by function

Income statement by nature		Income statement by function	
Sales of merchandise	17,000	Sales of merchandise	17,000
– Purchases of merchandise	−8,000	– Cost of goods sold	−9,000
– Inventory change of merchandise (a)	−1,000	= Gross margin	8,000
– Personnel expense (b)	−6,000	– Selling expenses (c)	−4,000
– Depreciation expense	−1,000	– Administrative expenses (d)	−3,000
= Operating income	1,000	= Operating income	1,000

(a) Beginning minus ending
(b) Sales personnel (4,000) plus administrative personnel (2,000)

(c) Sales personnel remunerations
(d) Administrative labor (2,000) + Depreciation (1,000)

2.3 Terminology

As early as Chapter 2 we made it clear that differences existed between US and UK terminology. For example, we pointed out that the income statement (in US terminology) is generally called 'Profit and Loss Account' (or P&L) in the UK. However, since the vocabulary is not standardized within most countries, there exist plenty of variations on a same theme as is the case in the United States. To make things somewhat more complex, the IASB tends to use its own terminology, which mixes both US and UK terminology and leaves a lot of room for individual choices. However, comparability implies that any terminology cover definitions that are essentially coherent and we will therefore try to stay with one set of terms.

Table 3.23 recapitulates the differences and defines the terminology we will use in this text. Our choice has been to stay as close as possible to the IASB terminology but to make a clear choice when the official terminology leaves some leeway. We opted for simple options that reflect practice as observed in the hundreds of annual reports we have consulted.

Table 3.23 Accounting terminology differences

USA	UK	IASB	Terminology used in this book
Financial statements	Accounts	Financial statements	Financial statements
Balance sheet			
Balance sheet (or statement of financial position)	Balance sheet	Balance sheet	Balance sheet
Long-term assets	Fixed assets	Non-current assets	Fixed assets
Real estate	Land and buildings	Land and buildings	Land and buildings
Property, plant, and equipment	Tangible fixed assets	Property, plant, and equipment	Tangible assets
Inventories	Stocks	Inventories	Inventories
Work in process (WIP)	Work in progress (WIP)	Work in progress (WIP)	Work in progress (WIP)
Receivables	Debtors	Receivables	Receivables
Accounts receivable	Trade debtors	Accounts receivable	Accounts receivable
Doubtful accounts	Bad debts, doubtful debts	Bad debts	Doubtful accounts
Allowance for doubtful accounts	Provision for doubtful debts	Allowance for bad debts	Provision for doubtful accounts
Treasury stock	Own shares	Treasury shares	Treasury shares
Stockholders' equity	Shareholders' equity, shareholders' funds (or capital and reserves)	Shareholders' equity	Shareholders' equity
Common stock	Ordinary shares	Share capital	Share capital
Preferred stock	Preference shares	–	Preference shares
Additional paid-in capital	Share premium	–	Share premium
Retained earnings, retained income	Reserves, retained profit, profit and loss account	Reserves, accumulated profits (losses)	Retained earnings, retained income, reserves
Loans	Debts	Loans	Borrowings
Bonds, notes payable	Debenture loan	–	Bonds
Long-term liabilities	Creditors: amounts falling due after more than one year	Non-current liabilities	Long-term liabilities
Payables	Creditors	Payables	Payables
Current liabilities	Creditors: amounts falling due within one year	Current liabilities	Current liabilities
Accounts payable	Trade creditors	Accounts payable	Accounts payable
Income statement			
Income statement, statement of operations	Profit and loss account	Income statement	Income statement
Sales	Turnover	Revenue	Sales or sales revenue
Expense	Charge	Expense	Expense
Interest expense	Interest payable	Finance cost	Interest expense
Interest income	Interest received	–	Interest income
Income	Profit	Profit	Income
Others			
Statement of cash flows	Cash flow statement	Cash flow statement	Cash flow statement
Leverage	Gearing	–	Leverage
Stock	Share	Share	Share
Residual value, salvage value, terminal value	Scrap value	Residual value	Residual value
Declining balance method	Reducing balance method	–	Declining balance method
Pay check	Pay slip	–	Pay slip
Corporation	Company	–	Company
Conservatism	Prudence	Prudence	Prudence

Key points

- Financial statements include, as a minimum, a balance sheet, an income statement, and notes to financial statements. Additionally, they tend to also comprise a cash flow statement and a statement of changes in shareholders' equity.
- The several possibilities of presentation that exist for the balance sheet do not affect its generic content.
- There are several ways of presenting an income statement. They all provide the same bottom line.
- The choice between a presentation by nature or by function is always debatable.
- The notes to the financial statements (often called 'footnotes') are an essential component of the information provided through financial statements.
- The cash flow statement reflects the timing difference existing between the recognition of revenues and expenses and their impact on cash, as well as any transaction affecting cash but not the income statement.
- An annual report includes information on the activity of a company as well as financial information.

Review (solutions are at the back of the book)

Review 3.1 Orkla*

Topic: Constructing a balance sheet
Related part of the chapter: Core issues

Orkla is a Norwegian-based group operating in the branded consumer goods, chemicals, and financial investment sectors. Listed below are in alphabetical order items and amounts taken from the group's consolidated balance sheet for the accounting year ended on 31 December 2004. All numbers are in millions of NOK (*source*: Annual report 2004). The consolidated financial statements have been prepared in accordance with laws and regulations, as well as Norwegian GAAP.

Accumulated profit	24,068	Other financial long-term assets	4,919
Cash and cash equivalents	2,232	Other short-term liabilities	8,223
Equity	26,304	Paid-in equity	2,007
Equity and liabilities	41,755	Portfolio investments, etc.	12,837
Intangible assets	3,647	Provisions	1,657
Inventories	2,869	Receivables	4,449
Investments in associates	1,716	Short-term assets	22,387
Long-term assets	19,368	Short-term interest-bearing liabilities	199
Long-term interest-bearing liabilities	5,372	Short-term liabilities	8,422
Long-term liabilities and provisions	7,029	Tangible assets	9,086
Minority interests	229	Total assets	41,755

Note:

- Minority interests represent the part of the net assets of a subsidiary attributable to interests, which are not owned, directly or indirectly through subsidiaries, by the parent company (minority shareholders). This item will be presented in a more detailed manner in the Chapter 13 devoted to Consolidation.
- 'Provisions' are assimilated to long-term liabilities.

Required

1. Reconstruct the balance sheet in a vertical, single-step and increasing liquidity/maturity format (check figure: total assets in balance sheet = 41,755).
2. Is the balance sheet organized by nature or by term?

Review 3.2 Holcim*

Topic: Constructing an income statement
Related part of the chapter: Core issues

Holcim is a Swiss-based group producing and selling cement and clinker, as well as aggregates. It is closely linked to the building industry. Listed below are in alphabetical order items and amounts taken from the group's consolidated statement of income for the accounting year ended on 31 December 2004. All numbers are in millions of Swiss Francs (*source*: Annual report 2004). The consolidated financial statements have been prepared in accordance with International Financial Reporting Standards (IFRS).

Administration expenses	(1,050)	Net income before minority interests	1,153
Distribution and selling expenses	(2,980)	Net income before taxes	1,663
EBIT (Earnings Before Interest and Taxes)	2,175	Net sales	13,215
Financial expenses net	(512)	Operating profit	2,251
Gross profit	6,598	Other depreciation and amortization	(317)
Income taxes	(510)	Other income (expenses)	(76)
Minority interests	(239)	Production cost of goods sold	(6,617)
Net income after minority interests	914		

Note: Minority interests, see note to Review 3.1.

Required

1. Prepare the income statement in a multiple-step format (check figure: bottom line = 914).
2. Is the income statement organized by nature or by function?

Review 3.3 Beethoven Company

Topic: Link between balance sheet, income statement and cash flow statement
Related part of the chapter: Core issues

Beethoven Company, a limited liability company that was incorporated in X1, has a commercial activity. It buys and sells books and CDs devoted to the learning of foreign languages. (The founder of the Company speaks at least 10 languages fluently.)

The balance sheet as at 31 December X1 is presented below.

Balance sheet as at 31 December X1 (in 000 CU)

ASSETS		SHAREHOLDERS' EQUITY AND LIABILITIES	
Fixed assets		*Shareholders' equity*	
Equipment (net value)	800	Capital	710
		Reserves	300
		Net income for X1 (a)	216
Current assets		*Liabilities*	
Merchandise inventory	150	Financial debt	110
Accounts receivable (b)	400	Accounts payable (c)	120
Cash at bank	250	Income tax payable (c)	144
Total	1,600	Total	1,600

(a) to be appropriated in X2: one third will be distributed.
(b) to be received in X2.
(c) to be paid in X2.

The following budgeted activities are envisaged for the year X2 (in 000 CU):

1. Sales budget: 1,600 (1,400 will be received from customers during the year).
2. Purchases budget (merchandise): 510 (400 will be paid to suppliers during the year).
3. Planned merchandise-ending inventory: 130.
4. Finance budget: repayment of financial debt for 80.
5. Salaries and social expenses budget: 430 (paid during the year).

6. Advertising expenses budget: 250 (paid during the year).
7. Miscellaneous taxes budget (other than income tax): 120 (paid during the year).
8. Depreciation budget: 40.
9. Additional fixed assets will be purchased: 300 (paid during the year).

The income tax rate is 40%.

Required

Prepare the following documents: income statement, balance sheet, and cash flow budget for the year X2.

Assignments

Assignment 3.1
Industry identification[2]

Related part of the chapter: Core issues

Common-size statements (see more on this concept in Chapter 15) and selected ratio values, related to the same financial year, are provided in Exhibit 1 for six well-known French companies. The name and some characteristics of these companies are given in Exhibit 2.

Required

Use your knowledge of general business practices to match the industries to the company data.

Exhibit 1 Common-size consolidated balance sheets

Company	A %	B %	C %	D %	E %	F %
Balance sheet						
Assets						
Intangible fixed assets	10.4	10.6	25.4	4.6	69.1	2.6
Tangible fixed assets (net)	20.9	40.9	33.1	19.0	7.7	35.7
Financial fixed assets	2.3	10.6	6.0	0.7	4.4	3.6
Inventories	47.7	2.4	16.0	30.7	4.0	17.7
Accounts receivable	1.4	14.5	7.8	27.1	5.9	18.1
Other receivables	14.1	7.4	4.2	6.4	5.7	12.1
Cash	3.2	13.6	7.5	11.5	3.2	10.2
Total assets	100.0	100.0	100.0	100.0	100.0	100.0
Equity and liabilities						
Capital and reserves	31.5	17.3	17.8	24.7	51.5	25.7
Net income	−2.7	2.9	3.6	2.0	−4.7	3.2
Provisions for risks	1.3	23.3	4.5	3.2	7.5	18.5
Financial liabilities	24.8	31.9	24.9	43.9	20.9	30.2
Accounts payable	33.9	20.2	36.8	13.9	3.6	9.9
Other debts	11.2	4.4	12.4	12.3	21.2	12.5
Total equity and liabilities	100.0	100.0	100.0	100.0	100.0	100.0
Financial ratios						
Net income/sales (%)	−1.5	4.4	1.9	1.5	−24.0	3.3
Sales/total assets (%)	182	65	186	131	20	97
Salaries and social charges/total assets (%)	27	12	17	22	N/A	30
Average collection period (days)	2.7	81.6	5.3	75.5	109.2	67.9

Exhibit 2 Name and characteristics of the companies

(Based on WVB Business Summaries and Multex Business Summaries – *source*: www.infinancials.com)

Carrefour

Carrefour is a French company, incorporated in 1959, primarily engaged in retail distribution. The Company manages hypermarkets, supermarkets, hard discounters, convenience stores, and cash-and-carry and food service. Headquartered near Paris, the company is present in 32 countries worldwide. It has enjoyed a dazzling growth with a high level of profitability.

Go Sport

Go Sport retails sports shoes, sportsgear, and related accessories. It operates 136 shops throughout France, 99 of them located in shopping malls. Products sold include all leading sports brands, such as Nike, Adidas, Timberland, and Ellesse.

Michelin

The main activity of this company is the production and sale of tires. The company distributes under several brand names, including the following: Michelin, Kleber, and Uniroyal. It manages important capital investments and has recorded a high level of profitability.

Sanofi-Aventis

Sanofi-Aventis, formerly known as Sanofi-Synthélabo, is a pharmaceutical group engaged in the research, development, manufacture, and marketing of healthcare products. The company's business includes two activities: pharmaceutical (prescription drugs) and human vaccines; the latter is conducted through its wholly owned subsidiary, Sanofi Pasteur (formerly Aventis Pasteur). On 20 August 2004 Sanofi-Synthélabo acquired control of Aventis. On 31 December 2004 Aventis merged with and into the company. The group manages a large portfolio of patents.

Skis Rossignol

Well known by skiers, Skis Rossignol SA, together with its subsidiaries, operates in the sporting goods sector, with its focus on the winter sports business. The company manufactures winter sporting goods, and offers a full range of products for all disciplines (alpine, Nordic, and snowboard) and all product families (board, binding, boot, and pole). Its product range also includes textile goods and accessories. Its growth is supported by important capital investment.

Suez

Suez is a global industrial company promoting sustainable development and offering a range of solutions in the energy and environment sector for companies, individuals, and municipalities. It develops, designs, implements, and operates systems and networks in each of these areas to meet the needs of its customers. The company operates in four business areas. Suez Energy Europe provides electricity and gas in Europe. Suez Energy International provides electricity and gas outside Europe. Suez Energy Services provides industrial and energy services. The Suez Environment mainly provides water and waste services.

Assignment 3.2
Ona Group*

Topic: Constructing an income statement
Related part of the chapter: Core issues

Ona Group is an industrial and financial private Moroccan group. Operating in Morocco, France, and sub-Saharan

Financial information about Ona Group for financial year 2004

Capital allowances	1,441	Operating income	1,458
Consolidated net income	431	Other operating revenues	728
Current income	1,221	Personnel charges	1,944
Duties and taxes	146	Portion of the result of companies valued at equity	145
Financial income	(237)	Purchases and other external charges	18,462
Income before taxes	1,147	Taxes on incomes	(624)
Net capital allowances of goodwill	(237)	Total operating charges	21,993
Net turnover	22,723	Total operating revenues	23,451
Non-current income	(74)		

Note:
- Capital allowances represent depreciation expenses.
- Goodwill represents any excess of the cost of the acquisition over the acquirer's interest in the fair value of the identifiable assets and liabilities acquired as at the date of the exchange transaction. This item will be presented in a more detailed manner in Chapter 13 devoted to Consolidation.
- Portion of the result of companies valued at equity represents the share in companies where the group only exerts a significant influence (ownership between 20 and 50% of share capital). This item is also covered in Chapter 13.

Africa, the Ona Group is organized into five strategic areas: mines and construction materials; agribusiness and beverages; tourism; distribution and development; and financial activities. Items and amounts taken from the consolidated income statement for the accounting year ending on 31 December 2004 are listed in alphabetical order on the previous page (*source*: company's web site: www.ona.ma). All numbers are in millions of Moroccan Dirhams (MDH).

Required

1. Prepare the income statement in a multiple-step format (check figure: bottom line = 431).
2. Is the income statement organized by nature or by function?

Assignment 3.3
Adidas–Salomon*

Topic: Constructing a balance sheet
Related part of the chapter: Core issues

In March 1998 the company Adidas completed its acquisition of Salomon. The Adidas–Salomon group is a major international actor in the sporting goods market. The group manages brands like Adidas, Salomon, and Taylor Made. Adidas–Salomon has acquired Reebok in 2005. Pursuant to a request by the EU competition authorities, Adidas–Salomon will divest itself of the Salomon business segment to Amer Sports Corporation (transfer to be completed in mid-October 2005).

Listed below are in alphabetical order items and amounts taken from the consolidated balance sheet as of 31 December 2004. All numbers are in millions of €. Some items have been grouped, in order to simplify the balance sheet.

Financial information excerpted from Salomon financial year 2004 balance sheet

Accounts payable	591,689	Other non-current assets	262,734
Accounts receivable	1,046,322	Other non-current liabilities	220,020
Accrued liabilities and provisions	558,121	Property, plant and equipment, net	367,928
Cash and cash equivalents	195,997	Shareholder's equity	1,628,452
Goodwill, net	572,426	Short-term bank borrowings	185,837
Income taxes	167,334	Short-term financial assets	258,950
Inventories	1,155,374	Total assets	4,427,480
Long-term borrowings	862,845	Total current assets	3,034,946
Long-term financial assets	93,134	Total current liabilities	1,687,313
Minority interests	28,850	Total equity	1,657,302
Other current assets	378,303	Total liabilities, minority interests, and shareholders' equity	4,427,480
Other current liabilities	184,332	Total non-current assets	1,392,534
Other intangible assets, net	96,312	Total non-current liabilities	1,082,865

Note:
- Minority interests, see note to Review 3.1.
- Goodwill, see note to Assignment 3.2.
- These items will be presented in a more detailed manner in the Chapter 13 devoted to Consolidation.

Required

1. Prepare a vertical balance sheet, knowing that this German group refers to the US accounting principles (check figure: total assets = 4,427,480).
2. Is it possible, on the basis of the balance sheet you just prepared, to estimate the impact of the divestiture of the Salomon part of the business? Comment on your answer.

Assignment 3.4
Nokia* and others

Topic: Determination of financial statements format
Related part of the chapter: Core issues

You will find below in Appendixes 1 and 2 the balance sheets and income statements from seven different companies.

- **Nokia** (Finland) is a leader in the communication industry, with emphasis on cellular phones and other wireless solutions. The consolidated financial statements have been prepared in accordance with International Financial Reporting Standards (IFRS).
- **Aracruz Celulose** (Brazil) is the world's leading producer of bleached eucalyptus pulp. The consoli-

conformity with accounting principles generally accepted in the USA (US GAAP).

- **Metro** (Germany) is one of the most important international trading and retailing companies. Metro AG's consolidated financial statements have been prepared in accordance with the rules of the International Accounting Standards Board (IASB), and the interpretations of the Standing Interpretations Committee (SIC).
- **Trigano** (France) is a European leisure equipment (e.g., motor caravans) specialist. Trigano's consolidated financial statements have been drawn up in accordance with French legislation and pursuant to Regulation 99–02 of the French Accounting Standards Committee.
- **Easyjet** (UK) is a low-cost airline carrier. The consolidated financial statements have been prepared in accordance with applicable accounting standards in the UK.
- **Wipro** (India) is a group involved in three businesses: 'Global IT Services and Products', 'Infotech' and 'Consumer Care & Lighting'. The consolidated financial statements have been prepared by the company in accordance with the requirements of Accounting Standards Nos 21, 23 and 27, in respect of consolidation of financial statements, issued by the Institute of Chartered Accountants of India.
- **Telefónica**, a Spanish telecom group, prepares its financial statements in accordance with generally accepted accounting principles in Spain.

Required

Analyze the financial statements and classify each balance sheet and income statement as described in the following table.

Company	Balance sheet			
	Format	Classification		Presentation
	Vertical (V) Horizontal (H)	Single step (S) Multiple step (M)	Nature (N) Term (T)	Increasing (I) Decreasing (D)
Nokia (Finland)				
Aracruz (Brazil)				
Metro (Germany)				
Trigano (France)				
Easyjet (UK)				
Wipro (India)				
Telefónica (Spain)				

Company	Income statement		
	Format	Degree of simplification	Classification of expenses
	Vertical (V) Horizontal (H)	Single step (S) Multiple step (M)	Nature (N) Function (F)
Nokia (Finland)			
Aracruz (Brazil)			
Metro (Germany)			
Trigano (France)			
Easyjet (UK)			
Wipro (India)			
Telefónica (Spain)			

Appendix 1: Balance sheets

The balance sheets listed hereafter are excerpted from the actual annual reports of the companies. Some of the data were simplified for pedagogical reasons.

Nokia – Consolidated balance sheets (IFRS)
31 December 2004 (in € millions)

ASSETS	
Fixed assets and other non-current assets	
Capitalized development costs	278
Goodwill	90
Other intangible assets	209
Property, plant and equipment	1,534
Investments in associated companies	200
Available-for-sale investments	169
Deferred tax assets	623
Long-term loans receivable	–
Other non-current assets	58
	3,161
Current assets	
Inventories	1,305
Accounts receivable, net of allowances for doubtful accounts	4,382
Prepaid expenses and accrued income	1,429
Other financial assets	595
Available-for-sale investments	255
Available-for-sale investments, liquid assets	9,085
Available-for-sale investments, cash equivalents	1,367
Bank and cash	1,090
	19,508
Total assets	**22,669**
SHAREHOLDERS' EQUITY AND LIABILITIES	
Shareholders' equity	
Share capital	280
Share issue premium	2,272
Treasury shares, at cost	−2,022
Translation differences	−126
Fair value and other reserves	69
Retained earnings	13,765
	14,238
Minority interests	168
Long-term liabilities	
Long-term interest-bearing liabilities	19
Deferred tax liabilities	179
Other long-term liabilities	96
	294
Current liabilities	
Short-term borrowings	215
Current portion of long-term debt	–
Accounts payable	2,669
Accrued expenses	2,606
Provisions	2,479
	7,969
Total shareholders' equity and liabilities	**22,669**

Source: Nokia, annual report 2004

Aracruz – Consolidated balance sheets (in US$000)

ASSETS		LIABILITIES AND STOCKHOLDERS' EQUITY	
Current assets		**Current liabilities**	
Cash and cash equivalents	36,474	Suppliers	52,869
Short-term investments	412,110	Payroll and related charges	15,486
Accounts receivable, net		Income and other taxes	42,123
Related party	0	Current portion of long-term debt	
Other	208,336	Related party	51,567
Inventories, net	126,220	Other	89,706
Deferred income tax, net	9,853	Short-term borrowings – export financing and other	3,767
Recoverable income and other taxes	36,984	Accrued finance charges	7,894
Prepaid expenses and other current assets	3,136	Interest on stockholders' equity payable	10,433
	833,113	Other accruals	961
			274,806
Property, plant and equipment, net	2,133,896	**Long-term liabilities**	
Investment in affiliated	273,890	Long-term debt	
Goodwill	207,050	Related party	178,588
		Other	1,044,140
Other assets		Tax assessments and litigation contingencies	130,846
Long-term investments	1,601	Deferred income tax, net	50,645
Advances to suppliers	50,685	Suppliers	14,118
Deposits for tax assessments	17,369	Other	21,928
Recoverable income and other taxes	6,675		1,440,265
Other	5,379	**Minority interest**	300
	81,709	**Stockholders' equity**	
		Share capital	31,105
		Preferred stock	
		Class A	583,391
		Class B	297,265
		Common stock	(2,288)
		Total share capital	909,473
		Appropriated retained earnings	619,527
		Unappropriated retained earnings	285,287
			1,814,287
TOTAL	3,529,658	TOTAL	3,529,658

Source: Aracruz, annual report 2004

Metro – Balance sheet as per 31 December 2004 (in € millions)	
ASSETS	
Fixed assets	
Goodwill	3,932
Other intangible assets	395
Tangible assets	10,820
Financial assets	171
	15,318
Current assets	
Inventories	6,272
Trade receivables	355
Other receivables and assets	2,302
Cash and cash equivalents	2,130
	11,059
Deferred tax assets	1,527
Prepaid expenses and deferred charges	188
	28,092
LIABILITIES	
Equity	
Capital stock	835
Additional paid-in capital	2,551
Reserves retained from earnings	526
Group net profit	827
	4,739
Minority interests	207
Provisions	
Provisions for pensions and similar commitments	1,006
Other provisions	697
	1,703
Liabilities	
Financial debt	7,803
Trade payables	10,771
Other liabilities	2,245
	20,819
Deferred tax liabilities	509
Deferred income	115
	28,092

Source: Metro, annual report 2004

Trigano – Consolidated balance sheet as of 31 August 2004 (in €000)

ASSETS		LIABILITIES	
	Net values		Net values
Goodwill	**32,582**	Share capital	45,284
Intangible fixed assets	**2,984**	Reserves	51,578
Land and buildings	35,452	Profit carried forward	55
Other tangible fixed assets	15,347	Consolidated reserves	78,087
		Treasury shares	(2,806)
		Group share of net income	42,655
Tangible fixed assets	**50,799**	**Shareholders' equity**	**214,853**
Equity-method investments	7,678	**Minority interests**	**1,639**
Other equity shares	1,482	**Total equity**	**216,492**
Other long-term investments	1,858		
Long-term investments	**11,018**	**Provisions for risks and charges**	**11,612**
Total fixed assets	**97,383**		
Inventories and work in progress	146,865	Financial debt	64,845
Trade accounts and notes receivable	121,735	Trade accounts and notes payable	100,075
Other receivables	33,150	Tax and social liabilities	40,982
Short-term investments	26,721	Other payables	11,256
Cash at bank and in hand	17,789		
Total current assets	**346,260**	**Total debt**	**217,158**
Prepayments and accrued income	3,401	Accruals and deferred income	1,782
Total assets	**447,044**	**Total equity and liabilities**	**447,044**

Source: Trigano, annual report 2004

Easyjet – Consolidated balance sheet as at 30 September 2004 (in £ millions)

Fixed assets		
Intangible assets		309.6
Tangible assets		330.4
Investments		
Joint venture arrangements:		
Share of gross assets	0.6	
Share of gross liabilities	(0.4)	
Net		0.2
		640.2
Current assets		
Debtors	174.4	
Cash at bank and in hand	510.3	
	684.7	
Creditors: amounts falling due within one year	(314.7)	
Net current assets		370.0
Total assets less current liabilities		1,010.2
Creditors: amounts falling due after more than one year		(157.7)
Provisions for liabilities and charges		(63.1)
Net assets		789.4
Capital and reserves		
Called up share capital		99.8
Share premium account		554.2
Profit and loss account		135.4
Shareholders' funds – equity		789.4

Source: Easyjet, annual report and accounts 2004

Wipro – Balance sheet as of 31 March 2004 (in Rs 000)

SOURCES OF FUNDS	
Shareholders' funds	
Share capital	465,519
Share application money pending allotment	–
Reserves and surplus	34,610,396
	35,075,915
Loan funds	
Secured loans	947,466
Unsecured loans	59,408
	1,006,874
Total	36,082,789
APPLICATION OF FUNDS	
Fixed assets	
Goodwill	85,542
Gross block	13,251,222
Less: depreciation	6,786,590
Net block	6,550,174
Add: capital work-in-progress and advances	1,397,121
	7,947,295
Investments	24,560,332
Deferred tax assets	315,533
Current assets, loans and advances	
Inventories	1,020,791
Sundry debtors	10,623,367
Cash and bank balances	2,900,940
Loans and advances	5,523,442
	20,068,540
Current liabilities and provisions	
Liabilities	8,563,202
Provisions	8,245,709
	16,808,911
Net current assets	3,259,629
Total	36,082,789

Source: Wipro, annual report 2004

Telefónica – Group consolidated balance sheets as of 31 December 2004 (in € millions)

ASSETS	
A) FIXED AND OTHER NON-CURRENT ASSETS	43,982.13
I. Start-up expenses	**409.18**
II. Intangible assets	**8,430.02**
Research and development expenses	1,256.97
Administrative concessions	7,872.63
Rights on leased assets	55.51
Other intangible assets	5,184.70
Accumulated amortization and allowances	(5,939.79)
III. Property, plant and equipment	**23,348.14**
Land and structures	6,626.27
Plant and machinery	2,089.89
Telephone installations	59,094.46
Furniture, tools, and other items	3,067.04
Construction in progress	1,242.40
Advances on property, plant, and equipment	9.05
Installation materials	264.91
Accumulated depreciation and allowances	(49,045.88)
IV. Long-term investments	**11,794.79**
Investments in associated companies	1,159.08
Other investments	518.52
Other loans	1,331.57
Long-term deposits and guarantees given	558.85
Tax receivables	8,567.17
Allowances	(340.40)
B) CONSOLIDATION GOODWILL	7,409.36
C) DEFERRED CHARGES	432.23
D) CURRENT ASSETS	11,642.62
I. Inventories	**669.62**
Inventories	704.05
Advances	23.42
Allowances	(57.85)
II. Accounts receivable	**6,935.79**
Trade receivables	6,383.30
Due from associated companies	77.68

STOCKHOLDERS' EQUITY AND LIABILITIES	
A) STOCKHOLDERS' EQUITY	16,225.12
I. Capital stock	4,955.89
II. Additional paid-in capital	5,287.68
III. Revaluation reserves	**1,357.86**
IV. Other reserves of the Parent Company	**9,326.14**
Unrestricted reserves	7,840.62
Restricted reserves	1,485.52
V. Reserves at fully or proportionally consolidated companies	**(591.88)**
VI. Reserves at companies accounted for by the equity method	**(835.89)**
VII. Translation differences in consolidation	**(6,151.97)**
VIII. Income for the year	**2,877.29**
Income of the Parent Company and subsidiaries	3,258.30
Income attributable to minority interests	(381.01)
B) MINORITY INTERESTS	3,775.58
C) NEGATIVE CONSOLIDATION GOODWILL	4.97
D) DEFERRED REVENUES	328.97
E) PROVISIONS FOR CONTINGENCIES AND EXPENSES	7,574.21
F) LONG-TERM DEBT	16,003.71
I. Debentures, bonds and other marketable debt securities	**9,319.47**
Non-convertible debentures and bonds	9,221.20
Other marketable debt securities	98.27
II. Payable to credit institutions	**5,450.37**
III. Other payables	**373.55**
Other payables	256.69
Notes payable	116.86
IV. Taxes payable	**855.82**
V. Uncalled capital payments payable	4.50
G) CURRENT LIABILITIES	19,344.92
I. Debentures, bonds and other marketable debt securities	**5,539.67**
Debentures	3,350.95
Other marketable debt securities	1,892.65
Interest on debentures and other debt securities	296.07
II. Payable to credit institutions	**4,244.53**
Loans and other accounts payable	4,169.80

(*continued*)

ASSETS		STOCKHOLDERS' EQUITY AND LIABILITIES	
Sundry accounts receivable	563.93	Accrued interest payable	74.73
Employee receivables	45.80	**III. Payable to associated companies**	**36.20**
Tax receivables	1,424.23	**IV. Trade accounts payable**	**5,665.41**
Allowances for bad debts	(1,546.68)	Advances received on orders	78.31
Allowances for sundry accounts receivable	(12.47)	Accounts payable for purchases and services	5,569.60
III. Short-term investments	**2,288.35**	Notes payable	17.50
Loans to associated companies	344.44	**V. Other non-trade payables**	**3,314.55**
Short-term investment securities	1,054.22	Taxes payable	1,859.40
Other loans	1,005.43	Other non-trade payables	1,455.15
Allowances	(115.74)	**VI. Accrual accounts**	**544.56**
IV. Short-term treasury stock	**690.18**	**H) SHORT-TERM PROVISIONS FOR CONTINGENCIES AND EXPENSES**	**208.86**
V. Cash	**855.02**		
VI. Accrual accounts	**203.66**		
TOTAL ASSETS (A + B + C + D)	**63,466.34**	**TOTAL STOCKHOLDERS' EQUITY AND LIABILITIES (A + B + C + D + E + F + G + H)**	**63,466.34**

Appendix 2: Income statements

The income statements listed hereafter are excerpted from the actual annual reports of the companies. Some of the data were simplified for pedagogical reasons.

Nokia – Consolidated profit and loss accounts, IFRS Financial year ended 31 December 2004 (in € millions)	
Net sales	29,267
Cost of sales	−18,133
Research and development expenses	−3,733
Selling, general and administrative expenses	−2,975
Customer finance impairment charges, net of reversals	–
Impairment of goodwill	–
Amortization of goodwill	−96
Operating profit	4,330
Share of results of associated companies	−26
Financial income and expenses	405
Profit before tax and minority interests	4,709
Tax	−1,435
Minority interests	−67
Net profit	3,207

Source: Nokia, annual report 2004

Aracruz – Consolidated statements of income year ended 31 December 2004 (in US$000)

Operating revenues		
Sales of eucalyptus pulp		
Domestic	66,083	
Export	1,256,648	
	1,322,731	
Sales taxes and other deductions	(155,618)	
Net operating revenues	1,167,113	+
Operating costs and expenses		
Cost of sales	700,333	
Selling	53,850	
Administrative	31,072	
Provision for loss on ICMS credit	22,859	
Other, net	2,349	
	810,463	–
Operating income	356,650	=
Non-operating (income) expenses		
Equity in results of affiliated companies	11,568	
Financial income	(56,123)	
Financial expenses	119,976	
Gain on currency remeasurement, net	(16,197)	
Other, net	(76)	
	59,148	–
Income before income taxes and minority interest	297,502	=
Income tax expense (benefit)		
Current	42,746	
Deferred	27,510	
	70,256	–
Minority interest in losses (earnings) of subsidiary	(9)	+
Net income	227,237	

Source: Aracruz, annual report 2004
Note: The column with the signs '+' and '–' has been added by the authors, in order to facilitate the understanding of the different steps in the calculation of the net income.

Metro – Income statement for the financial year from 1 January to 31 December 2004 (in € millions)	
Net sales	56,409
Cost of sales	(43,851)
Gross profit on sales	12,558
Other operating income	1,511
Selling expenses	(11,110)
General administrative expenses	(1,047)
Other operating expenses	(103)
Earnings before interest, taxes and amortization (EBITA)	1,809
Goodwill amortization	–
Earning before interest and taxes (EBIT)	1,809
Net investment income	31
Net interest result	(484)
Other financial result	(12)
Net financial income	(465)
Earnings before taxes	1,344
Income taxes	(411)
Group net income	933
Minorities	(106)
Group net profit	827

Source: Metro, annual report 2004

Trigano – Consolidated income statement as of 31 August 2004 (in €000)	
Turnover	701,666
Change in stocks of finished goods and work in progress	7,328
Other operating income	4,295
Operating income	**713,289**
Raw materials and consumables	(450,491)
Other operating charges	(72,603)
Taxations	(5,212)
Payroll costs	(98,916)
Amounts written off	(15,074)
Amounts written back	11,300
Depreciation of tangible and intangible assets	(7,884)
Operating profit	**74,409**
Financial result	(3,958)
Profit before extraordinary items and taxes	**70,451**
Extraordinary income (expense)	(250)
Income tax	(23,039)
Net income from consolidated subsidiaries	**47,162**
Share of income from equity-accounted companies	906
Net profit before goodwill amortization	**48,068**
Goodwill amortization	(4,913)
Net income	**43,155**
Minority interests	500
Net income, group share	**42,655**

Source: Trigano, annual report 2004

Easyjet – Consolidated profit and loss account for the year ended 30 September 2004 (in £ millions)	
Turnover: Group and share of joint ventures	1,092.4
Less: Share of turnover of joint ventures	(1.4)
Group turnover	1,091.0
Cost of sales	(929.3)
Gross profit	161.7
Distribution and marketing expenses	(55.7)
Administrative expenses	(55.5)
Group operating profit	50.5
Share of operating profit of joint venture	0.2
Total operating profit: Group and share of joint ventures and associates	50.7
Interest receivable and similar income	14.2
Amounts written off investments	–
Interest payable	(2.7)
Profit on ordinary activities before taxation	62.2
Tax on profit on ordinary activities	(21.1)
Retained profit for the financial year	41.1

Source: Easyjet, annual report 2004

Wipro – Profit and loss account for the financial year ended 31 March 2004 (in Rs000)	
INCOME	
Gross sales and services	51,881,933
Less: excise duty	555,128
Net sales and services	51,326,805
Other income	1,269,922
	52,596,727
EXPENDITURE	
Cost of goods sold	34,200,968
Selling, general and administrative expenses	7,537,920
Interest	35,171
	41,774,059
PROFIT BEFORE TAXATION	
Continuing operations	10,822,668
Discontinuing operation	–
Total	10,822,668
PROVISION FOR TAXATION	
Continuing operations	1,673,868
Discontinuing operation	–
Total	1,673,868
PROFIT FOR THE PERIOD BEFORE EXTRAORDINARY ITEMS	
Continuing operations	9,148,800
Discontinuing operation	–
Total	9,148,800
Loss on discontinuance of ISP business	–
Tax benefit on above	–
Net loss on discontinuance of ISP business	–
PROFIT FOR THE PERIOD	9,148,800

Source: Wipro, annual report 2004

Telefónica – Group consolidated statement of income for the year ended 31 December 2004 (in € millions)

DEBIT		CREDIT	
A) EXPENSES		B) REVENUES	
Decrease in inventories	(32.97)	Net sales and services	30,321.90
Procurements and other external expenses	**7,558.69**	Variation in work-in-process	–
Purchases	3,384.22	Capitalized expenses of Group work on fixed assets	474.31
Work performed by other companies	4,174.47	**Other operating revenues**	**381.71**
Personnel expenses	**4,411.81**	Non-core and other current operating revenues	173.09
Depreciation and amortization expense	**5,980.15**	Subsidies	16.95
Property, plant and equipment	4,629.92	Overprovision for contingencies and expenses	191.67
Intangible assets	1,187.04		
Deferred charges	163.19		
Variation in operating allowances	**336.16**		
Variation in allowances for inventories	8.07		
Variation in allowances for bad debts	318.98		
Variation in other allowances	9.11		
Other operating expenses	**5,688.83**		
Outside services	5,082.47		
Taxes other than income tax	519.16		
Other operating expenses	87.20		
I. OPERATING INCOME	7,235.25	I. OPERATING LOSS	–
Interest on payables to associated companies	0.01	**Revenues from equity investments**	**29.17**
Interest on accounts payable and similar expenses	1,619.10	Other companies	29.17
Amortization of deferred interest expenses	39.71	**Other financial revenues**	**389.85**
Variation in investment valuation allowances	0.41	Associated companies	49.52
Exchange losses	111.98	Other companies	340.33
		Exchange gains	**168.39**
II. FINANCIAL INCOME	–	II. FINANCIAL LOSS	1,183.80
Share in losses of companies accounted for by the equity method	104.34	Share in the income of companies accounted for by the equity method	48.23
Amortization of consolidation goodwill	433.53	Reversal of negative consolidation goodwill	0.94
III. INCOME FROM ORDINARY ACTIVITIES	5,562.75	III. LOSS ON ORDINARY ACTIVITIES	–
Variation in fixed asset and investment valuation allowances	32.71	Gains on fixed asset disposals	81.50
Losses on fixed assets	49.71	Gains on disposals of investments in consolidated companies	65.39
Losses on disposal of investments in consolidated companies	33.23	Capital subsidies transferred to income for the year	94.90
Extraordinary expenses and losses	1,459.11	Extraordinary revenues and income	167.23
IV. EXTRAORDINARY INCOME	–	IV. EXTRAORDINARY LOSS	1,165.74
V. CONSOLIDATED INCOME BEFORE TAXES	4,397.01	V. CONSOLIDATED LOSS BEFORE TAXES	–
Corporate income tax	653.03		
Foreign taxes	485.68		
VI. CONSOLIDATED INCOME FOR THIS YEAR	3,258.30	VI. CONSOLIDATED LOSS FOR THE YEAR	–
Income attributed to minority interests	472.82	Loss attributed to minority interests	91.81
VII. INCOME FOR THE YEAR ATTRIBUTED TO THE PARENT COMPANY	2,877.29	VII. LOSS FOR THE YEAR ATTRIBUTED TO THE PARENT COMPANY	–

Assignment 3.5
Schumann Company

Topic: Link between balance sheet, income statement and cash flow statement

Related part of the chapter: Core issues

The Schumann Company is a small business that makes and sells computers on a limited national market. The balance sheet at 31 December X1 is presented below.

Balance sheet at 31 December X1 (in 000 CU)

ASSETS		SHAREHOLDERS' EQUITY AND LIABILITIES	
Fixed assets		*Shareholders' equity*	
Equipment (net value)	600	Capital	500
Current assets		Reserves	200
Inventories		Net income for X1 (a)	168
■ Raw materials	80	*Liabilities*	
■ Finished products	120	Financial debt	100
Accounts receivable (b)	140	Accounts payable (c)	110
Cash at bank	250	Income tax payable (c)	112
Total	1,190	Total	1,190

(a) to be appropriated in X2: one half will be distributed.
(b) to be received in X2.
(c) to be paid in X2.

The following budgeted activities are considered for period X2 (000 CU):

1. Sales budget: 1,300 (1,140 will be received from customers during the year).
2. Purchases budget (raw materials): 520 (380 will be paid to suppliers during the year).
3. Rent expenses budget: 220 (paid during the year).
4. Other (not income based) taxes budget: 100 (paid during the year).
5. Salaries and social charges budget: 400 (paid during the year).
6. Finance budget: repayment of financial debt for 60. Interest expense: 10 (paid during the year).
7. Investment budget: acquisition of fixed assets for 200 (paid during the year).
8. Depreciation budget: 20.
9. The capital has been increased in cash by 100, received from shareholders.
10. Budgeted inventory level:
    - ■ Finished products ending inventory: 140;
    - ■ Raw materials ending inventory: 120.

The income tax rate is 40% (paid in the following year).

Required

Prepare the following forecast documents: cash flow budget, income statement, and balance sheet for the year X2.

Assignment 3.6
Bach Company

Topic: Link between balance sheet, income statement and cash flow statement – notion of management
Related part of the chapter: Core/Advanced issues

1 Introduction

Bach Company is a business game created to give realistic training in the use of accounting and financial concepts, language, and the preparation of financial documents. To this end, the participants in the game are expected to prepare balance sheets, income statements, and cash flow budgets deriving from their decisions. All decisions are made on a yearly basis and are not modifiable. However, the actual volume of sales is not controllable by the company and will be determined by the instructor for each company.

2 Your company and its market

The company, of which you become manager on 1 January X3, is a rather small-sized business. It designs, assembles, and sells hairdryers on a limited domestic market. At the beginning of the game, the market is shared equally between five companies, all of similar size[3].

The overall market for the year X3 is estimated to be about 500,000 units (in the case of five companies – the formula for the total market size is 100,000 units times the number of companies selected for the game). It is reasonable to anticipate that the total market size will increase, beyond X3 at a rate of about 10% per year, but this will depend on the decisions taken by the companies in such matters as sales prices and their evolution, advertising and marketing expenses, and so on. The market is extremely sensitive to prices and to marketing expenses.

3 Manufacturing equipment

On the opening date (1 January X3), the production capacity of each company consists of nine assembly lines. Each one can assemble a maximum of 10,000 dryers per year. An additional assembly line would represent an investment of 400,000 CU. It would be depreciated over five years using the straight-line method, which implies a yearly depreciation expense of 80,000 CU for each new line acquired. Old lines, in this fictitious world with no inflation, were acquired, at different times, at the same price of 400,000 CU per line. They have been depreciated using the straight-line method on the basis of a useful life of five years.

The existing equipment (nine assembly lines) is broken down, for each company, as follows (values are in thousands of CU):

Number of lines		Years operated		Gross value		Accumulated depreciation		Net book value
2	Lines which have already operated for	4	Their accounting book value is therefore	(2 × 400)	–	(2 × 320)	=	(2 × 80)
3		3		(3 × 400)	–	(3 × 240)	=	(3 × 160)
3		2		(3 × 400)	–	(3 × 160)	=	(3 × 240)
1		1		400	–	80	=	320

Each company may invest in as many new assembly lines as it feels is necessary. Each new assembly line is operational immediately in the period of purchase. All purchases are assumed to take place at the beginning of the period and therefore a new line increases the capacity of production by 10,000 units. Once an assembly line is fully depreciated, it is scrapped and has neither residual value nor production capabilities.

4 Inventories

The companies acquire from outside suppliers the motors and parts, which enter into the assembly of the hair dryers. There is no shortage of motors or parts, and there is no competition to access the parts and motors markets. The motors are purchased for a cost of 30 CU per unit in X3 (each dryer requires one motor). The various other parts are acquired at a cost of 50 CU in X3 for a set of parts allowing the assembly of one dryer. The total material cost is therefore 80 CU for each hairdryer.

On 1 January X3 each company holds an inventory on hand of motors and parts, which would allow the production of 10,000 hairdryers without any additional purchases. In addition, the company has 5,000 finished dryers in inventory, ready for delivery, whose unit direct cost (materials and labor) amounts to 170 CU, which is calculated as follows:

Motor, per unit		30 CU
Parts, per unit		50 CU
Direct labor ■ Annual salary cost of one worker ■ Number of dryers made in a year (per worker) → Labor cost of one dryer	 180,000 CU 2,000 	 90 CU
Total cost		**170 CU**

5 Personnel

As of 1 January X3, 50 employees are working on the production lines in each company. Each worker can normally assemble up to 2,000 hairdryers in a year. As far as production is concerned, each company can hire additional personnel or dismiss redundant workers. Every dismissal must first be notified to an Inspector from the Ministry of Labor who may refuse the lay-off, and will be subject to the payment, to the worker, of a cash indemnity equivalent to four months of salary. No social charges will be applied to this indemnity. Dismissals are presumed to take place at the beginning of the period in which they take place.

In X3 the minimum annual salary will be 120,000 CU per assembly worker. In addition to the salary, the employer must pay social charges amounting to 50% of the employee's remuneration. Thus, the total labor cost incurred by the company is 180,000 CU per year for each employee. In each successive period, the management of each company is free to raise the base pay by whatever amount it feels is necessary.

Management and administrative personnel as a whole receive a total remuneration amounting to 1 million CU per year in X3. Once social charges are added at the rate of 50%, the payroll cost to the employer for management and administrative personnel is 1.5 million CU. This category of personnel will benefit from any percentage increase granted to production workers. Thus, the per person payroll cost for both assembly production personnel and management and administrative personnel would increase, in a company, by the exact same proportion if a raise were decided by management. The management and administrative personnel fulfils essential functions in the company and cannot be dismissed, regardless of the level of activity. Unlike the manual labor used in assembly work, this category of personnel uses a lot of computerized and automated routines, and can handle a significant increase in the workload without requiring any new hiring.

6 Financing

The opening balance sheet that follows indicates that the shareholders have paid in 1,600,000 CU of share capital and that the company has realized profits in the past, since the reserves amount to 680,000 CU.

A debt of 1,300,000 CU was contracted at the start of X1 with interest payable at the annual rate of 10%. It is repayable on 31 December X4. The interest is due every 12 months at the end of the accounting period (first interest payment at the end of X3). The amount of any new (medium- or long-term) debt financing you may require would have to be negotiated in light of your justified needs.

The banker(s) or the shareholders must clear any requests for additional debt financing or issuance of new capital. Their decision can only be taken after they have been provided with your pro forma financial statements and have been able to review the financial situation of your company.

Temporary financial needs can be covered by short-term overdrafts granted by the bank. Interest is charged at the rate of 12% on the overdraft needed at the end of the year.

Balance sheet at 31 December X2 (in 000 CU)			
ASSETS		LIABILITIES AND SHAREHOLDER'S EQUITY	
Fixed assets		*Shareholders' equity*	
Manufacturing equipment (net) (3,600 − 1,920)	1,680	Capital	1,600
		Reserves	680
		Net income for X2 (to be appropriated in X3)	400
Current Assets		*Liabilities*	
Inventories		Debts 10% X1 (due 31 December X4)	1,300
■ Raw materials (80 × 10,000)	800	Accounts payable	1,600
■ Finished products (170 × 5,000)	850	Income tax payable	200
Accounts receivable	2,000		
Cash at bank	450		
Total	5,780	Total	5,780

7 Other purchases and external expenses or charges (yearly amounts, for each company)

- Each company rents its buildings for 600,000 CU per year.
- The various utility services (water, gas and electricity) amount to 1,000,000 CU.
- Various (non-income related) taxes amount to 300,000 CU.

The amount of other expenses or charges, such as advertising, marketing, and promotion expenses, will result from your decisions. For the sake of simplicity, expenses of this nature are calculated as a percentage of sales; for instance: 2% or 5%. Future sales are sensitive to the level of spending for market development and maintenance.

8 Credit conditions

Investments in manufacturing equipment, personnel expenditure, other purchases, and external charges are paid for during the period concerned:

- 85% of the value of the purchases of motors and parts are paid in the period concerned;
- the remaining 15% (debts to suppliers) are paid in the immediately following period.

Customers pay the company 80% of the invoiced value of the sale in the period during which delivery takes place. The credit sales amount of 20% is included in accounts receivable and will be settled in the following year.

9 Income tax and dividends

If the income statement shows a profit, it is assessed for income tax at a rate of 40%. Income tax is due to the state at the end of the year and paid the following year. No fixed minimum income tax is due when the company incurs a loss.

The net after tax income may be distributed wholly or partially as a dividend to shareholders. The amount of the dividend (if any) distributed during any year cannot exceed the income of the preceding year, i.e., it has been agreed by shareholders that, once earnings have been retained, they should not be distributed.

10 Decisions to be taken by the board

See Appendix 1.

11 Procedure for a one-year simulation

A Prepare the batch of budget documents (balance sheet, income statement, and cash flow forecast) to test the validity of your decisions (see Appendix 2).

B Hand in your decision sheet to the instructor.

C The instructor will advise each company of the quantity of its actual potential sales for the period. This amount is a maximum figure. If a company has not planned to produce enough to meet the revealed potential demand, that company's sales will be limited to the quantities available for shipment (production plus available beginning inventory). The calculation of the potential maximum sales of any company reflects the decisions taken by both the company and its competitors.

D Once each company knows its actual demand, each company management team will prepare the resulting definitive accounting documents (balance sheet, income statement, cash flow statement), which will be presented to the shareholders. These documents have to be certified by the statutory auditor (see Appendix 2).

NAME OF THE COMPANY	YEAR

Appendix 1: Decision sheet

1 Sales

1.1 Unit sales price (in CU)

1.2 Quantities you intend to sell

2 Production

2.1 Investment (number of acquired new assembly lines)

2.2 Number of operational assembly lines: existing lines at the end of the previous period minus fully depreciated lines this period plus newly acquired lines = number of productive lines available this period

2.3 Production you will launch (quantity of hairdryers)

2.4 Outside purchases of motors and parts (quantity)

2.5 Consumption of motors and parts (quantity)

3 Personnel

3.1 New hires (number of persons)

3.2 Personnel dismissed (number of persons)

3.3 Annual total remuneration (excluding employers' social security charges) – in CU per employee

4 External charges (in 000s of CU)

4.1 Budget for advertising, marketing, and promotion

4.2 Auditing fees (of the past year)

5 Dividends and others (in 000s of CU)

5.1 Dividends distributed

5.2 Profit not distributed (and transferred to reserves)

5.3 Increase of capital in cash (on the basis of approval by shareholders)

5.4 Increase of capital by incorporation of reserves (on the basis of approval by shareholders)

5.5 New debt received (according to agreements made)

5.6 Interest expense on bank overdraft (of the past year)

Appendix 2: Summary financial statements

COMPANY	YEAR

CASH FLOW BUDGET/STATEMENT (in 000 CU)

Opening balance (1)	
Cash flows from operating activities	
Cash from sales (80%)	....
Cash from receivables (see preceding balance sheet)	....
Cash purchases: 85% of annual purchases	....
Accounts payable (see preceding balance sheet)	....
Income tax payable	....
Other taxes	....
Personnel expenses.	....
Rent expense.	....
Utility services.	....
Advertising expenses.	....
Auditing fees.	....
Financial expenses.	....
Net cash flows from operating activities (2)	
Cash flows from investing activities	
Investments (assembly lines)	....
Other (sale of fixed assets)	....
Net cash flows used in investing activities (3)	
Cash flows from financing activities	
Increase in capital	....
New debts	....
Repayment of debts	....
Dividends paid	....
Net cash flows used in financing activities (4)	
Net increase (decrease) in cash (5) = (2) + (3) + (4)	
Ending balance (6) = (1) + (5)	

INCOME STATEMENT (in 000 CU)

Operating expenses		**Operating revenues**	
Purchases of motors and parts	.....	Sale	.....
Change in inventory of raw materials (B-E)	.....	Change in inventory of finished products (E-B)	.....
External expenses	.....		
Other taxes	.....		
Personnel expenses	.....		
Depreciation	.....		
Financial expenses	.....	**Financial income**	.....
Exceptional expenses	.....	**Exceptional income**	.....
Subtotal	.....	Subtotal	.....
Income tax	.....		
Net income		Net loss	
Total		Total	

BALANCE SHEET (in 000 CU)

Fixed assets	....	*Shareholders' equity*	
Manufacturing equipment	....	Capital	....
		Reserves	....
Current Assets		Net income/loss	....
		Subtotal	....
Inventories			
■ Motors and parts	....	*Liabilities*	
■ Finished products	....		
Accounts receivable (20%)	....	Debt 10% X1	....
		Bank overdraft	....
Cash at bank	....	Accounts payable (15%)	....
		Income tax payable	....
Total		Total	

References

Colasse, B. (1993) *Gestion financière*, 3rd edn, PUF, Paris.

Drury, C. (2004) *Management and Cost Accounting*, 6th edn, Thomson Learning, London.

EU (European Union) (1978) 4th Directive on the annual accounts of certain types of companies no. 78/660/EEC. *Official Journal of the European Communities*, 14 August.

IASB (1989) Framework for the Preparation and Presentation of Financial Statements, London.

IASB (1992) International Accounting Standard No. 7: Cash Flow Statements, London.

IASB (2003) International Accounting Standard No. 1: Presentation of Financial Statements, London.

Further reading

Parker, R. H. (1996) Harmonizing the notes in the UK and France: a case study in *de jure* harmonization. *European Accounting Review*, 5(2), 317–37.

Additional material on the website

Go to http://www.thomsonlearning.co.uk/stolowylebas2 for further information.

The following appendix to this chapter is available on the dedicated website:

Appendix 3.1: Cost of goods sold

Notes

1. This presentation allows the calculation of the so-called 'value added' of the firm. This concept emanates essentially from a tax preoccupation (value added tax) and a national statistics viewpoint. It will be further explored in Chapters 10 and 15. Simply stated, this value added concept (not to be confused with that of 'economic value added' – developed in Chapter 15 – used in the rank ordering of firm performance – essentially operating profit minus cost of capital employed) measures the amount of value created by the firm beyond 'what it acquired from outside the economic entity'. The definition of the business perimeter, although provided by tax authorities, rarely reflects a decision-makers' preoccupation.
2. Based on idea developed by Colasse (1993). The figures have been updated and several companies are different.
3. The number of companies in the game will, in fact, vary according to the number of participants. The average quantity of units potentially sold by any company is always 100,000 in the first period. Thus, the market potential in period X3 is equal to the number of teams times 100,000 units.

C4

Chapter 4
The accounting process

Learning objectives

After studying this chapter, you will understand:

- How to use the concepts of debit and credit.
- That the accounting process consists in a structured multistep progressive classification and aggregation process of elemental data.
- That each accounting transaction originates in a source document.
- That the journal is the day-to-day chronological register of accounting information.
- That the general ledger is the grouping of all accounts (a ledger is a grouping of selected, homogeneous accounts).
- That all entries are transferred ('posted') from the journal to the appropriate specialized ledger (where they can be used, when needed, for further internal and managerial analyses) and, ultimately, to the general ledger.
- That the accountant must prepare a 'trial balance', which is a list of the debit and credit footings for each account in the general ledger. The trial balance is a method of internal control, which helps verify that all transactions have been recorded in accordance with the double entry bookkeeping principle.
- That all companies have a chart of accounts, which is a logically organized list of all recognized accounts used in recording transactions.
- That some countries have a standardized chart of accounts while others do not.
- That, in general, account codes are an extremely useful shortcut.

In order to establish financial statements a business needs to set up an organized accounting system. This system consists in a multistage process, illustrated in this chapter. The accounting process relies not only on the use of technical tools, but requires human intervention and interpretation (mainly in classifying the recording of each transaction in the proper categories). The importance of the human factor must never be underestimated in accounting.

1 Core issues

1.1 Double entry bookkeeping and the recording of transactions

1.1.1 Accounts

Chapter 2 provided a direct illustration of the impact of economic transactions on the balance sheet, or on both balance sheet and income statement. Business organizations deal with very large numbers of transactions, and some degree of systematic organization quickly becomes necessary to avoid chaos and to provide the ability for the users of accounting information to understand how the business works.

Each balance sheet or income statement item or line may undergo thousands or even millions of modifications during an accounting period. (At the extreme end of the spectrum, for example, Wal-Mart, the US-based largest retail chain in the world, is said to serve over 45 million customers per day, and to employ 1.6 million persons, an activity that generates millions of accounting entries.) Each of these successive modifications affects specialized accounts that result from subdivisions, according to the type of transaction, of balance sheet and income statement items. At year-end, only the net summary positions of the accounts, known as their balance, are used in establishing the balance sheet and income statement. Too much detail in reporting would make the accounting signals un-understandable or overwhelming and, therefore, useless.

In the Verdi Company example, discussed in Chapter 2 (Figures 2.2–2.10), the company's cash on 1 January X1, before the incorporation of the company, was 0 CU. This initial amount (or opening balance) underwent several modifications (entries) following transactions either raising this amount (+240) or lowering it (−325), such that the year-end cash showed a positive balance of 5 CU. This last figure (see Table 4.1) is reported in the balance sheet assets on 30 April X1: the cash balance is one of the components of the financial position of Verdi Company at the end of the accounting period (see Chapter 2, Table 2.3).

Table 4.1 Cash account of Verdi Company

Cash account			
Cash inflows		**Cash outflows**	
Beginning balance	*0*	Cash payment to suppliers	80
Capital contribution	90	Cash payment on equipment	125
Cash receipt from customers	180	Cash payment to employees	101
Cash receipt on debt	60	Cash payment on debt	15
		Cash payment on interest	4
Total cash inflows	330		
Ending balance[1]	5	Total cash outflows	325

Note: We have not specified what sort of 'cash' this account covers. Cash inflows and outflows refer, at this stage, indiscriminately to either cash in hand or cash at bank (or totally liquid assets at some financial institution).

1.1.2 The concept of debit and credit

Basic principles Since the concepts of increases and decreases to monetary amounts in the accounts can be confusing, the respective sides must be clearly defined. *By convention*, the left-hand side of a T-account is called the debit side, and the right-hand side the credit side. Thus, the 'cash' account (an asset account) increases on the debit side and decreases on the credit side. The initial positive amount is a debit balance. Similarly, a 'debt' account (part of shareholders' equity and liabilities) increases on the credit side (the right-hand side) and decreases on the debit side (the left-hand side). The balance of this account, when the borrowing is not totally repaid, is thus a credit balance.

In general, the asset side of the balance sheet is designed to summarize balance sheet accounts with debit balances, while the shareholders' equity and liabilities side contains the balance sheet accounts with credit balances. Since the balance sheet is always balanced, it means the total of debit balances (the assets) equals the total of credit balances (shareholders' equity and liabilities). Expense accounts function similarly to asset accounts, while revenue accounts function in the same way as shareholders' equity and liabilities.

A schematic presentation of these rules is shown in Figure 4.1, using the basic business equation.

It is important to note that the terms **'debit'** and **'credit'** correspond to the left- and right-hand sides. They are not synonymous with 'increase' and 'decrease'. To understand the meaning of debit and credit for accounts recording expenses and revenues, suffice it to remember that revenues increase shareholders' equity, but expenses reduce it. For this reason, revenue accounts 'behave' in a way similar to that of shareholders' equity accounts (credit = increase, and debit = decrease), while, for expense accounts, the opposite applies.

Figure 4.1 also shows that net income is the difference between revenues and expenses, and becomes a component of shareholders' equity (retained earnings).

Figure 4.1 Basic business equation and concepts of debit and credit

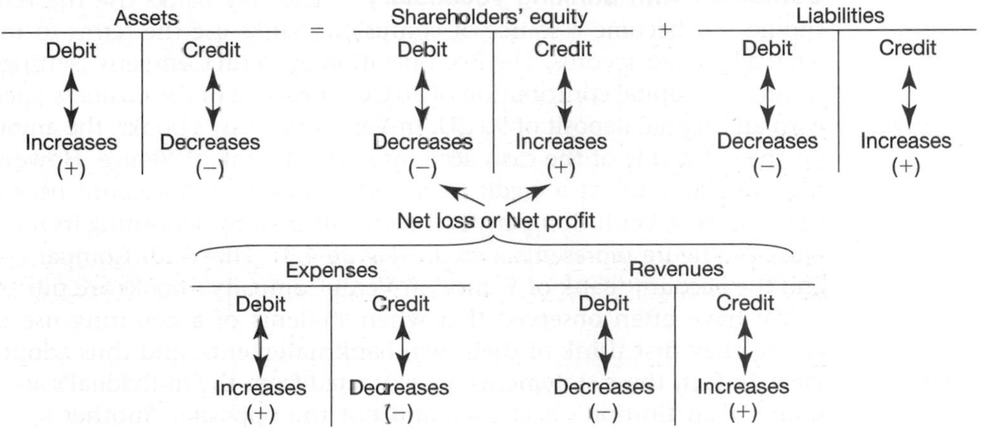

Origins of the concept To understand the concepts of debit and credit, we must go back to the origin of the terms. According to Vlaemminck (1979: 63), they 'are derived from the Latin words used in the Middle-Ages "debit" (verb *debere*: to owe) and "credit" (verb *credere*: to lend or to trust)'. The terms debit and credit refer to the other party's position in relation to the business. In other words, a debit means a claim ***of** the business* on something (equipment, inventory, or a promise to pay by a customer), while a credit reflects a claim of a third party ***on** the business*.

As an illustration, let us use the example of a sale of merchandise on credit by Romulus to his brother Remus for 100 sesterces (S). This transaction will be recorded in Figure 4.2.

In Romulus' books the sale, worth 100 S, is recorded on the credit side (Romulus is potentially getting richer, subject to the cost incurred by Romulus of what he sold to Remus and which is not involved in the recording of this transaction) and this is recorded by recognizing the counterbalancing entry which is a debit to accounts receivable called

Figure 4.2 Debit and credit

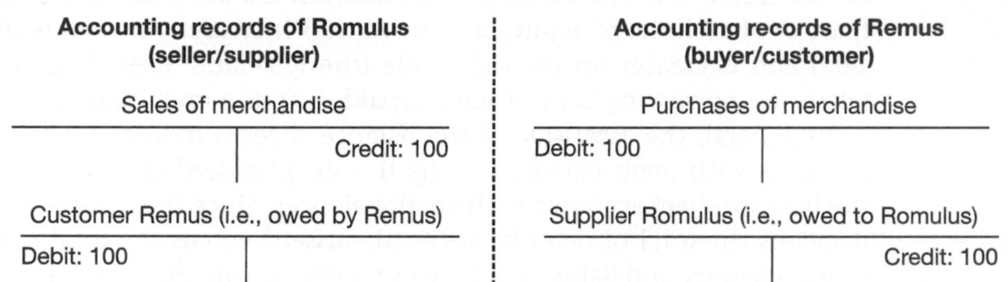

'customer Remus' which shows that Romulus holds a claim of 100 S over Remus. This entry in Romulus' books shows that: (a) a claim of Romulus' shareholders has been created for 100 S on the credit side of the 'sales' account; and (b) a claim of Romulus' business on Remus (reflecting the fact the cash or equivalent resources will be transferred later) is created as a debit to the accounts receivable. In a mirror image, the same amount is recorded on the credit side of the 'supplier' account in Remus' books, because the supplier, Romulus, trusts his buyer Remus.

By extension of this principle, the terms debit and credit are used to position the effect of any transaction even those that do not involve a third party such as the recognition of a depreciation expense, even though we can hardly say the old meanings of 'owes us' or 'trusts us' apply.

Confusion with banking vocabulary The way banks use the terms debit and credit should not become a source of confusion. Banks use the terms to mean the opposite of what a business records. The first operation by Verdi Company (setting up the company by means of a capital contribution of 90 CU) consisted of the business opening a bank account with an original deposit of 90 CU. In Verdi Company's books, the amount of 90 is recorded on the debit side of the cash account entitled Bank of Venice. However, the bank records the same amount as a credit to the Verdi Company's account because, from the bank's point of view, Verdi Company is showing its trust by depositing its money, and thus for the bank the figure represents a credit (Figure 4.3). The Verdi Company account at the bank and the account 'Bank of Venice' in Verdi Company's books are mirror accounts.

We have often observed that when students of accounting use the terms debit and credit, they first think of their own bank statements, and thus adopt the bank's point of view. In fact, these statements are extracted from the individual's account taken from the financial institution's accounts, and not the opposite. Another approach, based on the concepts of 'use' and 'source' is possible and presented in Appendix 4.1.

Figure 4.4 summarizes these basic rules in a diagram form.

In the end, the reader should use the vocabulary he or she finds most helpful. The most important thing is to translate the true impact of the transactions recorded on the position of the firm in an understandable and consistent way, regardless of the specific set of words used.

Figure 4.3 Debit and credit from a bank's perspective

Accounting records of Verdi Company		**Accounting records of Bank of Venice**	
Bank of Venice		Verdi Company	
D	C	D	C
Debit: 90			Credit: 90

Figure 4.4 Basic rules for debit and credit

Assets or expenses	
Debit	Credit
Left	Right
Increase	Decrease

Shareholders' equity, liabilities, or revenues	
Debit	Credit
Left	Right
Decrease	Increase

1.2 The accounting process

1.2.1 Description of the process

Double entry bookkeeping is entirely based on a fundamental idea: each individual accounting transaction has two sides, which are always balanced. In accounting for cash, for example, double entry describes, on the one hand, the reasons why money has been received (or paid out) and, on the other, which account (cash at bank or cash in hand) was increased (or decreased).

For practical reasons evoked earlier, it would be impossible to report the full effect of every transaction on the shareholders' equity. However, in order to leave a clear audit trail (i.e., a possibility of *ex post* verification), all transactions must be recorded. The accounting process consists of a structured multistep progressive aggregation of elemental data, which is designed to be both exhaustive and efficient. It is illustrated in Figure 4.5.

Figure 4.5 Accounting process/accounting system

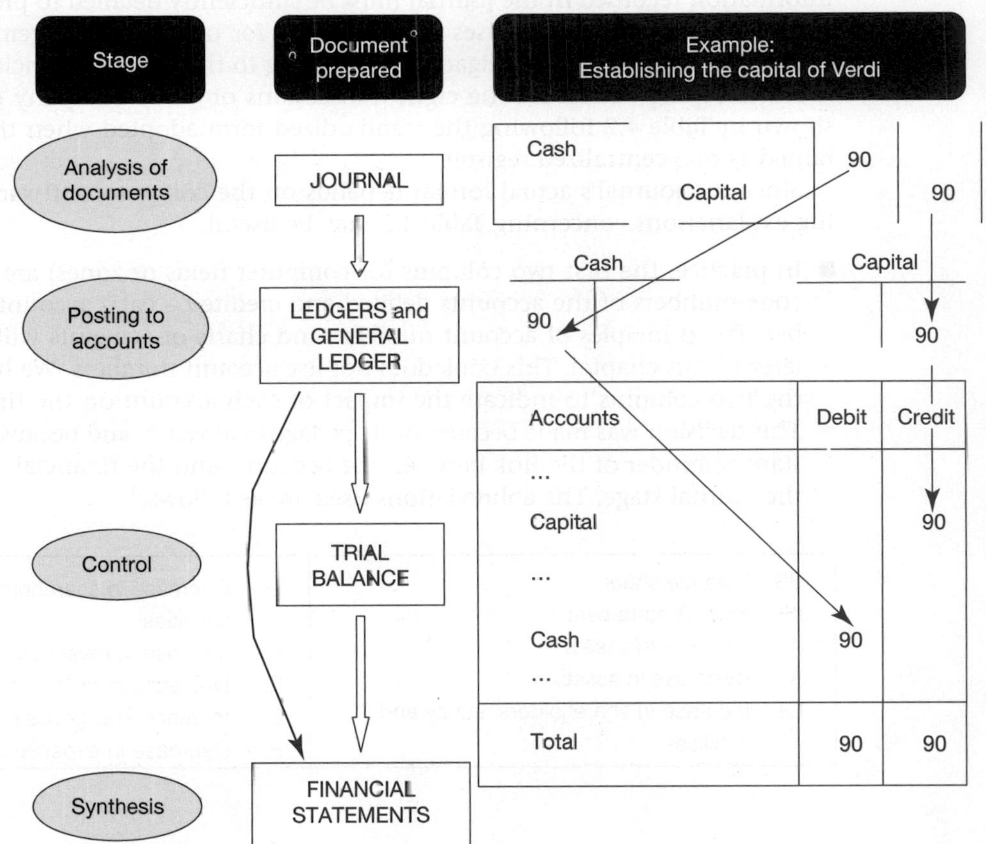

Each accounting transaction originates in a **document**. This document serves as the basis for an entry in a **journal**. The journal provides a chronological list of all transactions. The next step is to distribute the effects of events between specialized **ledger** accounts where they can be accumulated in homogenous classes of nature and type of transaction. The ledger balances (net sum of a class of effect of transactions) will in turn be aggregated in the two main components of the **financial statements** (balance sheet and income statement).

1.2.2 Documents

The documents (invoices, cheques, insurance premium receipts, contracts, tax and social security filings, etc.) formalizing each transaction are called 'supporting documents' or 'source documents'. The information they contain must be recorded in the accounts. In some cases (e.g., for depreciation and amortization, provisions, or adjusting entries), no specific document exists, and the operation is classified as 'miscellaneous'.

The accountant should verify that each source document specifically and unambiguously pertains to the business in whose accounts it will be recorded. This question is essential because of the need to clearly distinguish between the business entity (or a legal entity) and individual shareholders or employees (sometimes problematic in the case of a sole proprietorship – see Chapter 11). Recording personal expenses, unrelated to the company's business and objectives, is a misappropriation of company assets and a fraud, which is disallowed by legal and/or tax authorities and may give rise to litigation.

1.2.3 Journal

As its name implies, the journal is the day-to-day chronological register of accounting information found in the source documents of all allowable transactions. The journal is often referred to as the 'record of prime entry' or the 'book of original entry', since it is the first formal phase in the accounting process, frequently called 'journalizing'. The information recorded in the journal must be sufficiently detailed to provide management with the possibility of analyses required both for ongoing management needs and for complying with the legal obligations pertaining to the annual financial statements.

Bookkeeping entries for the eight transactions of Verdi Company (see Chapter 2) are shown in Table 4.2 following the standardized form adopted when the journal is maintained as one centralized register.

Since the journal's actual format depends on the computer software used, the following explanations concerning Table 4.2 may be useful.

- In practice, the first two columns (or computer fields or zones) are used to record the code numbers of the accounts debited and credited – each account has its own number. The principles of account numbers and charts of accounts will only be discussed later in this chapter. This book does not use account numbers. We have, however, kept the two columns to indicate the impact of each account on the financial statements. This decision was made because of its pedagogical value, and because it provides a constant reminder of the link between the accounts and the financial statements, even at the journal stage. The abbreviations used are as follows:

BS	Balance sheet	L−	Decrease in shareholders' equity and liabilities
IS	Income statement	R+	Increase in revenues
A+	Increase in assets	R−	Decrease in revenues
A−	Decrease in assets	E+	Increase in expenses
L+	Increase in shareholders' equity and liabilities	E−	Decrease in expenses

Table 4.2 Verdi Company journal

		(1) Establishing capital payment			
BS (A+)		Cash		90	
	BS (L+)		Capital		90
		(2) Borrowing from Bank of Venice			
BS (A+)		Cash		60	
	BS (L+)		Financial debt		60
		(3) Purchasing equipment			
BS (A+)		Equipment		125	
	BS (A−)		Cash		125
		(4) Sale to customer Sam Suffit			
BS (A+)		Accounts receivable		250	
	IS (R+)		Service revenue		250
		(5) Partial settlement of accounts receivable by customer Suffit			
BS (A+)		Cash		180	
	BS (A−)		Accounts receivable		180
		(6) Payment of workers remuneration			
IS (E+)		Payroll expenses		101	
	BS (A−)		Cash		101
		Payment of interest on debt (Bank of Venice)			
IS (E+)		Interest expense		4	
	BS (A−)		Cash		4
		Purchases of services			
IS (E+)		External expense		85	
	BS (L+)		Accounts payable		85
		(7) Partial settlement of accounts payable			
BS (L−)		Accounts payable		80	
	BS (A−)		Cash		80
		(8) Partial reimbursement of debt principal			
BS (L−)		Financial debt		15	
	BS (A−)		Cash		15
				990	990

- The two central columns are used for the names of the accounts debited or credited. By convention, the debited account(s) is (are) recorded first, to the left on the upper line, while the credited account(s) is (are) shown to the right on a line below (one single transaction may require that more than two accounts be used).
- The last two columns (one for debits and one for credits) show the amounts relevant to the entry.

Each transaction is described in words that allow the reader to understand the nature of the transaction and to identify the source document(s) (often numbered sequentially). The date of each transaction is also indicated in each entry, even if here, in this very simple illustration, we chose to omit the dates for reasons of simplicity.

The debit and credit columns must be totaled, and the absolute equality of the totals shows (and allows the accountant to verify) that double entry rules have been properly applied. At this stage no error, not even a difference of one currency unit, can be tolerated. A difference between the totals of two columns would signal an error in recording since, for each entry, debits equal credits.

The journal recording only recognizes the existence of the elements of the transaction. The subsequent steps will organize, classify, and aggregate the data in significant groupings (as on the balance sheet, for example) allowing comparison with prior information from the same company or with industry benchmarks. This is done in ledgers.

1.2.4 Ledger

Any set of homogeneously defined accounts used in a business is called a **ledger**[2] or **specialized ledger**. For example, all accounts pertaining to sourcing transactions on credit constitute, collectively, the payables ledger. A ledger is a classification category. It contains all the details of the relevant side of the journal entries and provides an ending balance, which is the net sum of all entries in this category.

The general ledger is the sum of all specialized numbered ledgers, each regrouping one relevant aspect of transactions (as defined by management in their quest for information assisting them in the effective and efficient running of the business – cash, purchases, sales, etc.). A specialized ledger is generally an 'intermediate' database, allowing the manager to analyze in detail that category of transactions. For example, the payables ledger will allow the management team to analyze their relationships with all or some categories of suppliers. The data recorded in the journal are integrally transcribed in the specialized ledgers and, ultimately, in the general ledger, still in chronological order in their category. Ledgers do not create data. Ledgers, however, reveal the informational content of data by creating (and archiving) meaningful aggregates. The advantage of a ledger is that, even if its current balance is zero (for example, its previous balance was – or all of its transactions were – transferred to the general ledger) all of its historical content is still available for analysis if needed.

The process of transferring entries from the journal to the ledger is called '**posting**'. Each account debited or credited in the journal is thus transferred as a debit or credit of the relevant account in the general ledger and the specialized ledgers. Posting is a purely mechanical task, with no analysis required. Indeed, one of the first advantages of dedicated accounting software is that they automate this task, saving businesses considerable time and eliminating errors (see the later section on 'Trial balance' for further discussion of errors).

The above-described system transfers balances from the specialized ledgers to accounts in the general ledger. For example, all the individual accounts receivable (from the specialized ledger 'receivables' or 'customers') are transferred to a general (aggregated) account entitled 'accounts receivable' in the general ledger. However, with the ease of electronic database management, most modern accounting software have preserved the intent of unbending rigorousness offered by the process we described and freed themselves from practices dating back to manual bookkeeping by simplifying the actual data manipulation. The specialized ledgers are not 'transferred' to the general ledger but simply added, in a single 'ledger-like' database where all accounts are recorded, whether they would have been detailed or not in a specialized ledger (e.g., share capital, fixed assets, etc., do not give rise to specialized ledgers in a traditional recording system and any transaction affecting them would be recorded directly in the general ledger). In this case, the large database can be considered the 'ledger' since it includes the traditional general ledger and all individual accounts appearing in the different specialized ledgers. If managers need a specialized analysis that would have required data from a specialized ledger, they simply extract from the ledger database the information they need. The process is simpler, but the logic is the same as the one used in the basic (essentially manual) system we described.

Table 4.3 shows Verdi Company's general ledger where each account (here the situation is extremely simplified) is listed according to its position in the financial statements.

1.2.5 Trial balance

Principle Before establishing the financial statements, the accountant will prepare a 'Trial balance', which is simply a list of the debit and credit entries and footings for each account in the general ledger. The object of this exercise is to check that the sum of all the debit entries or balances is equal to the sum of all the credit entries or balances. In other words, it is the verification that 'Total Debits' = 'Total Credits'.

The format of the trial balance varies from one business (or software) to another. Table 4.4 illustrates a model of trial balance, using the Verdi Company data.

Accounts are listed nearly always in the order of the company's account codes. To simplify matters, our example follows the order used in the financial statements, i.e., assets accounts first, followed by equity and liabilities accounts in the upper portion of Table 4.4, expenses accounts and revenues accounts are listed sequentially in the lower part of the table.

The trial balance is used to verify two fundamental equations:

Sum of debit entries = Sum of credit entries

Sum of debit balances = Sum of credit balances

The initial purpose of the trial balance was a straightforward arithmetical verification. Above all, it was used to check that the amounts in the journal had been correctly copied (posted) into the ledger, and that the double entry rules had been applied properly. Today, thanks to the use of computer software, both the above equations are (fortunately) always mechanically verified. And yet – perhaps surprisingly – the trial balance is still established, for, essentially, the following two reasons:

1. It is a useful instrument in auditing accounts, since the trial balance reveals potential errors (e.g., accounts with an abnormal type of balance, for instance a capital account with a debit balance or an equipment account with a credit balance – Table 4.5 lists 'normal' balances) and anomalies (for instance, balances that are higher or lower than usual or than during a previous relevant period, accounts missing or wrongly included, etc.).
2. It provides a simple determination of the net profit/loss without having to establish a balance sheet or income statement. Whatever the system of codes attributed to the accounts, the trial balance generally comprises two distinct parts (as in Table 4.4): balance sheet accounts, followed by income statement accounts. The following equations permit a rapid calculation of the income of the period:

Using only balance sheet accounts:

'Sum of debit balances' minus 'Sum of credit balances' = Net income

Using only income statement accounts:

'Sum of credit balances' minus 'Sum of debit balances' = Net income

Table 4.3 Verdi Company's ledgers

Balance sheet
(on the last day of the accounting period X1)

Assets

D	Equipment	C
125 (3)		
D balance = 125		

D	Accounts receivable	C
250 (4)	180 (5)	
D balance = 70		

D	Cash		C
90 (1)	125	(3)	
60 (2)	101	(6)	
180 (5)	4	(6)	
330	80	(7)	
	15	(8)	
	325		
D balance = 5			

Shareholders' equity and liabilities

D	Capital	C
	90 (1)	
	C balance = 90	

D	Financial debt	C
15 (8)	60 (2)	
	C balance = 45	

D	Accounts payable	C
80 (7)	85 (6)	
	C balance = 5	

Income statement
(for the accounting period X1)

Expenses

D	External expenses	C
85 (6)		
D balance = 85		

D	Payroll expense	C
101 (6)		
D balance = 101		

D	Interest expense	C
4 (6)		
D balance = 4		

Revenues

D	Sales	C
	250 (4)	
	C balance = 250	

Numbers in parentheses next to the entry refer to the transaction number in the journal (see Table 4.2).
D = debit and C = credit

Comments:

1. For transactions with customers and suppliers, one account alone (a 'collective' or 'general' account) is not enough. These accounts must be subdivided into one account per customer and per supplier, and all individual customer and supplier accounts taken together form the accounts receivable and accounts payable specialized ledgers (also called special or subsidiary ledgers).
2. The totals of each column of an account are called 'footings'. The difference between the debit footing and the credit footing is called the balance of the account.
3. For learning purposes, we chose to record transactions directly in T-accounts. Doing this has the advantage of providing a clear view of the impact of a transaction on each account.
4. In the summary of balance sheet accounts:
   - The total of debit balances (D) is 125 + 70 + 5 = 200.
   - The total of credit balances (C) is 90 + 45 + 5 = 140.
   - Therefore, since the total of debit balances and the total of credit balances must be equal, the shortfall of 60, on the equity and liabilities side, must, by construction, correspond to the net income of the period.

Table 4.3 Verdi Company's ledgers (*Continued*)

5. In the summary of the income statement accounts:
   - The total of debit balances (D) is 85 + 101 + 4 = 190.
   - The total of credit balances (C) is 250.
   - There is thus a positive net income of 60, which is by definition identical to the income found through the summary of the balance sheet debits and credits.
6. As expected, the amount (net profit/loss) to be added to the shareholders' equity is the same regardless of whether one uses the balance sheet or the income statement approach. It was easy in our example to calculate the net profit/loss both ways because very few accounts were involved. When a business' accounts comprise thousands of individual accounts, they must, first, be controlled by transcribing the balances in the trial balance.

Table 4.4 Verdi Company trial balance

	Entries		Balances	
Accounts	Debit	Credit	Debit	Credit
Balance sheet				
Equipment	125		125	
Accounts receivable	250	180	70	
Cash	330	325	5	
Capital		90		90
Financial debt	15	60		45
Accounts payable	80	85		5
Income statement				
External expenses	85		85	
Payroll expenses	101		101	
Interest expense	4		4	
Sales		250		250
Total	990	990	390	390

Table 4.4 was structured in this way. The net profit/loss is thus determined as follows:

Using only balance sheet accounts: Debit balances − Credit balances = 200 − 140 = 60

Using only income statement accounts: Credit balances − Debit balances = 250 − 190 = 60

Table 4.5 Examples of 'normal' account balances (this list is in no way exhaustive)

Accounts	Debit	Credit
Assets	*x*	
Set up expenses	x	
Land	x	
Plant, machinery or office equipment	x	
Accumulated depreciation of plant, machinery or office equipment		x
Investments	x	
Provision for depreciation of investments		x
Deposits and guarantees	x	
Merchandise inventories (inventories of goods acquired for resale)	x	
Provision for depreciation of merchandise		x
Accounts receivable	x	
Doubtful debt accounts	x	
Provision for doubtful debts		x
Advance payments made to suppliers	x	
Income tax receivable	x	
Prepaid rent	x	
Cash at bank	x	
Cash in hand	x	
Shareholders' equity		
Share capital		x
Retained earnings or reserves		x
Losses brought forward	x	
Profits brought forward		x
Liabilities		*x*
Long-term debt or bonds		x
Short-term debt or bonds payable		x
Bank overdrafts		x
Accounts payable		x
Advance payments received from customers		x
Salaries payable		x
Revenues		*x*
Sales of merchandise (goods purchased for resale)		x
Sales of finished products		x
Changes in finished (manufactured) products inventories (two possible normal balances)	x	x
Other trade revenues		x
Financial income		x
Exceptional revenues (or extraordinary revenue items)		x
Expenses	*x*	
Purchases of merchandise	x	
Change in merchandise inventory (two possible normal balances)	x	x
Purchases of raw materials, parts and components (RM, P, & C)	x	
Change in RM, P, & C inventories (two possible normal balances)	x	x
Cost of goods sold	x	
Selling and marketing expenses	x	
General and administrative expenses	x	
R&D expense	x	
External services – electricity, utilities	x	
Insurance and other services	x	
Miscellaneous payroll taxes	x	
Wages and salaries	x	
License fees	x	
Financial expense and interest	x	
Exceptional expenses (or extraordinary expense items)	x	

Figure 4.5 above showed, with a thin arrow, that the trial balance could, technically, be bypassed in the preparation of the financial statements, thus allowing the accountant to go directly from the ledgers to the financial statements. However, such a solution is not recommended because it sidesteps the essential internal control usage of the trial balance. Even if arithmetic errors are now technically impossible, the trial balance still will be used effectively to detect errors of logic in the choice of accounts used, which could be revealed, for example, by the unexpected algebraic sign of an account balance. The normal directionality of account balances is illustrated in Table 4.5 (see also Appendix 4.2).

Normal account balances Table 4.5 lists common accounts and indicates the expected nature of their balance (debit or credit).

Trial balance errors Appendix 4.2 provides some explanations regarding errors which might be found in a trial balance (debit or credit).

1.2.6 Financial statements

The establishment of the financial statements is the final stage of the accounting process. We have already discussed financial statements, principally in Chapter 3. Some operations are undertaken specifically to establish the year-end financial statements. These are known as 'end-of-period entries', and are discussed in Chapter 5.

Going back to the example of Verdi Company, we have a balance sheet on 31 December X1 (see Table 2.3 in Chapter 2) that summarizes the debit balances on the asset side (excess of debits over credits) and the credit balances on the liabilities side (excess of credits over debits) and an income statement for the accounting period X1 (see Tables 2.6 or 2.7 in Chapter 2).

As we have seen, thanks to the double entry system, it is possible to establish both the balance sheet and the income statement at the same time. The balance sheet registers profit of 60 CU, and the income statement explains how it was obtained.

2 Advanced issues

The accounts kept by a business serve three essential purposes:

1. They constitute legal evidence, and, as such, must be easily accessible to controllers (e.g., tax inspectors or auditors) and comply with laws and regulations.
2. They are instruments for business management. For example, the accounts payable should tell, with accuracy and timeliness, how much the company owes its suppliers; or the accounts receivable should reflect how much is owed by its customers, etc.
3. They are a source of management information. The accounting process, and the accounts that comprise it, allow reports on value creation (or subsets thereof, such as sales by market segment or costs by nature) at any desired interval, including the minimum legally required annual financial statements.

To be effective, the organization of the accounting system must therefore strike the best balance between these objectives or constraints, and the related operating costs.

2.1 Organization of the accounting system

Appendix 4.3 provides some developments on the organization of the accounting system, in terms of timing, specialized journals, and computer software. It also describes the accounting function within the company.

2.2 The chart of accounts

A chart of accounts is a pre-established, logically organized list of all recognized (and authorized) accounts used in recording all transactions in a firm. A chart of accounts generally assigns a unique code to each account.

2.2.1 Principles

As indicated earlier in this chapter, each account must be identified by a name or, most frequently, by a code. Several coding methods are possible, mainly: Alphabetical, Numerical, and Alphanumerical. Each account's unique code is necessary for quick reference in processing transactions to the accounts, and is absolutely vital for IT systems.

Alphabetical coding appears to be the most simple: no numbers to remember, and only the names of the accounts to know, in natural language. But in practice, it is not a good solution, because:

- it proved in the past to be complicated for programming IT systems;
- it may prove to be time-consuming to enter the full name of an account, unless the name is given a shortcut name, which makes matters more complex again;
- each account must have a specific name, and no variants (such as spelling errors or unspecified abbreviations) could be recognized. The practical difficulties associated with natural language codes have made pure alphabetical coding rather uncommon.

For these reasons, account codes are almost always numerical or alphanumerical. For example, 'accounts receivable' might be coded 142, and account '142Soprano' (a subsidiary account of account 142) would be used to record sales transactions with the Soprano family businesses, whereas '142Tessitura' would be used to record sales transactions with Tessitura Inc.

In general, charts of accounts are based on hierarchical classification, in which classes or groups of accounts are identified, and then subdivided as the need requires. There can be as many subclasses or nested subdivisions as the company requires. Figure 4.6 illustrates one possible chart of accounts.

2.2.2 Standardized chart of accounts

In countries such as Belgium, France, Portugal, Spain, and many African countries, the overall structure of the accounts code is laid down nationally whilst in several other countries the choice of structure is left entirely up to company management (e.g., Italy, the Netherlands, Switzerland, the UK, and the US).

Figure 4.6 A possible chart of account

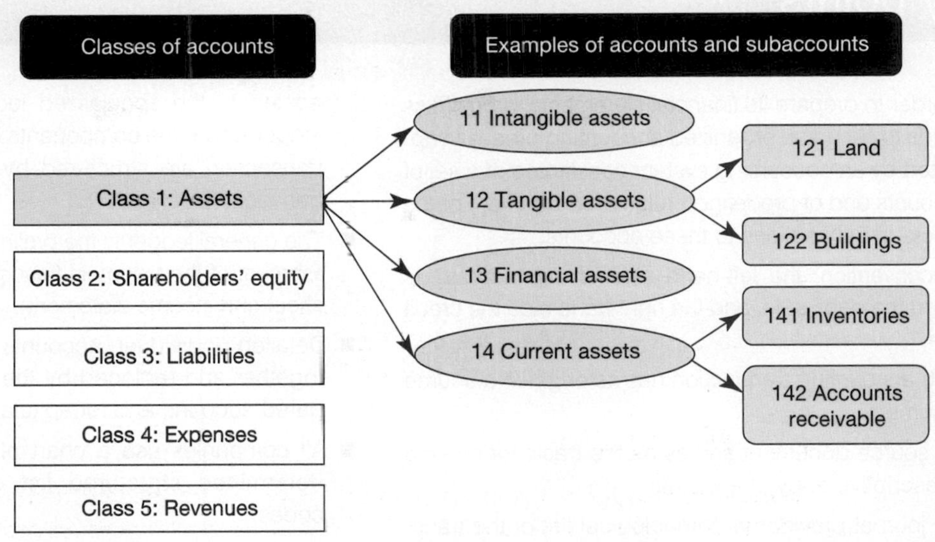

2.2.3 The importance of account codes

As stated above, some countries (but not many) have a standardized chart of accounts, while most other countries let the company decide on its own chart. Although the debate over standardization of charts of accounts is not a fundamental issue, the proponents of national standardized charts argue that:

- it facilitates the mobility of qualified accountants since all firms use the same basic account structure;
- it reduces the cost of designing accounting software packages;
- it facilitates intercompany comparability of published accounts.

The internal logic of a hierarchical numbering of accounts allows an immediate understanding of the nature and role of an account, often in a clearer way than words might. For example, an account called 'fees' can be unclear as it may refer either to fees received or to fees paid. If the account is numbered '4xxx-Fees' (using the basic chart of accounts introduced in Figure 4.6) it is clearly fees expensed, while if the code is 5yyy-Fees, it unambiguously refers to fees earned. The numerical part of the account allows for further decomposition into subsidiary accounts when needed. Any large organization with multiple establishments, plants and/or subsidiaries is sooner or later forced to create its own internal standardized chart of accounts (applicable throughout the world) to allow managerial discussions and facilitate consolidation (regrouping of the financial position and income of subsidiaries into the parent company accounts). The list of codes chosen either nationally or by any one firm has no intrinsic meaning and no classification is superior to any other. What matters is that the users understand the reasons for the choices made. We deliberately chose, in this book, to de-emphasize the use of codes in referring to accounts since there is no international standardization of charts of account.

Key points

- In order to prepare its financial statements, a business needs to set up an organized accounting process supported by an accounting system constituted of a set of accounts and of predefined rules of assignment of the effects of transactions to these accounts.
- By convention, the left-hand side of any account is called the debit side, and the right-hand side the credit side.
- Each accounting transaction has its origin in a source document.
- The source document serves as the basis for making a descriptive entry in a journal
- The journal provides a chronological list of the transactions. After journalizing accounting entries, they are posted in the specialized ledgers and the general ledger where the components of the description of the transaction are structured by nature and/or type of transaction.
- The general ledger is the preliminary step to the establishment of the two main financial statements (balance sheet and income statement).
- Detailed individual accounts entries are grouped together and replaced by the balance of the aggregated account, and recapitulated in the trial balance.
- All companies use a chart of accounts, i.e., a predetermined structured list of accepted account codes.

Review (solutions are at the back of the book)

Review 4.1 Grieg Company (1)

Topic: The accounting process: from the journal to the financial statements (purchases of merchandise are recorded first in inventory)
Related part of the chapter: Core issues

The Grieg Company was incorporated on 1 January X1. Grieg had five holders of share capital. The following events occurred during January X1.

1. The Company was incorporated. Common shareholders invested a total of 10,000 CU cash.
2. Equipment valued of 1,200 CU was acquired for cash.
3. Merchandise inventory was purchased on credit for 9,000 CU.
4. Cash was borrowed from a bank, 500 CU.
5. Merchandise carried in inventory at a cost of 7,000 CU was sold for 11,000 CU (cash for 6,000 CU and on credit for 5,000 CU).
6. Collection of the above accounts receivable, 4,000 CU.
7. Payment of accounts payable, 8,000 CU (see transaction 3).
8. Depreciation expense of 120 CU was recognized.

Required

1. Prepare an analysis of Grieg Company's transactions and record the entries in the journal, *assuming that the purchases of merchandise are first recorded in inventory* (see 'Advanced issues' in Chapter 2).
2. Post the entries to the ledger, entering your postings by transaction number.
3. Prepare a trial balance as of 31 January X1.
4. Prepare a balance sheet as of 31 January X1, and an income statement for the month of January.

Review 4.2 Grieg Company (2)

Topic: The accounting process: from the journal to the financial statements (purchases of merchandise are first recorded in the income statement)
Related part of the chapter: Core issues

The Grieg Company was incorporated on 1 January X1. Grieg had five holders of share capital.

Required

1. Prepare an analysis of Grieg Company's transactions (see Review 4.1) and record the entries in the journal, *assuming that the purchases of merchandise are first recorded in the income statement* (see 'Advanced issues' in Chapter 2). You are informed that ending inventory was valued at cost, i.e., 2,000 CU.
2. Post the entries to the ledger, entering your postings by transaction number.
3. Prepare a trial balance as of 31 January X1.
4. Prepare a balance sheet as of 31 January X1, and an income statement for the month of January.

Assignments

Assignment 4.1
Sibelius Company

Topic: The beginning of the accounting process: the journal
Related part of the chapter: Core issues

The Sibelius Company was incorporated on 1 March X1. It carries a commercial activity. The following transactions were undertaken during the first month of operation of Sibelius Co.

1. 1 March — Sibelius company was incorporated with a share capital of 600 CU. A bank account was opened with Commercial Credit Bank.
2. 6 March — Purchased merchandise on credit: 350 CU.
3. 12 March — Paid telephone expense for the month of March: 50 CU.
4. 20 March — Sold merchandise for 500 CU (260 CU cash and 240 CU on credit). (The purchase price of the merchandise sold was 300 CU.)
5. 29 March — Paid the supplier of merchandise (see transaction 2).
6. 30 March — Organized a physical inventory and computed an ending inventory of 50 CU.

Required

Prepare the journal entries for the month of March X1.
Note that:

- The company wants to compute the income that reflects the economic situation at 31 March. Consequently, the ending inventory must appear in the records of the company.
- In order to record purchases, sales, and inventory, you can choose to record the purchases of merchandise either in the inventory (balance sheet) or as a purchase (income statement). You must indicate your choice clearly at the top of your journal (see the appendix).
- A partial excerpt from the chart of accounts of Sibelius Co. is given in the table below (note that the authorized accounts are provided in alphabetical order without reference to their expected ending balance):

- Accounts payable
- Accounts receivable
- Capital
- Cash in bank
- Change in inventories (if purchases recorded in the income statement)
- Cost of goods sold (if purchases recorded in the balance sheet)
- Inventories
- Purchases of merchandise (if purchases recorded in the income statement)
- Sales of merchandise
- Telephone expenses

Recording of purchases, sales and inventory:
Indicate the system chosen (perpetual or periodic).

Model journal

Transaction number	Date	Accounts		Amounts	
		Debit	Credit	D	C

Appendix

Assignment 4.2
Internet-based exercise

Related part of the chapter: Advanced issues

- Search the Internet for job offers concerning vacancies for accounting and related personnel (auditor, financial director, management controller, treasurer, etc.).
- Using the offers located, draw up a list of the characteristics of each position.
- Compare and contrast the positions in accounting and related professions.

Assignment 4.3
Accounting history

Related part of the chapter: Advanced issues

- Prepare and give a 15-minute presentation on the history of charts of accounts, with particular reference to the French chart of accounts (dating from 1942).
- Prepare and give a 15-minute presentation of how accounts have been kept and presented in the past, to the present day.

References

Vlaemminck, J. H. (1979) *Histoire et doctrines de la comptabilité*, Pragnos (quoted by Colasse, B. (2005) *Comptabilité générale*, 9th edn, Economica, Paris, p. 165).

Further reading

Chauveau, B. (1995) The Spanish Plan General de Contabilidad: Agent of development and innovation? *European Accounting Review*, 4(1), 125–38.

Inchausti, B. G. (1993) The Spanish accounting framework: some comments. *European Accounting Review*, 2(2), 379–86.

Plan comptable général (General accounting plan), France, http://www.finances.gouv.fr/CNCompta/ (English version available).

Plan General de Contabilidad (General accounting plan), Spain, www.udg.es/fcee/professors/jmolins/Normativa/normativ.html (in Spanish).

Plano Oficial de Contabilidade (General accounting plan), Portugal, http://www.cnc.min-financas.pt/POC/PO Contabilidade.pdf (in Portuguese).

Richard, J. (1995) The evolution of accounting chart models in Europe from 1900 to 1945: some historical elements. *European Accounting Review*, 4(1), 87–124.

Additional material on the website

Go to http://www.thomsonlearning.co.uk/stolowylebas2 for further information.

The following appendices to this chapter are available on the dedicated website:

Appendix 4.1: Concepts of use and source
Appendix 4.2: Trial balance errors
Appendix 4.3: Organization of the accounting system

Notes

1. Which will be the beginning balance for the subsequent period. Also called 'balance carried forward'.
2. Before computerization, the general ledger was a large, bound volume with pre-numbered pages. The general ledger was a voluminous tome because a certain number of pages were

Chapter 5
Accounting principles and end-of-period adjustments

Learning objectives

After studying this chapter, you will understand:

- How accounting principles (conventions, broad guidelines, rules, and detailed procedures) structure and organize accounting and reporting.
- That the accounting principles can be classified around four objectives or requirements: objectivity, quality of information, prudence, and periodicity.
- That end-of-period adjustments (entries) must be recorded to give a true and fair view of both the financial position at the end of an accounting period, and the income statement for the accounting period.
- That adjusting entries originate in the passage of time.
- That end-of-period entries are adjusting entries that reflect uncompleted transactions (such as revenues earned but not recorded, revenues recorded but unearned, expenses consumed but not recorded, and expenses recorded but not consumed).
- That end-of-period entries are adjusting entries that also reflect changes in value of fixed assets.
- That end-of-period entries are adjusting entries that also reflect changes in value of current assets.
- That end-of-period entries also include some corrections of errors and recording of ending inventories.
- That these entries will be carried out every time one 'closes' the books (yearly, half-yearly, quarterly, monthly, etc.).
- That end-of-period entries are often mentioned and explained in the notes to financial statements.

The preceding chapter described how transactions are recorded during the year in the accounting process. We explained how data enter the accounting process and how they are recorded in the journal and ledger(s). The overall objectives of the accounting procedures during that phase of recording are to ensure that:

- All data recorded are relevant to the description of the financial performance of the entity.
- The descriptors of every transaction can be verified from source documents.

- The structure of the data in the ledgers is relevant to the business model held by management and to their decision-making needs.
- Accurate and significant data can be extracted rapidly from the ledgers on a periodical basis.

In order for the techniques introduced in Chapter 4 to deliver data that meet these objectives, transactions recording follows a certain number of guidelines or principles, which are accepted by accountants around the world.

This chapter will present these key principles (a broad term that encompasses conventions, broad guidelines, rules, and detailed procedures) around which accounting is organized. These principles apply to all accounting entries and provide a common foundation for greater understandability and comparability of financial statements.

One of these principles is the matching principle, introduced in Chapter 2, which is connected to the definition of the accounting period. The matching principle specifies that costs or expenses should be recorded at the same time as the revenues to which they correspond, i.e., costs and revenues that are linked during an accounting period should be reported in the same period. What we have recorded in Chapter 4 are the current operations of a business. However, the cut-off between periods (specifying to which of two sequential periods a revenue or an expense 'belongs') will require end-of-period adjustments to be carried out. These allow one to close the books of one period and open those of the next. This chapter will, therefore, also introduce these entries that are essential to the completion of the periodic accounting cycle.

1 Core issues

1.1 Accounting principles

As indicated in Chapter 1, accounting produces a social good: information. The output of accounting is aimed at a variety of users who use it in their decision making. It is therefore crucial that a large number of users be able to understand the meaning of the accounting reports, and that these describe fairly the situation of the economic entity. It is therefore necessary that 'rules of the game' be established and followed. These rules, as mentioned previously, are the accounting principles. These form a coherent set (see Figure 5.1) of behavioral rules and guidelines that range from pure concepts to very operational guidelines about practice.

Words used to refer to these principles vary between authors, between practitioners, and between countries. What we call principles is called elsewhere 'concepts', 'conventions', or 'assumptions'. In countries of Roman Law tradition, these principles are generally integrated in the body of business or company law and/or in legal accounting rules (see Chapter 1). It is notably the case in Belgium, France, and Switzerland where these principles have been adopted by the appropriate legislative bodies. In countries where the legal system is one of Common Law, such as in the Anglo-Saxon world, the power of these principles is most of the time derived from the consensus within the accounting profession and between it and the business world.

In a given country, the set of principles is referred to, in short, as the local GAAP (for Generally Accepted Accounting Principles, a concept defined in Chapter 1). We will therefore specify to which country's set of GAAP to refer to when it will be useful in understanding a specific real-world example. We will thus speak of US GAAP, or Dutch GAAP, or German GAAP. The trend is, however, to evolve towards a single GAAP (which would, in all likelihood, lead to increased international comparability between – and greater ease of consolidation of – financial statements). There are, however, to date, still two different main sets of GAAP: the US GAAP, largely influenced by the US financial market regulators; and the IFRS/IAS GAAP which reflects the views of a broad international community of users. Whether one of the leading two contenders will dominate in the end or whether some compromise will be found between the two sets is, however, pure speculation at this time (see Chapter 1).

It is useful to understand why these principles have been retained over time, as they help producers, and users as well, understand the value and the limits of accounting information. It also provides an opportunity to explore how the usefulness and quality of accounting information can be improved (the qualitative characteristics of useful information have been presented in Chapter 1 – see Figure 1.7).

Figure 5.1 aims at classifying the accounting principles in four broad categories based on four critical requirements or constraints information users place on accounting.

Figure 5.1 Accounting principles

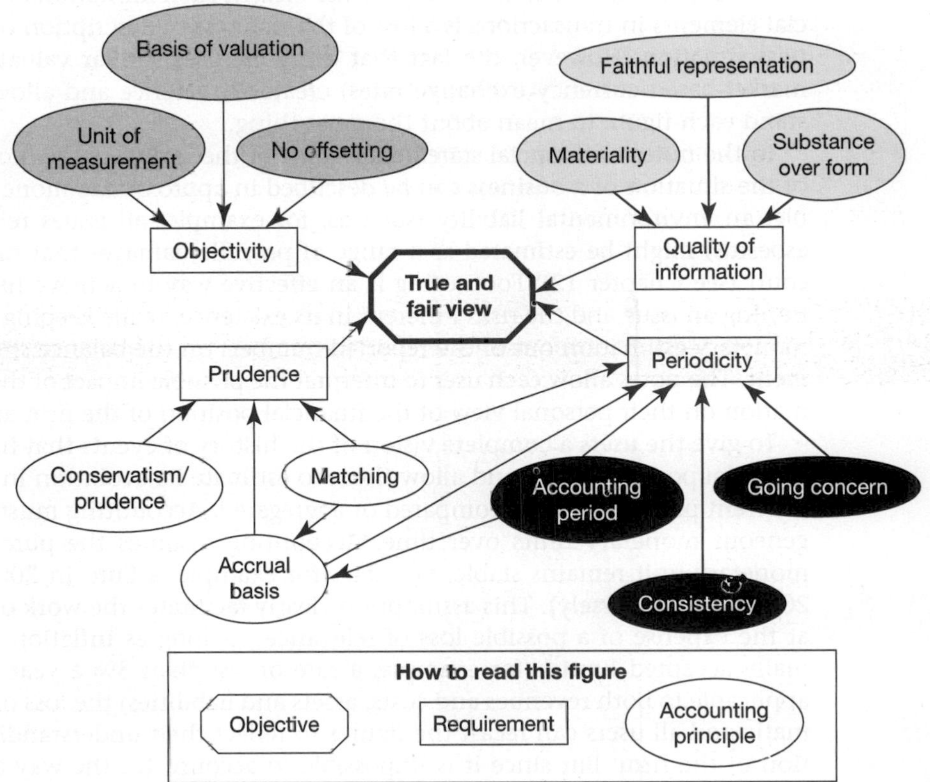

1.1.1 Main objective of accounting principles: give a true and fair view

We have used the term 'true and fair view' in Chapter 3. It does not really represent a principle per se but defines the intent of the adoption of the principles we list below, as shown in Figure 5.1.

True means that the financial statements do not falsify or dissimulate the financial situation of the company at period-end, or its profits (or losses) for the period then ended.

Fair applies to accounts that give accounting users complete and relevant information for decision making.

There is, as a matter of fact, no officially recognized and generally accepted definition of 'true and fair' as it applies to financial statements. The term is used but never precisely defined. For instance, IAS 1 (IASB 2003a: § 13) requires that financial statements 'present fairly the financial position, financial performance and cash flows of an entity'. The 4th EU Directive (1978: art. 2) prescribes that the annual accounts 'give a true and fair view of the company's assets, liabilities, financial position and profit or loss'. Neither, however, ever defines clearly the concepts they use. We can say that 'true and fair' is the result of the application of the principles we are now going to explore in further details.

1.1.2 Objectivity

Unit of measurement Financial accounting only records transactions expressed in financial units (Euro, Pound Sterling, US dollar, Renmimbi, Ruble, Dinar, etc.). No principle prevents accounting from keeping accounts of value creation and value consumption in terms other than financial[1]. For example, it is conceivable to account for the environmental effect of a firm's behavior or its impact on the health of a population, and some specialized accounting approaches exist to handle such issues. However, all alternative valuation bases have a subjective component. The most objective common denominator between events and transactions is the financial measure of their economic impact, which can be expressed only in monetary terms. Clearly, such limitation to recording only financial elements in transactions is a loss of the richness of description of the reality of a business situation. However, the fact that everyone uses similar valuation bases (subject to market-based currency exchange rates) creates coherence and allows all users to understand each figure to mean about the same thing.

In the notes to financial statements, some of the reality of the 'non-financial' elements of the situation of a business can be described in approximate monetary terms. For example, an environmental liability (such as, for example, all issues relating to past uses of asbestos) might be estimated as a range of possible damages that might be assessed by a court (see Chapter 12). Footnoting is an effective way to achieve full disclosure by mentioning an issue and the risks inherent in its existence, while keeping the ambiguity of any monetary estimation out of the reported numbers on the balance sheet and income statement. The notes allow each user to interpret the possible impact of the non-financial information on their personal view of the financial position of the firm and their decisions.

To give the users a complete vision of the history of events that have shaped the firm's financial position today and allow them to estimate its evolution in the future, figures of different periods must be compared or aggregated. Accounting must therefore use homogeneous monetary units over time. Accounting assumes the purchasing power of the monetary unit remains stable, i.e., that, for example, a Euro in 2006 is worth a Euro in 2004 (and conversely). This assumption clearly facilitates the work of the accountant, but at the expense of a possible loss of relevance. As long as inflation remains within 'normally accepted limits' (for example, a rate of less than 3% a year and is, more or less, applicable to both revenues and costs, assets and liabilities) the loss of relevance is not dramatic and all users can recast the figures to reflect their understanding of the 'real' situation of the firm. But since it is impossible to account for the way all people experience inflation, the accountant de facto ignores inflation. In cases where the hypothesis of modest inflation rate is not satisfied, specific methods will be required to keep the purchasing power of the monetary unit in line with reality, while attempting to separate the inflationary effects on profit and cash flows from the fruit of managerial decisions.

Basis of valuation and measurement 'Measurement is the process of determining the monetary amounts at which the elements of the financial statements are to be recognized and carried in the balance sheet and income statement' (IASB 1989: § 99). Defining the numbers that describe the effects of a transaction involves the selection of a particular basis of measurement. A number of different measurement bases can be employed and even mixed to different degrees in financial statements. They include the following (Conceptual framework, IASB 1989: § 100):

- '*Historical cost*: Assets are recorded at the amount of cash or cash equivalents paid or the fair value of the consideration given to acquire them at the time of their acquisition. Liabilities are recorded at the amount or proceeds received in exchange for the obligation, or, in some circumstances (for example, income taxes), at the amounts of cash or cash equivalents expected to be paid to satisfy the liability in the normal course of business.
- *Current* [or replacement] *cost*: Assets are carried at the amount of cash or cash equivalents that would have to be paid if the same or an equivalent asset were acquired cur-

rently. Liabilities are carried at the undiscounted amount of cash or cash equivalents that would be required to settle the obligation right now.

- *Realizable (settlement* [or liquidation]) *value*: Assets are carried at the amount of cash or cash equivalents that could currently be obtained by selling the asset in an orderly disposal. Liabilities are carried at their settlement values; that is, the undiscounted amounts of cash or cash equivalents expected to be paid to satisfy the liabilities in the normal course of business.
- *Present value*: Assets are carried at the net present value of the future net cash inflows that the item is expected to generate in the normal course of business. Liabilities are carried at the net present value of the future net cash outflows that are expected to be required to settle the liabilities in the normal course of business'.

The measurement basis most commonly adopted by enterprises in preparing the financial statements is historical cost since it is the one that requires the fewest hypotheses. This choice is coherent with the philosophy of 'better approximate, unchallengeable, and understandable than more descriptive but debatable and difficult to interpret'. Historical costing is usually combined with other measurement bases. For example, inventories are usually carried at the lower of (historical) cost and net realizable value. Such a choice makes sense, especially in high-tech fields where the cost of components (i.e., their price on the market) falls very rapidly. It would not be fair to shareholders to describe an asset at its purchase price if the replacement value (or the resale value) is lower than that, as is probably the case in the microelectronics field, given the rapid decrease in the market price of many components. We have to keep in mind that the objective of financial statements is to report to shareholders the financial situation of their investment. Overvalued inventories would misrepresent the actual situation, i.e., the potential future cash flows. As we will see below, accountants will always shy away from the possibility of overestimation (see: Prudence principle, § 1.1.4).

No offsetting Offsetting of opposite net effects of different transactions could hide some of the richness of the situation accounting is supposed to report on. Such practice would obscure the reality of the risks faced by the firm in each transaction. Two transactions may have the same absolute value effect with opposite algebraic signs. The net balance of these two transactions would, arithmetically, be zero. Such a presentation would not reflect the complete 'truth' or 'reality'. For example, an overdrawn account at one bank and a positive bank balance with another bank may have equivalent amounts, but the risks they carry (or the signals they communicate) are not equivalent.

Accountants have established the principle that 'assets and liabilities, and income and expenses should not be offset unless required or permitted by a Standard or an Interpretation' (IAS 1, IASB 2003a: § 32).

For this reason all ledgers and specialized ledgers provide the richness of records where all details of all transactions remain un-offset against one another. Accounting is not only the way to report on the financial position of the firm, it is also the way to create and maintain a full archive of how such a position was achieved. Such an archive is essential for better understanding what went right and what went wrong, so that more performance can be created in the future.

Example 1

If a business has two bank accounts, one in Acme Bank with a positive balance of 1,000 CU and a second one in Everyone Thrift Bank with a negative balance of 400 CU, offsetting would be to report a net balance of a positive cash at bank of 600 CU. However, the no-offsetting principle requires that the positive balance be reported on the asset side and the negative balance be reported on the liabilities side of the balance sheet.

Example 2

If a business owes a supplier 5,000 CU and simultaneously has a claim on that very supplier for the same amount (for example, as the result of a down-payment on another order) it would not make sense to offset the two events as they reflect different parts of the business. The debt will be on the liabilities side and the claim on the supplier will be an asset.

1.1.3 Quality of information

The usefulness of financial statements to decision makers rests on the reports being detailed enough, but not too detailed to be overwhelming (materiality and aggregation principle), providing a faithful description of the economic situation of the business, and being meaningful in the sense that they result from a choice of substance over form.

Materiality and aggregation 'Omissions or misstatements of items are material if they could, individually or collectively, influence the economic decisions of users taken on the basis of the financial statements' (IAS1, IASB 2003a: § 11). 'Each material class of similar items shall be presented separately in the financial statements. Items of a dissimilar nature or function shall be presented separately unless they are immaterial' (IAS 1, IASB 2003a: § 29).

Faithful presentation 'To be reliable, information must represent faithfully the transactions and other events it either purports to represent or could reasonably be expected to represent. Thus, for example, a balance sheet should represent faithfully the transactions and other events that result in assets, liabilities and equity of the enterprise at the reporting date (...). Most financial information is subject to some risk of being less than a faithful representation of that which it purports to portray. This is not due to bias, but rather to inherent difficulties either in identifying the transactions and other events to be measured or in devising and applying measurement and presentation techniques that can convey messages that communicate the full complexity of those transactions and events' (Conceptual framework, IASB 1989: §§ 33–34).

Substance over form 'If information is to represent faithfully the transactions and other events that it purports to represent, it is necessary that they are accounted for and presented in accordance with their substance and economic reality and not merely their legal form. The substance of transactions or other events is not always consistent with that which is apparent from their legal or contrived form. For example, an enterprise may dispose of an asset to another party in such a way that the documentation purports to pass legal ownership to that party; nevertheless, agreements to pay exist that ensure that the enterprise continues to enjoy the future economic benefits embodied in the asset. In such circumstances, the reporting of a sale would not represent faithfully the transaction entered into (if indeed there was a transaction)' (Conceptual framework, IASB 1989: § 35).

An operation such as the one described in the preceding paragraph is called a leaseback (see Chapter 12) and is commonly used by businesses to raise cash without having to go through the process of obtaining a loan from financial institution. For example, a business may sell the building in which their headquarters is housed, and lease it back immediately from the buyer. The proper way of recording such an operation should be to recognize, on the one hand, the sale and the cash it generated and, on the other hand, recognize the fact the business now has a commitment to pay rent, which can be measured through the net present value of the rental payments (a liability) and an asset of equivalent amount that recognizes the building is actually at the disposal of the firm and will therefore permit future economic benefits. The retained earnings are not affected since we have the same amount on both sides of the balance sheet, but now the document fully reflects the reality of the situation.

The substance over form principle, although logical and useful, is not universally accepted. To make an oversimplification, the substance over form principle is accepted and used mainly in the North American zone of influence. Many countries have adopted specific rules or principles for the recording of leases, which represent a major issue in this area (see Chapter 12). Other areas where substance over form can be a significant issue involve all trades related to intellectual property such as licensing or sale of patents.

1.1.4 Prudence

An accountant is prudent by nature. He or she does not wish to recognize profit (or loss) before it has been 'earned' with certainty. Three principles serve to achieve this requirement: conservatism, accrual, and matching.

Conservatism Preparers of financial statements 'have to contend with the uncertainties that inevitably surround many events and circumstances, such as the collectability of doubtful receivables, the probable useful life of plant and equipment, and the number of warranty claims that may occur. Such uncertainties are recognized by the disclosure of their nature and extent and by the exercise of prudence [or conservatism] in the preparation of the financial statements. Prudence [conservatism] is the inclusion of a degree of caution in the exercise of the judgments needed in making the estimates required under conditions of uncertainty, such that assets or income are not overstated and liabilities or expenses are not understated' (Conceptual framework, IASB 1989: § 37).

The exercise of prudence does not allow, for example, excessive provisions, or the deliberate (1) understatement of assets or income, (2) overstatement of assets or income, or (3) overstatement of liabilities or expenses, because the financial statements would not be neutral, and, therefore, not have the quality of reliability.

The 4th EU Directive (1978: art. 31) states that 'valuation must be made on a prudent basis, and in particular:

1. only profits concretely and definitively earned on the balance sheet date may be included;
2. account must be taken of all foreseeable liabilities and potential losses arising in the course of the financial year concerned or of a previous one, even if such liabilities or losses become apparent only between the date of the balance sheet and the date on which it is drawn up;
3. account must be taken of all depreciation whether the result of the financial year is a loss or a profit'.

Practically, this principle means that profits should not be anticipated. They should only be taken into the accounts when they are realized. For example, sales should be recorded only when the goods have been shipped and invoiced and not when the order was received.

As far as losses are concerned, however, they should be recognized as soon as the events giving rise to them take place. For example, when the resale value of an item in inventory decreases below its acquisition or manufacturing cost, the loss in value should be recognized immediately, even if the item is not sold. One example of a practice coherent with conservatism is that of always valuing inventories at the 'lower of cost or market'. Provisions or valuation allowances used to recognize these losses will be further explored later in this chapter.

Conservatism is, like the historical basis in the measurement unit, generally accepted but still controversial at times, as there are many situations in which its usefulness is debatable, as is the case in the valuation of marketable securities in a volatile market.

Accrual basis As we showed in Chapter 2, the accrual principle consists in recognizing or recording an event when it occurs and not when the cash transaction it induces has been completed. IAS 1 (IASB 2003a: § 25) stipulates that 'an entity shall prepare its financial statements, except for cash flow information, under the accrual basis of accounting'. Financial statements must only reflect revenues, expenses, and income that relate to a given accounting period. The resulting difference between cash transactions and amounts recognized under the accrual basis must be shown as either an accrued expense (liability), a prepaid expense (asset), accrued revenue (asset), or prepaid revenue (liability) (see the next section in this chapter).

Matching According to this principle, also introduced earlier, and coherently with the accrual basis, expenses are recognized in the income statement on the basis of their direct association with the revenues also recognized. Matching of costs with revenues is defined in the IASB Framework (IASB 1989: § 95) as the simultaneous or combined recognition of revenues and expenses that result directly and jointly from the same transactions or other events.

1.1.5 Periodicity

This requirement consists of three principles: accounting period, going concern, and consistency of presentation. It is also connected to the accrual and matching concepts introduced earlier.

Accounting period As stated in Chapter 1, reporting to shareholders occurs at regular intervals, these defining the accounting period. The yearly accounting period is generally some arbitrary segmentation of the life cycle of any business.

The outcome of the managers' decisions and actions (income) must be known for at least the following economical and legal reasons:

1. Need to: (a) know changes in the overall performance potential of the firm; and (b) evaluate the quality of the management and of their decisions as agents of the shareholders.
2. Need to know the amount of income (or wealth created) that is to be shared between shareholders or partners.
3. Need to provide a basis for the state to levy taxes based on income.

The only definitive measure of the income or value created by a business is the one that would be established through an income statement that would span the entire life of the firm. However, no shareholder or regulatory agency wants to have to wait that long to know: (a) how much wealth has been created; and (b) whether the managers, who are the shareholders' agents or representatives, are making the right decisions or at least decisions that the shareholders approve. Businesses are controlled by checking the outcome of decisions against the firm's strategic intent. If there is an unacceptable gap between intent and result, corrective actions are decided (both by investors and by managers) to bring the firm's financial position ever closer to fulfilling its strategic intent. A year-long accounting period is the longest periodicity that appears acceptable to all parties. However, many require more frequent information. In fact, most financial markets require reporting the financial position of listed firms on a quarterly basis.

The measurement of income is carried in sequential, yet clearly separated, time slices. The accrual principle and the end-of-period entries (see later in this chapter) permit this pairing of time and income in coherent sets useful for forecasting and decision making.

Going concern The ability to accrue revenues and expenses, and therefore income, in the appropriate time periods rests on the assumption that a business entity has a life expectancy that exceeds the accounting reporting period. This assumption of continuity is called the 'going concern principle'. Unless the accountant has specific knowledge to the contrary, he or she will assume continuity when establishing the financial statements. It is management's responsibility to take decisions so the business goes on as long as possible for the benefit of the shareholders. Failure in exercising this responsibility leads to bankruptcy, or to the business entity being bought out or liquidated.

The going concern principle is a key reason for valuing assets and resources or liabilities at their historical cost rather than at their liquidation value. During the next periods the company will be able to gain economic benefits from the existence of these assets. The least debatable proxy for the net present value of these future benefits remains the purchase price of the asset, eventually adjusted over time through depreciation to recognize reduction of the potential since acquisition.

IAS 1 (IASB 2003a: § 23) stipulates: 'When preparing financial statements, management shall make an assessment of an entity's ability to continue as a going concern. Financial statements should be prepared on a going concern basis unless management either intends to liquidate the enterprise or to cease trading, or has no realistic alternative but to do so. When management is aware, in making its assessment, of material uncertainties related to events or conditions which may cast significant doubt upon the entity's ability to continue as a going concern, those uncertainties shall be disclosed. When the financial statements are not prepared on a going concern basis, that fact shall be disclosed, together with the basis on which the financial statements are prepared and the reason why the entity is not considered to be a going concern'.

Similarly the EU 4th Directive (1978: art. 31) prescribes that 'the company must be presumed to be carrying on its business as a going concern'. In other words, this principle means that there is no reason to suppose that the company will not be carrying on its business throughout the following financial year and years.

Consistency of presentation Financial statements must be useful to decision makers. They must provide not only comparability with other firms involved in the same line of business (same risk factors) but also comparability from period to period to be able to detect trends and evolutions. It is therefore critical that the financial statements be presented in consistent fashion and over consistent parameters. If principles of presentation or parameters change following alterations of strategy or necessity, it will be essential, in order to give a true and fair view of the firm's situation, to recast the old data so that a minimum number of years are presented in homogeneous fashion for comparison purposes. This principle allows changes and regulates how these can be implemented (see Chapter 6 for more details).

IAS 1 (IASB 2003a: § 27) indicates that: 'the presentation and classification of items in the financial statements shall be retained from one period to the next unless:

(a) It is apparent, following a significant change in the nature of the entity's operations or a review of its financial statements, that another presentation or classification would be more appropriate having regard to the criteria for the selection and application of accounting policies in IAS 8 [Accounting policies, changes in accounting estimates and errors]; or

(b) A Standard or an Interpretation requires a change in presentation'.

The 4th EU Directive (1978: art. 31) states that: 'the methods of valuation must be applied consistently from one financial year to another'. In practice, this means that the valuation methods used at the end of a financial year must be the same as that applied at the end of the preceding year. The effect of this is that the comparative figures for the preceding year appearing in a balance sheet (which are required by IAS 1, by the 4th EU Directive and by many other national standards) are fully comparable with the figures for the current year. The importance of this principle will become apparent when we look later at the different methods of valuation used for various assets (concepts of depreciation and provision or valuation allowance).

1.1.6 The entity concept

Although not quite a 'principle', the entity concept, which we introduced in Chapter 1, is a key foundation of accounting and of financial reports. It specifies that regardless of the legal form of the economic entity (sole proprietorship, partnership, limited company, etc. – see Chapter 11) economic transactions carried by the entity must be recorded separately from that of the personal transactions of actors involved in or with the entity.

1.2 End-of-period entries

Accounting principles, and especially the matching, accrual, and periodicity principles, create the need to know exactly what pertains to a period (and provide the techniques to handle that requirement). Some events that took place during the period are linked to the passage of time or other causes such that they are not effectively documented through a transaction with a paper or electronic support. Other events straddle two periods and need to be partitioned between the two. Inventories and some asset values have to be adjusted if their market value has decreased below their cost, assets must be depreciated, etc.

End-of-period entries refer to any such entries that are necessary to give a true and fair view of both the financial position at the end of an accounting period and the income statement for the accounting period. These entries will be carried out every time one closes the books (yearly, half-yearly, quarterly, monthly, etc.).

Figure 5.2 outlines the main categories of end-of-period entries and identifies the principles that are at the source of the issue.

Figure 5.2 Main categories of end-of-period entries

End-of-period entries: Type of entries	Examples	Root principles
Adjusting entries	Unexpired costs, unearned revenues, unrecorded expenses, unrecorded revenues	Accounting period Matching Accrual basis
Change in value of fixed assets	Depreciation, amortization, depletion	Historical cost Conservatism
Change in value of current assets	Valuation allowances/provisions (accounts receivable, inventories, short-term investments)	Historical cost Conservatism
Other entries and adjustments	Correction of errors	(Internal and external) auditing
	Ending inventory (periodic system)	Accounting period Matching
	Closing entries	Accounting period

The accounting principles studied earlier in this chapter become particularly important when the year-end entries are recorded. In order to apply these principles, management has to exercise considerable judgment. This confirms that accounting cannot be considered an exact mathematical science.

1.2.1 Adjusting entries

The fundamental difficulty encountered with year-end financial statements is that the accounting period (generally the year, and even more so in the case of quarterly reporting) does not correspond to the duration of a normal operating cycle, whatever the company's activities. In manufacturing, distribution, services, utilities, etc., the economic cycle may be either longer or shorter than that of the reporting period.

However, in order to provide regular periodic information to shareholders, employees, financial institutions and markets, and, incidentally, to tax authorities, annual financial statements have to be prepared despite the economic entity continuing to carry on its operational activities on an ongoing basis. This means that a cut-off date has to be selected by company management in agreement with the shareholders. This date will be used as a watershed separating transactions pertaining to the closing period and those pertaining to the next one. As a result, many year-end adjustments are related to the influence of time: for example, an insurance premium invoice is probably not going to be received on the first day of a 12-month accounting period, and since it generally corresponds to an insurance coverage for a year, the amount of the premium must be partitioned between at least two accounting periods.

The 4th EU Directive (1978: art. 18) states: 'Expenditure incurred during the financial year but relating to a subsequent financial year, together with any income which, though relating to the financial year in question, is not due until after its expiry must be shown under Prepayments and Accrued Income'. Similarly article 21 mandates that: 'Income receivable before the balance sheet date but relating to a subsequent financial year, together with any charges which, though relating to the financial year in question, will be paid only in the course of the subsequent financial year, must be shown under Accruals and Deferred Income'.

The most common adjusting entries may be classified in four categories as shown in Figure 5.3.

Figure 5.3 Main adjusting entries

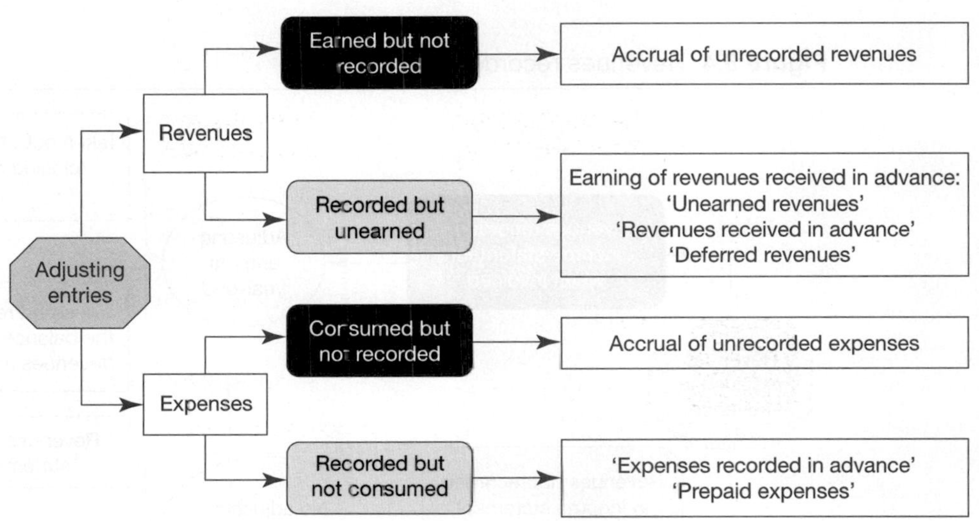

Revenues The principles of revenue recognition, which will be developed in Chapter 6, prescribe that revenues affect net income in the period during which they are earned, and not the period in which their cash equivalent are collected. In other words, net income must include all and only the revenues which have been earned during the accounting period. This principle has two major consequences:

1. Revenues which have been earned but not recorded, in particular because the triggering event has not occurred yet (for example, interest (on a loan) to be received after the closing date, sales delivered but not invoiced, etc.), must be recorded and 'attached' to the current net income.
2. Conversely, revenues which have been recorded in advance and which cover a service to be rendered at a later date (for example, rent received in advance, subscription received from a customer for a newspaper service) must be adjusted to 'leave in the period' only the relevant part.

Revenues earned but not recorded It is necessary to recognize revenues that have been earned but have not yet been recorded. No entry has been recorded, mainly due to the fact that the event, which would lead to the recognition of the revenue, will only happen in the future. For example, let us assume that annual interest revenue on a loan (for example, granted to a customer at the end of February X1) becomes due only on the anniversary of the loan. When the financial statements are drawn on the closing date of 31 December X1, the triggering event has not happened yet. However, during the period ending on that date, the firm has earned 10/12th of the annual interest on the loan. However, the interest revenue is not due by the customer. No source document will be issued saying the customer owes the firm 10/12th of the annual interest. But, because of the matching principle, it is essential to recognize, since interest is due to the passage of time, part of the annual interest revenue in this period even though it will be claimed and collected only during the next period. This unrecorded revenue will be accrued and recognized as revenue in period X1 and capitalized as an asset in the balance sheet at the end of X1 (see details in the Advanced issues section).

Revenues recorded but unearned When revenues are received in advance (for example, rent received in advance for several months, retainer fee, etc.) two alternative solutions can be used to record this event and to recognize the revenues in the appropriate accounting period. They are listed in Figure 5.4 and will be detailed in the Advanced issues section. In each country one of the alternatives is generally preferred, but the other one is often tolerated.

Figure 5.4 Revenues recorded but unearned

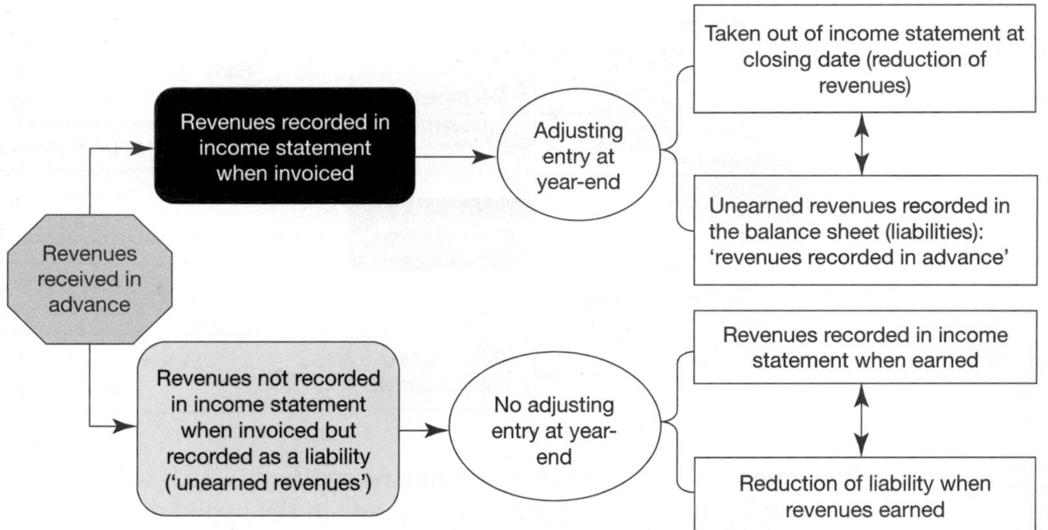

Expenses Expenses should affect net income in the period during which the resources they represent are consumed, and not the period in which their acquisition transaction is settled in cash or cash equivalent. In other words, net income must include all and only those expenses that have been consumed during the accounting period. This principle has two major consequences:

1. Expenses which have been consumed but not recorded, in particular because the triggering event has not occurred (interest to be paid after closing date, purchases received but invoice not received from supplier, etc.), must be recorded and 'attached' to the current net income calculation.

2. Conversely, expenses which have been recorded in advance (for example, rent paid in advance, retainer fee paid to lawyer) must be adjusted so as to recognize in the income statement only that part that is relevant for the accounting period.

Expenses consumed but not recorded It is necessary to recognize expenses that have been consumed but not yet recorded (because the triggering event that will create the source document which will initiate the recording has not yet occurred). This would, for example, be the case of an interest expense on debt which would be due, say, on 30 June X2 while the closing date is 31 December X1. Interest from 1 July X1 to 31 December X1 has actually built up and represents an expense of the closing period. However, it will not be due until 30 June of the next period. This accrued but unrecorded expense must be recognized as both an expense in the income statement and a liability as interest due in the balance sheet (see example later).

Expenses recorded but not consumed When an expense is paid in advance it often straddles two accounting periods. For example, the subscription fee to a software help line is generally paid in advance for the coming year, but these 12 months rarely correspond to the accounting period. Two solutions can be used to record such an event and to recognize the expense in the proper period. Figure 5.5 illustrates the choice. Although each country's accounting regulators generally indicate a preferred approach, it is not unusual to see both approaches coexist.

A comparison of the two methods is presented later in Advanced issues.

Figure 5.5 Expenses paid in advance

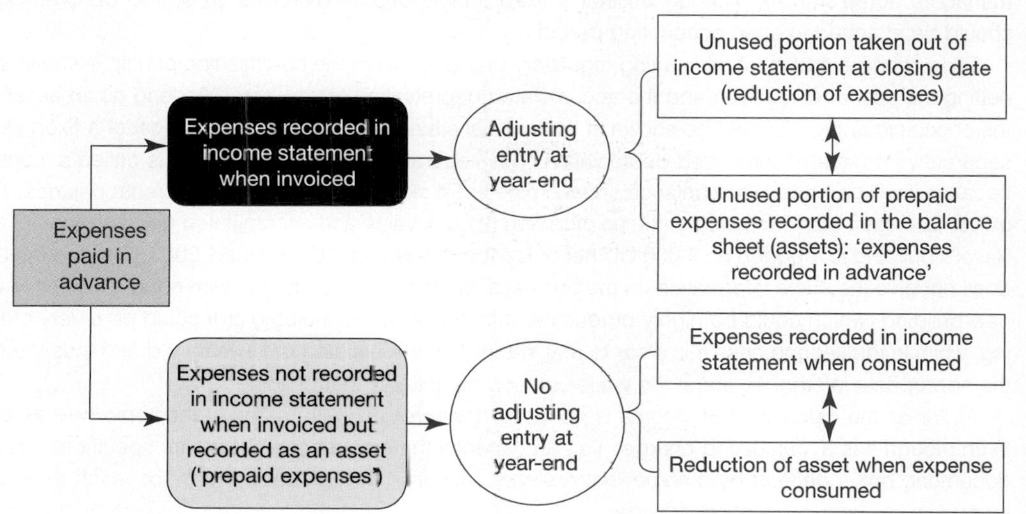

1.2.2 Value adjustments to fixed asset accounts

Principles Fixed or tangible assets are defined in IAS 16 (IASB 2003b: § 6) under the term of 'property, plant and equipment'. They 'are tangible items that:

(a) Are held for use in the production or supply of goods or services, for rental to others, or for administrative purposes; and

(b) Are expected to be used during more than one period'.

The value of fixed assets in the balance sheet is initially carried at their purchase price or acquisition cost (i.e., purchase price plus all costs incurred to make the asset useable in the context of the business strategy). This (book) value of the asset needs to be adjusted periodically to recognize either or both the wear and tear on the equipment (reduction of potential to create a stream of future economic benefits) and its technological obsolescence.

The 4th EU Directive defines fixed assets (1978: art. 15) as comprising 'those assets which are intended for use on a continuing basis for the purposes of the undertaking's activities'. It specifies that their accounting value ('the purchase price or production [cost]') 'must be reduced by value adjustments' (which we call depreciation) 'calculated to write off the value of such assets systematically over their useful economic lives' (article 35 b). This rule, it adds, should only be applied to assets with a limited economic life. For example, land is not considered subject to these downward value adjustments (although it satisfies all the criteria of definition of an asset) because the stream of future economic benefits is not affected by use. Incidentally, any increase in value of land is going to remain unrecorded in accounting because of the prudence principle.

Depreciation is the process of allocating the cost of a tangible or fixed asset (with the exception of land) over the period during which economic benefits will be received by the firm. The justification for this process is found in the matching principle because each period benefits from the existence of the asset and is therefore deemed to consume a share of the original cost. Depreciation has already been mentioned in Chapter 2. Chapter 7 will give us the opportunity to explore further the depreciation mechanisms and their implication in the management of the business (see the Ravel Company example).

Example Ravel Company

The local tax authorities have informed the accountant that the normal useful life for Ravel's buildings was 50 years. This means that the acquisition cost of the building (5,000 CU) should be distributed over that period of time. The managers agree with the accountant that a fixed annual depreciation charge of 100 CU (i.e., 5000 CU/50 years) should be attached to each accounting period.

Tax authorities and most accounting regulatory bodies endorse the no-offsetting principle whose application forbids netting the cost of acquisition and the accumulated depreciation of any asset. As long as an asset is the property of the economic entity, it should be shown in its financial statements. The acquisition cost of a fixed asset will be shown separately from the accumulated depreciation. This separate depreciation account is called a 'contra asset' account because it will be listed in the balance sheet on the asset side but with a negative (credit) balance. The financial information users are also interested in the no offsetting of book value and accumulated depreciation; for example, whether Ravel's building is reported as 4,000 CU net or is reported as 5,000 CU minus 1,000 CU of accumulated depreciation does not give the same information on the business. In the first case it might, with equal probability, be a small, brand new building (which could be highly productive with built-in IT technology) or it could be a very old, inefficient building, while in the second case it is clear to any reader that the building is 10 years old and thus the reader can derive the appropriate inferences about the value creation potential of that building.

As far as the calculation of income is concerned, depreciation is treated in the same way as any expense item, even though it is a 'calculated charge', i.e., an expense the amount of which is not specifically defined by a source document, but is defined by a somewhat arbitrary allocation of a global amount (for which there is a source document) over several accounting periods.

Figure 5.6 illustrates the entries required to account for depreciation related to the first year.

Figure 5.6 Accounting for depreciation

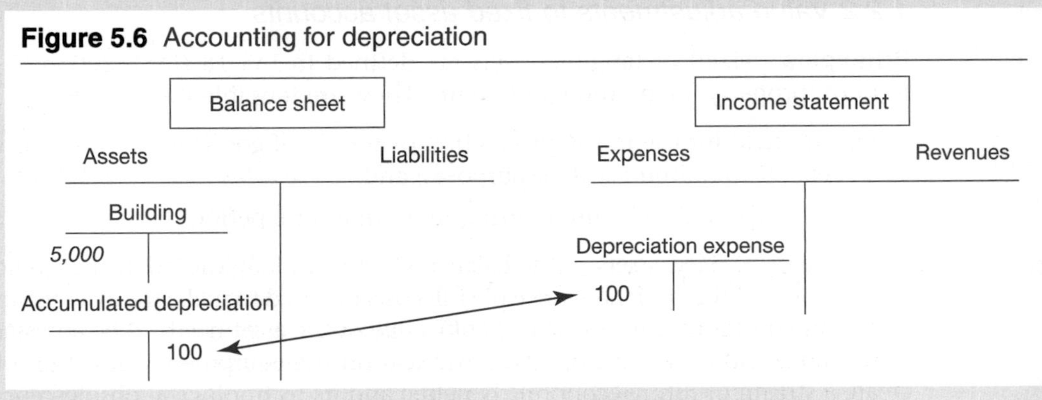

1.2.3 Value adjustments to current asset accounts

The application of the prudence/conservatism principle, so that information given in the annual accounts satisfies the true and fair view objective, implies that the accounting values recorded during the year for current assets must be validated against economic realities at year-end.

This implies checking that:

- assets really do physically exist;
- their value is not overstated in relation to the future benefits that they represent.

The first point, an asset protection issue, is addressed through carrying out a physical inventory of the existing current (and fixed) assets on a regular basis. The second point is an accounting issue. The 4th EU Directive (1978: art. 39b) states that, when necessary, 'value adjustments shall be made in respect of current assets with a view to showing them at the lower market value': that is, where the price that a willing purchaser is prepared to pay for an asset is below its original cost, its accounting value should be reduced to this lower value.

To ensure that the 'market value' of the current assets is equal to or greater than the value in the ledger accounts, the Ravel Company accountant (see above) had to study the underlying supporting documents and other data. As far as cash and bank balances are concerned there is usually no problem since both accounts are held in one given currency unit.

For inventories of finished products, the accountant confirmed with management that the current sales prices and the future sales forecasts gave every assurance that the future customers would pay an amount at least equal to the cost recorded in the inventories accounts. For inventories of raw materials, the production program indicated clearly that all the items held in inventory would be used and the invested cost recovered through future saleable products. Therefore, for these categories of current assets no value adjustment is, in this case, necessary.

The accountant also needs to evaluate the probability that Ravel Company will recover the full value of claims held by Ravel over its customers (accounts receivable). To do this, he or she studies the situation of each individual customer, looking for example at the following aspects:

- Has the customer challenged the validity of the receivable?
- Has the customer returned goods and/or complained about Ravel Company's service?
- Is the customer up to date with payments in accord with the agreed contractual terms governing the sales?
- Is there any correspondence (or other data) indicating that the customer has or had financial difficulties?
- Have any letters from Ravel Company been returned as undeliverable from the customer's address?

Although value adjustment to current assets will be developed more fully in Chapter 10, suffice it to say at this stage that a loss of value of a current asset will be recorded through contra asset accounts such as provisions or allowances for which the mechanism is very similar to that of depreciation. Such a process is illustrated in Figure 5.7. Provision or allowance entries conform to the no offsetting principle as well as the lower of cost or market value seen under the units of measurement principle.

1.2.4 Reporting for adjusting entries

Some illustrations of actual notes to financial statements follow that provide details, in conformance with the no-offsetting principle, of the elements affected by adjusting entries and which create the balances reported.

Figure 5.7 Recording of a provision expense

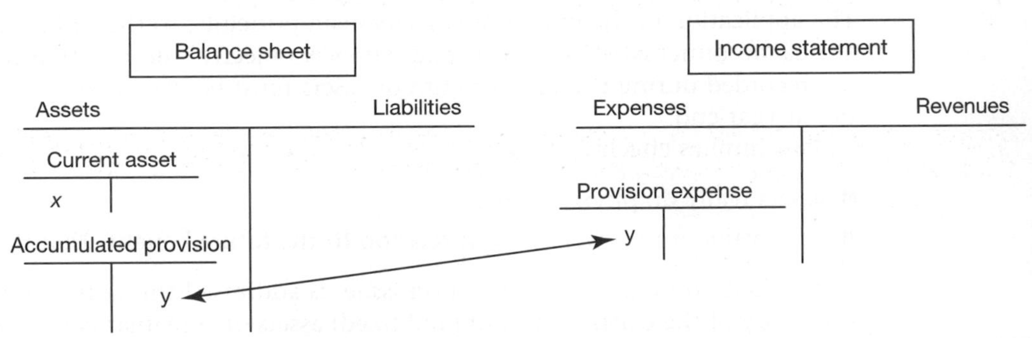

Real-life example Pirelli

(Italy – Italian GAAP – *Source*: Annual report 2004 – Tires, cables and systems)

Notes to the financial statements

'Accrued income' mainly relates to hedging revenues, interest income, insurance, and other minor items.

'Prepaid expenses' mainly relate to insurance, building rent, and other minor items.

'Accrued liabilities' (...) include the portion of exchange differences on hedging transactions, building leases payable, hedging costs, and other minor items.

'Deferred income' (...) include installment payments received in advance.

Real-life example Philips

(Netherlands – US GAAP – *Source*: Annual report 2004 – Consumer electronic products)

Note 18. Accrued liabilities

Accrued liabilities are summarized as follows:	2003	2004
Personnel-related costs:		
Salaries and wages	545	554
Accrued holiday entitlements	216	212
Other personnel-related costs	127	154
Fixed-assets-related costs		
(Gas, water, electricity, rent and other)	111	109
Taxes:		
Income tax payable	235	277
Other taxes payable	–	9
Communication and IT costs	84	66
Distribution costs	100	85
Sales-related costs:		
Commissions payable	52	29
Advertising and marketing-related costs	123	122
Other sales-related costs	371	309
Material-related costs	113	190
Interest-related accruals	168	135
Deferred income	250	486
Derivative instruments – liabilities	156	149
Liabilities for restructuring costs	115	114
Other accrued liabilities	399	307
Total	3,165	3,307

Comment: This example provides a very detailed list of components of accrued liabilities.

Real-life example Meritage Hospitality Group

(USA – US GAAP – *Source*: Annual report 2004 – Quick-service and casual dining restaurant industries)

Excerpts from the Balance sheet at year end

Year ended (amounts in dollars)	28 November 2004	30 November 2003
LIABILITIES AND STOCKHOLDERS' EQUITY		
(…)		
Accrued liabilities	2,119,037	1,966,280
(…)		

Notes to financial statements

D. Accrued liabilities

Accrued liabilities consist of the following at 28 November 2004 and 30 November 2003:

$	**2004**	**2003**
Payroll and related payroll taxes	1,193,505	1,056,294
Property taxes	324,622	316,522
Interest expense	115,802	123,547
Single business tax	165,000	155,000
Other expenses	320,108	314,917
	2,119,037	1,966,280

Comment: This example illustrates how to reconcile the amount reported in the balance sheet ($2,119,037 at the end of 2004) and the detail provided in the notes.

2 Advanced issues

At year-end, adjusting entries, correction of errors, entries relating to ending inventories, and closing entries will be recorded.

2.1 Recording of adjusting entries

After the introduction of the main types of adjusting entries, we will now explore the details of how each is being recorded in accounting.

Figure 5.8 Accrual of revenues at year-end – Year X1

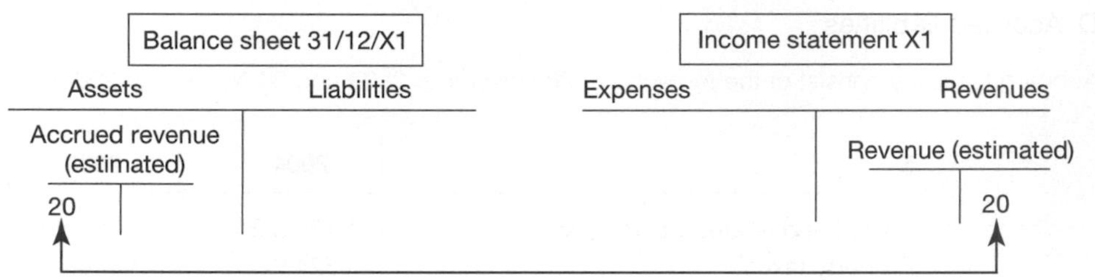

Figure 5.9 Accrual of revenues – Year X2

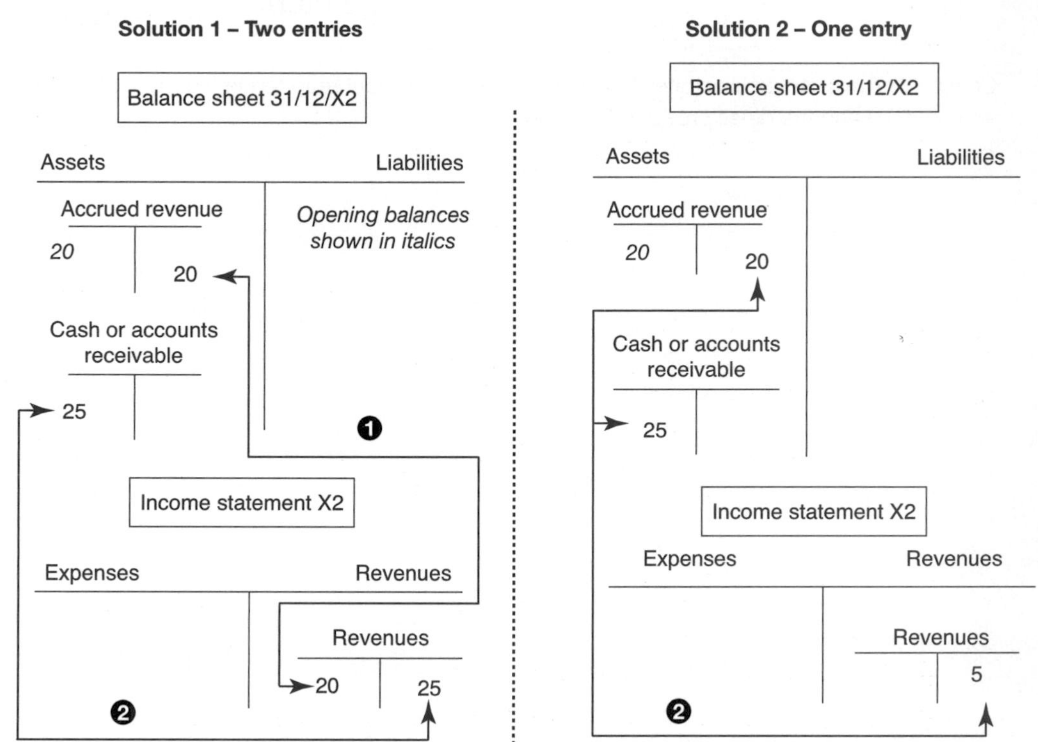

❶ Opening date (of the following accounting period)

❷ Date the source document is received or date of the event.

2.1.1 Revenues earned but not recorded

Let us use the example of royalty revenue not invoiced because the department in charge has been overworked and lags behind in invoicing. At the end of the year, the accountant records an amount of 20 CU as an estimate of the royalty to be recovered. During the next accounting period, when the royalty department has time to calculate the correct amount to claim, an invoice is issued for 25 CU. Figures 5.8 and 5.9 describe the way to handle the situation.

Two possible solutions for handling the completion of the transaction in the second period are illustrated in Figure 5.9.

Appendix 5.1 analyzes in more details these two alternative solutions.

2.1.2 Revenues recorded but unearned

The general principles for handling such an entry have been introduced in the first part of the chapter. Two possible methods have been mentioned. We now present an example comparing the two methods.

Example

Rent for 200 CU is received from a tenant on 15 December X1, in advance for the second half of December X1 of this current accounting period plus January X2 and the first half of February X2 of the next accounting period. The closing date for the books is 31 December X1. Figure 5.10 illustrates how accounting will record the situation.

Figure 5.10 Revenues recorded in advance – Year X1

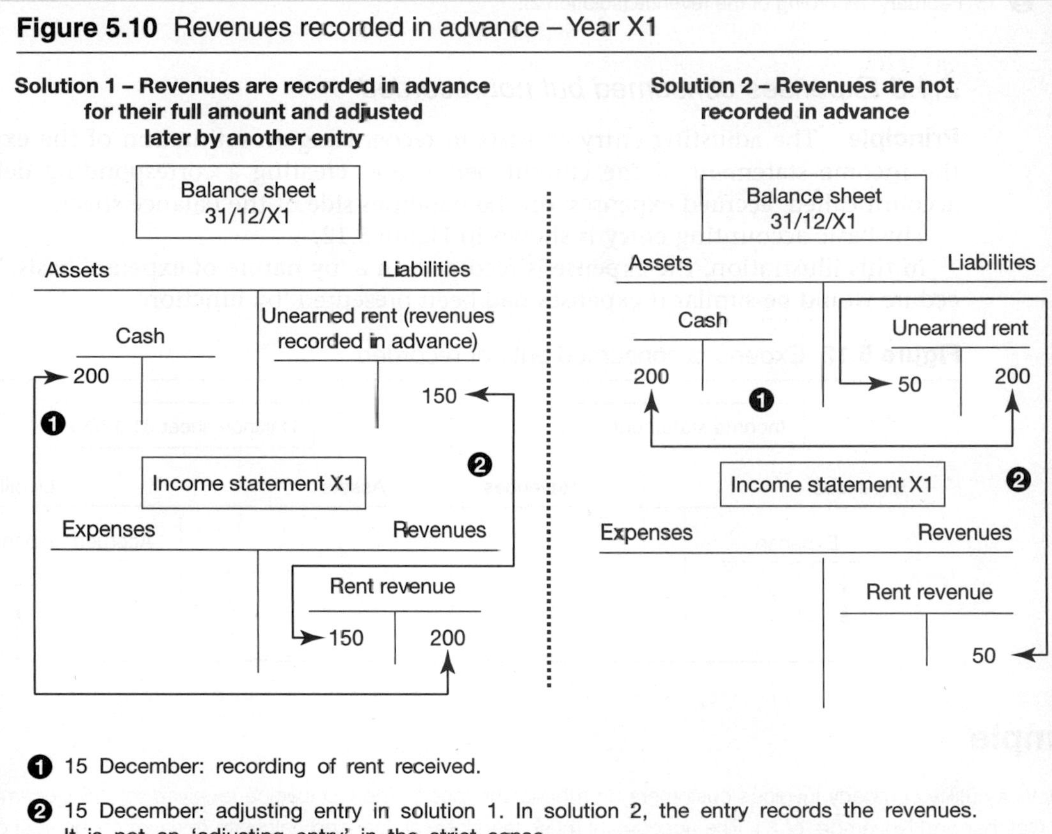

❶ 15 December: recording of rent received.

❷ 15 December: adjusting entry in solution 1. In solution 2, the entry records the revenues. It is not an 'adjusting entry' in the strict sense.

Entries for the following year are presented in Figure 5.11.

Figure 5.11 Accounting entries – Year X2

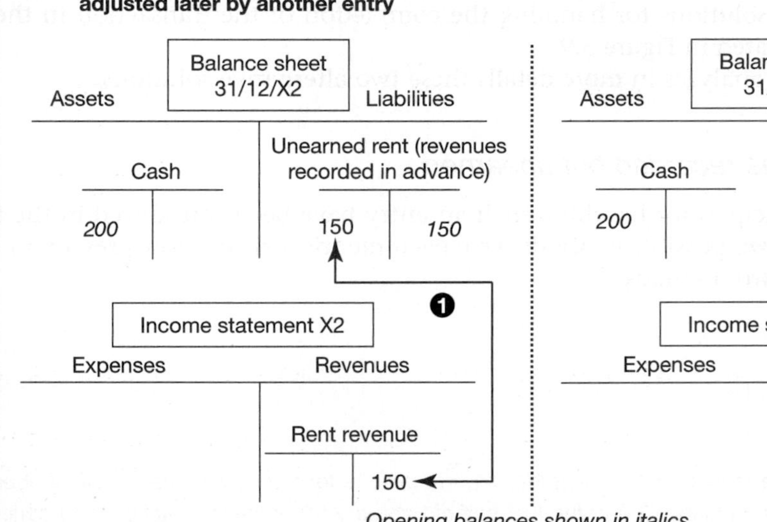

Opening balances shown in italics

❶ 1 January: reversal of adjusting entry.

❷ 15 February: recording of the revenue (solution 2).

2.1.3 Expenses consumed but not recorded

Principle The adjusting entry consists in recognizing an estimation of the expense in the income statement of the current period and creating a corresponding debt in an account called 'accrued expenses' on the liabilities side of the balance sheet.

The basic accounting entry is shown in Figure 5.12.

In this illustration, the expense is recorded on a 'by nature of expense' basis. The procedure would be similar if expenses had been presented 'by function'.

Figure 5.12 Expenses consumed but not recorded

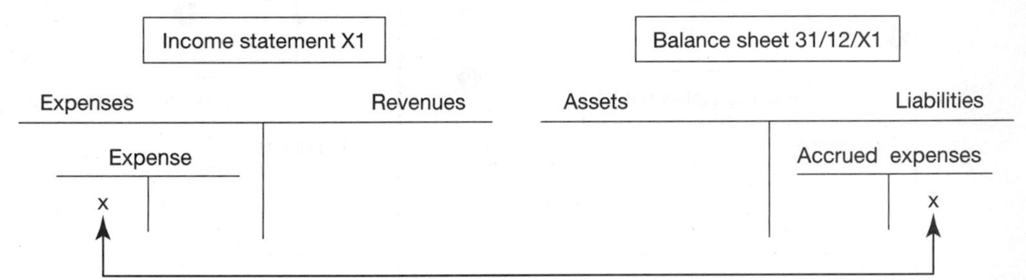

Example

The electricity utility company invoices customers on a bimonthly basis. The last invoice received, on 15 December X1 was for October and November of X1. The accountant must, therefore, at year-end calculate or estimate the cost of electricity consumed in December. From the business' own electrical engineer, he or she receives an estimate of the number of kWh (kilowatt hours) consumed in December. Thus, using the rate known from previous invoices, the accountant calculates that the estimated electricity expense for December X1 amounts to 175 CU (see Figure 5.13). The accountant will thus recognize both an expense of 175 CU in the income statement of X1 and an 'accrued electricity payable' for the same amount, indicating that the estimated expense will, in fact, be paid in February of X2 or later, after the invoice is received.

Figure 5.13 Accrual of electricity expense – Year X1

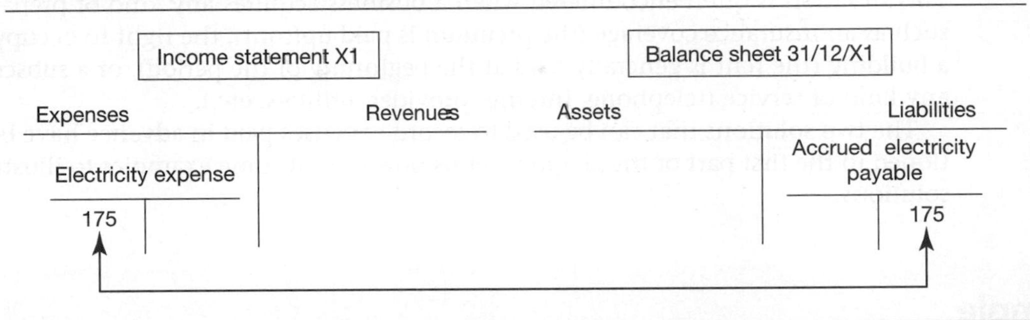

This example has illustrated the way to close the books at the end of the year for events that straddle the closing date.

The next issue is to see how to handle the second part of this transaction in the following year. Two solutions are possible: either we use two entries or we use a single entry. We continue the procedure with the last transaction. Let us assume further that an analysis of the detailed invoice received in mid-February shows the real cost of electricity for December of X1 was 180 CU (instead of the 175 estimated). Figure 5.14 illustrates how

Example

Figure 5.14 Recording – Year X2

Two entries
Balance sheet 31/12/X2
Assets
Liabilities
Cash
Accrued electricity payable
180
175 *175*
Income statement X2
Expenses
Revenues
Electricity expense
180 175

One entry
Balance sheet 31/12/X2
Assets
Liabilities
Cash
Accrued electricity payable
180
175 *175*
Income statement X2
Expenses
Revenues
Electricity expense
5

Opening balances shown in italics

❶ Opening date (beginning of the following year).

❷ Source document is received or date of the event.

accounting will handle the situation. Regardless of the method selected the underestimation of the electricity cost will be charged to the income statement of X2.

Appendix 5.3 presents some comments on this type of entry.

2.1.4 Expenses recorded in advance

This situation is often encountered when a business acquires any kind of prepaid service such as an insurance coverage (the premium is paid upfront), the right to occupy space in a building (the rent is generally paid at the beginning of the period), or a subscription to any kind of service (telephone, internet provider, utilities, etc.).

The two solutions that can be used to record expenses paid in advance have been mentioned in the first part of the chapter. Let us now look at some examples to illustrate these solutions.

Example

Insurance premium of 120 CU paid on 1 September for coverage during the next 12 months. The closing date for the accounts is 31 December.

Figure 5.15 Expenses recorded in advance – Year X1

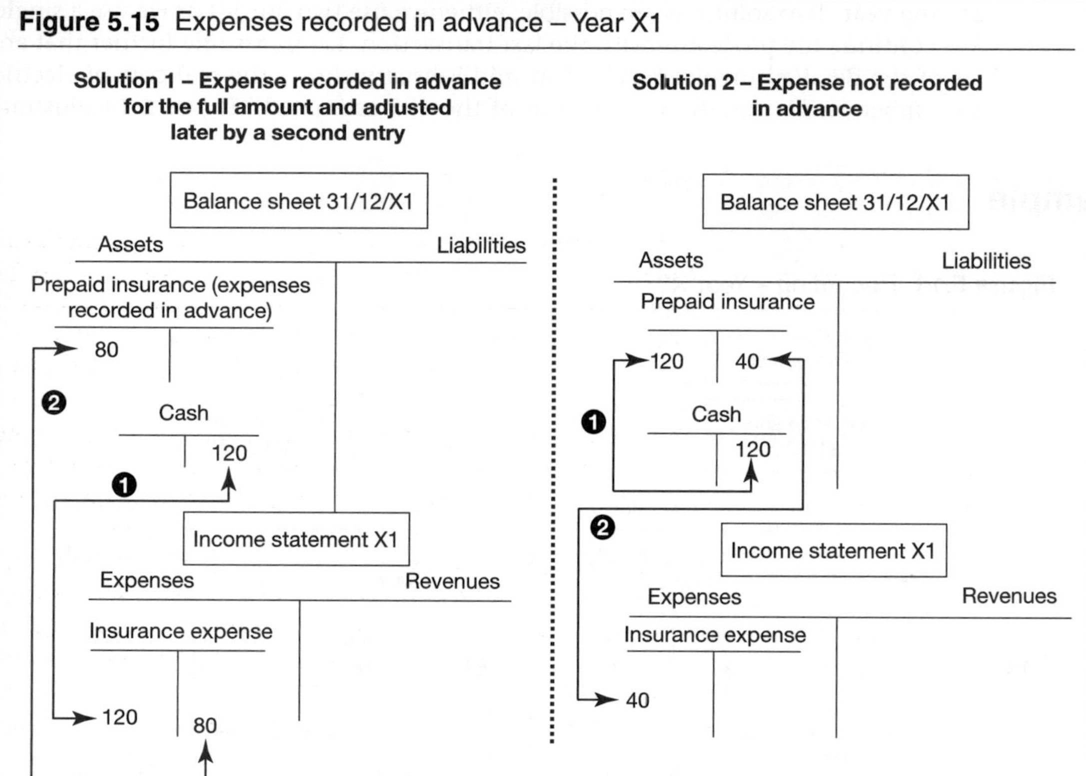

Year X2 entries are described in Figure 5.16. Either the adjustment takes place at the beginning of the year (method 1) or when the period during which the benefits received (insurance coverage) expire (method 2).

Entries are identical between the two methods but they are not recorded on the same date, thus quarterly financial statement would not be affected in the same way. Appendix 5.4 compares the two methods and comments on their implementation.

Figure 5.16 Expenses recorded in advance – Year X2

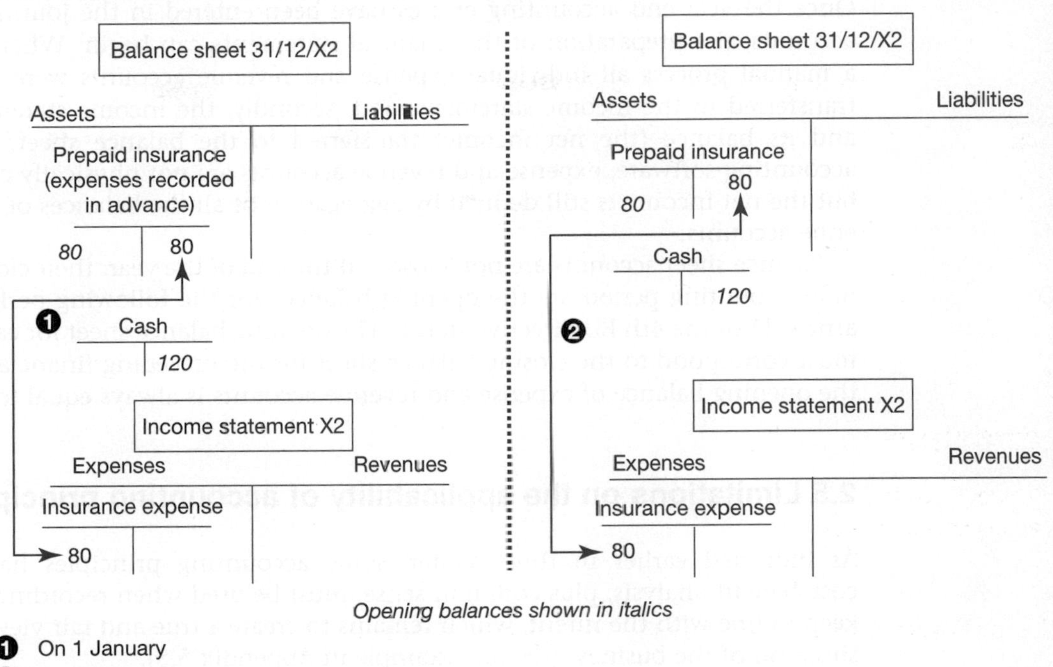

❶ On 1 January
❷ On 31 August

2.2 Correction of errors

Accounting records may contain errors. We said in Chapter 4 that computerization of accounting could guarantee a quasi-perfect reliability of transfers between accounts but errors in the original recording, generally involving a human intervention, may have been introduced without being immediately detected. It is part of normal procedures for all firms establishing financial statements to carry out an internal audit of their procedures and practices to create assurance that the figures are true and fair and devoid of mistakes. When carried out with rigor, this internal audit can detect the majority of errors and allow for their immediate correction. In addition, because financial statements are so important for a variety of users, especially the shareholders, these mandate an external accountant (external auditor) to carry an independent audit so as to make doubly sure that all figures are true and fair.

When an error is uncovered, the most common solution is the cancellation of the erroneous entry through a 'reversing entry' and the re-entry of the correct data for the same event. Some accounting software packages allow a pure and simple cancellation or modification of an entry until it has been validated and rendered 'definitive'. Such a possibility is convenient, but can be dangerous because it does not leave any trace of the original (erroneous) entry, the identification of which, in many cases, can be source of improvement and learning.

Errors and omissions that are uncovered after the books are definitely closed and the financial statements drawn require a special procedure, which will be dealt with in Chapter 6.

2.3 Ending inventory

Chapters 2 and 9 cover the end-of-period entries required for inventories when purchases are recorded directly in the income statement as if they can be presumed to be fully consumed in the period.

2.4 Closing entries

Once the year-end accounting entries have been entered in the journal and the ledger accounts, the preparation of the financial statements can begin. When accounting was a manual process all individual expense and revenue accounts were first 'closed' and transferred to the income statement, and, secondly, the income statement was 'closed' and its balance (the net income) transferred to the balance sheet. Nowadays, with accounting software, expense and revenue accounts are not physically closed any longer, but the net income is still defined by aggregation of all the balances of expense and revenue accounts.

Balance sheet accounts are not 'closed' at the end of the year: their closing balances for one accounting period are the opening balances for the following period. For instance, article 31 of the 4th EU directive states: 'The opening balance sheet for each financial year must correspond to the closing balance sheet for the preceding financial year'. However, the opening balance of expense and revenue accounts is always equal to zero.

2.5 Limitations on the applicability of accounting principles

As indicated earlier in this chapter, some accounting principles have limits and a cost–benefit analysis, plus common sense, must be used when recording a transaction to keep in line with the intent, which remains to create a true and fair view of the financial situation of the business (see one example in Appendix 5.5).

Key points

- Accounting for transactions follows a certain number of guidelines or principles, which are accepted by all accountants around the world.
- These principles apply to all accounting entries and provide a common foundation for improved understandability and comparability of financial statements.
- In order to reach the final objective of 'true and fair view', accounting information must respect four major requirements: (1) objectivity (unit of measurement, basis of valuation, and no offsetting); (2) quality of information (materiality, faithful representation, and substance over form); (3) prudence (conservatism, accrual basis, and matching); and (4) periodicity (accounting period, consistency, and going concern).
- The term 'end-of-period entry' refers to any entry that is necessary to give a true and fair view of both the financial position and the income statement. These entries will be carried out every time one closes the books (yearly, half-yearly, quarterly, monthly, etc.).
- The main categories of end-of-period entries are: adjusting entries, entries relating to changes in value of fixed assets (depreciation and amortization), entries concerning changes in value of current assets (provision), corrections of errors, entries relating to ending inventory (if necessary), and closing entries.
- One fundamental difficulty encountered with year-end financial statements is that the accounting period (generally the year, and more and more the quarter, for companies quoted on a stock exchange) does not correspond to the duration of a normal operating cycle. Consequently, a cut-off date has to be selected to allow proper matching and year-end adjustments must be recorded.
- The four categories of adjusting entries are: 'revenues earned but not recorded'; 'revenues recorded but unearned'; 'expenses consumed but not recorded'; and 'expenses recorded but not consumed'.

Review (solutions are at the back of the book)

Review 5.1 Adam

Topic: Accounting principles and end-of-period entries
Related part of the chapter: Core issues

Eve Adam, a newly hired graduate at the accounting firm Dewey, Billem and How, is puzzled by the preliminary balance sheet of four of the clients she is in charge of.

Company 1 – Balance sheet on 31 December (000 CU)

Assets		Shareholders' equity and liabilities	
Fixed assets (gross)	300,000	***Shareholders' equity***	
Less accumulated depreciation	–160,000	Share capital and reserves	330,000
Fixed assets (net)	140,000	Net income	20,000
Current assets		***Liabilities***	40,000
Inventories	120,000		
Accounts receivable	130,000		
Total assets	390,000	Total shareholders' equity and liabilities	390,000

Eve Adam has learned that a freeway is going to be built in the next year adjacent to one property the company had set aside to build housing for its employees. This piece of land is carried in the books at its historical acquisition cost of 100,000 CU. The market value of land in the area has fallen by 40% as soon as the news of the construction of the freeway became public.

Company 2 – Balance sheet on 31 December (000 CU)

Assets		Shareholders' equity and liabilities	
Fixed assets (gross)	250,000	***Shareholders' equity***	
Less accumulated depreciation	–130,000	Share capital and reserves	300,000
Fixed assets (net)	120,000	Net income	50,000
Current assets		***Liabilities***	20,000
Inventories	100,000		
Accounts receivable	150,000		
Total assets	370,000	Total shareholders' equity and liabilities	370,000

When analyzing the accounts receivable, Eve Adam finds out that the Lakme Corp. accounts receivable, has been in arrears for the past three years over an invoice of 60,000 CU. Company 2 has never handled the situation in accounting terms. Exploring a little further Eve Adam discovers that Lakme Corp. had actually filed for bankruptcy two years ago and that the probability of collecting on the receivable is probably nil.

Company 3 – Balance sheet on 31 December (000 CU)

Assets		Shareholders' equity and liabilities	
Fixed assets (gross)	500,000	***Shareholders' equity***	
Less accumulated depreciation	−240,000	Share capital and reserves	520,000
Fixed assets (net)	260,000	Net income	20,000
Current assets		***Liabilities***	200,000
Inventories	330,000		
Accounts receivable	150,000		
Total assets	740,000	Total shareholders' equity and liabilities	740,000

Eve Adam is rather surprised by the valuation of the inventory of 300,000 gold jewelry pieces. On average, the jewelry pieces were acquired at a cost of 1,000 CU each. On 31 December the market value of the jewelry pieces is 1,100 CU each. The head accountant seems to have valued the inventory at its replacement cost.

Company 4 – Balance sheet on 31 December (000 CU)

Assets		Shareholders' equity and liabilities	
Fixed assets (gross)	210,000	***Shareholders' equity***	
Less accumulated depreciation	−90,000	Share capital and reserves	150,000
Fixed assets (net)	120,000	Net income	10,000
Current assets		***Liabilities***	120,000
Inventories	40,000		
Accounts receivable	120,000		
Total assets	280,000	Total shareholders' equity and liabilities	280,000

Eve Adam observes that the income statement includes in the sales revenue one 100,000 CU sale to Godounov Inc. Despite being in an advanced stage of negotiation, the sale has not yet been concluded; however, the chief salesperson feels very strongly the sale will actually be signed in the first days of the year. The goods that would be sold to Godounov Inc. have been acquired for 70,000 CU and would be sold with a margin on sales of 30%.

Required

Establish the definitive balance sheet for each of the four companies by incorporating the information provided. For each case, specify both the accounting principle concerned and the journal entry that should be recorded to correct the preliminary balance sheet. The impact of taxation will be omitted.

Assignments

Assignment 5.1
Dukas Company

Type: Multiple-choice questions
Related part of the chapter: Advanced issues

1. On 1 June the Dukas Company paid three months rent in advance, for a total cost of 900 CU. At the time of payment, prepaid rent was increased by this amount. What adjusting entry is necessary as of 30 June (if financial statements are prepared on this date?)

(a) Prepaid rent (Increase in assets)	300	
Rent expense (Decrease in expenses)		300
(b) Rent expense (Increase in expenses)	300	
Prepaid rent (Decrease in assets)		300
(c) Rent expense (Increase in expenses)	600	
Prepaid rent (Decrease in assets)		600
(d) Prepaid rent (Increase in assets)	600	
Rent expense (Decrease in expenses)		600
(e) No adjusting entry is necessary		

2. The Dukas Company signed a 3,000 CU debit note to Bankix, their local bank on 1 September X3. At that time, the accountant of the company made the appropriate journal entry. However, no other journal entry relating to the note has been made. Given that the bank is charging interest at a yearly rate of 10%, what adjusting entry, if any, is necessary on Dukas Company's year-end date of 31 December X3?

(a) Interest expense (Increase in expenses)	300	
Interest payable (Increase in liabilities)		300
(b) Interest expense (Increase in expenses)	100	
Note payable (Increase in liabilities)		100
(c) Interest expense (Increase in expenses)	100	
Accrued interest payable (Increase in liabilities)		100
(d) Interest expense (Increase in expenses)	300	
Note payable (Increase in liabilities)		300
(e) Note payable (Decrease in liabilities)	100	
Interest expense (Decrease in expenses)		100
(f) Note payable (Decrease in liabilities)	300	
Interest expense (Decrease in expenses)		300

3. The Dukas Company owns offices that are rented to other companies. On 1 February Dukas rented some office space and received six months rent in advance, totaling 6,000 CU. At that time, the entire amount was recorded to increase unearned rent. What adjusting entry is necessary on 28 February if the company decides to prepare financial statements on that date?

(a) Unearned rent (Decrease in liabilities)	1,000	
Rent revenue (Increase in revenues)		1,000
(b) Rent revenue (Decrease in revenues)	1,000	
Unearned rent (Increase in liabilities)		1,000
(c) Unearned rent (Decrease in liabilities)	5,000	
Rent revenue (Increase in revenues)		5,000
(d) Rent revenue (Decrease in revenues)	5,000	
Unearned rent (Increase in liabilities)		5,000
(e) No adjusting entry is necessary		

4. The Dukas Company owns an interest-bearing note receivable with a nominal value of 1,000 CU. Interest at 8% per annum on the note receivable has accrued for three months and is expected to be collected when the note is due in July. What adjusting entry is necessary on 31 March if the company decides to prepare financial statements at that date?

(a) Interest revenue (Decrease in revenues)	20	
Accrued interest receivable (Decrease in assets)		20
(b) Note receivable (Increase in assets)	80	
Interest revenue (Increase in revenues)		80
(c) Interest revenue (Decrease in revenues)	80	
Note receivable (Decrease in assets)		80
(d) Accrued interest receivable (Increase in assets)	20	
Interest revenue (Increase in revenues)		20
(e) Note receivable (Increase in assets)	20	
Interest revenue (Increase in revenues)		20
(f) No adjusting entry is necessary		

Assignment 5.2
Gounod Company

Topic: Accounting principles
Related part of the chapter: Core issues

Guillemette Gounod is CEO of the Gounod Corporation, a manufacturer of smartcards and electronic personal identification devices. As chair of the annual meeting of shareholders she is reporting on the performance of the previous period and commenting on some of the key points revealed by the financial statements. Her remarks follow.

1. Despite the figures you can observe in the comparative income statements, sales activity of X1 is significantly greater than that of period X0. Several major customers, essentially government and semi-government agencies with unused budget allowances in X0 had paid in advance in X0 for deliveries that did not take place until X1. This shifted sales that really took place in X1 towards X0, thus creating the erroneous perception that X1 sales were only 10% greater than those of X0. In reality the sales of your company have increased brilliantly by 40%.
2. Further to this understatement of the X1 sales, our X1 purchases have been inflated because we accepted early delivery of about three months' worth of card readers we purchased from MG-Electronics. MG-Electronics is a subsidiary of Silver Electric International and the CEO of MG-E asked us, and we accepted, to help him meet his X1 sales growth target by accepting early delivery and invoicing. He has extended us a six-month credit term for the delivery so this will have no impact on our cash situation.

   These two events, deflated sales and inflated purchases, affect negatively the reported income of X1 as you can well understand.
3. You will observe that the balance sheet shows an asset called capitalized R&D, which is lower this year in comparison to last year. The R&D team is involved in a long-term project, a new-generation smartcard, which we do not expect to see hitting the market for another year at least. The headcount of our R&D team has been reduced this year by one person due to our seconding Dr Thaddeusz Czapik to PT-Microelectronics to work on the development of the new generation of microchips we will use in our new smartcard.
4. As you know we capitalize the work (engineering and legal) that leads to our taking patents to protect our intellectual capital. In X1 we are valuing the new patents registered in our name at 160,000 CU, down from 340,000 in X0. I have been worried by this downward trend and have investigated and found that our patents department has been understaffed due to two sick leaves and is way behind in filing applications for new patents.
5. Our company's reputation and market share have been increasing significantly. I have been asking our external auditor repeatedly to allow us to recognize this increase in value of the firm due to both our name and the quality of our products and labor force in the larger sense. The auditor refused once again to recognize this value creation, fruit of the labor of my team, and I will later propose a motion to change auditors.
6. Our tangible assets are essentially numerically controlled machines, which still work magnificently well in the manufacturing of our products. These machines have not lost any of the potential they had when we

bought them. However, I have had to reluctantly accept the demand by the CFO to depreciate them on the balance sheet. Fortunately, the machines were purchased before a price increase and therefore, despite that added cost, that makes us comparatively more competitive.

7. The chief accountant has told me that each year he chooses the best methods for depreciating the building and fixtures in order to minimize taxable income. This year I understand we used the straight-line method but last year we had used the declining balance method, a form of accelerated depreciation.
8. My last remark, that also leads me to be critical of our auditor, is to say that I strongly feel our financial statements are overly prudent, bordering on pessimism. I still do not understand why we are not allowed to build a provision for the cost of laying-off all or most of our personnel. Such a provision would, of course, reduce taxes if it were allowed by the tax authority but mainly it would give us a true and fair view (accountants have been using this buzzword around me too much) of the situation of our company in case of a downturn in the economy.

Required

Ms Guillemette Gounod seems to have an incomplete understanding of some key accounting principles. For each of the points of her speech to the shareholders, identify the accounting principle(s) that was (were) ignored or applied improperly and explain to her the correct position she should accept.

Assignment 5.3
Lalo Company

Topic: End-of-period entries
Related part of the chapter: Core issues

The company

Lalo Company, headquartered in Vaduz, is a company listed in Amsterdam, Paris, and Zurich. It is the third largest small home appliance manufacturer in Europe. The company was founded in 1955 by Patrick O'Share, a self-made millionaire, whose family emigrated from Ireland during the 1930s. Despite Lalo being a public company, the O'Share family still holds a significant interest in the company through the ownership of 20% of the outstanding voting shares. The remainder of the shares is actively traded and the stock ownership is diversified. Patrick O'Share, now 70 years old, serves in the largely honorary position of Chairman of the Board. His eldest daughter, Minnie Mize (her married name), 45, is the current President and Chief Executive Officer.

The company has a 31 December fiscal year-end. Today is 10 January of year X2 and the books for year X1 are about to be closed. All normal and recurring transactions have been recorded in the accounts and a preliminary balance sheet and income statement have been prepared (see Appendices 1 and 2).

Eric Faithful, Vice President–Finance, has organized a meeting to discuss several issues concerning seven year-end adjustments and closing entries. All parties interested in the year-end adjusting entries have been invited to attend. The meeting will include, among others, Eric Faithful, Minnie Mize (CEO), Max E. Mumm (Vice President–Investor Relations), Celia Vee (Vice President–Sales) and Gunther Somday (Vice President–Production).

Key players

After graduating from a French Graduate School of Business, Eric Faithful passed the CPA exam. He worked as an Audit Supervisor for a 'Big Four' accounting firm in Frankfurt before joining Lalo two years ago. In his opinion, compliance with the letter and spirit of generally accepted accounting principles is essential. He is opposed to any form of manipulation of the accounts. He often declares: 'Our mission is to give a clear and truthful view of the financial position and results of operations of the company'.

Minnie Mize, being both the daughter of the founder of the company and having progressed through the ranks from being a salesperson to her current position as President and CEO, is a firm believer in reinvesting profits and generating enough operating cash flows to support growth without having to depend too much on external financing. Her philosophy is that the accounting experts should 'use conservative accounting methods and take advantage of all legal loopholes to minimize reported and taxable income and avoid unnecessary drains on the cash flow of the company. A better future for all comes from our ability to generate and reinvest as large a cash flow as possible'.

After five years in the Investor Relations Department of a large North American conglomerate, Max E. Mumm assumed the position of Vice President for Investor Relations at Lalo approximately 12 months ago. He has been critical of what he sometimes refers to as the 'lack of vision of the family'. He believes that presenting the company in the most favorable light, and maintaining effective communications with financial analysts and the investment community, are key to the company's success. 'If we are to continue expanding in the face of increased international competition and the consolidation trend in the industry, we are going to need to obtain additional equity capital. We must keep the loyalty of our shareholders and attract new ones. It is essential for a growing business like ours to earn a high return on equity in order to lower our cost of capital.'

Minutes of the meeting

Seven adjusting entries still need to be finalized and this is the major objective of the meeting.

1. *Depreciation*

Eric Faithful: 'Last 1 July, we purchased a new sheet metal press for 1 million CU. The cost of the press was added to property, plant and equipment, but no decision has been made yet about its useful life or depreciation. Gunther, what do you think of the useful life of this press?'

Gunther Somday (VP–Production): 'Technically the useful life of the press should be between 5 and 10 years. Although I do not want to interfere with your accounting discussion, I know we have to choose between a straight-line and an accelerated method of depreciation'.

Minnie Mize: 'This is a no-brainer, let's choose the accelerated method and let's do it over the shortest acceptable life, i.e., five years here. The machine will become obsolete in a few years and I'd rather depreciate it to the maximum before we have to scrap it, or at least, as soon as we have benefited from all the production that we're going to get from the machine. Eric, we should multiply the straight-line amount by two to get the accelerated amount, is that right?'

Eric Faithful: 'Yes, it would be two, in double-declining balance depreciation. That would give a depreciation rate equal to twice as much as straight-line. This rate would be applied to the remaining balance, until you have to switch back to straight-line when the amount of depreciation expense is lower than the straight-line amount calculated over the remaining years. Of course, whatever method of depreciation we choose, we must start depreciating as of 1 July X1'.

Max E. Mumm: 'I don't agree with that approach. This machine will have a remaining life expectancy of at least 10 years. With our projected sales demand we can use the machine's capacity for at least ten years to come. And, on top of that, I hear it's a good machine with a technology that will not become obsolete that soon. Based on these facts, I feel the straight-line method is the one that is most appropriate. In addition, analysts tell me that straight-line depreciation is the method that is most commonly used by our competitors. Furthermore, if we choose to depreciate the machine over 10 years, we will show a better bottom line. If the machine were to become obsolete, we could just expense the remaining un-depreciated book value at that point in time. Why penalize ourselves in the eyes of shareholders?'

Eric Faithful: 'I don't necessarily agree with either of you. Our accounting methods should reflect as faithfully as possible the actual position of the company. Gunther says that given the new products in the pipeline, he expects to use the machine for the next eight years, but beyond that he is not sure we'll still use this technology. I would therefore suggest we take the eight-year time frame into consideration in our decision about depreciation. As for the method of depreciation, the accelerated method seems to me to be the most appropriate because the market indicates that the resale value of the machine falls off dramatically after the first year of operation. I second Minnie's motion in favor of the double-declining balance method'.

2. *Allowance for doubtful accounts*

Eric Faithful: 'A 200,000 CU invoice for a sale of microwaves that we made last 15 May to Worldapart is still outstanding and the receivable is still unpaid. The sales people estimate that in all probability we will not collect more than 10 to 40%. Their best educated guess is that we will collect about 30%'.

Minnie Mize: 'How about creating a provision for 90%? It is conservative since, at worst, we'll collect only 10%, and it is easy to defend if we are criticized'.

Max E. Mumm: 'Why not provide a 60% allowance? The financial analysts are not happy if we signal that we might have collection problems that could lead to lower earnings numbers. It would raise our cost of capital at the worst time. Let's work hard on making sure we collect those 40 cents on the CU instead of giving up so easily'.

3. *Contingent liabilities*

Eric Faithful: 'We are also involved in a lawsuit brought against us by Fairprice for patent infringement. They are asking for damages of 200,000 CU. I really see no merit in the suit and we will definitely not settle out of court. I don't know which way the judge will go. I estimate we have a 50:50 chance of losing the case. I would suggest recording a liability for half the amount they are seeking'.

Minnie Mize: 'Absolutely not. Let's plan for the worst. What happens if our lawyers blow it? We should provide for the worst case: the full amount. We can reverse the accrual later if our lawyers get us off the hook'.

Max E. Mumm: 'I think that this is another unneeded accrual. The more you accrue, the less earnings you report. Let's face it, this is an era of global capital markets. You may not like it, but the view that the analysts have about the company can make or break it. In any case the amount of damages Fairprice is seeking is ridiculously high. In a lawsuit you know that you always ask for five if you want to get one. If we make the accrual, we would be admitting that we would be willing to pay that amount. So, I don't see any need to make an accrual here at this time'.

4. *Revenue recognition*

Celia Vee (VP–Sales): 'We may have a problem with determining the exact X1 sales revenue. We shipped a truckload of mini-ovens to Pricelead's warehouse on 28 December. I understand the bookkeeper did not have time to record the invoice until 2 January X2, and I am not sure whether the truck got to their warehouse before that date. We are talking here about an invoice for 500,000 CU; so it is not a small amount. The question is whether to record the sale in X1 or postpone its recognition into X2'.

Max E. Mumm: 'Since we shipped the goods in December X1, it seems logical to consider it as an X1 sale'.

Minnie Mize: 'But, wait a minute, the invoice was recorded and mailed in X2 and the goods may have been delivered in X2. The preliminary income figures I received show that the operating income for X1 will be great. Wouldn't it be better to shift the revenue into X2? Why make X1 even better? In addition, it would be good for the sales force to know they are starting the year X2 with a little plus, don't you think Celia? Competition is getting harder every day and we all know they have an uphill battle in front of them. Let's give them a push and record that sale in X2'.

Eric Faithful: 'Sorry to rain on your parade, but I think Celia forgot to tell you that our shipments are always made FOB Shipping Point, from our warehouse'.

5. *Accrued warranty expense*

Eric Faithful: 'Because of our quality control systems, we have relatively low warranty claims. However, we still need to record a liability for our potential warranty claims. Ramon Psikotic, in the sales department, has estimated the warranty expense for X1 at about 100,000 CU'.

Minnie Mize: 'Yes but the repair department thinks that the cost of warranties is going to increase. The total amount should be 120,000 CU. We can always adjust the figure downwards later if the real figure ends up being less than anticipated'.

Max E. Mumm: 'Personally, I've reviewed Ramon's calculations and I think that the accrual should only be 80,000 CU. That's the number I would go with'.

6. *Deferred revenue*

Eric Faithful: 'On 1 November, we received a 300,000 CU cash payment for the rent on the warehouse that we leased to Ready-Sol, our European distributor. This represents the rent for three months, i.e., through January X2. We recorded the full payment as rent revenue in the year X1'.

Max E. Mumm: 'I agree. Since the cash is in, it ought to be recorded as revenue in X1'.

Minnie Mize: 'Sorry, Max, I don't agree! One month of that rent relates to January and therefore only two thirds of the rent payment should be recognized as revenue for X1'.

7. *Deferred expenses*

Eric Faithful: 'On 1 September, we paid 90,000 CU for our annual liability insurance premium. We recorded the payment as insurance expense (external expense). The period of coverage extends from 1 September X1 to 31 August X2'.

Minnie Mize: 'What matters is when the payment took place. Keep it fully in X1 expenses'.

Max E. Mumm: 'Wait a minute, here! Since we had no liability claim in X1, the period during which we will receive the benefits from that premium can only be for X2. It would seem more logical to recognize the expense as belonging to X2'.

Required

The class has been divided into three subsections A, B, and C. Each subsection prepares the version of the financial statements (balance sheet as of 31 December, year X1 plus income statement for year X1) reflecting the point of view of one of the three protagonists on each of the seven points evoked during the meeting:

- Subsection A: The position held by Minnie Mize (profit minimization).
- Subsection B: The position held by Max E. Mumm (profit maximization).
- Subsection C: position held by Eric Faithful (middle view).

Appendices 1 and 2 present the preliminary balance sheet and income statement established by the accountant before any year-end adjusting entry. Appendices 3 and 4 present the financial statements using a different format: vertical, decreasing for the balance sheet and by function for the income statement. They can be used as an alternative.

- Whatever the format chosen by the course instructor, all calculations should ignore the impact of both income tax and value added or sales tax.
- The only adjustments that need to be made to the balance sheet and income statement are those relating to the issues that were discussed above. (The students should not attempt to record all of the entries that produced the preliminary balance sheet and income statement shown in the appendices.)
- Arguments advanced, and positions taken, should be backed up with references to the course textbook and accounting principles whenever possible.

Appendix 1: Preliminary balance sheet before year end adjustments (horizontal, increasing format) 31 December X1 (000 CU)

Assets		Shareholders' equity and liabilities	
Fixed assets (gross)	17,300	Capital	5,000
−Accumulated depreciation	−8,300	Reserves	3,000
Fixed assets (net)	9,000	Net income	200
Inventory	4,800		
Accounts receivable (gross)	2,400	Liabilities	8,705
−Accumulated provisions	−95		
Accounts receivable (net)	2,305		
Cash	800		
Total	16,905	Total	16,905

Appendix 2: Preliminary income statement for X1 before year-end adjustments (format by nature) (000 CU)

Sales	29,000
Rent revenue	300
Purchases	−20,000
External expenses	−230
Personnel expenses	−6,825
Depreciation expense	−1,100
Provision expense	−95
Operating income	1,050
Financial revenues	220
Financial expenses	−1,070
Financial income	−850
Income before income tax	200

Appendix 3: Preliminary balance sheet before year-end adjustments (vertical, decreasing format) 31 December X1 (000 CU)

Assets	
Cash	800
Accounts receivable (gross)	2,400
−Accumulated allowance	−95
Accounts receivable (net)	2,305
Inventory	4,800
Fixed assets (gross)	17,300
−Accumulated depreciation	−8,300
Fixed assets (net)	9,000
Total	16,905
Liabilities and shareholders' equity	
Current liabilities	8,705
Common stock	5,000
Retained earnings	3,200
Total	16,905

Appendix 4: Preliminary income statement for X1 before year-end adjustments (format by function) (000 CU)

Sales	29,000
Cost of goods sold	−20,000
Gross margin	9,000
S, G & A expenses	−8,250
Operating income	750
Rent revenue	300
Interest revenue	220
Interest expense	−1,070
Net interest expense	−850
Income before income tax	200

Assignment 5.4
Electrolux*

Topic: Reporting for adjusting entries
Related part of the chapter: Core issues

Electrolux is the world's largest producer of appliances and equipment for kitchen, cleaning and outdoor use, such as refrigerators, cooking ranges, washing machines, chainsaws, lawn mowers, and garden tractors. The financial statements are prepared in accordance with accounting principles generally accepted in Sweden. From the consolidated balance sheet (annual report 2004) we extracted the following data (amounts in millions of Swedish Krona, SEK):

Equity and liabilities	31 December 2004	31 December 2003	31 December 2002
(...)			
Operating liabilities			
Accounts payable	16,550	14,857	16,223
Tax liabilities	900	1,180	1,211
Other liabilities	2,153	1,935	2,535
Accrued expenses and prepaid income	8,002	8,024	8,259
	27,605	25,996	28,228

The notes to financial statements, provide, inter alia, the following information on accrued liabilities.

Note 25 Accrued expenses and prepaid income (in SEKm):

	2004	2003	2002
Accrued holiday pay	1,150	1,139	1,214
Other accrued payroll costs	1,280	1,267	1,217
Accrued interest expenses	168	202	199
Prepaid income	483	637	1,040
Other accrued expenses	4,921	4,779	4,589
Total	8,002	8,024	8,259

Required

1. What figures should be crosschecked (or 'reconciled')?
2. Explain the principle behind the first three items of accrued liabilities and illustrate your explanation showing the impact on the financial statements of the adjusting entries that have probably been recorded for each of these three items at the end of 2004.

Assignment 5.5
Poulenc Company

Topic: Adjusting entries
Related part of the chapter: Core/Advanced issues

Poulenc & Associates, a consulting firm, was incorporated on 1 June X1. On 30 June the trial balance shows the following balances for selected accounts:

- Notes payable (balance sheet) 20,000
- Unearned fees (balance sheet) 1,200
- Prepaid insurance (balance sheet) 3,600
- Fees earned (income statement) 1,800

Analysis reveals the following additional data relating to these accounts (no adjusting entry has been recorded):

1. A customer paid 1,200 CU towards a yearly subscription to a service which started in June.
2. Prepaid insurance is the cost of a nine-month insurance policy, effective 1 June.
3. The note payable is dated 1 June. It is a 12-month, 10% note.
4. Services rendered to customers but not billed at 30 June totaled 1,500 CU.

Required

Show the impact on balance sheet and income statement for Poulenc Company as of 30 June, for each of the above transactions.

Assignment 5.6
Debussy Company

Topic: End-of period entries and preparation of financial statements

Related part of the chapter: Advanced issues

Debussy Company has prepared a set of financial statements in accordance with US GAAP: balance sheet, income statement and statement of retained earnings (see Appendix 1). The accounting period X1 ends on 30 September X1. Due to the illness of the company's accountant, the end-of-period entries have not been recorded.

Appendix 1: Preliminary financial statements (000 CU)

Income statement for the year ended 30 September X1	
Sales	10,000
Cost of goods sold	−6,200
Gross profit	3,800
Operating expenses	
■ Salaries	−1,300
■ Advertising	−800
■ Insurance	−30
■ Telephone	−40
■ Maintenance	−20
■ Rent	−25
■ Miscellaneous expense	−21
Total operating expenses	−2,236
Operating income	1,564
Deduct interest expense	−26
Income before income taxes	1,538

Balance sheet – 30 September X1

Assets		**Liabilities and Shareholders' equity**	
Current assets		*Current liabilities*	
■ Cash	1,000	■ Accounts payable	600
■ Accounts receivable	1,178	■ Notes payable	300
■ Note receivable	400	■ Unearned rent revenue	60
■ Merchandise inventory	2,000	Total current liabilities	960
■ Unexpired insurance	20		
Total current assets	4,598		
Long-term assets		*Shareholders' equity*	
■ Land	1,700	■ Paid-in capital	5,000
■ Building	3,000	■ Retained income	3,038
■ Accumulated depreciation	−300		
Total assets	8,998	Total liabilities and shareholders' equity	8,998

Required

1. Show the impact on the financial statements of the end-of-period transactions or events which are described in Appendix 2.
2. Update the financial statements taking into account these transactions and events.

Statement of retained earnings	
Retained income, 1 October X0	1,500
Net income for X1	1,538
Total	3,038
Cash dividends declared	
Retained income, 30 September X1	3,038

Appendix 2: End-of-period entries (all amounts in 000 CU)

1. Depreciation expense on the building is 80 CU for X1.
2. Part of the building owned by the company has been rented to other companies with occupancy starting on 1 September X1. The amount invoiced to the tenants (60 CU in total) was paid in advance for three months and collected in cash. It has been recorded in the item 'Unearned rent revenue'.
3. Salaries are paid on a weekly basis. The amount corresponding to the last week of September (100) will be paid at the beginning of October.
4. Interest on the note receivable has accrued for one month. It will be collected when the note is due at the end of December. The rate is 6% per annum.
5. Income tax at the rate of 30% applies to X1. The tax owed will be paid in the following accounting period.
6. Cash dividends of 800 were declared in September X1. They will be paid-out in October X1. (Such an announcement is common in the USA, where quarterly dividend payments are generally decided by the board, announced by the CEO, and, sometimes, later ratified by shareholders. In many other countries, dividends are commonly decided and paid out on a yearly basis. Their amount can only be decided by the General Assembly and cannot be known before a vote is held.)

References

EU (European Union) (1978) 4th Directive on the annual accounts of certain types of companies No. 78/660/EEC. *Official Journal of the European Communities*, 14 August.

IASB (1989) Framework for the Preparation and Presentation of Financial Statements, London.

IASB (2003a) International Accounting Standard No. 1: Presentation of Financial Statements, London.

IASB (2003b) International Accounting Standard No. 16: Property, Plant and Equipment, London.

Further reading

Alexander, D., and Archer, S. (2000) On the myth of 'Anglo-Saxon' financial accounting, *The International Journal of Accounting*, 35(4), 539–57.

Brorstom B. (1998) Accrual accounting, politics and politicians. *Financial Accountability & Management*, 14(4), November, 319–33.

Colasse, B. (1997) The French notion of the *image fidèle*: the power of words. *European Accounting Review*, 6(4), 681–91.

Dunk, A. S., and Kilgore, A. (2000) The reintroduction of the true and fair override and harmonization with IASC standards in Australia: Lessons from the EU and implications for financial reporting and international trade. *The International Journal of Accounting*, 35(2), 213–26.

Evans, L., and Nobes, C. (1996) Some mysteries relating to the prudence principle in the Fourth Directive and in German and British Law. *European Accounting Review*, 5(2), 361–73.

Evans, L. (2003) The true and fair view and the 'fair presentation' override of IAS 1, *Accounting and Business Research*, 33(4), 311–25.

Gangolly, J. S., and Hussein, M. E. A. (1996) Generally accepted accounting principles: Perspectives from philosophy of law. *Critical Perspectives on Accounting*, 7(4), 383–407.

Jun Lin, Z., and Chen, F. (1999) Applicability of the conservatism accounting convention in China: Empirical evidence. *The International Journal of Accounting*, 34(4), 517–37.

Ordelheide, D. (1993) True and fair view: A European and a German perspective. *European Accounting Review*, 2(1), 81–90.

Van Hulle, K. (1997) The true and fair view override in the European accounting Directives. *European Accounting Review*, 6(4), 711–20.

Zeff, S. A., Buijink, W., and Camfferman, K. (1999) 'True and fair' in the Netherlands: *inzicht* or *getrouw beeld*? *European Accounting Review*, 8(3), 523–48.

Additional material on the website

Go to http://www.thomsonlearning.co.uk/stolowylebas2 for further information.

The following appendices to this chapter are available on the dedicated website:

Appendix 5.1: Revenues earned but not recorded

Appendix 5.2: Revenues recorded but unearned

Appendix 5.3: Expenses consumed but not recorded

Appendix 5.4: Expenses recorded in advance

Appendix 5.5: Limitations on the applicability of accounting principles

Note

1. It can be noted that the Hammurabi Code (circa 1750 BC, see http://www.wsu.edu/~dee/MESO/CODE.HTM) specified that payment in a drinking establishment could be paid either in currency or in 'corn', as long as the market price of the quantity of corn demanded by the owner of the establishment was equivalent to the amount of currency required to obtain the same level of service. Since market prices create equivalencies between goods and currency it can be said that, even in barter economies, accounting only uses monetary units.

Part 2

International and comparative accounting: A topical approach

C6

Chapter 6
Revenue recognition issues

Learning objectives

After studying this chapter, you will understand:

- What the concept of revenue recognition represents.
- When to recognize revenue.
- What accounting consequences result from divergences between tax regulation and financial reporting guidelines.
- How deferred taxation is recorded and reported.
- How losses can be carried forward or carried back.
- Which methods can be applied to revenue recognition for long-term contracts.
- How to distinguish between ordinary, extraordinary, and exceptional items in the income statement.
- What the different types of accounting 'changes' are and how to deal with them: changes in accounting policies, changes in estimates, and correction of errors.
- What is meant by 'comprehensive income' and why it was introduced.
- What accounting issues relate to recording and reporting government assistance.

Before exploring in detail the various accounts composing the balance sheet (Chapters 7–12), it is essential to gain a better understanding of one of the most important balance sheet accounts, namely the income statement. As we saw in Chapter 2, the income statement is conceptually a subset of the balance sheet, summarizing those entries related to operations that affect shareholders' equity.

Beside the handling of costs and expenses, which was covered in Chapters 4 and 5, three issues remain that need clarification:

1. Revenue recognition: when and how much revenue to recognize.
2. Issues arising: (a) from the existence of different purposes in tax and shareholder reporting; and (b) from the corollary different accounting rules used for tax and financial reporting. (Both these topics raise some fundamental and universal issues, which will be covered in the Core issues section, and some more complex or unusual issues that will be covered in the Advanced issues section.)
3. Handling of extraordinary events (i.e., events not occurring in the normal course of business), which will also be dealt with in the Advanced issues section.

1 Core issues

1.1 Issues of revenue recognition

Revenues represent 'the gross inflow of economic benefits during the period arising in the course of the ordinary activities of an entity when those inflows result in increases in equity, other than increases relating to contributions from equity participants' (IAS 18, IASB 1993b: § 7).

To recognize revenue is to record the impact of a transaction on the revenue component of the income statement. One major accounting issue, derived from the matching and periodicity principles (see Core issues in Chapter 5), is to determine when to recognize revenue. Some rules are specified in IAS 18 (IASB 1993b: §§ 1–5) guiding the revenue recognition process for the following three categories of transactions and events:

1. The sale of goods (goods purchased for resale or goods manufactured by the selling firm, or land and other property held for resale).
2. The rendering of services (performance by the enterprise of a contractually agreed task benefiting a customer over an agreed period of time).
3. The use by others of enterprise assets yielding:
   - interest (charges for the use of cash or cash equivalents or amounts due to the enterprise);
   - royalties (charges for the use of long-term assets of the enterprise, for example, patents, trademarks, copyrights, and computer software);
   - dividends (distributions of profits to holders of equity investments in proportion to their holdings of a particular class of capital).

Criteria for recognition vary according to each type of transaction. Although some implementation differences may exist between countries, IAS 18 offers a set of generally accepted practices for revenue recognition. We will essentially adopt, in this chapter, the position presented in that standard.

1.1.1 Sale of goods

Principles Revenue from the sale of goods should be recognized (IAS 18, § 14) when all the following conditions 'have been satisfied:

(a) The entity has transferred to the buyer the significant risks and rewards of ownership of the goods;

(b) The entity retains neither continuing managerial involvement to the degree usually associated with ownership nor effective control over the goods sold;

(c) The amount of revenue can be measured reliably;

(d) It is probable that the economic benefits associated with the transaction will flow to the enterprise;

(e) The costs incurred or to be incurred in respect of the transaction can be measured reliably'.

These five criteria call for several comments. The assessment of when an enterprise has transferred the significant risks and rewards of ownership to the buyer requires an examination of the circumstances of the transaction. In most cases, this transfer coincides with the transfer of the legal title or of possession to the buyer. This is the case for most retail sales.

However, the seller, especially in business-to-business transactions, may retain a significant risk of ownership in a number of ways, such as:

- When the enterprise retains an obligation in the case of unsatisfactory performance not covered by normal warranty provisions (for example, a sale conditional on a specific performance-level clause).
- When the receipt of the revenue from a particular sale is contingent on the derivation of revenue by the buyer from its sale of the goods (for example, consignment sales).
- When the goods are shipped subject to installation, and that installation is a significant part of the contract, which has not yet been completed by the selling enterprise or on its behalf.
- When the buyer has the right to rescind the purchase for a reason specified in the sales contract and the enterprise is uncertain about the probability of return (for example, a sale on approval).

If an enterprise retains an insignificant risk of ownership, the transaction is considered to be a finalized sale and revenue should be recognized. An example would be a retail sale for which a refund is offered if the customer is not satisfied. Revenue in such a case would be recognized at the time of the sale, provided the seller can reliably estimate future returns, and recognizes a liability for probable returns, calculated on the basis of previous experience and other relevant factors.

The rules that govern revenue recognition are all practical applications of the matching principle. They are conceived to facilitate the co-temporal recognition of revenues and expenses that are related to the same transaction or other event.

Cost associated to the sale Some expenses or costs, including, for example, warranty work or recycling costs, are incurred after the shipment of the goods takes place and ownership changes hands. That is why co-temporality is an issue if we want to strictly respect the matching principle. These expenses or costs can generally be estimated with some statistical reliability and therefore appropriately provisioned so as to be matched with the corresponding revenue.

A provision is an estimation of the future probable cost created by an uncertain or risky situation (see Chapter 12). A provision allows the recognition of an expense at the time of the triggering event, therefore matching it to revenue. A provision is a cost or reduction in shareholders' equity. In order to keep the balance sheet balanced, the provision expense will lead to the creation of a liability for the very same amount. The provisioned liability will be used to 'compensate' or offset the actual expense when it is actually incurred. This way the expense, when incurred, will not affect profit, at least up to the provisioned amount. If it becomes established the actual expense will be less than what was provisioned or will not happen at all, the amount of the provision must be, at the time this 'knowledge' becomes available, reintegrated in the current profit (the provision is said to be 'reversed').

Example

Assume a sale generates a gross margin (revenue minus cost of goods sold) of 150 CU. This sale carries a 100% chance that the seller will need to provide additional services at a cost of 40 CU two years from the date of the sale. The gross profit from the sale is recognized as 150 CU and a provision is constituted for 40 CU. In keeping with the no offsetting principle, the net effect of that sale in the income statement is 110 CU and, simultaneously, a liability is created for 40 CU, which acknowledges the anticipated recording of a future expense. When the actual cost of 40 CU is incurred it might appear to have all the characteristics of an expense, but this cannot be the case since that amount has already been deducted from revenue as an anticipated expense. Therefore, that cost will be compensated by the cancellation of the provision taken as a liability two years before. With this procedure the matching principle has been fully respected, and the shareholders' equity has only been affected at the time of the triggering event, not when the actual cost is incurred.

If, however, it were difficult or impossible to estimate these post-sale expenses, the revenue should not be recognized at all at the time of shipment (and postponed until the uncertainties about these future costs are sufficiently reduced). Any cash or consideration received for the sale of the goods or service should, in this case, be recognized as a debt towards the customer (if we increase cash and create a liability of the same amount, there is no impact on shareholders' equity).

1.1.2 Rendering of services

Services rendered contracts such as long-term construction or consulting contracts, legal cases, or research contracts tend to span several accounting periods. This creates specific problems of measurement of both periodic revenue and completion. We will cover these later in the Advanced issues section.

IAS 18 (§ 20) states that, 'when the outcome of a transaction involving the rendering of services [such as in long-term contracts] can be estimated reliably, revenue associated with the transaction shall be recognized by reference to the stage [or percentage] of completion of the transaction at the balance sheet date. The outcome of a transaction can be estimated reliably when all the following conditions are satisfied:

(a) The amount of revenue [that will be obtained upon completion] can be measured reliably [i.e., the terms of the sales contract are clear];
(b) It is probable that the economic benefits associated with the transaction will flow to the entity;
(c) The stage [or percentage] of completion of the transaction at the balance sheet date can be measured reliably; and
(d) The costs incurred for the transaction and the costs to complete the transaction can be measured reliably'.

The recognition of revenue by reference to the degree of completion of a transaction is often referred to as the percentage of completion method. Under this method, a portion of the final revenue is recognized in each of the accounting periods in which the services are rendered, in proportion to the increase in the degree of completion (total fulfillment of the contract) that took place during the period.

The percentage of completion of a transaction may be determined by a variety of methods. Each enterprise uses the method that, in their view, best measures reliably the services performed and gives what they feel is the fairest representation of the actual financial situation of the firm. Some methods are more suited for certain type of transactions. Methods include:

(a) Actual measurement of work performed (a feasible option when only one activity is performed and the resources or work required to completion are known without ambiguity).
(b) Quantity of services performed to date as a percentage of total services to be performed (a feasible option when the completed, possibly complex service can be decomposed in small discrete and measurable sections or segments separated by clearly defined milestones).
(c) The proportion that costs incurred to date represent as a percentage of the re-estimated total costs of the transaction at completion, i.e., actual costs plus committed costs plus re-estimated costs remaining to be incurred until completion. (This is the preferred option when the service rendered is complex and requires the cooperation of several different types of expertise.)

Progress payments and advances received from customers often do not reflect the services performed. Even though agreed milestones of completion generally trigger invoicing for a predefined portion of the contractual revenue, it would be a rare case to find that the cumulative costs to date represent the same proportion of the total cost as the cumulative invoicing (cumulative revenue to date) does. Given possible interpretations of the matching principle, three situations can occur at any point during the life of a long-term contract:

1. Cumulative actual costs exceed cumulative revenue: the seller finances the difference. It is equivalent to a hidden discount, granted by the seller, on the selling price. Defining the relevant revenue figure becomes a matter of discussion and of availability of proper traceability systems: the relevant revenue should be equal to [sales price minus (costs plus financing cost incurred due to the negative contract cash balance in the seller's books)]. However, all too often the inability (or unwillingness[1]) to match cash inflows and outflows relevant to a given contract leads to misreporting of the profit on a given contract. The lack of tracing financial costs attached to a contract leads to overestimating a given contract's revenue.
2. Cumulative revenue exceeds cumulative actual costs: the customer finances the difference. It is equivalent to a hidden premium on the agreed upon sales price paid by the buyer. The issue of defining the relevant revenue stream is the converse of that mentioned in point 1 above. Simply, this time, revenue is underestimated since there should be a financial revenue on the positive cash balance on the contract's cash flow.
3. The two streams are pretty well balanced. The agreed sales price includes neither discount nor premium. Profitability of the contract is straightforward.

Clearly, the recognition of revenue leaves some room to choice. That is why long-term contracts are such an important subject in today's economy.

'When the outcome of the transaction involving the rendering of services cannot be estimated reliably, revenue shall be recognized only up to the extent of the expenses recognized that are recoverable' (IAS 18: § 26) (i.e., no profit should be recognized).

1.1.3 Interest, royalties, and dividends

When (a) it is probable that the economic benefits associated with the transaction will flow to the entity, and (b) the amount of the revenue can be measured reliably, revenue arising from the use by others of entity assets yielding interest, royalties, and dividends should be recognized on the following bases (see IAS 18: §§ 29–30):

- **Interest**: Proportionately to the length of the period during which the asset was actually made available and on the basis of the agreed interest rate.
- **Royalties**: On an accrual basis in accordance with the substance of the relevant agreement.
- **Dividends**: When the shareholders' right to receive payment is established (decision of the shareholders' general meeting).

1.1.4 Revenue recognition and reporting

Principles The revenue recognition policy of a firm may have a significant impact on its income and on the image it will communicate of its future economic potential (going concern principle) to the variety of users of accounting information and especially to the financial markets. The rules can be applied with more or less flexibility. Managers and accountants alike can use this flexibility to anticipate or delay recognition of profit or losses. Such a deliberate action on the timing of recognition of revenue (and of expenses) creates 'income smoothing' (i.e., attempts to avoid reporting peaks and troughs in revenue and or income which the manager or accountant thinks might give an alarming message to financial markets – see Chapter 15).

Although financial markets can generally 'see' through most income smoothing practices and are not fooled by them, these may have a significant impact in terms of taxation and, therefore, on cash outflows. The consistency accounting principle is theoretically designed to prevent such abuses of flexibility, but the recognition criteria have such a large built-in subjectivity component that flexibility always legitimately exists.

This is probably a reason why shareholders require (in keeping with full disclosure) that the notes to the financial statements reveal the methods of recognition retained and highlight any deviation from these. IAS 18 (§ 35) defines the minimum that 'an entity shall disclose:

(a) The accounting policies adopted for the recognition of revenue, including the methods adopted to determine the stage [or percentage] of completion of transactions involving the rendering of services;
(b) The amount of each significant category of revenue recognized during the period, including revenue arising from: (i) the sale of goods, (ii) the rendering of services, (iii) interest, (iv) royalties, (v) dividends; and
(c) The amount of revenue arising from exchanges of goods or services [bartering] included in each significant category of revenue'.

Real-life examples of revenue-recognition-relevant notes to financial statements
Some illustrative notes excerpted from the financial statements of some large international corporations follow.

Real-life example Bull

(France – French GAAP – *Source*: Annual report 2004 – International IT group)

Groupe Bull sells and leases computer equipment and [provides] data-processing services under various contractual arrangements. Regular sales are recognized upon full performance, by Groupe Bull, of the terms of the contract, which generally coincides with delivery or acceptance. Sales contracts generally include a clause reserving title to the goods in countries where this is permitted by law.

Revenue from one-time charge licensed software is recognized upon performance of the license agreement and delivery of the software. Revenue from monthly software licenses is recognized as license fees accrue.

Services are either of a recurring nature invoiced periodically or contracts with progress deliveries. Recurring contracts generally cover maintenance and outsourcing services while progress delivery contracts mainly involve systems integration activities. As from 1 January 2002, progress delivery contracts partially completed at the year-end are now recorded using the percentage of completion method. Previously revenue was recorded at the end of each invoice period in the first instance and on each progress delivery in the second.

Real-life example Ericsson

(Sweden – Swedish GAAP – *Source*: Annual report 2004 – Communications solutions)

Sales are recorded net of value added taxes, goods returned, trade discounts, and rebates. Revenue is recognized with reference to all significant contractual terms when the product or service has been delivered, when the fee is fixed and determinable and when collection is reasonably assured.

Real-life example China Unicom

(China – Hong Kong GAAP – *Source*: Annual report 2004 – Cellular telephone business)

Revenue is recognized when it is probable that the economic benefits associated with a transaction will flow to the Group and when the revenue and cost can be measured reliably, on the following basis:

- Usage fees are recognized when the service is rendered;
- Monthly fees are recognized as revenue in the month during which the services are rendered;
- Revenue from telephone cards, which represent prepaid service fees received from customers for telephone services, is recognized when the related service is rendered upon actual usage of the telephone cards by customers;
- Leased line rental income is recognized on a straight-line basis over the lease term; and
- Sales of telecommunications products, such as handsets, SIM cards, UIM cards, and accessories, etc., are recognized when title has been passed to the buyers.

1.2 Accounting for differences in net income calculations originating from diverging financial reporting and tax regulations

In most countries an income tax is levied on taxable income, which is generally defined as the difference between taxable revenues and deductible (or tax-deductible) expenses or costs. In principle, all sources of revenue are taxable and all ordinary and necessary expenses of doing business are deductible. But there are notable, large exceptions to this generalization.

In addition, the rules used for reporting to shareholders and for accounting for taxation do not have similar or coherent intents.

Accounting rules and policies are designed to support a true and fair reporting of the financial situation of a firm (i.e., measuring and reporting fairly and usefully the wealth created in a period of time) to the shareholders and to other users.

Tax policies regarding calculation of the income tax base (i.e., taxable income) are a practical compromise between stimulating the economy by encouraging certain behavior in a context of industrial policies, income redistribution, and the need for any state administration to obtain sufficient resources for its own policies. It is not within the scope of this book to explore exhaustively the tax regulations about costs deductibility and revenues taxability. Each country has its own rules, recorded, for example, in the Internal Revenue Code in the USA, the *Code général des impôts* in France, or different sections of tax law in the UK (Income and Corporation Taxes Act, Value Added Tax Act, etc.)[2].

This section deals with accounting for generic differences between reporting and taxation in unconsolidated financial statements. Accounting for income tax effects in consolidated financial statements will be covered in Chapter 13.

1.2.1 Pre-tax income and taxable income

Pre-tax income and taxable income do not derive from the same purposes and set of principles. Examples of differences in policies and practices include:

- **Depreciation** is generally computed on a straight-line basis for financial reporting purposes, while an accelerated method is often used for tax purposes. This tax-accepted acceleration of depreciation actually postpones the taxation of profits. A common argument supporting accelerated depreciation methods is that it provides larger deductions from taxable revenue in the early life of the asset. This creates a larger cash flow from operations available early for reinvestment[3] and hopefully growth, thus encouraging the acquisition of assets and boosting the economy, which is generally in the interest of the government.

- **Warranty costs** are most often recognized for financial reporting purposes in the period in which the sale took place (matched with the sales revenue through the use of provisions for future warranty costs), while they are often deductible for tax purposes only when actually incurred. Here tax authorities do not want to leave open the door to possible easy abuses of provision expenses used to postpone paying taxes.
- **Expenses benefiting several years** can sometimes be immediately deductible for tax purposes but can be amortized over several years for reporting purposes.

Differences between income tax rules and accounting rules lead to different figures for income. Since only one uniquely defined figure can serve as the actual tax basis (and thus affect the cash flow), it is important to reconcile the two income figures for the same period so as to give a true and fair view of the financial position.

Revenue and expense recognition rules for tax purposes can differ from accounting rules in two ways:

- whether or not an item is recognized (taxable or deductible);
- the date on which an item is recognized (the current period, when the triggering event takes place, or one or several subsequent periods).

These differences in rules create two types of differences between tax-basis income and pre-tax accounting income:

- permanent differences (linked to recognition or non-recognition);
- temporary differences (linked to the timing of recognition).

Figure 6.1 illustrates how these differences arise.

Tables 6.1 and 6.2 illustrate the two methods for the calculation of taxable income: either a 'direct dedicated' approach, or one based on a 'reconciliation' starting from the accounting income.

Figure 6.1 Differences between taxable and pre-tax income

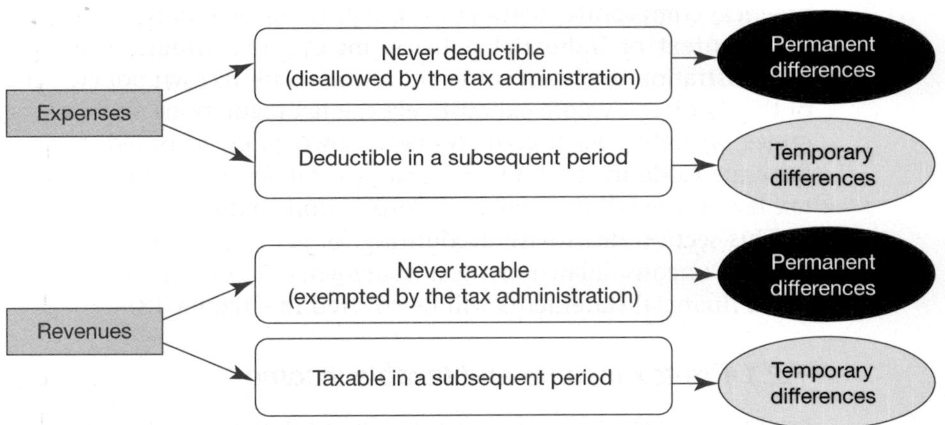

'The direct dedicated' approach This approach is used in some countries where tax and financial accounting rules are largely or totally similar (generally at the cost of a loss of relevance to the other users of financial information). It is also frequently used in unlisted small and medium enterprises where they do not wish to go through the reconciliation, and keep only a set of required tax books, applying tax rules for all recognition issues. Since the users are generally limited to the banker, the owners, or a limited group

Table 6.1 Method 1 – Direct computation

Taxable revenues
– Deductible expenses
= Taxable income = Reported income

Table 6.2 Method 2 – Reconciliation in Year X1

Pre-tax (i.e., reported accounting) income for the year X1
Positive tax adjustments
+ Expenses X1 never deductible
+ Expenses X1 deductible in X2 or after
+ Revenues X0 not taxable in X0 but taxable in X1
Negative tax adjustments
– Revenues X1 never taxable
– Revenues X1 taxable in X2 or later
– Expenses X0 not deductible in X0 but deductible in X1
= Taxable income X1

of close-knit shareholders, they often have an intimate knowledge of the reality of the situation of the firm and do not rely greatly on financial statements for interim information. Thus, the loss of information created by the merger of tax and reporting accounting is not significant. However larger businesses, and especially listed companies, must use the reporting format required by financial markets and thus may deviate from tax rules in their reporting.

'Reconciliation and detailed description of steps' approach In this second approach, the steps describing the differences of rules and practices are detailed so that one can go, step by step, from the pre-tax income of the period to the taxable income. The interest of this method, when it is disclosed, is that it allows the reader of financial statements to better understand the choices made by the firm and to therefore better anticipate the future cash flows from operations.

1.2.2 Impact of permanent differences

Permanent differences are created by revenue and expense items that are recognized for accounting purposes, but not for tax purposes, or the converse, such as:

- interest revenue on state and municipal bonds are, in some countries, not taxable;
- life insurance premiums (taken on the head of executives) paid by a company that is the designated beneficiary of the life insurance in case of death are not always tax deductible;
- penalties and fines for violation of laws or regulations are rarely tax deductible;
- depreciation on certain assets may not be tax deductible (for instance, on cars of a value in excess of certain tax-specified amount);
- interest expense on shareholders' current accounts in excess of certain tax-specified limitation can be non-tax deductible in some countries;

- provisions for doubtful accounts receivables are not always tax deductible;
- non-deductibility of charitable contributions in excess of a tax-specified ceiling.

We will see how these permanent differences affect accounts through the example of non-tax deductible parking violation fines for a firm whose main activity is the on-site maintenance of photocopying equipment in a small medieval town without much public parking. From an accounting point of view, they are legitimate expenses because repair persons have no choice but to often park illegally while visiting their customers. The tax authorities cannot condone the violation of the law and thus legitimately deny the deductibility of these parking violation fines. There is therefore a divergence between the two sets of rules. The pre-tax income before deducting the non-deductible fines is 110 CU. The amount of parking fines is 20 CU. The tax rate is 40%.

Table 6.3 illustrates the detailed steps followed to calculate the income tax applicable to both the tax basis and the reporting basis income.

Any other permanent difference would be handled in a similar way. Thus, we can state that 'permanent differences' do not impair reporting (as long as the non-deductible penalty is fully reported, as was the case here in the financial statements side of Table 6.3):

- permanent differences do not reverse themselves over time;
- they have no future tax consequences.

Table 6.3 Permanent differences

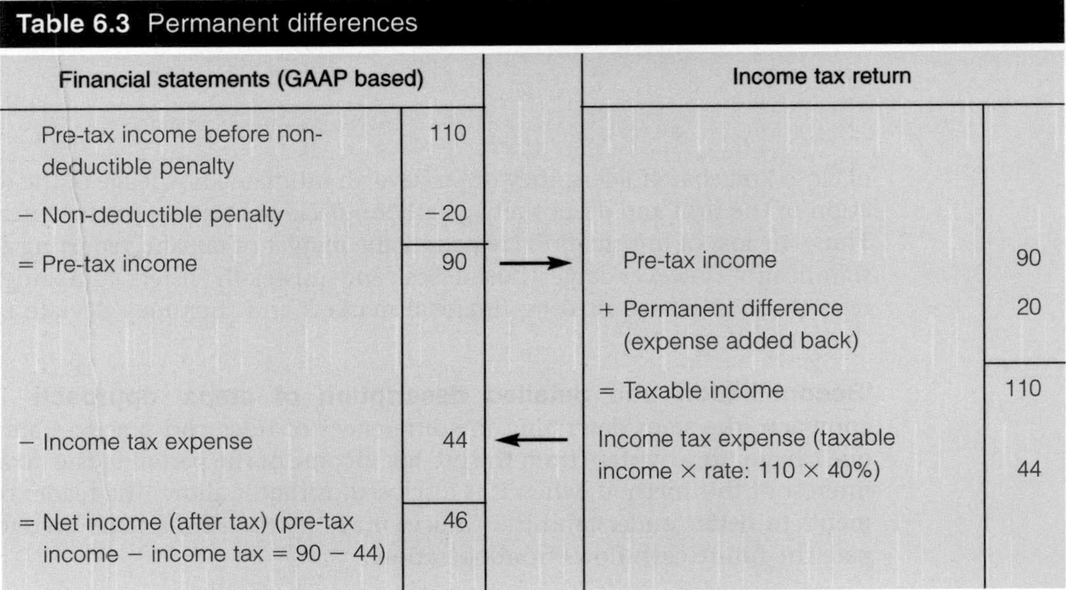

Financial statements (GAAP based)			Income tax return	
Pre-tax income before non-deductible penalty	110			
– Non-deductible penalty	–20			
= Pre-tax income	90	→	Pre-tax income	90
			+ Permanent difference (expense added back)	20
			= Taxable income	110
– Income tax expense	44	←	Income tax expense (taxable income × rate: 110 × 40%)	44
= Net income (after tax) (pre-tax income – income tax = 90 – 44)	46			

1.2.3 Temporary differences

As we mentioned before in the case of warranty costs, the impact of the divergence between tax and accounting rules is on the timing of the recognition, not on the amount recognized as was the case for permanent differences.

Temporary differences arise when some expenses are recognized immediately for reporting to shareholders and at a later date for tax purposes, or the reverse. If the tax rules lead to a later recognition of the tax burden than under financial accounting rules, a tax liability is created which is called deferred tax liability, often shortened to 'deferred taxes'. It is the most common case. If, on the contrary, the tax rules lead to recognizing taxes earlier than would have been found according to financial accounting rules, a prepaid tax asset is created that is called 'deferred tax asset'. Temporary differences also arise with regard to revenues (see below).

Figure 6.2 summarizes the process of creation of these deferred tax assets and liabilities (numbers refer to the examples that follow).

The basic principle of deferred taxation is that the difference is expected to be reversed in future periods. These differences are said to originate in one period and be 'capable of reversal' in one or more subsequent periods.

Temporary differences arise not only from different rules of recognition of revenues and expenses in the income statement, but also from differences in tax and accounting bases of valuation of either assets or liabilities.

IAS 12 (IASB 2000, § 5) states that 'temporary differences are differences between the carrying amount of an asset or liability in the balance sheet and its tax base'. They 'may be either:

(a) *Taxable temporary differences*, which are temporary differences that will result in taxable amounts in determining taxable profit (tax loss) of future periods when the carrying amount of the asset or liability is recovered or settled; or

(b) *Deductible temporary differences*, which are temporary differences that will result in amounts that are deductible in determining taxable profit (tax loss) of future periods when the carrying amount of the asset or liability is recovered or settled'.

The tax base of an asset or liability is the value attributed to that asset or liability for tax purposes. For instance, if a provision for doubtful accounts receivables (see Chapter 10) is considered by tax authorities to have been overstated, the tax administration might disallow part of it. As a consequence, the tax value of the asset (accounts receivable net of accumulated provision) is greater than the carrying amount (net book value). This situation leads to the recording of a deferred tax asset, as the 'excess' provision expense will be reversed when (assuming the provision for doubtful receivables was based on realistic estimates, and that the tax authorities had simply placed some arbitrary ceiling on this type of provision) the actual bad debt will be recognized, but the excess actual cost over the tax-allowed provision will not affect the taxable income at the time of reversal.

For pedagogical purposes, we prefer to focus our analysis of deferred taxation by reference to only revenues and expenses, as we believe that the approach based on assets and liabilities is less common and might lead to confusion, especially for beginners.

Temporary differences are essentially 'timing differences'. In practice, many accountants use the terms 'temporary' and 'timing' interchangeably when discussing differences between tax accounting and accounting for reporting to shareholders.

Let us now illustrate some of the sources of temporary differences (numbered cases refer to Figure 6.2).

Figure 6.2 Temporary differences and income

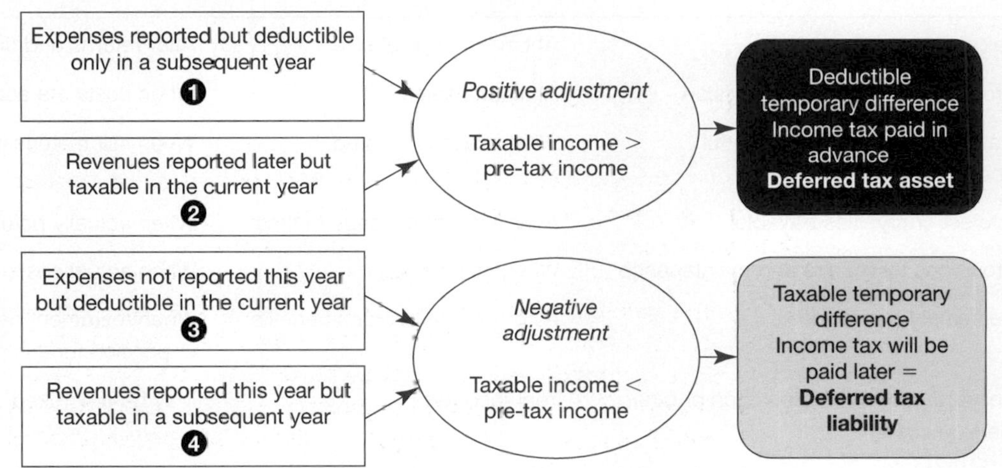

Case ❶ – Expenses that are tax deductible in a later period than they are recorded under financial accounting rules Table 6.4 provides examples of situations of this type that abound in the life of any business.

A quantified warranty provision example will provide an illustration. Lorentz Co. sells products with a short life cycle. Every year a new product replaces the previous year's product. In year X1, product A is still pretty experimental and Lorentz Co. feels it is appropriate to create a provision of 10 CU for future warranty costs on product A. Product B is introduced in year X2, completely replacing product A, which is no longer sold. B is a second-generation product and is considered to be extremely robust and, thus, in year X2, Lorentz Co. sees no need to create a provision for future warranty costs. In year X2, however, all the fears about the warranty service to be provided on product A materialize and the actual warranty service cost is 10 CU. The tax rate in this illustration is assumed to be 40%. We assume the company has a pre-tax income before warranty expense and provision of 100 CU each year. The provision is tax deductible only in the year of the actual expense (year X2 in our example).

Two alternative accounting solutions exist: either the firm does report taxes as they are owed (no use of the deferred tax mechanism) as shown in Table 6.5, or they use the deferred tax mechanism as shown in Table 6.6.

First solution: the local GAAP do not allow (or require) the deferred tax mechanism In year X2 the actual expense of 10 CU is compensated by the pre-existing provision. The recognition of the expense goes along with the cancellation of the provision, thus creating no impact on the income statement of year X2 as can be seen in Table 6.5.

Since no deferred taxes mechanism is used, the left-hand panel of Table 6.5 shows what is recorded according to the local GAAP. The tax accrued in each year is the same in the fiscal calculation (right-hand panel) and in the GAAP statements.

Second solution: the local GAAP accept or require the use of deferred tax accounting Table 6.6 shows, in the left-hand panel, that the tax recorded in the financial accounting books is calculated on the basis of the GAAP-based pre-tax income. It is, in a way, a 'theoretical' amount since the taxes that will really be owed to the tax authority are calculated as a function of the taxable income in the right-hand panel of the table. There is a timing difference between the recorded tax expense, calculated on the basis of pre-tax income

Table 6.4 Examples of expenses that are tax deductible in a period later than they are recorded under financial accounting rules

Examples	Accounting timing	Tax timing
Tax on net sales revenue	At time of original sale	After returns and claims are known
Product warranty-costs provision	At time of sale	When costs are actually incurred
Bad debt expense (or doubtful accounts) provision	When claim is created	When risk materializes
Interest or royalties payable	Accrued with passage of time	When actually paid
Provisions for repairs and maintenance	When established	When actual costs incurred
Retirement benefit costs	As employee accrues benefits	When retirement benefit or contribution to pension fund is paid out
Research costs (incorporation or other start-up costs)	Year incurred	May be amortized over a few years

Table 6.5 Effect of a provision when local GAAP do not allow deferred tax accounts

GAAP financial statements			Income tax return		
	Year X1	Year X2		Year X1	Year X2
Pre-tax income before actual warranty expense	100	100			
Actual warranty expense	0	−10			
Pre-tax income before accounting for product warranty provision	100	90	Pre-tax income	90	100
Product warranty provision expense	−10	0	Provision added back	+10	
Reversal of provision	0	+10	Reversal of provision		−10
Pre-tax income	90	100	Taxable income	100	90
Income tax expense	−40	−36	Income tax expense	40	36
Net reported income after tax	50	64			

Table 6.6 Accounting for deferred income taxes

Tax expense based on financial reporting			Reminder: Tax expense based on tax return		
	Year X1	Year X2		Year X1	Year X2
Pre-tax income (from Table 6.5)	90	100			
(Theoretical) Income tax expense (40% of pre-tax income)	36	40	(Actual) Income tax expense (40% of taxable income from Table 6.5)	40	36
Net income	54	60			
	Year X1	Year X2			
Deferred tax	+4	−4			

(36 CU for year X1), and the tax due (40 CU for year X1). The actual tax liability for year X1 is greater than the tax recorded in the books. Note that, if cumulated over the two years of the illustration, both the after tax income and the taxes due are the same (in nominal CU) regardless of whether one takes the GAAP or the tax basis. The difference between the two approaches is only one of timing.

The accounting tax expense is, like any expense, a reduction of the shareholders' equity. Thus, in order to keep the financial accounting balance sheet balanced (the cash outflow for taxes in year X1 was indeed 40 CU, while the 'books' only show it theoretically should have been 36 CU), the firm must recognize the creation of a 'deferred tax asset', which is equivalent to it saying it has 'prepaid taxes' in the amount of 4 CU (i.e., 40 − 36 = 4) (see Figure 6.3).

The deferred tax asset records the temporary differences due to using differing rules and regulations between accounting for taxes and accounting for reporting. This example shows

Figure 6.3 Recording a deferred tax asset in the financial accounting (GAAP-based) books

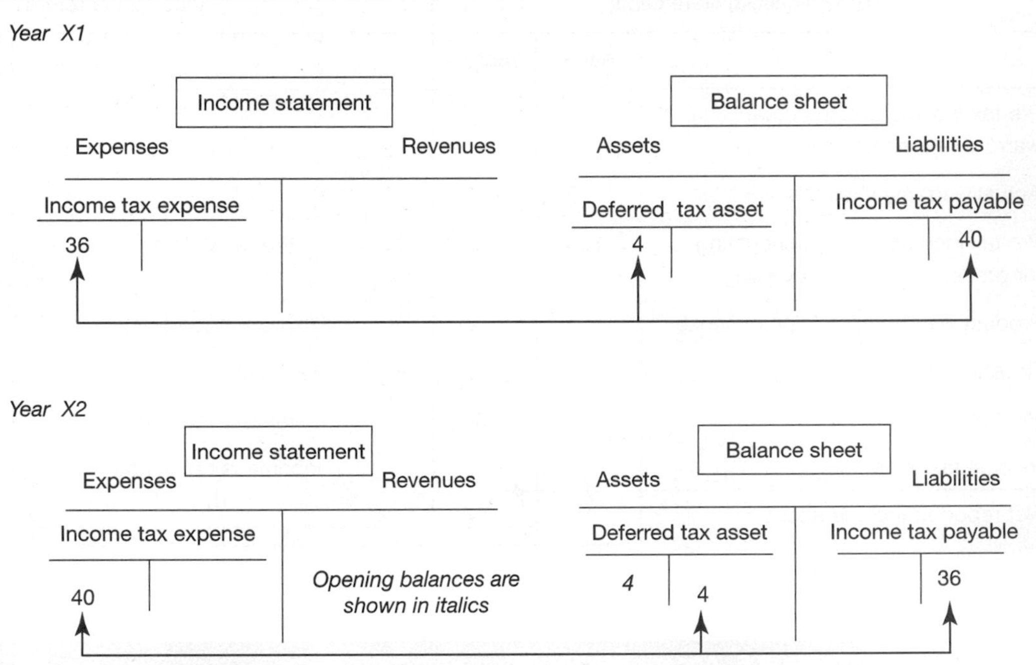

that the deferred tax assets do, indeed, reverse in the second period. The deferred taxation mechanism's impact is only to modify the timing of the recognition of taxes on income.

Not all countries allow the deferred taxation mechanism. Some countries (see Table 6.9 later) require that the tax calculated according to tax rules be the one reported in financial accounting statements. In this case, the reported tax liability would be 40 CU for year X1 and 36 CU for year X2 in our example.

Case ❷ – Revenues or gains that are taxable in an earlier period than they are recognizable under financial accounting rules Several such situations may occur in the normal course of business:

- A latent gain on marketable securities (see Chapter 10) is, in fact, taxable in some countries in the period incurred, but is reported under GAAP only at the time of the sale of these marketable securities. (Remember, the logic of taxation is sometimes just an expedient to get the cash into the coffers of the government sooner.)
- Cash received in advance for rent is sometimes taxable in the year received while it generally must be accrued under the local GAAP. Only that part of the cash payment relevant to the period is recognized as revenue under financial reporting rules and the remainder is recognized as 'prepaid rent received', i.e., a liability.

These temporary differences will generate a deferred tax asset because, as was the situation in the previous example, there is a timing difference between the GAAP and the tax calculation.

Case ❸ – Expenses or losses that are deductible in earlier periods for tax purposes than they are recorded under financial accounting rules This is, for example, the case for:

- Expenses spread over several years according to the local GAAP (in application of the matching principle) but that are tax deductible for the full amount in the year initially incurred. This is, for example, the case for product development costs that can be capitalized in some countries and, thus, will be amortized in the income statement over several periods covering the life expectancy of the product, while the full amount of such an expense may be tax deductible in the period in which the development costs were incurred.

- Greater depreciation for tax purposes than for financial reporting purposes in the early periods of an asset's life, as is the case when accelerated depreciation is used for tax reporting while straight-line depreciation is used for reporting to shareholders or when the depreciation period used for tax purposes is shorter than the useful economic life of the asset.

Such situations create a tax liability as is shown in the following very simple example of Gade Company. The firm's business requires the acquisition of an asset worth 20 CU. The pre-tax income before accounting for depreciation expense is 180 CU in both years X1 and X2. Let us further assume that, for tax purposes, the asset can be fully depreciated in the year of acquisition (i.e., the tax deductible depreciation expense will be fully incurred in year X1) while, under local GAAP, the asset depreciation is recognized over two years for reporting purposes.

The data can be summarized as follows:

Income before depreciation and taxes	180
Asset purchased	20
Depreciation for tax purposes (asset is depreciated in one year)	20
Depreciation for reporting purposes (asset is depreciated over two years)	10
Income tax rate	40%

The impact of the different accounting and tax rules regarding depreciation expense is described in Tables 6.7 and 6.8. Two alternative treatments exist:

(a) The financial accounting report to shareholders shows the actual tax expense (with an income before tax figure calculated according to tax rules); or

(b) the financial statements report to shareholders the tax that would have been owed if tax rules regarding income determination had been identical to GAAP rules (i.e., a theoretical amount different from the actual income tax paid) and, thus, requires a deferred tax liability account to reconcile the two ways of calculating the net income after tax.

First alternative: GAAP indicate that financial statements report (or are allowed to report) as tax expense the real tax owed (calculated according to tax rules) The left-hand panel of Table 6.7 shows the reported statement while the right panel of Table 6.7 shows the calculation mechanism for the taxes on income that will actually be paid to the local fiscal administration.

Second alternative: local GAAP allows or states that reported tax expense should be calculated according to GAAP rules, and not according to tax rules (thus creating a deferred taxation issue) Table 6.8 shows the calculations required for the establishment of the financial statements.

There will exist a timing difference between the two flows: in year X1, for example, the tax expense actually owed to the fiscal administration is only 64 CU, while under GAAP it will appear as 68 CU. In the first year Gade Company actually pays 4 CU less in taxes than it reports to shareholders. The situation is the reverse in year X2. Over the two years taken together, the taxes owed are, of course, the same (136) in nominal CU. Therefore, it is essential for the financial statements to inform the shareholders that a debt to the tax authorities has been created by the use of GAAP rules to calculate the reported income tax owed in year X1. The accountant does so by recognizing a deferred tax liability of 4 CU at the end of year X1 (see Figure 6.4).

In Figure 6.4 the deferred tax liability is indeed the result of a temporary difference since it clearly was reversed in the second year. Once again this illustrates the fact that the

Table 6.7 Case of an expense which is deductible, under tax rules, earlier than under GAAP

Financial statements			Income tax return		
	Year X1	Year X2		Year X1	Year X2
Pre-tax income before accounting for depreciation expense	180	180	Pre-tax income	170	170
Depreciation expense (GAAP based)	−10	−10	Reported depreciation expense added back	+10	+10
Pre-tax income	170	170	Deductible expense (full depreciation in year X1)	−20	
			Taxable income (under tax rules)	160	180
Income tax expense	−64	−72	Income tax expense	64	72
Net income reported	106	98			

Table 6.8 Accounting for deferred income taxes

Tax expense based on financial reporting			Reminder: Tax expense based on tax return		
	Year X1	Year X2		Year X1	Year X2
Pre-tax income based on local GAAP (see Table 6.7)	170	170			
Income tax expense (40% of pre-tax reported income)	68	68	Income tax expense (40% of taxable income) (Table 6.7)	64	72
Net income reported	102	102			
	Year X1	Year X2			
Deferred tax	−4	+4			

deferred tax mechanism only impacts the timing of recognition of the tax expense. The deferred tax liability may be classified as long-term or current liability (when the balance sheet distinguishes the time horizon of liabilities – see Chapter 3) as a function of the expected timing of the reversal.

Case ❹ – Revenues or gains that are taxable in later periods than they are recognized under GAAP This is the case for example in the following situations:

- In some countries, the revenue from credit sales (that give rise to an account receivable) may be fully recognized under GAAP when the sale takes place, but only be taxable for tax purposes on a cash basis, i.e., only when the customer settles his/her debt.
- Interest revenue is generally received in arrears and is included in GAAP accounting profit on a time-apportioned accrual basis (in application of the matching principle) but is included in taxable profit only on a cash basis.

These differences are only temporary as their effect will reverse over time. They generate a deferred tax liability.

Figure 6.4 Recording a deferred tax liability

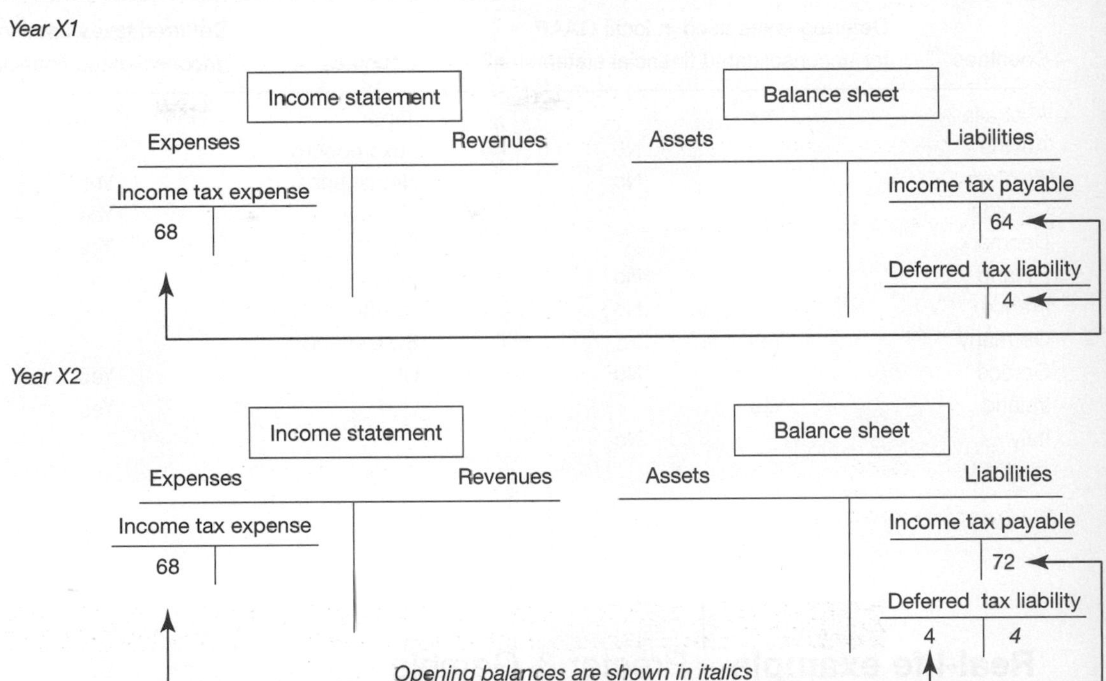

1.2.4 Accounting for and reporting income taxes

Principles The choice of reporting method for income taxes should answer the fundamental question: Should the expected tax consequences of the existing temporary differences be recognized in financial statements? In other words, should deferred taxation be reported?

Two basic alternatives can be identified:

1. **Taxes payable accounting** (or **flow-through method** or **integrated model**): This approach consists of ignoring temporary differences, recognizing income tax expense (in the financial statements for shareholders) as identical to the actual income tax payable. This view is defended by experts and countries (see Table 6.9) who hold the position that taxation is, in fact, a sharing mechanism in which the tax is the share of income that should go to the state, government, or fiscal administration (in return for granting the business the right to exist and providing the conditions for existence, such as the enforcement of the rule of law and open markets for resources and output) rather than a cost of doing business that needs to be recorded on an accrual basis in the income statement. This view is in opposition to the matching principle since, in the reported net income to shareholders, the link between the tax recognized and the triggering event is weak or non-existent.
2. **Deferred taxation accounting** (or **full provision method** or **deferred tax model**): This approach consists in recognizing the tax consequences of the temporary differences by including its tax effect as income tax expense on the income statement and as an asset or a liability (called a deferred tax asset or a deferred tax liability) in the balance sheet. This method actually reports an economic tax expense based on the (financial accounting) pre-tax income. This method is in full compliance with the matching principle.

While reporting deferred taxation in the consolidated financial statements is an almost universal practice, many countries' GAAP do not include or require the use of deferred taxes in the unconsolidated financial statements, as shown in Table 6.9.

Table 6.9 Reporting for deferred income taxes in unconsolidated financial statements

Countries	Deferred taxes used in local GAAP for unconsolidated financial statements?		Countries	Deferred taxes used in local GAAP for unconsolidated financial statements?	
Australia	Yes		Japan		No
Austria		No	Luxembourg		No
Belgium		No	Netherlands	Yes	
Canada	Yes		Norway	Yes	
Denmark	Yes		Portugal	Yes	
Finland		No	Spain		No
France		No	Sweden		No
Germany	Yes		Switzerland		No
Greece		No	UK	Yes	
Ireland	Yes		USA	Yes	
Italy		No			

Real-life example Procter & Gamble

Procter & Gamble, a diversified personal and home care US group involved, among other activities, in fabric and home care (Ariel, Mr. Clean), feminine protection (Always), healthcare, food and beverage, beauty care (Head & Shoulders), and baby care (Pampers), publishes in its annual report 2004 the following figures relating to income taxes:

Procter and Gamble
Consolidated Statement of Earnings (in millions of US$)
for the Years Ended June 30 2002–2004 (*source*: Annual report 2004)

In millions of US$	2004	2003	2002
Income taxes	2,869	2,344	2,031

In note 10 to the financial statements, the following information appears:

In millions of US$	2004	2003	2002
Current tax expense			
US federal	1,508	1,595	975
International	830	588	551
US state & local	116	98	116
	2,454	2,281	1,642
Deferred tax expense			
US federal	348	125	571
International	67	(62)	(182)
	415	63	389
Income taxes	2,869	2,344	2,031

2 Advanced issues

Earlier sections of this chapter dealt with the general principles of revenue recognition. We will now examine the specific revenue recognition issues raised by some business practices.

2.1 Long-term contracts

As shown earlier in this chapter, long-term contracts represent a very common situation in which the revenue and cost recognition principles find all their usefulness.

2.1.1 Principles

Long-term contracts are referred to by IASB as 'construction contracts' (IAS 11, IASB 1993a). We will, however, keep using the expression long-term contracts since contracts that span several accounting periods include many other categories of contracts than construction contracts. For example, research contracts, contracts for the delivery of a series of locomotives or aircraft, facilities management contracts, computer service contracts, law suits, consulting contracts, etc., are all long-term contracts which span several accounting periods.

This section is largely inspired by IAS 11, which states the problems arising with the accounting for long-term contracts in a very clear way. The primary issue with long-term contracts is the allocation of contract revenues and contract costs to the accounting periods in which work is performed. The general rules of revenue recognition introduced in the 'Core issues' section of this chapter apply.

IAS 11 (§ 3) distinguishes two types of long-term contracts based on the revenue determination formula:

- A *fixed price contract* is one 'in which the contractor agrees to a fixed contract price, or a fixed rate per unit of output, which in some cases is subject to cost escalation clauses' to reflect inflation on the cost of resources consumed.
- A *cost plus contract* is one 'in which the contractor is reimbursed for allowable or otherwise defined costs, plus a "margin" represented by a percentage of these costs or a fixed fee'.

'When the outcome of a [long-term contract] can be estimated reliably, contract revenue and contract costs associated with [this] contract shall be recognized as revenue and expenses respectively by reference to the stage of completion of the contract activity at the balance sheet date' (IAS 11: § 22). The IASB and a majority of countries prefer the 'percentage of completion method' over any other. It consists in recording costs and revenues associated with the contract in increments linked (generally proportionally) to the degree of completion of the contract during the period.

The IASB endorses this method if several stated conditions are met. In the case, for example, of a fixed price contract (see IAS 11: § 23), 'the outcome of the contract can be considered to have been reliably estimated when all the conditions mentioned earlier for recognition of services are satisfied'. If any one of these conditions cannot be met, IAS 11 recommends a prudent approach for the recognition of revenue, which is a variation on the percentage of completion method (IAS 11: § 32):

(a) 'Revenue shall be recognized only to the extent of contract costs incurred that it is probable will be recoverable; and

(b) Contract costs shall be recognized as an expense in the period in which they are incurred'.

An alternative method exists that is not endorsed under IAS 11 but which is still used by many enterprises in countries that accept its use: the 'completed contract method'. Its mechanism consists of waiting until the contract is fully completed to recognize all of its revenues and costs. Under this method the costs pertaining to the contract are capitalized as an asset and revenue received from interim billing are capitalized as a liability, and thus they do not impact the income of the firm until completion. This method is extremely simple to apply. It is built on the premise that the final outcome of a long-term contract cannot be known until the contract is fully completed, because too many uncertainties taint any attempt at estimating the end result. While the 'percentage of completion method' is a direct application of the matching principle, the 'completed contract method' is a direct application of the prudence principle. The completed contract method has been used in the past, when it was allowed and where it is still acceptable, as a powerful income-smoothing instrument. Such blatant abuses of the prudence principle are likely to be reason enough for most countries to have banned its use and for the IASB to have not endorsed it.

Regardless of the method used for the recognition of income pertaining to a long-term contract, both require immediate recognition of potential losses on a contract as soon as they can be legitimately established. Appendix 6.1 provides a detailed illustration of both methods of recording long-term contracts.

Real-life examples Some excerpts of long-term contract revenue recognition issues now follow as they appear in the financial statements of two large international businesses.

Real-life example Ericsson

(Sweden – Swedish GAAP – *Source*: Annual report 2004 – Communications solutions)

Revenue from construction-type contracts are recognized using the percentage-of-completion method. The degree of completion is measured using either the milestone output method or, to a very limited extent, the cost-to-cost method. The terms of construction-type contracts generally define milestones for progress billing to the customer, which also well reflect the degree of completion of the contract. (...). The profitability of contracts is periodically assessed and adjusted, if necessary, based on changes in circumstances. Provisions for losses are made when such losses become known.

Inventories (in millions of Swedish Kroner)

	2004	2003
(...)		
Contract work in process	7,278	9,275
Less advances from customers	−2,784	−3,158
(...)		

Real-life example Atos Origin

(France – French GAAP – *Source*: Annual report 2004 – IT business processes)

Consulting and Systems Integration revenue from fixed-price contracts is recognized in line with the technical completion of projects. Income from fixed-price contracts to develop individual applications or integrated systems is recorded over the course of several fiscal years and recognized using the percentage of completion method. Work in progress is recorded in the balance sheet under 'Trade accounts and notes receivable' and the excess of billings over costs under 'Deferred income'.

2.2 Installment sales

Installment sales are developed in Appendix 6.2.

2.3 Deferred taxation

2.3.1 Recognition of a net deferred tax asset

The recognition of a net deferred tax asset (excess of deferred tax assets over deferred tax liabilities) raises an issue of both value and reality and is developed in Appendix 6.3.

2.3.2 Accounting for net operating losses

Some tax regulations allow the recording of carry-back and/or carry-forward of net operating losses. It means that the losses of one period can be carried back, i.e., used to offset profits made in previous periods (thus calling for a tax refund), or carried forward to be offset against future profits, so as to avoid paying taxes in the future. The carry-back/carry-forward issue can affect greatly the cash flow of any business and is a major way of supporting start-up companies (the accumulated tax losses can be offset against future profits thus maintaining cash inside the firm when it needs it the most), and a significant element of financing in mergers and acquisitions (a profitable firm buys a business with large accumulated losses to shield its current and possibly future profits against taxation, thus reducing the net cash cost of the acquisition).

Table 6.10 indicates whether such practice is allowed in a given country (the list is not exhaustive and does not identify special cases).

Appendix 6.4 illustrates the mechanism of carry-back and carry-forward. A loss carry-back allows the business to carry the net operating loss back a certain number of years (generally between 1 and 3 years – see Table 6.10) and receive refunds for income taxes already paid in those years.

A **loss carry-back** is not a complex accounting issue as the claim on the tax authority is definite and real. Thus, the following entry is perfectly legitimate: increase in assets (Income tax refund receivable) and increase in revenues (Benefit due to loss carry-back) [or, in some countries, decrease in expenses (Income tax expense)].

A **loss carry-forward** allows the enterprise to offset future taxable income against the accumulated losses for up to a certain number of years (20 in the USA) or during an unlimited period (Australia or France, for example). The tax effect of a loss carry-forward represents future tax savings. Contrary to a carry-back, the carry-forward encompasses a certain degree of uncertainty because the claim against future taxes can only be used if taxes payable result from future profits. In this context, the key accounting issue is whether the requirements for recognition of a deferred asset for operating loss carry-forwards should be different from those for recognition of a deferred tax asset for deductible temporary differences.

Table 6.10 Net operating losses[4]

Country	Loss carry-forward	Loss carry-back
Australia	Unlimited	No
Austria	Unlimited	No
Belgium	Unlimited	No
Canada	7 years	3 years
Denmark	Unlimited	No
Finland	10 years	No
France	Unlimited	3 years
Germany	Unlimited	1 year
Greece	5 years	No
Ireland	Unlimited	1 year
Italy	5 years	No
Japan	5 years	1 year
Luxembourg	Unlimited	No
Netherlands	Unlimited	3 years
Norway	10 years	2 years (if ceased activity)
Portugal	6 years	No
Spain	15 years	No
Sweden	Unlimited	No
Switzerland	7 years	No
United Kingdom	Unlimited	1 year
United States	20 years	2 years

According to IAS 12 (IASB 2000: § 35): 'the criteria for recognizing deferred tax assets arising from the carry-forward of unused tax losses and tax credits are the same as the criteria for recognizing deferred tax assets arising from deductible temporary differences. However, the existence of unused tax losses is strong evidence that future taxable profits may not be available. Therefore, when an entity has a history of recent losses, the entity recognizes a deferred tax asset arising from unused tax losses or tax credits only to the extent that the entity has sufficient taxable temporary differences or there is convincing other evidence that sufficient taxable profit will be available against which the unused tax losses or unused tax credits can be utilized by the entity'.

The US answer is that there should not be different requirements. Different solutions have, however, been adopted in other countries. When local GAAP and regulation authorize the recognition of a deferred tax asset in the case of loss carry-forward, an entry similar to the one mentioned above for carry-back is recorded, with one difference: 'Income tax refund receivable' is replaced by 'Deferred tax asset'.

2.3.3 Changes in tax rates

Appendix 6.5 develops the impact of changes in tax rates on deferred taxation.

2.4 Extraordinary and exceptional items

Most country-specific GAAP include the principle that it is essential for an income statement to be useful in terms of evaluation of past performance and establishment of extrapolations concerning future performance. Consequently, an income statement presents separately and distinctly what pertains to 'normal' and recurrent business activities and what pertains to actions, decisions, and events that are occasional and unusual.

There are, however, some divergent views (reflected in the choice of terms used to refer to answers to this question) about what are 'normal' (in the course of carrying out the business activity) and what are 'abnormal' or unusual activities.

The IASC, actually followed in its choice by many countries, originally distinguished extraordinary items from ordinary items. The IASB, however, deviated from this initial position and prescribed that 'an entity shall not present any items of income and expense as extraordinary items, either on the face of the income statement or in the notes' (IAS 1, IASB 2003a: § 85).

The difficulty of defining the words 'ordinary' and 'extraordinary' in generic terms for any and all businesses is undoubtedly daunting, but one can nonetheless wonder whether the best remedy to this debatable categorization of events is the pure and simple suppression of any information about the subject. To make things worse and add to the confusion, the IASB, since its revision of IAS 1 in 2003, failed to define what is to be understood as 'ordinary or extraordinary' activities. At best one can still refer for guidance to the IASC's original Conceptual Framework (1989: § 72) which has not been invalidated, and in which one can read that 'when distinguishing between [ordinary and extraordinary] items (...) consideration needs to be given to the nature of the entity and its operations. Items that arise from the ordinary activities of one entity may be unusual in respect of another'. For example, selling productive assets such as machinery may unambiguously be recognized as an 'ordinary' activity for a business whose strategy implies they always have in their production process the machinery with the latest technology, while the sale of a similar machine, if sold by a company that has a strategy of using all machinery to the full extent of their useful life, would clearly be an extraordinary event. The distinction between the two terms is clearly not easy.

For lack of better rule, we will consider that events or transactions that give rise to truly extraordinary items for most enterprises are generally events over which the management of the firm has no control, such as an expropriation of assets, or an act of God such as an earthquake, a flood, or other natural disaster. Some countries introduce a slightly different meaning to the word extraordinary by choosing other words: for example, by distinguishing extraordinary from exceptional items and from current items (which means operating and financial).

Appendix 6.6 provides further developments on the concepts of extraordinary and exceptional items.

2.5 Reporting accounting changes

2.5.1 Changes in accounting policies

The consistency principle evoked in Chapter 5 states that identical accounting policies are normally adopted in each period in order to allow users to compare the financial statements of an enterprise over a period of time and to identify trends in its financial position, performance, and cash flows. Therefore, in this context, 'an entity shall change an accounting policy only if the change: (a) is required by a Standard or an Interpretation; or (b) results in the financial statements providing reliable and more relevant information about the effects of transactions, other events or conditions on the entity's financial position, financial performance or cash flow' (IAS 8, IASB 2003b: § 14).

IAS 8 prescribes the retrospective method as benchmark treatment: 'when an entity changes an accounting policy (...) it shall apply the change retrospectively' (§ 19b), i.e., 'as if the new accounting policy had always been applied' (§ 22). The entity 'shall adjust the opening balance of each affected component of equity for the earliest prior period presented and the other comparative amounts disclosed for each period presented' (§ 22).

When the retrospective method is impracticable, the 'entity shall adjust the comparative information to apply the new accounting policy prospectively from the earliest date practicable' (IAS 8: § 25), which means 'applying the new accounting policy to transactions, other events and conditions occurring after the date as at which the policy is changed' (IAS 8: § 5).

In the case of a voluntary change, IAS 8 (§ 29) prescribes disclosure of:

(a) 'The nature of the change in accounting policy;

(b) The reasons why applying the new accounting policy provides reliable and more relevant information;

(c) For the current period and for each period presented, to the extent practicable, the amount of the adjustment (...) for each financial statement line item affected (...);

(d) The amount of the adjustment relating to periods before those presented, to the extent practicable; and

(e) If retrospective application is impracticable for a particular prior period, or for periods before those presented, the circumstances that led to the existence of that condition and a description of how and from when the change in accounting policy has been applied'.

2.5.2 Changes in accounting estimates

'As a result of the uncertainties inherent in business activities, many items in financial statements cannot be measured with precision but can only be estimated. Estimation involves judgments based on the latest available, reliable information. For example, estimates may be required of: (a) [future] bad debts, (b) inventory obsolescence [rate] or (...) (d) the useful lives of, or expected pattern of consumption of the future economic benefits embodied in, depreciable assets (...). The use of reasonable estimates is an essential part of the preparation of financial statements and does not undermine their reliability' (IAS 8, IASB 2003b: §§ 32–33).

'An estimate may need revision if changes occur in the circumstances on which the estimate was based or as a result of new information, or more experience. By its nature, the revision of an estimate does not relate to prior periods and is not the correction of an error'.

IAS 8 (§ 36) prescribes that the 'effect of a change in an accounting estimate (...) shall be recognized prospectively'. According to this Standard (§ 38), 'a change in an accounting estimate may affect only the current period's profit or loss, or the profit or loss of both the current period and future periods. For example, a change in the estimate of the amount of bad debts affects only the current period's profit or loss and therefore is recognized in the current period. However, a change in the estimated useful life of, or the expected pattern of consumption of the future economic benefits embodied in, a depreciable asset affects depreciation expense for the current period and for each future period during the asset's remaining useful life. In both cases, the effect of the change relating to the current period is recognized as income or expense in the current period. The effect, if any, on future periods is recognized as income or expense in those future periods'.

'An entity shall disclose the nature and amount of a change in an accounting estimate that has an effect in the current period or is expected to have an effect in future periods, except for the disclosure of the effect on future periods when it is impracticable to estimate that effect' (IAS 8: § 39).

2.5.3 Prior period errors

'Errors can arise in respect of the recognition, measurement, presentation or disclosure of elements of financial statements' (IAS 8, IASB 2003b: § 41).

'A prior period error shall be corrected by retrospective restatement except to the extent that it is impracticable to determine either the period-specific effects or the cumulative effect of the error' (IAS 8: § 43). 'When it is impracticable to determine the cumulative effect, at the beginning of the current period, of an error on all prior periods, the entity shall restate the comparative information to correct the error prospectively from the earliest date practicable' (IAS 8: § 45).

IAS 8 adds that (§ 49) 'an entity shall disclose:

(a) The nature of the prior error;
(b) For each prior period presented, to the extent practicable, the amount of the correction: (...) for each financial statement line item affected (...);
(c) The amount of the correction at the beginning of the earliest prior period presented; and
(d) If retrospective restatement is impracticable for a particular prior period, the circumstances that led to the existence of that condition and a description of how and from when the error has been corrected'.

2.6 Reporting discontinued operations

Any business entity may, in the normal course of its activity, discontinue, spin-off, or cede some segments of its activity so as to, for example, reallocate its resources towards potentially more profitable markets. Entire sections of a business will therefore be either sold or discontinued. Since users need to be able to interpret the current performance of the firm by comparing it against previous periods' performance, it is critical to be able to reconstitute an equivalent economic perimeter so that the basis of comparability can be re-established. The handling of discontinued operations is therefore a very important element of quality reporting.

As defined in IFRS 5 (IASB 2004: § 32), which replaces IAS 35, 'a discontinued operation is a component of an entity that either has been disposed of, or is classified as held for sale, and:

(a) Represents a separate major line of business or geographical area of operations,
(b) Is part of a single coordinated plan to dispose of a separate major line of business or geographical area of operations, or
(c) Is a subsidiary acquired exclusively with a view to resale'.

The standard establishes principles for reporting information about discontinued operations, thereby enhancing the ability of users of financial statements to make projections of an enterprise's cash flows, earnings-generating capacity, and financial position by segregating information about discontinued operations from information about continuing operations.

According to IFRS 5 (IASB 2004: § 33), 'an entity shall disclose:

(a) A single amount on the face of the income statement comprising the total of: (i) the post-tax profit or loss of discontinued operations and (ii) the post-tax gain or loss recognized on the measurement to fair value less costs to sell or on the disposal of the assets or disposal group(s) constituting the discontinued operation.
(b) An analysis of the single amount in (a) [above] into: (i) the revenue, expenses and pre-tax profit or loss of discontinued operations; (ii) the related income tax expense as required by paragraph 81(h) of IAS 12; (iii) the gain or loss recognized on the measurement to fair value less costs to sell or on the disposal of the assets or disposal group(s) constituting the discontinued operation; and (iv) the related income tax expense as required by paragraph 81(h) of IAS 12.

The analysis may be presented in the notes or on the face of the income statement. If it is presented on the face of the income statement it shall be presented in a section identified as relating to discontinued operations, i.e., separately from continuing operations. (...)

(c) The net cash flows attributable to the operating, investing and financing activities of discontinued operations. These disclosures may be presented either in the notes or on the face of the financial statements (...)'.

Real-life example Saurer

(Switzerland – IFRS/IAS GAAP – *Source*: Annual report 2004 – Textile solutions and transmission systems)

Saurer operates in two segments: textile solutions and transmission systems. It used to have a third sector, surface technology, which was discontinued in 2004. The consolidated financial statements of Saurer are presented in Euros, although the parent company, Saurer Ltd, is domiciled in Switzerland. This reflects the fact that the Euro is the functional currency of the major part of Saurer's business.

Excerpts from the management's discussion of results

After the profitable sale of Xaloy's European businesses in 2003, the US and Asian business units were divested early in 2004, followed by the IonBond group in its entirety. The divestment of the Surface Technology division has now been completely and profitably concluded. The sale realized a total profit of €17 m (of which €1 m was realized in 2003). Saurer's consolidated figures for 2004 include revenue and costs of Surface Technology up to the date of sale. The sale proceeds have largely been received and have helped to reduce Saurer's net debt in 2004. The Surface Technology divestment has reduced Saurer's employee numbers by 871 in 2004.

Excerpts from the notes to financial statements

2 Discontinuing operations – Surface Technology	2004	2003
Sales	21,264	107,494
Operating profit before sale of discontinuing operations	2,891	2,213
Profit on sale of discontinuing operations	16,202	988
Operating profit	19,093	3,201
Financial expense (net)	−208	−889
Profit before income taxes	18,885	2,312
Income taxes on ordinary activities	−513	283
Income taxes on profit on sale of discontinuing activities	−161	–
Net profit	18,211	2,595
Total assets	–	113,209
Total liabilities	–	85,670
Cash flow from operating activities	8,851	5,003
Cash flow from investing activities (including proceeds from divestment)	87,334	−7,378
Cash flow from financing activities	−265	−3,154
Employees (full-time equivalents at year-end)	–	871

2.7 Comprehensive income

Comprehensive income is defined as the sum of all 'change[s] in equity of a business enterprise during a period [arising] from transactions and other events and circumstances', excluding those resulting from investments by owners and distributions to owners (FASB 1997: § 8).

2.7.1 Principles

Certain changes in assets and liabilities, which, according to accounting principles, are not considered as part of the business activity (i.e., neither ordinary nor exceptional or extraordinary), and thus are not part of the business net income, are sometimes not reported in the income statement for the period in which they are recognized but, instead, are included directly in a separate component of equity in the balance sheet. For example, the potential gain resulting from a rise in the market value of 'available-for-sale' marketable securities (see Chapter 10) would not be recorded in the income statement but directly in the shareholders' equity.

Some users of financial statement information have expressed concerns about the increasing number of items that bypass – or are not reported in – the income statement. In this context, the FASB issued in June 1997 the Statement of Financial Accounting Standard (SFAS) No. 130: Reporting Comprehensive Income that discusses how to report and display these items to arrive at a 'total comprehensive income'.

Those items 'bypassing' the income statement are referred to as 'other [elements of] comprehensive income'. Figure 6.5 presents the components of the total comprehensive income.

SFAS 130 encourages an enterprise to report 'the components of other comprehensive income and total comprehensive income [separately and] below the total for net income in a statement that reports results of operations' ('one-statement approach'), 'or in a separate statement of comprehensive income that begins with net income' ('two-statement approach') (FASB 1997: § 23). Comprehensive income and other comprehensive income may also be presented in a statement of changes in equity (see Chapter 11).

We should note that the IASB has been discussing the idea of reporting a comprehensive income for several years and is still in the process of discussion.

Figure 6.5 Components of the total comprehensive income

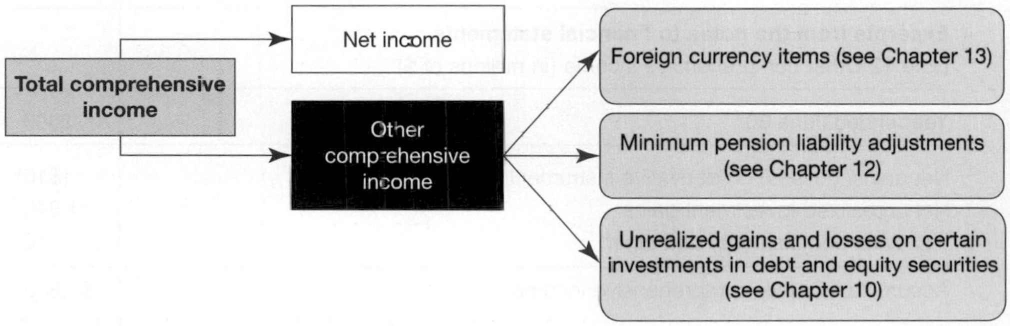

2.7.2 Examples

SFAS 130 SFAS 130 includes in its appendix an example of statement of income and comprehensive income. We are listing here the elements that are added to the net income to obtain the comprehensive income (see Table 6.11).

We will not delve into the details of the different items of the other comprehensive income. The interested reader is encouraged to consult SFAS 130.

Table 6.11 Comprehensive income in SFAS 130

Net income		63,250
Other comprehensive income, net of tax:		
Foreign currency translation adjustments		8,000
Unrealized gains on securities		11,500
Unrealized holding gains arising during period	13,000	
Less: reclassification adjustment for gains included in net income	(1,500)	
Minimum pension liability adjustment		(2,500)
Other comprehensive income		17,000
Comprehensive income		80,250

The following example illustrates the reporting for comprehensive income as a component of equity.

Real-life example Microsoft

(USA – US GAAP – *Source*: Annual report 2003–2004 – Industry: Software)

Balance sheet (excerpts) (in millions of $)

June 30	2003	2004
Stockholders' equity:		
(...)		
Retained earnings, including accumulated other comprehensive income of $1,840 and $1,119	15,678	18,429
(...)		

Excerpts from the notes to financial statements
Note 12 Other comprehensive income (in millions of $)

Year ended June 30	2003	2004
Net gains/ (losses) on derivative instruments	($16)	$85
Net unrealized investment gains	1,846	973
Translation adjustments and other	10	61
Accumulated other comprehensive income	$1,840	$1,119

2.8 Government assistance: grants and subsidies

Government direct financial support to businesses for special purposes (grants or subsidies) is a relatively common practice in many countries. IAS 20 (IASB: 1994) uses the term 'government assistance' to show that the aid provided takes many forms varying both in the nature of the assistance given and in the conditions which are usually attached to it. Such assistance creates a serious revenue recognition question, the answer to which can affect the interpretation of financial statements by users. Is government assistance revenue (or a compensation of costs, which is equivalent to a revenue), or a source of financing?

There are several categories of government assistance, and each category may require a different answer to this question. They are:

- grants related to assets;
- grants related to income;
- forgivable loans (i.e., loans that will not need to be reimbursed if certain conditions are met).

Let us analyze in turn the specificity of each type of assistance.

2.8.1 Grants related to assets

Grants related to assets are government grants whose purpose is to specifically encourage qualified enterprises to 'purchase, construct or otherwise acquire long-term assets' (IAS 20: § 3). These grants are mostly a targeted aid to investment in sectors or geographical areas selected for economic development. These grants, often called 'investment grants', can be used to finance greenfield operations as well as part of the cost of additions or modifications to existing fixed assets.

Figure 6.6 illustrates the several possible ways to account for such government assistance.

Figure 6.6 shows that the IAS 20 preferred solution consists of recognizing the grant as revenue in systematic and rational sections that allow matching, over the relevant periods, of the government assistance with the related costs (in practice the depreciation expenses).

Figure 6.6 Accounting and reporting for investment grant in IAS 20

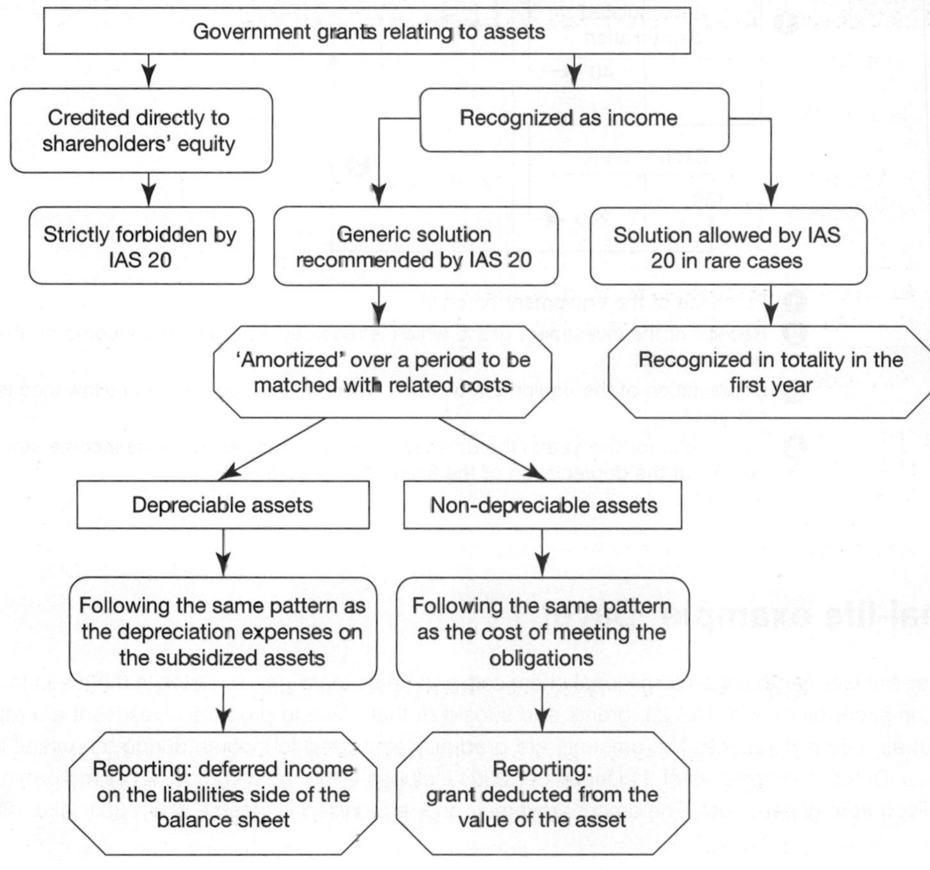

The full recognition of the whole investment grant in the first year would only be acceptable if no basis existed for allocating it to periods other than the one in which it was received.

Alternative solutions, however, exist without violating the intent of IAS 20. For example, under French GAAP, an investment grant is reported not in the income statement but in the balance sheet as a separate item within shareholders' equity (in the unconsolidated financial statements) or as a non-current liability (in the consolidated financial statements). The amount so recorded is 'amortized' following the method prescribed by IASB, i.e., a systematic and rational matching to revenue. The separate item is then equivalent to the 'deferred income' account prescribed by IASB as shown in Figure 6.6.

Theoretical example Kunzen SA acquires on 1 January X1 an asset in exchange for a cash payment of 200 CU. This asset will be depreciated over five years on a straight-line basis. Because Kunzen is located in a special economic zone, it qualifies for government assistance related to this asset for an amount of 150 CU. Figure 6.7 illustrates the accounting for the grant in year X1.

Figure 6.7 Accounting for an investment grant

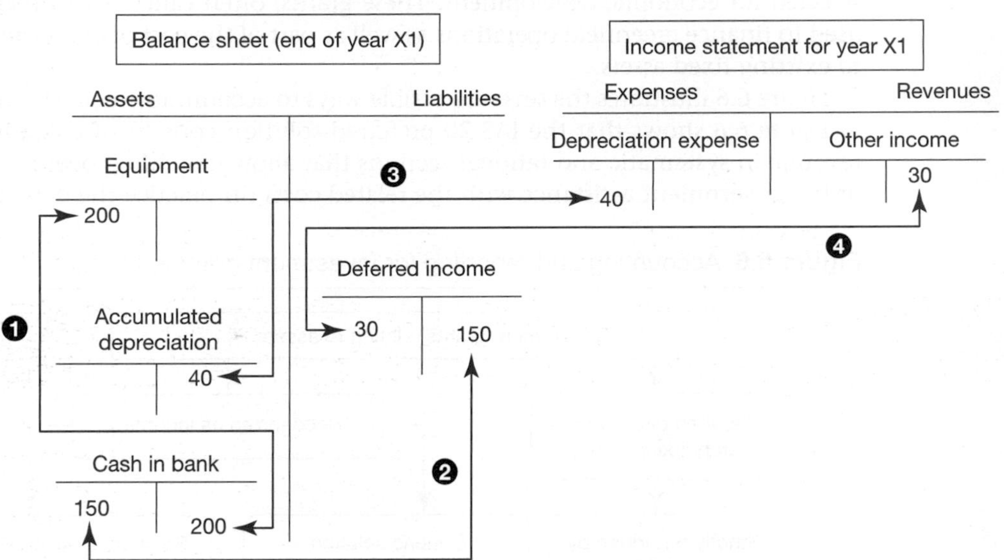

❶ Purchase of the equipment on cash.

❷ Receipt of the investment grant, which is recorded as a deferred income on the liabilities side of the balance sheet.

❸ Depreciation of the equipment over five years (annual depreciation allowance is 200 CU/5 = 40 CU per year).

❹ Every year, for five years, the deferred income is transferred to the income statement, following the pattern of the depreciation of the fixed asset (150/5 = 30).

Real-life example Bayer

Bayer, the German-based international chemicals and health care group, states in the notes to its annual report 2004 that, in accordance with IAS 20, grants and subsidies that serve to promote investment are reflected in the balance sheet as deferred income. The amounts are gradually amortized to income during the useful lives of the respective assets. Deferred income as of 31 December 2004 includes €106 million (2003: €121 million) in grants and subsidies received from government. The amount reversed and recognized in income was €33 million (2003: €23 million).

2.8.2 Grants related to income

These grants are defined by IAS 20 (§ 3) as government grants other than those related to assets. In practice, they are also called operating grants or subsidies. They include capacity development grants when the capacity refers to the development of competences or skills. An example of an operating subsidy could be that of an incentive grant awarded to a business that creates new jobs or provides gainful employment to certain categories of unemployed persons. Grants related to income are included in the income statement when they are received, as an income (in the category 'other income') or as a deduction of the related expense.

2.8.3 Forgivable loans and repayable grants

These loans are defined as loans for which the lender accepts to waive repayment under certain prescribed conditions such as, for example, the effective creation within a specified time span of a given number of jobs. If the conditions are not met, the grant is, in principle, repayable. Other grants are repayable in case of success, such as, for example, a grant to help in research and development or a grant to help develop a new market. These grants are recorded in the balance sheet (on the liabilities side) until the condition has been met or it is established that the conditions will not be met. They are recorded under the special caption 'conditional advances received from the state' that lists these grants immediately next to shareholders' equity. At the end of the life of such a grant, if the conditions are not met the grant is repayable and will be handled exactly as would a normal loan. If, conversely, the conditions are met, an operating revenue or an exceptional revenue will be recorded.

Key points

- The issue of revenue recognition deals with when and how much revenue to recognize.
- Criteria for recognition vary according to the type of transaction: sales of goods, rendering of services, or use of enterprise assets yielding interest, royalties, or dividends.
- Revenue from the sale of goods should be recognized when several conditions have been satisfied, and mainly when the enterprise has transferred to the buyer the significant risks and rewards of ownership of the goods.
- When the outcome of a transaction involving the rendering of services spanning several accounting periods (such as in long-term contracts) can be estimated reliably, revenue and costs associated with the transaction should be recognized on the balance sheet date as a function of the stage or percentage of completion of the transaction.
- There may be some divergences between tax regulation and accounting rules. When these differences relate to the timing of the recognition they are called 'temporary differences'.
- Deferred tax assets or liabilities are created when the income tax expense is based on the pre-tax reported income (defined according to accounting rules) and not on the taxable income (based on the tax rules).
- The 'percentage of completion method', which consists of recording costs and revenue associated with the contracts as the work proceeds, is the preferred method for the recognition of profit in long-term contracts.
- Accounting standards stipulate that for an income statement to be useful in terms of evaluation of performance and permitting extrapolations, it must present separately and distinctly what pertains to 'normal' and recurrent business activities, and what pertains to actions, decisions, and events that are occasional and unusual.
- The comprehensive income includes revenue and expenses that are usually excluded from net income (e.g., unrealized gains and losses on short-term investments). This concept aims at showing the global performance of the company.
- Government assistance (grants, subsidies, subventions or premiums) raises revenue recognition issues.

Review (solutions are at the back of the book)

Review 6.1 Schultz Accountancy Firm (1)

Topic: Revenue recognition
Related part of the chapter: Core issues

Mr Schultz, the managing partner of an accounting firm, is concerned by some of his clients who adopted specific rules in terms of revenue recognition. He provides the following list of some of the rules he has found in the notes to his customers' financial statements:

(a) An advertising agency records as revenue the full commission as soon as the advertisement campaign has been fully prepared.

(b) Atrium Auditorium Inc. (AA Inc.) sells subscription packages to several series of concerts to be held between October X1 and September X2. Most concerts will take place in the fall and the spring and a sprinkling of events will take place during the summer. Customers are expected to pay cash for their subscription. AA Inc.'s reporting year ends on 31 December. In its income statement for period X1, AA Inc. records as revenue 3/12 (three months) of the amounts received as subscription from paying customers. The remaining 9/12 of the cash intake will be recognized in X2.

(c) Boticcelli Markets is specialized in home delivery of groceries, fruit, and produce. It expects cash on delivery. It recognizes revenue at the time of payment.

(d) The Olympic Sports Club is a membership-only club. The yearly admission fee allows the members to enter the premises. Members have the possibility of paying the membership fee in installments for a small surcharge. All services within the club are billed to the members at about 20% below the open enrolment market prices of competing clubs. Membership fees are recognized in the income statement in equal installments over the duration of the membership (generally one year, although discounts are granted to members who pay upfront for longer periods). Membership fees already paid cannot be reimbursed.

Required

Evaluate whether the accounting policies adopted by the different companies are acceptable or not. If you feel they are not, which policy should have been adopted?

Review 6.2 Schall Company

Topic: Deferred taxation
Related part of the chapter: Core issues

Schall Company realized in the year X1 a fiscal pre-tax income of 100 CU. This income includes taking into account a one-off royalty fee expense for 10 CU (which was paid upfront in X1). The royalty fee is for the use by Schall Co. of a new technology for two years. Accordingly, Schall Co.'s accountant chose to recognize as an expense, for reporting purposes, half the fee in year X1, and the second half in year X2. However, tax regulations require an immediate deduction in tax accounts. The income tax rate is 40%.

The following table summarizes the data:

Pre-tax income before recording the royalty fee	110
Royalty fee expense recorded for tax purposes	10
Pre-tax income after recording the fee	100
Royalty fee expense to be split over two years	10
Amortization of the fee expense over two years	5
Income tax rate	40%

Required

1. Compute the deferred taxation, assuming that the pre-tax income before recording the royalty fee expense is the same in X2 as in X1.
2. Record the deferred taxation at the end of X1 and at the end of X2.

Assignments

Assignment 6.1
Schultz Accountancy Firm (2)

Topic: Revenue recognition
Related part of the chapter: Core issues

Mr Schultz, the managing partner of an accounting firm, is concerned by some specific rules of revenue recognition adopted by some of his clients. The following list contains some of the rules he found in their notes to financial statements:

(a) DPS Business School Inc. (DPSBS Inc.) invoices its students at the beginning of each quarter for the quarterly tuition fees. DPSBS Inc. recognizes revenue only when tuition is actually paid by the students (or whomever, on their behalf). The first quarter X2 tuition invoices were mailed on 1 December X1 and all the tuition fee payments have been received in full by 15 December X1. No adjusting entry has been recorded.

(b) The *Commercial Times* is a newspaper, which receives payment for subscriptions. *Commercial Times* has a circulation of 750,000 copies and sells over three-quarters of these through annual subscription. Readers subscribe at any time during the year and there seems to be no clear seasonality in new subscriptions or cancellations. The *Commercial Times*' accountant is in the habit of recognizing as revenue for any year half of the cash received for annual subscriptions in that year plus half the subscriptions payments received in the previous year.

(c) A bridge club invoices a membership fee to its members who receive in return the magazine *Bridge Forever* and are entitled to special prices on other magazines. The club, in order to simplify its recording of fees, spreads the fee revenue on a straight-line basis over the period of membership.

(d) A seller (shipper) transfers goods to a buyer (recipient) who undertakes to sell the goods on behalf of the seller (consignment sales). The shipper recognizes the revenue at the time of delivery to the buyer.

Required

Evaluate whether the policies adopted by the different companies are acceptable or not. In the latter case, which policy should have been adopted?

Assignment 6.2
Nielsen Company

Topic: Deferred taxation
Related part of the chapter: Core issues

During year X1 the Nielsen Company reported sales of 2,400 CU and total expenses of 1,800 CU. It has no preexisting deferred tax liability or tax asset. The following information is provided in relation to year X1:

1. Marketable securities held by Nielsen Co. have a market value at the end of the year which exceeds their book value by an amount of 8 CU. This potential gain is taxable as pertaining to year X1, but will be reported to shareholders only at the time of the sale.
2. The company accrued interest due on a bank loan for 16 CU. This interest (included in the expenses mentioned) will be tax deductible only when paid (which will be the case in year X2).
3. Nielsen Co. uses an accelerated method of depreciation for certain assets. The depreciation allowance for year X1 for tax purposes exceeds that reported to shareholders (included in the total expenses mentioned above) by 250 CU.
4. During year X1 a fine for an accidental pollution occurrence (included in the total expenses mentioned above) was paid for a total amount of 10 CU.
5. Part of the liquidity of Nielsen Co. is invested in tax-free municipal bonds. During year X1 these yielded a return of 40 CU (not included in the sales revenue mentioned above).
6. Warranty costs are provisioned at the level of 1.5% of sales. The corresponding amount has been included in the total expenses mentioned above. Actual expenses incurred during year X1 for services and repairs included in the warranty contract amounted to 15 CU.

   Assume the tax rate is 40%.

Required

1. Compute the income before income tax for shareholder reporting.
2. Analyze each event with regard to taxation in terms of permanent and timing differences.
3. Compute the income tax payable to the tax authorities and income tax expense for shareholder reporting. (Local GAAP allow that reported tax expense be calculated according to GAAP rules.)
4. Record the income tax expense for year X1.

Assignment 6.3
Repsol YPF*

Topic: Extraordinary/exceptional items
Related part of the chapter: Advanced issues

Repsol YPF, a Spanish oil and gas company, publishes the following information (*source*: Annual report 2004). The detail of the extraordinary revenue and expenses included in the accompanying consolidated statements of income for 2004 and 2003 is as follows:

	Revenues/(Expenses)	
€ millions	2004	2003
Extraordinary expenses:		
Labor force restructuring (1)	(76)	(32)
Losses on fixed assets	(36)	(6)
Provision for commitments and contingent liabilities (2)	(422)	(69)
Extraordinary provisions future losses (3)	(343)	(318)
Other extraordinary expenses	(125)	(147)
	(1,002)	(572)
Extraordinary revenues:		
Gains on fixed asset disposals	9	13
Gains on disposals of Equity Investment (4)	61	76
Variation in fixed asset provisions (5)	121	249
Subsidies and other deferred revenues transferred to income	5	5
Revenues from reversal of provisions for contingencies and expenses	17	36
Other extraordinary revenues (6)	107	39
	320	418
	(682)	(154)

(1) In 2004, this included the cost of restructuring after a number of senior executives terminated their working relationships with the Group. This restructuring was agreed and those affected informed at end-2004.

(2) In 2004, this included part of the provisions for tax contingencies of Group companies, basically in Spain and Argentina.

(3) The main items included in 2003 are the provision arising from the valuation of a commitment to transport certain quantities of crude oil through an oil pipeline in Ecuador (€162 million), the provision for litigation (€35 million), the provision for major repairs (€30 million), the provision to the key employee loyalty allowance (€28 million), and the special provision arising from the modification of the actuarial variables used in the calculation of the provision for pensions of Maxus Energy Corporation, a subsidiary of YPF (€27 million). The main items included in 2004 are: (i) an €84 million provision representing the discount to present value of an undertaking to transport certain quantities of crude oil through an oil pipeline in Ecuador (as a result of events in 2004 this item is reviewed at each year-end); (ii) a €56 million provision for the estimated loss on termination of an asset swap contract between Repsol YPF Brasil, S.A. and several Petrobras Group companies as a result of changes in the values specified in the contract over 2004; (iii) a €61 million provision for litigation; and (iv) a €25 million extraordinary provision in respect of loyalty programs for key personnel.

(4) In 2003 this account includes the gains arising from the sale of 6.78% of CLH to Oman Oil Company. This transaction completed the sale process stipulated by Royal Decree 6/2000, under which the individual holding in CLH of each shareholder cannot exceed 25% and the aggregate holding of Repsol YPF, Cepsa, and BP cannot exceed 45% of CLH's capital stock. In 2004, this caption basically covers the proceeds from Gas Natural SDG's sale of a 12.5% stake in Enagas, S.A. and the sale of Global Companies LLC.

(5) In 2004 and 2003 this caption includes, among other items, €208 million and €275 million, respectively, relating to the writeback of some of the provision recorded in past years as a result of the comparison between fair value or cash-flows, discounted as appropriate, from proved and unproved reserves (the latter are subject to a risk effect) of oil and gas and the net book value of the corresponding assets.

This revaluation, basically reflecting changes in crude prices and reserves, is carried out at every year-end. Also, in 2004, changes in the Brazilian market led to a diminution in value of the Brazilian service stations business, giving rise to a provision of €58 million.

(6) In 2004, this account includes €51 million for upcoming adjustments to the prices in CLH's sale contracts signed in previous years.

Required

1. Compare the expenses and income with the definitions of extraordinary items given in the Advanced issues section of this chapter.
2. What do you think of the terminology used by the Repsol group?
3. Explain the item 'Subsidies and other deferred revenues transferred to income'.

References

AICPA (1973) Accounting Principles Board Opinion No. 30: Reporting the Results of Operations – Reporting the Effects of Disposal of a Segment of a Business, and Extraordinary, Unusual, and Infrequently Occurring Events and Transactions. New York, NY.

FASB (1997) Statement of Financial Accounting Standards No. 130: Reporting Comprehensive Income, Norwalk, CT.

IASB (1989) Framework for the Preparation and Presentation of Financial Statements, London.

IASB (1993a) International Accounting Standard No. 11: Construction Contracts, London.

IASB (1993b) International Accounting Standard No. 18: Revenue, London.

IASB (reformatted 1994) International Accounting Standard No. 20: Accounting for Government Grants and Disclosure of Government Assistance, London.

IASB (2000) International Accounting Standard No. 12: Income Taxes, London.

IASB (2003a) International Accounting Standard No. 1: Presentation of Financial Statements, London.

IASB (2003b) International Accounting Standard No. 8: Net Profit or Loss for the Period, Fundamental Errors and Changes in Accounting Policies, London.

IASB (2004) International Financial Reporting Standard No. 5: Non-current Assets Held for Sale and Discontinued Operations, London.

Skousen F., Stice J., and Stice E. K. (2003) *Intermediate Accounting*, South-Western College Publishing, Cincinnati, CH.

Further reading

Artsbert, K. (1996) The link between commercial accounting and tax accounting in Sweden. *European Accounting Review*, 5(Supplement), 795–814.

Ballas, A. A. (1999) Valuation implications of exceptional and extraordinary items. *British Accounting Review*, 31(3), 281–95.

Bauman, C. C., Bauman, M. P., and Halsey, R. F. (2001) Do firms use the deferred tax asset valuation allowance to manage earnings? *Journal of the American Taxation Association*, 23(Supplement), 27–48.

Christiansen, M. (1996) The relationship between accounting and taxation in Denmark. *European Accounting Review*, 5(Supplement), 815–33.

Eberhartinger, E. L. E. (1999) The impact of tax rules on financial reporting in Germany, France, and the UK. *The International Journal of Accounting*, 34(1), 93–119.

Eilifsen, A. (1996) The relationship between accounting and taxation in Norway. *European Accounting Review*, 5(Supplement), 835–44.

Frydlender, A., and Pham, D. (1996) Relationships between accounting and taxation in France. *European Accounting Review*, 5(Supplement), 845–57.

Holeckova, J. (1996) Relationship between accounting and taxation in the Czech Republic. *European Accounting Review*, 5(Supplement), 859–69.

Holland, K., and Jackson, R. H. G. (2004) Earnings management and deferred tax, *Accounting and Business Research*, 34(2), 101–23.

Hoogendoorn, M. N. (1996) Accounting and taxation in Europe – A comparative overview. *European Accounting Review*, 5(Supplement), 783–94.

Hoogendoorn, M. N. (1996) Accounting and taxation in the Netherlands. *European Accounting Review*, 5(Supplement), 871–82.

Jaruga, A., Walinska, E., and Baniewicz, A. (1996) The relationship between accounting and taxation in Poland. *European Accounting Review*, 5(Supplement), 883–97.

Järvenpää, M. (1996) The relationship between taxation and financial accounting in Finland. *European Accounting Review*, 5(Supplement), 899–914.

Jorissen, A., and Maes, L. (1996) The principle of fiscal neutrality: The cornerstone of the relationship between financial reporting and taxation in Belgium. *European Accounting Review*, 5(Supplement), 915–31.

Lamb, M. (1996) The relationship between accounting and taxation: The United Kingdom. *European Accounting Review*, 5(Supplement), 933–49.

Pierce, A. (1996) The relationship between accounting and taxation in the Republic of Ireland. *European Accounting Review*, 5(Supplement), 951–62.

Pfaff, D., and Schröer, T. (1996) The relationship between financial and tax accounting in Germany – the authoritativeness and reverse authoritativeness principle. *European Accounting Review*, 5(Supplement), 963–79.

Rocchi, F. (1996) Accounting and taxation in Italy. *European Accounting Review*, 5(Supplement), 981–89.

Additional material on the website

Go to http://www.thomsonlearning.co.uk/stolowylebas2 for further information.

The following appendices to this chapter are available on the dedicated website:

Appendix 6.1: Illustration of the two methods for reporting of long-term contracts
Appendix 6.2: Installment sales
Appendix 6.3: Recognition of a net deferred tax asset
Appendix 6.4: Illustration of the principle of carry-back and carry-forward
Appendix 6.5: Deferred taxation and changes in tax rates
Appendix 6.6: Extraordinary and exceptional items

Notes

1. When a business simultaneously manages several contracts, some generating a positive cash balance and some generating a negative one, the management may choose, erroneously, to blur the results of each contract and consolidate the cash flows. This bad practice is depriving both management and shareholders of relevant information about the risks and profitability of the types of contracts the firms manages.
2. For more detail, see *Corporate Taxes 2004–2005, Worldwide Tax Summaries*, PricewaterhouseCoopers, Wiley.
3. The link between depreciation and cash flow is developed in Chapter 7, Advanced issues.
4. From *Corporate Taxes 2004–2005, Worldwide Tax Summaries*, PricewaterhouseCoopers, Wiley.

C7

Chapter 7

Tangible fixed assets

Learning objectives

After studying this chapter, you will understand:

- That tangible assets represent a significant portion of both total and fixed assets. This proportion is heavily industry-related. The depreciation expense on tangible fixed assets often represents a large expense item in the income statement.
- That tangible assets are physically observable items that are held for use in the production, sale, or supply of goods or services, for rental to others, or for administrative purposes, and are expected to be used during more than one period.
- That tangible assets are different from inventories.
- How to distinguish capital expenditures (which are capitalized as assets) and revenue expenditures (which are included in expenses).
- What the concept of depreciation represents.
- What the main methods of depreciation are.
- What the main concepts are that allow the preparation of a depreciation schedule (residual value, depreciable amount, useful life).
- How to record internally constructed tangible assets.
- How to handle financing or borrowing (interest) costs.
- How to integrate tangible assets and depreciation in financial statement analysis.

The asset side of the balance sheet comprises both current and long-term – or fixed – assets. Current assets are those that are created or used in the operating cycle of the firm. They turn over rather rapidly (the speed of rotation is, of course, specific to each industrial or commercial sector), and, in the case of a well-managed firm, their turnover cycle is generally much shorter than the accounting period. Fixed assets are those that reflect the facilities and 'capacity' provided by the firm that allow the operating cycle to take place. These assets create economic benefits over several periods, and represent significant investments that must be put in place before any activity can take place.

Among fixed assets, tangible assets represent a significant portion of total assets and the related depreciation expense can be a large expense item, thus impacting the income calculation greatly. Table 7.1 illustrates the diversity of the proportions that tangible assets represent in balance sheets of an illustrative, but non-representative, sample of industries and countries. The importance of tangible assets in financial statements is generally defined through two ratios:

net tangible assets/total net assets, and

depreciation expense/net sales.

...7.1 Weight of tangible assets

Company (country – activity)	Currency	Tangible assets (net amount)	Total assets (net amount)	% of total assets	Depreciation expense	Sales	% of sales
Irish Continental (Ireland – Shipping, transport)	€m	320	377	84.9	25	293	8.5
Stora-Enso (Finland – Paper production)	€m	9,755	16,412	59.4	1,172	12,396	9.5
China Petroleum & Chemical Corporation (China – Oil and chemistry)	RMBm	270,136	460,081	58.7	30,766	397,789	7.7
Club Méditerranée (France – Leisure)	€m	761	1,482	51.3	431	9,690	4.4
Repsol (Spain – Oil and gas)	€m	19,677	38,943	50.5	2,396	40,585	5.9
Heineken (Netherlands – Brewery group)	€m	5,127	10,418	49.2	773	10,005	7.7
Temple-Inland (USA – Paper packaging products)	$m	1,843	4,638	39.7	238	3,501	6.8
Elkem (Norway – Metals and materials [production])	NOKm	7,252	18,951	38.3	936	22,043	4.2
Interbrew (Belgium – Brewery group)	€m	5,298	18,596	28.5	621	8,568	7.2
Pirelli (Italy – Tires, cables and systems)	€000	2,065,211	10,385,732	19.9	265,387	7,114,085	3.7
Honda Motor Co. (Japan – Automobile and motorcycle industry)	¥m	1,435,531	8,328,768	17.2	213,445	8,162,600	2.6
Philips (Netherlands – Consumer products)	€m	4,997	30,723	16.3	1,402	30,319	4.6
Securitas (Sweden – Security systems)	SEKm	5,820	36,231	16.1	1,540	59,687	2.6
Taylor Nelson Sofres (UK – Market information)	£m	84	853	9.8	24	929	2.6
ISS (Denmark – Support services)	DKKm	1,793	29,676	6.0	535	40,355	1.3

All data are extracted from 2004 annual reports. The currency is the one used in the annual report.

Companies are classified in decreasing order of percentage of net tangible assets over net total assets. The table shows that this ratio is heavily influenced by the sector of activity, services companies appearing at the bottom. The ratio varies from 84.9 to 6.0%.

After a short presentation of the various categories of fixed assets, this chapter will mainly deal with reporting and accounting issues (valuation and income effects) regarding tangible fixed assets.

The qualifier 'tangible' distinguishes assets from those that are called 'intangible' (see Chapter 8) or financial (see Chapter 13). A tangible asset is one that has a physical reality or substance such as a building or a piece of equipment, while an intangible asset does not have a physical substance but represents an idea or knowledge (for example, the capitalized costs incurred in developing a patented product, technique, or technology) or a right (for example, the price paid for a license to use a technology developed by someone else, or a leasehold). A financial fixed asset (neither tangible nor intangible) is generally representing the historical value of acquiring a participation in the capital of some other business or enterprise.

Fixed assets are, by nature, the most illiquid assets on the balance sheet. In countries where the accounting tradition is more 'patrimonial' they will be shown at the top of the list of assets, while in countries where the accounting culture emphasizes operations or liquidity, the tangible fixed assets will be listed at the bottom of the list.

1 Core issues

1.1 Categories of fixed assets

Fixed assets can be divided into three categories: tangible, intangible (see Chapter 8), and financial (see Chapter 13).

The first two categories are sometimes confused since their difference is not one of purpose or life cycle but only one of physical substance. Table 7.2 presents the common and distinguishing characteristics of the three categories of fixed assets.

Since all three categories of fixed assets are long lived, a distinguishing feature is also the way their historical cost is allocated (distributed) over time. The distribution over time of the cost of acquisition of an asset is called depreciation or amortization. The matching principle calls for the depreciation pattern over time to, more or less, reflect the consumption of the 'productive[1] capacity' or 'productive potential' of the asset (at least in principle, as we will see below, there are exceptions to this rule). Table 7.3 highlights how each category's and subcategory's cost of consumption of the productive capacity provided by the asset (i.e., depreciation expense) is recorded for reporting income to shareholders.

Systematic allocation of the acquisition cost of an asset (i.e., depreciation, amortization, or depletion) reflects an ongoing process of consumption of the potential offered by that asset (in the course of business and in a way reflecting as much as possible the pace of activity), while an unsystematic allocation (called impairment) reflects the recognition of some form of random, unpredictable, or catastrophic (often external) event that modifies the value of the asset rather than reflecting the consumption of the potential of economic benefit generation provided by the fixed asset.

Table 7.2 Tangible, intangible, and financial assets compared

Tangible assets	Intangible assets	Financial assets
Used in the course of the operations of the business (production, sale or distribution of goods and services) and not acquired for the purpose of resale		
Long-term (long-lived) in nature and usually subject to 'consumption' reflected by depreciation, amortization, depletion, or impairment		Long-term (long-lived) in nature and are generally not susceptible to depreciation
Possess physical substance	Lack physical substance	

1.2 Accounting issues relating to tangible assets

Figure 7.1 summarizes the various accounting issues that arise when reporting truly and fairly on tangible fixed assets. (The diagram also indicates in which part of this chapter each issue will be dealt with.)

Table 7.3 Fixed assets and cost allocation

Asset classification	Examples	Systematic cost allocation	Unsystematic cost allocation
Tangible assets	Buildings, equipment, furniture, machinery	Depreciation	Impairment (rare)
	Land	No systematic cost allocation	Impairment (rare)
	Natural resources (oil and gas reserves, mineral deposits – e.g., mines and quarries)	Depletion	Impairment (rare)
Intangible assets	With a finite useful life: patents, copyrights, franchises, leaseholds, software	Amortization	Impairment (possible)
	With an indefinite useful life: brands, trademarks, goodwill	No systematic cost allocation	Impairment (common when appropriate)
Financial fixed assets	Investments	No systematic cost allocation	Impairment (common when appropriate)

Figure 7.1 Accounting issues in reporting tangible assets

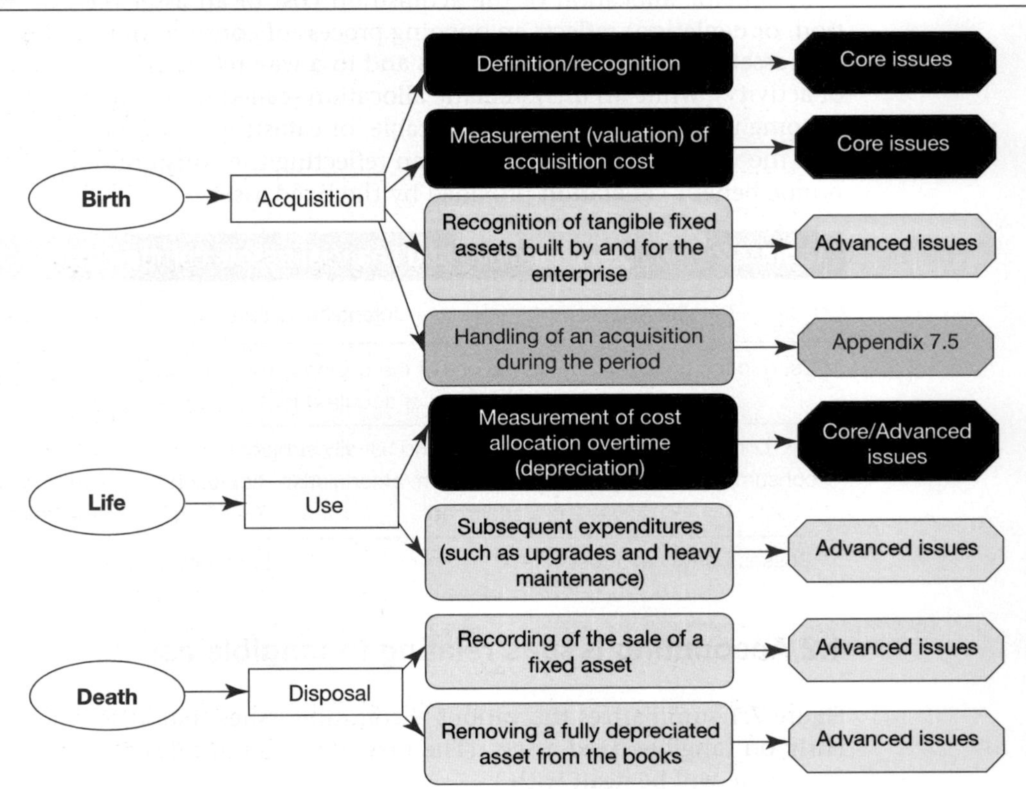

The acquisition of a tangible fixed asset raises many other issues, which will not be developed in this book such as the valuation of an asset acquired (1) with deferred payments, (2) through the issuance of securities, (3) by donation, or (4) in exchange of other assets.[2]

1.3 Definition of tangible fixed assets

1.3.1 General definition

The vocabulary used in businesses to refer to tangible fixed assets tends to be diverse and even sometimes misleading: terms like 'property, plant and equipment' (PPE), and the less appropriate 'plant assets', 'operational assets', or 'fixed assets', are often used interchangeably with the proper term of tangible fixed assets. IAS 16 (IASB 2003) defines (§ 6) as 'property, plant and equipment' the 'tangible items that:

(a) Are held for use in the production or supply of goods or services, for rental to others, or for administrative purposes; and

(b) Are expected to be used during more than one period'.

In the remainder of this chapter, we will use the term 'tangible assets' as synonymous with 'property, plant, and equipment' and all the other equivalent terms. Tangible assets include:

- land, freeholds, and leaseholds;
- building structures (stores, factories, warehouses, offices);
- equipment (machinery, tools, fixtures);
- vehicles;
- furniture and fittings;
- payments on account (payments made by a company towards the acquisition of as yet undelivered tangible assets);
- tangible assets during their construction (cost of purchasing, constructing, and installing tangible assets ahead of their productive use).

From the preceding definition, it would appear that the identification of a tangible asset should pose no problem. However, asset valuation and revenue recognition require that a clear distinction be made between fixed assets and inventories, on the one hand, and fixed assets and expenses, on the other.

1.3.2 Difference between tangible assets and inventories

The principal criterion used for making the distinction between tangible assets and inventories is the nature of the company's activity, which determines the purpose for which the asset is held – own use, transformation, or resale without transformation. Thus, any type of tangible asset may be a fixed asset in one company and an inventory in another. The distinction is, of course, important because it affects the timing of income recognition. Tangible assets are subject to an annual depreciation expense over their normal useful life, while inventories are not. Interesting definitional issues can arise, for example, in the treatment of livestock. What kind of asset is an ox?

- A dray ox is a tangible asset (just like a tractor would be).
- An ox reared for meat is an inventory (work-in-process inventory while on the hoof, and sellable inventory after slaughter).
- A stud ox may be either a tangible asset (if the owner owns a few such oxen and does not trade them) or an inventory (if the owner is in the business of selling and buying stud oxen)!

However, items that are carried in inventory are not all for resale. It is normal for businesses to have inventories of supplies, consumables, and maintenance parts. For example, for the latter, withdrawals from inventory will normally be expensed (consumed and recognized as such in the income statement) as repair and maintenance costs. However, when the unit cost of a spare part is intrinsically large and is an integral part of the business process' ability to remain operational, it may be accounted for as a fixed asset. For example, an airplane jet engine in working order kept in inventory to be used, as a temporary replacement, during maintenance operations (off line) on the original engine would be treated as a tangible asset (no scheduled airline can operate effectively unless it has access to available replacement engines), and, as such, the spare engine should be subject to an annual depreciation expense, even before being brought into operational use.

1.3.3 Difference between tangible assets and expenses (expenditures)

'An asset is a resource (a) controlled by an entity as a result of past events and (b) from which future economic benefits are expected to flow to the entity' (IASB 1989: § 49 and IASB 2004b: § 8).

Revenue and capital expenditure A 'Revenue expenditure' is a consumption of resources for the purpose of generating revenue. They include the costs of production and transformation, costs of marketing and distributing, and costs of administering the enterprise. Following the matching principle, all expenses incurred in creating and satisfying demand are called revenue expenditures and, as such, recognized (expensed) in the income statement when incurred.

Some expenses or expenditures are incurred in: (1) the course of bringing an asset 'online'; or (2) in upgrading it; or (3) in carrying a major maintenance operation required to ensure or extend the economic life of the asset. Any of these expenses change (modify and, hopefully, extend) the potential for future economic benefits of the asset. In the first case, the expenditure could be either considered as a normal consumption of resources in the course of doing business (and, as such, recognized as an expense of the period), or, and it probably would be more logical to do so, considered as an increase in the value of the original book value of the asset (the asset cannot be brought in operations without these upfront preparation costs). The latter two cases [(2) and (3)] call unambiguously for a capitalization of the expense. The book value of the asset to date is increased by the amount of the expense (and probably leading to a recalculation of the depreciation schedule).

The ambiguity of the materiality of an upgrade or maintenance expense (proportion of the expenditure to the value of a new asset) leads sometimes to debate as to the proper handling of that expense. Some businesses argue they serve their shareholders best in expensing (in the period incurred) these upgrading or maintenance expenses, while others prefer to capitalize them and depreciate them over the periods during which benefits will be derived. Table 7.4 summarizes the distinction between 'Capital expenditure', which are recorded as assets (i.e., capitalized), and 'Revenue (generating) expenditure', which will be recognized in the period in which they are incurred.

Focus on capital expenditure Capital expenditure should meet at least one of the following criteria:

1. The quantity of economic benefits or services received from using the asset will be increased through a longer useful life.
2. The quantity of economic benefits received from using the asset will be increased with more units of output.
3. The quality of the services received from using the asset will be increased.

An expense or expenditure that meets at least one of these three conditions is considered a capital expenditure.

Table 7.4 Capital and revenue expenditure

Type of expenditure	Definition	Accounting	Depreciation
Capital expenditure	Expenses incurred for the purpose of generating future economic benefits	Recorded as assets	Yes
Revenue expenditure	Expenses caused by the short-term usage – or normal maintenance – of the revenues generating potential of an asset (examples: minor spare parts, oil and cooling fluids, maintenance expenses, minor repairs expenses)	Charged as expense as incurred	No

'Small' equipment The decision of whether a specific expenditure should be handled as either the creation of a tangible asset or an expense is often made solely on grounds of materiality. Many countries' GAAP and tax regulations have established minimum threshold amounts (arbitrary, thus not necessarily coherent between the two sources of regulation) to facilitate the distinction between expense (expensing) and asset (capitalizing). Thus, acquired resources of small unitary value that may benefit future periods (such as off-the-shelf software packages, small tools, furniture, and office equipment) may be fully expensed in the year of acquisition and not ever be listed as a fixed asset at all. For example, French tax law states that any industrial or office equipment with an invoiced price below €500 can be expensed, but must be dealt with as an asset if its amount is above that threshold. Thresholds are often relative to the size of the firm (however defined). For example, in the USA, practice acknowledges the following thresholds: $100 (for a 'small' company) and $10,000 (for a 'large' company).

As regulatory texts or practice allow companies to expense capital expenditures and revenue expenditures of an amount below a certain limit, most enterprises have generally opted for immediately expensing all those below that threshold. Doing so has two advantages:

1. It will reduce taxable profit in the year of acquisition by an amount much greater than would have an allowance for depreciation expense. Less taxable profit early means a higher immediate cash flow, all things being equal and larger cash flows are generally considered to be good for the company. Of course, if the expense is recognized this year, the taxable profit next year will be higher, but 'sooner is always better than later' when it comes to cash flow. … (This leads, at times, some businesses to request that their suppliers break-up large purchases of maintenance contracts with a value above the threshold into several smaller invoices, so as to be able to expense each individual invoice immediately, and thus reduce their immediate tax burden. Such a practice is, of course, misleading to the shareholders and other financial information users and should not be condoned.)
2. There will be no fiscal obligation to maintain, for these items, the detailed records of acquisition cost and accumulated depreciation that are usually mandated by tax regulations.

1.4 Cost of acquisition

1.4.1 Definition

Acquisition 'cost is the amount of cash or cash equivalents paid or the fair value of the other consideration given to acquire an asset at the time of its acquisition or construction'

(IAS 16: § 6). In general, the cost of acquisition is the cash or cash equivalents paid to obtain the asset and to bring it to the location and condition necessary for its intended use.

More precisely, IAS 16 (§ 16) states: 'The cost of an item of property, plant and equipment comprises (a) its purchase price, including import duties and non-refundable purchase taxes, after deducting trade discounts and rebates; (b) any costs directly attributable to bringing the asset to the location and condition necessary for it to be capable of operating in the manner intended by management; (c) the initial estimate of the costs of dismantling and removing the item and restoring the site on which it is located, the obligation for which an entity incurs either when the item is acquired or as a consequence of having used the item during a particular period for purposes other than to produce inventories during that period'.

1.4.2 Recording of the acquisition of an asset

Let us take the example of a piece of equipment with a cost of acquisition, which can be broken down as follows (in CU):

Purchase price	40
Import duties	3
Transportation	5
Professional fees	2
Total	50

The acquisition cost is therefore 50 CU. Figure 7.2 describes the recording procedure when the asset is acquired.

Figure 7.2 Recording of the acquisition

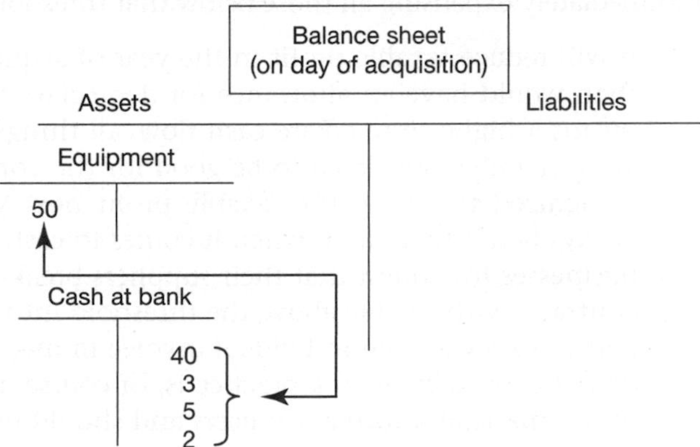

1.4.3 Examples of components of the acquisition cost

Examples of directly attributable costs (i.e., which should be included in the cost of acquisition) are provided in IAS 16 (§ 17): '(a) costs of employee benefits (...) arising directly from the construction or acquisition of the item of property, plant and equipment; (b) costs of site preparation; (c) initial delivery and handling costs; (d) installation and assembly costs; (e) costs of testing whether the asset is functioning properly, after deducting the net proceeds from selling any items produced while bringing the asset to that location and condition (such as samples produced when testing equipment); and (f) professional fees' (such as for architects and engineers).

However, according to IAS 16 (§ 19), 'examples of costs that are not costs of an item of property, plant and equipment are:

(a) Costs of opening a new facility;
(b) Costs of introducing a new product or service (including costs of advertising and promotional activities);
(c) Costs of conducting business in a new location or with a new class of customer (including costs of staff training); and
(d) Administration and other general overhead costs'.

Appendix 7.1 lists some examples of components of the acquisition cost of tangible assets as reported in notes to financial statements.

1.5 Depreciation

IAS 16 (§ 6) defines depreciation as 'the systematic allocation of the depreciable amount of an asset over its useful life'. In other words, depreciation is the process of allocating the cost of a long-term asset in a **rational and systematic manner** over its useful life in order to achieve a matching of expenses and revenues. The yearly depreciation allowance ('depreciation expense') is therefore a normal component of the expense side of the income statement.

With the notable exception of land, the book value (acquisition cost minus accumulated depreciation) of each and all tangible fixed assets will diminish irreversibly due to the effect of the passage of time, use, and any other reason, reflecting the diminution of the productive potential of the assets. When the obsolescence of the potential for future benefits is unpredictable (unsystematic reduction in value due to unexpected or catastrophic events), the loss of value of an asset is not recognized through depreciation but will lead to a write-down (see the concept of 'impairment' in Advanced issues).

In the definition of depreciation, two concepts are important:

- *Rational manner*: The depreciation expense is related to the flow of benefits expected to arise from the asset.
- *Systematic manner*: The computation of the depreciation expense is based on a formula, which was decided at the time of acquisition or before, and cannot be modified during the life of the asset. This characteristic is designed to prevent any possibility of income smoothing that might have happened if the amount of the periodic depreciation allowance had been left to the whim of the management or of the accountant.

In order to establish the systematic and rational schedule of depreciation of a tangible asset, several parameters need to be documented:

- existence of different 'components' ('parts') of the asset (see below § 1.5.1);
- residual value of the asset;
- depreciable amount;
- useful life duration;
- choice of a depreciation method.

They will lead to:

- a depreciation schedule (or several, in case of the existence of different 'components' of the asset, each having, for example, a specific life duration);
- a book value, which is periodically updated.

Each of these points will be covered in succession. The last section of the Core issues will introduce the procedures for recording depreciation. Some unusual methods of depreciation, as well as impairment, the impact of depreciation on financial statements, and the problem of partial years will be dealt with in the Advanced issues section of the chapter. 'Depletion' (depreciation recorded for mineral deposits) is a specific topic especially relevant for countries with important exhaustible natural resources. It is not, however, covered in detail in this book.[3]

1.5.1 Components of a tangible asset

'Each part of an item of property, plant and equipment with a cost that is significant in relation to the total cost of the item shall be depreciated separately' (IAS 16: § 43). 'An entity allocates the amount initially recognized in respect of an item of property, plant and equipment to its significant parts and depreciates separately each such part. For example, it may be appropriate to depreciate separately the airframe and engines of an aircraft' (IAS 16: § 44). What the IASB calls 'part' of an asset is often referred to by practitioners as 'component' of that asset. The method required by the IASB is thus called 'depreciation by component' or 'component accounting'.

An asset can, if appropriate, be separated between its 'structure' and its 'components', each part having its own depreciation schedule. For example, a long-haul truck is generally separated in at least three parts: the structure (the truck itself, with a life expectancy of about five years) and two components, the engine plus transmission and the tires. The first component is depreciated, for example, over 500,000 kilometers, while the tires are depreciated, for example, over 80,000 kilometers. Depreciation by components does not modify the total depreciable cost of the asset. If a tangible asset is acquired and it appears depreciation by component would be appropriate, the depreciable cost of the structure is often found by deduction. If a 40-ton truck is acquired for 100 CU and the cost of a replacement engine plus transmission is 25 CU and the cost of a set of tires is 15 CU, by deduction the depreciable cost of the structure would be 60 CU. The full 100 CU cost of the whole truck would be depreciated through three different depreciation schedules.

1.5.2 Residual value

IAS 16 (§ 6) defines 'residual value' as 'the estimated amount that an entity would currently obtain from disposal of the asset, after deducting the estimated costs of disposal if the asset were already of the age and in the condition expected at the end of its useful life'. Note, however that the estimated costs of disposal which should be deducted from the residual value, and, therefore, depreciated, could not include costs relating to dismantling, removing the asset, and restoring the site if they were already included in the depreciable cost of acquisition (see above: IAS 16: § 16).

The actual depreciable cost of an asset can only be the actual cost incurred to create the economic benefits over its life expectancy. The residual value is not depreciated because the company will, eventually, recover it. If an asset, at the end of its useful economic life, still has a residual value (through, for example, scrap, resale, or reuse), the depreciable asset value should conceptually be the cost of acquisition minus the residual value.

The residual value (also called salvage value, terminal value, end-of-life salvage value, or scrap value) is often difficult to estimate. As a consequence, it is often neglected in the computation of the depreciation expense, i.e., assumed to be zero. IAS 16 explicitly allows this possibility: 'In practice, the residual value of an asset is often insignificant and therefore immaterial in the calculation of the depreciable amount' (§ 53). Another possibility, often found in practice, is to adopt a discretionary standard percentage of the acquisition cost to determine the residual value, or to assume by convention the residual value is one currency unit (practice, for example, in Argentina, Austria, Germany, and Switzerland).

1.5.3 Depreciable amount

IAS 16 (§ 6) defines the 'depreciable amount' as the 'cost of an asset, or other amount substituted for cost in the financial statements, less its residual value':

Depreciable amount = Acquisition cost − Estimated residual value

It is in the interest of the firm to select as high a depreciable amount as possible as the depreciation expense generally reduces taxable profit and thus creates a higher cash flow[4] potentially retained in the firm.

1.5.4 Useful life (or service life) for accounting purposes

IAS 16 (§ 6) defines the 'useful life' as 'either:

(a) The period of time over which an asset is expected to be available for use by an entity; or

(b) The number of production [output] or similar units expected to be obtained from the asset by an entity'.

Useful life = Time period over which an asset is available for use
or
Maximum expected number of units of output before the asset is declared unproductive

'The useful life of an asset is defined in terms of the asset's expected utility to the entity. The asset management policy of the entity may involve the disposal of assets after a specified time or after consumption of a specified proportion of the future economic benefits embodied in the asset. Therefore, the [accounting] useful life of an asset may be shorter than its [true] economic life. The estimation of the [accounting] useful life of the asset is a matter of judgment based on the experience of the entity with similar assets' (IAS 16: § 57). The estimation of the duration of the useful life of a type of asset can vary from country to country, but this is frequently due to companies adopting depreciation rates consistent with that allowed for taxation purposes and these allowances vary between countries. Table 7.5 presents the most commonly accepted useful lives for a selection of classes of tangible assets.

Long-haul truck tires are generally not depreciated *prorata temporis* (i.e., on the basis of time elapsed) but on the basis of mileage covered. For a tractor-trailer, the expected mileage for a set of tires varies from country to country, but is generally in the range of 60,000–80,000 kilometers (37,290–49,720 miles).

In practice, as it is often difficult to forecast the real useful life of a fixed asset, the selected useful life may prove, *ex post* (i.e., after complete use of the asset), to be shorter than the real life of the asset. The principle of prudence (combined with the desire to create as much cash flow as early as possible) may explain the fact that many businesses deliberately choose shorter useful lives than they really expect to experience. The choice of a useful life may have a great impact on net income and on cash flows. Sometimes, however the reverse may be true and the entity may choose to lengthen its original estimate of the useful life as shown in the example below.

Table 7.5 Common useful lives

Tangible assets	Useful life (in years)	Corresponding straight-line annual rate (in %)
Commercial buildings	20–50	5–2
Industrial buildings	20	5
Equipment	8–10	12.5–10
Industrial equipment (tooling)	5–10	20–10
Transportation (trucks, vans, cars)	4–5	25–20
Furniture	10	10
Computers	3	33.33
Office equipment	5–10	20–10
Fixtures and fittings	10–20	10–5

Example EDF Group

For example, at 1 January 2003, EDF Group, the French national electrical utility (production and distribution), decided to increase the depreciation period of its nuclear installations in France from 30 to 40 years. The annual report specified that this change was 'prompted by operating experience, technical surveys, the renewal in the United States of operating licences for nuclear installations using the same technology and the application filed by the Group with the Nuclear Safety Authority to define the operating conditions of installations after a 30-year term. This change is recognized prospectively and therefore has no impact on equity at 31 December 2002. The extension of the period of useful life of nuclear power stations affected the amortization of nuclear power stations by €853 million. In addition the change in amortization method affected the depreciation of these assets by €(224) million. The extended useful life of nuclear power stations introduced with effect from 1 January 2003 has deferred decommissioning and last core disbursements by ten years' (*Source*: Annual report 2003).

1.5.5 Choice of a depreciation method

Several methods have been developed. According to IAS 16 (§ 60), 'the depreciation method used shall reflect the pattern in which the asset's future economic benefits are expected to be consumed by the entity'. The choice of the appropriate method should therefore be specific to each class of tangible asset.

Classification of methods Table 7.6 presents a classification of the main depreciation methods in two families: time-based and activity level-based methods.

The methods most commonly used are the straight-line method and the declining balance method. They will be presented in this section. The three other methods will be developed in the Advanced issues section. All these methods will be first described, and then illustrated through the same example, with data pertaining to a piece of

Table 7.6 Main depreciation methods

Time-based depreciation methods	Depreciation methods based on activity level (or service level or level of use)
1. Straight-line	3. Productive output
2. Accelerated (reducing charge)	4. Service quantity
2.1 Declining (reducing) balance	
2.2 Sum-of-the-years' digits (sum of digits)	
Depreciation expense will be determined regardless of the level of activity during the period	*Depreciation expense is the result of the multiplication of a constant depreciation (expense) rate per unit of activity times the number of units of activity consumed or produced during the period*

equipment purchased by the Purcell Company on 1 January X1. The data (in thousands of CU) we will use is as follows:

Basic data	
Acquisition cost	6,000
Residual value	1,000
Depreciable amount	5,000
Estimated useful life (in years)	5

Straight-line method This method is appropriately used if the decline in service potential relates primarily to the passage of time rather than to the level of activity, and if it can be assumed the asset will be equally productive each year.

Principles The asset is depreciated evenly over its useful life. In other words, the company allocates an equal amount of depreciation expense to each year of the asset's estimated useful life. Periodic depreciation expense is computed as follows:

Annual depreciation expense = (Acquisition cost − Residual value)/Number of years of useful life
= Depreciable amount/Estimated useful life
= Depreciable amount × Depreciation rate

(with Depreciation rate = 1/Number of years of useful life of the asset)

The straight-line method is the most frequently used method because of its simplicity of application and because it often reflects accurately the schedule of consumption of the productive potential.

Illustration: Purcell Company Table 7.7 shows an example of depreciation using the straight-line method. The annual depreciation rate = 1/5 years = 20%.

Table 7.7 Depreciation schedule – Straight-line method

End of year	Depreciable amount	Depreciation rate	Depreciation of the year	Balance: accumulated depreciation	Year-end book value
Date of acquisition					6,000
Year 1	5,000	20%	1,000	1,000	5,000
Year 2	5,000	20%	1,000	2,000	4,000
Year 3	5,000	20%	1,000	3,000	3,000
Year 4	5,000	20%	1,000	4,000	2,000
Year 5	5,000	20%	1,000	5,000	1,000

Depreciable amount = 6,000 (acquisition cost) – 1,000 (residual value) = 5,000

Yearly depreciation expense = 5,000 (depreciable amount) × 20% (depreciation rate) = 1,000
Year-end book value (year 1) = 6,000 (year-end book value of the preceding year) – 1,000 (depreciation of the year).

Declining balance method The objective of any **accelerated** (or **reducing charge**) method is to recognize greater amounts of depreciation in the early years of an asset's life and smaller amounts in the later years. The logic behind using an accelerated method of depreciation is twofold. First, it is a way of recognizing the loss of resale value that is incurred in the first period of use (for example, the market resale value of a car is, according to published sales records in many countries, reduced by up to 15–20% in the first few months after acquisition – i.e., the market offers a premium for a pristine car). Second, it is also a way of shielding more income from taxation, thus leaving more cash in the firm in the early years to be used, hopefully, for the development of the firm.

However, depreciation methods are supposed, in keeping with the matching principle, to be first and foremost ways to allocate the cost of the asset to the periods during which the economic benefits are derived from the use of the asset.

Accelerated depreciation may be conceptually sound if the declining pattern of expense recognition is consistent with the actual contribution the asset makes to the revenue-generating process. Accelerated depreciation methods are conceptually attractive when an asset is believed to provide superior performance (i.e., operate with greater efficiency or provide more benefits) in the early years of its life, or if repairs and maintenance costs will burden the last years of the useful life more than the earlier years and the manager wishes to even out, over time, the cost of operating that asset.

Of the several variations of accelerated depreciation, the most widely used is the declining balance method (it consists in applying a constant rate to a declining base). A second method, known as 'the sum-of-the years' digits method' (it consists in applying a declining rate to a constant base), is, despite its simplicity, rarely applied outside North America. In this method, for example, in the case of an asset with a life expectancy of five years, the sum of the years' digits is 1 + 2 + 3 + 4 + 5 = 15; the first year 5/15 of the depreciable amount will be expensed (depreciated), 4/15 of the depreciable amount the second year, etc. until 1/15 for the fifth year.

Determination of a multiple in the declining balance method The percentage applied to the base is defined as some multiple of the straight-line rate. The selection of the multiple is highly variable from country to country. In some countries, the choice of a multiple is totally open, subject to some unspecified criterion of reasonableness. In the USA, where the choice is essentially open, the most common application of this method is the double-declining balance, in which the accelerated percentage is twice the straight-line rate. By way of contrast, in some countries, such as France, the tax authorities have defined, for each class of assets, a standardized multiple.

Most accelerated methods (with the notable exception of the sum-of-the-years' digits method) have to switch, at some point in time, to a straight-line method, so as to arrive at a book value equal to the residual value at the end of the useful life. In order to avoid this switching, a method, mainly used in the UK, called 'fixed percentage of book value method' or 'fixed percentage of declining balance method' has been devised that selects a rate that depreciates the asset exactly down to the residual value. The formula for this method is shown in Table 7.8 along with some illustrations of practice in other countries.

Table 7.8 Examples of multiples

Country	Determination of the multiple M (or rate of depreciation) Where N = asset's useful life, expressed in years
Belgium	M = 2 (usual practice). Declining balance rate limited to 40% of the depreciable amount
France	M = 1.25, if N = 3 or 4 years M = 1.75, if N = 5 or 6 years M = 2.25, if N > 6 years
Germany	Limitation of application of the accelerated rate to 30% of the depreciable amount
UK	Rate of depreciation $= 1 - \sqrt[n]{(\text{Residual value/Cost of acquisition})}$ If the residual value is 0, assume a residual value of 1
USA	M = 2 (common practice). However, 1.5 is also used

Application to the declining book value This fixed percentage is applied to the book value of the asset, giving a depreciation figure that declines throughout the life of the asset.

Declining balance (DB) depreciation expense = (DB rate) × (book value)

or

DB depreciation expense = (DB rate) × (Depreciable cost minus accumulated depreciation)

Table 7.9 provides an illustration of the method.

How to end the depreciation process If applied consistently, the mathematics of the method are such that the book value would never be equal to the residual value. If the

Table 7.9 Method 1: Double-declining balance (DDB) with reversal to straight line (SL) when rate of SL over remaining life exceeds that of DDB

End of year	Depreciable basis	Depreciation expense of the year	Balance: accumulated depreciation	Year-end book value
Date of acquisition				6,000
Year 1	6,000	2,400	2,400	3,600
Year 2	3,600	1,440	3,840	2,160
Year 3	2,160	864	4,704	1,296
Year 4	1,296	148	4,852	1,148
Year 5	1,296	148	5,000	1,000

Depreciable amount = 6,000 (initial book value).
Depreciation expense of year 1 = 6,000 (depreciable amount) × 40% (DDB rate) = 2,400.
Depreciation expense of year 2 = 3,600 (ending book value of the preceding year) × DDB rate = 1,440.
In year 4, because the DDB approach would lead to a lower residual value than agreed upon ([1,296 − (1,296 × 40%)] = [1,296 − 518 = 778 < 1,000]), there is a reversal to straight line over the remaining useful life (two years at 50%). Note that we could also have said the switch to SL was due to the straight-line rate over the remaining useful life, i.e., 50% exceeding the DDB rate i.e., 40%. Thus, since we switch to straight line for the remaining two years, the annual depreciation expense for each of these years is 148 = [1,296 (the depreciable basis) − 1,000 (residual value)]/2.

Real-life example Siemens

Siemens AG, the German group which is one of the world's largest electrical engineering and electronics companies, offers an example of application of this method. The notes to the financial statements (annual report 2004) state that 'Depreciation expense is recognized either using the declining balance method until the straight-line method yields larger expenses or the straight-line method'.

method were applied without adjustments, not only would the asset never be fully depreciated but also its book value would eventually end up below the residual value. It is, therefore, important to decide beforehand how to terminate the depreciation to end up exactly at the level of the residual value.

In this context, several possibilities exist. They consist of either:

- Switching to a straight-line method (over the remaining useful life) at the point where the straight-line rate (calculated over the remaining useful life) exceeds the declining balance rate selected (illustrated in Table 7.9).
- Switching to a straight-line method (over the remaining useful life) at the midpoint of the life of the asset (illustrated in Table 7.10).
- Defining the depreciation expense as the difference between the preceding book value and the residual value in the year in which the accelerated depreciation expense would bring the book value to be lower than the residual value (illustrated in Table 7.11).

The 'fixed percentage of book value method' used mainly in the UK for computing the depreciation rate (see Table 7.8) avoids the entire problem of how to reach the residual value.

In choosing a method, the most important thing is to be rational and systematic. These conditions are met if the method for handling the end of depreciation is selected at the time of acquisition and applied to all assets of one homogeneous category.

Tables 7.9–7.11 illustrate the three possibilities as applied to the Purcell Company. If we choose a multiple equal to 2, we have: double-declining balance (DDB) rate = straight-line (SL) rate × 2 = 20% × 2 = 40%.

Table 7.10 Method 2: Declining balance with switch to straight line in mid-life

End of year	Depreciable basis	Depreciation expense of the year	Balance: accumulated depreciation	Year-end book value
Date of acquisition				6,000
Year 1	6,000	2,400	2,400	3,600
Year 2	3,600	1,440	3,840	2,160
Year 3	1,160	387	4,227	1,773
Year 4	1,160	387	4,614	1,386
Year 5	1,160	386	5,000	1,000

Switch to straight line at the midpoint of the life of the asset (2.5 years is conventionally translated as third year).
Depreciable basis at the time of the switch to straight line = 2,160 (book value at the end of year 2) – 1,000 (residual value) = 1,160.
Depreciation allowance for years 3, 4 and 5 = 1,160 (the depreciable basis)/3 = 387 (or 386, due to rounding).

This method, although simple, does not give the entity the full benefit of the cash flow impact of the accelerated depreciation and is thus less frequently used than method 1.

Table 7.11 Method 3: Double-declining balance with switch to SL as soon as DDB would lead to a book value lower than the residual value

End of year	Depreciable basis	Depreciation expense of the year	Balance: accumulated depreciation	Year-end book value
Date of acquisition				6,000
Year 1	6,000	2,400	2,400	3,600
Year 2	3,600	1,440	3,840	2,160
Year 3	2,160	864	4,704	1,296
Year 4	1,296	296	5,000	1,000
Year 5	0	0	5,000	1,000

In year 4, the depreciation expense would bring the book value to be lower than the residual value [1,296 – (1,296 × 40%)] = [1,296 – 518 = 778 < 1,000]. The depreciation expense is then set as the difference between the preceding book value and the residual value: 1,296 – 1,000 = 296.
No depreciation in year 5.

This method is not recommended because it leads to the violation of the agreed upon expected useful life of five years.

1.5.6 Depreciation schedule

The depreciation schedule is the pre-established list of depreciation amounts for each year of an asset's useful life. The elaboration of a depreciation schedule is based on the choice of depreciation method as illustrated in Tables 7.7 and 7.9–7.11.

1.5.7 Book value (also called 'net book value' or 'carrying amount')

The book value is the difference between the asset's cost (cost of acquisition) and the balance of its accumulated depreciation. After the book value has reached the residual value (even equal to zero), the asset might not be taken out of service if it is still reliable and usefully productive. It will be reported (carried) in the balance sheet at the residual value or for a book value of zero so that the asset remains identified.

1.5.8 Recording the depreciation expense

Principle In countries where the income statement is organized by nature of expenses, depreciation is recorded as shown in Figure 7.3 below.

The 'accumulated depreciation' is a reduction of assets and is called a 'contra-asset' account, i.e., is displayed in the assets side of the balance sheet with a negative sign or by placing the amount in parentheses.

In countries where the income statement is presented by function (see this concept in Chapter 3), the depreciation expense on a manufacturing asset is included in the cost of the goods manufactured[5] at the stage of the manufacturing process when that asset is used. The depreciation expense is recorded as an increase in the 'work in progress' account of that stage. The depreciation expense will flow to the cost of goods sold account (and thus be matched against revenue) after having transited through the various levels of inventories. The depreciation expense ends up, therefore, being distributed over the cost of goods sold and the various inventories (if there has been an increase of the inventory levels). For non-manufacturing equipment (such as a computer used in the accounting department), the depreciation expense is a period cost that does not flow through inventory accounts, and the accounting entries are similar to the ones described for countries using a by nature income statement structure.

Illustration: Purcell Company Figure 7.3 illustrates the accounting entries for the recording of depreciation (year 1 only), using the straight-line method.

Figure 7.3 Recording the depreciation expense in a by-nature income statement

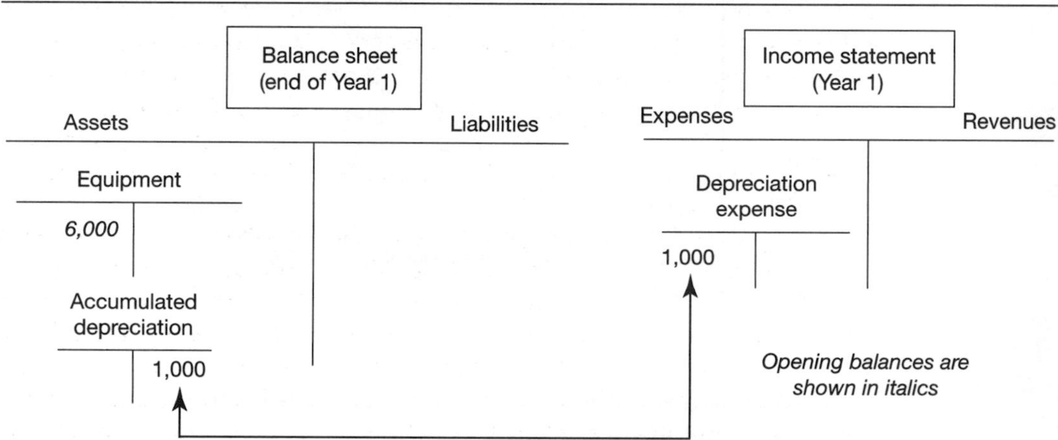

1.5.9 Reporting depreciation policies

Real-life example Weyerhaeuser

(USA – US GAAP – *Source*: Annual report 2004 – International forest products company)

Excerpts from the notes.

Property and Equipment. The company's property accounts are maintained on an individual asset basis. Improvements to and replacements of major units are capitalized. Maintenance, repairs, and minor replacements are expensed. Depreciation is provided on the straight-line method at rates based on estimated service lives. Amortization of logging railroads and truck roads is provided generally as timber is harvested and is based upon rates determined with reference to the volume of timber estimated to be removed over such facilities. The cost and accumulated depreciation of property sold or retired is removed from the accounts and the gain or loss is included in earnings.

Timber and Timberlands. Timber and timberlands are carried at cost less depletion charged to disposals. Depletion is the cost of standing timber and is charged to fee timber disposals as fee timber is harvested, lost as a result of casualty, or sold. Generally, all initial site preparation and planting costs are capitalized as reforestation. Reforestation is transferred to a merchantable (harvestable) timber classification after 15 years in the south and 30 years in the west. Generally, costs incurred after the first planting, such as fertilization, vegetation and insect control, pruning and pre-commercial thinning, property taxes, and interest, are considered to be maintenance of the forest and are expensed as incurred. Accounting practices for these costs do not change when timber becomes merchantable and harvesting commences. Depletion rates used to relieve timber inventory are determined with reference to the net carrying value of timber and the related volume of timber estimated to be available over the growth cycle.

2 Advanced issues

2.1 Definition and recognition of tangible assets

2.1.1 Particular issues relating to reporting land and buildings

Because they cannot be depreciated, land assets must always be reported separately from buildings that are constructed on them. Even if a purchase contract provides only one global acquisition cost for a property comprising land and buildings, the firm acquiring the property has to obtain the necessary information to split the sum between two separate accounts. Such a correction is necessary not only to provide correct information on the assets (the market value of land and construction do not evolve in parallel), but also because buildings and constructions are depreciable assets, unlike land.

Buildings shown in the tangible asset category on the balance sheet include only those that are held as long-term investments, thus excluding short-term or speculative holdings. This means that, in principle, all industrial, commercial, and administrative buildings should give rise to the recognition of an annual depreciation expense throughout their expected useful life.

During a very inflationary period, depreciation of buildings might not be coherent with truthful reporting because the residual value of the asset might increase to the point of exceeding the acquisition cost or the book value. Since the depreciable base is the difference between the cost of acquisition and the residual value, there might not be anything to depreciate in such a context. Such a situation is very rare in developed economies but was not uncommon in the 1980s in countries with high inflation rates such as Brazil or Argentina, and would require, in any case, full disclosure in a note to the financial statements.

2.1.2 Assets constructed by and for the enterprise (internally generated assets)

Businesses often use their own resources to build an asset for their own use. These can be machinery, buildings, or fixtures. The issue of valuation of such assets is especially problematic since there is no 'at arm's length' relation in the acquisition which would remove any and all ambiguity and arbitrariness in the valuation of the asset. We will approach this valuation issue in three steps:

1. Definition of the term 'asset constructed by and for the enterprise'.
2. Valuation of such asset (cost measurement).
3. Recording of such asset in the accounting system.

Definition – Principle In certain circumstances, companies construct or build their own tangible assets instead of acquiring them from other companies. This practice happens frequently in certain industrial sectors such as construction, automotive, railroad, utilities (building a power plant or a water treatment facility, or laying the network of pipes for gas distribution), etc. For instance, when Bouygues Company, a French-based global construction and civil engineering firm, built their showcase headquarters near Paris, they did it with their own human and physical resources. It would not have made sense to ask a competitor to develop such a building that is meant to showcase all the best facets of Bouygues' *savoir faire*. Similarly, a machine tool manufacturer might develop its own machines to make the machine tools it sells, or an automotive manufacturer might make the dies for its body shop, or an airplane manufacturer might create a dedicated lift to hoist the tail reactor (for power and air conditioning) in place. Assets built by and for the firm are extremely common occurrences in many businesses.

Valuation Tangible assets, which are created or developed internally, must be valued at their production cost. The production cost of an object is generally broken down into several components, which can be traced to the object with varying degrees of accuracy:

- Cost of raw materials and components.
- Cost of the labor that was directly involved in the creation of the object (whether it is in the research and development phase or the manufacturing and testing phase).
- Overhead (or indirect) costs that include supplies, energy and fluids, supervisory labor, and all the costs of the facilities and support functions that permitted the creation of the object.
- Financial costs, which can be very significant when the asset is extremely costly and the construction process spans a long period, as is the case, for example, in the building of a power plant or the construction of a large office building.

Overhead While there are generally few problems arising from the tracing of direct materials and components or direct labor cost to the object, allocation of overhead costs is a difficult issue (see Appendix 7.2).

Financing costs: interest costs (or borrowing costs) While the asset is being constructed, resources are consumed but no revenue is generated. The revenue will be generated when the asset will be operational and for the duration of its useful life. The firm must, therefore, finance the cost of the resources consumed, either out of its own funds (possibly losing an opportunity to earn revenue) or by borrowing funds to cover the need. There is, therefore, little doubt that there is a causal link between the construction and the financing costs, but it is not so clear how much of it should be attached to the cost of the asset.

IAS 23 (IASB 1993) states that borrowing costs ('interest and other costs incurred by an entity in connection with the borrowing of funds' [§ 4]) 'shall be recognized as an expense in the period in which they are incurred' (§ 7). However, the interest costs can, under certain circumstances, be included in the cost of the construction (§ 11). This possibility is referred to as the 'capitalization' of borrowing/interest costs. Directly attributable interest costs are capitalized as part of the cost of the asset 'when it is probable that they will result in future economic benefits to the entity and the costs can be measured reliably' (§ 12).

An example of computation of capitalized interest costs is provided in Appendix 7.3. Capitalized interest may represent a very large share of the asset cost and, thus, a big stake in the determination of income.

Real-life example Bayer

(Germany – IFRS/IAS – *Source*: Annual report 2004 – Biotechnology)

If the construction phase of property, plant, or equipment extends over a long period, the interest incurred on borrowed capital up to the date of completion is capitalized as part of the cost of acquisition or construction. (...) Interest expense incurred to finance the construction phase of major investment projects is not included [in the interest expense]. Such interest expense, amounting in 2004 to €4 million (2003: €18 million), is capitalized as part of the cost of acquisition or construction of the property, plant, or equipment concerned, based on an average capitalization rate of 4% (2003: 5%).

Recording of the transactions

Example Let's take the example of a piece of machinery constructed by the Purcell Company for its own use. The production cost includes the following cost items (all are assumed to be paid cash, for simplicity sake):

- materials and components (already in inventory): 30 CU;
- labor (personnel expense): 55 CU;
- overhead (various expenses): 15 CU.

The new machine will be depreciated over five years.

One way of recording the capitalization of the costs incurred in the construction is presented in Figure 7.4.

Recording procedures Across countries, several alternative solutions are possible at the time of capitalization. The most common three approaches are described below:

1. To record, in the income statement, an increase in the costs or expenses incurred for the capitalized asset (step ❶), and, to neutralize the income effect of such an entry, increase a revenue account (production capitalized), with a counterpart for that same amount to the balance sheet, thus creating the capitalized asset (step ❷). (This is the solution followed in Figure 7.4.)
2. To record, in the income statement, an increase in the costs or expenses incurred for the capitalized asset (step ❶) and decrease the same accounts, thus creating the capitalized asset (second step). (This solution is not illustrated in Figure 7.4.)
3. To open a 'project account' (directly in the balance sheet) in which all expenses pertaining to the new asset being developed are transferred, thus creating directly the value of the asset without having to go through the income statement. This solution is very simple, but does not give the same visibility for shareholders to see what their business is really doing with its resources. (This solution is not illustrated here.)

Figure 7.4 Accounting for tangible assets constructed by and for Purcell Company

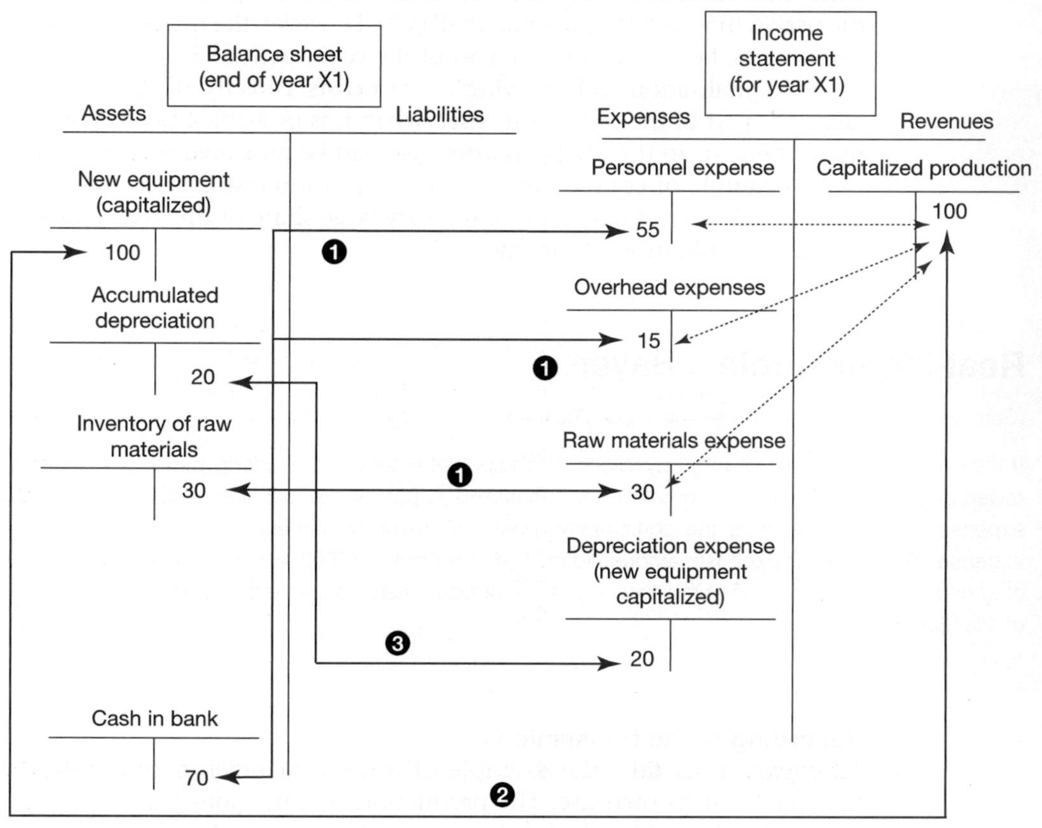

In all three cases, regardless of the capitalization process adopted, depreciation will have to be recognized for the year. Here, assuming a depreciation of the new equipment over five years (100/5 = 20 if we choose straight line) the annual depreciation expense of the asset is recognized through step ❸.

After capitalization, the impact of the new machine on income for the first year is limited to the depreciation expense, i.e., 100/5 = 20. If the machine built in-house had not been capitalized and considered to be an asset, the impact on the first-year income would have been the full 100 CU, i.e., the full cost of constructing the asset.

2.2 Depreciation: additional methods

This section will illustrate the three methods of depreciation mentioned but not covered in detail in the Core issues of this chapter. They are:

- sum-of-the-years' digits method;
- depreciation methods based on activity level (two cases):
  - units-of-output method;
  - service-quantity method.

We will use the same data as used previously of an acquisition by Purcell Company of a piece of equipment for 6,000 CU. Table 7.12 summarizes the data (in thousands of CU, unless otherwise specified).

Table 7.12 Basic data

Cost	6,000
Residual value	1,000
Depreciable amount	5,000
Estimated useful life	5 years

Expected units of output over the life of the asset	25,000 units	Expected number of machine hours over the life of the asset	50,000 hours
Year 1	8,000	Year 1	12,000
Year 2	7,000	Year 2	12,000
Year 3	6,000	Year 3	12,000
Year 4	3,000	Year 4	8,000
Year 5	1,000	Year 5	6,000

2.2.1 Sum-of-the-years' digits method (sum of the digits method)

This method belongs to the category of accelerated (reducing charge) methods of depreciation. Tax authorities rarely allow it and its use in reporting to shareholders is declining. It is presented in Appendix 7.4.

2.2.2 Depreciation methods based on activity level

The use of such methods, matching the depreciation schedule with the 'consumption' of the potential of economic benefits the asset can provide, is appropriate only if the asset's output is discretely and distinctly measurable and if the useful life of the asset is better expressed in terms of maximum number of units of output than in terms of time periods.

Productive-output method (units-of-output method)

Principle The depreciation schedule matches the timing of the output of the asset expressed in units of products or services such as miles or kilometers driven, units shipped, or tons produced. A depreciation cost per unit of output is calculated by dividing the depreciable amount by the total potential expected of that asset. This depreciation rate per unit is then applied to the actual output for the period to determine the depreciation expense of the period.

The amount of depreciation expense cannot be determined in advance for any given period, because it is dependent on the level of output during the period.

$$\text{Depreciation expense} = \frac{\text{Depreciable amount}}{\text{Life expressed in units of output}} \times \text{Units of output for the period}$$

$$= \text{Depreciation rate per unit} \times \text{Units of output for the period}$$

This method is easy to apply when the required information is readily available as, for example, for a bottling machine whose quantity of output (number of bottles filled and capped) would automatically be recorded.

One of the advantages of this method is that it allows the enterprise to record the depreciation expense in proportion to the intensity of use of the asset. It is clear that a machine that produces 48,000 containers of yogurt per hour during one eight-hour shift for five days a week will not wear out as quickly as it would if it were used 20 hours a day for 6½ days a week (five shifts).

However, the determination of the rated lifetime output is not completely objective: the difficulty of choosing the useful economic life is compounded with that of defining the output per period (generally estimated by the manufacturer or production engineers). For example, the yogurt-packaging machine just mentioned was rated by the manufacturer at 36,000 containers per hour but the dairy's maintenance and production engineers were able to increase the rated output to 48,000 containers per hour after only three months of operation. Which is the appropriate figure in determining the denominator number: 36,000 or 48,000?

Another major source of ambiguity concerning the number of units constituting the total life potential of the machine comes from the fact that there is no guarantee the market will absorb the whole output potential over the expected useful life of the machine. If the cumulated market demand does not materialize and does not match the expected output, the asset may be completely obsolete much before it is fully depreciated. This method thus requires that the accountant use, as the denominator, only the total cumulated output that will reasonably be absorbed by the market.

The productivity of many plant assets, such as buildings and fixtures, however, cannot be measured in terms of a unit of output. For such classes of assets, this method of depreciation is inappropriate.

Table 7.13 offers an illustration of this method for the Purcell Company.

Table 7.13 Depreciation schedule – Productive-output method

End of year	Annual output in units	Depreciation rate per unit	Annual depreciation expense	Balance: accumulated depreciation	Year-end book value
Date of acquisition					6,000
Year 1	8,000	0.20	1,600	1,600	4,400
Year 2	7,000	0.20	1,400	3,000	3,000
Year 3	6,000	0.20	1,200	4,200	1,800
Year 4	3,000	0.20	600	4,800	1,200
Year 5	1,000	0.20	200	5,000	1,000

Depreciable amount: 5,000 CU (cost of acquisition of 6,000 minus the residual value of 1,000).
The expected normal number of units of output the asset can create, and which are expected to be sold, has been estimated at 25,000 units.
The estimated depreciation rate per unit of output is therefore 0.20 CU (5,000/25,000 = 0.20).
Depreciation of year 1 = 8,000 (units produced and sold) × 0.20 (depreciation rate per unit) = 1,600 CU.

Service-quantity method

Principle While the mechanics of applying the service-quantity (or unit depreciation) method are similar to those of the productive-output method, the concepts underlying the methods are somewhat different. Under the service-quantity method, the contribution to operation is stated in terms of productive-output factors rather than physical sellable output of the production process. This method is commonly employed in air or ground transportation businesses. Aircraft are depreciated on the basis of flying hours (but the landing gear should logically be depreciated on the basis of the number of landings), locomotives or trucks are depreciated on the basis of kilometers (or miles) driven. The same issue arises as was found in the case of the productive-output method, namely the definition of the accumulated number of units of service the equipment can handle. A truck may be rated for half a million miles for use over 'normal roads under normal driving conditions', but the actual mileage that will be obtained from the same truck may vary greatly with the load factor and road conditions as well as with the driving style and intensity of use. For example, the mileage wear and tear cannot be equivalent between a truck driven over dirt roads in the Sahel and one driven over modern freeways in the Netherlands or over mountain roads in Switzerland or Austria. The actual number of useful productive unit is a strategic choice: the same aircraft can produce a different number of flight hours depending on whether it is used by a low cost carrier or used on a feeder line by a legacy airline using the hub and spoke system in a long-haul route system.

The depreciation rate per unit of productive service is determined as follows:

$$\text{Depreciation expense} = \frac{\text{Depreciable amount}}{\text{Total quantity of productive service}} \times \text{Productive service for the period}$$

$$= \text{Depreciation rate per unit of services} \times \text{Units of output for the period}$$

Table 7.14 provides an illustration using the Purcell Company data.

Table 7.14 Depreciation schedule – Service-quantity method

End of year value	Life-time number of units of service	Depreciation rate per unit of service	Annual depreciation expense	Balance: accumulated depreciation	Year-end book
Date of acquisition					6,000
Year 1	12,000	0.10	1,200	1,200	4,800
Year 2	12,000	0.10	1,200	2,400	3,600
Year 3	12,000	0.10	1,200	3,600	2,400
Year 4	8,000	0.10	800	4,400	1,600
Year 5	6,000	0.10	600	5,000	1,000

Depreciable amount: 5,000 CU (cost of acquisition of 6,000 minus the residual value of 1,000).
Estimated life-time number of units of service: 50,000 units of service.
Estimated cost per unit of service = 0.10 (5,000/50,000).
Depreciation expense for year 1 = 12,000 (number of units of service) × 0.10 (depreciation rate per unit of service) = 1,200.

Limitations of the methods based on activity level The unit depreciation methods are not widely used outside of small niches, probably for two major reasons:

- These methods produce schedules of depreciation for the first years of the asset that are often not very different from those that would be obtained through the use of either the straight-line or accelerated depreciation methods.
- As mentioned in the text, the ambiguity linked to the definition of the reference figures can be rather large and the data collection costs might prove to be high.

2.2.3 Summary of the income statement impact of the different methods

Table 7.15 summarizes in the illustrative case of the Purcell Company the depreciation expense and the closing book value of the same asset under the five main depreciation methods described above (in both parts of this chapter, including Appendix 7.4).

Figure 7.5 shows evolution of the annual depreciation expense over time under each of the alternative depreciation methods and Figure 7.6 shows the resulting book value at each year-end.

In practice, tangible assets are rarely purchased or sold on the first day of the accounting period. The issues which arises for a purchase or sale during the year are dealt with in Appendix 7.5.

Table 7.15 Summary of the different methods

	Straight-line (see Table 7.7 in Core issues)		Sum-of-years' digits (see Appendix 7.4)		Double-declining balance (see Table 7.9 in Core issues)		Productive output (see Table 7.13 in Advanced issues)		Service quantity (see Table 7.14 in Advanced issues)	
Year	Depreciation expense	Book value	Depreciation expense	Book value	Depreciation expense	Book value	Depreciation expense	Book value	Depreciation expense	Book value
At acquisition		6,000		6,000		6,000		6,000		6,000
Year 1	1,000	5,000	1,667	4,333	2,400	3,600	1,600	4,400	1,200	4,800
Year 2	1,000	4,000	1,333	3,000	1,440	2,160	1,400	3,000	1,200	3,600
Year 3	1,000	3,000	1,000	2,000	864	1,296	1,200	1,800	1,200	2,400
Year 4	1,000	2,000	667	1,333	148	1,148	600	1,200	800	1,600
Year 5	1,000	1,000	333	1,000	148	1,000	200	1,000	600	1,000

Figure 7.5 Annual depreciation expense

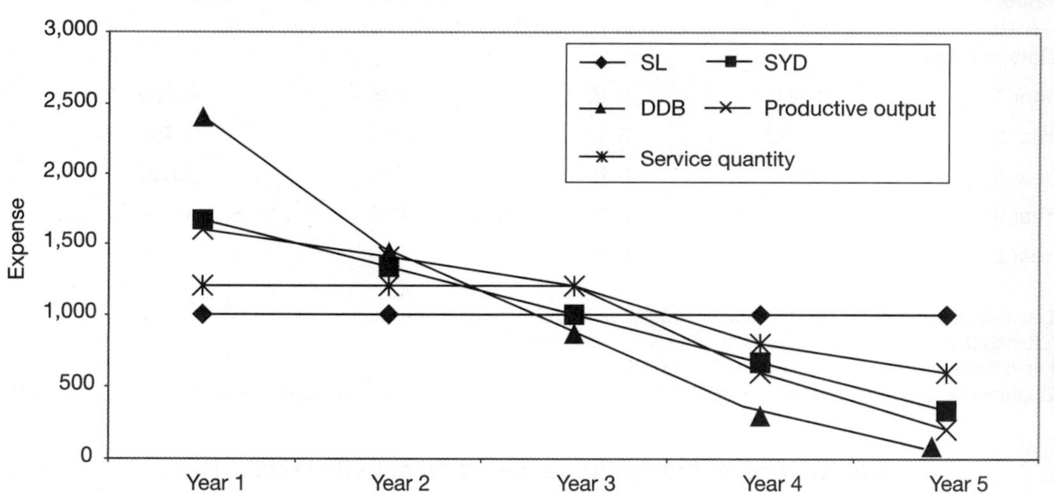

2.2.4 Impairment

Principle IAS 16 (IASB 2003: § 6) defines an 'impairment loss' as 'the amount by which the carrying amount of an asset exceeds its recoverable amount'. IAS 36 (Impairment of Assets

Figure 7.6 Closing book value

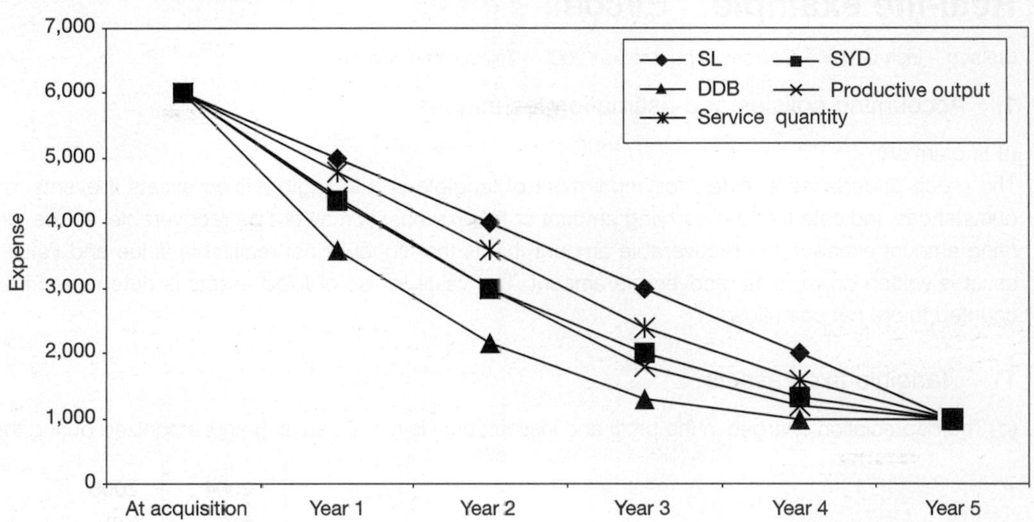

[IASB 2004a)] provides the guidelines to determine whether an item of property, plant, and equipment should be impaired by the entity. It explains how an entity reviews the carrying amount of its assets, how it determines the recoverable amount of an asset and when it recognizes an impairment loss, or reverses a previously recognized impairment loss (§ 63).

Practically, if the fair market value of a tangible asset is less than its book value, such asset should be written down and a loss recognized (this practice, also known as 'lower of cost or market' is a consequence of the prudence principle) as an 'impairment loss' expense or 'loss from write-down expense' or 'provision expense'. If and when the impairment is no longer required, a reversal could and should be recorded as a negative expense or through a revenue account such as 'write-back on impairment' or 'reversal of provisions' (it is, however, rarely done in practice, essentially to keep in line with the prudence principle).

Practice and regulation regarding impairment have varied over time and between countries in the world. Apart from IAS 36 (IASB 2004a), rules for impairment exist now in many countries, such as the USA (SFAS 121, Accounting for the Impairment of Long-lived Assets and for Long-lived Assets to Be Disposed Of) and the UK (FRS 11, Impairment of Fixed Assets and Goodwill).

The topic of impairment may become increasingly relevant, with the change of rules relating to impairment of intangibles (see Chapters 8 and, especially, 13). In practice, tests for impairment are very difficult to implement.

Real-life example Eircom

(Ireland – Irish GAAP – *Source*: Annual report 2005 – Telecommunications)

1. Accounting policies and estimation techniques

(l) Impairment

The group undertakes a review for impairment of tangible and intangible fixed assets if events, or changes in circumstances, indicate that the carrying amount of the fixed asset may not be recoverable. To the extent that the carrying amount exceeds the recoverable amount that is the higher of net realizable value and value in use, the fixed asset is written down to its recoverable amount. The value in use of fixed assets is determined from estimated discounted future net cash flows.

11. Tangible fixed assets

(c) The depreciation charged in the profit and loss account is net of capital grants amortized during the year as follows:

	2004 €m	2005 €m
Depreciation	362	317
Impairment charge included in depreciation	9	–
Amortization of capital grants (note 20)	(3)	(1)
	368	316

The impairment charge of €9 million, included in depreciation in the year ended 31 March 2004, relates to Eircom's investment in Global Crossing, International Cable and Synchronous Digital Hierarchy ('SDH') equipment, which has been written off.

2.2.5 Depreciation of 'land'

Normally, land is accounted for at its acquisition cost and is not subject to any depreciation, since it theoretically neither gets consumed through use nor wears out, or becomes obsolete. However, where land has been purchased as a natural resource for a productive activity – such as a quarry, a mine, oil field, or natural gas well – the acquisition cost relates not to the land surface but to the volume of non renewable riches which are hidden beneath it. In such cases, depreciation will be calculated on a unit consumption basis (proportional to the output extracted compared to the estimated life capacity of the deposit) since exploitation of the resource reduces the potential of future exploitation. This depreciation is recognized under the specific name of 'depletion'.

Another situation in which the land acquisition costs will be subject to value adjustment at the end of a financial year is when its current market value has fallen below the cost of acquisition. The required value adjustment will be recognized as an impairment.

Example Britten Corp.

Britten purchased a well-located piece of suburban farmland for 850,000 CU (much higher than the price of land for farming but much lower than the price of constructible land) in the anticipation that it could be re-zoned and developed as a shopping center. However, three years later the company learns formally from its lawyer that, despite her efforts to obtain that the zoning regulations be changed, there will be no possibility of obtaining a building permit. As a consequence the market value of the land is not more than 305,000 CU (farmland price). In this case the company should take an impairment loss expense of 545,000 CU in the income statement of the year.

2.3 Costs subsequent to acquisition

The way to handle costs subsequent to acquisition is based on the rule, mentioned earlier about the distinction between capital and revenue expenditure (see Core issues), that 'the cost of an item of property, plant and equipment shall be recognized as an asset if, and only if: (a) it is probable that future economic benefits associated with the item will flow to the entity; and (b) the cost of the item can be measured reliably' (IAS 16: § 7). The text of IAS 16 refers constantly to this rule to distinguish, among costs incurred after acquisition, between those that must be capitalized and those that should be expensed (see IAS 16: §§ 12–14).

Therefore, costs incurred after the acquisition of an asset, such as additions, improvements, or replacements, are added to the asset's depreciable cost base if they provide future service potential, extend the useful life of the asset, or increase either the quantity or quality of service rendered by the asset. Otherwise, they are expensed immediately.

Examples of improvements that result in increased future economic benefits are the following:

- Modification of an asset to extend its useful life, including an increase in its capacity.
- Upgrading machine parts to achieve a substantial improvement in the quality of output.
- Adoption of new production processes enabling a substantial reduction in previously assessed operating costs.
- Relining of a blast furnace required after a specified number of hours of use, or replacement of aircraft interiors such as seats and galleys (example given in IAS 16: § 13).

However, 'an entity does not recognize in the carrying amount of an item of property, plant and equipment the costs of the day-to-day servicing of the item' (IAS 16: § 12). An expenditure on repairs or maintenance of a tangible asset is made only to maintain or restore the stream of future economic benefits. As such, it is usually recognized as an expense when incurred. For example, the cost of servicing or repairing plant and equipment is usually an expense since it maintains, rather than increases, the originally assessed standard of performance.

The developments (in Core issues) relating to the difference between an asset and an expense can be applied to the concept of 'subsequent expenditure', especially in the case of small expenditures.

2.4 Disposal of long-term assets

Tangible assets are disposed of for many different reasons and in a variety of ways: sale, abandonment, and loss (flood, fire, natural disaster, etc.).

We will mainly deal with the sale of tangible assets, knowing that the other two categories of disposal can be assimilated to a sale without the entry recognizing the proceeds of the sale (see later).

2.4.1 Recording of the sale of an asset

When long-term assets are sold before their useful lives are completed, the difference between the book value and the disposition proceeds (sales proceeds or selling price) is treated as a gain or a loss.

Some countries (e.g., the USA) record the net impact from the sale in a single line (gain or loss, depending on the nature of this difference) directly in the income statement. Other countries record separately in the income statement the selling price as revenue and the book value as an expense (e.g., France) or open an asset disposal account, the balance of which is transferred to the income statement account (e.g., the UK). Of course, the reported impact on net income is the same, whichever method is chosen. Depreciation must be recorded for the period of time between the date of the last depreciation entry and the date of sale. An illustration of the recording of a sale of fixed asset is given in Appendix 7.6 and the treatment of the removal of a fully depreciated tangible asset from the book is provided in Appendix 7.7.

2.4.2 Classification in the income statement

Gains and losses from the sale of long-term assets need to be reported to shareholders. The choice of where in the income statement to report these items (exceptional, extraordinary, or ordinary income) differs from country to country. In the USA, gains and losses from asset sales do not satisfy criteria for the extraordinary item treatment (see Chapter 6). They are included in the income statement 'above the line', i.e., they are considered to be part of the normal business of the firm. In continental Europe, the book value of fixed assets sold and the sales price are classified as exceptional items. In the UK, profits and losses on disposals (sales) of fixed assets must be disclosed after the operating profit as an exceptional item.

2.5 Financial aspects of tangible assets

2.5.1 Depreciation and cash flow

Depreciation expenses (and impairment losses) are non-cash expenses. This means that they have no direct impact on the cash balance, but an indirect one arising from the income tax effect of expenses. This is illustrated through the example of the Purcell Company summarized in Table 7.16.

Assume that the company sales (all for cash) were 200 CU and the corresponding cash operating expenses (materials, labor, and overhead excluding depreciation) amounted to 120 CU. In addition, since Purcell Company used its tangible fixed assets (which amounted to 100 CU and had a useful economic life of five years), depreciation expense (a component of the class of costs called 'overhead') is another expense to be matched with the revenue. If Purcell Company uses the straight-line method, the depreciation expense for the first year amounts to 20 CU, while if it uses the double-declining balance depreciation method, the first year depreciation expense amounts to 40 CU. In both cases we assume the income tax rate to be 40%. Table 7.16 presents the income statement and the operating cash flow (extracted from the cash flow statement – see Chapters 3 and 14).

Table 7.16 illustrates some important points:

- The choice of method of depreciation impacts both income before tax and income after tax.
- Cash flow (either before or after tax) from operating activities is not influenced by depreciation expense because its calculation does not include the depreciation expense.
- The higher the depreciation expense in one year, other things being equal otherwise, the larger the net after tax cash flow. This is due to the different income tax shield provided by each method. (In reality, this is, of course, the case only where tax regulation allows the use of accelerated depreciation methods).

2.5.2 Reporting movements in tangible assets

Principle In most countries, the notes to financial statements must include two separate statements, one reporting the movements in the gross value of tangible assets and the other with the changes in accumulated depreciation (with the exception of the USA and Canada where both are merged). One example of such statement is provided in Table 7.17.

Table 7.16 Depreciation and cash flow

	Straight-line depreciation	Double-declining balance depreciation
Income statement		
Sales 200	200	
Cash operating expenses	(120)	(120)
Earnings before interest, taxes and depreciation or amortization (EBITDA)	80	80
Depreciation expense	(20)	(40)
Income before income tax (EBIT)	60	40
Income tax expense (40%)	(24)	(16)
Net income after tax	36	24
Cash flow statement		
Cash received from customers	200	200
Cash paid for operating expenses	(120)	(120)
Cash flow before tax from operating activities	80	80
Cash paid for income tax	(24)	(16)
Cash flow after tax provided from operating activities	56	64
Alternative presentation of the cash flow statement		
Net income after tax	36	24
Plus Depreciation expense (a non-cash expense)	20	40
Equals Cash flow (after tax) from operating activities	56	64
Plus Cash paid for income tax	24	16
Equals Cash flow (before tax) from operating activities	80	80

According to IAS 16 (§ 73), 'the financial statements shall disclose, for each class of property, plant and equipment:

(a) The measurement bases used for determining the gross carrying amount;
(b) The depreciation methods used;
(c) The useful lives or the depreciation rates used;
(d) The gross carrying amount and the accumulated depreciation (aggregated with accumulated impairment losses) at the beginning and end of the period; and
(e) A reconciliation of the carrying amount at the beginning and end of the period showing:
   (i) Additions;
   (ii) Assets classified as held for sale or included in a disposal group classified as held for sale in accordance with IFRS 5 and other disposals;
   (iii) Acquisitions through business combinations;
   (iv) Increases or decreases resulting from revaluations under paragraphs 31, 39, and 40 and from impairment losses recognized or reversed directly in equity in accordance with IAS 36;

(v) Impairment losses recognized in profit or loss in accordance with IAS 36;

(vi) Impairment losses reversed in profit or loss in accordance with IAS 36;

(vii) Depreciation;

(viii) The net exchange differences arising on the translation of the financial statements from the functional currency into a different presentation currency, including the translation of a foreign operation into the presentation currency of the reporting entity; and

(ix) Other changes'.

Table 7.17 Movements in tangible assets

Beginning value	+	Increases	−	Decreases	=	Ending value
Gross value	+	Acquisitions	−	Disposals	=	Gross value
Beginning accumulated depreciation	+	Depreciation expense	−	Cancellation of depreciation of fixed assets sold or disposed off	=	Ending accumulated depreciation

Real-life example Atos Origin

(France – French GAAP – *Source:* Annual report 2004 – IT business processes)

(in € millions)	Land	Buildings	Computer hardware	Other assets	Fixed assets in progress	Payments on account	Total
Gross value at 31 December 2003	1.1	112.5	468.5	113.6	0.4	0.1	696.2
Additions		16.8	50.2	31.9	0.5	0.1	99.5
Disposals		(8.1)	(45.9)	(45.7)	–	–	(99.7)
Changes in Group structure	2.5	54.5	133.2	156.8	8.4	(0.1)	355.3
Gross value at 31 December 2004	3.6	175.7	606.0	256.6	9.3	0.1	1,051.3
Accumulated depreciation at 31 December 2003	0.0	(55.1)	(394.3)	(90.8)	0.0	0.0	(540.2)
Charge		(20.0)	(73.1)	(31.9)			(125.0)
Release		5.4	40.2	44.5			90.1
Changes in Group structure		(27.5)	(89.7)	(126.0)			(243.2)
Accumulated depreciation at 31 December 2004	0.0	(97.2)	(516.9)	(204.2)	0.0	0.0	(818.3)
Net value at 31 December 2004	3.6	78.5	89.1	52.4	9.3	0.1	233.0

- It should be noted that the movements are presented in line and the assets in columns.
- The book value is computed as the difference between the gross value and the accumulated depreciation at year-end.
- The line 'changes in group structure' represents the impact of acquisitions and sales of group companies on the movements in tangible assets.
- Fixed assets in progress are fixed assets being constructed but not completed at year-end.
- Payments on account are advance payments made to suppliers of fixed assets.

2.5.3 Financial statement analysis

Several ratios may be computed to help the user of financial information gain a better understanding of the financial position of the business regarding its ability to use its tangible fixed assets.

Capital intensity ratios There are two key ratios:

Rate of return on tangible assets = Net income/Net tangible assets

Tangible asset turnover = Net sales/Average net tangible assets (book value)

They answer the questions 'how much profit does the business create per CU invested in tangible assets' or 'how much sales are generated per CU originally invested in tangible assets'. These ratios are essential for extrapolating the consequences of an investment strategy. Their value is clearly influenced by the depreciation method chosen.

Although commonly used, these ratios are somewhat misleading in that when the *book value* is used as the denominator, the ratio increases with the passage of time, even if the firm does nothing (the ratio may even improve when things go bad if the speed of depreciation of the denominator exceeds the rate of decline of income!). More relevant denominator values that are sometimes used, especially in business communication with the financial community, are (most commonly) the historical book value (before accumulated depreciation) or (still unusual) the replacement value of the tangible fixed assets.

Average age and life of tangible assets Shareholders (potential or actual) and financial analysts need to evaluate the risk of obsolescence of the assets of the firm. Failing to have exact, engineering-based knowledge of the average age or life of the assets, a quick estimate can be found by exploiting the fact that financial statements report both the gross value of the assets and their accumulated depreciation.

Average age = Accumulated depreciation at year-end/Depreciation expense for the year

Average life = Gross value of depreciable assets at year-end/Depreciation expense for the year

These two ratios suffer several limits since the depreciation allowance (and thus the timing of the accumulated depreciation) varies with the method of depreciation selected:

- They provide reasonably good information only in the case of use of the straight-line depreciation method.
- They assume the cost of acquisition of equivalent assets over time is stable.
- They are influenced by acquisitions and disposals during the year.

A further problem with the meaningfulness of these ratios derives from the fact managers could manipulate tangible assets valuation and depreciation expense in order to increase (or decrease) net income. The three major sources of manipulation are:

- increase (or decrease) an asset's useful life;
- change the depreciation method (from straight-line to declining balance or the opposite, for example) (with the limitation of the consistency accounting principle);
- decide to capitalize (or not) elements of the acquisition cost (such as financial expenses) or upgrade of the asset (by decomposing the upgrade in slices that all fit under the capitalization threshold).

The notes to financial statements, in particular the first part devoted to accounting policies, are very helpful for the user of financial statements. Managers must use them to reveal the accounting choices they have made during the year and thus allow the analyst or any reader to recast the figures in the light that suits them.

The impact of the choice of a depreciation method on the financial statements is dealt with in Appendix 7.8.

Key points

- Tangible fixed assets ['property, plant, and equipment' (PPE), 'plant assets', 'operational assets', or 'fixed assets'] create economic benefits over several periods and represent significant investments that must be put in place before any economic activity can take place.
- Fixed assets are, by nature, the most illiquid assets on the balance sheet. In countries where the accounting tradition is more 'patrimonial' they will appear at the top of the list of assets, while in countries where the accounting culture favors liquidity the tangible fixed assets will be listed at the bottom of the list.
- Fixed assets can be divided into three categories: (1) tangible assets; (2) intangible assets (see Chapter 8); and (3) financial fixed assets (see Chapter 13).
- The various accounting issues that arise when dealing with tangible fixed assets are related to their acquisition (definition, recognition, measurement), use (depreciation), and disposal (sale or removal).
- Depreciation is 'the systematic allocation of the depreciable cost of an asset over its useful life'.
- Several depreciation methods have been developed. The choice of the most appropriate method for reporting to shareholders should theoretically be made so as to best reflect the pattern of decline in the asset's service potential and should therefore be specific to each class of tangible assets.
- Two categories of methods are available: (1) time-based depreciation methods (straight-line, declining balance, and sum-of-the-years' digits); and (2) methods based on activity level (productive output and service quantity).
- In any given year, depreciation expenses are 'non-cash expenses' (the tangible assets have already been paid for, and depreciation expenses are only a time-based allocation of that original cost, as mentioned above). This means that the depreciation expenses have *no direct impact* on the cash balance (the *impact is only indirect*, through the tax deductibility of the depreciation expenses). The indirect impact on after-tax cash is even greater when an accelerated depreciation method is allowed for tax purposes.

Review (solutions are at the back of the book)

Review 7.1 Gibbons

Topic: Determining the cost of acquisition
Related part of the chapter: Core issues

Gibbons Co., a coffee shop, purchases a new coffee machine. The list price for the machine is 1,500 CU. However, the manufacturer is running a special offer, and Gibbons Co. obtains the machine for a price which is 20% lower than the list price. Freight expenses for the delivery of the machine are 150 CU, and installation and testing expenses amount to 100 CU. During installation, uninsured damages are incurred resulting in repair expenses of 200 CU.

Required

1. Compute the acquisition cost of the machine.
2. Record the acquisition in the format of your choice ('ledger–financial statements', ledger, journal, impact on financial statements).

Assignments

Assignment 7.1
Multiple-choice questions

Related part of the chapter Core issues

Select the right answer.

1. The most appropriate method of depreciation of land is
   (a) The straight-line method
   (b) The declining balance method
   (c) Either method
   (d) None of these

2. Depreciation will directly generate
   (a) An increase in cash
   (b) An increase in liabilities
   (c) A decrease in liabilities
   (d) A decrease in assets
   (e) A decrease in cash

3. At the end of the useful life of a tangible asset originally purchased for 100 CU and fully depreciated over five years, the gross value is
   (a) 0
   (b) 100
   (c) 20
   (d) None of these

4. Which of the following items would not be considered a tangible asset?
   1. Land
   2. Trademark
   3. Building
   4. Oil well
   5. Software

   (a) 1, 3, and 4
   (b) 2 and 4
   (c) 2 and 5
   (d) 2, 3, 4, and 5
   (e) 3 and 5

5. Examples of tangible assets include land, buildings and equipment
   (a) True
   (b) False

6. All tangible assets are charged to expense over a period of years in some systematic and rational manner
   (a) True
   (b) False

7. Companies can only use one method of depreciation for all of their depreciable assets
   (a) True
   (b) False

8. The Carthage Company acquired a building for its new head office. The following cash outlays were associated with the acquisition

Amount paid for the building	300,000
Legal fees	30,000
Property title search	3,000
Realtor's commissions	10,000

How should the Carthage Company record the acquisition? Allocate the total cash outlays between the book value of the asset (to be depreciated) and expenses recognized in the current year

	Building	Expenses
(a)	300,000	43,000
(b)	330,000	13,000
(c)	333,000	10,000
(d)	343,000	0
(e)	310,000	33,000

9. When using the double-declining balance method, in calculating the annual depreciation expense, the depreciation rate is multiplied by the
   (a) Purchase cost of the asset
   (b) Fair value of the asset at beginning of the period
   (c) Depreciable amount
   (d) Book value at beginning of that year
   (e) None of these

10. The share of a natural resource deposit's cost of acquisition that is expensed each year is called
   (a) Depreciation
   (b) Amortization
   (c) Depletion
   (d) Exhaustion
   (e) None of these

Assignment 7.2
Discussion questions

Related part of the chapter: Core/Advanced issues

1. Give some arguments in favor of at least four different methods of depreciation.
2. Does depreciation provide or consume cash?

3. Give some arguments in favor of each method of reporting the sale of tangible assets.
4. Does the acquisition of a tangible asset influence net income?

Assignment 7.3
Reporting in different sectors of activity

Related part of the chapter: Core issues

On the Internet, or in the library, find the annual reports of four companies from different sectors of activity in a given country.

Required

1. How are tangible fixed assets presented in their balance sheets? What decisions on the basis of this information can investors or shareholders take? What decisions would be difficult to take on the basis of just this information?
2. Are there any notes relating to tangible fixed assets? How do they enlarge the decision analysis possibilities offered to shareholders and investors?
3. What are the accounting treatments applied to these assets?
4. What appear to be the estimated useful lives of the major categories of tangible assets?
5. What is the weight of tangible fixed assets as a percentage of total assets? What strategic implications do you derive from this ratio?
6. What is the weight of depreciation expense as a percentage of sales?

Assignment 7.4
Reporting in the same sector of activity

Related part of the chapter: Core issues

On the Internet, or in the library, find the annual reports of three companies essentially in identical or similar industries in a given country or in different countries.

Required

Use questions from Assignment 7.3.

Assignment 7.5
Choice of depreciation methods

Related part of the chapter: Core/Advanced issues

Choose a country you know well, either because you come from this country or have worked there.

Required

Identify the depreciation methods which are most commonly used in practice. You can base your presentation on official statistics (if they exist) or on a sample of annual reports you will survey.

Assignment 7.6
Tippett

Topic: Popular depreciation methods
Related part of the chapter: Advanced/Core issues

Tippett Company acquired new machine tools for 10 million CU. Their aggregate predicted useful lives is four years and predicted residual value is 1 million CU.

Depreciation expense of this class of asset can be computed through one of five methods:

- Straight-line
- Double-declining balance
- Sum-of-the-years' digits
- Units of output basis
- Service hours basis.

Units of output and service hours for each year and in total are listed in the following table.

	Annual	Total
Units of output		15,000
■ Year 1	7,000	
■ Year 2	4,000	
■ Year 3	2,000	
■ Year 4	2,000	
Service hours		36,000
■ Year 1	12,000	
■ Year 2	9,000	
■ Year 3	8,000	
■ Year 4	7,000	

Required

- Variation 1: Prepare a depreciation schedule comparing the first two depreciation methods, assuming that the acquisition date was 1 January X1.
- Variation 2: Prepare a depreciation schedule comparing the five depreciation methods, assuming that the acquisition date was 1 January X1.

Assignment 7.7
Britten Inc.

Topic: Determining the cost of acquisition – recording the acquisition and the depreciation
Related part of the chapter: Advanced/Core issues

Britten Inc. is a large European civil engineering and construction enterprise. They have just finished building, for their own use, a large hangar that will serve as both a warehouse for their inventory of raw construction materials and as a garage for idle equipment between assignments. Construction began on 14 July X1 and was completed on 1 October of the same year. Resources consumed by the construction projects were:

- raw materials which were already in inventory for an amount of 10,000 CU;
- labor costs amounting to 20,000 CU.

This type of light construction is generally depreciated over 10 years and Britten Inc. chose to use the double-declining balance method. The residual value of the building will be essentially zero. The hangar will be fully depreciated by:

- either switching to the straight-line method when the double-declining rate on the balance becomes smaller than the straight-line rate over the remaining years;
- or switching to straight-line method at the mid-point of useful life of the hangar.

The closing date is 31 December.

Required

1. Record the cost of the hangar (depreciable amount).
2. Prepare the depreciation schedule under both possibilities for switching to straight-line, assuming that the hangar is fully depreciated at the end of year X10.
3. Record the depreciation allowance pertaining to the hangar in the income statement of Britten Inc. for the year ended 31 December X1.

Assignment 7.8
Saint-Gobain*

Topic: Reporting for movements of tangible assets
Related part of the chapter: Core issues

Founded in France in 1665 as a manufacturer of flat glass, Saint-Gobain has undergone several major transformations of its operations. The group is currently operating in five core sectors (construction material distribution, construction products, high-performance materials, flat glass, and packaging), and operates in over 49 countries around the world.

Note 5 in the 2004 consolidated annual report – prepared under French GAAP – pertains to property, plant, and equipment. It states the following:

Note 5 excerpted from Saint-Gobain's 2004 consolidated annual report

In millions of €	At 31 December 2003	Changes in Group structure	Acquisitions	Disposals	Transfers	Translation adjustments	Depreciation charge	At 31 December 2004
At cost:								
Land	1,195	30	33	(35)	0	(3)	–	1,220
Buildings	5,234	109	99	(168)	150	(27)	–	5,397
Machinery and equipment	13,911	196	449	(675)	742	(101)	–	14,522
Construction in progress	859	48	956	(8)	(892)	(19)	–	944
Total at cost	21,199	383	1,537	(886)	0	(150)	0	22,083
Depreciation:								
Land	(99)	(6)	–	4	–	1	(10)	(110)
Buildings	(2,596)	(38)	–	91	–	13	(232)	(2,762)
Machinery and equipment	(9,816)	(127)	–	623	–	31	(976)	(10,265)
Construction in progress	(2)	(3)	–	0	–	1	(3)	(7)
Total depreciation	(12,513)	(174)	0	718	0	46	(1,221)	(13,144)
Book value	8,686	209	1,537	(168)	0	(104)	(1,221)	8,939

References

EU (European Union) (1978) 4th Directive on the annual accounts of certain types of companies, No. 78/660/EEC. *Official Journal of the European Communities*, 14 August.

IASB (1989) Framework for the Preparation and Presentation of Financial Statements, London.

IASB (revised 1993) International Accounting Standard No. 23: Borrowing Costs, London.

IASB (2003) International Accounting Standard No. 16: Property, Plant and Equipment, London.

IASB (2004a) International Accounting Standard No. 36: Impairment of Assets, London.

IASB (2004b) International Accounting Standard No. 38: Intangible Assets, London.

Skousen F., Stice J., and Stice E. K. (2003) *Intermediate Accounting*, South-Western College Publishing, Cincinnati, OH.

Further reading

Burlaud, A., Messina, M., and Walton, P. (1996) Depreciation: concepts and practices in France and the UK. *European Accounting Review*, 5(2), 299–316.

Chambers, D., Jennings, R., and Thompson, R. (1999) Evidence on the usefulness of capital expenditures as an alternative measure of depreciation. *Review of Accounting Studies*, 2(3–4), 169–95.

Collins, L. (1994) Revaluation of assets in France: the interaction between professional practice, theory and political necessity. *European Accounting Review*, 3(1), 122–31.

Paterson, R. (2002) Impairment. *Accountancy*, 130(1312), 105.

Additional material on the website

Go to http://www.thomsonlearning.co.uk/stolowylebas2 for further information.

The following appendices to this chapter are available on the dedicated website:

Appendix 7.1: Examples of components of the acquisition cost

Appendix 7.2: Overhead

Appendix 7.3: Calculation of capitalized interest costs

Appendix 7.4: Sum-of-the-years' digits method

Appendix 7.5: Depreciation for partial years (fractional year problems)

Appendix 7.6: Accounting for a sale of fixed asset: Illustration: Purcell Company

Appendix 7.7: Removing a fully depreciated tangible asset from the book

Appendix 7.8: Impact of the choice of a depreciation method on the financial statements

Notes

1. Productive, here, refers to the potential of economic benefit generation provided by the fixed asset
2. The reader can read Skousen *et al.* (2003) to find an explanation referring to US GAAP.
3. The interested reader can consult the following US textbook: Skousen *et al.* (2003).
4. The concept of non-cash item and the mechanism linking the depreciation expense to the cash flow are developed in Chapter 14.
5. Without wanting to get into too many details – that would be the purpose of a Cost Accounting book – let us say that the cost of an object, at any point in the manufacturing to distribution cycle of the object, is the sum of all services (represented by materials costs, components costs, labor costs, and the cost of various and assorted overhead) that the object has received at that point. These aggregated costs 'travel' with the object as it physically moves from workshop to warehouse, to another workshop to storage to the delivery truck, etc. These costs are matched against revenue when the object is sold. The depreciation cost is one the services received by the object in that it represents the consumption, by the object, of the productive capacity of the tangible asset.

C8

Chapter 8 Intangible assets

Learning objectives

After studying this chapter, you will understand:

- That intangible assets are usually divided in three categories: research and development (R&D); goodwill; and other intangible assets.
- That intangible assets may represent a significant proportion of total assets.
- That intangible assets raise issues of definition, recognition, and recording of their change in value.
- How the concept of goodwill is defined and what it represents.
- That some accounting principles favor recognition of intangible assets while others oppose it.
- What the criteria are for recognition of an intangible asset.
- How accounting handles changes in value of intangible assets after their recognition.
- What the conditions are for appropriate R&D capitalization.
- What the arguments are in favor and against R&D capitalization.
- What accounting rules apply to reporting development of computer software.

As defined in Chapter 7, intangible assets are long-lived (long-term) assets that lack physical sub-stance and whose acquisition and continued possession represent rights to future economic benefits. Intangible assets comprise patents, franchises, licenses, trademarks, brands, copyrights, etc., and, if certain conditions are met, capitalized R&D.

The valuation and reporting of intangibles has been controversial and a source of debate for many years, mainly because it is very difficult to objectively define and value future economic benefits derived from such assets. How can one establish an 'objective' value for a brand, especially if the brand was developed by the firm itself and not purchased from someone else in an 'at arm's length' transaction? Unlike with physical assets where the value is linked to ownership, it is the 'quality' of the usage made of the intangible by a management team that creates the stream of future economic benefits.

For example, when a pharmaceutical laboratory with a cosmetics division acquired a firm owning a well-known perfume brand, their intention was to use the well-known brand as a locomotive for the rest of their cosmetics division and develop the stream of future economic benefits of both the newly acquired firm and also, by ricochet and osmosis, of the other pre-existing products and brands in the portfolio of that division. Right after the acquisition, the value of the 'brand' was clearly the market price paid for it. However, the culture of that pharmaceutical laboratory was so different from that of a cosmetics and perfume business that it drowned the image of the acquired brand and the management was unable to capitalize on its acquisition. It ended up choosing to sell the whole cosmetics division a couple of years later at a loss (i.e., at a selling price below the book value of the division, including valuing the acquired brand below its original purchase price). The buyer, in turn, having a culture that proved to be more coherent with the potential of the brand was able to reap significant profit from the acquisition. Although it listed the brand only at its (deflated) purchase price, the reality of the future economic benefits would have called for a higher valuation had the firm sought a new buyer for that brand. Of course, the prudence principle did not allow the new owner of the brand to revaluate upwards that intangible asset in its books. 'Same' intangible asset, different values, depending on in whose hands it is held.

Accountants and financial analysts have long been quite cautious about intangible assets. Accountants tended to expense the cost of any intangibles acquisition (or development) in the period incurred. Financial analysts, when faced with financial statements in which these costs had been recorded as assets, tended to consider them as 'virtual' assets and excluded them from their analyses.

However, today's economy relies heavily on intangibles (see Table 8.1 later) and these assets have to be reported accurately if the financial statements are to give the shareholders a true and fair view of the business. Both the accountants and financial analysts communities are therefore reconsidering their positions. The development of brands or the sale of rights to patents may, in some cases, represent the major source of value creation by a business (for example, in retail, cosmetics or luxury products, biotechnology, or software development).

The reporting of intangible assets raises three major issues listed in Figure 8.1. Each will be dealt with in turn in the Core issues of this chapter.

Among the various intangible assets, capitalized research and development costs and computer software deserve special attention, and will be covered in the Advanced issues of this chapter.

Figure 8.1 Intangible assets issues

Intangible assets issues → Definition of what constitutes an intangible asset; Recognition of intangible assets and their valuation in the balance sheet; Handling of changes in value in case of such recognition

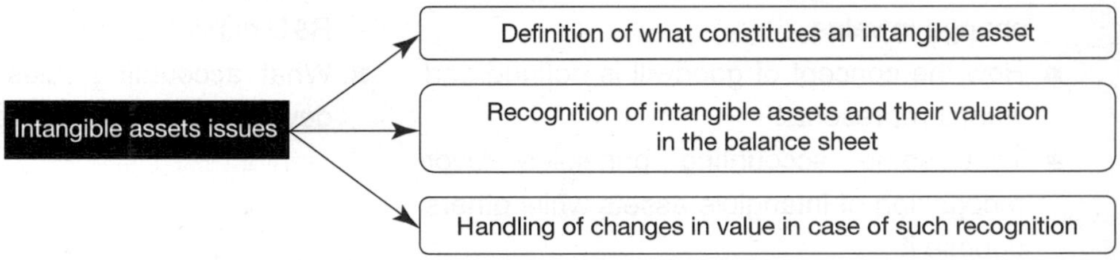

1 Core issues

Most businesses report at least some intangible assets in their year-end 2004 balance sheet, as exemplified by the sample of firms listed in Table 8.1.

1.1 Definition of intangibles

The definition of intangibles has evolved over the last few years trying to provide a better understanding of the concept, allow reliable measurement of intangible investments, and promote understanding, and communication between researchers, managers, users of financial information, and policy makers. Intangible assets are usually considered to have no physical substance and to be linked to legal rights (trademarks, patents, copyrights).

Table 8.1 Weight of intangible assets in balance sheets

Company (country – activity)	Currency	Types of intangibles	Intangible assets (net amount)	Total assets (net amount)	Intangibles as % of total assets
RC2 (USA – Racing replicas)	$000	Goodwill Intangible assets, net	282,367 58,243		48.2 9.9
		Total intangible assets	340,610	585,748	58.1
ISS (Denmark – Support services)	DKKm	Goodwill Software and others	15,494 175		52.2 0.6
		Total intangible assets	15,669	29,676	52.8
Interbrew (Belgium – Brewery group)	€m	Intangible assets Goodwill	7,459 246		40.1 1.3
		Total intangible assets	7,705	18,596	41.4
Securitas (Sweden – Security services and alarm systems)	SEKm	Goodwill Other intangible fixed assets	14,508.3 431.9		40.1 1.2
		Total intangible assets	14,940.2	36,203.8	41.3
EMI (UK – Music)	£m	Music copyrights Goodwill	402.8 33.2		23.5 1.9
		Total intangible assets	436.0	1,713.0	25.4
Saint-Gobain (France – Glass, building materials, and high-performance industrial materials)	€m	Goodwill Other intangible assets	5,170 1,883		16.7 6.1
		Total intangible assets	7,053	30,887	22.8
Roche (Switzerland – Pharmaceuticals, chemicals)	CHFm	Goodwill Patents, licenses, trademarks and other	5,532 6,340		9.5 10.9
		Total intangible assets	11,872	58,076	20.4
Club Méditerranée (France – Leisure)	€m	Goodwill Intangible assets	79 104		5.3 7.0
		Total intangible assets	183	1,482	12.3
Repsol (Spain – Oil and gas)	€m	Start-up expenses Intangible assets Goodwill	1 1,345 2,677		0.0 3.5 6.9
		Total intangible assets	4,023	38,943	10.4
Philips (Netherlands – Consumer and professional electronics)	€m	Intangible assets Goodwill	989 1,818		3.2 5.9
		Total intangible assets	2,807	30,723	9.1
Pirelli (Italy – Tires, cables and) broadband systems)	€000	Formation costs Patents and design patent rights Concessions, licenses, trademarks and similar rights Goodwill Difference on consolidation Intangible assets in progress and payments on account Other intangible assets	13,993 2,293 24,756 39,370 392,448 2,012 55,386		0.1 0.0 0.2 0.4 3.8 0.0 0.5
		Total intangible assets	530,258	10,385,732	5.1
EVN (Austria – Electricity and gas production and retail, and wholesale distribution, heating services)	€000	Goodwill Other intangible assets	34,030.0 90,823.3		0.9 2.4
		Total intangible assets	124,853.3	3,731,967.4	3.3
Aluminum Corporation of China (China – Aluminum production)	RMB000	Goodwill Mining rights	406,686 322,467		0.8 0.7
		Total intangible assets	729,153	48,980,363	1.5

Generally, the definition of intangibles is based on the existence of the following four criteria:

1. identifiability;
2. lack of physical substance;
3. the entity claiming it as an asset must have control over the asset; and
4. existence of defined future economic benefits deriving from the asset.

1.1.1 Principles

The IASB defines an intangible asset as 'an identifiable non-monetary asset without physical substance' (IASB 2004b, IAS 38: § 8). Remember that an asset is 'a resource: (a) controlled by an entity as a result of past events; and (b) from which future economic benefits are expected to flow to the enterprise', while 'monetary assets are money held and assets to be received in fixed or determinable amounts of money' (IAS 38: § 8).

All countries' GAAP acknowledge the existence and the importance of intangible assets. However, each may have its own specific definition of the concept with more or fewer details than contained in the IASB definition. For example, in the United States, intangible assets are 'assets (not including financial assets) that lack physical substance' (FASB 2001, SFAS 142, Appendix F). In the UK, intangible assets are 'non-financial fixed assets that do not have physical substance but are identifiable and are controlled by the entity through custody or legal rights' (ASB 1997: § 2).

1.1.2 Main categories of intangibles

Intangible assets are usually divided in three categories: research and development (R&D), goodwill, and other intangible assets.

Research and development In certain circumstances, R&D expenses may be capitalized, i.e., recorded as an asset. This topic will be developed in the second part of this chapter.

Goodwill The term *goodwill* has been adopted around the world to refer to the difference between the purchase price of an acquired business and the 'value' of its identifiable assets (minus identifiable liabilities). The term goodwill has two somewhat different meanings depending on whether it is reported in consolidated financial statements (corresponding to the group – see Chapter 13) or in unconsolidated (individual company) financial statements.

'Goodwill acquired in a business combination [i.e., which will be recorded in consolidated financial statements] represents a payment made by the acquirer in anticipation of future economic benefits from assets that are not capable of being individually identified and separately recognized' (IAS 38: § 11). Goodwill represents any excess of the cost of the acquisition over the acquirer's interest in the fair value of the identifiable assets and liabilities acquired as of the date of the exchange transaction (IASB, 2004c: based on § BC 122). The calculation of goodwill is presented in Chapter 13.

Figure 8.2 below explains the difference between the purchase price and the book value of assets and liabilities acquired.

Figure 8.2 Goodwill and valuation differences

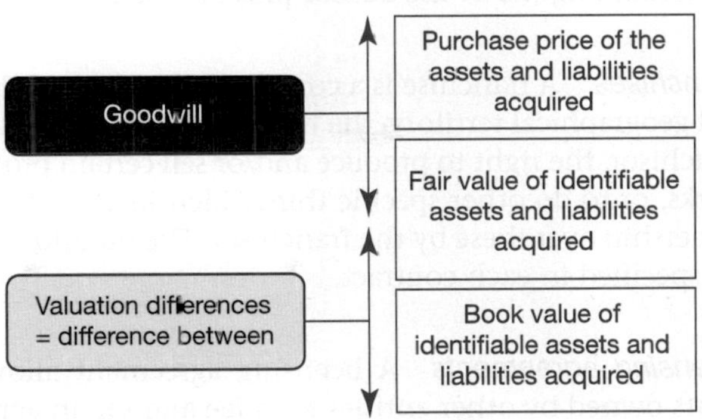

The difference between the fair value of each identifiable asset or liability and their book value is called a 'valuation difference' (see Figure 8.2). Unlike goodwill, the valuation differences are not explicitly reported in the balance sheet. Since each asset or liability is recorded in the acquirer's books at fair value, the valuation differences are not reported as such. They are included in the new book value of the item in the acquirer's accounts (fair value in the acquirer's books equals book value in the seller's books plus valuation difference). We consider that it is important to conceptually identify these valuation differences because we feel it is crucial to avoid overestimating the goodwill. We agree with the IASB's position that goodwill should only represent the value of the unidentified intangible assets acquired (see below).

In consolidated financial statements, goodwill is often referred to in the balance sheet as 'consolidation goodwill'. In the unconsolidated financial statements, some countries' GAAP recognize goodwill and call it 'purchased goodwill'.

Goodwill, whether in consolidated or unconsolidated financial statements, often represents the value of intangible elements of the value of the firm such as the loyal customer base of the enterprise, the brand name or the reputation of the firm, the 'pipeline' of R&D projects or new products, the expertise of the personnel, etc.

Other intangible assets

Patent A patent is a document granted by a government or an official authority bestowing on the inventor of a product or manufacturing process the exclusive right to use or sell the invention or rights to it. The duration of the protection offered by a patent varies between countries (17 years in the USA, 20 in France, etc.). A patent cannot be renewed, but obtaining a new patent on modifications and improvements to the original invention may extend its effective life.

Trademark A trademark (or trade name, brand or brand name) is a distinctive identification (symbol, logo, design, word, slogan, emblem, etc.) of a family of manufactured products and/or services that distinguishes it from similar families of products or services provided by other parties. Legal protection for trademarks is usually granted by registration with a specialized (government regulated or supervised) office. This registration is effective for an initial duration which varies from country to country (for example, 20 years in the USA or 10 years in France) and which can be renewed periodically for the same period under specified conditions (mainly that the trademark be effectively used by the entity in carrying out its business).

Copyright A copyright provides the holder with exclusive rights to the publication, production, and sale of the rights for an intellectual creation, be it a musical, artistic, literary, or dramatic work (and often, by extension, software). Usually, the protection is granted for the remaining life of the author plus 50 years.

Franchises A franchise is a contractual agreement that grants, for a fee and within a limited geographical territory, the holder (franchisee), with or without direct support from the franchisor, the right to produce and/or sell certain products or services, to use certain trademarks, or to do other specific things identified in the franchise agreement without loss of ownership over these by the franchisor. The duration and terms of the franchise agreement are specified in each contract.

Licensing agreements A licensing agreement allows a company to use properties or rights owned by other entities for a fee and for an agreed upon duration. It applies specifically to patents and trademarks.

Organization (or set-up) costs Organization costs (incorporation or set-up costs) are the costs incurred during the process of establishing or incorporating a business. They include incorporation fees, legal fees (such as those incurred for the writing of by-laws or articles of incorporation), underwriting fees, accounting fees, and promotional fees. Some countries allow these costs to be recorded as intangible assets. If these costs have been capitalized, they must be amortized over a fairly short period (up to five years), generally using a straight-line approach.

IASB (IAS 38) prohibits the recognition of such organization costs as an intangible asset because they do no meet the asset recognition criteria (future economic benefits and cost measured reliably, see IAS 38: §§21–23). If a business entity reports in accordance with IASB, the organization or incorporation costs are expensed as incurred.

For example, Albeniz NA was created on 1 January X1. The cost incurred during the incorporation process amount to a total 200 CU. The manager decides to capitalize these costs and amortize them over four years. Figure 8.3 describes the ensuing accounting entries.

Figure 8.3 Accounting for organization costs

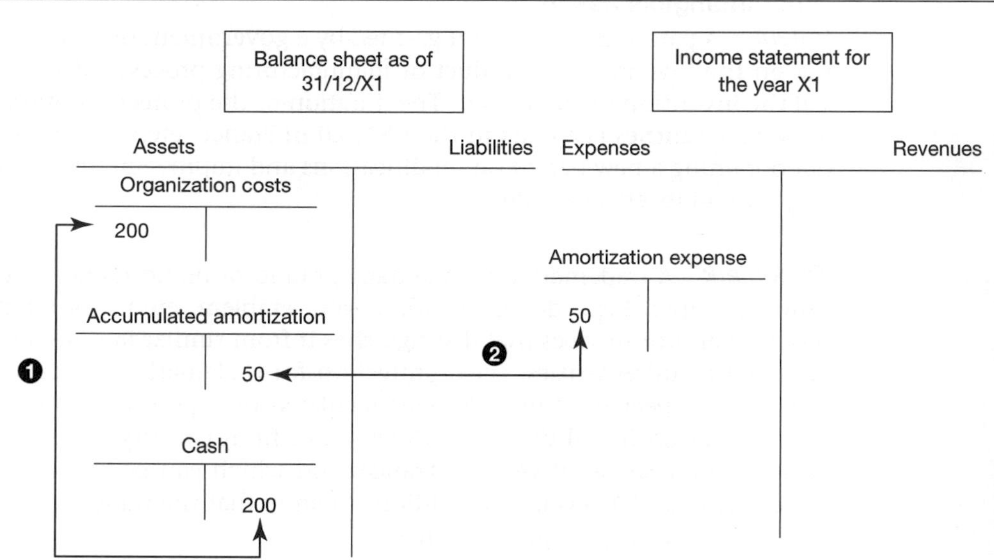

❶ Payment of organization costs.

❷ Amortization: 200/4 years = 50 CU per year.

Computer software costs Under certain circumstances, computer software can be considered to be an 'intangible asset'. (See more on this point in the Advanced issues section.)

Soccer player transfer fees In the UK, for example, incorporated soccer (football) clubs are allowed, although not required, to reflect the acquisition value of their players on their balance sheets and to amortize such value over the length of their contract. Until recently, these clubs had no choice but to charge transfer fees against profits in the year they occurred, thus leading to wild fluctuations in yearly reported income without fairly representing the situation of the business.

Similar dispositions exist in other countries. For example, in France (CRC ruling 2004–07), amounts paid by a sports team to another in order to obtain the transfer of a player are grounds for the creation of an intangible asset because the new team controls the employment of the player and expects to derive future economic benefits from the player being a member of the team. Such an asset can be amortized over the life of the contract or over five years, whichever is the shortest.

Deferred charges (deferred assets) Deferred charges are sometimes considered to be intangible assets. They are conceptually identical to prepaid or deferred expenses but they have longer-term economic benefits and must therefore be recognized over several periods to be coherent with the matching principle. Examples of such deferred charges are debt issuance costs (e.g., fees paid to banks or brokerage firms for a new flotation of stock or bonds) or fixed assets acquisition costs (when they are not included in the cost of the asset). Accountants often use this category as a catchall for items hard to classify anywhere else. Deferred charges, therefore, deserve significant attention on the part of any user of financial information to understand what is actually covered in this category. However, as IASB prohibits their recognition (IAS 38) because they do not meet the asset recognition criteria, the use of deferred charges should decrease in world practice.

Real-life example EVN AG (Energie Versorgung Niederösterreich)

(Austria – IFRS/IAS GAAP – *Source*: Annual report 2003/04 – Energy, gas, heating services)

Notes to financial statements

Other intangible assets [see Table 8.1] include electricity procurement rights, transportation rights on natural gas pipelines, and other rights, in particular software licenses, as well as capitalized future profit contributions from the order backlog of the WTE Group at the date of initial consolidation.

Real-life example Club Méditerranée

(France – French GAAP – *Source*: Annual report 2004 – Leisure)
This company provides an interesting detailed list of its intangible assets.

Note 3-1-2 to the consolidated financial statements

Other intangible assets

Millions of euros	31 October 2004		
	Cost	Amortization and provisions	Net
Start-up costs	1	(1)	–
Jet tours trademark	23	–	23
Club Med Gym purchased goodwill	33	(4)	29
Other trademarks, licenses	5	(3)	2
Booking [and reservation software] system	44	(28)	16
Other software	59	(40)	19
Leasehold rights and purchased goodwill	9	(2)	7
Other intangible assets	9	(4)	5
Intangible assets in progress	3	–	3
	186	(82)	104

Comment: The reader will have noted that this example illustrates the point made earlier of the existence of two kinds of goodwill. Club Méditerranée distinguishes purchased goodwill (which is included in the note above) from consolidation goodwill (which is mentioned in Table 8.1 and does not appear in the note 3-1-2, which only deals with intangible assets other than consolidation goodwill).

Real-life example Saint-Gobain

(France – French GAAP – *Source*: Annual report 2003/2004 – Production, processing, and distribution of glass, high-performance materials, and construction supplies)

Note 1 to the consolidated financial statements

Other intangible assets [see Table 8.1] are represented by purchased goodwill, trademarks, patent, computer software, and debt issuance costs.

Comment: Here again, purchased goodwill is distinguished from consolidation goodwill (which was mentioned in Table 8.1). The inclusion of debt issuance costs should be noticed.

Real-life example Volvo Group

(Sweden – Swedish GAAP – *Source*: Annual report 2004 – Car industry)

Intangible assets (31 December 2004) (net amounts)	In millions of Swedish Kroner (SEK)
Goodwill	14,184
Entrance fees, aircraft engine programs	2,758
Product and software development	6,569
Other intangible assets	1,734
Total	25,245

Comment: The second item in the list of intangible assets is relatively rare and is directly connected to the industrial activity of Volvo Group. It reflects the fact that, when joining an existing international, multicompany R&D program such as the one referred to here, each new partner must provide some capital to buy into the program, i.e., compensate the pre-existing partners for the investment they have already incurred and which they are willing to share, thus seeing a dilution of their future returns.

Real-life example Pirelli

(Italy – Italian GAAP – *Source*: Annual report 2004 – Tires, cables and broadband systems)

The detail of intangible assets is given directly in the balance sheet (see Table 8.1). The notes provide for information on the nature of the items, which require such an explanation:

- Formation costs: capital increase costs of consolidated companies.
- Goodwill: amount paid for this purpose by the Group companies for the acquisition of companies or other corporate transactions [purchased goodwill].
- 'Difference on consolidation', relating to the acquisition of investments [consolidation goodwill].
- Other intangible assets: applied software acquisition costs, leasehold improvements, image awareness costs benefiting future periods, loan acquisition costs.

1.2 Recognition of intangible assets

Different accounting principles favor or oppose recognition of intangible assets.

Matching principle: The recognition of intangible assets allows their amortization over the period during which economic benefits are derived.
Prudence principle: Since economic benefits derived from intangible assets are uncertain, the cost should be expensed in the period when incurred.

The recognition of intangible assets is the result of an informativeness trade-off between relevance and reliability or conservatism and prudence (see Høegh-Krohn and Knivsflå, 2000). Accounting standards in local GAAP generally provide recognition criteria for each of the three categories of intangible assets: research and development costs (R&D); goodwill (G); and other intangible assets (O).

Figure 8.4 illustrates the possibilities of recognizing (R) or not recognizing (NR) intangible assets.

Figure 8.4 Recognition of intangible assets

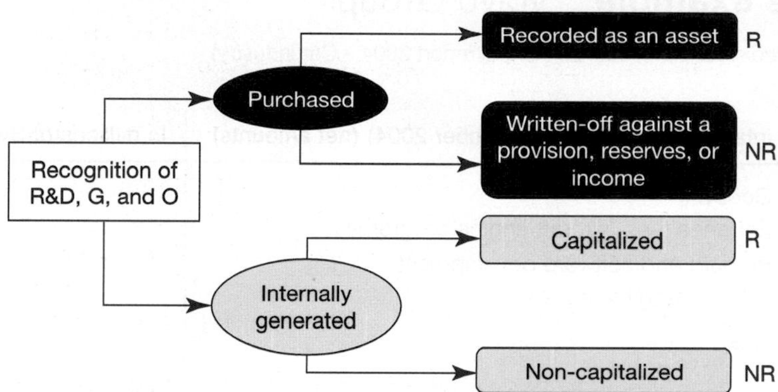

According to IASB (IAS 38): 'the recognition of an item as an intangible asset requires an entity to demonstrate that the item meets: (a) the definition of an intangible asset (...); and (b) the recognition criteria (...)' (§ 18). More precisely, 'an intangible asset shall be recognized if, and only if:

(a) It is probable that the expected future economic benefits that are attributable to the asset will flow to the entity; and
(b) The cost of the asset can be measured reliably' (§ 21).

In the case of an acquisition of a discrete asset, the issue is simple; the probability of attributable future economic benefits, mentioned in the recognition criterion (...) 'is always considered to be satisfied for separately acquired intangible assets' (IAS 38: § 25).

In the case of an acquisition as part of a business combination, the situation is more complex. IAS 38 and IFRS 3 state that: 'an acquirer recognizes at the acquisition date, separately from goodwill, an intangible asset of the acquiree if the asset's fair value can be measured reliably, irrespective of whether the asset had been recognized by the acquiree before the business combination' (§ 34). One example of such a situation could be the valuation of the air-rights over a piece of real estate in a dense urban environment. The use of a real estate property represented by, say, a railroad station can hardly be modified, but the right to build over the railroad can prove to be vary valuable when urban constructible land is scarce; the railroad company owning the land probably never valued the air-rights in its books. The new owner of the Pennsylvania Railroad real estate, after the railroad's bankruptcy was entitled to value – and develop – the air-rights over both Penn station and Grand Central Station in central Manhattan in New York.

The writing-off of goodwill against reserves in business combinations, even if it was used only exceptionally, is no longer supported by the IASB (see IFRS 3, 2004c), and is therefore more rarely recommended in national GAAPs. Denmark, Germany, the Netherlands, and Switzerland are, at the date of this writing, the only remaining European countries allowing goodwill to be written off against reserves. The United Kingdom, a proponent for many years of goodwill write-off, has reversed its position, and standard FRS 10 (adopted in 1997 by the ASB) disallows this possibility.

IAS 38 also states clearly: 'internally generated goodwill shall not be recognized as an asset' (§ 48).

Finally, IAS 38 acknowledges that: 'it is sometimes difficult to assess whether an internally generated intangible asset qualifies for recognition'. An entity should assess if the asset meets the criteria for recognition. The Standard provides some specific developments concerning research and development (see Advanced issues).

1.3 Reporting of changes in intangible assets value

As seen in Chapter 7, the process of allocation of the cost of an intangible asset over its useful life is called amortization instead of depreciation.

1.3.1 Different possibilities exist of changes in intangible assets value

In principle, three possibilities for reporting changes in value of intangible assets exist and are summarized in Figure 8.5. Either the asset cost is amortized (over different periods: e.g., five years, 20 years, or the useful life), or a decrease in value is recognized through impairment, if necessary. A revaluation based on the fair value of the intangible asset is allowed by some countries' GAAP and represents the third possibility of recording a change in value of intangible assets.

Duration and practices of amortization, when the method is allowed, vary between countries, rendering international comparisons often difficult without considerable rework. Some local GAAP simply indicate that amortization must be recorded over the useful life of the asset without any further specification; others require amortization over the useful life up to an upper limit (five, 20 years or even 40 years in the USA, before the reform of 2001 – see below).

In the USA, the Statement of Financial Accounting Standard No. 142, Goodwill and Other Intangible Assets, adopted in June 2001, abolished amortization over 40 years and replaced it by an impairment test. The same modification has been adopted in Canada. The new regulation has been implemented in the majority of cases in 2002. Following this move, the IASB has revised IAS 38 (IASB 2004b) on intangible assets and issued IFRS 3 (IASB: 2004c) on business combinations.

In IAS 38, the treatment of changes in value after recognition concerning intangible assets (excluding goodwill) is now based on the following distinction: intangible assets with finite or indefinite useful lives.

- Finite useful life: 'The depreciable amount of an intangible asset with a finite useful life shall be allocated on a systematic basis over its useful life' (IAS 38: § 97).
- Indefinite useful life: 'An intangible asset with an indefinite useful life shall not be amortized' (IAS 38: § 107). 'In accordance with IAS 36 Impairment of Assets, an entity is required to test an intangible asset with an indefinite useful life for impairment by comparing its recoverable amount with its carrying amount' (IAS 38: § 108).

Figure 8.6 summarizes the treatment of changes in intangible assets value after recognition, according to the IASB.

Figure 8.5 Processes of changes in value of intangible assets (different theoretical possibilities)

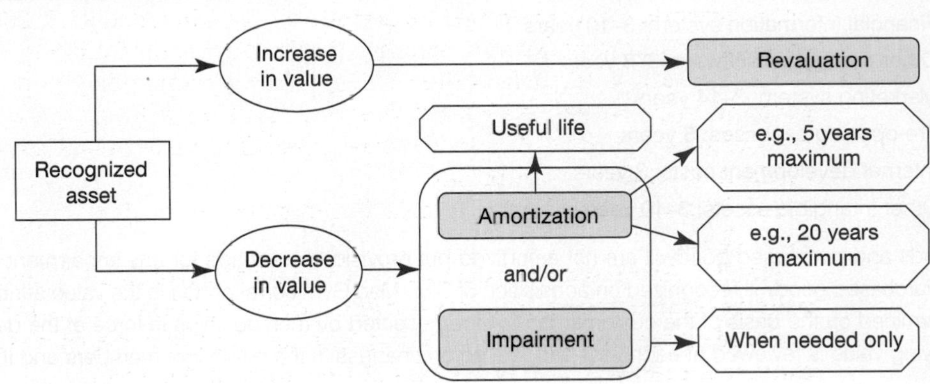

Figure 8.6 Processes of changes in value of intangible assets (IASB)

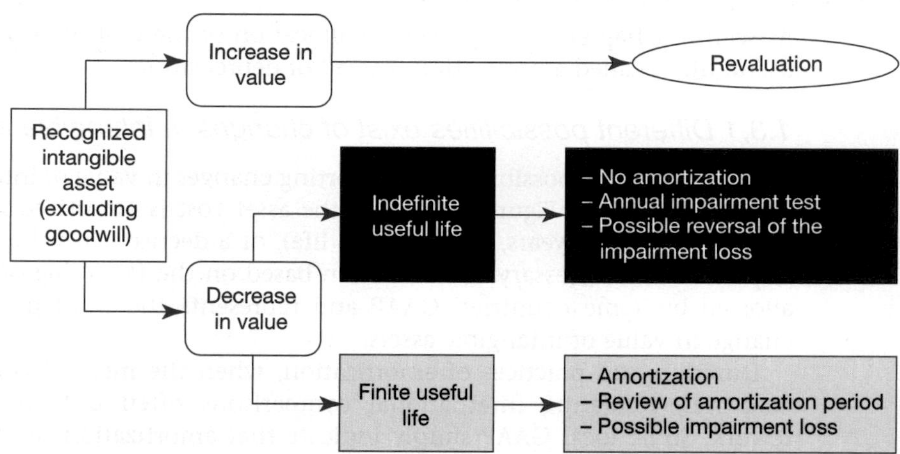

The handling of changes in value of goodwill is somewhat different from that applied to all other intangible assets, and dealt with in IFRS 3 (§§ 51 and 54). It is based on the following rules:

- no amortization;
- annual impairment test (in accordance with IAS 36: 2004a);
- no reversal of any impairment loss.

This latest element should be highlighted: the reversal of the impairment loss is not possible for goodwill, whereas it is still an open possibility for other intangible assets.

In the case of intangible assets with a finite useful life, amortization and impairment are not exclusive of each other. The impairment amount can be added to the predefined amortization expense if the accountant feels the environment has changed and the pattern of depreciation does not offer a fair net value of the asset (the principle of the 'lower of cost or market' applies here). Many countries, including the Netherlands, Canada, Ireland, the United Kingdom and France, have adopted this position. In addition, the IASB allows the possibility of revaluation for intangible assets (IAS 38: § 75).

Real-life example Club Méditerranée

(France – French GAAP – *Source*: Annual report 2003/2004 – Leisure)

Note 1.3.1 to the financial statements: Intangible assets (other than goodwill)

Amortization is charged by the straight-line method over the following estimated useful lives:

- Travel management module: 3 years
- Financial information system: 3–10 years
- Other purchased software: 3–8 years
- Marketing system: 3–14 years
- Pre-opening expenses: 5 years
- Internet development costs: 3 years
- Other intangible assets: 3–10 years

Brands and purchased goodwill are not amortized but provisions are made for any impairment in value.

Purchased goodwill recognized on acquisition of Club Med Gym corresponds to the value attributed to market share, determined on the basis of the customer portfolio represented by memberships in force at the date of acquisition. The carrying value is reviewed at each year-end, based on changes in the number of members and the membership fee.

Real-life example Saint-Gobain

(France – French GAAP – *Source*: Annual report 2004 – Production, processing and distribution of glass, high-performance materials, and construction supplies)

Note 1 to the consolidated financial statements states that trademarks other than retail and wholesale trademarks are amortized on a straight-line basis over a period not exceeding 40 years. Trademarks pertaining to the wholesale and retail business are not amortized. Patents are amortized over their useful estimate lives, not exceeding 20 years. Purchased software is amortized over a period of 3–5 years.

Debt issuance costs relating to bonds or other long-term borrowings are capitalized and amortized over the term of the debt.

Real-life example Repsol YPF

(Spain – Spanish GAAP – *Source*: Annual report 2004 – Oil and gas)

According to notes 2 and 4 to the consolidated financial statements, the following periods are adopted:

Purchased goodwill	10 years, the average years of useful life of the facilities
Contracts for purchase of service management rights	Related contract terms (from 15 to 25 years)
Exclusive rights to use gas pipelines	Term of the related right (currently 25 years)
Computer software and intellectual property	From 4 to 10 years
Administrative concessions	Concession term
Rights under long-term time-charter agreements	Useful life of methane vessels (currently 20 years)

Real-life example EVN (Energie Versorgung Niederösterreich)

(Austria – IFRS/IAS GAAP – *Source*: Annual report 2003/04 – Energy, gas, heating services)

As a result of the impairment tests completed during the period under review, a value adjustment was required for the intangible assets. This was met by exceptional depreciation on intangible assets of €2,184,800.

2 Advanced issues

2.1 Accounting for research and development

2.1.1 Definition

IAS 38 (IASB 2004b: § 8) states that:

(a) Research is 'original and planned investigation undertaken with the prospect of gaining new scientific or technical knowledge and understanding'. 'Examples of research activities are:

- Activities aimed at obtaining new knowledge;
- The search for, evaluation and final selection of, applications of research findings or other knowledge;
- The search for alternatives for materials, devices, products, processes, systems, or services; and
- The formulation, design, evaluation, and final selection of possible alternatives for new or improved materials, devices, products, processes, systems, or services' (IAS 38: § 56).

(b) Development is 'the application of research findings or other knowledge to a plan or design for the production of new or substantially improved materials, devices, products, processes, systems or services before the start of commercial production or use' (IAS 38: § 8). 'Examples of development activities include:

- The design, construction, and testing of pre-production or pre-use prototypes and models;
- The design of tools, jigs, molds, and dies involving new technology;
- The design, construction, and operation of a pilot plant that is not of a scale economically feasible for commercial production; and
- The design, construction, and testing of a chosen alternative for new or improved materials, devices, products, processes, systems, or services' (IAS 38: § 59).

Some countries distinguish between fundamental and applied research within the category of research and development, and recommend differentiated reporting:

- Pure research is experimental or theoretical work undertaken primarily to acquire new scientific or technical knowledge for its own sake, rather than directed towards any specific aim or application.
- Applied research is original or critical investigation undertaken in order to gain new scientific or technical knowledge and directed towards a specific practical aim or objective.

2.1.2 Accounting for R&D expenses or costs

The default position, because of the prudence principle, is to expense research and development costs when incurred. This principle applies, with no exception, to research costs: 'No intangible asset arising from research (or from the research phase of an internal project) shall be recognized. Expenditure on research (or on the research phase of an internal project) shall be recognized as an expense when it is incurred' (IAS 38: § 54). However, under certain circumstances and if specified criteria are met, some development (and applied research – when the distinction is made) costs may be capitalized and recorded as an intangible asset.

Conditions for capitalization According to IAS 38 (IASB: 2004b: § 57), 'an intangible asset arising from development (or from the development phase of an internal project) shall be recognized if, and only if, an entity can demonstrate all of the following criteria are met:

(a) The technical feasibility of completing the intangible asset so that it will be available for use or sale.

(b) Its intention to complete the intangible asset and use or sell it.

(c) Its ability to use or sell the intangible asset.

(d) How the intangible asset will generate probable future economic benefits. Among other things, the entity can demonstrate the existence of a market for the output of the intangible asset or the intangible asset itself or, if it is to be used internally, the usefulness of the intangible asset.

(e) The availability of adequate technical, financial and other resources to complete the development and to use or sell the intangible asset.

(f) Its ability to measure reliably the expenditure attributable to the intangible asset during its development'.

The wording 'shall' is important here as it might lead the reader to think that capitalization of R&D is required if the six above-mentioned criteria are met. In practice, we believe that there is still maneuvering room for companies; given that some criteria are extremely subjective in their application, it is fairly easy to claim that, even with the same facts, a condition has not been met or has been met.

Table 8.2 summarizes the six necessary criteria stated in the IAS 38 that must be met for capitalization (in addition to general recognition criteria) and provides examples of excerpts from accounting standards around the world, corresponding to these criteria. Each country standard for capitalization can be defined, as shown in Table 8.3, as a specific mix of the six IASB criteria.

Table 8.2 Criteria for R&D capitalization

(1)	Identifiability	■ 'The projects concerned are clearly identifiable' ■ 'A detailed description has been made of the product and process' ■ 'The R&D work and the expenditures accrued on the work shall be well defined and the R&D work should have a fixed application'
(2)	Evaluation	■ 'Their respective costs are distinctly evaluated in order to be allocated over time' ■ 'Costs to be allocated are determinable' ■ 'Ability to measure the expenditure attributable to the intangible asset during its development'
(3)	Technical feasibility	■ 'Proof exists of technical feasibility of the product or process' ■ 'The technical feasibility of the product or process has been established' ■ 'The technical feasibility of completing the intangible asset so that it will be available for use or sale'
(4)	Commercial success	■ 'Each project has a serious chance of commercial success at the date of closing of financial statements' ■ 'The new product or process will be introduced in the market' ■ 'There is a clear market potential or other beneficial use' ■ 'The enterprise should demonstrate the existence of a market for the output of the intangible asset' ■ 'Ability to use or sell the intangible asset'
(5)	Future economic benefits	■ 'It will generate future economic benefits over several years'
(6)	Financial feasibility	■ 'The development process can be completed (i.e., is financially feasible)' ■ 'There must be resources both for the completion of the R&D work and for the marketing of the product or process if it is intended for sale' ■ 'Adequate resources exist, or are expected to be available, to complete the project'
(7)	Intention to complete	■ 'Intention to complete the intangible asset and use or sell it'

Table 8.3 Examples of countries and conditions

Country/organization	Minimum set of criteria required in local GAAP to allow capitalization of R&D expenses
Canada	(1) (2) (3) (4) (6)
Denmark	(1) (5)
France	(1) (2) (4)
Ireland/UK	(1) (2) (3) (4) (5) (6)
Netherlands	(1) (2) (3) (4) (6)
Sweden	(1) (3) (4) (5) (6)
Switzerland	(1) (2) (5) (6)
IASB	(1) (implicit in the general recognition criteria) (2) (3) (4) (5) (6) (7)

Arguments favoring capitalization of R&D Many users of financial statements (financial analysts and banks being among the most vocal[1]) see capitalization of R&D as a grave violation of the prudence principle (see Chapter 5). Any position on the subject is therefore controversial. Arguments for and against are traded by both sides, arguing matching versus prudence.

Arguments in favor R&D expenses, in case of a favorable outcome, should be related to future periods when the benefits will accrue (matching principle). Therefore, R&D expenses should be accrued (capitalized) and not expensed immediately.

Arguments against Future economic benefits potentially derived from R&D are not sufficiently objectively defined or certain to flow to the enterprise at the time the expense is incurred to justify capitalization. The principle of prudence militates therefore in favor of expensing R&D costs as incurred.

The impact of capitalization Let us take an example. Albeniz NA has incurred a development cost for a total amount of 150 CU (80 for labor expenses and 70 of depreciation expense for equipment and facilities used in carrying the development project). The manager of Albeniz NA has decided to capitalize the expenditure and to amortize it over the next five years as she feels the economic benefits will be derived for that period. Figure 8.7 illustrates the accounting entries required to record the first year of the project.

The impact of capitalization on the bottom line can be broken down as shown in Table 8.4.

The impact on net income of the choice of method for handling R&D over the amortization period is shown in Table 8.5.

Comments In practice, the impact of R&D is more complex than in this simple illustration because R&D is rarely limited to a one-time project and it is likely that additional R&D costs will be incurred in year 2 and capitalized (to be coherent – principle of consistency of accounting methods – see Chapter 5) and thus amortized, and so on. A business whose bottom line is not exactly prosperous may be tempted to improve its situation by

Figure 8.7 Accounting for R&D

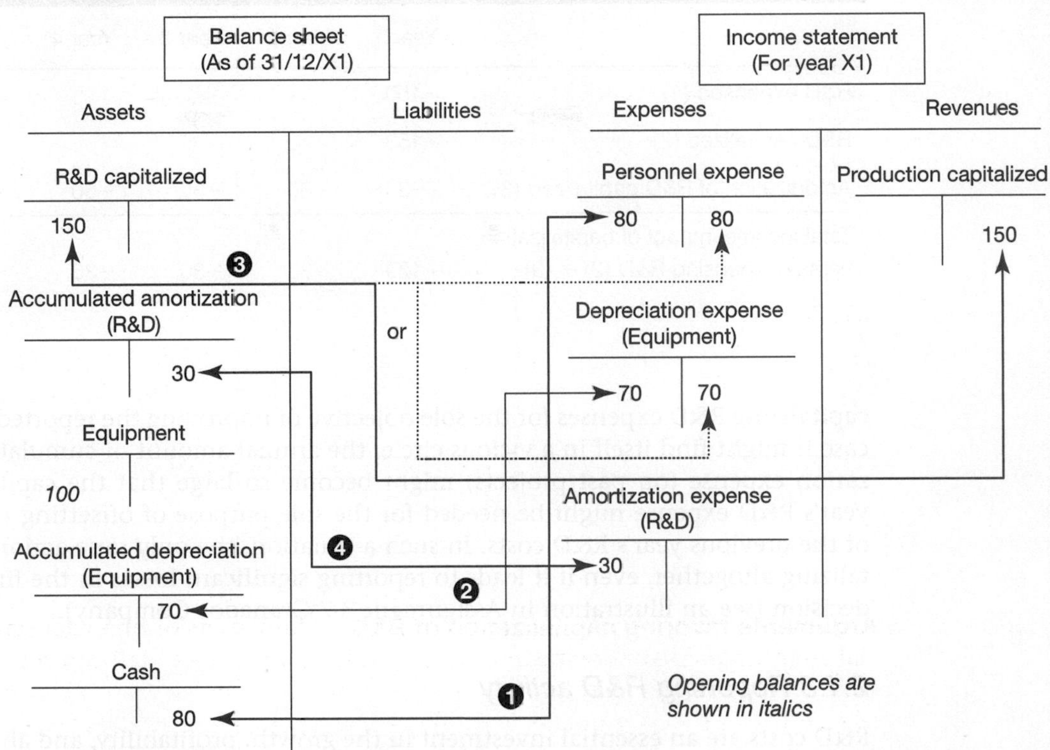

Entries ❶ and ❷ record the cost of the development project. If the conditions for capitalization are met, the total cost of the project is transferred to the asset side of the balance sheet ❸.

Two solutions are available in order to carry out this transfer:

- cancel (through a reduction of expenses) the original expense accounts (labor expense and depreciation expense) (dotted lines); or
- create (through an increase in revenue) a revenue account (production capitalized).

Each country GAAP recommends either one, and on a large sample of countries neither one seems to show dominance.

❹ Amortization is calculated on the basis of a useful life of five years (150/5 = 30).

Table 8.4 Simulation: impact of capitalization

		Simulation 1 R&D expensed	Simulation 2 R&D capitalized
Net income before R&D		500	500
R&D expenses	Personnel expense	−80	−80
	Depreciation expense	−70	−70
Net income after R&D expenses		350	350
Capitalization of R&D		0	150
Net income after R&D capitalized		350	500
Amortization of capitalized R&D		0	−30
Income before income tax		350	470
Differential net income due to treatment of R&D		+120	

Table 8.5 Impact on net income over the life of the project

	Year 1	Year 2	Year 3	Year 4	Year 5	Total
R&D expensed (1)	−150					−150
R&D capitalized (2)	+150					+150
Amortization of R&D capitalized (3)	−30	−30	−30	−30	−30	−150
Total income impact of capitalization versus expensing R&D (2) + (3)	+120	−30	−30	−30	−30	0

capitalizing R&D expenses for the sole objective of improving the reported income. In this case it might find itself in a vicious circle: the annual amount of cumulated R&D amortization expense (on past projects) might become so large that the capitalization of the year's R&D expense might be needed for the sole purpose of offsetting the amortization of the previous year's R&D costs. In such a situation, the only sane action is to stop capitalizing altogether, even if it leads to reporting significant losses in the first year after the decision (see an illustration in Assignment 8.7 Granados Company).

2.1.3 Reporting R&D activity

R&D costs are an essential investment in the growth, profitability, and ability to remain a going concern. It should therefore be essential to report their amount as accurately and truthfully as possible, in all parts, financial and non-financial of the annual statements.

Income statement by function The income statement presentation by function (Chapter 3) is the only one in which R&D expenses can be reported as such. The following examples show that business entities use three possibilities:

- R&D expenses reported as a separate function, item or line (e.g., Mitsubishi Electric).
- R&D is not identified as such but is included in another function, such as selling, general, and administrative expenses (e.g., Saint Gobain).
- R&D is not reported as such but since it is expensed as incurred, it becomes a part of the cost of goods sold (e.g., Sandvik).

Real-life example Bayer

(Germany – IFRS/IAS GAAP – *Source*: Annual report 2004 – Pharmaceuticals, chemicals)

Basic principles of the consolidated financial statements

Research and development expenses. According to IAS 38 (Intangible Assets), research costs cannot be capitalized; development costs can only be capitalized if specific conditions are fulfilled. Development costs must be capitalized if it is sufficiently certain that the future economic benefits to the company will cover not only the usual production, selling and administrative costs but also the development costs themselves. There are also several other criteria relating to the development project and the product or process being developed, all of which have to be met to justify asset recognition. As in previous years, these conditions are not satisfied.

Real-life example Sandvik

(Sweden – Swedish GAAP – *Source*: Annual report 2004 – Engineering group in tooling and materials technology)

Note 4. Research, development and quality assurance

SEKm	2004	2003
Expenditure on		
Research and development	1,403	1,425
Quality assurance costs	467	435
Total	1,870	1,860
of which, expensed	1,761	1,733

Research and quality assurance expenditures are expensed as incurred. Expenditures for development are reported as an intangible asset if they meet the criteria for recognition as an asset in the balance sheet.

Note 4 relates to the caption 'Cost of goods sold' in the income statement.

Real-life example Saint-Gobain

(France – French GAAP – *Source*: Annual report 2004 – Production, processing, and distribution of glass, high-performance materials, and construction supplies)

NOTE 1. ACCOUNTING PRINCIPLES AND POLICIES – Research and development costs.

Research and development costs are expensed as incurred and recorded in selling, general and administrative expenses.

NOTE 22. RESEARCH & DEVELOPMENT AND ADVERTISING COSTS

Selling, general, and administrative expenses include research and development costs of €304 million, €306 million and €312 million for the years ended 31 December 2004, 2003, and 2002, respectively.

2.2 Accounting for computer software

2.2.1 Accounting rules

Reporting computer software costs has long been a debated issue but today's practice is stabilized along the lines described in Figure 8.8.

As can be expected, the most delicate issue is deciding on the accounting treatment of internally developed software for use by the developing firm itself. The costs that can be capitalized in this case vary between countries (see the illustration in Appendix 8.1).

Figure 8.8 Accounting for computer software

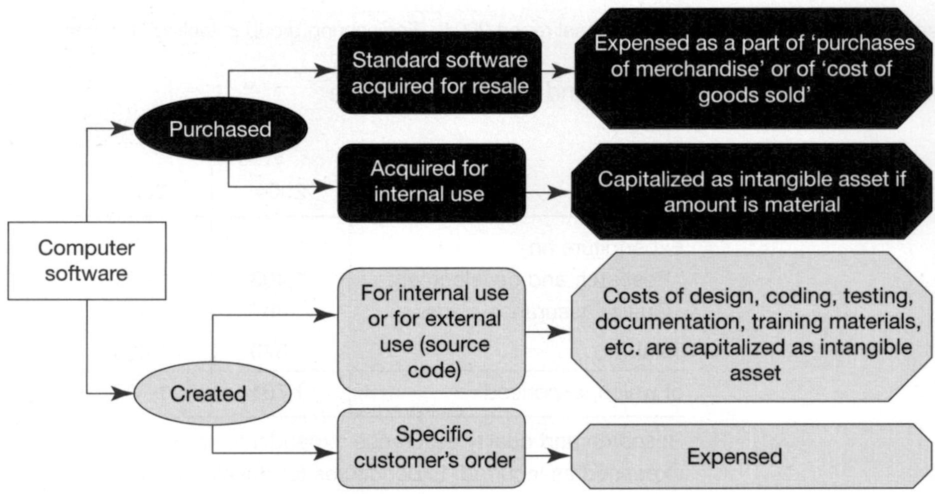

2.2.2 Reporting computer software costs

Table 8.6 provides some examples of notes relating to computer software issues (excerpted from year 2004 annual reports).

Table 8.6 Examples of reporting for computer software

Company	Type of software and comments	Period of amortization
Bayer (Germany – IFRS/IAS GAAP)	Self-created intangible assets generally are not capitalized. Certain development costs relating to the application development stage of internally developed software are, however, capitalized in the Group balance sheet. These costs are amortized over the useful life of the software from the date it is placed in service.	Useful life
Bull (France – French GAAP)	Intangible assets mainly include capitalized development costs for software products with identified markets which have reached a stage in their development at which there are no longer any major technical or commercial risks. Capitalized development costs are amortized on a straight-line basis from the moment of capitalization over the estimated useful life of the product, subject to a maximum of three years.	Useful life Maximum 3 years
VimpelCom (Vimpel – Communications) (Russia – Russian/US GAAP)	Software costs Under the provision of Statement of Position No. 98-1, 'Accounting for the Costs of Computer Software Developed or Obtained for Internal Use', VimpelCom capitalizes costs associated with software developed or obtained for internal use when both the preliminary project stage is completed and VimpelCom management has authorized further funding of the project which it deems probable will be completed and used to perform the function intended. Capitalization of such costs ceases no later than the point at which the project is substantially complete and ready for its intended purpose. Research and development costs and other computer software maintenance costs related to software development are expensed as incurred. Capitalized software development costs are amortized using the straight-line method over the expected life of the product.	Expected life

2.3 Financial statement analysis

Many financial analysts feel too many would-be intangible assets are often omitted from the balance sheet due to 'excessive' prudence on the part of accountants. As the economy is moving gradually into a knowledge-based, technology-intensive world, intangibles become ever more important in the competitive strategy of a firm. Investments in information technology, research and development, human resources, and advertising have become essential in order to strengthen the firm's competitive position and ensure its future viability (see Cañibano *et al.* 2000). Because some intangibles are not reflected in the balance sheet, a loss of relevance of accounting information has been highlighted by many studies and one evidence of this phenomenon is the gap existing between the book value and the market value of companies (Hope and Hope 1998; Lev and Zarowin 1999).

Among intangibles, R&D has received special attention on the part of financial analysts as it helps describe the effort of the firm to be innovative and build its future competence. Numerous academic studies (Lev and Sougiannis 1996, for example) have documented the positive relationship between a company's R&D investment and its market value both in the USA and in the UK.

Several ratios are often used in such evaluation, which we will explore further in turn. They are:

- R&D expenses/sales [or R&D expenses/operating expenses], often called 'R&D intensity'.
- R&D expenses/number of employees: R&D per employee.
- Annual growth rate of R&D expenses [(R&D expenses year 2 – R&D expenses year 1)/ R&D year 1].

2.3.1 R&D intensity

Table 8.7 provides some examples of R&D intensity based on 2004 annual reports (unless otherwise specified).

Table 8.7 confirms that the R&D intensity is clearly a function of the line of business of the firm. In industries with short product life cycle (Baltimore Tech) or requiring gigantic relative steps in innovation (Roche or Bayer), the need to invest in R&D is much greater than it is in industries where products and processes have a long life cycle and innovation is incremental (Sandvik or Saint-Gobain, for example). The average R&D intensity for a sample of 700 international firms (R&D Scoreboard) reported by the UK Department of Trade and Industry (DTI) is 4.2% for 2004, with very large standard deviations both between and within countries (see further developments on this topic in Appendix 8.2).

Table 8.7 R&D intensity

Companies	Currency	R&D expenses	Sales	R&D/sales
Baltimore Technologies (UK – Security for e-commerce) (annual report 2003)	£000	6,325	18,171	34.8%
Roche (Switzerland – Pharmaceuticals, chemicals)	CHFm	5,093	31,273	16.3%
Bayer (Germany – Chemicals, health care)	€m	2,107	29,758	7.1%
Bull (France – IT group)	€m	54	1,138.7	4.7%
Procter & Gamble (USA – Consumer products)	$m	1,802	51,407	3.5%
Sandvik (Sweden – Tools and engineering)	SEKm	1,403	54,610	2.6%
Saint-Gobain (France – Glass and building materials)	€m	304	32,025	0.9%

2.3.2 Link between R&D and growth

Several surveys showed that R&D intensity is linked to subsequent sales growth. For instance, Morbey (1988) demonstrated that companies sustaining R&D investment over 4% of sales were particularly likely to achieve higher long-term growth. The R&D Scoreboard reaches a similar conclusion.

2.3.3 Link between R&D and market value

The success of the NASDAQ as an effective market has drawn attention to the market value of technology-based companies. Numerous academic studies (Lev and Sougiannis 1996) have shown the relationship between a company's R&D investment and its market value both in the USA and in the UK. It is therefore quite important, in a spirit of true and fair view, to inform the shareholders of the R&D expenditures of their company.

Key points

- Intangible assets are long-lived (long-term) assets that lack physical substance and whose acquisition and continued possession represent rights to future economic benefits.
- Intangible assets comprise patents, franchises, licenses, trademarks, brands, copyrights, etc., and may include R&D costs if these are capitalized.
- It is very difficult to be objective in the valuation of intangible assets as their value may be a function of the firm's ability to use them.
- Intangible assets raise three major questions: (1) What is an intangible asset? (2) Recognition? (3) How to treat a change in value?
- When purchased, intangibles are valued without any ambiguity; the valuation of internally generated intangibles is a highly debated issue among accountants and analysts, as well as between them.
- The choice of capitalization versus expensing is the result of a trade-off between the matching and the prudence principles.
- Intangible assets may be amortized and/or impaired over an appropriate horizon regulated by local GAAP.
- Research and development costs are usually expensed when incurred. However, under certain circumstances, some development expenses may be capitalized and recorded as an intangible asset if specified 'capitalization criteria' are met.
- R&D intensity, R&D per employee, and R&D growth rate are ratios that help analysts and investors monitor the policies of a management team regarding its investment in the future.

Review (solutions are at the back of the book)

Review 8.1 Turina

Topic: Various intangibles
Related part of the chapter: Core issues

The following information is given by the head accountant of the Turina Company.

1. The Turina Company acquired a franchise on 1 July X3 by paying an initial franchise fee of 160,000 CU. The franchise term is eight years.
2. The Turina Company incurred advertising expenses amounting to 300,000 CU related to various products. According to the marketing department, these expenses could generate revenue for approximately four years.
3. During X3, Turina incurred legal fees of 40,000 CU in connection with the unsuccessful defense of a patent. The patent had been acquired at the beginning of X2 for 150,000 CU and was being amortized over a five-year period. As a result of the unsuccessful litigation, the patent was considered to be worthless at the end of year X3.

Required

Analyze each piece of information and show its impact on financial statements (or record the journal entries).

Review 8.2 De Falla

Topic: Accounting for R&D
Related part of the chapter: Advanced issues

During X1, the De Falla Company incurred the following costs in relation to its R&D activities (all figures in 000 of CU):

- Wages and salaries of researchers, technicians and R&D managers: 100.
- Supplies used in R&D activities (all drawn from existing inventory): 20.
- Depreciation of the building where R&D activities take place: 30.
- Depreciation of machinery and equipment specifically devoted to R&D: 50.
- Allocation of general and administrative expenses: 60.

Required

Assuming that the income statement is presented by function, show the impact of R&D on the financial statements.

Assignments

Assignment 8.1 Multiple-choice questions

Related part of the chapter: Core issues

Select the right answer.

1. An example of an item that is not an intangible asset is
   (a) Patent
   (b) Goodwill
   (c) Computer
   (d) Computer software
   (e) Trademark
2. An example of a trademark which should unambiguously be capitalized is
   (a) The logo of a business school designed and created by the school
   (b) The trademark 'Chivas' acquired by Pernod Ricard within its purchase of the whole Seagram company
   (c) The name 'Oneworld', referring to a group of airlines including, among others, American Airlines, British Airways and Cathay Pacific
   (d) None of these

3. Albeniz company bought a patent for 100 CU on 2 January X1. The legal protection granted by the patent is 17 years. Albeniz estimated that the economic life of the patent is five years. What amount should be recognized for the year ended 31 December X1?
   (a) Depreciation expense for 20
   (b) Amortization expense for 5.88
   (c) Depletion expense for 20
   (d) Amortization expense for 20
   (e) Depreciation expense for 5.88
   (f) None of these

4. All recorded intangible assets should be amortized to match their cost with revenues
   (a) True
   (b) False

5. Albeniz company spent 500 CU throughout X1 in promoting a not well-known trademark it created internally during that same year. This trademark is supposed to have an indefinite life. The company applies IFRS/IAS GAAP in its financial statements. It should be
   (a) Capitalized and amortized over 40 years
   (b) Capitalized and not amortized but tested for impairment
   (c) Not capitalized and expensed in X1
   (d) Capitalized and amortized over 20 years
   (e) None of these

6. Same question as (5) but Albeniz applies US GAAP
   (a) Capitalized and amortized over 40 years
   (b) Capitalized and not amortized but tested for impairment
   (c) Not capitalized and expensed in X1
   (d) Capitalized and amortized over 20 years
   (e) None of these

7. Same question as (5) but Albeniz purchased the trademark (instead of having developed it internally a long time ago) and applies US GAAP
   (a) Capitalized and amortized over 40 years
   (b) Capitalized and not amortized but tested for impairment
   (c) Not capitalized and expensed in X1
   (d) Capitalized and amortized over 20 years
   (e) None of these

8. Training costs are
   (a) Capitalized and amortized over 40 years
   (b) Capitalized and not amortized but tested for impairment
   (c) Not capitalized and expensed
   (d) Capitalized and amortized over 20 years
   (e) None of these

9. Deferred assets are equivalent to
   (a) Prepaid revenues
   (b) Prepaid expenses
   (c) Deferred tax assets
   (d) Deferred revenues
   (e) None of these

10. In IAS 38 of IASB ('Intangible assets'), all intangible assets should be amortized over their useful life
    (a) True
    (b) False

Assignment 8.2
Discussion questions

Related part of the chapter: Core/Advanced issues

Required

1. Accounting for intangible assets. Discuss relevance versus reliability as they apply to reporting on the intangible assets of the firm.
2. Goodwill. Discuss the pros and cons of the choice between the different possible methods of handling goodwill over time in the financial statements (no amortization, amortization, impairment, immediate write-off).
3. Research and development costs. Discuss the choice between capitalization versus expensing or R&D costs.

Assignment 8.3
Reporting for intangibles

Related part of the chapter: Core/Advanced issues

On the Internet, or in the library, find the recent annual reports of four companies from one or different countries in approximately the same activity.

Required

1. How are intangible assets presented in the balance sheet? What decisions on the basis of this information can investors or shareholders take? What decisions would be difficult to take on the basis of just this information?
2. Are there any notes relating to intangible assets? How do they enlarge the decision analysis possibilities offered to shareholders and investors?

3. How are these assets being reported? What method is used in reporting?

Assignment 8.4
Searching for specific intangibles

Related part of the chapter: Core issues

Required

On the Internet, or in the library, find recent illustrations or examples of industry-specific intangible assets in the annual reports of four companies from different sectors of activity in a single country or in different countries (for example, electricity procurement rights in the energy sector).

Assignment 8.5
R&D intensity

Related part of the chapter: Advanced issues

On the Internet, or in the library, find the recent annual reports of four companies from sectors of activity in a given country or in different countries for which you anticipate that R&D expenses may be quite important.

Required

Compare and contrast the firms in your sample.

1. Look for the data relating to R&D expenses and sales.
2. Compute the ratio R&D expenses/sales revenue.
3. Look for the data relating to the workforce.
4. Compute the ratio R&D expenses/number of employees.

Assignment 8.6
CeWe Color*

Topic: Accounting for changes in intangibles
Related part of the chapter: Advanced issues

CeWe Color is a German group operating in the development of films and color prints business. From the notes to the consolidated financial statements (annual report 2004), we extracted the following information (in thousands of €):

	Industrial property rights and similar rights	Goodwill
Additions	4,424	0
Amount carried forward 01.01.2004	23,815	36,618
Amount carried forward 01.01.2004 (depreciation)	16,512	24,994
Balance on 31.12.2004	28,125	36,627
Balance on 31.12.2004 (depreciation)	19,612	30,384
Book transfers/reorganization	261	0
Book transfers/reorganization (depreciation)	43	0
Book value 31.12.2003	7,303	11,624
Book value 31.12.2004	8,513	6,243
Depreciation	3,362	5,390
Disposals	475	0
Disposals (depreciation)	364	0
Exchange rate adjustment	100	9
Exchange rate adjustment (depreciation)	59	0

Required

1. From the information given, which is presented in alphabetical order, prepare a statement showing the movements in intangible assets using the format presented in Chapter 7 for tangible assets.
2. Show which figures could be used as check figures in this exercise.
3. Explain briefly the meaning of each line.

Assignment 8.7
Granados Company

Topic: Accounting for Research and Development
Related part of the chapter: Advanced issues

Granados Company's accounting policies call for the expensing of R&D expenditures in the year incurred. The following table presents the amount of R&D expenses from Year 1 to Year 5.

Year 1	Year 2	Year 3	Year 4	Year 5
200	150	150	100	50

The managers of the company are considering modifying their accounting policies and capitalize R&D with an amortization over five years.

Required

1. Compute the impact of capitalization on net income for each year of the period.
2. Compute from which year the amount of amortization of past R&D will be at least equal to R&D expensed during the year.
3. What would you suggest to the managers of the company, with regard to possible modifications in accounting policies?

Assignment 8.8
Sanofi–Aventis*

Topic: R&D intensity
Related part of the chapter: Advanced issues

Sanofi-Synthelabo and Aventis are two French-based groups, heavily involved in the pharmaceutical business. On 20 August 2004, Sanofi-Synthelabo acquired control of Aventis, and the two groups were merged on 31 December 2004 under the name of Sanofi–Aventis.

We present below the following income statements:

- Before merger:
  - Sanofi-Synthelabo (years 2001, 2002 and 2003);
  - Aventis (years 2001, 2002 and 2003).
- After merger: Sanofi–Aventis (year 2004).

The consolidated financial statements of the three structures have been prepared in accordance with French law, and more specifically with Rule 99-02 of the Accounting Regulatory Committee (*Comité de la Réglementation Comptable*, 'CRC') issued 29 April 1999.

Sanofi–Synthelabo – Consolidated statements of income

(in € millions)	Year ended 31 December 2003	Year ended 31 December 2002	Year ended 31 December 2001
Net sales	8,048	7,448	6,488
Cost of goods sold	(1,428)	(1,378)	(1,253)
Gross profit	6,620	6,070	5,235
Research and development expenses	(1,316)	(1,218)	(1,031)
Selling and general expenses	(2,477)	(2,428)	(2,306)
Other operating income/(expense), net	248	190	208
Operating profit	3,075	2,614	2,106
Intangibles – amortization and impairment	(129)	(129)	(68)
Financial income/(expense), net	155	85	102
Income before tax and exceptional items	3,101	2,570	2,140
Exceptional items	24	10	281
Income taxes	(1,058)	(746)	(842)
Net income before income from equity investees, goodwill amortization and minority interests	2,067	1,834	1,579
Income from equity investees, net	20	20	14
Goodwill amortization	(8)	(8)	(7)
Net income before minority interests	2,079	1,846	1,586
Minority interests	(3)	(87)	(1)
Net income	2,076	1,759	1,585

Aventis – Statements of operations

(in € millions)	2003	2002	2001
Net sales	17,815	20,622	22,941
Co-promotion income	252	161	
Production costs and expenses	(5,377)	(6,578)	(7,943)
Selling, general and administrative costs, and other operating income (expenses)	(5,365)	(6,866)	(7,178)
Research and development	(2,924)	(3,420)	(3,481)
Restructuring expenses	(251)	(68)	(50)
Goodwill amortization	(480)	(1,021)	(650)
Operating income	3,670	2,830	3,639
Equity in earnings of affiliated companies	(107)	51	85
Interest (expense) income – net	(151)	(309)	(704)
Miscellaneous non-operating income and expenses – net	(501)	1,120	(134)
Income before taxes and minority interests	2,911	3,692	2,886
Provision for income taxes	(929)	(1,430)	(1,111)
Minority interests	(29)	(86)	(142)
Preferred remuneration	(52)	(85)	(128)
Net income	1,901	2,091	1,505

Sanofi–Aventis – Statement of income

(in € millions)	2004
Net sales	15,043
Cost of goods sold	(3,753)
Gross profit	11,290
Research and development expenses	(7,455)
Selling and general expenses	(4,500)
Other operating income/(expense) – net	360
Operating profit	(305)
Amortization and impairment of intangibles	(1,563)
Financial income/(expense) – net	25
Income before tax and exceptional items	(1,843)
Exceptional items	(402)
Income taxes	(819)
Net income before income from equity investees, goodwill amortization, and minority interests	(3,064)
Income from equity investees, net	(261)
Goodwill amortization	(292)
Net income before minority interests	(3,617)
Minority interests	7
Net income	(3,610)

In the notes to the financial statements of the three groups (Sanofi-Synthelabo, Aventis and Sanofi–Aventis) we can read that research and development expenses are charged as an expense as incurred.

Required

1. Compute the R&D intensity over the period for each company.
2. Comment on the evolution of the figures you have calculated.

References

ASB (1997) Financial Reporting Standard No. 10: Goodwill and Intangible Assets, London.

Cañibano, L., García-Ayuso, M., and Sánchez, M. P. (2000) Accounting for intangibles: A literature review. *Journal of Accounting Literature*, 19, 102–30.

FASB (2001) Statement of Financial Accounting Standards No. 142: Goodwill and Other Intangible Assets, Norwalk, CT.

Høegh-Krohn, N. E. J., and Knivsflå, K. H. (2000) Accounting for intangible assets in Scandinavia, the UK, the US, and by the IASC: Challenges and a Solution. *The International Journal of Accounting*, 35(2), 243–65.

Hope, T., and Hope, J. (1998) *Managing in the Third Wave*, Harvard Business Press, Cambridge, MA.

IASB (2004a) International Accounting Standard No. 36: Impairment of Assets, London.

IASB (2004b) International Accounting Standard No. 38: Intangible Assets, London.

IASB (2004c) International Financial Reporting Standard No. 3: Business Combinations, London.

Lev, B. and Sougiannis, T. (1996) The capitalization, amortization and value relevance of R&D. *Journal of Accounting and Economics*, 21, 107–38.

Lev, B. and Zarowin, P. (1999) The boundaries of financial reporting and how to extend them. *Journal of Accounting Research*, 37(2) (Autumn), 353–85.

Morbey G. K. (1988) R&D: Its relationship to company performance. *The Journal of Product Innovation Management*, 5(3), 191–201.

Power, M. (1992) The politics of brand accounting in the United Kingdom. *European Accounting Review*, 1(1), 39–68.

Stolowy, H., Haller, A. and Klockhaus, V. (2001) Accounting for brands in France and Germany compared with IAS 38 (intangible assets) – An illustration of the difficulty of international harmonization. *The International Journal of Accounting*, 36(2), 147–67.

Stolowy, H., and Jeny-Cazavan, A. (2001) International accounting disharmony: The case of intangibles. *Accounting, Auditing and Accountability Journal*, 14(4), 477–96.

Further reading

Nixon, B. (1997) The accounting treatment of research and development expenditure: Views of UK company accountants. *European Accounting Review*, 6(2), 265–77.

Additional material on the website

Go to http://www.thomsonlearning.co.uk/stolowylebas2 for further information.

The following appendices to this chapter are available on the dedicated website:

Appendix 8.1: Accounting for computer software

Appendix 8.2: R&D intensity

Note

1. However, the capitalization of R&D expenses is one of the major adjustments to income suggested by Stern & Stewart, the firm that invented EVA (Economic value added – a variation on return on capital employed) and promotes its use for the evaluation of the return on capital invested by shareholders.

C9

Chapter 9
Inventories

Learning objectives

After studying this chapter, you will understand:

- That inventories play an important role in the operating cycle of a business entity.
- That inventories may represent a significant part of an entity's assets and, consequently, an important quantity of funds may be required to finance the inventories.
- That there are different categories of inventories (such a finished goods, semi-finished goods, components and materials, etc.).
- That there are different methods for valuing the cost of goods withdrawn from inventory.
- How to record movements in inventory.
- The choice of how to attach costs to objects that transit through an inventory before their sale affects profit.
- How inventory valuation methods affect cash flow.
- What the accounting consequences are of a decline in the value of an inventory.
- Why knowledge of detailed information about inventories is important to restate an income statement by nature into an income statement by function (and vice versa).
- How inventory valuation policies are disclosed.
- How to analyze inventory turnover.

Inventories play a critical role in the operating cycle of many organizations. They play the role of buffers between demand and production (supply). In accounting, an inventory helps in the application of the matching principle. An inventory is akin to a storage tank that can release its content (the costs attached to the objects held in inventory) when certain triggering events take place. For example, as long as a product has not been sold, all costs attached to it are withheld from the income statement. They are temporarily 'stored' in an inventory account, which is an asset, i.e., a potential source of future economic benefits.

Even if, in a world of just in time, the role of inventories is decreasing as a management tool for adjusting the needs of cost minimization and production smoothing to the randomness or seasonality of demand, inventories still create significant issues in reporting to shareholders: (a) inventories represent an immobilization of funds (required to finance the inventories); and (b) the choice of how to attach costs to objects that transit through an inventory before their sale affects profit. It is therefore important to examine how inventories are recorded and reported[1].

The three major issues relating to accounting for inventories valuation are shown in Figure 9.1. They are: periodicity of recording; costing of inflows and outflows; and valuation adjustments.

Figure 9.1 Inventories major issues

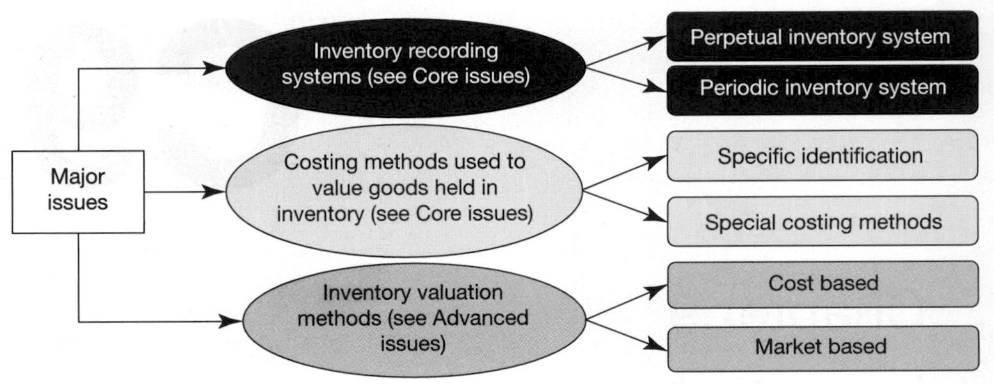

1 Core issues

1.1 Classification of inventories

1.1.1 Definition

According to IAS 2 (IASB 2003: § 6), 'inventories are assets:

(a) Held for sale in the ordinary course of business;
(b) In the process of production for such sale; or
(c) In the form of materials or supplies to be consumed in the production process or in the rendering of services'.

1.1.2 Different types of inventories

Figure 9.2 illustrates the six basic types of inventories found on a balance sheet, each reflecting a different degree of saleability of the items each contains.

The six inventory types shown in Figure 9.2 are shown in three shades: from the dark blue for inventories of goods closest to the customer (they represent potential sales and it is only a question of time until these inventories can be turned into receivables or cash), to light blue

Figure 9.2 Classification of inventories

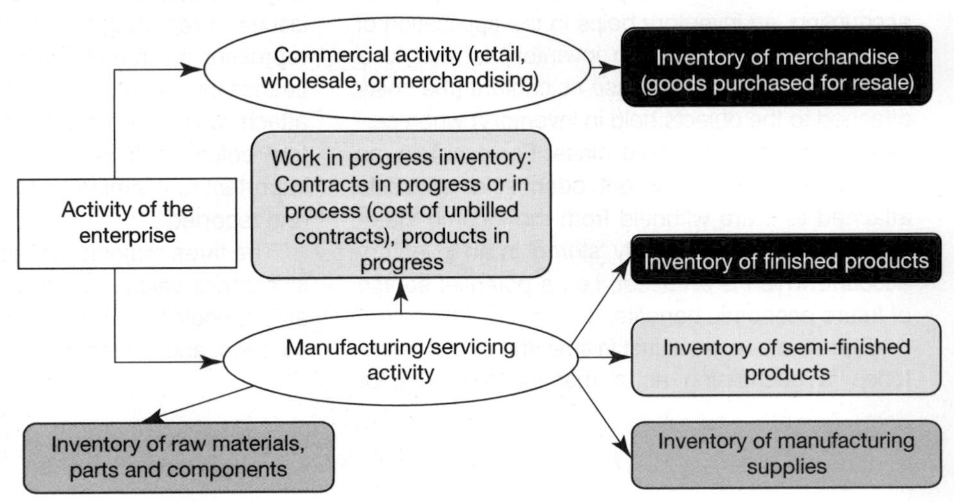

for inventories in the process of transformation that will eventually, but certainly, turn into sellable products, to grey to reflect the fact these last two categories of inventories are not potentially sellable in the condition in which they are held. The items in these last two inventory categories will require either transformation or integration in the products themselves (raw materials and supplies), or being used in supporting the production process or the machinery and devices that contribute to production (supplies).

Many businesses, as mentioned in Chapter 6, report in a single line their work in progress and their contracts in progress even though the two items are not of the same nature.

Work in progress measures the value of the resources attached to items that are still left in the process of production on the closing date. Normally, work in progress should be a pretty small investment, equal to, at the worst, less than the sum of the resources required to manufacture the quantity produced in half a product production cycle.

Contract(s) in progress (see Chapter 6) can legitimately represent large amounts of investment since that item on the balance sheet measures the amount of resources consumed in realizing all or part of a (long-term) contract but for which no invoicing has been issued to the customer. If invoicing takes place, for example, only every four months, the cost of up to four months of production may be listed under contracts in progress. As soon as an invoice is issued, all corresponding resources (application of the matching principle and subject to long-term contract rules) are carried, as cost of goods sold, to the income statement. On average, in the example of billing every four months, the contracts in progress account will represent about two months' worth of activity or 16% of the annual cost of goods sold, i.e., a significant amount invested.

Although the terms 'in progress' (UK usage) and 'in process' (North American usage) are clearly interchangeable as already mentioned, we will use the first one (which is adopted by IASB). The reader will take solace in the fact that most of the time the initials WIP are used to refer to either of these items.

Table 9.1 presents and illustrates the various categories of inventories.

Table 9.1 Main categories of inventories[2]

Activity	Name of the goods	Definition	Examples
Commercial activity	Merchandise	Goods purchased for resale without transformation	Wholesale and retail activities
Manufacturing activity	Raw materials, parts, components, and consumables	Goods that, once incorporated in the production process, become integrally and physically part of the product	Electronic parts in a computer manufacturing business
	Manufacturing supplies	Items used in supporting production and not part of the product	Machine fluids, cleaning materials, spare parts
	Work in progress (WIP)	Products still in the manufacturing process at the close of the day and services rendered but not invoiced	Chassis and parts of a computer still on the assembly line at the end of the day
	Semi-finished goods	Items that are finished with regard to one stage of production but are, nonetheless, not sellable in that condition. They will generally be integrated in a finished product at a later date	Subassembly of the chassis of a computer waiting to receive the microprocessor and the skirt, once the customer order is known
	Finished goods	Completed products ready for sale	Computers ready to be shipped
Service activity	Work in progress	Accumulated costs incurred in fulfilling a contract and not yet billed	Consultancy projects, law suit, engineering projects

Real-life example Siemens

(Germany – US GAAP – *Source*: Annual report 2004 – Energy, industry components, automotive systems, information, and communication products)

Excerpts from the notes to the consolidated balance sheet

Inventories (millions of euros)	30 September 2004
Raw materials and supplies	2,282
Work in process	2,261
Cost and earnings in excess of billings on uncompleted contracts	6,650
Finished goods and products held for resale	2,777
Advances to suppliers	651
Total inventories	14,621
Advance payments received	(3,263)
Inventories – net	11,358

Comments

- The amounts in the notes are net of allowances for provisions (see Chapter 5 and Advanced issues of this chapter).
- Finished products and merchandise are reported as a single item, thus not allowing the shareholders to understand the breakdown between inventories of finished products (manufactured in house) and inventories of merchandise (acquired from third-party suppliers, for resale without transformation).
- The large amount listed under 'work in process' possibly reflects a choice made by Siemens to pool together work in process and semi-finished products. That choice is not unreasonable since a large part of Siemens' activity is in heavy equipment and long-term contracts, and therefore much of the semi-finished products are probably part of a product that will take more than the interim reporting period to complete.

Real-life example Sony Corporation

(Japan – Japanese/US GAAP – *Source*: Annual report 2005 – Electronics [such as AV/IT products and components], games [such as PlayStation], entertainment [such as motion pictures and music], and financial services)

Excerpts from the notes to the consolidated balance sheet

Note 4: Inventories (millions of Yen)	31 March 2005
Finished products	405,616
Work in process	93,181
Raw materials, purchased components and supplies	132,552
	631,349
Note 5: Film costs (millions of Yen)	**31 March 2005**
Theatrical:	
Released (including acquired film libraries)	119,438
Completed not released	11,358
In production and development	118,271
Television licensing	
Released (including acquired film libraries)	29,894
In production and development	0
	278,961

Comments

Sony is a very complex organization dealing both in manufacturing and selling diversified electronic equipment and in creating and selling cultural material (music and films). In the past, it used to distinguish current from non-current inventories (a rather unusual situation but quite legitimate in the entertainment field). The first ones are used in the course of the operating cycle (i.e., within less than 12 months after acquisition or creation). This includes both manufactured goods and entertainment products whose release is expected within the next 12 months. The non-current inventories represent film rights, which are held for use over a period of time extending beyond one year. Technically one might have been tempted to consider non-current inventories as long-lived (fixed) assets, since they represent a right to future stream of economic benefits. However, such assets (films already released for which Sony holds future TV and DVD rights as well as films under development whose release date is not within 12 months, i.e., work in progress) do not qualify as tangible fixed assets since they have been acquired (or created) for the sole purpose of being sold as such. Sony has changed its reporting method and now discloses 'inventories' (note 4, formerly 'current' inventories) separately from 'film costs', (note 5, formerly 'non-current' inventories), which is a specific line between current assets and financial assets.

1.1.3 Weight of inventories in the balance sheet

Inventories sometimes represent a large portion of assets and therefore their correct valuation is essential for reporting shareholders' equity. The larger the proportion of total assets is represented by inventories, the more important it is to correctly estimate the physical inventories and their value.

For example, when Charbonnages de France (the now defunct French coal monopoly) was holding inventories of about one year's supply of coal in the early 1960s (and coal was still a major source of fuel in France), it was rumored that an error of estimation of less than 1% of the physical inventory of coal could either entirely wipe out the losses of the firm or double them. When one knows how difficult it is to estimate the physical quantity of coal in a coal storage bin (and even harder when we are talking about tens of millions of tons), one realizes that errors of more than 1% either way were very likely.

Each industry (and probably to some extent each firm's strategy) has its own appropriate level of inventory and there is a lot of diversity between industries (as can be seen in Table 9.2), but the interesting exercise is to compare firms in the same industry. However, the lower level of inventory is not always (but most of the time it probably is) synonymous with better management unless the services offered by the firm are completely comparable (a rare occurrence). In Table 9.2 Sony and Philips are not directly comparable because of the weight of the entertainment products in Sony's inventories, products which Philips no longer has. However, from the note on Sony's balance sheet (seen earlier) we know that the manufacturing inventories of Sony can be estimated at 631,349 million yen, thus giving an industrial inventory as a percentage of total assets of 6.6% which compares favorably to Philips' 10.5%. This is, of course, a first pass at an analysis but it is the way that financial reporting becomes useful.

Not surprisingly, a service industry like the telephone industry, in which Telefónica operates, shows little inventory compared to other assets (probably parts for repair of telephone exchanges and network infrastructure).

Table 9.2 Weight of inventories

Company	Currency (millions)	Inventory	Total assets	Inventories/ total assets
SEB (France – Small domestic appliances)	Euros	387	1,726	22.4%
Siemens (Germany – Energy, industry components, automotive systems, communication products)	Euros	11,358	79,518	14.3%
Kerry (Ireland – Consumer foods, agribusiness)	Euros	458	3,342	13.7%
Pirelli (Italy – Tires, cables and broadband systems)	Euros	1,338	10,386	12.9%
Volvo (Sweden – Cars, trucks, buses, construction equipment, aero, marine, and industrial engines)	SEK	28,598	222,896	12.8%
Bosch (Germany – Automotive equipment, consumer goods, communication technology, capital goods)	Euros	4,267	35,380	12.1%
Unilever (Netherlands – Food business, detergents, home and personal care)	Euros	3,758	33,875	11.1%
Aluminum Corporation of China (China – Aluminum production)	RMB'000	5,231,907	48,980,363	10.7%
Philips (Netherlands – Technological consumer products, components, semi-conductors)	Euros	3,230	30,723	10.5%
Hewlett-Packard (USA – Computers and printers)	USD	7,071	76,138	9.3%
L'Oreal (France – Beauty and cosmetic products, toiletries, and pharmaceuticals)	Euros	1,089	13,559	8.0%
Sony (Japan – Electronics, games, music, pictures)	Yen	631,349	9,499,100	6.6%
Norsk Hydro (Norway – Oil and energy, light metals, agribusiness)	NOK	12,851	195,180	6.6%
Telefónica (Spain – Telecommunications, media)	Euros	670	63,466	1.1%

1.2 Inventory recording systems

Chapter 2 introduced the two methods most commonly used to report inventory movements (whether they pertain to purchases of goods or raw materials or to addition of goods manufactured in-house): purchases recorded in the balance sheet and transferred to the income statement, or, conversely, purchases recorded in the income statement and transferred to the balance sheet. In practice, there are two methods for recording inventory movements: perpetual and periodic inventory systems. We will now study these two practices in detail as they impact differently on the profit and on the ending balance sheet structure. We will also examine the possibility that items carried in inventory are either so large, so valuable, and/or so specific that they cannot be considered fungible (a basic assumption of both perpetual and periodic inventories) and are therefore kept in inventory under the so-called 'specific identification method'.

1.2.1 Perpetual (or permanent) inventory system

Under a perpetual inventory system, a continuous record of changes in inventory quantities and values (entries as well as withdrawals) is maintained in the inventory account. Practically, all movements flow through an inventory account (in the general ledger). Purchases are recorded as increases of the inventory assets in the balance sheet, and all withdrawals and consumption are reduction of the inventory assets.

The inventory account is presented in the following way:

Perpetual inventory account	
Asset increase (debit) ■ Beginning inventory ■ Purchases (cost of goods purchased) or additions to the inventory (cost of goods manufactured)	Asset decrease (credit) ■ Withdrawals from inventory (cost of goods sold or cost of goods consumed in the next downstream segment of the 'manufacturing' process)
Balance: Ending inventory (by deduction)	

This system provides a continuous record of the balances in both the 'inventory account' and the 'cost of goods sold account'.

Let us illustrate the mechanism with an example. The relevant complete data for the Borodine Company are:

Inventory of goods for resale (merchandise) at beginning of year	200
Purchases of goods for resale (merchandise) during the year	900
Sales revenue from the sale of goods for resale (merchandise)	1,200
Cost of goods sold (valued at their purchase price)	800
Inventory of goods for resale (merchandise) at end of year	300

In a perpetual inventory system, the fundamental inventory equation is used to calculate the ending inventory as follows:

Beginning inventory	+	Purchases or additions	−	Withdrawals	=	Ending inventory (the unknown)
200	+	900	−	800	=	X

$$X = 200 + 900 - 800 = 300$$

This system has two main characteristics:

1. All additions to inventory through manufacturing or purchase are recorded as an increase of the inventory account (asset increase).
2. All withdrawals for sale or further manufacturing are recorded as a decrease of the inventory account (asset decrease) and are eventually charged to the income statement as cost of goods sold.

Dedicated accounting software will help any company record purchases, additions, and withdrawals nearly instantaneously at an acceptable cost if a proper system of control and measurement is introduced. However, creating a closed storeroom with rigorous controls counting all movements (in and out) can be a complex and expensive procedure, even if bar coding has often simplified recording (and the reduction in the cost of Radio Frequency Identification – RFID – will soon make manual or optical tracking obsolete for most businesses). Many small companies do not have the administrative and technical capacity and resources to record all movements in and out of inventory. These companies, in particular, take advantage of the simplification allowed under the periodic inventory system.

1.2.2 Periodic inventory system

This method is minimalist. It simply follows the general requirement that at least once every period (commonly the year) a business physically counts – and attests to – what is really in inventory and what assets and liabilities really exist (opportunity to record impairment or provisions when needed). The periodic inventory system relies on the required periodic (annual) physical counting to establish the quantities in the ending inventory so that they can be valued.

This system has two main characteristics:

1. All beginning inventories and additions to inventory (through manufacturing or purchase) are, in a first step, presumed consumed and recorded directly as an expense in the income statement.
2. In a second step, the presumed consumption cost is adjusted at the end of the period (adjusting entry) by deducting the independently measured ending inventory(ies).

The cornerstone of the periodic inventory method is therefore the physical inventory figures (always assumed to be measured on the balance sheet date[3]). Appendix 9.1 deals with differences between physical and accounting inventory count. The balance shown on an inventory account in the ledger is only changed when a new physical inventory is taken.

The inventory account is presented in the following way (purchases or acquisitions are not presumed to transit through the inventory account):

Periodic inventory account	
Asset increase (debit)	Asset decrease (credit)
■ Beginning inventory (opening balance)	■ Beginning inventory (assumed consumed)
■ Ending inventory (measured at year end)	
Balance: Ending inventory (measured at year end)	

The fundamental inventory equation is expressed as follows (continuing the Borodine Company example):

Beginning inventory	+	Purchases or additions	−	Ending inventory (independently measured)	=	Costs of goods sold or cost of goods transferred (deducted or consumed)
200	+	900	−	300	=	X
X = 200 + 900 − 300 = 800						

1.2.3 Comparison of recording

As the example shows, profit and inventory values are the same under either method, as long as the basic data do not show any inflation or deflation. The preference of most businesses for the perpetual inventory (subject to cost-benefit criteria applied to the information the system generates) comes from the superior managerial information and internal control it provides. (A more detailed comparison of advantages and limits of both methods is presented in Appendix 9.2.)

Figure 9.3 illustrates side by side the impact of the perpetual and periodic inventory methods on the financial statements of the Borodine Company.

- The ending inventory value, 300 CU, is the same under either method. It is calculated as follows:
  - Perpetual inventory: Beginning inventory (i.e., 200) + Purchases or additions (i.e., 900) − Withdrawals (cost of goods sold or consumption) (i.e., 800) = 300.
  - Periodic inventory: The ending inventory is declared to be 300 after an end-of-period physical inventory count.
- Both methods provide the same cost of goods sold (or cost of goods consumed) which is calculated as follows:
  - Perpetual inventory: Directly by summing the withdrawal or requisition slips that recorded the movements.
  - Periodic inventory (by deduction): Purchases (i.e., 900) + Change in inventory (i.e., 200 − 300).

Figure 9.3 Recording of inventory – Impact on the financial statements

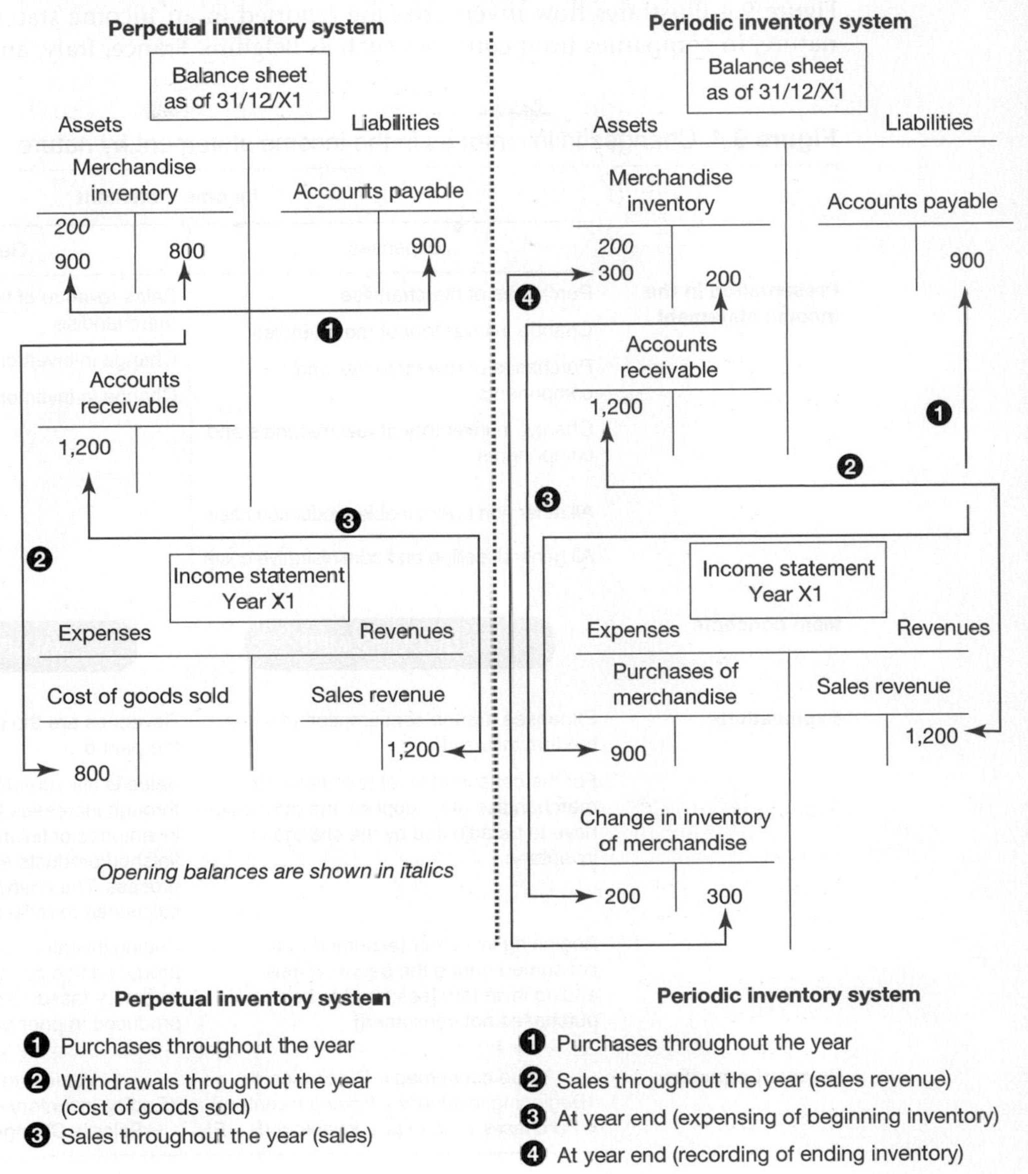

- The periodic inventory system is the by default minimum recommendation of the 4th European Union Directive for a retail business or for raw material and components in a manufacturing firm:

Purchases of goods for resale or used in manufacturing	900	This is considered an expense
Adjusted by the change in inventory of goods for resale or for use in production	−100	Here the sign is negative because the inventory actually increased, thus it is equivalent to a reduction of the expense
Withdrawals (cost of goods consumed or cost of goods sold)	=800	The expense recognized either as cost of goods sold or as a cost consumed in the manufacturing process

1.2.4 Presentation of changes in inventories in the income statement by nature

Figure 9.4 illustrates how inventories are reported in an income statement presented by nature, in companies from countries such as Belgium, France, Italy, and Spain.

Figure 9.4 Changes in inventories in the income statement by nature

	Income statement	
	Expenses	Revenues
Presentation in the income statement	Purchases of merchandise Change in inventory of merchandise Purchases of raw materials and components Change in inventory of raw materials and components All other non inventoriable production costs All general, selling and administrative costs	Sales revenue of finished products and merchandise Change in inventory of finished products Change in inventory of work in progress
Main concepts	VALUE CONSUMED	VALUE CREATED
Explanations	Expenses are the consumption of value the firm incurred. For the consumption of raw materials, merchandise and supplies, the purchases have to be adjusted by the change in inventory: Beginning inventory [assumed to be consumed during the period] minus ending inventory [assumed to be purchases not consumed]	Revenues are the creation of value during the period. Value is also created [or destroyed] through increases [or decreases] in inventories of finished products, semi-finished products and work in progress/in process. The change in inventory is calculated to reflect this value creation: Ending inventory [assumed to have been produced this period] minus beginning inventory [assumed to have been produced in prior periods]
Relevant equation	Value consumed = Purchases + (Beginning inventory – Ending inventory) = Purchases + Change in inventory (B – E)	Value created = Sales + (Ending inventory – Beginning inventory) = Sales + Change in inventory (E – B)

1.3 Inventory valuation and reported income

1.3.1 The basic issue

The value of the cost of goods sold (which, by definition, is linked to the value of the ending inventory in the balance sheet) directly impacts on the gross margin, and, consequently, on net income. As a consequence, inventory valuation and costing methods have a great impact on net income.

IAS 2 (IASB 2003: § 10) states: 'the cost of inventories shall comprise all costs of purchase, costs of conversion and other costs incurred in bringing the inventories to their present condition and location' (i.e., historical cost of acquisition). IAS 2, like most accounting standards, defines the value of the inventory as the critical element (i.e., taking a balance sheet view of the firm), while to a manager whose responsibility is to allocate resources in order to manage a product and customer portfolios it is the value of the cost of goods sold that is the most important element (and inventory valuation is residual information).

Any cost that flows to the income statement by being attached to a 'product' (following the physical flow of goods in their production, transformation, and conversion process) is called a 'product cost'. Some components of the acquisition cost, such as supplier qualification, sourcing, purchasing, ordering, receiving, in-bound transportation, and warehousing costs, may be difficult to trace in businesses with weak or non-extant cost-accounting systems. If these items are not included in the acquisition cost they will flow directly to the income statement of the period when incurred. Any cost, regardless of its cause or purpose, that does not flow to the income statement by way of a cascade of inventory accounts is recognized in the period incurred and is thus called a 'period cost'.

The cost of goods manufactured (production cost) is the sum total of the acquisition cost of raw materials, components and supplies consumed, direct production costs (mainly labor and conversion costs), and a reasonable proportion of production support and infrastructure costs (called 'overheads'). The tracing of overheads to products is a key topic in cost accounting[4] and is not guided by one unambiguous dominant solution.

The cost of acquisition or of manufacturing of an item is not stable over time, even over the course of a year as the market price of any and all resources change in response to the evolution of their supply and demand.

1.3.2 Methods for the valuation of inventory outflows (costing formulae for withdrawals)

Four procedures exist for the valuation of withdrawals, but only three are outlined and allowed in IAS 2 (IASB 2003: §§ 23–27). The issue is about the relative fungibility of items in inventory. Either they are not fungible and we have the method of specific identification or they are partially fungible (within a batch received or produced) and the issue is that of time-ordering of entries and withdrawals (first-in, first-out (FIFO) versus last-in, first-out (LIFO); it should be noted that this latest method is no longer allowed by the IASB – see below), or they are completely fungible and an average cost will be used.

Specific identification method Items that are not ordinarily interchangeable or fungible (such as jewels, diamonds, paintings, custom orders, etc.), and goods that were produced for a specifically identified project or customer, will keep their specific cost when carried in inventory. This means that their cost upon withdrawal is absolutely identical to the one they had when entering in inventory (cost of acquisition or cost of goods manufactured). This method is known as the 'specific identification method'. When this method is used, the distinction between periodic or perpetual inventory system is not needed since the item will be entered or withdrawn only once during the accounting period. This method is simple but extremely costly to implement when the individual value of the items involved is moderate or small. It is also a method that could be used deliberately to affect (manipulate) the bottom line by carefully selecting those items that are sold and those that remain in inventories. Usually, this method is reserved for high-priced items or items that must not be considered to be fungible for legal reasons, such as cars at a dealer's showroom (cars from the point of view of the car manufacturer are generally considered to be fungible within their production series), heavy equipment, farm equipment, works of art, furs, jewelry.

Methods used for fungible and semi-fungible items When items are fungible to some degree, it is not simple (quasi-impossible?) to trace the cost of acquisition of a given item. The specific identification method is unworkable if large quantities of items flow through an inventory account, as it would be impractical to maintain individualized inventory records for each item. Specific identification would be impossible and unnecessary for generic microprocessors, nails, or cans of beer, difficult for a hand-finished motor vehicle, necessary for a classical antique piece of furniture, and essential for an item produced to contractually defined customer specifications. In other words, it is rarely feasible to trace the cost of a specific item in inventory.

As a consequence, businesses recognize the partial or total fungibility of products and make assumptions about the timing sequence according to which inventory items enter and leave an inventory account to either become part of goods consumed in a further step of transformation (manufacturing) or become part of the cost of goods sold. There are two sets of hypotheses. Either products are totally fungible, or they are fungible only within a batch defined by a date of acquisition.

When products are considered partially or totally fungible, three possibilities for time-ordering withdrawals exist[5], each reflecting a specific assumed pattern of goods flow:

1. Goods withdrawn are valued batch by batch in the order they entered inventory (first-in, first-out, or FIFO).
2. Goods withdrawn are valued batch by batch in the reverse order from the one they followed when entering inventory (last-in, first-out, or LIFO).
3. Goods withdrawn (considered totally fungible) are valued at the average cost of available goods (weighted average cost method, or WAC).

Both the FIFO and LIFO approaches require that a record of each acquisition be kept by date and that the withdrawals be valued by adding complete (or parts of) batches. The WAC is simpler and potentially less costly to operate. It consists of using a continuously updated weighted average for the unit cost of any item in inventory.

In periods of inflation the price (and thus the cost of acquisition) of resources does go up. FIFO or WAC methods do not give a true view of the financial condition of the business. Especially, they may lead to an overestimation of the real value created. If goods purchased three months ago for 100 CU, are sold for 150, the apparent profit margin is 50 CU. But if the replacement of these units (required if the business is to remain a going concern) requires that 120 CU be spent, the 'real' (sustainable) profit is only 30 CU. The LIFO method is more reactive to the evolution (up or down) of the market price of resources and is often preferred to FIFO or WAC in the context of managerial decisions. However, the historical costing and prudence principles would tend to favor FIFO or WAC for reporting purposes. Some other LIFO considerations are shown in Appendix 9.3.

LIFO is permitted as a valid basis for the valuation of withdrawal flows by the European Union but is no longer allowed by the IASB for consolidated accounts (reporting purpose) in the latest revision of the accounting standard IAS 2 (2003): 'The cost of inventories, other than those dealt with in paragraph 23 [subject to specific identification], shall be assigned by using the first-in, first-out (FIFO) or weighted average cost formula' (§ 25).

Some European countries' local GAAP do not allow the use of LIFO in reporting unconsolidated accounts, while others (Belgium, Germany, Greece, Italy, Netherlands, Portugal, and Spain) allow it. Many businesses in the USA and Japan legitimately use LIFO reporting, authorized by their local GAAP.

The three main reasons for not using LIFO are:

- **Reporting**: Inflation is very limited today in developed economies and there is often simultaneously inflation and deflation on different products or resources, thus the reporting benefit might not be significant.
- **Taxation**: With even a small inflation, the LIFO-based taxable income of a growing business would be less than it would be under FIFO or WAC and, if there is a reversal of inflation, LIFO might create larger swings in taxable income levels than would WAC or FIFO. In fact, the use of LIFO is forbidden for tax purposes in many countries.
- **Accounting**: LIFO in periods of heavy inflation may lead to a valuation of an inventory that is physically and concretely real but is valued at meaningless costs, thus giving less credibility to the balance sheet.

Figure 9.5 summarizes the different costing methods.

Figure 9.5 Costing inventories

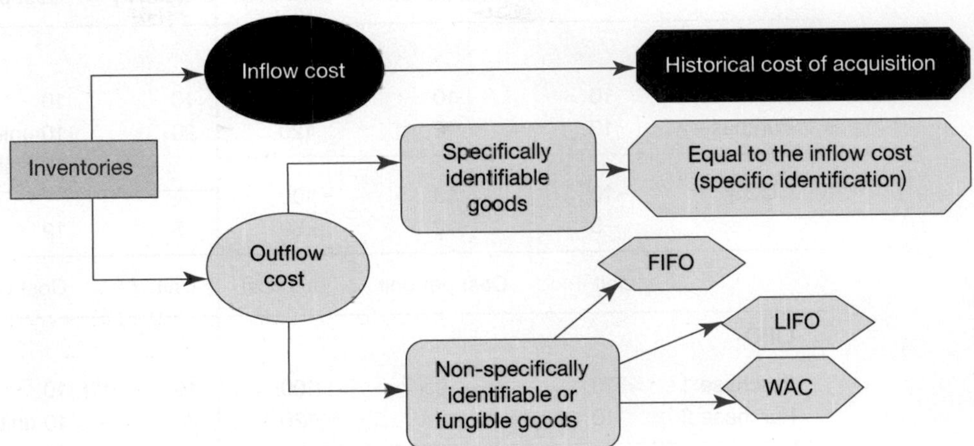

The Glinka Company example summarized in Tables 9.3 and 9.4 illustrates the effect on income and the balance sheet of using FIFO, LIFO, or WAC. In this illustration we assume, without loss of generality, no beginning inventory. Glinka's relevant data for the period under scrutiny were the following:

- 1st purchase: 10 units are purchased and are recorded for an acquisition cost of 10 CU per unit.
- 2nd purchase: 10 units are purchased and are recorded for an acquisition cost of 12 CU per unit.
- 15 units are sold at the end of the period for a unit selling price of 18 CU per unit.

In this example, the sum of 'cost of goods sold plus ending inventory' is equal to the sum of 'purchases plus beginning inventory' as a consequence of the fundamental inventory equation which can be reformulated:

Beginning inventory + Purchases − Cost of goods sold = Ending inventory

Beginning inventory + Purchases = Cost of goods sold + Ending inventory

The example confirms that, in an inflationary world, LIFO gives the highest cost of goods sold (COGS) of the three methods and thus the lowest value for ending inventory and the lowest reported income. The situation would be the exact opposite if Glinka had operated in a deflationary world. The effect of LIFO is that, after a period of years in an inflationary world, the balance sheet might no longer present a true and fair view of the company's real assets. However, over the same years the LIFO method has provided management with a true and fair measure of the COGS and thus allowed them to appropriately manage both products and customers to create more value for the shareholders. The debate between the various methods is thus a question of whether one prefers to have a 'correct' income statement or a 'correct' balance sheet.

Table 9.3 Cost of consumption and value of remaining inventory

	Transactions (in and out)			Ending inventory		
	Quantity	Cost per unit	Total cost	Quantity	Cost per unit	Total cost
FIFO						
Purchase 1	10	10	100	10	10	100
Purchase 2	10	12	120	20	10 units at 10	100
					10 units at 12	120
COGS	−10	10	−100			
	−5	12	−60	5	12	60
	Unit	Cost per unit	Total cost	Unit	Cost per unit	Total cost
LIFO						
Purchase 1	10	10	100	10	10	100
Purchase 2	10	12	120	20	10 units at 12	120
					10 units at 10	100
COGS	−10	12	−120			
	−5	10	−50	5	10	50
WAC						
Purchase 1	10	10	100	10	10	100
Purchase 2	10	12	120	20	20 units at 11	220
COGS	−15	11	−165	5	11	55

Table 9.4 Impact on income statement

	FIFO	LIFO	WAC
Sales	270	270	270
Cost of goods sold (direct computation)	160	170	165
Alternatively the COGS can be obtained by applying the full equation:			
Purchases	*220*	*220*	*220*
Plus beginning inventory	*0*	*0*	*0*
Equals cost of goods available for sale	*220*	*220*	*220*
Minus ending inventory	*−60*	*−50*	*−55*
Equals cost of goods sold	*160*	*170*	*165*
Gross margin (before tax)	110	100	105
− Income tax (assuming a 40% rate)	−44	−40	−42
Gross margin (after tax)	66	60	63
Control:			
Cost of goods sold + Ending inventory	220	220	220
Purchases + Beginning inventory	220	220	220

Table 9.5 summarizes the impact on income and ending inventory of the three methods in the context of rising or falling costs of acquisition.

Table 9.5 Impact on net income and ending inventory

Context	Impact on net income	Impact on ending inventory
Rising prices of resources used	FIFO → higher income reported WAC → medium income reported LIFO → lower income reported	FIFO → higher ending inventory reported WAC → medium ending inventory reported LIFO → lower ending inventory reported
Falling prices of resources used	FIFO → lower income reported WAC → medium income reported LIFO → higher income reported	FIFO → lower ending inventory reported WAC → medium ending inventory reported LIFO → higher ending inventory reported

2 Advanced issues

2.1 Effect of an inventory misstatement

Inventory misstatements may have an impact on net income (see Appendix 9.4).

2.2 Inventories and cash flow

The choice of inventory valuation methods has no impact on the cash flow before tax. However, it has an impact on the tax expense that will accrue (because of the differences in gross margins). It will thus change the cash flow after tax. The effect of the choice of a method of cost flow (i.e., inventory valuation) on cash flows is illustrated in Table 9.6 using the data from the Glinka Company example (see earlier) assuming that sales and purchases are both paid in cash.

Table 9.6 illustrates that, in an inflationary resources market with stable market prices for units sold, it is the use of LIFO that generates the highest cash flow after tax because it provides the lowest income before income tax (Table 9.4).

Table 9.6 Impact on cash flow

	FIFO	LIFO	WAC
Cash inflow from sales	270	270	270
Minus Cash outflows for purchases	−220	−220	−220
Equals Cash flow before tax	50	50	50
Minus Income tax (40% rate) (see Table 9.4)	−44	−40	−42
Equals Cash flow after tax	6	10	8

2.3 Decline in value of inventories (end of year adjustments)

Decline in replacement prices, physical deterioration, or obsolescence are some of the reasons why the inventory at the end of the year may be worth less than its value shown in the books (assuming all physical discrepancies have been accounted for already). The rule of 'lower of cost or market' is outlined in IAS 2 (§ 9): 'Inventories shall be measured at the lower of cost and net realizable value'. Net realizable value is defined as the 'estimated selling price in the ordinary course of business less the estimated costs of completion and the estimated costs necessary to make the sale' (IAS 2: § 6). This rule requires that a business 'realigns' the books when it finds itself in a situation in which the book value of inventories is greater than their market value (expressed either in terms of disposal or liquidation cost or in terms of sale price that the business hopes to obtain from customers for the goods in inventory). If the 'market value' is lower than the recorded cost, the inventory is written-down to current market value. The corresponding unrealized loss must be recognized in the income statement.

Let us illustrate this point with an example. Glazunov GmbH purchased 1,000 stuffed wombats at a unit cost of acquisition of 20 CU. There has been a huge shipment from South East Asia of inexpensive stuffed wombats to all retailers competing with Glazunov GmbH. The wholesale market unit price of these stuffed wombats has dropped to 15 CU for the products that had been purchased for 20 CU. Glazunov GmbH still holds 100 units in inventory at the end of the accounting period. A provision for loss of value of inventory must be recorded. It amounts to $(20 - 15) \times 100 = 500$ CU. Figure 9.6 illustrates the year-end adjusting entries.

The 'inventory' account is reduced in the form of a contra-asset account ('Provision for depreciation of inventories') so as to not lose information. If the market value recovers by year-end, the write-down (provision) should be reversed either by reversing the expense itself or creating an income or a revenue.

Figure 9.6 End-of-year adjustments

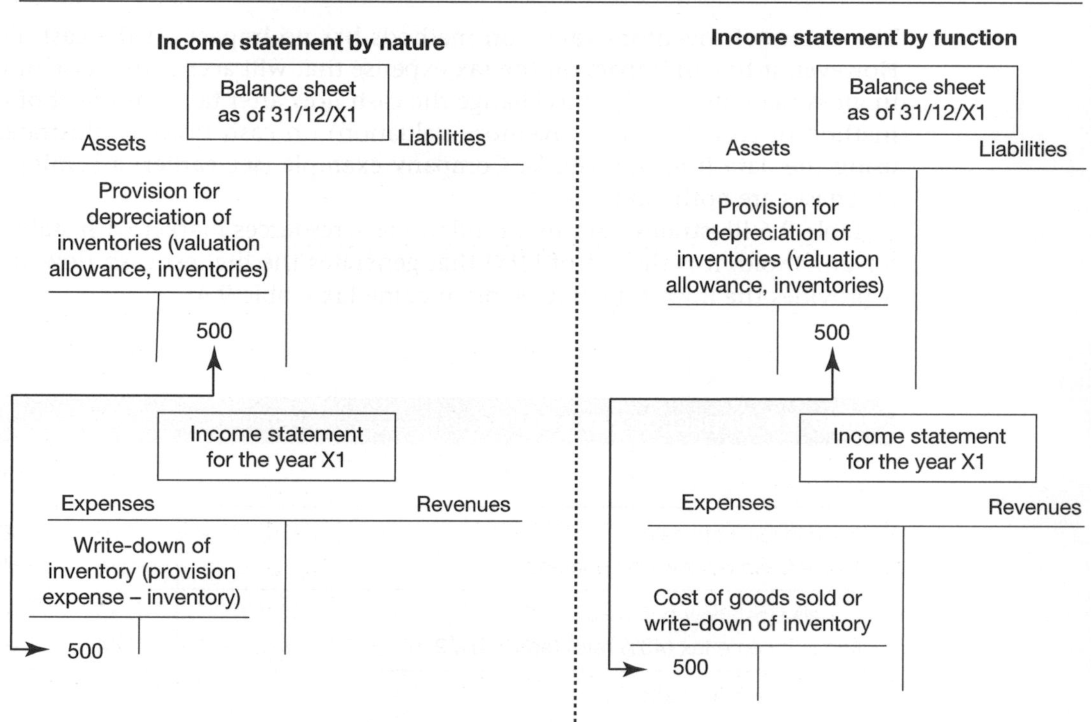

2.4 Income statement by nature and income statement by function

Expenses in the income statement can be classified either by nature or by function. In Chapter 3 we illustrated how to go from one presentation to the other for Brahms Company, a retailer. We can now illustrate the passage from one presentation to the other for a manufacturing company. Our illustration will be about the Moussorgski Company. The relevant data are provided in Table 9.7 (in thousands of CU).

Table 9.8 shows side by side the calculation of the operating income by nature and by function (we assume, for the sake of simplicity, that no general and administrative overhead is allocated to the production costs). The operating income is mechanically exactly the same under both approaches. The difference in presentation offers different possible interpretation and uses of the information contained in the income statement.

Table 9.7 Data

Beginning inventory of raw materials	20	Depreciation expenses	
		■ Production equipment	19
Purchases of raw materials	40	■ Sales equipment	5
Sales revenue (finished products sold)	100	■ Administrative equipment	3
Raw materials consumed in manufacturing	50	Rent expenses	
		■ Production	3
Ending inventory of raw materials	10	■ Administration	1
Personnel expenses		Beginning inventory of work in process	2
■ Direct labor	20		
■ Supervisory labor	6	Cost of units transferred into finished goods inventory during the period	88
■ Sales personnel	4		
■ Accounting and administration personnel	3	Ending inventory of work in process	12
Total cost of units sold during the period	80	Beginning inventory of finished products	3
		Ending inventory of finished products	11

2.5 Disclosure of inventory valuation policies

Although disclosure practices in the notes to financial statements may vary between countries, the following minimum information should be given according to IAS 2 (§ 36):

- Accounting policies adopted in measuring inventories, including the cost formula used.
- Total carrying amount of inventories and carrying amount in classifications appropriate to the entity.
- Carrying amount of inventories carried at fair value less costs to sell.
- Amount of any write-down of inventories recognized as an expense in the period (...).
- Amount of any reversal of any write-down of inventories that is recognized as a reduction in the amount of inventories recognized as expense in the period (...).
- Circumstances or events that led to the reversal of a write-down of inventories (...).
- Carrying amount of inventories pledged as security for liabilities.

Table 9.8 Income statement by nature and by function

Income statement by nature	
Sales revenue from finished products	100
+ Change in inventory of finished products (a)	8
+ Change in inventory of work in process (a)	10
− Purchases of raw materials	−40
− Change in inventory of raw materials (b)	−10
− Rent expenses (c)	−4
− Personnel expenses (d)	−33
− Depreciation expense (e)	−27
= Operating income	4

(a) Ending minus beginning
(b) Beginning minus ending (subtraction of the change)
(c) 3 + 1
(d) 20 + 6 + 4 + 3
(e) 19 + 5 + 3

Income statement by function	
Sales revenue from finished products	100
− Cost of goods sold (f)	−80
= Gross margin	20
− Selling expenses (g)	−9
− Administrative expenses (h)	−7
= Operating income	4
(f) Cost of goods sold	
+ Raw materials consumed	50
+ Direct labor	20
+ Supervisory labor	6
+ Depreciation (production equipment)	19
+ Rent expense (production overhead)	3
= Production costs incurred this period	98
− Change in inventory of finished products (a)	−8
− Change in inventory of work in process (a)	−10
= Cost of goods sold (f)	80
(g) Selling expenses	
+ Personnel expenses (sales person)	4
+ Depreciation (sales equipment)	5
= Selling expenses (g)	9
(h) Administrative expenses	
+ Personnel expenses (administration)	3
+ Depreciation (administration)	3
+ Rent expense (administration)	1
= Administrative expenses (h)	7

Real-life example Saurer

(Switzerland – IFRS/IAS GAAP – *Source*: Annual report 2004 – Full service solutions in textile machinery and mechanical power transmission systems)

Income statement (excerpts)

(EUR 000)	2004	%	2003	%
Sales	1,614,364	100	1,745,874	100
Cost of goods sold	−1,264,867	−78.4	−1,348,164	−77.2
Gross profit	349,497	21.6	397,710	22.8

Note to the financial statements

Note 9: Inventories	31.12.04	31.12.03
Raw materials	141,019	128,877
Work in process	190,286	160,771
Finished goods	87,528	90,108
Provision for slow-moving and obsolescent inventories	−40,828	−46,045
Total inventories before customer payments on account	378,005	333,711
Customer payments on account	−144,569	−126,500
Total inventories (net)	233,436	207,211

Inventories. Raw materials are valued at the lower of cost and market, using the FIFO or weighted average cost method. Finished goods and work in process are valued at production cost, reduced to net realizable value should this be lower than cost. Provisions are made for items of reduced salability and excess stocks. Customer payments on account are deducted from inventories.

Several comments can be made on this note.

- Advances received on orders are subtracted here from inventories. Usually, this item is reported as a liability. We could say the presentation adopted by Saurer, if the offset were not mentioned explicitly in note 9, might be considered in violation of the 'non-offsetting principle'.
- The notes allow the calculation of the change in inventories of raw materials and supplies, which could not be obtained from the income statement because Saurer reports the cost of goods sold and therefore these variations are hidden in the COGS.
- The financial statements allow the calculation of the net variation of the provision for slow-moving and obsolescent inventories. However, there is no indication about added provisions expenses or reversed provisions during the year 2004, thus depriving the user of key information about the meaningfulness of the net reduction by 5,217 million Euros of that provision.

Real-life example Sauer-Danfoss

(USA – US GAAP – *Source*: Annual report 2004 – Design, manufacture, and sale of highly engineered hydraulic systems and components for off-highway mobile equipment)

In the notes to consolidated financial statements for the year 2004, we find the following information:

Inventories are valued at the lower of cost or market, using various cost methods, and include the cost of material, labor, and factory overhead. The last-in, first-out (LIFO) method was adopted in 1987 and is used to value inventories at the US locations which existed at that time. Inventories at all of the non-US locations and the US locations obtained through acquisition after 1987, which produce products different than those produced at US locations existing at 1987, are valued under the inventory valuation method in place prior to acquisition, either weighted average or first-in, first-out (FIFO). The percentage of year-end inventory using LIFO, FIFO, and average cost methods was 17%, 42%, and 41%, respectively, for 2004, and 18%, 39%, and 42%, respectively, for 2003.

Comment: The fact the note gives the opportunity to the reader of the financial statements to recast the income statement according to any of the three basic inventory valuation methods is rather unusual. It helps identify better the earnings potential of the firm in allowing one to understand what comes from past events (FIFO) and what comes from current competitive edge (LIFO), which is a good indicator of future earnings potential. It would appear that the choice of inventory valuation methods favors avoiding the tax effect of switching old LIFO inventories to a FIFO or WAC basis over a coherent presentation of inventories throughout the group. Thus only newly acquired businesses are using the FIFO or WAC methods. This reflects the fact, as mentioned above, that under LIFO, the value of the inventories in the balance sheet might end-up being completely disconnected from the reality of the value of the goods held on hand. If Sauer-Danfoss were to convert these 'old' inventories to a FIFO or WAC basis, it would have to acknowledge an unrealized gain on the inventory, which would be taxable in the year of conversion.

2.6 Financial statement analysis pertaining to inventories

The financial analysts' main concern is with the coherence between the actual level of inventory and the one they feel would be desirable, given the operating cycle, the firm's strategy, and its competitive business environment. Two metrics are commonly used in this respect:

- *Inventory turnover*: This metric is defined as the number of times the inventory 'turns' during the accounting period. The shorter the operating cycle, the higher the turnover. This ratio is obtained by dividing the cost of goods sold by the average value of the relevant inventory (beginning inventory plus ending inventory divided by 2). For a given industry, the higher the turnover ratio, the more likely the management of the physical flows is efficient. With the development of just in time relations between suppliers and customers, ratios of 26 (equivalent to an inventory sufficient to meet the needs of two weeks of average demand or consumption) or even 52 (one week) are no longer unusual in the automotive industry or the assembly of washing machines.

- *Average days of inventory available*: This metric is the inverse of the turnover ratio. It expresses the inventory in terms of number of days of activity that can be 'supplied' without having to purchase (or produce) any new products or materials. It is obtained as the 'number of activity days in the year divided by the turnover ratio'.

The choice of presentation of the income statement (by nature or by function) facilitates or hinders the calculation of these ratios. In an income statement by nature, extensive information is available describing the inventories for each type of good (finished, intermediate, raw materials, or merchandise) (see Table 9.9).

Table 9.9 Formulae for the calculation of the inventory turnover in the income statement by nature

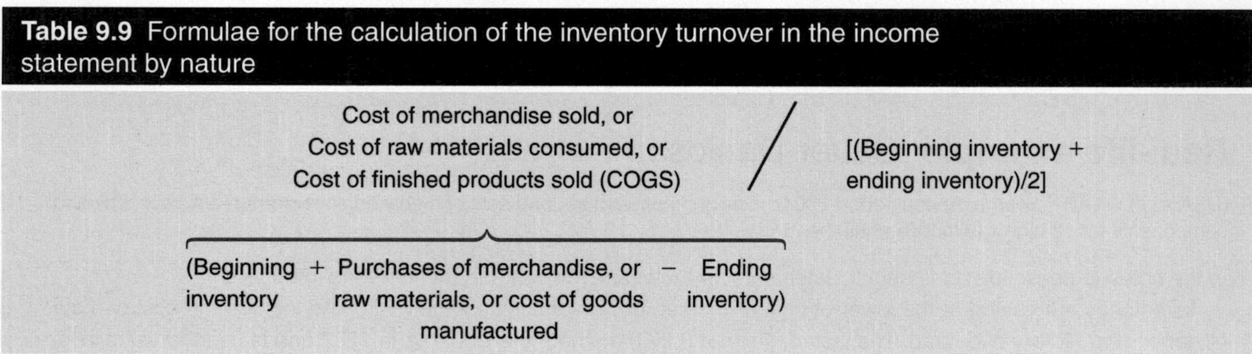

In an income statement presented by function, the cost of goods sold does not distinguish between merchandise, raw materials, and finished products. A general inventory turnover is then calculated by dividing the cost of goods sold (obtained from the income statement) by the average inventory (obtained from the balance sheet).

Real-life example Toray Industries

(Japan – Japanese GAAP – *Source*: Annual report 2003–04 – Manufacturer of synthetic fibers and textiles)

		Millions of yen	
Note 3 to financial statements		2004	2003
Balance sheet			
Finished goods and work in process		165,729	167,879
Raw materials and supplies		41,339	45,102
		(A) 207,068	(B) 212,981
Income statement			
Cost of goods sold	(1)	850,881	
Computation			
Average inventory	(2) = [(A) + (B)]/2 = 210,025		
Inventory turnover	(3) = (1)/(2) = 4.1 times		
Average days of inventory available	(4) = 1/(3) × 365 = 90 days		

Key points

- Inventories are essential assets (potential source of future economic benefits): (1) held for sale in the ordinary course of business; (2) in the process of production for such sale; or (3) in the form of materials or supplies to be consumed in the production process or in the rendering of services.
- As long as a product has not been sold, all costs attached to it are withheld from the income statement and essentially stored in an inventory account.
- The three major issues relating to accounting for inventories are: (1) inventory recording systems; (2) inventory costing methods; and (3) inventory valuation methods.
- The main categories of inventories are: (1) merchandise (commercial activity); and (2) raw materials, manufacturing supplies, work in progress and process, and semi-finished goods and finished goods (manufacturing activity).
- Inventories sometimes represent a large portion of assets, and therefore their correct valuation is essential for reporting accurately and fairly the value of the shareholders' equity.
- The fundamental inventory equation is [withdrawals are equal to purchases or additions plus beginning inventory minus ending inventory].
- A perpetual inventory system is a continuous record of changes in inventory (additions as well as withdrawals).
- The periodic inventory system relies on the required periodic (annual) physical counting to establish and value the quantities in the ending inventory.
- Inventory valuation and costing methods have a great impact on net income.
- There are four methods for costing items withdrawn from inventory: 'specific identification method'; FIFO (first-in, first-out); LIFO (last-in, first-out); and WAC (weighted average cost).
- The IASB no longer allows the use of LIFO for external reporting of a business financial position.
- Financial analysts are mainly concerned with the coherence between the current or actual level of inventory of a business with that which would appear to be appropriate given the firm's business's environment and strategy. Their measures to evaluate this coherence are: (1) inventory turnover (number of times the inventory 'turns' during the accounting period); and (2) average days of inventory available (inverse of the turnover ratio).

Review (solutions are at the back of the book)

Review 9.1 Ericsson*

Topic: Reporting for inventory
Related part of the chapter: Core/Advanced issues

Based in Sweden, Ericsson is a leading provider in the telecom world, with communication solutions that combine telecom and datacom technologies with freedom of mobility for the user.

The 2004 annual report shows inventories to be as follows:

31 December, SEK million	Note	2004	2003
Assets			
(...)			
Inventories	13	14,003	10,965

The notes to the consolidated financial statements contain the following information:

Note 13: Inventories	2004	2003
Raw materials, components and consumables	5,557	4,332
Manufacturing work in progress	232	245
Finished products and goods for resale	3,720	271
Contract work in progress	7,278	9,275
Less advances from customers	−2,784	−3,158
Inventories – net	14,003	10,965

Reported amounts are net of obsolescence reserves by SEK 3,146 million (SEK 3,658 million 2003).

Movements in obsolescence reserves	
Opening balance	3,658
Additions	533
Utilized	−976
Translation difference for the year	−69
Closing balance	3,146

Of the total obsolescence reserve, a large portion is due to slow moving items related to phased-out products, where Ericsson still has contractual commitments to be able to supply spare parts during a number of years. To satisfy such commitments, some inventories are set aside when products with long life cycles in use are phased out.

Of net inventories, SEK760 million are valued at net realizable value.

Contract work in progress includes amounts related to construction type contracts as well as other contracts with ongoing work in progress.

Required

1. What are 'obsolescence reserves' usually called?
2. What do the 'Additions' in these reserves represent?
3. What does the item 'Utilized' in these reserves refer to?
4. What restatement is necessary to obtain the gross amount of inventories?
5. What business anomaly should worry the financial statement users when comparing the 2004 figures with those of 2003? How could you explain it?

Assignments

Assignment 9.1
Multiple-choice questions

Related part of the chapter: Core/Advanced issues

1. Raw materials and merchandise are included in
   (a) Expenses
   (b) Fixed assets
   (c) Cash
   (d) Current assets
   (e) None of these

2. Ending inventory is reported in the liabilities side of the balance sheet
   (a) True
   (b) False

3. In an income statement by nature, change in inventory of finished products is reported
   (a) On the revenues side, under the sales of finished products
   (b) On the expenses side, under the purchases of raw materials
   (c) Both solutions are possible
   (d) None of these

4. In an income statement by nature, change in inventory of merchandise is reported
   (a) On the revenues side, under the sales of merchandise
   (b) On the expenses side, under the purchases of merchandise
   (c) Both solutions are possible
   (d) None of these

5. In the balance sheet, the item 'inventories' may be subject to
   (a) Depreciation
   (b) Amortization
   (c) Depletion
   (d) Provision
   (e) None of these

6. The following inventory costing method provides a value for *ending inventory* which approximates most closely the current replacement cost
   (a) FIFO
   (b) LIFO
   (c) None of these

7. The following inventory costing method provides a value for *cost of goods sold* which approximates most closely the current replacement cost
   (a) FIFO
   (b) LIFO
   (c) None of these

8. An audit shows that the beginning inventory at 1 January X1 had been overstated by 1,000 CU and the ending inventory (31/12/X1) was overstated by 400 CU. As a consequence, the cost of goods sold for X1 was
   (a) Overstated by 1,000
   (b) Understated by 1,000
   (c) Overstated by 400
   (d) Understated by 400
   (e) Overstated by 1,400
   (f) Understated by 1,400
   (g) Overstated by 600
   (h) Understated by 600
   (i) None of these

9. In periods of steadily decreasing prices, the following method will give the highest ending inventory value (assuming quantities purchased exceed quantities withdrawn)
   (a) FIFO
   (b) LIFO
   (c) Weighted average cost (WAC)

10. The average day's inventory available is defined as: (Cost of goods sold/Average inventory) × 365
   (a) True
   (b) False

Assignment 9.2
Discussion questions

Related part of the chapter: Core/Advanced issues

1. Give at least three arguments in favor of each of the three basic methods of inventory valuation (FIFO, LIFO, and WAC).
2. Provide at least three arguments in favor of perpetual and three for periodic inventory accounting methods.

Assignment 9.3
Taylor Nelson Sofres* and Irish Continental*

Topic: Nature of inventory
Related part of the chapter: Core issues

Taylor Nelson Sofres is a UK group specialized in market information, providing continuous and custom research and analysis. It is active in managing consumer panels and measuring television audience.

Irish Continental Group is a shipping, transport, and leisure group (Irish Ferries) principally engaged in the transport of passengers and cars, freight, and containers.

Both companies have in common the fact that their inventories are very low, particularly in relation to total assets as shown in the following table where figures have been extracted from the 2004 annual reports of each company.

Taylor Nelson Sofres	2004 £m	2003 restated £m
Stocks (a)	75	76.3
Total assets	852.7	848.8
Inventories/total assets	8.8%	9.0%

Irish Continental Group	2004 €m	2003 €m
Stocks (a)	0.6	0.7
Total assets	376.7	399.0
Inventories/total assets	0.16%	0.18%

(a) Inventories are also called 'Stocks' in the United Kingdom and Ireland.

Required

Provide a list of possible items that could be included under the item 'inventories' (stocks) for each of these companies.

Assignment 9.4
Stravinsky

Topic: FIFO, LIFO and WAC
Related part of the chapter: Advanced issues

Stravinsky Company, a retailer selling a single product, opened shop on 3 April. The first months' transactions were as follows:

April 02: Purchase of 220 units @ 22 CU each
April 08: Purchase of 180 units @ 18 CU each
April 17: Sale of 240 units @ 25 CU each.

Required

Using successively each of the three costing methods (FIFO, LIFO, and WAC), prepare a table allowing you to compare the impact of the three methods on:

1. the ending inventory;
2. the net income, assuming a 40% income tax rate;
3. the cash flow.

Assignment 9.5
Repsol*

Topic: Reporting for inventory
Related part of the chapter: Core issues

Repsol is a Spanish group involved in the oil and gas sector. From the financial statements (annual report 2004), which are prepared in accordance with Spanish GAAP, we extracted the following information relating to inventory:

Consolidated statements of income, as of 31 December 2004 and 2003 (excerpts)

Expenses	2004	2003
Millions of euros		
Materials consumed and other external expenses	33,420	29,917
Revenues	**2004**	**2003**
Millions of euros		
Net sales	40,585	36,069
Variation in finished product and work-in-process inventories	283	54
Capitalized expenses of Group work on fixed assets	90	68
Other operating revenues	731	1,015
	41,689	37,206

Consolidated balance sheets as of 31 December 2004 and 2003 (€ millions) (excerpts)

Assets	2004	2003
Inventories (Note 9)	2,652	2,109

Note to the financial statements (excerpts)

€ millions	Cost	Allowance for decline in value	Net
2004			
Crude oil and natural gas	798	(28)	770
Finished and semi-finished products	1,297	(45)	1,252
Supplies and other inventories	646	(16)	630
	2,741	(89)	2,652
2003			
Crude oil and natural gas	699	(13)	686
Finished and semi-finished products	1,007	(17)	990
Supplies and other inventories	444	(11)	433
	2,150	(41)	2,109

Required

1. Identify the links between the figures of the balance sheet and the figures in the notes.
2. Explain why some figures of the income statement cannot be double-checked.

Assignment 9.6
Tchaïkovsky

Topic: Income statement by nature and by function
Related part of the chapter: Advanced issues

Tchaïkovsky Company manufactures and sells various and assorted products. Information relating to year X1 is given below (in thousands of CU).

Required

Prepare an income statement by nature and an income statement by function. (Check figure (operating income) is 21.)

Beginning inventory of raw materials	18
Purchases of raw materials	60
Sales of finished products	150
Raw materials consumed	55
Ending inventory of raw materials	23
Personnel expenses	
■ Direct labor	16
■ Supervisory labor	5
■ Sales personnel	3
■ Accounting and administration	4
Depreciation expenses	
■ Production equipment	20
■ Sales equipment	6
■ Administrative equipment	4
Rent expenses	
■ Production	4
■ Administration	5
Beginning inventory of work in process	10
Units completed during the period	105
Ending inventory of work in process	5
Beginning inventory of finished products	3
Cost of units sold during the period	107
Ending inventory of finished products	1

Assignment 9.7
McDonald's* and others

Topic: Comparative inventory turnover
Related part of the chapter: Advanced issues

The following information concerns eight US companies operating solely or mainly restaurants.

McDonald's Corporation*

The company primarily operates and franchises McDonald's restaurants in the food service industry. The company also operates Boston Market and Chipotle Mexican Grill in the USA and has a minority ownership in UK-based Prêt A Manger. In December 2003, the company sold its Donatos Pizzeria business. All restaurants are operated either by the company, by independent entrepreneurs under the terms of franchise arrangements (franchisees), or by affiliates operating under license agreements.

Extracted from the consolidated balance sheet and income statement (annual report 2004) the following data are provided.

Millions of US$	31 December 2004	31 December 2003
Inventory (balance sheet)	147.5	129.4
Company-operated restaurant expenses – Food and paper (income statement)	4,852.7	–

There is no note to the financial statements indicating the details of the inventory.

Benihana*

Benihana Inc. is the leading Asian restaurant chain in the USA. As of October 2004 it owned and operated 55 teppanyaki, eight RA Sushi restaurants, seven Haru sushi restaurants, and one Sushi Doraku restaurant, and franchised 22 other teppanyaki restaurants. From the consolidated balance sheet and income statement (annual report 2005), the following data were extracted.

Thousands of US$	27 March 2005	28 March 2004
Inventories (balance sheet)	6,571	6,147
Cost of food and beverage sales (income statement)	53,372	–

A note to the financial statements indicates that inventory consists principally of restaurant operating supplies and food and beverage. The company has a 52/53-week fiscal year. The company's first fiscal quarter consists of 16 weeks and the remaining three quarters are 12 weeks each, except in the event of a 53-week year with the final quarter composed of 13 weeks. Because of the differences in length of these accounting periods, results of operations between the first quarter and the later quarters of a fiscal year are not comparable.

Dave & Buster's*

Dave & Buster's owns and operates restaurant/entertainment complexes. Each Dave & Buster's offers food and beverage items, combined with an array of entertainment attractions such as pocket billiards, shuffleboard, state-of-the-art flight simulators, virtual reality, and traditional carnival-style amusements and games of skill. Whereas food and beverage represent 53.7% of sales revenue, amusement and other revenues represent 46.3%. From the consolidated balance sheet and income statement (annual report 2004), the following data were extracted.

Thousands of US$	30 January 2005	1 February 2004
Inventories (balance sheet)	28,935	26,233
■ Food and beverage	2,249	1,809
■ Amusements	2,467	2,393
■ Smallware supplies	17,535	16,715
■ Other	6,684	5,316
Cost of food and beverage (income statement)	51,367	–

A note to the financial statements indicates that inventory consists principally of food, beverage, merchandise, and supplies, and also provides the breakdown between these four categories (see above). The closing date is the Sunday after the Saturday closest to 31 January. The fiscal year consists of 52 weeks. Approximately every sixth or seventh year, a 53rd week is added.

Diedrich Coffee*

Diedrich Coffee, Inc. is a specialty coffee roaster, wholesaler, retailer, and franchiser whose brands include Diedrich Coffee, Gloria Jean's, and Coffee People. The company owns and operates 56 retail locations and is the franchiser of 426 retail locations as of 30 June 2004. The retail units are located in 34 states and 13 foreign countries. The company also has over 460 wholesale accounts with businesses and restaurant chains. In addition, the company operates a coffee-roasting facility in central California that supplies freshly roasted coffee beans to its retail locations and to its wholesale customers.

From the consolidated balance sheet and income statement (annual report 2004), the following data were extracted.

US dollars	30 June 2004	2 July 2003
Inventories (balance sheet)	2,815,000	2,611,000
Cost of sales and related occupancy costs (income statement)	25,112,000	–

Note to financial statements indicates that inventory consists principally of unroasted coffee beans, roasted coffee, accessory and specialty items, and other food, beverage and supplies. The company's fiscal year ends on the Wednesday closest to 30 June.

Frisch's Restaurants*

Frisch's Restaurants, Inc. is a regional company that operates full service family-style restaurants under the name 'Frisch's Big Boy'. It also operates grill buffet style restaurants under the name 'Golden Corral' pursuant to certain licensing agreements. All restaurants operated by the company during the three years ended 29 May 2005 were located in various regions of Ohio, Kentucky, and Indiana. From the consolidated balance sheet and income statement (annual report 2005), the following data were extracted.

US dollars	29 May 2005	30 May 2004
Inventories (balance sheet)	4,592,093	4,381,814
Cost of sales – Food and paper (income statement)	98,569,774	–

A note to the financial statements indicates that inventory consists principally of food items. The closing date is the Sunday nearest to the last day of May. The first quarter of each fiscal year contains 16 weeks, while the last three quarters each normally contain 12 weeks. Every fifth or sixth year, an additional week is added to the fourth quarter, which results in a 53-week fiscal year.

Meritage Hospitality Group*

Meritage Hospitality Group currently conducts its business in the quick-service and casual dining restaurant industries. At 28 November 2004, the company operated 47 Wendy's Old Fashioned Hamburgers quick service restaurants under franchise agreements with Wendy's International Inc., and one O'Charley's full service casual dining restaurant under franchise agreements with O'Charley's, Inc. All operations of the company are located in Michigan. From the consolidated balance sheet and income statement (annual report 2004), the following data were extracted.

US dollars	28 November 2004	30 November 2003
Inventories (balance sheet)	288,951	262,058
Cost of food and beverages (income statement)	14,661,710	–

A note to the financial statements indicates that inventory consists principally of restaurant food items, beverages and serving supplies. The company has elected a 52/53-week fiscal period for tax and financial reporting purposes. The fiscal period ends on the Sunday closest to 30 November.

Morton's Restaurant Group*

Morton's Restaurant Group, Inc. is engaged in the business of owning and operating restaurants under the names Morton's The Steakhouse ('Morton's') and Bertolini's Authentic Trattorias ('Bertolini's'). As of 2 January 2005, the company owned and operated 69 restaurants (65 Morton's and four Bertolini's). From the consolidated balance sheet and income statement (annual report 2004), the following data were extracted.

Thousands of US dollars	2 January 2005	4 January 2004
Inventories (balance sheet)	9,302	9,094
Food and beverage (income statement)	93,222	–

A note to the financial statements indicates that inventory consists principally of food, beverages, and supplies. The company uses a 52/53-week fiscal year which ends on the Sunday closest to 1 January. Approximately every sixth or seventh year, a 53rd week will be added.

Rare Hospitality International*

Rare Hospitality International, Inc. is a multiconcept restaurant company operating the following restaurants in the District of Columbia and 28 states located primarily in the eastern half of the United States: LongHorn Steakhouse (210), Bugaboo Creek Steak House (28), The Capital Grille (20), and other specialty concepts (2). From the consolidated balance sheet and income statement (annual report 2004), the following data were extracted.

Thousands of US dollars	26 December 2004	28 December 2003
Inventories (balance sheet)	12,564	9,820
Cost of restaurant sales (income statement)	299,448	–

A note to the financial statements indicates that inventory consists principally of food and beverages. The company's fiscal year is a 52- or 53-week year ending on the last Sunday in each calendar year.

Required

1. Compute the inventory turnover for each company.
2. Compute the average days' inventory available for each company.
3. Compare and contrast the figures obtained.

Assignment 9.8
Toyota*

Topic: Inventory ratios
Related part of the chapter: Advanced issues

Toyota Motor Corporation (the 'parent company') and its subsidiaries (collectively 'Toyota') are primarily engaged in the design, manufacture, assembly, and sale of passenger cars, recreational and sport-utility vehicles, minivans, trucks, and related parts and accessories throughout the world. In addition, Toyota provides retail and wholesale financing, retail leasing, and certain other financial services primarily to its dealers and their customers related to vehicles manufactured by Toyota.

The parent company and its subsidiaries in Japan maintain their records and prepare their financial statements in accordance with accounting principles generally accepted in Japan, and its foreign subsidiaries in conformity with those of their countries of domicile. Certain adjustments and reclassifications have been incorporated in the accompanying consolidated financial statements to conform with accounting principles generally accepted in the United States of America.

From the consolidated balance sheet and income statement (annual reports 2005, 2004, 2003, and 2002), we extracted the following information.

Required

1. Compute the inventory turnover.
2. Compute the average days inventory available.
3 Comment on the results of your computations.

	31 March				
Yen in millions	2001	2002	2003	2004	2005
Inventories	876,252	961,840	1,025,838	1,083,326	1,306,709
Cost of products sold	10,218,599	10,874,455	11,914,245	13,506,337	14,500,282

References

Drury, C. (2004) *Management and Cost Accounting*, 6th edn, Thomson Learning, London.

IASB (2003) International Accounting Standard No. 2: Inventories, London.

Further reading

Ahmed, M. N., and Scapens, R. W. (2000) Cost allocation in Britain: Towards an institutional analysis. *European Accounting Review*, 9(2), 159–204.

Jennings, R., Simko P. J., and Thompson, II, R. B. (1996) Does LIFO inventory accounting improve the income statement at the expense of the balance sheet? *Journal of Accounting Research*, 34(1), 85–119.

Knapp, M. C., and Knapp, C. A. (2000) Perry Drug Stores, Inc.: Accounting and control issues for inventory in a retail environment. *Issues in Accounting Education*, 15(2), 237–55.

Pfaff, D. (1994) On the allocation of overhead costs. *European Accounting Review*, 3(1), 49–70.

Additional material on the website

Go to http://www.thomsonlearning.co.uk/stolowylebas2 for further information.

The following appendices to this chapter are available on the dedicated website:

Appendix 9.1: Differences between physical and accounting inventory count

Appendix 9.2: Comparison of advantages and limits of perpetual and periodic inventory systems

Appendix 9.3: Other LIFO considerations

Appendix 9.4: Effect of an inventory misstatement

Notes

1. The reader wishing to explore the topics of inventory management or 'costing' of inventory inflows is encouraged to consult books respectively on production management and managerial accounting. See, for example, Drury (2004).
2. Inventories related to long-term contracts have been developed in Chapter 6, Appendix 6.1.
3. Even if the physical inventory is not taken on the very date of closure of the books, the modification of said inventory between the two dates only requires minor adjustments, which can be handled by keeping track, exceptionally, of each movement between inventory and closing dates.
4. See Drury (2004) for example.
5. In a physical inventory management system the first-in, first-out approach is the only one to make sense so as to avoid the build-up of obsolete inventories.

C10

Chapter 10

Current assets (other than inventories)

Learning objectives

After studying this chapter, you will understand:

- What 'accounts receivable' or 'receivables' represent.
- That their weight in the balance sheet varies according to the firm's activity.
- What are the different categories of 'risky' accounts receivable.
- How to record a decrease in the probability of collectibility of accounts receivable.
- How accounts receivable are reported.
- What 'current investments' represent.
- How they are recorded and reported.
- What 'cash and cash equivalents' represent and how they are reported.
- What 'notes receivable' represent and how they are reported.
- How to analyze accounts receivable for decision making.

Current assets, excluding inventories, comprise essentially three types of accounts: receivables, current investments (marketable securities or short-term investments), and cash and cash equivalents.

These three categories of assets are defined by the IASB as 'financial assets': 'A financial asset is any asset that is:

(a) cash;
(b) an equity instrument of another entity;
(c) a contractual right:
   (i) to receive cash or another financial asset from another entity; or
   (ii) to exchange financial assets or financial liabilities with another entity under conditions that are potentially favorable to the entity; or a contract that will or may be settled in the entity's own equity instruments (…)' (IAS 32, IASB 2003a: § 11).

The valuation of receivables on the asset side of the balance sheet is strictly linked to the choice of revenue recognition rules (Chapter 6). These current assets are essential in the operating cycle of the firm and their valuation affects the way a user estimates how a firm would fare in a business downturn and evaluates the possible consequences on both income statement (provision expenses) and balance sheet of possible strategic actions.

In this first section, we will review sequentially the three main types of accounts: receivables, marketable securities, and cash. The Advanced issues section will deal with special cases of receivables called 'notes receivables' or 'commercial paper' as well as with the handling of customer returns.

1 Core issues

1.1 Accounts receivable or 'receivables'

Accounts receivable (A/R) often represent a sizeable component of the asset side of a balance sheet, as shown in Table 10.1, which lists companies in decreasing percentage of accounts receivable (or, more broadly, receivables) over total assets in their 2004 annual financial statements. The percentage represented by receivables is, of course, much higher for a service activity (few fixed assets) than in a business involved in a heavy industry (large fixed assets components).

Table 10.1 Weight of accounts receivable (A/R)

Company (country – activity)	Currency (millions)	Account name	Receivables (rounded)	Total assets	A/R/ total assets
Elkem (Norway – Metals and materials)	NOK	Receivables from customers (net)	4,201	18,951	22.2%
ISS (Denmark – Support services)	DKK	Trade accounts receivable	6,376	29,676	21.5%
Bull (France – IT group)	€	Trade receivables (less allowances for doubtful accounts)	213	1,073	19.9%
Sulzer (Switzerland – High-tech material technologies and fluid dynamics applications)	CHF	Trade accounts receivable	462	2,495	18.5%
Saurer (Switzerland – Textile solutions and transmission systems)	€	Accounts receivable, trade	227	1,300	17.5%
Pernod Ricard (France – Beverages)	€	Current receivables	1,132	7,044	16.1%
RC2 corporation (USA – Production and sales of collectibles)	US$	Accounts receivable, net of allowances for doubtful accounts	94	586	16.0%
Boc (UK – Production and distribution of industrial gases)	UK£	Debtors	722	4,597	15.7%
Philips (Netherlands – Consumer and professional electronic products)	€	Accounts receivable (net)	4,528	30,723	14.7%
Iberia (Spain – Airline)	€	Accounts receivable	600	4,854	12.4%
Stora-Enso (Finland – Paper production)	€	Short-term operative receivables	1,865	16,412	11.4%
Sony (Japan – Music, movies, games, and consumer and professional electronics)	Yen	Notes and accounts receivable, trade (net)	1,025,362	9,499,100	10.8%
Fiat (Italy – Car manufacturer)	€	Trade receivables	3,928	57,243	6.9%
China Petroleum & Chemical Corporation (China – Oil and chemistry)	RMB	Trade accounts receivable and bills receivable	17,568	460,081	3.8%

This table, like equivalent tables in previous chapters, is provided for the sole purpose of illustrating the diversity of situations. It is interesting to note the variety of terms used in annual accounts to describe a similar reality. In continental Europe, companies often explicitly distinguish accounts receivable (or trade receivables) from other receivables. On the other hand, Anglo-American practice often reports all receivables under one single caption in the balance sheet.

Several accounting issues affect the reporting of receivables:

- non-offsetting principle;
- subsidiary ledgers;
- probability that the claim will effectively be collected (collectibility) leading to 'bad debts' and 'doubtful accounts';
- reporting;
- handling of value added tax (VAT) (covered in Appendix 10.1).

1.1.1 Application of the non-offsetting principle to accounts receivable

Accounts receivable are the result of credit sales, whether they relate to individuals, retailers, wholesalers, or manufacturers. In principle, accounts receivable should show an excess of assets as a balance (on the left-hand side of the account = debit balance), since the account represents an increase of assets when the sale (increase of revenues in the income statement) is recorded. In a second step, the account is reduced when the amount receivable is actually settled by the customer (increase in cash). However, accounts receivable can show a 'negative' balance (i.e., a credit balance on the right-hand side of the account) in the case of payment by anticipation (down-payment, for example) or an error on the part of the customer (for example, a payment in excess of the amount owed, or a duplicated payment).

When an accounts receivable shows a 'negative' (i.e., credit) balance, it must be shown on the liabilities side of the balance sheet (with a 'positive' balance). Such an account represents a debt towards the customer. The 'no-offsetting principle' states that 'positive' (debit) balances and 'negative' (credit) balances in accounts receivable cannot, under any circumstances, be compensated.

1.1.2 Subsidiary ledgers

In previous chapters we have recorded credit sales by increasing the assets with a generic 'accounts receivable'. For accounting to be useful to managers, such a generic account is not a sound basis for monitoring transactions with customers. Although reports to outside users of accounting information contain only one (or very few) line(s) for accounts receivable, internally the firm will generally use one account (or subsidiary ledger) per customer.

Most accounting software programs code accounts on an alphanumeric basis (see Chapter 4). At the end of the accounting period, individual subsidiary ledger accounts are centralized (accumulated) and transferred to the controlling 'accounts receivable' in the general ledger.

1.1.3 Collectibility of receivables

The development of credit sales or sales on account is a legitimate way for reaching new customers and growing sales. The existence of receivables leads to the necessity of evaluating, at the end of each accounting period, the probability that the account will effectively be collected. This evaluation is based on both commercial information (customer satisfaction, returns, complaints, etc.) and external information pertaining to the economic or financial situation of the debtor. Figure 10.1 highlights the four categories of accounts receivable that will result from such an analysis.

Figure 10.1 Different categories of claims

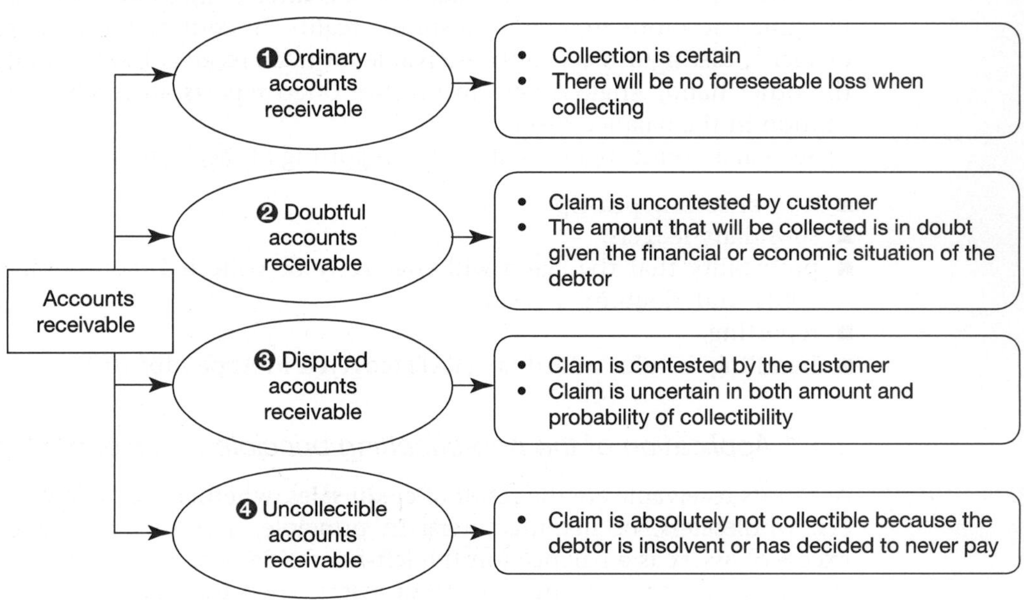

Doubtful ❷ or disputed ❸ accounts, which are partly or totally uncollectible, are referred to as 'bad' or 'doubtful' debts.[1] The value of these accounts will have to be written-down by taking a provision expense – or valuation allowance – in the income statement. Uncollectible accounts ❹, must be written-off through a bad debt expense in the income statement. Sometimes, both written-down and written-off amounts are called 'bad debt expense'.

The write-down or write-off procedures are highlighted in Figure 10.2 and described subsequently.

❶ Identification of doubtful or disputed accounts The balances of each individual customer account are individually reviewed and structured by due date in an aged balance[2]. Any transaction whose age is considered to fall outside the customary credit terms for this type of clientele is potentially a doubtful or a disputed account. Further research about the cause of the lateness will establish whether the account should be considered doubtful or disputed.

The range of credit terms shown in Table 10.2 illustrates, in increasing order, the range of average credit terms observed in several European countries.

The more a receivable exceeds the 'normal' credit terms, the higher the likelihood of its uncollectibility.

❷ Evaluation of the probability of uncollectibility

Global estimation (percentage of sales or percentage of receivables) The uncollectibility probability can be estimated globally using statistical elements as long as these are specific to the firm. The most commonly used methods consist of applying a historically based selected percentage to either total sales or total receivables. This method is, however, less and less used in practice since the generalization of efficient accounting software permits the specific write-down (provision expense) or write-off (bad debt expense) of individualized transactions.

Figure 10.2 Doubtful accounts receivable

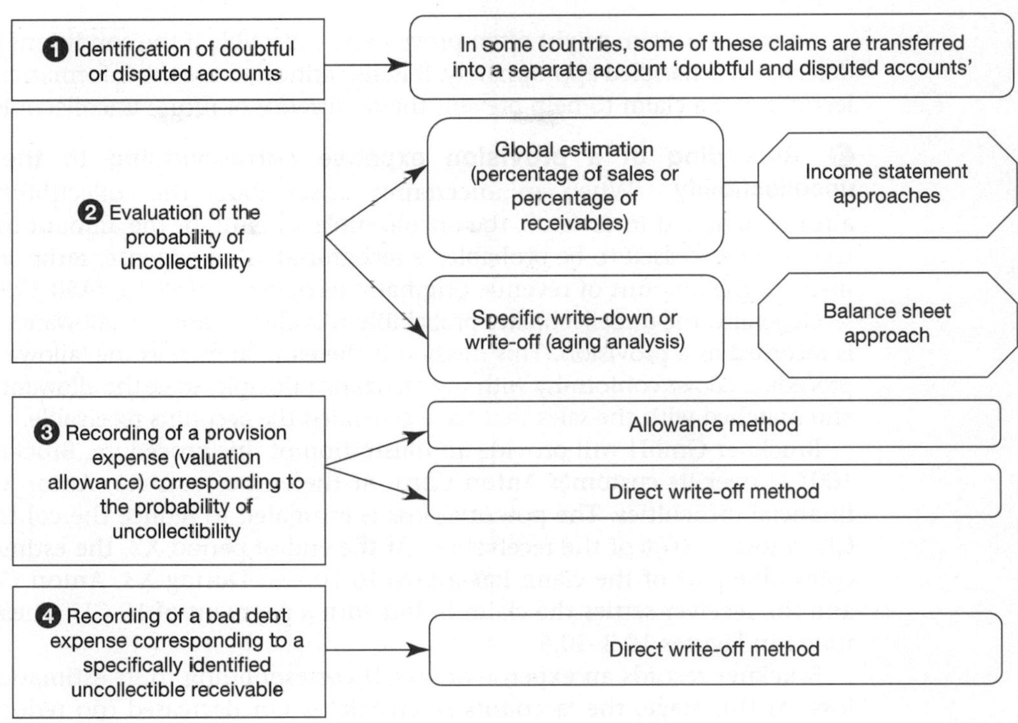

Table 10.2 Average credit terms in some European countries in 2004[3]

Country	Number of days	Country	Number of days
Finland	26.0	Lithuania	47.0
Norway	27.1	Czech Republic	47.5
Estonia	31.3	Austria	48.4
Latvia	34.9	United Kingdom	50.5
Iceland	35.0	Belgium	52.3
Denmark	35.2	Ireland	54.2
Sweden	35.7	France	67.4
Germany	39.7	Spain	82.3
Netherlands	41.6	Portugal	85.3
Poland	43.5	Cyprus	96.0
Hungary	44.4	Italy	96.2
Switzerland	45.2	Greece	102.2

Specific write-down or write-off (aging analysis) The aging analysis permits a transaction by transaction decision. The situation of each individual customer (or transaction) determined to be problematic is further documented through questions like the following:

- Has the customer challenged the validity of the receivable?
- Is the customer up to date in their payments according to the specifically agreed schedule pertaining to this transaction?
- Has there been any correspondence or other piece of information indicating that the customer had financial difficulties?

- Have any letters from the company been returned undelivered from the customer's address?

An overdue claim might often prove to be collectible if the conditions for its lateness are detected and handled appropriately. It is also critical to use the information about the uncollectibility of a claim to help prevent the occurrence of future uncollectible receivables.

❸ Recording of a provision expense corresponding to the probability of uncollectibility 'When an uncertainty arises about the collectibility of an amount already included in revenue, the uncollectible amount, or the amount in respect of which recovery has ceased to be probable, is recognized as an expense, rather than as an adjustment of the amount of revenue originally recognized' (IAS 18, IASB 1993: § 22).

Generally, the uncollectibility probability is evaluated and an 'allowance for uncollectibles' is recorded as a provision. This method is therefore known as the 'allowance method'. This procedure allows conformity with the matching principle, since the allowance will be expensed and matched with the sales that have generated the accounts receivable.

Brückner GmbH will provide an illustration of this procedure. Brückner has a claim of 100 CU over its customer Anton Corp. At the end of year X1, Anton Corp. experiences financial difficulties. The potential loss is estimated to reduce the collectible claim to 60 CU (a loss of 40% of the receivable). At the end of period X2, the estimation of the non-collectible part of the claim has grown to 70 CU. During X3, Anton Corp. is liquidated and the receiver settles the claim in full with a payment of 10 CU. These events are illustrated in Figures 10.3–10.5.

Brückner records an expense of 40 CU corresponding to its estimation of the possible loss. At this stage, the 'accounts receivable' is not decreased (no reduction of assets). A contra-asset account is used: 'provision' (or 'allowance') for 'bad debts' (or 'for doubtful accounts'). One should absolutely not reduce directly the individual customer account as it would give the impression that the receivable has been settled. As a matter of fact, the claim Brückner holds over Anton remains integral as long as Anton Corp. has not been liquidated. What is at stake here is the probability of collection, not the claim itself.

In X2, the possible loss is now estimated to be 70 CU. The allowance must be raised to recognize the further devaluation of the claim. An additional allowance amounting to 70 − 40 = 30 (40 was the estimation of the possible loss at the end of X1) should be recorded. The accumulated provision (recorded on the balance sheet) is now raised to 70 CU.

When the customer finally settles the account (even if it is not for the full amount remaining due and not yet provisioned), one must:

- cancel the cumulated provisions pertaining to this account or this receivable by recognizing the equivalent amount as revenue (or as a negative expense);
- record a bad debt expense corresponding to the difference between the original claim (here it is 100 CU) which is settled and the amount actually collected (here it is 10 CU).

Figure 10.3 Doubtful accounts – Year X1

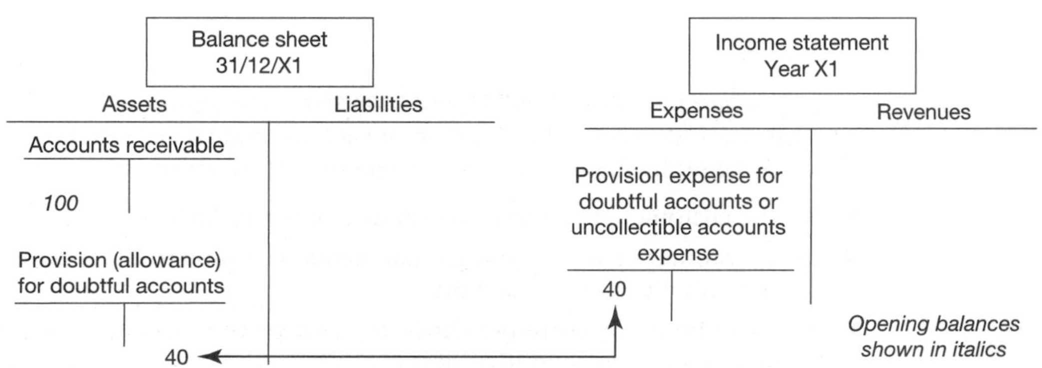

Figure 10.4 Doubtful accounts – Year X2

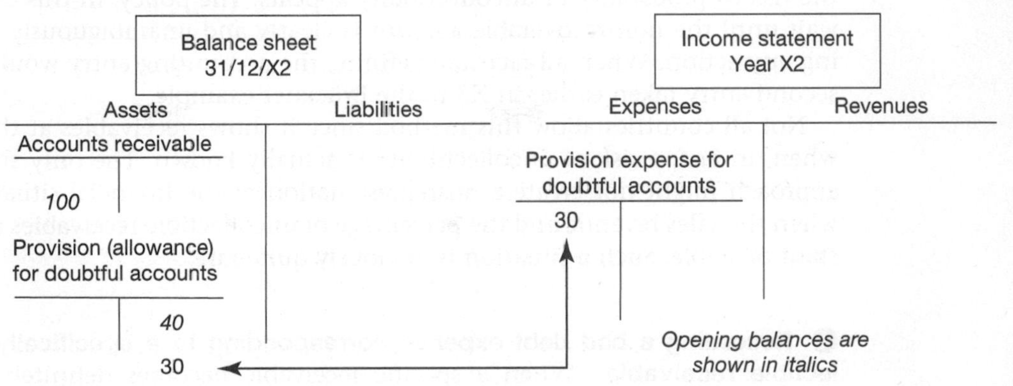

Figure 10.5 Doubtful accounts – Year X3

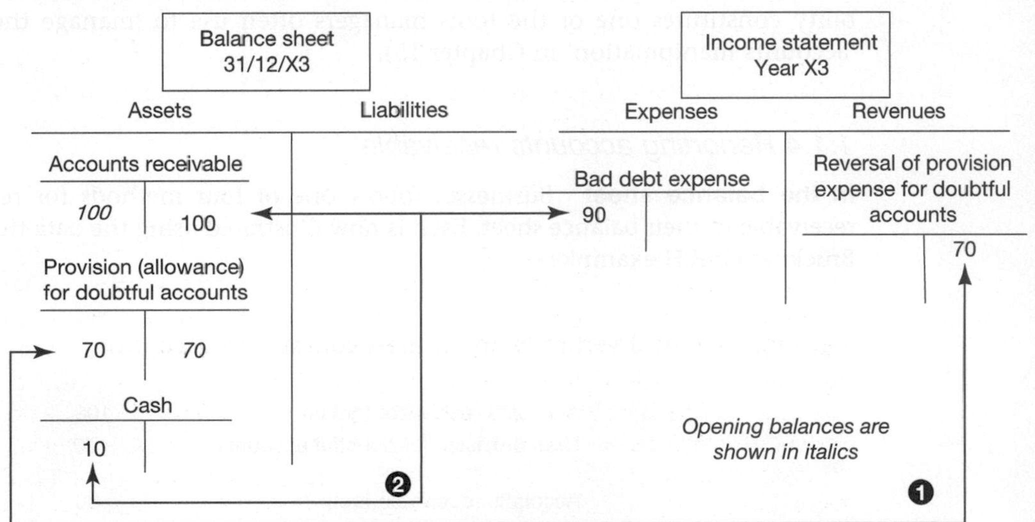

Impact on income of each of the year's entries

Year X1	Provision expense	−40		
Year X2	Provision expense	−30		−90
Year X3	Reversal of provision expense	+70	−20	
	Bad debt expense	−90		

Comments

- The mechanism of allowance (provision) has the effect of distributing the net charge (here 90 CU) over the years it takes to clear the receivable.
- The net impact is always equal to the 'bad debt'.
- The possible loss was originally difficult to evaluate (as shown in the case here, first evaluated at 40 CU and later revised to 70 CU). The difference between the total expense and the cumulated provisions (here it amounts to 20 CU) is always recorded in the year during which the bad debt expense is finally recognized (here it is X3). In practice, there is almost always a difference (one way or another) between the estimated bad debt expense (which led to provisioning) and the accounts receivable written-off (actual bad debt expense).

Direct write-off method Under this method, no provision (or allowance) is created when the risk or probability of uncollectibility appears. The policy, in this case, is, however, to wait until the non-recoverable amount is clearly and unambiguously known before taking any action. When all facts are definite, the accounting entry would be similar to the second entry taken earlier in X3 in the Brückner example.

Not all countries allow this method since it shows receivables at their nominal value when, in fact, a risk of uncollectibility is actually known. The only situation where this approach might not create a misrepresentation of the financial situation of the firm is when the sales revenue and the percentage of uncollectible receivables are essentially constant or stable. Such a situation is obviously quite rare.

❹ Recording a bad debt expense corresponding to a specifically identified uncollectible receivable When a specific receivable becomes definitely uncollectible, an expense is recorded. If a provision (allowance) had been created for this specific receivable this provision has to be canceled (reversed), as was done in the Brückner GmbH example.

A concluding remark to this section is that the valuation of the uncollectibility probability constitutes one of the tools managers often use to 'manage their earnings' (see 'accounts manipulation' in Chapter 15).

1.1.4 Reporting accounts receivable

In the balance sheet Businesses follow one of four methods for reporting accounts receivable in their balance sheet. Each is now illustrated using the data from year X2 of the Brückner GmbH example:

Method 1 (detailed vertically and using a contra-asset account):

Accounts receivable (gross)	100
Less provision for doubtful accounts	−70
Accounts receivable (net)	30

Method 2 (synthetic with detail in the balance sheet):

Accounts receivable (net of provision for doubtful accounts: 70)	30

Method 3 (synthetic with detail in a note to the balance sheet):

Accounts receivable (net) (see note X) 30

Notes to the financial statements:

Note X – Accounts receivable

The accumulated amount of provision for doubtful accounts is equal to 70.

Method 4 (detailed horizontally):

	Gross value	Amortization and provisions	Net value
Accounts receivable	100	70	30

Whichever method is used, the most important is, for the user of financial information, to get access to the gross amount of receivables, which is used to compute ratios (see developments on financial statement analysis later in this chapter).

Real-life example Ericsson

(Sweden – Swedish GAAP – *Source*: Annual report 2004 – Telecommunications and network solutions)

December 31, SEK million	2004	2003
Balance sheet (excerpts)		
Current assets		
Receivables		
Accounts receivable – trade (note 14)	32,644	31,886
Short-term customer financing	1,446	979
Other receivables	12,239	12,718
Notes to the consolidated financial statements		
14. Accounts receivable–trade	2004	2003
Trade receivables excluding associated companies	33,906	33,725
Provision for impairment of receivables	−1,782	−2,051
Trade receivables, net	32,124	31,674
Trade receivables from associated companies and joint ventures	520	212
Total	32,644	31,886

Reporting movements in provision for doubtful accounts In Chapter 7 we evoked the changes in valuation of fixed assets concerning the evolution of the gross value of fixed assets and also of accumulated depreciation. It is possible to create a similar table to report the changes in the provision account. For example, Bayer, the German chemical group, published such a table in its 2004 annual report:

[22] Trade accounts receivable

Trade accounts receivable include a reserve of €299 million (2003: €302 million) for amounts unlikely to be recovered. Trade accounts receivable as of 31 December 2004 include €5,561 million (2003: €5,066 million) maturing within one year and €19 million (2003: €5 million) maturing after one year. Of the total, €9 million (2003: €16 million) is receivable from non-consolidated subsidiaries, €44 million (2003: €42 million) from other affiliated companies, and €5,527 million (2003: €5,013 million) from other customers.

Changes in write-downs of trade accounts receivable are as follows:

€ million	31 December 2003	31 December 2004
Balance at beginning of year	(345)	(302)
Additions charged to expense	(106)	(103)
Exchange differences	13	2
Changes in scope of consolidation	1	(1)
Deductions due to utilization	135	105
Balance at end of year	(302)	(299)

- Additions charged to expense: they are provision expenses for the year (i.e., provisions on new receivables plus additional provisions on receivables for which the probability of uncollectibility is considered to have increased).
- Deductions due to utilization: cancellation of provisions taken in previous years because the probable loss is perceived to have decreased on some of the receivables or cancellation of provisions because the receivable has been settled. This cancellation can be recorded as either a reduction in expenses or a revenues (reversal of provision).
- Other movements: they are movements linked to the consolidation of subsidiaries, such as:
  - exchange differences on the conversion of financial statements of subsidiaries labeled in a currency other than the one of the parent company (see Chapter 13);
  - changes in the scope of consolidation resulting from acquisition or sale of subsidiaries (see Chapter 13).

1.2 Current investments

1.2.1 Definitions

'Current investments' included in current assets are investments that are by their nature readily realizable and are intended to be held for not more than one year. IASB does not make any distinction between current investments included in financial fixed assets and those included in current assets.

IAS 39 (IASB 2003b: § 9) defines four different categories of financial assets:

- 'Financial asset (...) at fair value through profit or loss': This category corresponds to financial assets that meet either of several conditions. One of them is the classification as 'held for trading', i.e., the assets are 'acquired (...) principally for the purpose of selling or repurchasing [them] in the near term'.
- 'Held-to-maturity investments': 'financial assets with fixed or determinable payments and fixed maturity that an entity has the positive intent and ability to hold to maturity'.
- 'Loans and receivables': 'non-derivative financial assets with fixed or determinable payments that are not quoted in an active market'.
- 'Available-for-sale financial assets': financial assets which do not properly belong in one of the three other categories.

We will limit our discussion of current investments to 'marketable securities' often called 'short-term investments', which correspond to 'held for trading' financial assets (see more on financial assets in Chapter 13). These assets can be sold readily and are held by

Table 10.3 Subsequent measurement of financial assets

	IASB (IAS 39)[4]	
Category	Valuation or measurement of the current investment in the balance sheet	Treatment of potential (unrealized) gains and losses measured by comparing cost to fair market value
Loans and receivables	At cost	N/A
Held-to-maturity investments		
Available-for-sale financial assets	At 'fair value' (unless the asset has no quoted market price in an active market or the fair value cannot be reliably measured)	Recognized (recorded) directly in equity
Financial assets at fair value through profit or loss		Included in net profit or loss of the period in which it arises

the firm as a cash substitute with the intention of protecting the purchasing power of a liquid asset and possibly earning a return on the capital invested.

The valuation of current investments is critical as their value is constantly changing, thus creating potential (unrealized) gains or losses. The way these losses or gains are recognized, if at all, and handled in the reporting process may affect both the risk evaluation and the measurement of the value created by the business.

According to IAS 39 (IASB 2003b: §§ 45–46), the measurement of financial assets subsequent to initial recording will depend, as shown in Table 10.3, on the choice of classification selected between the four above-mentioned categories.

According to IAS 39 (§ 9), financial assets classified as held for trading should be valued at fair value through profit or loss: 'Fair value is the amount for which an asset could be exchanged, or a liability settled, between knowledgeable, willing parties in an arm's length transaction'. 'The existence of published price quotations in an active market is the best evidence of fair value' (IAS 39: § AG71). But let us keep in mind that the ability to evaluate the market or fair value of many financial assets is a highly debated topic.

In other words, the IASB states that unrealized gains or losses on current financial investments held for trading should be recognized in the income statement of the period for which the gain or loss was calculated. Some countries, such as France and Belgium, do not allow the recognition of unrealized gains.

Table 10.4 Data of Mozart Company's current investment example

Date of purchase	Security	Quantity	Unit cost	Total cost	Market value at year-end	Total market value	Period-end adjustment (individual basis)	Period-end adjustment (aggregate portfolio basis)
25 October X1	Shares Alpha Company	10	150	1,500	160	1,600	100	
23 November X1	Shares Beta Company	20	100	2,000	90	1,800	−200	
Total		30		3,500		3,400	−100	−100

1.2.2 Accounting for current investments

Let us illustrate. Mozart Company holds in current investment equity securities of two other businesses (Alpha Company and Beta Company). Let us examine the key operations that can affect this current investment using data displayed in Table 10.4.

Although the no-offsetting principle would normally call for the recording of unrealized gains and losses for each separate security (individual basis), IAS 39 has endorsed the portfolio basis approach in which only the aggregate portfolio unrealized gains or losses are reported. One can surmise that the choice made results from the observation that since the financial instruments involved in this category are traded, the specific nature of each item is not relevant to the analyst.

Let us pursue the example using the aggregate portfolio basis method required by IAS 39. Potential losses on Beta Company are offset against potential gains on Alpha Company. The difference is a net loss and recorded as such (see Figure 10.6). In this example, we record the change in fair value as a provision expense. In keeping with IFRS/IAS usual policy of not mentioning which accounts should be used, IAS 39 states only that the change in fair value should be recognized 'in profit or loss'. The provision mechanism thus seems to be adequate to handle the situation. In the case of a potential gain (not dealt with in our example), a revenue account should be created for this purpose.

Figure 10.6 Accounting for current investments – Year X1

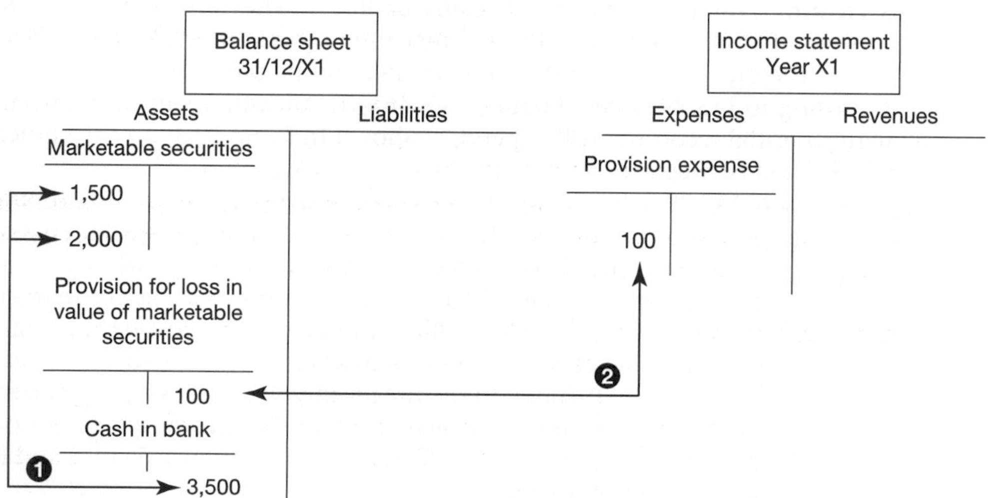

❶ Purchase of marketable securities

❷ At year-end, accounting for a potential loss (computed on an aggregate basis). The loss is only potential as long as the securities have not been sold. The terminology for unrealized losses or potential losses is not settled and several alternative terms can be found in financial statements.

On 20 April X2 10 shares of Beta Company are sold at a unit price of 90. Since they had been purchased for 100 each, there is a total loss of 100 on the sale. The appropriate entries are illustrated in Figure 10.7.

Some countries merge the two entries by recording in the income statement the difference between the reversal of the provision and the loss on the sale. In our example, no entry would have been recorded (100 – 100 = 0).

As mentioned above, several countries do not allow the offsetting of unrealized (potential) gains and losses, at least in non-consolidated financial statements which are often not concerned by IFRS/IAS. The individual basis is applied and the potential gain on Alpha Company shares is not taken into account. In that case, the entries shown in Figure 10.6 are still applicable with the exception that the amount of the provision expense is different: 200 instead of 100. In Figure 10.7, the reversal of provision also equals 100 as it corresponds to one half of the provision recorded in year X1 (remember that only one half of Beta shares were sold).

Figure 10.7 Accounting for current investments – Year X2

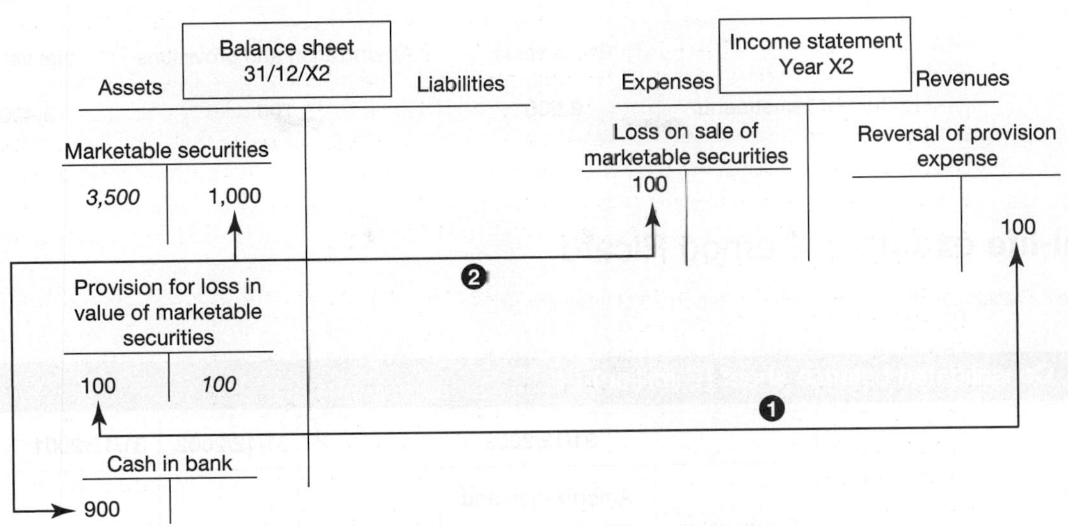

❶ The computation of the net potential loss or gain is the following: potential gain on Alpha (+100) minus potential loss on Beta (−100 for 10 remaining shares) equals zero. The provision is no longer necessary and the provision (allowance) is canceled (reversed).
❷ The sale is recorded without taking the provision into account. The loss is: 1,000 − 900 = *(10 x 100)* − *(10 × 90)* = 100.

1.2.3 Reporting current investments

Current investments are found in annual statements to be reported in four different ways. If we use the Mozart company data for year X1, the current investments can be reported in one of the four following formats:

Format 1 (detailed vertically and using a contra-asset account):

Current investments (gross – at cost)	3,500
Minus provision for potential loss	−100
Current investments (net)	3,400

Format 2 (synthetic with detail in the balance sheet):

Current investments (net of provision for potential loss: 100)	3,400

Format 3 (synthetic with detail in a note to the balance sheet):

Current investments (net) (see note X)	3,400

Notes to the financial statements:

Note X – Current investments:

The accumulated amount of provision for potential losses is equal to 100.

Format 4 (detailed horizontally):

	Gross value	Amortization and provisions	Net value
Current investments	3,500	100	3,400

Real-life example Pernod Ricard

(France – French GAAP – *Source*: Annual Report 2003 – Beverages)

Consolidated balance sheet (€ million)

	31/12/2003			31/12/2002	31/12/2001
	Gross value	Amortization and provisions	Net value	Net value	Net value
Marketable securities	158.2	2.2	156.0	90.4	152.0

Notes to the financial statements

Note 1.11 Marketable securities
Marketable securities are recorded in the balance sheet at their historical cost. A provision for write-down is established when the year-end market value of a marketable security is less than its historical cost.

Real-life example Toray Industries

(Japan – Japanese GAAP – *Source*: Annual Report 2004 – Manufacturer of synthetic fibers and textiles)

Consolidated balance sheet – 31 March 2005 and 2004 (in millions of yen)

	2005	2004
(...)		
Current assets		
Short-term investment securities (Note 6)	1,088	5
(...)		

Note to the financial statements

1. Significant accounting policies
Securities
Other securities [than held-to-maturity debt securities] for which market quotations are available are stated at fair value. Net unrealized gains or losses on these securities are reported as a separate item in stockholders' equity at a net-of-tax amount. Other securities for which market quotations are unavailable are stated at cost, except as stated in the paragraph below. In cases where the fair value of (...) other securities has declined significantly and such impair-

ment of the value is not deemed temporary, those securities are written-down to fair value and the resulting losses are included in net income or loss for the period.

6. Securities

At 31 March 2005 (...), the carrying amount and aggregate fair value of the securities classified as (...) other securities for which market quotations were available were as follows:

Millions of yen	2005			
	Cost	Unrealized gains	Unrealized losses	Fair value
Other securities	36,302	65,941	260	101,983

At 31 March 2005 and 2004, the carrying amount of the securities classified as (...) other securities for which market quotations were unavailable were as follows:

Millions of yen	2005	2004
Other securities	7,338	4,488

The difference between the above fair value, carrying amount, and the amounts shown in the accompanying consolidated balance sheets principally consisted of subscription certificates.

Comment: We can observe that the notes of Toray Industries do not make a distinction between securities included in current assets and those included in financial fixed assets. This makes a reconciliation between balance sheet and figures in the notes impossible.

1.3 Cash and cash equivalents

IAS 7 (IASB 1992) states that 'cash comprises cash in hand' (coins, banknotes, and currency available) and 'demand deposits' (deposits in bank accounts that are available on demand). 'Cash equivalents are short-term, highly liquid investments that are readily convertible to known amounts of cash and which are subject to an insignificant risk of changes in value' (§ 6). If the concept of 'cash' is easily understandable, that of 'cash equivalents' is more fuzzy. This is why IAS 7 specifies that cash equivalents are held for the purpose of meeting short-term cash commitments rather than for investment or other purposes. An investment normally qualifies as a cash equivalent only when it has a short maturity of, say, three months or less from the date of acquisition.

The concept of 'net cash', which is not defined in IAS 7, represents the difference between 'cash and cash equivalents' (defined above) and liabilities accounts corresponding to negative cash (essentially bank overdrafts).

The proportion of cash and cash equivalents in a balance sheet can vary greatly between companies (see Table 10.5). Unlike what we said before about other balance sheet items, there appears to be no link between the nature of the industrial sector the firm is involved in and its level of cash and cash equivalents. The level of cash and cash equivalent plus current investments is, in fact, considered to be the cash reserve a firm chooses to build in order to be able to strike rapidly in case opportunities appear. For example

Table 10.5 Proportion of cash and cash equivalents (C&CE)

Company (country – activity)	Currency millions)	Name of the account	Cash and cash equivalents	Total assets	Cash and cash equivalents/ total assets
Saurer (Switzerland – Textile solutions and transmission systems)	€	Cash	216.2	1,300.3	16.6%
Sulzer (Switzerland – Advanced materials technologies and fluid dynamics applications)	CHF	Cash and cash equivalents	408.0	2,495.0	16.4%
Philips (Netherlands – Consumer and professional electronics)	€	Cash and cash equivalents	4,349.0	30,723.0	14.2%
ISS (Denmark – Support services)	DKK	Liquid funds	3,121.0	29,676.0	10.5%
Sony (Japan – Music, entertainment, games, and professional and consumer electronics)	Yen	Cash and cash equivalents	779,103.0	9,499,100.0	8.2%
Bull (France – IT group)	€	Cash	66.0	1,073.0	6.2%
Heineken (Netherlands – Brewery)	€	Cash	628.0	10,418.0	6.0%
Fiat (Italy – Car manufacturer)	€	Bank and post office accounts, checks, cash in hand	3,164.0	57,243.0	5.5%
Elkem (Norway – Metals and materials)	NOK	Cash and short-term deposits	875.0	18,951.0	4.6%
China Petroleum & Chemical Corporation (China – Oil and chemistry)	RMB	Cash at bank and in hand	18,280	460,081	4.0%
RC2 corporation (USA – Racing cars replicas)	US$	Cash and cash equivalents	20.1	585.7	3.4%
Pernod Ricard (France – Beverages)	€	Cash	152.4	7,043.6	2.2%
Stora-Enso (Finland – Paper production)	€	Cash and cash equivalents	274.3	16,411.9	1.7%
Iberia (Spain – Airline)	€	Cash	30.9	4,853.6	0.6%

Microsoft's 'cash and cash equivalent plus current investments' as at 30 June 2004 was equal to US$60.6 billion. It is a strategic reservoir of resources coherent with a strategy of major acquisitions in a very turbulent world in which an exchange of shares may no longer be considered as attractive as it may have been in the previous year(s).

Real-life example of cash and cash equivalents Rare Hospitality

(USA – US GAAP – *Source*: Annual Report 2004 – Restaurants)

Consolidated balance sheet as of 26 December 2004 and 28 December 2003 (in US$ thousands)

		2004	2003
	(...)		
	Current assets		
11	Cash and cash equivalents	17,088	20,508
	(...)		

Note to the financial statements

Cash equivalents

The company considers all highly liquid investments which have original maturities of three months or less to be cash equivalents. Cash equivalents are comprised of overnight repurchase agreements and totaled approximately $14.4 million at 26 December 2004, $16.0 million at 28 December 2003 and $9.8 million at 29 December 2002. The carrying amount of these instruments approximates their fair market values. All overdraft balances have been reclassified as current liabilities.

Financial instruments

The carrying value of the company's cash and cash equivalents (...) approximates their fair value. The fair value of a financial instrument is the amount for which the instrument could be exchanged in a current transaction between willing parties. The following methods and assumptions were used to estimate the fair value of each class of financial instruments: For cash and cash equivalents (...) the carrying amounts approximate fair value because of the short maturity of these financial instruments.

The topic of cash and cash equivalents is developed in greater detail in Chapter 14.

2 Advanced issues

Notes receivable and sales returns deserve special attention, as well as the impact of value added taxes on the valuation of receivables (Appendix 10.1) and bank reconciliation (Appendix 10.2).

2.1 Notes receivable

2.1.1 Principle

Credit sales sometimes are settled through specific monetary instruments called 'notes' or 'commercial paper'. These instruments are either a 'draft' or 'bill of exchange' when issued by the seller or a 'promissory note' when issued by the purchaser. Such instruments are an extensively used practice mainly in southern Europe in countries such as Spain, Italy,

France, and Greece. They are also found in other countries such as Japan, Finland, and the UK. Commercial paper or notes are defined as follows:

- A draft (or bill of exchange) is a written order by a first party (the drawer, i.e., the seller) instructing a second party (the drawee, i.e., the buyer) to pay a third party (the payee or beneficiary, who may be the drawer himself) a specified amount at a specified date (maturity) without conditions. It is common practice to have the draft prepared by the seller and sent to the buyer along with the invoice as a suggested preferred method of payment. The buyer then returns the signed ('accepted') draft to the seller, thus creating the contract by their signature.
- A promissory note is a written document in which a person or business (generally known as the 'maker') promises to pay a given amount to a third party (individual or business), referred to as the 'beneficiary', on a specified date (maturity date). The maker is the customer and the beneficiary is generally the supplier.

Since the accounting handling is the same for a draft, a bill of exchange, or a promissory note, we will refer to this class of financial instruments by using the generic term of 'notes receivable' on the supplier side and 'notes payable' on the buyer side (the latter is covered in Chapter 12).

Notes receivable offer three advantages to the seller over the traditional credit sale in which an invoice leads the recording of a receivable:

- A note is a contract since it has been 'accepted' by the buyer. It offers a higher level of guarantee of payment to the seller than a simple combination 'order, delivery, acknowledgement of receipt plus invoice'.

Figure 10.8 Notes receivable discounted (sold) before maturity (draft emitted by the seller and accepted by the buyer)

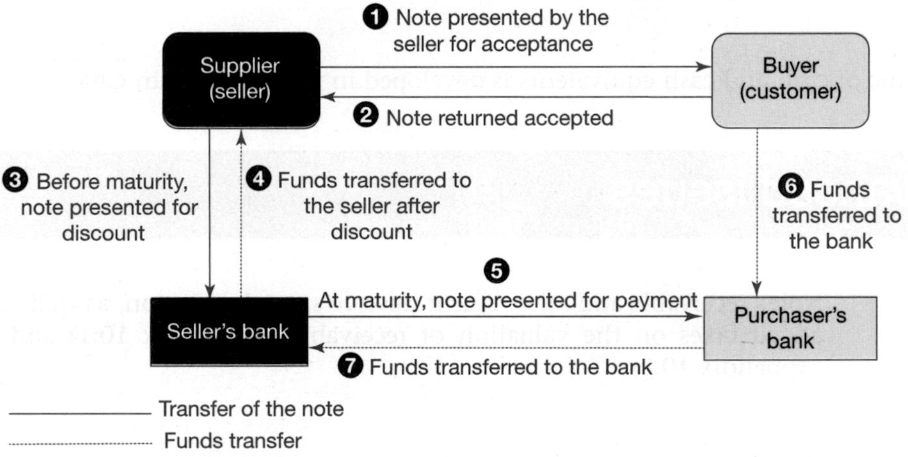

- Any holder of a note (even after an endorsement) can sell it whenever they feel the need.
- In case of a discounting, in phase 4 the holder of the note does not receive the full face amount of the note. The bank keeps a discounting fee which represents: (1) the interest for the period separating the date of discounting and the maturity date; (2) an administrative fee; and eventually (3) a risk premium.
- Discounting a note can be done in two ways that involve different risk levels:
  - *without recourse*: the note is sold with complete transfer to the buyer of the note of the default risk of the drawer;
  - *with recourse*: i.e., a conditional sale. If the drawer defaults on the maturity date, the discounting financial institution will demand full reimbursement of the note plus fees from the seller of the note who discounted it in the first place.

- A note is a regular financial instrument. A note can be endorsed over to a third party (not limited to financial institutions).
- A note is a negotiable credit instrument. The seller can sell a note (commercial paper) to a financial institution before its maturity date. The financial institution charges a fee for its services (generally proportional to the face value of the note plus a fixed administrative fee). The act of selling a note to a financial institution is referred to as 'discounting' it.

The life cycle process of a draft or bill of exchange is illustrated in Appendix 10.3 for a payment on the maturity date and in Figure 10.8 for a sale (also called discounting) of the note before that date.

2.1.2 Recording of notes receivable

The recording of notes receivable is developed in Appendix 10.4 and several accounting methods coexist. If the note is discounted, the notes receivable is canceled, and the cash account is increased, net of discounting fees which are recorded as expenses. The amount of discounted notes that have been removed from the assets but which still carry a possibility of recourse should be reported in the footnotes to financial statements, in the 'commitments' or the 'accounts receivable' sections. For example, Michelin's annual report for the year 2004 discloses the following information in the section 'Off-balance sheet commitments' of the notes: 'Discounted bills: 5,392 (€ thousands) (2004) and 5,808 (€ thousands) (2003)'. It means that the accounts receivable represented by notes (or drafts) to that amount have been taken out of the assets at the time of discounting but still could represent a latent liability.

Another solution is possible: the notes receivable, although discounted, remain as an asset and a matching liability (representing the debt towards the bank) is recorded. IAS 39 (IASB 2003b: § 20) favors this second solution if the discounting is with recourse: 'When an entity transfers a financial asset (...) if the entity retains substantially all the risks and rewards of ownership of the financial asset, the entity shall continue to recognize the financial asset'.

The amount of discounted notes is a necessary information to compute the average days of sale on credit in a financial statement analysis (see later).

2.2 Sales returns

When a customer is not satisfied for any reason with the product that was delivered (such as non-conformity of delivery with order, defects, etc.), the product can generally be returned to the seller for credit or reimbursement. The original sale must therefore be reversed. Two methods exist for recording a sales return: cancellation of the sale directly in the sales ledger account or indirectly through a 'contra-revenue' account, which offers a better way than direct cancellation of monitoring the important operating parameter represented by sales returns (see Figures 10.9 and 10.10).

The sales returns account (a rarely reported, essentially internal, account) creates a measure used by management to monitor the evolution of returns so as to better be able to research and manage their causes. Gross sales (before discounts and other price adjustments) are most of the time reported net of returns in the income statement.

When goods have been returned, they must be entered in inventory before resale or destruction. Accounting entries here depend on whether the firm is using a periodic or perpetual inventory[5].

If the firm uses a periodic inventory system (see Chapters 2 and 9), no specific entry is required at the time of the return since the returned goods will automatically be counted

Figure 10.9 Method 1: Recording of a sales return with direct cancellation

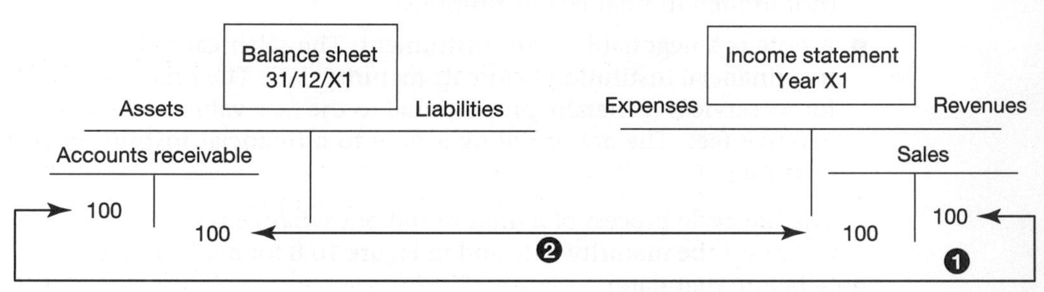

Figure 10.10 Method 2: Recording of a sales return with use of a contra account

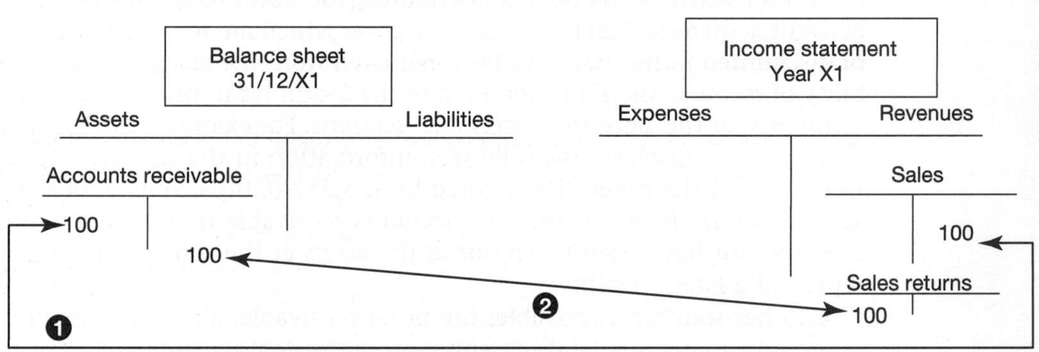

in the year-end physical inventory unless they have, by then, already been resold or destroyed.

If the firm uses a perpetual inventory system (see Chapters 2 and 9), and the goods are still in a sellable condition, the goods must be re-entered in the inventory account so as to adjust the cost of goods sold by the appropriate amount, and if they are not sellable they are simply 'ignored' (in that case only the negative revenue (i.e., cost) element of the return is recorded without the offset of an increase in inventory).

2.3 Financial statement analysis

Managers as well as many users are interested in monitoring the operating and cash cycles of a business. The credit policy of a firm has an impact on sales revenue (credit terms can be a key attribute in the customer's decision to buy), on the level of receivables, and the length of the cash collection cycle. Two ratios, actually linked, are commonly used to monitor the effects of a credit policy. They are the 'average days of sales' and the 'receivables turnover'. They are defined as follows:

Average days of sales (in receivables) (or **Average collection period**) =

(Average accounts receivable/Net sales) × 365 days

This ratio provides the average duration of credit terms offered to customers.

Receivables turnover = Net sales/Average accounts receivable

This second ratio, which is proportional to the inverse of the previous one, measures the number of times receivables turned over during the year.

Observations about these ratios:

- The gross value of accounts receivable should be considered as it represents the real credit granted to customers. In other terms, the net value – after deduction of valuation allowances for doubtful accounts – artificially minimizes the average days of sales in receivables. However, in practice, many companies do not disclose the gross amount of accounts receivable. Consequently, financial analysts often compute the two above-mentioned ratios with the net amount of accounts receivable. This practice can be admitted but it should always be borne in mind that it is a by-default solution and could provide misleading figures if amounts of valuation allowances are significant or vary from period to period. If gross amounts are available, they should, of course, be taken into account.
- The accounts receivable are generally averaged between beginning and end of year in an attempt to minimize seasonal variations. External analysts generally only have, in the worst case, annual and, in the best case, quarterly data to build the averages, thus not freeing themselves completely of seasonal variations within the period. An internal manager probably uses rolling averages over 12 months based on monthly balances for a better vision of the impact of the interaction of the credit policy and the state of the economy on the behavior of customers.
- Some analysts suggest that only credit sales be used in the calculation in order to not introduce a favorable bias due to cash sales. Although theoretically more accurate than the averaging of total sales versus total receivables, this approach is difficult to implement as the breakdown between cash and credit sales is rarely reported in annual statements.
- Notes receivable that have been discounted to a bank or other financial institution and have been removed from accounts receivable (but are mentioned in the notes) should be added back to the net book receivables in order to get as accurate a picture of the real situation as possible. In fact, the possibility for the seller to sell their notes to a financial institution is an encouragement to feel free to extend credit without having to bear the requisite increase in working capital it would involve.
- When sales are eligible for VAT (or sales tax) the accounts receivable balance includes VAT (see Appendix 10.1). Therefore, in order to use coherent figures in the calculation of ratios, one must verify that numerator and denominator are expressed coherently either VAT-included or VAT-excluded. However, such coherence is not always easy to achieve as, for example, export sales are generally not submitted to VAT in the country of origin and each country tends to have a specific VAT rate for its domestic sales. Current practice calls for ignoring VAT and accept that the figures do not give the true value of the ratio. It is not, however, a dramatic error in that the general trend of evolution is still the same as long as no major changes in the mix of sales (cash versus credit, as well as domestic versus export) take place.

In the Ericsson example overleaf, we have chosen to not extract the VAT, which is included in the receivables, because the proportion of total sales originating from domestic operations is very small. The credit term appears to be intrinsically long but, as we will see in Chapter 15, no ratio can ever be interpreted on its face value, but only by analyzing its evolution over time and comparing its value to equivalent ratios pertaining to other comparable firms in the same line of business.

Real-life example Ericsson

Ericsson, the Swedish telecommunications network solutions manufacturer shows an excellent example of the difficulty of evaluating the average days of sales when a large proportion of sales are export sales or sales not realized by the parent country's operations. In its 2004 annual report they report their average days of sales at approximately 90 days:

		Millions of SEK
Net sales	2004	131,972
Net sales in Sweden	2004	6,180
Accounts receivable – trade	2004	32,644
Accounts receivable – trade	2003	31,886
Accounts receivable – trade	Average	32,265
Average days' sales (32,265/131,972) × 365		89.2
Receivables turnover (131,972/32,265)		4.1

Key points

- Current assets, excluding inventories, comprise receivables, marketable securities (or short-term investments), and cash.
- The percentage of total assets represented by receivables is generally related to the business activity in which the company is involved: higher for a service activity, lower in a heavy industry, because of the relative importance of fixed assets.
- The probability that an account receivable will effectively be collected must be evaluated at the end of each accounting period. Doubtful or disputed accounts, which are partly or totally uncollectible, are referred to as 'bad' or 'doubtful' debts, or 'doubtful accounts'. Their value has to be written-down by recognizing a provision expense.
- Uncollectible accounts must be written-off by recognizing a bad debt expense.
- 'Current investments' are semi-liquid assets that are readily realizable and are intended to be held for not more than one year.
- According to IASB, current investments held for trading should be carried in the balance sheet at fair value through profit or loss.
- Cash comprises 'cash in hand' (coins, banknotes, and currency available) and 'demand deposits' (deposits in bank accounts that are available on demand).
- Cash equivalents are short-term, highly liquid investments that are readily convertible to known amounts of cash and which are subject to an insignificant risk of changes in value.
- The two main indicators relevant with regard to accounts receivable are: (1) the average days of sales; and (2) the receivables turnover.

Review (solutions are at the back of the book)

Review 10.1 Berg

Topic: Accounting for provision on receivables
Related part of the chapter: Core issues

At the end of their accounting period, on 31 December X3, Berg Enterprises have reviewed their receivables and found two doubtful accounts.

Customer	A/R Balance	Comments	Probable loss
Alban	200	Filed for protection from creditors	25%
Zizou	300	Filed for protection from creditors	40%

As of 31 December X4, these doubtful accounts are as follows:

Customer	A/R balance	Comments	Probable (or real) loss
Alban	200	Filed for protection from creditors	70%
Zizou	300	Paid 50 in total settlement of account.	250

Required

1. Prepare the doubtful accounts provisions at the end of X3.
2. Prepare the appropriate entries at the end of X3.
3. Prepare the doubtful accounts provisions at the end of X4.
4. Prepare the appropriate entries at the end of X4.

Assignments

Assignment 10.1
Multiple-choice questions

Related part of the chapter: Core/Advanced issues

Select the right answer (only one possible answer, unless otherwise stated).

1. Doubtful debts represent
   (a) Liabilities which are challenged by one of the parties
   (b) Receivables which might not be collected
   (c) All of these
   (d) None of these

2. Accounts receivable is equivalent to (several answers possible)
   (a) Trade creditors
   (b) Trade debtors
   (c) Trade accounts payable
   (d) Trade accounts receivable
   (e) All of these
   (f) None of these

3. A bank overdraft should be
   (a) Included in the financial fixed assets
   (b) Reported as a current asset
   (c) Reported as a current liability
   (d) Netted against positive cash balances at other banks
   (e) None of these

4. The direct write-off method is consistent with the matching accounting principle while the allowance method is not
   (a) True
   (b) False

5. Accounts receivable are generally valued at the
   (a) Amounts invoiced to customers
   (b) Net realizable value
   (c) Present value of future cash flows
   (d) None of these

6. Given the following information, determine the accounts receivable turnover (two possible answers):

Beginning accounts receivable	20
Ending accounts receivable	40
Beginning cash	50
Ending cash	60
Cash sales	40
Credit sales	300
Net income	35

   (a) 15
   (b) 7.5
   (c) 10
   (d) 17
   (e) 8.5
   (f) 11.33
   (g) 1
   (h) 2
   (i) 2.5
   (j) 3
   (k) None of these

7. An accounts receivable with a 100% probability of being collected is a cash equivalent
   (a) True
   (b) False

8. When a note receivable is discounted
   (a) The note is removed from the assets
   (b) The note is maintained in the assets and a liability is recorded
   (c) The note is removed from the assets or maintained in the assets with a liability recorded, depending on the national GAAP
   (d) None of these

9. When a provision (allowance) is no longer necessary
   (a) An expense account is decreased (credited)
   (b) A revenue account is increased (credited)
   (c) Both solutions are possible, it depends on the country
   (d) None of these

10. In a monthly bank reconciliation, the statement begins with
   (a) The cash balance per books at the end of the month
   (b) The cash balance per books at the beginning of the month
   (c) The cash balance on the bank statement at the beginning of the month
   (d) The cash balance on the bank statement at the end of the month
   (e) None of these

Assignment 10.2
Mahler

Topic: Estimating provision for doubtful accounts
Related part of the chapter: Core issues

Mahler Company provides the following information relating to sales, accounts receivable, and the provision for doubtful accounts for year X2 (000 CU omitted).

Sales for X2 (80% on credit)	3,000
Sales returns on credit sales	100
Accounts receivable balance, on 1 January X2	400
Provision for doubtful accounts balance, on 1 January X2	40
Cash collected on accounts receivable during X2	1,000
Accounts written-off as bad debt expenses during X2	30

Required

1. Record the write-off of uncollectible doubtful accounts during X2.
2. Prepare the adjusting entry required on 31 December X2 to record the provision on doubtful accounts for each of the following *independent* assumptions:
   (a) The provision for doubtful accounts is based on the ending balance of accounts receivable. Eighty percent of the sales during X2 were credit sales. The accountant of Mahler Company, Mr Gustav, estimates, from past experience, that 10% of the 31 December X2 accounts receivable will prove to be doubtful.
   (b) The provision for doubtful accounts is based on net credit sales. The accountant estimated that 80% of the sales are credit sales, and that 5% of the net credit sales will prove to be doubtful.
   (c) The provision for doubtful expense is based on aging of accounts receivable. The following aging schedule has been prepared by the accountant:

Days outstanding	Amount	Probability of collection
0–30 days	900	95%
31–60 days	500	90%
61–90 days	250	80%
More than 90 days	20	70%

Assignment 10.3
Bosch*

Topic: Reporting for receivables
Related part of the chapter: Core issues

Bosch is a German group producing automotive equipment, power tools, and home appliances. The consolidated balance sheet and notes to financial statements 2004 show the following elements relating to receivables (*source*: Annual report 2004):

Figures in millions of euros

Balance sheet as per 31 December 2004	Per 31 December 2004	Per 31 December 2003
Current assets		
Receivables and other assets (Note 8)		
– Accounts receivable	6,315	5,687
– Other receivables and other assets	3,902	3,432
Note 8 Receivables and other assets	**2004**	**2003**
[a] Accounts receivable	6,315	5,687
– thereof due in more than one year	2	3
Other receivables and other assets		
Receivables from affiliated companies [1]	194	178
– thereof due in more than one year	3	15
Receivables from companies in which interest are held [2]	172	142
Other assets [3]	3,536	3,112
– thereof due in more than one year	2,176	2,367
[b] Subtotal [1] + [2] + [3]	3,902	3,432
Receivables and other assets [sum of (a) + (b)]	10,217	9,119
Other assets contain deferred tax assets of EUR 2,463 million.		

Required

1. Relate the balance sheet items shown to the information contained in the notes.
2. What plausible conclusion can be drawn about the format of presentation of the balance sheet from the existence of the line 'thereof in more than one year'?
3. In your best judgment, are the amounts reported in the notes gross or net? Explain your position and, eventually, its possible implications.
4. What are affiliated companies and is it normal that receivables pertaining to trade with these companies still appear on a consolidated balance sheet (see Chapter 13)?

Assignment 10.4
Bayer*

Topic: Financial statement analysis of receivables
Related part of the chapter: Advanced issues

Bayer is a German chemical group, The consolidated balance sheet and income statement (*source*: Annual report 2004) include the following data:

Consolidated balance sheets € million	31 December 2003	31 December 2004
Current assets		
Receivables and other assets		
Trade accounts receivable	5,071	5,580
Consolidated statements of income € million	**2003**	**2004**
Net sales	28,567	29,758

The notes, as mentioned earlier in this chapter, provide the following table concerning changes in write-downs of trade accounts receivable as follows:

€ million	31 December 2003	31 December 2004
Balance at beginning of year	(345)	(302)
Additions charged to expense	(106)	(103)
Exchange differences	13	2
Changes in scope of consolidation	1	(1)
Deductions due to utilization	135	105
Balance at end of year	(302)	(299)

Required

1. Compute the average days of sales (also called the number of days' revenue outstanding) and receivables turnover on the sole basis of the information provided in the balance sheet and income statement.
2. Compute the same ratios incorporating data disclosed in the notes.
3. Explain the difference you find between the two methods of computations.
4. Comment on these ratios.

Assignment 10.5
Holmen*

Topic: Reporting for receivables
Related part of the chapter: Advanced issues

Holmen (formerly MoDo) is a Swedish paper and cardboard manufacturer. In the notes to their 2004 consolidated financial statements (*source:* Annual report 2004), the company disclosed the following data with regard to operating receivables:

	Group		Parent company	
	2004	2003	2004	2003
Accounts receivable	2,324	2,176	1,853	1,733
Receivables from Group companies	–	–	103	52
Receivables from associate companies	–	4	–	45
Prepaid costs and accrued income	112	95	83	73
Other receivables	291	238	202	173
	2,727	2,513	2,241	2,076

In the income statement, the net turnover (net sales) amounts to:

	2004	2003
Net turnover	15,653	15,816

Required

1. Explain why the 'receivables from Group companies' do not appear in the 'Group' financial statements.
2. Compute the average days of sales (in receivables) for 2004 and 2003.
3. Comment on these figures.

References

FASB (1993) Statement of Financial Accounting Standard No. 115: Accounting for Certain Investments in Debt and Equity Securities, Stamford, CT.

IASB (1992) International Accounting Standard No. 7: Cash Flow Statements, London.

IASB (1993) International Accounting Standard No. 18: Revenue, London.

IASB (2003a) International Accounting Standard No. 32: Financial Instruments: Disclosure and Presentation, London.

IASB (2003b) International Accounting Standard No. 39: Financial Instruments: Recognition and Measurement, London.

Lymer A., and Hancock, D. (2003/04) Taxation: Policy & Practices, 10th edn, Thomson Learning, London.

Nexia International (1994) *VAT in Europe,* Tolley Publishing, Croydon.

Additional material on the website

Go to http://www.thomsonlearning.co.uk/stolowylebas2 for further information.

The following appendices to this chapter are available on the dedicated website:

Appendix 10.1: Value added tax
Appendix 10.2: Bank reconciliation
Appendix 10.3: Notes receivable paid at maturity
Appendix 10.4: Recording of notes receivable

Notes

1. The term 'debt' is still often used in practice. A more accurate (but rarely used) term ought to be 'bad' or 'doubtful receivables'. Some countries use the term 'doubtful accounts' or 'uncollectible accounts'.
2. Aging accounts receivable is the process of classifying individual receivable transactions by the time elapsed since the claim came into existence. Most accounting software programs provide an automatic partitioning of the accounts receivable by age class, i.e., due date or overdue delay (30 days, 31–60 days, etc.).
3. *Source*: MOCI (France) no. 1763, 19 May 2005, p. 60.
4. After the revision of IAS 39 in 2003, the treatment shown in Table 10.3 is similar to the one stated by FAS 115 (FASB 1993).
5. See Chapter 9.

Chapter 11
Shareholders' equity

Learning objectives

After studying this chapter, you will understand:

- The differences between the legal forms of business organization.
- What share capital is.
- How changes in share capital (increase or reduction) are reported.
- What different categories of shares exist.
- What a share premium is and how it is reported.
- How profit appropriation is recorded.
- What kinds of different categories of reserves are found in the balance sheet.
- How stock options plans are recorded.
- How changes in shareholders' equity are reported.
- How shareholders' equity can be analyzed.

As shown in Figure 1.3 (in Chapter 1), in order to create value or wealth for its creators, a business must finance upfront the acquisition of its initial means of 'production' so it can deliver its value proposition to its customers and thus activate the cash pump. The two main sources of seed financial resources of a firm are:

1. capital provided by the entrepreneur or by investors in exchange for a claim on the future returns of the business venture; and
2. borrowed funds, generally provided, for a predefined and limited period of time, by financial institutions in a contract specifying the principal will be returned by an agreed upon date plus a fee (interest) which is not conditional on the success of the venture.

Additional financial resources will be generated, on an ongoing basis, through operations, but, if these are not sufficient to support growth, further calls on external sources of financing might be required.

Capital can be provided in the form of cash contributions, contribution of tangible or intangible assets (including intellectual property), or even of labor (in lieu of remuneration). Capital, unlike borrowed financial resources, has no specified reimbursement date to the provider(s) and generally no return is guaranteed.

The term used to refer to investors (providers of capital) is a function of the legal form of the business organization. In a corporation they are shareholders (or stockholders), in a partnership they are partners or associates. A sole proprietor is the investor in a business she or he owns entirely. Whatever the legal organizational format, the separation of private and business rights and responsibilities is essential.

Capital is an investment at risk that implies the investor's participation (even if sometimes such participation remains only theoretical or virtual) in managerial decision making. Investors are therefore liable for the consequences of the actions of 'their' business. That liability may be limited to their contribution to the capital of the firm, for example in 'limited liability corporations', or it may be unlimited, for example in an unincorporated sole proprietorship or entrepreneurship.

Since capital, in limited liability companies, represents the upper limit of the potential liability assumed by investors, its nominal or face value must be communicated to all persons dealing (or potentially dealing) with the business. It cannot be modified without public notice and without conforming to the rules defined in the business's by-laws or their equivalent.

Understanding what capital and shareholders' equity are and how they are recorded and reported is crucial in the definition of standardized key investment return metrics (such as earnings per share, cash flow per share, share yield, dilution, share (stock) options, etc.) that are used by financial market investors to inform their investment decisions.

This chapter is devoted to business owners' equity: definitions and processes through which equity and capital can be increased (whether it be through operation of the business or through additional capital contributions) or modified (for example, through the payment of dividends or the, hopefully rare, absorption of accumulated losses).

1 Core issues

The IASB Framework (1989) defines equity as: 'the residual interest [of the investors] in the assets of the entity after deducting all its liabilities' (§ 49). The term equity refers to the concept of 'net worth', i.e., the difference between total assets and liabilities.

Because businesses that are incorporated represent a much larger part of the global gross wealth creation (measured, for example, by gross national products) than do the unincorporated firms, the most important form of equity or 'net worth', from an economic point of view, is that of 'shareholders' equity'. For simplicity sake, we will use in this text the term shareholders' equity to refer to any investor's residual claim on the worth of the company regardless of the organizational form retained in the by-laws by the founders of the firm. The alternative forms of organization are evoked briefly first as they are important for understanding the extent of the responsibility assumed by the investors in each case.

The two principal components of shareholders' equity will then be reviewed: (share) capital and retained (accumulated) earnings (or reserves). The mechanism of their modification will subsequently be examined: decrease or increase of capital as well as payment of dividends are some of the most common events that impact on the shareholders' equity.

1.1 Forms of business organization

Three generic and alternative legal forms of organization specify the roles and responsibilities of the capital providers: (1) sole proprietorship; (2) partnership; and (3) limited liability company. Each country's legal system defines precisely the rules applying to each generic form. It would be beyond the scope of this book to explore the more detailed specific elements of any country.

A business represents a legal or economic entity that is separate from the individual or corporate capital provider(s). Any business must report on its economic activity by issuing periodic financial statements, even if only for tax purposes. If incorporated as a legal entity, a business can possess wealth, own property, make decisions, contract debts, pay money in its own right, go to court, or be taken to court, etc.

It is essential that the accounting and the reporting systems completely separate economic transactions that concern the business exclusively from those that concern its individuals or corporate capital providers. Capital providers are distanced and separated from the firm in which they invested. This separation suffers one exception pertaining to risk sharing (assumption of liability for the firm's actions) as mentioned before: some legal organizational forms limit responsibility while others do not.

1.1.1 Sole proprietorship

In a sole proprietorship, the single capital provider holds claim to 100% of the future wealth creation of the business and bears all the risks of the venture. This legal form is not well adapted to the needs of large businesses. Creating a sole proprietorship generally is simple. This simplicity and the corollary low organizational costs may explain its common usage in the creation of small enterprises.

1.1.2 Partnership

A partnership is a business with two or more owners. In many countries, a partnership is not incorporated and each of the associates or partners is fully responsible for all the consequences of the actions of the business. Some countries do not specifically offer the partnership form as such, but generally offer other forms approximating the partnership format such as the 'unlimited liability company', also called 'incorporated partnership'. Examples of such national variations on the theme are: *Société en nom collectif* (SNC) in Belgium, France, and Switzerland; *Interessentskab* (I/S) in Denmark; *Offene Handelsgesellschaft* (OHG or oHG) in Germany; *Omorrythmos Etairia* (OE) in Greece; *Unlimited company* in Ireland and the UK; *Società in nome collettivo* (SNC) in Italy; *Vennootschap Onder Firma* (VOF) in the Netherlands; *Sociedad regular colectiva* (SRC) in Spain; and *Sociedade em nome colectivo* in Portugal.

This form of organization is best suited for a limited number of associates or partners. Each country's legislation specifies the minimum number of partners and sometimes an upper limit to that number. Both lower and, occasionally, upper limits vary greatly between countries. This form of legal organization is flexible enough to allow a significant expansion of the business activities. New partners (i.e., additional capital providers) can often be added on with minimal formality. The organizational costs of setting up a partnership are greater than those incurred in setting up a sole proprietorship, but the procedures are nonetheless not very complex or burdensome.

1.1.3 Limited liability company

The limited liability company, also called corporation in North America, is the most common form of organization for larger businesses. The liability assumed by the investors does not extend beyond their investment. The capital is partitioned in small homogeneous and tradable increments called shares. Each share represents both a contribution to the capital and a claim on future profits. Investors are called shareholders. Shares can generally be traded independently of the enterprise.

Most countries require a minimum level of capital funds be provided by investors as this type of organization is meant to grow and expand, and their level of responsibility of potential liability with them. Since capital measures the maximum level of liability an incorporated enterprise assumes, its trading partners (suppliers, customers, banks, etc.) generally require that the capital be brought to a level coherent with the size of the business activities.

Limited liability companies generally raise capital in the open market. They have an obligation of reporting to their shareholders. An auditor generally is required to certify that the financial statements have been prepared in accordance with the rules and requirements of the country, and also that they represent fairly the financial situation of the business. Corporations are generally highly regulated and the incorporation process is often complex, leading to significant organizational costs.

Many countries distinguish two types of limited liability companies:

- *Private limited companies*: They generally have a fairly low minimum level of capital and at least two distinct share capital providers, although there are exceptions such as in Belgium (SPRLU), France (EURL), Germany (*Einmann* GmbH), and Portugal (EIRL) where a single capital provider (individual or corporate entity) may incorporate her, his, or its business as a private limited company. Country-specific business legislation generally specifies a maximum number of capital providers. For example, it is 50 shareholders in India, Ireland [Private limited company], Spain [*Sociedad de responsabilidad limitada* (SL)], and the UK [Private limited company], and 100 shareholders in France [*Société à responsabilité limitée* (SARL)]. There is no requirement for a maximum number of proprietors in Germany [*Gesellschaft mit beschränkter Haftung* (GmbH)]. Because the number of shareholders is often small, the shares are not traded on a financial market and their sale may even require approval (as is the case for partnerships) by a majority of the remaining shareholders. These shares are thus not very liquid and often represent a cumbersome investment instrument for the capital provider.

- *Public limited companies*: A minimum number of capital providers is required, but no maximum is ever specified. The minimum number of shareholders varies greatly between countries (two in Argentina, Belgium [*Société anonyme* (SA)], Greece [*Anonymos eteria* (AE)], Italy [*Società per azioni* (Spa or SpA)], the Netherlands [*Naamloze vennootschap* (NV)], and the UK [public limited company (PLC)], three in Denmark [*Aktieselskab* (AS], Spain [*Sociedad anonima* (SA)], and Switzerland [*Société anonyme* (SA)], five in Germany [*Aktien Gesellschaft* (AG)], and Portugal [*Sociedad anonima* (SA)], and seven in France [*Société anonyme* (SA)], India [public limited company (PLC)], and Ireland [public limited company (PLC)], etc.). Each country's legislation also specifies a minimum amount of capital and such minimum is generally higher for the public limited companies than it is for the private limited companies. Most of the time, shares of public limited companies can be traded freely on open financial markets. When such a market exists, these shares are liquid and offer a preferred medium of investment for capital providers who can go in and out of an investment with a low transaction cost. A side benefit of such liquidity is that it generally provides the enterprise with a lower cost of capital than the one incurred by businesses where the capital is not as liquid.

Figure 11.1 summarizes the principal characteristics of the various forms of legal organization.

Figure 11.1 Forms of business organization

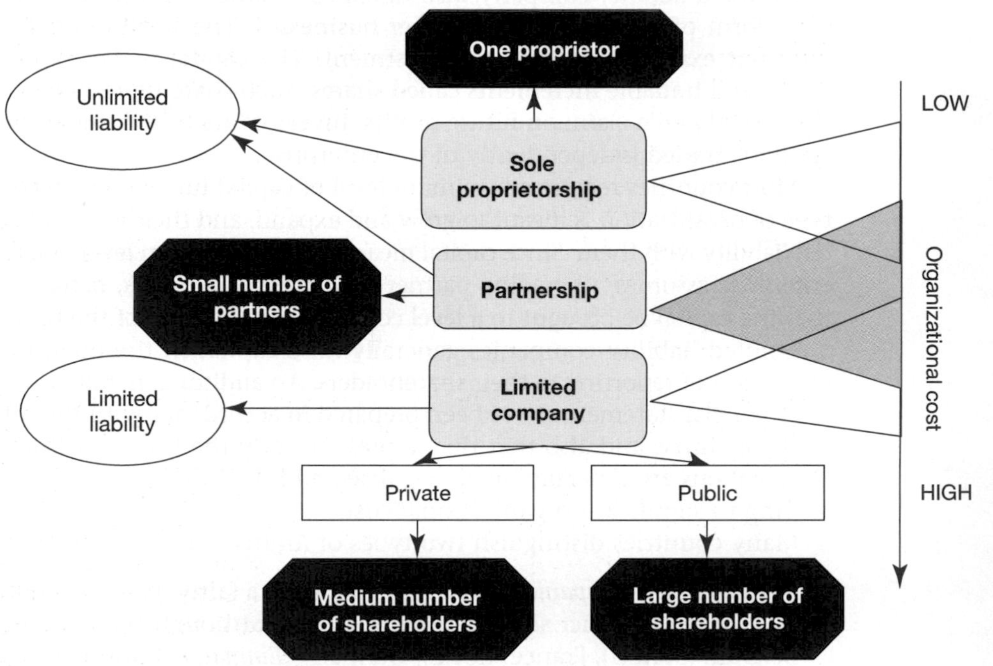

Although shareholders' equity is defined by the IASB as a residual, its framework states that it 'may be sub-classified in the balance sheet [i.e., for reporting purposes]. For example, in a corporate [i.e., incorporated] entity, funds contributed by shareholders, retained earnings, reserves representing appropriations of retained earnings and reserves representing capital maintenance adjustments may be shown separately. Such classifications can be relevant to the decision-making needs of the users of financial statements when they indicate legal or other restrictions on the ability of the entity to distribute or which apply to its equity. They may also reflect the fact that parties with ownership interests in an enterprise have differing rights in relation to the receipt of dividends or the repayment of contributed equity' (IASB 1989: § 65). The following sections will explore these subcategories of shareholder's equity.

1.2 Share capital

1.2.1 Definition

Shares or stock certificates represent the capital. They are evidence of the contribution of the shareholders to the formation of the capital. Shares are attributed to investors proportionately to the value of the resource they provided. A share is a certificate of property. It can generally be sold, bought or transferred by the shareholder without the consent of the corporation. Each shareholder has the right to:

- influence management decision making by participating in and voting in general assembly meetings;
- receive dividends and a proportionate share of any eventual liquidations surplus;
- have first pass at acquiring additional shares (proportionately to the current holding) in the case of the business deciding to issue new shares.

1.2.2 Nominal or par value

Generally, at the time of a business' incorporation, its by-laws specify (within the constraints specified by law) the face value of the unitary share, which represents the metric that will determine how many shares constitute the capital. The face value of a share is called the nominal or par value. The capital is therefore equal to the number of shares multiplied by the par value. The market value of the share has generally no relation to the par value. Some countries' regulation, like that of the United States, allows 'no-par' shares. We will ignore this unusual situation here.

The par or nominal value of the capital represents an 'official' measure of the minimum monetary extent of liability assumed by the corporation. The total capital 'at par' is often mentioned in official documents of the firm addressed to the general public. As a general rule, capital cannot be issued below par.

1.2.3 Payment of share capital

Investors are not always required to hand over to the corporation the full amount of their investment as represented by par value of the number of shares they receive. This is due to the fact a newly created business often does not need to have all the capital available right at the beginning and would not be able to provide the shareholders a return that would be competitive. Corporations can therefore offer their shareholders the possibility to subscribe to (or buy on credit) their shares by delivering their funds or resources to the corporation over a period specified by the board of directors, but generally not exceeding five years. This subscription process is useful to shareholders as it gives them time to accumulate the funds or resources they will use to pay for the shares they have purchased upon issuance. The 2nd European Directive states that at least only one-quarter of the capital needs be handed over to the corporation upon incorporation and initial issuance of shares.

The vocabulary reflects the complexity of this situation:

- **Authorized capital** is the maximum amount of capital (at par) the charter (or by-laws) states the corporation can issue when needed. It is the maximum number of shares authorized multiplied by the par value.
- **Subscribed** or **issued capital** is that part of the authorized capital that the shareholders have agreed to purchase and pay for when called to do so. Some countries require that subscribed capital be equal to authorized capital. The fact that there are authorized shares in excess of subscribed shares, however, gives great flexibility to the management of the business in issuing new shares as they see fit, as is for example the case when the compensation package of executives or senior personnel includes stock options or share options. For example, British Telecom's 2005 annual report in the notes to consolidated financial statements (note 34) states that 'Of the authorized but unissued share capital at 31 March 2005, 26 million ordinary shares (2004 – 26 million) were reserved to meet options granted under employee share option schemes described in note 31'.
- **Called-up capital** is the fraction of the subscribed capital that the corporation's board decided to collect from the investors (the amount of the par or only a portion of the par).
- **Paid-in capital** or **contributed capital** is the part of the capital that has been actually contributed by the shareholders and is available to the corporation.
- **Uncalled capital** is the part of the subscribed capital that has not been called up. It will represent a declining balance as the investors actually deliver on their promise to fund the company.
- **Capital receivable** is the part of the subscribed capital that has been called up and remains unpaid. It will represent a declining balance as the investors actually deliver on their promise to fund the company.
- **Outstanding capital** (outstanding shares times the par value) is subscribed capital (at par) minus the par value of any share that has been bought back by the corporation (treasury shares).

To sum up:

Outstanding shares ≤ Issued shares ≤ Authorized shares

and

Subscribed capital = Paid-in capital + Capital receivable + Uncalled capital

1.2.4 Different categories of shares

Shares are negotiable instruments that grant certain rights to their owner. However, a corporation may find an interest in giving different rights to different categories of shareholders in order, for example, to make the capital subscription more attractive to certain types of investors or more attractive at certain times such as when the ongoing nature of the business is not fully assured. Shares carrying special rights are called 'preferred shares' or 'preference shares'. They form a category distinct from 'ordinary shares'.

Preferred versus ordinary shares The special rights of preferred shares that make them more (or less) attractive to purchase when issued than ordinary shares can take many forms, which can be combined:

- pecuniary advantage such as fully or partially guaranteed dividend, larger dividend than common (ordinary) shares, priority dividend, cumulative dividends[1], etc.;

- different voting rights in the general assembly (often double, but occasionally no voting right at all) than those held by the ordinary shares.

The basic idea behind preferred shares is that they allow raising of capital without necessarily creating a proportional dilution or without creating a shift in stewardship away from the original shareholders (case of no voting shares), or, on the contrary, shifting control towards a certain class of shareholders (case of multiple voting rights).

Preferred shares generally represent a trade off between return and control: either higher dividends but reduced voting rights, or higher voting rights but lower returns. The common or ordinary shareholders are the residual owners of the corporation after the preferred shareholders have received their dues. Shares carrying the same rights are organized in homogeneous classes.

Real-life example Barloworld

(South Africa – IFRS and South African GAAP – *Source*: Annual report 2004 – Capital equipment, materials handling, motor, cement and lime)

Barloworld has created preference shares as indicated in Note 12 to its financial statements (the currency is the Rand):

For the year ended 30 September 2004		Company	
		2004 R'm	2003 R'm
Authorized share capital			
500,000	6% non-redeemable cumulative preference shares of R2 each	1	1
300,000,000	ordinary shares of 5 cents each	15	15
		16	16
Issued share capital			
375,000	6% non-redeemable cumulative preference shares of R2 each (2003: 375,000)	1	1
222,892,403	ordinary shares of 5 cents each (2003: 215,430,249)	11	11
		12	12
The above figures have been rounded by the company in its annual report.			

Redeemable or convertible preference shares When the special rights attached to preferred shares are only temporary, these shares may be redeemable or convertible. In this first case, the preferred shares can be retired or redeemed at the initiative of the corporation at a price and under conditions that were mentioned in the preference share contract (such as the exchange price is conditional on the market performance of common shares). In the second case, convertible shares can be converted, within a certain time range and at the initiative of the bearer, into bonds or ordinary shares.

Shares with amended voting rights The voting power of a common shareholder is strictly proportional to the number of common shares she or he holds. Preferred shares may hold voting rights that deviate from the normal 'one share one vote' rule. Preferred shares with special voting rights are often used in new share issuance when the original shareholders are willing to incur a dilution of earnings but not of their power to direct the affairs of the firm. They are also used as defensive or offensive tactics in acquisitions, mergers, or takeover bids.

For example, Quebecor Inc., a Canadian company operating in the fields of communications, printing, and forest products, reports the existence of multiple voting rights shares in the note 19 on capital stock in its 2004 annual report:

(a) Authorized capital stock
An unlimited number of Class A Multiple Voting Shares (herein referred to as 'A shares') with voting rights of 10 votes per share, convertible at any time into Class B Subordinate Voting Shares (herein after referred to as 'B shares'), on a one-for-one share basis.
An unlimited number of B shares convertible into A shares on a one-for-one basis only if a takeover bid regarding A shares is made to holders of A shares without being made concurrently and under the same terms to holders of B shares.
Holders of B shares are entitled to elect 25% of the Board of Directors of Quebecor Inc. Holders of A Shares may elect the other members of the Board of Directors.

Other illustrations:

- Volvo Group (Swedish car and truck manufacturer): 'The share capital of the Parent Company is divided into two series of shares: A and B. Both series carry the same rights, except that each Series A share carries the right to one vote and each Series B share carries the right to one tenth of a vote' (Note 20 to the 2004 consolidated financial statements).
- Ericsson (Swedish telecommunications network solutions provider): As of 31 December 2004, 'the 16,132,258,678 shares [par SEK 1] were divided into 1,308,779,918 (656,218,640 [in 2003]) Class A shares, each carrying one vote, and 14,823,478,760 (15,476,040,038 [in 2003]) Class B shares, each carrying one-tenth of a vote. As of 31 December 2004, Ericsson held 299,715,117 of its Class B shares. No Class C shares, each carrying one-thousandth of a vote, are outstanding' (Annual report 2004, Share information, page 39 of the Summary Annual Report).

1.2.5 Share premium

The par value of a share is only a way of defining the number of shares in the legal capital and thus the relative power of decision of each shareholder. A share is valued by the market as the net present value of the estimated future cash flows (or dividends plus liquidation value) of the business venture. Most shares are issued at par at the time of incorporation (i.e., the issuance price equals the nominal value) and above their par for subsequent issuances, to reflect the market values that the investment has already realized.

The share premium is the difference between the issue price and the par value. It records a contribution from the 'new' shareholders in excess of the legal share capital. The share premium is also called 'additional paid-in capital' or 'capital in excess of par' or, in the USA, 'capital surplus'. It is reported as a part of the shareholders' equity.

1.2.6 Accounting for share capital

Accounting for capital issuance follows the same rules whether it is when the capital is first issued or when further capital is raised through a flotation of new shares. It is illustrated here through the entries required to record the issuance of capital by Gershwin Corporation. This business entity was incorporated at the beginning of year X0. Its authorized capital is 100,000 ordinary shares with a par of 1 CU. The initial issue was for 10,000 ordinary shares sold at par. This issue was entirely subscribed (paid-in) for a total cash inflow of

10,000 CU. During year X1, 90,000 additional shares were floated at the price of 1.2 CU per share. The terms of the flotation are that the acquirers of the new shares must contribute immediately 50% of the par (the rest to be contributed when called) and 100% of the share premium. This flotation creates a share premium for a total of 18,000 CU [90,000 shares × (1.2 CU − 1 CU at par)]. Of the par value of the 90,000 shares (i.e., 90,000 CU), only 45,000 CU will be contributed while another 45,000 CU will remain uncalled for the time being. The total cash raised immediately is therefore 63,000 CU through the issuance of the new shares.

Figure 11.2 illustrates the accounting mechanism required for recording both transactions (000 CU).

The capital is increased by the par value of the 90,000 shares issued, even though one-half has not yet been contributed and remains uncalled. However, in some countries (e.g., the USA), the uncalled portion of capital ('uncalled capital' or 'subscriptions receivable') is not shown as an asset as here but as a reduction of share capital, i.e., a contra-liability account. However, the end result is the same and the two different approaches, giving full disclosure, provide a true and fair view of the financial situation of the firm. When the uncalled capital is called and the shareholders pay in the rest of their contribution, the only additional entry required will be to balance cash against either the uncalled capital (receivable) or the contra-liability of uncalled capital.

Figure 11.2 Accounting for issuance of share capital

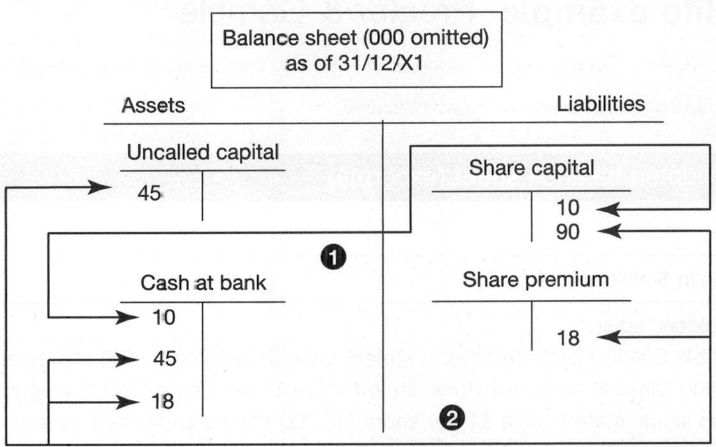

❶ Recording of the capital issued at the time of the incorporation of the company (year X0).

❷ Issuance of additional shares for cash.

1.2.7 Reporting share capital

International standard IAS 1 (IASB 2003a) stipulates rather detailed rules for the reporting of share capital in financial statements. Paragraph 76 states that 'an entity shall disclose the following, either on the balance sheet or in the notes:

(a) For each class of share capital

(i) The number of shares authorized;

(ii) The number of shares issued and fully paid, and issued but not fully paid;

(iii) Par value per share, or that the shares have no par value;
(iv) A reconciliation of the number of shares outstanding at the beginning and at the end of the period;
(v) The rights, preferences and restrictions attaching to that class including restrictions on the distribution of dividends and the repayment of capital;
(vi) Shares in the entity held by the entity or by subsidiaries or associates; and
(vii) Shares reserved for issue under options and sales contracts for the sale of shares, including the terms and amounts; and

(b) A description of the nature and purpose of each reserve within equity'.

IAS 1 (§ 125) adds that 'all entity shall disclose in the notes:

(a) The amount of dividends proposed or declared the financial statements were authorized for issue but not recognized as a distribution to equity holders during the period, and the related amount per share; and
(b) The amount of any cumulative preference dividends not recognized'.

'An entity without share capital, such as a partnership or trust, shall disclose information equivalent to that required by paragraph 76(a), showing changes during the period in each category of equity interest, and the rights, preferences and restrictions attaching to each category of equity interest' (IAS 1: § 77).

Real-life example Procter & Gamble

(USA – US GAAP – *Source*: Annual report 2005 – Beauty and personal care, family health, household care)

Procter & Gamble reports several types of shares.

Consolidated balance sheet (excerpts)

	30 June	
Amounts in $millions	2005	2004
Shareholders' equity		
Convertible Class A preferred stock, stated value $1 per share (600 shares authorized)	1,483	1,526
Non-Voting Class B preferred stock, stated value $1 per share (200 shares authorized)	–	–
Common stock, stated value $1 per share (10,000 shares authorized; shares outstanding: 2005 – 2,472.9, 2004 – 2,543.8)	2,473	2,544
Additional paid-in capital	3,142	2,425
(...)		

1.3 Profit appropriation

As mentioned in Chapter 2, all earnings generated by a business are theoretically available for appropriation and distribution to shareholders. However, although the right of ownership by shareholder over all after-tax earnings is not challenged, yearly earnings are partitioned in two categories: some will be 'retained' in the business as retained earnings (i.e., a voluntary reinvestment), also called reserves, and some will effectively be distributed as dividends.

1.3.1 Dividends

A dividend is a distribution of the earnings of the business to its shareholders. Dividends are allocated proportionately to the rights attached to the shares held by the shareholders on a date of record[2]. The management team of the business generally proposes the dividend pay-out ratio for approval by the general assembly of shareholders once the financial statements have been approved. Shareholders have the final say (through the general assembly) in what to do with the earnings. Dividends are paid to the shareholders following a schedule that varies with the traditions of each country: monthly or quarterly and mostly by anticipation in the USA, or annually and *ex post* in most European countries.

1.3.2 Reserve accounts

According to the IASB Framework (IASB 1989: § 66): 'The creation of reserves is sometimes required by statute or other law in order to give the entity and its creditors an added measure of protection from the effects of losses. Other reserves may be established if national tax law grants exemptions from, or reductions in, taxation liabilities when transfers to such reserves are made. The existence and size of these legal, statutory and tax reserves is information that can be relevant to the decision-making needs of users. Transfers to such reserves are appropriations of retained earnings rather than expenses'.

All required reserve accounts must be funded before dividends can be paid out. It means that the earnings available to the shareholders for distribution or voluntary reinvestment is equal to:

Annual earnings minus sum of the allocations to reserve accounts =
Earnings available for distribution

The 'distributable earnings' are either distributed or transferred to reserves (called optional reserves) or retained (retained earnings) until further decisions concerning their possible distribution.

For example, as of 31 December 2004, Ericsson (Swedish telecommunications network provider) described its 'restricted equity' (SEK million 56,302) as the sum of capital stock (SEK million 16,132) plus 'Reserves not available for distribution' (SEK million 40,170) out of a total 'stockholders' equity' of SEK million 77,299.

In summary, the main categories of reserves are the following: legal reserve, statutory reserve, regulated reserve, revaluation reserve, reserve for own shares, optional (or voluntary) reserves, and profit/loss brought forward (also called unappropriated retained earnings, i.e. which will be added to appropriatable earnings in the next period). These different categories are presented in Appendix 11.1.

1.3.3 Reporting retained earnings/reserves

A balance sheet may be presented 'before' or 'after appropriation'. The term 'appropriation' here refers to the decision taken by the shareholders or directors to distribute dividends and/or to transfer all or part of the income of the period to retained earnings (or to reserves if so required by by-laws or covenants)[3]. In the 'after appropriation' method, the earnings of the year are not reported explicitly in the balance sheet; only additions to the retained earnings will be reported. The earnings of the period are added to the 'retained earnings/reserves'. The formula defining retained earnings/reserves at any point in time is presented in Table 11.1.

Table 11.1 Retained earnings/Reserves

	Retained earnings/Reserves (up to end of the previous period)
plus	Net income (after tax) of the year
minus	Dividends declared
minus	Transfers to reserves
=	Retained earnings/Reserves (at year-end)

Table 11.1 is a bare-bone template for the 'statement of retained earnings' that is required in the USA, in Canada, and generally in the annual statements of financial position of any business reporting under the US GAAP (most firms quoted on the New York Stock Exchange) or under a local GAAP that is based on the US GAAP. That statement explains how the retained earnings of the previous year are transformed, in a recurring fashion, into the retained earnings of the current year.

Most of the time the term 'retained earnings' is a part of 'shareholders' equity'. However, an analyst of the financial position of the firm must beware of the fact that the term 'retained earnings' may cover different realities depending on the country whose laws and practices are followed (see more on this topic in Appendix 11.2).

1.3.4 Reporting and accounting for shareholders' equity

Simple example of reporting of reserves and retained earnings Gershwin Corporation's income and dividend payment for years X1 and X2 are as follows (000 CU):

	Year X1	Year X2
Profit	50	70
Dividends	0	30

Table 11.2 illustrates the presentation of shareholders' equity according to each of the two methods commonly used by corporations.

Comments

- The choice of method has no impact on the actual total shareholders' equity plus liabilities.
- When method 1 is used, there is a 'dividends payable' only as long as the dividends have not actually been paid out at balance sheet date. If they had already been paid out by the date the financial statements are approved, in our example the 30 CU of the paid-out dividend would already have reduced the cash account and would not need to be reported as a liability.

Accounting for profit appropriation Figure 11.3 illustrates the impact of profit appropriation for year X2 on the balance sheet of Gershwin Corporation. Since the accounting entries for methods 1 and 2 are essentially the same (but the timing is different), we chose to only illustrate method 2, i.e., reporting before appropriation, which appears to be the most frequently used method in Europe.

Table 11.2 Presentation of shareholders' equity in the balance sheet

	Year X1	Year X2
Method 1 (after appropriation)		
Share capital	100	100
Share premium	18	18
Retained earnings	50	90*
Shareholders' equity	168	208
Dividends payable (liabilities)	0	30
Total shareholders' equity and liabilities	168	238
Method 2 (before appropriation)		
Share capital	100	100
Share premium	18	18
Retained earnings (beginning balance)	0	50
Net income	50	70
Shareholders' equity	168	238

*[50 (beginning balance) + 70 (income of the period) − 30 (dividends payable)]

Figure 11.3 Accounting for profit appropriation

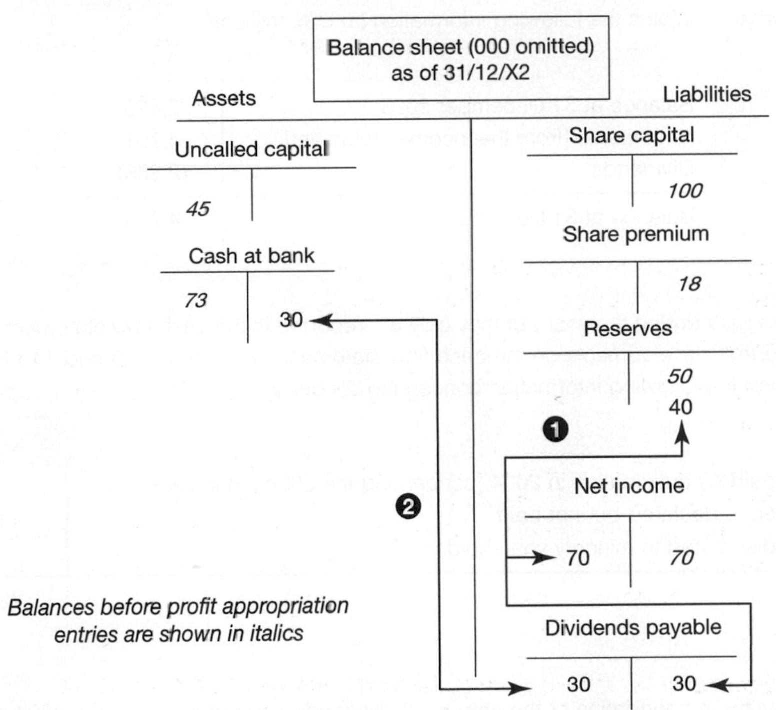

❶ Cancellation of net income, and transfer to reserves and to dividends payable. Dividends have been declared but not paid.

❷ Payment of dividends.

Real-life examples

Method 1 – Balance sheet after appropriation

Mittal Steel (formerly Ispat International) N.V.

(Netherlands – US GAAP – *Source*: Annual report 2004 – Steel company)

Excerpts from the consolidated balance sheet – 31 December, US$ millions

	2003	2004
Shareholders' equity		
Common shares	59	59
Treasury stock	(110)	(123)
Additional paid-in capital	584	552
Retained earnings	2,423	4,739
Accumulated other comprehensive income	(395)	619
Total shareholders' equity	2,561	5,846

- The topic 'Accumulated other comprehensive income' was introduced in Chapter 6 and is further developed in the Advanced issues section of this chapter.
- The topic 'Treasury stock' is further developed in the Advanced issues section of this chapter.
- The evolution of retained earnings between 2003 and 2004 is explained in the statement of changes in shareholders' equity, which contains the following information (in US$ millions):

Balance at 31 December 2003	2,423
Net income [from the income statement]	4,701
Dividends	(2,385)
Balance at 31 December 2004	4,739

Dividends have been paid during the year but they only are reported in the cash flow statement (financing activities). (For refresher and further developments on the cash flow statement, see Chapters 3 and 14.) In the 2004 cash flow statement, we can find the following information concerning dividends:

Dividends paid by anticipation in 2004 [concerning the 2004 net income]	(763)
Cash dividends declared but not paid	(1,650)
Dividends distributed to minority shareholders	27
Total	(2,386)

These elements allow the reconciliation of the amount of dividends corresponding to the 2004 net income (see US$ millions 2,385 in the statement of changes in shareholder's equity) and the amount computed on the basis of the cash flow statement (US$ millions, 2,386 – the difference is due to rounding).

Kerry Group Plc

(Ireland – Irish/UK GAAP – *Source*: Annual report 2004 – Food industry)

Excerpts from the consolidated balance sheet – 31 December, €000

	Notes	2004	2003
Capital and reserves			
Called-up equity share capital	18	23,356	23,234
Capital conversion reserve fund	20	340	340
Share premium account	19	375,032	365,229
Profit and loss account	20	645,177	531,149
		1,043,905	919,952
Consolidated profit and loss account (excerpts)			
For the year ended 31 December 2004	**Note**	**2004**	**2003**
Profit after taxation and attributable to ordinary shareholders		145,785	160,977
Dividends – paid	8	8,483	7,625
– proposed	8	17,751	15,985
		26,234	23,610
Retained profit for the year		119,551	137,367
Note 20. Reconciliation of movements in equity shareholders' funds			
Profit and loss account	**Notes**	**2004**	
At beginning of year		531,149	
Profit after taxation and attributable to ordinary shareholders		145,785	
Dividends	8	(26,234)	
Exchange translation adjustment	24	(5,523)	
At end of year		645,177	

Comments:

- The existence of a caption 'profit and loss account' in the balance sheet could lead one to think, wrongly, that the balance sheet is presented before profit appropriation. In reality, this caption represents the non-distributed part of the net income, which is transferred to reserves. In other terms, the dividends have already been deducted. The 'profit and loss account' caption is then a reserve account and the balance sheet is definitely presented after profit appropriation.
- The coherence of the 2003 and 2004 'profit and loss account' is explained in note 20 to financial statements (see in the table above).
- The topic of 'exchange translation adjustment' is covered in Chapter 13.

Method 2 – Balance sheet before appropriation

Ericsson

(Sweden – Swedish GAAP – *Source*: Annual report 2004 – Telecommunications network solutions)

Excerpts from the consolidated balance sheet – 31 December, SEK millions

	2004	2003
Stockholders' equity		
Capital stock	16,132	16,132
Reserves not available for distribution	40,170	40,298
Restricted equity	56,302	56,430
Retained earnings	1,973	14,895
Net income [from the income statement]	19,024	−10,844
Non-restricted equity	20,997	4,051
	77,299	60,481

- Ericsson's annual report indicates clearly restricted and unrestricted equity. (This distinction is developed in Appendix 11.3.)
- The 'retained earnings' only represent accumulated earnings in unrestricted reserves.

Repsol YPF

(Spain – Spanish GAAP – *Source*: Annual report 2004 – Oil and gas)

Excerpts from the consolidated balance sheet – 31 December, in € millions

Millions of euros	2004	2003
Shareholders' equity (Note 11)		
Capital stock	1,221	1,221
Paid-in surplus	6,428	6,428
Other reserves of the parent company:		
Revaluation reserves	3	3
Other reserves	4,141	3,914
Reserves of consolidated companies	6,240	4,940
Translation differences	(5,133)	(4,650)
Income for the year [same as in income statement]	1,950	2,020
Interim dividend [paid during the year]	(305)	(244)
Total shareholders' equity	14,545	13,632

- This excerpt of a balance sheet is a good illustration of a rather detailed description of shareholder's equity.
- The topic 'translation differences' is covered in Chapter 13.
- An interesting detail in this statement can be found in the fact that the interim dividends are shown and deducted, as is to be expected, from shareholders' equity.

2 Advanced issues

This part of the chapter will address special situations that deviate from the general principles presented in Core issues. Issues that are covered in this section are:

- Issuance of (new) shares may be the result of non-cash contributions.
- Share issuance costs need to be recorded and reported appropriately.
- Shareholders' equity is affected by the possibility that most corporations have to purchase their own shares and cancel them. This is used when no investment alternatives exist to increase the return on equity for the shareholders (by reducing the denominator, while productive investment opportunities would have increased the numerator).
- The comprehensive income (discussed in Chapter 6) may appear in the shareholders' equity.
- The statement of changes in shareholders' equity is an important document.

2.1 Accounting issuance of shares for non-cash capital contributions

Not all shares are issued against cash. There are three basic situations that may lead to the issuance of shares in return for something other than cash:

1. Shares can be issued in return for a capital contribution in kind.
2. New shares may be issued as the result of a 'capitalization' of reserves or of retained earnings.
3. New shares may be the result of the conversion by a creditor of their claim into shares.

2.1.1 Issuance of shares for capital contributions in kind

Shareholders may contribute assets other than cash. For example, intangible assets such as patents, specific knowledge, provision of access to a market, or tangible assets such as fixed assets, inventories, or receivables (all net of attached liabilities) are often important capital contributions, especially in the early phases of the life of a corporation. Shares issued for capital contributions in kind are also frequent in the case of business combinations such as acquisitions or mergers (see Chapter 13). The contributed value is theoretically the 'fair value' of the net assets, but such a value is often difficult to estimate since their value may be a function of their coherence with the strategy of the buyer.

The mechanism of recording is similar to that of a cash capital contribution, with the only difference being that an asset account different from cash is increased.

To illustrate the mechanism of recording a contribution in kind, let us go back to the Gershwin Corporation. In year X3, new shareholders contribute a patent valued at 15,000 CU. In exchange for the property transfer of the patent, these new shareholders receive 10,000 ordinary shares with a par of 1 CU. A 5,000 CU share premium therefore needs to be recorded. Figure 11.4 describes the mechanism.

2.1.2 Issuance of new shares due to capitalization of reserves or of retained earnings

To incorporate reserves or retained earnings into the share capital is called capitalization. When the balance of the accumulated undistributed earnings becomes very large in

Figure 11.4 Accounting for a share issuance in kind

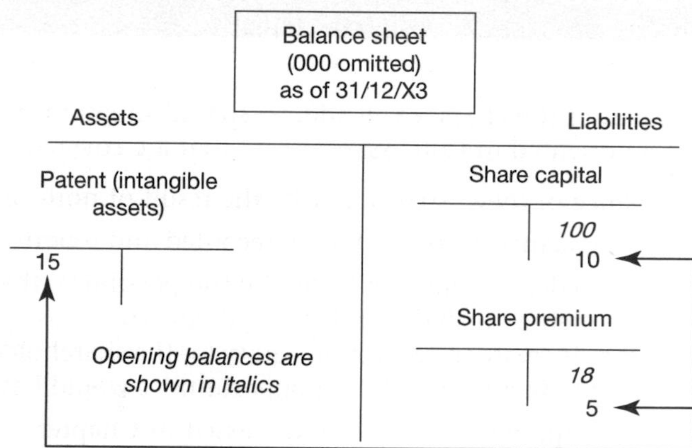

proportion to the share capital, it may be a good idea to incorporate all or part of the reserves or retained earnings into the capital. It is so because: (1) it may improve the liquidity of the shares if new shares are issued; and (2) it increases the protection of creditors to a higher level of responsibility assumed by the shareholders.

After the incorporation of reserves or retained earnings in the share capital (restructuring and consolidation of the shareholders' equity), the total book value of the shareholders' equity is unchanged but the number or par value of shares has been modified. Such an operation is called by different names: 'stock split'[4], mainly in North America (where an increase of the par value would be extremely unusual), and 'bonus issue' or 'capitalization of reserves' elsewhere (depending on whether or not new shares are issued).

Unless the corporation chooses to reflect this action by increasing the par value of the share, the procedure will lead to the issuance of new shares that will generally be given to the current shareholders. It leads to a 'bonus issue' and the shareholders of record on the date of the issue receive the new shares in proportion to their previous holdings.

Most reserves or retained earnings that are unambiguously the property of the shareholders (essentially all reserves and retained earnings) can be incorporated into share capital. Although each country may have its own specific rules regarding the incorporation of reserves or retained earnings, the eligible reserves are generally composed of (see the definition of each reserve in Appendix 11.1):

- legal reserve (after its capitalization, this reserve must be reconstituted);
- statutory reserves;
- regulated reserves;
- optional (voluntary) reserves;
- revaluation reserves;
- profit brought forward;
- net income of the year;
- share premium.

While some countries allow either or both an increase of the par value of the existing shares and the issuance of bonus shares, at the initiative of the corporation, others forbid either one or the other.

To illustrate the mechanism of incorporation of reserves in the share capital, let us revisit the Gershwin Corporation example. In year X4, the board of directors decides (and the decision is approved by the general assembly) to incorporate 30,000 CU worth of reserves in the share capital. Some 30,000 new shares of par 1 CU are created and attributed to the shareholders proportionately to their current holdings (i.e., 3 new shares for 11 old ones – let's keep in mind that Gershwin Corporation had 110,000 shares outstanding after the capital contribution in kind in year X3). The appropriate entry is shown in Figure 11.5.

Such an entry involves a mere transfer from reserves to capital. The beginning balance of the reserves account (150 CU) is the sum of the undistributed earnings up to and including those of year X3.

Figure 11.5 Share issuance by capitalization of reserves

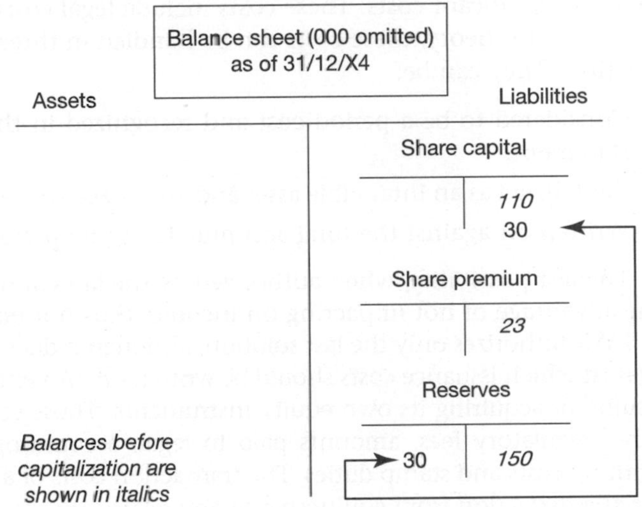

2.1.3 Issuance of shares resulting from an increase in capital due to a conversion of liabilities

Creditors of the corporation (suppliers or bankers) may accept to receive shares of capital as a counterpart for canceling their claim. In this case the shares they receive are new shares, thus creating an increase of the share capital.

Any combination of the following three reasons may explain the decision of the creditors to surrender a fixed claim in exchange for a conditional claim:

- The debtor corporation is experiencing serious cash difficulties and/or the total interest charge is not compatible with the current operational possibilities of the business. In order to avoid bankruptcy of their debtor, the creditors may find the conversion of loans or payables a less risky operation than the significant loss that the failure of their client might entail. In many cases the creditors use this opportunity to effectively take control of the board of directors to reorient the business activities in a way that provides for what they feel might be a more secure future for their investment.
- The corporation had issued convertible debt. The choice of issuing convertible debt is often the result of a bad image of the corporation on the share market. It allows lenders to reduce the risks they are taking: they receive a fixed remuneration if things do not go so well, and could receive a dividend remuneration – which may be greater than the original fixed return – if things do go well and they decide to convert their debt to capital. This way the lender can take the time to see how the business is evolving before deciding to become a shareholder.

- The lender is, for example, the parent company of the borrower and such an operation belongs to the long-term strategy of the parent. It may, for example, be an opportunity for the parent to increase its control over the subsidiary, or even to create a possibility for a de facto transfer of the debt to an outside party when it is easier to raise capital by selling shares of the subsidiary than it is for the subsidiary to raise funds through debt.

The increase in capital is recorded by a simple accounting entry in which debt is eliminated and 'share capital at par' is increased and 'capital surplus' or 'share premium' is incremented for the balance.

2.2 Accounting for share issuance costs

Incorporating a corporation or increasing its capital are operations that cause the incurrence of significant costs. These costs include legal costs, auditors' fees, bankers' commissions, etc. In theory, these costs can be handled in three different ways at the initiative of the firm. They can be:

- Considered to be a period cost and recognized in the corresponding period's income statement.
- Capitalized as an intangible asset and amortized (in general over a maximum of 5 years).
- Written off against the total accumulated share premium.

The last possibility, when authorized by the laws and regulations of the country, offers the advantage of not impacting on income, thus not biasing the time series of earnings.

IASB authorizes only the last solution, although it does not explicitly mention the caption against which issuance costs should be written off: 'An entity typically incurs various costs in issuing or acquiring its own equity instruments. Those costs might include registration and other regulatory fees, amounts paid to legal, accounting and other professional advisers, printing costs and stamp duties. The transaction costs of an equity transaction are accounted for as a deduction from equity (net of any related income tax benefit) to the extent they are incremental costs directly attributable to the equity transaction that otherwise would have been avoided. The costs of an equity transaction that is abandoned are recognized as an expense' (IAS 32, 2003b: § 37). In practice, the costs are deducted from the share premium.

2.3 Capital reduction

A corporation may be led to reducing its capital for essentially either of two reasons:

- Taking into account the reality created by accumulated losses (see Appendix 11.5).
- Cancellation of shares to acknowledge the reduction in the total liability assumed by the population of shareholders because, for example, the business has repurchased its own shares.

The second case is so important that we will devote the following section to the issues such a practice raises. As a reduction of share capital reduces the maximum liability assumed, company laws in most countries strictly regulate reductions of share capital to protect creditors.

2.4 Treasury shares (or own shares, or treasury stock)

Treasury shares occur when the corporation acquires its own shares.

2.4.1 Why repurchase one's own shares?

Corporations generally do not normally acquire or hold their own shares. However, in most countries such a practice is perfectly legal. Corporations are allowed to purchase their own shares (i.e., create treasury stock, in North American terminology) under certain circumstances. The following situations offer a far from exhaustive list of such conditions:

- A corporation can repurchase its shares so as to reduce its capital by canceling the repurchased shares. This is generally done with the intent of boosting the earnings per share ratio when no better alternative exists to developing the numerator (earnings) of that ratio.
- Shares can be repurchased and given to employees in the context of a profit-sharing plan or in their exercising the stock options they have received. Such a policy would be coherent only if: (a) the remaining shareholders do not want to see any dilution take place due to the distribution; or (b) all the authorized shares have already been issued and it would be difficult to increase the number of authorized shares.
- A listed corporation may repurchase its own shares with the intent of smoothing the market value of its shares in a turbulent environment.
- A listed corporation may wish to repurchase its own shares as a preventive measure if it fears a potential takeover. If fewer shares are on the open market, it may be harder for the 'predator' to obtain a majority of the voting rights.
- In some countries, the by-laws may require that the sale of a block of shares by a shareholder be made conditional on the approval of the new shareholder by the remaining previous shareholders. In such a situation, the corporation may act as a broker and thus allow the shareholder wanting to sell to find an acceptable candidate.

Among these five possible situations, the first one does not, strictly speaking, lead to the creation of 'own shares' or 'treasury stock' since the shares are rapidly canceled and taken off the books.

2.4.2 Purchase of treasury shares to reduce the share capital

As we have seen, the main reason for such action, called retirement of shares, is generally a way of boosting the earnings per share or to stabilize the market price of the share. However, it may be used in other circumstances. Retirement of shares may take place, for example, in a small corporation, when one of the shareholders wants to leave the group of shareholders for whatever reason. For example, let us assume that the shareholders of Gershwin Corporation have a falling-out. One of the shareholders, Mr George, owns 20% of the shares and wants out. The remaining shareholders wish neither to buy George's shares nor to welcome an outside buyer of his shares.

The total share capital amounts 140,000 (at par). Mr George's claim on the par capital amounts to 28,000 CU, but the equity book value of Mr George's shares is 20% of (140 + 23 + 120), i.e., 56.6 thousand CU (56,600 CU). The remaining shareholders and Mr George have agreed to value the shares at only 56,000 CU. The simplest solution is to have the corporation repurchase Mr. George's shares and cancel them. As shown in Figure 11.6, this transaction is carried out in two steps. The difference between the market value of the shares in the transaction and their par value will be taken out of the reserves and share premium accounts (the former for 20% of the reserves and the latter only for the balance). In this simplified example, we assume that the share premium and the reserves are unrestricted (see Appendix 11.3).

2.4.3 Purchase of treasury shares held by the corporation

When own shares are purchased and held for some time for whatever purpose (regulating the market of the share, anti-takeover bid strategy, employees profit-sharing plan, etc.), the accounting transaction recording the purchase is identical to that of phase ❶ in Figure 11.6.

Figure 11.6 Accounting for retirement of shares to reduce share capital

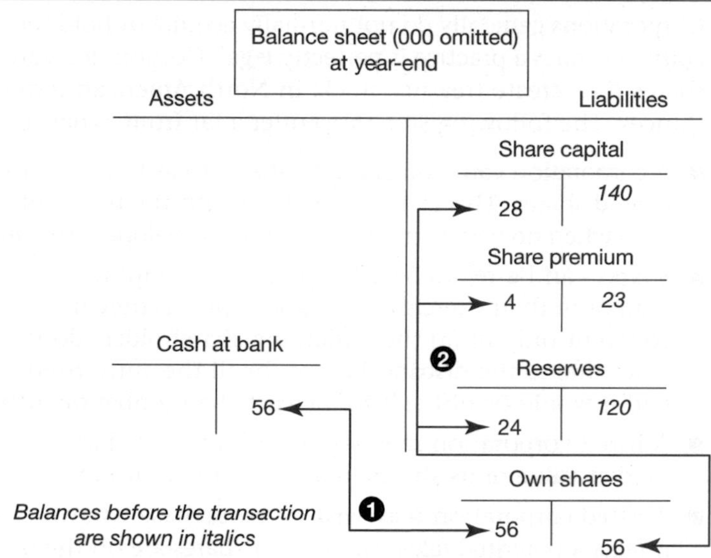

❶ Purchase of the corporation's own shares for the amount accepted by the seller and the remaining shareholders. According to IAS 32 (IASB, 2003b: § 33) and North American practice the own shares are reported as a negative entry in the shareholders' equity. We followed this method in the above figure. Another approach is possible and applied in several European countries: own shares are recognized (positively) on the asset side.

❷ Reduction of the capital by canceling these shares and all the rights pertaining to them.

- Generally, phase 2 (entry ❷) happens simultaneously with phase 1.
- In some countries, both entries are merged into only one and the account 'own shares' is not used.
- In some European countries, the law requires that despite canceling shares, the total amount of the restricted reserves/capital remain unmodified. In such a case a special restricted reserve ('reserve for own shares') must be created for the amount by which the capital was reduced. Here such a reserve would compensate the reduction of capital, i.e., 28 CU, as we assume that reserves and the share premium are unrestricted. The following entry would be recorded: decrease of 'reserves' and increase of 'reserves for own shares'.

When the shares are eventually sold (or, for example, handed over to employees under a profit-sharing plan), the entry is simply reversed as long as the amounts are the same. However, the amounts are rarely identical. When the resale value is different from the purchase value, the difference is recorded, varying between countries, following either:

- Solution 1: in the income statement, as an income or a loss.
- Solution 2: in the shareholders' equity, as an increase or decrease of the share premium (this is notably the case in North America).

If the company reporting follows IFRS/IAS, IAS 32 (§ 33) applies: 'If an entity reacquires its own equity instruments, those instruments ("treasury shares") shall be deducted from equity. No gain or loss shall be recognized in profit or loss on the purchase, sale, issue or cancellation of an entity's own equity instruments. Such treasury shares may be acquired and held by the entity or by other members of the consolidated group. Consideration paid or received shall be recognized directly in equity'. In other terms, when own shares are finally resold or attributed to employees, the gain or loss on sale is recorded as an increase or decrease of equity. (IAS 32 does not mention explicitly which caption to use for the offset. In practice, share premium is often used as the balancing entry.)

It must be noted that the IASB authorizes only the above-mentioned solution 2.

2.4.4 Reporting for treasury shares

There are many ways to report the ownership of one's own shares and we have already seen one in the Core issues (real-life example Barloworld). Some examples of practice will illustrate that point.

Real-life example Club Méditerranée

(France – French GAAP – *Source*: Annual report 2004 – Leisure)

General information about the company's capital

Authorization to trade in the company's shares

The authorization given to the Executive Board to trade in the company's shares on the stock market, as provided under Articles L. 225–209 et seq. of the Commercial Code, was renewed at the Annual Shareholders' Meeting of 11 March 2004 (9th resolution) for a further period of eighteen months. Under the terms of this authorization, the number of shares purchased may not exceed 10% of the capital stock.

The authorization may be used, in the following order:

- To purchase and sell shares to stabilize the stock price by trading against the market.
- To purchase shares for allocation on exercise of stock options granted by the company or other Group entities.
- To purchase and sell shares based on market conditions.
- To purchase shares for allocation in settlement of amounts due under employee profit-sharing plans or for allocation to employee share ownership plans.
- To purchase shares to be exchanged for stock in other companies or in connection with the issue of share equivalents.
- To purchase shares in connection with the management of the company's assets and liabilities and financial position.
- To purchase shares to be held or, if appropriate, sold or transferred by any appropriate method in connection with the active management of the company's equity funds, taking into account its financing needs.

As of 3 January 2005, the company had used the 11 March 2004 authorization to purchase 264,765 shares and sell 291,269 shares. The total amount of these transactions, including taxes and other transaction costs, was €17,590.

As of 31 October 2004, a total of 257,000 shares were held in treasury. At the Annual Meeting on 16 March 2005, shareholders will be asked to approve a new authorization, based on an information memorandum to be filed with the Autorité des Marchés Financiers.

Comment: This footnote is interesting in that it explains what happened during the period and what were the safeguards placed by the Executive Board on these treasury stock transactions.

Real-life example Toray Industries

(Japan – Japanese GAAP – *Source*: Annual report 2005 – Manufacturer of synthetic fibers and textiles)

Excerpts from the consolidated balance sheet – 31 March 2005 and 2004

	2005 Millions of yen	2004 Millions of yen
Stockholders' equity		
Common stock		
Authorized: 4,000,000,000 shares		
Issued: 1,401,481,403 shares	96,937	96,937
Capital surplus	85,800	85,792
Retained earnings	270,489	245,267
Unrealized gain on securities	38,785	29,731
Foreign currency translation adjustment	(39,031)	(43,326)
	452,980	414,401
Treasury stock, at cost	(461)	(154)
Total stockholders' equity	452,519	414,247

Comment: The own shares (treasury stock) are shown as a reduction of stockholders' equity, as is required by IAS 32 and is common in a North American balance sheet.

2.5 Stock options plan ('Share options plan')

2.5.1 Definition

A stock options plan is a motivational device in which the corporation grants employees the right to acquire a specified personalized number of shares of the corporation at a predetermined invariant price or at a specified discount over a moving average of the share value and for a specified time window. These options are generally granted only after a given number of months or years of employment (the vesting period) and if the performance of either or both the employee and the business have met pre-specified levels. The implementation of such a plan is at the discretion of the management of the firm.

Employees exercise their option to buy only when the current market price is sufficiently high for the difference between the exercise price and the current market price to cover the transaction costs (often the employee must borrow funds to exercise her/his options[5]) and leave an appreciable surplus.

The shares sold to the employees can be new shares or shares acquired by the firm on the market to be re-sold to employees. International accounting standards do not make a clear distinction between these two situations and, in both cases, there is an increase in equity.

2.5.2 Accounting for stock options plan

IFRS 2 (IASB 2004) deals with accounting for stock options plan. The general principle is the following: 'When the goods or services received or acquired in a share-based payment transaction do not qualify for recognition as assets [which is the case with the service provided by employees], they shall be recognized as expenses' (§ 8). The procedure applicable to the attribution of stock options to employees is then the following:

- At the date the option is granted to employees, an option pricing model must be applied. The option's value is recorded as an increase in expenses (personnel expense) and an increase of an equity account (share premium). This entry is definitive, whether the option is exercised or not.
- When the option is exercised, one should record the sale of own shares or the issuance of new shares, in exchange of the exercise price.

For example, let us assume that in year X4, the Gershwin Corporation board grants its General Manager, Mrs Claire, an option to subscribe 1,000 shares at the exercise price of 1.80 CU per share. This option can be exercised after 1 July X5. On the date of the granting of the option, the market value of a Gershwin share is 2 CU. A valuation model estimates the value of the option thus granted to be 215 CU. The value of an option is the sum of the intrinsic value plus a speculative value. Here the intrinsic value is equal to the difference between the actual market value of the share and the exercise price: $(2 - 1.80) \times 1,000 = 200$ CU. The speculative value (here 15 CU) reflects the possibility of additional gain given the exercise date for the option is nine months to a year hence (the speculative value is based on the estimated volatility of both earnings and the share market value – i.e., a highly subjective measure, generally grounded on past statistics). When Mrs Claire exercises her option, the business will create an additional 1,000 shares. The entries required by such a transaction are shown in Figure 11.7.

2.6 Share dividend and dividend in kind

Normally, dividends are paid out in cash. However, they could also be paid out by giving assets to the shareholders (known as 'dividend in kind'). For example, the corporation may distribute third-party securities held in portfolio or may hand over some real property. Such

Figure 11.7 Accounting for stock options

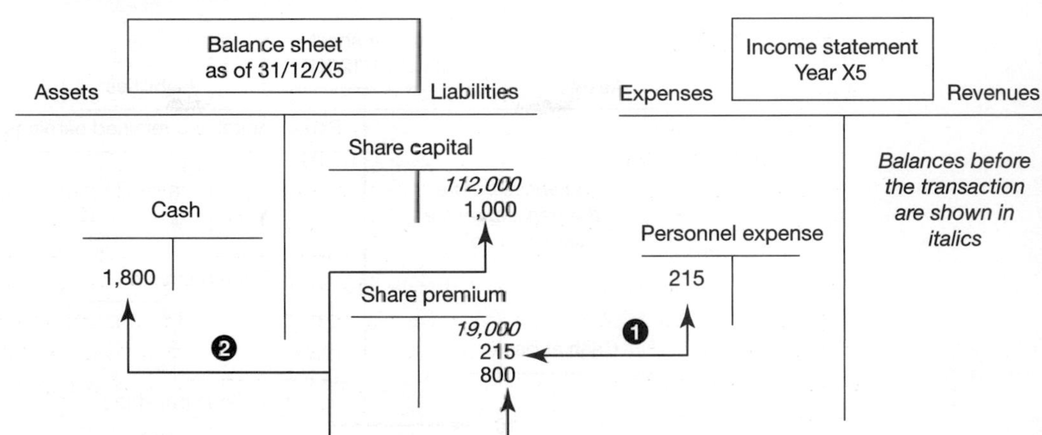

❶ Recording of the fair value of the option at the date of attribution.

❷ When the option is exercised, issuance of 1,000 shares in cash at an issuance price of 1.8 (including 1 of nominal value and 0.8 of share premium).

an approach, although perfectly conceivable, encounters significant legal issues about property rights and is, therefore, very rarely used.

More frequently corporations issue dividends by giving their own shares to their shareholders without requiring any additional contribution on their part (share dividend or stock dividend). This method is interesting to an organization because it allows the 'payment' of dividends without placing any strain on the cash situation of the firm. This is an especially attractive approach for often cash-strapped new ventures or fast growing businesses.

By-laws often allow the shareholders to elect, individually or collectively (in the general assembly), whether they prefer their dividend to be paid out in cash or in the form of additional shares.

In the calculation of the number of shares to be given as dividends, there are several valuation options and the actual choice varies from country to country. The possibilities are:

- par value;
- fair value (i.e., market value);
- par value or fair value, at the discretion of the management team;
- par value or fair value depending on the size of the dividend distribution. (In the United States the choice is essentially based on the size of the distribution relative to shareholder's equity. If it is a 'small stock distribution' fair value is to be used; if it is a large stock distribution, par value is to be used.)

When it distributes its dividends in the form of shares, the corporation has to record a capital increase and a share premium (capital surplus).

The accounting recording of the payment of a share dividend is illustrated below. MacDowell Corporation has a shareholders' equity composed of a capital of 100 shares with a par value of 1 CU plus 900 CU in retained earnings. For period X1, the annual general meeting has decided to vote a dividend of 100 CU in total and to give the choice to the individual shareholders between a payment in cash or as a share dividend. Shareholders holding a total of 10 shares prefer payment in cash while the others, holding a total of 90 shares, prefer to receive a share dividend.

The average market quote over the six weeks prior to the distribution was 15 CU per share. Figure 11.8 illustrates the recording of these share dividends.

Figure 11.8 Accounting for share dividends

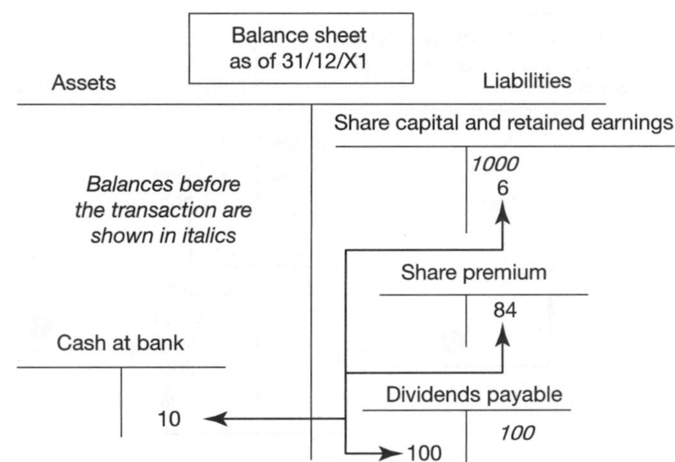

Comments

- The dividends owed to those shareholders who prefer a share dividend amounts to 90 CU. The fair value of that dividend is equivalent to 6 shares at fair market value (90 CU/15 CU per share = 6 shares).
- A share dividend is essentially similar to a share issuance by capitalization of reserves.

The practice may be different in North America (see Appendix 11.6).

2.7 Comprehensive income

In Advanced issues in Chapter 6, comprehensive income was defined. It was also stated that the comprehensive income could be detailed either directly in the income statement or in the shareholders' equity. According to SFAS 130 (FASB 1997: § 26): 'The total of "other comprehensive income" for a period shall be transferred to a component of equity that is displayed separately from retained earnings and additional paid-in capital in a balance sheet at the end of the accounting period. A descriptive title such as "accumulated other comprehensive income" could be used for that component of equity'. It is also important to highlight the non-distributable nature of the 'other comprehensive income'.

An illustration of reporting for comprehensive income is developed in Appendix 11.7.

2.8 Changes in shareholders' equity

Given the complexity of the shareholders' equity account and the many changes that can affect its composition during the year, IAS 1 (IASB 2003a) and the GAAP of many countries require (or suggest) that a table be provided that explains changes in shareholders' equity.

2.8.1 The prescriptive content of IAS 1

IAS 1 (IASB 2003a: § 96) states that: 'An entity shall present a statement of changes in equity showing on the face of the statement:

(a) Profit or loss for the period;

(b) Each item of income and expense for the period that, as required by other Standards or by Interpretations, is recognized directly in equity, and the total of these items;

(c) Total income and expense for the period (calculated as the sum of (a) and (b)), showing separately the total amounts attributable to equity holders of the parent and to minority interest; and

(d) For each component of equity, the effects of changes in accounting policies and corrections of errors recognized in accordance with IAS 8.

A statement of changes in equity that comprises only these items shall be titled a statement of recognized income and expense'.

IAS 1 (§ 97) adds that: 'An entity shall also present, either on the face of the statement of changes in equity or in the notes:

(a) The amounts of transactions with equity holders acting in their capacity as equity holders, showing separately distributions to equity holders;
(b) The balance of retained earnings (i.e. accumulated profit or loss) at the beginning of the period and at the balance sheet date, and the changes during the period; and
(c) A reconciliation between the carrying amount of each class of contributed equity and each reserve at the beginning and the end of the period, separately disclosing each change'.

2.8.2 Presentation of the changes in equity

The requirements of IAS 1 (see §§ 96–97) or of the local national regulations may be met in a number of ways. IAS 1 offers the possibility of reporting in two formats:

- A broad one, cumulating all the elements mentioned in paragraphs 96 and 97: the 'statement of changes in shareholders' equity' or 'statement of changes in equity'.
- A reduced version corresponding to the items mentioned in paragraph 96 only: the 'statement of recognized income and expense'.

Statement of changes in equity IAS 1 provides in its appendix (§ IG4) an illustration of a statement of changes in equity. We consider it to be an illustration of best practice. Table 11.3 is a simplified abstract of that example.

Table 11.3 XYZ Group – Statement of changes in equity for the year ended 31 December X2 (in thousands of CU)

	Share capital	Other reserves	Translation reserve	Retained earnings	Total
Balance at 31 December X1	x	x	(x)	x	x
Changes in accounting policy				(x)	(x)
Restated balance	x	x	(x)	x	x
Changes in equity for X2					
Gain on property revaluation		x			x
Exchange differences on translating foreign operations			(x)		(x)
Net income recognized directly in equity		x	(x)		x
Profit for the period				x	x
Total recognized income and expense for the period		x	(x)	x	x
Dividends				(x)	(x)
Issue of share capital	x				x
Balance at 31 December X2	x	x	(x)	x	x

Statement of recognized income and expense IAS 1 (§ IG4) provides an example of a statement, which presents those changes in equity that represent income and expense (see a simplified version in Table 11.4).

Table 11.4 XYZ Group – Statement of recognized income and expense for the year ended 31 December X2 (in thousands of CU)

	X2	X1
Gain/(loss) on revaluation of properties	(x)	x
Available-for-sale investments:		
Valuation gains/(losses) taken to equity	(x)	(x)
Transferred to profit or loss on sale	x	(x)
Exchange differences on translation of foreign operations	(x)	(x)
Net income recognized directly in equity	x	x
Profit for the period	x	x
Total recognized income and expense for the period	x	x
Attributable to:		
Equity holders of the parent	x	x
Minority interest	x	x
	x	x
Effect of changes in accounting policy		
Equity holders of the parent		(x)
Minority interest		(x)
		(x)

Real-life example Aluminum Corporation of China (Chalco)

(China – Hong Kong GAAP – *Source*: Annual report 2004 – Production, sales and research of alumina and primary aluminum)

The detail of the shareholders' equity (consolidated balance sheet) is reproduced below:

	2004 RMB'000	2003 RMB'000
Share capital	11,049,876	10,499,900
Reserves	8,696,143	4,649,293
Retained earnings		
Proposed final dividend	1,944,778	1,060,788
Un-appropriated retained earnings	5,465,346	2,532,360
Issued capital and reserves	27,156,143	18,742,341

continued

After the income statement and balance sheet, the Group publishes a 'Consolidated statement of changes in equity':

	Share capital	Capital reserve	Statutory surplus reserve	Statutory public welfare fund	Retained earnings	Total
	RMB'000	RMB'000	RMB'000	RMB'000	RMB'000	RMB'000
As of 1 January 2004	10,499,900	3,493,594	592,682	563,017	3,593,148	18,742,341
Issue of shares	549,976	2,750,672	–	–	–	3,300,648
Share issue expenses	–	(49,998)	–	–	–	(49,998)
Profit for the year	–	–	–	–	6,223,940	6,223,940
Transfer to						
– Capital reserve	–	9,777	–	–	(9,777)	–
– Statutory surplus reserve	–	–	685,107	–	(685,107)	–
– Statutory public welfare fund	–	–	–	651,292	(651,292)	–
Dividend paid	–	–	–	–	(1,060,788)	(1,060,788)
As of 31 December, 2004	11,049,876	6,204,045	1,277,789	1,214,309	7,410,124	27,156,143
Retained earnings represented by:						
2004 final dividend proposed					1,944,778	
Un-appropriated retained earnings					5,465,346	
Retained earnings as of 31 December 2004					7,410,124	

One can easily reconcile the beginning (18,742,341) and ending (27,156,143) equity disclosed in the statement of changes in equity with the figures reported in the consolidated balance sheet (see above).

Real-life example Hilton Group

(United Kingdom – UK GAAP – *Source*: Annual report 2004 – Leisure sector, hotels, health clubs, betting and gaming services)

We disclose below an excerpt of the consolidated balance sheet corresponding to the detail of total equity

Shareholders' equity

At 31 December	2004 £m	2003 £m
Capital and reserves		
Called up share capital		
Share premium account	158.6	158.2
Revaluation reserve	1,729.6	1,722.2
Other reserves	243.3	241.5
Profit and loss account	143.7	150.3
Equity shareholders' funds	276.0	171.5
	2,551.2	2,443.7

continued

After the primary financial statements (income statement, balance sheet, cash flow statement), Hilton Group publishes two separate documents: a 'Statement of total recognized gains and losses' and a 'Reconciliation of movements in shareholders funds'.

Statement of total recognized gains and losses For the year ended 31 December	2004 £m	2003 £m
Profit attributable to shareholders	260.8	112.0
Currency translation differences on foreign currency net investments net of taxation	(2.2)	6.5
Total recognized gains and losses for the period	258.6	118.5
Reconciliation of movements in shareholders' funds **For the year ended 31 December**	**2004** **£m**	**2003** **£m**
Opening equity shareholders' funds	2,443.7	2,465.8
Total recognized gains and losses	258.6	118.5
Dividends	(152.3)	(141.1)
New share capital subscribed	7.8	3.9
Net decrease due to shares held in ESOP trusts	(6.6)	(3.4)
Closing equity shareholders' funds	2,551.2	2,443.7

The reconciliation table begins with the opening balance of shareholders' funds and ends by the closing balance of shareholders' funds. The figures that appear as 'Total recognized gains and losses' are in fact extracted from the 'Statement of total recognized gains and losses'.

2.9 Financial statement analysis

2.9.1 Impact on financial structure

Table 11.5 summarizes the different possible key types of capital increase. It also describes their impact on the structure of the balance sheet. In order to facilitate the understanding of the right-most column, the following definitions may prove useful to the reader (the concepts are fully defined in Chapter 15):

- Working capital = Equity + Long-term liabilities − Fixed assets (also equals Current assets including cash − Current liabilities)
- Working capital need (simplified definition) = Current assets (excluding cash) − Current liabilities (excluding bank overdrafts) = Inventories + Receivables − Payables
- Cash = Cash at bank and in hand − Bank overdrafts.

2.9.2 Ratios

The share yield (earnings per share divided by market value of the share – see the definition of the earnings per share in Chapter 15) is a key ratio for analysts and investors alike in deciding whether to move their investment or not. However, many other ratios help analysts evaluate shareholders' equity.

Table 11.5 Different types of capital increases

Types of increases	Objectives	Procedure	Impact on the balance sheet	Impact on the financial structure
In cash	To obtain additional long-term financial resources without term limits in order to buttress the development potential of the firm	Issuance of new shares either at a price greater than the par value (thus creation of a 'share premium' for the difference) or Increase in the par value of the existing shares	*Increase* of current asset, and *Increase* of the capital account on the liability side	Increase in working capital, and Increase in cash
Capitalization of reserves	Reconcile the level of legal capital with the actual value of the assets and/or strengthen the capital as a gesture of responsibility towards the firm's trading partners	Distribution of shares or Increase of the par value	*Reduction* of the reserves on the liabilities side, and *Increase* of capital on the liabilities side	Financial structure unchanged
In kind	Reinforce the growth potential of the firm by adding new tangible and intangible assets that will enhance the firm's future development	New shares are valued close to their fair market value	*Increase* on the assets side (the contributed asset) and, possibly, *Increase* on the liabilities side if the contribution is not net of debt, and *Increase* of the capital	If the contribution is a fixed asset, the financial structure is not modified If the contribution is a current asset: ■ Increase in working capital ■ Increase in working capital need If the contribution includes a financial (i.e., long-term) debt the financial structure is unchanged If the contribution includes operating (i.e., short-term) or non-operating debts: ■ Increase in working capital ■ Increase in working capital need
Conversion of liabilities	Reimburse debt without impacting on cash: the creditor abandons its claim in exchange for shares	New shares are valued close to their fair market value	*Decrease* in liabilities, and *Increase* of shareholders' equity	If the canceled debt was long-term debt, the financial structure is unchanged If the canceled debt was short-term (operating or non-operating): ■ Increase in working capital ■ Increase in working capital need If the conversion is one of short-term bank credit such as overdraft: ■ Increase in working capital ■ Increase in cash
Share dividend	Reinforce the capital structure without strapping either the firm or the shareholders for cash	New shares are valued close to their fair market value	*Reduction* of the debt (dividends payables), and *Increase* of the capital	Increase in working capital Increase in working capital need

Return on equity The most common shareholders' equity ratio is undoubtedly the return on equity (ROE). The formula is as follows:

Net income/Average equity

Managers use this ratio to compare investments opportunities, hopefully from the point of view of the shareholders.

A variant, called 'return on common equity', is sometimes used when only the point of view of the common shareholders needs to be taken into account:

(Net income minus preferred dividends)/Average common equity

Economic value added This metric, designed by and proprietary to the financial consulting firm Stern Stewart, and developed in Chapter 15, addresses the concept of return on equity from a slightly different point of view by restating both the income (to reflect the long-term dynamics of the firm) and the equity to show the real investment (beyond the book value of equity) of the shareholders in the firm.

Equity ratio This ratio measures the contribution of the shareholders in providing the resources required by the firm's operations.

Shareholders' equity/Total shareholders' equity and liabilities (or total assets)

Debt/equity ratio This ratio describes the financial leverage the shareholders have obtained. This ratio has many different definitions as will be shown in the real-life examples below.

Long-term debts/Shareholders' equity

Market to book ratio Shareholders' equity defines the book value of the company. However, the amount at which equity is shown on the balance sheet is dependent on the valuation of assets and liabilities. Since (a) assets and liabilities are recorded in accounting systems at their historical cost and (b) the market value of a firm (and thus of its shares) is largely a function of its intangible assets (expertise, legitimacy, knowledge base, customer loyalty, employee loyalty, etc.), the market value of a firm is generally much greater than the book value of its equity. Even the resale value of the assets in the context of liquidation often exceeds their book value by a large amount.

The 'market to book' ratio measures the under-valuation represented by the book value of equity. The higher the ratio, the higher the intangible assets are likely to be (since they are not recorded in the balance sheet – see Chapter 8). The formula is very simple:

Market price per share/Book value per share

This ratio represents the amount investors appear to be willing to pay for each CU of a firm's net assets.

Real-life examples Table 11.6 compares three ratios as published by three industrial companies in the same country so as to minimize discrepancies that might be due to

Table 11.6 Examples of ratios based on equity

Company	Name of the ratio	Computation	2004	2003
Holmen (newsprint and magazine paper)	Return on equity (in %)	Profit/loss for the year, expressed as a percentage of the average equity calculated on the basis of quarterly data	8.4	9.7
Rottneros (production of pulp)	Return on equity after full tax (in %)	Net profit as a percentage of average yearly shareholders' equity	Neg.	5
Sandvik (engineering)	Return on shareholders' equity (in %)	Net profit for the year as a percentage of average shareholders' equity during the year	20.2	12.8
Holmen	Equity ratio (in %)	Equity plus minority interests expressed as a percentage of the balance sheet total	52.1	58.3
Rottneros	Equity/assets ratio (in %)	Shareholders' equity including minority as a percentage of balance sheet total	66	73
Sandvik	Equity ratio (in %)	Shareholder's equity and minority interests in relation to total capital	45	46
Holmen	Debt/equity ratio	Net financial debt divided by the sum of equity and minority interests	0.36	0.22
Rottneros	Debt/equity ratio (multiple)	Interest-bearing liabilities divided by shareholders' equity	0.2	0.0
Sandvik	Net debt/equity ratio (times)	Interest-bearing current and long-term debts (including provision for pensions) less liquid assets divided by the total of shareholders' equity and minority interests	0.6	0.5

differing GAAP (all data are from the companies' own 2004 annual reports). Even in the same country, here Sweden, discrepancies exist because technologies (thus assets required), markets, financing, and reporting strategies are different. This diversity implies that when ratios are being used to compare companies around the world, great care must be taken to ensure comparability. We should also note that Sandvik calls 'equity ratio' a ratio that is significantly different from the same ratio computed by the two other companies: the denominator is 'total capital' for Sandvik instead of 'total assets' for the others. A direct comparison is thus impossible.

Key points

- The two main sources of seed long-term financial resources of a firm are: (1) the entrepreneur or investors; and (2) the providers of borrowed funds.
- The wealth contributed by the entrepreneur or by investors as capital to a business can be in the form of cash contributions, contribution of tangible or intangible assets, of intellectual property, or even of labor, etc.
- Investors bring in capital to the business venture in return for a claim on a portion of the wealth potentially created by the enterprise over the years following the investment.
- Equity is 'the residual interest [of the investors] in the assets of the enterprise after deducting all its liabilities'.
- The two principal components of shareholders' equity are (share) capital and retained earnings (reserves).
- Shares or stock certificates represent the capital of incorporated firms. They are evidence of the contribution of the shareholders to the formation of capital.
- The face value of a share is called the nominal or par value. The capital is, therefore, equal to the number of shares multiplied by the par value.
- 'Ordinary' (or common) shares are distinct from 'preferred' shares. The latter carry rights different from those of common shares.
- The share premium is the difference between the issuance price and the par value.
- The profit of a period can be either distributed to the shareholders in the form of dividends or kept in the organization either as a voluntary re-investment by the shareholders as retained earnings (reserve) or as a legally required reserve for a purpose specified by the law.
- The statement of changes in shareholders' equity is an important document that details how the current year's decisions (beyond operating decisions) have affected shareholder's equity.
- Several important ratios are related to shareholders' equity: return on equity, equity ratio, debt/equity ratio, and market to book ratio.

Review (solutions are at the back of the book)

Review 11.1 Copland Company

Topic: Share issuance in cash
Related part of the chapter: Core issues

Copland has a capital of 300,000 CU, divided into 3,000 shares each with a par of 100 CU. It issues 1,000 new shares (par 100) for a price of 170 each. The legislation of the country in which Copland operates requires that the full share premium (here 70 CU per share) be paid up at the time of the new shares subscription but only requires that a minimum of 25% of the par value be paid up. The share issuance costs pertaining to this issuance (legal fees, auditors fees, printing costs, financial commissions, and sundry fees) are offset against share premium. All providers, whose bills are summed up under issuance costs for an amount of 5,000 CU, have been paid immediately by check.

Required

1. Prepare the accounting entries necessary to record this capital increase.
2. Prepare a comparison of the relevant excerpts of the balance sheet before and after the issuance of new shares.

Review 11.2 Menotti Company

Topic: Profit appropriation
Related part of the chapter: Core issues

As of 1 January X1, Menotti's capital comprised 4,000 shares of 100 CU par. These shares are divided in two classes: 1,000 class-A shares and 3,000 class-B shares. Class-A shares enjoy a 5% of par preference dividend over and above the ordinary dividends.

Before appropriation of the annual earnings, the books show the following year-end data (in CU).

Capital	400,000
Legal reserve	39,000
Regulated reserves	8,000
Losses brought forward	−5,000
Net income after tax (year ending 31/12/X0)	40,000

Tax regulations require that the regulated reserve be incremented by 2,000 CU in X1.

The by-laws contain the following stipulations:

- Each year the legal reserve must be incremented by an amount of 5% of the net income for the year net of any loss carry-forward (if the net is positive) as long as the legal reserve is less than 10% of the par capital.
- Class-A shares must receive a preference dividend of 5% of their par value.
- All A and B shares are equally entitled to the payment of ordinary dividends.

The board of directors proposes that: (a) an optional reserve be created for an amount of 10,000 CU; and (b) that an ordinary dividend of 4 CU per share be paid out. The general assembly approves these propositions.

The balance of income after appropriation will be carried forward.

Required

1. Prepare a table detailing the profit appropriation calculations (including the per share dividend for each class of shares).
2. Prepare the appropriation accounting entries.
3. Prepare a table detailing the shareholders' equity and liabilities before and after appropriation.

Assignments

Assignment 11.1
Multiple-choice questions

Related part of the chapter: Core issues

Select the right answer (only one possible answer, unless otherwise mentioned).

1. The sale by a shareholder of shares of a company to another shareholder should be recorded by the company
   (a) True
   (b) False
2. A company received cash subscriptions for 5,000 shares of 20 CU nominal (par) value at 100 CU per share. A downpayment of 50% of the issuance price is required. The remainder of the purchase price is to be paid the following year. At the time that the share is subscribed, share capital should be credited for

(a) 500,000
(b) 250,000
(c) 100,000
(d) 50,000
(e) 400,000
(f) 200,000
(g) None of these

3. Dividends cannot be distributed if net income is not greater than zero

(a) True
(b) False

4. The difference between the price paid for a company's common share and the par value of each share can be called (several possible answers)

(a) Capital surplus
(b) Share premium
(c) Additional paid-in capital
(d) Paid-in capital
(e) Additional contributed capital
(f) Ordinary share capital
(g) Capital in excess of par value
(h) Premium fund
(i) All of these
(j) None of these

5. A company's board has authorized 20,000 shares and 10,000 shares were issued and are outstanding. On April X2, the company declared a 2 CU per share ordinary dividend. Which of the following journal entries would be necessary at the time of the declaration?

		Dr	Cr
(a)	Decrease in Net income (or retained earnings)	20,000	
	Decrease in Cash		20,000
(b)	Decrease in Net income (or retained earnings)	40,000	
	Increase in Dividend payable		40,000
(c)	Decrease in Net income (or retained earnings)	40,000	
	Decrease in Cash		40,000
(d)	Decrease in Net income (or retained earnings)	20,000	
	Increase in Dividend payable		20,000
(e)	Decrease in Dividend payable	40,000	
	Increase in Net income (or retained earnings)		40,000
(f)	Decrease in Dividend payable	20,000	
	Increase in Net income (or retained earnings)		20,000
(g)	None of these		

6. A company has the following shareholders' equity section:

Ordinary shares: par = 2 CU; 250,000 shares authorized; 100,000 shares issued and outstanding	200,000
Share premium	30,000
Reserves	50,000
Net income	20,000
Shareholders' equity	300,000

The market price per share is 15 CU. What is the book value per share?

(a) 2
(b) 1.2
(c) 3
(d) 0.8
(e) 15
(f) 2.3
(g) 0.92
(h) None of these

7. In all types of limited liability companies, it is possible to defer the payment of one part of the subscribed capital

(a) True
(b) False

8. The number of authorized shares is greater than the amount of issued shares which might be greater than the amount of outstanding shares

(a) True
(b) False

9. A share may grant a voting right greater than one but never lower than one

(a) True
(b) False

10. The main objective of the legal reserve is to protect the shareholders of the company

(a) True
(b) False

Assignment 11.2
Ives Company

Topic: Impact on shareholders' equity
Related part of the chapter: Core/Advanced issues

Transactions related to Ives Company's shareholders' equity (far left column) are listed in the following table. For each line you are provided with three choices of impact of the transaction on the total of shareholders' equity: increase, decrease, or no impact.

Required

Indicate by a checkmark the impact of each transaction.

	Impact on shareholders' equity		
	Increase	Decrease	No impact
Core Issues			
Issuance of ordinary shares in cash at par value			
Issuance of preference shares in cash at par value			
Declaration of the year's cash dividend			
Payment of the above mentioned cash dividend			
Issuance of ordinary shares in cash at a price greater than par value			
Issuance of preference shares in cash at a price greater that nominal value			
Conversion of preference shares to ordinary shares			
Advanced Issues			
Issuance of share dividends			
Issuance of ordinary shares at par (nominal) value by capitalization of reserves (retained earnings)			
Issuance of ordinary shares by conversion of bonds for a price greater than nominal value			
Issuance of shares in kind for a price greater than nominal value			
Repurchase and retirement of shares by the company			
Purchase of treasury shares (own shares)			

Assignment 11.3
Bernstein Company

Topic: Share issuance in cash
Related part of the chapter: Core issues

Bernstein Company is a limited liability company. The annual general assembly, held on 6 May X1, voted to issue an additional 2,500 shares (each with a par of 550 CU). The public offering price is set at 700 CU. The capital will be called for the full amount of the legal minimum. Bank X received the subscriptions from 7 to 30 May. On 30 May, the bank issued a certificate stating that the sale was complete and all funds had been collected.

Required

Under both of the following hypotheses:

1. The legal minimum that must be called is half of the issuance price
2. The legal minimum that must be called is half the par value and the entire share premium

prepare the appropriate entries, in any one of the following formats:

- balance sheet entries
- journal entries
- T-accounts entries.

Assignment 11.4
Gilbert Company

Topic: Profit appropriation
Related part of the chapter: Core issues

Gilbert Company was created in early X1. Its original capital was 2,500 shares with a par value of 100 CU. The composition of the capital as of 31 December X9 is described in article 7 of the amended by-laws (see exhibit).

At the end of X9 the shareholders' equity account before appropriation stands as shown in the table.

Share capital	3,780,000
Share premium	7,560,000
Legal reserve	370,000
Optional reserve	2,000,000
Profit/loss brought forward	−100,000
Net income for X9	1,000,000
Total	14,610,000

The board of directors has approved a motion in which, in addition to the appropriation of the earnings from X9, there will be a second dividend, which will be paid to shares of all classes. This second dividend will be the maximum legally possible without, however, exceeding 10 CU per share. The remaining balance, if there is any, will be transferred to the optional reserve account.

The prime rate mentioned in the by-laws and applicable to the year X9 is 6% per annum.

The amount of the legal reserve may be limited to 10% of the share capital.

Required

1. Prepare a suggested appropriation of the X9 net income.
2. Prepare the appropriate accounting entries that your suggested appropriation requires.
3. Prepare a table describing the shareholders' equity after appropriation.

Exhibit

Article 7 – **Share capital**

The capital of Gilbert is 3,780,000 (three million seven hundred eighty thousand) CU.

The capital is composed of 37,800 (thirty seven thousand eight hundred) fully subscribed shares, each with a par of 100 (one hundred) CU.

The shares are partitioned in two classes:

- 27,000 A Shares, numbered 1–27,000, and
- 10,800 B Shares, numbered 27,001–37,800.

The B shares are preference shares with a preference dividend for the fiscal years X9 to X15 inclusive. This preference dividend will be calculated as a fixed remuneration on the basis of the prime rate minus 1% for fiscal year X9, prime rate plus 2% for fiscal year X10, and prime rate plus 5% for years X11 to X15.

The fixed remuneration rate will be applied to the full subscription price (including the capital surplus), i.e., 800 CU per share of 100 CU. All holders of B shares will receive this dividend. The dividend will be payable in keeping with the conditions defined by law.

(...)

Assignment 11.5
Gerry Weber*

Topic: Reporting for profit appropriation
Related part of the chapter: Core issues

Gerry Weber International AG is a German group active in the design, manufacture and retail of woman clothing. The following data concerning the parent company were excerpted from the 2004 annual report.

Balance sheet (excerpts)	31.10.2004 €	31.10.2003 €
Capital stock		
Subscribed capital	23,443,200.00	23,443,200.00
Capital reserve	33,668,025.21	33,668,025.21
Revenue reserves		
1. Reserve for own shares	540,000.00	0.00
2. Other revenue reserves	32,460,000.00	28,000,000.00
Net profit for the year	10,045,034.22	9,340,758.09
	100,156,259.43	94,451,983.30
Income statement (excerpts)	**2003/2004 €**	**2002/2003 €**
Profit for the year	13,909,396.13	6,000,402.16
Profit carried forward	1,135,638.09	3,340,355.93
Allocation to revenue reserves	5,000,000.00	0.00
Net profit for the year	10,045,034.22	9,340,758.09

Required

1. Explain the computation of the 'net profit for the year' in the income statement.
2. What does this net profit for the year represent? Is the balance sheet presented before or after profit appropriation?
3. On 28 June 2004, Gerry Weber International AG acquired 75,000 of its own shares at a price of €7.20 per share. How can you use this information in relation to the 'reserve for own shares'?
4. Explain the change in the 'other revenue reserves'. Relate this change to the 'Allocation to revenue reserves' disclosed in the income statement.

5. From the data excerpted from the balance sheet and income statement provided above, find the amount of the dividends distributed in 2004 with regard to 2003.
6. The annual report indicates that the dividends distributed in 2004 relating to the 2003 profit amounted to €0.35 per share. It also states that the share capital includes 23,443,200 shares. Double-check the amount of dividends paid in 2004 as found in question 5.

Assignment 11.6
Holmen*

Topic: Statement of changes in equity
Related part of the chapter: Advanced issues

Holmen (formerly MoDo), is a Swedish group manufacturing and selling newsprint and magazine paper, as well as paperboard. Its financial statements are prepared in accordance with Swedish GAAP. The 2004 financial statements contain the following information on 'equity' for the year ended 31 December 2004 (*source*: Annual report 2004).

Group balance sheet (excerpts)
(MSEK = millions of Swedish krona)

At 31 December; MSEK	2004	2003
Equity		
Restricted equity		
Share capital	4,238	3,999
Restricted reserves	4,349	4,249
Non-restricted equity		
Non-restricted reserves	3,939	5,555
Profit for the year	1,211	1,451
	13,737	15,254

Conversion and subscription of shares have taken place in 2004 with an impact of 239 MSEK on share capital and 235 MSEK on restricted reserves. Profit for the year 2003 has been appropriated and transferred to non-restricted reserves. At the same time, dividends taken from these non-restricted reserves have been distributed: 800 MSEK (ordinary dividends) and 2,399 MSEK (extra dividends). Some currency differences affect negatively the restricted reserves (3 MSEK). Finally, an accounting transfer of 132 MSEK has occurred from restricted reserves to non-restricted reserves.

Required

Prepare the statement of changes in shareholders' equity for the year 2004 using the format recommended in IAS 1 (see the example of Aluminum Corporation of China in Advanced issues earlier in this chapter).

Assignment 11.7
Nokia*

Topic: Ratios based on equity
Related part of the chapter: Advanced issues

Nokia (Finland) is among the leaders in the telecommunication industry, with emphasis on cellular phones and other wireless solutions. The consolidated financial statements are prepared in accordance with International Financial Reporting Standards. We disclose below the consolidated balance sheets at 31 December 2003 and 2004 (*source*: Annual report 2004) as well as some additional information (2003 and 2004).

Consolidated balance sheet (Assets)

As of December 31	2004 € millions	2003 € millions
ASSETS		
Fixed assets and other non-current assets		
Capitalized development costs	278	537
Goodwill	90	186
Other intangible assets	209	185
Property, plant, and equipment	1,534	1,566
Investments in associated companies	200	76
Available-for-sale investments	169	121
Deferred tax assets	623	743
Long-term loans receivable	–	354
Other non-current assets	58	69
	3,161	3,837
Current assets		
Inventories	1,305	1,169
Accounts receivable, net of allowances for doubtful accounts (2004: €361 million, 2003: €367 million)	4,382	5,231
Prepaid expenses and accrued income	1,429	1,106
Other financial assets	595	465
Available-for-sale investments	255	816
Available-for-sale investments, liquid assets	9,085	8,512
Available-for-sale investments, cash equivalents	1,367	1,639
Bank and cash	1,090	1,145
	19,508	20,083
Total assets	22,669	23,920

Consolidated balance sheet (Shareholders' equity and liabilities)

As of December 31	2004 € millions	2003 € millions
SHAREHOLDERS' EQUITY AND LIABILITIES		
Shareholders' equity		
Share capital	280	288
Share issue premium	2,272	2,272
Treasury shares, at cost	−2,022	−1,373
Translation differences	−126	−85
Fair value and other reserves	69	93
Retained earnings	13,765	13,953
	14,238	15,148
Minority interests	168	164
Long-term liabilities		
Long-term interest-bearing liabilities	19	20
Deferred tax liabilities	179	241
Other long-term liabilities	96	67
	294	328
Current liabilities		
Short-term borrowings	215	387
Current portion of long-term debt	–	84
Accounts payable	2,669	2,919
Accrued expenses	2,606	2,468
Provisions	2,479	2,422
	7,969	8,280
Total shareholders' equity and liabilities	22,669	23,920

Additional information

Additional information	2004 € millions	2003 € millions
Net profit (income statement)	3,207	3,592
Advance payments from other companies (notes)	133	4

In addition the annual report 2003 mentions that the amount of shareholders' equity on 31 December 2002 was equal to 14,281 millions euros.

Required

Compute the three following ratios based on equity, as defined by the company in its annual report:

1. Return on shareholders' equity (%): Net profit/average shareholders' equity during the year.
2. Equity ratio (%): (Shareholders' equity plus minority shareholders' interests)/(Total assets minus advance payments received).
3. Net debt to equity (gearing ratio) (%): (Long-term interest-bearing liabilities [including the current portion thereof] plus short-term borrowings minus cash and other liquid assets)/(Shareholders' equity plus minority shareholders' interests).
4. Comment on the evolution of these ratios.

References

FASB (1997) Statement of Financial Accounting Standards No. 130: Reporting Comprehensive Income, Norwalk, CT.

IASB (1989) Framework for the Preparation and Presentation of Financial Statements, London.

IASB (2003a) International Accounting Standard No. 1: Presentation of Financial Statements, London.

IASB (2003b) International Accounting Standard No. 32: Financial Instruments: Presentation and Disclosure, London.

IASB (2004) International Financial Reporting Standard No. 2: Share-based Payment, London.

Further reading

Dhaliwal, D., Subramanyam, K R., and Trezevant, R. (1999) Is comprehensive income superior to net income as a measure of firm performance? *Journal of Accounting & Economics*, 26(1–3), 43–67.

Maines, L. A., and McDaniel, L. S. (2000) Effects of comprehensive-income characteristics on nonprofessional investors' judgments: The role of financial-statement presentation format, *The Accounting Review*, 75(2), 179–207.

Additional material on the website

Go to http://www.thomsonlearning.co.uk/stolowylebas2 for further information.

The following appendices to this chapter are available on the dedicated website:

Appendix 11.1: Different categories of reserves
Appendix 11.2: Differences in the meaning of retained earnings
Appendix 11.3: Unrestricted and restricted reserves
Appendix 11.4: Share (stock) split
Appendix 11.5: Reduction of the share capital due to accumulated losses
Appendix 11.6: Share dividends in North America
Appendix 11.7: Reporting comprehensive income

Notes

1. A *cumulative* dividend means that if there are not enough earnings to pay out the guaranteed dividend during one period, the dividends in arrears (i.e., that were not paid) will be carried over to the next period and paid in priority before any other dividend can be paid out.
2. The date of record is a cut-off: investors who acquired shares beyond this date do not receive dividends emanating from earnings relating to the period(s) during which they were not actually shareholders.
3. This topic has been introduced in Chapter 2.
4. The concept of "stock split" (or 'share split') is developed in Appendix 11.4.
5. Borrowing the funds, exercising the option, and reselling all or enough shares to reimburse the loan in full may all be done in a 24- to 48-hour window.

C12

Chapter 12
Liabilities and provisions

Learning objectives

After studying this chapter, you will understand:

- How to define a liability.
- How liabilities are usually classified and reported in the balance sheet.
- How to record current and non-current liabilities.
- How to distinguish between liabilities, accrued liabilities, provisions, and contingent liabilities.
- How to record bonds issue.
- That the distinction between finance and operating leases is important.
- How to record leased assets.
- How to report leased assets.
- How to record employee benefits.
- How to analyze liabilities.

Liabilities (in a broad sense) are one of the major components of the balance sheet. They include:

- Liabilities (in a strict sense), i.e., debts with a defined face amount and a specified timing for interest payments and reimbursement of the principal.
- Provisions: liabilities of uncertain timing or amount.

In the rest of this chapter we will apply this distinction: liabilities (in a strict sense) and provisions.

Liabilities represent, beside shareholders' equity, the other source of funding for any business (through either direct contribution of cash, such as in the case of a loan, or postponement of cash outlays, such as in the case of suppliers' credit). A liability is the result of a business' past transactions that recognizes an obligation to transfer, in the future and for the benefit of 'liability holders' (for example, lenders), some of the business' resources such as assets – and particularly cash – or provide services.

The liability funds providers can be persons or organizations whose main activity is to do so (such as bond holders – private or institutional – or financial institutions such as banks or insurance firms) or business 'partners' such as customers (who prepaid for services, as would be the case, for example, of a subscription to a magazine), suppliers (accounts payable), tax or para-fiscal authorities (such as a social security authority, for example), or even salaried employees (who get paid – or receive a bonus – after they provided the work and thus are owed their salary or bonus until payday and thus provide some cash float to the business). The same issues that applied to assets apply to liabilities. They are issues of definition (what constitutes a liability), recognition (when to recognize the obligation), valuation (what is the amount of the obligation), and classification in reporting.

The principles of liabilities reporting, as well as the handling of provisions and equivalent, will be addressed in the Core issues section, while a certain number of special issues including those created by bonds and 'quasi-liabilities' like leases will be dealt with in the Advanced issues section.

1 Core issues

A liability reflects an obligation to pay or deliver in the future. However, the definitions of what an obligation is and how definitive it is or to how much it amounts are difficult points that the IASB has attempted to clarify. Liabilities or obligations are generally divided between current and non-current. The weight of these obligations in the financing of a business, as well as the mix of current and non-current, varies from business to business and between industrial or service sectors.

1.1 Definitions

International Accounting Standard 37 (IASB 1998: § 10) defines a liability as a 'present obligation of the entity arising from past events, the settlement of which is expected to result in an outflow from the entity of resources embodying economic benefits'. In this definition, several concepts are important. Each will be reviewed in turn.

1.1.1 Present obligation

The IASB Framework (IASB 1989: § 60) specifies that an 'essential characteristic of a liability is that the entity has a present obligation'. The concept of obligation is then defined as: 'A duty or responsibility to act or perform in a certain way. Obligations may be legally enforceable as a consequence of a binding contract or statutory requirement. This is normally the case, for example, with amounts payable for goods and services received. Obligations also arise, however, from normal business practice, custom and a desire to maintain good business relations or act in an equitable manner. If, for example, an entity decides as a matter of policy to rectify faults in its products even when these become apparent after the warranty period has expired, the amounts that are expected to be expensed in respect to goods already sold are liabilities'.

1.1.2 Past events

'Liabilities result from past transactions or other past events. Thus, for example, the acquisition of goods and the use of services give rise to trade payables (unless paid for in advance or on delivery) and the receipt of a bank loan results in an obligation to repay the loan. An entity may also recognize future rebates based on [accumulated] annual purchases by customers (*ex post* quantity discount) as liabilities; in this case, the sale of the goods in the past was the transaction that gave rise to the liability' (IASB 1989: § 63).

1.1.3 Settlement of the obligation

'The settlement of a present obligation usually involves the entity giving up resources embodying economic benefits in order to satisfy the claim of the other party'. This settlement 'may occur in a number of ways, for example, by: (a) Payment of cash; (b) Transfer of other assets; (c) Provision of services; (d) Replacement of that obligation with another obligation; or (e) Conversion of the obligation to equity [see Chapter 11]. An obligation may also be extinguished by other means, such as a creditor waiving or forfeiting its rights' (IASB 1989: § 62).

1.2 The current/non-current distinction

As seen in Chapter 3, IAS 1 (IASB 2003a: § 51) states: 'an entity shall present (...) current and non-current liabilities (...) except when a presentation based on liquidity provides information that is reliable and is more relevant. When that exception applies, all assets and liabilities shall be presented broadly in order of liquidity'. In practice, businesses are relatively free to choose their format for reporting liabilities as separate classifications on the balance sheet. Alternative acceptable classifications to the current/non-current classification include order of maturity [called 'liquidity' in IAS 1] (short term versus long term) and distinguishing interest-bearing liabilities from non-interest-bearing ones (and possibly ranking liabilities by order of maturity within each category). Reporting of liabilities is aimed at informing investors, partners, and analysts. Any classification is a choice reflecting an emphasis on a given focus. For example, the distinction financial/operating (❶ in Figure 12.1) emphasizes the operating cycle, while the distinction short term/long term (❷ in Figure 12.1) refers to a preoccupation with solvency.

IAS 1 (IASB 2003) specifies (§ 60) that: 'a liability shall be classified as current when it satisfies any of the following criteria:

(a) It is expected to be settled in the entity's normal operating cycle;
(b) It is held primarily for the purpose of being traded;
(c) It is due to be settled within twelve months after the balance sheet date; or
(d) The entity does not have an unconditional right to defer settlement of the liability for at least twelve months after the balance sheet date.

All other liabilities shall be classified as non-current'.

IAS 1 does not provide a definition of the presentation 'by liquidity' described as an exception in § 51. It simply mentions that this presentation could be used 'for some entities, such as financial institutions (...) because the entity does not supply goods or services within a clearly identifiable operating cycle' (§ 54). Consequently, we will not explore the 'by liquidity' classification and will concentrate on the common rule, the 'current/non-current' distinction.

If we concentrate on the four alternative definitions provided in § 60 of IAS 1, two main alternative criteria emerge:

- The realization/settlement in the operating cycle: we call this classification 'by nature' (financial liabilities versus operating liabilities) (point (a) in § 60); or
- The realization/settlement within 12 months after the balance sheet date: we call this second classification 'by term' (short term versus long term) (point (b) in § 60).

Figure 12.1 summarizes the two classifications of liabilities. It shows that the expressions 'current' and 'non-current' are used to refer either to the operating/financial classification or to the short term/long term distinction. This makes the understanding of the liabilities side of the balance sheet more difficult and it is necessary to study the detail of the captions to know which classification is actually used behind the terms 'current' and 'non-current' (this topic was covered in detail in Chapter 3).

The concept of 'operating cycle' was introduced in Chapter 3. 'Some current liabilities, such as trade payables and accruals for employee costs and other operating costs, form part of the working capital used in the normal operating cycle of the business. Such operating items are classified as current liabilities even if they are due to be settled after more than twelve months from the balance sheet date' (IASB 2003a: § 61). This paragraph is rather ambiguous. It should be understood that liabilities such as trade payables can be classified as 'current' (in the sense of IAS 1), i.e., 'operating', with our definition, even if they are long term. This rule applies if the entity has decided to adopt the 'operating/financial' classification. Otherwise, a long-term trade payable should remain in long-term liabilities, if this classification 'by term' is used.

Figure 12.1 Classification of liabilities

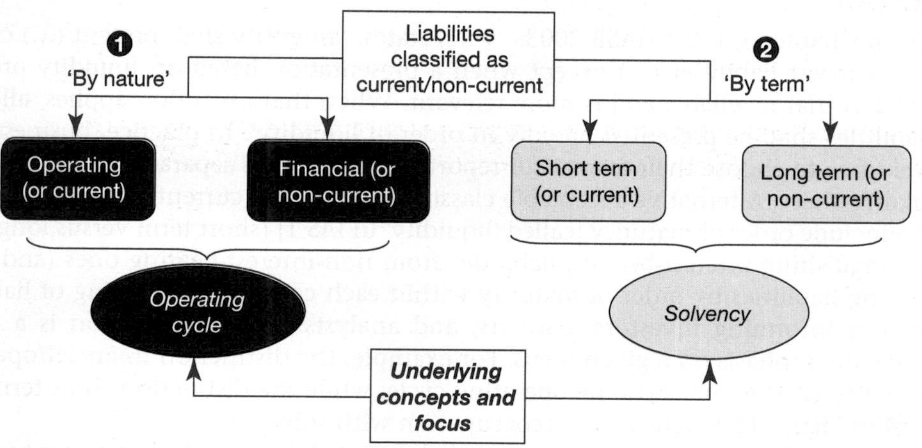

Real-life example Sandvik

(Sweden – Swedish GAAP – *Source*: Annual report 2004 – Engineering in tooling and materials technology)

Consolidated balance sheet (excerpts)

Amounts in Swedish Krona (SEK) millions	2004	2003
Shareholders' equity and liabilities		
Total shareholders' equity	21,856	21,440
Minority interests in shareholders' equity	959	846
Provisions	7,285	7,544
	30,100	29,860
Long-term interest-bearing liabilities	1,722	2,373
Loans from financial institutions	–	1,022
Convertible debenture loans	4,344	3,909
Other liabilities	6,066	7,304
Current interest-bearing liabilities		
Loans from financial institutions	4,956	3,001
Other liabilities	170	136
	5,126	3,137
Non-interest-bearing liabilities		
Advance payments from customers	583	330
Accounts payable	3,731	3,002
Bills payable	60	60
Due to associated companies	57	30
Income tax liabilities	749	363
Other liabilities	984	1,003
Accrued expenses and deferred income	3,775	3,338
	9,939	8,126
Total shareholders' equity and liabilities	51,231	48,397

Comment: This excerpt of the Sandvik balance sheet illustrates a presentation of liabilities first according to their interest-bearing and non-interest-bearing nature, and second, within the first category by range of maturity date (long term versus short term). We can note that Sandvik calls 'current' its short-term liabilities. This presentation is equivalent to an operating (i.e., non-interest-bearing)/financial (i.e., interest-bearing) classification.

Real-life example Sony Corporation

(Japan – Japanese/US GAAP – *Source*: Annual report 2005 – Electronics, games, music, motion pictures)

Consolidated balance sheet (excerpts)

	Yen in millions	
	2004	2005
Liabilities		
Current liabilities		
Short-term borrowings	91,260	63,396
Current portion of long-term debt	383,757	166,870
Notes and accounts payable, trade	778,773	806,044
Accounts payable, other and accrued expenses	812,175	746,466
Accrued income and other taxes	57,913	55,651
Deposits from customers in the banking business	378,851	546,718
Other	479,486	424,223
Total current liabilities	2,982,215	2,809,368
Long-term liabilities		
Long-term debt	777,649	678,992
Accrued pension and severance costs	368,382	352,402
Deferred income taxes	96,193	72,227
Future insurance policy benefits and other	2,178,626	2,464,295
Other	286,737	227,631
Total long-term liabilities	3,707,587	3,795,547

Comment: This excerpt of the balance sheet of this company illustrates the classification presenting liabilities in a decreasing order of maturity (short term [called here 'current'] versus long term).

Concerning disclosure, IAS 1 (§ 52) adds that 'whichever method of presentation is adopted, for each asset and liability line item that combines amounts expected to be recovered or settled (a) not more than twelve months after the balance sheet date and (b) more than twelve months after the balance sheet date, an entity shall disclose the amount expected to be recovered or settled after more than twelve months'. In practice, this paragraph means that if the operating/financial distinction is adopted, some liabilities might mix short-term and long-term portions. In this case, the long-term part should be disclosed explicitly in the notes.

1.3 Relative weight of liabilities in the balance sheet

Between businesses, countries, and even between firms in the same economic sector, liabilities (and provisions) represent different weights in the balance sheet. Such diversity is illustrated in Table 12.1 based on the 2004 annual reports of a non-statistically significant sample of companies.

When looking at a single economic sector, it is interesting to notice that not all business entities have similar approaches to trade indebtedness (short-term liabilities), even if they operate essentially in similar markets, and often with the same suppliers. Table 12.2 illustrates the percentage trade creditors represent out of retail inventory in 11, essentially UK-based, supermarkets or drugstore chains (excerpted from the *Financial Times*, 7 December 2005, page 13).

From Table 12.2 it is clear that the profitability of the various chains will be very different because they neither use trade credit in the same way nor manage to have the same inventory turnover (see Chapter 9).

The recourse to liabilities as a source of funding for a business is a very strategic decision. It is therefore essential for the users of financial information to be well informed about what the situation of the firm is.

1.4 Non-current (long-term or financial) liabilities

Figure 12.2 illustrates the fact that businesses have both non-current (long-term or financial liabilities – depending on the presentation adopted) and current liabilities (short-term or operating). The operating cycle (the cash pump introduced in Chapter 1) requires that the entity's financial needs be met not only by short-term (or current or operating) liabilities but also by long-term resources. If the current liabilities were to dry up (for example, if the suppliers were to refuse any trade credit), the long-term resources offer a safe financing, giving the business the opportunity to continue operating its cash pump and thus have a chance to 'get back on its feet'.

A business' financing needs come essentially from a combination of three factors:

- **Growth**: In order to grow, a business must invest in both long-term fixed assets (tangible or intangible) and in operating assets.
- **The operating cycle**: Inventories, receivables, and payables will generally grow with the expansion of the business activity unless the speed (turnover) of the operating cycle can be increased faster than the rate expansion (which is a highly improbable occurrence). Because the need for operating assets is recurrent, a large part of the growth in these items should be financed through long-term (permanent or semi-permanent) funds.
- **Temporary imbalances in the equilibrium** between the various components of the operating cycle (for example, due to a strong seasonality factor). Although such imbalances are generally short lived and self-correcting, they tend to reoccur on a regular basis and often require long-term funding as a way of avoiding the transaction costs that would be incurred in securing appropriate short-term funding each time the problem occurs.

The long-term financing need (Figure 12.2) is equal to: Fixed assets + Current assets − Current liabilities. It is satisfied (or covered) by two sources of funds:

- shareholders' equity (see Chapter 11);
- long-term (or financial) liabilities (developed later).

The relative interest of funding through shareholders' equity or long-term liabilities is an issue constantly debated in all businesses. The leverage effect[1] it creates is generally a

Table 12.1 Weight of liabilities in the balance sheet

Company (country – activity)	Currency	Types of liabilities	Liabilities	Total equity and liabilities	% of total equity and liabilities
Easynet (UK – Internet provider)	£000	Creditors: amounts falling due within one year	76,277		43.7
		Creditor: amounts falling due after more than one year	115,004		66.0
		Provisions for liabilities and charges	14,607		8.4
		Total	205,888	174,370	**118.1**
Sony (Japan – Music)	¥m	Current liabilities	2,809,368		29.6
		Long-term liabilities	3,795,547		40.0
		Total	6,604,915	9,499,100	**69.5**
Iberia (Spain – Airline)	€000	Deferred revenue	25,705		0.5
		Provisions for contingencies and expenses	1,241,921		25.6
		Long-term debt	414,066		8.5
		Current liabilities	1,519,818		31.3
		Total	3,201,510	4,853,597	**66.0**
Morton's Restaurant (USA – Restaurants)	$000	Current liabilities	38,192		14.6
		Senior secured notes	91,717		35.0
		Obligations to financial institutions, less current maturities	6,636		2.5
		Deferred income taxes	23,004		8.8
		Other liabilities	7,546		2.9
		Total	167,095	26,436	**63.2**
Mittal Steel (Netherlands – Steel)	$m	Current liabilities	6,230		32.5
		Long-term debt	1,639		8.6
		Deferred tax liabilities	955		5.0
		Deferred employee benefits	1,931		10.1
		Other long-term obligations	809		4.2
		Total	11,564	19,153	**60.4**
Elkem (Norway – Metals and materials production)	NOK m	Provisions	1,674		8.8
		Interest-bearing long-term debt	4,772		25.2
		Current liabilities	4,725		24.9
		Total	11,171	18,951	**58.9**
Sinopec (China – Oil and chemistry)	RMB m	Current liabilities	143,910		31.3
		Long-term liabilities	98,407		21.4
		Deferred tax liabilities	198		0.0
		Total	242,515	460,081	**52.7**
Fielmann (Germany – Glasses)	€000	Other liable capital	128		0.0
		Accruals	45,623		10.2
		Liabilities	64,417		14.4
		Deferred income	355		0.1
		Total	110,523	446,660	**24.7**
Mountain Province Diamonds (Canada – Mining)	C$	Current liabilities	94,976		0.3
		Total	94,976	36,038,157	**0.3**

Table 12.2 Relative weight of trade creditors as a percentage of retail inventories

	2000	2001	2002	2003	2004
Wm Morrison	288	301	362	343	264
J Sainsbury	167	194	187	165	255
Tesco	189	201	196	203	216
Tesco UK	200	202	199	219	n/a
Asda (Wal-Mart UK)	163	196	209	262	206
Wal-Mart Group	71	69	69	72.5	74
Alliance Unichem	138	148	149	159	163
John Lewis Partnership	89.5	95.5	88	72.5	88.5
Waitrose	n/a	169	153	128	150
Marks and Spencer	44	61.5	55.5	53	57.5
Boots	56	57	59	58.5	51

Figure 12.2 Financing of a business is met by both short-term and long-term resources

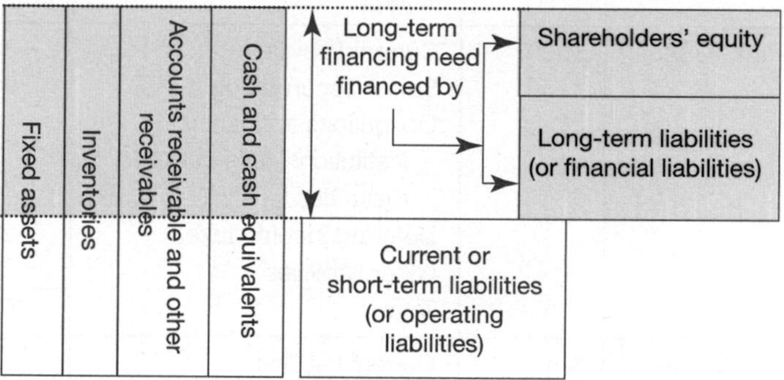

major topic in corporate finance or financial statement analysis textbooks[2]. Table 12.3 summarizes some of the key issues looked at when choosing whether to go the equity or the liability route.

Long-term liabilities are generally divided between two categories:

- **Bank loans or borrowings**: Each loan represents a lump sum liability, generally from a single source.
- **Bonds**: In this case, the debt is broken up in small (generally equal) increments represented by certificates. The holder of a debt certificate (bond) can trade it on a financial market. Each certificate has a face value (or par value), a specific coupon rate (interest rate) that indicates the periodic interest paid to the bond bearer, and a mention of the date by which the principal must be repaid (and under what condition it will be repaid – such as either at the end of the specified life of the bond, or mentioning the possibility of an early retirement of the debt at the initiative of the borrower).

The specificities of accounting for bonds will be dealt with in the Advanced issues section of this chapter.

Bank loans or borrowings can take on many different forms depending on whether or not they are secured. For example, a mortgage liability is a debt secured by real property.

Table 12.3 Comparative characteristics of liabi ities and shareholders' equity

	Liabilities	Shareholders' equity
Repayment term	Repayment of principal is required	No repayment required
Flexibility	Highly flexible (duration, amount, ease of obtaining additional funds, possibility to refinance, etc.)	Not flexible and high transaction costs. Decision is not reversible
Cost of funds	Interest must be paid regardless of the economic outcome of the use of the funds. Rates are market based	No direct required remuneration. Dividends paid only if there is enough net income or accumulated previously undistributed income. Part of the remuneration may come from a market appreciation of the shares. Given shareholders are taking risks with their investment, their implicit remuneration is generally expected to be much higher than the cost of borrowed funds
Deductibility of the cost of funds	Interest expense is generally tax-deductible	Regular dividends are never tax-deductible.
Rights of the funds providers	Debt-holders generally have no influence or control over the decisions or the management of the firm New debt holders affect previous debt holders only because the interest expense of the new liability may overburden the earnings and increase the likelihood of bankruptcy	Shareholders generally have influence and control over decisions and management Additional shareholders may cause a dilution of the power of current shareholders
Use of funds	Funds obtained and specific projects may be linked explicitly (for example, through specific securing or guarantee agreements such as mortgages)	Funds obtained cannot be targeted to a specific project

1.5 Accounting for current liabilities

Current liabilities are liabilities that relate to the operating cycle or that will be settled within 12 months after the balance date. They include accounts payable, notes payable, employee benefits payable, income taxes payable, sales or value added taxes payable, and the current portion of long-term liabilities.

1.5.1 Accounts payable

An 'account payable' (or 'trade payable') represents the obligation of a business to a creditor (generally a supplier or vendor) usually arising from the purchase of goods and services on credit. Most businesses around the world show their accounts payable (the sum of all individual accounts payable) as a separate line item under current liabilities on their balance sheet.

Figure 12.3 illustrates the accounts payable mechanism. Larsson Company, a video equipment manufacturer, acquires electronic components, on credit, from Gynt AB. The components will be kept in inventory for a few days before being consumed in the manufacturing process. The purchase of these components amounts to 100 CU. It will be settled in two installments: a first payment of 90 CU after 30 days and the balance after 45 days. Figure 12.3 illustrates both the acquisition ❶ and the first payment ❷.

Figure 12.3 Accounts payable

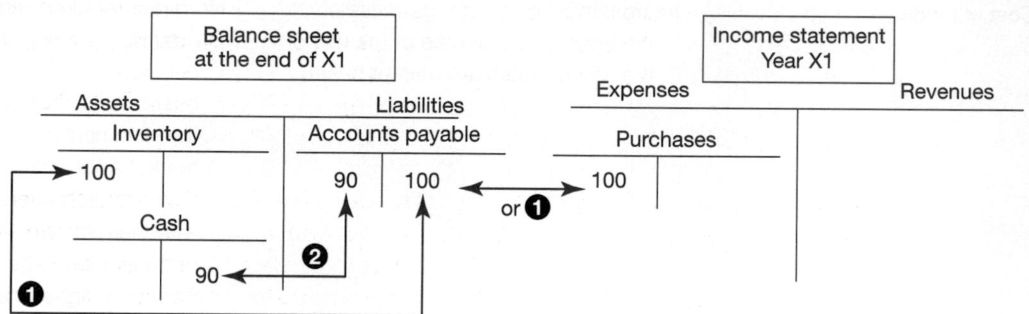

The transaction recorded as ❶ happens on the date of the purchase. It either involves recognizing the transaction as a purchase (i.e., in traditional financial accounting that assumes all purchases are presumed consumed and the cost of materials consumed is obtained by deducting the net increase/decrease in inventory between two physical inventories) or incrementing the inventory if the cost of part of merchandise consumed is calculated by accumulating the requisitions for withdrawals from inventory (see Chapters 2 and 9).

Entry ❷, recorded on the date of the first settlement, accounts for the first payment.

1.5.2 Notes payable

Chapter 10 introduced 'notes receivable' (bills of exchange and promissory notes) in the accounts of the seller. Notes payable are the equivalent items in the buyer's books. Figures 10.8 and 10.2A (Chapter 10 and corresponding appendix) are applicable without complexity (as a mirror image) to notes payable.

When notes are payable within the next 12 months, they are shown in the balance sheet as current liabilities. Otherwise, they are reported as long-term liabilities (if a presentation by maturity term is adopted). An illustration of the recording of notes payable is given in Appendix 12.1.

1.5.3 Short-term employee benefits

Employers compensate their employees (salaries, wages, or some other form of remuneration) in exchange for their 'labor'. Salaries are paid on a periodic basis (generally every two weeks or every month) as a fixed installment of an agreed upon total amount defined as the remuneration for the person making her or his services available to the employer for an agreed upon annual number of hours, regardless of the level of occupation the employer will be able to provide. Wages refer to the payment (daily, weekly, biweekly, or monthly) of an amount defined by an agreed hourly rate or piecework applied to the actual number of units of labor provided during the period for which the wages are calculated. In accounting terms, wages and salaries are handled in the same way and are recorded as 'compensation expense'.

Employers often withhold part of their employee's total compensation to pay the worker's share of the contributions due for such things as health insurance premiums, social security contributions, labor union dues, and even, in some countries, income tax. In that case, the employer is assuming the role of an intermediary in the settlement of otherwise personal employees' obligations. The cost (to the employer) of compensation also includes the employer's share of the same and possibly other contributions (such as payroll taxes and fringe benefits) that derive from either the benefits package applicable to their workforce or (and) from legal obligations imposed by regulatory agencies. These expenses increase the cost of the workforce to the employer beyond the take-home pay of the employee.

Compensation expense Figure 12.4 is an illustration of the recording of the compensation expense for Larsson Company. The total of the employees' monthly pay-slips amounts to 300 CU. This amount corresponds to a net payment to the workers of 235 CU, a total of employee withholdings of 20 CU for contribution to the social security program, and a withholding of 45 CU, which will be paid to the fiscal authorities in the name of the employees in settlement of personal income taxes.

The amounts withheld are not an additional employer cost. The gross salary (300 CU) is the compensation cost to the employer.

Payroll taxes and fringe benefits Payroll taxes and fringe benefits are employee-related costs that are paid by the employer in addition to the compensation package (wages or salaries). They are sometimes called 'social expenses' or 'social charges'.

Payroll taxes are amounts paid to the tax authorities for items such as the employer's portion of social security, unemployment taxes (federal and state taxes as the case may be), and

Figure 12.4 Accounting for compensation expense

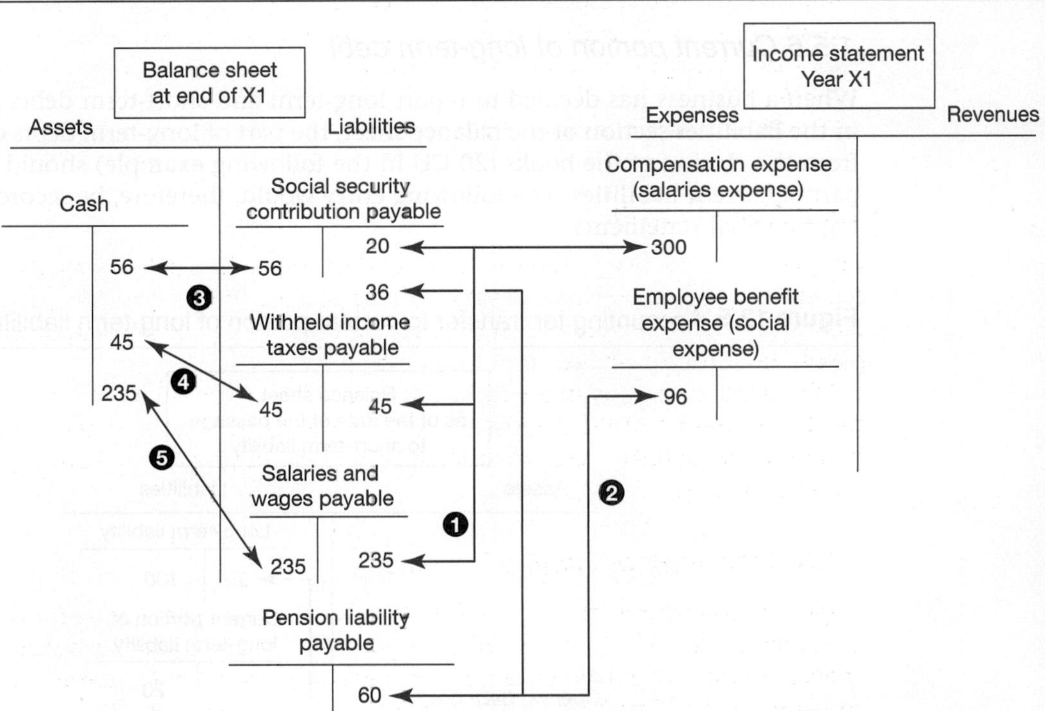

❶ Compensation expense. The net amount due to the employees is recorded in the 'salaries payable' account, but the expense that will eventually be recognized in the income statement is the compensation expense.

❷ Recording of the employer's contribution.

❸, ❹, and ❺ Payment (separately) of each liability on the appropriate date when it is due. (The social security withheld from the employees (20 CU) and the social security charged to the employer (36 CU) are often paid at the same time.)

The total amount of personnel expenses amounts to 300 (gross salary) + 96 (social expenses) = 396 CU.

workers' compensation taxes. Fringe benefits include the employer's share of employees' pension contributions, life and health insurance premiums, and vacation pay.

The Larsson Company, in its country of operation, is required: (a) to pay an employer's social security contribution equal to 12% of the gross salary; and (b) to contribute to the workforce's retirement account recording an employer's contribution amounting to 20% of gross salaries. The total compensation cost (to the employer) is thus $300 + 300 \times (12\% + 20\%) = 396$ CU with 300 CU as the compensation expense and 96 CU as the employees fringe benefits expense.

The necessary entry is recorded in Figure 12.4.

1.5.4 Income taxes payable

The recording of income taxes has been presented in Chapter 6.

1.5.5 Sales tax and value added tax (VAT) collected

Value added tax (VAT) or sales tax collected has been introduced and developed in Chapter 10 (Appendix 10.1). VAT and sales tax collected follow similar mechanisms. When sellers (whether retailers or business to business enterprises) collect VAT or sales tax, they are agents of the state or local government. Appendix 12.2 illustrates the sales tax payable accounting entries.

1.5.6 Current portion of long-term debt

When a business has decided to report long-term and short-term debts as separate items in the liabilities section of the balance sheet, the part of long-term debts due within a year from the closing of the books (20 CU in the following example) should be reclassified as part of current liabilities. The following entry would, therefore, be recorded when preparing financial statements:

Figure 12.5 Accounting for transfer to current portion of long-term liabilities

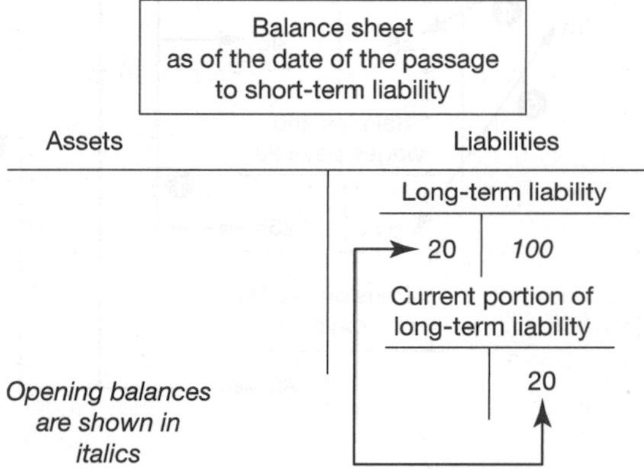

1.6 Reporting liabilities

The degree of detail provided by any firm in reporting their liabilities in both the balance sheet and the notes will assist (or hinder) the ability of the analyst or of the investor to understand the financial position of the firm, the potential dynamics of its evolution, and the risks they are taking.

1.6.1 No separation between short-term and long-term liabilities on the balance sheet

When the balance sheet is presented along the distinction operating/financial liabilities, it does not separate short-term and long-term liabilities. In that case, the annual report often provides, in the notes to the statements, a fairly detailed table listing the liabilities by date of maturity. Such a disclosure is essential since the liabilities are not structured by relative maturity dates in the balance sheet. For example, Continental, a global German-based manufacturer of tires, brake systems, and chassis modules for the automotive industry, discloses the following figures in its financial statements (*Source*: Annual report 2004):

Consolidated balance sheets (excerpts)

in € millions	31 December 2004	31 December 2003
Shareholders' equity and liabilities		
(...)		
Indebtedness	1,834.4	1,916.2
Trade accounts payable	1,235.8	1,035.5
Other liabilities	854.1	708.9
(...)		

The liabilities are presented by nature, i.e., separating the operating liabilities (trade accounts payable and other liabilities) from financial ones (indebtedness). Note 21 to the financial statements discloses the detail of indebtedness (bonds, bank loans, and overdrafts, etc.) by degree of maturity.

Note 21. Indebtedness in € millions		Thereof with a term of			Thereof with a term of	
	31 December 2004	up to one year	more than five years	31 December 2003	up to one year	more than five years
Bonds	1,152.0	42.8	400.0	1,295.5	273.9	–
Bank loans and overdrafts	478.2	169.5	17.9	419.5	153.6	21.8
Lease liabilities	69.6	4.2	17.7	64.9	1.8	55.6
Liabilities on bills drawn and payable	0.6	0.6	–	0.2	0.2	–
Other indebtedness	134.0	140.1	0.0	136.1	72.0	0.7
	1,834.4	357.2	435.6	1,916.2	501.5	78.1

Comment: The details of the liabilities maturity ranges are provided in note 21. The liabilities with a maturity date between one and five years are not explicitly indicated and can only be obtained by deduction.

A similar detail is provided in note 22 concerning 'Other liabilities'.

1.6.2 Short-term and long-term liabilities reported separately on the balance sheet

The most common situation is to report liabilities separately by showing the short-term liabilities distinctly from the long-term liabilities with the expression 'long-term' meaning a date of maturity of more than one year. A typical example is provided by the Elkem annual report.

Real-life example Elkem

(Norway – Norwegian GAAP – *Source*: Annual report 2004 – Metals and materials – production)

This company discloses in its balance sheet the following categories of liabilities, in decreasing order of maturity date:

- provisions;
- interest-bearing long-term debt;
- interest-bearing short-term debt;
- other short-term liabilities.

Notes to the financial statements provide some information on these four categories. As an example, we show below notes 29 and 30, which provide more information about the last two categories of liabilities in Elkem's balance sheet.

Note 29. Interest-bearing short-term debt

Norwegian Krone (NOK) millions	2004	2003	2002
Bank overdrafts	84	93	77
Short-term loans	238	229	572
First year's installment on long-term debt	317	533	274
	639	855	923

Note 30. Other short-term liabilities

NOKm	2004	2003	2002
Payable to suppliers	2,339	2,048	1,790
Value added tax, vacation pay, and employee taxes payable	526	545	435
Dividends	375	395	320
Taxes payable	255	132	304
Deferred income	–	–	162
Provision for restructuring	69	86	47
Advances from external customers	30	32	32
Other short-term liabilities	492	505	553
	4,086	3,743	3,643

1.7 Liabilities, provisions, and contingent liabilities

Quasi-liabilities often render 'liabilities' reporting complex. Liabilities are the materialization of a future obligation. However, the reality and immediacy of that obligation may be subject to debate. Quasi-liabilities are obligations for which either the triggering event may not come from a transaction with a third party, or the timing of which may not be clear, or the amount may not be well defined, or any combination of the three. Liabilities (in the broad sense) include:

- liabilities (strict sense);
- provisions;
- accrued liabilities;
- contingent liabilities.

The distinction between these four categories is not always straightforward. Figure 12.6 illustrates the characteristics of each and summarizes the differences on the basis of the certainty of three distinguishing characteristics of the obligation they represent: principle creating the obligation, timing, and valuation or amount of the obligation.

Figure 12.6 Liabilities and related concepts

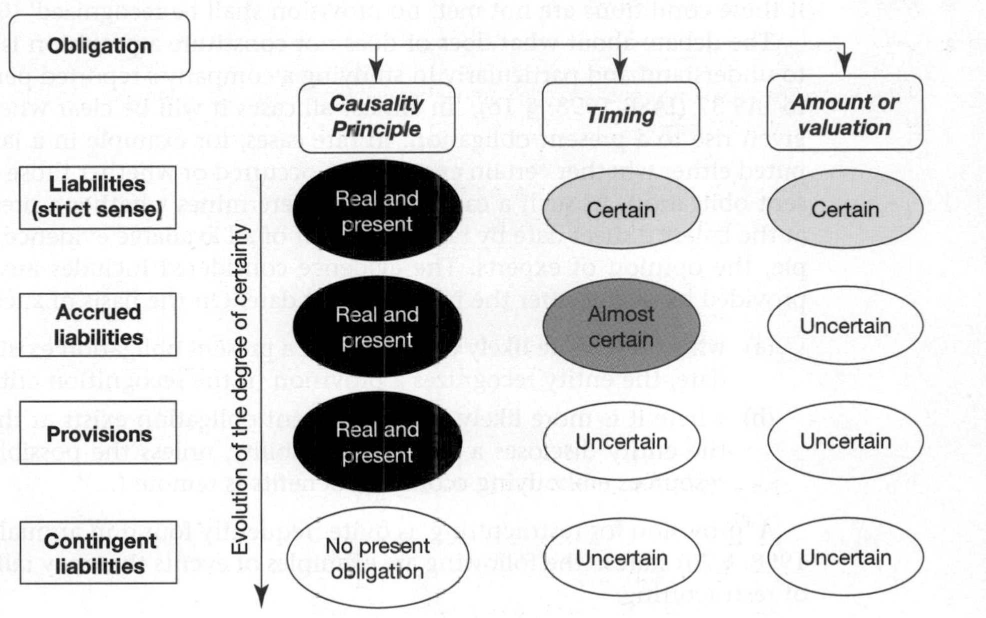

1.7.1 Provision versus liability (in the strict sense of the word)

A provision is an obligation that could eventually be reversed because some degree of estimation is involved in its amount and timing (Figure 12.6). It represents an obligation whose object is real although potential, the amount of which cannot easily be determined with precision at the time. A liability (in the strict sense of the word), however, is generally irreversible. Both its timing and principal amount are known with certainty, and can only be settled according to the terms of the contract or event that created it.

The Anglo-American terminology, partly adopted by the IASB, uses the term 'provision' in the case of liabilities (in a broad sense). The potential reduction of the value of an asset is called 'impairment' for fixed assets (see Chapter 7) and 'valuation allowance' for current assets (see Chapter 10). However, some countries and/or practitioners use the term 'provision' to also cover other reduction in assets and increase in liabilities. In that case, the second category is often called 'provisions for risks and charges' to avoid any ambiguity.

Principle and definition The IASB Framework (IASB 1989: § 64) explains that: 'Some liabilities can be measured only by using a substantial degree of estimation. Some enterprises describe these liabilities as provisions. In some countries, such provisions are not regarded as liabilities because the concept of a liability is defined narrowly so as to include only amounts that can be established without the need to make estimates'. The IASB definition of a liability favors the broader approach. Thus, according to the IASB, 'when a provision involves a real and present obligation and satisfies the rest of the definition, it is a liability even if the amount has to be estimated' (Conceptual Framework: § 64). Examples include provisions for payments to be made under existing warranties provided to customers and provisions to cover pension obligations.

For IASB (1998: § 10), a provision is 'a liability of uncertain timing or amount'. A provision shall therefore be recognized 'when:

(a) An entity has a present[3] obligation (legal or constructive) as a result of a past event;
(b) It is probable that an outflow of resources embodying economic benefits will be required to settle the obligation; and
(c) A reliable estimate can be made of the amount of the obligation.

If these conditions are not met, no provision shall be recognized' (§ 14).

The debate about what does or does not constitute a provision is extremely important to understand and particularly in studying a company's reported performance. According to IAS 37 (IASB 1998: § 16), 'in almost all cases it will be clear whether a past event has given rise to a present obligation. In rare cases, for example in a law-suit, it may be disputed either whether certain events have occurred or whether those events result in a present obligation. In such a case, an entity determines whether a present obligation exists at the balance sheet date by taking account of all available evidence, including, for example, the opinion of experts. The evidence considered includes any additional evidence provided by events after the balance sheet date. On the basis of such evidence:

(a) where it is more likely than not that a present obligation exists at the balance sheet date, the entity recognizes a provision (if the recognition criteria are met); and
(b) where it is more likely that no present obligation exists at the balance sheet date, the entity discloses a contingent liability, unless the possibility of an outflow of resources embodying economic benefits is remote (...)'.

A 'provision for restructuring' is quite frequently found in annual reports. IAS 37 (IASB 1998: § 70) states: 'the following are examples of events that may fall under the definition of restructuring:

- Sale or termination of a line of business;
- Closure of business locations in a country or region or the relocation of business activities from one country or region to another;
- Changes in management structure, for example, eliminating a layer of management;
- Fundamental reorganizations that have a material effect on the nature and focus of the entity's operations'.

IASB has adopted a very strict position when it comes to provisions for restructuring. IAS 37 (§ 71) adds: 'a provision for restructuring costs is recognized only when the general recognition criteria for provisions set out in paragraph 14 are met'. Some detailed conditions are then defined (IAS 37: § 72): 'A constructive obligation to restructure arises only when an entity:

(a) Has a detailed formal plan for the restructuring identifying at least:
  (i) The business or part of a business concerned;
  (ii) The principal locations affected;

(iii) The location, function, and approximate number of employees who will be compensated for terminating their services;

(iv) The expenditures that will be undertaken; and

(v) When the plan will be implemented; and

(b) Has raised a valid expectation in those affected that it will carry out the restructuring by starting to implement that plan or announcing its main features to those affected by it'.

The restructuring provision amount shall be calculated so as to reflect estimates of 'only the direct expenditures arising from the restructuring, which are those that are both (a) necessarily entailed by the restructuring; and (b) not associated with the ongoing activities of the enterprise' (IAS 37, 1998: § 80).

Because estimates of future costs are often difficult to establish objectively, many managers have long used 'provisions for restructuring' as a preferred tool of earnings management or income smoothing. An overestimation of the amount of the provision (for example, decided by a new management team) offers the possibility of improving future earnings when the actual expense reveals itself to be lower than anticipated (i.e., lower than the amount provisioned) since the excess provision will be reversed and added to the income of the following period.

Movements in the provision accounts are generally reported in the notes to the financial statements. Since the appropriate reporting is similar to that of accounts receivable variations as described in Chapter 10, this topic will not be developed further.

Real-life example ISS – International Service System

(Denmark – Danish GAAP – *Source*: Annual report 2004 – Support services)

The consolidated balance sheet and notes include the following elements:

Consolidated balance sheet (excerpts)

In millions of Danish Krone (DKK)	2004	2003
Pensions and similar obligations	263	253
Deferred tax liabilities	318	310
Other provisions	646	530
Total provisions	1,227	1,093

Note 21. Other provisions

In DKK m	2004	2003
Labor-related items	71	83
Self-insurance	36	38
Acquisitions	115	61
Other	424	348
	646	530

Labor-related items: The provision mainly relates to obligations in Belgium, France, the Netherlands, and Spain.

Self-insurance: In the UK and Ireland, ISS carries an insurance provision on employers' liability. ISS is self-insured up to DKK 41 m for employers' liability.

Acquisitions: The provision includes obligations incurred in the normal course of acquisitions mainly related to transaction costs, redundancy payments, and [costs of] termination of [leases on] rental of properties.

Other: The provision comprises various obligations incurred in the normal course of business, e.g., costs related to changes in local working and social regulations, etc., provision for dismantling costs, operational issues, closure of contracts, and legal cases.

The 'pensions and similar obligations', also called 'provision for pensions' or 'pension liability', will be developed in the Advanced issues section of this chapter. 'Deferred taxes' were introduced in Chapter 6. The details of 'Other provisions' are provided in note 21 to the consolidated financial statements.

As the effect of time value of money (see Appendix 12.3) is not considered to be material, the provisions are not discounted.

1.7.2 Provision versus accrued liabilities

Accrued liabilities are the results of both the accrual process and the time lag between an event and its complete resolution in the course of the cycle of operations.

Principle and definition IAS 37 states (IASB 1998: § 11): 'Provisions can be distinguished from other liabilities such as trade payables and accruals because there is uncertainty about the timing or amount of the future expenditure required in settlement. By contrast:

(a) Trade payables are liabilities to pay for goods or services that have been received or supplied and have been invoiced or formally agreed with the supplier; and

(b) Accruals are liabilities to pay for goods or services that have been received or supplied but have not been paid, invoiced or formally agreed with the supplier, including amounts due to employees (for example, amounts relating to accrued vacation pay). Although it is sometimes necessary to estimate the amount or timing of accruals, the uncertainty is generally much less than for provisions.

Accruals are often reported as part of trade and other payables, whereas provisions are reported separately'.

Accrued liabilities are usually recorded as part of the end-of-period entries (Chapter 5). Many annual reports do not distinguish clearly between 'liabilities' and 'accrued liabilities', and merge them under only one category in the balance sheet. However, it is clear that such a distinction could considerably help the analyst or the investor in understanding the effect of the operating cycle on the liquidity and solvency of the firm. Notes often provide much needed details.

Real-life example Sulzer

(Switzerland – IAS GAAP – *Source*: Annual report 2004 – Medical technology, mechanical applications in the oil, gas, and chemical industries, pumps)

Notes to the consolidated financial statements

Other current and accrued liabilities in millions of Swiss francs (CHF)	2004	2003
Other current liabilities		
Notes payable	2	3
Employee accounts	11	10
Social security institutions	7	8
Taxes	13	10
Derivative financial instruments	4	2
Other liabilities	24	20
Total other current liabilities	61	53
Accrued liabilities		
Interest payable	0	1
Vacation and overtime claims	26	26
Salaries, wages and bonuses	32	26
Contract-related costs	36	47
Other accrued liabilities	50	47
Total accrued liabilities	144	147
Total other current and accrued liabilities	205	200

Comment: While only the 'Total other current and accrued liabilities' is reported on the balance sheet, Sulzer discloses the details of this category of liabilities, separating the current and the accrued liabilities.

Real-life example China Eastern Airlines Corporation

(China – Hong Kong GAAP/IFRS – *Source*: Annual report 2004 – Airline company)

Notes to the consolidated financial statements

Note 24. Accrued aircraft overhaul expenses in thousands of Renminbi (RMB)	2004	2003
At 1 January 2004	576,552	547,813
Additional provisions	244,625	123,213
Over provision	(20,814)	(59,456)
Utilized during the year	(85,154)	(35,018)
At 31 December 2004	715,209	576,552
Less: current portion	(539,249)	(385,168)
Long-term portion	175,960	191,384

Accrued aircraft overhaul expenses represent present value of estimated costs of major overhauls for aircraft and engines under operating lease as the Group has the responsibility to fulfill certain return conditions under relevant leases.

Comment: China Eastern discloses the movements in accrued aircraft overhaul expenses. It also provides the split between long-term and short-term accruals. We can note that the company report mixes two terminologies: 'accrued expenses' and 'provisions'.

1.7.3 Contingent liabilities

Contingent liabilities, as shown in Figure 12.6, are the liabilities for which there is uncertainty simultaneously about causing principle, timing, and amount. Contingent liabilities, as their name implies, are obligations that are contingent (conditional) on events that are not entirely under the control of the firm.

IAS 37 (IASB 1998: § 10) defines a contingent liability as:

(a) 'A possible obligation that arises from past events and whose existence will be confirmed only by the occurrence or non-occurrence of one or more uncertain future events not wholly within the control of the entity; or

(b) A present obligation that arises from past events but is not recognized because:
   (i) It is not probable that an outflow of resources embodying economic benefits will be required to settle the obligation; or
   (ii) The amount of the obligation cannot be measured with sufficient reliability'.

1.7.4 Provisions versus contingent liabilities

Discussion The borderline between provisions and contingent liabilities is not always clear-cut. IAS 37 (§ 12) explains that, 'in a general sense, all provisions are contingent because they are uncertain in timing or amount'. In this context, IAS 37 explains in its paragraph 13 the distinction 'between provisions and contingent liabilities:

1. Provisions are recognized as liabilities (assuming that a reliable estimate can be made) because they are present obligations and it is probable that an outflow of resources embodying economic benefits will be required to settle the obligations; and
2. Contingent liabilities are not recognized as liabilities because they are either:
   (i) Possible obligations, as it has yet to be confirmed whether the enterprise has a present obligation that could lead to an outflow of resources embodying economic benefits; or
   (ii) Present obligations that do not meet the recognition criteria in this Standard (because either it is not probable that an outflow of resources embodying economic benefits will be required to settle the obligation, or a sufficiently reliable estimate of the amount of the obligation cannot be made)'.

An illustration of the difficulty of distinguishing between accrued liabilities, provisions, and contingent liabilities will be given in the Advanced issues section of this chapter using an environmental liability as an example. IAS 37 does not address the recognition issue of obligations derived from 'commitments' (such as loan repayment guarantees given by a solid parent for the benefit of helping a fledgling subsidiary secure a lower cost of financing). These commitments actually and conceptually represent an obligation that meets the same criteria as a contingent liability. In fact, most businesses report commitments in the same footnote to the financial statements in which they give the details pertaining to their 'contingent liabilities'.

Litigation liabilities The provisions created in anticipation of the possible worst outcome of litigation cases are often mentioned as contingent liabilities. Since litigation takes a significant amount of time to settle, creating such a provision as close as possible in time to the triggering event is coherent with the matching principle. Litigation provisions are often mentioned as part of the contingent liabilities as exemplified by the following excerpt from the Stora Enso annual statement.

Real-life example Stora Enso

(Finland – IAS GAAP – *Source*: Annual report 2004 – Production of paper)

Note to the consolidated financial statements

Note 26 Commitments and contingent liabilities

Contingent Liabilities

Stora Enso is party to legal proceedings that arise in the ordinary course of business and which primarily involve claims arising out of commercial law. The Group is also involved in administrative proceedings relating primarily to competition law. The Directors do not consider that liabilities related to such proceedings, before insurance recoveries, if any, are likely to be material to the Group financial condition or results of operations.

In May 2004 Stora Enso was the subject of inspections carried out by the European Commission and the Finnish Competition Authority at locations in Europe and received subpoenas issued by the US Department of Justice as part of preliminary anti-trust investigations into the paper industry in Europe and the US. The investigations by the authorities in both jurisdictions are at a fact-finding stage only and no formal allegations have been made against the Group or any of its employees. Coincident with these investigations, Stora Enso was named in a number of class action lawsuits filed in the US. No provisions have been made.

Stora Timber Finance B.V. has been found responsible for soil pollution at the Port of Amsterdam, but has appealed the decision to the Court of Appeal in Amsterdam; EUR 2.4 million was recorded as a provision at 31 December 2003.

Comment: The information reported by Stora Enso is very precise. Reporting precise information about a litigation or lawsuit places the business in a conundrum: if detailed quantified information is published, such as an estimate of the possible out-of-court settlement or court verdict or award, such reporting might be construed by the opposing party as an acknowledgment of responsibility. By the same token, if there is not enough information about the case and the risks involved, users of financial information might consider themselves maligned if events turn to the disadvantage of the entity (and, in turn, these users of financial information might sue the business!).

Contingent liability derived from discounted notes or bills of exchange We have seen in Chapter 10 that one way to record the discount of bills of exchange and notes receivable is to cancel the account 'notes receivable'. In that case, the discount mechanism for notes creates a contingent liability if the discount is 'with recourse' (see Chapter 10). This liability is often mentioned in the footnote pertaining to the notes payable. The mention of such a liability is critical in the calculation of the average days' sales ratio that must take into account the notes discounted in the denominator since the final responsibility is still borne by the company in case the discounted note is not paid in the end.

However, there is no contingent liability if the firm follows the rules of IAS 39 (2003c: § 20) that require that the discounted notes remain in the assets of the balance sheet, with a bank debt recorded in the liabilities of the balance sheet.

Real-life example Mitsubishi Electric

(Japan – US GAAP – *Source*: Annual report 2005 – Electrical and electronic equipment used in home products, and commercial and industrial systems, and equipment)

Note to consolidated financial statements

Note 17 Commitments and contingent liabilities

(...) It is common practice in Japan for companies, in the ordinary course of business, to receive promissory notes in settlement of trade accounts receivable and to subsequently discount such notes at banks. At 31 March 2005, the companies were contingently liable on trade notes discounted in the amount of ¥593 million ($5,542 thousand). Notes discounted are accounted for as sales. The aggregate amounts of proceeds from notes discounted for the years ended 31 March 2005, 2004, and 2003 are not available; however, based on its financing policy, the company believes that the balance of such contingent liabilities should not have significantly fluctuated during the year ended 31 March 2005.

Comment: There is no established or normalized terminology for reporting discounted notes. For example, Toray Industries, a Japanese company, reports the amounts of discounted notes-related contingent liabilities as 'buyback obligations associated with securitization[4] of receivables'.

Other contingent liabilities A variety of other contingent liabilities are found in annual reports, e.g., contingent liability as loan guarantor, contingent liability to cover product warranty obligations.

2 Advanced issues

Among financial liabilities, several offer specific accounting challenges. Bonds, financial leases, environmental liabilities as well as pension liabilities are examples of specific liabilities that require specific solution for quality reporting. In this part of the chapter we will also cover the importance of liabilities in financial statement analysis.

2.1 Bonds

2.1.1 Definition

In order to attract interest-bearing funds from investors, a company may issue bonds. A bond is a certificate allowing the division of a debt between large numbers of investors (bondholders), each of whom can contribute only a small amount of the debt (the face value, or the selling price if sold at a discount or with a premium). If the face value of a bond is small, it makes this lending instrument accessible to a large public and thus may be useful to raise funds from a broad spectrum of possible lenders. In the aggregate a bond issue may represent a very large amount of borrowed funds to cover all or part of the company's financing needs. The larger the bond issue, the larger the number of bonds that can be sold individually or in blocks.

The bond or certificate shows the evidence of the claim held by the bondholder. The claim is based on a lending agreement between the provider of funds who purchases the bond (bondholder or investor) and the business (the borrower or the issuer of the bond). Each bond has a par or face value, a coupon rate (interest rate), and a maturity or redemption date. Bond issuance offers businesses an alternative to bank loans. Instead of dealing with a single (or a limited pool of) financial institution(s), the business choosing to float a bond issue goes to the open financial markets (generally through financial institutions for placement) to collect funds from a variety of sources (institutional as well as private) who value the liquidity offered by the tradability of bonds.

A company that issues bonds assumes two obligations:

1. To pay investors a specified amount of cash on an agreed upon maturity date (when the bond will be redeemed) – which may be either a specified and unmodifiable date or a date which can be established later at the initiative of the borrower, generally after a period during which early retirement of the bond is not allowed. The amount that will be given to the bondholder on the date of redemption is called principal, par value, face value, or maturity value.
2. To pay investors a cash interest at periodic intervals on specified dates (generally before the maturity date) at a rate of interest defined on the date of issuance (fixed rate or conditional rates linked, for example, to the evolution of the prime rate or to the market price of some commodity).

Bonds are most of the time traded on financial markets, thus providing the lender with the possibility of making their investment liquid if needed.

There are at least two basic types of bonds:

- **Term bonds** in one bond issue mature all on the same date. All the bonds are repaid *in fine*, i.e., at the end of the maturity period. For example, 500 term bonds of 1,000 CU each with a maturity date of five years from the date of issuance represent a total maturity value of 500,000 CU that will be paid on the fifth anniversary of the issuance.
- **Serial bonds** mature in predetermined installments (but the specific bonds called in a given installment are often drawn through a lottery). For example, 500 serial bonds, with a 1,000 CU face value each, would, in this case, for example, mature at the rate of 100,000 CU per year over a five-year period.

Zero-coupon bonds (or Zeroes) are bonds that do not pay interest during their life and for which the maturity value is the result of the compounding of the specified interest rate over the maturity period of the bond. Such bonds sell for an amount that is, of course, much reduced compared to the maturity value and offer a tax advantage to the holder as no taxable interest is earned by the lender during the entire life of the bond until it matures. Such bonds are also interesting for growing firms that may be cash-strapped at some point (often early phases) of their development and thus need not divert cash to pay a periodic interest.

2.1.2 Interest, discount, and premium

Bonds are generally issued with a fixed or variable stated interest rate. The main concepts related to bonds issue will be illustrated through the example of Berwald Company. The data for this illustration are given in Table 12.4.

In this example, the bond is a term bond. Its principal will be repaid *in fine*, at the end of year X5. The selling price of a bond should be equal to the present value of the future cash flows the lender will receive, i.e., all the interest payments (during the lending period) and the reimbursement of the principal (at the end). (Time value of money and present value are developed in Appendix 12.3.)

In this computation, the interest rate (also called discount rate) used is the market rate of interest at the issue date for like instruments with similar risk. Table 12.6 shows the value of the bond issue described in Table 12.4 for market interest rates of 8%, 6%, and 10%.

Table 12.4 Berwald Company – Basic data

Date of issuance	1 January X1
Term	5 years
Principal at face value (1)	500,000
Stated interest rate (2)	8%
Annual interest expense (1) x (2)	40,000
Payment of interest	Annually, 31 December
Maturity date	31 December X5

Table 12.5 summarizes the current cash flows (in CU), while Table 12.6 illustrates the present value of those cash flows.

Table 12.5 Cash flows linked to the bond

	1 Jan. X1	31 Dec. X1	31 Dec. X2	31 Dec. X3	31 Dec. X4	31 Dec. X5
Interest payment		40,000	40,000	40,000	40,000	40,000
Repayment of the principal						500,000
Total		40,000	40,000	40,000	40,000	540,000
Value of bonds = Net present value of future payments						

Table 12.6 Present value of the cash flows from Table 12.5

If the market rate on 1 January X1 is:				8%	6%	10%
	Basis	Number of years				
Present value of repayment of principal	500,000	5	(1)	340,292	373,629	310,461
Present value of interest payments	40,000/year	5	(2)	159,708	168,495	151,631
Selling price			(3) = (1) + (2)	500,000	542,124	462,092
Stated value of principal			(4)	500,000	500,000	500,000
Premium/(discount)			(5) = (3) − (4)	0	42,124	(37,908)
Effective yield on the selling price				8%	6%	10%

(1) Present value $= \dfrac{\text{Principal}}{(1 + \text{assumed discount rate})^5}$ (see Appendix 12.3 and Table 12.1A).

(2) Present value of an ordinary annuity (see Appendix 12.3 and Table 12.3A).

In this table no issuance cost is assumed. Such cost would, of course, have to be covered by the funds received and the issuer of the bonds would receive less than the amount stated as the selling price in Table 12.6. The three assumed possible interest rates represent three generic cases we now review in detail.

Case 1: Interest assumed in discounting is 8% or the same as in the bond issue. When the rate that investors can earn on investments of similar risk is 8%, the same as the stated rate, the bonds will sell at par (face) value and yield 8%.

Case 2: Assumed discount rate of 6%. When the market rate of interest is 6% (i.e., investors can earn only 6% on bond issues or other investments of comparable level of risk), investors will bid up the price of the bonds (face value of 500,000 CU) to 542,124 CU because the stated rate of 8% is more favorable than the current (opportunity) market rate. In this case, the effective yield will correspond to the market rate of 6% and the bonds will sell at a premium of 42,124 CU (i.e., above face value).

Case 3: Assumed discount rate is 10%. When the market rate of interest is 10%, (i.e., investors could earn 10% on bond issues or other investments of comparable level of risk) the price of the bonds will be only 462,092 CU (even though the face value is 500,000 CU) because the stated rate of 8% is less favorable than the current (opportunity) market rate. In this case, the effective yield will correspond to the market rate of 10% and the bonds will sell at a discount of 37,908 CU (i.e., below face value) to attract investors.

The difference between what was received at the date of issue and what must be paid at maturity is a premium (if the market rate is lower than the stated rate) or a discount (if the market rate is higher than the stated rate).

2.1.3 Accounting for bonds

The mechanism is illustrated in Figures 12.7, 12.8, and 12.3A.

Bonds issued at par

Figure 12.7 Accounting for bonds issued at par

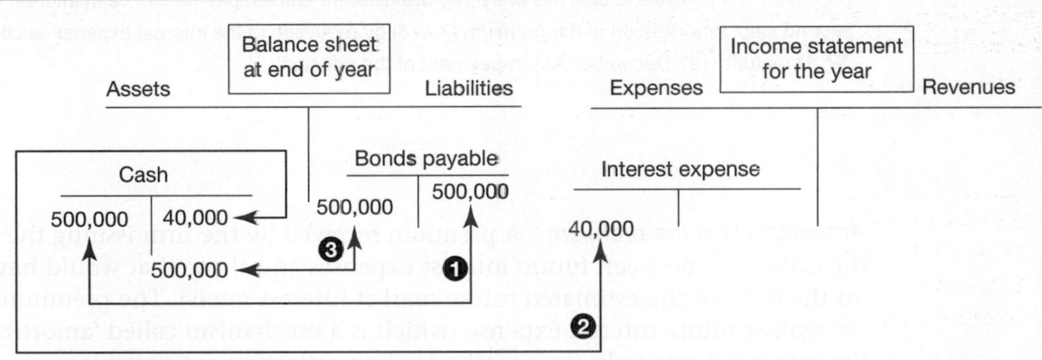

❶ On 1 January X1. At issuance: receipt of the selling price (equal to the principal of the bond).
❷ On 31 December X1 (and on 31 December for each of the four following years): payment of the interest due.
❸ At maturity (31 December X5): repayment of the principal.

Bonds issued at a premium

Figure 12.8 Accounting for bonds issued at a premium

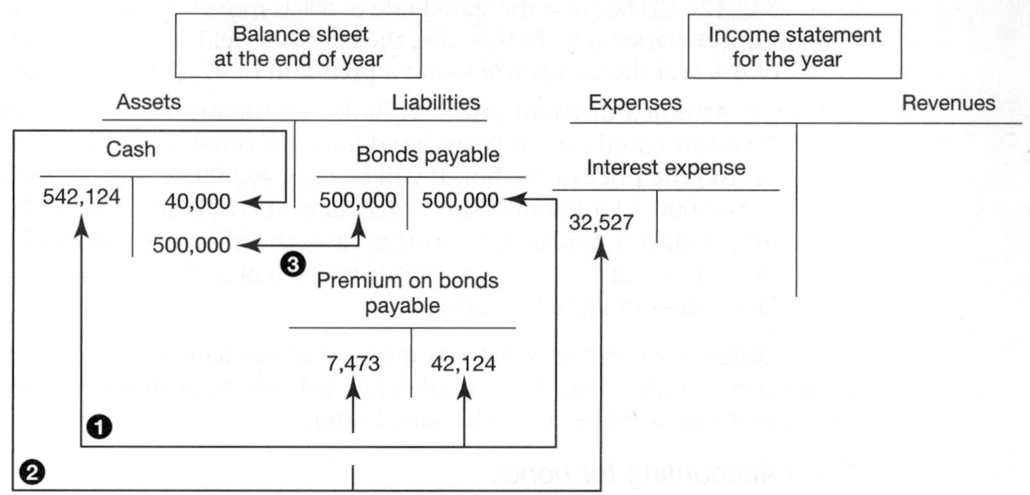

❶ On 1 January X1, at issuance date: receipt of the selling price, which is higher than the principal. (It is also possible to record the bonds in one account, including the premium.)

❷ On 31 December X1 (and on 31 December for each the four following years): payment of the interest and amortization of the premium (see Table 12.7 later). (In this context, the term 'amortization' does not have exactly the same meaning as the term used in Chapter 8 when discussing the amortization of intangible assets. However, both are methods of distributing a cost over a period of time in application of the matching principle.) It is possible to split this entry into two different entries: payment of cash interest (40,000) and, in a second step, amortization of the premium (7,473) by reduction of the interest expense account.

❸ At maturity (31 December X5): repayment of the principal.

Amortization of the premium A premium received by the firm issuing the bond represents the difference between future interest expenses and those that would have been incurred on the basis of the estimated future market interest rate(s). The premium needs to be offset against future interest expense (which is a mechanism called 'amortization') to follow the matching principle. Two methods of amortization are possible:

- effective interest method;
- straight-line method.

Effective interest method The effective interest method considers the issuance price (including the premium) as the amount to be 'amortized' (to be repaid). The periodic interest expense is determined by multiplying this amount to be amortized (book value at the beginning of each period) by the 'effective' (market) interest rate at the time the bonds were issued (6%). As the issuing business entity pays an interest expense (40,000 CU), which is higher than the effective interest (32,527 CU if the interest rate had been 6%), the 'excess' interest paid partly amortizes the amount of the premium. In other terms, the premium amortization for each (interest) period is the difference between the interest calculated at the stated rate (8%) and the interest calculated at the effective rate (6%). Table 12.7 presents an illustration of such a calculation.

Table 12.7 Schedule of interest and book value – Effective interest method, in the case of a premium

Year ending expense	Effective interest expense (1) = (4) [i.e. previous line] × 6%	Cash (interest paid) (2)	Premium amortization expense (decrease in book value) (3) = (1) − (2)	Book value of bonds (4)
				542,124
31 Dec. X1	32,527	40,000	−7,473	534,651
31 Dec. X2	32,079	40,000	−7,921	526,730
31 Dec. X3	31,604	40,000	−8,396	518,334
31 Dec. X4	31,100	40,000	−8,900	509,434
31 Dec. X5	30,566	40,000	−9,434	500,000
Total	157,876	200,000	−42,124	

Straight-line method The interest expense is a constant amount each year, equal to the cash interest minus the annual premium amortization (total premium divided by the number of years the bond will live): 31,575.2 CU, representing the interest [40,000 CU] minus a constant part of the premium [42,124 CU/5 years = 8,424.8 CU].

The interest patterns under the effective interest method conform more closely to economic reality. In most countries, the effective interest method must be used if the results are materially different from those of the straight-line method.

Bonds issued at a discount

The mechanism for an issuance at a discount is the reverse of one with a premium (see developments in Appendix 12.4).

2.2 Leased assets

A company may choose to enjoy the benefits of having a long-term asset at its disposal without necessarily wanting (or having the means) to own it. In this case, the user (lessee) will enter into a leasing contract with the supplier or a specialized financial institution (the lessor).

In a leasing contract, title to the asset does not change hands. An analyst or an investor would want to know what lease agreement the business has entered into, both because the access to the assets involved is a potential source of value creation, and because the lease contract creates an obligation to pay a rent for the equipment, property, or building. Leases are therefore an important element in the description of the financial situation of a firm at any point in time and must be reported to the users of financial information.

IAS 17 (IASB 2003b: § 4) defines a 'lease' as 'an agreement whereby the lessor conveys to the lessee, in return for a payment or series of payments, the right to use an asset for an agreed period of time'. This Standard further distinguishes between:

- finance leases, which are 'leases that transfer substantially all the risks and rewards incidental to ownership of an asset. Title may or may not eventually be transferred' (IASB 2003b: § 4); and
- operating leases which are 'lease[s] other than a finance lease' (IASB 2003b: § 4).

In this definition,

- risks include the possibilities of losses from idle capacity or technological obsolescence and of variations in return due to changing economic conditions;
- rewards may be represented by the expectation of profitable operation over the asset's economic life and of gain from appreciation in value or realization of a residual value.

Concretely, a finance lease is essentially equivalent to the acquisition of a fixed asset with debt financing.

2.2.1 Accounting recording of leased assets

The distinction between the concepts of 'finance' and 'operating' leases plays a major role in the way leased assets will be reported. Figure 12.9 illustrates the issues at hand.

We will only examine here the accounting issues from the point of view of the lessee. Leases in the financial statements of lessors will not be developed and the reader interested in this topic can consult IAS 17 (§§ 36–57).

Figure 12.9 Accounting treatment of leased assets

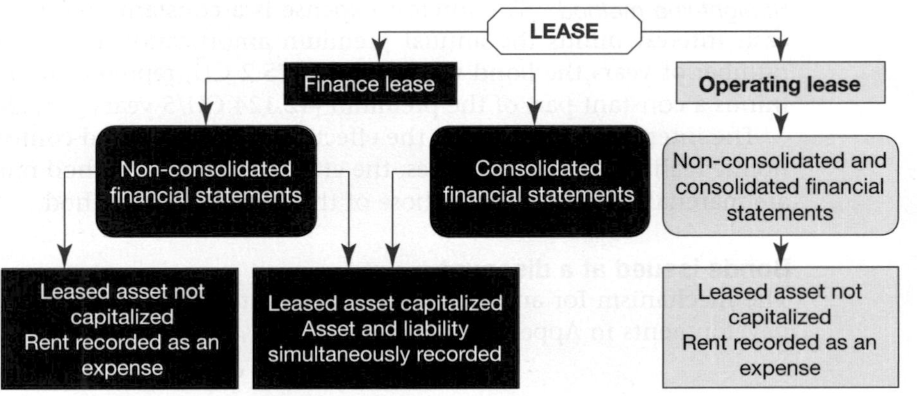

2.2.2 Finance and operating leases

IAS 17 (IASB 2003b, § 10) states that 'whether a lease is a finance lease or an operating lease depends on the substance of the transaction rather than the form of the contract. Examples of situations that individually or in combination would normally lead to a lease being classified as a finance lease are:

(a) The lease transfers ownership of the asset to the lessee by the end of the lease term;

(b) The lessee has the option to purchase the asset at a price that is expected to be sufficiently lower than the fair value at the date the option becomes exercisable for it to be reasonably certain, at the inception of the lease, that the option will be exercised;

(c) The lease term is for the major part of the economic life of the asset even if title is not transferred;

(d) At the inception of the lease the present value of the minimum lease payments amounts to at least substantially all of the fair value of the leased asset; and

(e) The leased assets are of such a specialized nature that only the lessee can use them without major modifications'.

In these situations, several terms are defined in the IASB standard (§ 4):

'*Fair value* is the amount for which an asset could be exchanged, or a liability settled, between knowledgeable, willing parties in an arm's length transaction'.

'*Economic life* is either:

(a) The period over which an asset is expected to be economically usable by one or more users; or

(b) The number of production or similar units expected to be obtained from the asset by one or more users'.

'The *inception* of the lease is the earlier of the date of the lease agreement and the date of commitment by the parties to the principal provisions of the lease'.

'*Minimum lease payments* are the payments over the lease term that the lessee is, or can be required, to make, excluding contingent rent, costs for services and taxes to be paid by and reimbursed to the lessor, together with:

(a) For the lessee, any amounts guaranteed by the lessee or by a party related to the lessee; or

(b) For the lessor, any residual value guaranteed to the lessor by (i) the lessee, (ii) a party related to the lessee, or (iii) a third party unrelated to the lessor that is financially capable of discharging the obligations under this guarantee.

However, if the lessee has an option to purchase the asset at a price that is expected to be sufficiently lower than the fair value at the date the option becomes exercisable for it to be reasonably certain, at the inception of the lease, that the option will be exercised, the minimum lease payments comprise the minimum payments payable over the lease term to the expected date of exercise of this purchase option and the payment required to exercise it'.

'The *lease term* is the non-cancelable period for which the lessee has contracted to lease the asset together with any further terms for which the lessee has the option to continue to lease the asset, with or without further payment, when at the inception of the lease it is reasonably certain that the lessee will exercise the option'.

When a contract meets even only one of the criteria laid out by the IASB, it should be considered as a finance lease. The IASB criteria are different from the criteria laid out by SFAS 13 (FASB 1976) under US GAAP. In IAS 17, the key differences between financial and operational leases pertain mainly to the two following criteria: 'the major part of the economic life of the asset' criterion and the 'present value of the minimum [accumulated] lease payments amounts to at least substantially all of the fair value of the leased asset'.

The IASB favors a professional appreciation of the situation over specifying precise conditions. Any precise list of conditions could always be bypassed or interpreted in borderline cases so as to avoid reporting a useful piece of information to investors and analysts. A **principles-based approach** in providing guidance for reporting is generally more effective than a **rules-based approach** if the intent is to be as informative as possible.

In the United States, SFAS 13 lists the four conditions that create a finance lease (meeting only one of these conditions is enough, however):

1. The lease transfers ownership of the asset to the lessee by the end of the lease term.
2. The lease contains a bargain purchase option.
3. The non-cancelable lease term is 75% or more of the estimated economic life of the leased asset.
4. The present value of the minimum lease payments equals or exceeds 90% of the fair value of the leased asset.

Under condition 3, 'the major part' (IAS 17) is replaced by 75% (SFAS 13), and under condition 4, 'substantially' (IAS 17) is replaced by 90% (SFAS 13).

2.2.3 Capitalization of finance leased assets

IAS 17 (§ 20) recommends that finance leases be recognized as assets (the use of the leased object is to create future economic benefits) and liabilities (representing future lease payments) on the balance sheet. Such recording of finance leases is often known as the 'capitalization' of the leased asset. As shown in Figure 12.9, capitalization is generally adopted in the consolidated financial statements. However, in the non-consolidated financial statements, some countries' GAAP do not follow the IAS recommendation and do not recognize leased assets at all in the balance sheet (it is the case for France and Italy, for example). In fact, legally the property belongs to the owner throughout the duration of the lease and for that reason EU countries with accounting systems based on commercial law do not capitalize leases and consider the rental payments as expenses in the income statement. The 4th Directive does not formulate a recommendation on the capitalization of leases. Some European countries, for example Belgium, Netherlands, Switzerland, and the UK, prefer to respect the accounting principle of 'substance over form' and require that the assets held under a finance lease agreement be reported in the balance sheet, following, implicitly or explicitly, the prescription of IAS 17.

If a company decides to capitalize leased assets, it can follow the IAS 17 prescriptions (§ 20): 'At the commencement of the lease term, lessees shall recognize finance leases as assets and liabilities in their balance sheets at amounts equal to the fair value of the leased property or, if lower, the present value of the minimum lease payments, each determined at the inception of the lease. The discount rate to be used in calculating the present value of the minimum lease payments is the interest rate implicit in the lease, if this is practicable to determine; if not, the lessee's incremental [marginal] borrowing rate shall be used. Any initial direct costs of the lessee are added to the amount recognized as an asset'. This 'incremental borrowing rate' is 'the rate of interest the lessee would have to pay on a similar lease or, if that is not determinable, the rate that, at the inception of the lease, the lessee would incur to borrow over a similar term, and with a similar security, the funds necessary to purchase the asset' (IASB 2003b: § 4).

If leased assets are capitalized, lease payments must be apportioned between finance expense and reduction of the outstanding liability. Simultaneously, the asset must be depreciated consistently with the depreciable assets that are owned by the company. 'If there is no reasonable certainty that the lessee will obtain ownership by the end of the lease term, the asset shall be fully depreciated over the shorter of the lease term and its useful life.' (IAS 17: § 27). Otherwise, the period of expected use is the useful life of the asset.

In practice, 'the sum of the depreciation expense for the asset and the finance expense for the period is rarely the same as the lease payments payable for the period, and it is, therefore, inappropriate simply to recognize the lease payments payable as an expense. Accordingly, the asset and the related liability are unlikely to be equal in amount after the commencement of the lease term' (IAS 17: § 29). In this context, it is necessary to restate the lease payment (The Lindblad Company example, below, illustrates how this is done.)

2.2.4 Example of accounting for leased assets

The Lindblad Company leases equipment (worth 600 CU at fair market value) under a finance lease. The contract is for a five-year period. The annual lease payment amounts to 150 CU. The purchase option at the end of the lease has been established at 10 CU. Such equipment would usually, if owned outright, be depreciated over an eight-year period.

The interest rate implicit in the lease may be determined by applying the method described below (and see additional information in Appendix 12.3).

Value of the equipment	600 CU
Total payments (5 × 150 + 10)	760 CU

The value of the asset is provided by the following formula (solving for i):

$$\text{Value of the leased equipment} = \text{lease payment} \times \sum_{t=1}^{5} \frac{1}{(1+i)^t} + \frac{\text{Purchase option}}{(1+i)^5}$$

$$= 150 \times \sum_{t=1}^{5} \frac{1}{(1+i)^t} + \frac{10}{(1+i)^5}$$

In this formula, the factor

$$\sum_{t=1}^{5} \frac{1}{(1+i)^t}$$

can be replaced by the following formula

$$\frac{1-(1+i)^{-n}}{i}$$

where n represents the duration of the contract, i.e., in this case five years.

Since the purchase value of the asset is known, one can solve the above equation for i. The interest rate i may be obtained from a statistics table (such as the one provided in Appendix 12.3) or by using some advanced handheld calculators, spreadsheet, or statistics software. Our example yields an implied rate of interest $i = 8.357\%$. In the case where the implicit rate is impossible to determine mathematically, the lessee's incremental borrowing rate may be used. Table 12.8 shows the schedule of financial amortization of the implicit debt.

It is important to note that the beginning lease liability equals the value of the equipment (600 CU) and not the total payments (760 CU).

The depreciation of the equipment will follow the depreciation schedule shown in Table 12.9. Given that the useful life is eight years, the depreciation rate is 12.5% (1/8) if straight line is used.

Figure 12.10 illustrates the accounting of the leased asset in year 1 as both an asset and a liability, using the information from both Tables 12.8 and 12.9.

Because the time schedule of the expense paid (lease payment of 150) differs from that of the reported expense (Depreciation expense + Interest expense = 75 + 50.14 = 125.14, for example in year 1), a deferred taxation situation arises (see Chapters 6 and 13).

Table 12.8 Repayment schedule of the implicit debt

Year	Beginning lease liability	Interest expense	Repayment of liability	Lease payment	Ending lease liability
	(1)	(2) = (1) × 8.357%	(3) = (4) − (2)	(4)	(5) = (1) − (3)
Year 1	600.00	50.14	99.86	150.00	500.14
Year 2	500.14	41.80	108.20	150.00	391.94
Year 3	391.94	32.75	117.24	150.00	274.70
Year 4	274.70	22.96	127.04	150.00	147.66
Year 5	147.66	12.34	137.66	150.00	10.00
Purchase	10.00		10.00	10.00	0.00
Total		160.00	600.00	760.00	

Table 12.9 Depreciation schedule of the leased equipment (assuming straight-line depreciation)

Year	Depreciable basis	Depreciation expense	Book value
Year 1	600	75	525
Year 2	525	75	450
Year 3	450	75	375
Year 4	375	75	300
Year 5	300	75	225
Year 6	225	75	150
Year 7	150	75	75
Year 8	75	75	0

Figure 12.10 Capitalization of leased equipment

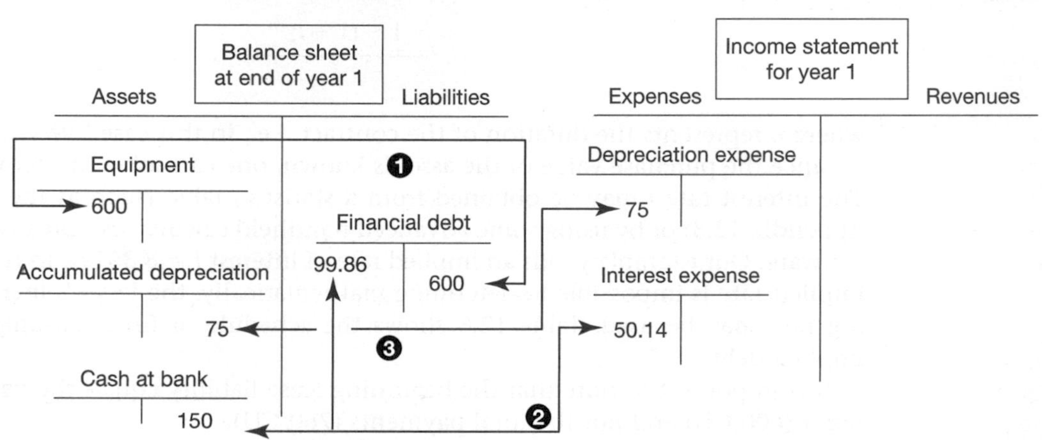

❶ The leased equipment is recorded as both an asset and a liability (for the same amount).
❷ The leased payment (150) is split between interest expense and repayment of the financial debt (figures are derived from Table 12.8).
❸ The leased asset is depreciated over eight years (figures are derived from Table 12.9).

2.2.5 Operating leases

According to IAS 17 (§ 33): 'Lease payments under an operating lease shall be recognized as an expense on a straight-line basis over the lease term unless another systematic basis is more representative of the time pattern of the user's benefit'.

2.2.6 Sale [of an asset] and leaseback transactions

Sale and leaseback transactions are developed in Appendix 12.5.

2.2.7 Reporting lease agreements to the users of financial information

Since leases are a very important way through which a business acquires control over assets (alternative to outright acquisition), it is very important to agree on how the commitment created by the lease is reported.

The IASB position IAS 17 (§ 31) states that lessees should disclose the following elements regarding their finance leases:

(a) 'For each class of asset, the net carrying amount at the balance sheet date;

(b) Reconciliation between the total of future minimum lease payments at the balance sheet date, and their present value. In addition, an entity shall disclose the total of future minimum lease payments at the balance sheet date, and their present value, for each of the following periods: (i) not later than one year; (ii) later than one year and not later than five years; (iii) later than five years.

(c) Contingent rents recognized in income for the period;

(d) (...)

(e) A general description of the lessee's significant leasing arrangements including, but not limited to, the following: (i) the basis on which contingent rent payable are determined; (ii) the existence and terms of renewal or purchase options (...), and (iii) restrictions imposed by lease arrangements, such as those concerning dividends, additional debt, and further leasing'.

Real-life example Benihana

(USA – US GAAP – *Source*: Annual report 2005 – Japanese style restaurants essentially in the US: Tepanyaki-style and sushi)

Excerpts from the notes to consolidated financial statements

Note 10 Leases

The company generally operates its restaurants in leased premises. The typical restaurant premises lease is for a term of between 15 to 25 years with renewal options ranging from 5 to 25 years. The leases generally provide for the payment of property taxes, utilities, and various other use and occupancy costs. Rentals under certain leases are based on a percentage of sales in excess of a certain minimum level. Certain leases provide for [built-in] increases based upon changes in the consumer price index. The company is also obligated under various leases for restaurant equipment and for office space and equipment.

Minimum payments under lease commitments are summarized below for capital and operating leases. The imputed interest rates used in the calculations for capital leases vary from 9.75% to 12% and are equivalent to the rates which would have been incurred to borrow, over a similar term, the amounts necessary to purchase the leased assets.

The amounts of operating and capital lease obligations are as follows (in [$] thousands):

Fiscal year ending:	Operating leases	Capital leases [i.e., finance leases]
2006	10,079	27
2007	10,365	
2008	10,342	
2009	10,423	
2010	10,050	
Thereafter	92,218	
Total minimum lease payments	143,477	27
Less amount representing interest		1
Total obligations under capital leases		26
Less current maturities		26
Long-term obligations under capitalized leases at 27 March 2005		0

Comment: This example also illustrates the required disclosure for operating leases.

2.3 Environmental liability

More and more businesses are aware that their business activity may create environmental risks. They not only explicitly manage such risk but also want to report the potential liabilities this creates (both as a signaling move to customers and other stakeholders, and for the sake of completeness of reporting to shareholders, analysts, and investors). This 'environmental liability' is presented in Appendix 12.6.

2.4 Employee benefits and pension accounting

Employee benefits give rise to complex future obligations. International Accounting Standard 19 (IASB 2002) deals with this topic. Its paragraph 4 distinguishes short-term employee benefits (while being employed), post-employment benefits, other long-term employee benefits and termination benefits. It defines the first three categories as:

(a) 'Short-term employee benefits, such as wages, salaries and social security contributions, paid annual leave and paid sick leave, profit-sharing and bonuses (if payable within twelve months of the end of the period) and non-monetary benefits (such as medical care, housing, cars and free or subsidized goods or services) for current employees;

(b) Post-employment benefits such as pensions, other retirement benefits, post-employment life insurance and post-employment medical care;

(c) Other long-term employee benefits, including long-service leave or sabbatical leave, jubilee or other long-service benefits, long-term disability benefits and, if they are not payable wholly within twelve months after the end of the period, profit-sharing, bonuses and deferred compensation'.

Figure 12.11 summarizes, in a simplified way, the accounting issues arising from the handling of employee benefits.

Figure 12.11 Accounting for employee benefits

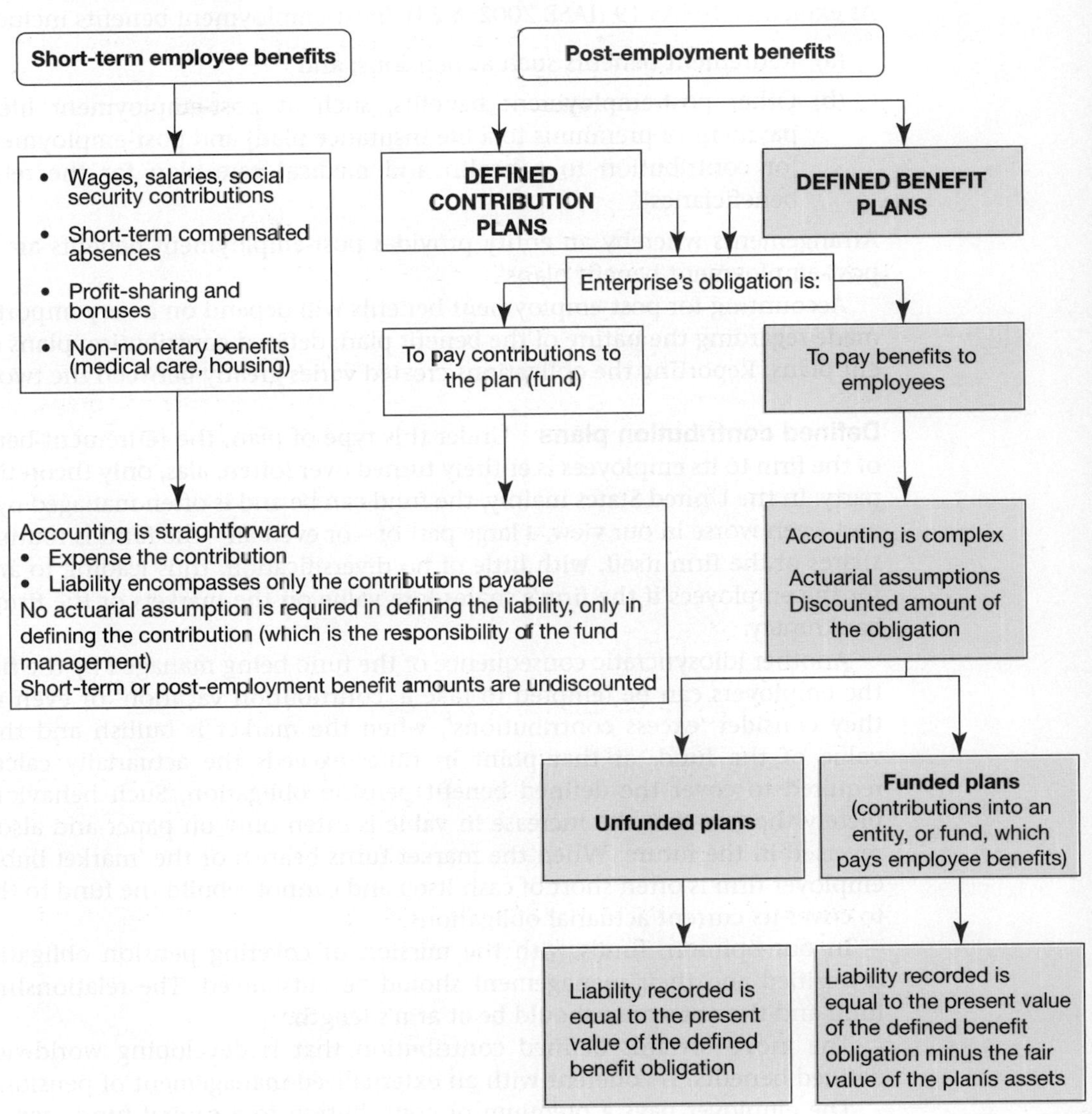

Let us now examine the various components of Figure 12.11.

2.4.1 Short-term employee benefits

Accounting for short-term employee benefits, as seen earlier, is generally straightforward because no actuarial assumption is required to evaluate the obligation and its cost. A business should recognize the undiscounted amount of short-term employee benefits expected to be paid in exchange of the service rendered by employees:

- as an expense for the amount paid whenever payment takes place;
- as a liability (accrued expense) for the amount accrued and still due (the expense of the period minus any amount already paid).

2.4.2 Post-employment benefits

As explained in IAS 19 (IASB 2002: § 24), 'post-employment benefits include, for example:

(a) Retirement benefits such as pensions; and

(b) Other post-employment benefits, such as post-employment life insurance [or payment of premiums to a life insurance plan] and post-employment medical care [or contribution to a health and medical care plan for the retirees and their beneficiaries].

Arrangements whereby an entity provides post-employment benefits are [referred to as] post-employment benefit plans'.

Accounting for post-employment benefits will depend on a very important distinction made regarding the nature of the benefit plan: defined contribution plans or defined benefit plans. Reporting the obligations created varies greatly between the two types of plans.

Defined contribution plans Under this type of plan, the retirement benefit obligation of the firm to its employees is entirely turned over (often, alas, only theoretically) to a third party. In the United States mainly, the fund can be and is often managed by the firm itself, and, even worse in our view, a large part of – or even all – the fund is routinely invested in shares of the firm itself, with little of no diversification, thus leading to an increased risk for the employees if the firm's shares lose value on the markets or the firm has to declare bankruptcy.

Another idiosyncratic consequence of the fund being managed by the firm itself is that the employers can be tempted to take a 'contribution vacation' or even withdraw what they consider 'excess contributions', when the market is bullish and thus the current value of the fund, at that point in time, exceeds the actuarially calculated amount required to cover the defined benefit pension obligation, Such behavior ignores completely the fact that the increase in value is often only on paper and also that it can be reversed in the future. When the market turns bearish or the 'market bubble' bursts, the employer firm is often short of cash itself and cannot rebuild the fund to the level needed to cover its current actuarial obligations.

In our opinion, funds with the mission of covering pension obligations should be diversified and their management should be outsourced. The relationship between the fund and the enterprise should be at arm's length.

The move towards defined contribution that is developing worldwide, away from defined benefits, is coherent with an externalized management of pension funds.

The employer pays a premium or contribution to a capital fund managed by a third party that will provide the service contractually agreed with the employee(s) (capital or annuity). The business need not recognize any obligation, provision, or liability. Accounting for the contribution expenses to a defined contribution plan is absolutely identical to that of short-term employee benefits such as salaries or wages.

Defined contribution plans are quite common in Europe where many state-run, -controlled or -appointed agencies have been created specifically to be the third party relieving the employer from any post-employment benefit obligation management beyond the payment of the contributions.

Defined benefit plans In defined benefit plans, the enterprise itself assumes the obligation to provide in the future the agreed benefits to current and former employees. This obligation needs to be measured (quantified), managed, and reported in the balance sheet. However, 'accounting for defined benefit plans is complex because actuarial assumptions are required to measure the obligation and expense and there is a possibility of actuarial gains and losses. Moreover, the obligations are measured on a discounted basis because they may be settled many years after the employees render the related service' (IASB 2002: § 48).

In addition to providing retirement pay until the former employee, or his beneficiaries decease, many businesses have chosen or negotiated the payment of a retirement bonus (at the time of retirement) that is most of the time proportional to the length of employment in the firm. Since the calculation method of the bonus is public knowledge[5] and cannot be modified without negotiation, such bonuses are considered to be defined benefits and should be recognized as an expense (and funded) throughout the period of employment since they are part of the compensation package for services rendered.

An enterprise has a choice of alternatives in handling defined benefit plans:

- *The plan may be unfunded.* In this case the business bears the sole responsibility of the obligation and pays the agreed upon benefits to the employees, either on a pay-as-you-go basis (the expense is covered as incurred – a very risky proposition either when the active workforce headcount reduces faster than the population of beneficiaries does, or when an economic downturn affects the profitability and liquidity of the firm), or by saving privately to cover the obligation and managing the fund inside the firm itself. In addition, unfunded pension plans tend to create ethical issues: when the savings created by the enterprise have increased in value (due to a bull market, for example) the value of the fund may vastly exceed the actuarially needed funds; the enterprise may be tempted to recapture the contributions it appears to have paid in excess of the need. Such situations have not been uncommon in the past. They have potentially dramatic consequences when the market turns bearish. For all these reasons, unfunded plans tend to become unusual because of the risks they offer.
- *The plan may be funded*, either partly or completely. In this case the enterprise pays a contribution premium to an entity (or fund) that is (in theory) legally and completely separate and independent from the reporting business. The contribution premiums will be managed by the fund so as to create enough capital to allow future payment of the agreed benefits. This type of plan is the most common. The contribution premium expenses are equivalent to a 'forced' saving plan for the firm. Insurance companies have made a specialty of managing this type of fund as they have the actuarial expertise in establishing the level of the contributions that will guarantee the ability to honor the contractual obligation of the fund to the employer and the employees.

In a simplified way, the amount recognized as a defined benefit liability in the balance sheet will be the net total of the following amounts:

(1) net present value of the defined benefit obligation as of the balance sheet date
minus (2) the fair value on the balance sheet date of the plan's assets (if the plan is funded).

In practice, the calculations required for the quantification of defined benefits obligations are rather complex. They require the use of the services of actuaries. Such a topic is generally well covered in an intermediate accounting course[6].

2.5 Financial statement analysis

The choices made regarding how to value, record, and report the business future obligations to a variety of constituencies impact on the understanding of and the ability to decode the firm's situation through its financial statements. Choices made about liability reporting affect also the asset side (through the capitalization of leases) and the value of various ratios.

2.5.1 Capitalized leased assets

Even if the firm does not capitalize its leases (the frontier between finance and operational leases is fuzzy at times), analysts generally restate the published financial information and treat any ambiguous lease as a finance lease to create the financial statement that would have been obtained if the asset had been acquired and 100% financed by debt. In the restated income statement, the interest portion of the lease payment is classified as 'interest expense' and the depreciation expense of the lease payment is a part of the depreciation expense. Both the balance sheet and the income statement are affected by the handling of leases and thus many ratios are also affected.

2.5.2 Ratios

Although ratios will be covered extensively as part of Chapter 15, Table 12.10 lists some of the key ratios pertaining to liabilities. These ratios are especially important in evaluating both the risk and the return on investment a business can offer to investors. All these ratios can be affected greatly by the choices made in handling the recognition of liabilities. Provisions (which, as mentioned, can sometimes be used for income smoothing) are generally included in liabilities for the computation of debt ratios. Some analysts exploit the notes to the financial statements to eventually restate the provisioned amounts and the income statement or simulate the range of values the ratios could take if the provisions were either accepted at face value or restated under specified hypotheses.

These ratios are critical for a potential lender or investor who may need to evaluate the risk attached to a transaction with another firm. One critical element of the dynamics of the risk evaluation is that the larger the shareholders' equity is, the lower are the liabilities to third parties and thus the less risky the business appears to be to a lender (and conversely). The first three ratios in Table 12.10 relate to that aspect of the evaluation of the firm's risk. They reflect the weight of third-party liabilities in the long-term financial resources of the firm. The fourth ratio in Table 12.10 (interest coverage) reflects the likely capability of the firm to face its interest obligation. This ratio is often considered to be a good proxy for the ability of the firm to cover its short-term or current liabilities or obligations. The fifth ratio is an indication of the power of the entity over its suppliers and indicates whether or not suppliers contribute to more than funding inventories.

Table 12.10 Debt ratios

Name of the ratio	Computation	Interpretation or meaning
Debt ratio or Debt to total assets ratio	Total debt/Total assets	Firm's long-term debt-paying ability The lower this ratio, the better the company's position
Debt to equity ratio	Debt[7]/Shareholders' equity or Debt/(Shareholders' equity + Debt)	
Long-term debt to equity ratio	Long-term debt/Shareholders' equity or Long-term debt/(Shareholders' equity + Debt)	Firm's degree of financial leverage
Interest coverage ratio	Operating income (before interest expense and income taxes)/ Interest expense	Number of times that a firm's interest expense is covered by operation earnings Rule of thumb: minimum of five
Inventory trade financing	Accounts payable/Inventory	How much do suppliers contribute to financing the operational cycle. If the ratio is greater than 1, suppliers are contributing to the possible growth of the firm

The generic definitions of the ratios presented in Table 12.10 are subject to many variations and adaptations to serve the specific needs of the analyst. Amendments can be made to either or both of the numerator or the denominator. For example, some practitioners restrict long-term liabilities in their ratio calculations to long-term interest-bearing liabilities.

Minority interests in consolidated statements (percentage of a subsidiary's shareholders' equity held by shareholders different from the parent company) add a little complexity to the calculation of the key liability-based ratios. Chapter 13 deals with these issues. A key question is to decide whether minority interests are part of liabilities or part of shareholders' equity. Both choices are possible in reporting the financial position of the firm.

Key points

- Liabilities are obligations to pay cash or to provide goods and services to third parties in the future. They represent a major source of financing in any business.
- Liabilities are classified as current versus non-current, which encompasses two presentations: operating versus financial (emphasis on operating cycle); or short-term versus long-term (emphasis on solvency).
- Weight represented by liabilities in the balance sheet as well as liabilities reporting practices are extremely variable across countries, business sectors, and firms.
- Liabilities should be distinguished from related but different concepts: (1) accrued liabilities; (2) provision; and (3) contingent liabilities on the basis of their varying degrees of certainty in (1) the principle causing the obligation, (2) its timing, and (3) its amount.
- The value of bonds depends on the market rate at the time of issuance. Bonds may be issued with a premium (sold above par if the interest rate is higher than the market rate) or with a discount (sold below par, in the opposite case).
- Leasing is a very convenient and flexible medium for obtaining the right to use a fixed asset. Operating leases and finance leases respond to different business needs, follow different business models and need to be handled differently in the accounting and the reporting systems. A finance lease is equivalent to the acquisition of an asset completely financed by a loan. Most countries require that financial leases be reported in the balance sheet as both a fixed asset and a financial liability.
- Costs relating to short-term employee benefits and defined contribution plans for post-employment benefits are expenses as incurred.
- Defined benefits plans for post-employment benefits open complex issues of valuation and accounting. They mainly require provisioning (or recognizing the (ever) increasing pension liability) during the period of employment of the eligible workforce.

Review (solutions are at the back of the book)

Review 12.1 Stenborg

Topic: Repayment of a bank loan
Related part of the chapter: Core issues

The Stenborg Company obtained a bank loan on 30 June X1, with the following terms and conditions:

- Amount: 100,000 CU.
- Annual interest: 10%.
- Reimbursement by ordinary annuities starting on 30 June X2 (annual payment).
- Term to maturity of the loan: 5 years.
- Closing date used by Stenborg in its books: 31 December.

Required

1. Compute the amount of the constant annuity (interest expense plus part of the principal)
2. Present the repayment schedule of the debt.
3. Show the accounting entries:
   - On the date of subscription
   - On the first closing date
   - On the first repayment date.

Review 12.2 Haeffner PLC (1)

Topic: Provisions and contingent liabilities
Related part of the chapter: Core issues

Haeffner PLC is an accounting firm. Some of its clients face the following situations. For each, it is assumed that a reliable estimate can be made of any outflows expected:

1. Acme Manufacturing Enterprises Ltd (AME) provides a warranty on its products at the time of sale. Under the terms of the warranty contract, AME undertakes to make good, by repair or replacement, any manufacturing defect that becomes apparent within three years from the date of sale. Based on past experience, it is probable that there will be some claims under the warranties.
2. Stone Oil Industries Co. (SOI) has been a medium-size oil producer and refiner for the past 50 years. It operates in many parts of the world. On occasions, SOI units have incurred spills of crude or refined products that have contaminated land and water. It is SOI's management philosophy that clean up should be organized only when the firm is required to do so under the laws of the country in which the spill took place. One country in which SOI operates has, until now, not had any legislation requiring cleaning up. SOI has been contaminating land and water in that country for several years without taking any corrective action. On 31 December X1 it becomes virtually certain that a draft law mandating retroactive cleaning up of land and waterways already contaminated will be enacted shortly after the year-end.
3. Sudstrom AB is a large upscale retail store established in most major consumer market areas. It has built its reputation on selection and quality of its products and on a well-advertised policy of refunding purchases to dissatisfied customers without asking any question as long as Sudstrom carries the product, even in cases where the store may not be under any legal obligation to do so.
4. On 18 December X1, the board of Zygafuss Agglomerated Enterprises Co. (ZAE) decided to close down one of its industrial divisions. By closing date (31 December) the decision had not yet been communicated to any of those affected (not even to the Works Council), and no other steps had been taken to implement the decision.

5. During X1 Mutter GmbH had provided a loan guarantee for the benefit of Scout AG, a trading partner (in which Mutter does not hold any share interest) opening the market for Mutter products in Transmoldavia. Scout's financial condition at that time is considered to be sound and its economic prospects bright. Bankers have, however, requested a loan guarantee because of the short history of Scout in this market and the possible instability of the Transmoldavian market. During X2 the market in Transmoldavia experiences a serious economic downturn and Scout's financial condition deteriorates. On 30 June X2 Scout AG actually files for protection from its creditors.

Required

Analyze each of these five situations and make a recommendation for each as to the necessity of recording (and reporting) or not an appropriate provision.

Assignments

Assignment 12.1
Multiple-choice questions

Related part of the chapter: Core issues

Select the right answer (one possible answer, unless otherwise mentioned).

1. Provisions for risks and liabilities are recorded
   (a) In the expenses
   (b) In the revenues
   (c) In the shareholders' equity and liabilities
   (d) As a contra-asset
   (e) None of these
2. An example of financial liabilities is
   (a) Income tax payable
   (b) Unearned revenues
   (c) Bank borrowings
   (d) Salaries payable
   (e) None of these
3. An example of a current liability is
   (a) Bank loan or borrowing (long-term portion)
   (b) Unearned revenues
   (c) Share capital
   (d) Retained earnings
   (e) None of these
4. An example of an item that is not a current liability is
   (a) Accrued expenses
   (b) Prepaid expenses
   (c) Salaries payable
   (d) Accounts payable
   (e) Unearned revenues
   (f) None of these
5. Warranty costs are recognized as an expense
   (a) At the time the products covered by the warranty are sold
   (b) At the time the costs are really incurred
   (c) Neither of the above
6. When the balance sheet is presented by nature, the current portion of a long-term liability is still included in the financial liabilities section of the balance sheet
   (a) True
   (b) False
7. Notes payable represent bills of exchange or promissory notes
   (a) True
   (b) False
8. The net salary (after deduction of withholdings) is recorded as an expense
   (a) True
   (b) False
9. A contingent liability is recorded
   (a) As part of the assets
   (b) As part of the shareholders' equity and liabilities
   (c) As part of the revenues
   (d) As part of the expenses
   (e) None of these

10 A provision for restructuring can be recorded as soon as a company has decided to close a business entity
   (a) True
   (b) False

Assignment 12.2
Reporting liabilities in different sectors of activity

Related part of the chapter: Core issues

On the Internet, or in the library, find the annual reports of four companies from different sectors of activity in a given country or in different countries.

Required

1. How are liabilities presented in their balance sheet? What decisions on the basis of this information can investors or shareholders take? What decisions would be difficult to take on the basis of just this information?
2. Are there any notes relating to liabilities? How do they enlarge the decision analysis possibilities offered to shareholders and investors?
3. What are the accounting treatments applied to these liabilities?
4. What is the weight of liabilities as a percentage of total shareholders' equity and liabilities? What strategic implications do you derive from this ratio?

Assignment 12.3
Reporting liabilities in the same sector of activity

Related part of the chapter: Core issues

On the Internet, or in the library, find the annual reports of four companies essentially in identical or similar industries in a given country or in different countries.

Required

Use questions from Assignment 12.2.

Assignment 12.4
Club Méditerranée*

Topic: Bonds, bank loans, and debts
Related part of the chapter: Core issues

Club Méditerranée, a French leisure company, reports the following information relating to its financial liabilities (*source*: Annual report 2004, financial year ended 31 October 2004):

Consolidated balance sheets at 31 October (excerpts)

Millions of €	Notes	31 Oct 2003	31 Oct 2004
Liabilities and shareholders' equity			
(...)			
Borrowings	3.13	564	550
(...)			

Note 3.13: Bonds, bank loans and other debt

Millions of €	31 Oct 2003	31 Oct 2004
OCEANE convertible/ exchangeable bonds	144	144
Total bonds	144	144
Short-term bank loans and overdrafts	20	27
Current maturities of long-term debt	22	250
Long-term debt	378	129
Total bank loans and debts	420	406
Total	564	550

Note 3-13-1: Analysis of debt by category

	31 Oct 2003	31 Oct 2004
Bonds	144	144
Obligations under capital leases	47	89
Bank borrowings	352	282
Other borrowings, deposits received and accrued interest	1	8
Bank overdrafts	20	27
Total	564	550

Required

1. Reconcile the figures provided in the notes with those provided in the balance sheet.
2. What do 'convertible bonds' represent?
3. What do 'obligations under capital leases' represent?
4. What does 'accrued interest' represent? Why is it included in 'borrowings'?
5. What is the difference between 'current maturities of long-term debt' and 'short-term bank loans'?
6. Are 'short-term bank loans' and 'overdrafts' equivalent?
7. In terms of presentation, what is the major difference between the two tables excerpted from the notes?

Assignment 12.5
Haeffner PLC (2)

Topic: Provisions and contingent liabilities
Related part of the chapter: Core issues

Haeffner PLC is an accounting firm. Some of its clients face the following situations. For each, it is assumed that a reliable estimate can be made of any outflows expected:

1. On 9 December X1 the board of Shankar Inc. decided to close down its defense division, effective 1 June X2. On 20 December X1 a detailed plan for closing down the division was agreed by the board. The plan was further discussed and amended during a scheduled meeting of the Works Council on 21 December. In the following week, letters were sent to customers warning them to seek alternative sources of supply and redundancy notices were sent to the staff of the division who would not be offered other positions in the company. The accounting closing date of Shankar Inc. is 31 December.
2. The government introduces a number of changes in legislation, which will generate the need for Acme Amalgamated Enterprises Co. to retrain its security and quality control staff. At closing date, no retraining of staff has taken place.
3. Five people were severely injured in an industrial accident in which machinery and equipment sold by Lang Sein Enterprise Inc. was involved. The injured parties' lawyers have started legal proceedings against Lang Sein Enterprise, seeking damages. Lang Sein disputes its liability. As of the date of approval for publication of the financial statements for the year ending 31 December X1, Lang Sein's lawyers are of the opinion that the evidence will probably show that the enterprise will not be found liable. However, one year later, due to new developments in the case, the Lang Sein lawyers believe that it is probable the enterprise will be found at least partially liable.

Required

Analyze each situation and conclude about the necessity to record a provision or not.

Assignment 12.6
Stora Enso*, Repsol YPF*, Barlow*, Cobham* and Thales*

Topic: Reporting movements in provisions
Related part of the chapter: Core issues

You are provided with excerpts from notes to consolidated financial statements of five companies reporting movements in provisions.

Stora Enso

(Finland – IAS GAAP – *Source*: Annual report 2004 – Production of paper)

	Other provisions			
€ million	Environmental	Reorganization	Other obligatory	Total provisions
Carrying value at 31 December 2003	47.2	48.6	31.8	127.6
Translation difference	0.1	−1.5	0.1	−1.3
Reclassification	–	4.6	−4.6	0.0
Disposals	–	–	−14.7	−14.7
Charge in Income Statement				
New provisions	2.7	6.2	–	–8.9
Increase in existing provisions	1.3	3.1	3.8	8.2
Reversal of existing provisions	–	−1.1	−0.2	−1.3
Payments	−5.9	−28.9	−11.0	−45.8
Carrying value at 31 December 2004	45.4	31.0	5.2	81.6

Repsol YPF

(Spain – Spanish GAAP – *Source*: Annual report 2004 – Oil and gas)

Note 14. Provisions for contingencies and expenses

€ Millions	Provision for pension	Provision for labor force restructuring	Dismantling of fields	Commitments and contingent liabilities	Reversion reserves	Other provisions	Total
Balance as of 31 December 2003	75	12	151	326	40	850	1,454
Period provisions charged to income	9	3	34	443	6	439	934
Provision released with credit to income	(1)	–	(1)	(7)	–	(27)	(36)
Provision used due to payment	(8)	(7)	(3)	(25)	–	(122)	(165)
Variations in scope of consolidation	–	2	–	14	–	6	22
Translation differences	(5)	–	(10)	(12)	–	(43)	(70)
Reclassifications and other variations	6	(2)	17	24	–	(40)	5
Balance as of 31 December 2004	76	8	188	763	46	1,063	2,144

The 'Other provisions' caption includes mainly technical reserves for insurance, provisions for environmental contingencies, provisions for litigation in progress, and other provisions for future contingencies.

Barloworld

(South Africa – IFRS/South African GAAP – *Source*: Annual report 2004 – Heavy equipment, material handling equipment, motors, cement, and lime)

Movement of provisions

(Millions of Rands) ZARm	Total 2004	Environmental rehabilitation	Onerous contracts	Insurance claims	Maintenance contracts	Post-retirement benefits	Warranty claims	Rights to Avis shares	Other
Balance at beginning of year as previously reported	758	103	46	69	126	271	85		58
Amounts added	1,023	2	10	43	456	57	155	166	134
Amounts used	(663)		(20)	(30)	(262)	(29)	(158)	(65)	(99)
Amounts reversed unused	(111)		(2)		(1)	(102)	(1)		(5)
Unwinding of discount in present valued amounts	2	2							
Translation adjustments	(10)				(4)	(4)	(1)		(1)
Other	3	1	(1)		(1)	(1)	2		3
Balance at end of year	1,002	108	33	82	314	192	82	101	90

Cobham

(United Kingdom – UK GAAP – *Source*: Annual report 2004 – Equipment, systems, and components for aerospace and defense industries)

Note 18. Provisions for liabilities and charges

Group: £m	Deferred taxation	Contingent consideration	Other	Total
At 1 January 2004	18.4	7.6	13.3	39.3
Re-analysis from creditors	–	5.5	0.2	5.7
Provisions created	2.2	–	4.3	6.5
On acquisitions in the year	(0.4)	–	0.3	(0.1)
Adjustment to contingent consideration in respect of prior year acquisitions	–	(0.5)	–	(0.5)
Provisions released	–	–	(2.9)	(2.9)
Expenditure charged against provisions	–	(5.3)	(4.4)	(9.7)
Foreign exchange adjustments	–	(0.2)	–	(0.2)
At 31 December 2004	20.2	7.1	10.8	38.1

The provisions for liabilities and charges, excluding deferred taxation, represent:

Class of provision	Estimated repayment period	Amount £M
Legal claims	Within one year	0.8
Onerous trading contracts	Over the next three years	9.0
Warranty claims	Over the next three years	1.0
Contingent consideration	Within one year	1.4
Contingent consideration	Over one to two years	0.5
Contingent consideration	Over two to three years	1.4
Contingent consideration	Over three to four years	3.8
		17.9

Thales

(France – French GAAP – *Source*: Annual report 2004 – Electronic systems and industrial electronics)

Note 18.2 Provisions for restructuring – Provisions on contracts and other provisions

	Opening balance	Changes in scope of consolidation, exchange rate, and other variations	Charges	Recoveries	Year-end balance
Restructuring	127.7	1.8	89.1	(84.5)	134.1
Estimated losses on long-term contracts	294.9	(29.6)	89.3	(112.9)	241.7
Accrued costs on completed contracts	32.6	(16.3)	7.8	(6.7)	17.4
Accrued penalties claims	130.1	3.9	56.1	(46.3)	143.8
Litigation	95.9	9.5	24.9	(54.1)	76.2
Guarantees and performance obligations	151.3	(8.7)	45.0	(41.9)	145.7
Other	164.4	(13.7)	70.1	(52.6)	168.2
Total	869.2	(54.9)	293.2	(314.5)	793.0
Net Total	996.9	(53.1)	382.3	(399.0)	927.1

For the five studied companies, all the figures mentioned in the caption 'total' or 'balance at end of period' have been recorded in the balance sheet.

Required

1. What is (are) the main formal difference(s) you can notice in the presentation of the tables between the five companies?
2. Identify and comment on the differences in the terminology used to name each table.
3. Explain each component of the movements for the five studied companies.
4. Explain the nature of each provision.
5. What difference(s) do you notice in the way these companies record reductions in provisions?

Assignment 12.7
Nilsson Company

Topic: Leasing
Related part of the chapter: Advanced issues

Nilsson Company closes its books on 31 December each year. During the past year they have taken a three-year lease on a computer web server to support the development of their e-business activities. The terms and conditions of the lease agreement are provided as Exhibit 1. The lease contract itself is summarized in Exhibit 2. In the case of an outright acquisition of the web server, Nilsson would have depreciated it on a straight-line basis over five years.

Required

1. Explain how this contract should be recorded in Nilsson's books if the company does not capitalize the lease.
2. Calculate the implicit interest rate in this lease contract. Prepare the schedule of amortization of a loan that would have the same principal, the same semi-annual reimbursements and the same residual value. Break down each semi-annual reimbursement between interest expense and principal reimbursement for the 3 years.
3. Illustrate the accounting entries required if the lease were capitalized (year one only).
4. Prepare the relevant information that should be placed in the notes to the financial statements if the leased equipment were not capitalized.

Exhibit 1: Everylease PLC

26 December X0
Customer: Nilsson Company
Object: File no. 982 (Nilsson)

Characteristics of the equipment provided by Everylease PLC to Nilsson Company:

- Price of the Web Server (in CU) 1,500
- Date of availability 1 January X1
- Purchase residual value of the Web server at the end of the contract (in CU) 10

Schedule of payments and terms of the contract (all payments are due at the end of the relevant period): There will be six semi-annual rent payments of 280 CU each on the following dates: 30 June X1, 31 December X1, 30 June X2, 31 December X2, 30 June X3, 31 December X3.

Exhibit 2: Lease contract

The following lease agreement is between, on one hand, Everylease, Public Limited Company, with a capital of 2,000,000 CU; Headquarters address: 15, Lost Rents Avenue, London, UK, hereafter called 'the lessor' and Nilsson Company, on the other hand, hereafter called 'the lessee'. The parties agree to the following:

1 Order and commitment to lease

The lessor has ordered from:

Micro Server Incorporated (hereafter called 'the supplier'), the equipment selected directly by the lessee from the supplier. Equipment consists of the following: Microcomputer Server Hexium V, 1,200 Mhz purchased at a price of 1,500 CU.

- The lessee has committed to take delivery of the equipment as ordered.
- The actual price in the lease will reflect the prices practiced by the supplier and the lessee acknowledges knowing what this price is going to be or accept what it will be.
- Delivery of the equipment will take place in accordance to the terms and conditions enumerated in Article 1 of the General Conditions of Lease Contracts and on the date agreed to by both supplier and lessee.

2 Lease date and duration

- The lease agreement is for an irrevocable 36-month period and will be effective as of the signing of the contract pursuant to the terms and conditions of Article 1 of the General Conditions of Lease Contracts.
- Residual value: The residual value at the end of the irrevocable lease period pursuant to Articles 5, 9, and 10 of the General Conditions of Lease Contracts granting the lessee an option to buy is set at 0.67% of the actual price of the equipment.
- If the purchase option is exercised by the lessee, the residual value will be paid by lessee to lessor on 31 December X3.

3 Schedule and amount of the rent

- The first semi-annual rent payment is due at the end of the semester during which the delivery took place as attested by the invoice of the supplier and the signed delivery notice; a copy of each shall be forwarded to lessor.
- The lease payments will be in six semi-annual payments of equal amount.

Signed	*Signed*
The lessor	The lessee

Assignment 12.8
Easynet*

Topic: Reporting for leasing
Related part of the chapter: Advanced issues

Easynet, a British Internet service provider, reports in its financial statements for the year ended 31 December 2004 the following simplified balance sheet (*source*: annual report 2004).

Easynet – Simplified balance sheet

	2004 £'000	2003 £'000
Fixed assets	99,859	67,788
Current assets	74,511	113,203
Creditors: amounts falling due within one year	(76,277)	(74,476)
Net current liabilities	(1,766)	38,727
Total assets less current liabilities	98,093	106,515
Creditors: amounts falling due after more than one year	(115,004)	(115,439)
Provisions for liabilities and charges	(14,607)	(16,440)
Total net assets	(31,518)	(25,364)
Shareholders' funds	(31,518)	(25,364)

In the notes to the accounts, the detail of creditors is provided:

Note: Creditors: amounts falling due within one year	2004 £'000	2003 £'000
Bank loans and overdrafts	1,770	–
Obligations under finance leases	173	324
Trade creditors	25,520	23,876
Amounts owed to Group undertakings	–	–
Corporate taxation	31	63
Other taxation and social security	2,562	2,727
Other creditors	1,661	1,810
Accruals	15,664	20,349
Deferred income	28,896	25,327
	76,277	74,476

Creditors: amounts falling due after more than one year	2004 £'000	2003 £'000
Bank loans	2,842	–
Obligations under finance leases (note 16)	59,302	59,469
Other creditors	1,552	942
Deferred income	51,308	55,028
	115,004	115,439

The notes also report special information on leases:

Assets held under finance leases and hire purchase contracts are capitalized at their fair value on the inception of the leases and depreciated over their estimated useful lives. The finance charges are allocated over the period of the lease in proportion to the capital amount outstanding.

Rentals under operating leases are charged to the profit and loss account as they accrue.

Note 16: Finance lease obligations	2004 £'000	2003 £'000
Net obligations under finance leases:		
Within one year	173	324
Between one and two years	192	173
Between two and five years	713	642
In more than five years	58,397	58,654
	59,475	59,793

Note 6 Net finance costs (excerpts)	2004 £'000	2003 £'000
Interest payable and similar charges		
Bank loans, overdrafts and associated banking charges	(360)	(164)
Finance leases	(6,347)	(6,393)
	(6,707)	(6,557)

Required

1. Reconcile the figures reported for creditors in the notes and the figures given in the balance sheet.
2. Identify in the notes the figures relating to finance leases.
3. Reconcile the detail of creditors and the special information given on finance leases.
4. In the notes, what information relating to interest implicit in lease payments and to finance leases in general is not given?

Assignment 12.9
Mittal Steel*

Topic: Debt ratios
Related part of the chapter: Advanced issues

Mittal Steel is a global steel producer. It is registered in the Netherlands. The balance sheet and income statement for the years 2003 and 2004 (*Source*: Annual report 2004), prepared in accordance with US GAAP, are provided as follows.

Consolidated balance sheets

Year ended 31 December Millions of US dollars	2003	2004
Assets		
Current assets	3,683	9,625
Property, plant, and equipment	4,654	7,562
Investment in affiliates and joint ventures	967	667
Deferred tax assets	536	855
Intangible pension assets	117	106
Other assets	180	338
Total assets	10,137	19,153
Liabilities and shareholders' equity		
Current liabilities	2,619	6,230
Long-term debt – net of current portion	2,193	1,639
Loan from shareholder	94	–
Deferred tax liabilities	263	955
Deferred employee benefits	1,933	1,931
Other long-term obligations	213	809
Total liabilities	7,315	11,564
Minority interest	261	1,743
Shareholders' equity	2,561	5,846
Total liabilities and shareholders' equity	10,137	19,153

Consolidated statements of income

Year ended 31 December Millions of US dollars	2003	2004
Net sales	9,567	22,197
Costs and expenses:		
Cost of sales	7,568	14,694
Depreciation	331	553
Selling, general, and administrative	369	804
	8,268	16,051
Operating income	1,299	6,146
Other income (expense) – net	70	128
Income from equity method investments	162	66
Financing costs:		
Interest expense	(200)	(265)
Interest income	25	78
Net gain (loss) from foreign exchange transactions	44	(20)
	(131)	(207)
Income before taxes, minority interest, and cumulative effect of change in accounting principle	1,400	6,133
Income tax expense	184	817
Income before minority interest and cumulative effect of change in accounting principle	1,216	5,316
Minority interest	(35)	(615)
Income from continuing operations	1,181	4,701
Cumulative effect of change in accounting principle	1	–
Net income	1,182	4,701

Required

1. Compute for the years 2003 and 2004 the first four 'debt ratios' introduced in the Advanced issues of this chapter: debt ratio, debt to equity ratio, long-term debt to equity ratio, and interest coverage ratio.
2. Analyze these ratios. Notice that minority interests[8] are often included in equity in the computation of ratios based on this concept.

References

FASB (1976), Statement of Financial Accounting Standard No. 13: Accounting for Leases, Norwalk, CT.

IASB (1989), Framework for the Preparation and Presentation of Financial Statements, London.

IASB (2003a) International Accounting Standard No. 1: Presentation of Financial Statements, London.

IASB (2003b) International Accounting Standard No. 17: Leases, London.

IASB (2003c) International Accounting Standard No. 39: Financial Instruments: Recognition and Measurement, London.

IASB (1998) International Accounting Standard No. 37: Provisions, Contingent Liabilities and Contingent Assets, London.

IASB (2002) International Accounting Standard No. 19: Employee Benefits, London.

Plender, J., Simons, M., and Tricks, H. (2005), Cash benefit: how big supermarkets fund expansion by using suppliers as bankers, *Financial Times*, Wednesday 7 December 2005, 13

Skousen F., Stice J., and Stice E. K. (2003) *Intermediate Accounting*. South-Western College Publishing, Cincinnati, OH.

Vernimmen, P., Quiry, P., Dallocchio, M., Le Fur, Y., and Salvi, A. (2005) *Corporate Finance – Theory and Practice*. Dalloz–Wiley, Chichester.

Walton, P. (2000) *Financial Statement Analysis – An International Perspective*. Business Press Thomson Learning, London.

Further reading

Cravens, K.S. and Goad Oliver, E. (2000) The influence on culture on pension plans. *The International Journal of Accounting*, 35(4), 521–537.

Fisher, J. G., Maines, L. A., Peffer, S. A. and Sprinkle, G. B. (2005) An experimental investigation of employer discretion in employee performance evaluation and compensation. *The Accounting Review*, 80(2), 563–583.

Garrod, N. and Sieringhaus, I. (1995) European Union accounting harmonization: the case of leased assets in the United Kingdom and Germany. *European Accounting Review*, 4(1), 155–164.

Moneva, J.M. and Llena, F. (2000) Environmental disclosures in the annual reports of large companies in Spain. *European Accounting Review*, 9(1), 7–29.

Additional material on the website

Go to http://www.thomsonlearning.co.uk/stolowylebas2 for further information.

The following appendices to this chapter are available on the dedicated website:

Appendix 12.1: Accounting for notes payable
Appendix 12.2: Accounting for sales tax
Appendix 12.3: Interest and time value of money
Appendix 12.4: Bonds issued at a discount
Appendix 12.5: Sales and leaseback transactions
Appendix 12.6: Environmental liability

Notes

1. Leverage can be illustrated by the following small example: Two firms A and B are exactly identical in all respects, except the structure of their long-term funding. Each has, during last accounting period, earned an income before interest of 100 CU. The market based interest rate for long-term funds they both face is 5%. Firm A's shareholders' equity is 200 CU while long-term debt amounts to 1,000 CU. The before tax return on equity for firm A is (200 – 5% × 1,000)/200 = 75%. Meanwhile, firm B's equity is 500 CU and its long-term debt amounts to 700 CU. The return on equity before taxes for firm B is (200 – 5% × 700)/500 = 33%. Firm A is more leveraged than firm B in that a CU of shareholders' equity yields a higher return than an equivalent CU in firm B. Higher leverage means higher shareholders' return on equity, but too much leverage (too little shareholders' equity) may lead to interest expenses that may reduce dramatically the income (or the cash flow) from operations and thus put the firm in danger (either through higher interest rates or through insufficient cash to keep the operating cycle going).
2. See, for example, Walton (2000), or Vernimmen *et al.* (2005).
3. We chose in Figure 12.6 to use the term 'real and present' rather than simply 'present' because we feel it is more explicit regarding the causality principle.
4. The process of gathering a group of debt obligations such as receivables into a pool, and then dividing that pool into portions that can be sold as securities in the secondary market. (Adapted from www.investordictionary.com)
5. The method of calculation is either firm specific or industry specific.
6. See, for example, Skousen *et al.* (2003).
7. 'Debt' represents long-term and short-term interest-bearing liabilities.
8. They represent the part of the net results of operations of a subsidiary attributable to interests that are not owned, directly or indirectly through subsidiaries, by the parent company (minority shareholders). This item will be presented in a more detailed manner in Chapter 13 which is devoted to Consolidation.

C13

Chapter 13

Financial fixed assets and business combinations

Learning objectives

After studying this chapter, you will understand:

- That there are several and different types of financial assets.
- How financial assets are valued.
- What a business combination is.
- Why consolidated financial statements are useful.
- That three methods of consolidation coexist and that the choice of the appropriate one depends on the nature of the relation between the parent and its related or subsidiary businesses.
- What minority interests and goodwill represent.
- How the consolidation process works.
- That deferred taxes may arise from specific consolidation rules and procedures that may differ from tax rules and procedures.
- How the translation of financial statements labeled in a foreign currency is recorded.
- How mergers are recorded.

Enterprises create value for their owners by utilizing and transforming resources to satisfy solvent customer demand. This means extracting more resources from the customer in exchange for the services or products provided than it took to create these and make them available to the customer.

We have seen that financial statements, and especially the income statement and the cash flow statement, reflect the transformation process that is implemented through the operations of a firm. However, the process of value creation may require that the firm look (and be proactive) beyond the frontiers of the 'legal entity' and start developing a network of relationships in order to secure a superior ability to deliver customer satisfaction in a sustainable way, and thus a return to its investors higher than other investments in the same risk class.

Beside strategic alliances that are beyond the scope of this text, the development of such a network organization can lead a business to engage in intercorporate investments. These are the focus of this chapter.

We saw in Chapter 10 that when excess resources (cash or equivalents) are created through operations, investing in marketable securities is one way (at least in the short run) to create value for the shareholders (alternative solutions being own-share repurchase and/or the issuance of large dividends). Such investments are passive (the investing firm has no right or possibility to influence the behavior of the enterprise whose marketable securities it purchased), and short lived in general. They are coherent with a position of 'wait and see' until an active (and strategically coherent) investment opportunity presents itself or is created.

This chapter deals with active investment of the resources of the firm in financial assets (as opposed to tangible or intangible assets). We use the term active in the sense that the investing firm chooses to apply its resources to deliberately grow its value creation potential and do so with a long-term, strategic view, requiring that it take an active role in the decision-making process of the firm in which it has invested. In this category of investments we find close-knit and loose networks, often built around a 'leader firm' specialized in production or distribution or both. The aerospace and automotive industries, with their long established system of concentric first-, second- and third-tier suppliers are examples of such networks, but networks of small businesses are also more and more common (a general contractor in the construction industry is a traditional example of such a loose network of medium to small enterprises). The idea here is to partition the risk and increase the speed of reactivity of the whole network to the needs and opportunities of both technology and markets while focusing each firm on its core competence and thus improving the efficiency of use of resources in delivering effectively the value proposition.

Such active financial investments are the product of a deliberate strategy on the part of the leading (investing) firm. They can take several forms. Three generic models or approaches can easily be combined to create customized 'solutions' fitting any tactical or strategic need:

1. **The lender approach**: The simplest solution to create a preferred relationship is probably to lend resources to another corporate entity (controlled or not) in order to foster its development in a strategically targeted way so as to, for example, create a reliable supplier (possibly using a defined technology) or a reliable customer. Under the lender approach the entity does not behave as a substitute to a financial institution, but actively encourages, by providing loan funds, a third-party enterprise to develop a certain technology, carry out a focused research program, increase quality or capacity, acquire facilities or equipment, etc. that will, *in fine*, benefit the lending enterprise.
2. **The joint business creation approach**: A business can also create another corporate entity either alone or in active partnership with one or several already existing firms sharing a similar interest. The new entity would be expected to be more nimble and reactive, or able to deal more effectively, than the investing firm(s) with regards to a core competence or core market (for example by being 'closer' to the technology, the resources, or the customers, or any combination of the three), or have access to less expensive resources. The issue here becomes one of degree of strategic control held by the reporting enterprise (provider of capital) over the third-party entity. Two levels of strategic control (i.e., integration in the value creation process of the investing firm) lead to different types of reporting. Accountants traditionally distinguish between influence[1] and control[2].

   IAS 28 defines influence as having between 20 and 50% of the capital – the implicit assumption being that owning less than 20% of the capital of an entity does not give significant influence to the investor[3].

   The term control is used to describe the relationship when the investing firm has more than 50% of the capital of the new entity. In the case of control, the reporting issues and practices are identical to those evoked under the acquisition approach below.
3. **The acquisition approach**: The third approach consists of acquiring a controlling interest in – or combining with – an already existing entity (thus, hopefully, reducing the risks inherent in the creation of a new venture), either to gain access to a technique or a market segment or to grow the size of the business to enjoy greater economies of scale and/or scope. Recent examples abound in the financial press of business entities creating closer links between their activities: Alcan/Péchiney, Exxon/Mobil, Crédit Agricole/Crédit Lyonnais, Pernod-Ricard/Allied-Domecq, Sanofi/Aventis, Sprint/Nextel, etc.

A fourth strategy exists that has no reporting implication in that it consists of creating a network of gentleman's agreement between firms that agree to cooperate freely (and often seal their agreement to work together through contracts, but without financial investment changing hands) either because of family or friendship ties between their leaders or because they feel all members of the network will benefit from their cooperation. Since such strategy has no reporting implications beyond mentioning them in the footnotes, we will not explore the issues raised by this approach.

The focus of this chapter is about reporting to shareholders the financial links created by – and, more importantly, the value creation potential of – these sometimes complex, more or less close-knit but formal networks of firms.

If the organizing firm (or 'pivot' of the network) were to only report its own economic activities without acknowledging the value created and the value creation potential (and obligations) resulting from these preferred linkages its active financial investments have built, it would not give true and fair information to the shareholders or potential investors. The pivot firm's only visible assets might be the loans granted or the shares acquired. The nature of the business and its potential, opportunities, obligations, and correlated risks would thus not be apparent from the figures reported in its balance sheet.

Consolidated financial statements create a description of the financial position of an economic entity that is the agglomeration or conglomeration of diverse and, often, distinct legal entities headed by a common management and connected by relations of intercorporate investments or lending relationships. A subsidiary, however, is generally not individually liable for the liabilities of another. Issues of degree of autonomy of each member of the 'group' and definition of rules partitioning the wealth created by the networked entity must be addressed if one is to provide relevant financial statements to financial information users. Such issues are central to this chapter.

The fact that complex, more or less loosely coupled 'groups' are now often more the norm than are the pre-1970s-style 'integrated' single legal entity firms, has led countries such as the USA and Canada to even cease asking the pivot firm to report as a stand-alone entity since its balance sheet would, as a rule, be largely meaningless to a potential investor.

We first look, in the Core issues section, at the method of establishment and interpretation of consolidated financial reports. The Advanced issues section explores more technical points created in the process of acquisition, merger, or consolidation such as deferred taxation, currency translation of financial statements established in foreign currency or currencies (i.e., different from the currency used by the consolidating firm), and the reporting of advanced forms of combination of entities such as absorption or legal merger.

1 Core issues

Consolidated financial statements describe the financial position of an economic entity resulting from the existence of active intercorporate financial investments or fixed financial assets. The latter can take different forms.

1.1 Types and definition of financial fixed assets

The three combinatorial strategies evoked in the introduction lead to the existence of five types of financial fixed assets:

- shares in subsidiaries;
- shares in associated (also called affiliated) companies;
- shares in other investments (including joint ventures);
- loans to subsidiaries, associated companies and other investments;;
- other loans.

We will clarify later in this chapter the difference between subsidiary, associate, and interest in a joint venture.

1.1.1 Definition of financial assets

We saw in Chapter 10 that the IASB does not make any distinction between fixed and current financial assets. IAS 32 (IASB 2003e: § 11) defines a financial asset as: 'any asset that is:

(a) Cash;

(b) An equity instrument of another entity;

(c) A contractual right:
- to receive cash or another financial asset from another entity; or
- to exchange financial assets or financial liabilities with another entity under conditions that are potentially favorable to the entity; or

(d) A contract that will or may be settled in the entity's own equity instruments and is:
- a non-derivative[4] for which the entity is or may be obliged to receive a variable number of the entity's own equity instruments; or
- a derivative that will or may be settled other than by the exchange of a fixed amount of cash or another financial asset for a fixed number of the entity's own equity instruments. For this purpose the entity's own equity instruments do not include instruments that are themselves contracts for the future receipt or delivery of the entity's own equity instruments'.

If we consider more precisely financial *fixed* assets, they include, from the above definition, both 'equity instruments of another entity' (which are generally securities [shares] in another business [subsidiary, associate or joint venture]) and 'contractual rights to receive cash or another financial asset from another entity' (which corresponds to long-term loans granted by the entity).

1.1.2 Definition of types of financial fixed assets

IAS 39 (IASB 2004b, as amended in June 2005: § 9) defines four categories of – assets or liabilities – financial instruments. As this chapter focuses only on assets (issues about liabilities were addressed in Chapter 12), we chose here to only retain from the above-mentioned paragraph of IAS 39 the implied following four categories of financial assets:

- financial asset at fair value through profit or loss [i.e., held at fair value];
- held-to-maturity investments;
- loans and receivables;
- available-for-sale financial assets.

IAS 39 does not apply directly to investments in subsidiaries, associates, and joint ventures, which constitute, in our mind, a fifth category. These investments are recorded in accordance, respectively, with IAS 27 (2003b), IAS 28 (2003c), and IAS 31 (2003d), because, as we will show later, they will be eliminated in the consolidation process (for subsidiaries and joint ventures) or revalued according to specific rules (for associates). It is, however, important to understand the definition and valuation rules of these financial assets.

Financial asset at fair value through profit or loss[5] This category includes two subcategories: financial assets designed as such on initial recognition and financial assets 'held for trading'.

IAS 39 (§ 9, as amended in June 2005 stipulates that a 'financial asset at fair value through profit or loss' could be 'upon initial recognition (...) designated by the entity as at fair value through profit or loss. An entity may use this designation only when permitted by paragraph 11A [which concerns 'embedded derivatives'], or when doing so results in more relevant information[6] (...)'. This amended version of what has been called the 'fair value option' is a much more restrictive version, compared to the original standard, which had not been accepted by the European Union. However, the EU Commission, following the Accounting Regulatory Committee (ARC), the EU advisory body on the endorsement of individual IFRS for use in the European Union, accepted on 15 November 2005 an amended version of IAS 39 relating to the fair value option (FVO):

'A financial asset (...) is classified as "held for trading" if it is:

(i) Acquired or incurred principally for the purpose of selling or repurchasing it in the near term;

(ii) Part of a portfolio of identified financial instruments that are managed together and for which there is evidence of a recent actual pattern of short-term profit-taking (...)' (IAS 39: § 9).

This emphasis on the short term and the characteristics of current assets were addressed in Chapter 10. A financial fixed asset is, by nature, not a current asset since it is held for the long term (a value adding network exists only if the financial relationships between its entities are long term). Thus, long-term financial assets listed in this category will be so as the result of a deliberate decision by the management of the entity at the time of acquisition (their intent may change later if, for example, the network does not produce the results expected).

Held-to-maturity investments Held-to-maturity investments are 'non-derivative financial assets with fixed or determinable payments and fixed maturity that an entity has the positive intention and ability to hold to maturity (...)' (IAS 39: § 9).

Loans and receivables Loans and receivables are 'non-derivative financial assets with fixed or determinable payments that are not quoted in an active market' (IAS 39: § 9). Through securitization[7], though, receivables or loans can be transformed into 'available-for-sale' financial assets.

Available-for-sale financial assets Available-for-sale financial assets 'are those non-derivative financial assets that [either] are [formally] designated as available for sale, or are not classified as (a) loans and receivables, (b) held-to-maturity investments or (c) financial assets at fair value through profit or loss' (IAS 39: § 9).

This class of financial assets is thus partly a residual category defined by opposition to the other three categories. In practice, two main types of investment will be found under this available-for-sale heading:

1. All equity securities except those classified as at fair value.... These can represent, for example, long-term equity investments, held for return, without intention to influence the business whose shares are held as an asset.
2. Investments in non-consolidated companies (because they do not meet the required threshold), or (speculative) investments (i.e., not part of an 'industrial strategy') included in the parent company's, or any subsidiary's, stand-alone balance sheet.

1.2 Valuation of financial fixed assets

1.2.1 Initial recognition

IAS 39 (§ 43) states that: 'When a financial asset (...) is recognized initially, an entity shall measure it at its fair value plus, in the case of a financial asset (...) not at fair value through profit or loss, transaction costs that are directly attributable to the acquisition or issue of the financial asset (...)'.

1.2.2 Subsequent measurement for reporting

The measurement of a financial asset after its initial recognition will depend on how it will have been classified between the four above-mentioned categories.

According to IAS 39 (§ 46), 'after initial recognition, an entity shall measure financial assets, (...) at their fair value, without any deduction for transaction costs it may incur on sale or other disposal, except for the following financial assets:

(a) Loans and receivables (...), which shall be measured at amortized cost using the effective interest method;

(b) Held-to-maturity investments (...), which shall be measured at amortized cost using the effective interest method; and

(c) Investments in equity instruments that do not have a quoted market price in an active market and whose fair value cannot be reliably measured (...)'.

From this paragraph, it stems that, in complement to 'financial assets at fair value through profit or loss', 'available-for-sale financial assets' should also be measured at fair value. However, IAS 39 (§ 55) introduces an important difference between these two categories of financial assets regarding the measure and reporting of gains and losses incurred after initial recognition: 'A gain or loss arising from a change in the fair value of a financial asset (...) shall be recognized, as follows:

(a) A gain or loss on a financial asset (...) classified as "at fair value through profit or loss" shall be recognized in profit or loss [i.e., in the income statement].

(b) A gain or loss on an available-for-sale financial asset shall be recognized directly in equity, through the statement of changes in equity [see Chapter 11] (...)'.

Table 10.3 in Chapter 10 summarizes the rules of subsequent valuation of financial instruments.

In practice, value adjustments should be made mainly when the market value falls below the acquisition cost (potential loss). In this case, a provision for depreciation should be recorded in the balance sheet to reduce the book value of the investment to its market level. As a counterpart, a provision (or valuation allowance) expense should be recognized in the income statement (for 'financial assets classified as at fair value through profit or loss') or a reduction in equity is recorded (for 'available-for-sale financial assets'). These entries could (conceptually) be partly or completely reversed in any subsequent year to the extent that the market value increases.

The first type of entry (provision expense) is essentially identical to the one shown in Chapter 10 with current investments. The reader may revisit the Mozart Company example (Chapter 10) to have an example of provision expense and reversal of provision. Appendix 13.1 illustrates this procedure applicable to long-term financial assets.

1.3 Business combinations: principles

1.3.1 Types of business combinations

A business combination is 'the bringing together of separate entities or businesses into one reporting entity. The result of nearly all business combinations is that one entity, the acquirer, obtains control of one or more other businesses, the acquiree' (IASB 2004b: § 4).

A variety of scenarios can be followed in order to create a business combination. The following list is illustrative of some of the most commonly observed scenarios but is in no way exhaustive. Merger and acquisition specialists (financiers and lawyers alike) compete in creativity in designing approaches best tailored to each specific situation. Essentially all solutions are variations on (or, even, combinations of) the generic five scenarios that are described below:

- **Acquisition of an interest in another entity**: Company X obtains control over Company Y by acquiring enough shares of Y in exchange for cash or in exchange of shares of X or a combination of the two. In this case, Company Y continues to exist as a separate legal entity (and thus may still be required to produce its own financial statements) but becomes a subsidiary of X. The financial statements of Y are integrated in the consolidated financial statements of X, which becomes the meaningful reporting entity.
- **Legal (or statutory) merger**: Company X acquires all the shares of Company Y. The latter is dissolved as a legal entity and all its assets and liabilities are merged in the accounts of Company X.
- **Statutory consolidation**: Company X and Company Y decide jointly to combine all their activities to become the Z Company entity. Both Company X and Company Y are dissolved as legal entities and their assets and liabilities are entirely integrated in the accounts of the Z entity.
- **Creation of a holding entity**: Company X and Company Y decide jointly to combine all their activities but, unlike in the previous case, neither of the combining companies is dissolved. The shareholders of each company exchange their shares against those of a newly formed holding company, Company H (formation of a holding company). Holding company H becomes the sole shareholder of both Company X and Company Y. These in turn become subsidiaries of H and their activities, assets and liabilities are consolidated in the accounts of the holding Company (the reporting company).
- **Acquisition of assets and liabilities**: Company X acquires directly all the assets of Company Y, without acquiring its shares (acquisition of assets). Company Y is essentially liquidated as it currently exists and the cash it receives in exchange for its assets is first used to settle its liabilities and secondly company Y either returns the surplus cash to its shareholders before dissolving itself or becomes a totally different business by investing the available funds in a new venture.

The method used to record any of the above business combinations is known as 'purchase accounting' (consolidation or merger). This method is based on the basic assumption that one of the combining enterprises (the acquirer) obtains control over the other combining enterprise (the acquired). However, in the recent past, when, in exceptional circumstances, it was not possible to identify an acquirer – the shareholders of the combining enterprises joining in a substantially equal arrangement to share control over the whole, or effectively the whole, of their net assets and operations – another accounting method was allowed: the 'uniting of interests' (also known as 'pooling of interests'). The use of this method, developed in Appendix 13.2, has been forbidden in the USA since June 2001 and is now prohibited in IFRS 3 (IASB 2004c). Occurrences of its use should therefore dwindle rapidly towards extinction.

1.3.2 Usefulness of consolidated financial statements

A corporation owning shares of another holds power over the second. The economic entity resulting from the combination of two or more enterprises linked by intercorporate investments of sufficient importance to warrant effective control of one over the other is called a 'group', which is defined by IASB (IAS 27, 2003b: § 4) as 'a parent and all its subsidiaries'. In most countries (with the notable exception of Germany) a group is generally not a legal entity as such, and the parent company (pivot of the combination) and each controlled corporation are the only legal entities.

In order to allow investors or shareholders to shape their opinion about the financial position and the performance potential of a group, it is essential for the management of the combined entities to develop and provide group accounts, also called consolidated accounts or consolidated financial statements.

Group or consolidated accounts are needed because the accounts of the pivot company (parent or holding company) contain, as mentioned earlier (and developed below), little useful information about the performance potential and the resources and obligations of the group. Some of the reasons for the lack of representativeness of the unconsolidated accounts of the parent are listed as follows. Each is a justification for developing consolidated statements:

1. *If the parent company is a 'pure' holding company* (i.e., the case of a corporation whose sole purpose is to own – hold and manage – the shares of the members of the group and coordinate their activities without directly exercising any industrial, commercial, or service activity itself).
   (a) The unconsolidated income statement of the holding company is very 'simple' and characterized by the following elements:
      (i) It does not include any of the 'traditional' items such as 'sales revenue', 'cost of goods sold', or 'purchases'.
      (ii) Revenues are essentially comprised of 'management fees' (internal billing of 'services' to each group member company) and 'investment income', which is the sum of all dividends received.
      (iii) Expenses include mainly administrative expenses (personnel expenses, depreciation of equipment) of an often very light coordination team. For example, the headcount at the Saint-Gobain headquarters (a holding company based in Paris with subsidiaries operating essentially in the building [materials] distribution, high-performance materials, flat glass, packaging, and construction products sectors) averages 237 people, while the whole group employs around 175,760 persons! (*source*: Annual report 2004).
   (b) The unconsolidated balance sheet is also somewhat unusual in its structure:
      (i) It probably does not include any significant (or relevant for evaluating the financial position) amounts under accounts receivable, accounts payable, and inventories.
      (ii) The value of tangible and intangible assets is often low.
      (iii) However, financial investments represent an unusually high percentage of total assets. These are the shares of group companies owned by the parent (holding) company. Since, in our opinion, IAS 39 does not address the valuation of these investments, they are generally reported at their acquisition cost. Some GAAP allow or encourage reporting these investments valued at equity.
2. *If the parent company is a 'mixed' holding company* (i.e., a corporation that both exercises a significant economic activity of its own and, in addition, administers a group of companies), the unconsolidated financial statements of the parent may have a more informative content (than the equivalent balance sheet of a 'pure' holding) since they reflect at least the stand-alone economic activity of the parent as well as the financial result of the holding activity. Despite their somewhat greater relevance than those of a pure holding company, the unconsolidated financial statements of the parent would still be very far from giving a true and fair view of the performance potential of the group and of its risks, assets and obligations: importance of financial investments, importance of investment income and management fees hide the reality of the relationships of the group with its markets.

Given each and all of these weaknesses and insufficiencies of unconsolidated statements, it appears judicious, so as to inform investors, to require such businesses to prepare financial statements that reflect the economic activity at the group level. As stated in IAS 27 (IASB 2003b: § 4): 'Consolidated financial statements are the financial statements of a group presented as those of a single economic entity'.

1.3.3 Nature of relations between parent company and group entities

The nature of the relation(s) existing between the parent company and the different group entities is a determinant of the way the financial statements of each of the individual group entities will be taken into account in the consolidation process to create the group financial statements.

Table 13.1 lists the definitions suggested by the IASB of the three types of group companies that result from a classification and a qualification of the subsidiarity[8] relationship that exists between a parent and another corporation. Any corporation whose relation to the 'parent' does not fall in one of the three types shown in Table 13.1 will not be considered as a group company (i.e., it will not be within the scope of consolidation) and thus will not be consolidated.

Table 13.1 Relations between a 'parent' and another group entity

Type of relation		Type of group company	
Control	'Power to govern the financial and operating policies of an entity so as to obtain benefits from its activities' (IAS 27: § 4).	Subsidiary	'Entity (...) that is controlled by another entity (known as the parent)' (IAS 27: § 4).
Significant influence	'Power to participate in the financial and operating policy decisions of the investee but it is not control or joint control over those policies' (IAS 28: § 2).	Associate	'Entity (...) over which the investor has significant influence and that is neither a subsidiary nor an interest in a joint venture' (IAS 28: § 2).
Joint control	'Contractually agreed sharing of control [between two or more legal entities] over a [third] economic activity' (IAS 31: § 3).	Joint venture	'Contractual arrangement whereby two or more parties undertake an economic activity that is subject to joint control' (IAS 31: § 3).

Detailed definition of the three types of relations

Control According to IAS 27 (IASB 2003b: § 13), 'control is presumed to exist when the parent owns directly, or indirectly through subsidiaries, more than one half of the voting power of an entity (...). Control also exists even when the parent owns one half or less of the voting power of an entity when there is:

(a) Power over more than one half of the voting rights by virtue of an agreement with other investors;

(b) Power to govern the financial and operating policies of the enterprise under a statute or an agreement;

(c) Power to appoint or remove the majority of the members of the board of directors or equivalent governing body and control of the entity is by that board or body; or

(d) Power to cast the majority of votes at meetings of the board of directors or equivalent governing body and control of the entity is by that board or body'.

'Control' may sometimes exist even though less than a majority of the capital is held by the parent, since voting rights alone define control (as seen in Chapter 11, multiple voting rights or no voting rights may be attached to shares). What matters is the actual ability to exercise control. The concepts, vocabulary, and procedure put forward in IAS 27 are more or less identical to those of the 7th European Directive of 1983 which covers consolidated accounts.

Significant influence According to IAS 28, entitled 'Investment in Associates' (IAS 2004b: § 6): 'If an investor holds, directly or indirectly through subsidiaries, twenty per cent or more of the voting power of the investee, it is presumed that the investor has significant influence, unless it can be demonstrated that this is not the case. Conversely, if the investor holds, directly or indirectly (...) less than twenty per cent of the voting power of the investee, it is presumed that the investor does not have significant influence, unless such influence can be clearly demonstrated'. The standard adds: 'A substantial or majority ownership by another investor does not necessarily preclude an investor from having significant influence'.

In practice: 'The existence of significant influence by an investor is usually evidenced in one or more of the following ways:

(a) Representation on the board of directors or equivalent governing body of the investee;
(b) Participation in policy-making processes including participation in decisions about dividends or other distributions;
(c) Material transactions between the investor and the investee;
(d) Interchange of managerial personnel; or
(e) Provision of essential technical information' (IAS 27: § 7).

Joint control Joint ventures take on many different forms and structures and are described in IAS 31 (IASB 2003d). All joint ventures result from a contractual arrangement between two or more economic entities which establish joint control of a (most of the time newly created) third company.

Percentage of control and percentage of interest The percentage of control and the percentage of interest affect the way that the accounts will be consolidated and how the value created will be shared:

1. **Percentage of control** (also called percentage of voting rights) is the term used to reflect the degree of dependency in which a parent company holds its subsidiaries or associates. The higher the percentage, the higher the dependency of the group company. This percentage measures the proportion of total voting rights held by the parent in its related company. This percentage will be used to determine which method of consolidation will be used in establishing the consolidated financial statements (the three methods are full consolidation, equity method, and proportionate consolidation; they are described below).
2. **Percentage of interest** (also called percentage of ownership or of stake) represents the claim held by the parent company over the shareholders' equity (including net income) of its subsidiaries or associates. This percentage is used in the process of consolidation of accounts and calculations to define majority and minority interests.

The percentage of control held by a parent may be different from the percentage of interest it holds in a given subsidiary or associate. This is the case, for example, when there is a cascade of dependency links. Figure 13.1 illustrates a situation in which a parent company P is linked to corporation C2 both directly and indirectly by way of another corporation C1 in which the parent holds a non-controlling interest.

Figure 13.1 Percentages of control may differ from percentages of interest

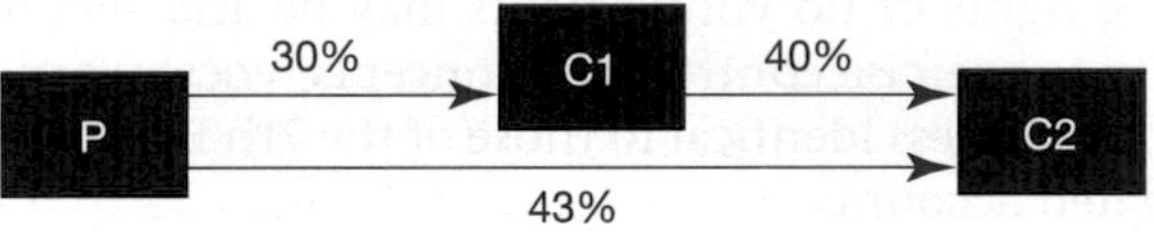

The *percentage of control* of the parent P over C2 is equal to only 43% and not to 83% (43% + 40%) because P does not have control over C1 (30% only), thus the 'possible influence' branch that goes through C1 gives zero control to P over C2. With 43% control by the parent and without any additional element qualifying the relationship between P and C2, we can only say that there is significant influence.

The *percentage of interest* of P in C2, however, is equal to 55% [43% + (30% × 40%), i.e., (43% + 12%)]. Even with a percentage of interest equal to 55% (which is higher than 50%), there is nonetheless not more than significant influence as the insufficient percentage of control dominates (43%, which is lower than 50%).

Note that the percentage of control equals the percentage of interest in case of a direct link (30% between P and C1, 40% between C1 and C2, and 43% between P and C2 [for the direct link only]).

1.4 Reporting the acquisition of a financial interest: addition method or consolidation methods

When the relevant regulatory body does not require consolidation (for example, because the lead entity and its related businesses do not meet certain size criteria), or when the investment is so small that no control or influence exists over the investee, a simple addition of the balance sheets and income statements may suffice to inform investors.

However, when there is control and/or influence, consolidation is generally required. Table 13.1 introduced the three main types of control or influence relationships and to each corresponds a method of consolidation as shown in Figure 13.2.

Figure 13.2 Consolidation methods

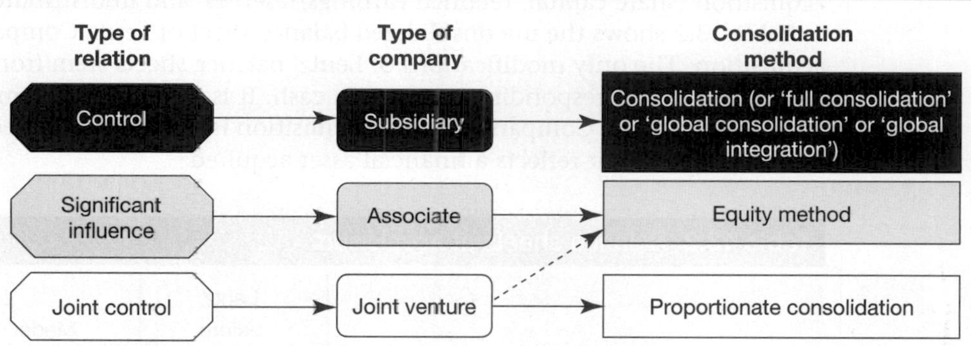

In Figure 13.2, the dotted arrow between 'joint venture' and 'equity method' arises from IAS 31 (2003d: § 38), which states that: 'as an alternative to proportionate consolidation (...), a venturer shall [can, in our opinion] recognize its interest in a jointly controlled entity using the equity method'. The text of that standard, however, adds that the IASB 'does not recommend the use of the equity method because proportionate consolidation better reflects the substance and economic reality of a venturer's interest in a jointly controlled entity, that is to say, control over the venturer's share of the future economic benefits. Nevertheless, this Standard permits the use of the equity method, as an alternative treatment, when recognizing interests in jointly controlled entities' (§ 40).

1.4.1 Impact of an acquisition on reporting

Each method described in Figure 13.2 will be analyzed below from a conceptual viewpoint and its mechanism illustrated both in a schematic diagram and through a quantified (running) example based on the Lentz Company acquiring an interest in Meder Company.

At the end of year X1 Lentz Company acquires an interest in the Meder Company which continues to exist, and becomes its subsidiary.

We will look at six situations: firstly, the reporting of the impact of the acquisition when no consolidation is required or mandated, and, secondly, when consolidation is required. We will cover this second case through 'simulations' of the consolidated statements in the following five alternative situations:

1. an interest of 100% is acquired for a price equal to the book value of the acquired equity (full consolidation);
2. an interest of only 90% is acquired (with the same assumption of price equals book value) (full consolidation);
3. an interest of 100% is acquired for a price that is larger than the book value of the equity acquired (full consolidation);
4. an interest of 30% is acquired for a price equal to the book value of the acquired equity (equity method);
5. an interest of 50% is acquired for a price equal to the book value of the acquired equity (proportionate consolidation).

1.4.2 When no consolidation is required

Lentz Company is headquartered in a country where consolidation is compulsory only if the group size exceeds a certain threshold. At the time of acquisition, Lentz Company does not meet the threshold level.

The price paid in cash (320 CU) is equal to the shareholders' equity (book value of the subsidiary). It corresponds to 100% of the subsidiary's shareholders' equity at the time of acquisition (share capital, retained earnings/reserves, and undistributed net income).

Table 13.2 shows the unconsolidated balance sheet of Lentz Company before and after acquisition. The only modifications of Lentz' balance sheets stem from the investment in Meder and the corresponding decrease in cash. It is important to remember that the balance sheet of Lentz Company after the acquisition is not a consolidated balance sheet, just a balance sheet that reflects a financial asset acquired.

Table 13.2 Balance sheets at acquisition

Balance sheets as of 31 December X1	Lentz before acquisition	Meder (stand-alone)	Lentz after acquisition
Assets			
Investment in Meder	0		320
Other assets (including cash)	2,000	500	1,680
Total	2,000	500	2,000
Equity and liabilities			
Share capital	600	200	600
Retained earnings/Reserves	460	100	460
Net income	30	20*	30
Liabilities	910	180	910
Total	2,000	500	2,000

*The net income will not be distributed.

1.4.3 When full consolidation is required

Figure 13.3 illustrates the basic principles of full consolidation.

The founding principle of full consolidation is that all assets and liabilities of the subsidiary are added to those of the parent (excluding, of course, the investment the parent holds in the subsidiary, which is eliminated in the process). Technically, if the percentage of interest of the parent is not 100%, part of the assets and liabilities (and thus of the equity) of the subsidiary belongs to 'minority shareholders' and will be identified as such in the consolidated statements (see Lentz Company, Simulation 2 below).

Two years later (at the end of X3), because of the growth of Lentz Company's business over the previous two years, the size threshold is crossed and providing shareholders with consolidated financial statements is now required (financial statements as of 31 December X3 to be published in early X4).

The unconsolidated (stand-alone) financial statements of both companies at the end of X3 are shown in Table 13.3.

Figure 13.3 Full consolidation

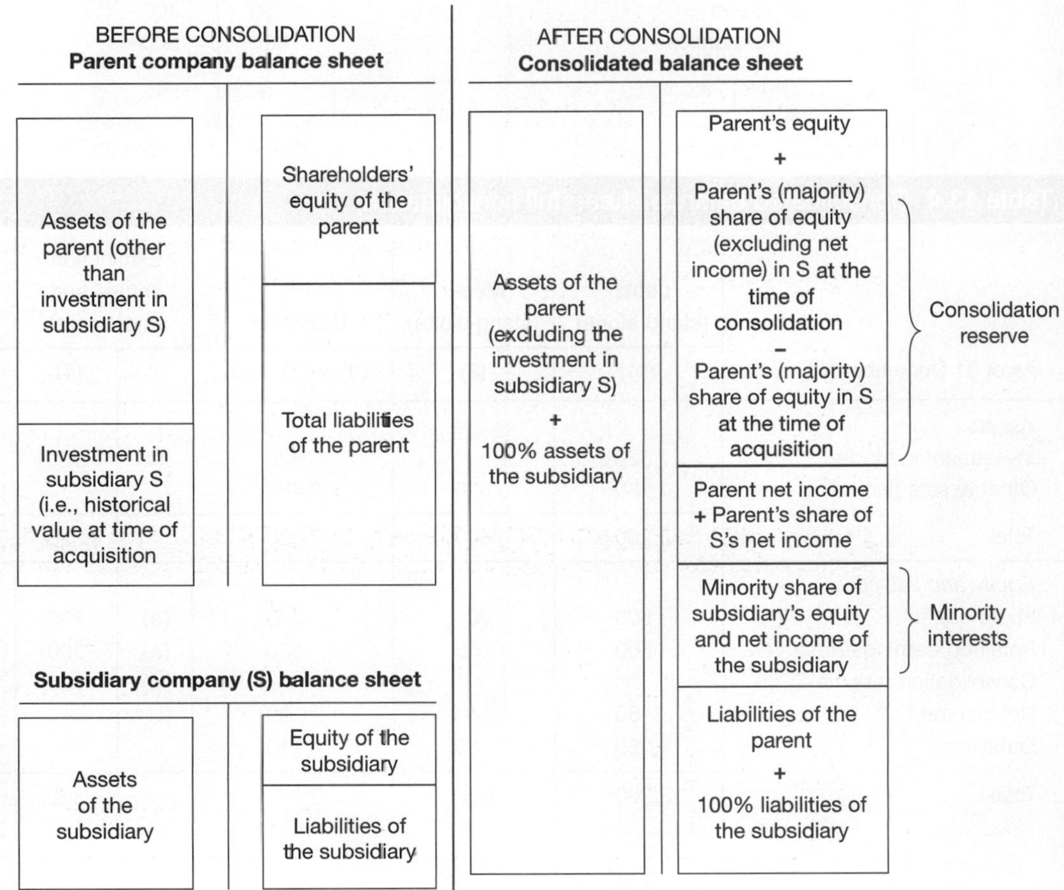

Simulation 1: Consolidation – 100% of interest – full consolidation The 'full consolidation' method consists in a series of eliminations and adjusting entries that create the consolidated financial statements. Table 13.4 illustrates the consolidated balance sheet in Simulation 1 and Table 13.5 illustrates the consolidated income statement.

When applying the full consolidation mechanism, as stated in IAS 27 (IASB 2003b: § 22): 'an entity combines the financial statements of the parent and its subsidiaries line by line by adding together like items of assets, liabilities, equity, income and expenses'. However,

Table 13.3 Financial statements as of 31 December X3

Balance sheets as of 31 December X3	Lentz	Meder
Assets		
Investment in Meder	320	
Other assets (including cash)	1,880	600
Total	2,200	600
Equity and liabilities		
Share capital	600	200
Retained earnings/Reserves	500	300
Net income	50	40
Liabilities	1,050	60
Total	2,200	600
Income statements – Year X3	**Lentz**	**Meder**
Sales	1,000	400
Expenses	950	360
Net income	50	40

Table 13.4 Consolidated balance sheet (full consolidation)

	Lentz (stand-alone)	Meder (stand-alone)	Combined	Elimination entries and adjustments		Consolidated balance sheet
As of 31 December X3	(1)	(2)	(3) = (1) + (2)		(4)	(5) = (3) + (4)
Assets						
Investment in Meder	320		320	(a)	−320	0
Other assets (including cash)	1,880	600	2,480			2,480
Total	2,200	600	2,800		−320	2,480
Equity and liabilities						
Share capital	600	200	800	(a)	−200	600
Retained earnings/Reserves	500	300	800	(a)	−300	500
Consolidation reserve				(a)	180	180
Net income	50	40	90			90
Liabilities	1,050	60	1,110			1,110
Total	2,200	600	2,800		−320	2,480

such direct addition of balance sheets (column (3) in Table 13.4) does not provide a 'true and fair view' of the group because it still includes the investment in Meder as an asset and in the equity the corresponding share of equity of the subsidiary, which belongs to the parent company. In other words, the combined balance sheet shows an investment of the group in itself. This investment must be eliminated along with the corresponding share of equity of the carrying amount of the parent's investment in each subsidiary.

This elimination is carried out as operation (a) in Table 13.4. Consequently, the consolidated equity represents only the share capital and reserves of the parent company (plus the undistributed net income of both parent and subsidiary companies).

Table 13.5 Consolidated income statement (full consolidation)

Year X3	Lentz (stand-alone)	Meder (stand-alone 50%	Combined	Elimination entries and adjustments	Consolidated income statement
Sales	1,000	400	1,400		1,400
Expenses	950	360	1,310		1,310
Net income	50	40	90		90

Figure 13.3 and Table 13.4 both show a 'consolidation reserve'. This reserve is the difference between:

- at the time of consolidation: the share (i.e., percentage of interest) of the subsidiary equity held by the consolidating parent (majority share of subsidiary's equity) *excluding* undistributed net income; and
- at the time of acquisition: the share (i.e., percentage of interest) of the subsidiary equity held by the consolidating parent *including* undistributed net income.

In our example, the consolidation reserve amounts to:

$$(200 + 300) \times 100\% - (200 + 100 + 20) \times 100\% = 180$$

An alternative description of the full consolidation process is to say that the investment in the subsidiary is mathematically and mechanically replaced by the book value of assets and liabilities of the subsidiary reflecting the percentage of interest of the parent. (As we will see in Simulation 2, had the interest been less than 100%, there would have been minority interests, which would be shown on the equity and liabilities side of the balance sheet.)

Intra-group balances and intra-group transactions (i.e., transactions between the parent and the subsidiary or between subsidiaries) should be eliminated in full. For example, if Lentz Company had held accounts receivable in the amount of 50 CU on Meder Company – which would mean the latter had recorded accounts payable to Lentz for the same amount – both balances would have been eliminated when calculating the consolidated assets and liabilities since these balances would have been of equal amount and opposite sign.

Table 13.5 illustrates the resulting consolidated income statement, which can be used to report the profit generation potential of the combined businesses.

As Table 13.5 shows, the preparation of the consolidated income statement requires no adjusting or eliminating entry (we have assumed no intra-group trade). The consolidated income statement is thus the result of combining mechanically the parent and subsidiary income statements with, of course, the elimination of any intra-group transactions. Such elimination has, in fact, no impact on net income of the group since the sales revenue recognized in one firm's stand-alone income statement is part of the costs incurred in the other's stand-alone income statement. However, it is critical to explicitly cancel out all intra-group transactions to avoid the risk of biasing operating ratios involving sales revenue and cost of sales separately (by artificially inflating the balances).

Simulation 2: Consolidation – 90% of interest – full consolidation with existence of minority interests

Principles Let us now assume that Lentz Company had not acquired a 100% interest in Meder Company but had acquired only 90% of its shares. In this simulation, we will assume the purchase price had been established at 90% of the book value of the shareholders' equity of the acquired firm (share capital, retained earnings/reserves, and undistributed current net income of Meder Company). [The (more common) case of a purchase price different from the book value of the share of equity will be dealt with in Simulation 3 below.] This means that the purchase price was (200 + 100 + 20) × 90% = 288 CU, which is assumed, for the sake of simplicity, to have been paid out in cash.

As mentioned earlier, the parent company must integrate 100% of the assets and liabilities of the subsidiary in its consolidated accounts because it holds effective economic control over the decisions of the subsidiary company. However, 10% of the Meder shareholders (the 'minority shareholders') still hold a (proportional) claim to the assets, liabilities, and past and future profits of Meder Company. The consolidated statements must explicitly recognize the existence of these claims as 'minority interests' or 'third-party interests'.

Minority interests are defined in IAS 27 (§ 4) as: 'That portion of profit or loss and net assets of a subsidiary attributable to equity interests that are not owned, directly or indirectly through subsidiaries, by the parent'. Table 13.6 illustrates the calculation and reporting of minority interests in the consolidated balance sheet at the end of X3.

Table 13.6 Consolidated balance sheet (full consolidation with minority interests)

As of 31 December X3	Lentz (stand-alone)	Meder (stand-alone)	Combined	Elimination entries and adjustments		Consolidated balance sheet
	(1)	(2)	(3) = (1) + (2)		(4)	(5) = (3) + (4)
Assets						
Investment in Meder	288		288	(a)	−288	0
Other assets (including cash)	1,912	600	2,512			2,512
Total	2,200*	600	2,800		−288	2,512
Equity and liabilities						
Share capital	600	200	800	(a)	−180	
				(b)	−20	600
Retained earnings/Reserves	500	300	800	(a)	−270	
				(b)	−30	500
Consolidation reserve				(a)	162	162
Net income	50	40	90	(b)	−4	86
Minority interests				(b)	54	54
Liabilities	1,050	60	1,110			1,110
Total	2,200	600	2,800	0	−288	2,512

*For the sake of simplicity, we have assumed that the balance sheet total of Lentz (stand-alone) is here, as it was in Simulation 1, equal to 2,200. The amount of 'other assets' has been calculated by the difference between the assets total and the carrying, historical, value of the investment in Meder.

In this example, two elimination entries will be required to carry out the full consolidation. Entry (a) in Table 13.6 serves to eliminate the investment of Lentz in Meder (for the same reasons as those mentioned in Simulation 1).

The purchase price of the 90% interest in Meder was 288 CU, established as follows (remember that in this simulation we assume the purchase price is based on book values only, not on market values of assets or equity):

- 180 CU (90% of the 200 CU share capital of Meder);
- plus 90 CU (90% of the 100 CU accumulated retained earnings/reserves of Meder at the time of acquisition);

- plus 18 CU (90% of the 20 CU undistributed net income of Meder at the time of acquisition);
- = 288 CU.

The adjustment to retained earnings/reserves amounting to 270 CU corresponds to the elimination of 90% of the retained earnings/reserves of Meder at the end of X3. A consolidation reserve is thus created amounting to 162 CU, which can be calculated as follows: ([200 + 300] × 90%) − [200 + 100 + 20] × 90% = 450 − 288 = 162 CU).

Entry (b) establishes the claim of the minority shareholders regarding both shareholders' equity and current income. The minority rights over Meder's equity amount to 54 CU. Minority interests include 20 CU (10% of share capital of 200) plus a 10% claim on the accumulated retained earnings/reserves of 300 CU, and a claim of 10% over the undistributed income of the period (10% of 40 CU). The minority interests thus represent a total amount of 20 + 30 + 4 = 54 CU.

As in the previous simulation, assets and liabilities are added to create their consolidated balances (with the elimination of intra-group loans or trade transactions if there had been any). The consolidated share capital and retained earnings/reserves represent the share capital and retained earnings/reserves of the parent company. The minority interest line item in the balance sheet acts as a mechanism to offset the mechanical 'over-incorporation' of assets and liabilities resulting from their mere addition and helps calculate, by deduction, the net claim held by the combined entity over the assets and liabilities it effectively 'owns'.

Table 13.7 presents the mechanism of establishing the consolidated income statement when there are minority interests. The net income attributable to the group differs from the net income of the combined operation by the amount of the claim held by minority interests over income. This claim is established by the third component of the (b) entry mentioned earlier.

Table 13.7 Consolidated income statement (full consolidation with minority interests)

Year X3	Lentz (stand-alone)	Meder (stand-alone)	Combined	Eliminations and adjustments	Consolidated income statement
Sales	1,000	400	1,400		1,400
Expenses	950	360	1,310		1,310
Net income	50	40	90		90
Minority interests (10%) in subsidiary's net income				−4	−4
Net income of consolidated entity					86

Reporting minority interests: How to report minority interests? Should minority interests be reported as part of shareholders' equity or of liabilities? They appear to be some kind of hybrid between the two. Choosing under which of the two categories to report minority interests will affect the ratios and financial analysis that users carry out on the consolidated financial statements. It is therefore a question for which the answer is important.

The way minority interests are reported (either as a liability to a third party, or as a part of shareholders' equity, or even ignored altogether) stems from the beliefs of – and perception by – each company of the purpose of consolidated financial statements in reporting to shareholders and investors. Three types of beliefs (property, parent, and entity) lead to four reporting positions (three 'pure' positions and a 'hybrid' one).

- *Property approach (or property concept)*: Its foundation is that consolidated financial statements are meant to describe what shareholders have invested in the company. In this case what is of foremost interest is the description of their shareholders' ownership in the subsidiary company. Thus, no minority interests would need to be reported.
- *Financial approach (or parent company concept)*: Its conceptual foundation is that the consolidated statements must focus mainly on informing the shareholders of the parent company because they are the ones who control the managerial decisions and orientations. In this case, minority shareholders are considered as residual (i.e., third party) and thus minority interests would be considered to be part of the business' liabilities (to third parties).
- *Economic approach (or entity concept)*: Its foundation is that the consolidated financial statements are established mainly for internal decision-making purposes. Consolidated financial statements should therefore give a fair view of what the consolidated entity actually controls, i.e., assets, shareholders' equity, and liabilities of the whole group, without making any reference to the specificity of the legal claim of some special class of shareholders (minority or majority). Minority interests would thus be reported as an unidentified or undistinguishable part of shareholders' equity.
- *Mixed approach (or parent company extension concept)*: This fourth case is a hybrid of two previous cases in that the minority shareholders are considered as a special and distinct class of shareholders and not dealt with as if they had been a third party. Minority interests are reported in shareholders' equity (i.e., in line with the economic approach) but are identified as a specific item (i.e., coherent with the financial approach). The IASB has adopted this approach (position), which states in IAS 27 (IASB 2003b: § 33): 'Minority interests shall be presented in the consolidated balance sheet within equity, separately from the parent shareholders' equity. Minority interests in the profit or loss of the group shall also be separately disclosed'.

Each set of beliefs regarding the foundations of consolidated financial statements leads to a specific way of reporting minority interests. These are summarized in Table 13.8.

Table 13.8 Minority interests and theories of consolidation

Theory	Reporting of minority interests
Property approach (Property concept)	No minority interests are reported (theory implies proportionate consolidation)
Financial approach (Parent company concept)	Minority interests are part of liabilities of consolidated entity
Economic approach (Entity concept)	Minority interests are included as a part of shareholders' equity
Mixed approach (Parent company extension concept)	Minority interests are reported as a specific category of shareholders' equity listed after the shareholders' equity of the parent and before liabilities

Real-life example Stora Enso

(Finland – IAS GAAP – *Source*: Annual report 2004 – Production of paper)

In the following tables only selected and aggregated relevant data are provided. A slight difference should be noted between the format adopted by Stora Enso and the requirement of IAS 27. Minority interests are reported separately between shareholders' equity and liabilities and not 'within equity, separately from the parent shareholders' equity' (IAS 27: § 33).

Consolidated balance sheet

€ million – as at 31 December Shareholders' equity and liabilities	2003	2004
Shareholders' equity	8,083.7	8,051.1
Minority interests	60.3	136.1
Long-term liabilities	6,137.8	5,500.6
Current liabilities	3,660.3	2,724.1
Total shareholders' equity and liabilities	17,942.1	16,411.9

Consolidated income statement

€ million – year ended 31 December	2003	2004
(...)		
Profit/(loss) after tax	143.7	747.8
Minority interests	−5.8	−8.1
Net profit/loss for the period	137.9	739.7

Simulation 3: Consolidation with 100% of interest but the purchase price of the controlling interest is different from that of the book value of the assets being purchased

Principles This hypothesis is closer to everyday life than the previous cases, which were oversimplified for pedagogical purposes. Most of the time the acquired entity's book value of net assets (i.e., equity) is, indeed, lower than the amount paid by the acquiring firm (otherwise the acquiree's shareholders would have little incentive to enter into a cession agreement). In this example, we consider that Lentz Company had acquired 100% of the outstanding shares of Meder Company in X1 (the same as in Simulation 1); however, whereas the purchase price in Simulation 1 had been 320 CU (equal to the book value of equity), we now make the hypothesis that Lentz had to pay 420 CU in cash on 31 December X1 to acquire a 100% interest in Meder Company. As seen before, at the time of acquisition, the book value of the shareholders' equity (including net income) of Meder Company was 320. There was therefore a premium of 100 CU paid by Lentz Company which resulted from the difference between the price paid (420 CU) and the book value of equity of the acquired subsidiary (320 CU). This 'premium' is called the 'difference arising on first consolidation'. The term 'first consolidation' refers to the fact that the difference is calculated – and analyzed – only the first time that the subsidiary's financial statements are integrated in consolidated financial statements, whenever such action takes place (and the difference will not change ever after). Consequently, at the time of consolidation, even if such action takes place several years after acquisition, it will be necessary to go back to archived data and extract the fair values of all the assets and liabilities at the time of acquisition (these, of course, were known at the time of the acquisition.)

The premium over book value paid by the investor for the investee finds its roots in two sources, as shown in Figure 13.4.

A first component of the premium comes from the difference between fair and book values of identifiable assets and liabilities: this component is called the 'valuation differences'.

The other component reflects the excess value embedded in the purchase price over and above the fair market value of the identifiable assets and liabilities. This second part of the premium, which is not explained by valuation differences, is called 'goodwill' (as seen in Chapter 8).

Goodwill is defined in IFRS 3 (IASB 2004c: § 51) as the 'cost [of acquisition] of the business combination [i.e., the acquiree] over the acquirer's interest in the net fair value of the identifiable assets, liabilities and contingent liabilities' [of the acquiree]. IFRS 3 adds: 'Goodwill acquired in a business combination represents a payment made by the acquirer in anticipation of future economic benefits from assets that are not capable of being individually identified and separately recognized' (§ 52). As mentioned in Chapter 8, goodwill represents such intangible 'assets' as customer loyalty, existing relationships with customers or distributors, etc.

Figure 13.4 Analysis of the difference arising on first consolidation

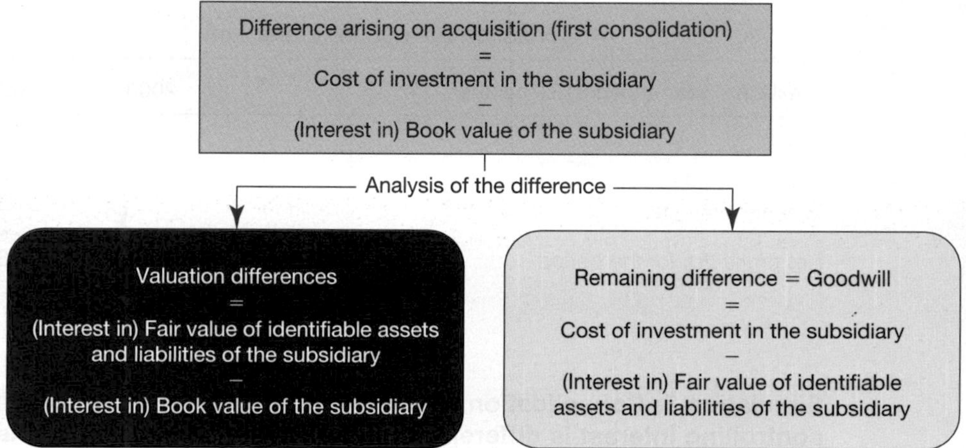

For the sake of our example, let us assume that the fair market value of Meder's identifiable assets (tangible or intangible), net of liabilities, amounts, in X1, to 390 CU. The global gross difference (100 CU) between cost of acquisition and book value of what was acquired (computed at the time of acquisition in X1) can be broken down in two components as shown in Figure 13.4. (The same principle has been explained in Chapter 8, Figure 8.2.) This difference arising on first consolidation of the acquisition of Meder by Lentz is broken down in Table 13.9.

Table 13.10 presents the consolidated balance sheet that results from the acquisition of the shares of Meder Company by Lentz Company for 420 CU.

If we refer to the consolidated balance sheet (see Table 13.10), transaction (a) is similar to the one described in Simulation 1 (elimination of investment in Meder). Let us emphasize here that the elimination entry concerns only the book value of equity of Meder (320). In a second step (transaction (b)), the difference arising on first consolidation (100 CU) is broken up and distributed between 'other assets' for an amount of 70 CU and 'goodwill' for an amount of 30 CU.

We will not cover in this text the complexity introduced by the coexistence of goodwill and minority interests. The reader wishing to explore this situation is encouraged to consult advanced textbooks[9].

Measurement of goodwill in the reporting posterior to its initial recording The measurement of goodwill has been presented in detail in Chapter 8. It suffices, here, to recall that, pursuant to the prescriptions of IFRS 3 (§ 54), 'After initial recognition, the acquirer shall measure goodwill acquired in a business combination at cost less any accumulated impairment losses'. The next paragraph (§ 55) adds: 'Goodwill (...) shall not be amortized. Instead, the acquirer shall test it for impairment annually, or more frequently if events or changes in circumstances indicate that it might be impaired (...)'. The reasons that had

Table 13.9 Breakdown of the difference arising on first consolidation

Purchase price	420	(1)
Book value of shareholders' equity (including net income) of subsidiary at the time of acquisition (in X1)	320	(2)
Interest in book value of shareholders' equity (including net income) of subsidiary at the time of acquisition (in X1)	320	(3) = (2) × 100%
Difference arising on first consolidation (calculated in X3 when consolidation is carried out)	100	(4) = (1) − (3)
Fair value of identifiable assets and liabilities of subsidiary (historical fair value as of X1)	390	(5)
Interest in fair value of identifiable assets and liabilities of subsidiary (historical fair value as of X1)	390	(6) = (5) × 100%
Valuation difference (reported in X3, when consolidation is carried out)	70	(7) = (6) − (3)
Goodwill (is only reported as of X3)	30	(8) = (4) − (7)

Table 13.10 Consolidated balance sheet (full consolidation with goodwill)

As of 31 December X3	Lentz (stand-alone)	Meder (stand-alone)	Combined		Elimination entries and adjustments	Consolidated balance sheet
	(1)	(2)	(3) = (1) + (2)		(4)	(5) = (3) + (4)
Assets						
Investment in Meder	420	0	420	(a)	−320	
Of which: difference arising on first consolidation (based on fair values dating back to X1)	100			(b)	−100	0
Goodwill				(b)	30	30
Other assets (including cash)	1,780	600	2,380	(b)	70	2,450
Total	2,200*	600	2,800		−320	2,480
Equity and liabilities						
Share capital	600	200	800	(a)	−200	600
Retained earnings/Reserves	500	300	800	(a)	−300	500
Consolidation reserve				(a)	180	180
Net income	50	40	90		0	90
Liabilities	1,050	60	1,110			1,110
Total	2,200	600	2,800	0	−320	2,480

*For the sake of simplicity, we have assumed that the balance sheet total of Lentz (stand-alone) was, here again, equal to 2,200 CU. The amount of other assets has been calculated by difference between the assets total and the purchase price (420 CU) of the investment in Meder.

originally led the firm to pay a premium over and above the fair value of the identifiable assets and liabilities of the acquired entity might have weakened, or even disappeared. It is then necessary to record the goodwill decrease in value by acknowledging its 'impairment'.

The determination of a possible impairment is carried out in accordance with IAS 36 (IASB 2004a). An impairment loss cannot be reversed, contrary to the rule applicable to other intangibles (see Chapter 8).

The USA's Statement of Financial Accounting Standard (SFAS) No. 142, 'Goodwill and Other Intangible Assets' (FASB 2001b), has led the way and was largely followed by the IASB. SFAS 142, adopted in June 2001, had already abolished the previously accepted amortization over 40 years and replaced it by an impairment test. The same modification had also been adopted in Canada before 2004. The EU, through IFRS 3, adopted the position of the IASB and since 2005 all business combinations reporting in the EU must follow the IASB position[10].

In the case of the Lentz Company all calculations have ignored, for the sake of simplicity, amortization of any goodwill.

1.4.4 When equity method is required

When the interest acquired in the subsidiary is 50% or less, there is no requirement for consolidation in the strict sense seen in the previous section, but the annual financial statements of the combined entities statements will be built using the equity method.

Principles The equity method consists of re-evaluating, in the accounts of the parent company, the investment in the associate (or affiliated) company over which the parent company exerts a significant influence. This method, therefore, excludes any idea of cumulating assets and liabilities. This method is not, in the strict sense, a consolidation since there is no 'integration' of the financial statements of the associate. IAS 28 (IASB 2003c: § 2) defines the equity method as: 'A method of accounting whereby the investment is initially recognized at cost and adjusted thereafter for the post-acquisition change in the investor's share of the net assets of the investee. The profit or loss of the investor includes the investor's share of the profit or loss of the investee'. The IASB adds in the same paragraph: 'the profit or loss of the investor includes the investor's share of the profit or loss of the investee'. The asset value of the intercorporate investment will therefore be called 'at equity' since it will reflect the share of the shareholders' equity controlled by the 'parent'.

Figure 13.5 illustrates schematically the application of the basic principles on the equity method.

In Figure 13.5, the term 'consolidated' as applied to the balance sheet of the combined businesses is placed between quotation marks to emphasize the fact that it is not a true consolidation but more a revaluation.

Simulation 4: 30% of interest Going back to the Lentz Company example, let us now assume that Lentz acquires, in X1, only 30% of the outstanding shares of Meder Company. Meder Company can no longer be called a subsidiary; it is called an associated company or associate. The 'consolidated' balance sheet, i.e., in which the investment is valued at equity, is shown in Table 13.11.

Investment in the associate has been paid 96 CU [(200 + 100 + 20) × 30%]. We do not cover in this book the situation when the investment in the associate has been acquired for a price higher than the book value of the associate. In practice, the same mechanism of calculation of the goodwill would be used as the one shown in Simulation 3 above (full consolidation).

The consolidation reserve is the difference between the interest in the equity of the associate (excluding net income) *at the time of consolidation* and the interest in the equity of the associate (including net income) *at the time of acquisition*.

Figure 13.5 Equity method

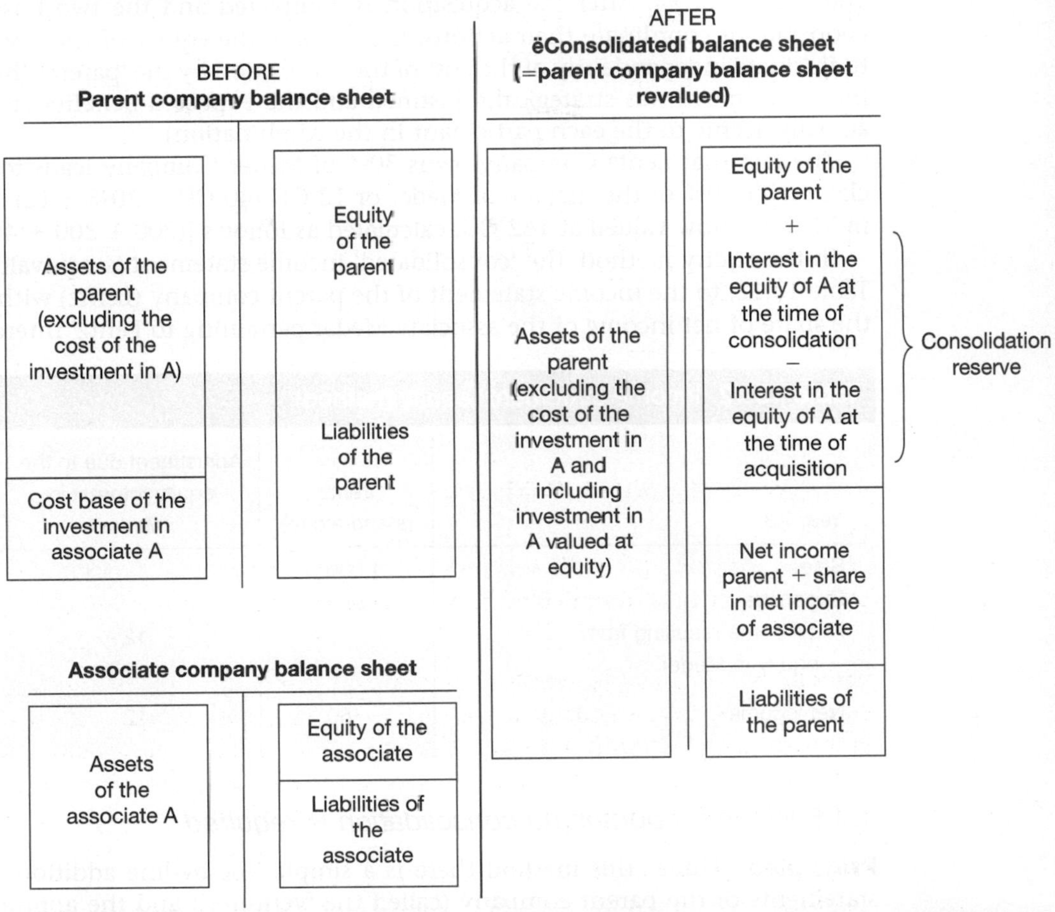

Table 13.11 Consolidated balance sheet (equity method)

As of 31 December x3	Lentz with investment valued at cost	Lentz with investment valued at equity
Assets		
Investment in Meder	96	162*
Other assets (including cash)	2,104	2,104
Total	2,200**	2,266
Equity and liabilities		
Share capital	600	600
Retained earnings/Reserves	500	500
Consolidation reserve		54
Net income	50	50
Share of Meder's net income resulting from Lentz owning 30% of Meder's equity		12
Liabilities	1,050	1,050
Total	2,200	2,266

* Valued at equity

**For the sake of simplicity, we have assumed that the balance sheet total of Lentz (stand-alone) was, here again, equal to 2,200 CU. The amount of other assets has been calculated by difference between the assets total and the (historical) price of the investment in Meder.

Here, given our hypotheses, this reserve is 54 [(200 + 300) × 30% – (200 + 100 + 20) × 30%]. After the acquisition is completed and the two businesses begin to cooperate or coordinate their actions, the value of the equity of the associate has begun to fluctuate independently of the cost of the acquisition by the 'parent' (hopefully increasing if the move was strategically justified and the expected benefits of the cooperation actually accrue to the each participant in the combination).

The fact that Lentz Company owns 30% of Meder Company leads to Lentz having a claim over 30% of the income of Meder or 12 CU (40 CU × 30% = 12). The investment in Meder is now valued at 162 CU, calculated as follows [(200 + 300 + 40) × 30%].

In the equity method, the 'consolidated' income statement is equivalent, as shown in Table 13.12, to the income statement of the parent company (Lentz) with the addition of the share of net income of the associate Meder pertaining to Lentz' interest.

Table 13.12 Income statement (equity method)

Year X3	Lentz (stand-alone)	Adjustment due to the equity interest in Meder	Consolidated income statement
Sales	1,000		1,000
Expenses	950		950
Net income resulting from equity in Meder		12	12
Net income	50	12	62

1.4.5 When proportionate consolidation is required

Principles Under this method there is a simple line-by-line addition of the financial statements of the parent company (called the 'venturer') and the appropriate part (proportion) of each of the corporate entity whose shares are owned by the parent in the context of a joint control. Such a corporate entity is generally referred to as a joint venture or JV. A joint venture, by definition, has at least two parents. In this text, we concentrate on the position of only one of the parents whom we call 'Parent 1' in Figure 13.6.

IAS 31 (IASB 2003d: § 3) defines proportionate consolidation as: 'A method of accounting whereby a venturer's share of each of the assets, liabilities, income and expenses of a jointly controlled entity is combined, line by line, with similar items in the venturer's financial statements or reported as separate line items in the venturer's financial statements'.

Figure 13.6 illustrates the mechanism of this method.

As shown in Figure 13.6, proportionate consolidation is a true consolidation method in that the investment in the joint venture is eliminated at the same time as is the share of parent company in the equity of the joint venture at the time of acquisition. There is, however, a major difference between proportionate consolidation and full consolidation: the assets and liabilities of the joint venture are integrated only proportionately to the interest held by the venturer in the JV, hence the absence of minority interests.

Simulation 5: 50% of interest (joint control) Let us now assume Lentz Company shares joint control over Meder Company with Marcus SA, which is an equal partner. Lentz company acquired its 50% control over the joint venture by paying 160 CU. The price of the investment, at the time of acquisition, was equal to 50% of the shareholders' equity: 160 = [(200 + 100 + 20) × 50%]. The consolidated balance sheet that resulted is illustrated in Table 13.13.

The consolidation reserve is computed as in the two previous methods: [(200 + 300) × 50% – (200 + 100 + 20) × 50%].

Figure 13.6 Proportionate consolidation

BEFORE CONSOLIDATION
Parent 1 company balance sheet

Assets	Equity and liabilities
Assets of the Parent 1 (other than investment in the JV)	Equity of Parent 1
Investment in the JV	Liabilities of Parent 1

JV company balance sheet

Assets	Equity and liabilities
Assets of the joint venture	Equity of the joint venture
	Liabilities of the joint venture

AFTER CONSOLIDATION
Consolidated balance sheet

Assets	Equity and liabilities
Assets of the Parent 1 (excluding the investment in the JV) + Interest in the assets of the joint venture	Equity of Parent 1 + [Interest in the equity of the JV at the time of consolidation − Interest in the equity of the JV at the time of acquisition] = Consolidation reserve
	Parent 1's net income + Share of net income of the JV
	Liabilities of Parent 1 + Interest in the liabilities of the joint venture

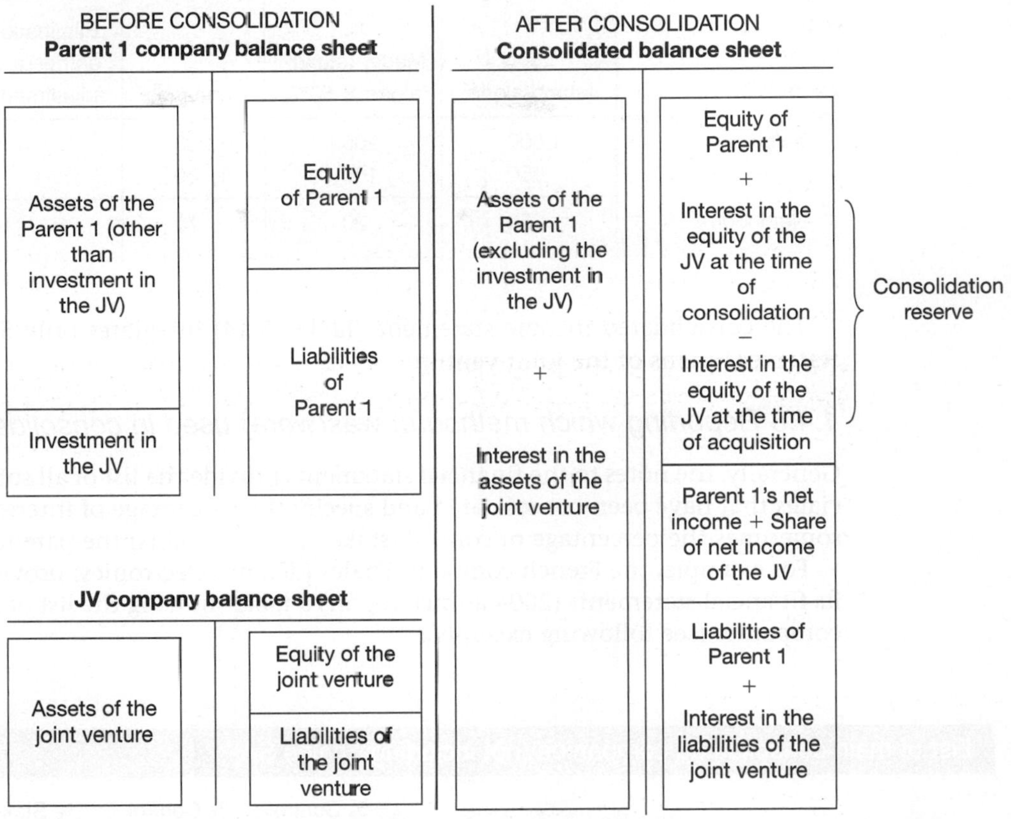

Table 13.13 Consolidated balance sheet (proportionate consolidation)

As of 31 December X3	Lentz (stand-alone) (1)	Meder (Lentz's interest) in Meder's assets and liabilities (2)	Combined (3) = (1) + (2)	Elimination entries and adjustments (4)		Consolidated balance sheet (5) = (3) + (4)
Assets						
Investment in Meder	160		160	(a)	−160	0
Other assets (including cash)	2,040	300	2,340			2,340
Total	2,200*	300	2,500		−160	2,340
Equity and liabilities						
Share capital	600	100	700	(a)	−100	600
Retained earnings/Reserves	500	150	650	(a)	−150	500
Consolidation reserve				(a)	90	90
Net income	50	20	70			70
Liabilities	1,050	30	1,080			1,080
Total	2,200	300	2,500		−160	2,340

*For the sake of simplicity, we assumed that the balance sheet total of Lentz was, once again, equal to 2,200 CU. The amount of other assets has been calculated by difference between the assets total and the (historical) price of the investment in Meder.

Table 13.14 Consolidated income statement (proportionate consolidation)

Year X3	Lentz (stand-alone)	Meder (stand-alone × 50%	Combined	Elimination entries and adjustments	Consolidated income statement
Sales	1,000	200	1,200		1,200
Expenses	950	180	1,130		1,130
Net income	50	20	70		70

The consolidated income statement (Table 13.14) integrates only 50% of the income statement items of the joint venture.

1.4.6 Reporting which method(s) was(were) used in consolidation

Generally, the notes to the financial statements provide the list of all subsidiaries and associates that have been consolidated and specify the percentage of interest (ownership) and sometimes the percentage of control (stake or voting rights) the parent holds in each.

For example, the French company Thales (defense electronics) provides in the notes to its financial statements (2004 annual report) a table showing the list of main consolidated companies (see following excerpts):

List of main consolidated companies (not including Thales SA)

	% Control 31/12/2004	% Control 31/12/2003	% Stake 31/12/2004	% Stake 31/12/2003
1. Consolidated subsidiaries				
African Defence Systems (South Africa)	80%	80%	60%	60%
Australian Defence Industries (Australia)	100%	100%	50%	50%
(...)				
2. Accounted for under the proportionate method				
Aircommand Systems International SAS (ACSI) (France)	50%	50%	50%	50%
(...)				
Navigation Solutions (USA)	35%	60%	35%	60%
(...)				
3. Accounted for under the equity method				
Arab International Optronics (Egypt)	49%	49%	49%	49%
Aviation Communications & Surveillance Systems (USA)	30%	30%	30%	30%
Camelot (UK)	20%	20%	20%	20%
(...)				

Groups' financial statements often contain a section on 'Changes in scope of consolidation', providing a list of newly consolidated and deconsolidated companies, and also a list of companies for which the consolidation method has changed.

For example in the case of Thales:

'a) In 2004
As from January 2004, Stesa has been consolidated under the proportionate method. The company was previously consolidated under the equity method. (...)'

1.4.7 Impact of each of the three methods on reported group sales revenue and net income

Tables 13.15 and 13.16 below provide a synthesis of the impact of each consolidation method on consolidated sales and consolidated income (share of the group). From a financial statement analysis viewpoint, understanding this impact is important.

Table 13.15 Integration of a subsidiary, associate, or joint venture company in the consolidated sales revenue (for the consolidated income statement)

Consolidation method [For companies consolidated using: ...]	Integration of sales revenue	Percentage (if applicable)
Full consolidation	Yes	100%
Proportionate consolidation	Yes	% of interest
Equity method	No	–

Table 13.16 Content of the consolidated income – share of the group

Consolidation method	Share of the group (to be added to the net income of the parent to create the consolidated income)
Full consolidation	100% of revenues – 100% of expenses = 100% of income – Minority interests = % of interest of the group in the net income
Proportionate consolidation	% of interest in the revenues – % of interest in the expenses = % of interest of the group in the net income
Equity method	Share of income in associates (% of interest of the group times the net income of associates)

2 Advanced issues

The consolidation process follows a rigorous methodology, which will be covered in the first section. We then will address two particularly sticky points in the consolidation process: deferred taxation arising from consolidation entries (due, among other reasons, to timing differences as seen in Chapter 6) and translation of financial statements established in a currency different from the one used by the reporting entity (the parent company). We will go on to cover the reporting issues resulting from a 'legal merger' in which the two or more combining entities literally disappear into a third entity.

2.1 Consolidation process

The consolidation process is a complex and rigorous sequential process that requires good organization. Preliminary steps include:

- Creating a detailed record of all companies that could be included in the scope of consolidation so that all relevant information will be located in the same database or file.

- Setting up a consolidation guide, continuously updated and describing the various steps in the consolidation activities, the procedures to be followed, and an allocation of responsibilities, etc.
- Issuance of a group accounting guide setting down the principles, rules, and methods of valuation the group companies involved in the consolidation perimeter or scope must follow to facilitate the consolidation work. The accounting guide will also specify the types of adjustments needed when required local practice or principles are not coherent with the group's principles and methods.
- Preparation of the 'consolidation package', i.e., the work documents, files, and tables that each group company must prepare following strict rules to prepare the consolidation calculations.

The consolidation process follows four standard steps:

Step 1: Identification of the economic entities to be consolidated Decide for each firm in which the parent holds an investment whether they should be included in the scope of consolidation. Based on the finding as to control and interest, decide on the method of consolidation that will be retained for each company.

Step 2: Pre-consolidation This step is generally carried out locally as it consists essentially of restatements of the local statements to align them with the accounting policies of the parent:

- Individual financial statements of all companies included in the scope of consolidation are restated so they present their financial position in a homogeneous way and follow the prescriptions of the group accounting guide.
- If the need exists, the restated financial statements must be converted to the currency used by the parent.

Step 3: Consolidation entries and operations

- Preparation of a comprehensive balance of all restated accounts.
- Elimination of intra-group operations and entries (between subsidiaries or between a subsidiary and the parent). The consolidation process retains only the operations and results arising from transactions with (third) parties external to the consolidation scope. Transactions that generate trivial or immaterial amounts are generally ignored as the potential benefit in improved reporting that would be obtained rarely balances the cost of their elimination activity.
- Elimination of the intra-group investments (in group companies) and partition of equities and net income of each consolidated company between the group and minority interests if the need arises.

Step 4: Preparation of the consolidated financial statements The trial balance of consolidated accounts (as they stand after step 3) serves to prepare a consolidated balance sheet, a consolidated income statement, and consolidated notes to financial statements, and sometimes both consolidated cash flow statement and statement of changes in consolidated shareholders' equity.

The elimination of intra-group transactions (step 3) represents a very important part of the consolidation process, and the key elimination entries are generally reported in the notes.

Real-life example China Eastern Airlines

(China – IFRS/Hong Kong GAAP – *Source*: Annual report 2004 – Airline company)

We provide below a few excerpts from the notes of China Eastern Airlines related to the consolidation process.

Subsidiaries

Intercompany transactions, balances and unrealized gains on transactions between group companies are eliminated. Where necessary, accounting policies of subsidiaries have been changed to ensure consistency with the policies adopted by the Group.

Associates

Unrealized gains on transactions between the Group and its associates are eliminated to the extent of the Group's interest in the associates; unrealized losses are also eliminated unless the transaction provides evidence of an impairment of the asset transferred.

2.2 Deferred taxation on consolidation

The consolidation operations bring together companies that may not follow the same tax calendar as the parent, or whose financial statements have been established in accordance with local tax or reporting rules that may differ from those selected in the group accounting guide or that apply to the parent. Chapter 6 showed that these differences create deferred taxation issues. Appendix 13.3 develops the specificity of deferred taxation arising on consolidation. In summary, deferred taxation may arise from:

- tax issues arising from restatements carried out in accordance with intra-group harmonization procedures: taxable revenues and deductible expenses, which are valued differently in individual group companies (for example, the most common differences arise from the choice of depreciation methods and the recording of leased assets);
- restatements incurred in order to eliminate entries that were required by tax regulations; and, at last,
- the tax consequences of eliminating intra-group profit (which may not have been taxed homogeneously between countries where the various group companies operate).

2.3 Foreign currency translations

Once each of the individual non-consolidated (stand-alone) financial statements have been restated and harmonized in keeping with the prescriptions of the group accounting guide, and before they can be aggregated, it is essential to express all accounts in the same currency. The unique currency or 'reporting currency' used in establishing the consolidated accounts is generally the parent's reporting currency. Foreign exchange rates therefore affect the translation of financial statements, established originally in foreign currencies, for all entities that are included in the perimeter of either a full or proportionate consolidation or the application of the equity method. The treatment of foreign currency translations is further developed in Appendix 13.4.

2.4 Legal mergers

A 'legal merger' between two companies may take two different forms. Either:

- The assets and liabilities of one company (the merged company) are transferred to the other company (the merging company) and the former (merged) company is dissolved.

- Or the assets and liabilities of both companies are transferred to a new company and both original companies are dissolved.

The major accounting issues pertaining to a legal merger are:

- determination of the value of each business;
- determination of the rate of exchange of shares;
- determination of the number of shares to issue;
- determination of the merger premium;
- accounting entries for recording for the merger so as to be able to produce a relevant new balance sheet.

Let us illustrate and discuss these points around an example.

Hol Company merges with Van Rennes Company. Table 13.17 presents the balance sheet of each firm before the merger (in thousands of the same CU).

Table 13.17 Balance sheets of merging and merged companies

Assets (000 omitted)	Hol	Van Rennes	Equity and liabilities (000 omitted)	Hol	Van Rennes
Assets	1,500	500	Capital	400	200
			Retained earnings/ Reserves	800	50
			Liabilities	300	250
Total	1,500	500	Total	1,500	500
Number of shares included in the capital:				4,000	2,000
Par value				100	100

The facts of the merger are as follows:

- Hol merges with (acquires) Van Rennes, which is dissolved. The 'purchase accounting' method is applied.
- However, the book values of assets do not reflect the economic (fair) values of the different Van Rennes balance sheet items, as indicated in the following table:

Van Rennes assets (excerpts)	Book value	Fair value	Difference
Assets	500	520	20 (potential gain on assets)
Other non-recorded or identifiable elements	–	30	30 (potential goodwill)

We should note that, in this example, we assume, for the sake of simplicity, that book values of Hol equal their fair values. Had we faced a different situation, we could have used these fair values to compute the 'rate of exchange of shares' (see below). However, the fair values of the acquirer are not taken into account in the preparation of the merged financial statements (this disparity of treatment is one more reason for stating clearly which firm is the acquirer and which is the acquiree).

2.4.1 Determination of the value of both companies

Table 13.18 shows the determination of the value of each company.

The determination of the value of each company is rather flexible and the market value can also be used. In this example, we can assume that neither of these two companies is listed and the approach implemented is therefore possible and plausible.

Table 13.18 Value of companies

		Hol	Van Rennes
Capital (000 omitted)	(1)	400	200
Retained earnings/Reserves (000 omitted)	(2)	800	50
Shareholders' equity (000 omitted)	(3) = (1) + (2)	1,200	250
Number of shares	(4)	4,000	2,000
Book value of a share	(5) = (3)/(4) × 1,000	300	125
Potential gain on assets (000 omitted)	(6a)		20
Goodwill (000 omitted)	(6b)		30
Shareholders' equity at fair value (000 omitted)	(7) = (3) + (6a) + (6b)	1,200	300
Fair value per share	(8) = (7)/(4) × 1,000	300	150

2.4.2 Determination of the rate of exchange of shares

The ratio of the per share values is:

$$\frac{\text{Value of a share Van Rennes}}{\text{Value of a share of Hol}} = 150/300 = 1/2$$

The rate of exchange is thus equal to one share of Hol for two shares of Van Rennes. We can check that one Hol share has the same value as two Van Rennes shares: 300 × 1 = 150 × 2.

2.4.3 Determination of the number of shares to issue in the merger

Hol, the merging company, should issue: 2,000 × (number of shares in Van Rennes) × 1/2 = 1,000 new shares of Hol to be awarded to the former shareholders of Van Rennes so they will retain the same value as they gave up in agreeing to the merger.

2.4.4 Determination of the merger premium

The capital increase is equal to 100 CU (par value) × 1,000 × (number of new shares) = 100,000 CU. The difference between net assets of Van Rennes (300,000 CU) and the capital increase is the merger premium (see Table 13.19).

Table 13.19 Determination of the merger premium

(000 omitted)	Computations	Share capital Hol	Merger premium
Capital Hol		400	
Net assets at fair value of Van Rennes	300		
Share capital increase	−100	100	
Merger premium	200		200
Total		500	200

2.4.5 Accounting for the merger

Table 13.20 illustrates the balance sheet after the merger.

The resulting balance sheet calls for several observations that affect the decision-making usefulness of the merged financial statements:

- A merger is a business combination which, as such, 'shall be accounted for by applying the purchase method' (IFRS 3, IASB 2004c: § 14). According to this method, 'the acquirer purchases net assets and recognizes the assets acquired and liabilities and contingent liabilities assumed, including those not previously recognized by the acquiree' (IFRS 3: § 15).
- Since IFRS 3 (§ 15) states that 'the measurement of the acquirer's assets and liabilities is not affected by the transaction', the reported assets of the merged entity end up being valued by mixing assets at fair value (from Van Rennes) and assets at book value (from Hol). This position of IASB creates a weakness in the meaningfulness of the book values of the consolidated financial statements. Financial analysts often spend considerable effort in correcting the book values to be able to determine a fair evaluation of the real financial position of the group.
- The retained earnings and reserves of the merged company are only those of Hol Company.
- The merger premium is the difference between the fair value of the assets contributed to the merger (300) and the nominal (or par value) of the shares of capital issued by Hol (100).
- 'The cost of a business combination is the aggregate of: (a) the fair values, at the date of exchange, of assets given, liabilities incurred or assumed, and equity instruments issued by the acquirer, in exchange for control of the acquiree; plus (b) any costs directly attributable to the business combination' (IFRS 3: § 24). This 'cost' is the amount 'paid' by the acquirer to control the acquiree. However, in practice, and especially in the case of a merger, the acquirer is not always required to 'pay' something. It can create new shares given to the shareholders of the acquiree to obtain the control of the acquiree. In our example, the 'cost' of the business combination equals the fair value of the Hol shares issued, i.e., 300 × 1,000 = 300,000 CU. This cost is allocated to net identifiable

Table 13.20 Balance sheet of Hol after the merger

(000 omitted)	Hol	Merger entries (see notes below)		Balance sheet after merger
Assets	1,500	520	(a)	2,020
Goodwill		30	(a)	30
Total	1,500	550		2,050
Capital	400	100	(b)	500
Merger premium		200	(b)	200
Retained earnings/Reserves	800			800
Liabilities	300	250	(a)	550
Total	1,500	550		2,050

(a) Integration of the net assets of the merged company at fair value:

	Identifiable assets of the merged company at fair value	520
minus	liabilities of the merged company	(250)
plus	non identifiable difference (goodwill)	30
	Total (net assets of the merged company at fair value)	300

(b) Increase of the capital of the merging company (100 + merger premium of 200).

assets of Van Rennes up to an amount of (520 − 250) = 270 CU (000 omitted). The unallocated difference (300 − 270 = 30 CU (000 omitted)) is recorded in the assets as goodwill.

- 'The acquirer shall, at the acquisition date, allocate the cost of a business combination by recognizing the acquiree's identifiable assets, liabilities and contingent liabilities' (IFRS 3: § 36).
- 'Any difference between the cost of the business combination and the (...) fair value of the identifiable assets, liabilities and contingent liabilities so recognized shall be accounted [as goodwill in the assets]' (IFRS 3: §§ 36 and 51).

Appendix 13.2 presents the 'pooling of interests' method and compares it to the 'purchase method'.

Key points

- Consolidated financial statements create a description of the financial position of an economic entity which is the agglomeration or conglomeration of diverse and often distinct legal entities connected by relations of intercorporate investments, control or lending relationships.
- Financial assets include mainly: (1) shares in subsidiaries; (2) shares in associated companies; (3) shares in other investments; (4) loans to subsidiaries, associated companies, and other investments; and (5) other loans.
- IAS 39 defines four categories of financial instruments: financial assets at fair value through profit or loss, held-to-maturity investments, loans and receivables, and available-for-sale financial assets.
- A *subsidiary* is an enterprise that is controlled by another enterprise (known as the parent) and an *associate* is an enterprise in which the investor has significant influence.
- When market value of a financial asset falls below its acquisition cost, an exceptional provision (or valuation allowance) expense is recognized in the income statement to reduce the value to market.
- A business combination is the bringing together of separate enterprises into the economic entity as a result of one enterprise uniting with or obtaining control over the net assets and operations of another enterprise.
- Accounting for business combinations is based on two exclusive generic hypotheses: purchase and uniting of interests. The latter is now forbidden by the IASB and in the USA.
- Usefulness of consolidated financial statements partly arises from the lack of representativeness of the unconsolidated accounts of the parent (holding) company.
- The nature of subordination and control relationship linking group companies to the parent drives the choice of the consolidation method.
- There are three main types of relationships (control, significant influence, and joint control) and to each corresponds a method of consolidation (full consolidation, equity method, and proportionate consolidation).
- In full consolidation, if the percentage of interest is below 100%, minority interests must be reported. They represent that part of the net results of operations and of net assets of a subsidiary attributable to interests which are not owned directly, or indirectly through subsidiaries, by the parent.
- If the purchase price of a subsidiary exceeds the interest in the book value of the acquired company, the difference arises from both valuation differences on identifiable assets and liabilities of the subsidiary and 'goodwill'.
- The consolidation process follows a rigorous methodology.
- Consolidation often gives rise to deferred taxation.
- The financial statements of all group companies should be expressed in the same currency. Financial statements of group companies prepared in a currency which is different from the one used for reporting should be translated into the reporting currency.
- A legal merger raises accounting issues regarding value of each business, rate of exchange of shares, number of shares to issue, merger premium, etc.

Review (solutions are at the back of the book)

Review 13.1 Mater & Filia

Topic: Consolidated balance sheet (three methods)
Related part of the chapter: Core issues

The balance sheet of the Mater & Filia companies, as of 31 December X1, are given in the following table (Mater Co. is the parent company and Filia Co. is the subsidiary company).

Balance sheets as of 31 December X1 (in thousands of CU)

	Mater	Filia
Assets		
Fixed assets (net)	1,500	550
Investment in Filia Company (1)	160	–
Inventories	930	510
Other current assets	1,210	740
Total Assets	3,800	1,800
Liabilities and shareholders' equity		
Capital	500	200
Retained earnings and reserves	780	600
Net income (2)	220	150
Debts	2,300	850
Total Liabilities and shareholders' equity	3,800	1,800

(1) Mater acquired 80% of the capital of Filia when the latter was first incorporated.
(2) Net income will not be distributed.

Required

Prepare the consolidated balance sheet by each of the following methods:

- Full consolidation
- Proportionate consolidation
- Equity method.

Assignments

Assignment 13.1 Multiple-choice questions

Related part of the chapter: Core issues

Select the right answer (one possible answer, unless otherwise mentioned).

1. The percentage of interest
   (a) Is used to define the dependency link
   (b) Is used to decide about the inclusion of a company in the consolidation scope
   (c) Reflects the interests that are controlled directly and indirectly
   (d) None of these
2. In the situation described in the diagram below, the percentage of control (voting rights, vote) of P in C2 is:

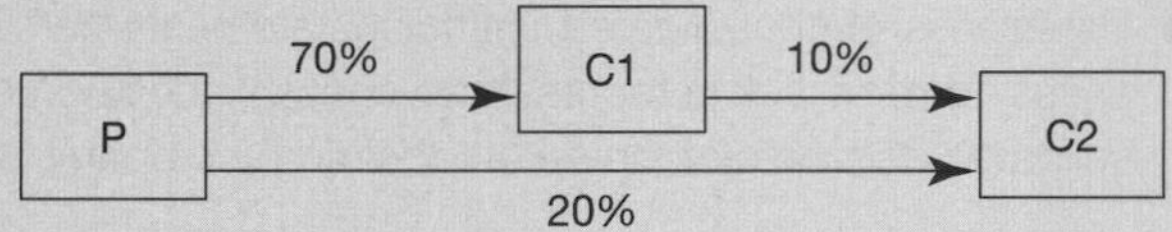

(a) 10%
(b) 20%
(c) 30%
(d) 27%
(e) None of these

3. In the diagram of question 2 above, the percentage of interest (ownership, stake) is:
   (a) 10%
   (b) 20%
   (c) 30%
   (d) 27%
   (e) None of these
4. Minority interests can be reported (several possible answers):
   (a) As a part of shareholders' equity
   (b) As a part of long-term liabilities
   (c) As a part of current liabilities
   (d) Between shareholders' equity and long-term liabilities
   (e) As a negative liability within financial fixed assets
   (f) None of these
   (g) All of these
5. Associate and affiliate are often considered as synonymous
   (a) True
   (b) False
6. The only possibility to hold control of a company is to own more than 50% of the voting rights of this entity
   (a) True
   (b) False
7. Minority interests are reported when which method is used?
   (a) Full consolidation
   (b) Equity method
   (c) Proportionate consolidation
   (d) None of these
8. Goodwill is the difference between the purchase price (cost of investment) of shares and the book value of these shares
   (a) True
   (b) False
9. Before the adoption and implementation of SFAS 141 and IFRS 3, the study of annual reports showed that goodwill was generally amortized over 20 or 40 years
   (a) True
   (b) False
10. The equity method should be used when the percentage of control is more than 30% and less than 50%
   (a) True
   (b) False

Assignment 13.2
Mutter & Tochter

Topic: Preparation of a consolidated balance sheet
Related part of the chapter: Core issues

The balance sheet of Mutter and Tochter companies, as of 31 December X1, is given in the following table (Mutter Co. is the parent and Tochter Co. is the subsidiary).

Balance sheet as at 31 December X1 (000 CU)

	Mutter		Tochter	
Fixed assets (net)	22,000		16,000	
Investment in Tochter Company	10,000	(1)	–	
Inventories	34,000		10,000	
Other current assets	25,700	(2)	9,200	
Total assets	91,700		35,200	
Capital	40,000		15,000	
Retained earning/Reserves	14,000		6,000	
Net income	7,000		4,000	
Debts	30,700		10,200	(3)
Total shareholders' equity and liabilities	91,700		35,200	
(1) When Mutter acquired 60% of the capital of Tochter, the shareholders' equity (capital, retained earnings/reserves and net income) of the subsidiary was valued at 16,000.				
(2) Includes a loan to Tochter	1,000			
(3) Includes a debt to Mutter			1,000	

Required

Prepare the consolidated balance sheet by using successively each of the following methods:

- Full consolidation
- Proportionate consolidation
- Equity method.

Assignment 13.3
Saint-Gobain*

Topic: Presentation of the consolidated income statement
Related part of the chapter: Core issues

Founded in France in 1665 as a manufacturer of flat glass, Saint-Gobain has undergone a major transformation of its operations. The group is now operating in three core sectors: glass, high-performance materials, and construction materials.

Excerpts from the consolidated income statement (*Source*: Annual report 2004 – French GAAP) show the following figures.

Consolidated statements of income

In € millions	2004	2003	2002
(...)			
Gross margin	8,096	7,327	7,604
(...)			
Operating income	2,632	2,442	2,582
(...)			
Income before profit/(loss) on sales of non-current assets and taxes	1,914	1,722	1,848
(...)			
Net operating income from consolidated companies before amortization of goodwill	1,267	1,213	1,239
Amortization of goodwill	(155)	(154)	(169)
Net operating income from consolidated companies	1,112	1,059	1,070
Share in net income of equity investees	8	6	4
Net income before minority interests	1,120	1,065	1,074
Minority interests in consolidated companies	(37)	(26)	(34)
Net income	1,083	1,039	1,040

Required

1. Which item of the income statement should disappear in the 2005 financial statements when Saint-Gobain will have applied the IAS/IFRS? Given any loss of information is detrimental to the users of financial statements, how could the information content of this item be possibly replaced?
2. What is the meaning of the item 'amortization of goodwill'? What questions does it raise for an analyst or an investor?
3. What is the meaning of the line item 'share in net income of equity investees'?
4. What is the meaning of the line item 'net income before minority interests'?
5. What is the meaning of the line item 'minority interest in consolidated companies'?
6. What is the real meaning of the item 'net income'? How useful is this item for an analyst or an investor?

Assignment 13.4
China International Marine Container*, Honda*, EVN*, and Serono*

Topic: Reporting for minority interests
Related part of the chapter: Core issues

The following are excerpts of the equity and liabilities section of the balance sheet (with notes when applicable) of four companies.

China International Marine Containers

(China – IFRS – *Source*: Annual report 2004 – Production of marine containers)

Balance sheet (aggregated version) In thousands of renminbi (RMB)	2004	2003
Share capital	1,008,483	630,302
Reserves	6,512,793	4,665,351
Total equity attributable to equity holders of the parent	7,521,276	5,295,653
Minority interests	854,499	659,804
Total equity	8,375,775	5,955,457
Total liabilities	8,610,540	4,302,899
Total equity and liabilities	16,986,315	10,258,356

Honda Motor Co.

(Japan – US GAAP – *Source*: Annual report 2005 – Manufacturer of automotive vehicles, motorcycles, and light farming equipment)

Consolidated balance sheet (aggregated version)

31 March 2004 and 2005 in Yen (millions)

Liabilities and Stockholders' Equity	2004	2005
Total current liabilities	3,334,819	3,748,564
Long-term debt	1,394,612	1,559,500
Other liabilities (note 8)	724,937	719,612
Total liabilities	5,454,368	6,027,676
Stockholders' equity		
Common stock	86,067	86,067
Capital surplus	172,719	172,531
Legal reserves	32,418	34,688
Retained earnings	3,589,434	3,809,383
Accumulated other comprehensive income (loss)	(854,573)	(793,934)
Treasury stock, at cost 33,498,264 shares in 2004 and 3,543,788 shares in 2005	(151,665)	(19,441)
Total stockholders' equity	2,874,400	3,289,294
Total liabilities and stockholders' equity	8,328,768	9,316,970

Note 8. Other liabilities (excerpts)	2004	2005
Minority interest	59,185	70,001

EVN AG

(Austria – Austrian GAAP – *Source*: Annual report 2003/04 – Energy and water services)

Balance sheet (aggregated version)	30.9.2004 000 €	30.9.2003 000 €
Equity and liabilities		
Equity		
Share capital	99,069.4	91,072.4
Capital reserves	309,361.9	186,789.5
Retained earnings	965,284.9	875,723.4
Valuation reserve according to IAS 39	159,514.0	−15,459.7
Currency translation differences	−419.9	−633.7
Minority interests	22,857.9	22,669.8
	1,555,668.2	1,160,161.7
Long-term liabilities	1,776,549.0	1,413,547.6
Current liabilities	399,750.4	420,092.5
Total equity and liabilities	3,731,967.6	2,993,801.8

Serono

(Switzerland – Swiss GAAP – *Source*: Annual report 2004 – Biotechnology)

Consolidated balance sheets (aggregated version)	2004 US$ 000	2003 US$ 000
Current liabilities	869,203	753,391
Non-current liabilities	1,083,866	936,408
Total liabilities	1,953,069	1,689,799
Minority interests	3,343	1,614
Shareholders' equity	2,447,878	2,880,190
Total liabilities, minority interests, and shareholders' equity	4,404,290	4,571,603

Required

- Compare and contrast the way minority interests are reported in the four companies.
- Suggest a coherent set of arguments that support the solution that has been adopted by each firm. How robust is your set of arguments? In other words, what hypotheses could be challenged that might change the outcome in terms of reporting the minority interests?

Assignment 13.5
Bosmans and Badings

Topic: Legal merger
Related part of the chapter: Advanced issues

Bosmans Company merges with the Badings Company, which will be dissolved after the merger. The balance sheet of each company is provided here (in 000 of CU).

Balance sheets of the merging companies (in 000 of CU)		
	Bosmans	Badings
Assets		
Fixed assets	700	500
Inventories	600	400
Receivables and cash	150	200
Total	1,450	1,100
Equity and liabilities		
Capital	400	600
Retained Earnings/ Reserves	500	280
Liabilities	550	220
Total	1,450	1,100
Number of shares	4,000	6,000
Par value	100	100

You are informed that, for some assets of Badings Company, the fair value is different from the book value, as indicated in the following table.

Assets (excerpts)	Book value	Fair value
Fixed assets	500	560
Inventories	400	390
Receivables and cash	200	170

Required

Prepare, step by step, the balance sheet of Bosmans after its merger with (absorption of) Badings under the following two sets of hypotheses:

(a) The net assets of Badings are integrated at fair value.

(b) The net assets of Badings are integrated at book value.

Discuss the pros and cons of each method, using the data of the Bosmans–Badings merger.

References

Alexander, D., and Britton, A. (2004) *Financial Reporting*, 7th edn, Thomson Learning, London.

EU (European Union) (1978) 4th Directive on the annual accounts of certain types of companies, No. 78/660/EEC. *Official Journal of the European Communities*, 14 August.

EU (European Union) (1983) 7th Directive on consolidated accounts of companies, No. 83/349/EEC. *Official Journal of the European Communities*, 18 July.

FASB (1981) Statement of Financial Accounting Standard No. 52: Foreign Currency Translation, Norwalk, CT.

FASB (2001a) Statement of Financial Accounting Standards No. 141: Business Combinations, Norwalk, CT.

FASB (2001b) Statement of Financial Accounting Standards No. 142: Goodwill and Other Intangible Assets, Norwalk, CT.

IASB (2003a) International Accounting Standard No. 21: The Effects of Changes in Foreign Exchange Rates, London.

IASB (2003b) International Accounting Standard No. 27: Consolidated and Separate Financial Statements, London.

IASB (2003c) International Accounting Standard No. 28: Investments in Associates, London.

IASB (2003d) International Accounting Standard No. 31: Interests in Joint Ventures, London.

IASB (2003e) International Accounting Standard No. 32: Financial Instruments: Disclosure and Presentation, London.

IASB (2004a) International Accounting Standard No. 36: Impairment of Assets, London.

IASB (2004b) International Accounting Standard No. 39: Financial Instruments: Recognition and Measurement, London.

IASB (2004c) International Financial Reporting Standard No. 3: Business Combinations, London.

Skousen, F., Stice, J., and Stice, E. K. (2003) *Intermediate Accounting*, South-Western College Publishing, Cincinnati, OH.

Further reading

Busse von Colbe, W. (2004) New accounting for goodwill: Application of American criteria from a German perspective, in *The Economics and Politics of Accounting* (eds, Leuz, C., *et al.*), Oxford University Press, pp. 201–18.

Feige, P. (1997) How 'uniform' is financial reporting in Germany? – The example of foreign currency translation. *European Accounting Review*, 6(1), 109–22.

Higson, C. (1998) Goodwill. *British Accounting Review*, 30(2), 141–58.

Kothavala, K. (2003) Proportional consolidation versus the equity method: A risk measurement perspective on reporting interests in joint ventures. *Journal of Accounting and Public Policy*, 22(6), 517–38.

Mora, A., and Rees, W. (1998) The early adoption of consolidated accounting in Spain. *European Accounting Review*, 7(4), 675–96.

Additional material on the website

Go to http://www.thomsonlearning.co.uk/stolowylebas2 for further information.

The following appendices to this chapter are available on the dedicated website:

Appendix 13.1 Value adjustment to lower of cost or market
Appendix 13.2 Uniting of interests and the pooling of interest method
Appendix 13.3 Deferred taxation on consolidation
Appendix 13.4 Foreign currency translations

Notes

1. *Significant influence* is the power to participate in the financial and operating policy decisions of the investee but implies not having control or joint control over those policies.
2. *Control* is the power to govern the financial and operating policies of an entity, so as to obtain benefits from its activities.
3. However, examples abound where a stake of significantly less than 20% still grants significant influence to the investor. For example, Kirk Kerkorian (through his private investment firm Tracinda Corporation), even after reducing, in December 2005, his stake in General Motors from 10% to 7.8% (a move that negatively impacted the share value on the NYSE) still holds a significant influence over the strategy of GM by his public comments and by seeking a seat on the board for a person close to him. The threshold of 20% may be a remnant of the past, but accountants need to have clear rules to avoid discretionary behavior in reporting (and a rule, even if imperfect, is better than no rule): under 20%, the investment is considered just that, i.e., an investment without influence, but above 20% it is considered that the influence on the value creation of the firm is significant and must be reported as such. Most countries require that the financial statements (or the publicly accessible filings with regulatory agencies) list the major stockholders and most stock exchanges require that investors signal to the market when their investment exceeds 5% and successively higher thresholds.
4. A derivative is any financial instrument derived from securities or physical markets. The term has become a generic term that is used to describe all types of new and old financial instruments. The most common types of derivatives are *futures, options, warrants,* and *convertible bonds*. Beyond these traditional derivatives instruments, 'the derivatives range is only limited by the imagination of investment banks' (adapted from 'derivatives' in www.numa.com/ref/faq.htm).
5. The notion of 'through profit or loss' refers to the fact that since the fair value may change from period to period, the investing business will recognize the potential gain or loss on its investment in its income statement on an as-you-go basis.
6. For example, it would be the case if such designation were to eliminate or significantly reduce, in further reporting, a measurement or recognition inconsistency (sometimes referred to as 'an accounting mismatch') that would otherwise arise from measuring assets [or liabilities] or recognizing the gains and losses on them on different bases.
7. Securitization consists in aggregating similar, generally not individually negotiable financial instruments, such as receivables, loans, or mortgages, into a negotiable security, which can be partitioned into 'shares' that can be sold and traded on financial markets.
8. The EU defines subsidiarity as the principle that decisions should always be taken at the lowest possible level or closest to where they will have their effect, for example in a local area rather than nationally. By extension, a well-managed group should delegate to its subsidiaries the responsibilities that allow the group to most effectively and rapidly respond to market demands and opportunities. Decisions should be made as close to the market as possible as long as they remain coherent with the higher level strategy defined by supervisors above. We use the term here to refer to the degree of autonomy over operations, strategy and financing granted by a parent to one of its subsidiaries. The concept therefore covers issues of delegation, control, and strategic autonomy,
9. See, for example, Alexander and Britton (2004).
10. An interesting presentation of the advantages of retrospective adoption of IFRS 3 (restatement of accounts for the years prior to 2005) can be found at the following URL: http://www.intangiblebusiness.com/Content/750.

Part 3

Financial statement analysis

C14

Chapter 14
Cash flow statement

Learning objectives

After studying this chapter, you will understand:

- What a cash flow statement is.
- That the cash flow statement is a very useful statement, from many perspectives.
- That the publication of a cash flow statement is required in many countries, especially for listed firms.
- What the content of each of the three categories of activities described in the cash flow statement is.
- What the direct and indirect methods of computation of the operating cash flow are.
- What the 'potential cash flow' is and what its role is in the determination of the operating cash flow.
- That, although the format of the cash flow statement is relatively harmonized in the world, there are still some differences of classification of the sources of flows of cash.
- How to deal with non-cash investing and financing cash flows.
- How the cash flow statement can be analyzed.
- The importance of 'available cash flow' and 'free cash flow' in financial statement analysis.

Neither balance sheet nor income statement provides a dynamic view of the evolution of the financial structure of a business, i.e., the changes in structure in general and changes in the cash position in particular. Yet, understanding such evolution over a period of time is of interest to both the company's management and external financial analysts. As IAS 7 puts it (IASB 1992: § 3): 'Users of an entity's financial statements are interested in how the entity generates and uses cash and cash equivalents. This is the case regardless of the nature of the entity's activities and irrespective of whether cash can be viewed as the product of the entity, as may be the case with a financial institution. Entities need cash for essentially the same reasons, however different their principal revenue-producing activities might be. They need cash to conduct their operations, to pay their obligations, and to provide returns to their investors'.

The 'cash flow statement' (IASB terminology) or 'statement of cash flows' (US terminology) was developed to meet these informational needs. A rudimentary cash flow statement was presented in Chapter 3, showing how it related to both balance sheet and income statement. In this chapter the Core issues section develops the model of cash flow statement adopted by the IASB and many countries. The Advanced issues section looks at differences in classification of certain cash flows and at a model called the statement of changes in financial position, which is still used in several countries.

1 Core issues

According to IAS 7 (IASB 1992: § 1): 'An entity shall prepare a cash flow statement (...) and shall present it as an integral part of its financial statements for each period for which financial statements are presented'. In some countries (the USA, the UK and France [for the consolidated financial statements], for instance) publishing a cash flow statement is compulsory, whereas in others (France [for stand-alone or individual financial statements] and Italy, for instance), it is optional. However, since 2005, with the required application of IFRS/IAS by listed firms in Europe and some other countries (such as Australia), the publication of a cash flow statement has become compulsory for these firms. In practice, most major listed companies already included a cash flow statement in their annual report, even if it was not required.

1.1 Structure of the cash flow statement

One of the objectives of a cash flow statement is, by definition, to provide information on those transactions that affect the cash position. The cash flow statement reports cash generated or provided and used during a given period. It classifies cash flows into three categories of activities: operating, investing, and financing, as shown in Table 14.1.

This classification by activity, as mentioned in IAS 7 (IASB 1992: § 11) 'provides information that allows users to assess the impact of those activities on the financial position of the entity and the amount of its cash and cash equivalents. This information may also be used to evaluate the relationships among those activities'.

Table 14.1 Cash flow statement structure

Net cash provided by/used in **operating** activities	A
Net cash provided by/used in **investing** activities	B
Net cash provided by/used in **financing** activities	C
Net increase/decrease in **cash and cash equivalents**	D = A + B + C
Cash and cash equivalents at beginning of year	E
Cash and cash equivalents at end of year	F = D + E

1.2 Usefulness of the cash flow statement

'A cash flow statement, when used in conjunction with the rest of the financial statements, provides information that enables users to evaluate [a] the changes in net assets of an entity, [b] its financial structure (including its liquidity and solvency) and [c] its ability to affect the amounts and timing of cash flows in order to adapt to changing circumstances and opportunities' (IAS 7: § 4). The cash flow statement is a useful statement in its own right, explaining the changes in the cash position, just as the income statement explains the components of net income.

1.2.1 The importance of cash

As early as in Chapter 1, we highlighted the fact that cash is the 'blood' of the enterprise and we presented the cash pump as the most basic business model of an economic entity. IAS 7 (IASB 1992: § 4) stresses the fact that 'cash flow information is useful in assessing the ability of the entity to generate cash and cash equivalents'. The cash position is a key indicator for management and financial analysis, both in the short (assessing solvency) and the long term (measuring financing requirements). The importance of the cash position, in both absolute and relative terms, and its sign (positive or negative) may reveal the company's situation: financially healthy, vulnerable, struggling, etc. Cash is a valuable indicator in forecasting business difficulties and possible bankruptcy, as the triggering event of bankruptcy is the inability to cover, with available cash and cash equivalents, the repayment of debt that is due.

1.2.2 Cash is objective

Cash flow statements enhance the comparability of reported operating performance by different enterprises because they eliminate the effects of using different accounting rules or procedures for the same transactions and events.

1.2.3 A valuable forecasting tool

The cash flow statement is well suited for both retrospective analysis (where did funds come from and what were they used for) and forecasting (where will funds come from and are they sufficient to implement the entity's strategy, thus starting an adjustment loop if, for example, funds from operations are not sufficient). It is therefore an essential part of any business planning process and is critical in the preparation of annual budgets.

In addition, cash flow statements enable users of financial information to assess and compare both the predictability of future cash flows and the present value of future cash flows of different enterprises.

1.2.4 Developments in international practice

There is currently a clear movement towards the adoption of a relatively uniform cash flow statement format, replacing a variety of previously used statements such as the 'funds flow statement' or the 'statement of changes in financial position', which are discussed later in the chapter. Table 14.2 lists the countries that allow or have adopted the publication of a cash flow statement as part of the annual report (other possible models may coexist in any given country). Even in countries where the standards do not require a cash flow statement, many companies still publish one if they apply IFRS/IAS in their annual report or if they are quoted on a major stock exchange.

1.3 Definition of the three categories of activities impacting on cash flows

Clear partitioning of the cash flow statement between the various 'activities' creating or consuming cash (operating, investing, and financing) is vital.

Each activity is defined by IAS 7 and we will follow that position. These definitions are used in international accounting practice and are coherent with the principal national standards regarding cash flow statements (SFAS 95 in the USA, FRS 1 in the UK, Regulation CRC 99-02, articles 4260 and 4261 in France, etc.).

The classification of certain operations is sometimes difficult. For example, deciding where financial expenses should be classified has been a hotly debated subject as the

Table 14.2 Countries allowing or requiring a cash flow statement

Date of first adoption	Date of revision	Country	Reference of the standard	Title of the document (translated in English, if necessary)
1985	1998	Canada	Section 1540 of the CICA handbook	Cash flow statement
1987	*	USA	SFAS 95	Statement of cash flows
1987	1994	New Zealand	SSAP 10 superseded by FRS 10	Statement of cash flows
1988	2004	South Africa	AC 118 superseded by GRAP 2	Cash flow statement
1988	1997 and 1999	France	Individual financial statements: Recommendation 1.22 superseded by Opinion 30	
			Consolidated financial statements: Regulation 99–02 (§§ 4260–4261).	Statement of cash flows
1991	1996	UK/Ireland	FRS 1	Cash flow statement
1992	–	IASB	IAS 7	Cash flow statement
1997	2004	Australia	AASB 1026 superseded by AASB 107	Cash flow statement
1999	2004	Germany	GAS 2	Cash flow statement

* Standard affected by several subsequent standards.

answer impacts on the very philosophy of what a business does. In addition, a single transaction may include cash flow components that belong to two or more distinct categories. For example, the monthly or quarterly cash repayment of an installment loan generally includes both an interest component and a partial reimbursement of the capital or principal. The interest element is generally classified as an operating activity, while the reimbursement of the principal is classified as a financing activity.

1.3.1 Operating activities

Cash flows from operating activities (often referred to as 'operating cash flows', in short, or 'cash flows from operations') are primarily derived from the main or core revenue-producing undertakings (activities) of the enterprise. They generally result from the transactions and other events that enter into the determination of net profit or loss. The amount of cash flows from operating activities is a key indicator of the extent to which the operations of the enterprise have generated sufficient cash flows to keep it afloat (in both the short and the long term). That implies the ability to maintain the operating capability of the enterprise, repay loans, pay dividends without needing recourse to external sources of financing, and, possibly, make new investments for the development of the firm.

Examples of cash flows from operating activities, as given in IAS 7 (§ 14) are provided in Table 14.3 and in Appendix 14.1. Some transactions, such as the sale of a fixed asset, may give rise to a gain or loss, which will be included in the determination of net profit or loss. However, the cash flows relating to such transactions should be included in cash flows from 'investing activities' since the business of the entity is not to sell its assets. The sale of an asset is a way for the firm to obtain funds that will therefore not need to be obtained from lenders or shareholders. A later section is dedicated to the methods and approaches to calculating operating cash flows.

1.3.2 Investing activities

Investing activities refer to the buying and selling of long-lived assets. These assets can be physical, such as land, buildings, machinery, equipment, etc., intangible, or financial, such as long-term securities, loans granted (and collecting their repayment), and equity in third parties.

The separate disclosure of cash flows arising from investing activities is important because these cash flows represent 'the extent to which expenditures have been made for resources intended to generate future income and cash flows' (IAS 7: § 16) (see examples of investing cash flows in Table 14.3 and Appendix 14.1).

1.3.3 Financing activities

Financing activities consist of: (1) obtaining funds from existing or new shareholders and providing them with dividends; and of (2) obtaining long-term loans or long-term funds through bond issues and managing their repayment.

The separate disclosure of cash flows arising from financing activities is important because it is useful in predicting claims on future cash flows by providers of capital to the enterprise. It also helps understand how much of the cash available in a business comes from influxes of 'fresh capital' by shareholders or financial partners of the firm (see examples of financing cash flows in Table 14.3 and Appendix 14.1).

Table 14.3 summarizes the contents of each cash-related activity. As will be seen later in this chapter, the classification of certain items is subject to debate. Our table reflects current standard practice.

Table 14.3 Classification of cash flows

Activities	Cash inflows (receipts)	Cash outflows (payments)
Operating activities	■ Sale of goods and rendering of services to customers ■ Royalties, fees, commissions, and other revenues ■ Interests on loans and investments	■ Purchase of goods and services ■ Salaries, fringe benefits, and social expenses ■ Taxes ■ Interests on borrowings
Investing activities	■ Sale of fixed assets (intangible, tangible, financial – securities which are not cash equivalents) ■ Receipt of repayment of loans and advances	■ Purchase of fixed assets (intangible, tangible, financial – securities which are not cash equivalents) ■ Loans and advances made
Financing activities	■ Proceeds from issuing shares ■ Proceeds from issuing debts	■ Repayment of shares ■ Repayment of debts ■ Payment of dividends

1.4 Calculating cash flows from operating activities

There are two ways of determining cash flows from operating activities: the *direct method* and the *indirect method*.

The **direct method** calculates the cash flows by grouping cash effects of transactions classes. In other words, it presents receipt and payment flows separately for each category of operating activities: selling, purchasing, securing employees, labor, etc. In practice, there are two subcategories of the direct method:

- A 'semi-direct' method, where accounting flows (sales, purchases, labor costs, etc.) are adjusted for changes in inventories and operating or trade receivables and payables to give cash flows of the period. For instance, cash received from customers equals 'sales revenue' minus 'change in accounts receivable' (X2 minus X1).
- A 'true' direct method, where cash flows are entered directly into the cash flow statement from the accounting records of cash movements in the 'cash at bank' and 'cash in hand' accounts.

The **indirect method** calculates the net cash flow from operating activities by adjusting net profit or loss for the effects of:

- changes during the period in inventories and operating receivables and payables;
- non-cash items such as depreciation, provisions, deferred taxes (see Chapter 6), unrealized foreign currency gains and losses, undistributed profits of associates, and minority interests (see Chapter 13);
- all other items for which the cash effects relate to investing or financing cash flows. For instance, the gain or loss from the sale of fixed assets is adjusted because it will be included in the investing activities (see later).

Figure 14.1 summarizes these methods.

Figure 14.1 Reporting cash flows from operating activities

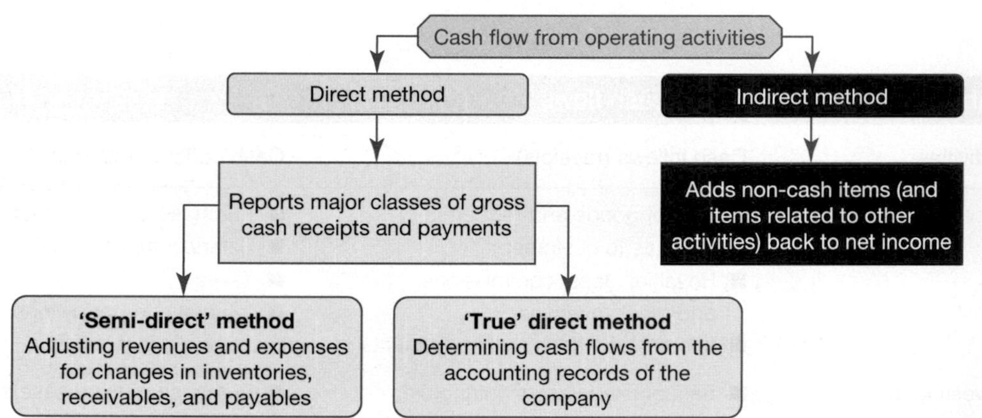

The computation of the operating cash flow using both methods is detailed later in this chapter.

Most standards (IAS 7, SFAS 95 in the USA, FRS 1 in the UK, etc.) recommend using the direct method in reporting, while allowing the use of the indirect method. Although the direct method provides information that may be useful in estimating future cash flows and which is not available under the indirect method, it is, however, difficult to implement. Managers may also see it as too revealing of the actual operations of their firm. The implementation of the 'semi-direct' method is also relatively complex. Thus, the vast majority of businesses – with the important exception of Australian and Chinese firms – report cash flows from operating activities using the indirect method, which is much simpler to implement. Unfortunately, the information thus provided by the cash flow statement is also, as a result, much less valuable.

To conclude on this issue, we should stress the difference between the determination of the cash flows from operating activities and reporting of that cash flow. A given company may be able to, internally, determine the operating cash flow with a semi-direct, or even true direct, method, and nevertheless decide to report the operating cash flow using the indirect method presentation. In other words, the format adopted for reporting does not allow any assumption as to which method is actually used in practice to determine the reported operating cash flow.

1.5. Cash and cash equivalents

1.5.1 Definitions

According to IAS 7 (IASB 1992: § 6): '*Cash* comprises cash on hand and demand deposits. *Cash equivalents* are short-term, highly liquid investments that are readily convertible to known amounts of cash and which are subject to an insignificant risk of changes in value'. An investment normally qualifies as a cash equivalent only when it has a short maturity of, say, three months or less from the date of acquisition. Equity investments are excluded from cash equivalents unless they are, in substance, cash equivalents, for example in the case of preferred shares with a specified redemption date acquired within a short period of their maturity.

'Bank borrowings are generally considered to be financing activities' (IAS 7: § 8). However, IAS 7 (§ 8) leaves the decision of classification of bank overdrafts open. For instance, 'in some countries, [such as Germany, France, and the UK], bank overdrafts, which are repayable on demand, form an integral part of a [business] entity's cash management' approach (IAS 7: § 8). IAS 7 states that when bank overdrafts are considered to be cash equivalents they should be recorded as a negative component of cash. (A characteristic of such banking arrangements is that the bank balance often fluctuates from being positive to being overdrawn.)

The inclusion of bank overdrafts in the category 'cash equivalents' is not without its flaws. For example, the separation of short-term credits from other debts makes it impossible to fully explain the total change in debt and to measure the leverage on the debt accurately. Another flaw arises from the fact that some (mostly fast growing) entities have a quasi-permanent overdraft situation: this normally short-term financial instrument can be used by some businesses, as was the case of payables, for medium- or even long-term financing.

In practice, many companies believe that there is a room for interpreting IAS 7 and treat bank overdrafts as short-term borrowings[1] (therefore included in financing activities).

1.5.2 Disclosure

Principles 'An entity shall disclose the components of cash and cash equivalents and shall present a reconciliation of the amounts in its cash flow statement with the equivalent items reported in the balance sheet' (IAS 7: § 45).

Real-life example The Vermont Teddy Bear Co., Inc.

(USA – US GAAP – *Source*: Annual report 2005 – Designer, manufacturer, and direct marketer of teddy bears and related products)

Notes to Financial Statements – 30 June 2005

Cash, Cash Equivalents and Restricted Cash

All highly liquid investments with initial maturities of three months or less are considered cash equivalents. At 30 June 2005 and 2004, approximately $475,000 and $471,000 of the company's cash was restricted, respectively. This cash has been restricted as part of the company's sale–leaseback transaction.

Comment: The first sentence of this note is pretty much boiler-plate wording and can be found in many annual reports. The remainder, however, is more interesting because it describes the company's specific circumstances. (Leaseback operations are discussed in Chapter 12.)

Real-life example Aluminum Corporation of China (Chalco)

(China – Hong Kong GAAP – *Source*: Annual report 2004 – Production, sales, and research of alumina and primary aluminum)

Notes to the financial statements

Cash and cash equivalents

Cash and cash equivalents are carried in the balance sheet at cost. For the purpose of the cash flow statement, cash and cash equivalents comprise cash on hand, deposits held at call with banks, cash investments with an original maturity of within three months and bank overdrafts.

Comment: This company reports bank overdrafts in line with one of the two formats allowed in IAS 7: a negative component of cash.

Real-life example Stora Enso

(Finland – IFRS/IAS GAAP – *Source*: Annual report 2004 – Production of paper)

Notes to the financial statements

Cash and cash equivalents

Cash and cash equivalents comprise cash in hand, deposits held at call with banks and other liquid investments with original maturity of less than three months. Bank overdrafts are included in short-term borrowings under current liabilities.

Comment: This company explicitly includes bank overdrafts in its financing activities.

Real-life example Coles Myer

(Australia – Australian GAAP – *Source*: Annual report 2004 – Department stores, discount stores, food stores, and specialty retail operations)

Note C. Reconciliation of cash

For the purposes of the statements of cash flows, cash includes cash on hand and at bank, net of bank overdraft. Cash at the end of the year as shown in the statements of cash flows is reconciled to the relevant statements of financial position items as follows:

$ million	2004	2003
Cash assets	849.0	905.5
Bank overdraft	(7.1)	(10.8)
	841.9	894.7

Comment: This excerpt from the notes illustrates a correct application of the requirement of IAS 7 (§ 45).

1.6 Example of a cash flow statement

Table 14.4 presents an example of a generic cash flow statement template for the year X2 reflecting the most common practices. The third column in Table 14.4 would not

Table 14.4 Example of a cash flow statement for the year X2

		Source of the information
Cash flow from operating activities *(indirect method)*		
Net income/loss	±	IS X2
Adjustments to reconcile net income/loss to net cash provided by/used in operating activities		
Depreciation and amortization (excluding those applying to current assets [inventories and accounts receivable])	+	IS X2
Gain/loss on sale of fixed assets	±	IS X2
Potential cash flow	=	
Changes in operating assets and liabilities		
Change in accounts receivable (net amount)	±	BS X1/X2
Change in inventories (net amount)	±	BS X1/X2
Change in prepaid expenses	±	BS X1/X2
Change in accounts payable and accrued expenses	±	BS X1/X2
Net cash provided by/used in operating activities = (A)	=	
Alternative		
Cash flow from operating activities *(direct method)*		
Cash received from customers	+	IS X2;BS X1/X2
Cash paid to suppliers*	–	IS X2;BS X1/X2
Cash paid to employees*	–	IS X2;BS X1/X2
Cash dividend received	+	IS X2;BS X1/X2
Other operating cash receipts	+	IS X2;BS X1/X2
Other operating cash payments	–	IS X2;BS X1/X2
Interest paid in cash	–	IS X2;BS X1/X2
Income taxes paid in cash	–	IS X2;BS X1/X2
Net cash provided by/used in operating activities = (A)	=	
Cash flows from investing activities		
Purchase of fixed assets	–	BS X1/X2;AI X2
Proceeds from sale of fixed assets	+	IS X2;AI X2
Loans granted	–	BS X1/X2;AI X2
Repayment of loans	+	BS X1/X2;AI X2
Net cash provided by/used in investing activities = (B)	=	
Cash flows from financing activities		
Proceeds from issuance of long-term debt	+	BS X1/X2;AI X2
Proceeds from issuance of shares	+	BS X1/X2;AI X2
Dividends paid	–	BS X1/X2;AI X2
Payment on long-term debt	–	BS X1/X2;AI X2
Payment on reduction of share capital (repayment of shares)	–	BS X1/X2;AI X2
Net cash provided by/used in financing activities = (C)	=	
***Net increase in cash and cash equivalents* = (A) + (B) + (C) = (D)**	=	
Cash and cash equivalents at beginning of year = (E)		
Cash and cash equivalents at end of year = (F) = (E) + (D)		

IS, income statement; BS, balance sheet; AI, additional information.
* These two lines are often merged.

normally be found in a published cash flow statement. It is presented, for pedagogical reasons only, to show the source of information for each line.

Table 14.4 shows, for pedagogical purposes, both the direct and the indirect methods for the cash flows from operating activities. Of course, in practice, only one of these methods is applied in the presentation of any cash flow statement.

This table also displays the 'potential cash flow', which is often not included in the official versions of the cash flow statement but is useful in understanding the basic mechanism of the indirect method. 'Potential cash flow' is calculated by adjusting net income for non-cash items and correcting for gains or losses on sales of fixed assets. Potential cash flow is illustrated in subsection 1.7.1.

1.7 Preparation of a cash flow statement

Tables 14.5 and 14.6, pertaining to the published statements of the Liszt Company, a retail and wholesale commercial business, provide the raw material for the construction of a cash flow statement.

Additional events took place during the year that are relevant for the preparation of the cash flow statement for the year X2 (all monetary figures in 000 CU):

- New equipment was purchased for 175.
- Equipment with an original cost of 20 and accumulated depreciation of 14 was sold for 9.
- No new loan was either granted or obtained.
- 135 were raised from the issue of shares in cash (share capital of 66 plus share premium of 69).
- Convertible bonds were converted into capital for 30 (share capital for 16 and share premium for 14).
- Other bonds were repaid at face (nominal) value at maturity for 60.
- Dividends (relating to net income of X1) were paid in cash for 8.

1.7.1 Cash flows from operating activities

The indirect method and direct method will be used successively. Although we believe that the direct method is more relevant, from a financial statement analysis standpoint, we start our explanation with the indirect method, which is, by far, the most frequently reported method.

Indirect method The indirect method consists in adjusting net income for non-cash expenses and revenues (such as depreciation expense), also called non-cash items, gain/loss on sale of fixed assets, and changes in receivables and payables. We will develop each of these elements, starting with the concept of 'non-cash items' and potential cash flow.

Non-cash items and potential cash flow The cash flows from operating activities cannot be obtained directly from the income statement because the latter records revenues and expenses, not receipts (cash inflows) and payments (cash outflows). Therefore, the first step is to determine a 'potential cash flow'. This is done by separating revenues and expenses in two categories: first, those which, by nature, will eventually generate a real cash flow (they are called by convention cash items or monetary items); second, those which will not generate a real cash flow (by convention, non-cash items or non-monetary items). Cash items

Table 14.5 Liszt Company – Comparative balance sheets before appropriation – years ended 31 December X2 and X1

000 CU	X2	X1	Changes (X2 – X1)
Assets			
Fixed assets			
Tangible assets			
Equipment (gross)	615	460	155
Accumulated depreciation	−116	−70	−46
Equipment (net)	499	390	109
Financial assets (loans granted)	115	174	−59
Total fixed assets	614	564	50
Current assets			
Inventory	144	100	44
Accounts receivable	44	63	−19
Cash and marketable securities	25	15	10
Prepaid expenses*	4	7	−3
Total current assets	217	185	32
Total assets	831	749	82
Shareholders' equity and liabilities			
Shareholders' equity			
Share capital	282	200	82
Share premium	198	115	83
Retained earnings/Reserves	124	122	2
Net income of the period (before appropriation)	9	10	−1
Total shareholders' equity	613	447	166
Liabilities			
Long-term liabilities (loans received and bonds)	155	245	−90
Current liabilities			
Accounts payable	62	54	8
Income taxes payable	1	3	−2
Total current liabilities	63	57	6
Total liabilities	218	302	−84
Total shareholders' equity and liabilities	831	749	82

* Related to 'Other operating expenses' in the income statement.

make up most of the income statement (sales, cost of merchandise sold, compensation expenses, operating expenses, etc.). Non-cash items include depreciation expense, amortization expense, depletion expense, provision expense (non-cash expenses), and reversal of provision (non-cash revenues). Figure 14.2 illustrates the fact that the income statement can be converted easily into the needed format for the calculation of the potential cash flow.

Table 14.6 Liszt Company – Income statement – year X2

000 CU	
Sales	800
Cost of merchandise sold	−570
Gross profit	230
Depreciation expense	−60
Other operating expenses	−162
Operating profit	8
Interest expense	−15
Investment income	18
Gain on sale of equipment	3
Profit before taxes	14
Income taxes	−5
Net profit	9

Figure 14.2 Cash and non-cash items in the income statement

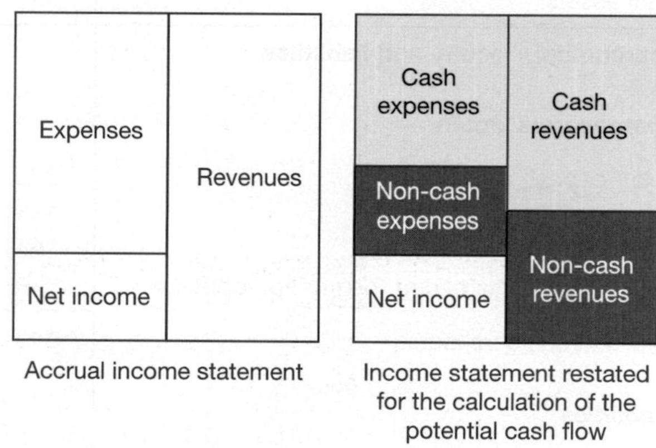

There are two ways of calculating the potential cash flow, since the sum of the expenses plus net income is, by definition, equal to the sum of revenues:

Potential cash flow = Cash revenues − Cash expenses

or

Potential cash flow = Net income + Non-cash expenses − Non-cash revenues

The first formula (Cash revenues − Cash expenses) is the one used in the direct method (see more details below). The second formula (Net income + Non-cash expenses − Non-cash revenues) is applied in the indirect method. It highlights the difference between cash flow generated and net income: the latter must be adjusted for non-cash items in order to provide the potential cash flow. The 'potential cash flow' is sometimes referred to as the 'Funds obtained from operations' by some businesses (see the example of Repsol in Appendix 14.4).

Gain on sale of equipment In our example (all monetary figures in 000 CU), equipment with an original cost of 20 and accumulated depreciation of 14 was sold for 9. A gain of 3 on the sale will contribute to the period's income. It is computed in the following way:

Sale price		9
Original cost	20	
Accumulated depreciation	−14	
Book (or net) value	6	−6
Gain on sale		3

The cash inflow from the sale of equipment (here amounting to 9) is recorded as part of the cash from investing activities ('proceeds from sale of equipment').

If the gain on the sale had considered as a part of operating activities, it would end up being recorded twice in the cash flow statement: once under operating activities (for an amount of 3), and once in investing activities (since it is, by construction, included in the sale price of 9). The gain on the sale of an asset must, therefore, never be considered as belonging to operating activities. As a matter of fact, many, if not most, businesses consider gains/losses on sales of fixed assets as a non-cash item, and, thus, include them in the calculation of their potential cash flow. We adopted this position in Figure 14.4, and throughout this chapter.

Changes in inventory, receivables, and payables As we will show later in the direct method, the 'potential cash flow' determined by adjustment of net income for non-cash items, then corrected for gains or losses on sales of fixed assets, now has to be adjusted by the amount of changes in inventory, receivables, and payables.

Changes in balance sheet items are calculated by a simple method: Year X2 balance minus Year X1 balance. However, increases or decreases of assets or liabilities impact cash differently, as shown below in Table 14.7.

Table 14.7 Sign of changes in assets and liabilities and impact on cash

	Change (ending minus beginning balances)	Impact on cash
Assets	Increase	−
	Decrease	+
Liabilities	Increase	+
	Decrease	−

The determination of the operating cash flow in the indirect method can thus be shown as follows in Figure 14.3.

Figure 14.3 From 'potential' cash flow to 'real' cash flow

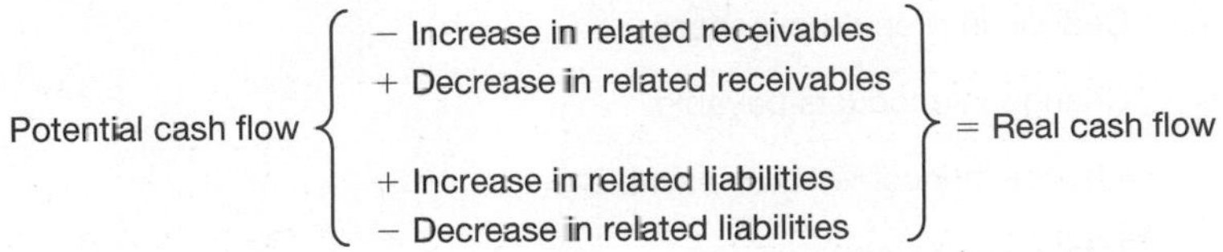

The change in inventories, accounts receivable, prepaid expenses, accounts payable, and income taxes payable are taken from the 'changes' column of the comparative balance sheet (see Table 14.5). The nature of the change (positive or negative) in one of these accounts is important. If we take the example of accounts receivable, a negative figure in the comparative balance sheet indicates a decrease, and this has a positive impact on cash (it means that more customers paid off their trade debt than new customers added to the trade receivable balance).

Summary of the indirect method Figure 14.4 summarizes the determination of the operating cash flow with the indirect method.

Figure 14.4 Indirect method

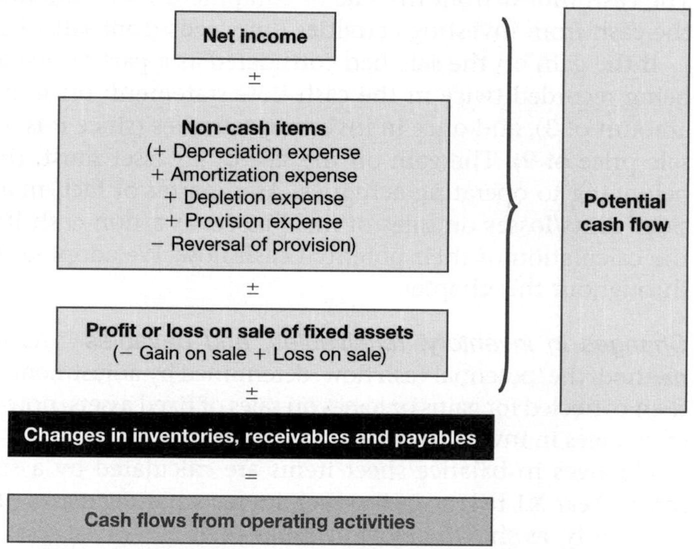

Liszt Company's schedule of cash flows from operating activities (indirect method) The cash flows from operating activities for Liszt Company are computed in Table 14.8.

Table 14.8 Cash flows from operating activities (indirect method)

Net income		9
Adjustments to reconcile net income/loss to net cash provided by/used in operating activities		
Depreciation expense	60	
Gain on sale of fixed assets	−3	
Changes in operating assets and liabilities		
Change in accounts receivable	19	
Change in inventories	−44	
Change in prepaid expenses	3	
Change in accounts payable	8	
Change in income taxes payable	−2	
Total adjustments	41	41
Net cash provided by/used in operating activities		50

Since the cash flows from operating activities must be the same under both methods, we will have to check after completion of the direct method that we find the same operating cash flow.

Direct method We use the 'semi-direct' method described earlier, where income statement items are adjusted for changes in inventories and operating receivables and payables to give cash flows[2]. This, in effect, transforms a *fund* flow (a transaction), calculated on an accrual basis (income statement item), into a *cash* flow. This calculation can be systematized into the equation shown as Figure 14.5.

Figure 14.5 Determination of cash flows using the semi-direct method

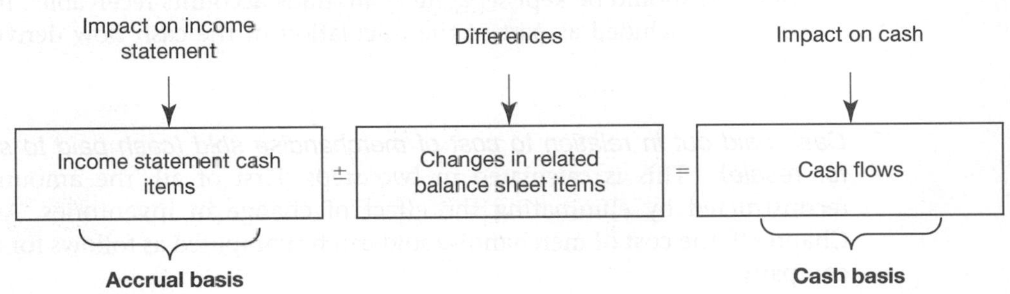

One difficulty is the correct association of related income statement and balance sheet items for inventories, receivables, and payables. Another difficulty is the determination of the sign of the change in related balance sheet items. (This issue has been covered above with the indirect method – see Figure 14.3 and Table 14.7.)

The determination of the operating cash flow with the direct method is shown in a simplified way in Figure 14.6, which represents a variation of Figure 14.3 (indirect method).

The equation in Figure 14.6 shows that each cash flow item is determined in the following way: a potential cash flow (represented by each income statement cash item) is adjusted by a change in inventories, receivables, or payables to obtain the real cash flow.

Figure 14.6 From income statement to 'real cash flow'

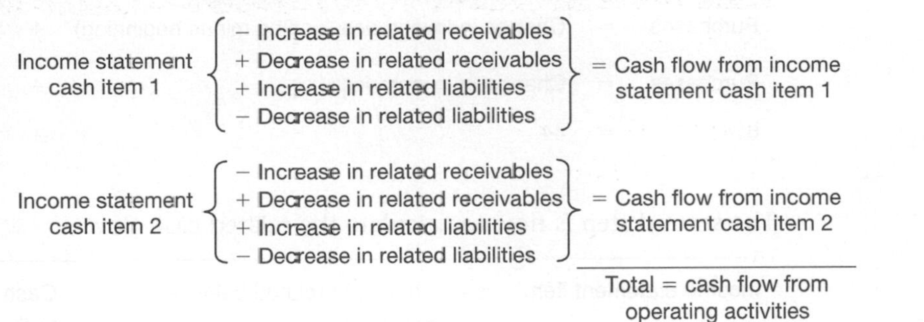

The equation is illustrated with the calculation of each component of the cash flow.

Cash received from customers

Income statement item	±	Change in related balance sheet item	=	Cash flow from customers
Sales revenue		Change in accounts receivable		Cash received from customers
800	+	19 (decrease)	=	819

- 'Sales revenue' is obtained from the income statement. It flows through the 'accounts receivable' before becoming cash.
- The change in accounts receivable is taken from the 'changes' column of the comparative balance sheet.
- The nature of the change in accounts receivable (positive or negative) is important. A negative figure in the comparative balance sheet indicates a decrease, and this has a positive impact on cash.
- The cash flow, in this example, exceeds sales revenue by the amount of the change in accounts receivable.
- The receivable arising on the sale of a fixed asset (if there were one – which is not the case here) should be kept separate from 'trade accounts receivable'. If there were one it would be included as part of the calculation of the cash flow derived from investing activities.

Cash paid out in relation to cost of merchandise sold (cash paid to suppliers of goods for resale) This is calculated in two steps. First of all, the amount of purchases is reconstructed by eliminating the effect of change in inventories. As already seen in Chapter 9, the cost of merchandise sold can be computed as follows for a trading (retailer) company:

Purchases + Change in inventories (i.e., beginning minus ending) = Cost of merchandise sold

Given that in Table 14.5 the balance sheet changes are calculated by deducting Year X1 figures from Year X2 figures (i.e., ending – beginning), this formula becomes:

Purchases – Change in inventories (i.e., ending minus beginning) = Cost of merchandise sold

Purchases are consequently calculated as follows:

Purchases	=	Change in inventories (ending minus beginning)	+	Cost of merchandise sold
Purchases	=	Change in inventories	+	Cost of merchandise sold
614	=	44	+	570

The second step is now to calculate the related cash flow.

Income statement item	±	Change in related balance sheet item	=	Cash flow related to the acquisition of merchandise
Purchases		Change in accounts payable		Cash paid out for purchases
–614	+	8 (increase)	=	–606

We assume here that all accounts payable relate to purchases of merchandise.

Special case of manufacturing firms Keep in mind the Liszt example is a retailing/wholesaling firm. If an analyst or an outside user of financial information wants to calculate the cash flows from operating activities created by a manufacturing firm that uses 'cost of goods sold' in its income statement (by function), the computation will be a little more complex than it is here in the case of a retailing or a service business (the problem, of course, does not exist if the entity reports its income statement by nature, since, in that case, the total depreciation expense will be clearly identified). The depreciation expense that will be used may be an approximation because the cost of goods sold does include part of the manufacturing depreciation expense (and the other part of the depreciation expense is attached to inventories which means less – increase in inventory level – or more – decrease in inventory level – than the depreciation of the period may have been, in fact, included in the cost of goods sold).

The following equations (ignoring, for the sake of simplicity, work in process) need to be kept in mind when looking at a manufacturing entity. They illustrate the reason why the total depreciation expense is not available directly in an income statement by function:

Raw materials and components (RM) consumed = Purchases + Beginning inventory of RM – Ending inventory of RM

Cost of goods manufactured = Cost of RM consumed + Cost of manufacturing labor + **Manufacturing depreciation** + Manufacturing overhead (i.e., supervision and support costs)

Cost of goods sold = Cost of goods manufactured + Beginning inventory of finished goods – Ending inventory of finished goods.

The total depreciation expense (manufacturing plus non-manufacturing depreciation expenses), which must be known to be able to use the indirect method of cash flow calculation, is not available directly from reading the income statement. An approximate value can be extracted through an analysis of the balance sheet.

The difference in accumulated depreciation between the beginning and ending balance sheets provides an approximation of the total depreciation expense of the period. It must be adjusted appropriately if the notes to the financial statements mention any sale of assets during the period (the sale should be reported, and should mention both the revenue from the sale and the book value and relevant accumulated depreciation of the assets sold). In a case like this, the depreciation expense that will thus be used in calculating the cash flows from operating activities will not be the depreciation expense reported in the income statement (that figure pertains only to non-manufacturing assets, since the manufacturing depreciation expense is buried in the cost of goods sold and in the inventories fluctuations), but it will be the estimated depreciation expense calculated on the basis of comparing balance sheets.

Cash paid for other operating expenses (cash paid to suppliers of other operating expenses)

Income statement item	±	Change in related balance sheet item	=	Cash flow related to other operating expenses
Other potentially cash impacting operating expenses		Change in prepaid expenses		Cash paid out for other operating expenses
−162	+	3 (decrease)	=	−159

- If there had been any accrued liabilities, or salaries, fringe benefits, and social expenses payable in the balance sheet, then these items would have been included in the adjustment of other operating expenses.

- Depreciation expense (and amortization expense, which does not exist in this example) has no impact on cash. These expenses are therefore not included in the direct method calculation.

Cash paid for interest In our example there is no accrued interest payable on the balance sheet. The cash outflow is thus equal to the interest expense: −15. In general, cash paid for interest is equal to the interest expense adjusted for the change in accrued interest payable.

Cash received from investment income Our example does not include any accrued interest receivable on the balance sheet. The cash inflow is thus equal to the investment income (dividends received): 18.

Cash paid for income taxes This is calculated as was done for 'other operating expenses'.

Income statement item	±	Change in related balance sheet items	=	Cash flow related to taxes
Income taxes expense		Change in income taxes payable		Income taxes paid
−5	−	2 (decrease)	=	−7

Gain on sale of equipment The gain on sale of equipment is not included in the direct method. The proceeds from the sale of fixed assets are included in investing activities.

Summary of adjustments Table 14.9 shows balance sheet items (receivables and payables) related to income statement items.

Depreciation expense and amortization expense are not included in this table because they have no impact on cash. Any given income statement item may be related, at the same time, to both assets and liabilities.

Liszt Company's schedule of cash flows from operating activities (direct method) Table 14.10 shows how cash flows from operating activities are calculated.

At this stage, we can cross-check the cash flow figure obtained with the direct method (50) with the one determined previously with the indirect method. As expected, we find the figures from each method to be identical.

1.7.2 Cash flows from investing activities

The flow of cash to be calculated is the 'cash flow from investing activities'. The relevant data for this activity for Liszt Company are (all monetary figures in 000 CU):

- Equipment was purchased for 175.
- Equipment with an original cost of 20 and accumulated depreciation of 14 was sold for 9.
- No new loans were granted.

Table 14.9 Income statement items and related balance sheet items

Income statement items	Related receivables (and inventory)	Related liabilities
Sales	Accounts receivable	Advances received from customers Revenues recorded in advance (unearned revenues)
Financial revenues	Interests receivable Accrued interests receivable	Unearned interests
Cost of merchandise sold	Inventory Advances paid to suppliers	Accounts payable
Rent expense	Prepaid rent (Expenses recorded in advance)	Rent payable Accrued rent payable
Salaries and social expenses	Prepaid salaries and social expenses (Expenses recorded in advance)	Salaries and social expenses payable Accrued salaries and social expenses payable
Other operating expenses	Prepaid other operating expenses (Expenses recorded in advance)	Other expenses payable Accrued other expenses payable
Taxes Income taxes	Prepaid taxes – prepaid income taxes (Expenses recorded in advance)	(Income) Taxes payable Accrued (income) taxes payable
Financial expenses	Prepaid interests	Interests payable Accrued interests payable

Table 14.10 Cash flows from operating activities (direct method)

Cash received from customers	819
Cash paid in relation to cost of merchandise sold	−606
Cash paid in relation to other operating expenses	−159
Cash paid on interest	−15
Cash received from investment income	18
Cash paid on income taxes	−7
Net cash provided by/used in operating activities	50

For balance sheet items affected by investing activities, the following equation is key (the same equation applies to any balance sheet item). It allows the calculation of any one of the four items when the other three are known.

Beginning balance	+	Increases	−	Decreases	=	Ending balance
A	+	B	−	C	=	D

An application of this equation is illustrated below.

Purchase of equipment

Beginning balance	+	Increases	−	Decreases	=	Ending balance
Equipment (gross value)	+	New equipment purchased (at cost)	−	Value of equipment sold at its original cost	=	Equipment (gross value)
460	+	175	−	20	=	615

Sale of equipment As stated earlier, the selling price of the equipment (9) must be included in the cash flow statement, since it represents a cash inflow. If the sale had been (partially or in its entirety) on credit, the price would represent a potential cash flow and should be adjusted by the changes in the specific accounts receivable (distinct from trade accounts receivable) to give the net cash flow from that transaction.

The change in accumulated depreciation between the beginning and end of the year should be verified (but that element has no impact on the cash flow).

Beginning balance	+	Increases	−	Decreases	=	Ending balance
Accumulated depreciation	+	Depreciation expense	−	Accumulated depreciation of fixed assets sold	=	Accumulated depreciation
70	+	60	−	14	=	116

Repayment of loans (previously) granted to third parties In our example, no new loan was granted, but the ending balance of loans granted to third parties is lower than the beginning balance. We therefore know that some borrowers have repaid their loans. As an external user of financial information we can deduct the amounts that were reimbursed and were therefore cash inflows for Liszt Company. The equation yields the missing piece of data:

Beginning balance	+	Increases	−	Decreases	=	Ending balance
Loan	+	New loan granted	−	Repayment of loan	=	Loan
174	+	0	−	?	=	115

$174 + 0 - X = 115$, thus $X = 174 - 115 = 59$. Borrowers have repaid a total amount of 59 CU of the loans previously granted by Liszt Company.

Liszt Company schedule of cash flows from investing activities Table 14.11 summarizes the cash flows from investing activities.

Table 14.11 Cash flows from investing activities

Purchase of equipment	−175
Proceeds from sale of equipment	9
Repayment of loan by borrowers	59
Net cash provided by/used in investing activities	−107

1.7.3 Cash flows from financing activities

The relevant information available is (all monetary figures in 000 CU):

- 135 were raised from the issuance of new shares in cash (66 of share capital and 69 of share premium).
- Convertible bonds with a face value of 30 were converted into capital: thus creating additional share capital for 16 and an increase in share premium of 14.
- Other bonds were repaid at face value at maturity for 60.
- Dividends (relating to net income of X1) were paid in cash in the amount of 8.

Issuance of new share capital The changes in share capital and share premium are due to both issuance of new shares and conversion of bonds:

Beginning balance	+	Increases	−	Decreases	=	Ending balance
Share capital	+	Issued	−	Repayment	=	Share capital
200	+	66 + 16 = 82	−	0	=	282
Share premium	+	Issued	−	Repayment	=	Share premium
115	+	69 + 14 = 83	−	0	=	198

These two transactions are separated in Table 14.12.

Table 14.12 Share issues

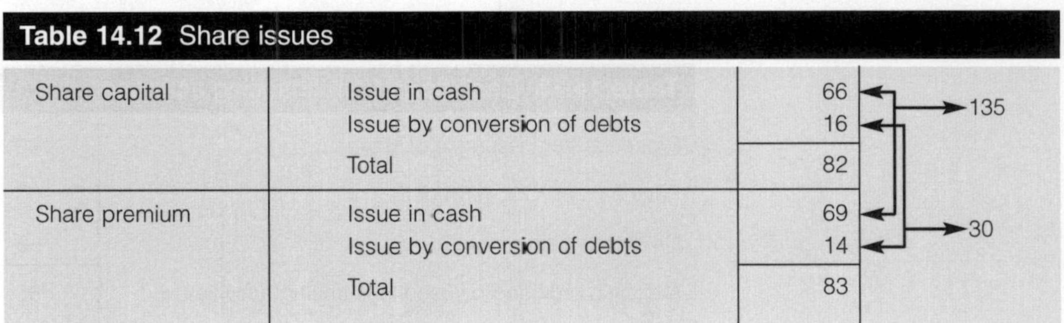

Share capital	Issue in cash	66	→ 135 (66 + 69)
	Issue by conversion of debts	16	→ 30 (16 + 14)
	Total	82	
Share premium	Issue in cash	69	→ 135 (66 + 69)
	Issue by conversion of debts	14	→ 30 (16 + 14)
	Total	83	

Only the issuance of new shares in cash can be included in the cash flow statement. The debt-conversion issue is a non-cash 'financing' activity and will be mentioned in a separate schedule as a footnote to the cash flow statement.

Beginning balance	+	Increases	−	Decreases	=	Ending balance
Bonds	+	New issue	−	Repayment Conversion	=	Bonds
245	+	0	−	(60 + 30)	=	155

The decrease of the balance of bond debt is the result of the following two actions:

- Repayment: 60.
- Conversion into capital: 30.

Dividends When the balance sheet is presented before profit appropriation, changes in retained earnings/reserves can be explained as follows:

Beginning balance	+	Increases	−	Decreases	=	Ending balance
Retained earnings/ Reserves	+	Net income of year X1	−	Dividends paid in year X2 or capitalization to Retained earnings/ Reserves	=	Retained earnings/Reserves
122	+	10	−	8	=	124

The dividends paid in year X2 are usually related to the net income of year X1. However, they could also represent advance payments on dividends related to net income of year X2. As the amount of dividends paid (8) fully explains the movements in retained earnings/reserves, we can infer that there was no capitalization of retained earnings/reserves during the period. (We also know from the study of share issues that the movement in capital was arising from an increase in cash and not from a transfer from retained earnings/reserves.)

Table 14.13 shows how cash flows from financing activities are computed.

Table 14.13 Cash flows from financing activities

Proceeds from issuance of shares	135
Payments on long-term debt	−60
Dividends paid	−8
Net cash provided by/used in financing activities	67

1.7.4 Full cash flow statement

Since we have calculated its three components, the cash flow statement can now be constructed by adding the three components. For the sake of simplicity, Table 14.14 uses the indirect method. The direct method would be obtained by replacing, in Table 14.14, the

Table 14.14 Cash flow statement of Liszt Company – Year X2 (indirect method)

Cash flows from operating activities (indirect method)	
Net income	9
Adjustments to reconcile net income to net cash provided by operating activities	
Depreciation expense	60
Gain on sale of fixed assets	−3
Changes in operating assets and liabilities	
Change in accounts receivable	19
Change in inventories	−44
Change in prepaid expenses	3
Change in accounts payable	8
Change in income taxes payable	−2
Total adjustments	41
Net cash provided by/used in operating activities	50
Cash flows from investing activities	
Purchase of equipment	−175
Proceeds from sale of equipment	9
Repayment of loan	59
Net cash used in investing activities	−107
Cash flows from financing activities	
Proceeds from issuance of shares	135
Payments on long-term debt	−60
Dividends paid	−8
Net cash provided by financing activities	67
Net increase in cash and cash equivalents	10
Cash and cash equivalents at beginning of year	15
Cash and cash equivalents at end of year	25
Schedule of non-cash investing and financing transactions	
Conversion of bonds into capital	30

operating cash flow (obtained by the indirect method) by the details of Table 14.10, which summarized the cash flow from operating activities using the direct method.

The total cash flow (net increase in cash and cash equivalents) is equal to the sum of the flows of cash from the three activities: 50 − 107 + 67 = 10. This figure corresponds to the changes in cash as reported in the balance sheet (25 − 15 = 10).

1.8 Reporting

Companies often report additional relevant information on events that have or could have impacted on the cash balance such as:

- non-cash investing and financing transactions;
- other [more detailed] cash flow information (for example, by indicating clearly the amount of interest and taxes paid);
- business acquisitions, net of cash acquired.

Examples of such disclosures follow, along with comments.

Real-life example Mitsubishi Electric

(Japan – US GAAP – *Source*: Annual report 2005 – Electrical equipment)

Notes to consolidated financial statements (year ended 31 March 2005)

(Note 21) Supplementary Cash Flow Information

	Yen (millions)		
	2005	**2004**	**2003**
Cash paid during the year for:			
Interest	10,744	14,332	23,789
Income taxes	21,552	36,406	35,085

'The company contributed certain marketable equity securities, not including those of its subsidiaries and affiliated companies, to an established employee retirement benefit trust, with no cash proceeds thereon in the years ended 31 March 2004 and 2003. The fair values of these securities at the time of contribution were ¥29,233 million and ¥10,676 million for 2004 and 2003, respectively. Upon contribution of these available-for-sale securities, the net unrealized gains amounting to ¥9,378 million and ¥3,845 million were realized for the years ended 31 March 2004 and 2003.

In April 2003, the company acquired shares in Renesas Technology Corp., which was a joint venture established with Hitachi, Ltd, amounted to ¥88,096 million, by contributing assets of ¥285,537 million, liabilities of ¥196,081 million, and minority interests of ¥1,360 million, with no cash proceeds (...)'.

Comment: The 'cash paid' information is given because the company used the indirect method to compute the cash flows from operating activities. As a result, the statement does not show interest- and tax-related cash flows separately, and so the company provides these additional details. Non-cash financing activities (transfer of securities to a retirement benefit plan, contribution to a joint venture in kind), as mentioned before, are not included in the cash flow statement but disclosed separately (see the Advanced issues section in this chapter).

Real-life example Benihana Inc.

(USA – US GAAP – *Source*: Annual report 2005 – Japanese style restaurants, operating mainly in the US)

Consolidated statements of cash flows

In thousands of US dollars	27 March 2005	28 March 2004	30 March 2003
(...)			
Investing activities			
Business acquisition, net of cash acquired	(2,816)		(11,353)
(...)			
Supplemental cash flow information			
Cash paid during the fiscal year for:			
Interest	386	484	423
Income taxes	3,380	2,305	3,055
Business acquisitions, net of cash acquired:			
Fair value of assets acquired, other than cash	2,816		2,346
Liabilities assumed			(1,646)
Purchase price in excess of the net assets acquired			10,653
		2,816	11,353

During fiscal 2005, 159,000 shares of common stock were converted into 159,000 shares of Class A Common stock. (...)
During fiscal 2003, a stock dividend of 1,141,050 shares of Class A Common stock was paid.

Comment: Benihana Inc. provides some information concerning interest and taxes paid for the same reasons as Mitsubishi. The table provides details of the acquisition of another business. The footnote to the table describes the conversion of some shares to a different class of common shares (in 2005) and the payment of a stock dividend in 2003 (see Chapter 11) even if both events have no impact on cash.

2 Advanced issues

2.1 Differences in classification

Most events in the life of a business fold neatly into one of three classes: operating, investing, and financing activities. 'Operating activities' reflect, in most local GAAP, one common line of thinking, namely that cash flows from operations are the result of the cash effect of transactions and other events that enter into the determination of net income. Consequently, operating activities include managerial actions and decisions that are required by operations in the strictest sense (procurement, manufacturing, selling, and distributing, for example), trade financing and cash management, as well as taxes and employee profit sharing. All affect operating cash flows.

Some events are, however, difficult to assign clearly and unambiguously to one particular class of sources or uses of cash. They include interests paid, dividends paid, interests received, dividends received, and taxes paid. As shown in Table 14.15, most countries give clear instructions, favoring a particular solution for some events while leaving maneuvering room for others (such as partitioning a given triggering event between categories as can be the case for interests paid: interests on trade financing, for example, could be thought of as being part of cash from operations, while interests on long-term financing would be considered as part of the financing activities). Meanwhile, the IASB leaves the choice to the reporting entity.

Appendix 14.2 provides some developments on the contents of Table 14.15. The best reporting practice, regardless of the classification adopted, is to provide as much specific information to allow users of financial statements to make any reclassifications they judge useful and to assess the effect of the company's classification policy. Appendix 14.3 presents the model adopted in the UK and Ireland.

Table 14.15 Differences in classification

	Interests paid	Interests received	Dividends paid	Dividends received	Taxes paid
IASB	OPE or FIN	OPE or INV	OPE or FIN	OPE or INV	OPE or INV or FIN
Australia	OPE or FIN	OPE or INV	FIN	OPE or INV	OPE (or INV or FIN)
Canada	OPE or FIN	OPE or INV	OPE or FIN	OPE or INV	OPE or INV or FIN
France	OPE	OPE	FIN	OPE	OPE
Germany	OPE (FIN)	OPE (INV)	FIN	OPE (INV)	OPE (INV/FIN)
South Africa	OPE or FIN	OPE or INV	OPE or FIN	OPE or INV	OPE (or INV or FIN)
UK/Ireland (see Appendix 14.3)	RETURNS	RETURNS	EQUITY DIVIDENDS PAID	RETURNS	TAXATION
USA	OPE	OPE	FIN	OPE	OPE

OPE = operating activities
INV = investing activities
FIN = financing activities
RETURNS = returns on investments and servicing of finance
Parentheses indicate that classifying in this or that category may be used only if the cash flow can be specifically identified to fit the requirements of such a category.

2.2 Non-cash investing and financing transactions

Some transactions affecting the capital and asset structure of an enterprise do not have any direct impact on current cash flows. They are, however, part of the investing and financing activities. Examples of such transactions are:

- The acquisition of assets either by assuming directly related liabilities or by means of a finance lease (see Chapter 12).
- The acquisition of an enterprise exclusively by means of an equity issue.
- The conversion of debt to equity (see Chapter 11).
- The issuance of shares by capitalization of retained earnings/reserves (bonus issue) (see Chapter 11).

Under IAS 7 (§ 43), and, accordingly, under most national standards, 'investing and financing transactions that do not require the use of cash or cash equivalents shall be excluded from a cash flow statement. Such transactions shall be disclosed elsewhere in the financial statements [generally in the Notes] in a way that provides all the relevant information about these transactions' (see examples earlier in this chapter).

2.3 Funds flow statement or statement of changes in financial position

Certain countries, and certain enterprises, are in the habit of publishing a 'funds flow statement' (or 'statement of changes in financial position'), built around a break down of the change in working capital (defined as the difference between equity and long-term debts, on one hand, and fixed assets, on the other, or the difference between current assets [including cash] and current liabilities). Some developments on this statement are presented in Appendix 14.4.

2.4 Different titles and different models

Cash flow statements are known by a wide variety of names:

- Financing statement (*Cuadro de Financiación* in Spain);
- Capital flows statement (*Kapitalflussrechnung* in Germany and German-speaking Switzerland);
- *Statement of cash flows* (in the USA);
- *Funds flow statement*;
- *Statement of sources and applications of funds* (former name in the UK);
- *Statement of changes in financial position* (in Canada).

Appendix 14.5 provides some remarks on the implications of these different titles for essentially the same document.

2.5 Analysis of the cash flow statement

There are several possible ways in which users of financial statements can analyze a cash flow statement.

2.5.1 Algebraic sign of cash flows

Generally, the operating cash flow is expected to be positive[3]. In fact, many financial and business analysts believe it *should* be positive: in other words, the core activity of the entity should generate a positive cash flow. A negative operating cash flow is generally seen as a serious indicator of potential weakness (and an important indicator that bankruptcy may be looming on the horizon) or of a need to generate rapid growth to reach the more stable situation created by a positive cash flow from operations. However, it is understood that in the early phase of the life cycle of a business the cash flow from operations may legitimately be negative, as the firm establishes its position in the market and has not yet reached a 'steady state' implying sufficiency for maintaining the status quo.

The investing cash flow is almost always negative, as a business generally invests more in new assets than it receives on sales of its underused or obsolete fixed assets. However, the investing cash flow can be (significantly) positive in the case of divestment, i.e., sale of a part of a group often representing a whole business segment. However, a positive investing cash flow is generally short lived since the funds thus raised are most of the time intended either to finance another investment (which may not take place in the same year) or to allow payment of an exceptional dividend (this second possibility is often seen as a sign that the management team has run out of investment opportunities, not a good prognostication of the entity being a 'going concern').

The financing cash flow can be positive or negative in any one year, depending on specific circumstances.

2.5.2 Available cash flow and free cash flow

Available cash flow The 'available cash flow' is the sum of the cash flow from operating activities and the cash flow from investing activities. Table 14.16 (later) illustrates how the available cash flow is linked to the change in cash position.

Since the (total) net cash flow is normally positive in a well-managed successful business, when the 'available cash flow' is positive the financing cash flow can, without endangering the ongoing nature of the business, be negative. For example, it allows the firm to engage in a policy of repayment of its long-term debt and/or of distribution of dividends. When, however, the available cash flow is negative, the business will need to compensate this situation by creating a positive financing cash flow. This would be achieved, for example, by issuing new shares or by contracting new debt. The anticipated evolution of the available cash flow is, therefore, a very important tool for understanding the likely future financing policy of a business, as well as its long-term developmental and survival potential.

Excess cash flow Some companies also report 'excess cash flow' (sometimes called 'free cash flow'), which is cash flow from operating activities minus the minimum investing cash flow required to maintain the competitive position of the firm. This minimum investing cash flow is difficult to define by an outsider to the firm. Thus, the common proxy used is generally 'purchases of fixed assets minus proceeds from sales of fixed assets', assuming the business management did actually take the appropriate decisions to keep the business competitive. However, any development-oriented investing is also included in this proxy measure. Analysts tend to use direct contact with managers in order to estimate the part of the investing activity pertaining to maintenance of competitiveness and that pertaining to developing it. This 'excess' cash flow conceptually represents the amount available for development (internal or external through acquisitions of third-party businesses) and for supporting financing activities. The possible strategic moves of a firm can be guided by the existence of such truly available cash flow.

Free cash flow Some analysts and the (mainly European) press often refer to the 'free cash flow' of a business as a metric in the evaluation of its performance. These analysts consider that an annual payment of dividends is a recurring obligation for the firm and thus they consider it to be a part of maintaining the competitive position of the enterprise. The free cash flow is, thus, a further variation on 'available' or 'excess cash flow'. It is equal to the available or excess cash flow minus dividends paid. Its reconciliation with the change in cash position is illustrated in Table 14.16.

Table 14.16 Liszt Company – Available and free cash flows

Net cash provided by operating activities	50
Net cash used in investing activities	−107
Available cash flow	−57
Dividends paid	−8
Free cash flow	−65
Other financing cash flows	75
Net increase in cash and cash equivalents	10

The free cash flow is seen by many financial statement users as more useful than the available cash flow because, since the payment of a dividend is a requirement for keeping the support of shareholders, the free cash flow represents the only amount of cash truly unencumbered and available for a possible reimbursement of debt.

Because he or she has access to more detailed information, a manager often will use a slightly different definition of free cash flow. The manager will also deduct from the available cash flow the minimum amount of operating investments required to maintain the capacity of the firm. This internal information is, however, not available to external users of financial statements.

Underlying hypothesis Excess cash flow, available cash flow, and free cash flow assume that the investing activity is supposed to be financed first by cash from operating activities, and that, therefore, the financing strategy is the consequence of any insufficiency in cash from operating activities. Such a hypothesis is pretty robust in a reasonably non-inflationary economy.

Illustration of the calculation process of available and free cash flows Going back to the Liszt Company example (see Table 14.14), we have determined the available and free cash flows in Table 14.16.

Given that the available cash flow is negative, the free cash flow is not surprisingly negative. This means the operating cash flow is not sufficient to finance the investing strategy of the firm, and it must therefore obtain new sources of financing (capital issuance will be the answer in this example) to balance its cash flows.

2.5.3 Ratios

Several ratios are particularly appropriate for analyzing cash flow statements. They allow users of financial information to obtain answers to legitimate questions such as:

- What is the relationship between cash flows and sales?
- What is the relationship between cash flows and earnings?
- What is the ability of the firm to reimburse its liabilities?

Cash flow as percentage of sales

Operating cash flow/Sales

By comparing the operating cash flow to net sales over several years, the 'transformation of sales into cash' can be measured and evaluated. For Liszt Company, this ratio is (50/800) = 6.25% in the year examined (Liszt Company is no 'cash machine': for example, Microsoft's operating cash flow to sales revenue was 50% in 2002, 49% in 2003, and was still 40% in 2004). Knowing the evolution of this ratio over time gives a good understanding of the prospects of the firm. For example, it is clear that, even if Microsoft's sales did increase by 22% over three years, the additions to cash remained essentially stagnant, an indicator of the difficulty Microsoft faces in creating new cash-cows with its new products.

Operating cash ratio or cash flow yield

Operating cash flow/Net income

For Liszt Company, this ratio is equal to (50/9) = 5.56, which indicates a very good yield. For Microsoft this ratio in 2004 was 14.6/8.2 = 1.78.

This ratio partly reflects the impact of depreciation policy of the business since one of the differences between income and operating cash flow derives from non-cash items, depreciation expense being the most important element of that category. (The other difference relates to changes in inventories, accounts receivable, and accounts payable.) In comparing two firms, identical except for their using different depreciation policies, it is a useful ratio in determining when the cash advantage of accelerated depreciation over straight-line depreciation will cease. Knowledge of the depreciation policy of the firm is an essential element in the ability to use this ratio effectively.

Cash liquidity ratio

Operating cash flow/Average current liabilities

This ratio indicates the company's ability to repay its current liabilities using its operating cash flows. For Liszt Company, the ratio is 50/[(63 + 57)/2] = 83.3%.

Cash leverage ratio

Operating cash flow/Average total liabilities

This ratio indicates the company's ability to repay its total liabilities using its operating cash flows. For Liszt Company, it is 50/[(218 + 302)/2] = 19.2%.

Other ratios

Investment ratio

Capital expenditures/(Depreciation plus sales of long-term assets)

This ratio indicates the ability of the business to maintain its competitive potential (depreciation expense is a proxy for the loss of productive capability of long-term assets). A growing firm will have a ratio greater than 1.

Cash flow adequacy

Cash flow from operations/(Long-term capital expenditures + Dividends + Scheduled debt reimbursements)

When the ratio is greater than 1, it is an indication that the firm is self-sufficient in its ability to maintain its productive capability. If the ratio is less than 1, it indicates a financing need that will be met by bringing in new cash from shareholders or lenders or by selling some assets.

Structure of each of the cash flows In order to examine the contents of each activity, it is possible to divide each cash flow by the total cash flow of the activity. For example, the proceeds from issuance of shares can be divided by the financing cash flows, over several years if required, to understand how much the business relies on issuing new shares for its financing and the evolution of that policy. It is also important for a user of financial statements to know the relative percentage that each cash flow source contributes to the total net cash increase.

Key points

- Users of an enterprise's financial statements are interested in how the enterprise generates and uses cash and cash equivalents.
- The cash flow statement or statement of cash flows is the tool designed to help users understand better how a firm creates and uses cash.
- The cash flow statement is an integral part of a firm's financial statements. In some countries, it is compulsory to publish a cash flow statement, whereas, in others, it is optional. In practice, most major listed companies include a cash flow statement in their annual report.
- The cash flow statement classifies cash flows of a period in three activities: operating, investing, and financing.
- Cash flows from operating activities are primarily derived from the principal revenue-producing activities of the enterprise. Therefore, they generally result from the transactions and other events that enter into the determination of net profit or loss.
- The cash flows arising from investing activities represent the expenditures that have been made in order to obtain resources intended to generate future income and cash flows.
- The financing cash flows help predict claims on future cash flows by providers of capital to the enterprise. They are the net result of cash proceeds from issuing shares or debt, cash repayments of amounts borrowed, and dividends paid.
- There are two ways of determining cash flows from operating activities: the detailed direct method (which discloses major classes of gross cash receipts and gross cash payments); and the aggregated indirect method (which discloses the net cash flow from operating activities by adjusting net profit or loss for the effects of several items including non-cash items and is thus created by an outside user).
- The 'excess cash flow' (often called in practice 'free cash flow') is the cash flow from operating activities minus the minimum investing cash flow required to maintain the competitive position of the firm.
- The 'available cash flow' is the 'excess cash flow' minus any additional discretionary investments.
- The 'free cash flow' equals the 'available cash flow' minus dividends paid. It represents cash flow available for the possible reimbursement of debt.
- Several ratios capture the dynamics of the cash flow statement. They include the 'cash flow as percentage of sales' and 'cash flow yield' (Operating cash flow/Net income).

Review (solutions are at the back of the book)

Review 14.1 Dvorak Company

Topic: Preparation of a cash flow statement
Related part of the chapter: Core issues

The balance sheets and income statements of Dvorak Company for the years X1 and X2 are presented in the following tables.

Dvorak Company Balance sheet		
ASSETS	*X1*	*X2*
Fixed assets (gross amount)	12,000	14,950
Less accumulated depreciation	−3,700	−4,300
Fixed assets (net amount)	8,300	10,650
Inventories (gross amount)	2,300	2,000
Less accumulated provision	0	0
Inventories (net amount)	2,300	2,000
Accounts receivable	1,650	2,300
Cash at bank	190	80
TOTAL ASSETS	*12,440*	*15,030*
LIABILITIES	*X1*	*X2*
Share capital	3,000	3,200
Reserves	3,600	3,800
Net income/loss	2,780	2,560
Shareholders' equity	9,380	9,560
Financial liabilities (1)	3,000	4,350
Accounts payable	60	870
Fixed assets accounts payable	0	250
TOTAL LIABILITIES	*12,440*	*15,030*
(1) Including bank overdrafts	200	950

Dvorak Company Income statement	
EXPENSES	*X2*
Purchases of merchandise	3,700
Change in inventory of merchandise	300
Other purchases and external expenses	550
Taxes and similar expenses	70
Personnel expenses	4,310
Depreciation expenses	1,400
Provision expenses	0
Total operating expenses	10,330
Financial expenses	580
Exceptional expenses (1)	250
Income tax	1,280
Net income	2,560
TOTAL EXPENSES	*15,000*
REVENUES	*X2*
Sales of merchandise	14,100
Other operating revenues	150
Total operating revenues	14,250
Financial revenues	300
Exceptional income (2)	450
Net loss	0
TOTAL REVENUES	*15,000*
(1) Book value of sold items	250
(2) Sales price of fixed assets	450

The following additional information was taken from the company's record:

Additional information				
	31/12/X1	+	–	31/12/X2
Fixed assets (gross amount)	12,000	4,000	1,050	14,950
Accumulated depreciation	3,700	1,400	800	4,300
Accumulated provision	0			0
Financial liabilities (excluding overdrafts)	2,800	1,000	400	3,400
Dividends paid in X2: 2,580				

Required

Prepare a cash flow statement for the year X2, using the direct or the indirect method.

Review 14.2 Mitsubishi Electric*

Topic: Understanding and analyzing a cash flow statement
Related part of the chapter: Advanced issues

Mitsubishi Electric Corporation is a multinational concern headquartered in Japan (Tokyo). It develops, manufactures, and distributes a broad range of electrical equipment in fields as diverse as home appliances and space electronics.

The company's 2005 total sales revenue is broken down between its principal lines of business (or business segments) as shown in the following table:

Business segments sales revenue (2005)	Yen (millions)	%
Energy and Electric Systems	791,925	20.8
Industrial Automation Systems	781,867	20.6
Information and Communication Systems	614,091	16.2
Electronic Devices	164,383	4.3
Home Appliances	866,428	22.8
Others	581,685	15.3
Total sales revenue	3,800,379	100.0
Eliminations [of intra-segment transactions]	(389,694)	
Consolidated total	3,410,685	

The financial statements are reported in conformity to the US generally accepted accounting principles. The following table presents the cash flow statements of the group for the period 2003–2005 (*source*: annual reports 2005 and 2004).

Consolidated statements of cash flows for years ended March 31

Yen (millions)	2005	2004	2003
Cash flows from operating activities			
Net income (loss)	71,175	44,839	(11,825)
Adjustments to reconcile net income (loss) to net cash provided by operating activities:			
Depreciation	105,356	109,975	208,884
Impairment losses of property, plant and equipment	5,974	8,411	11,538
Loss from sales and disposal of property, plant, and equipment – net	1,737	3,362	796
Deferred income taxes	17,001	20,119	(27,669)
Loss (gain) from sales of securities and other – net	(5,986)	(3,123)	(7,204)
Devaluation losses of securities and other – net	3,892	1,701	51,055
Equity in earnings of affiliated companies	(17,029)	(5,653)	(2,032)
Decrease (increase) in trade receivables	(29,665)	(1,316)	(36,183)
Decrease (increase) in inventories	(41,223)	50,686	96,715
Decrease (increase) in prepaid expenses and other assets	18,855	(21,308)	(1,702)
Increase in trade payables	14,927	17,758	53,813
Increase in accrued expenses and retirement, and severance benefits	3,712	27,280	2,473
Increase (decrease) in other liabilities	30,768	(8,406)	(41,350)
Other – net	9,430	(814)	(58,844)
Net cash provided by operating activities	188,924	243,511	238,465
Cash flows from investing activities			
Capital expenditure	(125,657)	(96,253)	(133,223)
Proceeds from sales of property, plant, and equipment	16,492	17,722	17,449
Purchase of short-term investments and investment securities	(52,489)	(71,233)	(37,068)
Proceeds from sale of short-term investments and investment securities	58,978	75,252	56,463
Other – net	1,541	4,425	2,694
Net cash used in investing activities	(101,135)	(70,087)	(93,685)
Cash flows from financing activities			
Proceeds from long-term debt	49,590	97,183	304,814
Repayment of long-term debt	(116,698)	(274,355)	(415,445)
Increase (decrease) in bank loans – net	(94,214)	(15,280)	(118,853)
Dividends paid	(12,877)	(6,440)	–
Purchase of treasury stock	(58)	(310)	(491)
Reissuance of treasury stock	50	6	–
Net cash provided by (used in) financing activities	(174,207)	(199,196)	(229,975)
Effect of exchange rate changes on cash and cash equivalents	2,385	(7,227)	(6,100)
Net increase (decrease) in cash and cash equivalents	(84,033)	(32,999)	(91,295)
Cash and cash equivalents at beginning of year	330,596	363,595	454,890
Cash and cash equivalents at end of year	246,563	330,596	363,595

From the balance sheet and income statement, we have extracted the following information:

Yen (millions)	2005	2004	2003
Sales revenue	3,410,685	3,309,651	3,639,071
Net earnings	71,175	44,839	(11,825)
Current liabilities	1,277,662	1,315,739	1,589,322
Total liabilities	2,395,112	2,575,179	3,225,044

Required

Step one: Understanding

1. Which method (direct or indirect) was used to compute the operating cash flow?
2. Compute the 'potential cash flow'.
3. Why does the statement use the expression 'decrease (increase)' to describe changes in trade receivables, inventories, and prepaid expenses while it uses 'increase (decrease)' when referring to changes in trade payables and other liabilities?
4. How are short-term investments reported? What could have been another legitimate possibility? Any comment as to why they chose the method they did over another?
5. Bank loans can be considered equivalent to 'bank overdrafts'. Comment on the way they are reported in the above statements. What would have been another possibility?

Step two: Analyzing

6. Analyze the cash flow statements over the period.

Review 14.3 Bartok Company (1)

Topic: Comparative financial analysis – cash flow statement
Related part of the chapter: Advanced issues

You receive information extracted from the financial statements of three companies.

	Company 1	Company 2	Company 3
Increase in capital	800		700
Purchase of tangible fixed assets	900	900	1,400
Purchase of financial assets	700		400
Increase in long-term debts	100	1,500	1,100
Repayment of long-term debts		300	
Potential cash flow*	1,000	400	100
Dividends paid	200	600	

* Net income adjusted for non-cash items.

Required

1. From the information, prepare the cash flow statements.
2. Comment on the resulting statements.

Assignments

Assignment 14.1 Multiple-choice questions

Related part of the chapter: Core issues

Select the right answer (one possible answer, unless otherwise mentioned).

1. Which of the following cannot be the main objective of a cash flow statement?
   (a) To provide relevant information on the cash receipts and cash payments of an enterprise during a given period

(b) To explain changes in cash in the same way as the income statement explains the components that comprise the net income
(c) To provide information on the operating, financing and investing activities of an entity and the effects of those activities on cash resources
(d) To explain the changes in working capital between opening and closing balance sheets
(e) To report on a standard basis the cash generation and cash absorption for a period
(f) To provide relevant information to users of the cash inflows and cash outflows of an entity during a reporting period
(g) To provide information on the historical changes in cash and cash equivalents

2. Which of the following would not be integrated in the computation of the cash flow from operating activities?

(a) Cash received from customers
(b) Cash paid to suppliers
(c) Proceeds from sale of fixed assets
(d) Depreciation and amortization
(e) Gain on sale of fixed assets

3. Which of the following would not be included in investing activities? (more than one answer is possible)

(a) Repayment of a loan granted to a subsidiary
(b) Dividends paid
(c) Purchase cost of fixed assets
(d) Depreciation and amortization
(e) Gain on sale of fixed assets

4. Which of the following would not be included in financing activities? (more than one answer is possible)

(a) Proceeds from issuance of shares
(b) Dividends received
(c) Repayment of debt
(d) Issuance of share capital by capitalization of reserves
(e) Dividends paid

5. When using the indirect method to compute the operating cash flow, which of the following items will not be included?

(a) Change in inventory
(b) Depreciation expense
(c) Gain on sale of fixed assets
(d) Cash paid to employees
(e) Net income

6. When using the direct method to compute the operating cash flow, which of the following items will not be included?

(a) Cash received from customers
(b) Depreciation expense
(c) Cash paid to suppliers
(d) Cash paid to employees
(e) Cash paid on other operating expenses

7. Depending on the country, interest expenses are included in either operating activities or investing activities

(a) True
(b) False

8. Under IAS 7, bank overdrafts are reported either as a part of cash equivalents (as negative cash) or as a part of financing activities

(a) True
(b) False

9. Dividends received are usually included in

(a) Operating activities
(b) Investing activities
(c) Financing activities

10. Which of these stages are included in the indirect method? (more than one answer is possible)

(a) Add any increase in inventory
(b) Subtract any increase in accounts receivable
(c) Add any loss on sale of fixed assets
(d) Subtract depreciation expense
(e) Subtract any increase in accounts payable

Assignment 14.2
Janacek Company (1)

Topic: Preparation of cash flow statement
Related part of the chapter: Core issues

The Janacek Company has a commercial activity in the beauty cream business.

Required

- With the help of the following balance sheets, income statements, and additional information, prepare a cash flow statement for the years X2 and X3 using the direct method.
- Prepare a separate statement reconciling the net income and the net cash provided by/used in operating activities.
- Comment on the cash flow statement.

Janacek Company Balance sheet (000 CU)

ASSETS	X1	X2	X3
Fixed assets (gross amount)	15,000	22,000	27,400
Less accumulated depreciation	−4,900	−5,500	−6,000
Fixed assets (net amount)	10,100	16,500	21,400
Inventories (gross amount)	3,200	4,500	5,700
Less accumulated provision	0	0	−100
Inventories (net amount)	3,200	4,500	5,600
Accounts receivable	2,020	3,500	5,300
Cash at bank	1,150	250	240
TOTAL ASSETS	*16,470*	*24,750*	*32,540*
LIABILITIES	*X1*	*X2*	*X3*
Share capital	3,000	5,000	7,500
Reserves	3,800	4,200	4,400
Net income/loss	1,728	474	246
Shareholders' equity	8,528	9,674	12,146
Financial liabilities (1)	3,900	8,500	11,500
Accounts payable	4,042	6,126	5,094
Accounts payable to suppliers of fixed assets	0	450	3,800
TOTAL LIABILITIES	*16,470*	*24,750*	*32,540*
(1) Including bank overdrafts	100	1,000	2,000

Janacek Company Income statement (000 CU)

EXPENSES	*X1*	*X2*	*X3*
Purchases of merchandise	3,500	7,100	9,000
Change in inventory of merchandise	200	−1,300	−1,200
Other purchases and external expenses	750	1,000	1,530
Taxes and similar expenses	100	200	500
Personnel expenses	7,561	11,000	13,000
Depreciation expenses	800	1,000	1,500
Provision expenses	0	0	100
Total operating expenses	12,911	19,000	24,430
Financial expenses	717	1,149	1,931
Exceptional expenses (1)	145	600	100
Income tax	864	237	123
Net income	1,728	474	246
TOTAL EXPENSES	*16,365*	*21,460*	*26,830*
REVENUES	*X1*	*X2*	*X3*
Sales of merchandise	16,000	20,900	25,500
Other operating revenues	310	220	710
Total operating revenues	16,310	21,120	26,210
Financial revenues	55	140	220
Exceptional income (2)	0	200	400
Net loss	0	0	0
TOTAL REVENUES	*16,365*	*21,460*	*26,830*
(1) Book value of items sold	0	600	100
(2) Sale price of fixed assets	0	200	400

It should be noted that this income statement is presented by nature.

Janacek Company Additional information							
	31/12/X1	+	–	31/12/X2	+	–	31/12/X3
Fixed assets (gross)	15,000	8,000	1000	22,000	6,500	1,100	27,400
Accumulated depreciation	4,900	1,000	400	5,500	1,500	1,000	6,000
Accumulated provision	0			0	100		100
Financial liabilities (excluding overdrafts)	3,800	4,000	300	7,500	3,000	1,000	9,500

	X2	X3
Dividends paid:	1,328	274

Assignment 14.3
Smetana Company

Topic: Preparation of cash flow statement
Related part of the chapter: Core issues

Smetana Company is a manufacturing firm.

Required

- With the help of the following income statement, balance sheet, statement of retained earnings, and additional information, prepare a cash flow statement for the year X2 using the direct method.
- Prepare a separate statement reconciling the net income and the net cash provided by/used in operating activities.
- Comment on the cash flow statement.

Smetana Company – Income statement (000 CU) – Year X2	
Sales	1,000
Cost of goods sold	−600
Gross profit	400
Depreciation expense	−60
Other operating expenses	−150
Operating profit	190
Interest expense	−18
Investment income	16
Loss on sale of equipment	−5
Profit before taxes	183
Income taxes	−60
Net profit	123

Smetana Company – Comparative balance sheets (000 CU) – Years ended 31 December X2 and X1	X2	X1	Changes (X2 – X1)
Assets			
Current assets			
Cash	65	20	45
Accounts receivable	55	80	−25
Prepaid expenses*	8	10	−2
Inventory	131	80	51
Total current assets	259	190	69
Fixed assets			
Financial assets (loans)	150	140	10
Tangible assets			
Equipment	700	600	100
Accumulated depreciation	−110	−80	−30
Equipment (net)	590	520	70
Total fixed assets	740	660	80
Total assets	999	850	149
Shareholders' equity and liabilities			
Liabilities			
Current liabilities			
Accounts payable	136	135	1
Income taxes payable	40	35	5
Total current liabilities	176	170	6
Long-term liabilities (bonds)	160	180	−20
Total liabilities	336	350	−14
Shareholders' equity			
Share capital	300	250	50
Share premium	150	120	30
Retained earnings	213	130	83
Total shareholders' equity	663	500	163
Total shareholders' equity and liabilities	999	850	149

*Related to other operating expenses.

Smetana Company – Statement of retained earnings (000 CU) – Year ended 31 December X2	
Retained earnings (at end of Year X1)	130
Net income of Year X2	123
Dividends paid during Year X2	−40
Retained earnings (at end of Year X2)	213

The following additional information is also relevant for the preparation of the cash flow statement for the year X2 (all monetary figures in 000 CU):

- Equipment with an original cost of 50 and accumulated depreciation of 30 was sold for 15.
- A new loan was granted. No loan was repaid.
- 80 were raised from the issue of shares in cash (share capital of 50 plus share premium of 30).
- Some bonds were repaid at maturity; they had a total face value of 70.

Assignment 14.4
Ericsson (1)*

Topic: Comments on the reported cash flow statement
Related part of the chapter: Core/Advanced issues

With more than 15 billion SEK of sales in 2004 and more than 125 years of experience, Ericsson, Sweden-based group, is a leading provider in the telecom world, with communication solutions that combine telecom and datacom technologies with freedom of mobility for the user. At the end of 2004, with about 50,000 employees (versus about 100,000 three years earlier) in 140 countries, the Group operates in three business segments:

- Systems: Ericsson offers solutions for both mobile systems and wireline multiservice networks (mobile systems according to all mobile standards, third-generation 3G mobile systems, GPRS, mobile internet, others).
- Phones: Sales are realized through a 50%/50% joint venture with Sony, since October 2001. This joint venture markets a full range of advanced multimedia mobile handsets under the brand names 'Sony', 'Ericsson', and 'Sony Ericsson'.
- Other operations: This segment consists of technology licensing, business innovation and enterprise systems (core operations), and defense systems and network technologies (non-core activities).

The recent evolution of sales by business segments is displayed below.

Opposite is the cash flow statement for the years 2004, 2003, 2002, 2001, 2000, 1999, 1998, and 1997 (*sources*: Ericsson, Annual reports 2004, 2003, 2002, 2001, 2000, 1999, and 1998). The Ericsson financial statements comply with the recommendations of the Swedish Financial Accounting Standards Council.

Required

1. Which method is used for computing the cash flow from operating activities?
2. What does the 'Changes in operating net assets' represent?
3. Compute the potential cash flow.
4. What does the 'Cash flow before financing activities' represent?
5. Prepare an analysis of the cash flow statement.

Ericsson sales by business segments

Ericsson (in SEK billions)	2004	2003	2002	2001	2000	1999
Systems	122.9	108.7	131.9	188.7	194.1	149.9
Phones	0.0	0.0	0.0	0.0	56.3	46.4
Enterprise solutions	0.0	0.0	0.0	0.0	17.5	17.3
Other operations	11.4	10.6	23.5	31.7	19.0	16.8
Total	134.3	119.3	155.4	220.4	286.9	230.4
Less: Intersegment sales	−2.3	−1.6	−9.7	−9.6	−13.3	−15.0
Total net	132.0	117.7	145.7	210.8	273.6	215.4
Ericsson (in % of total)	2004	2003	2002	2001	2000	1999
Systems	92%	91%	85%	86%	68%	65%
Phones	0%	0%	0%	0%	20%	20%
Enterprise solutions	0%	0%	0%	0%	6%	8%
Other operations	8%	9%	15%	14%	7%	7%
Total	100%	100%	100%	100%	100%	100%

Appendix
Cash flow statement (SEK m)

	2004	2003	2002	2001	2000	1999	1998	1997
OPERATIONS								
Net income	19,024	−10,844	−19,013	−21,264	21,018	12,130	13,041	11,941
Adjustments to reconcile net income to cash								
Depreciation, amortization and write-downs on tangible assets, intangible assets, and other operating long-term receivables	4,797	8,395	6,537	7,828	11,020	7,382	6,081	5,756
Taxes	5,228	−2,352	−9,171	−16,983	1,873	−947	−2,301	619
Capital gains/losses on sale of fixed assets – net	−121	924	721	−6,126	−25,278	−1,399	−230	152
Other non-cash items	−899	−580	81	1,724	574	422	227	1,019
Changes in operating net assets								
Inventories	−3,432	2,286	8,599	20,103	−18,305	714	−2,056	−3,396
Customer financing, short term and long term	−65	7,999	−2,140	3,903	−2,752	722	−5,727	−347
Accounts receivable – trade	−1,403	4,131	9,839	19,653	−10,404	−9,911	−10,695	−15,828
Other operating assets, provisions, and liabilities – net	−650	12,908	−5,541	−7,420	8,135	3,812	9,054	14,986
Cash flow from operating activities	**22,479**	**22,867**	**−10,088**	**1,418**	**−14,119**	**12,925**	**7,394**	**14,902**
INVESTMENTS								
Investments in tangible assets	−2,452	−1,806	−2,738	−8,726	−12,643	−9,085	−8,965	−7,237
Sales of tangible assets	358	1,510	2,977	10,155	6,415	625	632	642
Acquisitions/sales of other investments – net	−1,549	−818	2,703	5,393	22,643	−4,768	−8,865	−69
Capitalization of development expenses	−1,146	−2,359	−3,442	0	0	0	0	0
Net change in capital contributed by minority	71	1	503	−83	13	134	35	21
Other	−70	60	2,981	−1,488	−1,959	−2,270	−56	−513
Cash flow from investing activities	**−4,788**	**−3,412**	**2,984**	**5,251**	**14,469**	**−15,364**	**−17,219**	**−7,156**
Cash flow before financing activities	**17,691**	**19,455**	**−7,104**	**6,669**	**350**	**−2,439**	**−9,825**	**7,746**
FINANCING								
Changes in current liabilities to financial institutions – net	−1,502	−854	−17,168	3,343	4,929	3,854	955	96
Issue of convertible debentures	0	0	0	0	1,048	58	19	4,875
Proceeds from issuance of other long-term debt	870	32	540	35,169	5,206	15,163	3,366	2,571
Repayment of long-term debt	−13,649	−10,904	−6,072	−8,470	−3,622	−1,515	−1,332	−2,672
Stock issue	0	158	28,940	155	0	0	0	0
Gain on sale of own stock options and convertible debentures	0	0	0	0	2,018	0	0	0
Sale/repurchase of own stock	15	−150	2	−156	−386	0	0	0
Dividends paid	−292	−206	−645	−4,295	−4,179	−4,010	−3,800	−2,805
Cash flow from financing activities	**−14,558**	**−11,924**	**5,597**	**25,746**	**5,014**	**13,550**	**−792**	**2,065**
Effect of exchange rate changes on cash	214	−538	−1,203	738	438	−336	−277	256
Net change in cash and cash equivalents	3,347	6,993	−2,710	33,153	5,802	10,775	−10,894	10,067
Cash and cash equivalents, beginning of period	73,207	66,214	68,924	35,771	29,969	18,233	29,127	19,060
Cash and cash equivalents, end of period	76,554	73,207	66,214	68,924	35,771	29,008	18,233	29,127

Assignment 14.5
Procter & Gamble*

Topic: Analysis of a cash flow statement
Related part of the chapter: Core/Advanced issues

Procter & Gamble, the US group involved in various sectors, such as fabric and homecare (Ariel, Mr. Clean), feminine protection (Always), healthcare, food, and beverages, beauty care (Head & Shoulders), and baby care (Pampers)[4], publishes the following consolidated statement of cash flows in its 2005 annual report.

Consolidated statements of cash flows for years ended June 30

Amounts in millions of US dollars	2005	2004	2003
Cash and cash equivalents, beginning of year	4,232	5,428	2,799
Operating activities			
Net earnings	7,257	6,481	5,186
Depreciation and amortization	1,884	1,733	1,703
Deferred income taxes	650	415	63
Change in accounts receivable	(86)	(159)	163
Change in inventories	(644)	56	(56)
Change in accounts payable, accrued and other liabilities	(128)	625	936
Change in other operating assets and liabilities	(498)	(88)	178
Other	287	299	527
Total operating activities	8,722	9,362	8,700
Investing activities			
Capital expenditures	(2,181)	(2,024)	(1,482)
Proceeds from asset sales	517	230	143
Acquisitions	(572)	(7,476)	(61)
Change in investment securities	(100)	(874)	37
Total investing activities	(2,336)	(10,144)	(1,363)
Financing activities			
Dividends to shareholders	(2,731)	(2,539)	(2,246)
Change in short-term debt	2,016	4,911	(2,052)
Additions to long-term debt	3,108	1,963	1,230
Reductions of long-term debt	(2,013)	(1,188)	(1,060)
Proceeds from the exercise of the stock options	478	555	269
Treasury purchases	(5,026)	(4,070)	(1,236)
Total financing activities	(4,168)	(368)	(5,095)
Effect of exchange rate changes on cash and cash equivalents	(61)	(46)	387
Change in cash and cash equivalents	2,157	(1,196)	2,629
Cash and cash equivalents, end of year	6,389	4,232	5,428

Required

1. What is unusual about this statement as regards its presentation of cash and cash equivalents at the beginning and the end of year?
2. Which method is used for computing the cash flow from operating activities?
3. Why are the operating cash flows larger than the net income each year?
4. With the help of the additional information provided below (*source*: Annual reports 2005, 2004, and 2003), prepare an analysis of the cash flow statement.

Amounts in millions of US dollars	2005	2004	2003	2002
Sales	56,741	51,407	43,377	40,238
Net earnings	7,257	6,481	5,186	4,352
Current liabilities	25,039	22,147	12,358	12,704
Total liabilities	44,050	39,770	27,520	27,070

Assignment 14.6 Sinopec*

Topic: Analysis of a cash flow statement
Related part of the chapter: Core/Advanced issues

China Petroleum & Chemical Corporation (known as 'Sinopec') is an integrated energy and chemical company. The principal operations of Sinopec Corp. and its subsidiaries include:

- Exploring for and developing, producing, and trading crude oil and natural gas.
- Processing crude oil into refined oil products, producing refined oil products, and trading, transporting, distributing, and marketing refined oil products.
- Producing, distributing, and trading petrochemical products.

On the basis of turnover in 2004, Sinopec Corp. is the largest listed company in China.

The significant accounting policies adopted by the Group are in conformity with the 'Accounting Standards for Business Enterprises' and 'Accounting Regulations for Business Enterprises', and other relevant regulations issued by the Ministry of Finance of the People's Republic of China.

Below is the cash flow statement of the Group for the years 2004 and 2003 (*source*: Annual report 2004).

Consolidated cash flow statement for the year ended 31 December 2004

	2004 RMB millions	2003 RMB millions
Cash flows from operating activities		
Cash received from sale of goods and rendering of services	712,682	505,489
Rentals received	368	370
Other cash received relating to operating activities	3,640	2,925
Subtotal of cash inflows	716,690	508,784
Cash paid for goods and services	(549,408)	(371,086)
Cash paid for operating leases	(6,871)	(4,224)
Cash paid to and on behalf of employees	(16,304)	(15,964)
Value added tax paid	(25,961)	(19,429)
Income tax paid	(16,858)	(9,486)
Taxes paid other than value added tax and income tax	(16,045)	(12,904)
Other cash paid relating to operating activities	(15,104)	(11,243)
Subtotal of cash outflows	(646,551)	(444,336)
Net cash flows from operating activities	70,139	64,448
Cash flows from investing activities		
Cash received from sale of investments	186	107
Dividends received	322	442
Net cash received from sale of fixed assets and intangible assets	315	380
Maturity of time deposits with financial institutions	2,217	1,700
Other cash received relating to investing activities	359	300
Subtotal of cash inflows	3,399	2,929
Cash paid for acquisition of fixed assets and intangible assets	(66,693)	(43,966)
Cash paid for acquisition of fixed assets and intangible assets of jointly controlled entities	(6,035)	(4,107)
Cash paid for purchases of investments	(1,225)	(1,545)
Increase in time deposits with financial institutions	(1,932)	(2,871)
Cash paid for acquisition of Sinopec Maoming, Xi'an Petrochemical and Tahe Petrochemical	(3,652)	–
Subtotal of cash outflows	(79,537)	(52,489)
Net cash flows from investing activities	(76,138)	(49,560)
Cash flows from financing activities		
Proceeds from contribution from minority shareholders	1,008	580
Proceeds from issuance of corporate bonds, net of issuing expenses	3,472	–
Proceeds from borrowings	391,832	228,654
Proceeds from borrowings of jointly controlled entities	3,014	1,450
Subtotal of cash inflows	399,326	230,684
Repayments of borrowings	(377,855)	(235,175)
Cash paid for dividends, distribution of profit, or interest	(13,538)	(12,520)
Dividends paid to minority shareholders by subsidiaries	(775)	(360)
Subtotal of cash outflows	(392,168)	(248,055)
Net cash flows from financing activities	7,158	(17,371)
Effects of foreign exchange rate	1	5
Net increase/(decrease) in cash and cash equivalents	1,160	(2,478)

Immediately after the consolidated cash flow statement, the annual report provides 'the notes to the consolidated cash flow statement'. The first note is the following:

Note (a) Reconciliation of net profit to cash flows from operating activities	2004 RMB millions	2003 RMB millions
Net profit	32,275	19,011
Add: Allowance for doubtful accounts	2,050	1,902
Provision for diminution in value of inventories	433	114
Depreciation of fixed assets	30,766	27,151
Amortization of intangible assets	476	520
Impairment losses on fixed assets	4,628	940
Impairment losses on long-term investments	88	115
Net loss on disposal of fixed assets and intangible assets	3,989	3,291
Financial expenses	4,331	4,129
Dry hole costs	2,976	2,789
Investment income	(843)	(515)
Deferred tax liabilities (less: assets)	(2,439)	(1,580)
(Increase)/decrease in inventories	(16,927)	676
Increase in operating receivables	(4,245)	(866)
Increase in operating payables	6,911	4,885
Minority interests	5,670	1,886
Net cash flows from operating activities	70,139	64,448

Required

Step one: Understanding

1. What is the method used to compute the cash flow from operating activities?
2. What does note (a) represent? How useful is it to users of financial information?
3. What particularity do you notice in the presentation of the investing and financing cash flows?
4. Compute the potential cash flow.

Step two: Analyzing

5. Analyze the cash flow statements over the period. You can use the additional information provided in the following table (*source:* Annual reports 2004 and 2003).

Additional information	2004	2003	2002
	RMB millions	RMB millions	RMB millions
Sales	590,632	417,191	Not necessary
Net earnings	32,275	19,011	Not necessary
Current liabilities	143,910	120,792	115,923
Total liabilities	242,515	201,190	192,549

References

ASB (1991, revised 1996) Financial Reporting Standard No. 1: Cash Flow Statements, London.

FASB (1987) Statement of Financial Accounting Standards No. 95: Statement of Cash Flows, Norwalk, CT.

IASB (1992) International Accounting Standard No. 7: Cash Flow Statements, London.

Further reading

Broome, O. W. (2004) Statement of cash flows: Time for change! *Financial Analysts Journal*, 60(2), 16–22.

Boussard, D., and Colasse, B. (1992) Funds-flow statement and cash-flow accounting in France: Evolution and significance. *European Accounting Review*, 1(2), 229–54.

Cheng, C. S. A., Liu, C. S., and Schaefer, T. F. (1997) The value-relevance of SFAS No. 95 cash flows from operations as assessed by security market effects. *Accounting Horizons*, 11(3), 1–15.

Clinch, G., Sidhu, B., and Sin, S. (2002) The usefulness of direct and indirect cash flow disclosures. *Review of Accounting Studies*, 7(4), 383–402.

Dhar, S. (1998) Cash flow reporting in India – A case study. *Indian Accounting Review*, 2(2), 39–52.

Haller, A., and Jakoby, S. (1995) Funds flow reporting in Germany: A conceptual and empirical state of the art. *European Accounting Review*, 4(3), 515–34.

Kinnunen, J., and Koskela, M. (1999) Do cash flows reported by firms articulate with their income statements and balance sheets? Descriptive evidence from Finland. *European Accounting Review*, 8(4), 631–54.

Krishnan, G. V., and Largay, J. A., III (2000) The predictive ability of direct method cash flow information. *Journal of Business Finance & Accounting*, 27(1/2), 215–45.

Kwok, H. (2002) The effect of cash flow statement format on lenders' decisions. *The International Journal of Accounting*, 37(3), 347–62.

Nissan, S., Kamata, N., and Otaka, R. (1995) Cash reporting in Japan. *The International Journal of Accounting*, 29, 168–80.

Rai, A. (2003) Reconciliation of net income to cash flow from operations: An accounting equation approach. *Journal of Accounting Education*, 21(1), 17–24.

Stolowy, H., and Walser-Prochazka, S. (1992) The American influence in accounting: Myth or reality? The statement of cash flows example. *The International Journal of Accounting*, Autumn, 185–221.

Wallace, R. S. O., Choudhury, M. S. I., and Pendlebury, M. (1997) Cash flow statements: An international comparison of regulatory positions. *The International Journal of Accounting*, 32(1), 1–22.

Wallace, R. S. O., Choudhury, M. S. I., and Adhikari, A. (1999) The comprehensiveness of cash flow reporting in the United Kingdom: Some characteristics and firm-specific determinants. *The International Journal of Accounting*, 34(3), 311–47.

Additional material on the website

Go to http://www.thomsonlearning.co.uk/stolowylebas2 for further information.

The following appendices to this chapter are available on the dedicated website:

Appendix 14.1: Content of activities according to IAS 7
Appendix 14.2: Differences in classification
Appendix 14.3: The UK/Ireland model
Appendix 14.4: Funds flow statement or statement of changes in financial position
Appendix 14.5: Different titles and different models

Notes

1. When a financial institution extends an overdraft authorization to a business, it is, de facto, equivalent to extending a 'line of credit' which would unambiguously be considered to be part of the financing activities of the business.
2. The 'true' direct method is not presented, since it requires access to internal company information, and this is not consistent with the users' perspective adopted in this book (users do not have access to inside information).
3. Known exceptions are start-up companies, and especially dot.com firms that require a large discretionary investment in operating facilities up front and build their business slowly. When speaking of many dot.com firms before the year 2000 crash or of weakened airlines like TWA (which disappeared in 2000) or United Airlines from 2003 to early 2006, or General Motors in 2005, their negative cash flow from operating activities (expressed on a per month basis) is referred to in the economic press as their 'cash burn rate'. Such firms either have a large stash of cash available (and then one can calculate how many months they can be expected to survive unless some serious reorganization takes place) or will require a constant influx of cash from either shareholders or financial institutions, or from selling assets. The question of their survival hinges on their ability to turn around a 'cash burn' situation into one with a positive cash flow from operating activities.
4. The group possesses many other brands besides the brands quoted.

C15

Chapter 15

Financial statement analysis

Learning objectives

After studying this chapter, you will understand:

- That the major tools of financial statement analysis are: ratio analysis, trend analysis, 'common-size' analysis, and financial statement structure analysis. These tools are used for both inter-firm comparisons and time-based analysis of a single firm.
- How users of financial information can use each of these tools to guide their decision making.
- How, more specifically, the 'statement of intermediate balances' and the 'cash equation' can lead to a more complete understanding of the dynamics of a business' financial performance.
- That these tools can be applied equally to income statements by nature or by function, or, if appropriate, to balance sheets by nature or by term, which allows the user to analyze any financial statement of any company, regardless of the GAAP used in its reporting.
- That ratios, although rich in useful information, should be used with caution.
- That there are many diverse available sources providing relevant information and data on which to perform a financial statement analysis.
- The definition and computation of earnings per share and what this key metric can be used for.
- Why residual income and its more modern version called EVA® are considered by many as useful metrics of the financial performance of a business (measures of 'value creation' for shareholders).
- That any analyst must be aware that published accounts, even if audited and respectful of GAAP, may, nonetheless, be affected by attempts at earnings management or be the result of any of possible manipulations.
- That models, called scoring models, may be used to detect an increased risk of corporate failure.

While, throughout previous chapters, we emphasized the decision-making potential and usefulness of reported financial information, this chapter focuses in more detail on the actual use of such information by decision makers. Data reported to shareholders, the financial community, and all interested parties are not meant to be directly useable in decision making. They are, first and foremost, descriptive. In order to bring their information content to light, they need to be analyzed, compared, decoded, and interpreted.

Financial statement analysis is a set of tools, practices, processes, and procedures that address the informational concerns of internal and external decision makers regarding a business' future performance and attached risks. It builds on understanding past financial performance or achievements as well as present financial and market condition(s) and opportunities. It uses various techniques integrating accounting and non-accounting data[1] and additional information, emphasizing comparative and relative analysis over time for one firm and between firms in a single period or over time.

Users are interested in understanding liquidity, solvency, leverage effects, and profitability of a firm as well as knowing its asset management policy and ability to deliver a return to investors in order to ground decisions about the future.

Although practical financial statement analysis may vary across countries, the main techniques used (and developed in the Core issues section in this chapter) include:

- Trend or horizontal analysis (comparison over time of the evolution of a specific expense or revenue item or of a particular asset or liability item).
- Common-size or vertical analysis (measurement of a particular item, in any of the financial statements, as a percentage of a reference item in the same statement and/or comparison of the evolution of the structure of the financial statements).
- Balance sheet structure and cash equation.
- Ratio analysis (evaluation of the relation between components of financial statements).

Additional specific instruments, such as earnings per share and economic value added, are presented in the Advanced issues section.

1 Core issues

1.1 Trend (horizontal or chronological) analysis

1.1.1 Definition and terminology

Since users are interested in gaining an understanding of the characteristics of the stream of future income of the firm, the analysis of the evolution over time of each or some constituent of its current and past income and financial risks represents a fundamental element of reflection. A measurement of the changes over the past accounting period (or over a longer period of time) of a limited number of items, or, by way of contrast, of the complete set of financial statements (income statement, cash flow statement, and balance sheet) can help the analyst or the user of the analysis understand the dynamics of the income (wealth) generation model and thus allow for extrapolations. Such a comparison over time is known as 'trend analysis'.

This comparison is carried line item by line item (in absolute values and/or in percentages) against the like value in a base year (often the previous year).

If the percentage change approach is used, the base year item amount (sales revenue, cost, liability, asset, etc.) is used as an index with a conventional base value of 100. Other periods are then measured against that index. For example: sales this year are 120% of last year's, cost of goods sold (COGS) is 125% of last year's, and commercial expenses are 150% of last year's. This example indicates that this firm appears to have been caught in a 'scissor effect' – costs, especially commercial expenses, have been rising faster than revenue did. An analyst, before formulating any conclusion, will need to identify the actions the firm did – and could – take about these evolutions (and their likelihood of success). In doing so, she/he will bring to bear additional knowledge about the market and the behavior of its players (suppliers, competitors, clients, regulators, etc.), and take into consideration what is known about the current strategy of the firm – are they, for example, in the process of launching one or several new products?, etc. Trend analysis must always be placed in context to be meaningful beyond the simple observation.

1.1.2 Advantages and limitations

This method allows the examination of short (two or three years) or long trends (evolution over 10 years, for example). Long trends are not always meaningful because the business model parameters (and the perimeter or the scope) of the enterprise and/or the environmental and competitive conditions may have changed significantly over that period.

For example, there would be very little meaning in carrying a trend analysis of Vivendi Universal from 1995 to 2005: this company evolved in less than 10 years, through acquisitions and divestitures, from Générale des Eaux (water distribution and environmental services) to become Vivendi (telecommunication and environmental services), and is now known as Vivendi Universal (telecommunication and entertainment products and services). For trends to be meaningful, the business model must have been stable over the period of comparison.

1.1.3 Example of trend analysis

Let us consider a fictitious firm, Bernstein AG, a provider of computer services (software and support) to medium and small enterprises. Its income statements for years X1 and X2 are compared in Table 15.1 (in millions of CU).

Table 15.1 Trend analysis

	X2	X1	Amount of change	% of change (X2/X1) – 1
Net sales revenue	28,500	25,000	3,500	14
Costs and expenses				
COGS (cost of goods sold)	14,700	12,000	2,700	23
Selling expenses	5,500	5,100	400	8
General and administrative expenses	5,000	5,000	0	0
Interest expenses	745	570	175	31
Interest income	−50	−90	40	−44
Income before tax	2,605	2,420	185	8
Income tax expense	1,042	847	195	23
Net income	1,563	1,573	−10	−1

This simple illustration shows that the components of income have varied from one year to the next in very different proportions. Some people may consider as positive the fact that income before tax (or net operating profit before tax or NOPAT) grew by 8%. But the situation has, possibly, deteriorated:

(a) COGS grew faster than sales leading to a reduction of the gross margin;

(b) interest expenses are higher in X2 than they were in X1;

(c) interest income is lower; and, consequently,

(d) profit declines, despite the growing volume of sales.

The fact that selling expenses grew less rapidly than sales revenue (not in itself an abnormal event as many such expenses, except for commissions, can generally be considered to be fixed costs, i.e., invariant with volume) deserves special attention in the light of the reduction of the gross margin. A series of questions need to be asked. The manager, of course, will have an easier time finding the answer to these than would an outside analyst (especially about a small- to medium-size firm), but, nonetheless, the questions are the same and need to be addressed squarely by both:

- Did the mix of services sold drift, unwittingly, towards lower margin ones?
- Was the customer base developed or enlarged towards customers whose resources lead them to prefer off-the-shelf (ready made and lower margin) products that require fewer (high margin) services?
- Linked to the previous point, we can observe the possible meaningfulness of the reduction of interest income. If we assume this revenue is derived from investing customer cash advances linked to developing customized software, and if we further assume this return came from investing the cash at a modest annual interest rate of, say, 3%, we can work backwards to find the amount of implied invested cash. In X1 this invested cash must have amounted to 3,000 CU (3,000 × 0.03 = 90). We can thus deduce that customized sales (on which Bernstein AG likely receives cash advances from customers) represented somewhere around 12% of sales revenue. But in X2 the same calculation indicates the cash advances (under the same hypotheses) amount to only 1,666 CU, i.e., sales assumed to be coming from high-margin customized products represent in X2 a percentage of total sales revenue of just under 6%. If the hypotheses are correct, the firm incurred a reduction of 50% of its sales of customized products. A dramatic evolution of the trend and a complete modification of the business model.
- Have credit terms been extended (by choice) or have they deteriorated (customer behavior) between X1 and X2? If this were the case it might explain why interest expenses have grown disproportionately: a larger working capital need (current assets [excluding cash] minus current liabilities [excluding bank overdrafts], see more on this concept later in this chapter) resulted from this evolution. The need was covered by additional borrowings. An alternative explanation of the rise in interest expense might also be that the firm engaged in a significant capital investment campaign (this could be verified by looking at either or both the balance sheets and cash flow statements for both years).
- Did the suppliers reduce their credit terms, thus creating a larger working capital need?
- Did labor expenses have to be increased in order to keep talent in the firm? (Such an event would explain part of the growth in the COGS.)
- Was there a change in market positioning of the firm's offering due to the entry of a new competitor in the market?
- We might even wonder whether the management of the firm did not sacrifice selling expenses (and even 'General and administrative expenses') in order to save (somewhat successfully in the short run) the bottom line, which was threatened by the runaway COGS. However, any coin has another side. The fact that selling expenses increased only by 8% while sales revenue increased by 14% means it costs the firm less in X2 than it did in X1 to create 1 CU of sales revenue. This increase in commercial productivity is, in itself, a good thing and needs to be replaced in the possible contexts evoked above.

This example shows the potential richness and also the difficulty and possible limits of trend analysis.

What is important is not only to measure the evolution of any one line item over time, but also to measure its evolution relative to other elements of the financial statements and to contextual elements, or to measure the evolution of its relative weight in the determination of income. What is important is the evolution of the structure of financial statements. It is important to confirm whether the causal relations creating the income (i.e., the business model) have been modified from one year to the next before appropriate actions can be taken on the basis of this analysis.

Difficulties and limits of trend analysis have led to the development of common-size analysis of financial statements.

1.2 Common-size (or vertical) analysis

1.2.1 Definition

Common-size analysis is based on the restatement of the income statement, balance sheet, and/or cash flow statement by presenting each line item as a proportion of a base figure (conventionally indexed as 100, thus the proportion is expressed as a percentage). Such restated statements are said to have been 'common sized' and are 'common-size statements'.

The base figure is generally net sales for the income statement, total assets (or total equity and liabilities) for the balance sheet, and cash flow from operating activities for a cash flow statement.

The common-size analysis provides an understanding of the relationships *between* items in the financial statements during a period. By combining vertical and horizontal analyses (trend analysis), assuming one has access to a series of financial statements, it is possible to additionally evaluate the evolution over time of such relationships, thus highlighting scissor effects (or 'squeeze effects').

The common-size financial statements are often referred to as 'income statement structure' or 'structural income statement', 'balance sheet structure' or 'structural balance sheet', and 'cash flow structure'. Since cash flow structure is changing dramatically from one period to the next due to investments and financing decisions, common-size analysis seems to be used less frequently for the whole cash flow statement. The focus is generally mainly on the evolution of the components of the cash flow from operating activities.

1.2.2 Illustration

The common-size income statements for Bernstein AG are shown in Table 15.2, revealing the evolution of the structure.

Table 15.2 confirms, for example, that the moderate (8%) increase in selling expenses we have observed in Table 15.1 (trend analysis) reveals a change in either strategy, market demand, or cost control over the consumption of this resource. The drift in COGS is confirmed by the fact that it increases to 52% of sales from a previous 48%.

Table 15.2 Common-size analysis

	X2	X1
Net sales revenue	100%	100%
Costs and expenses		
COGS (cost of goods sold)	52%	48%
Selling expenses	19%	20%
General and administrative expenses	18%	20%
Interest expenses	3%	2%
Interest income	ns	ns
Income before tax	9%	10%
Income tax expense	4%	3%
Net income (as a % of sales revenue)	5%	6%

ns, not significant.

Common-size analysis, just like trend analysis before, fails to give complete, sufficient, or final answers. Each method of analysis helps raise questions that need to be explored by the decision maker in seeking further data and information to interpret the financial data provided. Some of these additional data are of non-accounting nature.

For example, the same increase in COGS can be due to a variety of causes in Bernstein AG's actions or reactions to market factors. Examples of causes of the increase in COGS could be:

- Introduction of a large number of different and totally new services or products in X2.
- Possible birthing difficulties in 'production' of new products or services.
- Increase in the cost of complexity of new products or services (the more complex a product or service is, the more costly it is to effectively and successfully provide it to customers).
- Changes in the mix of sales.
- Growth in sales due mainly to lower margin, maturing products or to more successful standardized products, at the expense of custom-designed software.
- Possible difficulties in development efficiency or/and a saturation of the current development capacity.

As we see here, and have seen in the previous paragraphs, the growth in COGS as a percentage of sales must be related to its contextual circumstances before it can be interpreted and exploited to anticipate future bottom line or performance of Bernstein AG.

1.2.3 Usefulness of common-size analysis.

Common-size analysis, in addition to being a powerful internal analytical tool, also permits the analyst (or the manager) to compare and contrast more easily the financial statements of two and more companies in the same industrial sector or risk class.

It effectively reduces the problem of the size difference between companies. It helps the analyst formulate hypotheses about which business model, between the firms compared, appears to be the most effective in driving sustainable financial performance and identify possible thresholds in economies of scale.

The most frequent use of common-size financial statements, both by managers and analysts and users, is a comparison of an enterprise's financial data with industry norms or averages, or 'rules of thumb' about good management (such as the rule of the three-thirds for the equity and liabilities side of the balance sheet – one-third equity, one-third long-term debt, and one-third short-term debt – or such as the, debatable, rule in the restaurant business that states the cost of materials should be about one-third of revenue).

Figure 15.1 summarizes the uses of common-sized financial statements.

Figure 15.1 The use of common-sized financial statements

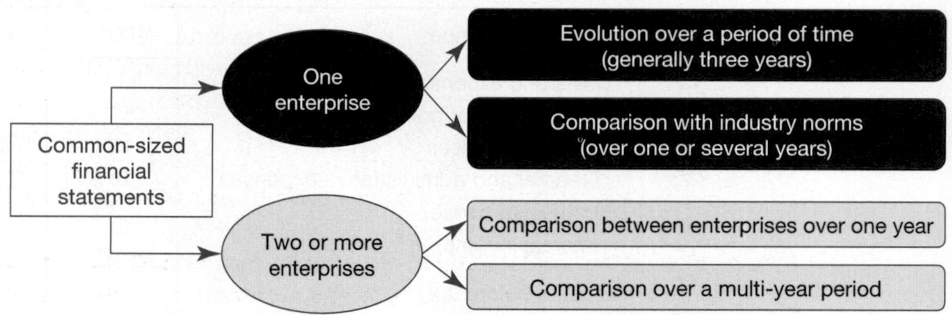

1.2.4 Common-sized income statement

As mentioned before, when analyzing the income statement the base line is the net sales figure. We examine separately the application of common-size analysis to income statements

Table 15.3 Procter & Gamble – Consolidated statement of earnings (in millions of US$) and common-sized income statements for the years ended 30 June 2001–2005 (*source*: Annual reports 2005 and 2003)

In millions of US$	2005	2004	2003	2002	2001
Net sales	56,741	51,407	43,377	40,238	39,244
Cost of products sold	27,804	25,076	22,141	20,989	22,102
Marketing, research, administrative, and other expense	18,010	16,504	13,383	12,571	12,406
Operating income	10,927	9,827	7,853	6,678	4,736
Interest expense	834	629	561	603	794
Other non-operating income, net	346	152	238	308	674
Earnings before income taxes	10,439	9,350	7,530	6,383	4,616
Income taxes	3,182	2,869	2,344	2,031	1,694
Net earnings	7,257	6,481	5,186	4,352	2,922
As percentages of net sales	2005	2004	2003	2002	2001
Net sales	100.0%	100.0%	100.0%	100.0%	100.0%
Cost of products sold	49.0%	48.8%	51.0%	52.2%	56.3%
Marketing, research, administrative, and other expense	31.7%	32.1%	30.9%	31.2%	31.6%
Operating income	19.3%	19.1%	18.1%	16.6%	12.1%
Interest expense	1.5%	1.2%	1.3%	1.5%	2.0%
Other non-operating income, net	0.6%	0.3%	0.5%	0.8%	1.7%
Earnings before income taxes	18.4%	18.2%	17.4%	15.9%	11.8%
Income taxes	5.6%	5.6%	5.4%	5.0%	4.3%
Net earnings	12.8%	12.6%	12.0%	10.8%	7.4%

presented by function and by nature (see Chapter 3) since each income statement structure reveals different aspects of performance.

Common-sized income statement by function Table 15.3 illustrates the common-sized consolidated income statements by function of the US company Procter & Gamble. In the upper part of the table absolute figures are provided. In the lower part of the table each line item of the income statement was divided by the net sales of the corresponding year and is shown as a percentage of net sales revenue.

Common-sized income statements are used to identify structural changes in a company's operating results. For example, it is quite significant to observe that the COGS is 49% of sales in 2005 while it was 56.3% in 2001. Clearly some large modification of the business model or of the product offering took place between these years. The case of Procter & Gamble will be studied in more detail in Assignment 15.2.

Statement of intermediate balances in common-sized income statement by nature: principles Given that common-sized statements are often used for comparing the enterprise with others, the income statement by nature offers a challenge in applying common sizing. There is a diversity of legitimate presentations by nature, often reflecting that charts of accounts are specific to each enterprise. Even if common sized, the resulting documents can hardly lead to useful inter-enterprises comparisons. A common or standardized presentation of the statement by nature has to be created first.

An income statement presented by nature must be restructured in order to identify the key intermediate balances (based on standardized definitions) that help describe the value creation process of the analyzed enterprises, which, then, become comparable. For example, some firms may use many subcontractors in their supply chain, while others may wish to control directly the resources required to create and deliver their value proposition to the markets. Intermediate balances such as commercial margin, value added, and gross operating profit highlight similarities and differences of the business process of any number of enterprises.

An income statement by nature, in which all intermediate balances have been clearly identified, is called a 'statement of intermediate balances'. We will now explain how such a statement is constructed to allow comparisons between firms. Once restructured, the income statement can be common sized without any difficulty. It suffices to choose a base line that will be used to calculate the percentages.

Figure 15.2 is an example of a statement of intermediate balances, which reports the sequence of 'levels' in the step-by-step formation of the income of the period. A more detailed definition of key terms is provided after Figure 15.2.

Figure 15.2 Structure of the income statement by intermediate balances of financial performance

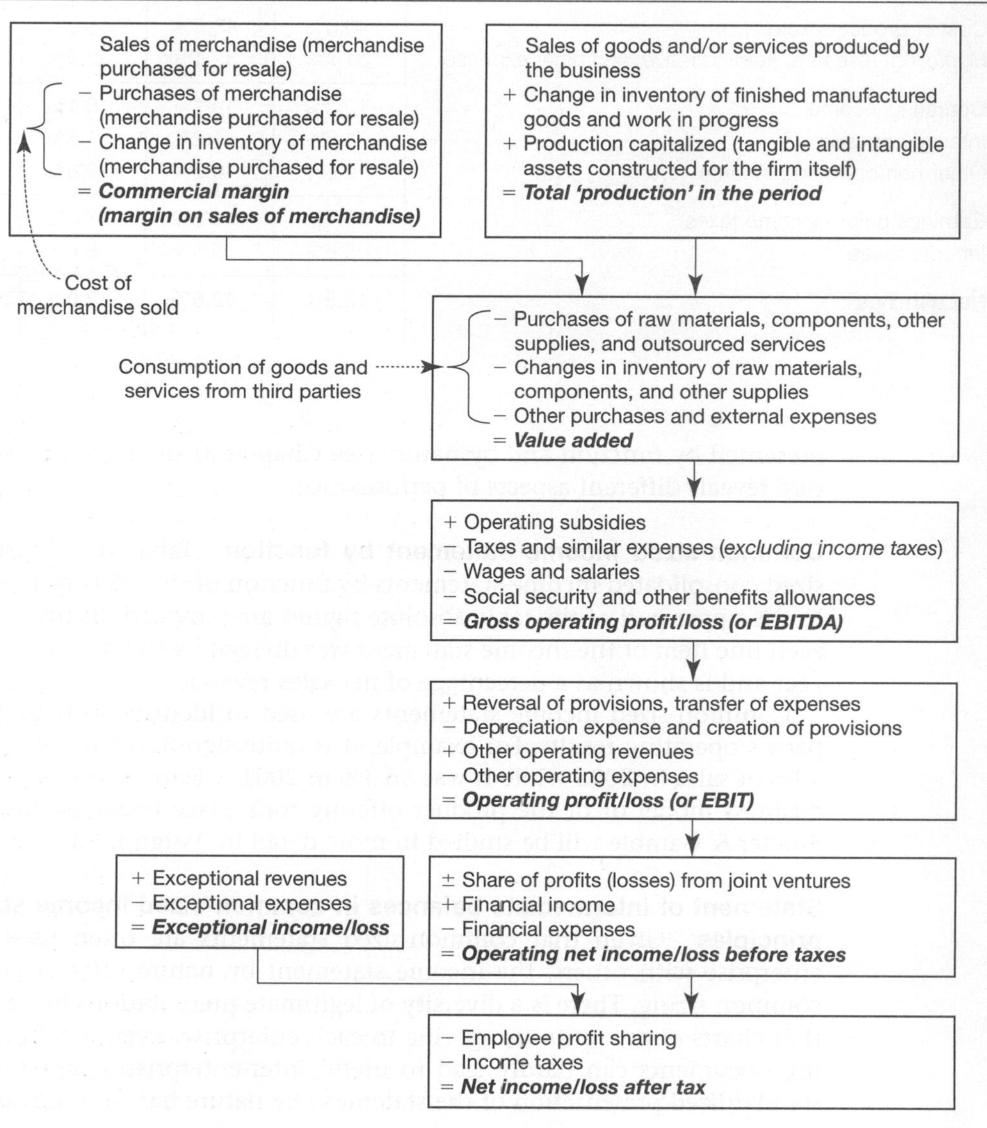

Essentially, such a statement dissects the income statement into meaningful blocks of data to help in the user's financial understanding and interpretation of the firm's economic activity. The intermediate balances may be presented in absolute monetary amounts, as percentages of variations from one period to another (trend analysis), or as percentages of some relevant in-period basis (i.e., common-size analysis, the most frequent use of this tool). This restructured income statement can prove to be particularly useful to the user when a company carries, side by side, diverse business lines such as a manufacturing activity (manufacture of goods or services for sale) and a dealership or brokerage activity (merchandise purchased for resale).

The following will develop the meaning and decision-making implications of the main terms (i.e., intermediate balances) used in a 'restructured' income statement (that was 'by nature' in the first place).

Commercial margin (margin on sales) The commercial margin expresses the difference between the sales revenue and the cost of merchandise sold. It is useful to separate the resale segment from other segments since this line of business often requires specific resources and is subject to different growth drivers than the main business of a manufacturing firm.

Total 'production' in the period (Current period 'production') The term 'production' used in Figure 15.2 may prove to be somewhat ambiguous to some readers. It is the commonly used term, drawn from economics and refers to the net potential wealth created by the activity of the firm, before considering *how* this additional potential wealth was created.

The enterprise's industrial output during the period is the total of units it sold, valued at their sales price (i.e., the sales revenue), plus (minus) increases (decreases) in absolute value of the finished goods and work-in-progress inventories, valued at cost plus the cost of any self-produced fixed assets.

Value added The term value added is a basic concept used in macroeconomics (Gross National Product accounting), which refers to the amount contributed by a particular enterprise to the national wealth. It is the creation or increase in 'value', resulting from the enterprise's current business activities, over and above the value of goods and services consumed by the enterprise that were provided by third parties. Roughly speaking, the firm's strategy does, de facto, partition the value added between employees, maintenance of the productive capacity (depreciation or provisions creation), the State (taxes), and shareholders. Although infrequently used in reporting to shareholders, the measurement of an enterprise value added is a basic tool used by financial analysts (often used by union leaders in their wages or benefits negotiations) and is frequently mentioned in business communication and the specialized press in several countries, such as Australia, Belgium, France, Germany, South Africa, Switzerland, and the UK. It is developed in Appendix 15.1.

Gross operating profit or EBITDA The gross operating profit, or EBITDA (***E***arnings from operations ***B***efore ***I***nterests, ***T***axes, ***D***epreciation, and ***A***mortization, and provisions), measures the wealth created by the enterprise from its operations, independently of its financing strategy (financial income and expenses), depreciation policy (charges for depreciation and amortization), and other firm specific income adjustments such as provisions for doubtful accounts.

EBITDA is also looked at as a proxy measure of the cash flow generated by operations since it only considers those revenues and expenses that have an impact on cash (cash items, as defined in Chapter 14). This indicator helps in evaluating the firm's management's short-term ability to create wealth, since it is not affected by long-term strategic decisions regarding financing (capital structure) and capital investment or fiscal policies. The ratio of EBITDA to sales (or accounting 'production') is often considered to be one of the most relevant measures of the intrinsic 'business (potential for) profitability' of the firm, allowing meaningful inter-enterprise comparisons (independently of the policies that are specific to a management team's choices, such as depreciation methods or provisioning, and thus the best proxy – and easiest to calculate – to the true cash flow generation potential of the firm).

The ratio comparing EBITDA to the value of the enterprise (net market value of equity) serves as a measure of the vulnerability of the firm to a takeover. This ratio (Value/EBITDA) provides, in fact, an estimate of the number of years of operations that would be needed for an acquirer to get to a payback, i.e., to recover the capital invested in an acquisition of the firm (even before taking into consideration the likely synergies behind the acquisition). The lower the ratio, i.e., the smaller the number of years until payback, the more attractive the business is, all things being equal, to a potential buyer.

Operating profit or EBIT Operating profit, or EBIT (***E***arnings from operations ***B***efore ***I***nterests and ***T***axes), represents the result of the firm's normal and current activity without taking into account income taxes or financial and extraordinary (exceptional) elements (see Chapter 6). This intermediate balance allows a comparison of firms while ignoring their financing strategies but taking into account their depreciation policies. It is a logical metric to use for comparison when businesses in an economic sector tend to use similar policies for the depreciation of their assets.

Operating net income before taxes Operating net income before taxes indicates economic and financial performance before consideration of extraordinary (exceptional) items and taxes.

Exceptional income The exceptional (sometimes called 'unusual') income is the profit or loss from activities that are not related to the firm's usual operations, and are, therefore, out of the ordinary or exceptional. In most cases, this income or loss is related to gains or losses on the sale of one or several fixed assets. This 'income' should be shown as a separate item on the statement of intermediate balances. It should never be hidden (by addition or subtraction) in any other main section of the statement.

Net income/loss The last line of the statement of intermediate balances is the net income/loss after tax, which is self-explanatory. It is also known as the 'bottom line'. This balance is useful, however, to double-check the equality between this restructured statement and the original income statement.

An income statement by nature can always be presented in a common-size format, even without the restructuring to identify the intermediate balances as we just did. Of course, without restructuring, its usefulness would be greatly reduced and would apply only to that firm as the metrics identified may not be comparable between two enterprises.

Statement of intermediate balances – Real-life example China Eastern Airlines (China – IFRS/Hong Kong GAAP – Air carrier) China Eastern Airlines Corporation Ltd ('China Eastern') is one of the largest Chinese air carriers. It was established in the People's Republic of China in 1995. It is headquartered in Shanghai. Although a majority of the shares are state owned, its shares are listed in Shanghai, Hong Kong, and New York. China Eastern Airlines Corporation Ltd and its subsidiaries provide civil aviation, air cargo, postal delivery, and other extended transportation services in the People's Republic of China. The company also offers aircraft maintenance, manufacturing and maintenance of aviation equipment, and agent services for airlines. As of 30 June 2005, it operated 116 aircraft (102 aircraft in May 2004), including 108 passenger jet aircraft and eight jet freighters. The company also operated a total of 221 routes, of which 144 were domestic routes, 15 were Hong Kong routes, and 62 were international routes, as of the same date. China Eastern carried 12 million passengers in 2003, 17.7 million in 2004, and 24.3 million in 2005.

China Eastern Airlines
Consolidated statements of income
For years ended 31 December 2004, 2003, 2002, 2001, and 2000

(in millions of RMB)	2004	2003	2002	2001	2000
Traffic revenues					
Passenger	15,358	10,261	10,038	9,587	8,644
Cargo and mail	4,428	3,187	2,445	2,092	2,124
Other operating revenues	1,253	829	596	474	452
Turnover	21,039	14,277	13,079	12,153	11,220
Other operating income	154	60	226	128	0
Operating expenses					
Wages, salaries and benefits	(1,866)	(1,449)	(1,036)	(773)	(798)
Take-off and landing charges	(3,020)	(2,254)	(1,988)	(1,703)	(1,572)
Aircraft fuel	(5,430)	(3,045)	(2,564)	(2,613)	(2,327)
Food and beverages	(758)	(542)	(606)	(567)	(499)
Aircraft depreciation and operating leases	(3,672)	(2,851)	(2,455)	(2,404)	(2,168)
Other depreciation and operating leases	(496)	(495)	(400)	(358)	(321)
Aircraft maintenance	(1,396)	(1,329)	(1,078)	(967)	(820)
Commissions	(772)	(465)	(380)	(487)	(645)
Office and administration	(1,338)	(1,058)	(1,044)	(849)	(724)
Revaluation deficit of fixed assets	(966)	0	(171)	0	0
Other	0	(628)	(520)	(563)	(568)
Total operating expenses	(19,714)	(14,116)	(12,242)	(11,284)	(10,442)
Operating profit	**1,479**	**221**	**1,063**	**997**	**778**
Finance costs, net	133	(712)	(731)	(814)	(814)
Exchange (loss)/gain, net	(763)	(70)	(38)	126	0
Other income, net	0	0	0	0	341
Share of results of associates before tax	(4)	(29)	(32)	5	0
Profit before taxation	**845**	**(590)**	**262**	**314**	**305**
Taxation	(181)	(247)	(54)	261	(100)
Profit after taxation	**664**	**(837)**	**208**	**575**	**205**
Minority interests	(150)	(112)	(122)	(33)	(29)
Profit attributable to shareholders	**514**	**(949)**	**86**	**542**	**176**

The 1999 annual report of the company indicates:

Revenues	1999 (in RMBm)
Passenger	8,031
Cargo and mail	1,730
Other operating revenues	402
Total revenues	10,163

China Eastern annual reports 2002 and 2001 indicate some changes in the presentation of the 'Other income, net' and 'Other operating income'. The following data (Additional information) will allow restating some elements of the income statement in order to ensure comparability throughout the period.

China Eastern also provided following information on government subsidy (Annual Report 2004, p. 76): in 2004, government subsidy was granted by the local government to the company in consideration of the relocation of the company's international flights and related facil-

Additional information (millions of RMB)	2004	2003	2002	2001	2000
Net exchange gain/(loss)				126	120
Gain on disposal of aircraft and engines				2	112
Rental income from operating subleases of aircraft				126	111
Other, net				(5)	(2)
Other income, net				249	341
Government subsidy	73	58			
Gain on disposal of aircraft and engines	(41)	(29)	116	2	
Rental income from operating subleases of aircraft	122	31	110	126	
Other operating income	154	60	226	128	
Operating lease rentals (aircraft)	1,720	1,238	1,026	925	769
Operating lease rentals (land and buildings)	147	116	99	90	83

ities from Hongqiao Airport to Pudong International Airport. In 2003, the mentioned government subsidy was granted for compensation of the impact of SARS[2] on air transport business.

Office and administration expenses mainly include training expenses, and expenses relating to overseas sales. Other operating expenses include maintenance expenses of other fixed assets, computer and telecommunications expenses, and other (unspecified) expenses. On 31 December 2002, the Group's fixed assets were revalued. The impact was charged to the income statement under the caption 'Revaluation deficit of fixed assets'.

As the income statement is presented by nature, it allows the preparation of the statement of intermediate balances (SIB) in value and in percentages (see below).

Statement of intermediate balances (millions of RMB)	2004	2003	2002	2001	2000
Passenger	15,358	10,261	10,038	9,587	8,644
Cargo and mail	4,428	3,187	2,445	2,092	2,124
Other operating revenues	1,253	829	596	474	452
Total production for the period	**21,039**	**14,277**	**13,079**	**12,153**	**11,220**
Take-off and landing charges	(3,020)	(2,254)	(1,988)	(1,703)	(1,572)
Aircraft fuel	(5,430)	(3,045)	(2,564)	(2,613)	(2,327)
Food and beverages	(758)	(542)	(606)	(567)	(499)
Aircraft maintenance	(1,396)	(1,329)	(1,078)	(967)	(820)
Commissions	(772)	(465)	(380)	(487)	(645)
Other	0	(628)	(520)	(563)	(568)
Operating lease rentals (aircraft)	(1,720)	(1,238)	(1,026)	(925)	(769)
Operating lease rentals (land and buildings)	(147)	(116)	(99)	(90)	(83)
Office and administration	(1,338)	(1,058)	(1,044)	(849)	(724)
Consumption from third parties	**(14,581)**	**(10,675)**	**(9,305)**	**(8,764)**	**(8,007)**
Value added	**6,458**	**3,602**	**3,774**	**3,389**	**3,213**
Wages, salaries and benefits	(1,866)	(1,449)	(1,036)	(773)	(798)
Gross operating income	**4,592**	**2,153**	**2,738**	**2,616**	**2,415**
Rental income from operating subleases of aircraft	122	31	110	126	111
Aircraft depreciation (excluding operating lease rentals)	(1,952)	(1,613)	(1,429)	(1,479)	(1,399)
Other depreciation (excluding operating lease rentals)	(349)	(379)	(301)	(268)	(238)
Earnings (loss) from operations	**2,413**	**192**	**1,118**	**995**	**889**
Finance costs, net	133	(712)	(731)	(814)	(814)
Exchange (loss)/gain, net	(763)	(70)	(38)	126	120
Share of results of associates before tax	(4)	(29)	(32)	5	(2)
Operating net income before taxes	**1,779**	**(619)**	**317**	**312**	**193**
Gain on disposal of aircraft and engines	(41)	(29)	116	2	112
Revaluation deficit of fixed assets	(966)	0	(171)	0	0
Government subsidy	73	58	0	0	0
Unusual income	**(934)**	**29**	**(55)**	**2**	**112**
Taxation	(181)	(247)	(54)	261	(100)
Minority interests	(150)	(112)	(122)	(33)	(29)
Profit attributable to shareholders	**514**	**(949)**	**86**	**542**	**176**

Statement of intermediate balances (in percentage – common-size income statements)	2004	2003	2002	2001	2000
Passenger	73.0%	71.9%	76.7%	78.9%	77.0%
Cargo and mail	21.0%	22.3%	18.7%	17.2%	18.9%
Other operating revenues	6.0%	5.8%	4.6%	3.9%	4.0%
Total production for the period	**100.0%**	**100.0%**	**100.0%**	**100.0%**	100.0%
Change in production over previous year	*47.4%*	*9.2%*	*7.6%*	*8.3%*	*10.4%*
Change in passenger revenues over previous year	*49.7%*	*2.2%*	*4.7%*	*10.9%*	*7.6%*
Change in cargo revenues over previous year	*39.0%*	*30.3%*	*16.9%*	*(1.5%)*	*22.8%*
Take-off and landing charges	(14.4%)	(15.8%)	(15.2%)	(14.0%)	(14.0%)
Aircraft fuel	(25.8%)	(21.3%)	(19.6%)	(21.5%)	(20.7%)
Food and beverages	(3.6%)	(3.8%)	(4.6%)	(4.7%)	(4.4%)
Aircraft maintenance	(6.6%)	(9.3%)	(8.2%)	(8.0%)	(7.3%)
Commissions	(3.7%)	(3.3%)	(2.9%)	(4.0%)	(5.7%)
Other	0.0%	(4.4%)	(4.0%)	(4.6%)	(5.1%)
Operating lease rentals (aircraft)	(8.2%)	(8.7%)	(7.8%)	(7.6%)	(6.9%)
Operating lease rentals (land and buildings)	(0.7%)	(0.8%)	(0.8%)	(0.7%)	(0.7%)
Office and administration	(6.4%)	(7.4%)	(8.0%)	(7.0%)	(6.5%)
Consumption from third parties	(69.3%)	(74.8%)	(71.1%)	(72.1%)	(71.4%)
Value added	**30.7%**	25.2%	28.9%	27.9%	28.6%
Wages, salaries and benefits	(8.9%)	(10.1%)	(7.9%)	(6.4%)	(7.1%)
Gross operating income	**21.8%**	**15.1%**	**20.9%**	**21.5%**	**21.5%**
Rental income from operating subleases of aircraft	0.6%	0.2%	0.8%	1.0%	1.0%
Aircraft depreciation (excluding operating lease rentals)	(9.3%)	(11.3%)	(10.9%)	(12.2%)	(12.5%)
Other depreciation (excluding operating lease rentals)	(1.7%)	(2.7%)	(2.3%)	(2.2%)	(2.1%)
Earnings (loss) from operations	**11.5%**	**1.3%**	**8.5%**	**8.2%**	**7.9%**
Finance costs, net	0.6%	(5.0%)	(5.6%)	(6.7%)	(7.3%)
Exchange (loss)/gain, net	(3.6%)	(0.5%)	(0.3%)	1.0%	1.1%
Share of results of associates before tax	(0.0%)	(0.2%)	(0.2%)	0.0%	(0.0%)
Operating net income before taxes	**8.5%**	**(4.3%)**	**2.4%**	**2.6%**	**1.7%**
Gain on disposal of aircraft and engines	(0.2%)	(0.2%)	0.9%	0.0%	1.0%
Revaluation deficit of fixed assets	(4.6%)	0.0%	(1.3%)	0.0%	0.0%
Government subsidy	0.3%	0.4%	0.0%	0.0%	0.0%
Unusual income	**(4.4%)**	**0.2%**	**(0.4%)**	**0.0%**	**1.0%**
Taxation	(0.9%)	(1.7%)	(0.4%)	2.1%	(0.9%)
Minority interests	(0.7%)	(0.8%)	(0.9%)	(0.3%)	(0.3%)
Profit attributable to shareholders	**2.4%**	**(6.6%)**	**0.7%**	**4.5%**	**1.6%**

Comments: Before analyzing the statement of intermediate balances (SIB), we should make the following comments:

- The 'Other income, net' and 'Other operating income' have been restated to ensure comparability throughout the period (see Additional information).
- Gains on disposal of aircraft and engines are reported under unusual items.
- The operating leases included in the items 'Aircraft depreciation and operating leases' and 'Other depreciation and operating leases' (see Additional information) have been separated and reported in the consumption from third parties.
- Because office and administration expenses mainly include training expenses and expenses relating to overseas sales, they have been included in the 'Consumption from third parties'.
- Other operating expenses include maintenance expenses of other fixed assets, computer and telecommunications expenses, and other (unspecified) expenses. They are appropriately listed as 'Consumption from third parties'.
- The 'Revaluation deficit of fixed assets' has been considered has an unusual item.

Revenues/production Even though the common-sized SIB is based on the principle of dividing all other figures in the statement by the total production for the year, we have added to the statement a line showing the change in revenues for each year as compared with the previous year. It can be seen that China Eastern experienced an increase from 2002. In 2004 China Eastern had a jump in revenues of 47.4%, reflecting the dynamism of Chinese market.

China Eastern's revenues are relatively diversified (see, in the introduction to this section, the diversity of business domains in which the airline is involved) but, nonetheless, 73% of China Eastern's revenues were derived from passengers in 2004.

Consumption of resources acquired from third parties The ratio of 'consumption from third parties' to 'total production' decreased from 74.8% in 2003 to 69.3% in 2004. Looking at the breakdown of consumption from third parties, we see that fuel cost represents the greatest expense. Fuel cost as a percentage of total production increased for China Eastern from 2002 to 2004. Common-sizing the SIB allows the user to separate the effect of growth in the revenue (which should be adjusted for the small increase in the load factor – a gain of about one to three points per year for an effective load factor of 66% in 2004) from the impact of the cost of fuel purchased. Here we can see that China Eastern experienced an increase in the average cost of aviation fuel. Not surprisingly, the 2004 oil price inflation turned fuel cost into a major issue for the company (as well as for all airlines).

China Eastern, probably due to the development of direct sales and of web-based sales combined with a lower level of remuneration of travel agents' efforts, experienced a reduction in the item called commissions (from 5.7% in 2000 to 3.7% in 2004).

China Eastern also reports an increase in the average take-off and landing fees (14.4% in 2004 versus 14.0% in 2000). This is possibly linked to the move of their operations to the new airport in Shanghai.

Value added While not widely used in North America, the value added figure shows the extent to which an enterprise contributes to the national wealth of the country and what amount of 'value' is to be shared between the various stakeholders. The value added figure for China Eastern improved in 2004. Given the ambitious plane acquisition plan implemented by China Eastern (implying future growth of depreciation expenses), this may imply that less of the 'value' may be available for shareholders. Given that the recruiting needs of the airline may cause the share of value added dedicated to salaries to increase, if both total remunerations and total depreciation expense increase, managers must address the challenge of creating a rate of growth of the value added such that it will allow the satisfaction of every stakeholder's growth expectations, lest they have to make heart-wrenching choices of favoring one stakeholder over the others.

Gross operating income The ratio of salaries, wages, and benefits to total production is low (8.9%). China Eastern has a high gross operating profit (21.8% in 2004), probably due to its low level of salaries. The growth of the airline and of its competitors might put pressure on the level of remuneration, thus placing China Eastern in front of a scissor effect and possibly squeezing its profit margin on top of the negative effect of the evolution of the price of aviation fuel.

As discussed previously, gross operating income reflects the return derived from the core activities of the enterprise. A negative gross operating income (i.e., a gross operating loss), which is not the case for China Eastern, would be a sign of financial distress.

Earnings from operations For China Eastern 'Aircraft depreciation and amortization' represents 9.3% of production in 2004 and has been declining over the recent past. Since sales increased faster than the investment in a new or larger fleet of aircraft, and the load factor improved, profit has increased. China Eastern shows a significant improvement of operating income (11.5% in 2004 in comparison with 1.8% in 2003).

Operating net income before taxes For the same reasons, in 2003, China Eastern's ratio of interest expense (net) to total production was high (5%), but it showed a decrease from 2000 (7.3%), which was a good sign. This item became positive (income instead of expense) in 2004. China Eastern came back from a negative operating net income before taxes (−4.3% in 2003) to a positive one (8.5% in 2004).

Unusual income (Loss) China Eastern recorded a huge loss under this heading (−4.4%) in 2004 because of the impairment of fixed assets probably due to the change of home airport.

Net income (Loss) China Eastern recorded a 2.4% profitability in 2004 after facing a loss in 2003 (−6.6% of total production).

Synthesis The preparation of an SIB confirms that focusing mainly on net income figures is not sufficient to gain a full understanding of what went on (and therefore to be able to forecast future results, and thus take appropriate actions). The other intermediate balances, such as value added and gross operating income, are also, as illustrated above, important to the analyst. In the present case, despite the wealth of knowledge and questions obtained through the SIB, we feel that, in addition, a comparison with other airline companies would have considerably enriched the analysis. Baker *et al.* (2005) compare the statement of intermediate balances of China Eastern, Southwest Airlines and Air France.

1.2.5 Common-sized balance sheet

In the case of the balance sheet, the selected common-size basis will generally depend on the reporting format adopted. The base line seems to be, more or less, culturally based. No basis is intrinsically superior to another. A survey of common practices indicates that:

- Total assets (or 'total equity plus total liabilities'; the two are identical by definition) seem to be preferred in the United States, in the majority of continental European countries, and in Japan.
- Shareholders' equity (total shareholders' funds) appears to be the favored base line in the UK and Ireland.
- Long-term capital employed (shareholders' equity plus long-term debts) appears to be the most frequently used base line in India and also by some Dutch companies.

Traditional common-size balance sheet The common-size balance sheet (in millions of US dollars) is illustrated in Table 15.4 through that of Procter & Gamble.

As is generally the case in a common-size presentation, the balance sheet reported in Table 15.4 is rather aggregated, and several items such as shareholders' equity, property, plant and equipment, goodwill, and intangibles are presented in more detail in the published balance sheet in the annual or quarterly reports.

Table 15.4 Procter & Gamble – Consolidated balance sheets (in millions of US$) and common-sized balance sheets for the years ended 30 June 2001–2005 (*sources*: Annual reports 2005 and 2003)

ASSETS	2005	2004	2003	2002	2001	2005	2004	2003	2002	2001
Current assets										
Cash and cash equivalents	6,389	4,232	5,912	3,427	2,306	10.4%	7.4%	13.5%	8.4%	6.7%
Investment securities	1,744	1,660	300	196	212	2.8%	2.9%	0.7%	0.5%	0.6%
Accounts receivable	4,185	4,062	3,038	3,090	2,931	6.8%	7.1%	7.0%	7.6%	8.5%
Inventories	5,006	4,400	3,640	3,456	3,384	8.1%	7.7%	8.3%	8.5%	9.8%
Deferred income taxes	1,081	958	843	521	397	1.8%	1.7%	1.9%	1.3%	1.2%
Prepaid expenses and other receivables	1,924	1,803	1,487	1,476	1,659	3.1%	3.2%	3.4%	3.6%	4.8%
Total current assets	20,329	17,115	15,220	12,166	10,889	33.0%	30.0%	34.8%	29.8%	31.7%
Property, plant and equipment (net)	14,332	14,108	13,104	13,349	13,095	23.3%	24.7%	30.0%	32.7%	38.1%
Goodwill and other intangible assets (net)	24,163	23,900	13,507	13,430	8,300	39.3%	41.9%	30.9%	32.9%	24.1%
Other non-current assets	2,703	1,925	1,875	1,831	2,103	4.4%	3.4%	4.3%	4.5%	6.1%
Total assets	61,527	57,048	43,706	40,776	34,387	100.0%	100.0%	100.0%	100.0%	100.0%
LIABILITIES AND SHAREHOLDERS' EQUITY	2005	2004	2003	2002	2001	2005	2004	2003	2002	2001
Current liabilities										
Accounts payable	3,802	3,617	2,795	2,205	2,075	6.2%	6.3%	6.4%	5.4%	6.0%
Accrued and other liabilities	7,531	7,689	5,512	5,330	4,631	12.2%	13.5%	12.6%	13.1%	13.5%
Taxes payable	2,265	2,554	1,879	1,438	907	3.7%	4.5%	4.3%	3.5%	2.6%
Debt due within one year	11,441	8,287	2,172	3,731	2,233	18.6%	14.5%	5.0%	9.1%	6.5%
Total current liabilities	25,039	22,147	12,358	12,704	9,846	40.7%	38.8%	28.3%	31.2%	28.6%
Long-term debt	12,887	12,554	11,475	11,201	9,792	20.9%	22.0%	26.3%	27.5%	28.5%
Deferred income taxes	2,894	2,261	1,396	1,077	894	4.7%	4.0%	3.2%	2.6%	2.6%
Other non-current liabilities	3,230	2,808	2,291	2,088	1,845	5.2%	4.9%	5.2%	5.1%	5.4%
Total liabilities	44,050	39,770	27,520	27,070	22,377	71.6%	69.7%	63.0%	66.4%	65.1%
Shareholders' equity	17,477	17,278	16,186	13,706	12,010	28.4%	30.3%	37.0%	33.6%	34.9%
Total liabilities and shareholders' equity	61,527	57,048	43,706	40,776	34,387	100.0%	100.0%	100.0%	100.0%	100.0%

1.3 Balance sheet structure and cash equation

1.3.1 Balance sheet structure

A company's simplified balance sheet can be structured: (a) by identifying two separate 'time horizons' within each side of the balance sheet (current or short term; and non-current or long term), each corresponding to different types of decisions for both assets, on one hand, and shareholders' equity and liabilities, on the other; and (b) by separating operating from financial activities. Table 15.5 illustrates such structure.

Table 15.5 Balance sheet structure

Assets	Shareholders' equity and liabilities
■ Fixed (non-current) assets (FA)	■ Shareholders' equity and long-term (financial) liabilities (=Long-term capital) (LTC)
■ Current assets (except cash) (CA)	■ Current liabilities (except bank overdrafts) (CL)
■ Cash and cash equivalents (positive cash) (PC)	■ Bank overdrafts (negative cash) (BO)
Total assets	Total shareholders' equity and liabilities

A firm's financial structure is sometimes analyzed through the use of the structurally simplified balance sheet just presented, but the best way probably remains the preparation of a common-sized simplified balance sheet.

1.3.2 Cash equation: working capital, working capital need, and net cash

Principles One extension of the simplified balance sheet described in Table 15.5, beyond subjecting it to a common-size analysis, is the calculation of 'net cash' (net cash refers here to totally liquid assets, i.e., cash plus cash equivalents, including marketable securities).

The simplified balance sheet of Table 15.5 can be restructured in turn to identify and highlight some critical and different balances, which are very useful in both managing the firm and evaluating its income growth potential and risks. Table 15.6 provides an illustration of these metrics which, when combined, form the 'cash equation'.

Table 15.6 Cash equation

	Shareholders' equity and long-term (financial) liabilities (long-term capital or LTC)
(−)	Net fixed (non-current) assets, i.e., net of accumulated depreciation (FA)
(=)	Working capital or WC
	Current assets (except cash) (CA)
(−)	Current liabilities (except bank overdrafts) (CL)
(=)	Working capital need (financing need arising from the operating cycle) or WCN
	Positive cash (i.e., cash and cash equivalents) (PC)
(−)	Bank overdrafts (BO)
(=)	Net cash (NC)

Given that 'shareholders' equity plus liabilities' always equal total assets, Table 15.6 can be summarized as the 'cash equation':

Working capital − Working capital need = Net cash
or
Working capital = Working capital need + Net cash
or
Working capital need = Working capital − Net cash

Working capital can be calculated in two ways (as shown in Table 15.7), each reflecting a different view of business risks:

(a) shareholders' equity *plus* long-term liabilities *minus* fixed assets (how much excess long-term capital does the firm have over and above the funding of fixed (production capacity) assets?), or

(b) current assets except cash (i.e., inventories plus receivables) *plus* cash *minus* current or short-term liabilities and bank overdrafts (how much of the resources *needed* for the operating cycle are funded by long-term capital?)

The managerial interest of the '*working capital need*' comes from the fact that, when looking at the future results of a business, cash is an unknown, while the evolution of fixed and current assets (excluding cash) can be fairly well anticipated given that their amount will result from known decisions that will be made: new equipment may need to be acquired, total receivables may grow with increased sales volume, or increase/decrease if credit terms are modified, inventories may be reduced by the decision of the management to go towards a just-in-time sourcing and selling policy, etc. Working capital need is a metric that allows any analyst to anticipate how much additional cash (if any) might be needed to support the growth of the firm and thus anticipate whether the enterprise might need additional long-term or short-term capital. The manager, like the analyst, is very interested, for the same reasons as the latter, in knowing how much additional funding might be required to implement an action plan. Of course, the manager has more specific answers than the analyst, but the reasoning remains the same. During 'road shows', where managers address the financial community about their enterprise's financial and

Table 15.7 Links between the balance sheet structure and the cash equation

Assets	=	Shareholders' equity and liabilities
FA + CA + PC	=	LTC + CL + BO
Or, without breaking the equilibrium, by moving FA to the right and BO and CL to the left, we have:		
(CA − CL) + (PC − BO)	=	(LTC − FA)
WCN + NC	=	WC
Or by moving WCN to the right, we have:		
(PC − BO)	=	(LTC − FA) − (CA − CL)
NC	=	WC − WCN

market performance, the managers will, most of the time, explain how they will meet the working capital need in the coming years.

Each approach selected for defining working capital, although it provides the very same figure in the end, communicates a different emphasis in the message.

The 'long-term financing minus net fixed assets' approach (called (a) in Figure 15.3) gives an indication of the financial solidity of the enterprise and its state of health: it essentially identifies how much long-term capital is available to finance the operating cycle (see Figure 15.3).

The availability of long-term financing reduces the risk that would result if, by some (undoubtedly dramatic but still possible) event, short-term financing were totally removed. It measures the probability that the business would still be viable in these (extreme) circumstances. The question is answered by looking at what would *remain available* to keep the operating cycle going once the required assets have been partially or completely liquidated. This approach is passive, while the (b) approach (see Figure 15.4) is, on the other hand, more proactive. The second approach looks at what would be needed if these circumstances were to occur, assuming the managers' job is to maintain a viable operating cycle. There are, of course, many different ways to address the problem of keeping the cash pump active. Both approaches, however, give the same end figures, but not with the same emphasis.

Figure 15.3 The (a) approach: WC (a) = Shareholders' equity + Long-term liabilities − Fixed assets

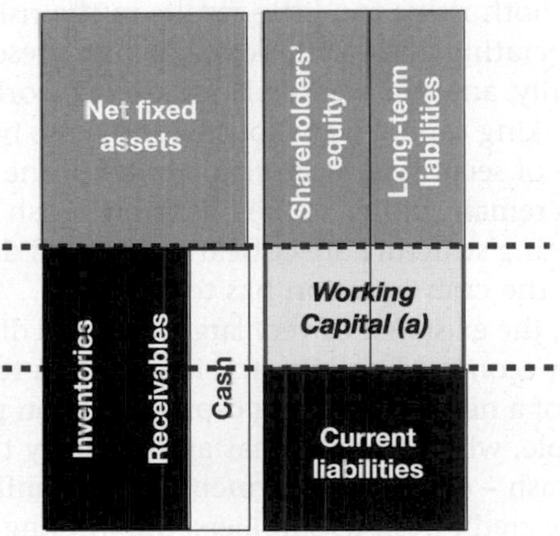

Figure 15.4 The (b) approach: WC (b) = Cash + Receivables + Inventories − Current liabilities

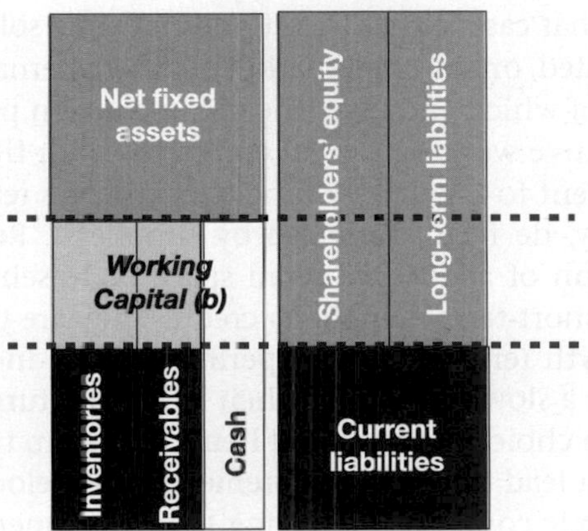

The approach in which the working capital is calculated by deduction of the current (short-term) financing from the current assets (the (b) approach mentioned above and in Figure 15.4) is the one most commonly used in North America. It highlights the capacity of the company to cover its short-term liabilities with its available cash, receivables, and inventories accounts, i.e. without needing to liquidate long-term (fixed) assets, a sale of which would endanger the going-concern nature of the firm. This approach emphasizes the ability of the firm to survive if it were to lose all short-term financial support. Clearly, if the operating cycle (cash pump) is to remain viable in the case of a (possibly total) short-term credit crunch, it is best to still have some cash, some receivables, and some inventories, a situation the working capital (approach (a) or (b)) illustrates well in both Figures 15.3 and 15.4.

From both approaches to the calculation of the working capital, it should be clear that there cannot be any generic normative, or rule-of-thumb value, for the level of working capital. The appropriate level of working capital is a function of the nature of the business, its opportunities and threats, its relationships with suppliers and customers, and of the specific business processes of the firm, which affect the speed and variance of the operating cycle.

The target working capital can be defined as the one that would keep the business afloat if all short-term financial supports were removed.

Working capital is a useful indicator, especially when viewed dynamically over time and in comparison with other enterprises operating in the same or similar economic or geographic sector of activity. The smaller the magnitude of the working capital, the less long-term capital is used to guarantee the security of the going concern. The larger the working capital, the more security the firm has in weathering storms. Too little or too much are both risky: too little results in the risk of bankruptcy; too much means financing the operating cycle with very expensive resources, thus reducing profitability.

Originally, analysts were only looking at working capital, ignoring the 'working capital need'. Working capital was expected to always be positive and was considered to represent a measure of security and survival ability of the firm. The structure of financing was considered to remain rather stable over time. Cash was not a critical issue. Today cash levels and financing structure are critical managerial decisions. They have become the unknown for which the cash equation has to be solved.

Further, the existence of very large retail and distribution enterprises and the development of the 'new economy' (service- and information-technology-based enterprises) have made the existence of a negative working capital situation perfectly acceptable in a growing economy. For example, when a retailer has an inventory that rotates 52 times a year, has customers that pay cash – credit card payment is very similar to cash payment – and obtains 45 days of effective credit from its suppliers, the working capital need will be, by construction, negative. In the retail business (unlike in a manufacturing enterprise), such a measure is not a sign of imminent danger (i.e., of possible inability to pay suppliers), as long as demand does not slow down. Of course, if demands slows down, or even plateaus, the incoming cash (current sales revenue) may not be sufficient to cover the accumulated short-term debt. In that case, either inventories must be sold at a large discount, or fixed assets must be liquidated, or any combination of other alternatives must be activated to raise the needed cash, all of which endanger the going-concern potential of the business.

A negative working capital computed with the (b) approach (negative working capital is equivalent to a source of funds) encourages retailers to continuously grow (that growth is actually, de facto, financed by suppliers). Retailers tend to finance long-term assets (acquisition of additional retail space or leaseholds in desirable locations, for example) through short-term (suppliers) credit. They are therefore simultaneously supporting their own growth (enlarging their perimeter) and increasing their risk in the case of a credit crunch or a slowing down of their inventory turnover (which could be due to events such as error in choice of the mix of items offered in the store, difficulty in sourcing, or increasingly long lead time for procurement from delocalized vendors) or a decline in sales (due to economic conditions affecting their customers or whatever other reason(s)).

The working capital need (working capital minus net cash) defines the financing need arising from the operating cycle. The cash equation establishes a critical liaison between the constituents of the balance sheet and allows users and analysts of financial information to evaluate the position of the firm with regard to its operating cycle.

Different scenarios of working capital need and net cash Every one of the three components of the cash equation defined above can be either positive or negative. The combination of the different signs leads to six different possible scenarios of (balance sheets) financial structures. These are illustrated in Figures 15.5(a) and (b).

Panel A illustrates the diverse combinations of working capital and working capital need. Panel B shows the three components of the cash equation relative to each other, following the same six cases as illustrated in panel A.

Working capital is illustrated in medium blue, while the working capital need is the difference between the current assets (minus cash), in dark blue, and current liabilities in light blue.

Figure 15.5(a) Panel A: Different types of financial structures of WC/NC

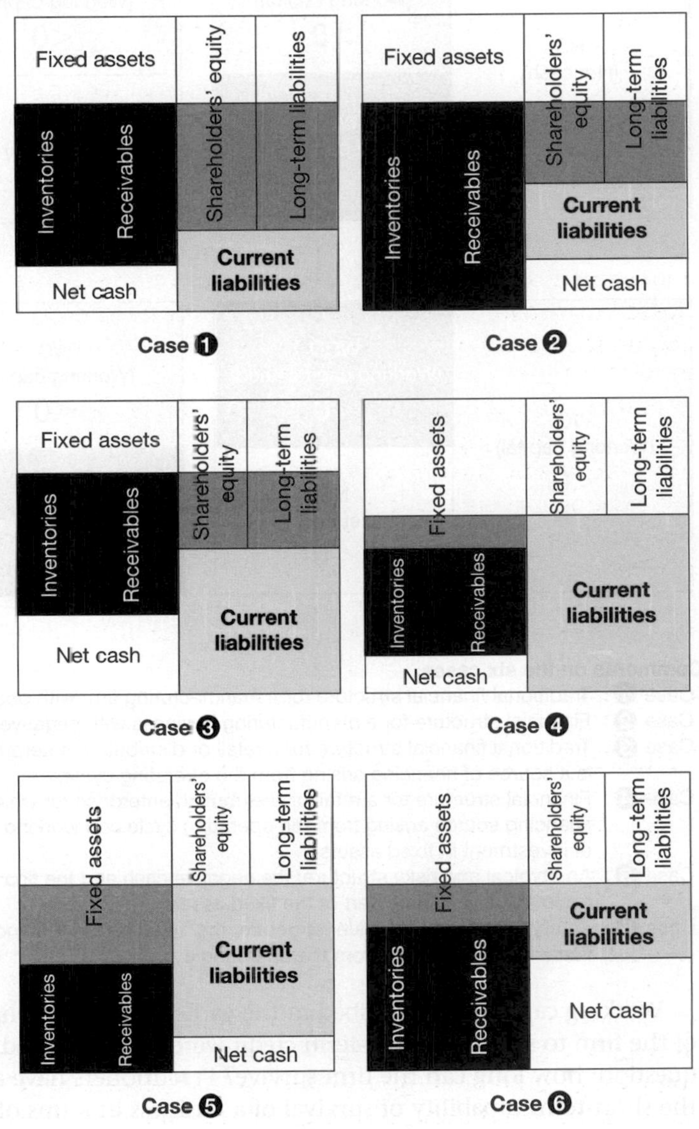

In Panel B three components of the cash equation are shown relative to each other, following in a more aggregated format, the six cases illustrated in Panel A.

Figure 15.5(b) Panel B: Different types of financial structures of WC/WCN/NC

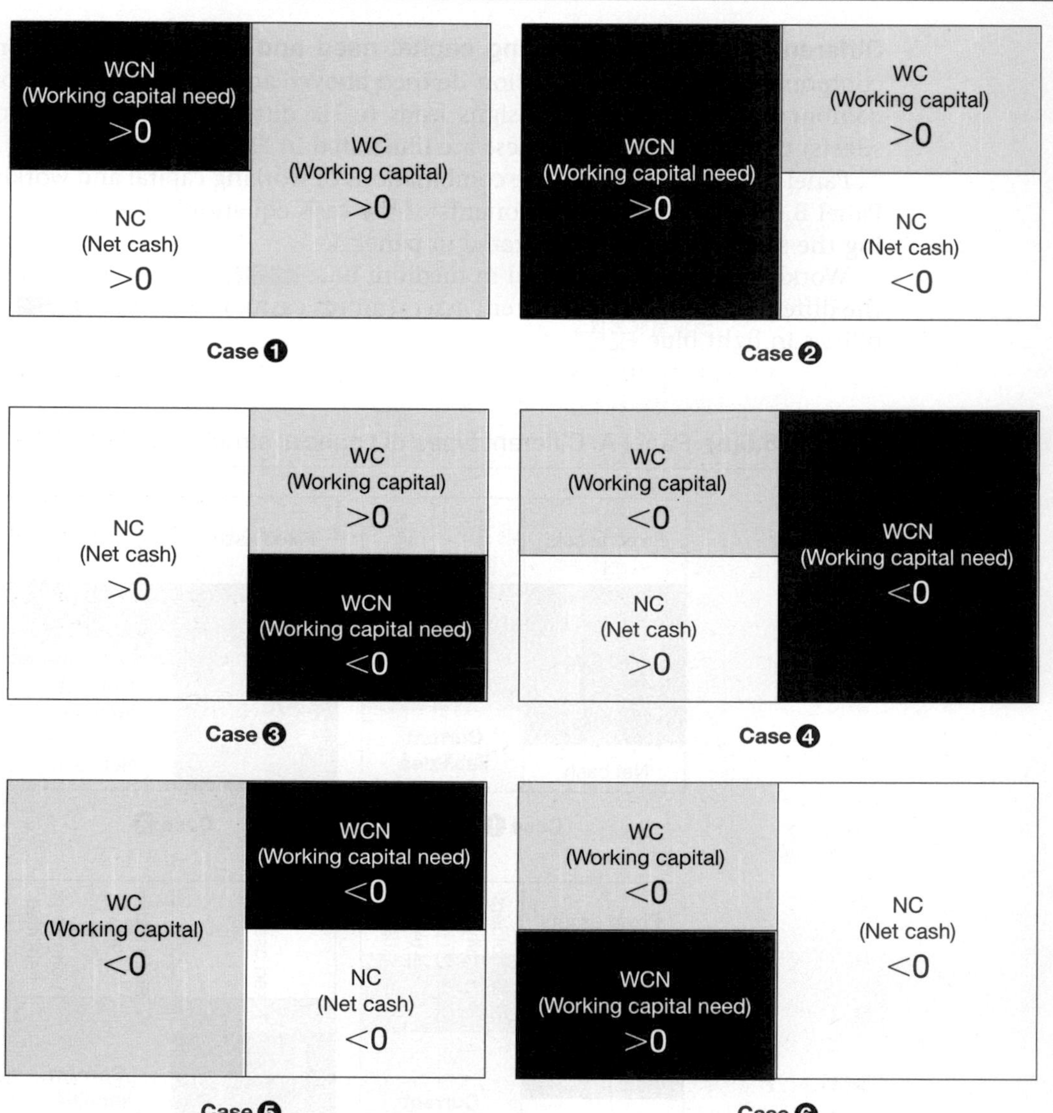

Comments on the six cases

Case ❶: Traditional financial structure for a manufacturing firm with positive net cash.
Case ❷: Financial structure for a manufacturing business with negative net cash.
Case ❸: Traditional financial structure for a retail or distribution enterprise for which the working capital need is a source of financing arising from the operating cycle.
Case ❹: Financial structure for a retail or distribution enterprise for which the working capital need is a financing source arising from the operating cycle and working capital is negative indicating an excess of investment in fixed assets.
Case ❺: An atypical and risky structure: the negative cash and the financing source arising from the operating cycle actually finance part of the fixed assets.
Case ❻: An atypical and even riskier structure: the negative cash finances both part of the fixed assets and the financing need arising from the operating cycle.

Working capital was described in the earlier part of the chapter as a measure of the ability of the firm to survive if short-term credit were to be canceled. It is therefore logical to ask the question: how long can the firm survive? Practitioners have acquired the habit of expressing the short-term capability of survival of a business in terms of numbers of days of sales.

Working capital need can also be expressed in terms of day of sales revenue. This metric highlights the survival potential of the firm in that it describes the number of sales activity days required to fund the working capital need. The essential definition of this metric is:

$$\text{Working capital need (in days of sales)} = \frac{\text{Working capital need}}{\text{Sales revenue}} \times 365$$

Appendix 15.2 presents some developments on this indicator and its usefulness.

1.4 Ratio analysis

A ratio is the quotient of two quantities, the numerator and the denominator. It assumes there is a relationship between the two elements of the quotient. The methods of computation and the interpretation of the meaning of any given ratio are more or less homogeneous between countries.

In financial analysis, quantities used in all ratio calculations come either from the financial statements or from descriptors of the business' activity (such as headcount, volume of units sold, share of market, etc.).

Ratio analysis is probably the most widely used analytical technique for interpreting financial statements for the benefit of decision makers and managers. However, caution should be exercised in using such tools.

1.4.1 Conditions of use of ratio analysis

A ratio assumes (reflects that) a meaningful relationship exists between two or more quantities descriptive of the business model. A causal interpretation of the variation over time of a ratio may weigh differently a variation of the numerator alone, of the denominator alone, or of both simultaneously.

It is also essential to verify both the logic of the relation assumed in the formula, and the coherence or homogeneity of the quantities that are being related in the ratio:

- they may not correspond to the same perimeter of analysis (possibly as the result of mergers, acquisition, closures or divestment, etc.);
- they may not result from similar accounting or classification rules (weighted average costing (WAC) versus FIFO costing of inventory flows, for example – see Chapter 9);
- they may not reflect the same operating assumptions (possibility of a divergence of views about the useful life of a tangible or intangible asset, or of the reality of its impairment);
- they may not be expressed in the same monetary units;
- they may have been calculated in different inflationary environments;
- they may not reflect the true underlying behavior of the relevant quantities as would be the case if there was a strong seasonality (for example, the average or opening and closing inventory may not reflect the impact on working capital need of the maximum inventory that was held during the peak of the season).

When using comparative ratio analysis, it is important to remember that the assumed causal relationship behind a certain value of a ratio may not have the same meaning in two different enterprises (Ford Motor Company relies heavily on outsourcing of many key car components, while Volkswagen believes in producing a much higher proportion of its own components, thus inventory-related ratios need to be interpreted only in the light of the specific strategy of each firm). It is also critical to consider that business practices between countries may be very different (supplier credit terms or the role of financial institutions as providers of long-term capital, for example).

Essentially, it is important to remember that ratios should be used to raise questions. They rarely allow a direct interpretation. A ratio calculation is generally the first step in an investigative research to get to the root cause of the situation described by the financial statements.

Some suggestions follow for an appropriate use of ratios in financial analysis.

- Base the analysis on appropriate comparisons (like risk factors, like industry, like markets, like size, etc.).
- Avoid 'information overload' that would likely result from computing seemingly different ratios, which, in reality, have the same informational content because, for example, they are the reverse of one another or the complement to 1. For example:
  - 'Equity/(Equity + Long-term debt)' is the complement to 1 of the ratio 'Long-term debt/(Equity + Long-term-debt)'.
  - The financial leverage ratio may be computed in two different but equivalent ways: 'Long-term debt/Equity' or 'Long-term debt/(Equity + Long-term debt)'.
  - The accounts receivable turnover ('Net sales/Average accounts receivable') is the reverse of the average collection period ('Average accounts receivable/Net sales × 365'). The same reasoning could be applied to inventory turnover, using COGS as the numerator rather than net sales revenue, of course.
- Some ratios are often referred to by somewhat standardized 'names' valid around the world such as 'current ratio' (Current assets/Current liabilities) or 'quick ratio' ([Cash equivalents plus Receivables]/Current liabilities). It is, however, essential to make sure that all parties in a discussion interpret each ratio to really mean the same thing and understand it to be constructed in the same way (especially given the mobility of personnel between firms). It may often prove best practice to provide the definition of the ratio next to the value reported, so as to avoid any ambiguity or misunderstanding.
- Be selective: avoid calculating too many ratios. Sometimes too many trees can hide the forest (the pattern) or the 'magnificent tree' you wanted to see (the ratio that could indicate whether or not there might be a serious problem needing to be addressed). A wisely selected number of relevant ratios will create a good picture of the prospects, performance, and financial position of a firm. Ratios should not be used in a 'fishing expedition'. The analyst should have an idea of what she or he is looking for before calculating ratios, and a few key ratios will always put the analyst on the path that will lead her or him to the problem issues if there are any. Only then is it useful to engage in drilling down in the facts.
- Be aware of the limits of ratios due to the timing of financial statements. The balance sheet gives figures valid on a given date, while the income statement or the cash flow statement gives figures that summarize a period. A ratio based on these figures may be misleading, in particular in the case of a seasonal or cyclical activity. One solution for balance sheet components consists, for example, in averaging figures: (a) from quarterly statements, if they are available, in a case of suspected seasonality; or (b) averaging beginning and ending balance sheet figures in the case of a large increase or decrease in the volume of business carried out by the enterprise over the period.
- Be aware that the validity of any ratio is limited by the quality of financial statements on which it is based.
- Be aware of the difficulty of interpreting negative ratios (because either the numerator or the denominator is negative – for instance, a loss or negative net income). In general, the negative sign of the ratio is meaningful and should be mentioned in any analysis, but the absolute value of the ratio is difficult to interpret and is often omitted altogether in reporting the analysis.

- Do not look for a standardized list of universally applicable ratios. Frustrating though it might feel, such a 'ready-to-use' list cannot exist. There are hundreds of possible different ratios, due to the existence of numerous items in the financial statements and the almost unlimited possibility of combinations. The ratios listed below, in subsection 1.4.3, are some examples of the most frequently used and discussed ratios. This list is not comprehensive, nor does it represent a sufficient or necessary set of ratios. These indicators may not be appropriate in a given strategic context or competitive environment, or for a specific enterprise or industry. Ratios often are economic-sector-specific, firm-specific, and always are time-specific. The analyst should first understand the business the firm is engaged in (i.e., its market strategy and business processes) before choosing the ratios that will prove to be relevant (rather than doing the opposite; although, sometimes, a few fundamental ratios may help the analyst identify some key additional questions that will allow her or him to understand the business).
- Ratios defined in a given country should only be used as a benchmark in analyzing financial statements of another country with great caution. Ratio analysis is dependent, among many other things, on accounting principles followed (although the generalization of IFRS/IAS adoption will somewhat reduce this difference), business practices, and local business culture. For instance, some ratios describing liquidity and solvency require a given presentation of the balance sheet (increasing liquidity or decreasing liquidity) (see Chapter 3), which may not be current reporting practice in that market. In countries where the balance sheet is presented by 'nature', the concepts of liquidity and solvency are more difficult to measure with the traditional ratios. Another example can be found in the diversity of practices in terms of accounts receivable credit terms in the world. A 90-day customer credit might be a good business practice in Greece and an indication of an abnormal relation with the customer in Denmark or Finland. It is not unusual in the US to hear furniture stores promote a policy of 12 months of 'free (customer) credit', while such a practice would be considered unusual and, possibly unethical, in France.
- Financial statement analysis is based on judgment calls and contextual interpretation on the part of the analyst. Never overestimate the explanatory power of any ratio. Always place ratio analysis within a more comprehensive analysis of the whole set of financial statements and of the business.

1.4.2 Comparisons of ratios

There are three possible different types of comparisons in the creation of ratios. They are mentioned in Figure 15.6.

Figure 15.6 Ratio comparisons

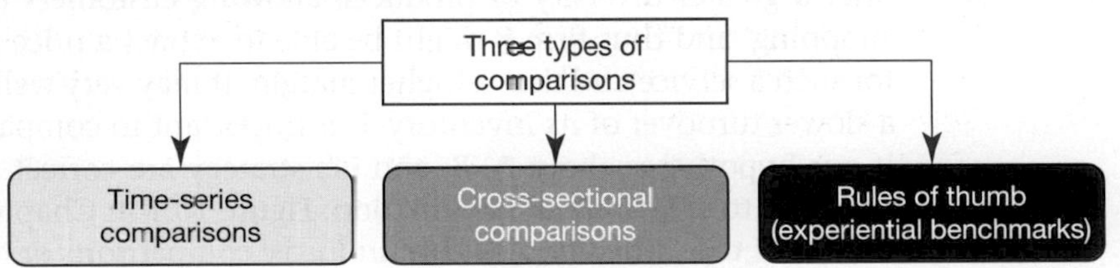

1. **Time-series comparisons** (or **longitudinal ratio analysis**): Ratios are computed yearly or more frequently and use data of a given period of time. When available, it is always a good idea to use quarterly data to be able to use sliding periods such as defining a running year as four quarters, dropping the oldest quarter and adding the new one each time a new quarterly data set is available. The ratios reflecting one year of activity are then compared to the historical ratios of the business for previous periods of equivalent duration. Although the length of the period over which the evolution

of ratio should be analyzed is not standardized, practice seems to imply that calculating and comparing ratios over a three-year sliding period generally provides enough relevant and useful information to decision makers, without running into the risk of a dramatic evolution of either business context or business processes.

Example:

	X1	X2	X3
COGS to sales (net of VAT or sales tax)	55%	57%	54%

It appears that in year X2 this business has experienced a deterioration of its gross margin and that, in year X3, it has benefited from an improvement. Further inquiry is required to understand why this happened. Neither a causal explanation nor a recommended action will rise directly from the data. The managers of this firm should not take solace in the fact that X3 did clearly show an improvement over X2. Unless they have a clear understanding of the reasons for the improvement, they know nothing. Once they know why the situation evolved positively, they will be able to create, or maintain, the conditions needed to ensure the continuation, or even further improvement, of the positive trend.

2. **Cross-sectional comparisons**: Ratios can be compared to equivalent ratios of other enterprises, a competitor for instance, or against industry averages. One limit of industry comparisons stems from the fact that there is no such thing as an 'average business process' or an 'average strategy'. Furthermore, the business process and activities of compared firms rarely offer a homogeneous or consistent basis for comparison. Another issue is the difficulty in obtaining the relevant ratios for competitors or businesses in the same economic sector (this topic will be developed in the second part of this chapter).

Example:

	Firm A	Firm B	Firm C
Average days of inventory available (Average inventory level /COGS) × 365	25	42	27

Firm B appears to be an outlier in this economic sector (in any sector a fast turnover of inventories is generally considered preferable to a slower one). However, firm B's strategy can be different from that of A and C. For example, A and C may offer little variety in their portfolio of products and sell, probably, at low margins, while B might offer a greater diversity of products, allowing customers to experience 'single stop shopping' and thus firm B might be able to extract a price premium from customers for such a service and thus a higher margin. It may very well be 'normal' for B to have a slower turnover of its inventory. It is important to compare only comparables and, if our hypotheses about A, B, and C's strategy are correct, the sample was not well designed to create useful information. Figure 10.1 in Chapter 10, offers another illustration of the difficulty of within-industry comparisons or of designing a meaningful sample (in that case about the ratio of accounts receivable over total assets).

3. **Rules of thumb (experiential benchmarks)**: Ratios can be compared to selected references. These can either be measures derived from competitors (such as comparing to the 'best in class' – with all the problems implied by the concept) or rules of thumb based on industry-wide 'experience'. For example, one often speaks of the rule of the three thirds for a 'sound' structure of equity and liabilities in the balance sheet: this rule implies shareholders' equity represent one third of total assets, long-term liabilities another third, and short-term liabilities the final third.

Such references for interpreting ratios can prove to be difficult to use effectively for any of the following reasons, and probably even many more:

- If the ratio is compared to industry-wide statistics or norms, all problems already raised about cross-sectional comparisons apply. For example, the rule that used to say that the working capital was supposed to be positive is continuously challenged (appropriately) in distribution and retail activities. Another rule of three thirds applies to the restaurant business in which one often hears that, in order to be 'normally' profitable, the price ought to be three times the cost of the raw materials. But even if this is often true, the same so-called rule of thumb probably cannot apply at the same time to fast-food establishments or institutional kitchens (here the rule of thumb is considered to be price should be 'twice' the cost of materials) or gastronomic restaurants (where the rule of thumb is closer to price equals four–six times the cost of raw materials and can even reach a 10-fold mark-up). The location of the restaurant may also have a great impact on the relevant benchmark: labor cost or rent per square meter in a capital city may be vastly different from that in rural areas.
- If the ratio is based on a 'rule of thumb' built over the years without any reasoned basis, the results of the meaningfulness of any analysis based on this ratio may be then subjected to doubt. For example, one often hears that a healthy firm is one that 'generates at least €150,000 of revenue (or some other figure) per person employed'. However, such a rule (or belief) does not take into account the fact enterprises differ vastly in their degree of value addition or in the intrinsic role of labor in the generation of revenue. Not only labor content may be different, but raw materials quality and price may also differ: seemingly similar raw materials in a three-star restaurant probably are more expensive than they are in a neighborhood diner, and both headcount and labor costs are probably vastly different between the two; brokers might have to handle a huge amount of trade to be able to cover the cost of their headcount; software or computer games manufacturers incur most of their costs in the design phase, not in the manufacturing and distribution phase of their products; oil refiners might see their raw material cost represent 90% of their costs, while an oil-based fine chemistry firm might see its cost of oil (as raw material) represent not more than 30% of its total costs, etc.

1.4.3 Some key ratios

Ratios are organized in four categories, each serving some of the needs expressed by shareholders or decision-makers: (a) evaluation of short-term liquidity and solvency; (b) evaluation of long-term solvency and financial leverage; (c) evaluation of profitability and generation of profitability; and (d) measures of shareholders' return.

Table 15.8 lists some key ratios, and the reader is reminded to remain very cautious in using such a list. The ratios mentioned may not all be appropriate or the best suited ones for any given situation. This list is a 'tool box', and the user must first identify the nature and issues of the business evaluated before selecting the appropriate tools from the box.

There are hundreds of possible different ratios, since the number of combinations of all the items on the financial statements, plus the possibility of relating these to non-financial activity descriptors, is almost limitless. As a consequence, ratios are frequently classified in subgroups that reflect a particular aspect of financial performance or position. For example, Sutton (2004) additionally distinguishes profitability ratios from financial risks ratios.

1.4.4 Additional remarks about ratios computation

Table 15.8 includes the 'average payment period' (Accounts payable/Purchases × 365), but it is not always easy for an outside analyst to calculate such a ratio, however useful it might be: the amount of the purchases is not provided in an income statement by function. However, in the case of businesses presenting their income statement by nature, this

Table 15.8 Some key ratios[3]

Name of the ratios	Computation	Comments
Short-term liquidity ratios (firm's ability to finance its day-to-day operations and to pay its liabilities as they fall due)		
Current ratio (or working capital ratio)	Current assets[4]/Current liabilities (creditors: amounts falling due within one year)[5]	Firm's ability to pay its current liabilities from its current assets Rule of thumb: 2:1 as an 'ideal'
Quick ratio (or quick asset or acid-test or liquidity)	(Cash + Marketable securities + Accounts receivable)/Current liabilities	Firm's ability to pay its current liabilities from its current assets excluding the sale of inventories
Cash ratio	(Cash + Marketable securities)/ Current liabilities	Firm's ability to pay its current liabilities from its cash and cash equivalents
Average collection period	[(Accounts receivable Year 2 + Accounts receivable Year 1)/2 × 365]/Sales	Average length of time to collect accounts receivable
Average payment period	[(Accounts payable Year 2 + Accounts payable Year 1)/2 × 365]/Purchases of goods and services	Average length of time to pay accounts payable
Inventory turnover	Cost of sales/[(Inventories Year 2 + Inventories Year 1)/2]	Number of times that a firm sells or turns over its inventories per year
Long-term solvency ratios (firm's ability to pay its long-term liabilities)		
Debt ratio	Total debt/Total assets	Firm's debt-paying ability
Debt to equity ratio	Debt[6]/Shareholders' equity or Debt/ (Shareholders' equity + Debt)	The lower this ratio, the better the company's position
Debt to tangible net worth	Debt/(Shareholders' equity – Intangible assets)	Firm's degree of financial leverage
Long-term debt to equity ratio	Long-term debt/Shareholders' equity or Long-term debt/(Shareholders' equity + Long-term debt)	Firm's long-term debt-paying ability The lower this ratio, the better the company's position Firm's degree of financial leverage
Interest coverage ratio (interest cover ratio)	Operating income (before interest expense and income taxes)/ Interest expense	Number of times that a firm's interest expense is covered by operation earnings Rule of thumb: minimum of 5
Profitability ratios (measure of the firm's performance)		
Return on shareholders' equity (ROE)	Net income/Average equity[7] or Income before interest and tax/Average equity	Return to shareholders
Return on investment (ROI) (return on capital employed or ROCE)	Net income/(Average long-term liabilities + Equity) = Net income/Capital employed or Earnings before interest and tax (EBIT)/ Capital employed	Measure of the income earned on the invested capital
Gross profit rate (gross profit margin)	Gross profit/Sales	Percentage of each sales currency unit not absorbed by the cost of sales
Return on sales (net profit margin)	Net income/Sales	Percentage of each sales currency unit that contributes to net income
Asset turnover	Sales/[(Assets Year 2 + Assets Year 1)/2]	Firm's ability to generate sales relative to its investment in assets

Table 15.8 *(Continued)*

Name of the ratios	Computation	Comments
Return on assets (ROA)	Net income/[(Assets Year 2 + Assets Year 1)/2]	Firm's ability to use its assets to create profits
Sales per employee	Sales/Number of employees	Measure of the sales productivity of the workforce
Market price and dividend ratios (capital markets' perception of the firm's share)		
Earnings per share	Net income/Average shares outstanding	Measure of share performance
Price/earnings ratio (P/E or PER)	Market price per share/Earnings per share	Amount that investors are willing to pay for each currency unit of a firm's earnings – Market confidence in a company
Market to book ratio	Market price per share/Book value per share	Amount that investors are willing to pay for each currency unit of a firm's net assets
Dividend yield ratio	Cash dividends per share/Market price per share	Cash return on the investment in a company
Dividend pay-out ratio	Cash dividends per share/Earnings per share	Proportion of earnings paid out in the form of dividends

ratio is easily and frequently computed. It is also a ratio that is pretty systematically calculated in any internal financial analysis, as it is a key element of the management of the speed of the operating cash cycle.

When net income is used in ratios, it is sometimes replaced by the earnings before interest and taxation (EBIT) because doing so takes away the financing policy effect as well as the income tax effects, thus facilitating cross-sectional and longitudinal comparisons.

There is a link between several 'return' ratios, as shown in Figure 15.7.

Developing a ratio into its components allows the manager and an analyst alike to understand better the trade-offs that are open to the firm. For example, return on sales and asset turnover can be combined as shown in Figure 15.8.

Figure 15.7 Pyramid of ratios

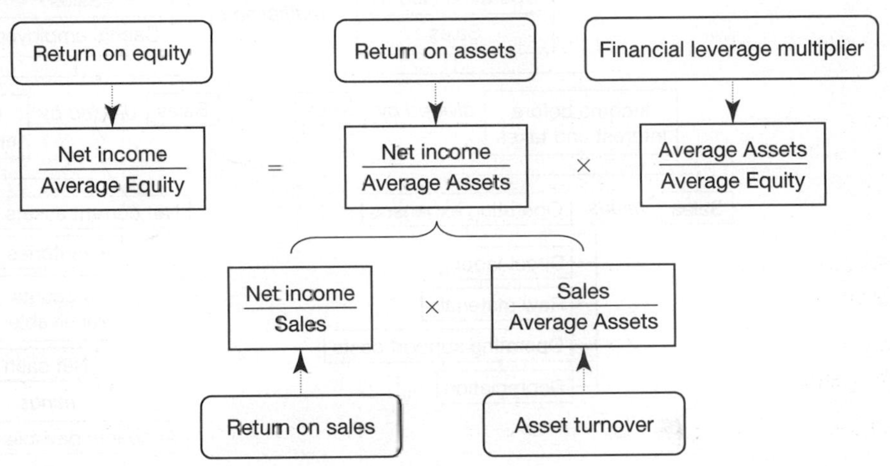

In Figure 15.8 we can see that very different strategies can lead to the same return on assets: one firm, with a high operating margin (Profit /Sales revenue) of 6% and a slow turnover of assets of 2, enjoys a ROA of 12%, and another firm with a low operating margin of 2% but a high turnover of assets of 6 also enjoys an ROA of 12%. We can see that either firm can improve their ROA by increasing either or both of the two decision variables. There is a real improvement in the situation of the firm only if it can move to a 'higher' iso-curve. The two firms may have the same ROA but their strategies are very different and managers and analyst need to understand what firm-specific actions can be taken to move to a higher iso-curve.

Figure 15.8 Iso-curves of ROA

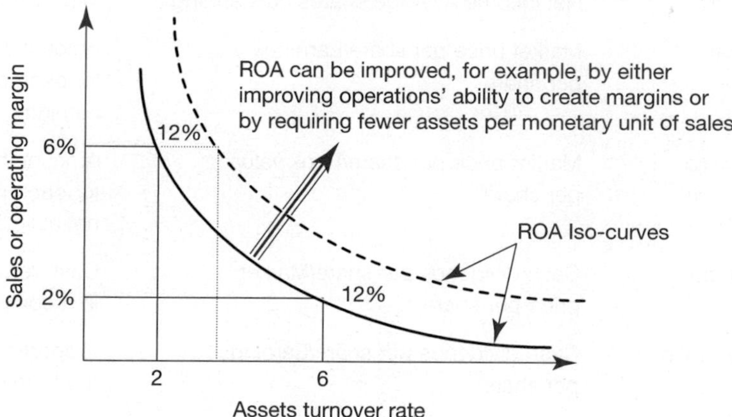

The pyramid of ratios was even developed as a management tool by Donaldson Brown for DuPont de Nemours in the US in the 1920s. It is illustrated in Figure 15.9, where ROCE stands for return on capital employed, and is thus applicable to almost any subset of a business entity.

Figure 15.9 The 'DuPont formula'

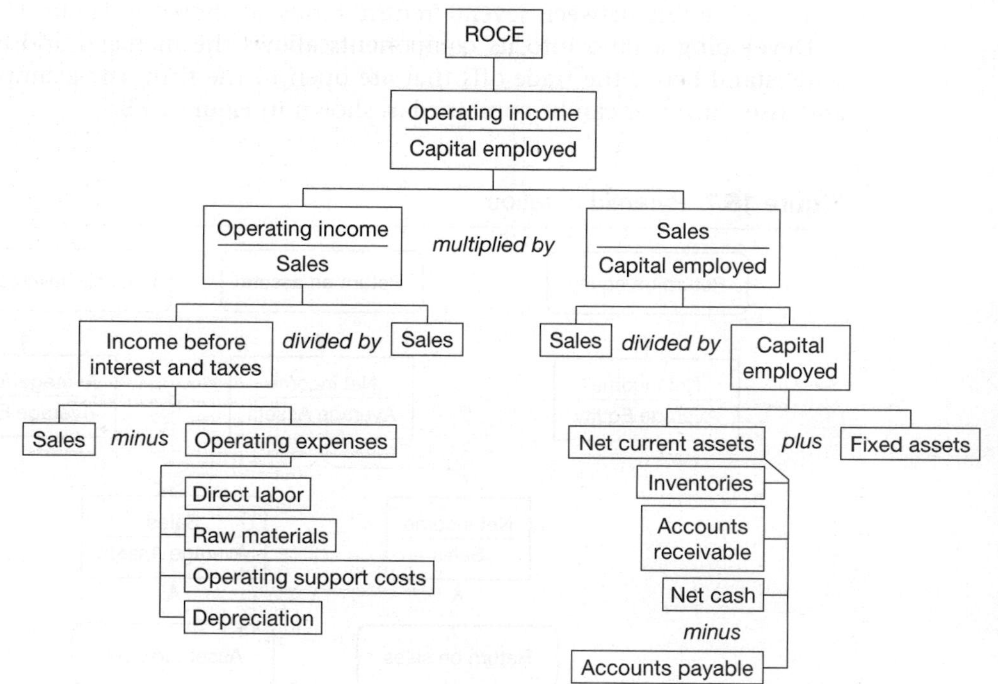

Figure 15.10 Financial footprint (An Excel version of this document is available on the book's dedicated website)

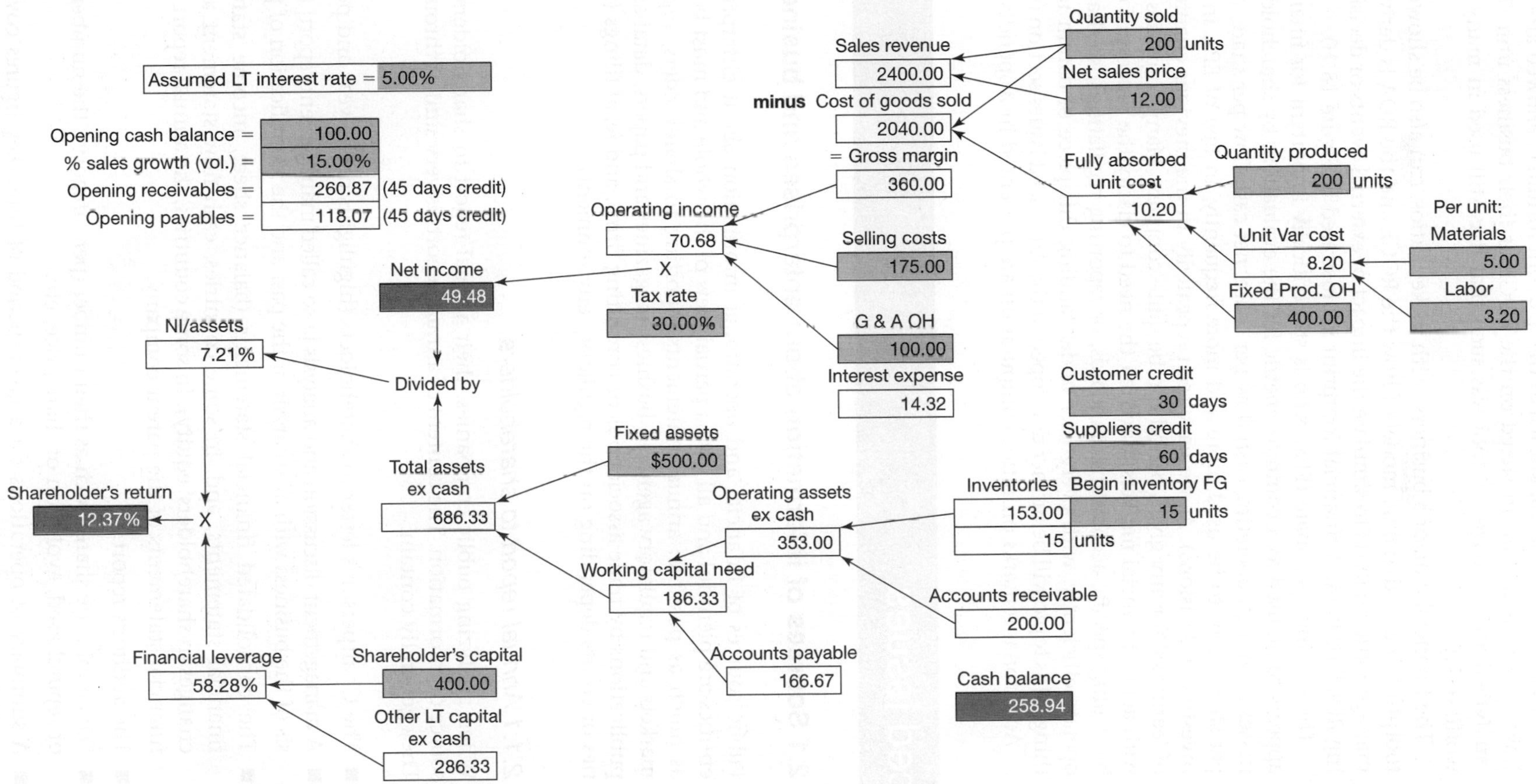

Assumed LT interest rate = 5.00%

Opening cash balance = 100.00
% sales growth (vol.) = 15.00%
Opening receivables = 260.87 (45 days credit)
Opening payables = 118.07 (45 days credit)

Quantity sold 200 units
Net sales price 12.00
Sales revenue 2400.00
minus Cost of goods sold 2040.00
= Gross margin 360.00
Fully absorbed unit cost 10.20
Quantity produced 200 units
Unit Var cost 8.20
Fixed Prod. OH 400.00
Per unit:
Materials 5.00
Labor 3.20
Selling costs 175.00
G & A OH 100.00
Interest expense 14.32
Operating income 70.68
X
Tax rate 30.00%
Net income 49.48
Divided by
NI/assets 7.21%
Customer credit 30 days
Suppliers credit 60 days
Begin inventory FG 15 units
Inventories 153.00
15 units
Accounts receivable 200.00
Operating assets ex cash 353.00
Accounts payable 166.67
Working capital need 186.33
Fixed assets $500.00
Total assets ex cash 686.33
Cash balance 258.94
Shareholder's capital 400.00
Other LT capital ex cash 286.33
Financial leverage 58.28%
X
Shareholder's return 12.37%

The set of linked ratios, known as the 'DuPont formula', allowed any manager to know how her or his action impacted on the ROCE of their business unit. The power of this 'analytical and managerial' tool was such that it is still used in many firms around the world today.

The financial data of a business, with its key ratios, can also be shown as the 'financial footprint', i.e., a dynamic model of how the ROCE and the ROA is derived, thus allowing managers and analysts to simulate the impact of external events or decisions on the resulting ROCE or ROA. A financial footprint is illustrated in Figure 15.10.

The earnings per share (EPS) ratio is still critically important for financial markets as it appears to be used as a common metric for the evaluation, by shareholders, of most businesses (although operating cash flow per share, net cash flow per share, and free cash flow per share seem to be used more and more frequently, in lieu of EPS, in making financial investment decisions). As we have seen repeatedly in the previous chapters, the definition of 'earnings' for any given period can be quite complex. Many countries (essentially those with active financial markets) have felt the need to clarify the process of calculation of EPS by issuing specific accounting standards, or reporting regulations, so that the markets can operate efficiently, with every user understanding this piece of datum to mean the same thing. This topic will be further developed in the Advanced issues section (see § 2.2.1 below).

Additional remarks on ratios computation are presented in Appendix 15.3.

2 Advanced issues

2.1 Sources of information about enterprises and business entities

Public sources of financial and operational information about enterprises and business entities are plentiful and all give a partial view of the whole and must be used conjointly, as much as possible: annual statements reporting to shareholders, reports to financial markets and regulatory agencies, business magazines and papers, databases and statistical publications by trade associations or consulting firms, and legal filings (with tax authorities or courts depending on the regulatory environment).

2.1.1 Annual report to shareholders

When analyzing public companies, their annual report to shareholders is an important source of information. The content of annual reports is very similar throughout the world. They generally contain:

- The Chairperson's letter to shareholders (highlights of the year and perspectives).
- A management discussion and analysis [also called management report] (segmental analysis of the business with an analysis of the past and the identification of perspectives).
- The consolidated financial statements (balance sheet, income statement, notes to financial statements, and, in some countries, cash flow statement and statement of changes in shareholders' equity). In some countries, the annual report also includes the financial statements of the parent company.
- The auditor's report.
- Data about the shares such as their number (per category), the number of shares issued or repurchased, evolution of share price, etc.
- A summary of operations for a given period of time (key figures covering a five-year period in general).

Annual reports can be obtained in an electronic format in different ways:

- Access to the company's website and the section 'financials' or 'investors relations' either through www.yahoo.com or www.google.com. Yahoo.com offers a particularly interesting finance section where core analyses of quoted firms can often be accessed freely. One easy way to reach directly the investor relations section of an enterprise's website is to use www.google.com, type the name of the company, and click on 'I'm feeling lucky' instead of 'Google search'.
- Access to the financial markets regulator's website, in countries where this regulator provides an access to annual reports filed by listed companies (e.g., in the USA, www.sec.gov and the Edgar database, in France through www.amf-france.org, or, in Spain at www.cnmv.es).
- Access to a commercial database, such as www.infinancials.com, which contains a collection of annual reports, including archives.

2.1.2 Business newspapers and magazines, specialized magazines

All countries have business and financial magazines and newspapers reporting news and current events about the financial and economic world. They represent a wealth of information, which can be helpful for financial analysts. Appendix 15.4 provides a partial list of such magazines and newspapers.

2.1.3 Databases and statistics publications

Appendix 15.5 lists several sources of government statistics or publications from private organizations.

2.1.4 Financial statements filed with tax or judicial authorities

In some countries (mainly European countries), there is an obligation for certain enterprises (in general limited liability companies) to file their financial statements with a government agency such as the fiscal administration or the judiciary. These filing obligations are described in Appendix 15.6 for several countries.

2.2 Measures of return to investors

The performance of an enterprise, both in terms of past results and in terms of potential or future prospects of value creation, is not all that the shareholders want to monitor. They want to see whether they earn enough to keep their money invested in this firm at that level of risk or whether they ought to move it to another business. Two families of indicators are used here: earnings per share and return on capital invested.

2.2.1 Earnings per share

As mentioned earlier, earnings per share (EPS) remain one of the prime metrics used by financial markets. It is the ratio of net income after taxes (and after preferred dividends if there are any)[8] to average number of shares during the period for which the income has been calculated. As we have seen, the calculation of earnings (income) for the numerator as well as the definition of the denominator (how to reflect the coexistence of ordinary, preference and treasury shares?) can be complex. Many countries have issued statements or standards aimed at clarifying how earnings, denominator shares, and, consequently, earnings per share ought to be calculated for public reporting. Examples of such regulations are FRS 14 in the UK (ASB 1998) and SFAS 128 in the US (FASB 1997). At the international level, IASB (2003) revised IAS 33 in 2003.

A particularly bothersome difficulty comes from the existence of 'share equivalents' such as stock options, stock warrants, or convertible instruments, for example convertible bonds which can be turned into shares any time the conditions specified when they were issued are met. The fully diluted earnings per share figure reveals the risk that the EPS may be much lower than currently calculated if all holders of options or warrants or convertible instruments were to effectively convert their rights into shares.

For example, let us assume a high-tech firm with a capital of one million CU (100,000 shares with a 10 CU par) has issued stock options to attract and retain managerial and creative talent. Options amount to a potential of 200,000 shares. Let us assume that today, for the most recent period of activity, the EPS was 2 CU per share (i.e., total earnings were 200,000 CU, thus EPS = 2 = 200,000 CU/100,000 shares). If total earnings were to increase by 50% to 300,000 CU in the next year, and all options were exercised, the original shareholders would see, at their great dismay, the EPS figure fall to only 1 CU:

$$\frac{200{,}000 \times 1.5}{100{,}000 + 200{,}000} = 1$$

Each above mentioned standard prescribes principles for the determination and presentation of earnings per share that improve comparisons of performance between enterprises in one period and between different periods for the same enterprise.

All regulations adopted apply to publicly traded companies and specifically to their consolidated financial statements. However, these rules and recommendations are common sense and may usefully be applied to not-publicly traded companies and to unconsolidated financial statements.

IAS 33 (IASB 2003) makes a distinction between basic and diluted earnings per share. Numerous companies compute adjusted earnings after the impact of both operating and non-operating exceptional items and amortization/impairment of goodwill in order to provide a better understanding of the underlying performance of the company on a normalized basis. By doing so, four earnings per share may be computed:

- basic EPS;
- diluted EPS;
- adjusted basic EPS;
- adjusted diluted EPS.

Basic earnings per share Basic earnings per share is defined as (IAS 33, IASB 2003: § 10):

$$\frac{\text{Profit or loss for the period attributable to ordinary equity holders of the parent entity}}{\text{Time-weighted average number of ordinary shares outstanding during the period}}$$

In this definition, the profit is computed after deduction of any preference dividends. The weighted average number of ordinary shares outstanding during the period is computed according to one of the two methods shown in Table 15.9.

'The time-weighting factor is the number of days that the shares are outstanding as a proportion of the total number of days in the period' (IAS 33: § 20). Moreover, as shown in Table 15.9, there are two different ways to compute the weighted average number of outstanding shares (both give the same result).

Table 15.9 Time-weighted average number of shares

Data:		Shares issued (1)	Treasury shares (2)	Shares outstanding	
1 January X1	Balance at beginning of year	3,100	400	2,700	= (1) − (2)
30 April X1	Issue of new shares for cash	900	–	3,600	
1 November X1	Purchase of treasury shares for cash	–	600	3,000	
31 December X1	Balance at end of year	4,000	1,000	3,000	= (1) − (2)

		Number of months shares Balance (1)	Weighted were held (2)	balance (1) × (2)/12
Method 1	1 January X1–30 April X1	2,700	4	900
	1 May X1–30 October X1	3,600	6	1,800
	1 November X1–31 December X1	3,000	2	500
	Weighted average number of shares			3,200
Method 2	1 January X1–31 December X1	2,700	12	2,700
	30 April X1–31 December X1	900	8	600
	1 November X1–31 December X1	−600	2	−100
	Weighted average number of shares			3,200

Diluted earnings per share

Principles As indicated in IAS 33 (IASB 2003: § 31): 'for the purpose of calculating diluted earnings per share, an entity shall adjust profit or loss attributable to ordinary equity holders of the parent entity, and the weighted average number of shares outstanding, for the effects of all dilutive potential ordinary shares'. The term 'potential ordinary share', as seen in Chapter 11, refers to a variety of financial instruments or other contracts that may entitle its holder to ordinary shares.

The amount of profit or loss pertaining to ordinary shares must be adjusted (§ 33) by the following after-tax elements:

- 'Any dividends or other items related to dilutive potential ordinary shares deducted in arriving at profit or loss attributable to ordinary equity holders (...);
- Any interest recognized in the period related to dilutive potential ordinary shares; and
- Any other changes in income or expense that would result from the conversion of the dilutive potential ordinary shares'.

In other words, the profit or loss of the period is increased (decreased) by the amount of dividends, interest, and other income or expense that would be saved (added) on the conversion of the dilutive potential ordinary shares into ordinary shares. Table 15.10 presents an example of computation of diluted earnings per share based on the conversion of bonds.

In our example, the shareholders took the risk of seeing their EPS diluted by 2.5% in order to attract bond financing at an attractive rate or in a market that was not favorable. Of course, if the dilution penalty for current shareholders evolves unfavorably (i.e., the dilution loss may become greater than 2.5%), they may decide (if the covenants covering

Table 15.10 Computation of diluted earnings per share

Reported net income (in CU) (net of all interest expenses)	(1)	5,000
Number of ordinary shares outstanding	(2)	2,500
Basic earnings per share (CU per share)	(3) = (1)/(2)	2
Number of convertible bonds (face value 5 CU, coupon rate 5%)	(4)	200
Conditions of conversion: 10 bonds for 4 shares	(5)	0.4
Number of new shares issued from the conversion	(6) = (4) × (5)	80
Interest expense for the current year relating to the liability component of the convertible bond (it would not be incurred if the conversion were to take place, so we'll have to add it back to (1))	(7) = 200 × 5 × 0.05	50
Current and deferred tax shield relating to that interest expense (tax rate 40%). We lose the tax deductibility of interests since interest expense would no longer exist from this source; this would reduce net reported income by that much.	(8)	20
Adjusted net profit (reflects the hypothetical complete conversion of the bonds)	(9) = (1) + (7) − (8)	5,030
Number of ordinary shares used to compute diluted earnings per share	(10) = (2) + (6)	2,580
Diluted earnings per share after assumed conversion	(11) = (9)/(10)	1.95
Effect of the potential dilution (1.95 − 2.00)/2.00 = −2.5%		2.5%

the bonds allow it) to either call the bonds and reimburse the lenders, or to force the conversion to lock-in the dilution risk.

Options, warrants and their equivalents are also covered in IAS 33: 'For the purpose of calculating diluted earnings per share, an entity shall assume the exercise of dilutive options and warrants of the entity. The assumed proceeds from these instruments shall be regarded as having been received from the issue of ordinary shares at the average market price of ordinary shares during the period. The difference between the number of ordinary shares issued and the number of ordinary shares that would have been issued at the average market price of ordinary shares during the period shall be treated as an issue of ordinary shares for no consideration' (IASB, IAS 33: § 45).

'Options and warrants are dilutive when they would result in the issue of ordinary shares for less than the average market price of ordinary shares during the period. The amount of the dilution is the average market price of ordinary shares during the period minus the issue price. Therefore, to calculate diluted earnings per share, potential ordinary shares are treated as consisting of both the following:

(a) A contract to issue a certain number of the ordinary shares at their average market price during the period. Such ordinary shares are assumed to be fairly priced and to be neither dilutive nor antidilutive. They are ignored in the calculation of diluted earnings per share.

(b) A contract to issue the remaining ordinary shares for no consideration. Such ordinary shares generate no proceeds and have no effect on profit or loss attributable to ordinary shares outstanding. Therefore, such shares are dilutive and are added to the number of ordinary shares outstanding in the calculation of diluted earnings per share' (IAS 33: § 46).

Real-life example Irish Continental Group

(Ireland – UK/Irish GAAP – *Source*: Annual report 2004 – Shipping, transport, and leisure group principally engaged in the transport of passengers and cars [Irish Ferries], freight, and containers)

Note 9 to the financial statements provides a detailed computation of earnings per share.

Note 9. Earnings per share unit

Basic earnings per share:		**2004**	**2003**
Basic earnings per share is calculated as follows:			
Numerator: Profit attributable to shareholders (€ millions)	(1)	8.0	17.4
Denominator: Weighted average number of shares in issue (millions of shares)	(2)	23.5	24.3
Basic earnings per share (cents of €)	(3) = (1)/(2) × 100	34.0	71.6
Diluted earnings per share:		**2004**	**2003**
Diluted earnings per share is calculated as follows:			
Numerator: Profit attributable to shareholders (€ millions)	(4)	8.0	17.4
Denominator: Weighted average number of shares in issue, including options exercisable at the date of this report (millions of shares)	(5)	23.6	24.4
Diluted earnings per share (cents of €)	(6) = (4)/(5) × 100	33.9	71.3

The weighted average [number of] shares used in the calculation of diluted earnings per share may be reconciled with the basic average [number of] shares as follows:

		2004	2003
Total options in issue (number of shares)	(7)	1,936,500	2,112,700
Non-dilutive options (number of shares)	(8)	(1,721,500)	(1,757,000)
Dilutive options (number of shares)	(9) = (7) + (8)	215,000	355,700
Average option exercise price (in cents of €)	(10)	561	565
Average fair value of share price during the year (in cents of €)	(11)	1097	855
Number of shares which would have to be issued at fair value (rounded figures on the basis of cents of €)	(12) = −[(9) × (10)]/(11)	(109,966)	(234,883)
Dilutive options (number of shares) [net amount]	(13) = (9) + (12)	105,034	120,817
Basic weighted average shares (number of shares)	(14)	23,503,473	24,296,694
Diluted weighted average shares (number of shares)	(14) = (13) + (14)	23,608,507	24,417,511

Adjusted earnings per share:
The numerator for adjusted earnings per share is the adjusted profit attributable to shareholders i.e., profit before goodwill and exceptional item of €19.9 m (2003: €22.2 m). The denominator for adjusted earnings per share is the weighted average number of shares in issue of 23.5 m (2003: 24.3 m). Adjusted earnings per share is reconciled to basic earnings per share as follows:

	€cents	2004	2003
Basic earnings per share		34.0	71.6
Exceptional items – restructuring provision		50.7	19.8
Adjusted earnings per share		84.7	91.4

The number of shares that would have been issued at fair value [line (12)] is computed by applying the ratio [average option price over average fair value] to the number of options exercisable.

2.2.2 Residual income and economic value added

Principles The idea behind these methods is that the profit reported in the accounting statements only accounts for the cost of borrowed capital when, in fact, shareholders also have provided capital and expect a return (higher even than that of borrowed capital because shareholders assume much more risk than banks or bond lenders do).

In this book, and in this section particularly, we separate the firm's decisions from those made by individual shareholders. A shareholder may acquire, or have acquired, on the financial market a share of the firm at a price that is different from the book value of equity divided by the number of shares. The difference between the market value of a share and book value of equity per share is the subject of market finance, a topic not covered here. In measuring whether a firm has created value during a period of time, we will only consider the book value of equity (the only one the managers actually have power to modify).

The original idea behind 'residual income' is that the 'real' profit of the firm is the income after taking into account the cost of all sources of capital, including a fair (but nominal) remuneration for the shareholders.

If we assume the shareholders place a risk-factor of 10% on this firm and the risk-free rate is 5%, the shareholders implicitly expect a minimum return of 15%. The residual income for a firm that earned an after-tax income of 1,000 CU and has a share capital of 10,000 CU is 1,000 – (10,000 × 0.15) = −500 CU. The firm, that showed a positive accounting profit, is, in fact, not returning enough, in that period, to meet the shareholders' expectations. Many businesses actually show a negative residual income, at least during some periods of their life.

The financial consulting firm Stern Stewart updated the old concept of residual income (it was introduced by R. Hamilton in 1777 in his *An Introduction to Merchandize*, Edinburgh) under the name of Economic Value Added® or EVA®. Their position is that many accounting elements used in the determination of income do not reflect a long-term view and thus the accounting bottom line does not reflect the ('true') point of view of the shareholders (interested more in the future than in the past and particularly interested in the ability of the enterprise to remain a going concern). In total they suggest some 150 adjustments to the income figure. Two such adjustments reflect the observation that R&D or advertising expenses are really investments to prepare the future and not outright period expenses (as decided on the basis of the prudence principle and as explained in Chapter 8). EVA® is illustrated in Figure 15.11. Other consulting firms have coined their own proprietary approaches.

Figure 15.11 Cascading from cash flow from operations to EVA®

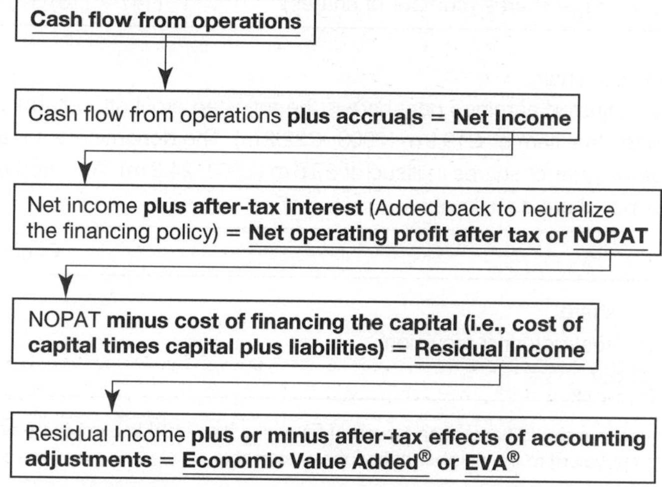

Stern Stuart extended their model to recognize the difference between book equity and market equity. It led to MVA (market value added) (see Figure 15.12). MVA measures the perception by the financial market of the capability of the firm to create value. It measures the excess market value of the shares beyond the requisite reward of long-term capital investment at that level of risk. MVA reflects the opinion of the financial market about past performance and, according to some authors, provides an estimation of the capability to create value in the future. The concept is illustrated in Figure 15.12 and the link between the two is illustrated in Figure 15.13.

Figure 15.13 illustrates the fact that, essentially, MVA can also be defined as the net present value of the stream of future EVAs®, thus reconciling the two approaches. However, while EVA® measures the excess value created during a period, MVA cannot distinguish between value created in the past from that created this current period.

Figure 15.12 The concept of MVA (market value added)

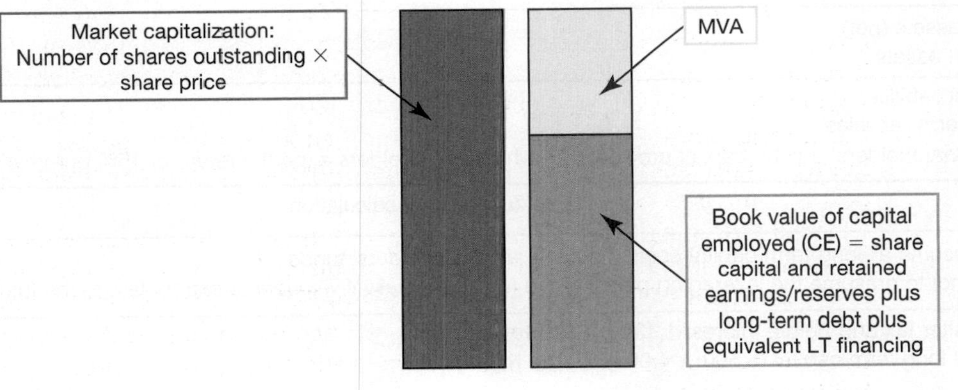

Figure 15.13 MVA and EVA® related

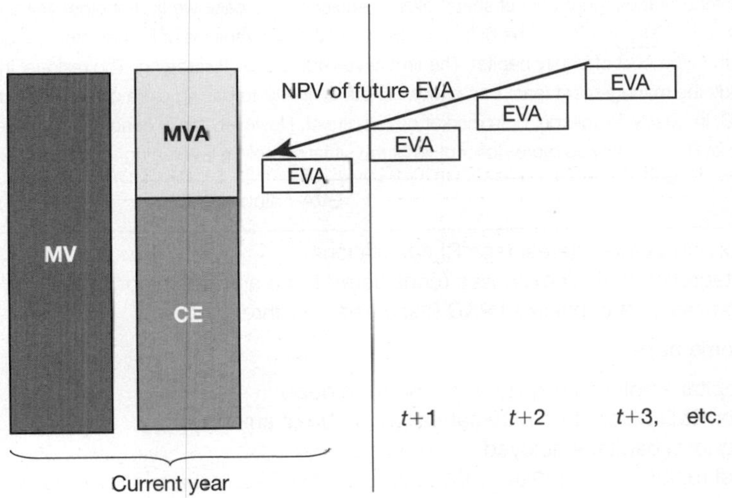

Example of residual income and EVA® calculation (assuming a shareholders' expectation of a 15% return) All methods, such as EVA® or residual income, try to provide what they feel is a 'better' answer to the question 'Did a business really create value?' than traditional financial analysis. As usual, no method provides a complete answer and each

Table 15.11 Example of economic value added

Income statement	
Sales revenue	6,500
COGS	3,500
Gross margin (after depreciation expense)	3,000
R&D expenses	500
Selling, general, and administrative expenses	600
EBIT	1,900
Interest expenses on long-term (LT) liabilities (interest rate = 5%)	200
Taxable income	1,700
Tax expense (assumed to be at 33% of taxable income)	561
Net income after tax	1,139
Balance sheet	
Fixed assets (net)	8,500
Current assets	5,500
Current liabilities	4,500
Long-term liabilities	4,000
Total Shareholders' equity (capital provided, on which shareholders expect a return of 15% per year)	5,500
Residual income calculation	
(We assume all long-term capital costs the same as shareholders' funds so as not to presume the leveraging policy of the firm, especially if we want to extrapolate to the future)	
Profit after tax and before interest 1,139 + 200 (1 − 0.33) =	1,273
Cost of long term capital (5,500 + 4,000) × 15%	1,425
Residual income (RI)	**−152**

The residual income indicates the firm was short by 152 CU of creating wealth over and beyond the cost of long-term capital (chosen here to be the minimum return expected by shareholders).

If we consider the leverage policy to be a given, we can use the weighted average cost of capital (10.79% = [4,000 × 5% + 5,500 × 15%]/9,500) instead of the higher cost of shareholders' equity. In that case we find another value for residual income of +248 CU (i.e. 1,273 − (9,500 × 10.79%) = +248). The difference between the two versions of RI indicates the benefit of leveraging long-term capital at a lower rate than the cost of equity capital. The firm saves 400 CU by leveraging. The residual income calculated in second (248 CU) is a pool of funds the management team can choose to affect 'freely' to paying extra dividends, to awarding bonuses to employees, or to invest in R&D, in quality, in volume, or in market development. However, this is conditional on keeping the long-term lenders happy, while the figure of RI = −152 was more descriptive of the situation before leveraging, and thus more meaningful for future decisions.

EVA calculation	
Profit after tax and before interest (see RI calculations)	1,273
After-tax reintegration of R&D expenses (considered to be an investment)* [500 × (1 − 0.33) = 335]	+335
After-tax amortization of capitalized R&D (assumed over three years)	−111
Adjusted income base	1,497
Long-term capital employed (equity plus long-term debt)	9,500
Adjustment for R&D before tax* (500 capitalized − 1/3 of amortization)	335
Adjusted long-term capital employed	9,835
Cost of capital (9,835 × 15%) (Rate of 15% is assumed to be applicable to any long term funds, for the same reasons as above)	1,475
EVA® (1,497 – 1,475)	+22

*The R&D expense is considered to be an investment. Consequently, the profit is increased and the shareholders' equity (included in the long-term capital) must also be adjusted by the same amount corresponding to the change in profit. (See capitalization of R&D, in Chapter 8.)

Source: Adapted from Lebas (1999)

metric sheds light on a different aspect of financial performance, especially as it pertains to an estimation of the potential for future profits. New methods appear continuously that try to compensate for the weaknesses or limitation of any previous method.

Very few of the items examined so far in this chapter account for the fact that the cash flow generation ability of a firm is essential to its survival and growth. Further, the accounting manipulations that are possible on income affect cash flow very little, or, at least, to a lesser extent.

Coherently with these observations, the Boston Consulting Group introduced a new metric, which they call the 'cash value added' or CVA. This metric attempts to measure the value generated by a business by looking at the cash influx (after-tax income before interest plus depreciation) minus the cost of *economic* depreciation (i.e., the minimum level of investment required to keep the production and commercial potential of the firm at its current level) minus the cost of long-term capital. Such a measure appears to be more appropriate than many of the other synthetic metrics for helping the decider in his or her decision to invest to grow the firm (by adding capacity, carrying out research, or by upgrading its value proposition and thus extracting a possible price premium).

A ratio of CVA to the market value of the shareholders' capital invested shows the cash flow return on investment or CFROI. An aggressively investing firm that chose the 'right' sectors to invest in (i.e., those in which the firm can generate excess cash flow over what is needed to maintain the firm at his current level of market acceptance) will be rewarded with a 'good' value of this indicator, while the management team that invested in the 'wrong' sector will be shown to be poor performers by this metric. These tools, designed to analyze the past, can, of course, also be used in the analysis of future action plans, business plans, and budgets, i.e., in deciding about the future.

2.3 Segment reporting

Segmenting the activity of a business means breaking it down into homogeneous subtotals or segments. Segmenting may be by markets, by customer profiles, by families of products or services, by families of technologies, by geographical areas, by type of currency exposure, by type of dependency on a given raw material, etc. Reporting financial information by segment may help the financial statements users in:

- better understanding the enterprise's operating model and thus better interpreting past performance as a leading indicator of future performance;
- better assessing the enterprise's risks and returns, opportunities, and threats, which may be vastly different in separate segments;
- making more informed judgments about the enterprise as a whole;
- estimating whether, in their mind, the firm is extracting enough synergies from its complexity or should be broken up and sold 'by apartments';
- etc.

Segments often yield differing profitability rates, experience different opportunities for growth, and present unequal future prospects and risks. Segment reporting is essential for both the management team of the firm (for resource allocation especially) and for shareholders. The principles and practices of segment reporting are documented through SFAS 131 (FASB 1997) in the USA and IAS 14 (IASB 1997) for the IASB. These standards, requiring reporting of segment information, apply mainly to publicly traded companies and especially to their consolidated financial statements. However, these standards promote good management and can be, without any difficulty and with great potential informational benefits, applied to not-publicly traded companies and to non-consolidated financial statements.

2.3.1 Definitions

IAS 14 (IASB 1997) on segment reporting defines a business segment (§ 9) as: 'A distinguishable component of an entity that is engaged in providing an individual product or service or a group of related products or services and that is subject to risks and returns that are different from those of other business segments. Factors that shall be considered in determining whether products and services are related include:

(a) The nature of the products or services;
(b) The nature of the production processes;
(c) The type or class of customer for the products or services;
(d) The methods used to distribute the products or provide the services; and
(e) If applicable, the nature of the regulatory environment, for example, banking, insurance, or public utilities'.

A geographical segment (IAS 14, IASB 1997: § 9) is: 'A distinguishable component of an entity that is engaged in providing products or services within a particular economic environment and that is subject to risks and returns that are different from those of components operating in other economic environments. Factors that shall be considered in identifying geographical segments include:

(a) Similarity of economic and political conditions;
(b) Relationships between operations in different geographical areas;
(c) Proximity of operations;
(d) Special risks associated with operations in a particular area;
(e) Exchange control regulations; and
(d) The underlying currency risks'.

2.3.2 Disclosure of segment information

Each enterprise may choose to report both a primary and, within this first classification, a secondary segment reporting format: for example, market or product or service-based business segments as primary information, and geographical segments as secondary information (or the opposite). The choice is based on the source and nature of the enterprise's perceived risks and returns.

Primary reporting format The following information should be reported for the primary segment(s):

- segment revenue (providing a clear distinction between revenue from sales to external customers and revenue from transactions with other segments);
- 'income' of the segment, which opens up the issue of whether it really is 'net' income – which would mean the simple consolidation of these amounts would give the total income of the firm – or simply a margin, which results from not allocating some costs, such as group level administrative costs or basic research, between the segments;
- total carrying amount (book value) of segment-specific assets;
- segment-specific liabilities;
- total cost incurred to acquire or develop segment tangible and intangible assets (capital expenditures);
- total depreciation and amortization of segment assets included in the calculation of the segment 'income';
- total amount of significant non-cash expenses (other than depreciation and amortization).

Reconciliation of segment data with enterprise-wide data must be carried out, so that any unassigned asset, liability, cost, or revenue is accounted for somewhere (generally, what cannot be attached unambiguously to a segment remains in the group-level cost pool and is deducted from the consolidated margins of the segments):

- Is the total of segment sales revenue equal to the total, firm-wide, sales revenue to external customers?
- Is the total of the segments 'income' equal to the enterprise-wide profit or loss (established on comparable bases)?
- Are segments' assets adding up to the enterprise's assets?
- Does the addition of all segment liabilities yield the same measure of total liabilities as the enterprise-wide liabilities?

Secondary reporting format The following information should be reported for the secondary segment(s):

- segment revenue from external customers;
- total carrying amount of segment assets;
- total cost incurred to acquire segment tangible and intangible assets (capital expenditures).

In general, this information is not required if the amount relating to a given segment represents less than 10% of the corresponding enterprise-level total amount.

Real-life example Toray Industries

(Japan – Japanese GAAP – *Source*: Annual report 2005 – Manufacturer of synthetic fibers and textiles)

The company operates principally in six industrial segments (see Table 15.12).

Table 15.12 Primary reporting by business segment – 2005 (in millions of Yen)

Year ended 31 March 2005	Fibers and textiles	Plastics and chemicals	IT-related products	Housing and engineering	Pharmaceuticals and medical products	New products and other businesses	Total	Elimination and corporate	Consolidated total
Sales to outside customers	513,354	300,404	219,142	148,661	44,356	72,689	1,298,606	0	1,298,606
Inter-segment sales	830	28,421	5,129	40,696	2	17,650	92,728	(92,728)	0
Total sales	514,184	328,825	224,271	189,357	44,358	90,339	1,391,334	(92,728)	1,298,606
Operating income	20,872	15,658	28,280	4,294	2,852	9,212	81,168	(116)	81,052
Assets	480,112	383,932	239,398	160,064	62,263	132,244	1,458,013	(55,749)	1,402,264
Depreciation and amortization	22,446	19,033	13,177	2,571	2,162	5,652	65,041	(753)	64,288
Capital expenditures	22,922	13,701	16,877	4,340	5,105	11,290	74,235	(1,141)	73,094

Although the term 'primary' is not used in the annual report, the information published refers obviously to the primary format.

The company operates in three major geographic segments (see Table 15.13).

Table 15.13 Secondary reporting by geographic segment – 2005 (in millions of Yen)

Year ended 31 March 2005	Japan	Asia	North America, Europe, and other areas	Total	Elimination and corporate	Consolidated total
Sales to outside customers	961,633	211,192	125,781	1,298,606	0	1,298,606
Inter-segment sales	81,145	34,161	4,975	120,281	(120,281)	0
Total sales	1,042,778	245,353	130,756	1,418,887	(120,281)	1,298,606
Operating income	65,793	10,269	5,103	81,165	(113)	81,052
Assets	1,055,154	225,510	146,550	1,427,214	(24,950)	1,402,264

Comment: The reader will notice that Toray Industries, although providing both a primary and secondary segmentation of their accounts, did not provide a matrix that would allow the user to know the presence of one primary segment in a geographical area. Reporting to the outside users such information would undoubtedly give too much knowledge, at a low cost of acquisition, to competitors, suppliers, or customers. It would be strategically unwise to reveal too much, even if, internally, that structuring of the data is likely to be readily available.

2.4 Accounts manipulation and quality of financial statements

2.4.1 Principles

A major part of financial statement analysis is based on figures including net income (the 'bottom line') or other intermediate levels of measurement of earnings (such as gross margin or value added). It is therefore important to evaluate the formal quality of such figures, in other words the 'quality of earnings[9]'. This quality is influenced by three factors:

- accounting methods;
- accounting estimates;
- classification of exceptional (or extraordinary) items in the income statement.

These three factors, joined together, have given rise to a practice known broadly as 'accounts manipulation' which encompasses earnings management (including income smoothing and 'big bath' accounting) and creative accounting. Copeland (1968: 101) defines manipulation as some ability to increase or decrease reported net income at will. At the same time, he implicitly acknowledges that the notion of manipulation may result from at least three types of behavioral patterns: 'income maximizers', 'income minimizers', and 'income smoothers'. However, we believe that accounts manipulation has a broader meaning than what Copeland describes. It also includes income statement classificatory practices, presented by Barnea *et al.* (1975, 1976) and Ronen and Sadan (1975), and also those related to the balance sheet, which are far less well described in the literature (Black *et al.*, 1998). Actually, these practices represent a more important phenomenon now than when Copeland published his seminal article. Such accounts manipulation practices are based on a common functional fixation view of share price determination, which states that accounting numbers contribute to the determination of share prices. Financial markets are essentially efficient and generally would 'see through' accounting manipulation engaged in by listed firms. However, unlisted firms are not subject to the scrutiny of market analysts and the functional fixation view of the world may well apply in their case. In any case, accounting manipulations may affect both cash flow and risks perceived by analysts (through the impact of any manipulation on the value of ratios).

We distinguish different streams of accounts manipulation, based on the fundamental principle that the aim of providing financial information is the reduction of the cost at which capital is obtained for the firm's endeavors. This reduction is related to the perception of the firm's risk by investors. The risk is technically measured, for listed companies, by the so-called '*beta*' factor, which measures the variance of earnings relative to that of a market-wide portfolio[10]. Moreover, there is a structural risk revealed by the equilibrium between debt and equity. As a consequence, the objectives of accounts manipulation are to alter at least one of the above and thus affect the variance of earnings per share and the debt/equity ratio.

Earnings per share can be modified in two ways:

- first, by adding or removing revenues or expenses (modification of net income); and,
- second, by listing an item 'before' or 'after' the profit definition used to calculate the earnings per share (classificatory manipulations, such as excluding or including some items as either extraordinary or not).

Figure 15.14 presents our framework for classifying accounts manipulation.

Regarding the nature of practices, the literature has mainly discussed manipulations that are legitimate interpretations of standards, for instance, decisions on the level of accruals. But manipulation can also be of dubious legitimacy and deliberate, i.e., transactions can be designed in order to allow a preferred accounting treatment yielding the

Figure 15.14 A framework for classifying accounts manipulation (see Stolowy and Breton, 2004)

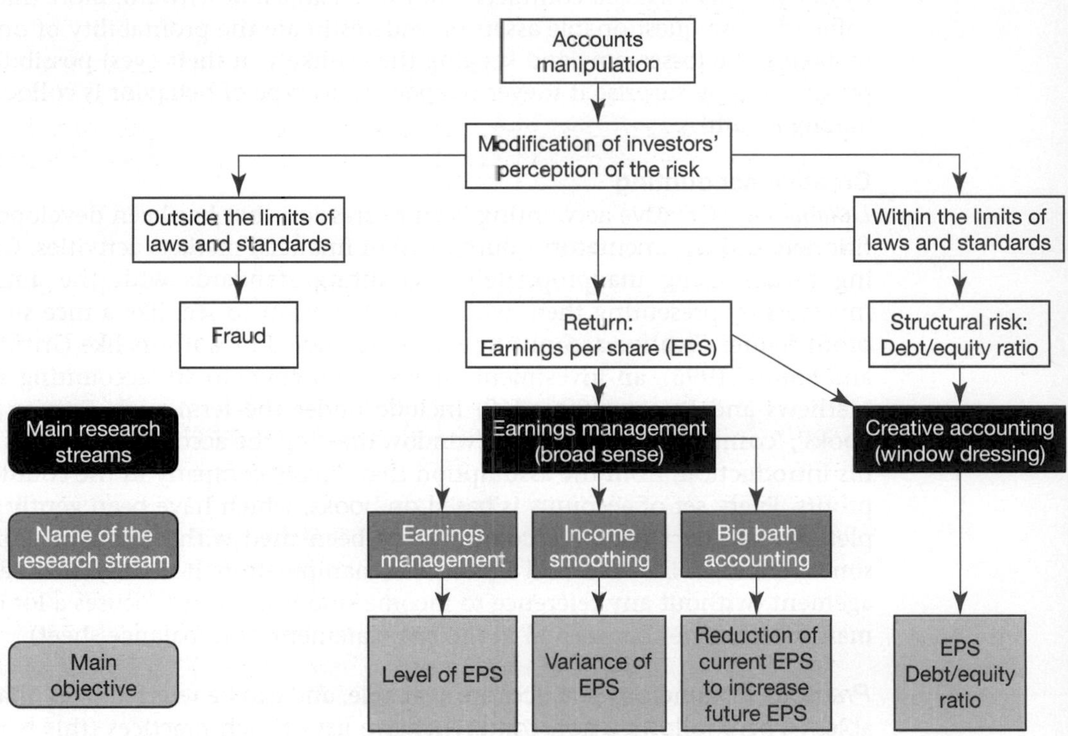

result desired. For instance, a leasing contract might be written in such a way that the leased equipment does not need to be capitalized, thus affecting the reporting of the lease expense (see Chapter 12).

2.4.2 The different streams of accounts manipulation

Earnings management In this family of manipulation practices, the firm's officers artificially manage earnings to achieve or meet some pre-established level of 'expected' earnings (e.g., analysts' expectations or forecasts, management's prior estimates, or continuation of some earnings trend) (Fern *et al.*, 1994).

Income smoothing Income smoothing has the clear objective of producing a steadily growing stream of profits by shifting the date on which some components of costs or revenues are recognized. This form of manipulation can be, for example, the result of creating and canceling provisions (which means that at some point profit was large enough to allow these – possibly unjustified – provisions), or through the appropriate choice of the date of recognition of profit on long-term contracts, or through the ad hoc sale of inventories or long-lived assets that were undervalued (as was the case for example for a firm that sold TV rights from the large inventory of (old) films it had obtained through an earlier acquisition and which were valued at little on the acquisition date because there was little demand for TV content at that time). Income smoothing is mainly a reduction of the variance of the profit.

Big bath accounting Intuitively, big bath accounting is easy to understand. When a new CEO is appointed, she or he may wish to 'clean up' the accounts: (a) to start on a sound base that will allow a growing income figure to obtain more easily; or (b) so as to create provisions, which will later be used to create some form of income smoothing. Such practices, consisting of reducing drastically earnings when the 'new' leadership takes over, are believed to be reassuring to the shareholders and facilitating the creation of a future positive stream of revenues. As Moore (1973: 100) explained, new management has a tendency to be very pessimistic about the value of certain assets or about the future profitability of currently engaged contracts. They often adjust downward, more than necessary, the value of these questionable assets or underestimate the profitability of ongoing contracts by taking the losses now and keeping the (unlikely in their eyes) possibility of profit as a possible happy surprise if it ever happens. This type of behavior is colloquially known as 'taking a bath'.

Creative accounting

Definitions Creative accounting is an expression that has been developed by both practitioners and commentators (journalists) of financial markets activities. Creative accounting means using inappropriately accounting standards with the aim of misleading investors by presenting them with what they want to see, like a nice steadily increasing profit figure. Creative accounting has been studied by authors like Griffiths (1986, 1995) and Smith (1996), an investment analyst, who refers to an 'accounting sleight of hand'. Mathews and Perera (1996: 260) include under the term such activity as 'fiddling the books', 'cosmetic reporting', and 'window dressing the accounts'. Griffiths (1986) starts, in his introduction, from the assumption that: 'Every company in the country is fiddling its profits. Every set of accounts is based on books, which have been gently cooked or completely roasted'. Creative accounting has been used with various meanings and brings some confusion into the field of accounts manipulation. It mainly includes earnings management (without any reference to income smoothing) and focuses a lot on classificatory manipulations (either related to income statement or to balance sheet).

Practices Numerous practices are available, and can be referred to as 'manipulating variables'. There follows a non-comprehensive list of such practices (this is not a hit parade and the order in which practices are listed is not particularly significant):

- Changes in accounting policies (this includes many possibilities and could be considered as a generic activity – see Chapter 6).
- R&D costs: capitalized or expensed? expenses deferred or anticipated? (see Chapter 8).
- Change from accelerated to straight-line depreciation (see Chapter 7).
- Capitalization (or not) of interest costs (see Chapter 7).
- Change in inventory valuation method (FIFO, WAC, LIFO – see Chapter 9).
- Accounting treatment of government grants (liability or revenue? – see Chapter 6).
- Long-term contracts: percentage of completion versus completed contract method (see Chapter 6).
- Treatment of unusual gains and losses (exceptional versus operating or extraordinary versus ordinary: classificatory manipulation; to anticipate or postpone: inter-temporal manipulation – see Chapter 6).
- Evaluation of provisions (inventories, doubtful accounts, long-term and marketable securities, loan loss, risks – see Chapters 9, 10, and 12).
- Capitalization of leases (see Chapter 12).
- Discretionary accounting decisions (expenses split over several years or deferred expenses, in countries allowing this practice – see Chapter 8).
- Purchase versus pooling decision (see Chapter 13) (although this possibility is no longer relevant, given the suppression of the pooling method in many countries, it was frequently used in the past. If an analyst carries out any historical research, he or she may encounter its occurrence).
- Merger recorded at fair value or at book value (see Chapter 13).
- Pension costs (see Chapter 12).
- Analysis of the difference arising on first consolidation (see Chapter 13).

Conclusion on accounts manipulation Some analysts believe that financial statements have no value because of the possibility of carrying out these manipulations (many anecdotes abound to support the reality of their existence). We do not agree with such a conclusion.

When prepared in accordance with GAAP, financial statements are always useful. The user must, however, be aware of the limitations placed on their reliability. The notes to financial statements are a very good source of information that can be used to cross-check and validate the reported figures, and to restate, if needed, the financial statements so as to perform comparative analyses. Moreover, the consistency accounting principle (see Chapter 5) often works as a good limitation to manipulations. One should also never forget that most of the manipulations, principally those based on 'cooking the books' with inappropriate provisions, will have an opposite effect at the time of their reversal. This is also an efficient source of limitation to the temptation a manager may feel in order to 'look better'.

Finally, the role of auditors is, among other things, to help verify that no manipulative practice took place during the period covered by the financial statements. We should also point out the responsibility of directors in conforming with standards and the increasing liability that rests with company directors for the content of the companies reports.

2.5 Governance

As we defined it in Chapter 1, accounting is the set of processes and procedures that create figures that reflect and depict the economic activity of an enterprise or economic entity.

Figures created by accounting result from a certain number of well-defined practices, developed throughout this book, which must be run in accordance with the accounting principles that were introduced in Chapter 5. Yet, as we have seen, a lot of leeway is still granted by all GAAP in coding, classifying, and reporting economic events. Particularly difficult questions are those of revenue and cost recognition and timing, or the creation of provisions.

The figures handled by the accounting system are the products of human endeavor. Ethical (or unethical) behavior, risk management practices, and the way to use the enterprise's resources in the business process affect the truthfulness and usefulness of the figures reported in an economic entity's accounts.

2.5.1 Enterprise governance defined

Governance is not a new topic. Adam Smith in his *Wealth of Nations* (1776) already mentioned the agency situation, albeit in a pessimistic tone, which creates the need for governance: 'Being managers of other people's money but their own, it cannot well be expected that they should watch over it with the same anxious vigilance with which ... [they] frequently watch over their own. Negligence and profusion, therefore must always prevail more or less in the management of the affairs of a company'.

Managers, and CEO and executive managers more directly than others, have received a mandate from the shareholders to be their agent (thus the term 'agency') in creating wealth with the resources they have handed over to the firm. In 1992, Sir Adrian Cadbury defined governance as 'the system for direction and control of the corporation'[11]. In 1999, the same author, in a work for the World Bank gave a broader definition of governance: 'Corporate governance is ... holding the balance between economic and social goals, and between individual and communal goals. The governance framework is there to encourage the efficient use of resources and equally to require accountability for the stewardship of these resources. The aim is to align as nearly as possible the interests of individuals, corporations and society. The incentive to corporations is to achieve their corporate aims and to attract investments. The incentive for states is to strengthen their economics and discourage fraud and mismanagement'[12].

Although we acknowledge the societal aspects of business enterprises and the need for societal governance, we will adopt a narrower definition of the term in the context of this section: 'Enterprise governance is the set of responsibilities and practices exercised by the board and executive management, with the goal of:

1. Providing strategic direction,
2. Ensuring that objectives are achieved,
3. Ascertaining that risks are managed appropriately, and
4. Verifying that the organization's resources are used responsibly'[13].

Enterprise governance, for the scope of this text, focuses mainly on the latter two parts of this definition. There are subsets or prerequisites of a larger question: is the image of the economic situation and value creation, past, present and future, of the business entity true and fair?

2.5.2 Corporate governance and internal controls, accountability, and assurance

Corporate governance builds on what used to be called 'internal control systems'. It includes all systems, practices, and procedures designed to ensure conformance with principles, regulations, and to create accountability assurance.

2.5.3 Business governance and value creation

Business governance addresses the question of responsible and strategically appropriate usage of resources of the firm, within a pre-defined, acceptable risk-taking policy. The purpose of business governance is to find whether the management team has actually created value.

Value creation can be measured, retrospectively, by cash flows and profits, but true value creation, in the logic of a going-concern entity, is when cash flows and profits generated (and reported) are effectively used to ensure the long-term development of the firm, i.e., to create the conditions for on-going success. In this context, 'risk management' becomes a major responsibility of executive management: risk evaluation and preparing for the occurrence of these risks is about preparing for the future.

2.5.4 Business governance metrics

The strategic vision of the executive management team is difficult to evaluate or measure. It is the role of the Board of Directors to exercise oversight to make sure risks are appropriately apprehended and managed.

Three families of measures exist to report on value creation, each addressing a different question:

1. **What is the current profitability of this business?** What is the ability of this business to generate positive and durable cash flows from the currently installed asset base? Examples of measures employed to answer this question are such as EPS, gross margin, free cash flow, return on capital employed (ROCE), EVA®, or plenty more.
2. **What is the value today of this business entity?** Examples of measures used here, in the absence of a market value, of course, are Price to Earning ratio multiples, shareholders' equity multiples, or discounted future cash flows.
3. **By how much have this business and management team increased the value from time *t* to *t* + 1?** (Value is defined by one of the measures cited above, or, for listed firms, by the market value of shareholders' equity.) The measure most frequently used to address this question is the total shareholders' return (TSR = $[(\text{Value}_{t+1} - \text{value}_t) + \text{dividends}]/\text{Value}_t$).

2.5.5 Regulating enterprise governance

After the fairly recent series of spectacular bankruptcies or scandals, including Enron, Parmalat, Tyco, Vivendi, or WorldCom, investors have begun doubting the validity of reported company accounts and the effectiveness of the oversight exercised by the Board of Directors (or its equivalent if the firm uses another format for oversight). Governments and regulators around the world have promulgated appropriate legislation or regulations to prevent further occurrences of such scandals that threaten all firms by casting a shadow over the fairness of information and thus the fairness of access to funds through financial markets.

One well-known and exemplary such piece of legislation is the Sarbanes–Oxley Act in the United States (applicable only to US firms or to any firm quoted on a US stock exchange). It is a complex piece of legislation but contains three key provisions that are directly relevant to the usefulness of reported accounts.

- Section 302: CEOs and CFOs must personally certify and guarantee the accuracy of quarterly and annual financial statements.
- Section 404: Businesses must: (1) clearly communicate the current managerial responsibilities for establishing and maintaining appropriate internal controls pertaining to the protection of assets and the establishment of financial statements; and (2) make public an assessment of the effectiveness of these internal controls (this second aspect is subject to an external audit report).
- Section 409: The firm is required to disclose in real time (within two days) any significant event that affects its financial position. Examples of such events would be the loss of a major customer, a change in the evaluation score issued by one of the financial-risk rating agencies or a modification to the benefit package that may result from labor negotiations.

These requirements are clearly quite strict. They can, however, if one so desires, be satisfied only to the letter, in a mechanical way (i.e., putting the emphasis on creating an 'audit trail' and only formally creating a responsibility chain, but with no accountability). They fail, in our view, to address some of the real issues that are behind the scandals that have cast a pall on financial reporting: greed and personal ambition, leading to excessive risk-taking and to accounting malpractice to cover one's own tracks.

Enron and other scandal-ridden firms have regularly and systematically abused the possibility of off-balance sheet commitments. They have under-reported (or reported in unclear ways) their off-balance sheet commitments (thus potentially creating real liabilities). Off-balance sheet commitments are not always fraudulent, but they always need to be understood to visualize the actual financial position of the firm. This is why, throughout this text, we have emphasized the notes are an integral and important part of financial statements. In an Associated Press wire quoted by IMA Online (10 August 2004), the financial statements of FedEx Corp. for 2003 reported $11.1 billion of debt but when exploring the footnotes one could find an additional $11 to $14 billion off-balance sheet (conditional) commitments, thus potentially doubling the actual liabilities reported. Transparency is one of the main accounting principles, but the complexity of today's business transactions makes it sometimes difficult to be fully transparent, even when no ill will is intended.

2.5.6 The causes of violations of the good governance principles

In 2003 the International Federation of Accountants (IFAC) mandated a research team to study governance frameworks in relation with the recent reporting scandals. Twenty-seven cases were studied around the world. The researchers distinguished two categories of issues: corporate governance, on one hand, and strategy definition and implementation issues, on the other.

Under corporate governance they listed the following sources of possible 'causes' for violation of the principle of true and fair view:

- The role of the chief executive (dominant, charismatic, authoritarian and not inclined to being challenged, focused on external growth though mergers and acquisitions (M&A), lack of clear strategy, etc.).
- The role of the Board of Directors (unable to challenge or direct the CEO because its members are too friendly with, or linked in one way or another with, the CEO or with key senior executive managers).
- Executive remuneration plans (non-congruent incentive or bonus programs, over-aggressive targets leading to earnings management to obtain the bonus).
- Ethics, culture, and tone at the top (poor ethical standards among senior executives, slowness in acknowledging and responding to difficulties in implementation of the strategy, particularly those pertaining to M&A).
- Internal controls (weak internal controls over the usage of assets and resources, including human resources).

The combination of these negative traits leads to earnings management, ethical violations, and generally leads to compromising with the truth.

2.5.7 Regulating ethics

The Sarbanes–Oxley Act attempts to create better oversight of these problems, but the spirit of the law is too often compromised in favor of respecting only its letter. Legislation like the Sarbanes–Oxley Act is not sufficient to prevent all attempts at fraudulent reporting (morality is a question of society), but, without it, there might be more such attempts. The three sections of the act we have highlighted above are essential to creating a good climate in the organization. However, no one can say, for example, whether a target or objective is too demanding or not, whether a leader is too charismatic or not, or whether a strategy is well formulated or not. It boils down to a question of morals and culture. As Peter Drucker is often quoted to have said: 'There is no such things as business ethics ... There is just ethics; and we all have to practice them every day in everything we do'.

Values in an organization begin with senior management and their oversight by a qualified and independent Board of Directors, truly representing the interests of shareholders. Shareholders have the responsibility to elect Board members who will really be stand-up people. Respect of the agency mandate received by both Board members and senior executives from the shareholders sets the condition for relevant financial accounts.

2.5.8 Corporate social responsibility

Without going into details on this subject, whole books are devoted to the theme, we would like to cite some good questions suggested by Djordjija Petkoski of the World Bank Institute (2004)[14]:

- What kind of impact does the firm, in its sector, can have on poverty, [health and education]?
- How is wealth created distributed? (Between profit reward to shareholders, remuneration to workers and suppliers, customers, the State, etc.)
- What kinds of activities constitute best practice in this area?
- Is the business aware of its impact?
- Is it doing something about it?
- If not, what are the issues the business needs to face, that have been faced effectively by others in the sector?

2.6 Scoring models

2.6.1 Principles

One main preoccupation of analysts is to identify the likelihood of a business failing, i.e., verifying whether the going-concern assumption is met. Several authors have developed models, called scoring models, generally based on a linear multivariate regression of several ratios and/or elements of the financial statements that create a unique 'score' for a firm at one point in time. If the score is (or drifts) above or below certain experiential thresholds, the likelihood of the business failing is declared to be high or low.

2.6.2 Example: the Altman's Z score

Altman's model is probably the original model and has become a classic of this genre. The original 'Z score', based on a limited sample of large manufacturing firms that had filed for bankruptcy, was created by the following equation where the coefficients had been determined by analyzing the data from the firms in the sample:

Z = 1.2 × (Working capital/Total assets) + 1.4 × (Shareholders' equity/Total assets) + 3.3 × (Earnings before income taxes/Total assets) + 0.6 × (Market value of equity/Book value of debt) + 1.0 × (Sales/Total assets)

To evaluate a firm's likelihood of bankruptcy (after, of course, verifying the firm analyzed is generally similar to those in the original sample or in redefining the coefficients of the equation for a relevant sample of firms), an analyst would compare the firm's Z score with the empirically determined thresholds. The thresholds for Altman's original Z factor study are shown below.

- If $Z < 1.81$, high probability of bankruptcy.
- If $1.81 < Z < 2.99$, one cannot tell (zone of ignorance).
- If $Z > 2.99$, low probability of bankruptcy.

The Z score approach has proven to be successful in the real world. Most applications confirm the findings of the original research, which showed the model correctly predicted 72% of bankruptcies two years prior to the event.

The values of the coefficients and of the thresholds have to be specified for each homogeneous group of businesses (size, industry, etc.). The coefficients for the Z score are not standardized, but most of the ratios combined in the Z score seem to be valid for all manufacturing industries[15].

Financial analysts rely heavily on scoring models and other models to help them anticipate risk. (For more details on scoring models, see Appendix 15.7.)

Key points

- Financial statement analysis processes, evaluates, and interprets the data reported to shareholders and the financial community to facilitate its usability in decision making.
- Financial statement analysis can be carried out by both managers and outsiders to the firm in order to assess a firm's past performance or achievements, present condition, and future prospects.
- It uses various techniques integrating accounting data and additional information, emphasizing comparative and relative analysis over time for one firm and between firms.
- Understanding current and past performance of a business helps users of financial statements, and principally investors, derive the firm's business model and its correlated risks.
- Users are interested in understanding liquidity, solvency, leverage, and profitability of a firm, as well as understanding its asset management policies and the resulting return to investors.
- The main techniques of financial statements analysis include: (1) trend or horizontal analysis (comparison over time of the evolution of a specific expense or revenue item or a particular asset or liability item); (2) common-size or vertical analysis (comparison of the evolution of the structure of the financial statements); (3) balance sheet structure and cash equation; and (4) ratio analysis (evaluation of the relation between items in the financial statements).
- 'Trend analysis' measures the changes over past accounting period(s) of a limited number of items or, conversely, of the whole financial statements (balance sheet, income statement, and cash flow statement). It reveals the dynamics of the income generation model.
- Common-size analysis is prepared by presenting each financial statement component in terms of its percentage of a selected base figure, generally indexed as 100, such as net sales for income statement items or total assets for balance sheet elements.
- The common-size analysis allows the analyst to compare and contrast more easily the financial statements of two or more companies in the same industrial sector or risk class.
- A company's simplified balance sheet can be structured by identifying two separate 'time horizons' (current or short term; and non-current or long term), each corresponding to different types of decisions about assets, on one hand, and shareholders' equity and liabilities, on the other.
- One extension of this simplified balance sheet, beyond the common-size analysis, is the 'cash equation' relating three major concepts: working capital, working capital need, and net cash.
- A ratio is the quotient of two quantities, the numerator and the denominator, showing (assuming) there is a relationship between them.

- Ratio analysis must be used cautiously as the numerator and denominator must be coherent within the business model and correspond to the same time period.
- Three types of comparison increase the information content of ratios: (1) time-series comparisons; (2) cross-sectional comparisons; and (3) comparisons against a competitive or rule of thumb-based benchmark.
- A financial analyst supplements the accounting data by additional information from a variety of sources. Earnings per share and return on capital invested help shareholders decide whether or not to keep their money invested in this firm. The economic value added measures the excess value (i.e., strategically available resources) generated by a business, after the cost of obtaining long-term capital has been covered (which includes shareholders' expected remuneration).
- Segmenting the activity of a business means breaking down its business model in homogeneous submodels or segments to help improve the predictability of future streams of economic benefits.
- The 'quality of earnings' is influenced by: (1) accounting methods changes; (2) accounting estimates, especially of required provisions; and (3) classification of exceptional (or extraordinary) items in the income statement.
- 'Accounts manipulation' is the result of earnings management including income smoothing and 'big bath' accounting, as well as a series of actions called creative accounting.
- Financial analysts strive to identify the risk of a business failing, i.e., going bankrupt. Scoring models establish, for each firm, a synthetic index or 'score' which, when benchmarked, indicates whether a firm should be considered as healthy or in difficulty.

Review (solutions are at the back of the book)

Review 15.1 Chugoku Power Electric Company*

Topic: Common-size income statements by nature
Related part of the chapter: Core issues

Chugoku Electric Power Company, Inc., was established in 1951 as one of 10 electric power companies in Japan. It maintains its head office in the city of Hiroshima and supplies electricity to the Chugoku region through an integrated structure that encompasses all stages of power supply, from generation to transmission and distribution. In fiscal year 2005, ended 31 March, it supplied 58.1 billion kWh of electricity.

The income statements of the parent company for the years 2003–2005 follow (**source**: Annual report 2005). Consolidated figures are very close to the non-consolidated ones because the parent is the heaviest actor in the group.

Non-consolidated statements of income

Millions of yen	2005	2004	2003
Operating revenues	956,690	912,813	965,499
Operating expenses			
Personnel	113,433	132,080	127,697
Fuel	128,076	100,058	110,466
Purchased power	154,910	134,488	141,496
Depreciation	144,622	156,469	166,822
Maintenance	92,717	86,261	86,855
Taxes other than income taxes	63,266	63,220	64,736
Purchased services	38,392	35,948	36,184
Other	101,513	104,850	104,949
	836,929	813,374	839,205
Operating income	119,761	99,439	126,294
Other expenses (income):			
Interest expense	36,727	36,771	56,646
Interest income	(61)	(82)	(88)
Loss on impairment of fixed assets	4,089	0	0
Other – net	4,325	1,556	(1,944)
	45,080	38,245	54,614
Income before special item and income taxes	74,681	61,194	71,680
Special item:			
Reserve for drought	1,747	712	0
Provision for income taxes:			
Current	25,061	28,457	31,368
Deferred	1,374	(7,504)	(5,382)
Net income	46,499	39,529	45,694

Required

1. Prepare common-size statements on the basis of the income statement, as published by the company.
2. Restate the income statement and prepare common-size intermediate balances following the format of Figure 15.2.
3. Comment on these different statements.

The item 'Other – net' in 'Other expenses (income)' can be assumed to refer to 'Financial expenses and income'.

Review 15.2 Elkem*

Topic: Balance sheet structure
Related part of the chapter: Core issues

Elkem, a Norwegian group based in Oslo, is one of the world's leading suppliers of metals and materials within its core areas. Its main products are silicon metal, aluminum, hydro-power, ferroalloys, carbon, and micro-silicon. Elkem has production plants in Europe, North America, South America, and Asia. It is listed on the Oslo and Frankfurt stock exchanges.

The consolidated balance sheet for the period 2002–2004 follows (*source*: Annual report 2004).

Consolidated balance sheet (aggregated version)

NOK million	31.12.04	31.12.03	31.12.02
ASSETS			
Intangible fixed assets	2,664	2,715	2,392
Tangible fixed assets	7,252	7,570	7,240
Investment in associates	454	75	5
Investment in other shares and interests	12	16	192
Long-term receivables	373	312	381
Financial fixed assets	839	403	578
Fixed assets	10,755	10,688	10,210
Inventories	3,054	2,982	2,316
Short-term receivables	4,201	3,911	3,718
Short-term financial assets	66	142	154
Cash and bank deposits	875	970	1,013
Current assets	8,196	8,005	7,201
TOTAL ASSETS	18,951	18,693	17,411
EQUITY AND LIABILITIES			
Paid-in capital	1,756	1,756	1,756
Other equity	4,892	4,505	4,258
Shareholders' equity	6,648	6,261	6,014
Minority interest	1,132	1,118	892
Shareholders' equity and minority interest	7,780	7,379	6,906
Pension liabilities	608	584	451
Deferred taxes liabilities	851	648	372
Other long-term liabilities	215	198	85
Provisions	1,674	1,430	908
Interest-bearing long-term debt	4,772	5,286	5,031
Interest-bearing short-term debt	639	855	923
Other short-term liabilities	4,086	3,743	3,643
Current liabilities	4,725	4,598	4,566
TOTAL EQUITY AND LIABILITIES	18,951	18,693	17,411

Required

1. Prepare a simplified balance sheet with three subheadings in the assets and three subheadings in the equity and liabilities (see the Core issues section in this chapter).
2. Compute working capital, working capital need, and net cash.
3. Comment on your findings.

Assignments

Assignment 15.1
Janacek Company (2)

Topic: Preparation of a statement of intermediate balances and statement of financial structure
Related part of the chapter: Core issues

The Janacek Company has a commercial activity in the sector of beauty products and cosmetics.

Required

1. With the help of the balance sheet, income statement, and additional information (see assignment Janacek Company (1), in Chapter 14), prepare a statement of intermediate balances for the years X1, X2, and X3.
2. Prepare a simplified balance sheet for the years X1, X2, and X3.
3. Prepare a statement showing the financial structure of the company for the years X1, X2, and X3.
4. Evaluate and comment these statements.

Assignment 15.2
Procter & Gamble*

Topic: Common-size income statements
Related part of the chapter: Core issues

The common-sized income statements of Procter & Gamble have been prepared for the years 2003–2005 (see Table 15.3 in this chapter).

Required

1. What financial performance intermediate balance does not appear in the income statement and would be useful to your analysis?
2. Comment on the common-size income statements over the period.

Assignment 15.3
Creaton AG*

Topic: Common-size income statements by nature
Related part of the chapter: Core issues

Creaton AG is one of Germany's leading clay roofing tile manufacturers. Its name stands for a uniquely broad product range, a strong exports focus, ultra-modern, ecologically friendly technologies, and a consistent brand image.

The annual financial statements for the Group have been compiled applying the provisions of the German Commercial Code and the German Stock Corporation Act.

You will find below the income statements for the periods 2001–2004 (*Source*: Annual reports 2004 and 2002). In the notes to financial statements, we learn that the 'Other operating income' includes mainly exceptional items.

Creaton – Consolidated income statements for the periods 1 January 2001–31 December 2004

	2004/€ 000	2003/€ 000	2002/€ 000	2001/€ 000
Sales revenue	133,147	130,225	112,243	125,124
Increase (or decrease) in finished goods and work in progress	2,620	(3,902)	1,179	470
Other own output capitalized	21	9	861	39
Other operating income	2,736	4,862	17,274	13,225
Total output	**138,524**	**131,194**	**131,557**	**138,858**
Cost of materials	(30,020)	(29,512)	(25,755)	(28,027)
Gross income	**108,504**	**101,682**	**105,802**	**110,831**
Personnel expense				
a) Wages and salaries	(28,672)	(27,545)	(25,622)	(27,272)
b) Social security, pension and other benefit costs	(5,938)	(5,837)	(7,212)	(6,042)
Scheduled amortization/depreciation	(12,941)	(12,640)	(22,274)	(20,104)
Other operating expense	(46,150)	(45,622)	(40,445)	(43,311)
Operating profits	**14,803**	**10,038**	**10,249**	**14,102**
Income from other securities and loans of financial assets	227	221	175	0
Other interest and similar income	88	137	156	284
Profit/(loss) attributable to associated companies carried at equity	(41)	39	0	0
Amortization on financial assets and marketable securities	(190)	(121)	(5,772)	0
Interest and similar expense	(2,769)	(2,682)	(2,657)	(2,163)
Earnings from ordinary activities	**12,118**	**7,632**	**2,151**	**12,223**
Extraordinary expenses	0	0	0	0
Taxes on income	(5,313)	(3,234)	(1,598)	(1,677)
Other taxes	(414)	(139)	(486)	(118)
Net income for the year	6,391	4,259	67	10,428

Required

1. Restate the income statement and prepare common-size intermediate balances as explained in the Core issues section earlier in this chapter.
2. Comment on the documents and information that result from your answer to question 1.

Assignment 15.4
Club Méditerranée*

Topic: Balance sheet structure
Related part of the chapter: Core issues

The French group Club Méditerranée is an active service provider in the field of leisure with, in particular, its famous resort 'villages'. The balance sheets for the period 2002–2004 follow (*Source*: Annual reports 2004 and 2003).

Required

1. What is the format of the balance sheet?
2. Prepare a simplified balance sheet with three subheadings in the assets and three subheadings in the equity and liabilities (see Table 15.5).
3. Compute the working capital, working capital need, and net cash.
4. Comment on the results and information created in your answers to questions 2 and 3.

Club Méditerranée – Consolidated balance sheet (€ million)

Years ended 31 October	2004	2003	2002
ASSETS			
Intangible assets	**183**	**194**	**222**
Goodwill	79	86	98
Other	104	108	124
Tangible assets	**761**	**805**	**958**
Land	89	92	105
Property and equipment	523	575	693
Other	149	138	160
Financial assets	**89**	**97**	**105**
Investments, loans and advances*	20	24	30
Deposits	58	65	65
Other	11	8	10
TOTAL FIXED ASSETS	**1,033**	**1,096**	**1,285**
Inventories	19	23	26
Trade receivables	61	67	78
Other receivables	59	56	70
Marketable securities	67	2	4
Bank and cash	93	173	77
TOTAL CURRENT ASSETS	**299**	**321**	**255**
Deferred taxes	74	76	56
Prepaid expenses and deferred charges	76	69	66
TOTAL ASSETS	**1,482**	**1,562**	**1,662**
LIABILITIES AND SHAREHOLDERS' EQUITY			
Common stock	77	77	77
Additional paid-in capital	562	562	562
Reserves	−175	−71	42
Group net income (loss)	−44	−94	−62
SHAREHOLDERS' EQUITY	**420**	**474**	**619**
MINORITY INTEREST	**24**	**14**	**12**
PROVISIONS FOR CONTINGENCIES AND CHARGES	**93**	**114**	**113**
Bonds	144	144	270
Bank loans and debts*	406	420	232
Trade payables	159	151	143
Amounts received for future vacations	77	93	90
Other	101	88	120
TOTAL DEBT	**887**	**896**	**855**
Deferred taxes	0	0	0
Accrued expenses and deferred income	58	64	63
TOTAL LIABILITIES AND SHAREHOLDERS' EQUITY	**1,482**	**1,562**	**1,662**
* Including current maturities of long-term debt, and	250	22	22
including bank overdrafts	27	20	28

Assignment 15.5
Vimpel Communications*

Topic: Comparative financial statement analysis
Related part of the chapter: Core issues

Vimpel Communications (VimpelCom) is a leading provider of wireless telecommunications services in Russia, operating under the 'Beeline' brand, which is one of the most recognized brand names in Russia.

The balance sheets for the period 2002–2004 follow (**source**: Annual reports 2004 and 2003). VimpelCom maintains its records and prepares its financial statements in accordance with Russian accounting and tax legislation and accounting principles generally accepted in the United States of America ('US GAAP'). The notes indicate the 2003 balance sheet was restated in 2004, but we believe the impact is not significant with regard to financial statement analysis.

Vimpel Com. – Consolidated balance sheets (in thousands of US dollars)

Assets	2004	2003	2002
Current assets:			
Cash and cash equivalents	305,857	157,611	263,657
Trade accounts receivable, net of allowance for doubtful accounts	119,566	113,092	75,399
Inventory	37,855	17,905	15,209
Deferred income taxes	64,706	21,377	15,742
Input value added tax	196,123	175,045	85,331
Other current assets	73,315	41,213	33,027
Total current assets	797,422	526,243	488,365
Property and equipment, net	2,314,405	1,439,758	957,602
Telecommunications licenses and allocations of frequencies, net of accumulated amortization	757,506	103,817	88,385
Goodwill	368,204	9,816	–
Other intangible assets, net	212,595	49,553	55,730
Due from related parties	534	1,171	2,083
Deferred income taxes	1,714	-	8,075
Other assets	327,861	151,090	92,504
Total assets	4,780,241	2,281,448	1,692,744

Liabilities and shareholders' equity	2004	2003	2002
Current liabilities:			
Accounts payable	345,187	158,467	80,241
Due to related parties	7,290	8,603	4,114
Due to employees	19,241	14,791	5,731
Accrued liabilities	21,429	10,153	10,455
Taxes payable	50,791	101,294	33,306
Deferred revenue	1,893	2,701	2,016
Deferred income taxes	11,785	1,451	–
Customer advances	242,064	140,756	53,469
Customer deposits	36,106	40,719	53,186
Capital lease obligations	2,851	6,587	3,868
Ruble denominated bonds payable	–	101,852	–
Bank loans, current portion	115,111	35,343	37,780
Equipment financing obligations, current portion	71,577	70,935	134,617
Total current liabilities	925,325	693,652	418,783
Deferred income taxes	296,967	28,943	35,227
Ruble denominated bonds payable	108,113	–	–
Bank loans, less current portion	1,240,199	330,112	306,080
5.5% Senior convertible notes due July 2005			85,911
Capital lease obligations, less current portion	5,004	9,154	899
Equipment financing obligations, less current portion	38,283	53,008	81,425
Accrued liabilities	6,837	4,046	3,265
Minority interest	2,380	174,882	98,491
Shareholders' equity:			
Common stock	92	90	90
Additional paid-in capital	1,365,978	569,828	528,914
Retained earnings	769,093	418,697	195,300
Accumulated other comprehensive income, net of tax	25,212	2,466	–
Treasury stock, at cost	(3,242)	(3,430)	(61,641)
Total shareholders' equity	2,157,133	987,651	662,663
Total liabilities and shareholders' equity	4,780,241	2,281,448	1,692,744

Required

1. What is the format of the balance sheet?
2. Prepare a simplified balance sheet with three subheadings in the assets and three subheadings in the equity and liabilities (see Table 15.5).
3. Compute the working capital, working capital need, and net cash.
4. Comment on the results and information created in questions 2 and 3.

Assignment 15.6
Ericsson (2)*

Topic: Analysis on the reported balance sheet and income statement
Related part of the chapter: Core/Advanced issues

The Ericsson group has been introduced in Chapter 14 (see Assignment 14.4).

Below are the income statements and balance sheets for the years 2004–1997 (**sources**: Annual reports 2004–1998). The Ericsson financial statements comply with the recommendations of the Swedish Financial Accounting Standards Council.

Required

1. What is the format of the income statement and balance sheet?
2. Analyze the income statement.
3. Analyze the balance sheet.
4. Prepare a synthetic analysis, including the cash flow statement if you have worked on Assignment 14.4 (Chapter 14).

Ericsson – Consolidated income statement

Years ended 31 December	2004 SEK m.	2003 SEK m.	2002 SEK m.	2001 SEK m.	2000 SEK m.	1999 SEK m.	1998 SEK m.	1997 SEK m.
Net sales	131,972	117,738	145,773	231,839	221,586	215,403	184,438	167,740
Cost of sales	−70,864	−78,901	−104,224	−173,900	−120,617	−125,881	−105,251	−97,868
Gross margin	**61,108**	**38,837**	**41,549**	**57,939**	**100,969**	**89,522**	**79,187**	**69,872**
Research and development and other technical expenses	−20,861	−27,136	−30,510	−46,640	−34,949	−33,123	−28,027	−24,242
Selling expenses	−9,693	−15,115	−21,896	−32,352	−26,563	−31,205	−24,108	−20,464
Administrative expenses	−6,551	−8,762	−9,995	−14,010	−12,004	−10,078	−8,922	−7,755
Total operating expenses	−37,105	−51,013	−62,401	−93,002	−73,516	−74,406	−61,057	−52,461
Share in earnings of joint ventures and associated companies	2,318	−604	−1,220	−715	−16,088	250	148	480
Other operating revenues and costs	2,617	1,541	773	8,398	27,463	2,224	995	866
Restructuring costs net, Phones	0	0	0	0	−8,000	0	0	0
Operating income	**28,938**	**−11,239**	**−21,299**	**−27,380**	**30,828**	**17,590**	**19,273**	**18,757**
Financial income	3,541	3,995	4,253	4,815	3,698	2,273	2,228	2,413
Financial expenses	−4,081	−4,859	−5,789	−6,589	−4,887	−2,971	−2,465	−2,365
Income after financial items	**28,398**	**−12,103**	**−22,835**	**−29,154**	**29,639**	**16,892**	**19,036**	**18,805**
Income taxes for the year	−9,077	1,460	4,165	8,813	−7,998	−4,358	−5,409	−5,755
Minority interest	−297	−201	−343	−923	−623	−404	−586	−1,109
Net income	19,024	−10,844	−19,013	−21,264	21,018	12,130	13,041	11,941

Ericsson – Consolidated balance sheet								
Financial year ended 31 December	2004 SEK m.	2003 SEK m.	2002 SEK m.	2001 SEK m.	2000 SEK m.	1999 SEK m.	1998 SEK m.	1997 SEK m.
Assets								
Fixed assets								
Intangible assets	10,415	11,210	12,609	13,066	12,833	10,548	6,354	748
Tangible assets	5,845	6,505	9,964	16,641	22,378	24,719	22,516	19,225
Financial assets								
Equity in joint ventures and associated companies	4,150	2,970	1,835	3,135	2,790	2,712	2,777	2,643
Other investments	543	433	2,243	3,101	2,484	1,751	1,438	1,434
Long-term customer financing	2,150	3,027	12,283	7,933	6,364	6,657	5,937	2,000
Deferred tax assets	21,815	27,130	26,047	6,980				
Other long-term assets	1,236	1,342	2,132	9,591	3,657	4,972	2,902	3,365
	46,154	52,617	67,113	60,447	50,506	51,359	41,924	29,415
Current assets								
Inventories	14,003	10,965	13,419	24,910	43,933	25,701	26,973	23,614
Receivables								
Accounts receivable – trade	32,644	31,886	37,384	57,236	74,973	63,584	53,900	46,151
Short-term customer financing	1,446	979	1,680	6,833	1,267	1,749	3,837	
Other receivables	12,239	12,718	23,303	39,171	44,029	31,227	22,589	19,133
Short-term cash investments	64,350	56,622	48,252	36,046	18,779	13,415	6,356	20,416
Cash and bank	12,204	16,585	17,962	32,878	16,827	15,593	11,877	8,711
	136,886	129,755	142,000	197,074	199,808	151,269	125,532	118,025
Total assets	183,040	182,372	209,113	257,521	250,314	202,628	167,456	147,440

Ericsson – Consolidated balance sheet (continued)

Financial Year ended 31 December	2004 SEK m.	2003 SEK m.	2002 SEK m.	2001 SEK m.	2000 SEK m.	1999 SEK m.	1998 SEK m.	1997 SEK m.
Stockholders' equity, provisions and liabilities								
Stockholders' equity								
Capital stock	16,132	16,132	15,974	8,066	7,910	4,893	4,878	2,436
Reserves not available for distribution	40,170	40,298	39,950	29,593	32,600	32,618	28,053	29,172
Restricted equity	56,302	56,430	55,924	37,659	40,510	37,511	32,931	31,608
Retained earnings	1,973	14,895	36,696	52,192	30,158	19,535	17,140	9,075
Net income	19,024	−10,844	−19,013	−21,264	21,018	12,130	13,041	11,941
Non-restricted equity	20,997	4,051	17,683	30,928	51,176	31,665	30,181	21,016
	77,299	**60,481**	**73,607**	**68,587**	**91,686**	**69,176**	**63,112**	**52,624**
Minority interest in consolidated subsidiaries	**1,057**	**2,299**	**2,469**	**3,653**	**2,764**	**2,182**	**2,051**	**4,395**
Provisions	**35,286**	**36,068**	**32,354**	**32,935**	**27,650**	**22,552**	**22,284**	**21,095**
Long-term liabilities								
Notes and bond loans	19,844	26,312	33,074	41,656	15,884	17,486	4,470	2,476
Convertible debentures	0	0	0	4,437	4,346	5,453	6,241	6,034
Liabilities to financial institutions	1,993	2,383	3,043	7,906	1,320	1,448	1,898	2,209
Other long-term liabilities	1,856	1,077	949	887	744	567	459	510
	23,693	**29,772**	**37,066**	**54,886**	**22,294**	**24,954**	**13,068**	**11,229**
Current liabilities								
Current maturities of long-term debt	781	7,262	11,083	3,622	3,188	1,491	1,188	742
Current liabilities to financial institutions	938	2,247	3,238	22,068	12,289	10,519	5,427	4,242
Advances from customers	3,390	3,297	2,672	4,803	6,847	6,437	8,398	7,633
Accounts payable – trade	10,988	8,895	12,469	19,511	30,156	21,618	18,246	14,803
Income tax liabilities	1,686	1,943	619	1,856	5,080	2,397	1,957	4,100
Other current liabilities	27,922	30,108	33,536	45,600	48,360	41,302	31,725	26,577
	45,705	**53,752**	**63,617**	**97,460**	**105,920**	**83,764**	**66,941**	**58,097**
Total stockholders' equity, provisions and liabilities	183,040	182,372	209,113	257,521	250,314	202,628	167,456	147,440
Bank overdraft	0	0	0	0	0	0	0	0

Assignment 15.7
4Kids Entertainment, Inc.*

Topic: Earnings per share
Related part of the chapter: Advanced issues

4Kids Entertainment is a US company that receives revenues from a number of sources, principally through licensing and media buying. It represents such well-known properties as Pokémon and Nintendo. The company's common stock is traded on the NASDAQ. The annual report 2004 (for the year ended 31 December) contains the following information. The company applies SFAS No. 128, which requires the computation and presentation of earnings per share (EPS) to include basic and diluted EPS. Basic EPS is computed based solely on the weighted average number of common shares outstanding during the period. Diluted EPS reflects all potential dilution of common stock.

The number of common shares, in 2004, is 13,683,756 and the number of stock options granted is 651,587 (if exercised, each option entitles the holder to one share of common stock). The income statement shows net income to be US$12,730,000.

Required

Prepare a statement showing the computation of basic and diluted earnings per share for the year 2004.

References

Altman, E. I. (1968) Financial ratios, discriminant analysis and the prediction of corporate bankruptcy. *The Journal of Finance*, (23), September, 589–609.

Altman, E. I., and McGough, T. P. (1974) Evaluation of a company as a going concern. *Journal of Accountancy*, December, 50–57.

ASB (1998) Financial Reporting Standard No. 14: Earnings Per Share, London, UK.

Baker, C. R., Ding, Y., and Stolowy, H. (2005) Using 'statement of intermediate balances' as tool for international financial statement analysis in airline industry. *Advances in International Accounting*, 18, 169–98.

Barnea, A., Ronen, J., and Sadan, S. (1975) The implementation of accounting objectives: An application to extraordinary items. *The Accounting Review*, January, 58–68.

Barnea, A., Ronen, J., and Sadan, S. (1976) Classificatory smoothing of income with extraordinary items. *The Accounting Review*, January, 110–22.

Black, E. L., Sellers, K. F., and Manly, T. S. (1998) Earnings management using asset sales: An international study of countries allowing noncurrent asset revaluation. *Journal of Business Finance & Accounting*, 25(9) & (10), 1287–317.

Copeland, R. M. (1968) Income smoothing. *Journal of Accounting Research, Empirical Research in Accounting, Selected Studies*, 6, Supplement, 101–16.

FASB (1997) Statement of Financial Accounting Standard No. 128: Earnings Per Share, Norwalk, CT.

FASB (1997) Statement of Financial Accounting Standard No. 131: Disclosures About Segments of an Enterprise and Related Information, Norwalk, CT.

Fern, R. H., Brown, B., and Dickey, S. W. (1994) An empirical test of politically-motivated income smoothing in the oil refining industry. *Journal of Applied Business Research*, 10(1) Winter, 92.

Griffiths, I. (1986) *Creative Accounting*, Irwin, London.

Griffiths, I. (1995) *New Creative Accounting*, Macmillan.

IASB (1997) International Accounting Standard No. 14: Segment Reporting, London.

IASB (2003) International Accounting Standard No. 33: Earnings Per Share, London.

Lebas, M. (ed.) (1999) *Management Accounting Glossary*, ECM, Paris and CIMA London.

Mathews, M. R., and Perera, M. H. B. (1996) *Accounting Theory and Development*, Nelson – ITPC, Melbourne.

Moore, M. L. (1973) Management changes and discretionary accounting decisions. *Journal of Accounting Research*, (Spring), 100–107.

Ronen, J., and Sadan, S. (1975) Classificatory smoothing: Alternative income models. *Journal of Accounting Research*, (Spring), 133–49.

Smith, A. (2003) *The Wealth of Nations (1776)*, New Edition Bantam Classics, New York.

Smith, T. (1996) *Accounting for Growth – Stripping the Camouflage From Company Accounts*, 2nd edn, Century Business, London.

Stolowy, H., and Breton, G. (2004) Accounts manipulation: A literature review and proposed conceptual framework, *Review of Accounting and Finance*, 3(1), 5–65.

Sutton, T. (2004) *Corporate Financial Accounting and Reporting*, 2nd edn, Financial Times Prentice Hall, London.

Further reading

Alford, A., Jones, J., Leftwich, R., and Zmijewski, M. (1993) The Relative Informativeness of Accounting Disclosures in Different Countries. *Journal of Accounting Research*, 31(Supplement), 183–223.

Cote, J. M., and Latham, C. K. (1999) The merchandising ratio: A comprehensive measure of working capital strategy. *Issues in Accounting Education*, 14(2), 255–67.

Deppe L. (2000) Disclosing disaggregated information. *Journal of Accountancy*, 190(3), 47–52.

Haller, A., and Park, P. (1994) Regulation and practice of segmental reporting in Germany. *European Accounting Review*, 3(3), 563–80.

Haller, A., and Stolowy, H. (1998) Value added in financial accounting: A comparative study of Germany and France. *Advances in International Accounting*, 11, 23–51.

Lainez, J. A., and Callao, S. (2000) The effect of accounting diversity on international financial analysis: empirical evidence. *International Journal of Accounting*, 35(1), 65–83.

Prather-Kinsey, J., and Meek, G. K. (2004) The effect of revised IAS 14 on segment reporting by IAS companies. *European Accounting Review*, 13(2), 213–34.

Prencipe, A. (2004) Proprietary costs and determinants of voluntary segment disclosure: Evidence from Italian listed companies *European Accounting Review*, 13(2), 319–40.

Street D. L., Nichols N. B., and Gray S. J. (2000) Segment disclosures under SFAS No. 131: Has business segment reporting improved? *Accounting Horizons*, 14(3), September, 259–85.

Additional material on the website

Go to http://www.thomsonlearning.co.uk/stolowylebas2 for further information.

The following appendices to this chapter are available on the dedicated website:

Appendix 15.1: Value added
Appendix 15.2: Working capital need in sales days
Appendix 15.3: Complementary remarks on ratios computation
Appendix 15.4: Business newspapers and magazines – specialized magazines
Appendix 15.5: Databases and statistics publications
Appendix 15.6: Filing of financial statements
Appendix 15.7: Scoring models

Notes

1. We distinguish data from information. A piece of data is a fact, a number, a descriptor. It has no specific meaning in and of itself. It is descriptive of something. Information is the result of a process applied to data (comparison with other pieces of data such as the construction of a ratio, calculation of the trend of the evolution over time of a given measure, replacing the piece of data in its historical or competitive context, etc.) that yields (potentially useful) metrics that can effectively be used in a decision model. These useful metrics are called information. Information has the *potential* of leading the decision maker to modify the decision he or she would have taken before the 'new' piece of information was provided. Data do not have such potential.
2. SARS or 'severe acute respiratory syndrome' is a health epidemic that caused a dramatic reduction in air travel within and towards South East Asia during the year 2003.
3. Assumed to be calculated for one year – should a different duration prove to be useful, replace 'year', where appropriate, by 'period'.
4. Current assets include cash.
5. Current liabilities include bank overdrafts.
6. 'Debt' represents long-term and short-term interest-bearing liabilities.
7. Average equity = (Beginning Shareholders' equity + Ending Shareholders' equity)/2.
8. The relevance of extraordinary items in the determination of the income integrated in the EPS computation has been discussed and the practice differs a lot.
9. We take here the meaning of 'earnings quality' to mean that it describes fairly and accurately the situation of the firm. Financial market analysts sometimes use the same expression but, in that case, they refer to the fact the earnings variance is proportionately small, thus that earnings are easily predictable and, most of the time, that the trend of earnings over time is ascending. We limit our analysis here to the formal quality (accurate descriptiveness) of the reported figures.
10. The *beta* (β) is a measure of the risk of the company's shares. It relates the variance of earnings of a company with the average variance of earnings of the market.
11. The Report on the Financial Aspects of Corporate Governance, 1992.
12. Sir Adrian Cadbury: 'Corporate governance: a Framework for Implementation', World Bank.
13. Information Systems Audit and Control Foundation, 2001.
14. 'Governance for young leaders: Understanding corporate governance', March 23, 2004.
15. For a quick introduction to Altman's Z score, see: 'Z scores – a guide to failure prediction', by Gregory J. Eidleman, *The CPA Journal*, February 1995 (The CPA Journal Online).

Solutions to review questions and problems

Review 1.1 Multiple-choice questions

Related part of the chapter: Core issues

1. (a), (c), (d) and in certain countries (b).

The statement of changes in shareholders' equity, which presents the changes in the 'net worth' (as described in the introduction to the chapter) has not been included in this list. It is, however, a compulsory financial statement in some countries. This statement will be explored further in Chapter 11.

2. False.

Many transactions have no impact on cash, either because the impact is postponed to a later date (as in the case of a sale on account) or because there never will be a direct cash impact, as we will see later (see Chapters 2 and 7) in the case of the recognition of the loss of value of physical assets or the consumption of the productive capacity of a fixed asset (depreciation).

3. False.

Financial accounting does not always have clear or complete documents supporting the exact value placed on a transaction. The value is often subjective. For example, the risk of uncollectibility on a credit sale may be estimated statistically (on the basis of past records) but cannot be known exactly for each transaction before final settlement or an incident actually occurs.

4. (b)

Bookkeeping means recording transactions. It is therefore part of financial accounting since recording of transactions is compulsory. Management accounting also uses the same recorded data for its own analyses.

Review 1.2 Discussion questions

Related part of the chapter: Core/Advanced issues

1. Why do decision makers use accounting information and for what purpose? Decision makers use accounting information for decisions regarding resource allocation. This allocation concerns management for internal purposes so as to increase the wealth creation of the firm. It concerns shareholders who may want to reconsider investing their wealth in this or that firm. Decision makers also use accounting to monitor the achievements of subordinate managers since accounting records their actions and the consequences of these.
2. Why have standards of reporting emerged that constrain the way events are recorded in accounting? To a large extent reporting standards have emerged to reduce the transaction cost borne by both producers and users of financial information. If the producer knows the recommended or preferred way to record an event, there is no need for the accountant to search for the most suitable way to do so. If the user receives data that come from a standardized coding method and agreed methods of aggregation and transformation, all users can interpret the same data to mean the same thing. Further, it improves the possibility of inter-firm comparisons without removing the possibility, for the user, of recoding the data in a preferred format.
3. What distinguishes financial accounting and reporting, from managerial accounting? This question is covered in Table 1.10.

Review 2.1 Vivaldi Company (1)

Topic: Transactions and the business equation
Related part of the chapter: Core/Advanced issues

1. Basic business equation

	Assets					=	Liabilities		+	Shareholders' equity (SE)		
	Cash	+ Accounts receivable	+ Merchandise inventory	+ Equipment	+ −Accumulated depreciation	=	Taxes payable	+ Salaries payable	+ Accounts payable	+ Retained earnings	+ Share capital	Details of SE transactions
(A)	+60			+40							+100	Initial investment
(B)									+40	−40		Purchases of merchandise
(C)									+7	−7		External expense
(D)		+120								+120		Sales of merchandise
(E)								+45		−45		Personnel expenses
(F)							+20			−20		Tax expenses
(G)	+60	−60										
(H)	−35								−35			
(I)	−30							−30				
(J)					−4					−4		Depreciation expenses
(K)			+10							+10		Change in inventory
Ending balance	55	+ 60	+ 10	+ 40	+ −4	=	20	+ 15	+ 12	+ 14	+ 100	

161

161

2. Preparation of the year-end balance sheet (as of 31 December X1)

Assets		Liabilities	
Fixed assets (equipment)	40	Capital	100
Equipment depreciation	−4	Net income	14
Fixed assets (net value)	36	Accounts payable (40 + 7 − 35)	12
Merchandise inventory	10	Salaries and social expenses payable (30 + 15 − 30)	15
Accounts receivable (120 − 60)	60		
Cash at bank (60 + 60 − 35 − 30)	55	Taxes payable	20
Total	161	Total	161

3. Preparation of the income statement (for the year X1)

Expenses		Revenues	
Purchases of merchandise	40	Sales of merchandise	120
Change in inventory of merchandise	−10		
Other purchases and external expenses	7		
Taxes	20		
Personnel expenses (30 + 15)	45		
Depreciation expenses	4		
Net income	14		
Total	120	Total	120

Remarks:

- The balance sheet is, itself, an account, which is comprised of the balances of all balance sheet subsidiary accounts. The profit or the loss is, itself, the balance of the balance sheet account.
- The income statement is the account that records the balances of all the expense and revenue accounts. Income (profit or loss) is the balance of the income statement.
- The income is the same, by construction, in the balance sheet and the income statement.

Review 2.2 Vivaldi Company (2)

Topic: Transactions and impact on the financial statements
Related part of the chapter: Core/Advanced issues

Balance sheet as of 31 December X1

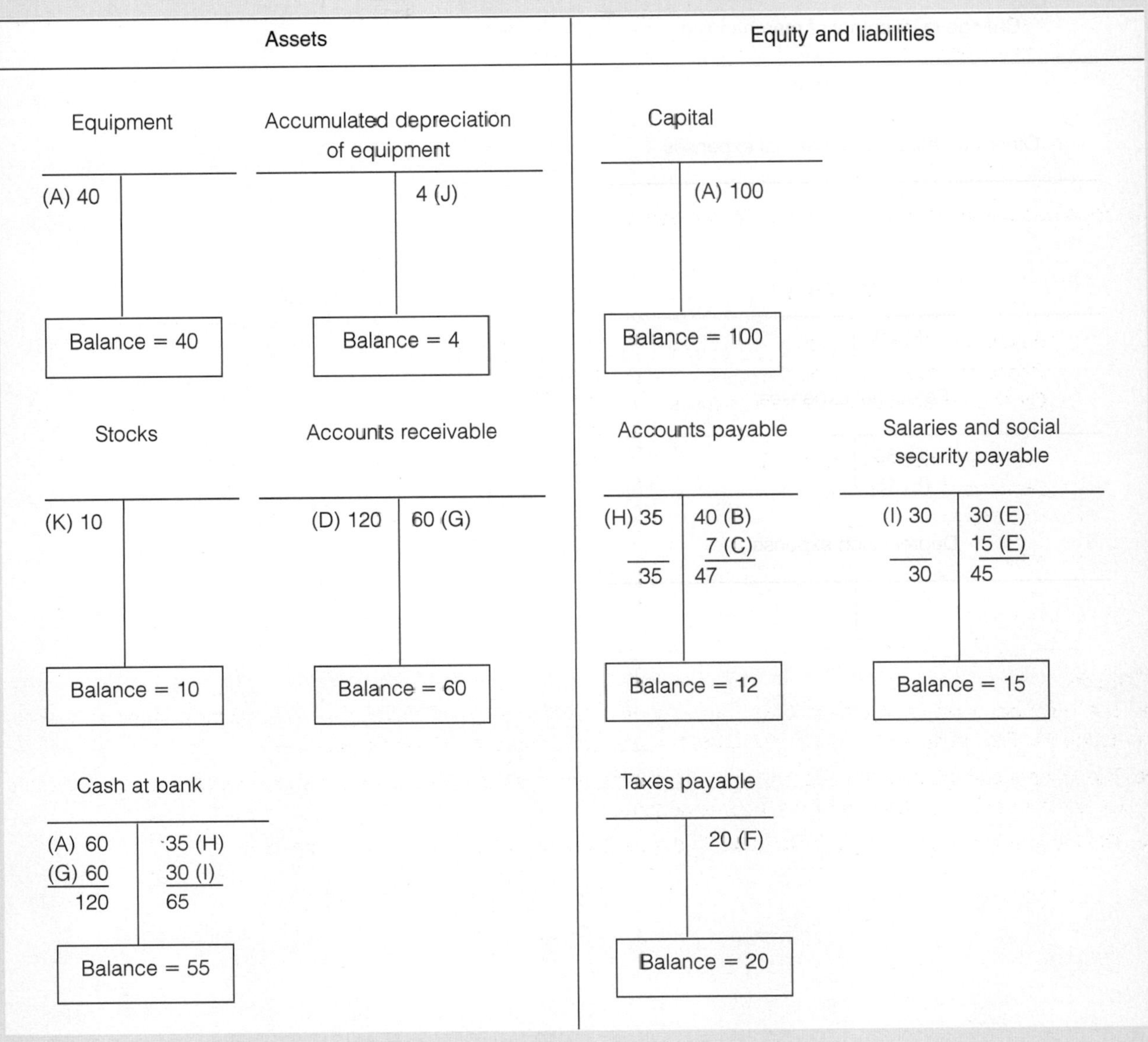

Income statement for the year X1

Expenses		Revenues	
Purchases of merchandise		**Sales of merchandise**	
(B) 40			120 (D)
Change in inventory of merchandise			
	10 (K)		
Other purchases and external expenses			
(C) 7			
Taxes			
(F) 20			
Personnel expenses			
(E) 30 (E) 15			
Depreciation expense			
(J) 4			

Review 2.3 Albinoni Company

Topic: Transactions and the business equation
Related part of the chapter: Core issues

Perpetual inventory

	Assets					= Liabilities		+ Shareholders' equity (SE)		
	Cash +	Accounts receivable +	Merchandise inventory	+ Equipment	+ Accumulated depreciation	= Financial debt	+ Accounts payable	+ Net income	+ Share capital	Details of SE transactions
(1)	30			80					110	Initial investment
(2)	200					200				
(3)	−40							−40		Taxes
(4)			50				50			
(5)	−10							−10		Legal fees
(6)	−30							−30		Personnel expenses
(7)	20	80						100		Sales
			−40					−40		Cost of merchandise sold
(8)	−30						−30			
(9)	70	−70								
(10)					−20			−20		Depreciation expense
(11)										
Ending balance	210 +	10 +	10	+ 80	+ −20	= 200	+ 20	+ −40	+ 110	

290 (total assets)   290 (total liabilities and shareholders' equity)

Periodic inventory

	Assets					= Liabilities		+ Shareholders' equity (SE)		
	Cash +	Accounts receivable +	Merchandise inventory	+ Equipment	+ Accumulated depreciation	= Financial debt	+ Accounts payable	+ Net income	+ Share capital	Details of SE transactions
(1)	30			80					110	Initial investment
(2)	200					200				
(3)	−40							−40		Taxes
(4)							50	−50		Purchase of merchandise
(5)	−10							−10		Legal fees
(6)	−30							−30		Personnel expenses
(7)	20	80						100		Sales
(8)	−30						−30			
(9)	70	−70								
(10)					−20			−20		Depreciation expense
(11)			10					10		Change in inventory
Ending balance	210 +	10 +	10	+ 80	+ −20	= 200	+ 20	+ −40	+ 110	

290 (assets total)

290 (liabilities and shareholders' equity total)

Review 3.1 Orkla*

Topic: Constructing a balance sheet
Related part of the chapter: Core issues

1. Reconstruct the balance sheet in a vertical, single-step, and increasing format (check figure: total balance sheet = 41,755).

Balance sheet as of 31 December 2004 (in millions of NOK)

Amounts in NOK million	2004
Intangible assets	3,647
Tangible assets	9,086
Investments in associates	1,716
Other financial long-term assets	4,919
Long-term assets	19,368
Inventories	2,869
Receivables	4,449
Portfolio investments, etc.	12,837
Cash and cash equivalents	2,232
Short-term assets	22,387
Total assets	41,755
Paid-in equity	2,007
Accumulated profit	24,068
Minority interests	229
Equity	26,304
Provisions	1,657
Long-term interest-bearing liabilities	5,372
Long-term liabilities and provisions	7,029
Short-term interest-bearing liabilities	199
Other short-term liabilities	8,223
Short-term liabilities	8,422
Equity and liabilities	41,755

2. Is the balance sheet organized by nature or by term?

The balance sheet is organized by term, as we find a clear distinction between long-term and short-term liabilities.

Review 3.2 Holcim*

Topic: Constructing an income statement
Related part of the chapter: Core issues

1. Prepare the income statement in a multiple-step format

Income statement as of 31 December 2004 (in millions of CHF)	
Million CHF	2004
Net sales	13,215
Production cost of goods sold	(6,617)
Gross profit	6,598
Distribution and selling expenses	(2,980)
Administration expenses	(1,050)
Other depreciation and amortization	(317)
Operating profit	2,251
Other income (expenses)	(76)
EBIT	2,175
Financial expenses net	(512)
Net income before taxes	1,663
Income taxes	(510)
Net income before minority interests	1,153
Minority interests	(239)
Net income after minority interests	914

2. Is the income statement organized by nature or by function?

The income statement is presented by function as we find the 'production cost of goods sold', the 'distribution and selling expenses' and the 'administration expenses'.

Review 3.3 Beethoven Company

Topic: Link between balance sheet, income statement, and cash flow statement
Related part of the chapter: Core issues

Income statement (000 CU) for the year X2			
Operating expenses		**Operating revenues**	
Purchases of raw materials	510	Sales	1,600
Inventory variation merchandise (B − E)	20		
External charges	250		
Miscellaneous taxes	120		
Personnel expenses	430		
Depreciation expense	40		
Financial charges	0	**Financial income**	0
Exceptional charges	0	**Exceptional income**	0
Subtotal	1,370	Subtotal	1,600
Income tax	92		
Net income	*138*	*Net loss*	*0*
Total	1,600	Total	1,600

Balance sheet (000 CU) at the end of year X2			
Fixed assets		**Shareholders' equity**	
Manufacturing equipment (net)	1,060	Capital	710
Manufacturing assets (Gross) = 800 + 300		Reserves	444
Minus accumulated depreciation = 40		Net income/loss	138
Current assets		Subtotal	1,292
		Liabilities	
Merchandise inventory	130	Financial debts	30
		Bank overdraft	0
Accounts receivable	200	Accounts payable	110
Cash at bank	134	Income tax payable	92
Total	1,524	Total	1,524

Cash flow budget (000 CU) for the year X2	
Cash flows from operating activities	
Cash from sales	1,400
Cash from receivables (see preceding balance sheet)	400
Purchases for the year	−400
Accounts payable (see preceding balance sheet)	−120
Payment of previous year's Income tax payable	−144
Miscellaneous taxes	−120
Personnel expenses	−430
Advertising expenses	−250
Financial expenses	0
Net cash flows from operating activities (1)	*336*
Cash flows from investing activities	
Investments	−300
Other (sale of fixed assets)	0
Net cash flows used in investing activities (2)	*−300*
Cash flows from financing activities	
Other (capital)	0
Repayment of debts	−80
Dividends paid	−72
Net cash flows used in financing activities (3)	*−152*
Net increase (decrease) in cash and cash equivalents (4) = (1) + (2) + (3)	−116
Opening balance (5)	250
Ending balance (6) = (4) + (5)	134

Review 4.1 Grieg Company (1)

Topic: The accounting process: from the journal to the financial statements (purchases of merchandise are recorded first in inventory)
Related part of the chapter: Core issues

Journal entries

1	BS (A+)		Cash in bank		10,000	
		BS (L+)		Shareholders' equity		10,000
2	BS (A+)		Equipment		1,200	
		BS (A−)		Cash in bank		1,200
3	BS (A+)		Merchandise inventory		9,000	
		BS (L+)		Accounts payable		9,000
4	BS (A+)		Cash in bank		500	
		BS (L+)		Debt		500
5	IS (E+)		Cost of goods sold		7,000	
		BS (A−)		Merchandise inventory		7,000
5	BS (A+)		Cash in bank		6,000	
	BS (A+)		Accounts receivable		5,000	
		IS (R+)		Sales		11,000
6	BS (A+)		Cash in bank		4,000	
		BS (A−)		Accounts receivable		4,000
7	BS (L−)		Accounts payable		8,000	
		BS (A−)		Cash in bank		8,000
8	IS (E+)		Depreciation expense		120	
		BS (A−)		Accumulated depreciation, Equipment		120
					50,820	50,820

General ledger

Assets accounts

Equipment

Debit	Credit
(2) 1,200	
D balance = 1,200	

Accumulated depreciation

Debit	Credit
	120 (8)
	C balance = 120

Merchandise inventory

Debit	Credit
(3) 9,000	7,000 (5)
D balance = 2,000	

Accounts receivable

Debit	Credit
(5) 5,000	4,000 (6)
D balance = 1,000	

Cash in bank

Debit	Credit
(1) 10,000	1,200 (2)
(4) 500	8,000 (7)
(5) 6,000	
(6) 4,000	
D balance = 11,300	

Equity and liabilities accounts

Capital

Debit	Credit
	10,000 (1)
	C balance = 10,000

Debt

Debit	Credit
	500 (4)
	C balance = 500

Accounts payable

Debit	Credit
(7) 8,000	9,000 (3)
	C balance = 1,000

Expense accounts

Cost of goods sold

Debit	Credit
(5) 7,000	
D balance = 7,000	

Depreciation expense

Debit	Credit
(8) 120	
D balance = 120	

Revenue accounts

Sales

Debit	Credit
	11,000 (5)
	C balance = 11,000

Comments

- The accounts have been divided into four main categories: assets, equity and liabilities, expenses, and revenues.

Trial balance

	Entries of the period		Ending balance	
	D	C	D	C
Equipment	1,200		1,200	
Accumulated depreciation		120		120
Merchandise inventory	9,000	7,000	2,000	
Accounts receivable	5,000	4,000	1,000	
Cash in bank	20,500	9,200	11,300	
Share capital		10,000		10,000
Accounts payable	8,000	9,000		1,000
Debt		500		500
Cost of goods sold	7,000		7,000	
Depreciation expense	120		120	
Sales		11,000		11,000
Total	*50,820*	*50,820*	*22,620*	*22,620*

Balance sheet and income statement

Balance sheet at 31 January X1			
ASSETS		LIABILITIES	
Fixed assets		Shareholders' equity	
Equipment	1,200	Share capital	10,000
Accumulated depreciation	−120	*Income for the month*	*3,880*
Net amount	1,080		
Current assets		Debts	
Merchandise inventory	2,000	Debt	500
Accounts receivable	1,000	Accounts payable	1,000
Cash in bank	11,300		
Total assets	*15,380*	*Total liabilities*	*15,380*

Income statement for the month ended 31 January X1	
REVENUES	
Sales	11,000
Total revenues (1)	11,000
EXPENSES	
Cost of goods sold	7,000
Depreciation expense	120
Total expenses (2)	7,120
Net income (1) – (2)	3,880

Comments

- The net income as calculated in the income statement is the same as that in the balance sheet.

Review 4.2 Grieg Company (2)

Topic: The accounting process: from the journal to the financial statements (purchases of merchandise are first recorded in the income statement)
Related part of the chapter: Core issues

Journal entries

1	BS (A+)		Cash in bank		10,000	
		BS (L+)		Shareholders' equity		10,000
2	BS (A+)		Equipment		1,200	
		BS (A−)		Cash in bank		1,200
3	IS (E+)		Purchase of merchandise for resale		9,000	
		BS (L+)		Accounts payable		9,000
4	BS (A+)		Cash in bank		500	
		BS (L+)		Debt		500
5	BS (A+)		Cash in bank		6,000	
	BS (A+)		Accounts receivable		5,000	
		IS (R+)		Sales		11,000
6	BS (A+)		Cash in bank		4,000	
		BS (A−)		Accounts receivable		4,000
7	BS (L−)		Accounts payable		8,000	
		BS (A−)		Cash in bank		8,000
8	IS (E+)		Depreciation expense		120	
		BS (A−)		Accumulated depreciation, Equipment		120
9	BS (A+)		Merchandise inventory		2,000	
		IS (E−)		Change in inventories		2,000
					45,820	45,820

General ledger

Assets accounts

Equipment

(2) 1,200	
D balance = 1,200	

Accumulated depreciation

	120 (8)
	C balance = 120

Merchandise inventory

(9) 2,000	
D balance = 2,000	

Accounts receivable

(5) 5,000	4,000 (6)
D balance = 1,000	

Cash in bank

(1) 10,000	1,200 (2)
(4) 500	8,000 (7)
(5) 6,000	
(6) 4,000	
D balance = 11,300	

Equity and liabilities accounts

Share capital

	10,000 (1)
	C balance = 10,000

Debt

	500 (4)
	C balance = 500

Accounts payable

(7) 8,000	9,000 (3)
	C balance = 1,000

Expense accounts

Purchase of merchandise

(3) 9,000	
D balance = 9,000	

Change in inventories

	2,000 (9)
	C balance = 2,000

Depreciation expense

(8) 120	
D balance = 120	

Revenue accounts

Sales

	11,000 (5)
	C balance = 11,000

Comments

- The accounts have been divided into four main categories: assets, equity and liabilities, expenses, and revenues.

Trial balance

	Entries of the period		Ending balance	
	D	C	D	C
Equipment	1,200		1,200	
Accumulated depreciation		120		120
Merchandise inventory	2,000		2,000	
Accounts receivable	5,000	4,000	1,000	
Cash in bank	20,500	9,200	11,300	
Share capital		10,000		10,000
Debt		500		500
Accounts payable	8,000	9,000		1,000
Purchase of merchandise	9,000		9,000	
Change in inventories		2,000		2,000
Depreciation expense	120		120	
Sales		11,000		11,000
Total	*45,820*	*45,820*	*24,620*	*24,620*

Balance sheet and income statement

Balance sheet at 31 January X1			
ASSETS		LIABILITIES	
Fixed assets		**Shareholders' equity**	
Equipment	1,200	Share capital	10,000
Accumulated depreciation	−120	*Income for the month*	*3,880*
Net amount	1,080		
Current assets		**Debts**	
Merchandise inventory	2,000	Debt	500
Accounts receivable	1,000	Accounts payable	1,000
Cash in bank	11,300		
Total assets	*15,380*	*Total liabilities*	*15,380*

Income statement for the month ended 31 January X1	
REVENUES	
Sales	11,000
Total revenues (1)	11,000
EXPENSES	
Purchase of merchandise	9,000
Change in inventories	−2,000
Depreciation expense	120
Total expenses (2)	7,120
Net income (1) − (2)	3,880

Comments

- The net income as calculated in the income statement is the same as that in the balance sheet.
- If we compare the Review problems Grieg (1) and Grieg (2), we notice that the total 'purchases + Change in inventories' is equal to the 'Cost of goods sold'. This is normal (see Chapters 2 and 9).

Review 5.1 Adam

Topic: Accounting principles and end-of-period entries
Related part of the chapter: Core issues

Company 1

Accounting principles involved: Prudence (conservatism) and 'lower of cost or market'.
Accounting entry:

- In the balance sheet: decrease of assets: (provision for depreciation).
- In the income statement (not displayed): increase in expenses (provision expense).

Company 1 – Modified balance sheet

Assets		Shareholders' equity and liabilities	
Fixed assets	300,000	*Shareholders' equity*	
Less accumulated depreciation (*−40,000*)	**−200,000**	Share capital and reserves	330,000
Fixed assets (net)	100,000	Net income (*−40,000*)	**−20,000**
Current assets		*Liabilities*	40,000
Inventories	120,000		
Accounts receivable	130,000		
Total assets	350,000	Total shareholders' equity and liabilities	350,000

In bold, modified figures; in italics, impact of the entry

Company 2

Accounting principle involved: Prudence (conservatism).
Accounting entry:

- In the balance sheet: decrease in assets (provision for depreciation).
- In the income statement (not displayed): increase in expenses (provision expense).

Company 2 – Modified balance sheet

Assets		Shareholders' equity and liabilities	
Fixed assets	250,000	*Shareholders' equity*	
Less accumulated depreciation	−130,000	Share capital and reserves	300,000
Fixed assets (net)	120,000	Net income (*−60,000*)	**−10,000**
Current assets		*Liabilities*	20,000
Inventories	100,000		
Accounts receivable (*−60,000*)	**90,000**		
Total assets	310,000	Total shareholders' equity and liabilities	310,000

Company 3

Accounting principle involved: Historical cost.
Accounting entry:

- In the balance sheet: decrease in assets (inventories).
- In the income statement (not displayed), decrease in revenues.
- Consequence: cancellation of the profit recorded (300,000 × 10% = 30,000).

Company 3 – Modified balance sheet

Assets		Shareholders' equity and liabilities	
Fixed assets	500,000	*Shareholders' equity*	
Less accumulated depreciation	−240,000	Share capital and reserves	520,000
Fixed assets (net)	260,000	Net income (*−30,000*)	**−10,000**
Current assets		*Liabilities*	200,000
Inventories (*−30,000*)	**300,000**		
Accounts receivable	150,000		
Total assets	710,000	Total shareholders' equity and liabilities	710,000

Company 4

Accounting principle involved: Accounting period and prudence.
Accounting entry:

- In the balance sheet: decrease in assets (accounts receivable: 100,000) and increase in assets (inventories: 70,000).
- In the income statement (not displayed): decrease in revenues (sales: 100,000) and decrease in expenses (change in inventory: 70,000).
- Consequence: cancellation of the profit recorded (100,000 × 30% = 30,000).

Company 4 – Modified balance sheet

Assets		Shareholders' equity and liabilities	
Fixed assets	210,000	*Shareholders' equity*	
Less accumulated depreciation	−90,000	Share capital and reserves	150,000
Fixed assets (net)	120,000	Net income (*−30,000*)	**−20,000**
Current assets		*Liabilities*	120,000
Inventories (*+70,000*)	**110,000**		
Accounts receivable (*−100,000*)	**20,000**		
Total assets	250,000	Total shareholders' equity and liabilities	250,000

In all four cases the net income of the period goes from positive (profit) to negative (loss) after end-of-period adjustments.

Review 6.1 Schultz Accountancy Firm (1)

Topic: Revenue recognition
Related part of the chapter: Core issues

Solution

(a) Media commissions should be recognized when the related advertisement or commercial appears before the public. The accounting treatment followed by this ad agency is not correct.

(b) Revenue from artistic performances, banquets, and other special events is recognized when the event takes place. When a subscription to a number of events is sold, the fee is allocated to each event, on a basis that reflects the extent to which services are performed at each event. The policy adopted by Altrium Auditorium is not correct, unless the events are distributed 1/4 and 3/4 over time, which does not appear to be the case on the basis of the problem data.

(c) Revenue is recognized when delivery is made and cash is received by the seller or its agent. The accounting treatment is correct.

(d) Revenue recognition depends on the uncertainty of the collection of the membership fee. The fee is recognized as revenue when no significant uncertainty about collection exists. In the present case, since the fee permits only membership (and must be paid before the member gains access to other services that will be paid separately), the club should not defer the recognition of the fee on a straight-line basis over the months of membership but recognize it when the contract is signed (generally when the cash payment to made).

Review 6.2 Schall Company

Topic: Deferred taxation
Related part of the chapter: Core issues

The impact on income tax calculations is as follows when no deferred tax account is to be used:

Financial statements			Income tax return		
	Year X1	Year X2		Year X1	Year X2
Pre-tax income before recording an expense	110	110	Pre-tax income before recording an expense	110	110
Expense recorded	−10	0	Deduction of expense	−10	0
Pre-tax income after recording the expense	100	110			
Expense split over two years	10	0			
Depreciation of the expense split over two years	−5	−5			
Pre-tax financial income	105	105	Taxable income	100	110
Income tax expense	−40	−44	Income tax expense	40	44
Net income	65	61			

In countries that authorize or require deferred taxation, the left-hand side of the table is not allowed because it mixes pre-tax income (coming from accounting for reporting calculations) and income tax, which is the result of a fiscal calculation.
The following table illustrates what needs to be done if the use of deferred taxes is required.

Accounting for deferred income taxes

Theoretical tax expense based on financial reporting			Actual tax expense based on tax return		
	Year X1	Year X2		Year X1	Year X2
Pre-tax income	105	105	Income tax expense (40% of taxable income)	40	44
Income tax expense (40% of pre-tax income)	42	42			
Reported net income	63	63			

Recording

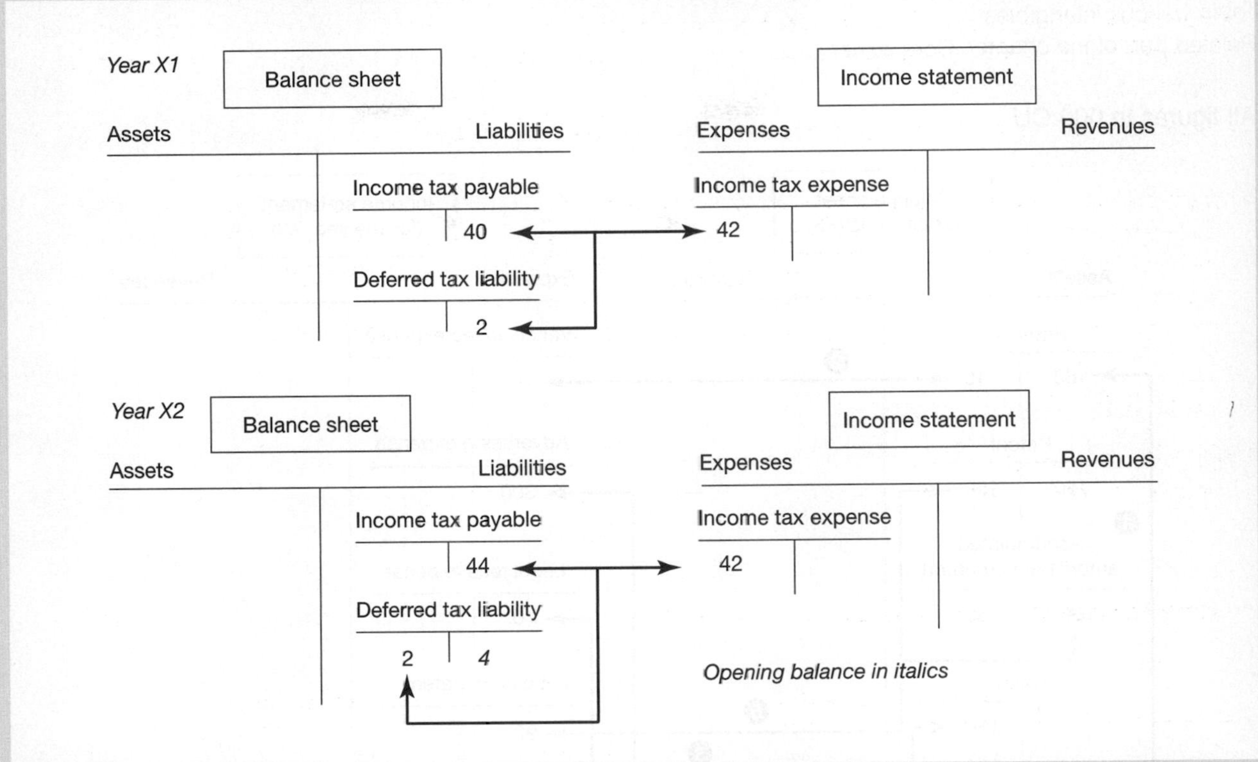

Review 7.1 Gibbons

Topic: Determining the cost of acquisition
Related part of the chapter: Core issues

1. Computation of the acquisition cost

Retail price		1,500
Discount	20%	– 300
Net invoice cost		1,200
Freight expenses		150
Installation expenses		100
Total acquisition cost		1,450

The repair expenses are not considered as a component of the machine's acquisition cost because those expenses are not necessary to obtain the machine.

2. Accounting entries

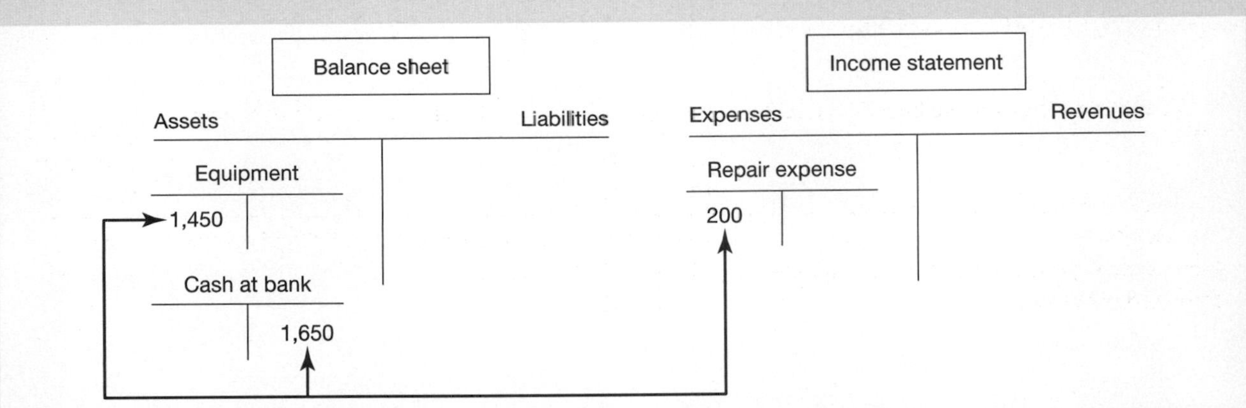

Review 8.1 Turina

Topic: Various intangibles
Related part of the chapter: Core issues

All figures in 000 CU

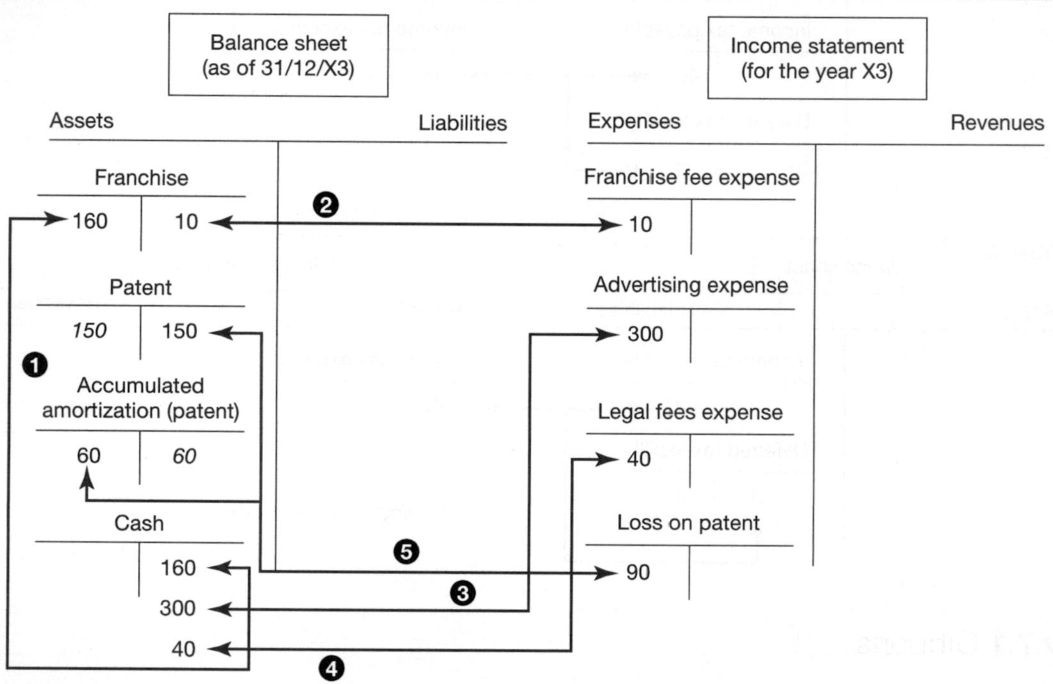

Question 1

❶ Recording of the franchise as an intangible asset.

❷ Franchise fee expense: 160 × 1/8 × 6 months. In the case of a franchise, a direct amortization (through the 'franchise fee expense' account) is possible. The 'franchise fee expense' is then equivalent to an amortization expense.

Question 2

❸ The advertising expense is not considered as an intangible asset.

Question 3

❹ The legal fees are recorded.

❺ The patent and accumulated amortization accounts are cancelled and a loss is recorded.

Review 8.2 De Falla

Topic: Accounting for R&D
Related part of the chapter: Advanced issues

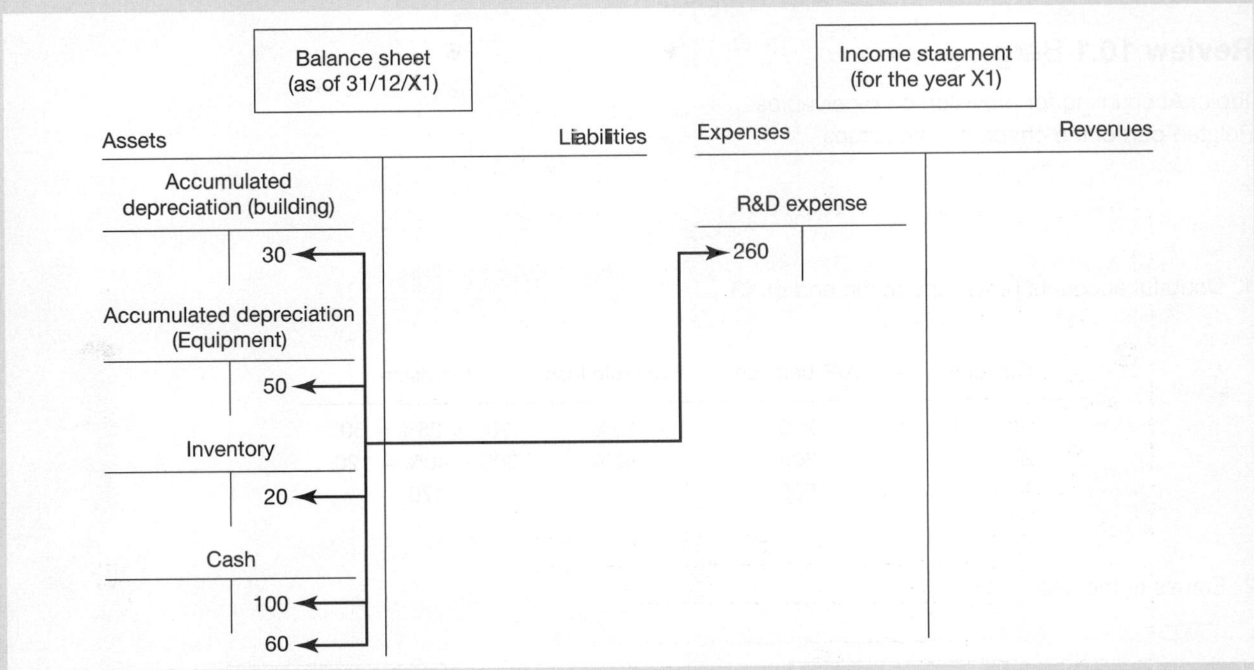

All these expenses can be included in R&D expense. We assumed that wages and salaries, as well as general and administrative expenses, are paid in cash. 'Payable' accounts could have been used instead of 'cash'.

Review 9.1 Ericsson*

Topic: Reporting for inventory
Related part of the chapter: Core/Advanced issues

Solution

1. What are 'obsolescence reserves' usually called? They are usually called 'provision for depreciation of inventories' or 'valuation allowance for depreciation of inventories'.

2. What do the 'Additions' in these reserves represent? They represent the provision expense of the year, charged against income.

3. What does the item 'Utilized' in these reserves refer to? It represents the reversal of provisions when the allowance is no longer necessary, for instance because inventories have been consumed or sold.

4. What restatement is necessary to obtain the gross amount of inventories? The amount reported in the balance sheet is a net amount, as confirmed in the notes (see the term 'Inventories, net' – the provision is shown separately in the notes). The gross amount can be obtained by adding the 'obsolescence reserve' to the net amount. At the end of 2004 the gross amount equals: 14,003 (net amount) + 3,146 (ending obsolescence reserve) = 17,149 (versus 10,965 + 3,658 = 14,623 in 2003).

   We should note that it is impossible to find the gross amount per category of inventory (raw materials, work in progress and finished goods, and goods for resale).

5. What business anomaly should worry the financial statement users when comparing the 2004 figures with those of 2003? How could you explain it? The total inventory of finished products and merchandise is more than 13 times larger in 2004 than it was in 2003. Such an anomaly can be explained by a drop in sales in the telecommunications sector that could not be matched by the similar reduction in production due to a possibly long production cycle from order to delivery (Cisco Systems suffered a similar mini-catastrophe when the Internet bubble burst). The observed reduction of 'work in progress' and of 'advances received from customers' are confirming indicators of the fact that, in 2004, Ericsson suffered a serious crisis (which has since been overcome).

Review 10.1 Berg

Topic: Accounting for provision on receivables
Related part of the chapter: Core issues

1. Doubtful accounts provisions at the end of X3

Customer	A/R balance	Probable loss	Provision
Alban	200	25%	200 × 25% = 50
Zizou	300	40%	300 × 40% = 120
Total	500		170

2. Entries at the end of X3.

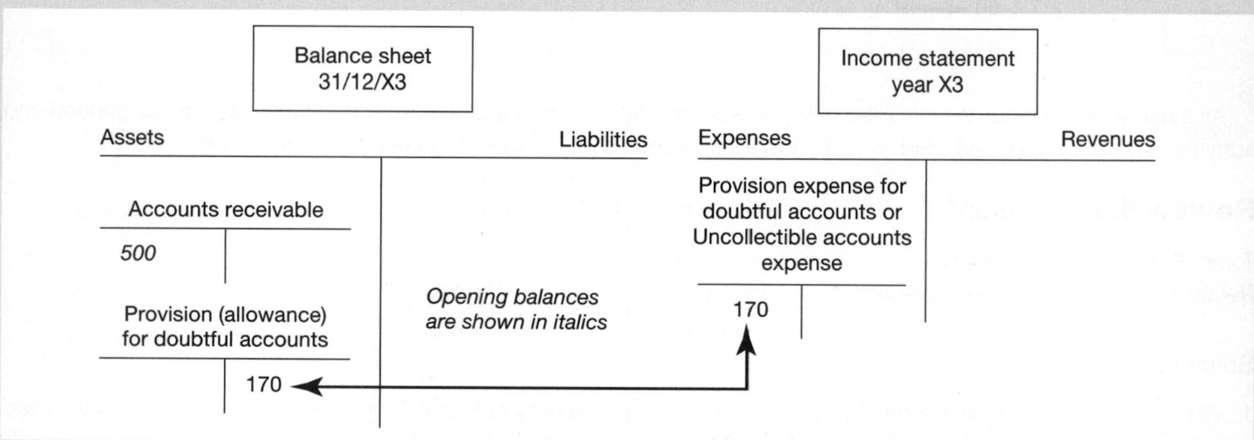

3. Doubtful accounts provisions at the end of X4

Customer	Accounts receivable	Probable loss	Provision
Alban	200	70%	200 × 70% = 140 − 50 (provision year X3) = 90
Zizou	300	–	Payment for 50. Reversal of provision (120)

4. Entries at the end of X4.

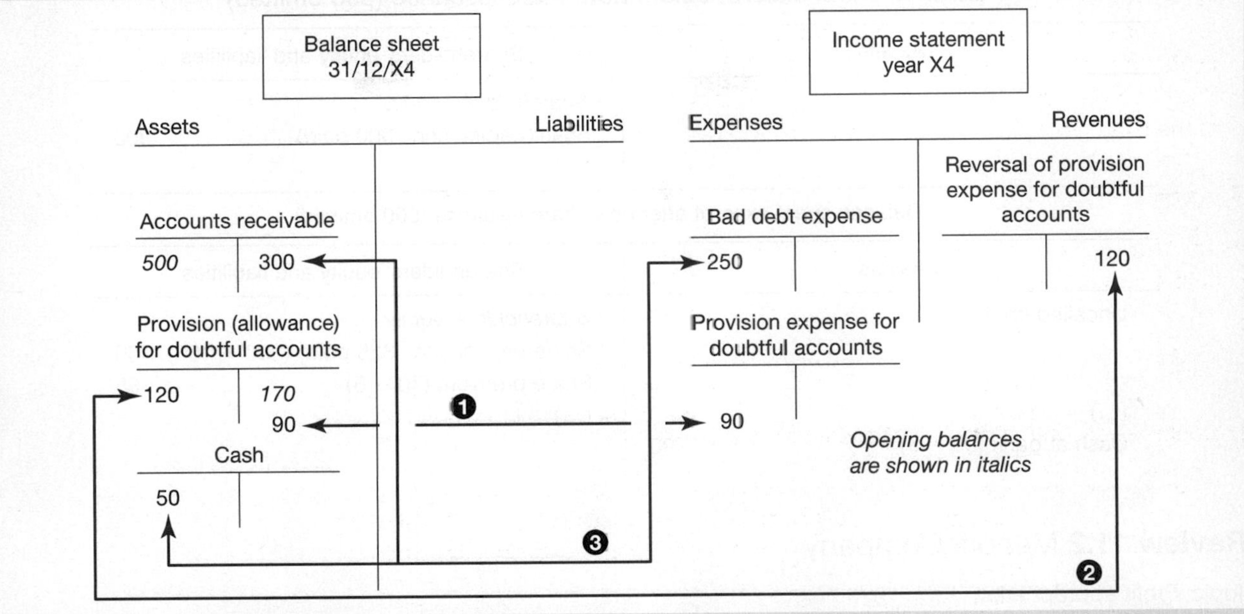

Review 11.1 Copland Company

Topic: Share issuance in cash
Related part of the chapter: Core issues

1. Accounting entries

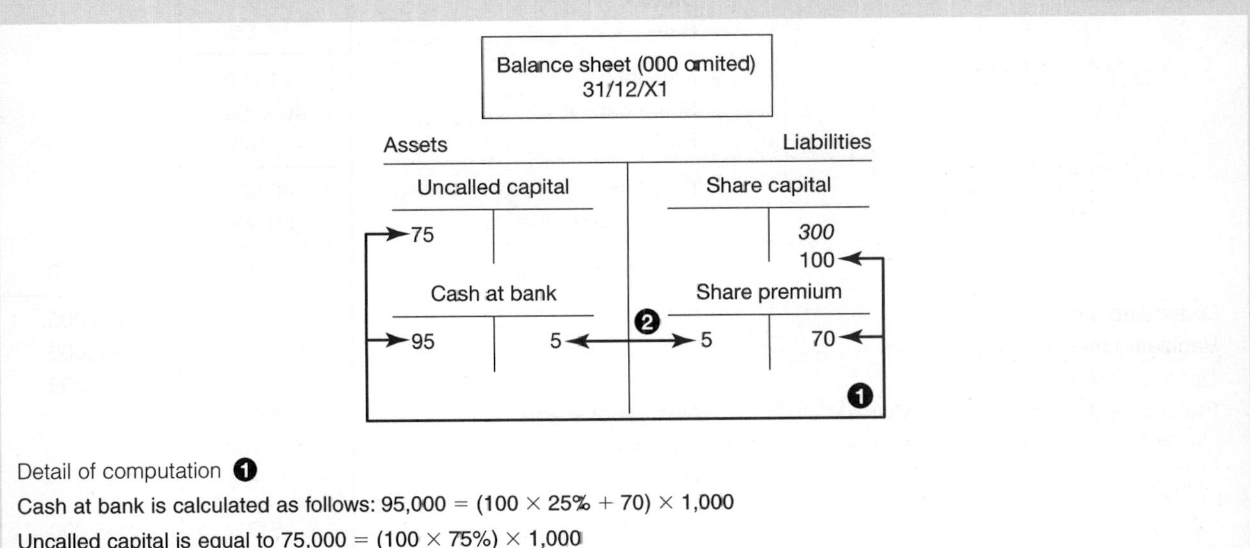

Detail of computation ❶

Cash at bank is calculated as follows: 95,000 = (100 × 25% + 70) × 1,000

Uncalled capital is equal to 75,000 = (100 × 75%) × 1,000

2. Balance sheet excerpts

Balance sheet excerpt before new share issuance (000 omitted)			
Assets		**Shareholders' equity and liabilities**	
		Shareholders' equity	
		Share capital (incl. 300 paid)	300
(...)		(...)	
Balance sheet excerpt after new share issuance (000 omitted)			
Assets		**Shareholders' equity and liabilities**	
Uncalled capital	75	*Shareholders' equity*	
		Share capital (incl. 325 paid) (300 + 100)	400
		Share premium (70 − 5)	65
(...)		(...)	
Cash at bank (95 − 5)	90		

Review 11.2 Menotti Company

Topic: Profit appropriation
Related part of the chapter: Core issues

1. Prepare a table detailing the profit appropriation calculations (including the per share dividend for each class of shares).

Net income			40,000
Losses brought forward			−5,000
Subtotal			35,000
Legal reserve	Basis	35,000	
	Rate	5%	
	Amount	1,750	
	Share capital	400,000	
	Rate	10%	
	Required legal reserve ceiling	40,000	
	Current legal reserve	39,000	
	Contribution required	1,000	−1,000
Distributable profit			34,000
Regulated reserve			−2,000
Optional reserve			−10,000
Preference dividend (Class A shares)	Number of shares	1,000	
	Par value	100	
	Rate	5%	
	Amount	5,000	−5,000
Ordinary dividends (Class A & B shares)	Number of shares	4,000	
	Amount per share	4	
	Amount	16,000	−16,000
Profit brought forward to retained earnings			1,000

Notes

- Since the legal reserve only requires an increment of 1,000 CU to reach the level of 10% of the capital at par, the amount appropriated to that purpose is limited (and will be nil for the next period).
- Legally, the increment of the regulated reserve is not truly compulsory. The creation of such a reserve is generally linked to a tax advantage. If the firm were to renounce the tax break, the regulated reserve would not have to be incremented. This is the reason why the distributable profit is calculated before the provision to increment the regulated reserve.
- All shares are entitled to receiving the ordinary dividend.
- The dividends per share are as follows:
  - Preference shares (class-A): 5 (preference dividend) + 4 (ordinary dividend) = 9 CU;
  - Ordinary shares (class-B): 4 CU (ordinary dividend).

2. Prepare the appropriation accounting entries.

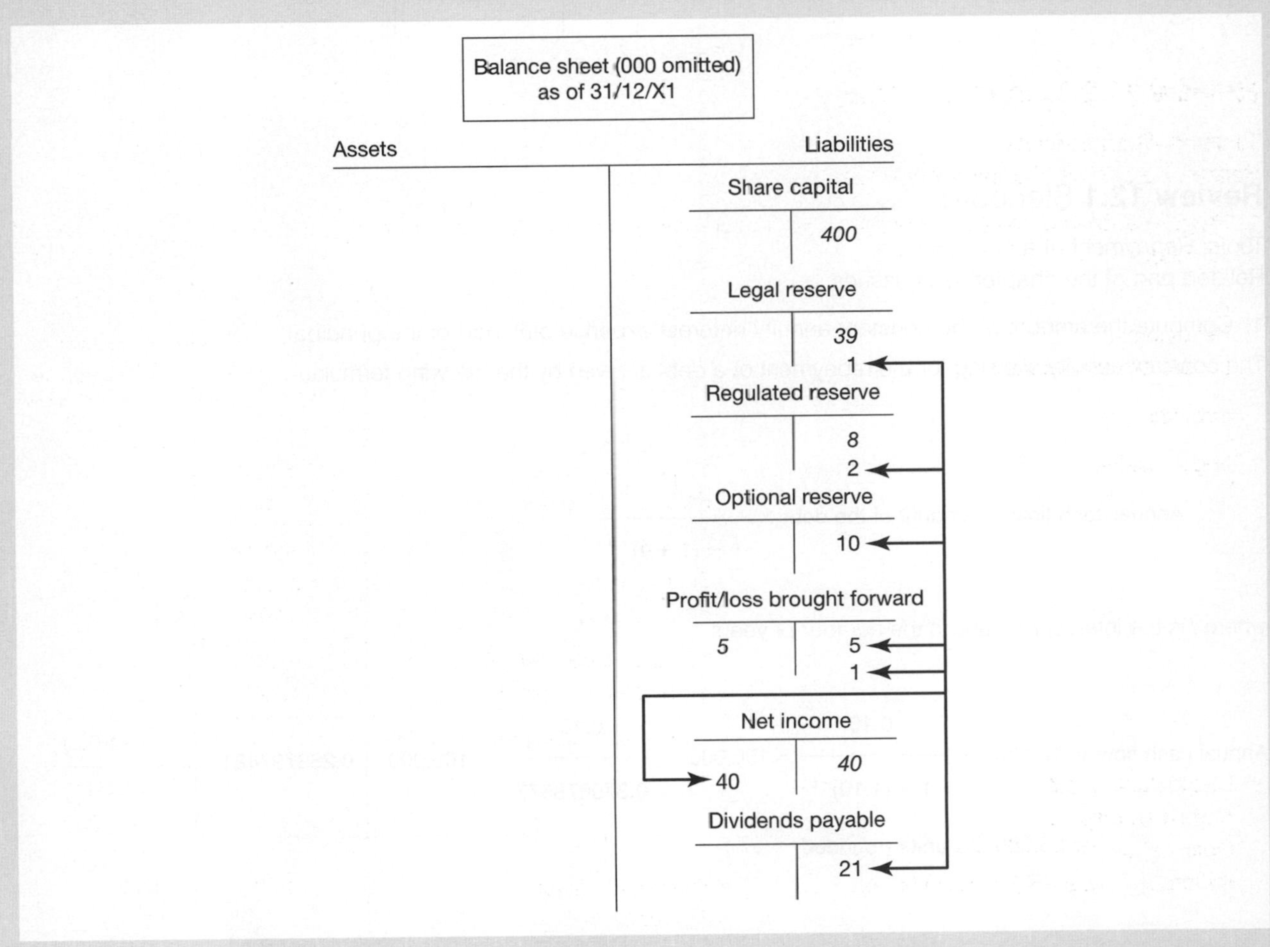

3. Prepare a table detailing the 'shareholders' equity and liabilities before and after appropriation.

000 omitted	Before appropriation	After appropriation
Shareholders' equity		
Share capital	400	400
Reserves		
Legal reserve	39	40
Regulated reserve	8	10
Optional reserve		10
Profit/loss brought forward	−5	1
Net income	40	0
Total shareholders' equity	482	461
Liabilities (dividends payable)		21
Total shareholders' equity and liabilities	482	482

Review 12.1 Stenborg

Topic: Repayment of a bank loan
Related part of the chapter: Core issues

1. Compute the amount of the constant annuity (interest expense plus part of the principal).

The constant annuity allowing for the repayment of a debt is given by the following formula:

$$\text{Annual cash flow} = \text{Amount of the debt} \times \frac{i}{1 - (1 + i)^{-n}}$$

where i is the interest rate and n the number of years.

$$\text{Annual cash flow} = 100{,}000 \times \frac{0.10}{1 - (1.10)^{-5}} = 100{,}000 \times \frac{0.10}{0.379078677} = 100{,}000 \times 0.263797481$$

$$= 26{,}380 \text{ CU units (rounded)}$$

2. Present the repayment schedule of the debt.

Repayment schedule

	Beginning balance	Interest expense	Repayment	Annuity	Ending balance
Years	(1) = (5) previous	(2) = (1) × 10%	(3) = (4) − (2)	(4)	(5) = (1) − (4)
30/6/X1	100,000	10,000	16,380	26,380	83,620
30/6/X2	83,620	8,362	18,018	26,380	65,602
30/6/X3	65,603	6,560	19,819	26,380	45,784
30/6/X4	45,783	4,578	21,801	26,380	23,982
30/6/X5	23,982	2,398	23,982	26,380	0
		31,898	100,000		

The addition of interest expense and repayment does not match perfectly with the annuity (26,380 CU) due to rounding.

3. Show the accounting entries: on the date of subscription, on closing date, on the first repayment date.

Year X1

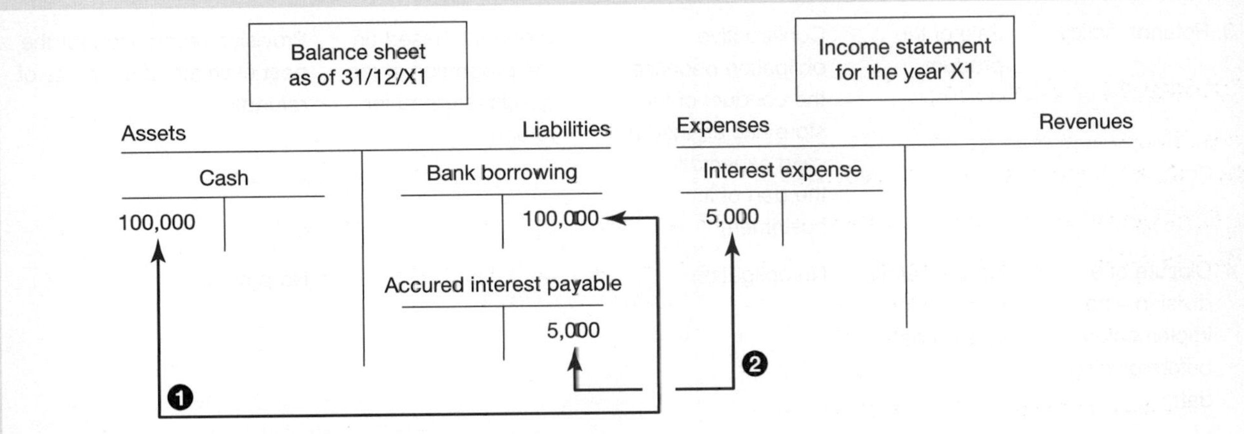

❶ On 30 June X1, subscription of the debt. Receipt of the principal.

❷ On the closing date (31 December X1), accrual of the interest relating to X1 (10,000 × 6 months from July to December = 5,000).

Year X2

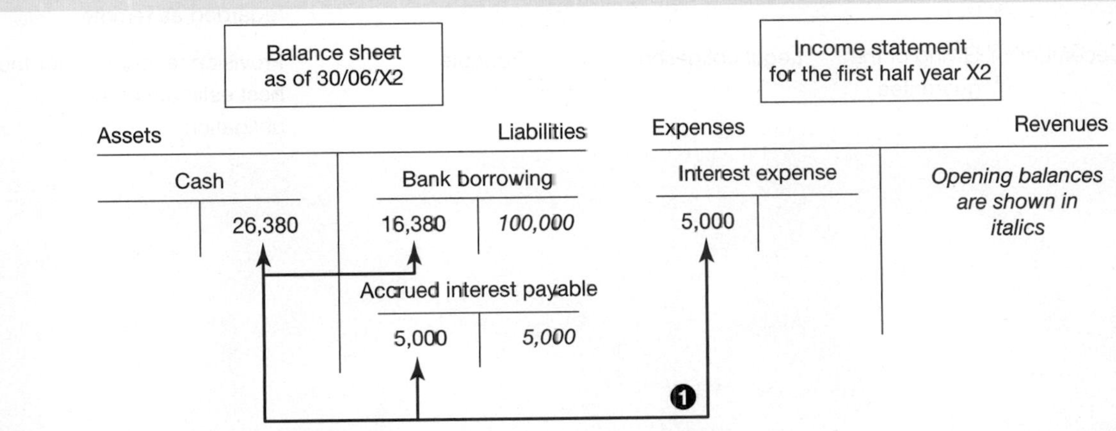

❶ At the first maturity date (30 June X2), repayment of the principal according to the schedule (16,380 CU), cancellation of the accrued interest payable (5,000 CU), and recording of the second part of the interest (10,000 CU × 6 months from January to June = 5,000 CU).

Review 12.2 Haeffner PLC (1)

Topic: Provisions and contingent liabilities
Related part of the chapter: Core issues

These review answers are based on the appendix of IAS 37.

Situations	Past obligating event...	...resulting in a present obligation	Outflow of resources embodying economic benefits in settlement	Conclusion
1. Warranties	Sale of the product with a warranty	Legal obligation	Probable for the warranties as a whole	Provision recognized for the best estimate of the costs of the warranty for products
sold before the balance sheet date				
2. Contaminated land – legislation virtually certain to be enacted	Contamination of the land	Virtual certainty of legislation requiring cleaning up	Probable	Provision recognized for the best estimate of the costs of the clean-up
3. Refunds policy	Sale of the product	Constructive obligation because the conduct of the store has created a valid expectation on the part of its customers	Probable, based on the proportion of the goods returned for refund	Provision recognized for the best estimate of the costs of refunds
4. Closure of a division – no implementation before closing date	No obligating event before closing date	No obligation	–	No provision
5. Simple guarantee At 31 December X1	Giving of the guarantee	Legal obligation	No outflow probable	No provision recognized, but disclosure of the guarantee as a contingent liability unless the probability of any outflow is regarded as remote
At 31 December X2	Giving of the guarantee	Legal obligation	Probable	Provision recognized for the best estimate of the obligation

Review 13.1 Mater & Filia

Topic: Consolidated balance sheet (three methods)
Related part of the chapter: Core issues

The requirement of application of the three consolidation methods is rather artificial here. In reality, only one of the three methods should be used and the method that is appropriate is defined by the percentage of control. Here full consolidation is the only legitimate consolidation method given the percentage of control – 80% – Mater holds in Filia.

However, this review problem has the pedagogical objective to show the differences between the three methods.

Full consolidation

	Mater	Filia	Combined statements	Elimination entries and adjustments		Consolidated balance sheet
				Elimination of investment	Minority interest	
Fixed assets (net)	1,500	550	2,050			2,050
Investment in Filia Company	160	–	160	−160		0
Inventories	930	510	1,440			1,440
Other current assets	1,210	740	1,950			1,950
Total assets	**3,800**	**1,800**	**5,600**	**−160**	**0**	**5,440**
Group interests						
Share capital	500	200	700	−160	−40	500
Retained earning/ Reserves	780	600	1,380	−480	−120	780
Consolidation reserve				480		480
Net income	220	150	370		−30	340
Minority interests						
Share capital of F					40	40
Reserves of F					120	120
Net income of F					30	30
Liabilities	2,300	850	3,150			3,150
Total equity and liabilities	**3,800**	**1,800**	**5,600**	**−160**	**0**	**5,440**

In the elimination of the investment in Filia, the investment (at cost) is canceled and the share of reserves of Filia belonging to the parent company, Mater, is transferred to the consolidation reserve. The minority interests are materialized by the transfer to that caption of the share of minority shareholders over the share capital, reserves, and net income of Filia.

Proportionate consolidation and equity method compared to full consolidation

Consolidated balance sheet as at 31 December X1 (000 CU)			
Comparison of the three methods			
	Full consolidation	Proportionate consolidation	Equity method
Fixed assets (net)	2,050	1,940	1,500
Investment in Filia Company	0	0	0
Investment valued at equity	–	–	760
Inventories	1,440	1,338	930
Other current assets	1,950	1,802	1,210
Total assets	5,440	5,080	4,400
Group interests (shareholders' equity)			
Share capital	500	500	500
Retained earnings/Reserves	780	780	780
Reserve from consolidation	480	480	480
Net income	340	340	340
Minority interests			
Share capital of Filia	40	0	0
Reserves of Filia	120	0	0
Net income of Filia	30	0	0
Liabilities	3,150	2,980	2,300
Total equity and liabilities	5,440	5,080	4,400

In the proportionate consolidation, all assets and liabilities would be the result of the combination of the Mater Company items + 80% of Filia items. For instance, for fixed assets, 1,500 + 550 × 80% = 1,500 + 440 = 1,940. However, the group interests (shareholders' equity) would be the same as with full consolidation.

In the equity method, there is no integration. Consequently, the assets (with the exception of investment) and liabilities would be taken from the parent (Mater) balance sheet. The share capital and reserves would also be those of the parent company. However, the investment in Filia (160 originally) would be revalued. The current value is: Shareholders' equity of Filia (including net income) × percentage of interest = (200 + 600 + 150) × 80% = 760. The difference between this value and the acquisition price (760 − 160 = 600) would be split between the consolidation reserve (480, which would represent the share of the reserves of Filia which did not exist at the time of acquisition: 600 × 80%) and net income (120, which would represent the share of the net income of Filia: 150 × 80%).

We notice that group equities are the same, whichever method is used.

Review 14.1 Dvorak Company

Topic: Preparation of a cash flow statement
Related part of the chapter: Core issues

We first present the solution with the indirect method.

Cash flow statement	
	X2
Cash flows from operating activities (indirect method)	
Net income/loss	2,560
Adjustments to reconcile net income/loss to net cash provided by/used in operating activities	
Depreciation and provision expense (excluding provision movements on current assets)	1,400
Gain/Loss on sale of fixed assets	−200
Potential cash flow	3,760
Change in operating assets and liabilities	
Change in inventories (net amounts)	300
Change in accounts receivable (net amounts)	−650
Change in accounts payable	810
Net cash provided by/used in operating activities (1)	4,220
Cash flows from investing activities	
Purchase of fixed assets	−4,000
Change in fixed assets payable	250
Cash paid on purchase of fixed assets	−3,750
Proceeds from sales of fixed assets	450
Net cash used in investing activities (2)	−3,300
Cash flows from financing activities	
Dividends paid	−2,580
Proceeds from issuance of share capital	200
Proceeds from issuance of financial liabilities	1,000
Repayment of financial liabilities	−400
Net cash provided by financing activities (3)	−1,780
Net increase/decrease in cash and cash equivalents (4) = (1) + (2) + (3)	−860
Cash and cash equivalents at beginning of year (5)	−10
Cash and cash equivalents at end of year (6) = (5) + (4)	−870
Cash and cash equivalents at end of year (balance sheet) (7)	−870
Control: (7) = (6)	

We now show the operating cash flow computed with the direct method.

Cash flows from operating activities (direct method)	
Sales of merchandise	14,100
Change in accounts receivable (net amounts)	−650
Cash received from customers	13,450
Purchases of merchandise	−3,700
Change in accounts payable	810
Cash paid to suppliers	−2,890
Other operating revenues	150
Financial revenues	300
Other purchases and external expenses	−550
Taxes and similar expenses	−70
Personnel expenses	−4,310
Financial expenses	−580
Income tax	−1,280
Net cash provided by/used in operating activities	4,220

In the cash flow statement, we assumed that the bank overdrafts formed an integral part of the cash management. As a consequence, they were excluded from the financing activities and included in the 'cash and cash equivalents' as a negative cash. Another solution is possible: to include the change in bank overdrafts in the financing activities. In this case, the cash and cash equivalents will only comprise the 'cash at bank'. The following table discloses this second solution.

Cash flows from financing activities	
Dividends paid	−2,580
Proceeds from issuance of share capital	200
Proceeds from issuance of financial liabilities	1,000
Repayment of financial liabilities	−400
Change in bank overdrafts*	750
Net cash provided by financing activities (3)	−1,030
Net increase/decrease in cash and cash equivalents (4) = (1) + (2) + (3)	−110
Cash and cash equivalents at beginning of year (5)	190
Cash and cash equivalents at end of year (6) = (5) + (4)	80
Cash and cash equivalents at end of year (balance sheet) (7)	80
Control: (7) = (6)	

* Line which is different from the first solution.

Review 14.2 Mitsubishi Electric*

Topic: Understanding and analyzing a cash flow statement
Related part of the chapter: Advanced issues

Solution

1. Which method (direct or indirect) was used to compute the operating cash flow? The method used to compute the operating cash flow is the indirect method, which starts from the net income and adjusts it by adding back non-cash expenses and gain on sale of fixed assets, subtracting non-cash revenues and loss on sale of fixed assets, and integrating the changes in inventories, receivables, and payables.

2. Compute the 'potential cash flow'. The potential cash flow is the net income adjusted with non-cash items. In this example, non-cash items are depreciation, impairment losses of property, plant and equipment, the deferred income taxes, devaluation losses of securities and other – net, and equity in earnings of affiliated companies. Net income is also adjusted with gain and loss of elements of investing activities: loss from sales and disposal of property, plant and equipment – net, and loss (gain) from sales of securities and other – net.

   We provide below, as a check, the computation of the potential cash flow but also compute the operating cash flow.

Yen (millions)	2005	2004	2003
Net income (loss)	71,175	44,839	(11,825)
Depreciation	105,356	109,975	208,884
Impairment losses of property, plant, and equipment	5,974	8,411	11,538
Loss from sales and disposal of property, plant, and equipment – net	1,737	3,362	796
Deferred income taxes	17,001	20,119	(27,669)
Loss (gain) from sales of securities and other – net	(5,986)	(3,123)	(7,204)
Devaluation losses of securities and other – net	3,892	1,701	51,055
Equity in earnings of affiliated companies	(17,029)	(5,653)	(2,032)
Potential cash flow	182,120	179,631	223,543
Changes in inventory, receivables, and payables	6,804	63,880	14,922
Operating cash flow	188,924	243,511	238,465

3. Why does the statement use the expression 'decrease (increase)' to describe changes in trade receivables, inventories, and prepaid expenses while it uses 'increase (decrease)' when referring to changes in trade payables and other liabilities?

   The statement indicates the changes having a positive impact on cash with a + sign and the changes having a negative impact with a – sign (or brackets).

   For the changes in inventories, trade receivables, and prepaid expenses (which are assets), an increase will generate less cash (minus sign) and a decrease means more cash (plus sign). Conversely, for the changes in trade payables and other liabilities, an increase is synonymous of more cash (plus sign) and a decrease leads to less cash (minus sign).

4. How are short-term investments reported? What could have been another legitimate possibility? Any comment as to why they chose the method they did over another?

   Short-term investments are reported under the investing activities. Alternatively, they could have been considered as cash equivalents, that are 'short-term, highly liquid investments that are readily convertible to known amounts of cash and which are subject to an insignificant risk of changes in value' (IAS 7: § 6).

5. Bank loans can be considered equivalent to 'bank overdrafts'. Comment on the way they are reported. What would have been another possibility?

   Bank loans are loans granted by banks. In other words, they represent a debt (liability) for the company. They are reported under the financing activities. They could have been included as negative cash in 'cash and cash equivalents'.

6. Analyze the cash flow statements over the period.

   Although the company showed a globally decreasing level of sales over the period (from 2003 to 2005), it has realized a significant increase in its net income. However, the change in cash and cash equivalents is negative and we will explain why.

The following table discloses the general structure of the cash flow statement.

Yen (millions)	2005	2004	2003
Net cash provided by operating activities (1)	188,924	243,511	238,465
Net cash used in investing activities (2)	(101,135)	(70,087)	(93,685)
Available cash flow (3) = (1) + (2)	87,789	173,424	144,780
Dividends paid (4)	(12,877)	(6,440)	0
Free cash flow (5) = (3) + (4)	74,912	166,984	144,780
Other financing cash flows (6)	(161,330)	(192,756)	(229,975)
Effect of exchange rates (7)	2,385	(7,227)	(6,100)
Change in cash and cash equivalents (8) = (5) + (6) + (7)	(84,033)	(32,999)	(91,295)

The available cash flow is positive over the period, but decreases from 2003 to 2005, which shows a deterioration. The operating cash flow is, in fact, able to finance the investing cash flow (in all years). This available cash allows the company to have a negative financing cash flow every year. In other words, the company is able to repay its debts (see below).

Operating activities

The operating cash flow has decreased significantly over the period for the following reasons:

- The potential cash flow (see question 2) has decreased, mostly because of the reduction of the earnings before depreciation (addition of net income and depreciation).
- There was, however, a positive impact of the changes in inventories, receivables, and payables, especially in 2004 (+63,880).
- This deterioration appears in the computation of the two following ratios.

	2005	2004	2003
Operating cash flow to sales	5.5%	7.4%	6.6%
Cash flow yield (operating cash flow/net earnings)	2.7	5.4	−20.2

Investing activities

Cash used in investing activities has remained almost stable over the period.

Financing activities

The financing cash flow is negative over the period, which shows that Mitsubishi was able to reduce its debt. In the cash flow statement, it appears that the proceeds from long-term debt has significantly decreased (from 304,814 in 2003 to 49,590 in 2005).

However, when we relate liabilities with the operating cash flow, the two following ratios provide an unfavorable evolution:

	2005	2004	2003
Cash liquidity ratio (operating cash flow/average current liabilities)	14.6%	16.8%	–
Cash leverage ratio (operating cash flows/average total liabilities)	7.6%	8.4%	–

Conclusion

We could say that the enterprise showed a decrease in cash, i.e., deteriorated its financial situation with regard to its cash flows by decreasing the operating cash flow and increasing the investing cash flow. However, a positive element can be seen in the repayment of debts.

Review 14.3 Bartok Company (1)

Topic: Comparative financial analysis – cash flow statement
Related part of the chapter: Advanced Issues

1. Cash flow statements

As an introduction, it should be stressed that the proposed exercise is intentionally simplified, and does not include the handling of any changes in inventory, receivables, or payables.

	Company 1	Company 2	Company 3
Cash flows from operating activities			
Potential cash flow	1,000	400	100
Net cash provided by operating activities	*1,000*	*400*	*100*
Cash flows from investing activities			
Purchase of tangible fixed assets	−900	−900	−1,400
Purchase of financial assets	−700	0	−400
Net cash used in investing activities	*−1,600*	*−900*	*−1,800*
Cash flows from financing activities			
Dividends paid	−200	−600	0
Proceeds from share issuance	800	0	700
New debt	100	1,500	1,100
Repayment of long-term debts	0	−300	0
Net cash provided by financing activities	*700*	*600*	*1,800*
Increase in cash and cash equivalents	100	100	100

Stage 1

It may be useful to draw up the following table summarizing the above information:

	Company 1	Company 2	Company 3
Net cash provided by operating activities (OCF)	1,000	400	100
Net cash used in investing activities (ICF)	−1,600	−900	−1,800
Available cash flow (ACF)	−600	−500	−1,700
Net cash provided by financing activities (FCF)	700	600	1,800
Change in cash	100	100	100

2. Comment on statements

All three companies have experienced the same change in cash, although their cash structures are very different.

Company 1

- It has the highest OCF of the three companies. This is a good sign.
- Its ICF is negative, as is almost always the case, since it represents investments.
- The ACF is negative, which means that the company will need financing to restore financial equilibrium. It does this through its FCF.

Company 2

- Its OCF is lower than for company 1. This is not as good, but not yet a real cause for concern.
- The ICF is negative but not as low as that of company 1. This is apparently logical, since company 2's investments are not as high.
- This is reflected in the ACF, which is almost identical to that of company 1.
- Once again, financing is necessary, hence the positive FCF.

Company 3

- The OCF is very low; this is an early warning of future difficulties.
- At the same time, the ICF is enormous, with the company making particularly large investments.
- The ACF is dramatically negative.
- The only solution is to use external financing, and this is reflected in the FCF.

Stage 2

After commenting on the main items in the cash flow statements, the contents of each function may be examined. For example, it might be interesting to point out that in its search for financing, company 3 uses loans but also, although to a lesser extent, calls on its shareholders.

Review 15.1 Chugoku Power Electric Company*

Topic: Common-size income statements by nature
Related part of the chapter: Core issues

The reader must pay attention to the signs of 'Other expenses (income)': Positive sign for expenses and negative sign for income.

1. Prepare common-size statements on the basis of the income statement, as published by the company.

Common-size income statements

Millions of yen	2005	2004	2003
Operating revenues	100.0%	100.0%	100.0%
Operating expenses			
Personnel	11.9%	14.5%	13.2%
Fuel	13.4%	11.0%	11.4%
Purchased power	16.2%	14.7%	14.7%
Depreciation	15.1%	17.1%	17.3%
Maintenance	9.7%	9.5%	9.0%
Taxes other that income taxes	6.6%	6.9%	6.7%
Purchased services	4.0%	3.9%	3.7%
Other	10.6%	11.5%	10.9%
	87.5%	89.1%	86.9%
Operating income	12.5%	10.9%	13.1%
Other expenses (income):			
Interest expense	3.8%	4.0%	5.9%
Interest income	(0.0%)	(0.0%)	(0.0%)
Loss on impairment of fixed assets	0.4%	0.0%	0.0%
Other – net	0.5%	0.2%	(0.2%)
	4.7%	4.2%	5.7%
Income before special item and income taxes	7.8%	6.7%	7.4%
Special item:			
Reserve for drought	0.2%	0.1%	0.0%
Provision for income taxes:			
Current	2.6%	3.1%	3.2%
Deferred	0.1%	(0.8%)	(0.6%)
Net income	4.9%	4.3%	4.7%

The income statement is drawn by nature and vertically. This second characteristic is very important because only a vertical statement can show the intermediate financial performance balances (see Chapter 3).

2. Restate the income statement and prepare common-size intermediate balances following the format of Figure 15.2.

Statement of intermediate balances

	Millions of yen			In percentage		
	2005	2004	2003	2005	2004	2003
Operating revenues	956,690	912,813	965,499	100.0%	100.0%	100.0%
Total production for the period	956,690	912,813	965,499	100.0%	100.0%	100.0%
Fuel	128,076	100,058	110,466	13.4%	11.0%	11.4%
Purchased power	154,910	134,488	141,496	16.2%	14.7%	14.7%
Maintenance	92,717	86,261	86,855	9.7%	9.5%	9.0%
Purchased services	38,392	35,948	36,184	4.0%	3.9%	3.7%
Consumption from third parties	414,095	356,755	375,001	43.3%	39.1%	38.8%
Value added	542,595	556,058	590,498	56.7%	60.9%	61.2%
Taxes other that income taxes	63,266	63,220	64,736	6.6%	6.9%	6.7%
Personnel	113,433	132,080	127,697	11.9%	14.5%	13.2%
Gross operating profit	365,896	360,758	398,065	38.2%	39.5%	41.2%
Depreciation	144,622	156,469	166,822	15.1%	17.1%	17.3%
Other	101,513	104,850	104,949	10.6%	11.5%	10.9%
Operating profit	119,761	99,439	126,294	12.5%	10.9%	13.1%
Interest expense	36,727	36,771	56,646	3.8%	4.0%	5.9%
Interest income	(61)	(82)	(88)	0.0%	0.0%	0.0%
Loss on impairment of fixed assets	4,089	0	0	0.4%	0.0%	0.0%
Other – net	4,325	1,556	(1,944)	0.5%	0.2%	−0.2%
Operating net income before taxes	74,681	61,194	71,680	7.8%	6.7%	7.4%
Reserve for drought	1,747	712	0	0.2%	0.1%	0.0%
Exceptional result	(1,747)	(712)	0	−0.2%	−0.1%	0.0%
Provision for income taxes	26,435	20,953	25,986	2.8%	2.3%	2.7%
Net income/loss after tax	46,499	39,529	45,694	4.9%	4.3%	4.7%

3. Comment on these different statements.

With regard to the different intermediate financial performance balances, many are the same as those in the non-restated income statement. The new information concerns mainly the upper part of the statement. A statement of intermediate balances is interesting and useful mainly because it offers an actionable decomposition of the operating profit:

- The added value rate decreased over the period. It may be an indication of a modification in the production structure (such as more reliance on outsourcing maintenance, at the expense of less internal maintenance), or a measure of the impact of the increase in the unit value of raw materials (fuel oil).
- This decrease of the value added percentage (61.2% down to 56.7%) appears, however, to have been compensated by savings before the income line: net income increased by 0.2%. This is a favorable signal, as it indicates that the management has been able to find actions to keep the impact of the decrease of the value added rate from impacting directly the income line.
- We can surmise some of the actions taken by management to preserve income when noting the reduction of the weight of the personnel expenses (down from 13.2% to 11.9%). The gross operating profit declined by the same proportion as the value added (a reduction from 41.2% to 38.2%). Therefore, not only was labor cost reduced significantly (almost a 10% reduction), but other expenses must have reduced also. Did these reductions endanger or enhance future prospects?

- We can notice the decrease of the depreciation expenses and of other operating expenses. We do not have enough information about fixed assets and investments during the period to know what the source of the decrease was. Only an analysis of the full annual report could let us know whether there was a decrease in investments, a change in the depreciation policy, or some key assets reached the end of their depreciation useful life.

  We can see in this very superficial analysis how the methods we have applied lead to a cascading of further questions. As we said earlier in the chapter, financial analysis is the beginning of a serious inquiry into the nature and policies of an enterprise.

Review 15.2 Elkem*

Topic: Balance sheet structure
Related part of the chapter: Core issues

1. Prepare a simplified balance sheet with three subheadings in the assets and three subheadings in the equity and liabilities (see the Core issues section in this chapter).

Simplified balance sheet

	Amounts (NOK million)			Structure (%)		
	31.12.04	31.12.03	31.12.02	31.12.04	31.12.03	31.12.02
Fixed assets	10,755	10,688	10,210	56.8%	57.2%	58.6%
Current assets	7,321	7,035	6,188	38.6%	37.6%	35.5%
Cash	875	970	1,013	4.6%	5.2%	5.8%
Total assets	18,951	18,693	17,411	100.0%	100.0%	100.0%
Equity and long-term liabilities	14,226	14,095	12,845	75.1%	75.4%	73.8%
Current liabilities	4,725	4,598	4,566	24.9%	24.6%	26.2%
Bank overdrafts	0	0	0	0.0%	0.0%	0.0%
Total equity and liabilities	18,951	18,693	17,411	100.0%	100.0%	100.0%

- The market-based financial current assets have been included in current assets and not in cash, because a note to the financial statements indicates that it represents shares of other companies.
- Apparently, the company has no bank overdraft.

2. Compute working capital, working capital need, and net cash.

Financial structure

NOK million	31.12.04	31.12.03	31.12.02
Equity and long-term liabilities	14,226	14,095	12,845
Fixed assets	−10,755	−10,688	−10,210
Working capital	3,471	3,407	2,635
Current assets	7,321	7,035	6,188
Current liabilities	−4,725	−4,598	−4,566
Working capital need	2,596	2,437	1,622
Cash	875	970	1,013
Bank overdrafts	0	0	0
Net cash	875	970	1,013
Control: Working capital less Working capital need = Net cash			
Net cash	875	970	1,013
Synthesis	31.12.04	31.12.03	31.12.02
Working capital	3,471	3,407	2,635
Working capital need	2,596	2,437	1,622
Net cash	875	970	1,013

The following graph shows the variation of the three items over the three years (do not forget that in the reported statements, the most current year was on the left; we have respected that presentation even if it may appear misleading: WC and WCN have both increased over the period).

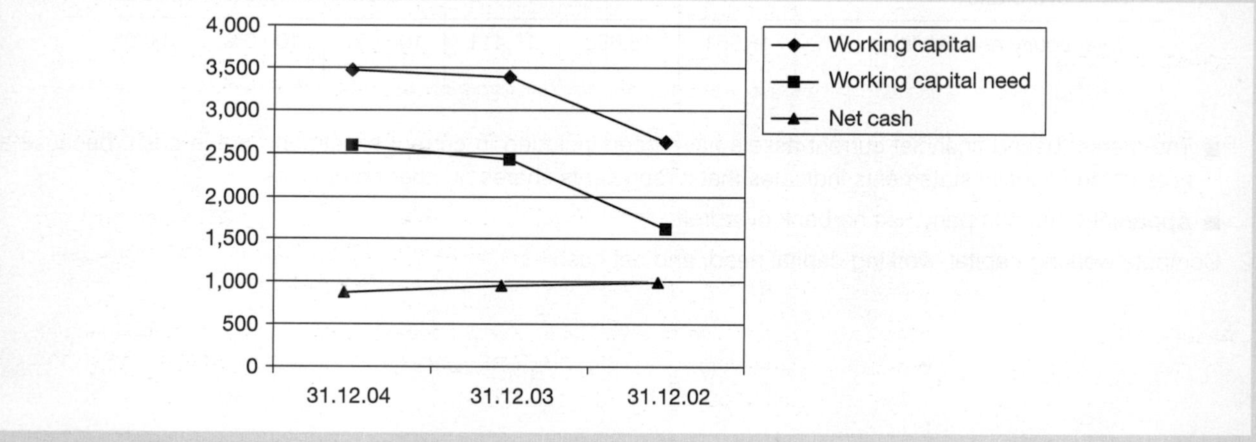

3. Comment on your findings.

Over the three years, the financial structure of the business corresponds to scenario 1 described in the Core issues section in this chapter. The structure can be considered to be sound. However, there was a slight decrease in cash over the period. The graph shows that this decrease in cash arose from the fact that the increase in working capital needs was larger than the increase in working capital. There is a signal here to the management to pay close attention in the upcoming months to the dynamics of the cash equation.

Glossary of key terms

Account payable Obligation of a business to a creditor (generally a supplier) usually arising from the purchase of goods and services on credit.

Accounting System of measurement ('to count') and reporting ('to account for') of economic events for the purpose of decision making.

Accounting changes Changes in accounting policies, changes in accounting estimates, and prior-period errors.

Accounting period The measurement of income is carried in contiguous yet clearly separated time slices. The duration of a 'time slice' is an accounting period. This duration is at most a year and is more and more frequently shorter than a year.

Accounting principles Coherent set of behavioral rules and guidelines that range from pure concepts to very operational guidelines about practice.

Accounting standards See Financial reporting standards.

Accrual basis 'An entity shall prepare its financial statements, except for cash flow information, under the accrual basis of accounting' (IAS 1, IASB 2003: § 25). Under this method, transactions and events are recognized when they occur (and not when cash or its equivalent is received or paid) and they are recorded in the accounting records and reported in the financial statements of the periods to which they relate.

Accrual principle A revenue (expense) is recorded in the income statement at the time of the transaction that causes it, and not at the time of the cash inflow (or outflow, for an expense).

Acquiree Legal and independent business entity of which an investor (or acquirer) acquires an interest (synonym: investee).

Acquisition cost 'Amount of cash or cash equivalents paid or the fair value of the other consideration given to acquire an asset at the time of its acquisition or construction' (IAS 16, IASB 2003: § 6).

Adjusting entries Year-end adjustments related to the influence of time (accrual of unrecorded revenues, unearned revenues, accrual of unrecorded expenses, prepaid expenses).

Annual accounts 'The balance sheet, the profit and loss account and the notes on the accounts' (4th European Directive).

Annual report Document published annually by listed companies (as well as some non-listed but large companies). It includes elements on business reporting (key financial information, management report, etc.) and financial reporting (financial statements).

Asset 'Resource (a) controlled by an entity as a result of past events and (b) from which future economic benefits are expected to flow to the entity' (Conceptual framework, IASB 1989: § 49 and IAS 38, IASB 2004: § 8).

Associate 'Entity (…) over which the investor has significant influence and that is neither a subsidiary nor an interest in a joint venture' (IAS 28, IASB 2003: § 2).

Authorized capital Maximum amount of capital (at par) that the charter states the corporation can issue when needed.

Available cash flow Addition of the cash flow from operating activities and the cash flow from investing activities.

Available-for-sale financial assets Financial assets other than 'financial assets at fair value through profit or loss', 'held-to-maturity investments', and 'loans and receivables'.

Average collection period [(Accounts receivable Year 2 + Accounts receivable Year 1)/2 x 365]/Sales.

Average days of sales (in receivables), or Average collection period Ratio providing the average duration of credit terms offered to customer: (Average accounts receivable/Net sales) x 365 days

Bad debt expense Expense corresponding to a specifically identified uncollectible receivable.

Balance sheet

- Set of two lists: resources on one side (also called assets) and obligations to external parties on the other side (liabilities to creditors and the residual due to shareholders or owners).
- 'Snapshot' of the financial position of the firm at a given point in time.

Basic business equation (Balance sheet equation) Equation representing the balance sheet: Resources (or assets) = obligations to third parties (liabilities) *plus* equity (shareholders' claims).

Bill of exchange See Notes receivable.

Bonds A bond is a certificate allowing the division of a debt between a large number of investors (bondholders), each of whom can contribute only a small amount of the debt (the face value, or the selling price if sold at a discount or with a premium).

Book value Difference between the asset's acquisition cost and the balance of its accumulated depreciation.

Borrowing costs 'Interest and other costs incurred by an entity in connection with the borrowing of funds' (IAS 23, IASB 1993: § 4).

Business 'Integrated set of activities and assets conducted and managed for the purpose of providing:

(a) a return to investors; or
(b) lower costs or other economic benefits directly and proportionately to policyholders or participants.

A business generally consists of inputs, processes applied to those inputs, and resulting outputs that are, or will be, used to generate revenues' (IASB Glossary).

Business combination 'Bringing together of separate entities or businesses into one reporting entity. The result of nearly all business combinations is that one entity, the acquirer, obtains control of one or more other businesses, the acquiree' (IFRS 3, IASB 2004: § 4).

Business segment 'A distinguishable component of an entity that is engaged in providing an individual product or service or a group of related products or services and that is subject to risks and returns that are different from those of other business segments' (IAS 14, IASB 1997: § 9).

By function (income statement) Income statement classified by reference to the function of expenses. The expenses are classified according to their role in the determination of income (e.g., cost of goods sold, commercial, distribution, or administrative expenses).

By nature (balance sheet) Balance sheet classified by reference to the operating cycle.

By nature (income statement) Income statement classified by reference to the nature of expenses (e.g., purchases of materials, transportation costs, taxes other than income tax, salaries and social expenses, depreciation, etc.).

By term (balance sheet) Balance sheet classified by reference to the realization/settlement within 12 months after the balance sheet date.

Capital Shares or stock certificates evidencing the contribution of the shareholders to the formation of the capital.

Capital expenditure Expenses incurred for the purpose of generating future economic benefits.

Capitalization of borrowing costs Inclusion of borrowing costs in the cost of the construction.

Capitalization of reserves (bonus issue) Incorporation of reserves into the share capital, generally giving rise to the issuance of additional shares to existing stockholders.

Carry-forward (or carry-back) Mechanism that allows the business to carry a net operating loss forward (or back) a certain number of years and offset it against future profits (or receive refunds for income taxes paid in the past).

Cash 'Cash in hand' (coins, banknotes, and currency available) and 'demand deposits' (deposits in bank accounts that are available on demand) (IAS 7, IASB 1992: § 6).

Cash account Cash in hand or cash at bank.

Cash equation Working capital – Working capital need = Net cash.

Cash equivalents 'Short-term, highly liquid investments that are readily convertible to known amounts of cash and which are subject to an insignificant risk of changes in value' (IAS 7, IASB 1992: § 6).

Cash flow adequacy Cash flow from operations/(Long-term capital expenditures + Dividends + Scheduled debt reimbursements).

Cash flow as percentage of sales Operating cash flow/Sales.

Cash flow statement 'The cash flow statement shall report cash flows during the period classified by operating, investing and financing activities' (IAS 7, IASB 1992: § 10).

Cash flow yield Operating cash flow/Net income.

Cash flows from financing activities Cash flows related to providers of capital and other funding to the enterprise.

Cash flows from investing activities Cash flows representing 'the extent to which expenditures have been made for resources intended to generate future income and cash flows' (IAS 7, IASB 1992: § 16).

Cash flows from operating activities Cash flows primarily deriving from the main or core revenue-producing activities of the enterprise.

Cash items Items of the income statement which, by nature, will eventually generate a real cash flow.

Cash leverage ratio Operating cash flow/Average total liabilities.

Cash liquidity ratio Operating cash flow/Average current liabilities.

Cash ratio (Cash + Marketable securities)/Current liabilities.

Change in inventory Difference between:

- beginning and ending inventory of raw materials or merchandises;
- ending and beginning inventory of finished products.

Chart of accounts Logically organized list of all recognized accounts used in recording transactions in a firm. A chart of accounts generally assigns a unique code to each account.

Commercial margin Difference between sales of merchandise and cost of merchandise sold.

Common-size or vertical analysis Comparison of the evolution of the structure of the financial statements.

Components of the tangible asset Each part of an item of property, plant and equipment with a cost that is significant in relation to the total cost of the item.

Comprehensive income Sum of all 'change[s] in equity of a business enterprise during a period [arising] from transactions and other events and circumstances', excluding those resulting from investments by owners and distributions to owners (SFAS 130, FASB 1997: § 8).

Conservatism 'Inclusion of a degree of caution in the exercise of the judgments needed in making the estimates required under conditions of uncertainty, such that assets or income are not overstated and liabilities or expenses are not understated' (Conceptual framework, IASB 1989: § 37).

Consistency of presentation Financial statements must be presented in consistent fashion and over consistent parameters over time.

Construction contract See Long-term contract.

Contingent liability '(a) Possible obligation that arises from past events and whose existence will be confirmed only by the occurrence or non-occurrence of one or more uncertain future events not wholly within the control of the entity or (b) a present obligation that arises from past events but is not recognized because (i) it is not probable that an outflow of resources embodying economic benefits will be required to settle the obligation; or (ii) the amount of the obligation cannot be measured with sufficient reliability' (IAS 37, IASB 1998: § 10).

Control 'Power to govern the financial and operating policies of an entity so as to obtain benefits from its activities' (IAS 27, IASB 2003: § 4).

Copyright Provides the holder with exclusive rights to the publication, production, and sale of the rights for an intellectual creation be it a musical, artistic, literary, or dramatic work (and often, by extension, software).

Cost of inventories 'All costs of purchases, costs of conversion and other costs incurred in bringing the inventories to their present condition and location' (IAS 2, IASB 2003: § 10).

Credit Right-hand side of a T-account.

Current investments Investments that are by their nature readily realizable and are intended to be held for not more than one year.

Current liability Liability which 'satisfies any of the following criteria: (a) it is expected to be settled in the entity's normal operating cycle; (b) it is held primarily for the purpose of being traded; (c) it is due to be settled within twelve months after the balance sheet date; or (d) the entity does not have an unconditional right to defer settlement of the liability for at least twelve months after the balance sheet date' (IAS 1, IASB 2003: § 60).

Current ratio Current assets/Current liabilities.

Debit Left-hand side of a T-account.

Debt ratio or Debt to total assets ratio Total debt/Total assets.

Debt to equity ratio Debt/Shareholders' equity or Debt/(Shareholders' equity + Debt).

Declining balance method Depreciation method which recognizes greater amounts of depreciation in the early years of an asset's life and smaller amounts in the later years.

Deferred taxation accounting Recognition of the tax consequences of the temporary differences by including its tax effect as income tax expense on the income statement and as an asset or a liability (called a deferred tax asset or a deferred tax liability) in the balance sheet.

Depreciable amount 'Cost of an asset, or other amount substituted for cost in the financial statements, less its residual value' (IAS 16, IASB 2003: § 6).

Depreciation Process of allocating the cost of a tangible or fixed asset (with the exception of land) over the period during which economic benefits will be received by the firm. The depreciation allowance or expense recognizes the fact that the potential of any asset is consumed through usage or passage of time.

Depreciation expense The consumption of a fixed asset. It reflects the gradual loss of value of this asset.

Derivative Any financial instrument derived from securities or physical markets such as futures, options, warrants, and convertible bonds.

Development 'Application of research findings or other knowledge to a plan or design for the production of new or substantially improved materials, devices, products, processes, systems, or services before the start of commercial production or use' (IAS 38, IASB 2004: § 8).

Direct method Computation of the net cash flow from operating activities by grouping cash effects of transactions classes.

Discontinued operation Component of an entity that either has been disposed of, or is classified as held for sale (IFRS 5, IASB 2004: § 32).

Discounting (of a note receivable) Endorsement of a note receivable towards a bank which, in exchange, transfers cash to the company. The bank keeps discounting fees.

Discounting fee Represents: (1) the interest for the period separating the date of discounting and the maturity date; (2) an administrative fee; and, eventually, (3) a risk premium.

Dividend Distribution of the earnings of the business to its shareholders.

Double entry accounting Each transaction impacts the basic equation in at least two ways that always keep the equation balanced.

Double entry bookkeeping Each individual accounting transaction has two sides, which are always balanced.

Doubtful or disputed accounts Accounts receivable partly or totally uncollectible.

Earnings Result of the difference between the resources created by the economic activity of the business (revenues) and the resources consumed in operating the firm (expenses).

Earnings per share (EPS) Ratio of net income after taxes (and after preferred dividends if there are any) to average number of shares during the period for which the income has been calculated.

EBIT Earnings from operations before interests and taxes.

EBITDA Earnings from operations before interests, taxes, depreciation and amortization, and provisions.

End-of-period entries Any such entries that are necessary to give a true and fair view of both the financial position at the end of an accounting period and the income statement for the accounting period. These entries will be carried out every time one closes the books (yearly, half-yearly, quarterly, monthly, etc.).

Entity concept Regardless of the legal form of the economic entity, economic transactions carried out by the entity must be recorded separately from that of the personal transactions of actors involved in or with the entity.

Equity method 'Method of accounting whereby the investment is initially recognized at cost and adjusted thereafter for the post-acquisition change in the investor's share of the net assets of the investee. The income statement reflects the investor's share of the net assets of the investee' (IAS 28, IASB 2003: § 2).

Equity

- Claim, right, or interest one has over some 'net worth'.
- Residual interest [of the investors] in the assets of the entity after deducting all its liabilities' (Conceptual framework, IASB 1989: § 49).

Expenses 'Decreases in economic benefits during the accounting period in the form of outflows or depletion of assets or incurrence of liabilities that result in decreases in equity, other than those relating to distributions to equity participants' (Conceptual framework, IASB 1989: § 70).

Fair value 'Amount for which an asset could be exchanged, or a liability settled, between knowledgeable, willing parties in an arm's length transaction' (IAS 39, IASB 2003: § 9).

Faithful presentation 'To be reliable, information must represent faithfully the transactions and other events it either purports to represent or could reasonably be expected to represent' (Conceptual framework, IASB 1989: § 33).

Finance leases 'Leases that transfer substantially all the risks and rewards incidental to ownership of an asset. Title may or may not eventually be transferred' (IAS 17, IASB 2003: § 4).

Financial accounting Process of description of the various events that take place in the life of a firm. It allows for the periodic creation of synthetic reports called financial statements.

Financial asset 'Any asset that is (a) cash; (b) an equity instrument of another entity; (c) a contractual right: (i) to receive cash or another financial asset from another entity; or (ii) to exchange financial assets or financial liabilities with another entity under conditions that are potentially favorable to the entity; or (d) a contract that will or may be settled in the entity's own equity instruments and is: (i) a non-derivative for which the entity is or may be obliged to receive a variable number of the entity's own equity instruments; or (ii) a derivative that will or may be settled other than by the exchange of a fixed amount of cash or another financial asset for a fixed number of the entity's own equity instruments. For this purpose the entity's own equity instruments do not include instruments that are themselves contracts for the future receipt or delivery of the entity's own equity instruments' (IAS 32, IASB 2003: § 11).

Financial asset at fair value through profit or loss 'Financial asset (...) that (...) is classified as held for trading' (IAS 39, IASB 2004: § 9) and for which the value in the balance sheet will be adjusted to market value leading to the recognition of a gain or a loss.

Financial asset classified as held for trading 'Asset (a) acquired or incurred principally for the purpose of selling or repurchasing it in the near term; (b) part of a portfolio of identified financial instruments that are managed together and for which there is evidence of a recent actual pattern of short-term profit-taking (...)' (IAS 39, IASB 2004: § 9).

Financial assets held for trading Financial assets 'acquired (...) principally for the purpose of selling or repurchasing [them] in the near term' (IAS 39, IASB 2003: § 9).

Financial reporting To report, in a somewhat aggregated way, the (economic) performance of the firm to essential external users such as shareholders, bankers, creditors, customers, unions, tax authorities, etc.

Financial reporting standards Also named 'Accounting standards'. Authoritative statements of how particular types of standards transaction and other events should be reflected in financial statements. These standards include specific principles, bases, conventions, rules, and practices necessary to prepare the financial statements.

Financial statements These generally comprise an income statement, a balance sheet, notes, and, in several countries, a cash flow statement.

'A complete set of financial statements comprises: a balance sheet; an income statement; a statement of changes in equity (...); a cash flow statement; and notes, comprising a summary of significant accounting policies and other explanatory notes' (IAS 1, IASB 2003: § 8).

Finished goods Completed products ready for sale.

First-in, first-out (FIFO) Goods withdrawn are valued batch by batch in the order in which they entered inventory.

Franchise Contractual agreement that allows, for a fee and within a limited geographical territory, the holder (franchisee), with or without direct support from the franchisor, to sell certain products or services, to use certain trademarks, or to do other specific things identified in the franchise agreement without loss of ownership over these by the franchisor.

Free cash flow Available cash flow minus the dividends paid.

Full consolidation Mechanism where 'an entity combines the financial statements of the parent and its subsidiaries line by line by adding together like items of assets, liabilities, equity, income and expenses' (IAS 27, IASB 2003: § 22).

GAAP Generally Accepted Accounting Principles.

General ledger Grouping of all accounts.

Going concern Assumption that a business entity has a long life expectancy. This concept separates a business from a project (which has a definite completion or termination date).

Goodwill [Acquired in a business combination]: 'payment made by the acquirer in anticipation of future economic benefits from assets that are not capable of being individually identified and separately recognized' (IAS 38, IASB 2004: § 11).

Grants related to assets Government grants whose purpose is to specifically encourage qualified enterprises to 'purchase, construct or otherwise acquire long-term assets' (IAS 20, IASB 1994: § 3).

Group 'A parent and all its subsidiaries' (IAS 27, IASB 2003: § 4).

Held-to-maturity investments 'Non-derivative financial assets with fixed or determinable payments and fixed maturity that an entity has the positive intention and ability to hold to maturity (…)' (IAS 39, IASB 2004: § 9).

Horizontal format (balance sheet or income statement) Two lists of accounts balances side by side.

IASB International Accounting Standards Board: independent, private sector body, formed in 1973, under the name of International Accounting Standards Committee (IASC), and restructured in 2001 when the name was changed. Its main objective is to promote convergence of accounting principles that are used by businesses and other organizations for financial reporting around the world.

Impairment loss 'Amount by which the carrying amount of an asset exceeds its recoverable amount' (IAS 16, IASB 2003: § 6).

Income statement

- Record of what happened during the period that caused the observed income (profit or loss).
- 'Film' of the activity of the business during a given period.

Indirect method Computation of the net cash flow from operating activities by adjusting net profit or loss for the effects of changes during the period in inventories and operating receivables and payables, and non-cash items such as depreciation and provisions.

Intangible asset 'An identifiable non-monetary asset without physical substance' (IAS 38, IASB 2004: § 8).

'Assets (not including financial assets) that lack physical substance' (SFAS 142, FASB 2001).

Interest coverage ratio Operating income (before interest expense and income taxes)/Interest expense.

Inventories 'Assets: (a) held for sale in the ordinary course of business; (b) in the process of production for such sale; or (c) in the form of materials or supplies to be consumed in the production process or in the rendering of services' (IAS 2, IASB 2003: § 6).

Inventory trade financing Accounts payable/Inventory.

Investee Legal and independent business entity in which an investor is acquiring an interest. Synonym with acquiree.

Investment ratio Capital expenditures/(Depreciation plus Sales of long-term assets).

Joint control	'Contractually agreed sharing of control [between two or more legal entities] over a [third] economic activity' (IAS 31, IASB 2003: § 3).
Joint venture	'Contractual arrangement whereby two or more parties undertake an economic activity that is subject to joint control' (IAS 31, IASB 2003: § 3).
Journal	Day-to-day chronological register of accounting information.
Last-in, first-out (LIFO)	Goods withdrawn are valued, batch by batch, in the reverse order from the one they followed when entering inventory.
Lease	'Agreement whereby the lessor conveys to the lessee in return for a payment or series of payments the right to use an asset for an agreed period of time' (IAS 17, IASB 2003: § 4).
Ledger	Grouping of accounts having homogeneous characteristics such as reflecting similar types of transactions.
Legal forms of organization	(1) Sole proprietorship; (2) partnership; and (3) limited [liability] company.
Liability	'Present obligation of the entity arising from past events, the settlement of which is expected to result in an outflow from the entity of resources embodying economic benefits' (Conceptual framework, IASB 1989: § 49).
Limited liability company	Incorporated business where liability assumed by the investors does not extend beyond their investment.
Loans and receivables	'Non-derivative financial assets with fixed or determinable payments that are not quoted in an active market (...)' (IAS 39, IASB 2004: § 9).
Long-term contract	Contract that spans several accounting periods.
Long-term debt to equity ratio	Long-term debt/Shareholders' equity or Long-term debt/(Shareholders' equity + Debt).
Long-term funding	Shareholders' equity + Long-term debt.
Managerial accounting	It deals with a rather detailed account of how resources are acquired, managed, and used in the various business processes constituting the firm and is thus of particular interest to managers inside the firm.
Market to book ratio	Market price per share/Book value per share.
Matching	'Simultaneous or combined recognition of revenues and expenses that result directly and jointly from the same transactions or other [linked] events' (Conceptual Framework, IASB 1989: § 95).
Materiality and aggregation	'Each material class of similar items shall be presented separately in the financial statements. Items of a dissimilar nature or function shall be presented separately unless they are immaterial' (IAS 1, IASB 2003: § 29).
Measurement	'Process of determining the monetary amounts at which the elements of the financial statements are to be recognized and carried in the balance sheet and income statement' (Conceptual framework, IASB 1989: § 99).
Merchandise	Goods purchased for resale without transformation.
Minority interests	'That portion of profit or loss and net assets of a subsidiary attributable to equity interests that are not owned, directly or indirectly through subsidiaries, by the parent' (IAS 27, IASB 2003: § 4).
Monetary assets	'Money held and assets to be received in fixed or determinable amounts of money' (IAS 38, IASB 2004: § 8).
Movements (changes) in tangible assets	Statement providing a reconciliation of the carrying amount at the beginning and end of the period by listing acquisitions and disposals.

Multiple-step format (balance sheet) List of subsets of the main categories of assets and liabilities. Identification of useful subtotals by subtracting relevant other subcategories of assets or liabilities.

Multiple-step format (income statement) Revenue and expense categories are paired so as to highlight the components of total net income.

Net assets Assets minus liabilities.

Net cash Difference between 'cash and cash equivalents' and liabilities accounts corresponding to negative cash (bank overdrafts).

Net income Remainder after all expenses have been deducted from revenues. Measure of the wealth created by an economic entity (increased shareholders' equity) during an accounting period.

Net value See Book value.

Net worth Difference between total assets and liabilities.

No offsetting 'Assets and liabilities, and income and expenses should not be offset unless required or permitted by a Standard or an Interpretation' (IAS 1, IASB 2003: § 32).

Nominal or par value Face value of a share.

Non-cash items Items of the income statement which, by nature, will never generate a real cash flow (depreciation expense, provision expenses, etc.).

Notes payable Equivalent to 'notes receivable' (see Chapter 10) in the seller's books.

Notes receivable Accounts receivable represented by a note issued by the seller and accepted by the customer or issued by the customer.

Notes to the financial statements 'Notes contain information in addition to that presented in the balance sheet, income statement, statement of changes in equity and cash flow statement. Notes provide narrative descriptions or disaggregations of items disclosed in those statements and information about items that do not qualify for recognition in those statements' (IAS 1, IASB 2003: § 11).

Obligation 'Duty or responsibility to act or perform in a certain way' (Conceptual framework, IASB 1989: § 60)

Operating cash ratio See Cash flow yield.

Operating leases 'Lease[s] other than a finance lease' (IAS 17, IASB 2003: § 4).

Organization costs, incorporation or set-up costs Costs incurred during the process of establishing or incorporating a business.

Partnership Business often not incorporated where associates or partners are fully responsible for all the consequences of the actions of the business.

Patent Document granted by a government or an official authority bestowing on the inventor of a product or manufacturing process the exclusive right to use or sell the invention or rights to it.

Periodic inventory system Periodic (annual) physical counting to establish the quantities in the ending inventory. This system implies that the cost of goods sold is found by deduction.

Permanent difference Difference between taxable income and pre-tax income linked to recognition or non-recognition

Perpetual inventory system Continuous recording of changes in inventory (entries as well as withdrawals). The cost of goods sold is the sum of all withdrawals and the theoretical ending inventory is found by deduction before being confronted with the physical count.

Post-employment benefits Pensions, other retirement benefits, post-employment life insurance, and post-employment medical care.

Posting	Process of transferring entries from the journal to a ledger.
Potential cash flow	Operating cash based on cash items.
Preferred shares	Shares granting a higher or guaranteed dividend or priority dividend.
Profit and loss account	See Income statement.
Profit appropriation	Decision taken by the shareholders to distribute dividends and/or to retain earnings.
Proportionate consolidation	'Method of accounting whereby a venturer's share of each of the assets, liabilities, income and expenses of a jointly controlled entity is combined line by line with similar items in the venturer's financial statements or reported as separate line items in the venturer's financial statements' (IAS 31, IASB 2003: § 3).
Provision	'Liability of uncertain timing or amount' (IAS 37, IASB 1998: § 10).
R&D intensity	R&D expenses/sales revenue.
R&D per employee	R&D expenses/number of employees.
Ratio analysis	Measure of the assumed relation between two or more components of financial statements.
Raw materials	Goods incorporated in the production process that become integrally and physically part of the product.
Receivables turnover	Ratio measuring the number of times receivables turned over during the year: Net sales/Average accounts receivable.
Recognition of in tangible assets	'An intangible asset shall be recognized if, and only if: (a) it is probable that the expected future economic benefits that are attributable to the asset will flow to the entity; and (b) the cost of the asset can be measured reliably' (IAS 38, IASB 2004: § 21).
Recourse	If the discounting of a note is without recourse, the note is sold with complete transfer to the buyer of the note of the default risk of the drawer. If it is made with recourse, i.e., a conditional sale: if the drawer defaults on the maturity date, the discounting financial institution will demand full reimbursement of the note plus fees from the seller of the note who discounted it in the first place.
Research	'Original and planned investigation undertaken with the prospect of gaining new scientific or technical knowledge and understanding' (IAS 38, IASB 2004: § 8).
Reserves (different types)	Legal reserve, statutory reserves, regulated reserves, optional (voluntary) reserves, revaluation reserves, profit brought forward.
Residual value	'Estimated amount that an entity would currently obtain from disposal of the asset, after deducting the estimated costs of disposal if the asset were already of the age and in the condition expected at the end of its useful life' (IAS 16, IASB 2003: § 6).
Retained earnings	Part of the value created through the firm's operations that shareholders have chosen not to take out of the firm. It is a *de facto* increase in their contribution to the ongoing activity of the firm.
Return on assets (ROA)	Net income/[(Assets Year 2 + Assets Year 1)/2].
Return on equity	Net income/Average equity
Return on investment (ROI)	Net income/(Average long-term liabilities 1 Average equity).
Return on sales (net profit margin)	Net income/Sales.
Return on shareholders' equity (ROE)	Net income/Average equity.

Revenue 'Gross inflow of economic benefits during the period arising in the course of the ordinary activities of an enterprise entity when those inflows result in increases in equity, other than increases relating to contributions from equity participants' (IAS 18, IASB 1993: § 7).

Revenue expenditure Expenses caused by the short-term usage – or maintenance – of the revenue generating potential of an asset (examples: minor spare parts, oil and cooling fluids, maintenance expenses, minor repairs expenses).

Revenue recognition Recording the impact of a transaction on the revenue component of the income statement.

Revenues 'Gross inflow of economic benefits during the period arising in the course of the ordinary activities of an entity when those inflows result in increases in equity, other than increases relating to contributions from equity participants' (IAS 18, IASB 2003: § 7).

Sales return Reversal of a sale when a customer is not satisfied for any reason with the product that was delivered (such as non-conformity of delivery with order, defects, etc.).

Semi-finished goods Items that are finished with regard to one stage of production but are, nonetheless, not sellable in that condition. They will generally be integrated in a finished product at a later date.

Share capital Historical value of the contributions to the firm all shareholders have made in the beginning and during the life of the firm by making external resources available to the firm and giving up control over these resources (cash, effort or ideas, physical assets, etc.).

Share dividend Dividends paid out by giving assets to the shareholders.

Share premium Difference between the issue price and the par value.

Significant influence 'Power to participate in the financial and operating policy decisions of the investee but it is not control or joint control over those policies' (IAS 28, IASB 2003: § 2).

Single-step format (balance sheet) Balance sheet presented with assets, on the one hand, and shareholders' equity and equity, on the other. No mix of assets and shareholders' equity and liabilities is performed.

Single-step format (income statement) Simplified version of the income statement. Expenses and revenues are each considered as one category.

Specific identification method The cost upon withdrawal of items that are not ordinarily interchangeable or fungible is absolutely identical to the one they had when entering in inventory.

Stakeholders Any party that has a 'stake' in the outcome and output resulting from the activity of an enterprise. They include a variety of parties: investors, employees, customers, suppliers … .

Statement of financial position Balance sheet.

Statement of intermediate balances Statement highlighting the key sequential intermediate balances that describe the value (income) creation process such as commercial margin, value added, and gross operating profit.

Stock option plan Motivational device in which the corporation grants employees the right to acquire a specified personalized number of shares of the corporation at a predetermined invariant price and for a specified time window.

Straight-line method The asset is depreciated evenly over its useful life.

Subscribed or issued capital Part of the capital authorized that the shareholders have agreed to purchase and pay when called to do so.

Subsidiary 'Entity (…) that is controlled by another entity (known as the parent)' (IAS 27, IASB 2003: § 4).

Substance over form 'If information is to represent faithfully the transactions and other events that it purports to represent, it is necessary that they are accounted for and presented in accordance with their substance and economic reality and not merely their legal form' (Conceptual framework, IASB 1989: § 35).

Tangible assets (also called 'tangible fixed assets', 'property, plant, and equipment', 'plant assets', or 'operational assets') 'Tangible items that: (a) are held for use in the production or supply of goods or services, for rental to others, or for administrative purposes; and (b) are expected to be used during more than one period' (IAS 16, IASB 2003: § 6).

Taxable income Difference between taxable revenue and deductible (or tax deductible) expenses or costs.

Temporary difference Difference between taxable income and pre-tax income linked to the timing of recognition of revenue or expenses.

Trademark (or trade name, or brand or brand name) Distinctive identification (symbol, logo, design, word, slogan, emblem, etc.) of a manufactured product or of a service that distinguishes it from similar products or services provided by other parties.

Transaction types Sale of goods, rendering of services, interest, royalties, dividends.

Treasury shares (own shares) Shares of a corporation acquired by itself.

Trend or horizontal analysis Comparison over time of the evolution of a specific expense or revenue item or a particular asset or liability item.

Trial balance List of the debit and credit footings for each account in the general ledger.

True and fair view Objective of financial statements not defined in the accounting standards.

Unit of measurement Financial accounting only records transactions expressed in financial units.

Useful life 'Either: (a) the period of time over which an asset is expected to be available for use by an entity; or (b) the number of production [output] or similar units expected to be obtained from the asset by an entity' (IAS 16, IASB 2003: § 6).

Users (of financial information) Managers and stakeholders.

Value added Creation or increase in value resulting from the enterprise's current professional activities over and above that of goods and services provided by third parties and consumed by the firm.

Vertical format (balance sheet or income statement) Continuous list of account balances.

Weighted average cost method (WAC) Goods withdrawn (considered totally fungible) are valued at the average cost of available goods.

Work in progress (WIP) Products still in the manufacturing process at the close of the day and services rendered but not invoiced.

Working capital 'Shareholders' equity plus Long-term (financial) debt minus Fixed (non-current) assets' or, alternatively, 'Currents assets (including cash) minus Current liabilities (including bank overdrafts)'.

Working capital need Current assets (excluding net cash) minus Current liabilities (excluding bank overdrafts).

Index

[A indicates an appendix (on the website)]

C

S